RAND McNALLY

Road Atlas 2015 LARGE SCALE

CONTENTS

TRAVEL INFORMATION

Mileage Chart 2
Driving distances between 77 North American cities.

Best of the Road® 3-5
Meet the winning towns from our Best of the Road search, celebrating the Best Small Towns in America.

6 Great Drives from Best of the Road 6-7
Find your way with these special road trips selected from our editor-crafted collection of nearly 300 on bestoftheroad.com

Mileage and Driving Times Map inside back cover
Distances and driving times between hundreds of North American cities and national parks.

MAPS

Map Legend inside front cover

United States Overview Map 8-9

States and Cities 10-235

INDEX 236-264

D1097579

Quick Map References

Photo credits:
Table of contents: top ©Bill Grant/ Alamy, center ©PhotoDisc; p. 3 (t to b), ©Lakov Kalinin/ istockphoto, ©dbimages/Alamy, ©age fotostock/Alamy, Courtesy B Street and Vine, ©George Oze/ SuperStock/Alamy; p. 4 (t to b) Courtesy Kewanee Economic Development Corporation, Courtesy Kewanee Economic Development Corporation, Courtesy Helena Tourism Alliance, Taplight/Alamy; p. 5 ©Bill Grant/Alamy, ©Dennis MacDonald/Alamy, ©Yaacov Daga/Alamy, ©Richard Cummins/ Alamy; back cover ©David R. Frazier Photolibrary, Inc./Alamy.

©2014-2015 RM Acquisition, LLC d/b/a Rand McNally. Rand McNally, the globe logo, and Best of the Road are registered trademarks of RM Acquisition. All other trademarks appearing in this publication are trademarks of third parties and are the responsibility of their respective owners.

For licensing information and copyright permissions, contact us at permissions@randmcnally.com

If you have a comment, suggestion, or even a compliment, please visit us at randmcnally.com/contact or e-mail us at consumeraffairs@ randmcnally.com.

or write to:
Rand McNally Consumer Affairs
P.O. Box 7600
Chicago, Illinois 60680-9915

Published in U.S.A.
Printed in China

1-2-3-LE-14-15

Alabama
Northern............................ 10-11
Southern............................ 12-13
Alaska 14-15
Arizona
Northern............................ 16-17
Southern............................ 18-19
Cities................................. 20-21
Arkansas
Western............................. 22-23
Eastern.............................. 24-25
California
Northern............................ 26-27
San Francisco 28
East-Central......................... 29
Northern Cities................. 30-31
Southern Cities................. 32-33
West-Central..................... 34-35
Southern............................ 36-37
Los Angeles...................... 38-41
Colorado
Western............................. 42-43
Eastern.............................. 44-45
Cities................................. 46-47
Connecticut...................... 48-49
Delaware 50-51
Florida
Cities................................... 51
Northern............................ 52-53
Southern............................ 54-55
Panhandle............................ 54
Cities................................. 56-57
Georgia
Northern............................ 58-59
Southern............................ 60-61
Atlanta................................ 62
Hawaii................................. 63
Honolulu.............................. 62
Idaho................................. 64-65
Illinois
Northern............................ 66-67
Southern............................ 68-69
Chicago.............................. 70-71
Cities................................. 72-73
Indiana
Cities................................. 72-73
Northern............................ 74-75
Southern............................ 76-77
Iowa
Western............................. 78-79
Eastern.............................. 80-81
Kansas
Western............................. 82-83
Eastern.............................. 84-85

Kentucky
Western............................. 86-87
Eastern.............................. 88-89
Louisiana............................ 90-91
Maine................................. 92-93
Maryland
Western................................ 94
Baltimore............................. 95
Eastern.............................. 96-97
Massachusetts
Western................................ 98
Boston.................................. 99
Eastern............................ 100-101
Michigan
Northern.......................... 102-103
Southern.......................... 104-105
Cities................................... 106
Detroit................................. 107
Minnesota
Northern.......................... 108-109
Southern.......................... 110-111
Minneapolis/St. Paul.... 112-113
Mississippi 114-115
Missouri
Western.......................... 116-117
Eastern........................... 118-119
St. Louis.............................. 120
Cities................................... 121
Montana
Western.......................... 122-123
Eastern........................... 124-125
Nebraska
Western.......................... 126-127
Eastern........................... 128-129
Nevada.......................... 130-131
Cities................................... 133
New Hampshire.............. 132-133
New Jersey
Northern.......................... 134-135
Southern.......................... 136-137
New Mexico.................... 138-139
New York
Southern.......................... 140-141
Northwestern.................. 142-143
Northeastern.................. 144-145
New York City 146-149
North Carolina
Western.......................... 150-151
Eastern........................... 152-153
Cities............................... 154-155
North Dakota.................. 156-157

Ohio
Northwestern.................. 158-159
Northeastern.................. 160-161
Southwestern.................. 162-163
Southeastern.................. 164-165
Oklahoma
Western.......................... 166-167
Eastern........................... 168-169
Oregon
Western.......................... 170-171
Eastern........................... 172-173
Pennsylvania
Northwestern.................. 174-175
Southwestern.................. 176-177
Northeastern.................. 178-179
Southeastern.................. 180-181
Philadelphia....................... 182
Pittsburgh.......................... 183
Rhode Island 184-185
South Carolina 186-187
South Dakota 188-189
Tennessee
Western.......................... 190-191
Eastern........................... 192-193
Cities................................... 195
Texas
Houston.......................... 194-195
Cities................................... 195
Dallas/Fort Worth 196-197
Southeastern.................. 198-199
Southwestern.................. 200-201
Northeastern.................. 202-203
Southeastern.................. 204-205
Utah
Western.......................... 206-207
Eastern........................... 208-209
Vermont.......................... 210-211
Virginia
Western.......................... 212-213
Eastern........................... 214-215
Cities............................... 216-217
Washington
Western.......................... 218-219
Eastern........................... 220-221
Cities............................... 222-223
Washington, DC 224-225
West Virginia 226-227
Wisconsin
Northern.......................... 228-229
Southern.......................... 230-231
Cities............................... 232-233
Wyoming.......................... 234-235

National Park Maps
Acadia National Park 93
Arches National Park 208
Black Hills Region
(Wind Cave National Park)...... 188
Bryce Canyon National Park 208
Canyonlands National Park 208
Capitol Reef National Park 208
Colonial National
Historical Park 216
Crater Lake National Park 172
Denali National Park
& Preserve 15
Gettysburg National
Military Park 177
Grand Canyon National Park........ 20
Great Smoky Mountains
National Park 155
Isle Royale National Park 102
Joshua Tree National Park 34
Mammoth Cave National Park 89
Mesa Verde National Park 42
Mount Rainier National Park........ 223
Petrified Forest National Park 21
Rocky Mountain National Park 46
Waterton-Glacier
International Peace Park 123
Yellowstone and
Grand Teton National Parks.... 234
Yosemite National Park 27
Zion National Park 207

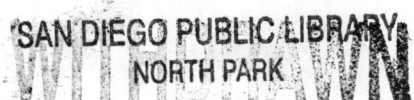

TELL RAND!
For over 155 years, Rand McNally has been collecting road travel information and publishing industry-leading maps and atlases. Each year our geographic information systems (GIS) specialists research road conditions and construction projects to update our atlas. Of course, conditions change quickly and new construction projects begin frequently.

If you see something that we haven't captured in our atlas, please let us know at **randmcnally.com/tellrand**.

Mileage Chart

This handy chart offers more than 2,400 mileages covering 77 North American cities and U.S. national parks. Want more mileages? Visit **randmcnally.com/MC** and type in any two cities or addresses.

	Albuquerque, NM	Atlanta, GA	Billings, MT	Boston, MA	Charlotte, NC	Chicago, IL	Cincinnati, OH	Dallas, TX	Denver, CO	Detroit, MI	Houston, TX	Indianapolis, IN	Kansas City, MO	Los Angeles, CA	Memphis, TN	Miami, FL	Milwaukee, WI	Minneapolis, MN	New Orleans, LA	New York, NY	Omaha, NE	Orlando, FL	Philadelphia, PA	Phoenix, AZ	Pittsburgh, PA	Portland, OR	Saint Louis, MO	Salt Lake City, UT	San Francisco, CA	Seattle, WA	Washington, DC	Wichita, KS
Albuquerque, NM		1386	998	2219	1626	1333	1387	647	446	1570	884	1279	784	786	1008	1952	1354	1225	1165	2001	863	1730	1924	462	1641	1363	1037	599	1086	1438	1885	591
Amarillo, TX	284	1102	965	1935	1342	1049	1103	363	424	1286	589	995	570	1072	720	1668	1132	1009	881	1716	647	1446	1640	746	1357	1669	752	883	1370	1743	1600	382
Atlanta, GA	1386		1831	1095	244	715	461	780	1404	722	794	533	800	2174	379	661	809	1127	468	882	992	440	780	1844	684	2603	555	1878	2472	2649	637	955
Atlantic City, NJ	1985	831	2072	338	590	818	632	1518	1792	644	1598	703	1187	2774	1063	1248	910	1232	1273	126	1272	1038	60	2447	365	2922	948	2201	2934	2889	188	1379
Austin, TX	705	920	1495	1959	1164	1121	1128	193	950	1358	157	1067	702	1381	643	1341	1204	1136	503	1737	839	1124	1658	1010	1411	2068	825	1304	1760	2143	1524	542
Baltimore, MD	1887	683	1953	400	442	699	513	1368	1673	524	1448	584	1068	2670	914	1082	792	1112	1124	192	1153	889	98	2349	246	2804	829	2081	2816	2771	39	1260
Billings, MT	998	1831		2236	1990	1246	1546	1425	551	1535	1652	1435	1026	1240	1477	2497	1173	838	1868	2041	845	2275	2011	1210	1713	891	1278	552	1173	818	1951	1064
Birmingham, AL	1241	146	1780	1177	390	660	466	636	1329	724	668	478	749	2030	235	746	754	1072	343	960	939	534	880	1700	748	2551	502	1826	2327	2598	745	810
Boise, ID	938	2177	621	2660	2336	1693	1943	1702	830	1960	1930	1835	1372	842	1825	2844	1732	1461	2216	2465	1225	2622	2435	914	2137	428	1622	339	639	503	2375	1338
Boston, MA	2219	1095	2236		841	983	870	1764	1970	724	1844	937	1421	2983	1312	1482	1074	1396	1520	207	1436	1288	306	2681	570	3086	1182	2365	3098	3054	439	1613
Branson, MO	864	652	1241	1433	868	545	601	435	806	784	602	493	209	1651	274	1284	630	643	597	1201	402	1062	1138	1326	851	2013	249	1288	1950	2060	1081	292
Calgary, AB	1542	2357	541	2615	2400	1627	1925	1967	1096	1916	2209	1814	1567	1557	2028	3018	1555	1221	2419	2439	1387	2797	2391	1524	2093	787	1820	869	1500	678	2334	1606
Charleston, SC	1703	317	2133	970	207	908	620	1099	1706	826	1105	726	1103	2491	696	583	1002	1324	742	768	1294	380	668	2165	654	2904	857	2180	2789	2951	532	1272
Charlotte, NC	1626	244	1990	841		769	477	1023	1566	616	1038	583	961	2414	619	728	867	1180	712	641	1151	526	539	2088	446	2761	714	2037	2712	2808	398	1092
Chicago, IL	1333	715	1246	983	769		289	926	1002	280	1085	181	526	2015	531	1381	90	408	923	787	470	1153	757	1795	459	2118	296	1398	2130	2063	697	724
Cincinnati, OH	1387	461	1546	870	477	289		934	1187	259	1055	108	584	2172	482	1127	381	703	804	637	722	905	571	1849	288	2369	348	1647	2380	2363	512	779
Cleveland, OH	1598	714	1597	638	514	342	248	1194	1330	168	1315	315	799	2342	729	1240	434	756	1057	460	797	1043	428	2060	131	2446	560	1725	2458	2414	370	992
Columbus, OH	1457	567	1606	763	426	354	106	1039	1261	191	1174	176	657	2244	587	1164	445	766	910	533	792	954	468	1920	184	2439	421	1718	2451	2425	411	851
Corpus Christi, TX	855	1001	1622	2051	1244	1338	1262	410	1077	1542	207	1228	919	1494	782	1394	1421	1353	554	1844	1056	1172	1754	1122	1561	2218	1042	1454	1873	2292	1619	758
Dallas, TX	647	780	1425	1764	1023	926	934		880	1163	228	873	489	1437	453	1307	1010	928	519	1548	656	1086	1467	1066	1221	2128	630	1403	1734	2193	1332	361
Denver, CO	446	1404	551	1970	1566	1002	1187	880		1270	1035	1083	603	1015	1097	2069	1042	913	1398	1775	534	1851	1732	908	1447	1256	854	533	1268	1320	1671	519
Des Moines, IA	983	902	946	1299	1057	332	580	683	670	599	938	474	193	1682	617	1567	371	242	1008	1105	137	1339	1074	1445	777	1786	354	1065	1798	1764	1015	391
Detroit, MI	1570	722	1535	724	616	280	259	1163	1270		1319	288	764	2281	742	1354	374	696	1066	613	736	1144	583	2032	285	2385	533	1664	2397	2353	522	964
Duluth, MN	1375	1187	860	1370	1239	466	760	1092	1063	754	1331	651	586	2076	963	1852	394	152	1354	1264	530	1632	1230	1838	932	1749	679	1458	2033	1677	1171	785
Edmonton, AB	1724	2391	722	2549	2443	1670	1968	2149	1278	1958	2391	1857	1626	1755	2147	3058	1598	1264	2538	2482	1445	2836	2434	1721	2136	966	1878	1069	1695	793	2377	1787
El Paso, TX	260	1418	1257	2373	1662	1455	1569	635	707	1702	744	1398	929	796	1089	1934	1497	1377	1095	2202	1004	1712	2102	424	1774	1630	1157	866	1175	1705	1967	730
Fargo, ND	1318	1361	607	1629	1414	641	937	1079	873	930	1321	825	600	1848	1054	2025	569	235	1445	1438	420	1807	1405	1780	1107	1497	841	1160	1781	1424	1348	685
Gatlinburg, TN	1439	196	1803	922	202	578	290	884	1376	552	964	396	773	2226	431	865	672	994	640	707	964	640	625	1901	493	2574	527	1850	2525	2621	490	905
Guadalajara, JA	1194	1739	2194	2789	1982	1954	1962	1028	1639	2191	948	1901	1535	1501	1482	2131	2037	1969	1292	2592	1672	1910	2492	1212	2261	2545	1658	1792	1963	2631	2356	1377
Gulfport, MS	1221	399	1912	1482	643	896	767	562	1386	1025	403	780	883	1949	365	792	988	1196	78	1266	1073	572	1180	1577	1052	2633	647	1909	2307	2730	1036	867
Houston, TX	884	794	1652	1844	1038	1085	1055	228	1035	1319		1021	732	1550	575	1186	1163	1171	347	1632	898	965	1547	1178	1354	2356	784	1634	1929	2431	1411	595
Indianapolis, IN	1279	533	1435	937	583	181	108	873	1083	288	1021		482	2068	464	1198	272	591	818	707	613	968	643	1742	359	2260	243	1541	2273	2253	582	674
Jacksonville, FL	1636	346	2183	1146	379	1068	796	992	1756	1002	871	874	1152	2421	677	349	1163	1474	547	939	1344	141	844	2050	825	2954	907	2230	2723	3001	706	1272
Kansas City, MO	784	800	1026	1421	961	526	584	489	603	764	732	482		1616	451	1466	565	436	844	1196	187	1246	1127	1246	840	1797	250	1073	1808	1844	1066	193
Key West, FL	2099	809	2646	1659	886	1534	1275	1455	2222	1515	1334	1348	1617	2884	1159	162	1632	1944	1010	1446	1807	387	1357	2514	1332	3417	1370	2693	3186	3464	1213	1735
Las Vegas, NV	572	1959	973	2714	2199	1746	1932	1220	747	2013	1457	1828	1349	270	1581	2525	1786	1656	1739	2518	1278	2303	2480	286	2190	1023	1600	419	569	1128	2428	1164
Lexington, KY	1371	369	1610	917	400	370	83	876	1186	344	996	184	581	2158	423	1030	464	782	745	701	771	817	638	1833	370	2381	334	1657	2392	2428	533	773
Little Rock, AR	877	515	1407	1447	754	650	617	319	965	885	439	583	381	1666	137	1147	724	815	425	1230	574	925	1150	1340	905	2211	345	1488	1963	2275	1015	446
Los Angeles, CA	786	2174	1240	2983	2414	2015	2172	1437	1015	2281	1550	2068	1616		1794	2735	2055	1925	1894	2787	1546	2515	2713	370	2428	963	1821	688	380	1134	2670	1377
Memphis, TN	1008	379	1477	1312	619	531	482	453	1097	742	575	464	451	1794		1012	622	831	394	1094	641	778	1014	1471	768	2245	283	1524	2095	2299	879	577
Mexico City, DF	1404	1718	2301	2768	1962	2017	1979	1090	1756	2254	924	1963	1598	1839	1500	2111	2100	2032	1272	2571	1735	1889	2471	1469	2279	2768	1721	2003	2218	2842	2336	1440
Miami, FL	1952	661	2497	1482	728	1381	1127	1307	2069	1354	1186	1198	1466	2735	1012		1475	1791	861	1288	1658	229	1180	2362	1173	3260	1221	2544	3038	3315	1044	1587
Milwaukee, WI	1354	809	1173	1074	867	90	381	1010	1042	374	1163	272	565	2055	622	1475		336	1015	879	509	1258	849	1817	551	2062	379	1437	2170	1990	788	763
Minneapolis, MN	1225	1127	838	1396	1180	408	703	928	913	696	1171	591	436	1925	831	1791	336		1223	1204	372	1573	1171	1687	874	1727	563	1308	2040	1655	1110	634
Mobile, AL	1234	328	1874	1427	571	917	721	589	1414	978	468	733	850	2014	382	719	1011	1224	144	1202	1038	497	1101	1643	1000	2661	645	1936	2320	2727	965	894
Montréal, QC	2129	1218	2099	310	980	847	824	1722	1832	560	1884	847	1330	2845	1314	1647	938	1262	1640	382	1302	1437	454	2591	603	2948	1092	2228	2960	2916	587	1529
Nashville, TN	1219	248	1586	1099	407	469	273	664	1158	534	786	287	555	2006	212	913	564	881	532	884	747	692	802	1682	560	2357	310	1633	2306	2404	667	688
New Orleans, LA	1165	468	1868	1520	712	923	804	519	1398	1066	347	818	844	1894	394	861	1015	1223		1304	1032	641	1222	1523	1090	2642	675	1920	2252	2716	1087	880
New York, NY	2001	882	2041	207	641	787	637	1548	1775	613	1632	707	1196	2787	1094	1288	879	1204	1304		1245	1089	97	2463	369	2891	954	2170	2902	2858	228	1391
Norfolk, VA	1910	558	2132	569	328	878	605	1350	1758	704	1362	720	1155	2707	898	950	969	1295	1026	370	1335	755	271	2373	425	2962	911	2238	2973	2949	189	1349
Oklahoma City, OK	542	844	1203	1678	1084	792	846	204	631	1029	437	739	348	1326	466	1476	876	788	722	1460	452	1254	1384	1005	1101	1922	496	1200	1627	1948	1344	158
Omaha, NE	863	992	845	1436	1151	470	722	656	534	736	898	613	187	1546	641	1658	509	372	1032	1245		1436	1212	1325	914	1650	439	930	1662	1663	1151	298
Orlando, FL	1730	440	2275	1288	526	1153	905	1086	1851	1144	965	968	1246	2515	778	229	1258	1573	641	1089	1436		986	2145	975	3048	999	2323	2816	3093	849	1365
Ottawa, ON	2039	1158	1768	428	920	760	732	1632	1748	471	1804	757	1240	2763	1230	1618	859	1032	1582	440	1213	1408	447	2501	546	2660	1002	2142	2877	2586	566	1439
Philadelphia, PA	1924	780	2011	306	539	757	571	1467	1732	583	1547	643	1127	2713	1014	1180	849	1171	1222	97	1212	986		2387	304	2861	888	2140	2873	2828	137	1319
Phoenix, AZ	462	1844	1210	2681	2088	1795	1849	1066	908	2032	1178	1742	1246	370	1471	2362	1817	1687	1523	2463	1325	2145	2387		2104	1332	1499	653	749	1414	2348	1053
Pittsburgh, PA	1641	684	1713	570	446	459	288	1221	1447	285	1354	359	840	2428	768	1173	551	874	1090	369	914	975	304	2104		2563	604	1842	2574	2530	244	1035
Portland, ME	2315	1192	2333	110	938	1079	967	1861	2067	825	1940	1034	1518	3082	1408	1585	1176	1492	1616	304	1533	1385	402	2778	666	3186	1279	2461	3196	3151	535	1710
Portland, OR	1363	2603	891	3086	2761	2118	2369	2128	1256	2385	2356	2260	1797	963	2245	3260	2062	1727	2642	2891	1650	3048	2861	1332	2563		2050	765	635	172	2800	1764
Rapid City, SD	843	1508	323	1900	1670	912	1208	1061	397	1200	1291	1100	704	1312	1160	2173	840	575	1551	1708	525	1956	1675	1305	1378	1215	959	649	1384	1142	1618	699
Reno, NV	1019	2396	958	2881	2555	1913	2163	1668	1051	2180	1904	2056	1591	470	2029	3063	1953	1818	2186	2685	1445	2841	2656	733	2357	578	1844	518	217	720	2595	1558
Richmond, VA	1832	532	2051	547	293	797	512	1278	1671	622	1329	627	1069	2620	824	944	888	1210	1002	334	1259	742	245	2294	344	2869	822	2145	2880	2868	108	1261
Saint Louis, MO	1037	555	1278	1182	714	296	348	630	854	533	784	243	250	1821	283	1221	379	563	675	954	439	999	888	1499	604	2050		1326	2061	2096	827	442
Salt Lake City, UT	599	1878	552	2365	2037	1398	1647	1403	533	1664	1634	1541	1073	688	1524	2544	1437	1308	1920	2170	930	2323	2140	653	1842	765	1326		735	839	2079	1042
San Antonio, TX	712	986	1480	2039	1230	1202	1210	276	935	1439	197	1149	766	1357	727	1379	1285	1205	541	1822	920	1160	1742	985	1495	2076	906	1311	1736	2150	1607	625
San Diego, CA	810	2138	1302	3046	2381	2080	2196	1359	1077	2346	1472	2089	1597	120	1819	2656	2118	1986	1816	2809	1613	2436	2738	352	2452	1083	1845	750	501	1256	2693	1401
San Francisco, CA	1086	2472	1173	3098	2712	2130	2380	1734	1268	2397	1929	2273	1808	380	2095	3038	2170	2040	2252	2902	1662	2816	2873	749	2574	635	2061	735		807	2812	1775
Santa Fe, NM	58	1379	943	2212	1618	1313	1379	640	391	1562	877	1272	766	846	998	1944	1336	1207	1158	1994	891	1723	1917	520	1634	1388	1029	625	1144	1463	1879	572
Sault Ste. Marie, ON	1777	1040	1273	923	947	471	577	1370	1428	347	1527	540	951	2465	972	1685	398	538	1355	921	850	1475	911	2240	614	2166	740	1848	2581	2090	854	1150
Seattle, WA	1438	2649	818	3054	2808	2063	2363	2193	1320	2353	2431	2253	1844	1134	2299	3315	1990	1655	2716	2858	1663	3093	2828	1414	2530	172	2096	839	807		2768	1828
Spokane, WA	1320	2369	541	2774	2528	1785	2084	1964	1091	2075	2192	1973	1564	1216	2018	3035	1712	1377	2409	2580	1383	2814	2550	1381	2252	351	1817	720	874	278	2490	1600
Tampa, FL	1746	451	2293	1342	578	1166	916	1102	1860	1178	980	984	1252	2525	779	255	1260	1578	651	1138	1445	84	1040	2153	1023	3064	1008	2340	2832	3111	904	1381
Toronto, ON	1800	963	1771	548	756	519	493	1393	1504	232	1551	518	1001	2517	983	1483	609	933	1306	489	974	1284	497	2262	316	2620	763	1899	2632	2588	486	1188
Tulsa, OK	645	782	1234	1576	1022	687	738	258	692	927	487	635	243	1433	402	1414	773	704	671	1350	380	1192	1282	1107	994	1938	392	1215	1731	2012	1234	173
Vancouver, BC	1575	2785	953	3188	2944	2198	2499	2338	1465	2487	2565	2389	1980	1275	2437	3451	2125	1790	2851	2993	1799	3229	2963	1550	2665	313	2232	973	947	141	2903	1973
Washington, DC	1885	637	1951	439	398	697	512	1332	1671	522	1411	582	1066	2670	879	1044	788	1110	1087	228	1151	849	137	2348	244	2800	827	2079	2812	2768		1258
Wichita, KS	591	955	1064	1613	1092	724	779	361	519	964	595	674	193	1377	577	1587	763	634	880	1391	298	1365	1319	1053	1035	1764	442	1042	1775	1828	1258	

Mileages in this chart are based upon the routes usually followed by motorists. Highway systems include interstate, U.S., and state highways.

Thirty finalist towns. Thirty compelling stories. Seven judges. Six winners . . .

Read on for the highlights of the small towns that were named **Most Fun**, **Best for Food**, **Friendliest**, **Best for Geocaching**, **Most Beautiful**, or **Most Patriotic** in Rand McNally's 3rd annual Best of the Road® contest. Find out more about all the towns—winners and finalists—at **bestoftheroad.com**.

★ *Winner Most Fun:* Corning, NY

It's not often you find a place and think, "Wow, there's something really special here!" But that's how many people feel about America's Crystal City. And it's not just the attractions in town and the natural beauty of the surrounding Southern Finger Lakes region that pull you in. No, it's something more. You feel excitement in the air and know you're in for a great time.

Surprising finds wait around every corner. In the historic Gaffer District—named for the community's master glass blowers—shoppers hunt for treasures in clothing boutiques, antiques shops, art galleries, and design stores. Restaurants, bistros, and cafes buzz with diners pairing whatever's freshest from area farms with wines from renowned Finger Lakes vineyards. Streets bustle with museum-goers heading between the world-class collections at the Rockwell Museum of Western Art and the Corning Museum of Glass, with exhibits that are fun for all ages.

Adding to the day-to-day fun, energy, and pull are the farmers markets, fairs, and festivals that fill the calendar—from May's GlassFest to December's Crystal City Christmas. It says a lot about a town when visitors return season after season, year after year; it says even more when some have so much fun that they decide to stay!

Corning Museum of Glass

> *Corning is a gem, where small town hospitality and charm mingle with urban flair! There's always something going on and plenty of fantastic shops and restaurants to enjoy. If you're visiting, Corning is a great base for exploring the Finger Lakes. If you're looking for a wonderful place to call home, Corning is it!* -Lwelles

Things to See and Do

One legacy of Corning Incorporated (formerly Corning Glass Works) is the **Corning Museum of Glass** (1 Museum Way, 607-937-5371, www.cmog.org), where the glass displays are dazzling. You can also watch contemporary glass artists at work and even fuse, blow, or sandblast your own beautiful piece during a Make Your Own Glass Experience.

Local department store owner Bob Rockwell's fascination with the American West began as a child on his family's Colorado ranch. His collection of Western-themed paintings, sculptures, and other works—including those by Frederic Remington and Charles M. Russell—now fills the **Rockwell Museum of Western Art** (111 Cedar St., 607-937-5386, www.rockwellmuseum.org).

The historic **Corning Gaffer District** (114 Pine St., 607-937-6292, www.gafferdistrict.com) has four self-guided, downloadable Experiences Trails geared to foodies, collectors, and kids. The **Steuben County Conference & Visitors Bureau** (1 W. Market St., 607-936-6544, www.corningfingerlakes.com) also has itineraries through Corning and the Southern Finger Lakes.

Scenic drive in the Finger Lakes area

★ *Winner Best for Food:* San Mateo, CA

B Street and Vine

In the tradition of Silicon Valley, San Mateo is a creativity hub. Set between San Francisco and San Jose, it's the birthplace of YouTube; AdMob; Epocrates; the high-tech Draper University; and the Draper Collective, a pop-up retail space that nurtures entrepreneurs. The community is equally well known for another innovative element: its food! Founded in 1894 as an agricultural community—in a state that, today, has more than 200 crops—you could say that food is embedded in San Mateo's DNA.

Of the 350 food establishments, three are Michelin rated, many are otherwise critically acclaimed, and all take full advantage of the region's fresh produce. Adding to the mix of restaurants, cafes, bistros, diners, and food trucks are green grocers, gourmet shops, bakeries, confectionaries, cheesemongers, and wine-tasting rooms. Menus here are extraordinarily diverse, with cuisines from across the globe. Weekly farmers markets and annual food-related festivals fill the calendar. All of these ingredients (and more) make San Mateo a great place for a California culinary experience—no small feat in a state known for its many fine epicurean offerings.

> *San Mateo is wonderful for foodies, from breakfast to after-dinner cocktails. . . . There's a diversity of ethnic food. There are cheap choices and fine restaurants . . . small bites and five-course meals. [We] rarely go in to San Francisco because we get such a variety and quality in San Mateo.* -rileyre

Things to See and Do

Amid the vitality of San Mateo's downtown—where history meets high-tech—is the tranquil oasis of **Central Park** (50 E. 5th Ave.) and its famous Japanese Tea Garden designed by Nagao Sakurai of the Imperial Palace of Tokyo. Walking amid the garden's cherry trees and bamboo grove before or after stopping at a downtown tea house or café is the perfect way to spend one of San Mateo's many sunny, mild afternoons.

Point Montara Lighthouse, Pacific coast near San Mateo

Founded in 1953, **Talbots Toyland and Cyclery** (445 S. B St., 650-931-8100 or 650-931-8120 to cyclery, www.talbotstoyland.com, www.talbotscyclery.com) not only has a great inventory of both toys and bicycles (including bikes for rent) it also has a doll department and a hobby shop that are renowned in the Bay Area. Even singer/songwriter Neil Young has reportedly been seen here adding to his collection of Lionel trains.

★ *Winner Friendliest:* Kewanee, IL

Dreamland Theatre Mural

Big-hearted Kewanee is a small factory and agricultural town roughly 150 miles southwest of Chicago. Folks here help each other out in bad times and celebrate with each other in good times. Take the annual Hog Days Festival, a Labor Day tradition during which family and friends from near and far gather for pork chops and beer. They're joined by as many as 30,000 visitors. Some become new friends who pledge to return . . . and do!

You'll find the same friendly, welcoming spirit during Fourth of July celebrations, Christmas in Kewanee, and other seasonal events. It was definitely present in 2013, during the five-day 20th Annual Walldogs Meet, when Kewanee hosted (and fed and assisted) more than 250 sign painters and muralists (aka Walldogs), who, in turn left behind 15 beautiful murals.

That friendly, welcoming spirit exists every day, too—with smiles and greetings from passersby on downtown streets and cheerful waves from folks in passing cars (or tractors) along rural routes. It's all part of a town where they simply choose to be friendly.

> *. . . Whether you grew up in Kewanee, or you're just passing through, you'll find friendly people willing and ready to share a smile, assist you with a purchase, give directions, and, perhaps, even tell a joke or engaging story. . .*
> -Lemans10

Things to See and Do

Get that Hog Days flavor year-round at **Cerno's Bar & Grill** (213 W. 3rd St., 309-853-3469), where they serve great pork tenderloin, among other amazing dishes, in a building that's been a tavern since the 1850s. Adding to the patina is the 50-foot-long bar, built and elaborately carved of red Belgian mahogany in 1898 just for the Pabst Brewing Company. On tap is plenty of camaraderie, not to mention 20 craft and classic drafts, including Pabst Blue Ribbon, which is just $1 all day, every day.

Old-time walldogs specialized in painting ads for tobacco, coffee, and cola on the sides of barns and other buildings. Today's Walldogs (thewalldogs.com) paint murals that promote civic pride. Their annual meets keep this art form alive and rejuvenate towns like Kewanee. During a walk of its 15 murals (kewaneewalldogs.com

A tractor ride passes Good's Furniture

has a downloadable map), stop by the **Country Morning Coffee Café** (205 W. 1st St., 309-540-5064, countrymorningcoffee.com), in an 1850s brick house, for a cup of java, a pastry or panini, and a hand-labeled bag (or two) of freshly roasted beans.

Good's Furniture (200 Main St. N., 309-852-5656, www.goodsfurniture.com), in business since 1895, has so much more than just a vast array of home furnishings. There's the Wine Cellar Restaurant, with its homemade soups, sandwiches, salads, breads, and pastries (carrot cake is a specialty) and its thoughtful wine and beer lists (try the Prairie Chicken Ale). There's also an indoor marketplace, with boutique-like displays showcasing a well-edited selection of clothing, jewelry, accessories, foodstuffs, and house wares. There's even an elegantly appointed B&B. It's all inside 12 historic, multilevel, downtown buildings—complete with a skywalk—just a block from the train station. Needless to say, people come from miles around!

★ *Winner Best for Geocaching:* Helena, MT

When it comes to treasure hunts, Helena is no novice. In July of 1864, four miners, down on their luck, gave things here one last chance—and struck it rich. The so-called Last Chance Gulch grew almost overnight, producing an estimated (in today's dollars) $3.6 billion in gold over 20 years. Nearly 150 years later, Helena's main street is still called Last Chance Gulch, but GPS units have replaced sluice boxes, and hidden caches and geocachers have replaced hidden veins of gold and prospectors.

In the heart of the Rocky Mountains, halfway between Yellowstone and Glacier national parks, Montana's capital of 30,000 residents has evolved into the region's geocaching leader. At the core of this is the GeoTour, which highlights the best of Helena and takes cachers to 38 destinations in and around town.

The Base Camp, a local outdoors store, rents GPS units with caches pre-loaded. Townsfolk freely provide tips and guidance. And everyone enjoys going after the coveted GeoCoin prize, locally crafted with an imprint of the Guardian of the Gulch, Helena's iconic fire tower. Although you don't have to geocache to enjoy the area's many historical, cultural, and natural sights, it is a great way to take everything in—so why not give it a try?

A bike and hiking trail above Helena

> *I've had a great time playing in my hometown with the Helena GeoTour. . . . I never expected to have so much fun learning, and I have converted several of my family members into geocachers. . .*
> -lkougl2011

Things to See and Do

Geocache

Helena is a great destination for hikers, trail runners, and mountain bikers (it's been designated a Bronze Level Ride Center by the International Mountain Bicycling Association). Many of the 70+ miles of area trails are accessible directly from downtown or via free shuttles. There's also access to the iconic Continental Divide Trail. And myriad bike lanes make the in-town cycling scene vibrant, too. **Bike Helena** (www.bikehelena.com) is a great resource for trail maps, rental listings, safety tips, and more.

Helena Tourism Alliance's Walking Tour App (105 Reeder's Alley, 800-743-5362, www.helenamt.com) guides you to in-town attractions and to trails. **Last Chance Tours** (406-442-1023, www.lctours.com) offers guided Segway

jaunts or train-like trolley tours that take in the Old Fire Tower, the Cathedral of St. Helena, and other historical sites. Outside town, glide through wilderness on a two-hour **Gates of the Mountains** (406-458-5241, www.gatesofthemountains.com) Missouri River cruise. Or bump along to a cabin in the woods for a prime rib dinner and some cowboy music with **Last Chance Wagon Ride Dinners** (406-442-2884, www.lastchanceranch.biz).

Exhibits at the **Montana Historical Society** (225 N. Roberts, 406-444-2694, www.montanahistoricalsociety.org) pull from 50,000 artifacts to showcase such things as the landscape during the time of Lewis & Clark; domestic life in Montana over the centuries; the paintings of Charles M. Russell, America's "cowboy artist;" and the rare white bison. The society also offers guided tours of the capitol and the original Queen Anne–style Governor's Mansion.

★ *Winner Most Beautiful:* Jefferson City, MO

Governor's Mansion and Gardens

Nearly 200 years ago, Lohman's Landing—a sleepy but centrally located and picturesque steamboat stop—was chosen as the site for a new state capital. The majesty of the Missouri River and its tree-lined bluffs are still captivating, but today's Jefferson City also has a vibrant culture identity, well-preserved historical districts, and stately landmarks.

The energy and optimism of the pioneer spirit are all palpable in downtown's restaurants, boutiques, and other entrepreneurial endeavors. Hanging baskets overflow with flowers. Patterned, tree-lined sidewalks invite strolling and window shopping. Benches and sidewalk cafes encourage lingering—to chat with locals or sit quietly and enjoy Missouri River breezes.

The Ash Street entertainment district to the east has the town's first microbrewery. To the south, the Old Munichburg district maintains its German heritage. Connecting these and other neighborhoods are walking and biking trails that take you through natural settings. Some even lead to the scenic Katy Trail, which follows a 200-mile-long abandoned stretch of the Missouri-Kansas-Texas rail line. Historical charm, pioneer spirit, and great scenery? What a beautiful combination.

> *We have one of the loveliest main streets (High Street) ever! Our thriving downtown has alfresco dining, hanging pots of flowers, shade trees with benches for resting, free parking, and so many other wonderful qualities! I'm proud to live here. . . . -JCLovers*

Things to See and Do

The **Missouri State Capitol** (201 W. Capitol Ave., 573-751-2854, mostateparks.com) was modeled after the U.S. Capitol and built in 1917 of locally quarried marble. A tour of its grounds, interior, and history museum is a great way to learn about both Missouri and Jefferson City. The **Missouri State Penitentiary Museum** (100 E. High St., 573-632-2820) lends insight into a famous (at times, infamous) prison that was built in 1836 and decommissioned in 2004.

Missouri State Capitol

The **Jefferson City Convention & Visitors Bureau** (100 E. High St., 800-769-4183, www.visitjeffersoncity.com) has a free, downloadable Historic Tours brochure that really showcases civic history and beauty. Sights include the capitol; the **Governor's Mansion and Gardens** (100 Madison St., 573-751-4141, missourimansion.org); and the **Jefferson Landing Historic Site** (100 Jefferson St., 573-751-2854, mostateparks.com).

Don't miss the two most delicious local landmarks: the ice cream shop at **Central Dairy** (610 Madison St., 573-635-6148, www.centraldairy.biz), in business since 1932, and **Whaley's East End Drug Store** (630 E. High St., 573-636-3733, www.whaleysrx.com), where a soda fountain serves traditional cherry cokes.

★ *Winner Most Patriotic:* Gallup, NM

John Wayne visited Gallup while filming. Bob Dylan claimed to be from here. Nat King Cole and John Mayer sang about it in "Route 66." The Indian Capital of the United States, so-called because of its many Navajo and Zuni residents, is a unique cultural hub; a strong, patriotic community; and an interesting place to live and to visit.

Gallupians stand together to protect what's right—referred to as being "Gallup Strong." From the Spanish American War to the wars in Iraq and Afghanistan, Gallupians have answered the call to duty in all branches of the armed forces. Among the community's veterans are Korean War Medal of Honor recipient, Hiroshi "Hershey" Miyamura and World War II's Navajo Code Talkers, Bataan Death March survivors, and Purple Heart Battalion members.

Folks here honor those who've served the country with monuments and parades and by enjoying every day to its fullest and never taking freedom for granted. You can join them in fully living each day, perhaps at the Saturday Flea Market or events like July's Wild Thing Bull Riding Championships or August's Inter-Tribal Indian Ceremonial Gathering. You can also cherish freedom while hiking or mountain biking in nearby Red Rock State Park. All this is part of Gallup—and part of what makes it strong.

Gallup parades celebrate Native American heritage and veterans alike

> *I'm a WWII veteran and member of the Gallup Veterans Helping Veterans. I've lived in many places, and, believe me, Gallup is the Most Patriotic Small Town in America. . . . I'm thankful to Gallup for all they do for veterans . . . . -strongbullnm1*

Things to See and Do

A statue at the Gallup Cultural Center honors WWII Code Talkers

A visit to the **Gallup Cultural Center** (201 E. Hwy. 66, 505-863-4131, www.southwestindian.com) is a great introduction to Zuni and Navajo culture—and to finding authentic Native American wares if you shop the trading posts along Route 66 (aka Main Street). Check out the bronze Code Talkers statue; view basketry, pottery, textiles, jewelry, kachina dolls, sand paintings, and other works; and take an "audio tour" of traditional songs and stories.

El Rancho Hotel (1000 E. Hwy. 66, 505-863-9311, route66hotels.org) honors classic American road travel and classic Hollywood Westerns. The lobby has photos of John Wayne and other movie stars who visited while filming nearby, and the restaurant serves celebrity-themed dishes like the Ronald Regan (a burger with a side of jellybeans). The acclaimed 49er Lounge, into which Errol Flynn once rode a horse, has notable selections of tequila and Mexican and New Mexican beer.

Another memorabilia-filled hangout is **Sammy C.'s Rockin' Sports Pub & Grille** (107 W. Coal Ave., 505-863-2220, www.sammycsgallup.com). Here, locals and visitors alike catch games, matches, races—or all three—over a cold one or two.

Most Fun: Corning, NY	Best for Food: San Mateo, CA	Friendliest: Kewanee, IL	Best for Geocaching: Helena, MT	Most Beautiful: Jefferson City, MO	Most Patriotic: Gallup, NM
Finalists:	**Finalists:**	**Finalists:**	**Finalists:**	**Finalists:**	**Finalists:**
Jim Thorpe, PA	Charlottesville, VA	Bradenton, FL	Merritt Island, FL	Punta Gorda, FL	Jonesborough, TN
Geneva-on-the-Lake, OH	Galesburg, IL	Macon, GA	Peachtree City, GA	Quincy, IL	Enterprise, AL
Lombard, IL	Roseville, MN	Murray, KY	West Bend, WI	Arvada, CO	Fairborn, OH
Nocona, TX	Walla Walla, WA	Keokuk, IA	Manhattan, KS	Cloudcroft, NM	Mandan, ND

6 Great Drives from Best of the Road®

Here are some road trips we thought you'd like. For more trips—and expanded versions of these—visit bestoftheroad.com/roadtrip. And look for the Rand McNally Trip Planning Tool, which lets you select road trips from our collection or map out your own with the attractions that interest you most. You can also print trips out, e-mail them, or take them with you on the Rand McNally mobile app.

High Tech to Steinbeck via Monterey Bay

The Golden State has always attracted explorers, adventures, and fortune-seekers. In native-son John Steinbeck's day, it beckoned Dustbowl migrants. Today it draws technology gurus. This trip takes you from San Jose, Silicon Valley's high-tech hub, along the Pacific Coast through Santa Cruz, Monterey (Steinbeck stomping grounds), Carmel, and inland again to Salinas—the author's hometown amid the so-called Salad Bowl of the World.

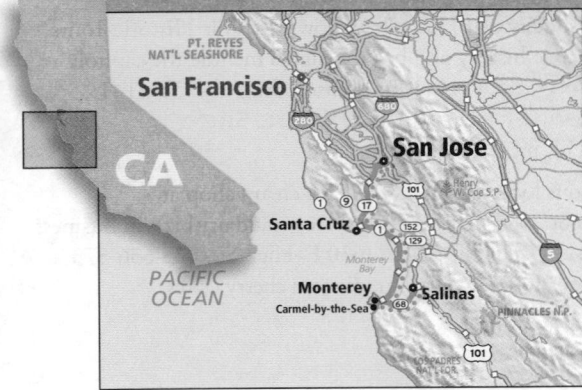

California see p. 34

Tech Museum Of Innovation
201 S. Market St., San Jose, (408) 294-8324, www.thetech.org
Immersive displays here show how technology affects and benefits our lives. Exhibits highlight robotics, health and biotech, energy, earth sciences, and space technology. There's also an IMAX theater, a café, and a gift shop with "only in Silicon Valley" items. TRAVEL TIP: **This museum pairs nicely with the nearby** San Jose Museum of Art **(110 S. Market St., 408-271-6840, www.sjmusart.org).**

Santa Cruz Beach Boardwalk
400 Beach St., Santa Cruz, (831) 423-5590, www.beachboardwalk.com
Among the 30-odd rides at California's only seaside amusement park are the 1911 Looff Carousel, the 1924 Giant Dipper coaster, and many state-of-the-art attractions. There's also bowling, laser tag, miniature golf, an arcade, shops, and restaurants.

Monterey Bay Aquarium
886 Cannery Row, Monterey, (831) 648-4800, www.montereybayaquarium.org
This Cannery Row aquarium is organized by area marine environments—a concept envisioned by marine biologist Edward F. Ricketts, a friend of John Steinbeck's and the inspiration for "Doc" in the 1945 novel, *Cannery Row*. Highlights of the 11 exhibits include the enormous Open Sea and Kelp Forest tanks.

Carmel Walks
1 Ocean Ave., Carmel (831) 642-2700, carmelwalks.com
Carmel is a sight in its own right, thanks to its storybook buildings; unique shops, wine-tasting rooms, and restaurants; and beautiful beaches. A two-hour guided tour with Carmel Walks is a great way to take it all in.

National Steinbeck Center
1 Main St., Salinas, (831) 775-4721, www.steinbeck.org
John Steinbeck once crossed the country in a camper with his dog, as documented in his 1962 book, *Travels with Charley*—just one more reason to love him. He was born in Salinas, educated at Stanford, and lived for a time in Pacific Grove. Learn all about his life and work (and even see his camper!) here. TRAVEL TIP: **Make lunch reservations at the** Steinbeck House **(132 Central Ave., 831-424-2735, www.steinbeckhouse.com), a restaurant in the writer's childhood home.**

Earth and Sky in Southern New Mexico

In southern New Mexico, things seem to center on either the earth or the sky. This trip covers both in equal measure. It takes you from Las Cruces—home to New Mexico State University (NMSU) and its Chile Pepper Institute—through White Sands and Alamogordo, with their glistening dunes and hard rocket science, to Roswell and its UFO "incident" and less-than-hard extraterrestrial science.

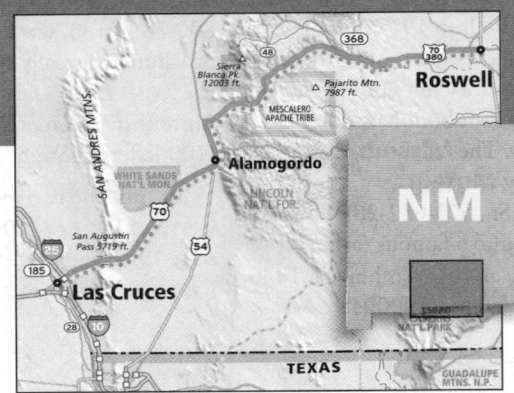

New Mexico see p. 139

NMSU Chile Pepper Institute
Gerald Thomas Hall, 945 College Ave., Las Cruces, (575) 646-3661, www.chilepepperinstitute.org
Learn about New Mexico's hottest crop; buy seeds, condiments, and cookbooks; and tour the gardens, with more than 200 varieties. By the end of your visit, you'll know your greens and jalapeños from your reds and cayennes.

White Sands Missile Range Museum
U.S. Hwy. 70, White Sands, (575) 647-1116, www.wsmr-history.org
This region was the site of the world's first atomic explosion and where scientists tested the German V-2 and other rockets. The Missile Park at this museum has more than 50 projectiles with plaques about each. Indoor exhibits highlight rocket and missile science. TRAVEL TIP: **To enter, stop at the visitors center near the gate and show your vehicle registration, driver's license, and proof of auto insurance.**

White Sands National Monument
19955 Hwy. 70 W., Alamogordo, (575) 479-6124, www.nps.gov/whsa.
Here, wave-like dunes of snow-white sand have engulfed 275 square miles of desert. You can explore them on foot, by car, or by sled! Pick up a plastic saucer (you *are* near Roswell, after all) and some tips at the visitors center. TRAVEL TIP: **Park roads close during missile tests at nearby White Sands Missile Range; check ahead.**

New Mexico Museum Of Space History
3198 State Rte. 2001, Alamogordo, (575) 437-2840, www.nmspacemuseum.org
Moon rocks, missiles, rockets, and "tours" of the night sky are all part of this ultra-modern, hillside museum and planetarium complex.

International UFO Museum
114 N. Main St., Roswell, (575) 625-9495, www.roswellufomuseum.com
Did a UFO really crash near Roswell in July 1947? Find out at this museum, founded in 1991 by two participants in the "Roswell incident." Through photographs, witness statements, and other items, you'll learn about reported extraterrestrials sightings—and purported government cover-ups of them.

Kentucky Bluegrass Country

Kentucky was not only the birthplace of bourbon, but also of both Abraham Lincoln and his wife, Mary Todd. This trip—from Hodgenville to Bardstown, Lexington, and Frankfort—is bookended with stops at both birth sites as well as at distilleries new and old. In the middle? Rolling green pastures dotted with grazing thoroughbreds. Nothing captures this aspect of Bluegrass Country quite like a visit to the Kentucky Horse Park.

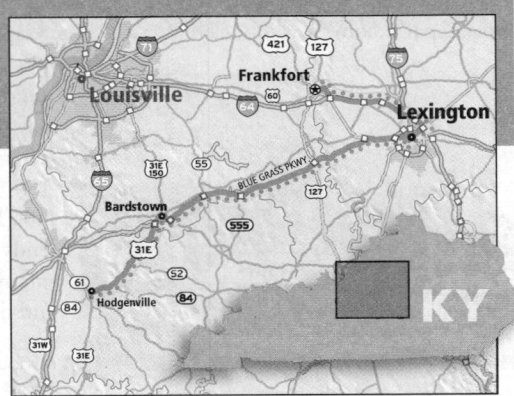

Kentucky see p. 87

Abraham Lincoln Birthplace
2995 Lincoln Farm Rd., Hodgenville, (270) 358-3137, www.nps.gov/abli
In 1809, Abraham Lincoln was born at Sinking Spring Farm. In 1811, the family moved 10 miles away to Knob Creek Farm. Today, both properties are part of this national historic site. To reach the granite memorial, climb the 56 steps, one for every year of Lincoln's life, or follow a boardwalk. A reproduction cabin marks where Lincoln was born. Knob Creek (7120 Bardstown Rd.) also has a reproduction cabin. TRAVEL TIP: **In town is Kentucky's official** Lincoln Museum **(66 Lincoln Sq., 270-358-3163, lincolnmuseum-ky.org).**

Heaven Hill Distilleries
1311 Gilkey Run Rd., Bardstown, (502) 337-1000, www.bourbonheritagecenter.com
Founded in 1934, this distillery is a "newcomer" compared with some operations. Still, it's the country's seventh-largest supplier of distilled spirits and the largest that's still family owned. Its Bourbon Heritage Center offers tours (fee, reservations a good idea) with tastings. TRAVEL TIP: **For more bourbon back story, visit the** Oscar Getz Museum of Whiskey **(114 N. 5th St., 502-348-2999, www.whiskeymuseum.com).**

Kentucky Horse Park & Training Grounds
4089 Iron Works Pkwy., Lexington, (859) 254-0253, www.kyhorsepark.com
Plan to spend at least a day at this enormous complex of show rings, barns, and other venues. Highlights include the International Museum of the Horse; the American Saddlebred Museum; horse-drawn carriage tours; and, of course, horseback riding!

Mary Todd Lincoln House
578 W. Main St., Lexington, (859) 233-9999, www.mtlhouse.org
Docents lead hour-long tours through this brick, 14-room, late-Georgian house. Mary's birthplace (in 1818) and home until she was 16 is filled with period furniture and personal items from both the Todd and Lincoln families.

Buffalo Trace Distillery
113 Great Buffalo Trace, Frankfort, (502) 696-5926, www.buffalotracedistillery.com
Buffalo Trace has been a successful distillery for more than two centuries! Free hour-long Trace Tours (no reservations needed) include tastings.

For more trips visit **bestoftheroad.com/roadtrip**

Ohio's Hocking Hills

By the time you hit Logan, an hour southeast of Columbus, Route 33 begins to wind up and down along S-curves through the Hocking Hills—a unique wooded landscape filled with gorges, caves, and waterfalls. In Logan and Nelsonville, you'll also find small town Americana. The same is true of Lancaster. To reach it from Nelsonville, consider looping back along Route 56, a stretch so curvaceous that Ford Motor Company has used it as a test road.

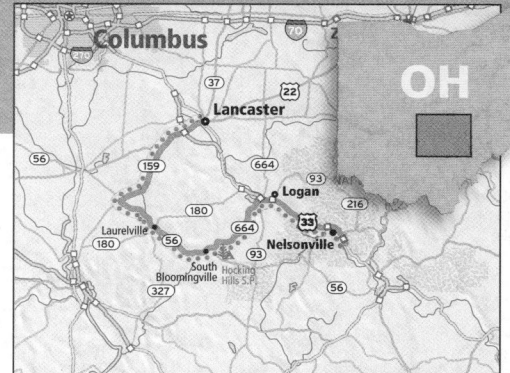

Ohio see p. 164

Hocking Hills State Park
19852 State Rte. 664 S., Logan, (740) 385-6842, parks.ohiodnr.gov/hockinghills
Here, you'll find hemlock shaded hollows, sandstone recesses, spellbinding waterfalls, and over 26 miles of trails. On the naturalist-led tours, you'll learn about the "magic tree," why Canadian hemlocks thrive here, and how the caves were formed.

Columbus Washboard Factory
14 Gallagher Ave., Logan, (740) 380-3828, www.columbuswashboard.com
Washboards do a great job removing stains from cuffs and collars. They're also rustically decorative and add rhythmic zing to bluegrass music. Here you can see them assembled by hand (in just 45 seconds) and see a 24-foot washboard, the world's largest.
TRAVEL TIP: while in Logan, visit the quirky Pencil Sharpener Museum (13178 State Rte. 664, 740-385-9706, www.explorehockinghills.com), just outside the Hocking Hills Regional Welcome Center.

Starbrick Gallery
21 W. Columbus St., Nelsonville, (740) 753-1011, www.starbrick.com
Nelsonville's main square is lined with restored Victorians. Several house galleries like the Starbrick, named after elegant paving stones once made in town. Look for pottery, handcrafted jewelry, and clothing as well as works in glass, wood, and paper.
TRAVEL TIP: Nearby is the outlet store for Rocky Boots (45 E. Canal St., 740-753-3130, www.rockyboots.com)– making footwear since 1932.

Ohio Glass Museum
124 W. Main St., Lancaster, (740) 687-0101, www.ohioglassmuseum.org
The decorative glassware exhibits and glass-blowing demonstrations here honor one of Lancaster's manufacturing traditions.

The Sherman House
137 E. Main St., Lancaster, (740) 687-5891, www.shermanhouse.org
Civil War General William Tecumseh Sherman was born in this house. The original 1811 section and an 1816 addition contain two parlors, a study, a kitchen/dining area, and bedrooms filled with family memorabilia and period furnishings. A brick 1870s addition has Civil War exhibits.

Florida's Cultural West Coast

It's more than just sun, sand, and Gulf waters that sparkle in western Florida. There are also many shining cultural, art, and historical attractions. Among the icons you'll encounter on this journey from Fort Myers to Sarasota, Bradenton, and St. Petersburg are Thomas Edison, Henry Ford, John Ringling, Salvador Dali, and Dale Chihuly. You'll also meet Snooty, the state's oldest manatee born in captivity.

Florida see p. 54

Edison and Ford Winter Estates
2350 McGregor Blvd., Fort Myers, (239) 334-7419, www.edisonfordwinterestates.org
Edison wintered at Seminole Lodge from 1886 until his death in 1931. His good friend, Henry Ford, bought the neighboring property—The Mangoes—in 1915. Here you can tour the estates, remarkable gardens, and a memorabilia-filled museum.

Circus Museum At The Ringling
5401 Bay Shore Rd., Sarasota, (941) 359-5700, www.ringling.org
Step right up to see circus costumes, props, banners, and posters at this museum on the estate of John and Mable Ringling. Check out the lavish railcar the couple used when traveling with the family business. Don't miss the 3,800-square-foot circus model.
TRAVEL TIP: The Ringling complex also includes John and Mable's mansion, Ca d'Zan, and the Museum of Art, housing their enormous collection.

South Florida Museum, Aquarium & Planetarium
201 10th St. W., Bradenton, (941) 746-4131, www.southfloridamuseum.org
Museum exhibits showcase prehistoric animal skeletons; Native American art; and colonial artifacts and Americana. At the 60,000-gallon Parker Aquarium, you'll learn about Florida's unique sea creatures and meet the beloved Snooty, the state's oldest captivity-born manatee. The Bishop Planetarium has astronomy and laser-light shows.

Dali Museum
1 Dali Blvd., St. Petersburg, (727) 823-3767, thedali.org
Who knew that South Florida had the world's most comprehensive collection of the Spanish surrealist master's oils, watercolors, drawings, graphics, photographs, sculptures, and objects d'art? Exhibits are organized to help you understand the artist and his work.

Chihuly Collection
400 Beach Dr. N.E., St. Petersburg, (727) 896-4527, www.moreanartscenter.org
What do Native American baskets, marine life, and Japanese flower arrangements have in common? They've all influenced Dale Chihuly's colorful, textural, blown-glass sculptures.

Connecticut River and Coast Tour

Absorb history on this tour down the Connecticut River and along the coast. You'll learn about a woman named Arnold who was thankful and a man named Hale who had only one regret. You'll discover the importance of the river and the coastal ports—from pre-colonial days through the Revolutionary War and beyond. You'll also experience the artistic legacy of later generations who were inspired by the area's landscapes—both wooded and watery.

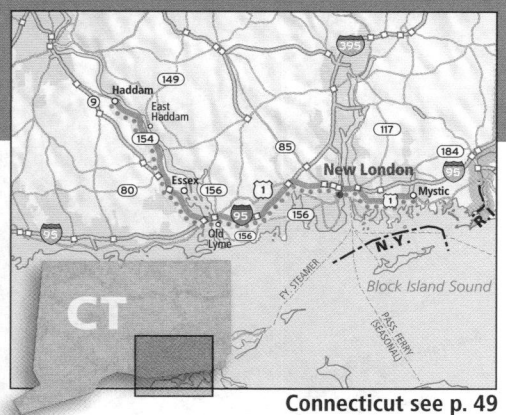

Connecticut see p. 49

Thankful Arnold House
14 Hayden Hill Rd., Haddam, (860) 345-2400, www.haddamhistory.org
Early New Englanders sometimes named their children for virtues. That's no doubt how Thankful Arnold (nee Clark) got her unusual moniker. On tours of this restored home, you'll learn about life in the late 18th and early 19th centuries as well as about the lives of Thankful, her husband, and their 12 children.

Nathan Hale School House
29 Main St., Rte. 149, East Haddam, (860) 873-3399, www.connecticutsar.org
In 1773, Nathan Hale spent five months teaching at this one-room schoolhouse (circa 1750). When the Revolution began, Hale joined the Continental Army. In 1776, the British executed him for spying in New York City. His last words were reportedly, "I only regret that I have but one life to live for my country."
TRAVEL TIP: To learn about another famous resident, visit Gillette Castle (67 River Rd., 860-526-2336, www.ct.gov/deep), an eccentric mansion built in 1919 by an actor noted for his Sherlock Holmes portrayals.

Connecticut River Museum
67 Main St., Essex, (860) 767-8269, www.ctrivermuseum.org
The exhibits in this 1878 steamboat-dock warehouse showcase life along the river. Before or after your visit, book a sail aboard the Mary E, a 75-foot schooner built in 1906. TRAVEL TIP: Ask about the museum tours that include a sail, a walk through Essex, or lunch at the historic Griswold Inn.

Florence Griswold Museum
96 Lyme St., Old Lyme, (860) 434-5542, www.flogris.org
Florence Griswold was the patron of many early 20th-century American landscape painters, some of whom boarded at her late-Georgian mansion and established one of the country's first Impressionist art colonies. Her home is now an art museum.

Mystic Seaport
75 Greenmanville Ave., Mystic, (860) 572-0711, www.mysticseaport.org
This maritime museum lets you experience 19th-century seafaring life in a recreated village. There's also a preservation shipyard, where craftsmen maintain reproduction tall ships.

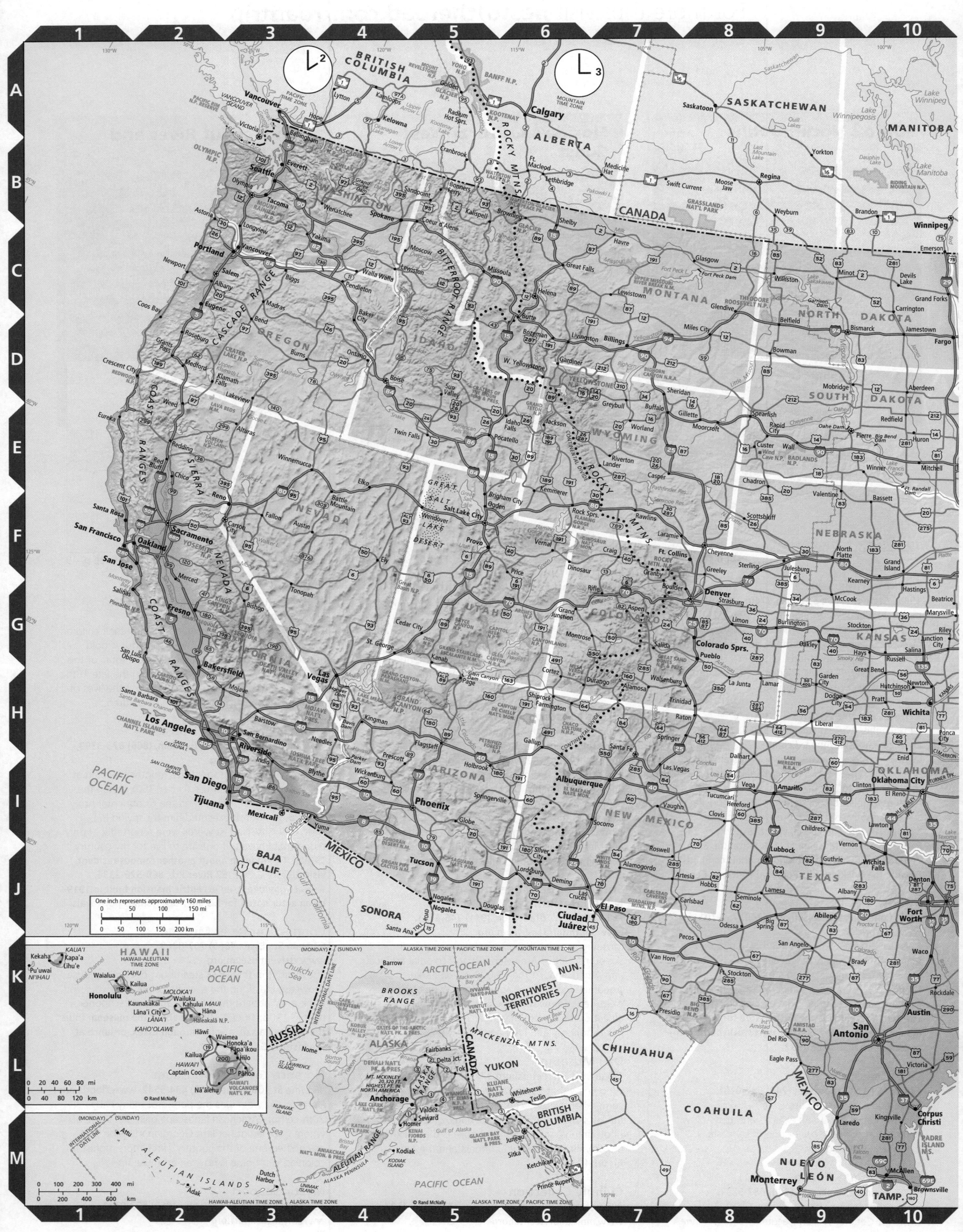

Selected places of interest

- Acadia National Park, C-20
- Arches National Park, G-6
- Badlands National Park, E-9
- Big Bend National Park, L-8
- Biscayne National Park, M-18
- Bryce Canyon National Park, G-5

- Canyonlands National Park, G-6
- Capitol Reef National Park, G-5
- Carlsbad Caverns National Park, J-7
- Channel Islands National Park, H-1
- Congaree National Park, I-17
- Crater Lake National Park, D-2

- Cuyahoga Valley National Park, F-16
- Death Valley National Park, G-3
- Denali National Park, L-4
- Dry Tortugas National Park, M-17
- Everglades National Park, M-17
- Glacier Bay National Park, M-5

- Glen Canyon National Recreation Area, G-5
- Grand Canyon National Park, H-4
- Grand Teton National Park, E-6
- Great Sand Dunes Nat'l Park & Pres., H-7
- Great Smoky Mountains Nat'l Park, H-15
- Guadalupe Mountains National Park, J-7

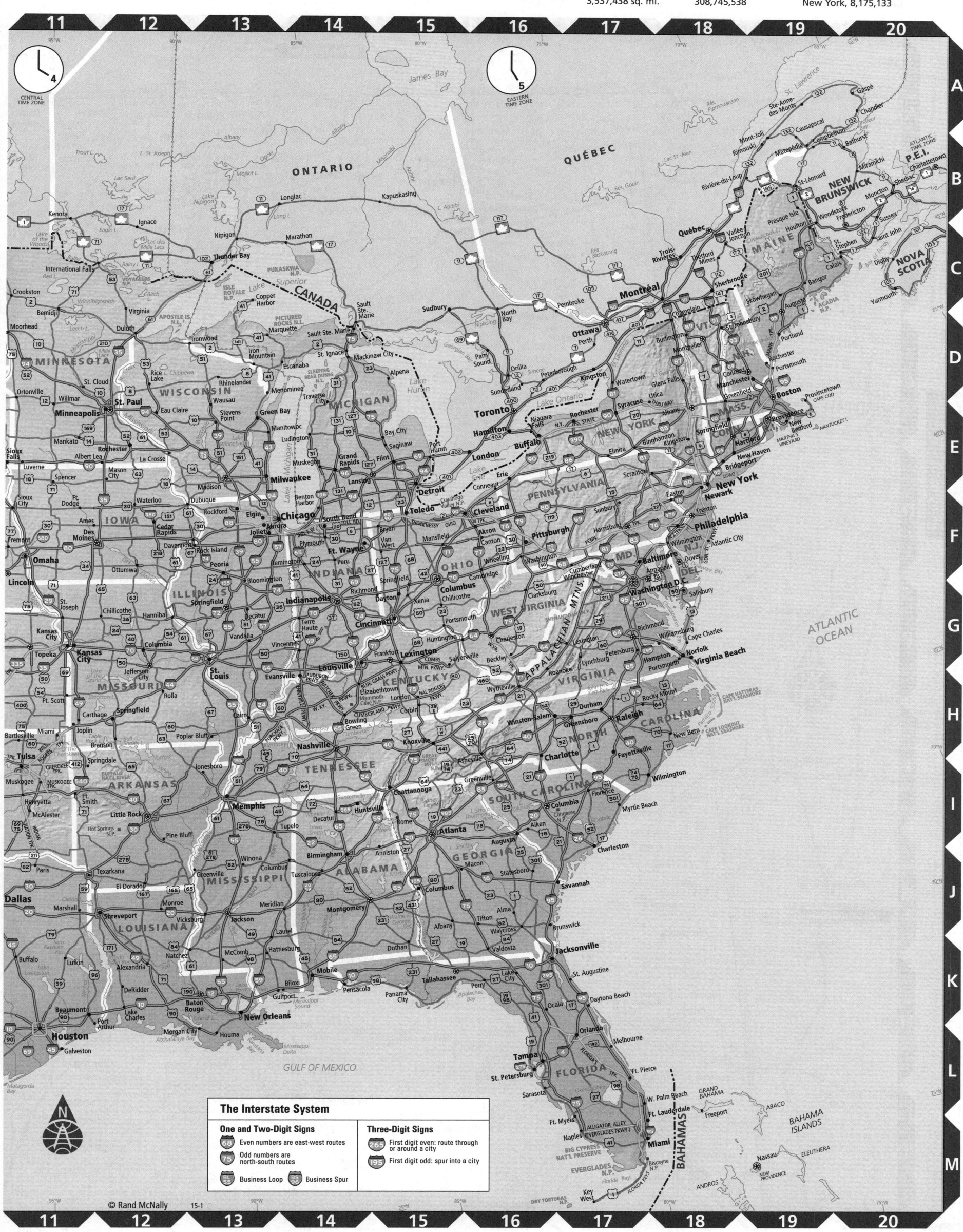

The Interstate System

One and Two-Digit Signs
- 68 — Even numbers are east-west routes
- 75 — Odd numbers are north-south routes
- Business Loop
- Business Spur

Three-Digit Signs
- 265 — First digit even: route through or around a city
- 195 — First digit odd: spur into a city

© Rand McNally   15-1

- Haleakalā National Park, K-2
- Hawai'i Volcanoes National Park, L-3
- Hot Springs National Park, I-12
- Isle Royale National Park, C-13
- Kings Canyon National Park, G-2
- Lake Mead National Recreation Area, H-4
- Lassen Volcanic National Park, E-2
- Mammoth Cave National Park, H-14
- Mesa Verde National Park, H-6
- Mount Rainier National Park, B-3
- North Cascades National Park, B-4
- Olympic National Park, B-3
- Petrified Forest National Park, I-5
- Redwood National Park, D-1
- Rocky Mountain National Park, F-7
- Sequoia National Park, G-2
- Shenandoah National Park, G-17
- Theodore Roosevelt National Park, D-8
- Voyageurs National Park, C-12
- Waterton-Glacier Int'l Peace Park, B-5
- Wind Cave National Park, E-8
- Yellowstone National Park, D-6
- Yosemite National Park, F-2
- Zion National Park, G-5

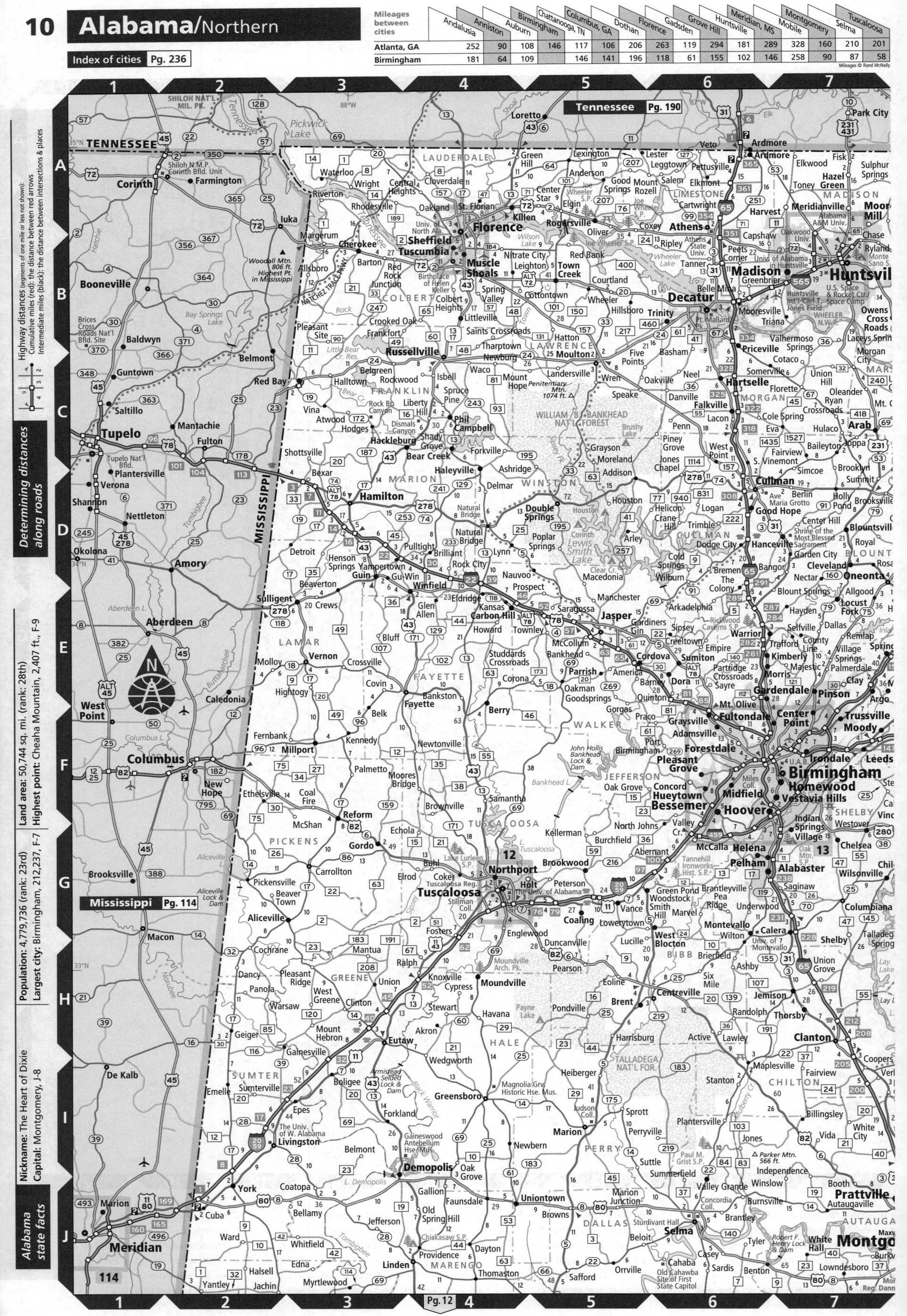

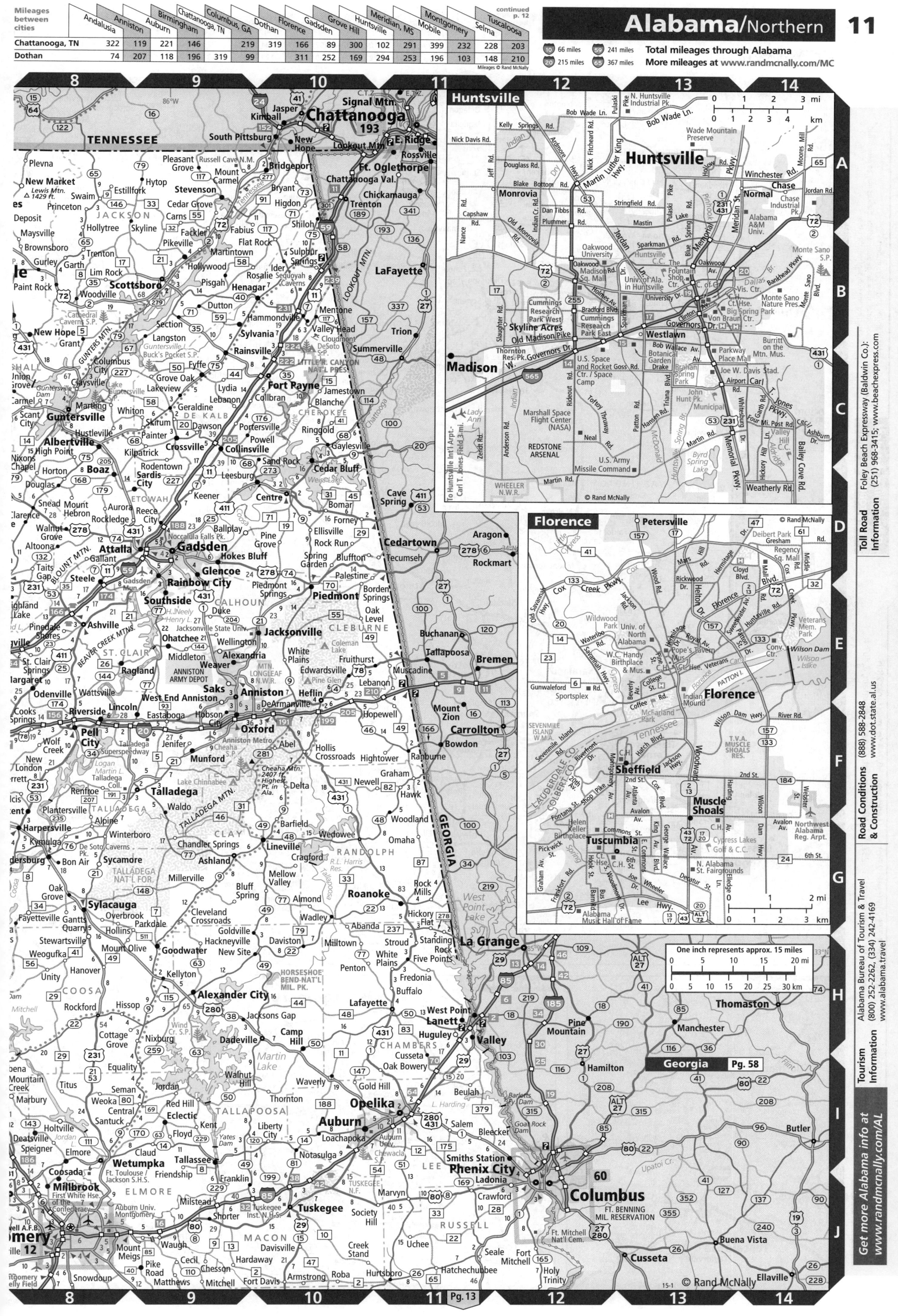

Mileages between cities	Andalusia	Anniston	Auburn	Birmingham	Chattanooga, TN	Columbus, GA	Dothan	Florence	Gadsden	Grove Hill	Huntsville	Meridian, MS	Mobile	Montgomery	Selma	Tuscaloosa
Chattanooga, TN	322	119	221	146		219	319	166	89	300	102	291	399	232	228	203
Dothan	74	207	118	196	319	99		311	252	169	294	253	196	103	148	210

Mileages © Rand McNally

continued p. 12

Total mileages through Alabama
More mileages at www.randmcnally.com/MC

Index of cities Pg. 236

Mileages between cities	Andalusia	Anniston	Auburn	Birmingham	Chattanooga, TN	Columbus, GA	Dothan	Florence	Gadsden	Grove Hill	Huntsville	Meridian, MS	Mobile	Montgomery	Selma	Tuscaloosa
Huntsville	279	104	210	102	102	243	294	64	72	254		244	356	189	188	155
Mobile	123	280	222	258	399	256	196	376	313	82	356	133		168	159	203

Mileages © Rand McNally

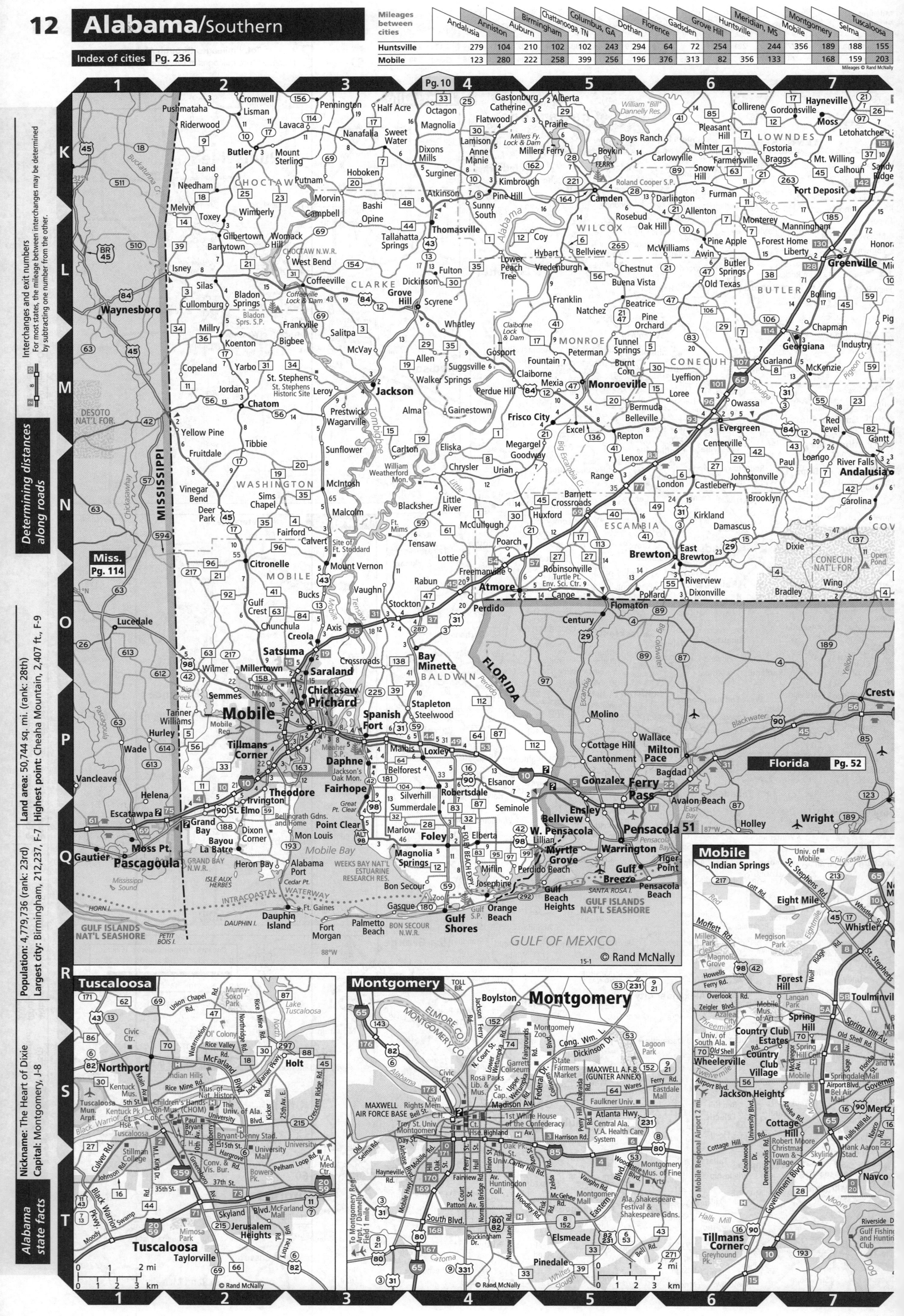

© Rand McNally

Alabama state facts

Nickname: The Heart of Dixie
Capital: Montgomery, J-8

Population: 4,779,736 (rank: 23rd)
Largest city: Birmingham, 212,237, F-7

Land area: 50,744 sq. mi. (rank: 28th)
Highest point: Cheaha Mountain, 2,407 ft., F-9

Determining distances along roads

Interchanges and exit numbers
For most states, the mileage between interchanges may be determined by subtracting one number from the other.

Tuscaloosa

Montgomery

Mobile

Mileages between cities	Andalusia	Anniston	Auburn	Birmingham	Chattanooga, TN	Columbus, GA	Dothan	Florence	Gadsden	Grove Hill	Huntsville	Meridian, MS	Mobile	Montgomery	Selma	Tuscaloosa
Montgomery	91	110	54	90	232	87	103	205	148	134	189	153	168		50	104
Tuscaloosa	194	118	159	58	203	192	210	123	118	121	155	93	203	104	75	

Mileages © Rand McNally

10 66 miles · 59 241 miles · 20 215 miles · 65 367 miles

Total mileages through Alabama
More mileages at www.randmcnally.com/MC

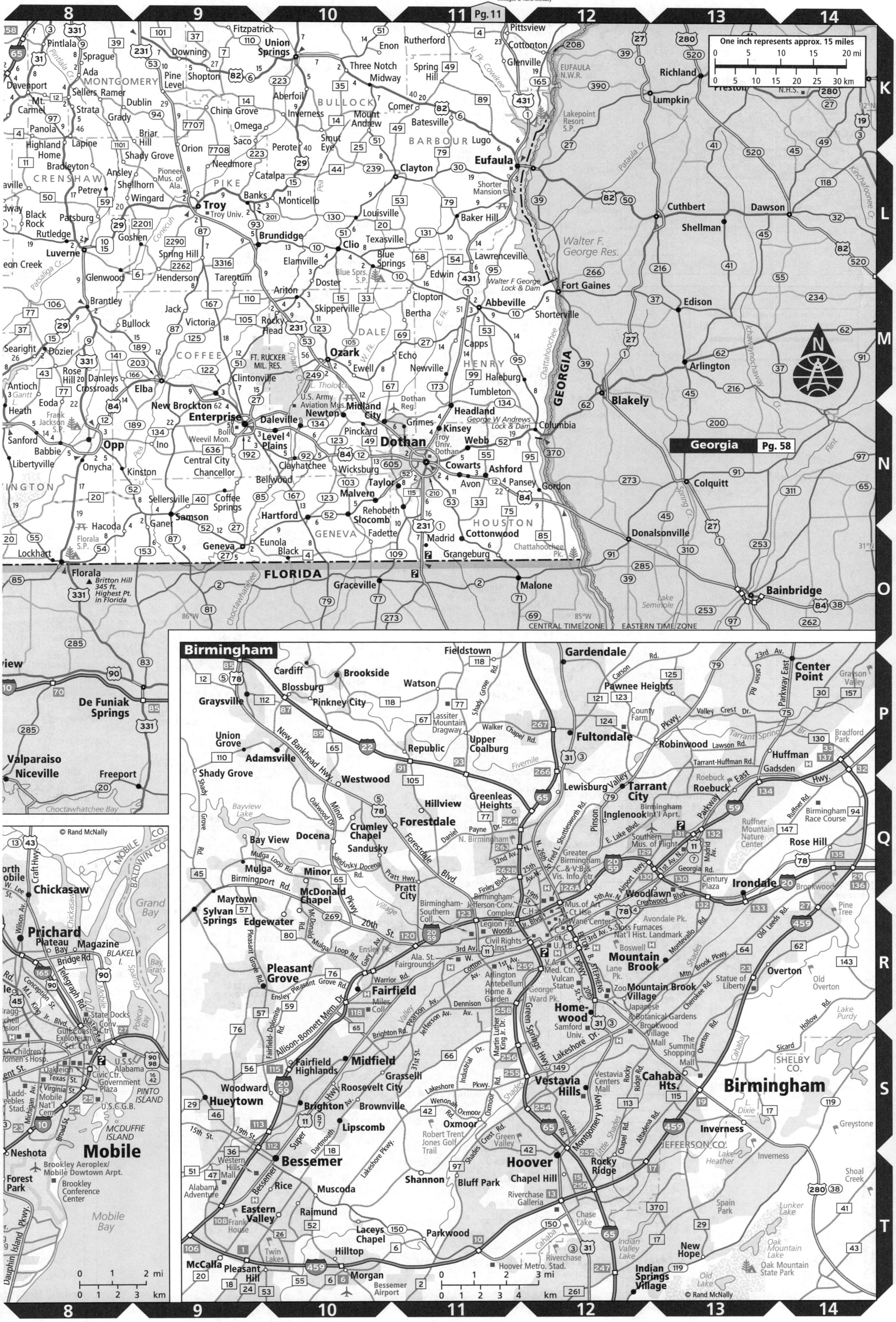

Pg. 11
One inch represents approx. 15 miles
GEORGIA
FLORIDA
Georgia Pg. 58
Birmingham
Mobile
CENTRAL TIME ZONE
EASTERN TIME ZONE
© Rand McNally

Toll Road Information Foley Beach Expressway (Baldwin Co.): (251) 968-3415; www.beachexpress.com

Road Conditions & Construction (888) 588-2848 www.dot.state.al.us

Tourism Information Alabama Bureau of Tourism & Travel (800) 252-2262, (334) 242-4169 www.alabama.travel

Get more Alabama info at www.randmcnally.com/AL

Index of cities Pg. 236

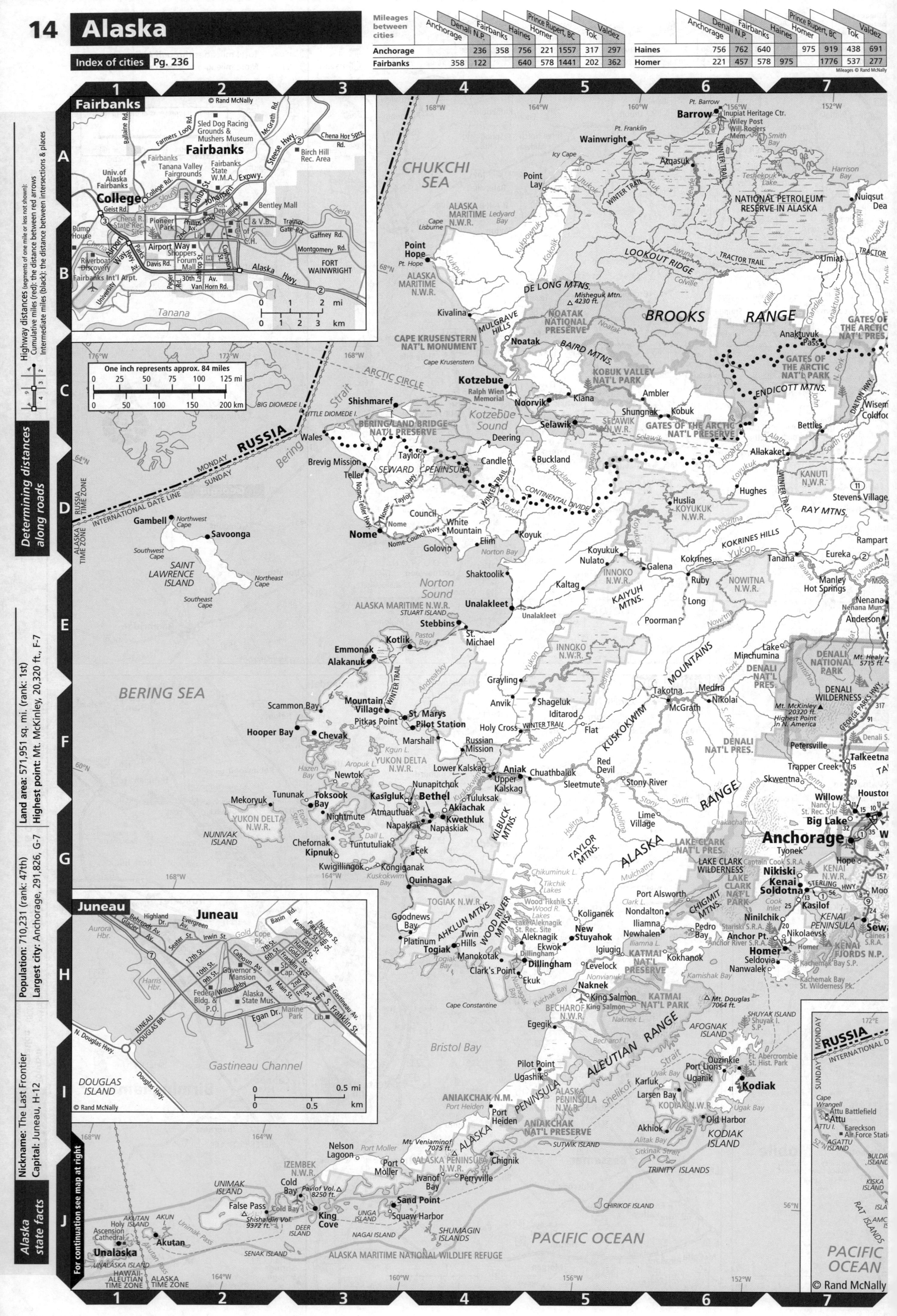

Mileages between cities	Anchorage	Denali N.P.	Fairbanks	Haines	Homer	Prince Rupert, BC	Tok	Valdez
Anchorage		236	358	756	221	1557	317	297
Fairbanks	358	122		640	578	1441	202	362
Haines	756	762	640		975	919	438	691
Homer	221	457	578	975		1776	537	277

© Rand McNally

Fairbanks

Juneau

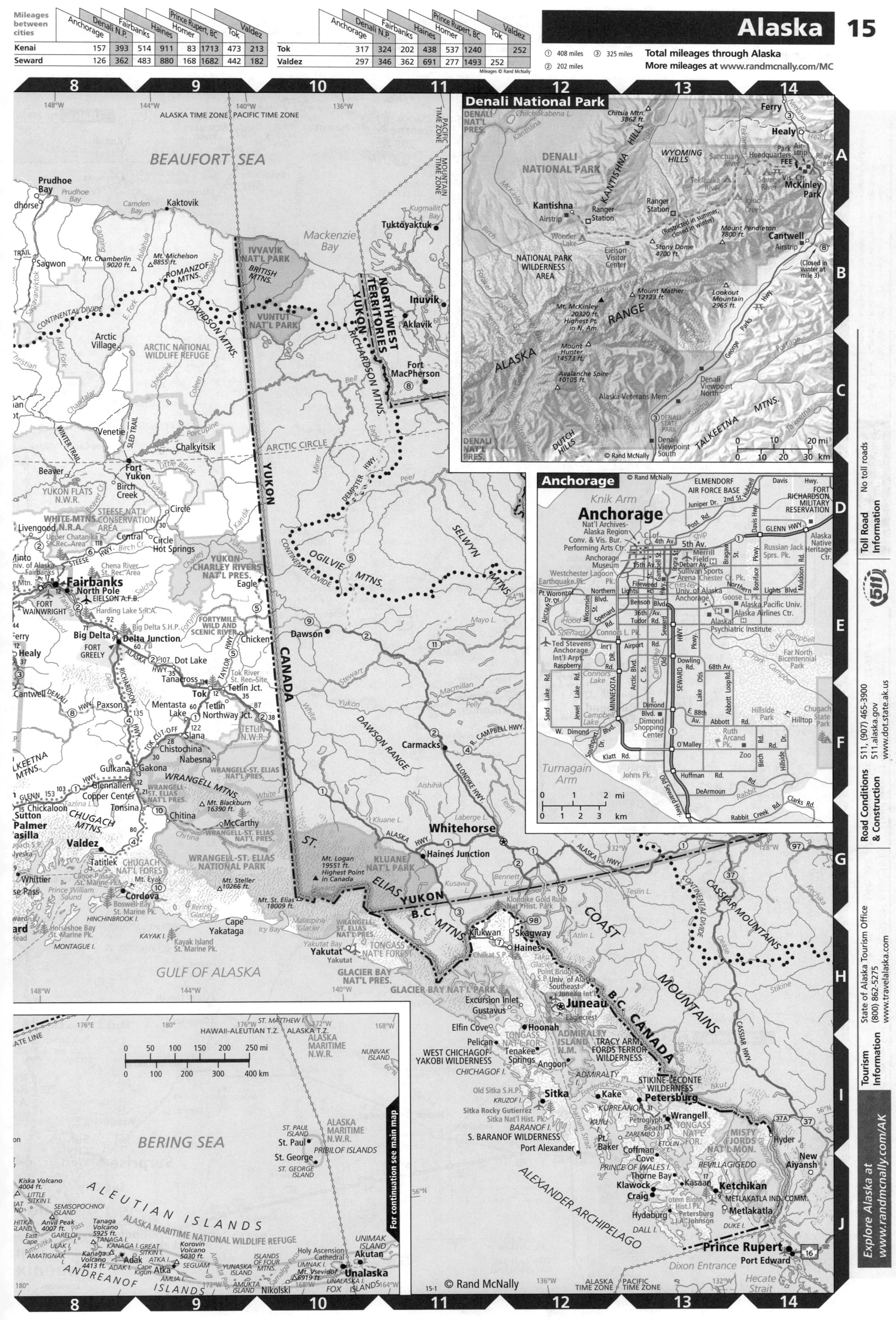

Mileages between cities	Anchorage	Denali N.P.	Fairbanks	Haines	Homer	Prince Rupert, BC	Tok	Valdez
Kenai	157	393	514	911	83	1713	473	213
Seward	126	362	483	880	168	1682	442	182

	Anchorage	Denali N.P.	Fairbanks	Haines	Homer	Prince Rupert, BC	Tok	Valdez
Tok	317	324	202	438	537	1240		252
Valdez	297	346	362	691	277	1493	252	

Mileages © Rand McNally

① 408 miles   ③ 325 miles
② 202 miles

Total mileages through Alaska
More mileages at www.randmcnally.com/MC

Denali National Park

Anchorage

© Rand McNally

511 (907) 465-3900
511.alaska.gov
511.dot.state.ak.us
Road Conditions & Construction

Toll Road Information   No toll roads

State of Alaska Tourism Office
(800) 862-5275
www.travelalaska.com
Tourism Information

Explore Alaska at www.randmcnally.com/AK

Mileages between cities	Casa Grande	Chinle	Eagar	Flagstaff	Gallup, NM	Grand Canyon	Holbrook	Kingman	Lake Havasu City	Las Vegas, NV	Lordsburg, NM	Nogales	Page	Phoenix	Tucson	Yuma
Flagstaff	191	213	176		185	79	90	146	204	250	374	321	133	139	255	318
Holbrook	220	123	86	90	94	167		237	295	340	264	304	214	230	238	409

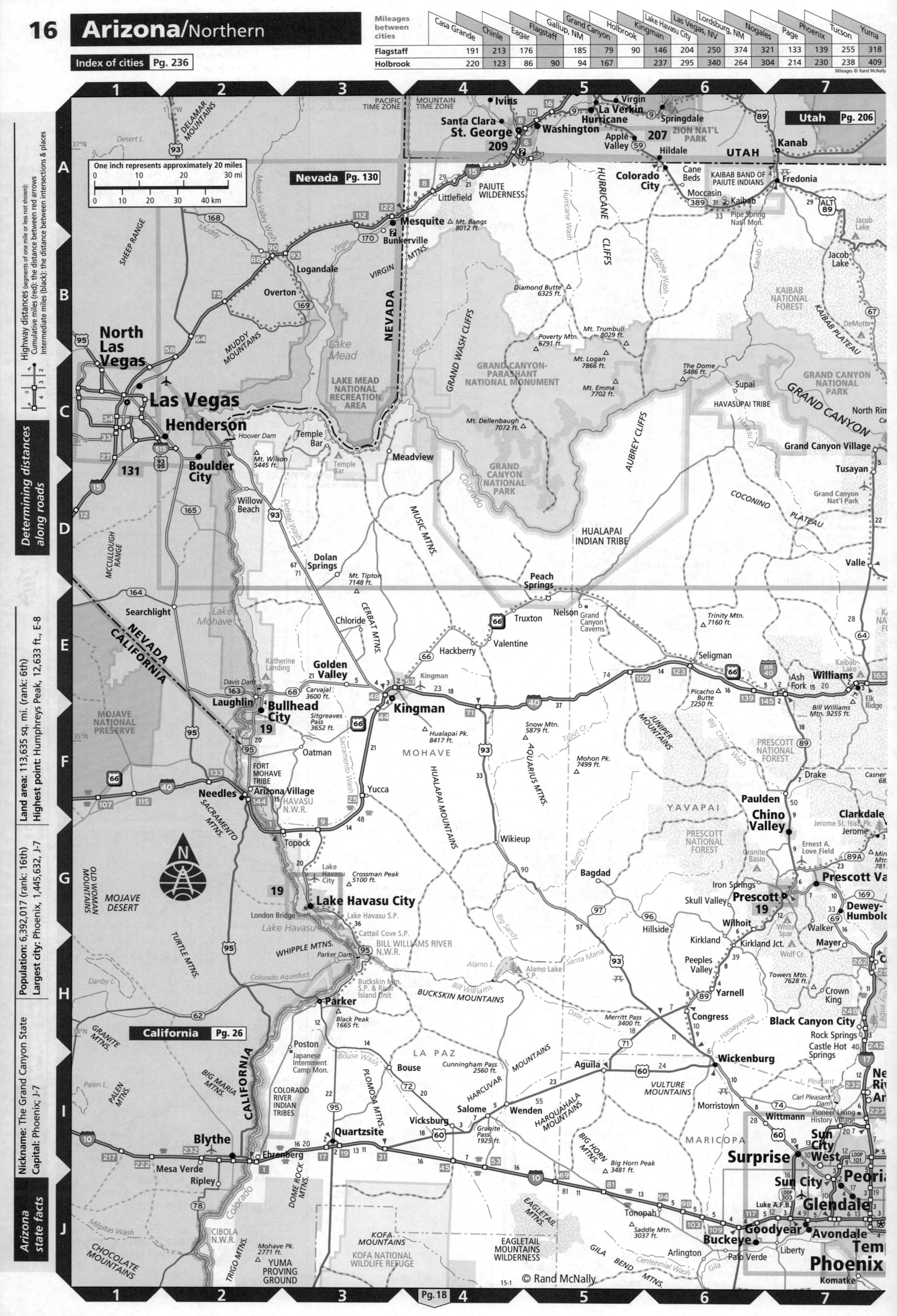

One inch represents approximately 20 miles

Nevada Pg. 130

Utah Pg. 206

California Pg. 26

Pg. 18

Arizona state facts

Nickname: The Grand Canyon State
Capital: Phoenix, J-7

Population: 6,392,017 (rank: 16th)
Largest city: Phoenix, 1,445,632, J-7

Land area: 113,635 sq. mi. (rank: 6th)
Highest point: Humphreys Peak, 12,633 ft., E-8

Determining distances along roads

Highway distances (segments of one mile or less not shown):
Cumulative miles (red): the distance between red arrows
Intermediate miles (black): the distance between intersections & places

Mileages between cities	Casa Grande	Chinle	Eagar	Flagstaff	Gallup, NM	Grand Canyon	Holbrook	Kingman	Lake Havasu City	Las Vegas, NV	Lordsburg, NM	Nogales	Page	Phoenix	Tucson	Yuma
Las Vegas, NV	336	463	427	250	435	275	340	104	152		558	467	271	285	401	292
Page	324	204	301	133	255	137	214	281	340	271		499	455		275	390	453

continued p. 18

Mileages © Rand McNally

Total mileages through Arizona

8 178 miles	**17** 146 miles		
10 392 miles	**40** 359 miles		

More mileages at www.randmcnally.com/MC

Colo. Pg. 42

N.M. Pg. 138

Pg. 19

Road Conditions & Construction — 511 / (888) 411-7623, (602) 523-0244 / www.az511.com, www.azdot.gov

Toll Road Information — No toll roads

Tourism Information — Arizona Office of Tourism / (866) 275-5816, (602) 364-3700 / www.arizonaguide.com

Plan an Arizona trip at www.randmcnally.com/AZ

Mileages between cities	Casa Grande	Chinle	Eagar	Flagstaff	Gallup, NM	Grand Canyon	Holbrook	Kingman	Lake Havasu City	Las Vegas, NV	Lordsburg, NM	Nogales	Page	Phoenix	Tucson	Yuma
Phoenix	48	353	226	139	324	218	230	182	198	285	268	179	275		116	181
Prescott	148	306	270	93	278	126	184	148	206	251	368	278	227	97	213	214

Mileages © Rand McNally

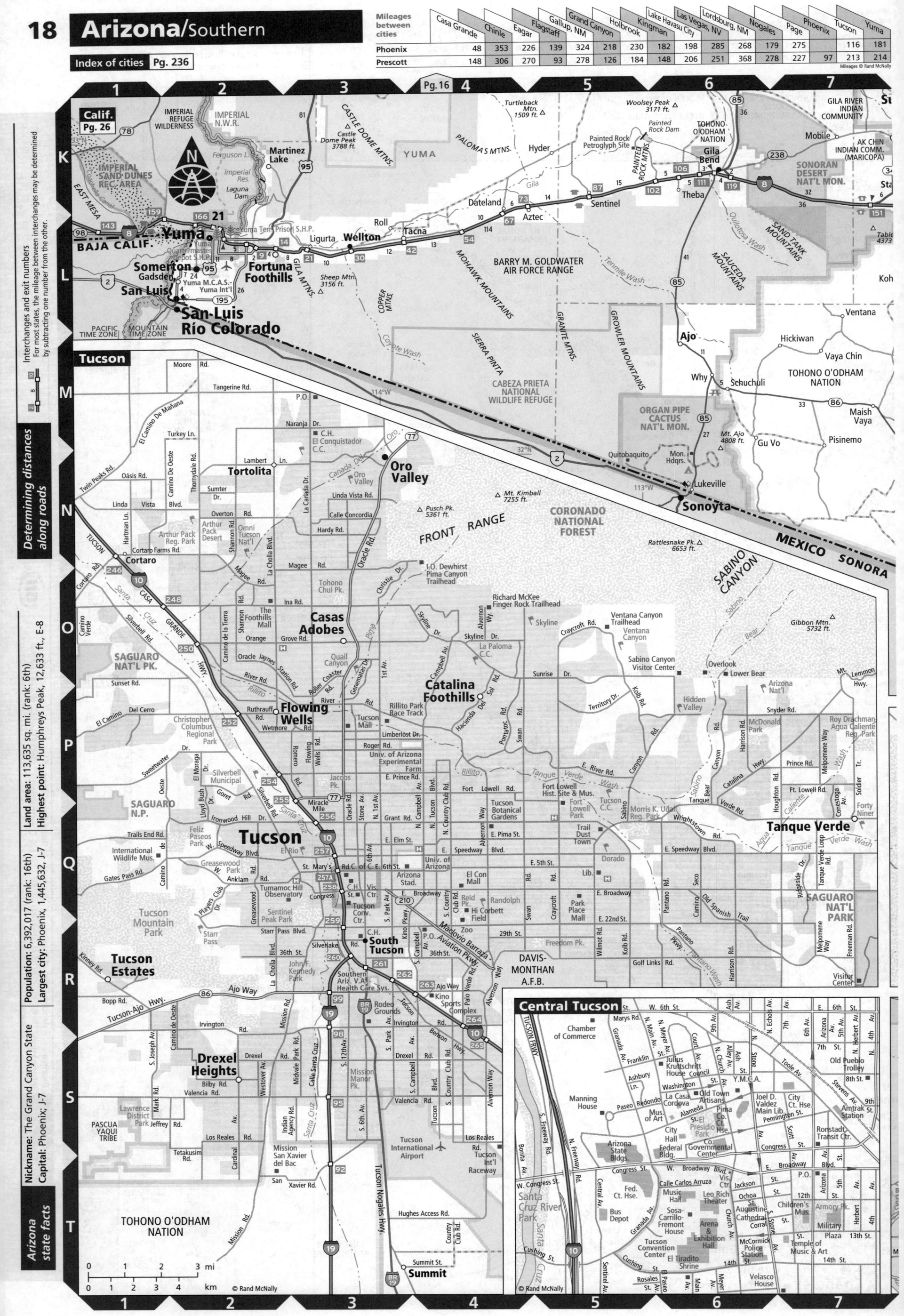

Arizona state facts

Nickname: The Grand Canyon State
Capital: Phoenix

Population: 6,392,017 (rank: 16th)
Largest city: Phoenix, J-7

Land area: 113,635 sq. mi. (rank: 6th)
Highest point: Humphreys Peak, 12,633 ft., E-8

Determining distances along roads

Interchanges and exit numbers
For most states, the mileage between interchanges may be determined by subtracting one number from the other.

© Rand McNally

Mileages between cities	Casa Grande	Chinle	Eagar	Flagstaff	Gallup, NM	Grand Canyon	Holbrook	Kingman	Lake Havasu City	Las Vegas, NV	Lordsburg, NM	Nogales	Page	Phoenix	Tucson	Yuma
Tucson	66	361	238	255	333	334	238	297	314	401	156	66	390	116		236
Yuma	172	532	399	318	502	397	409	213	155	292	392	301	453	181	236	

Mileages © Rand McNally

	Total mileages through Arizona	More mileages at www.randmcnally.com/MC
8 178 miles	17 146 miles	
10 392 miles	40 359 miles	

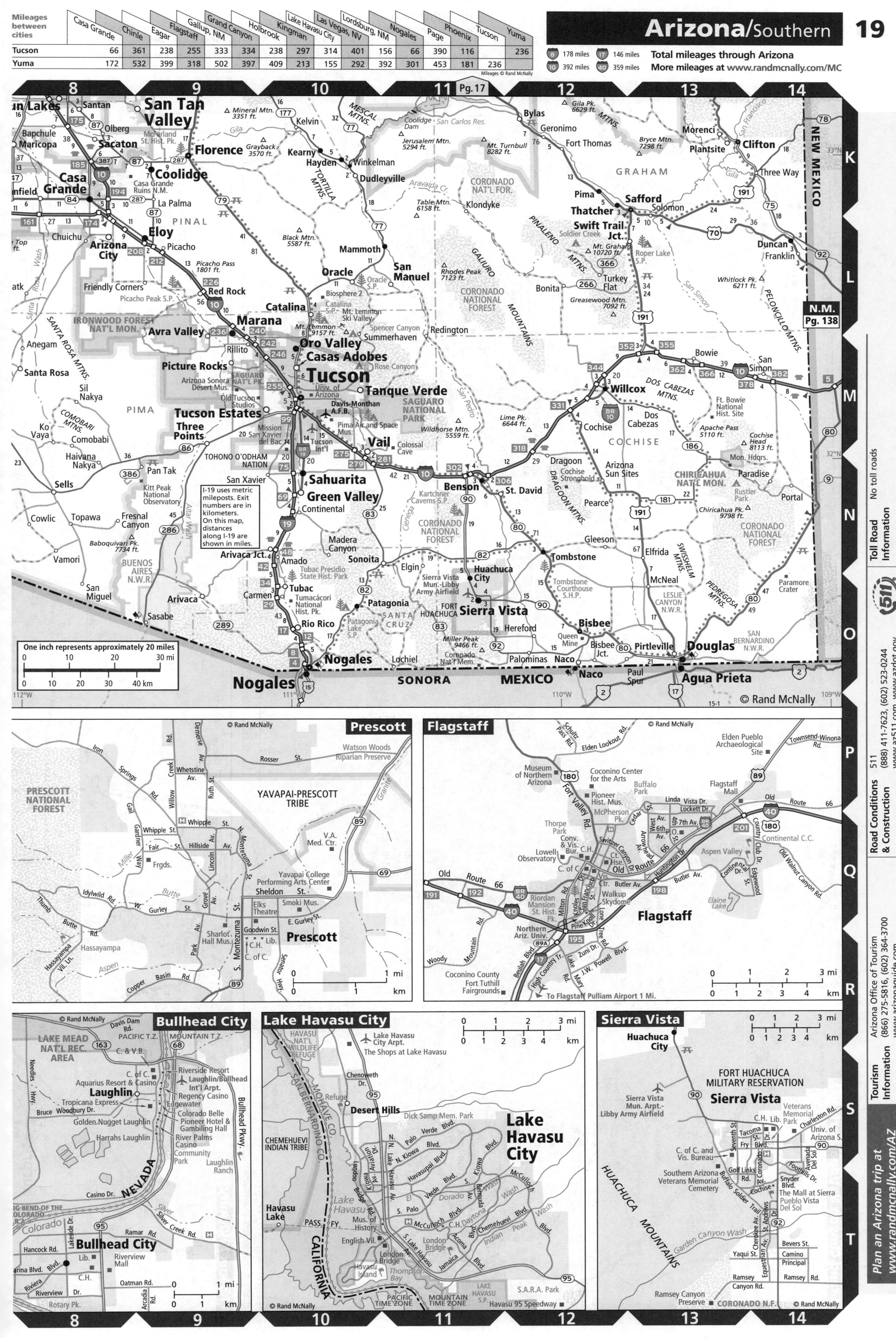

City sights to see
- Arizona Historical Society Sanguinetti House Museum, Yuma, L-6
- Arizona Museum of Natural History, Mesa, J-7
- Arizona Science Center, Phoenix, M-3
- Arizona State Capitol, Phoenix, M-1
- Heard Museum, Phoenix, L-2
- Painted Desert Inn Museum, Petrified Forest National Park, L-10

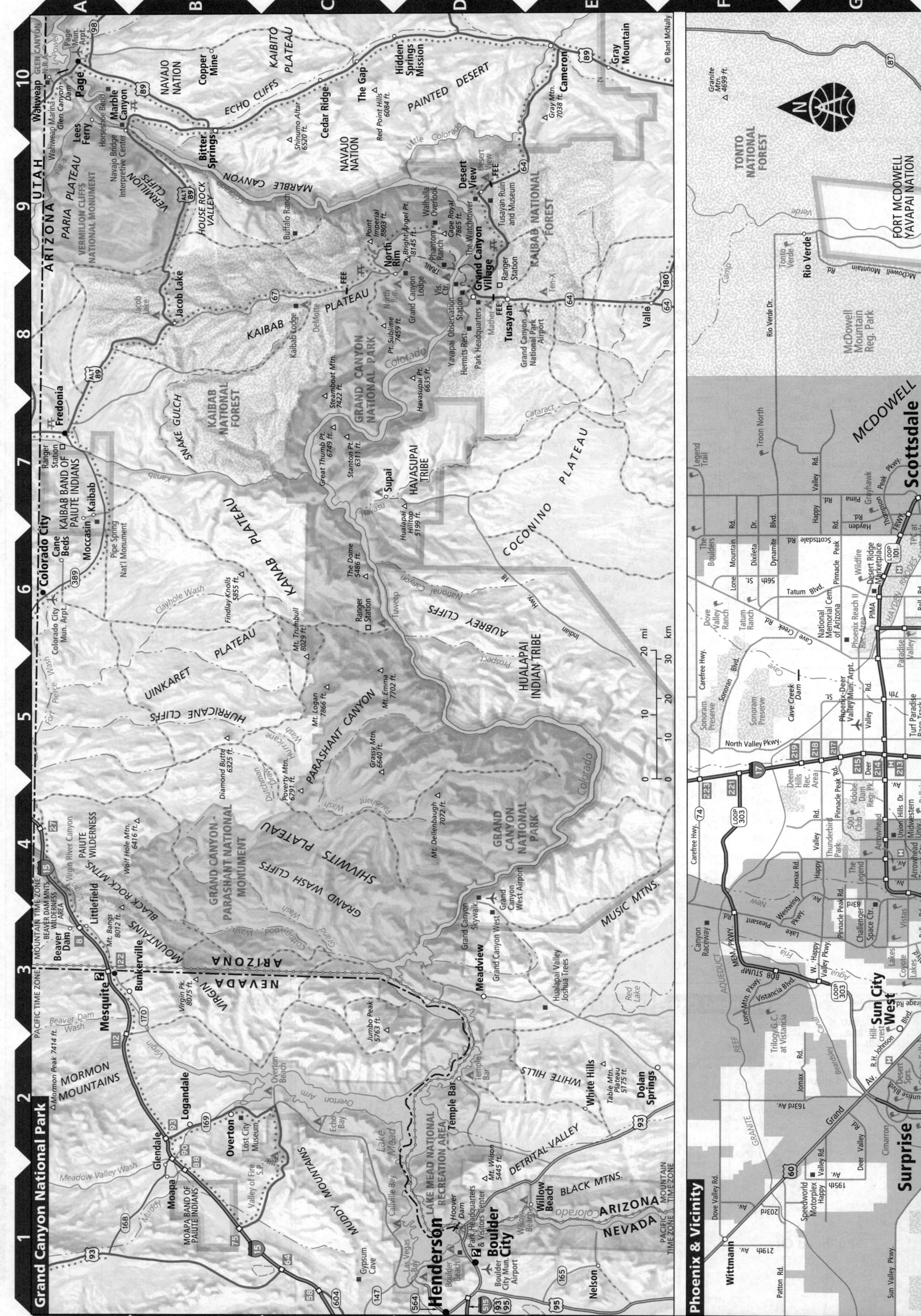

- Phoenix Art Museum, Phoenix, L-2
- Taliesin West, Scottsdale, H-7
- Tusayan Ruin and Museum, Grand Canyon National Park, D-9
- Yavapai Observation Station, Grand Canyon National Park, D-8
- Yuma Territorial Prison State Historic Park, Yuma, L-6

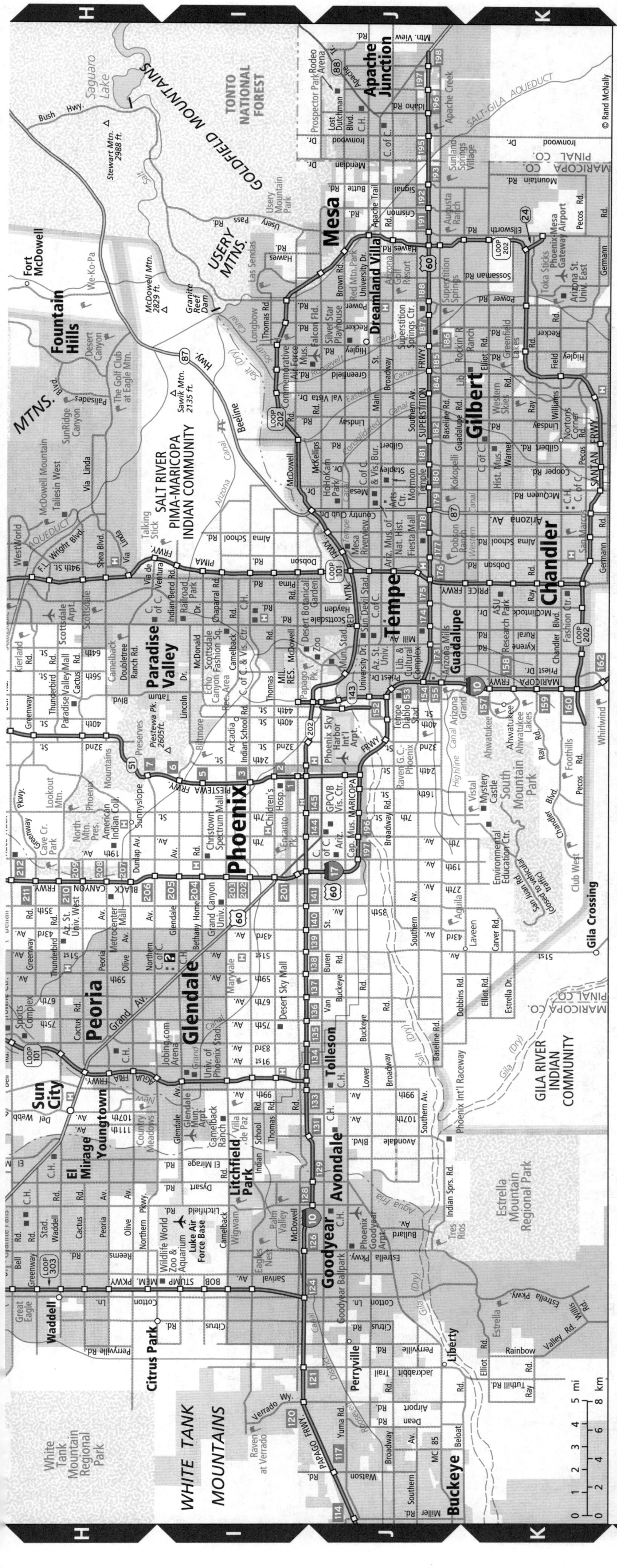

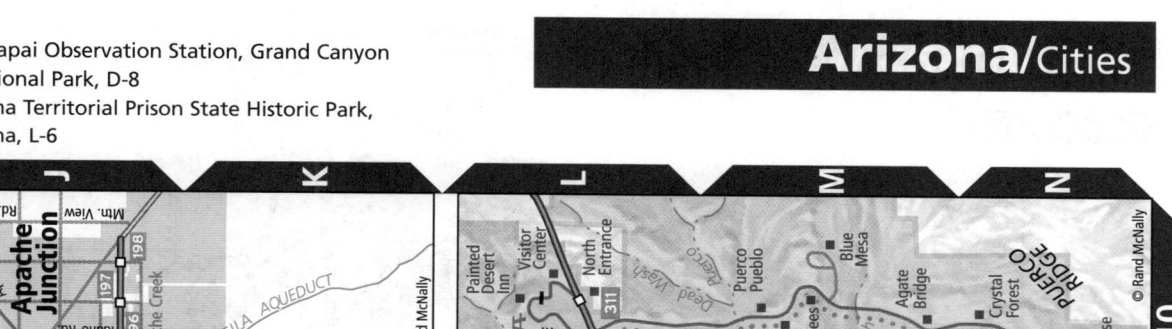

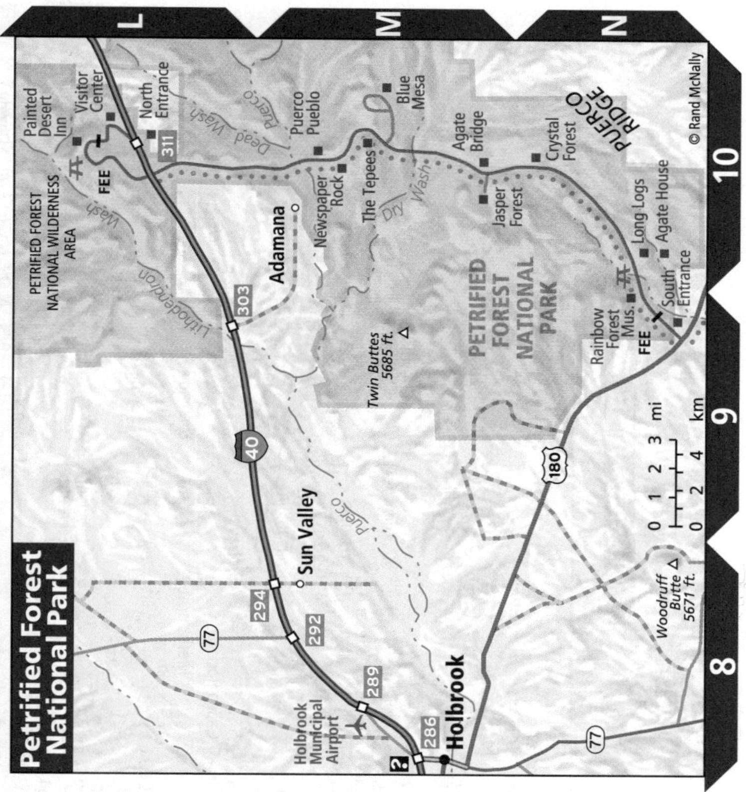

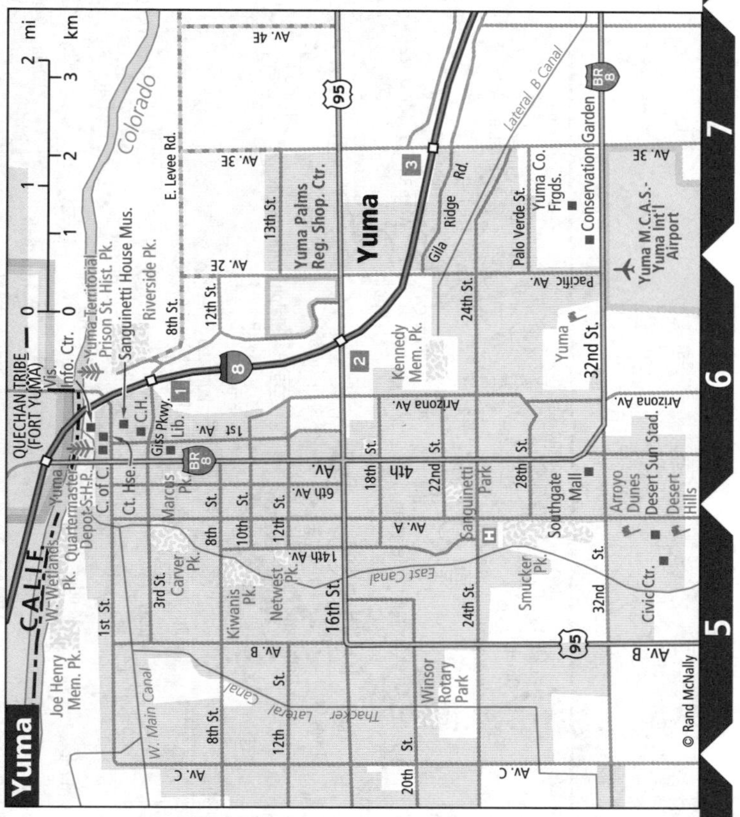

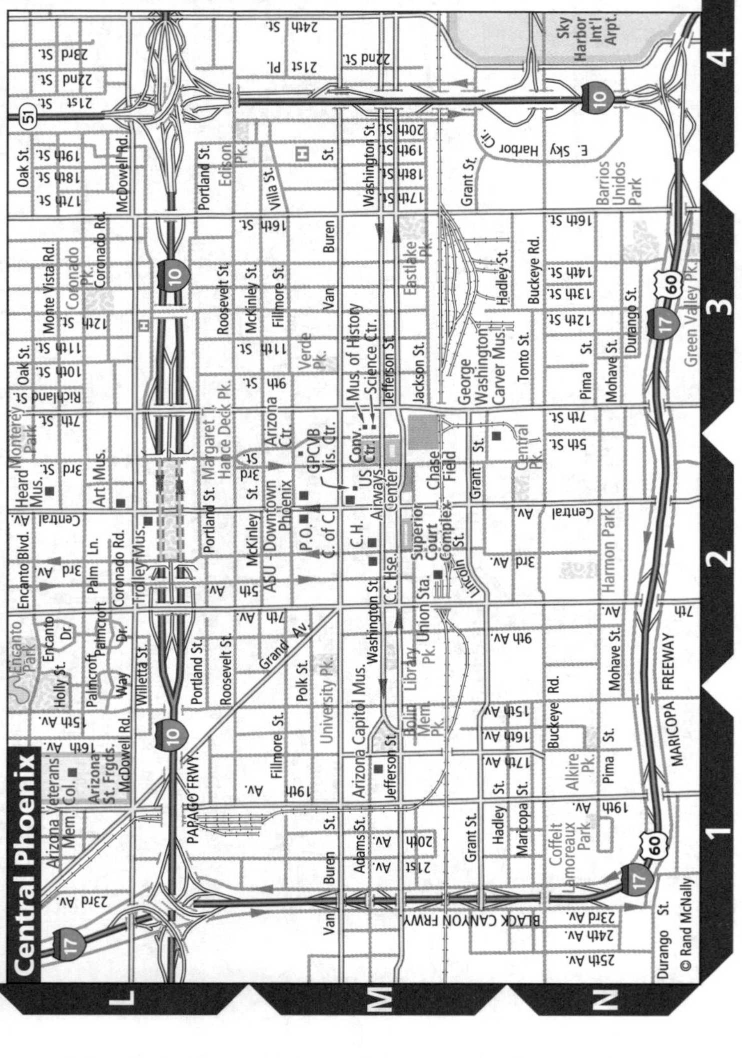

Pg.24

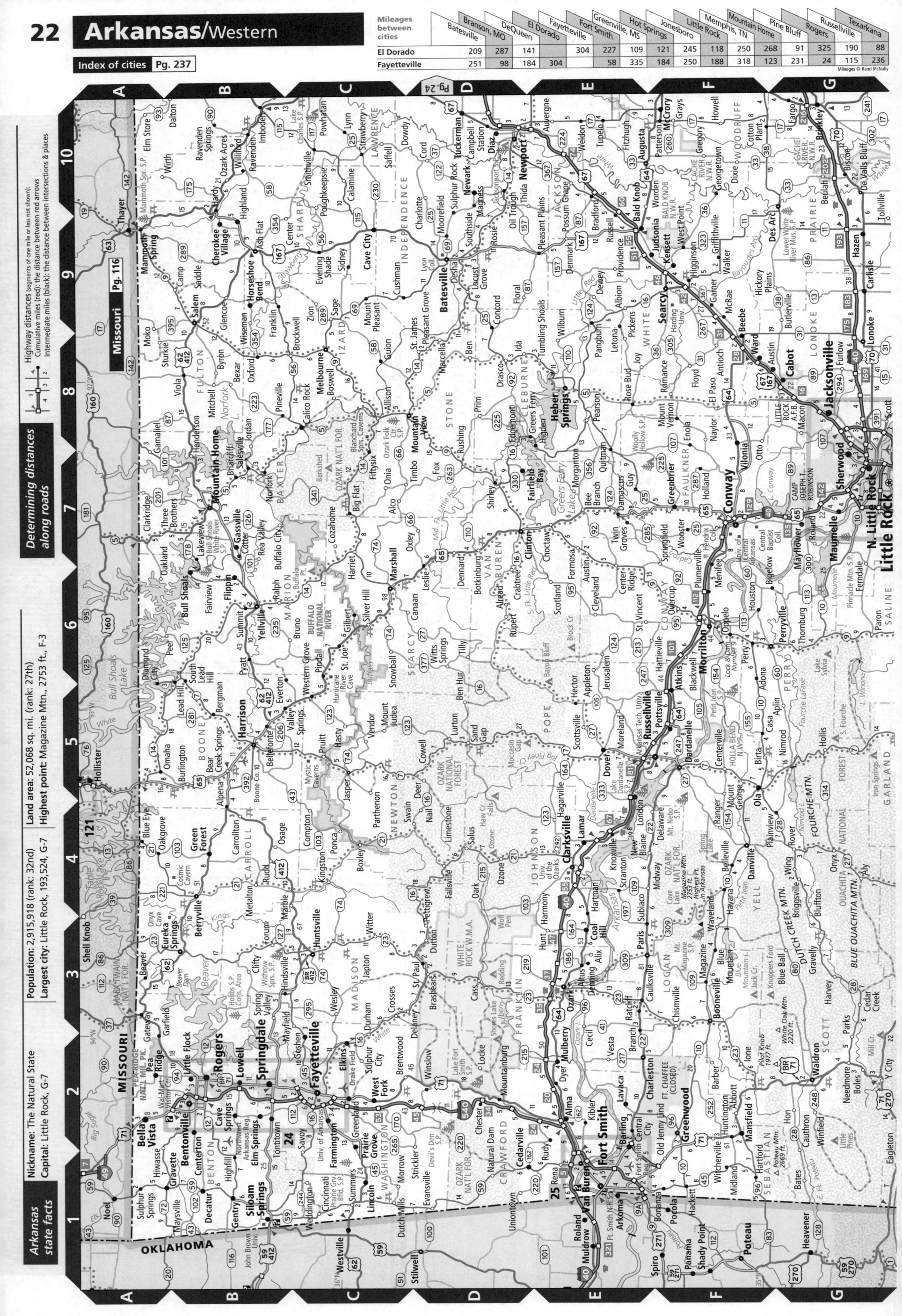

Mileages between cities	Batesville	Branson, MO	DeQueen	El Dorado	Fayetteville	Fort Smith	Greenville, MS	Hot Springs	Jonesboro	Little Rock	Memphis, TN	Mountain Home	Pine Bluff	Rogers	Russellville	Texarkana
El Dorado	209	287	141		304	227	109	121	245	118	250	268	91	325	190	88
Fayetteville	251	98	184	304		58	335	184	250	188	318	123	231	24	115	236

Mileages © Rand McNally

Arkansas state facts

Nickname: The Natural State
Capital: Little Rock, G-7

Population: 2,915,918 (rank: 32nd)
Largest city: Little Rock, 193,524, G-7

Land area: 52,068 sq. mi. (rank: 27th)
Highest point: Magazine Mtn., 2753 ft., F-3

Determining distances along roads

Highway distances (segments of one mile or less not shown):
Cumulative miles (red): the distance between red arrows
Intermediate miles (black): the distance between intersections & places

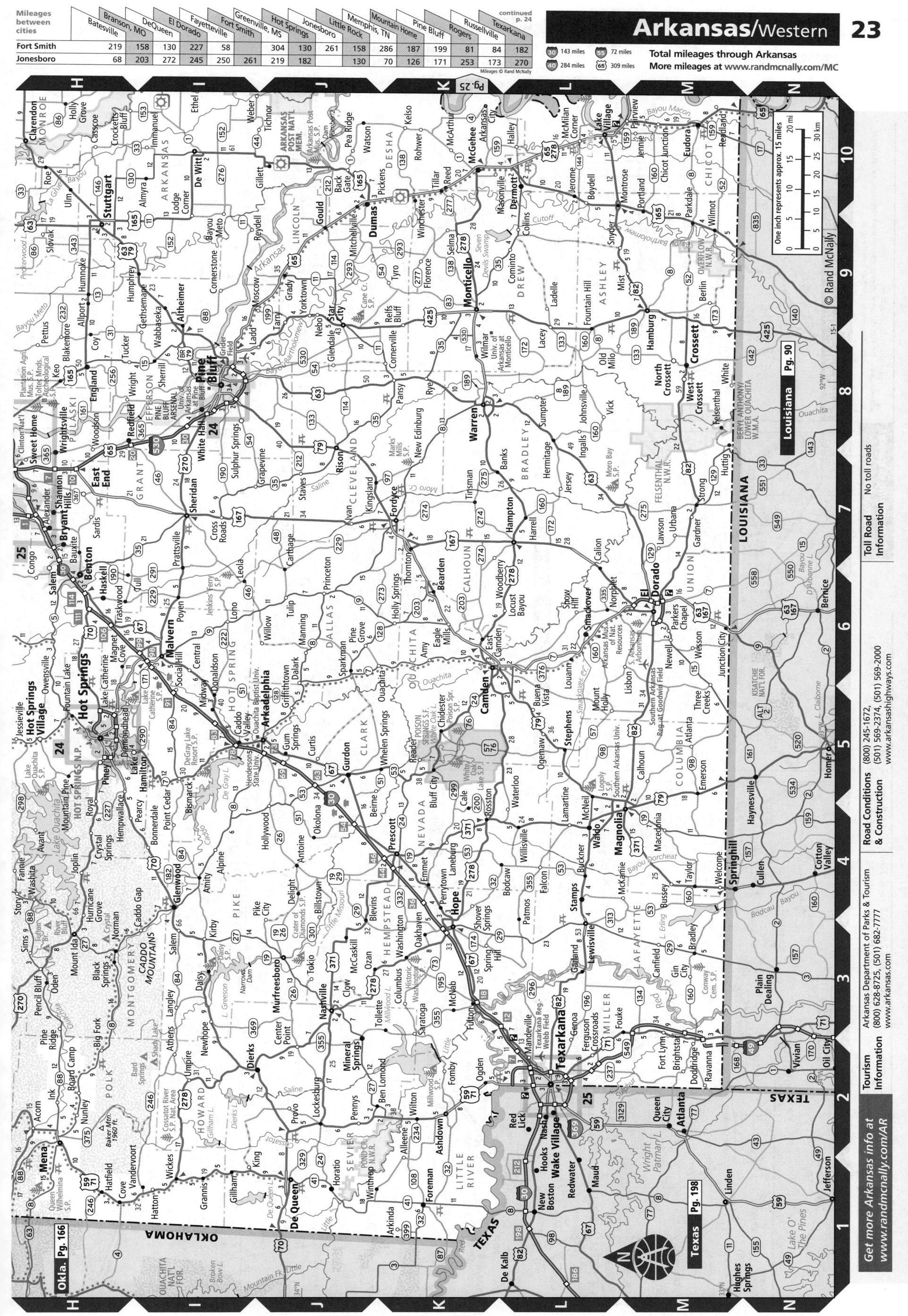

Mileages between cities

	Batesville	Branson, MO	DeQueen	El Dorado	Fayetteville	Fort Smith	Greenville, MS	Hot Springs	Jonesboro	Little Rock	Memphis, TN	Mountain Home	Pine Bluff	Rogers	Russellville	Texarkana
Fort Smith	219	158	130	227	58		304	130	261	158	286	187	199	81	84	182
Jonesboro	68	203	272	245	250	261	219	182		130	70	126	171	253	173	270

Mileages © Rand McNally

continued p. 24

One inch represents approx. 15 miles

© Rand McNally

Louisiana Pg. 90

Texas Pg. 198

Okla. Pg. 166

Get more Arkansas info at
www.randmcnally.com/AR

Tourism Information
Arkansas Department of Parks & Tourism
(800) 628-8725, (501) 682-7777
www.arkansas.com

Road Conditions & Construction
(800) 245-1672,
(501) 569-2374, (501) 569-2000
www.arkansashighways.com

Toll Road Information
No toll roads

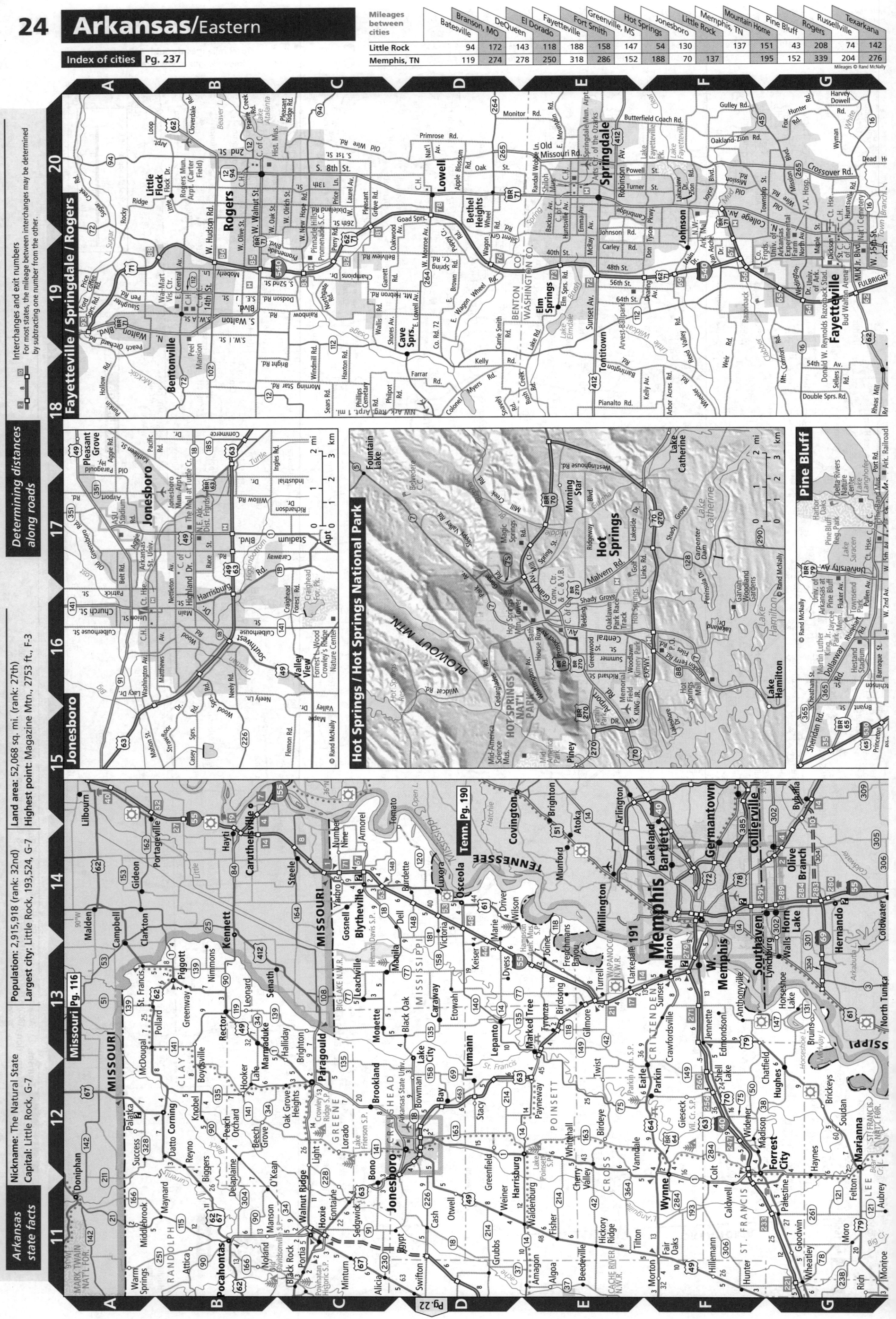

Mileages between cities	Batesville	Branson, MO	DeQueen	El Dorado	Fayetteville	Fort Smith	Greenville, MS	Hot Springs	Jonesboro	Little Rock	Memphis, TN	Mountain Home	Pine Bluff	Rogers	Russellville	Texarkana
Little Rock	94	172	143	118	188	158	147	54	130		137	151	43	208	74	142
Memphis, TN	119	274	278	250	318	286	152	188	70	137		195	152	339	204	276

Mileages by Rand McNally

Arkansas state facts

Nickname: The Natural State
Capital: Little Rock, G-7

Population: 2,915,918 (rank: 32nd)
Largest city: Little Rock, 193,524, G-7

Land area: 52,068 sq. mi. (rank: 27th)
Highest point: Magazine Mtn., 2753 ft., F-3

Determining distances along roads

Interchanges and exit numbers
For most states, the mileage between interchanges may be determined by subtracting one number from the other.

Fayetteville / Springdale / Rogers

Jonesboro

Hot Springs / Hot Springs National Park

Pine Bluff

Missouri Pg. 116

Tenn. Pg. 190

Pg. 22

Mileages between cities	Batesville	Branson, MO	DeQueen	El Dorado	Fayetteville	Fort Smith	Greenville, MS	Hot Springs	Jonesboro	Little Rock	Memphis, TN	Mountain Home	Pine Bluff	Rogers	Russellville	Texarkana
Mountain Home	78	83	287	268	123	187	298	198	126	151	195		194	126	125	287
Texarkana	234	306	54	88	236	182	198	110	270	142	276	287	152	258	209	

Mileages © Rand McNally

Total mileages through Arkansas
More mileages at www.randmcnally.com/MC

30 143 miles   55 72 miles
40 284 miles   65 309 miles

Get more Arkansas info at www.randmcnally.com/AR

Tourism Information
Arkansas Department of Parks & Tourism
(800) 628-8725, (501) 682-7777
www.arkansas.com

Road Conditions & Construction
(800) 245-1672, (501) 569-2374, (501) 569-2000
www.arkansashighways.com

Toll Road Information
No toll roads

Mileages between cities	Bishop	Crescent City	Los Angeles	Oroville	Redding	Sacramento	San Francisco	San Jose	Santa Rosa	S. Lake Tahoe	Stockton	Susanville	Ukiah	Vallejo	Yosemite N.P.	Yreka
Alturas	371	280	648	225	144	302	357	385	365	228	349	103	330	329	392	176
Bishop		614	265	326	400	269	295	290	364	176	224	286	418	328	138	454

Mileages ® Rand McNally

California state facts

Nickname: The Golden State
Capital: Sacramento, NK-7

Population: 37,253,956 (rank: 3rd)
Largest city: Los Angeles, NK-7

Land area: 155,959 sq. mi. (rank: 1st)
Highest point: Mt. Whitney, 14,494 ft., SC-11

Determining distances along roads

Highway distances (segments of one mile or less not shown):
Cumulative miles (red): the distance between red arrows
Intermediate miles (black): the distance between intersections & places

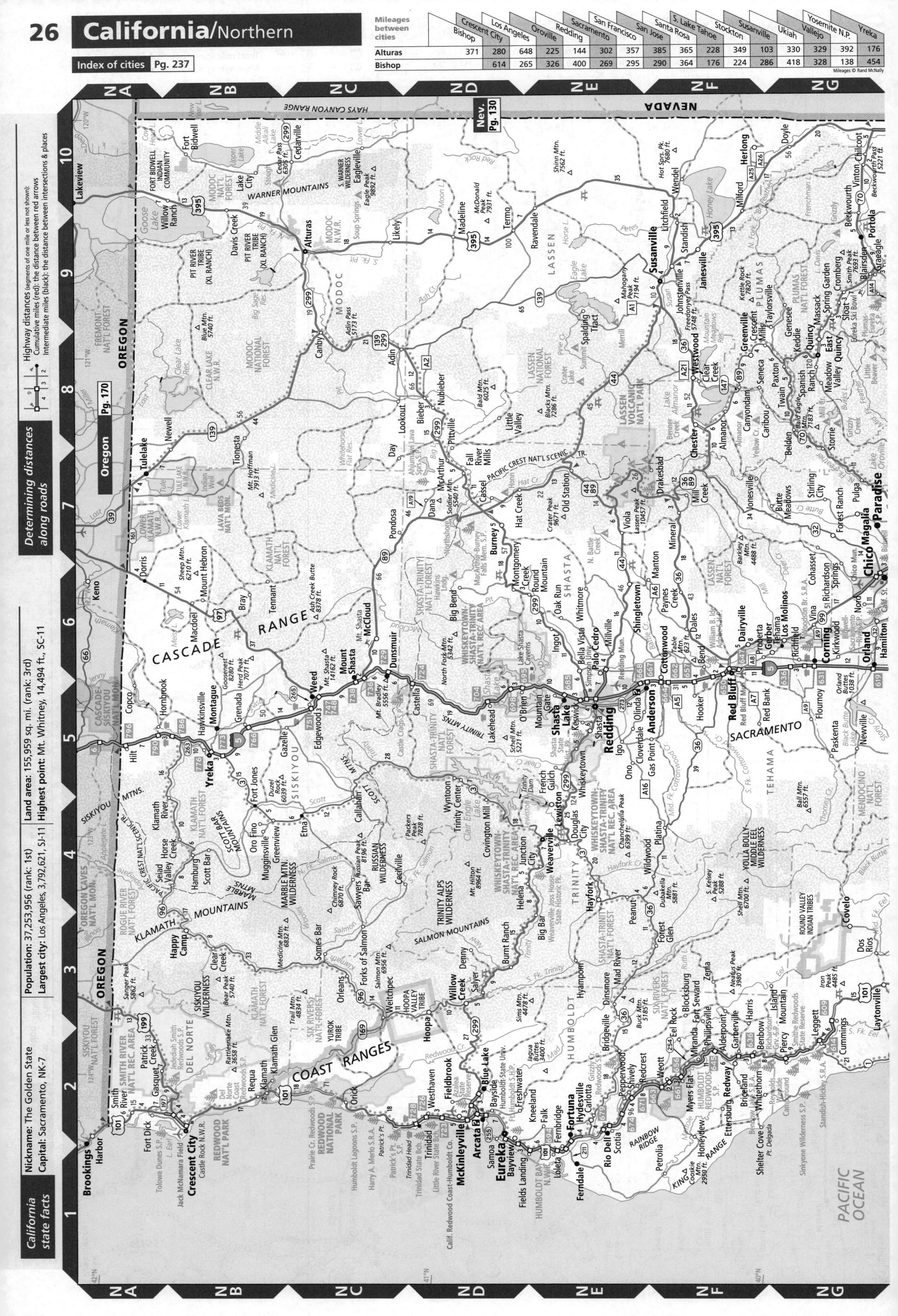

Mileages between cities	Bishop	Crescent City	Los Angeles	Oroville	Redding	Sacramento	San Francisco	San Jose	Santa Rosa	S. Lake Tahoe	Stockton	Susanville	Ukiah	Vallejo	Yosemite N.P.	continued p. 28 Yreka
Eureka	546	81	644	222	146	289	272	315	217	392	325	259	158	262	454	198
Redding	400	208	544	94		161	216	244	198	264	209	112	188	187	332	98

Mileages © Rand McNally

Total mileages through California
797 miles · 101 791 miles · 80 199 miles
More mileages at www.randmcnally.com/MC

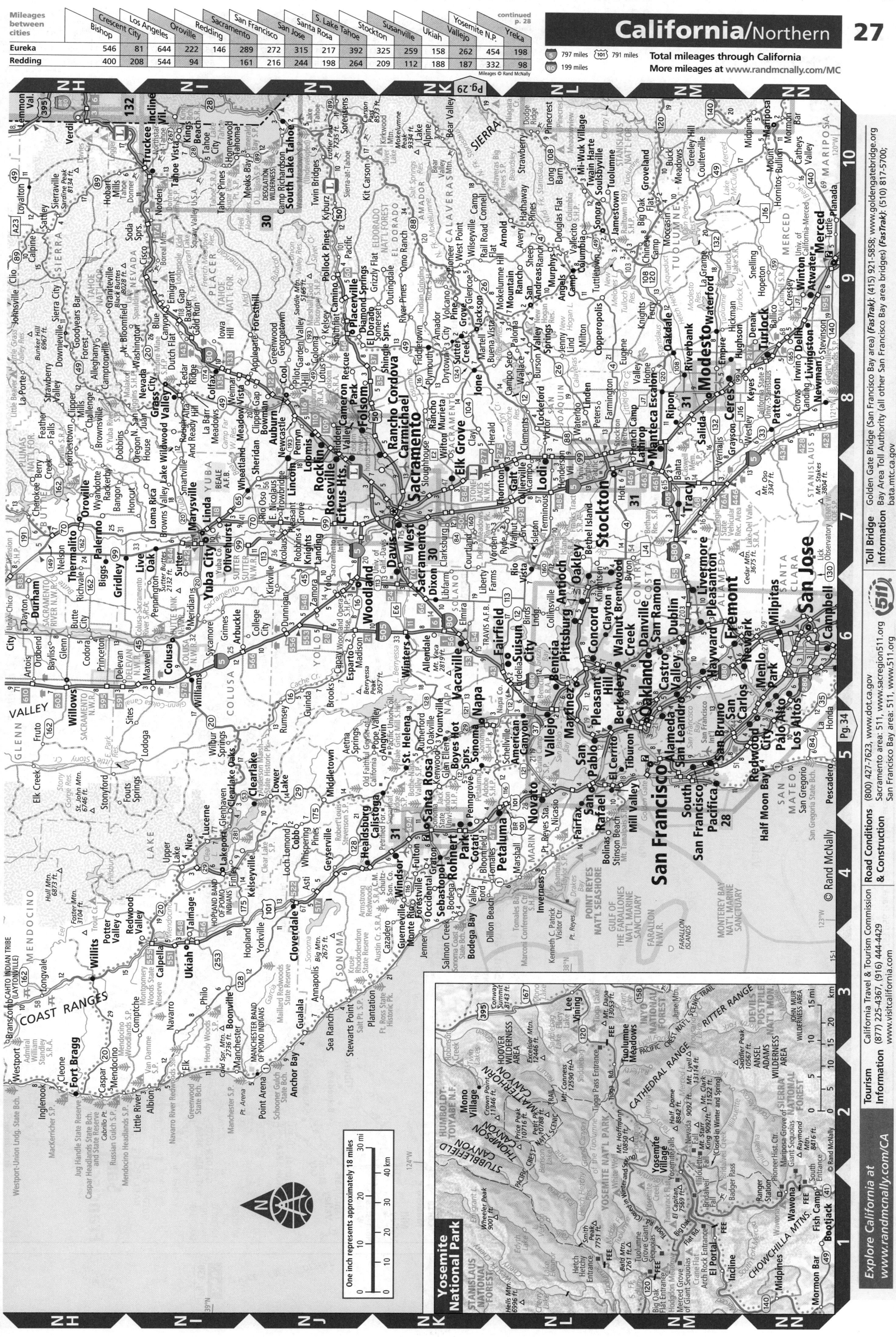

Explore California at www.randmcnally.com/CA

Tourism Information California Travel & Tourism Commission (877) 225-4367, (916) 444-4429 www.visitcalifornia.com

Road Conditions & Construction California Dept. of Transportation (800) 427-7623, www.dot.ca.gov Sacramento area: 511, www.sacregion511.org San Francisco Bay area: 511, www.511.org

Toll Bridge Information Golden Gate Bridge (San Francisco Bay area) (FasTrak): (415) 921-5858; www.goldengate.org Bay Area Toll Authority (all other San Francisco Bay area bridges) (FasTrak): (510) 817-5700; bata.mtc.ca.gov

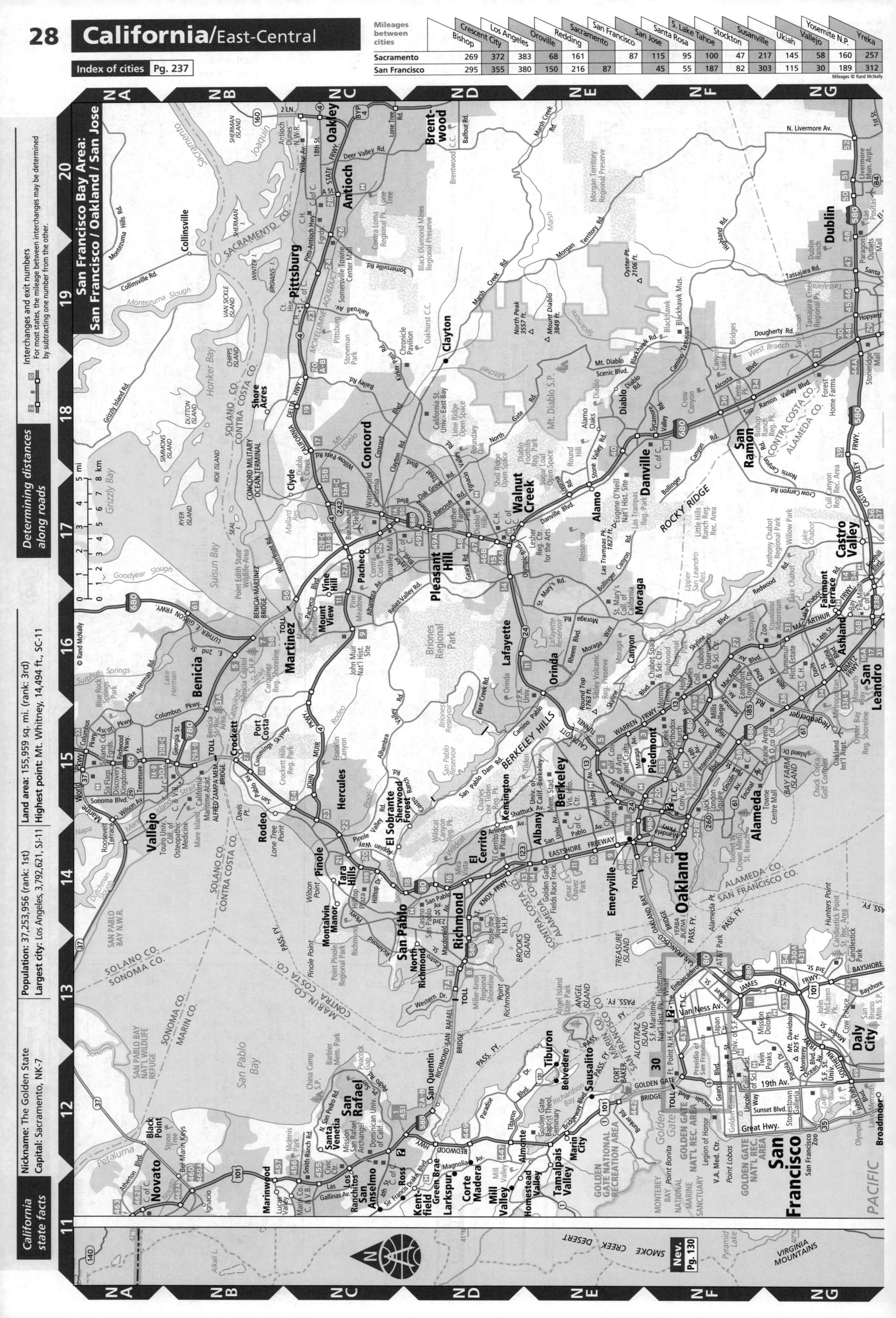

Mileages between cities	Bishop	Crescent City	Los Angeles	Oroville	Redding	Sacramento	San Francisco	San Jose	Santa Rosa	S. Lake Tahoe	Stockton	Susanville	Ukiah	Vallejo	Yosemite N.P.	Yreka
Sacramento	269	372	383	68	161		87	115	95	100	47	217	145	58	160	257
San Francisco	295	355	380	150	216	87		45	55	187	82	303	115	30	189	312

Mileages © Rand McNally

San Francisco Bay Area:
San Francisco / Oakland / San Jose

California state facts

Nickname: The Golden State
Capital: Sacramento, NK-7

Population: 37,253,956 (rank: 1st)
Largest city: Los Angeles, 3,792,621, SJ-11

Land area: 155,959 sq. mi. (rank: 3rd)
Highest point: Mt. Whitney, 14,494 ft., SC-11

Determining distances along roads

Interchanges and exit numbers
For most states, the mileage between interchanges may be determined by subtracting one number from the other.

Mileages between cities	Crescent City Bishop	Los Angeles	Oroville	Redding	Sacramento	San Francisco	San Jose	Santa Rosa	S. Lake Tahoe	Stockton	Susanville	Ukiah	Yosemite N.P. Vallejo	Yreka
San Jose	290	396	340	178	244	115	45	96	215	74	330	156	64	182	340
S. Lake Tahoe	176	472	445	157	264	100	187	215	195		147	143	248	159	189	311

Mileages © Rand McNally

Total mileages through California

5 797 miles   101 791 miles
80 199 miles

More mileages at www.randmcnally.com/MC

Explore California at www.randmcnally.com/CA

Tourism Information California Travel & Tourism Commission (877) 225-4367, (916) 444-4429 www.visitcalifornia.com

Road Conditions & Construction California Dept. of Transportation (800) 427-7623, www.dot.ca.gov Sacramento area: 511, www.sacregion511.org San Francisco Bay area: 511, www.511.org

Toll Road Information Golden Gate Bridge (San Francisco Bay area): (415) 921-5858; www.goldengatebridge.org Bay Area Toll Authority (all other San Francisco Bay area bridges) (FasTrak): www.bata.mtc.ca.gov

City sights to see

- AT&T Park, San Francisco, E-10
- California State Capitol, Sacramento, I-6
- California State Railroad Museum, Sacramento, H-6
- Chinatown, San Francisco, C-8
- Coit Memorial Tower, San Francisco, B-8
- Crocker Art Museum, Sacramento, I-5
- Fisherman's Wharf, San Francisco, A-7

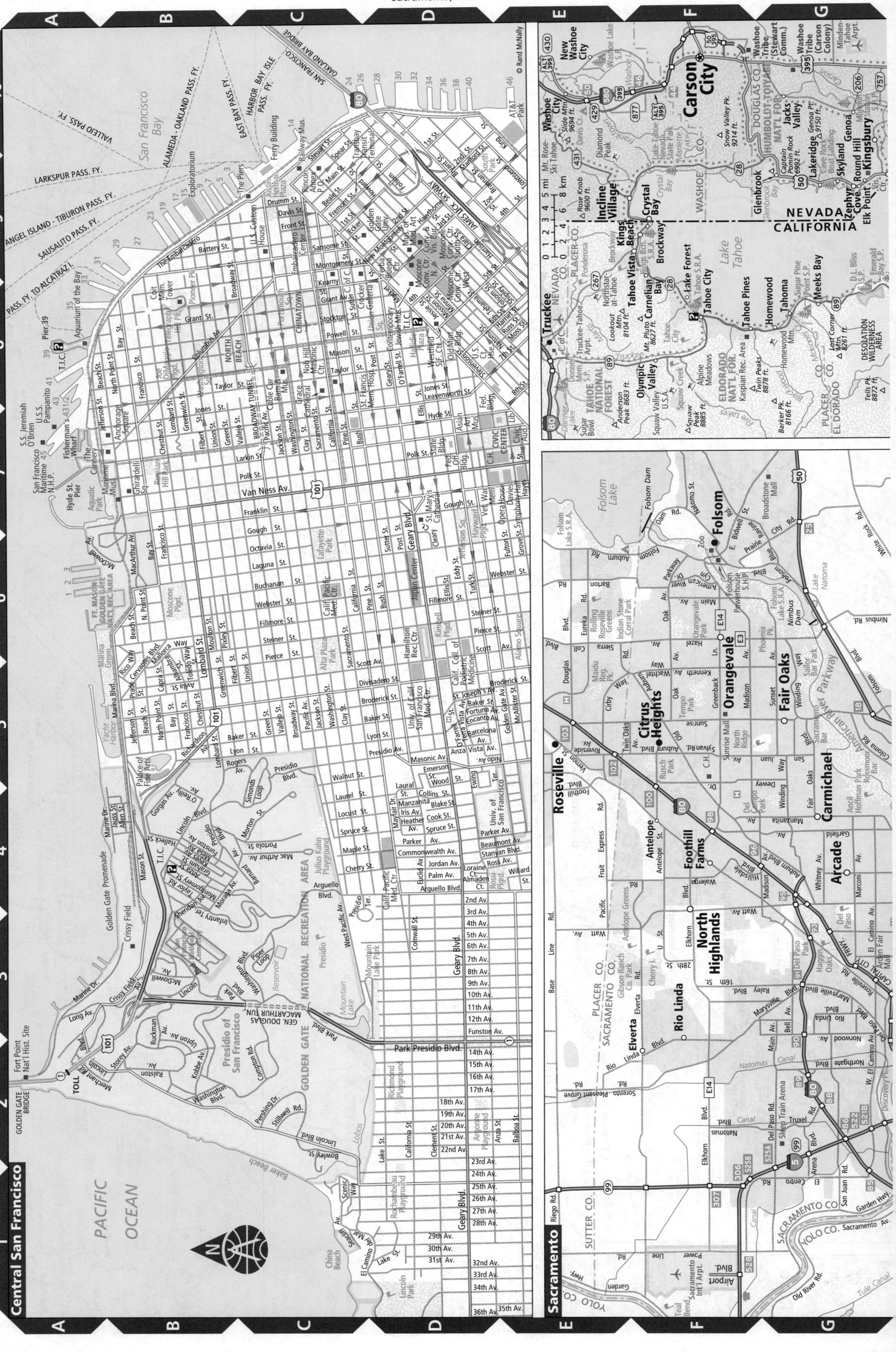

Central San Francisco

Sacramento

© Rand McNally

- Ghirardelli Square, San Francisco, B-7
- Golden Gate Bridge, San Francisco, A-2
- Monterey Bay Aquarium, Monterey, M-1
- National Steinbeck Center, Salinas, K-5
- Pier 39, San Francisco, A-8
- San Francisco Cable Car Museum, San Francisco, C-8
- Squaw Valley U.S.A., Olympic Valley, F-8

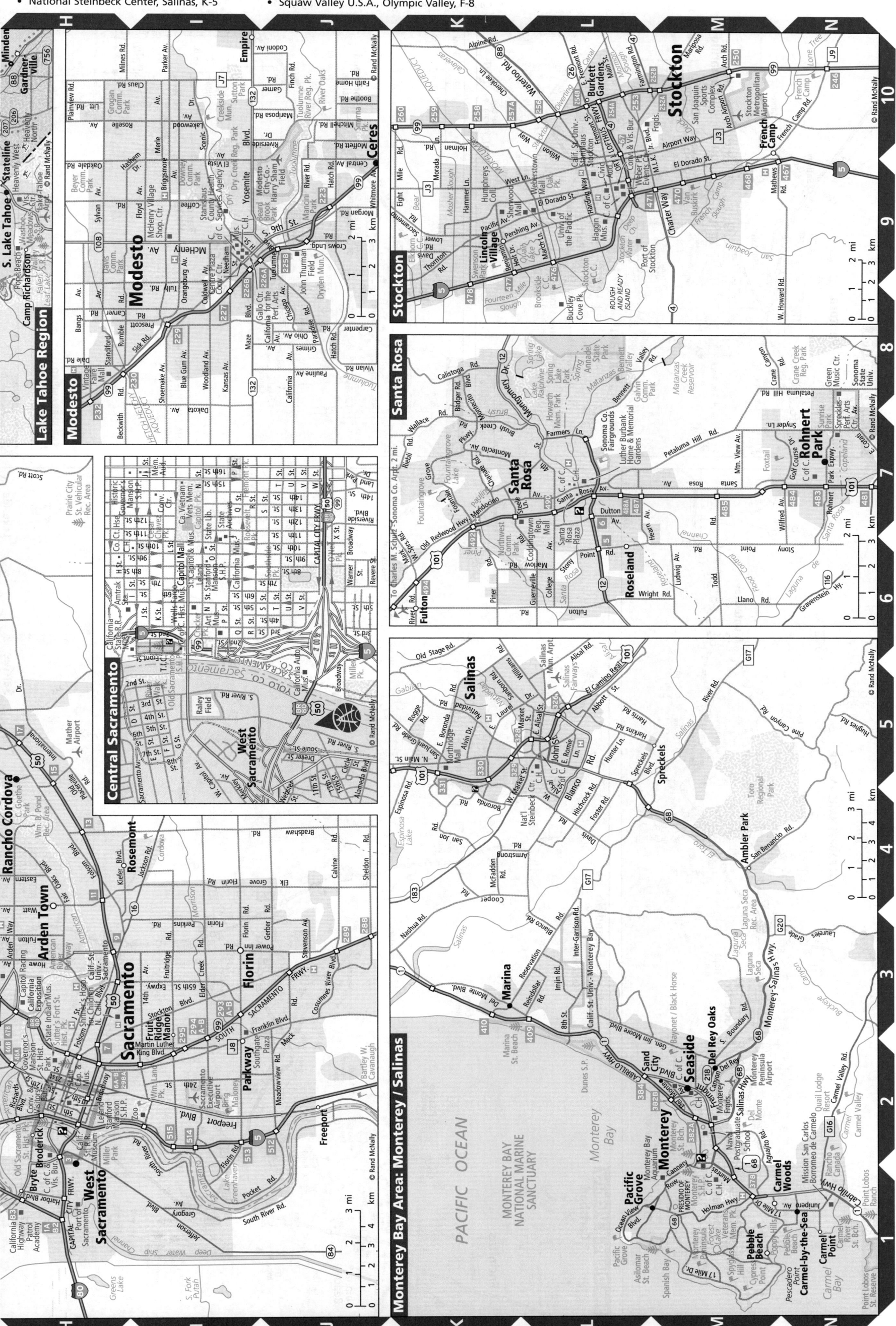

City sights to see
- Balboa Park, San Diego, K-10
- Birch Aquarium at Scripps Institute, San Diego, G-1
- Cabrillo National Monument, San Diego, K-1
- Channel Islands National Park Visitor Center & Headquarters, Ventura, B-8
- Gaslamp Quarter Historic District, San Diego, M-9

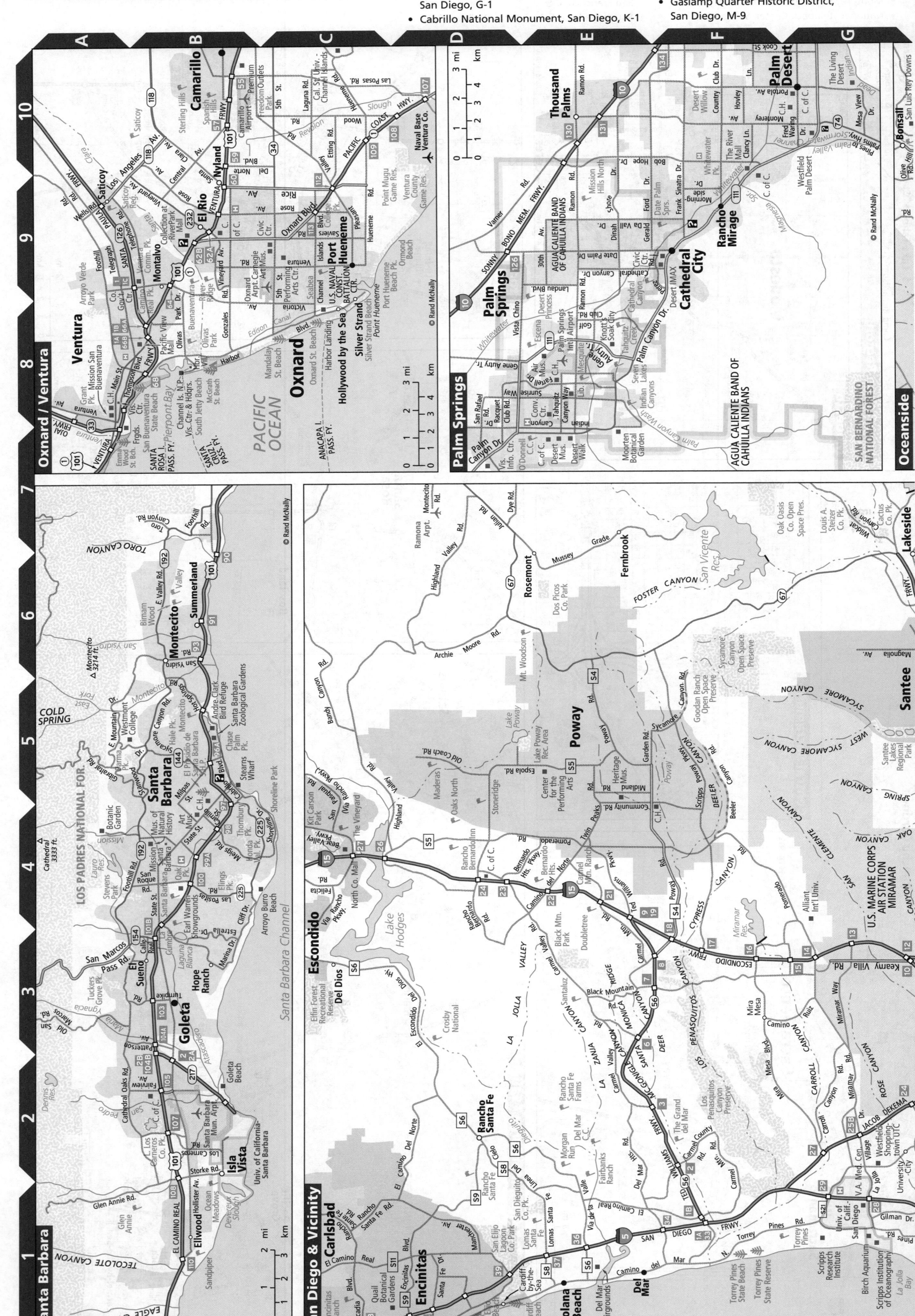

- LEGOLAND California, Carlsbad, J-8
- The Living Desert Nature Preserve, Palm Desert, G-10
- Museum of Contemporary Art, San Diego, L-8
- Palm Springs Desert Museum, Palm Springs, E-7
- San Diego Zoo, San Diego, J-3
- SeaWorld, San Diego, I-1
- Stearns Wharf, Santa Barbara, B-5

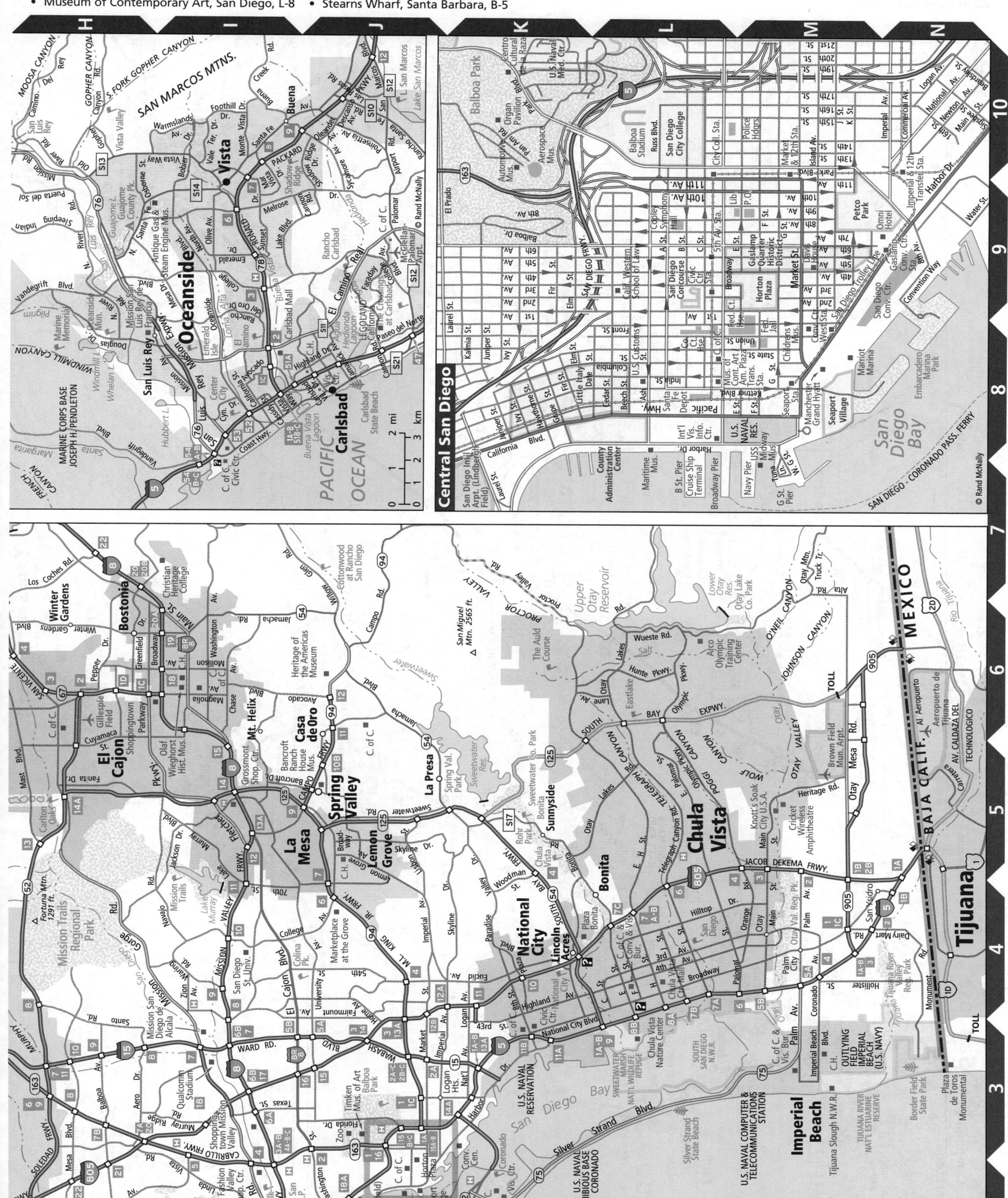

© Rand McNally

© Rand McNally

Mileages between cities	Bakersfield	Barstow	El Centro	Fresno	Las Vegas, NV	Los Angeles	Monterey	Needles	Palm Springs	Riverside	San Bernardino	San Diego	San Francisco	San Luis Obispo	Santa Barbara	Sequoia N.P.
Bakersfield		129	322	109	286	112	222	272	216	166	166	232	284	130	147	122
Fresno	109	239	429		395	218	150	381	323	271	273	339	183	130	254	77

Mileages © Rand McNally

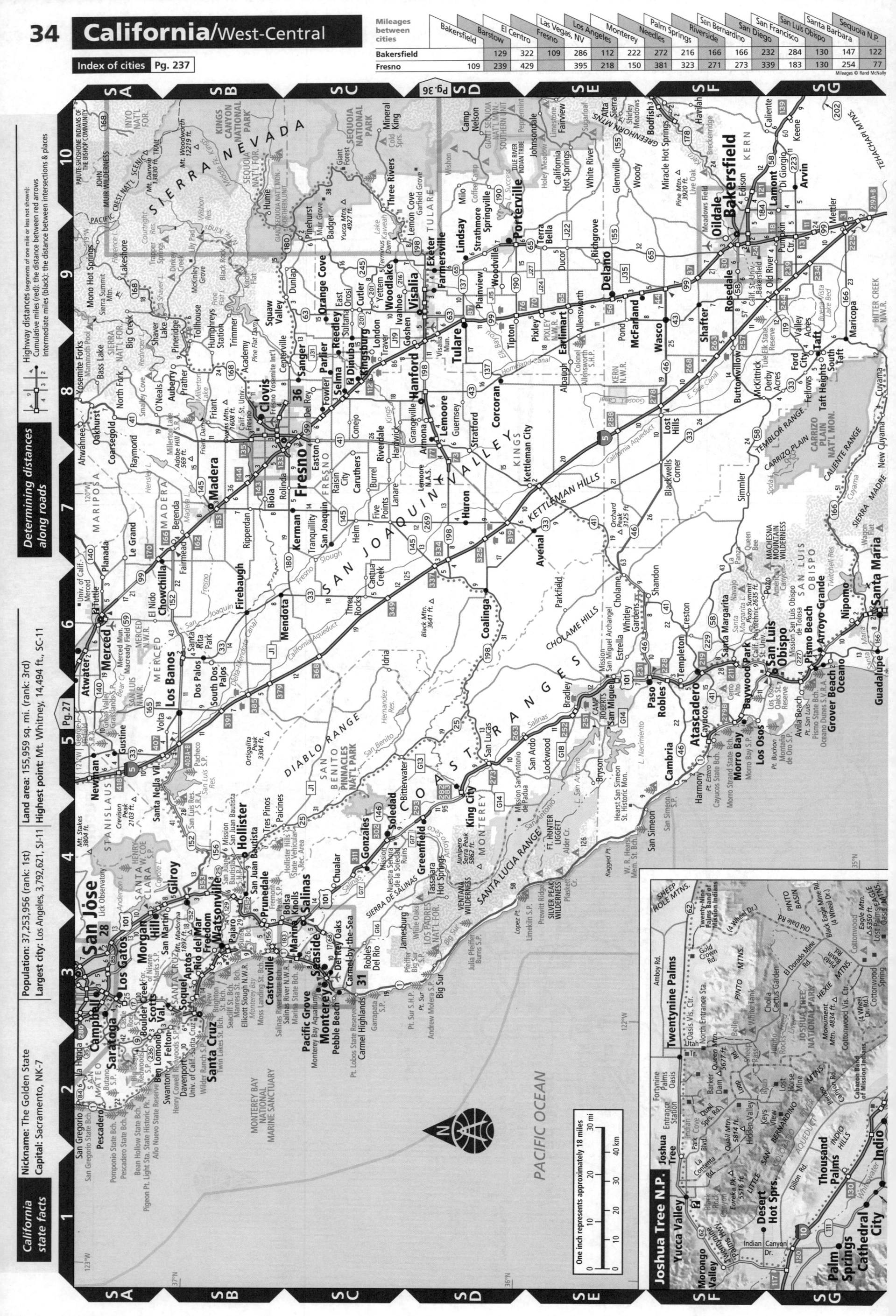

California state facts

Nickname: The Golden State
Capital: Sacramento, NK-7

Population: 37,253,956 (rank: 1st)
Largest city: Los Angeles, 3,792,621, SJ-11

Land area: 155,959 sq. mi. (rank: 3rd)
Highest point: Mt. Whitney, 14,494 ft., SC-11

Determining distances along roads

Highway distances (segments of one mile or less not shown):
Cumulative miles (red): the distance between red arrows
Intermediate miles (black): the distance between intersections & places

One inch represents approximately 18 miles

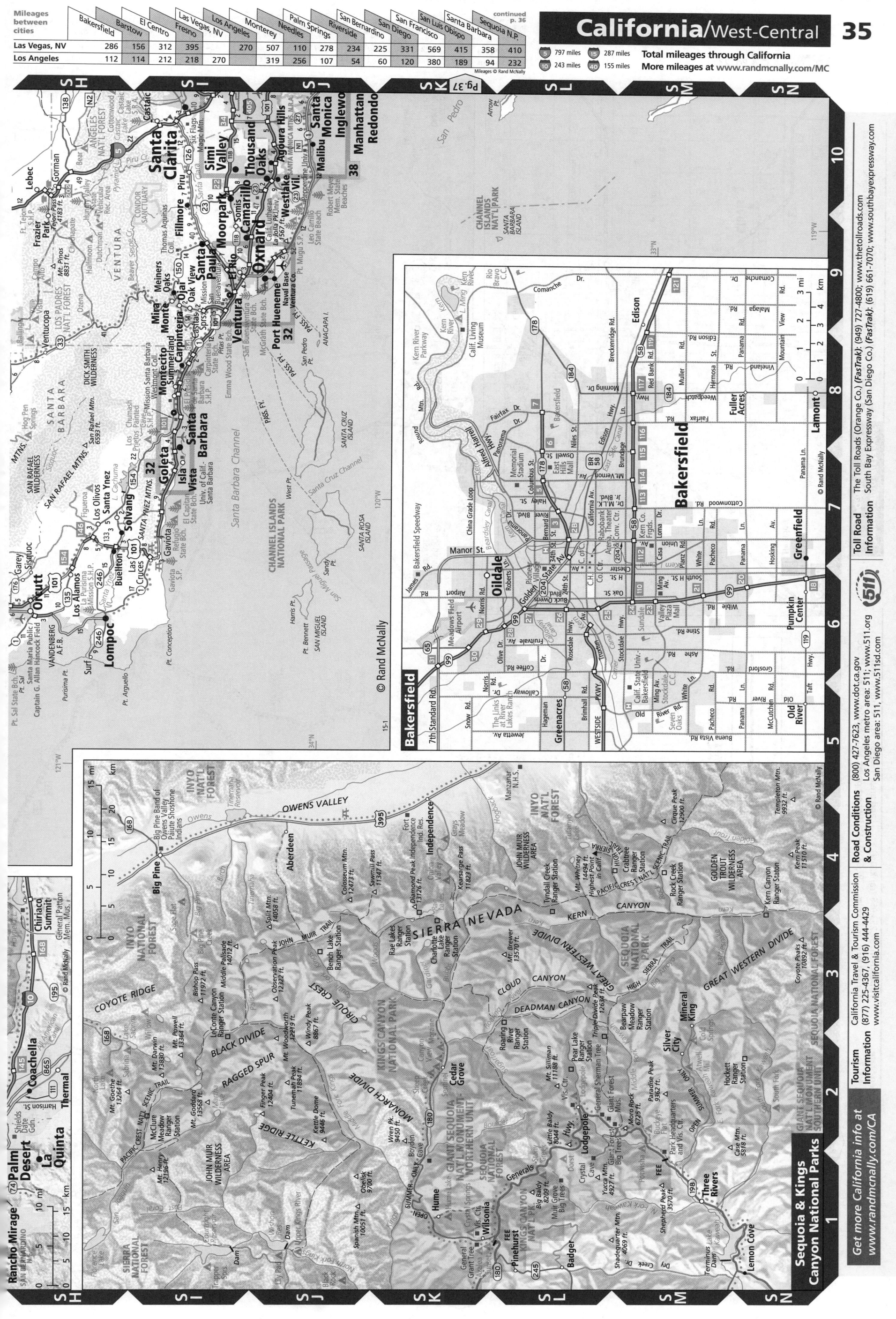

Mileages between cities	Bakersfield	Barstow	El Centro	Fresno	Las Vegas, NV	Los Angeles	Monterey	Needles	Palm Springs	Riverside	San Bernardino	San Diego	San Francisco	San Luis Obispo	Santa Barbara	Sequoia N.P.
Las Vegas, NV	286	156	312	395		270	507	110	278	234	225	331	569	415	358	410
Los Angeles	112	114	212	218	270		319	256	107	54	60	120	380	189	94	232

continued p. 36
Mileages © Rand McNally

Total mileages through California
More mileages at www.randmcnally.com/MC

| 5 | 797 miles | 15 | 287 miles |
| 10 | 243 miles | 40 | 155 miles |

© Rand McNally

Bakersfield

Sequoia & Kings Canyon National Parks

Get more California info at www.randmcnally.com/CA

Tourism Information	California Travel & Tourism Commission (877) 225-4367, (916) 444-4429 www.visitcalifornia.com
Road Conditions & Construction	(800) 427-7623, www.dot.ca.gov Los Angeles metro area: 511; www.511.org San Diego area: 511, www.511sd.com
Toll Road Information	The Toll Roads (Orange Co.) (949) 727-4800; www.thetollroads.com South Bay Expressway (San Diego Co.) (619) 661-7070; www.southbayexpressway.com

Mileages between cities	Bakersfield	Barstow	El Centro	Fresno	Las Vegas, NV	Los Angeles	Monterey	Needles	Palm Springs	Riverside	San Bernardino	San Diego	San Francisco	San Luis Obispo	Santa Barbara	Sequoia N.P.
Monterey	222	350	530	150	507	319		494	424	372	373	439	112	142	237	226
Palm Springs	216	123	108	323	278	107	424	188		52	54	139	486	296	201	338

Mileages © Rand McNally

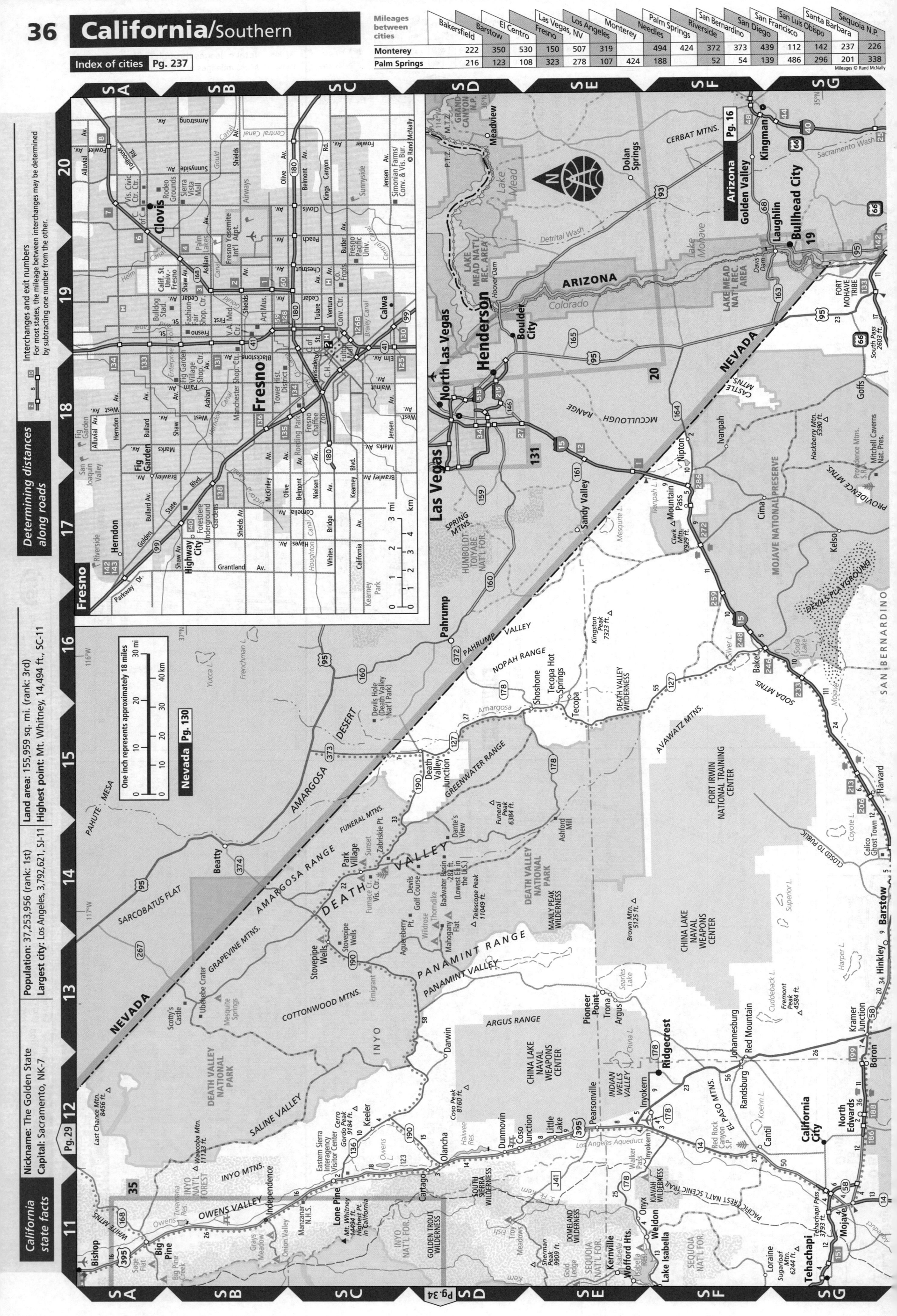

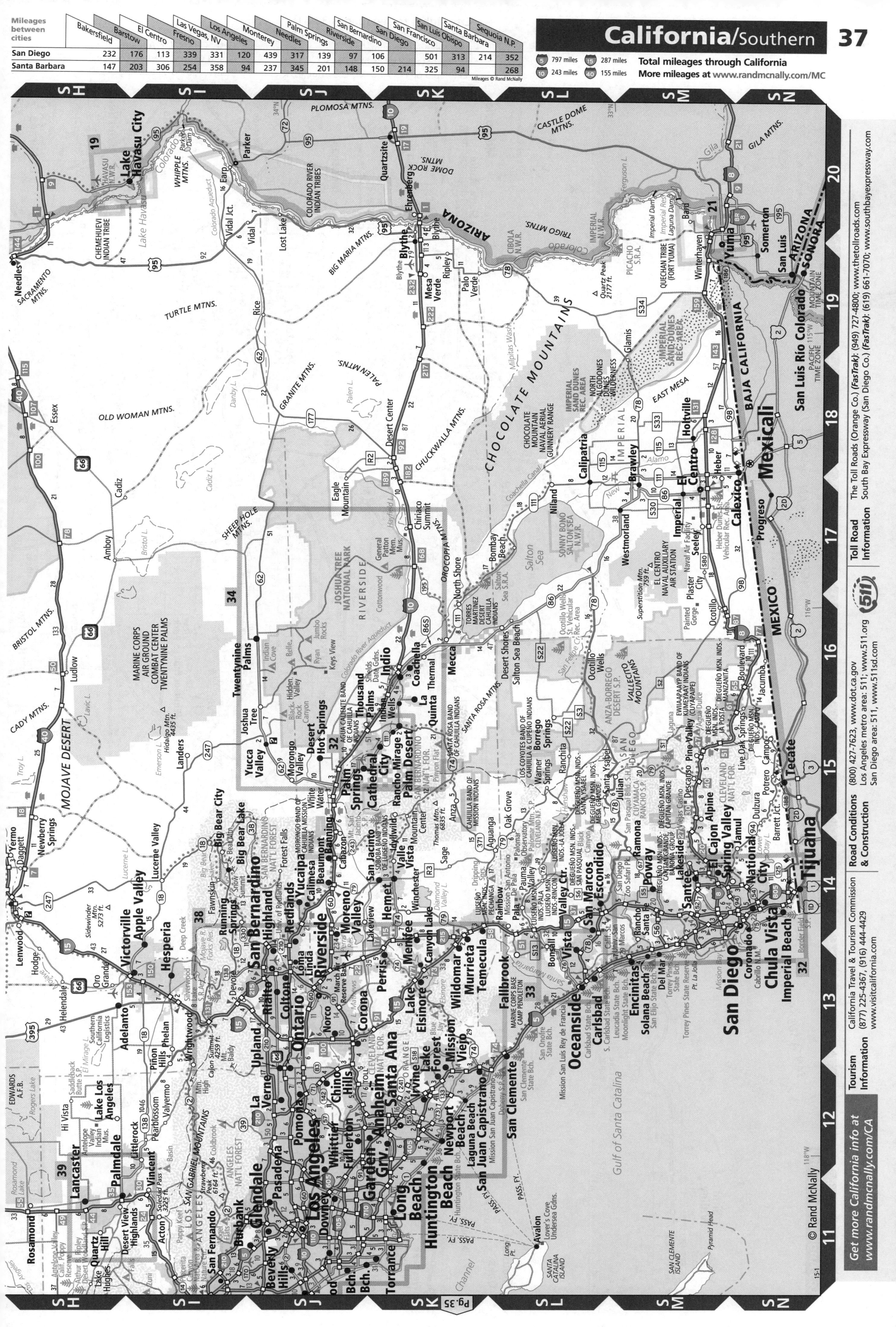

Mileages between cities	Bakersfield	Barstow	El Centro	Las Vegas, NV	Los Angeles	Monterey	Needles	Palm Springs	Riverside	San Bernardino	San Diego	San Francisco	San Luis Obispo	Santa Barbara	Sequoia N.P.
San Diego	232	176	113	339	331	120	439	317	139	97		106	501	313	214	352
Santa Barbara	147	203	306	254	358	94	237	345	201	148	150	214	325		94	268

Mileages © Rand McNally

Total mileages through California
More mileages at www.randmcnally.com/MC

5	797 miles	15	287 miles
10	243 miles	40	155 miles

City sights to see (pages 38-41)

- Aquarium of the Pacific, Long Beach, I-8
- Disneyland, Anaheim, I-11
- Dodger Stadium, Los Angeles, I-1
- El Pueblo de Los Angeles, Los Angeles, K-2
- Exposition Park, Los Angeles, F-7
- Getty Center, Los Angeles, E-4
- Grand Central Market, Los Angeles, L-2
- Hollywood Bowl, Los Angeles, D-6

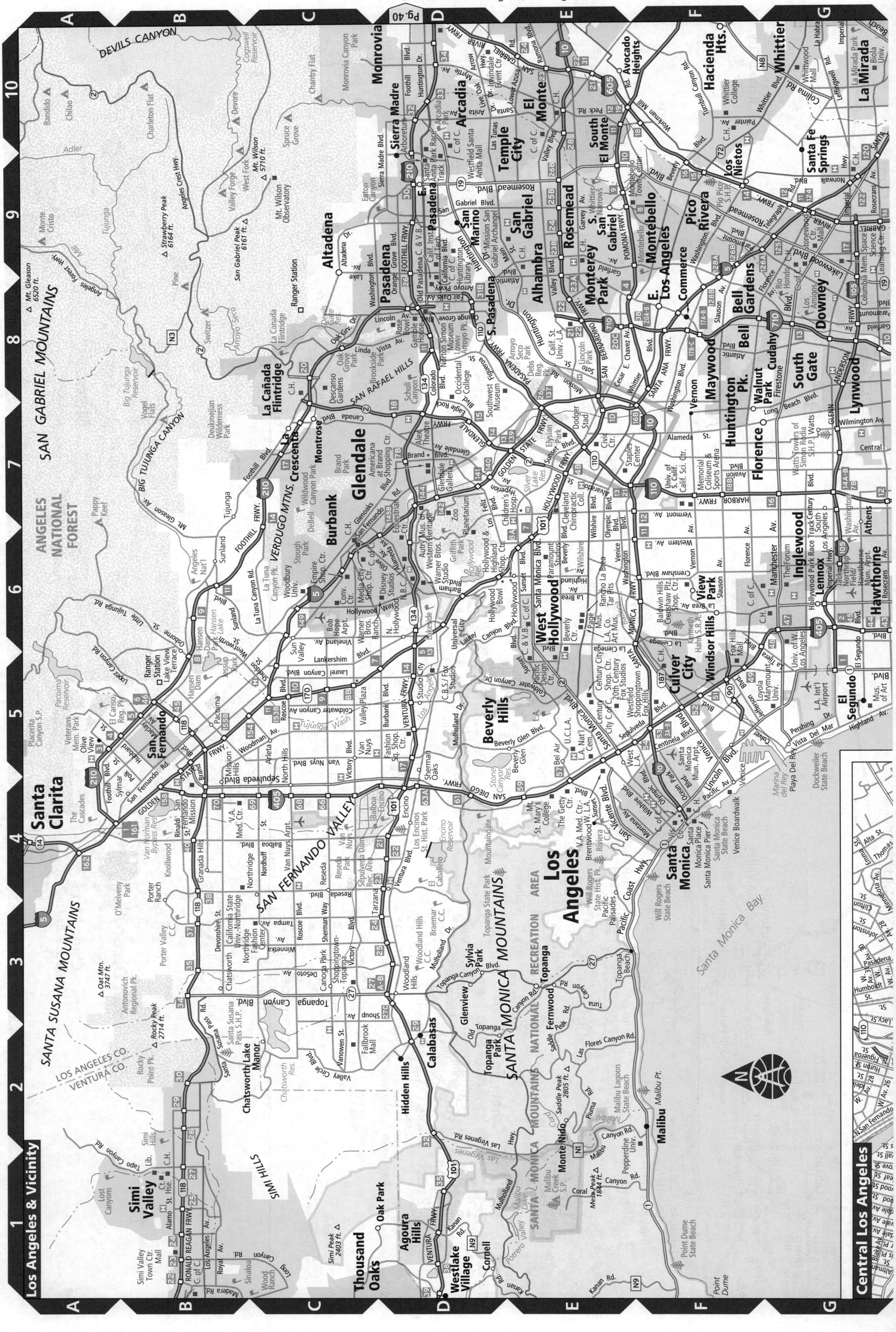

- Huntington Library, San Marino, D-9
- Japanese American National Museum, Los Angeles, K-3
- Knott's Berry Farm, Buena Park, H-10
- Los Angeles Co. Art Mus., Los Angeles, E-6
- Los Angeles Maritime Museum, Los Angeles, J-7
- Los Angeles Zoo and Botanical Gardens, Los Angeles, D-7

list continued p.40

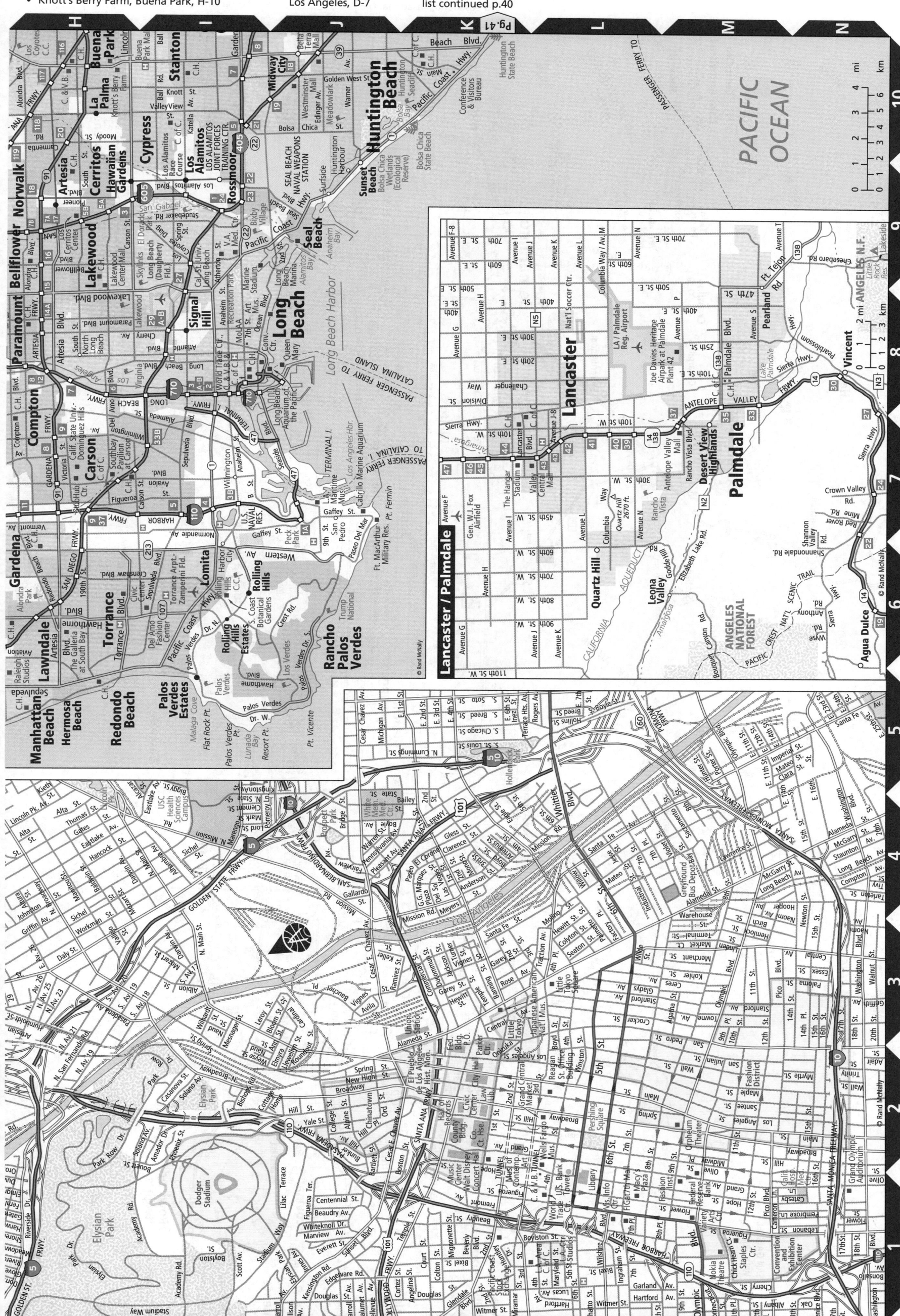

Pg.41

City sights to see (pages 38-41)
- Mission San Juan Capistrano, San Juan Capistrano, M-14
- Mount Wilson Observatory, Mt. Wilson, C-9
- Old Pasadena, Pasadena, D-8
- Oldest Winery in Calif., Rancho Cucamonga, D-15
- The Queen Mary, Long Beach, J-8
- Richard M. Nixon Library & Birthplace, Yorba Linda, H-12

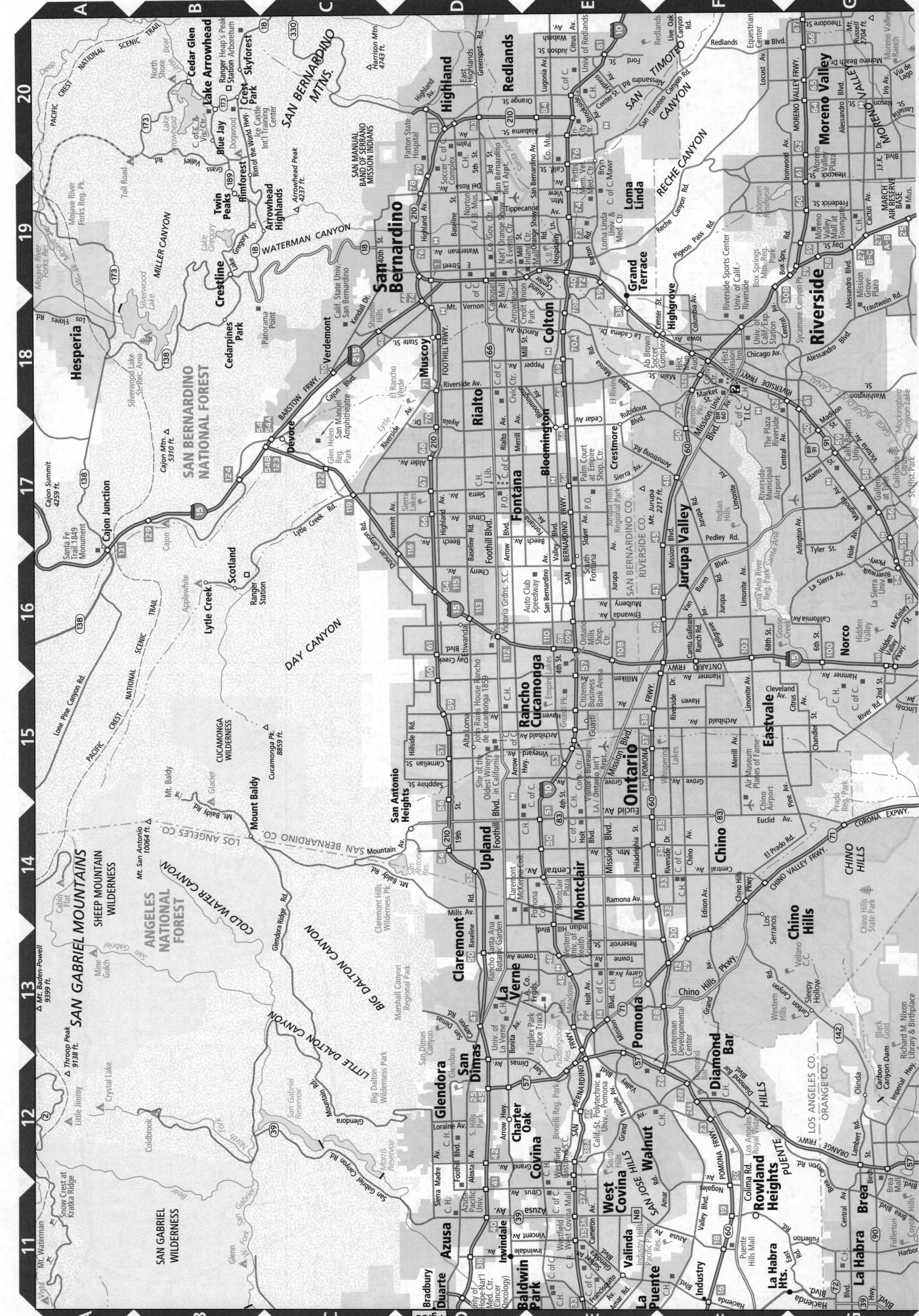

- Rose Bowl, Pasadena, D-8
- Santa Monica Pier, Santa Monica, F-4
- Universal City, Los Angeles, D-6
- Venice Boardwalk, Los Angeles, F-4
- Walt Disney Concert Hall, Los Angeles, K-2
- Warner Bros. Studio, Burbank, D-6
- Will Rogers State Historic Park, Pacific Palisades, E-4

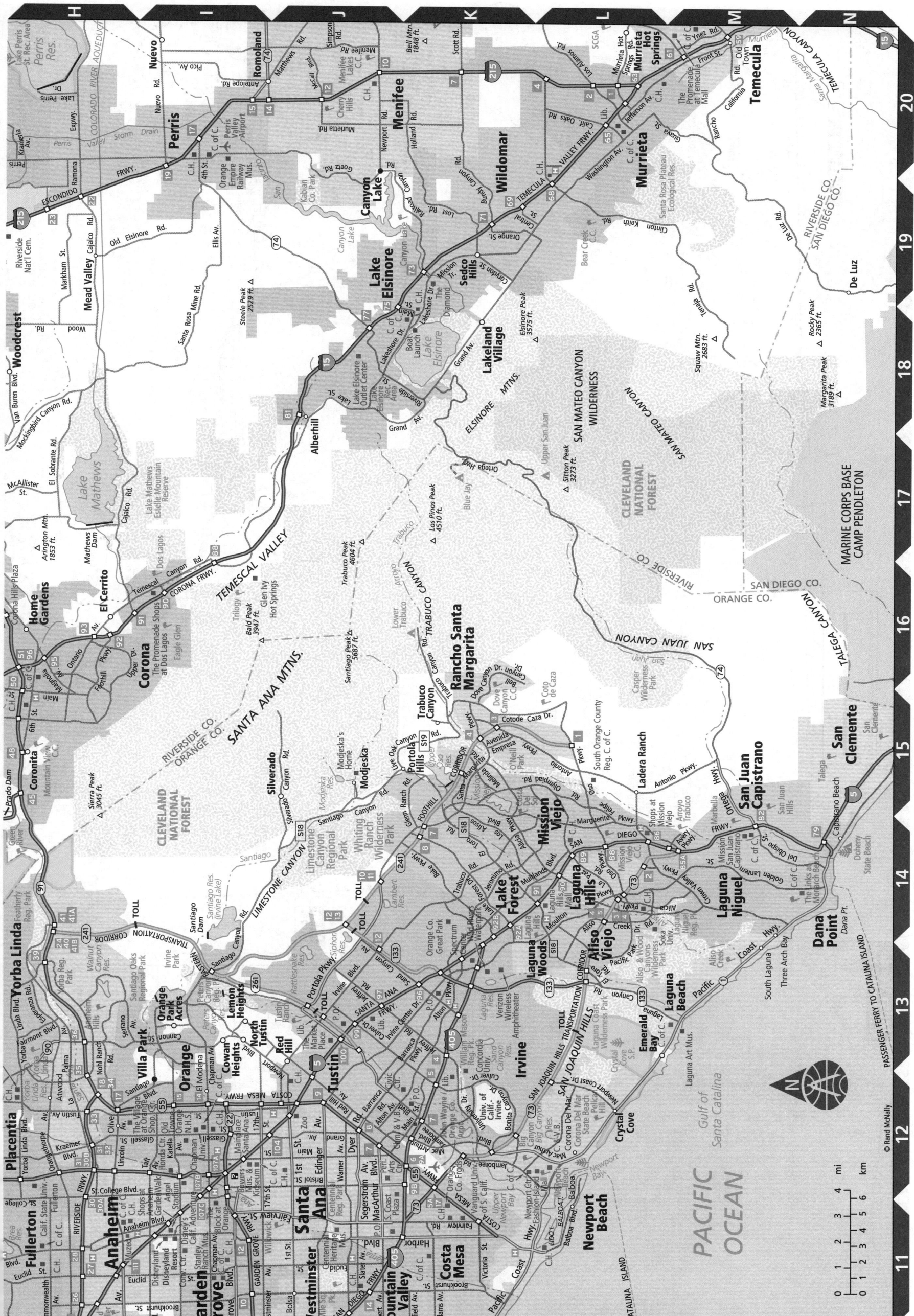

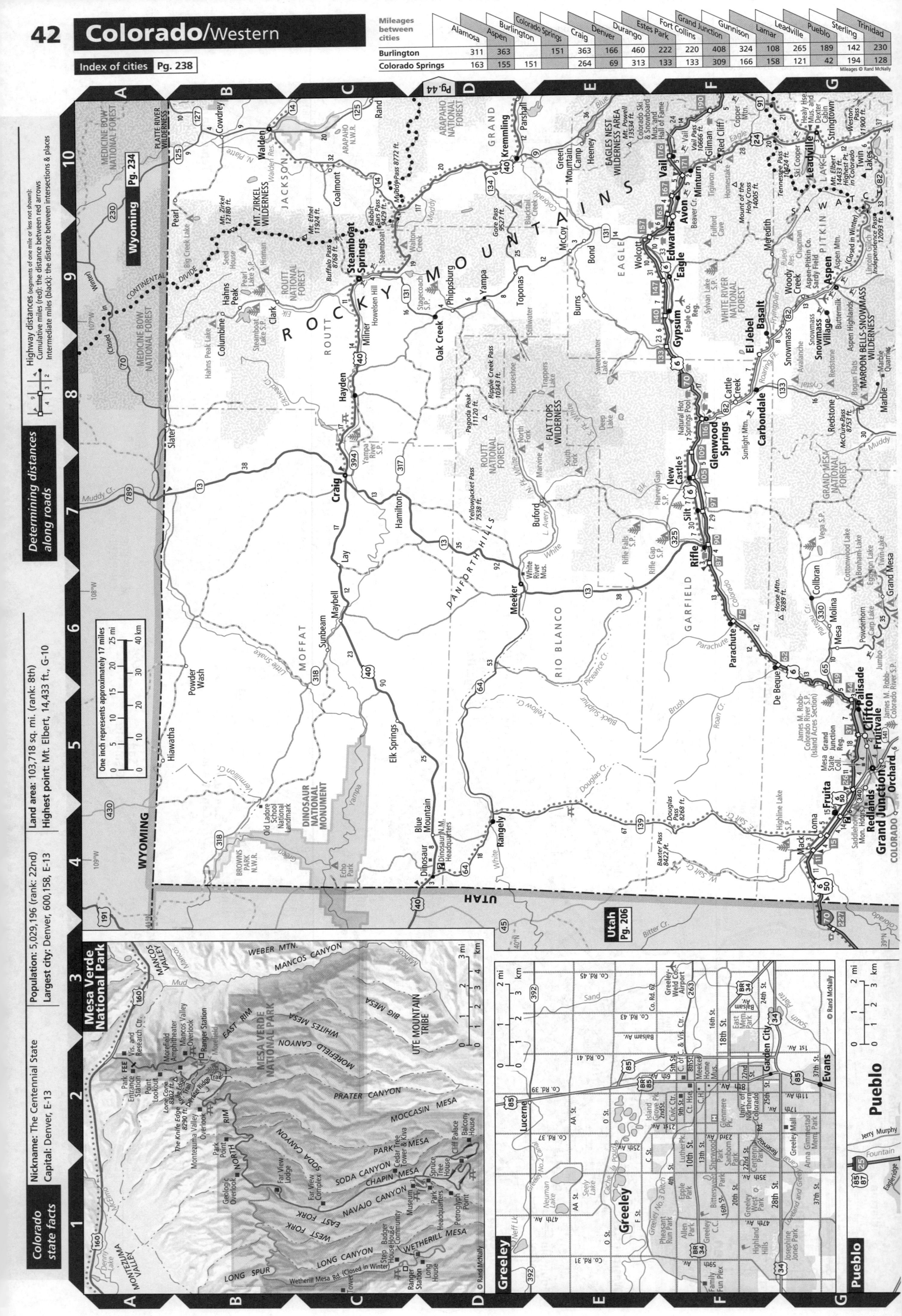

Mileages between cities	Alamosa	Aspen	Burlington	Colorado Springs	Craig	Denver	Durango	Estes Park	Fort Collins	Grand Junction	Gunnison	Lamar	Leadville	Pueblo	Sterling	Trinidad
Burlington	311	363		151	363	166	460	222	220	408	324	108	265	189	142	230
Colorado Springs	163	155	151		264	69	313	133	133	309	166	158	121	42	194	128

Mileages © Rand McNally

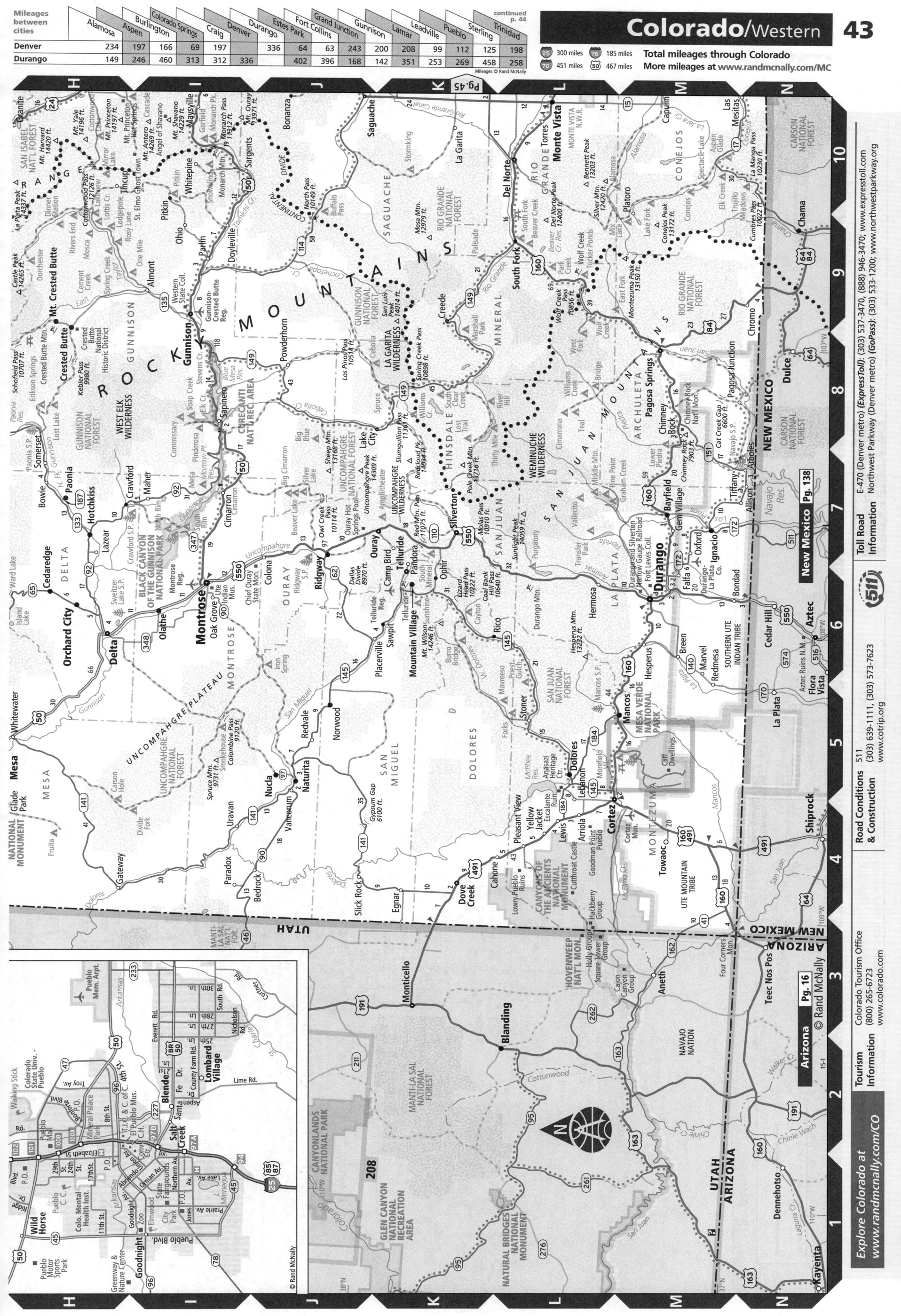

Mileages between cities	Alamosa	Aspen	Burlington	Colorado Springs	Craig	Denver	Durango	Estes Park	Fort Collins	Grand Junction	Gunnison	Lamar	Leadville	Pueblo	Sterling	Trinidad
Denver	234	197	166	69	197		336	64	63	243	200	208	99	112	125	198
Durango	149	246	460	313	312	336			402	396	168	142	351	253	269	458	258

continued p. 44

Mileages ©Rand McNally

Total mileages through Colorado
25 300 miles 76 185 miles
70 451 miles 50 467 miles
More mileages at www.randmcnally.com/MC

Tourism Information: Colorado Tourism Office (800) 265-6723 www.colorado.com

Road Conditions & Construction: 511 (303) 639-1111, (303) 573-7623 www.cotrip.org

Toll Road Information: E-470 (Denver metro) (ExpressToll): (303) 537-3470, (888) 946-3470; www.expresstoll.com Northwest Parkway (Denver metro) (GoPass): (303) 533-1200; www.northwestparkway.org

511

Explore Colorado at www.randmcnally.com/CO

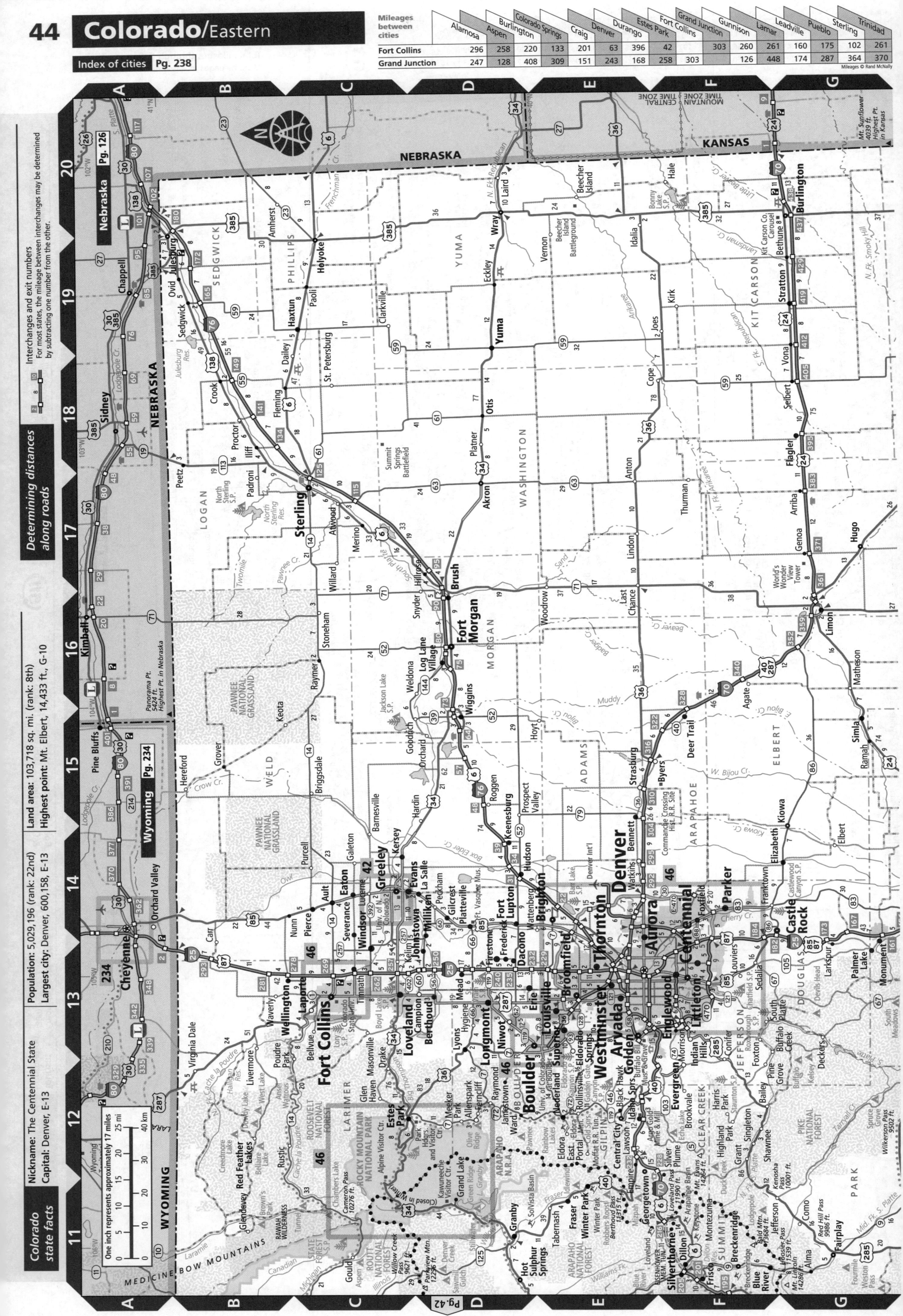

Mileages between cities	Alamosa	Aspen	Burlington	Colorado Springs	Craig	Denver	Durango	Estes Park	Fort Collins	Grand Junction	Gunnison	Lamar	Leadville	Pueblo	Sterling	Trinidad
Fort Collins	296	258	220	133	201	63	396	42		303	260	261	160	175	102	261
Grand Junction	247	128	408	309	151	243	168	258	303		126	448	174	287	364	370

Mileages by Rand McNally

Colorado state facts

Nickname: The Centennial State
Capital: Denver, E-13

Population: 5,029,196 (rank: 22nd)
Largest city: Denver, E-13

Land area: 103,718 sq. mi. (rank: 8th)
Highest point: Mt. Elbert, 14,433 ft., G-10

Determining distances along roads

Interchanges and exit numbers
For most states, the mileage between interchanges may be determined by subtracting one number from the other.

One inch represents approximately 17 miles

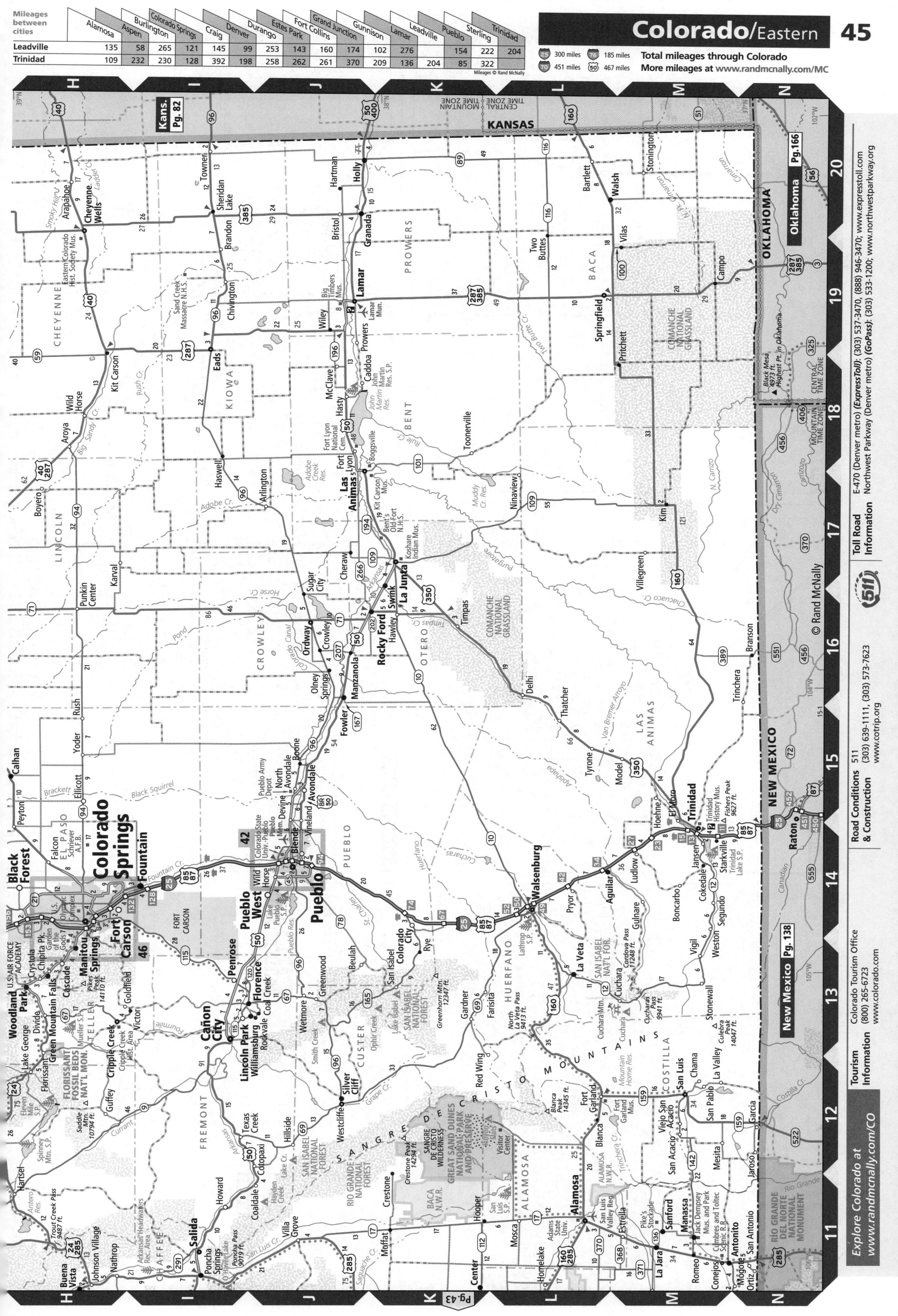

Mileages between cities	Alamosa	Aspen	Burlington	Colorado Springs	Craig	Denver	Durango	Estes Park	Fort Collins	Grand Junction	Gunnison	Lamar	Leadville	Pueblo	Sterling	Trinidad
Leadville	135	58	265	121	145	99	253	143	160	174	102	276		154	222	204
Trinidad	109	232	230	128	392	198	258	262	261	370	209	136	204	85	322	

Mileages © Rand McNally

Total mileages through Colorado
More mileages at www.randmcnally.com/MC

25 300 miles	76 185 miles		
70 451 miles	50 467 miles		

City sights to see

- Black American West Museum & Heritage Center, Denver, L-3
- Cave of the Winds, Colorado Springs, G-1
- Colorado History Museum, Denver, M-2
- Colorado State Capitol, Denver, M-2
- Denver Art Museum, Denver, M-2
- Denver Museum of Nature & Science, Denver, L-4
- Garden of the Gods, Colorado Springs, G-1

Fort Collins

Boulder

Denver & Vicinity

Rocky Mountain National Park

Colorado Springs

ROOSEVELT NAT'L. FOR.

ROCKY MOUNTAIN NATIONAL PARK

ARAPAHO NATIONAL FOREST

ROOSEVELT NAT'L FOREST

ARAPAHO NAT'L FOREST

ARAPAHO NAT'L REC. AREA

PIKE NATIONAL FOREST

ROCKY MOUNTAIN ARSENAL NAT'L WILDLIFE REFUGE

Denver International Airport

U.S. AIR FORCE ACADEMY

Estes Park

Grand Lake

Brighton

Westminster

Broomfield

Thornton

Northglenn

Federal Hts.

Western Hills

Welby

Dupont

Henderson

Wattenberg

Lochbuie

Barr Lake

Lafayette

Louisville

Superior

Laporte

Mountain View

Gunbarrel

Paragon Estates

Timnath

© Rand McNally

- National Center for Atmospheric Research, Boulder, D-4
- Old Town National Historic District, Fort Collins, B-9
- ProRodeo Hall of Fame, Colorado Springs, G-2
- Red Rocks Amphitheatre, Morrison, J-4
- U.S. Airforce Academy, Colorado Springs, F-1
- United States Mint, Denver, M-2
- World Figure Skating Hall of Fame, Colorado Springs, I-2

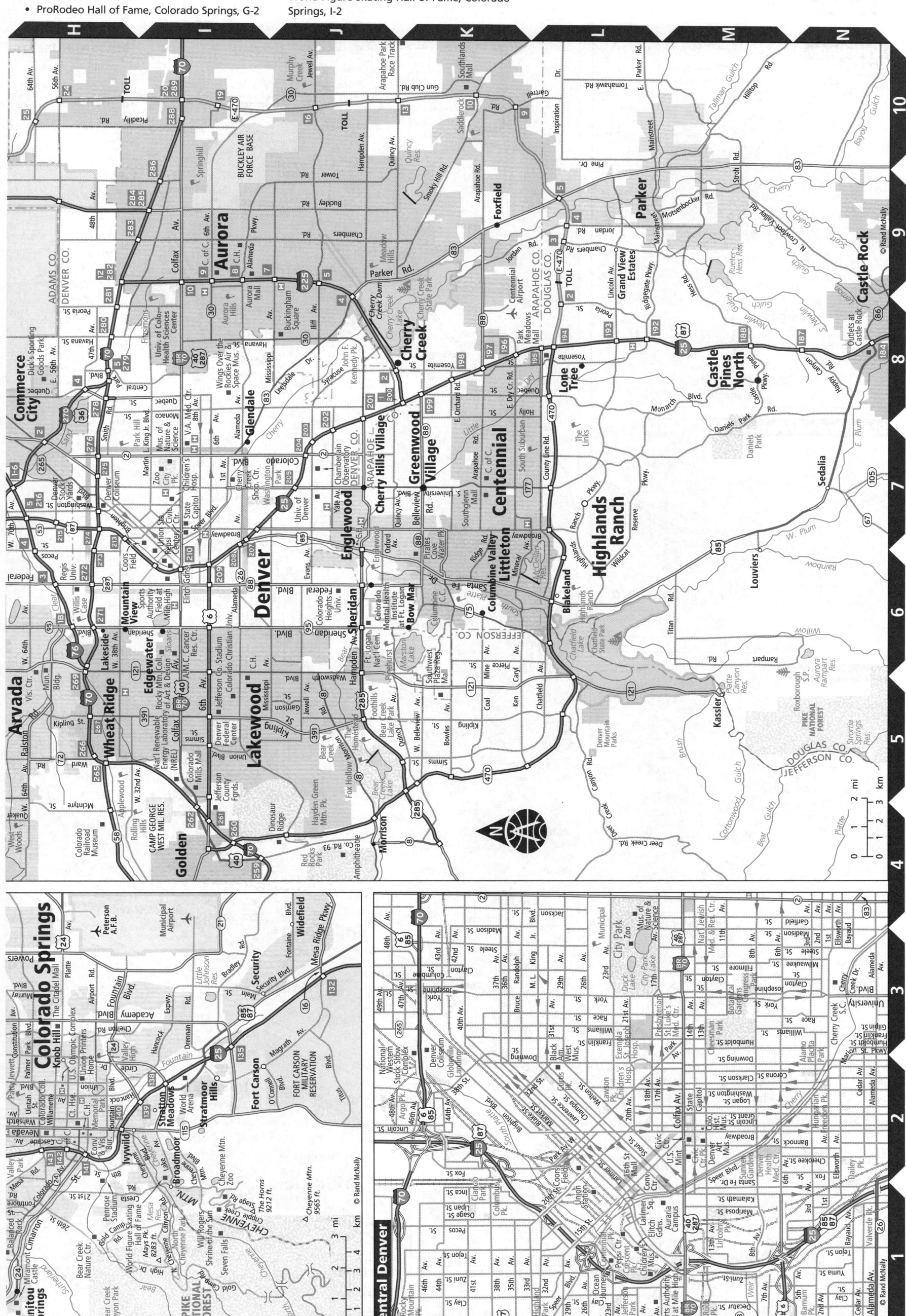

Mileages between cities	Bridgeport	Hartford	New Haven	New London, NY	New York, NY	Putnam	Torrington	Waterbury		Bridgeport	Hartford	New Haven	New London, NY	New York, NY	Putnam	Torrington	Waterbury
Bridgeport		55	18	64	54	107	50	30	Hartford	55		38	45	108	47	26	30
Danbury	29	57	35	81	62	104	47	27	New Haven	18	38		46	72	89	43	22

Mileages © Rand McNally

Connecticut state facts

Nickname: The Constitution State
Capital: Hartford, C-9

Population: 3,574,097 (rank: 29th) Land area: 4,845 sq. mi. (rank: 48th)
Largest city: Bridgeport, H-5 Highest point: Mt. Frissell, 2,380 ft., A-4

Determining distances along roads

Interchanges and exit numbers
For most states, the mileage between interchanges may be determined by subtracting one number from the other.

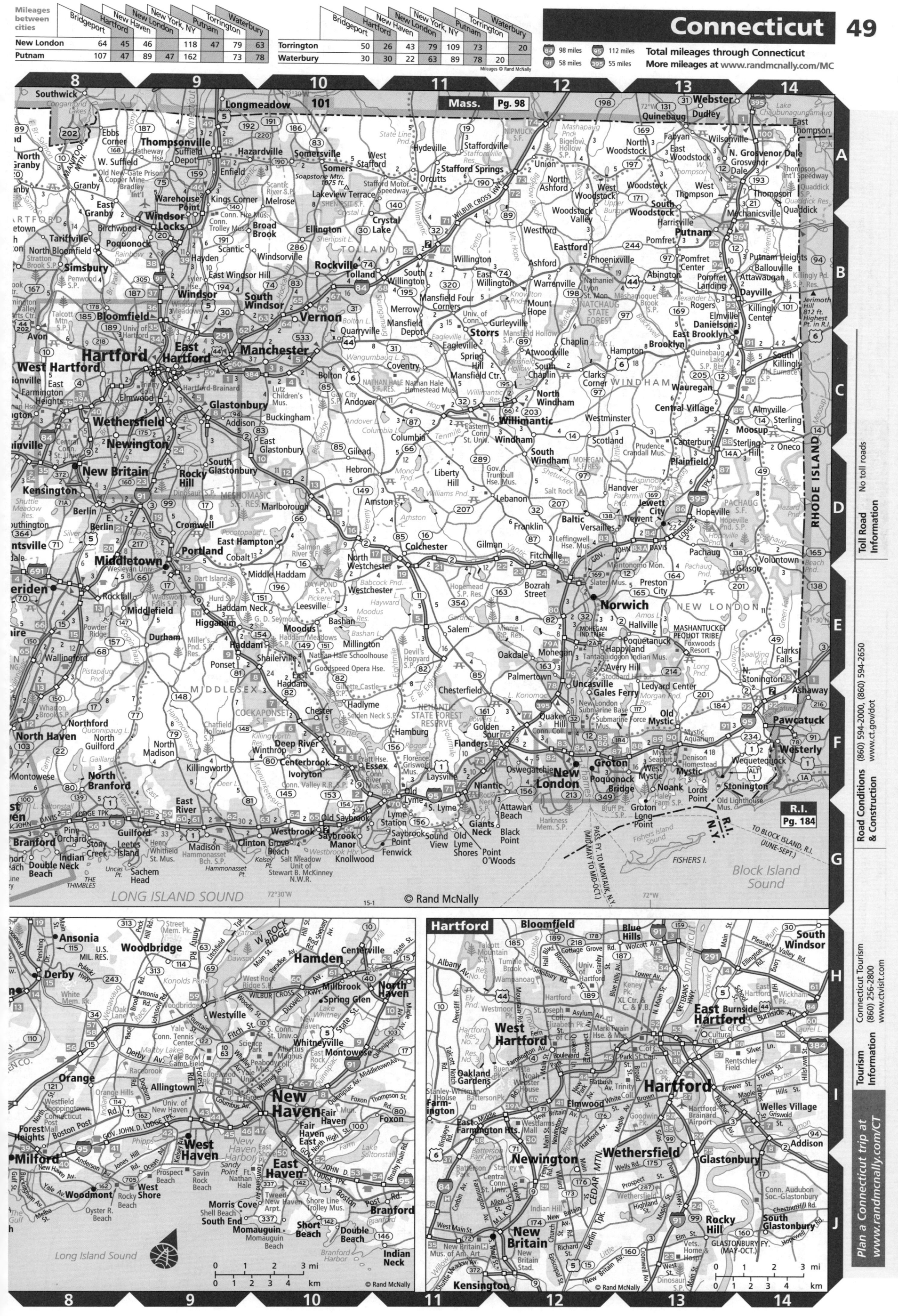

Mileages between cities

	Bridgeport	Hartford	New Haven	New London	New York, NY	Putnam	Torrington	Waterbury
New London	64	45	46		118	47	79	63
Putnam	107	47	89	47	162		73	78

	Bridgeport	Hartford	New Haven	New London	New York, NY	Putnam	Torrington	Waterbury
Torrington	50	26	43	79	109	73		20
Waterbury	30	30	22	63	89	78	20	

Mileages © Rand McNally

Total mileages through Connecticut
98 miles · 112 miles · 58 miles · 55 miles
More mileages at www.randmcnally.com/MC

Tourism Information — Connecticut Tourism (860) 256-2800 · www.ctvisit.com

Road Conditions & Construction — (860) 594-2000, (860) 594-2650 · www.ct.gov/dot

Toll Road Information — No toll roads

Plan a Connecticut trip at www.randmcnally.com/CT

© Rand McNally

Mileages between cities	Georgetown Dover	Lewes	Philadelphia Milford	Salisbury, PA	Selbyville MD	Wilmington		Georgetown Dover	Lewes	Philadelphia Milford	Salisbury, PA	Selbyville MD	Wilmington
Dover	36	40	20	80	56	55	50	Lewes	40	15	21	119	43	29	90
Georgetown	36		15	16	114	27	20	85	Middletown	26	62	66	46	56	84	81	27

Mileages © Rand McNally

Mileages between cities

	Georgetown Dover	Lewes Milford	Philadelphia, PA Salisbury, MD	Wilmington Selbyville	Wilmington
Millville, NJ	94 124	128 108	45 147	143 53	
Newark	46 80	85 64	43 102	99 14	
Selbyville	55 20	29 36	133 24		104
Wilmington	50 85	90 70	29 107		104

Mileages © Rand McNally

Total mileages through Delaware
More mileages at www.randmcnally.com/MC

- 23 miles
- 104 miles
- 108 miles

Toll Road Information
Delaware River & Bay Bay Authority (Del. Memorial Bridge & Lewes-Cape May Ferry) (E-ZPass):
(302) 571-6300; www.drba.net
Delaware Dept. of Trans. (all other toll roads) (E-ZPass): (888) 397-2773, www.ezpassde.com

(E-ZPass): www.ezpassde.com

Tourism Information
Delaware Tourism Office
(866) 284-7483
www.visitdelaware.com

Road Conditions & Construction
(302) 760-2080
www.deldot.gov
In DE: (800) 652-5600

Get more Delaware info at
www.randmcnally.com/DE

Pensacola

Tallahassee

Maryland Pg. 94

© Rand McNally

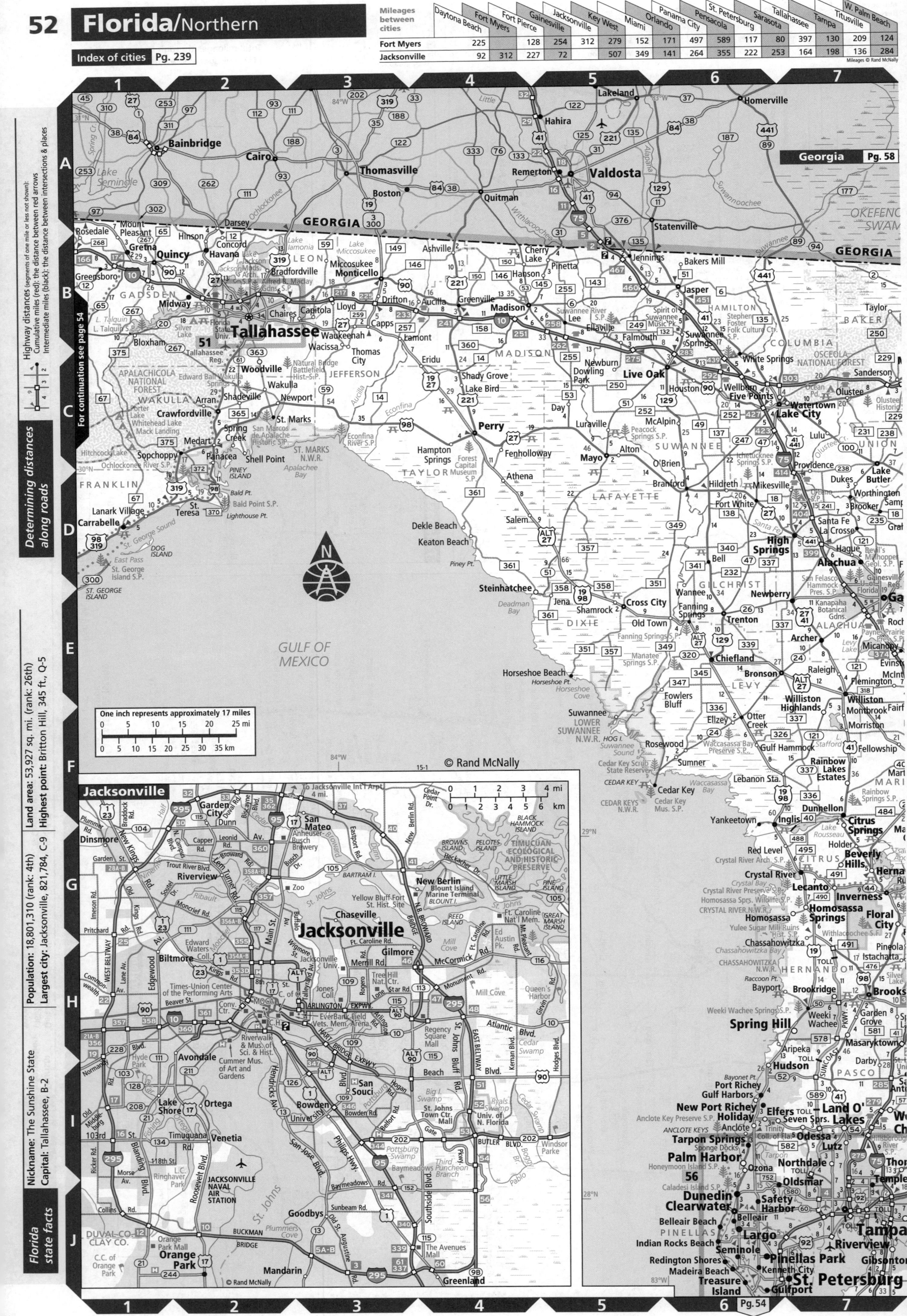

Mileages between cities	Daytona Beach	Fort Myers	Fort Pierce	Gainesville	Jacksonville	Key West	Miami	Orlando	Panama City	Pensacola	St. Petersburg	Sarasota	Tallahassee	Tampa	Titusville	W. Palm Beach
Fort Myers	225		128	254	312	279	152	171	497	589	117	80	397	130	209	124
Jacksonville	92	312	227	72		507	349	141	264	355	222	253	164	198	136	284

Mileages © Rand McNally

Mileages between cities	Daytona Beach	Fort Myers	Fort Pierce	Gainesville	Jacksonville	Key West	Miami	Orlando	Panama City	Pensacola	St. Petersburg	Sarasota	Tallahassee	Tampa	Titusville	W. Palm Beach
Key West	414	279	284	483	507		162	387	727	821	390	352	627	402	371	231
Miami	256	152	123	336	349	162		229	579	663	262	225	479	255	213	68

continued p. 54

Mileages © Rand McNally

Total mileages through Florida

| 4 | 132 miles | 75 | 471 miles |
| 10 | 362 miles | 95 | 382 miles |

More mileages at www.randmcnally.com/MC

© Rand McNally

Daytona Beach

Melbourne / Titusville

continued p. 54

Toll Road Information — Florida's Turnpike (SunPass): (800) 749-7453 floridasturnpike.com

511 — 511, (866) 374-3368, fl511.com, www.dot.state.fl.us

Road Conditions & Construction — 511, (866) 374-3368, (850) 488-5607

Tourism Information — Visit Florida (888) 735-2872, (850) 488-5607 www.visitflorida.com

Plan a Florida trip at www.randmcnally.com/FL

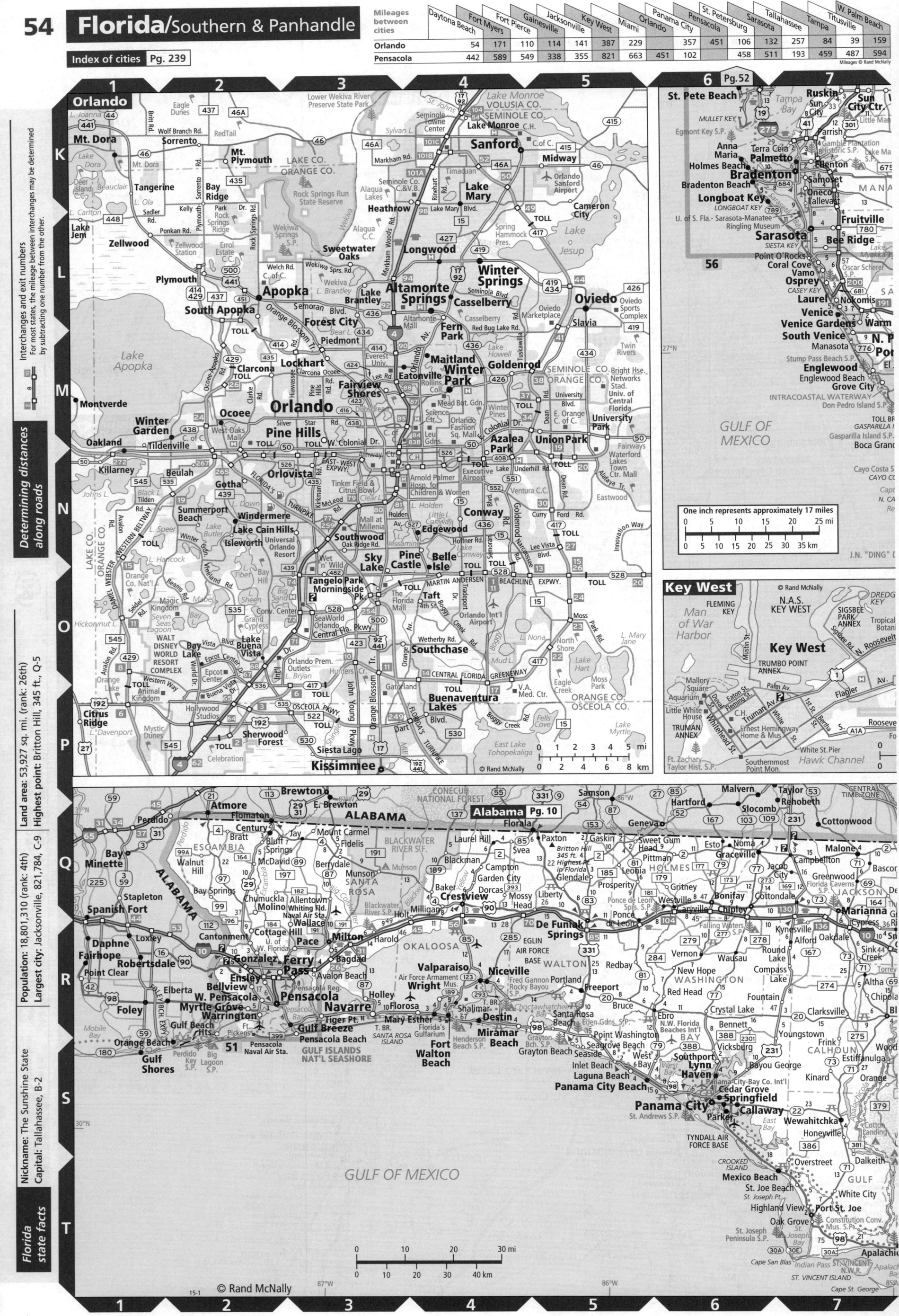

Mileages between cities	Daytona Beach	Fort Myers	Fort Pierce	Gainesville	Jacksonville	Key West	Miami	Orlando	Panama City	St. Petersburg	Sarasota	Tallahassee	Tampa	Titusville	W. Palm Beach
Tallahassee	253	397	364	148	164	627	479	257	96	193	257		273	295	413
Tampa	137	130	151	127	198	402	255	84	373	459	23	60		124	202

Mileages © Rand McNally

Total mileages through Florida

4 132 miles	**75** 471 miles
10 362 miles	**95** 382 miles

More mileages at www.randmcnally.com/MC

ATLANTIC OCEAN

THE EVERGLADES

EVERGLADES NATIONAL PARK

BIG CYPRESS NATIONAL PRESERVE

FLORIDA KEYS

GULF OF MEXICO

Pg. 53

For continuation see page 52

Ga. Pg. 58

Florida's Turnpike (SunPass):
(800) 749-7453
floridasturnpike.com

Toll Road Information

511
Road Conditions & Construction
(866) 374-3368
www.fl511.com, www.dot.state.fl.us

Visit Florida
(888) 735-2872, (850) 488-5607
www.visitflorida.com

Tourism Information

Plan a Florida trip at
www.randmcnally.com/FL

© Rand McNally

1 mi
1 km

City sights to see
- Art Deco National Historic District, Miami Beach, L-9
- Busch Gardens, Tampa, B-4
- Goodyear Blimp Base, Pompano Beach, G-9
- Hugh Taylor Birch State Park, Fort Lauderdale, H-9
- Marie Selby Botanical Gardens, Sarasota, H-3
- Miami Seaquarium, Miami, M-9

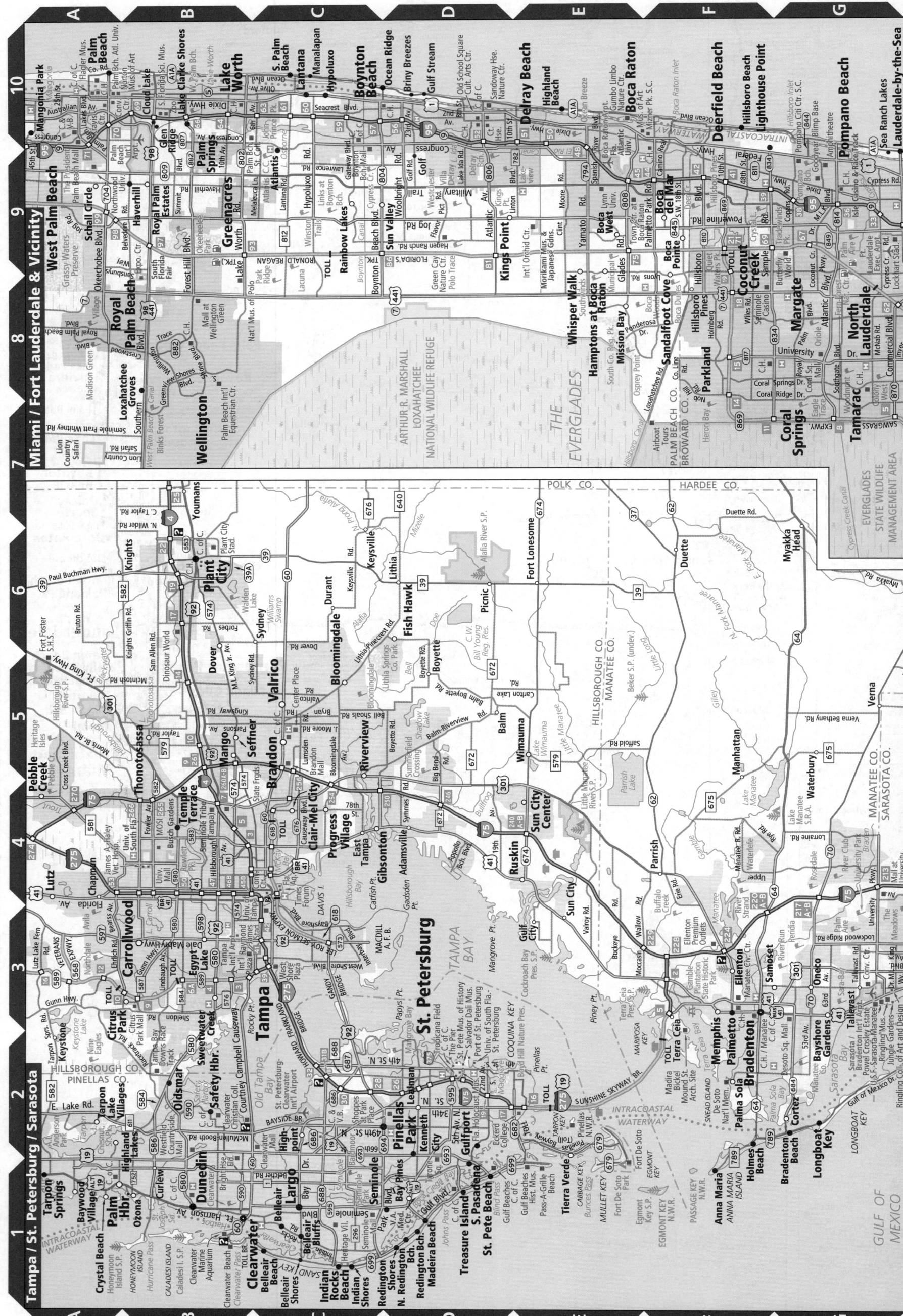

- Norton Mus. of Art, West Palm Beach, B-10
- Ringling Museum of Art / Ringling Center for the Cultural Arts, Sarasota, G-3
- Salvador Dali Museum, St. Petersburg, D-2
- St. Petersburg Mus. of Hist., St. Petersburg, D-2
- Thomas A. Edison & Henry Ford Winter Estates, Fort Myers, M-1
- Vizcaya Museum and Gardens, Miami, M-8

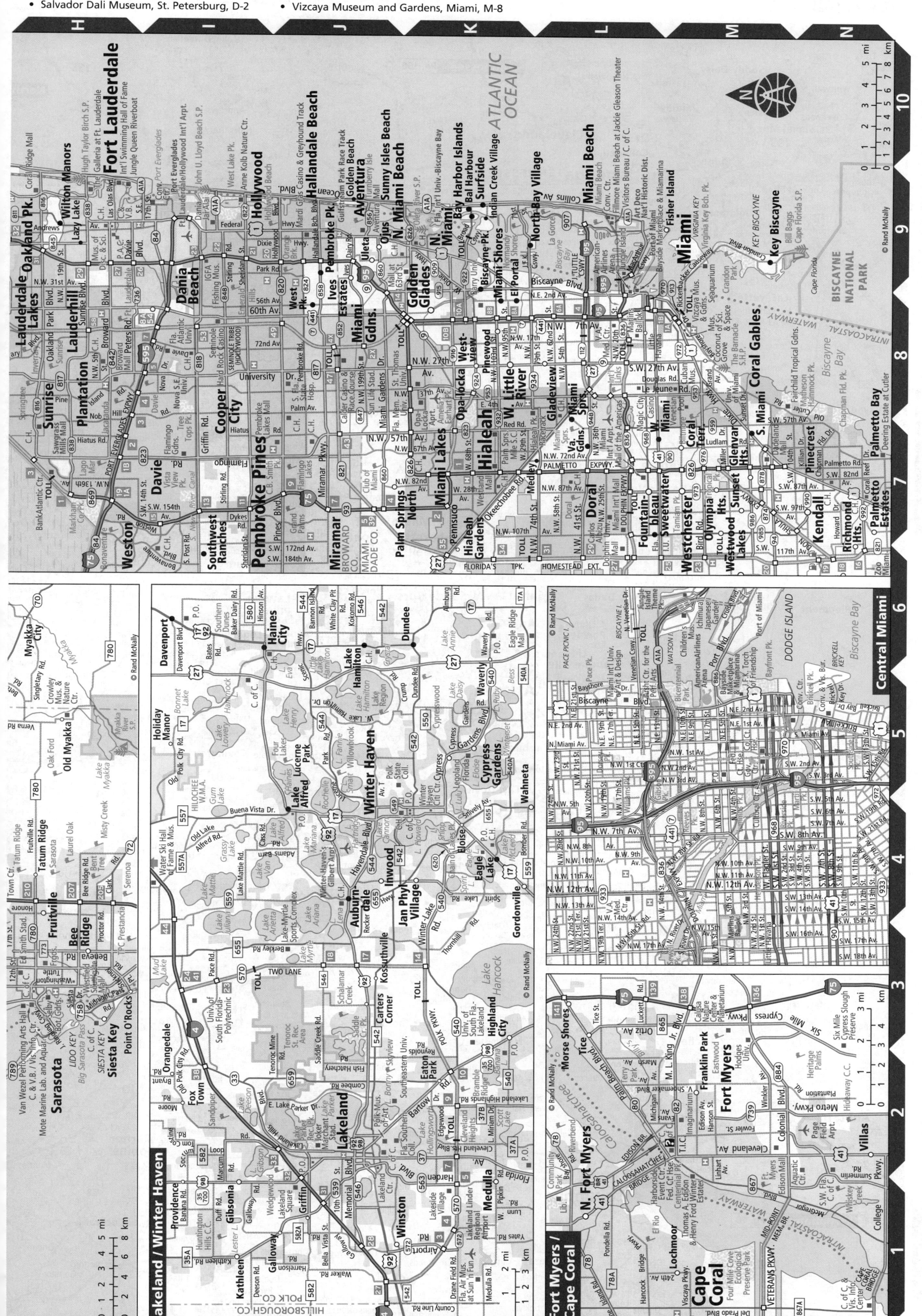

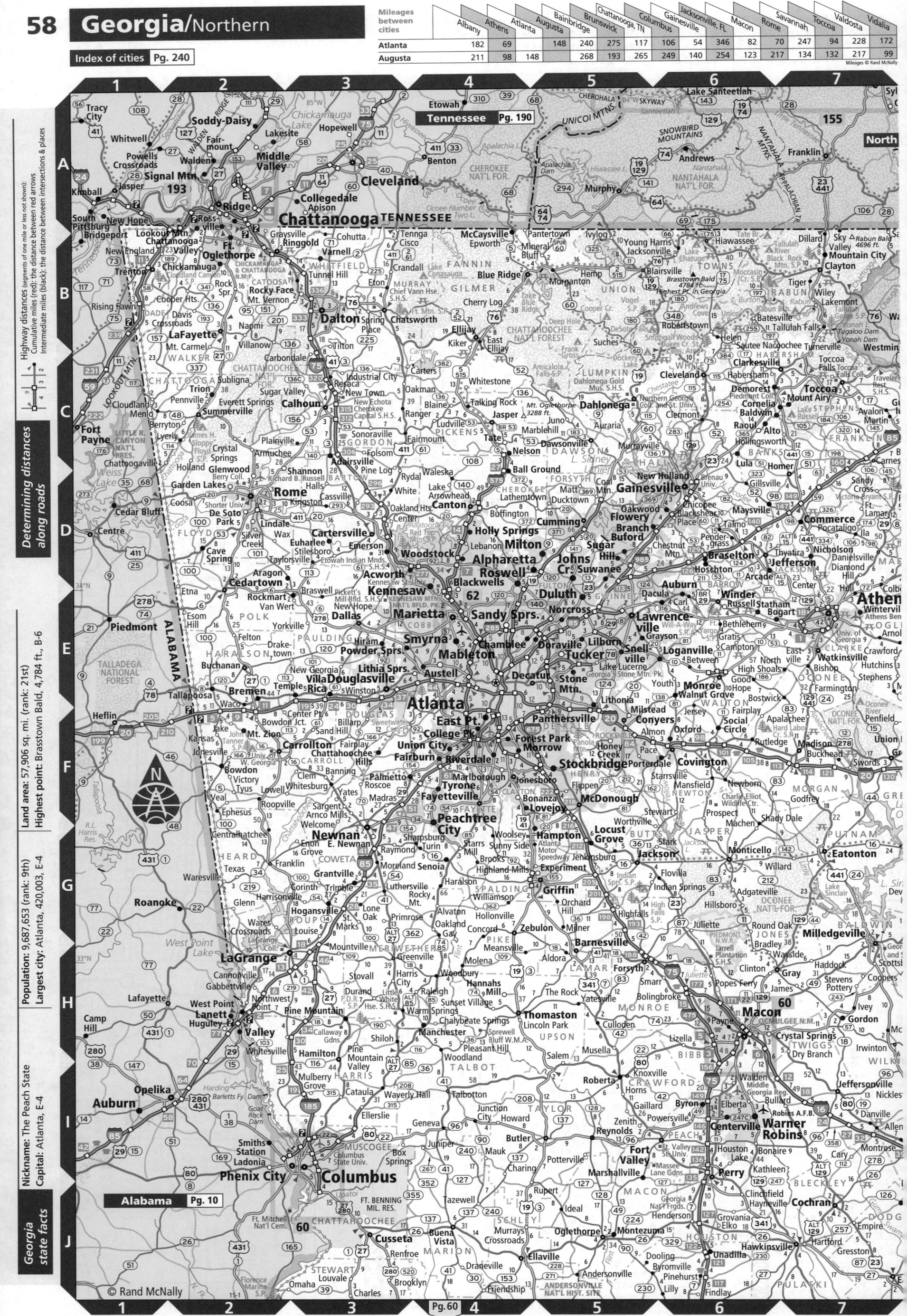

	Albany	Athens	Atlanta	Augusta	Bainbridge	Brunswick	Chattanooga, TN	Columbus	Gainesville	Jacksonville, FL	Macon	Rome	Savannah	Toccoa	Valdosta	Vidalia
Atlanta	182	69		148	240	275	117	106	54	346	82	70	247	94	228	172
Augusta	211	98	148		268	193	265	249	140	254	123	217	134	132	217	99

Mileages © Rand McNally

Georgia state facts

Nickname: The Peach State
Capital: Atlanta, E-4
Population: 9,687,653 (rank: 9th)
Land area: 57,906 sq. mi. (rank: 21st)
Highest point: Brasstown Bald, 4,784 ft., B-6
Largest city: Atlanta, 420,003, E-4

Determining distances along roads

Highway distances (segments of one mile or less not shown):
Cumulative miles (red): the distance between arrows
Intermediate miles (black): the distance between intersections & places

© Rand McNally

Mileages between cities	Albany	Athens	Atlanta	Augusta	Bainbridge	Brunswick	Chattanooga, TN	Columbus	Gainesville	Jacksonville, FL	Macon	Rome	Savannah	Toccoa	Valdosta	Vidalia
Chattanooga, TN	300	172	117	265	348	397		219	121	465	201	71	364	155	346	289
Columbus	85	171	106	249	128	258	219		161	292	98	144	249	201	173	175

continued p. 60

Mileages © Rand McNally

Total mileages through Georgia

20	203 miles	85	180 miles
75	355 miles	95	112 miles

More mileages at www.randmcnally.com/MC

One inch represents approximately 16 miles

No toll roads

Toll Road Information

Road Conditions & Construction — Georgia Dept. of Economic Development

Tourism Information — Georgia Dept. of Economic Development (800) 847-4842

Road Conditions & Construction — 511, (888) 635-8287, (877) 694-2511, (404) 635-8000, www.511ga.org

Explore Georgia at www.randmcnally.com/GA — www.exploregeorgia.org

Mileages between cities	Albany	Athens	Atlanta	Augusta	Bainbridge	Brunswick	Chattanooga, TN	Columbus	Gainesville	Jacksonville, FL	Macon	Rome	Savannah	Toccoa	Valdosta	Vidalia
Jacksonville, FL	198	310	346	254	204	66	465	292	396		270	416	135	375	121	164
Macon	106	91	82	123	163	193	201	98	132	270		152	165	143	152	90

Mileages © Rand McNally

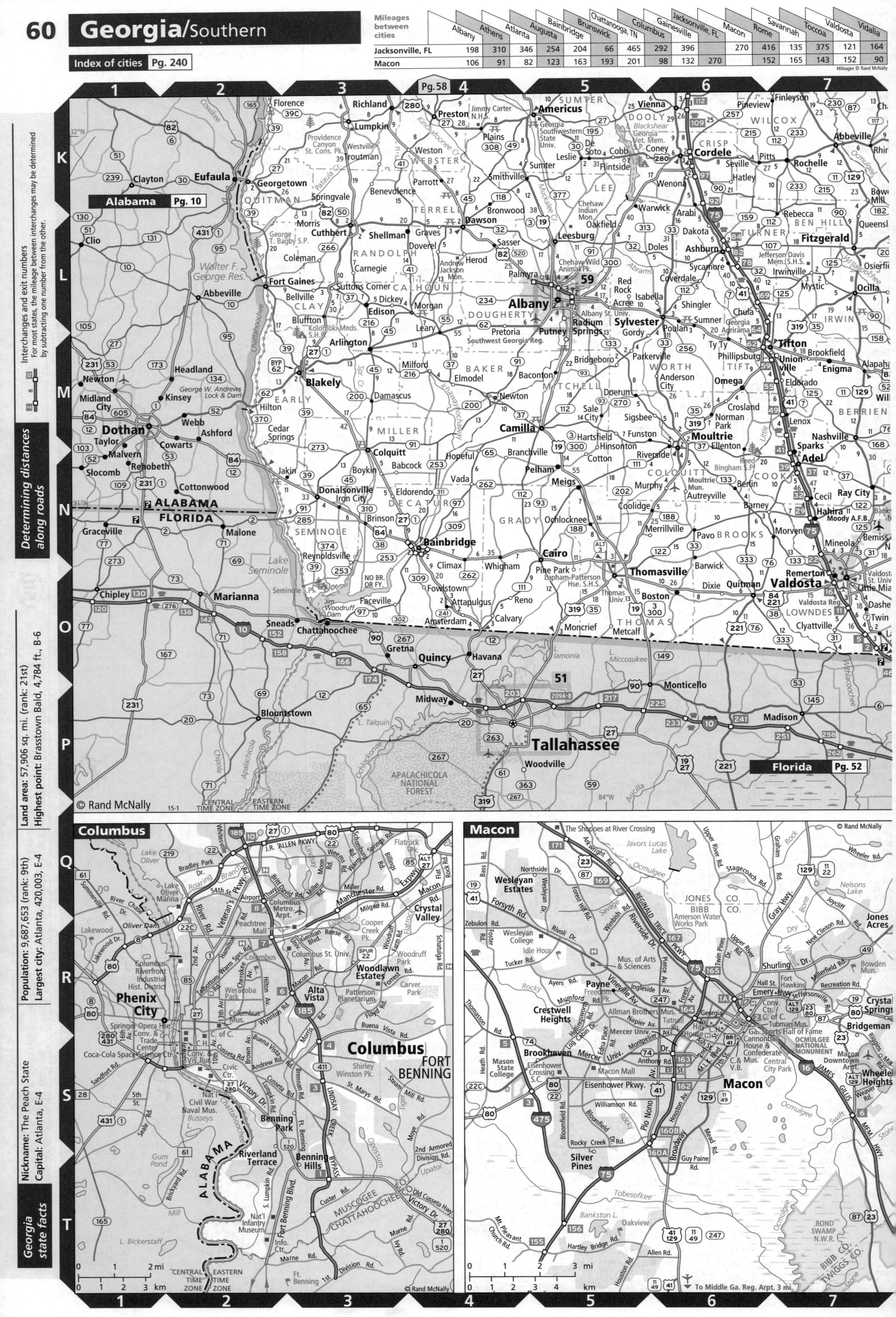

Georgia state facts

Nickname: The Peach State
Capital: Atlanta, E-4

Population: 9,687,653 (rank: 9th)
Largest city: Atlanta, 420,003, E-4

Land area: 57,906 sq. mi. (rank: 21st)
Highest point: Brasstown Bald, 4,784 ft., B-6

Determining distances along roads

Interchanges and exit numbers
For most states, the mileage between interchanges may be determined by subtracting one number from the other.

Mileages between cities

	Albany	Athens	Atlanta	Augusta	Bainbridge	Brunswick	Chattanooga, TN	Columbus	Gainesville	Jacksonville, FL	Macon	Rome	Savannah	Toccoa	Valdosta	Vidalia
Savannah	226	222	247	134	249	77	364	249	297	135	165	317		255	167	90
Valdosta	79	243	228	217	83	120	346	173	278	121	152	298	167	317		118

Mileages © Rand McNally

Total mileages through Georgia

| 20 | 203 miles | | 85 | 180 miles |
| 75 | 355 miles | | 95 | 112 miles |

More mileages at www.randmcnally.com/MC

Pg. 59

S. Car. Pg. 186

One inch represents approximately 16 miles
0 5 10 15 20 25 mi
0 5 10 15 20 25 30 40 km

511, (888) 635-8287,
(877) 694-2511, (404) 635-8000
www.511ga.org

Georgia Dept. of Economic Development
(800) 847-4842
www.exploregeorgia.org

Explore Georgia at
www.randmcnally.com/GA

Savannah

Brunswick

Mileages between cities	Hilo	Honolulu	Kahului	Kailua	Kailua Kona	Kapa'a	Lahaina	Wahiawa
Hilo		225*	127*	237*	74	337*	149*	236*
Honolulu	225*		108*	11	177*	116*	130*	20

	Hilo	Honolulu	Kahului	Kailua	Kailua Kona	Kapa'a	Lahaina	Wahiawa
Kahului	127*	108*		22*	93*	214*	22	119*
Kailua Kona	74	177*	93*		188*	283*	116*	188*

*via plane

Mileages © Rand McNally

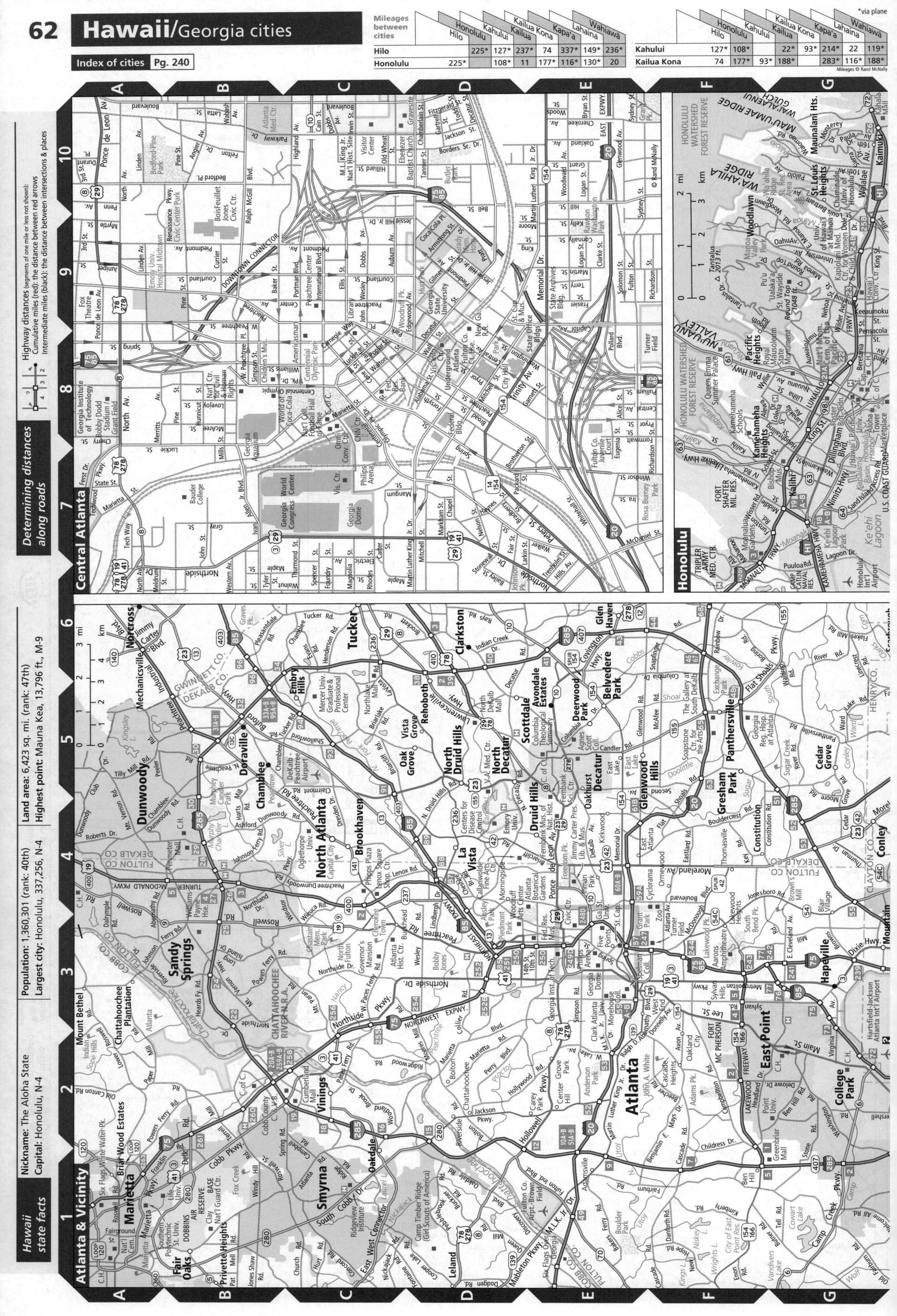

Central Atlanta

Honolulu

Atlanta & Vicinity

Hawaii state facts

Nickname: The Aloha State
Capital: Honolulu, N-4
Population: 1,360,301 (rank: 40th)
Largest city: Honolulu, 337,256, N-4
Land area: 6,423 sq. mi. (rank: 47th)
Highest point: Mauna Kea, 13,796 ft., M-9

Determining distances along roads

Highway distances (segments of one mile or less not shown); the distance between red arrows
Cumulative miles (red); the distance between intersections & places
Intermediate miles (black); the distance between intersections & places

Mileages between cities	Honolulu Hilo	Kahului	Kailua Kailua Kona	Kapa'a	Lahaina	Wahiawā
Kapa'a	337*	116*	214* 128*	283*	236*	128*
Kaunakakai	177*	68*	55* 79*	144*	174* 77*	79*

	Honolulu Hilo	Kahului	Kailua Kailua Kona	Kapa'a	Lahaina	Wahiawā
Lahaina	149*	130*	22 43*	116*	236*	141*
Wahiawā	236*	20	119* 26	188*	128*	141*

*via plane
Mileages © Rand McNally

Total mileages through Hawaii
More mileages at www.randmcnally.com/MC

H1 27 miles   H3 15 miles
H2 8 miles

Maui

O'ahu

Honolulu

Hawaii

Plan a Hawaii trip at www.randmcnally.com/HI

| Tourism Information | Hawaii Visitors & Convention Bureau (800) 464-2924, (808) 923-1811 www.gohawaii.com | Road Conditions & Construction | (808) 536-2150 www.hawaii.gov/dot | Toll Road Information | No toll roads |

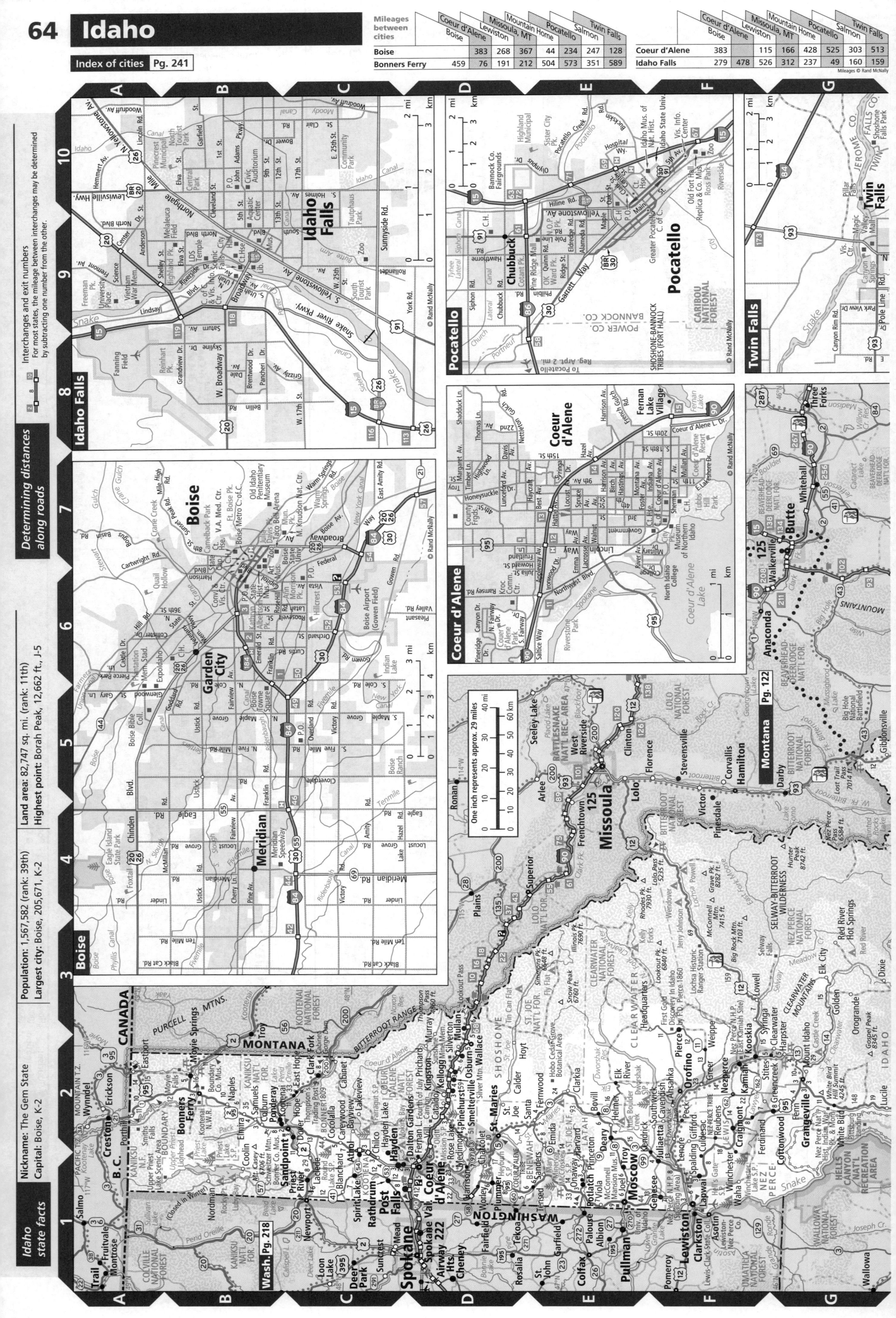

Mileages © Rand McNally

Mileages between cities	Coeur d'Alene	Lewiston	Missoula, MT	Mountain Home	Pocatello	Salmon	Twin Falls
Boise	383	268	367	44	234	247	128
Bonners Ferry	459	76	191	212	504	573	351	589

	Coeur d'Alene	Lewiston	Missoula, MT	Mountain Home	Pocatello	Salmon	Twin Falls
Coeur d'Alene	383	115	166	428	525	303	513
Idaho Falls	279	478	526	312	237	49	160	159

Idaho state facts

Nickname: The Gem State
Capital: Boise, K-2

Population: 1,567,582 (rank: 39th)
Largest city: Boise, 205,671, K-2

Land area: 82,747 sq. mi. (rank: 11th)
Highest point: Borah Peak, 12,662 ft., J-5

Determining distances along roads

Interchanges and exit numbers
For most states, the mileage between interchanges may be determined by subtracting one number from the other.

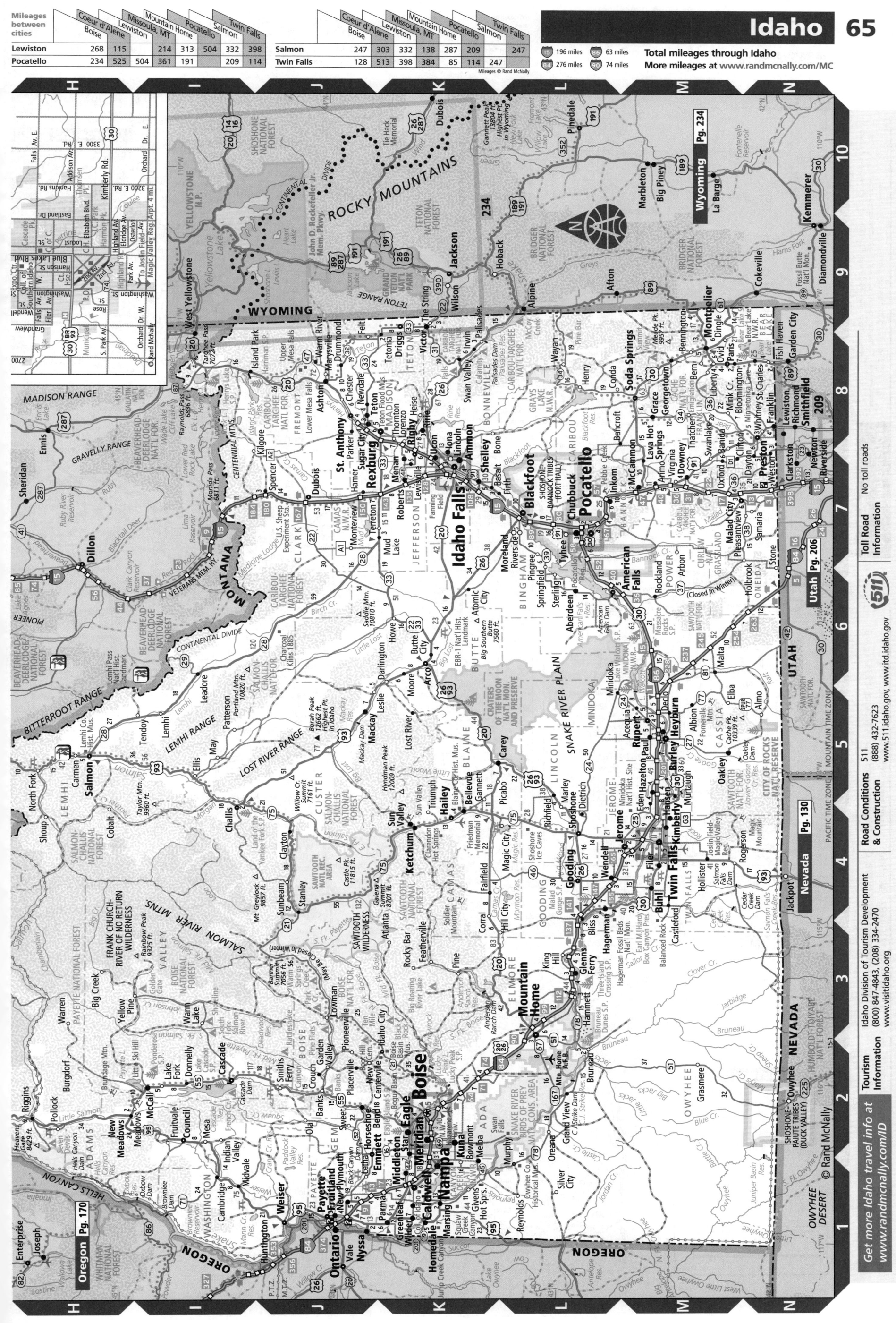

Mileages between cities	Coeur d'Alene Boise	Lewiston	Missoula, MT	Mountain Home	Pocatello	Salmon	Twin Falls
Lewiston	268	115		214	313	504	332	398
Pocatello	234	525	504	361	191		209	114

	Coeur d'Alene Boise	Lewiston	Missoula, MT	Mountain Home	Pocatello	Salmon	Twin Falls
Salmon	247	303	332	138	287	209		247
Twin Falls	128	513	398	384	85	114	247	

Mileages © Rand McNally

Total mileages through Idaho
More mileages at www.randmcnally.com/MC

15 196 miles   86 63 miles
84 276 miles   90 74 miles

Road Conditions & Construction 511 (888) 432-7623 www.511.idaho.gov

Tourism Information Idaho Division of Tourism Development (800) 847-4843, (208) 334-2470 www.visitidaho.org

Toll Road Information No toll roads

Get more Idaho travel info at www.randmcnally.com/ID

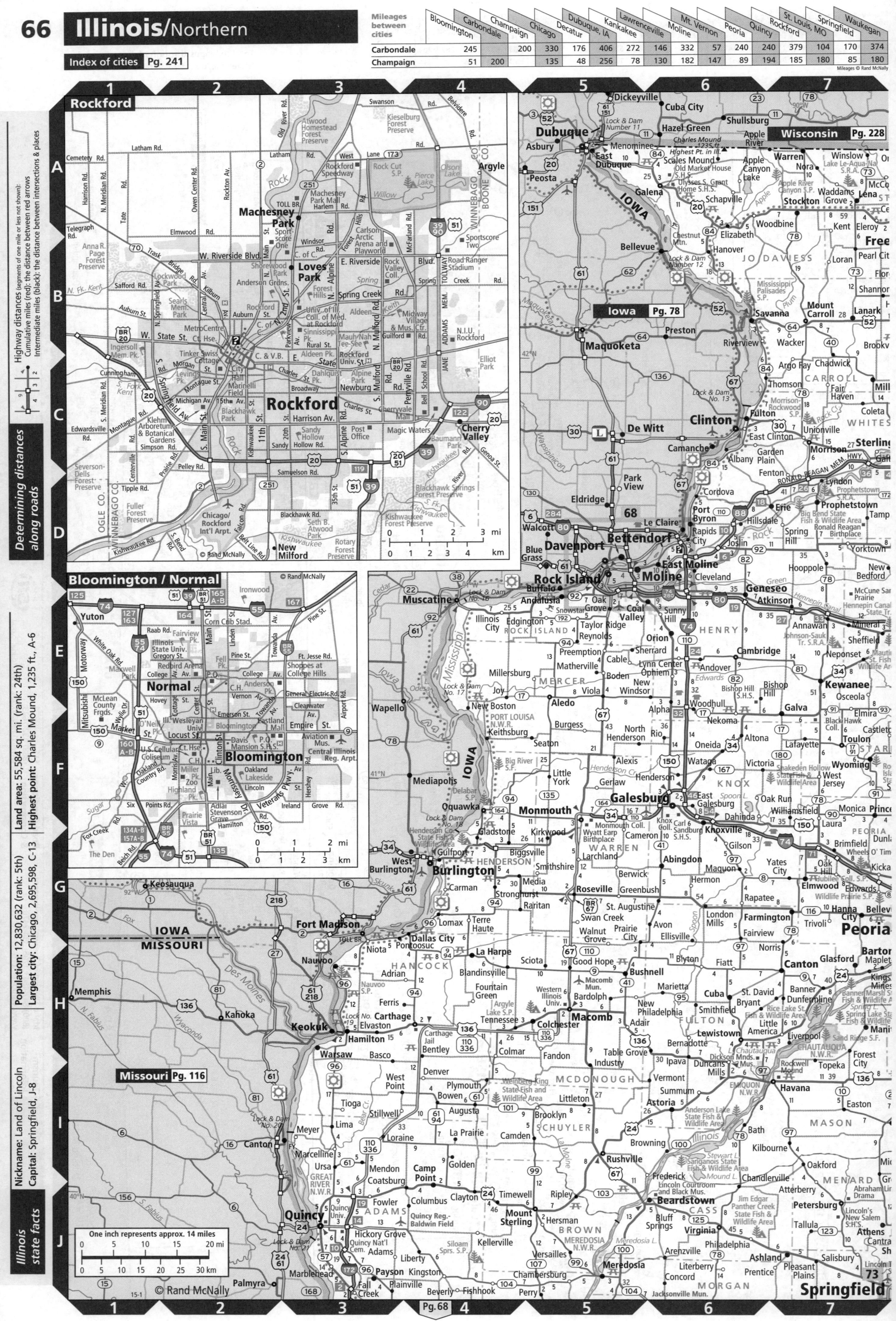

Mileages between cities	Bloomington	Carbondale	Champaign	Chicago	Decatur	Dubuque, IA	Kankakee	Lawrenceville	Moline	Mt. Vernon	Peoria	Quincy	Rockford	St. Louis, MO	Springfield	Waukegan
Carbondale	245		200	330	176	406	272	146	332	57	240	240	379	104	170	374
Champaign	51	200		135	48	256	78	130	182	147	89	194	185	180	85	180

Mileages © Rand McNally

continued p. 68

Mileages between cities	Bloomington	Carbondale	Champaign	Chicago	Decatur	Dubuque, IA	Kankakee	Lawrenceville	Moline	Mt. Vernon	Peoria	Quincy	Rockford	St. Louis, MO	Springfield	Waukegan
Chicago	132	330	135		179	177	58	247	166	277	154	309	84	296	198	38
Moline	131	332	182	166		171	75	158		307	308	93	148	120	261	164	190

Total mileages through Illinois
55 313 miles 80 164 miles
70 156 miles 90 124 miles
More mileages at www.randmcnally.com/MC

Mileages © Rand McNally

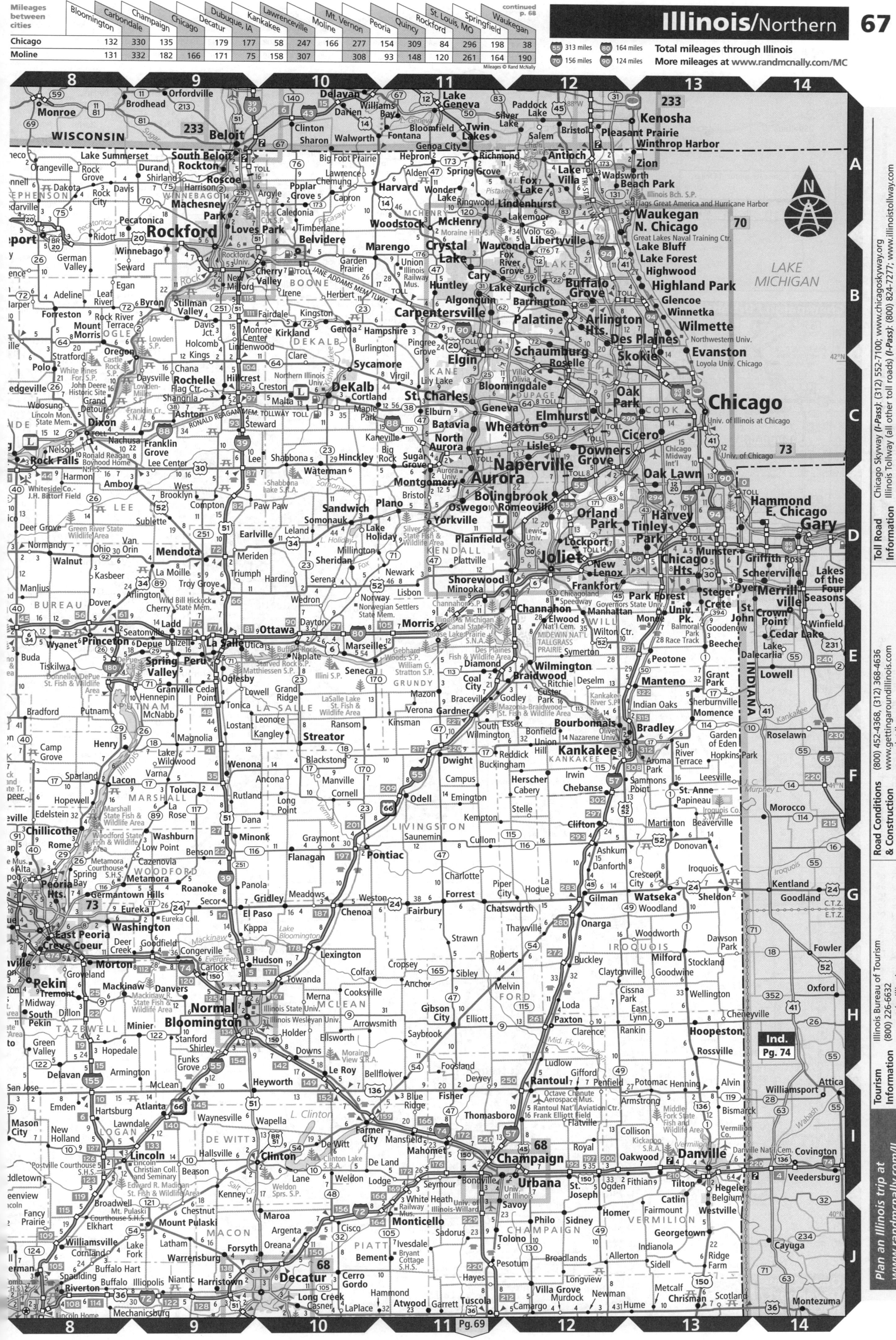

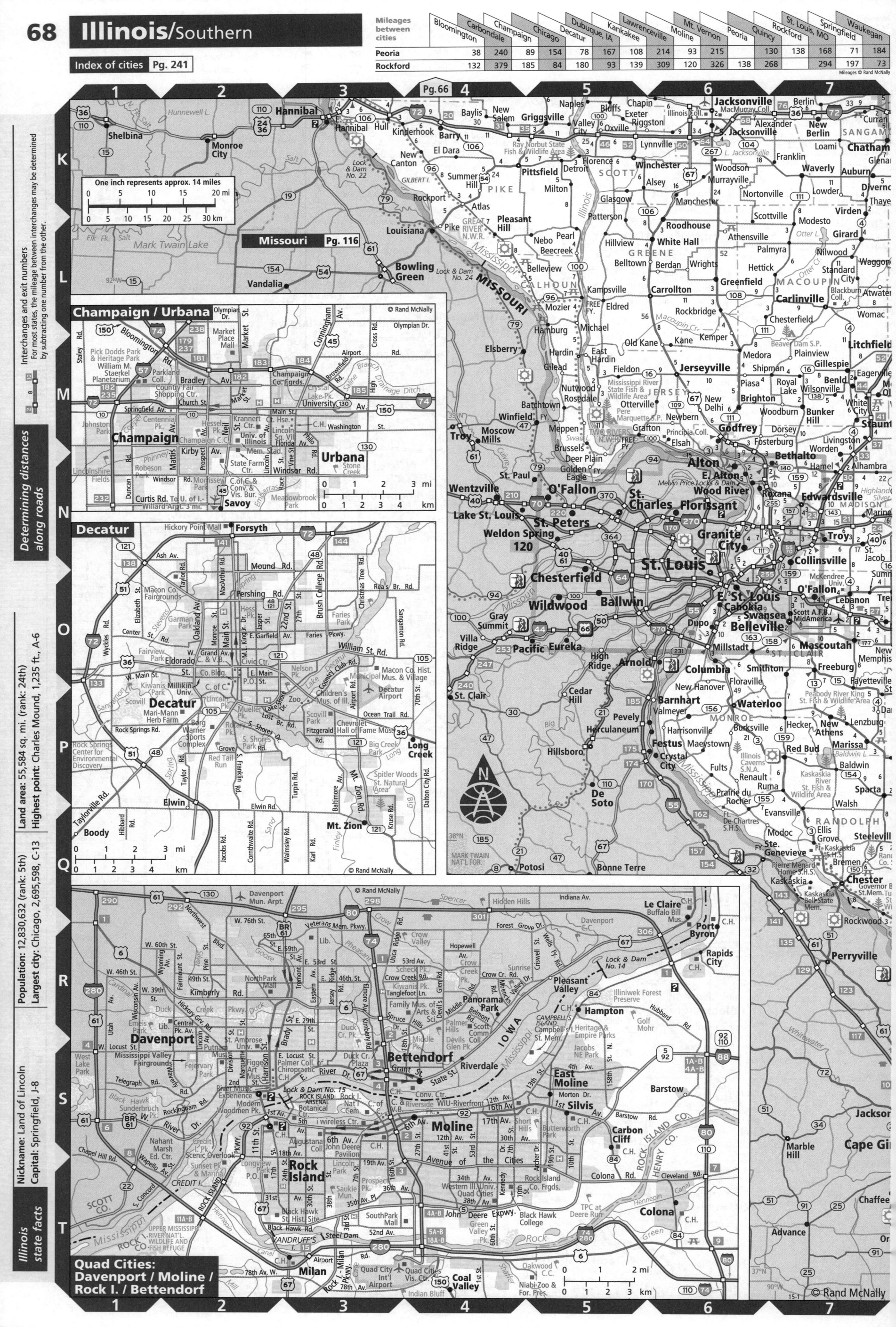

Mileages between cities	Bloomington	Carbondale	Champaign	Chicago	Decatur	Dubuque, IA	Kankakee	Lawrenceville	Moline	Mt. Vernon	Peoria	Quincy	Rockford	St. Louis, MO	Springfield	Waukegan
St. Louis, MO	162	104	180	296	135	335	252	144	261	79	168	139	294		98	326
Springfield	66	170	85	198	38	238	157	153	164	138	71	112	197	98		229

Mileages © Rand McNally

Total mileages through Illinois

55	313 miles	80	164 miles
70	156 miles	90	124 miles

More mileages at www.randmcnally.com/MC

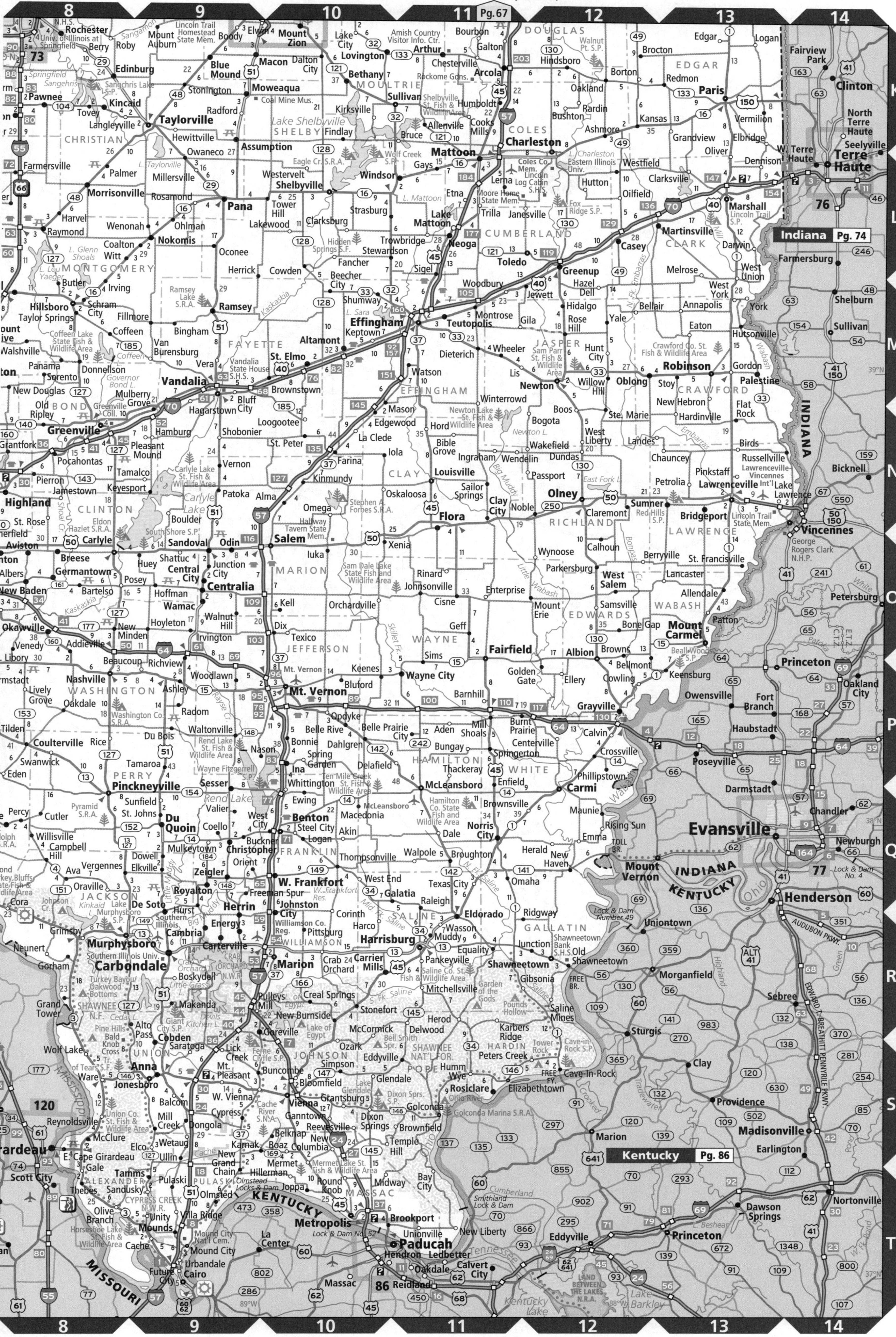

City sights to see

- Adler Planetarium, Chicago, G-15
- Art Institute of Chicago, Chicago, E-13
- Baha'i Temple, Wilmette, E-8
- Chicago Botanic Garden, Glencoe, D-8
- Field Museum, Chicago, G-14
- Frank Lloyd Wright Home & Studio, Oak Park, H-8
- Illinois Holocaust Museum, Skokie, F-8

- John G. Shedd Aquarium, Chicago, G-14
- John Hancock Center, Chicago, C-13
- Lincoln Park Zoo, Chicago, H-9
- Millennium Park, Chicago, E-13
- Museum of Science & Industry, Chicago, J-10
- Navy Pier, Chicago, D-14
- Willis Tower, Chicago, E-12
- Wrigley Field, Chicago, G-9

City sights to see

- Abraham Lincoln Presidential Library & Museum, Springfield, M-16
- Children's Museum of Indianapolis, Indianapolis, D-18
- Eiteljorg Museum, Indianapolis, E-17
- Fort Wayne Children's Zoo, Fort Wayne, L-19
- Illinois State Capitol Complex, Springfield, M-16
- Indiana State Capitol, Indianapolis, E-18

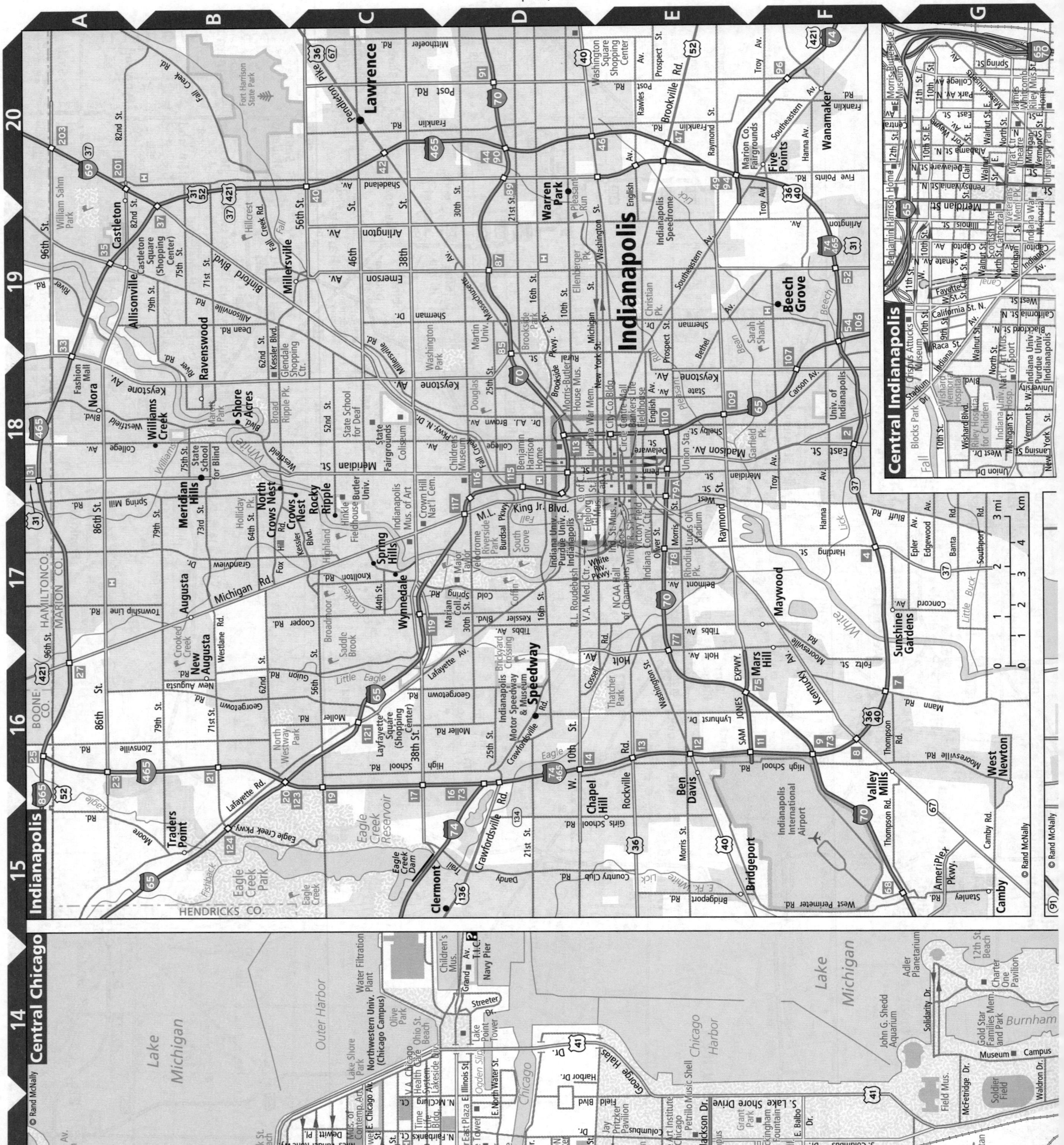

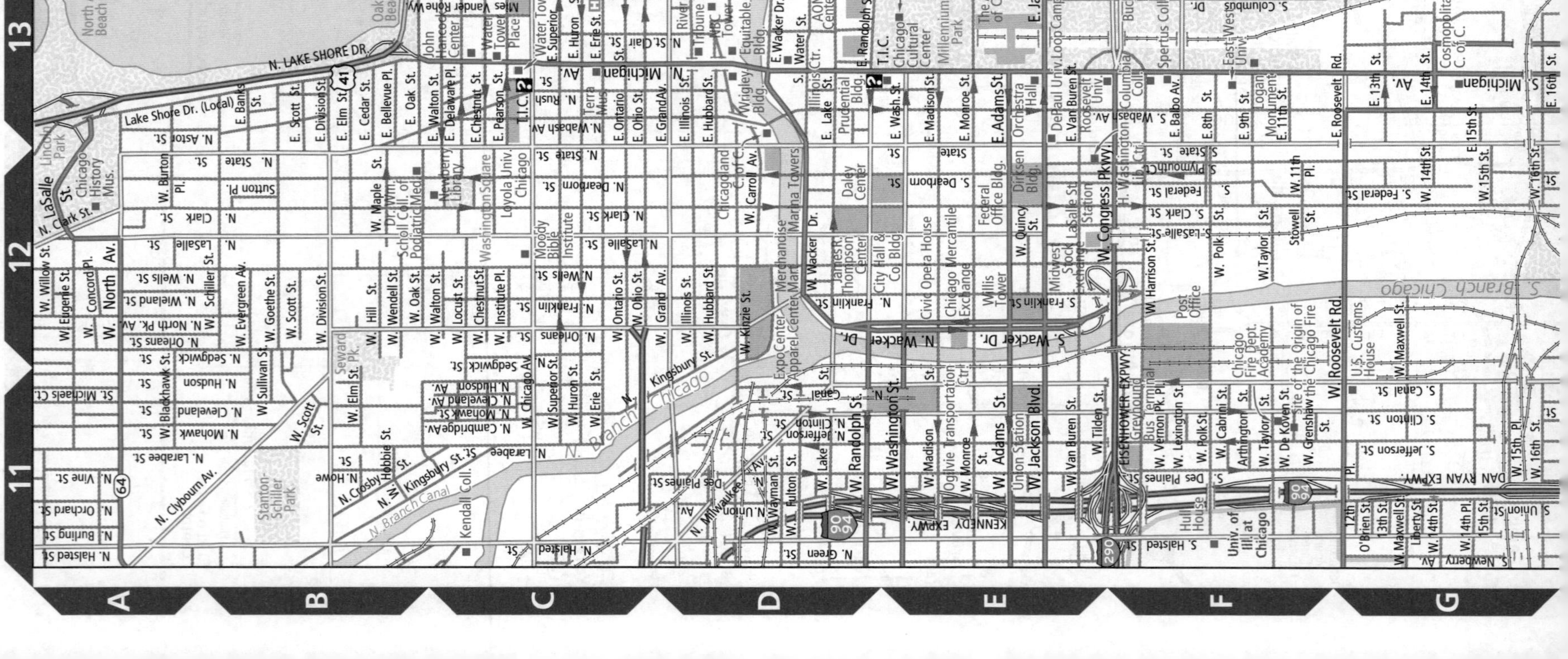

Indianapolis

Central Indianapolis

Central Chicago

© Rand McNally

- Indiana State Museum, Indianapolis, E-17
- Indianapolis Motor Speedway and Hall of Fame Museum, Indianapolis, D-16
- NCAA Hall of Champions, Indianapolis, H-18
- President Benjamin Harrison Home, Indianapolis, D-18

South Bend
Fort Wayne
Peoria
Springfield
LAKE MICHIGAN
El. 579 ft. above sea level
© Rand McNally
Pg. 71

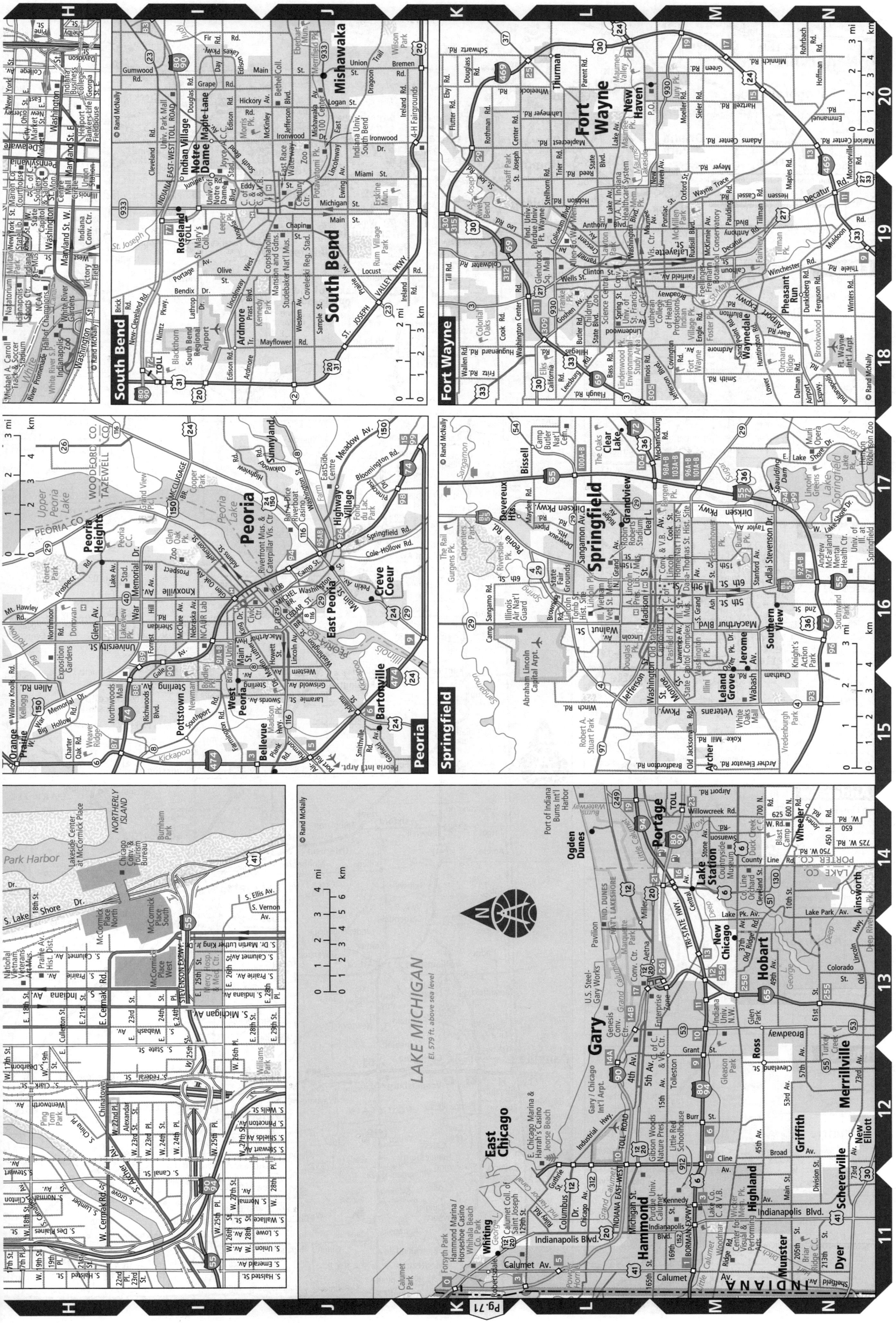

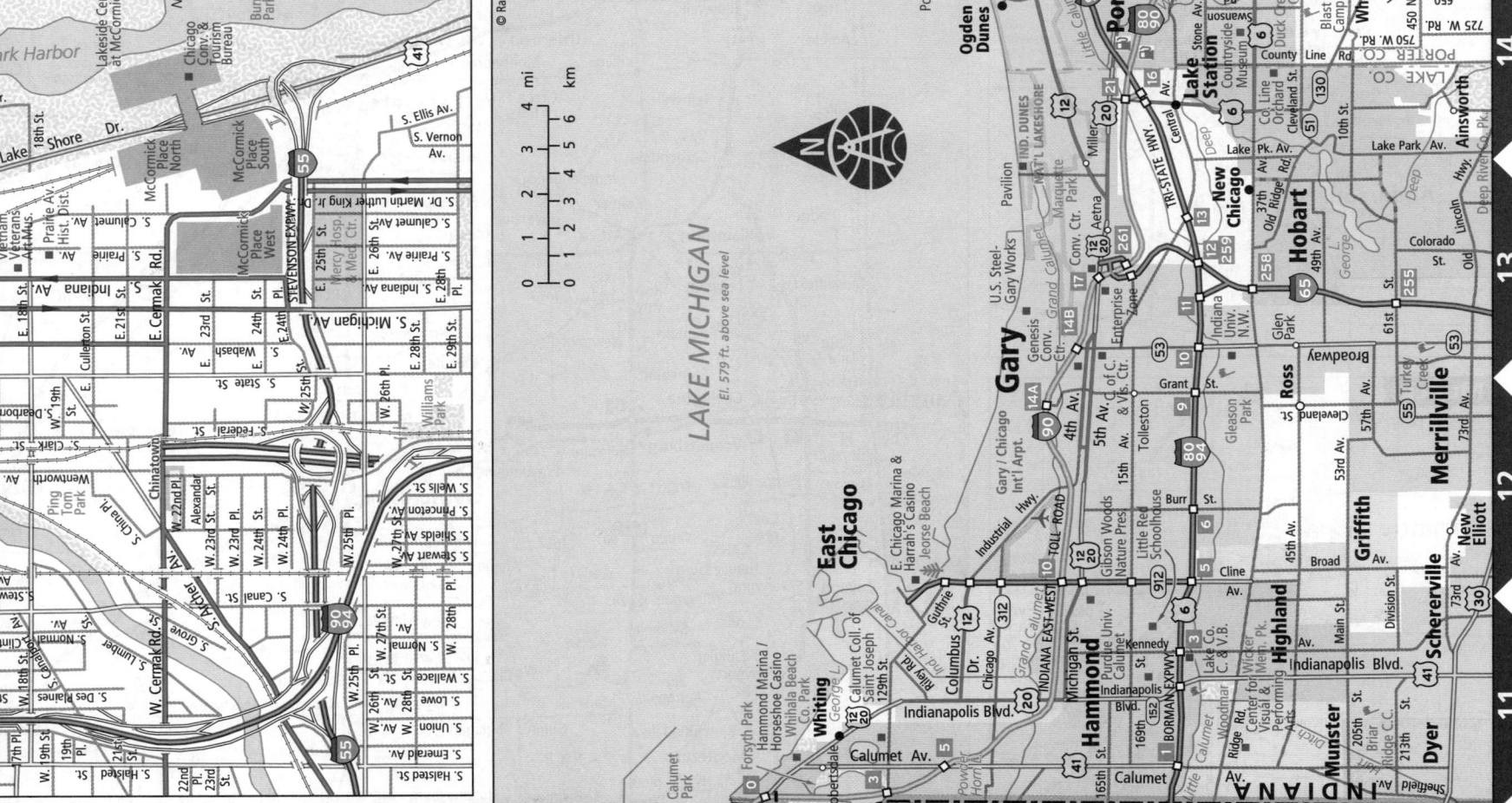

Mileages between cities	Angola	Bloomington	Chicago, IL	Crawfordsville	Evansville	Fort Wayne	Gary	Greensburg	Indianapolis	Kokomo	Lafayette	Muncie	New Albany	Richmond	South Bend	Terre Haute
Evansville	347	120	289	178		309	273	202	180	234	198	244	112	255	320	109
Fort Wayne	39	178	160	162	309		132	147	129	86	117	72	238	92	89	205

Mileages © Rand McNally

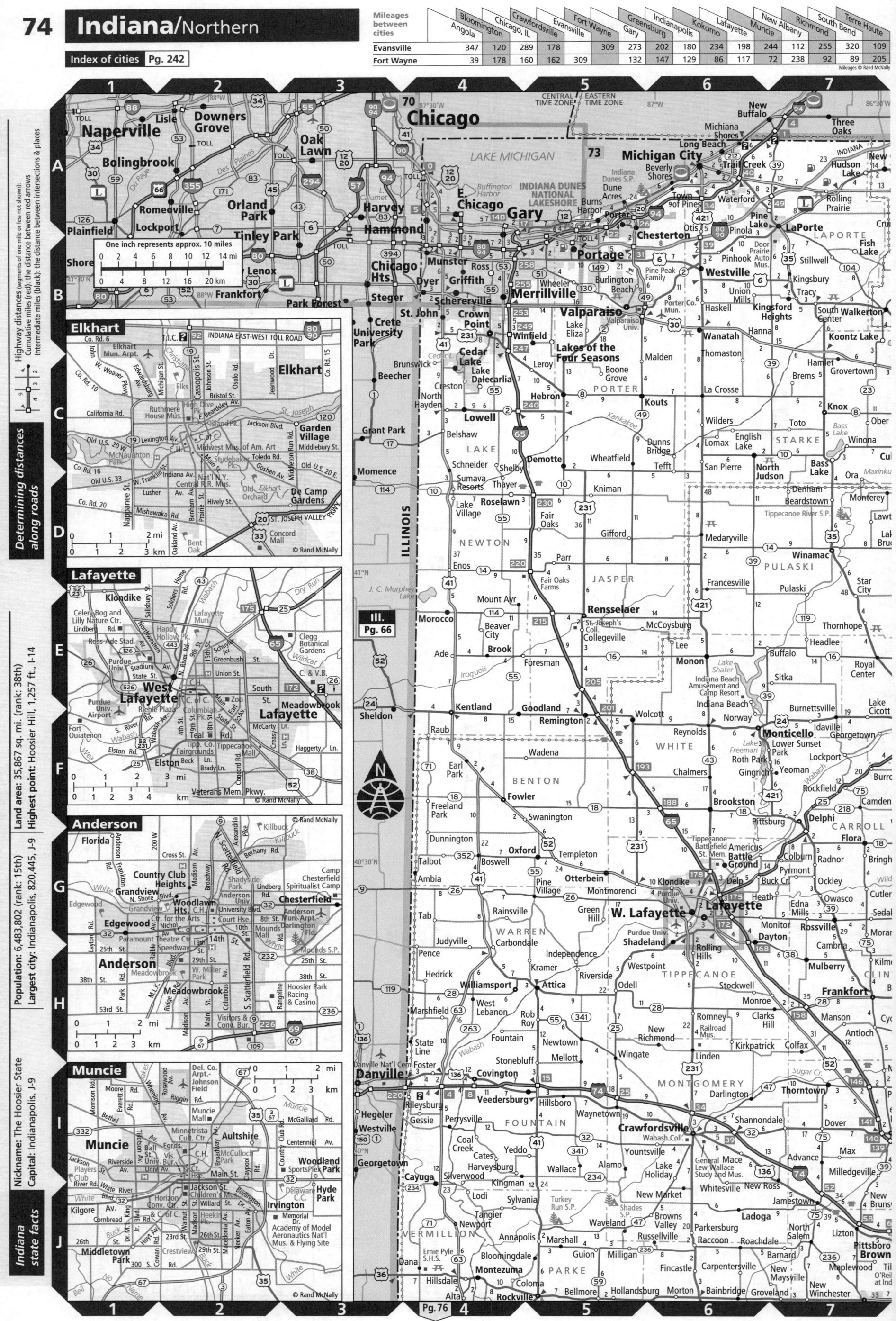

Determining distances along roads

Highway distances (segments of one mile or less not shown): Cumulative miles (red): the distance between red arrows. Intermediate miles (black): the distance between intersections & places

Indiana state facts

Nickname: The Hoosier State
Capital: Indianapolis, J-9

Population: 6,483,802 (rank: 15th)
Largest city: Indianapolis, 820,445, J-9

Land area: 35,867 sq. mi. (rank: 38th)
Highest point: Hoosier Hill, 1,257 ft., I-14

One inch represents approx. 10 miles

© Rand McNally

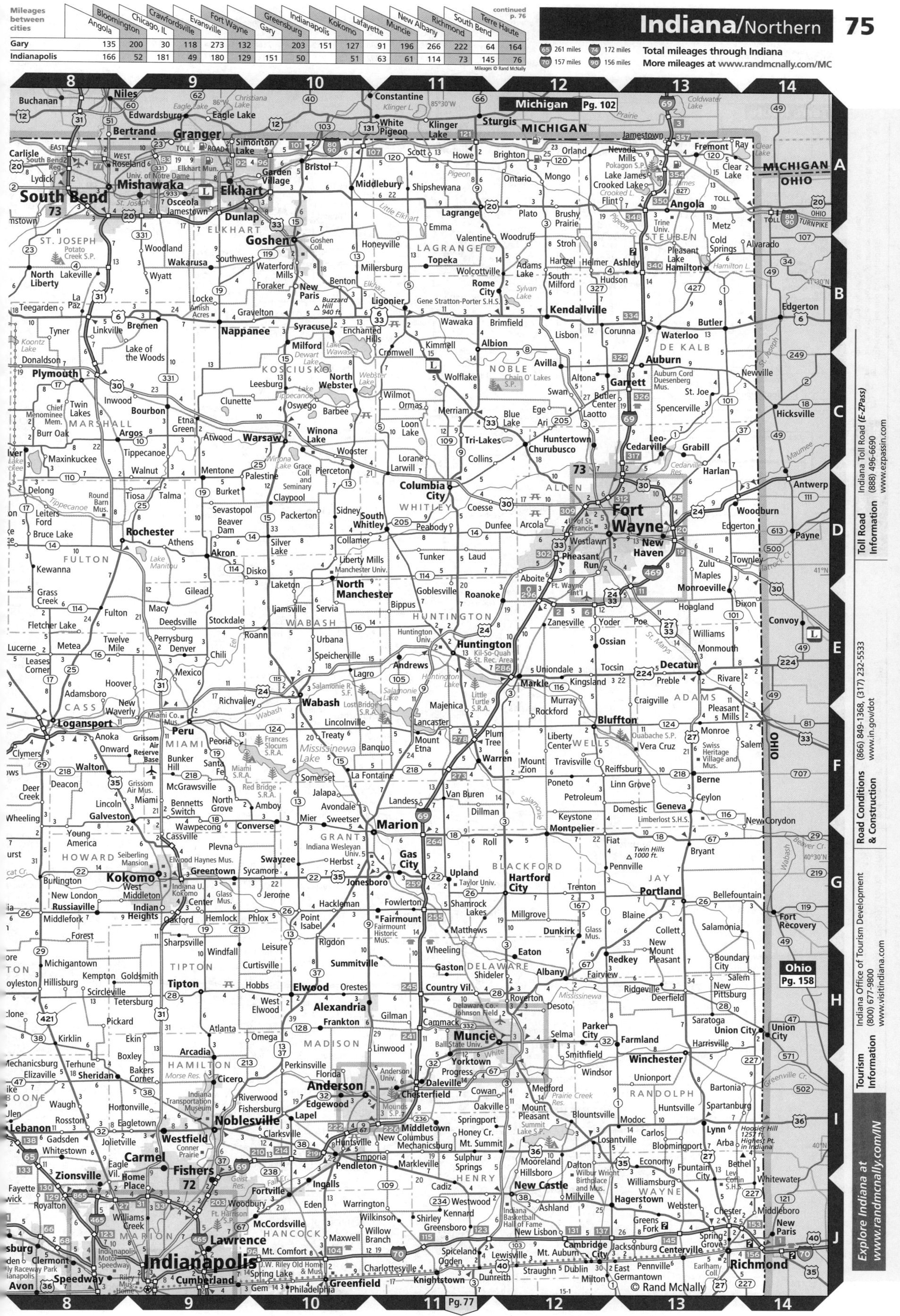

Mileages between cities	Angola	Bloomington	Chicago, IL	Crawfordsville	Evansville	Fort Wayne	Gary	Greensburg	Indianapolis	Kokomo	Lafayette	Muncie	New Albany	Richmond	South Bend	Terre Haute
Gary	135	200	30	118	273	132		203	151	127	91	196	266	222	64	164
Indianapolis	166	52	181	49	180	129	151	50		51	63	61	114	73	145	76

Mileages © Rand McNally

continued p. 76

Total mileages through Indiana

More mileages at www.randmcnally.com/MC

| 65 | 261 miles | 74 | 172 miles |
| 70 | 157 miles | 90 | 156 miles |

Toll Road Information: Indiana Toll Road (E-ZPass) (888) 496-6690 www.ezpassin.com

Road Conditions & Construction: (866) 849-1368, (317) 232-5533 www.in.gov/dot

Tourism Information: Indiana Office of Tourism Development (800) 677-9800 www.visitindiana.com

Explore Indiana at www.randmcnally.com/IN

© Rand McNally

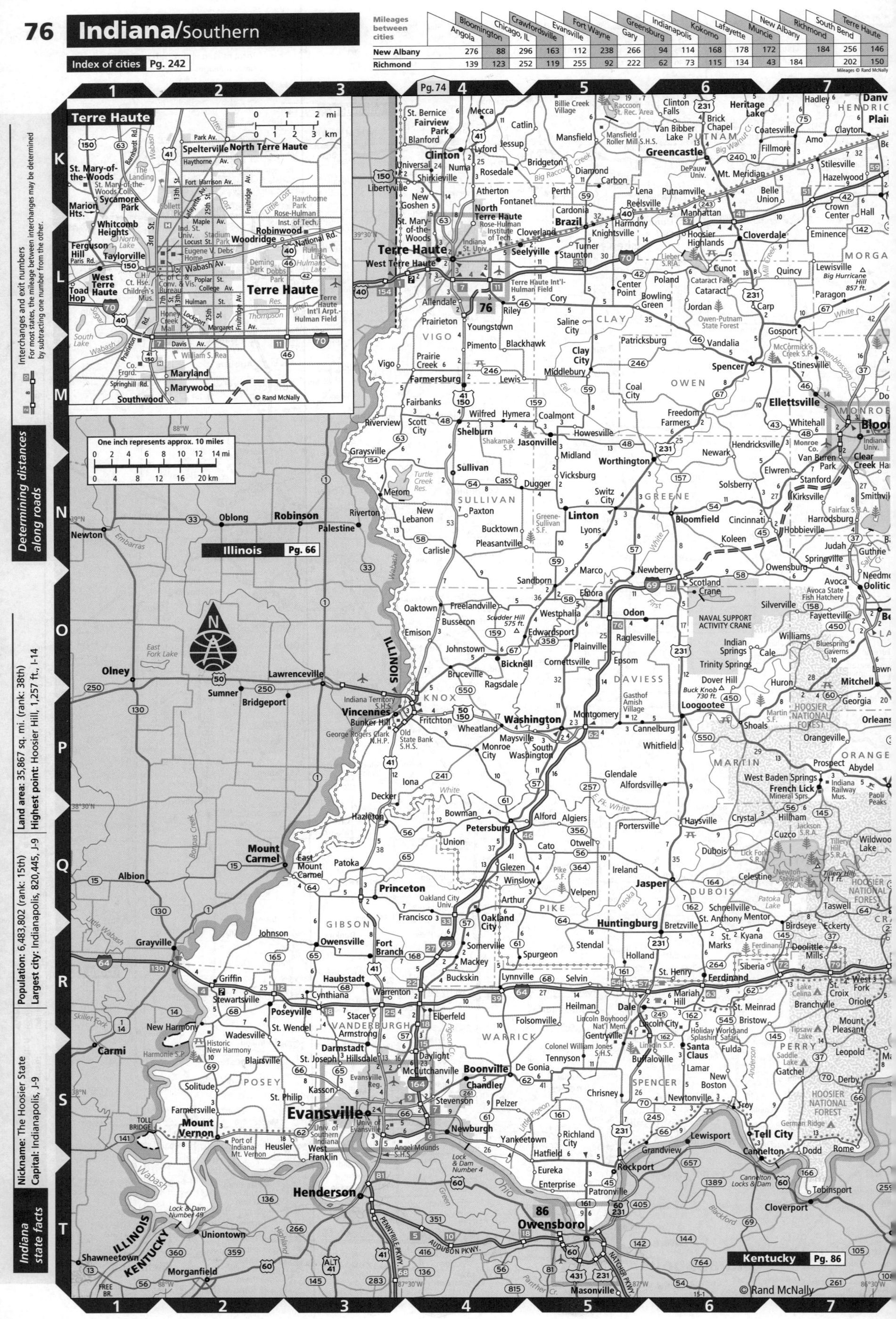

Mileages between cities

	Angola	Bloomington	Chicago, IL	Crawfordsville	Evansville	Fort Wayne	Gary	Greensburg	Indianapolis	Kokomo	Lafayette	Muncie	New Albany	Richmond	South Bend	Terre Haute
South Bend	77	195	93	135	320	89	64	183	145	87	106	143	256	202		216
Terre Haute	242	58	180	58	109	205	164	123	76	129	89	139	146	150	216	

Mileages © Rand McNally

Total mileages through Indiana
More mileages at www.randmcnally.com/MC

65	261 miles	74	172 miles
70	157 miles	90	156 miles

Ohio Pg. 158

Bloomington

Evansville

Toll Road — Indiana Toll Road (E-ZPass) (888) 496-6690 www.ezpassin.com

Road Conditions & Construction — (866) 849-1368, (317) 232-5533 www.in.gov/dot

Tourism Information — Indiana Office of Tourism Development (800) 677-9800 www.visitindiana.com

Explore Indiana at www.randmcnally.com/IN

© Rand McNally

Index of cities Pg. 243

Mileages between cities	Ames	Burlington	Cedar Rapids	Council Bluffs	Davenport	Decorah	Des Moines	Dubuque	Iowa City	Mason City	Ottumwa	Sioux City	Sioux Falls, SD	Spirit Lake	Storm Lake	Waterloo
Burlington	209		100	294	77	206	167	150	77	238	78	366	451	355	312	155
Cedar Rapids	108	100		253	82	105	126	70	28	136	110	268	357	252	212	53

Mileages © Rand McNally

Iowa state facts

Nickname: The Hawkeye State
Capital: Des Moines

Population: 3,046,355 (rank: 30th)
Land area: 55,869 sq. mi. (rank: 23rd)
Highest point: Hawkeye Point, 1,670 ft., B-4
Largest city: Des Moines, 203,433, I-10

Determining distances along roads

Highway distances (segments of one mile or less are not shown):
Cumulative miles (red); the distance between red arrows
Intermediate miles (black); the distance between intersections & places

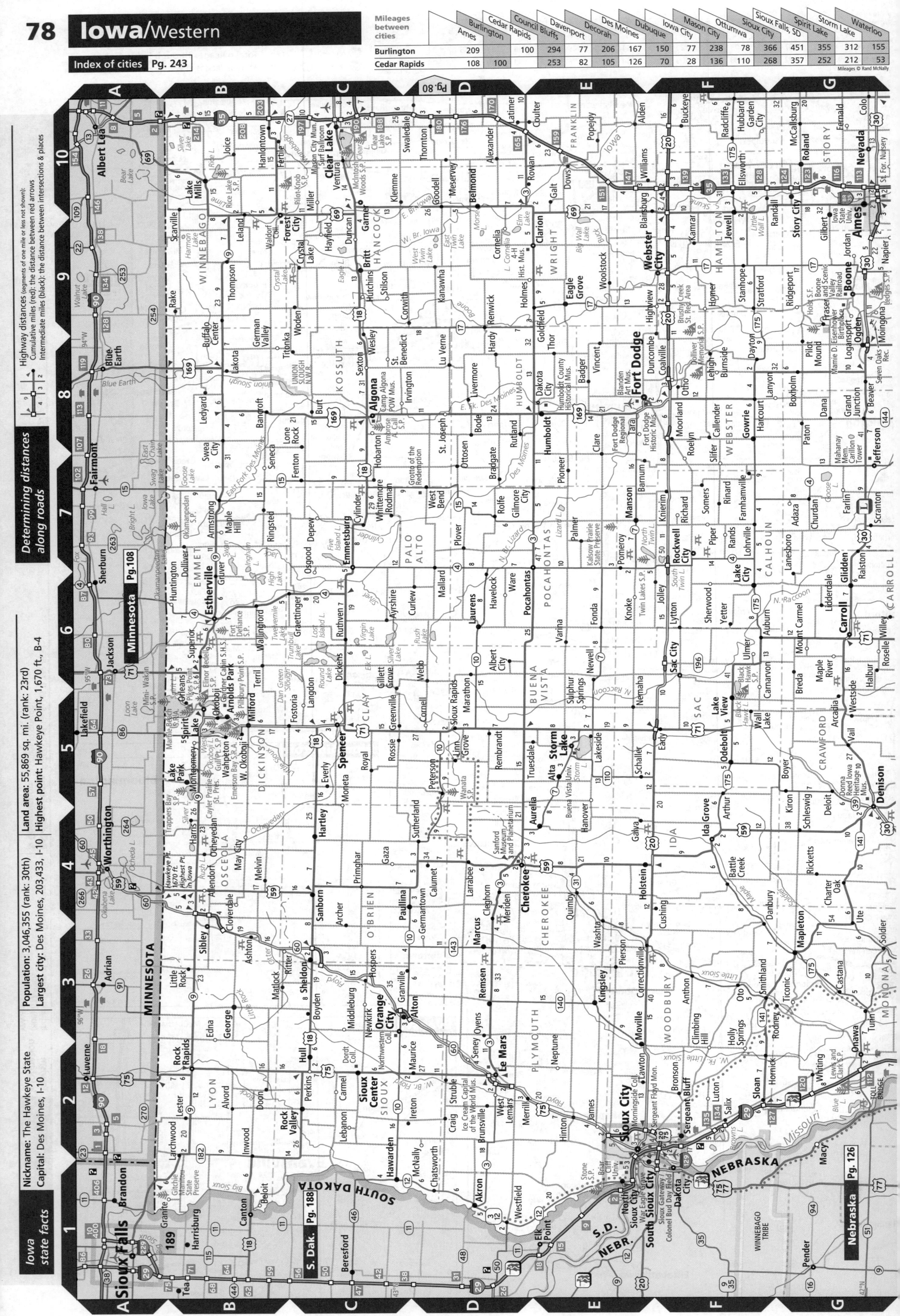

Mileages between cities	Ames	Burlington	Cedar Rapids	Council Bluffs	Davenport	Decorah	Des Moines	Dubuque	Iowa City	Mason City	Ottumwa	Sioux City	Sioux Falls, SD	Spirit Lake	Storm Lake	Waterloo continued p. 80
Council Bluffs	160	294	253		295	328	127	327	241	246	213	94	180	176	122	253
Davenport	191	77	82	295		167	167	71	57	220	133	366	441	336	294	136

Mileages © Rand McNally

Total mileages through Iowa
More mileages at www.randmcnally.com/MC

29 155 miles   80 303 miles
35 218 miles   218 257 miles

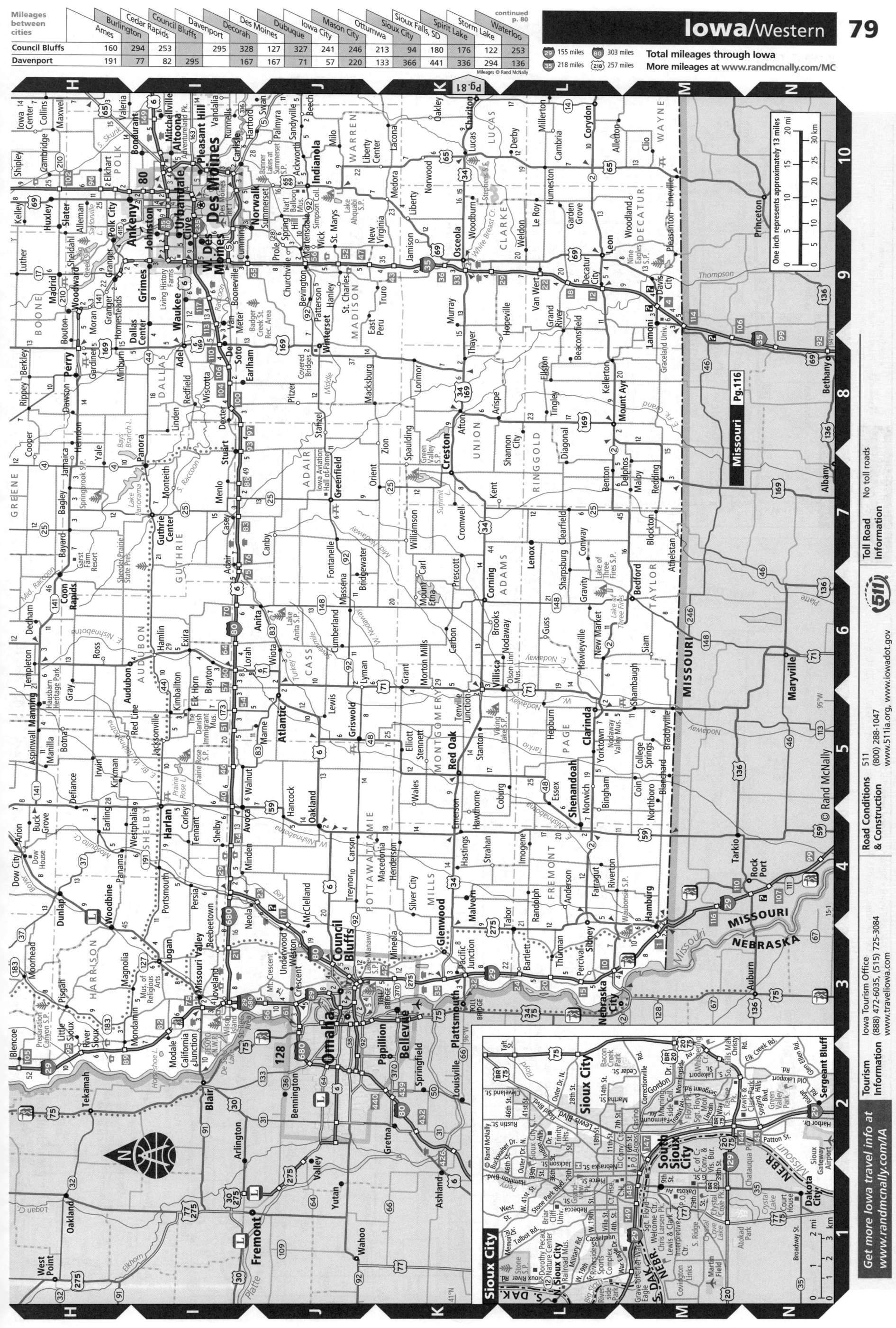

Pg. 81

Tourism Information
Iowa Tourism Office
(888) 472-6035, (515) 725-3084
www.traveliowa.com

Road Conditions & Construction
511
(800) 288-1047
www.511ia.org, www.iowadot.gov

511

Toll Road Information
No toll roads

Get more Iowa travel info at
www.randmcnally.com/IA

Mileages between cities	Ames	Burlington	Cedar Rapids	Council Bluffs	Davenport	Decorah	Des Moines	Dubuque	Iowa City	Mason City	Ottumwa	Sioux Falls, SD	Spirit Lake	Storm Lake	Waterloo
Des Moines	33	167	126	127	167	201		199	114	119	86	198	283	200	154	126
Dubuque	185	150	70	327	71	96	199		84	174	184	305	395	290	249	91

Mileages © Rand McNally

Iowa state facts

Nickname: The Hawkeye State
Capital: Des Moines, I-10

Population: 3,046,355 (rank: 30th)
Largest city: Des Moines, 203,433, I-10

Land area: 55,869 sq. mi. (rank: 23rd)
Highest point: Hawkeye Point, 1,670 ft., B-4

Determining distances along roads

Interchanges and exit numbers
For most states, the mileage between interchanges may be determined by subtracting one number from the other.

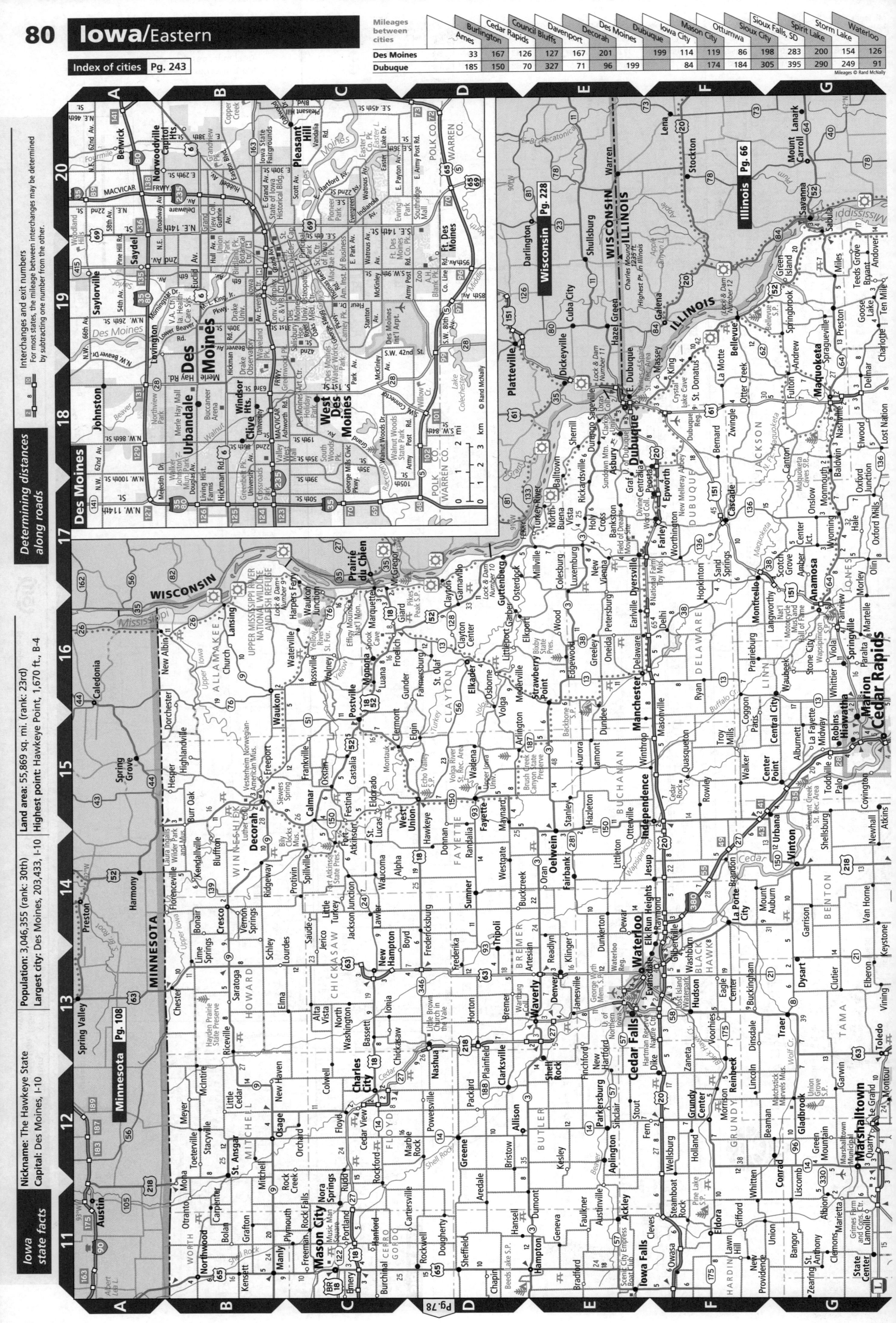

Mileages between cities	Ames	Burlington	Cedar Rapids	Council Bluffs	Davenport	Decorah	Des Moines	Dubuque	Iowa City	Mason City	Ottumwa	Sioux City	Sioux Falls, SD	Spirit Lake	Storm Lake	Waterloo
Mason City	91	238	136	246	220	88	119	174	165		203	200	222	118	135	83
Sioux City	175	366	268	94	366	304	198	305	312	200	285		85	109	78	218

Mileages © Rand McNally

Total mileages through Iowa
More mileages at www.randmcnally.com/MC

155 miles   303 miles
218 miles   257 miles

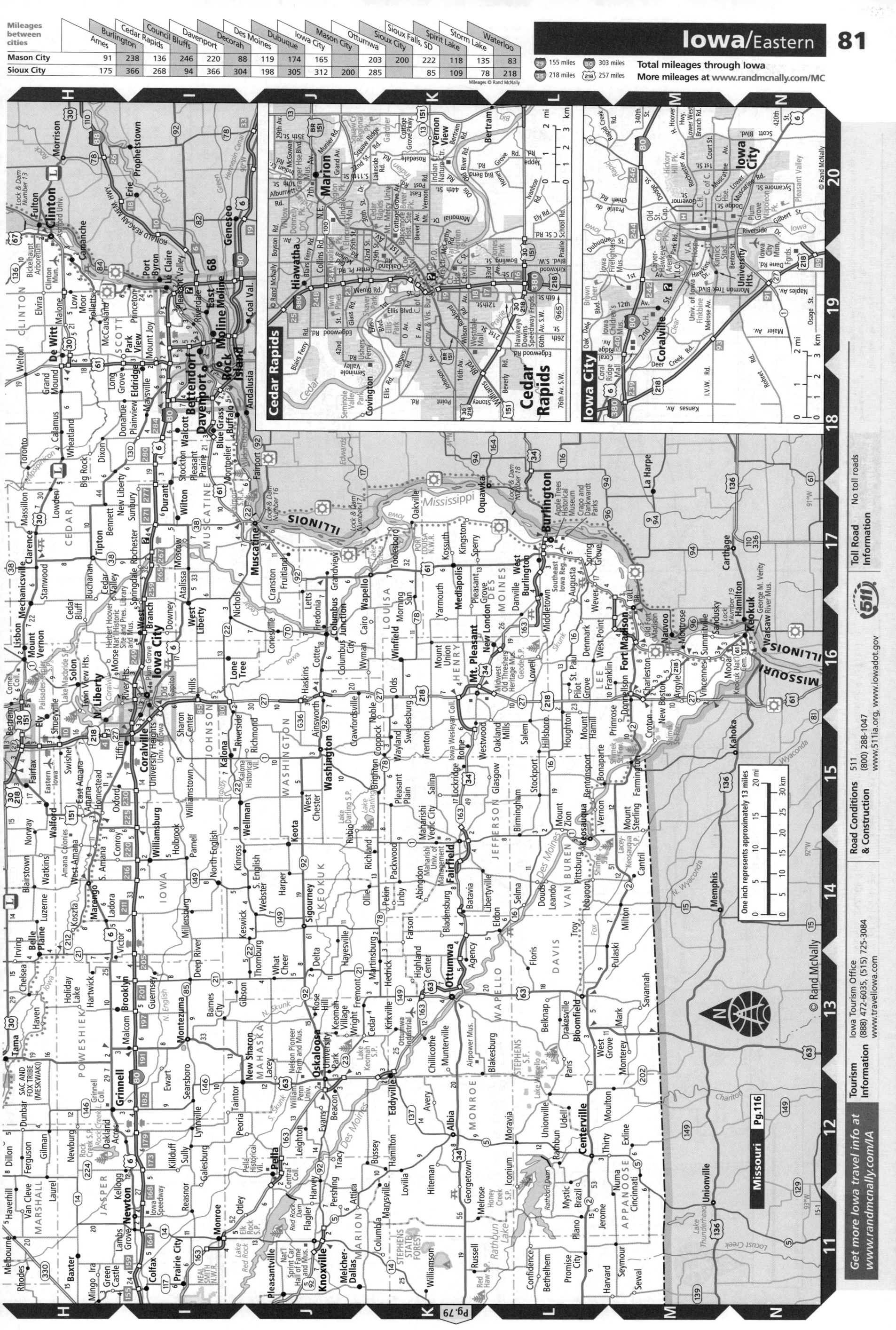

Toll Road Information
No toll roads

Tourism Information
Get more Iowa travel info at www.traveliowa.com/IA
www.randmcnally.com/IA

Iowa Tourism Office
(888) 472-6035, (515) 725-3084
www.traveliowa.com

511
Road Conditions & Construction
511
(800) 288-1047
www.511ia.org, www.iowadot.gov

One inch represents approximately 13 miles

Missouri Pg.116

Mileages between cities	Arkansas City	Atchison	Coffeyville	Dodge City	Emporia	Fort Scott	Goodland	Hays	Hutchinson	Joplin, MO	Kansas City	Liberal	Manhattan	Salina	Topeka	Wichita
Dodge City	212	323	288		240	304	192	104	122	337	333	82	227	164	273	154
Goodland	384	395	455	192	349	472		144	268	505	406	209	299	235	344	323

Mileages © Rand McNally

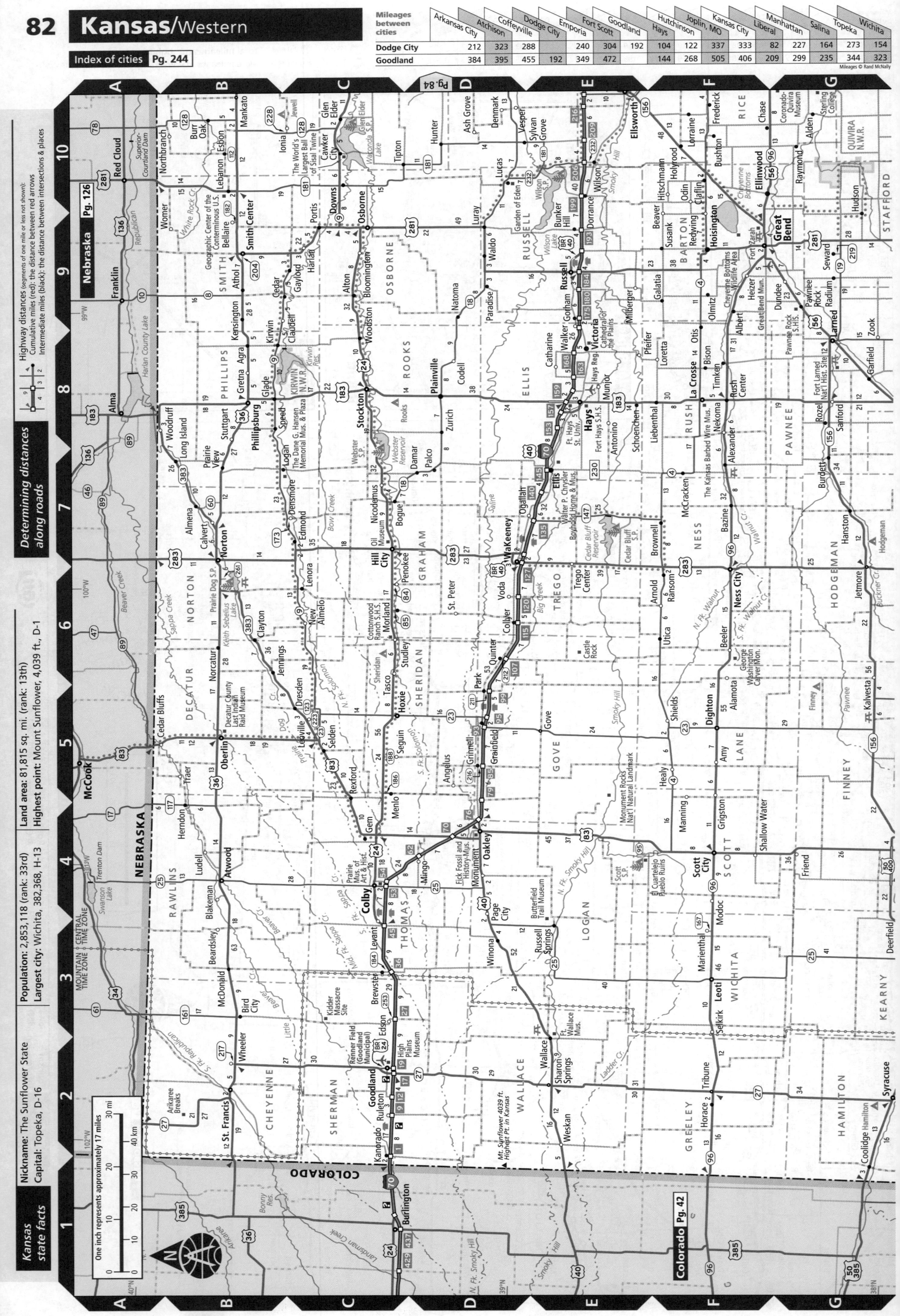

Determining distances along roads

Highway distances (segments of one mile or less not shown):
Cumulative miles (red): the distance between red arrows
Intermediate miles (black): the distance between intersections & places

Mileages between cities	Arkansas City	Atchison	Coffeyville	Dodge City	Emporia	Fort Scott	Goodland	Hutchinson / Hays	Joplin, MO	Kansas City	Liberal	Manhattan	Salina	Topeka	Wichita
Joplin, MO	150	196	65	337	177	60	505	366	233	—	154	395	252	274	196	183
Kansas City	228	58	172	333	109	94	406	266	220	154	—	406	117	173	62	196

continued p. 84

Mileages © Rand McNally

35	235 miles	56	464 miles	**Total mileages through Kansas**
70	424 miles	81	220 miles	More mileages at www.randmcnally.com/MC

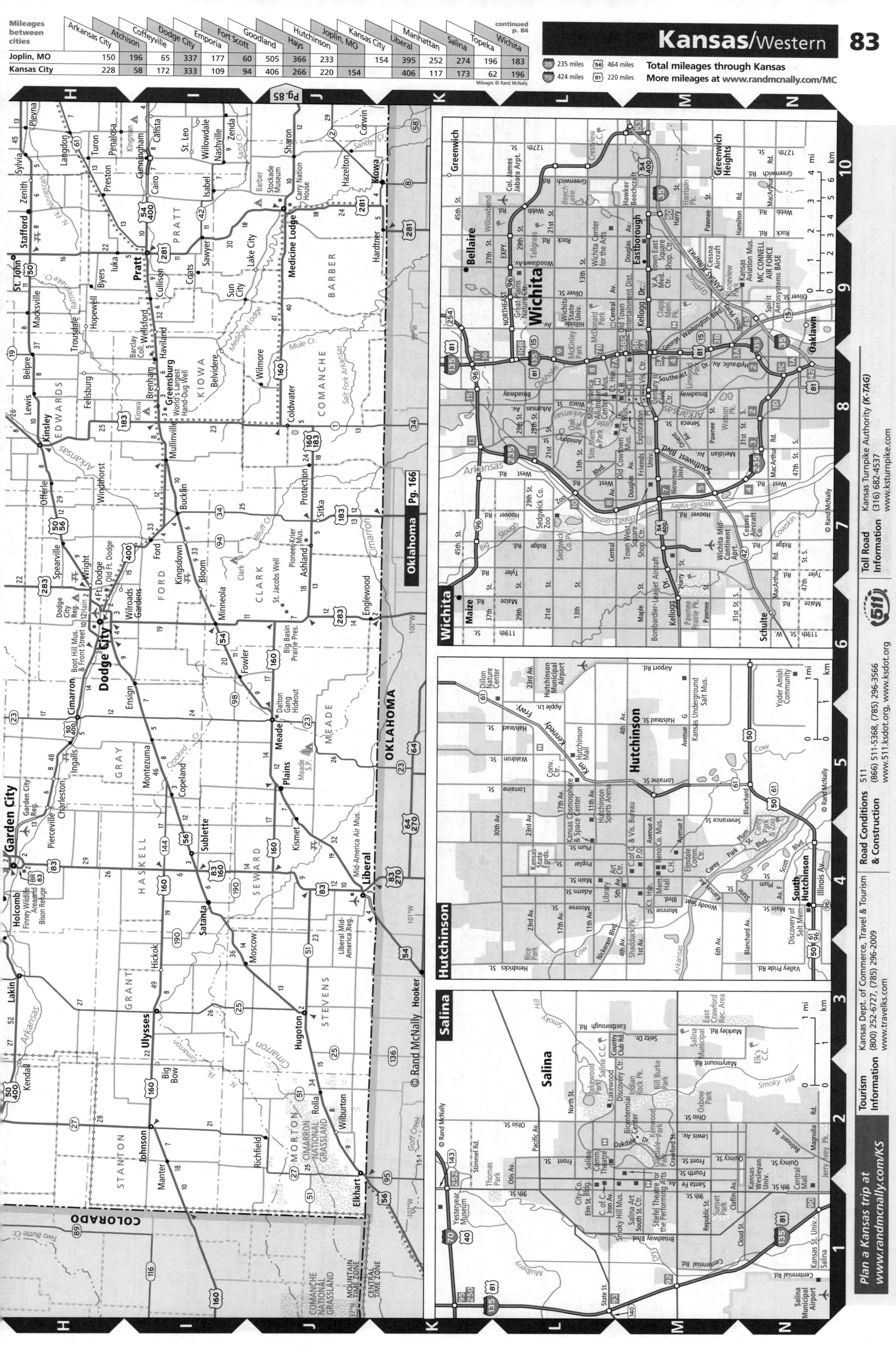

Wichita

Hutchinson

Salina

Oklahoma Pg. 166

Plan a Kansas trip at www.randmcnally.com/KS

Tourism Information	Kansas Dept. of Commerce, Travel & Tourism (800) 252-6727, (785) 296-2009 www.travelks.com
	511 (866) 511-5368, (785) 296-3566 www.511.ksdot.org, www.ksdot.org
Road Conditions & Construction	511 511.ksdot.org, www.ksdot.org
Toll Road Information	Kansas Turnpike Authority (K-TAG) (316) 682-4537 www.ksturnpike.com

Mileages between cities	Arkansas City	Atchison	Coffeyville	Dodge City	Emporia	Fort Scott	Goodland	Hays	Hutchinson	Joplin, MO	Kansas City	Liberal	Manhattan	Salina	Topeka	Wichita
Salina	151	160	224	164	117	238	235	96	65	274	173	246	65		109	90
Smith Center	266	213	338	195	231	342	175	91	155	387	263	277	150	117	206	205

Mileages © Rand McNally

Determining distances along roads

Interchanges and exit numbers
For most states, the mileage between interchanges may be determined by subtracting one number from the other.

One inch represents approximately 17 miles

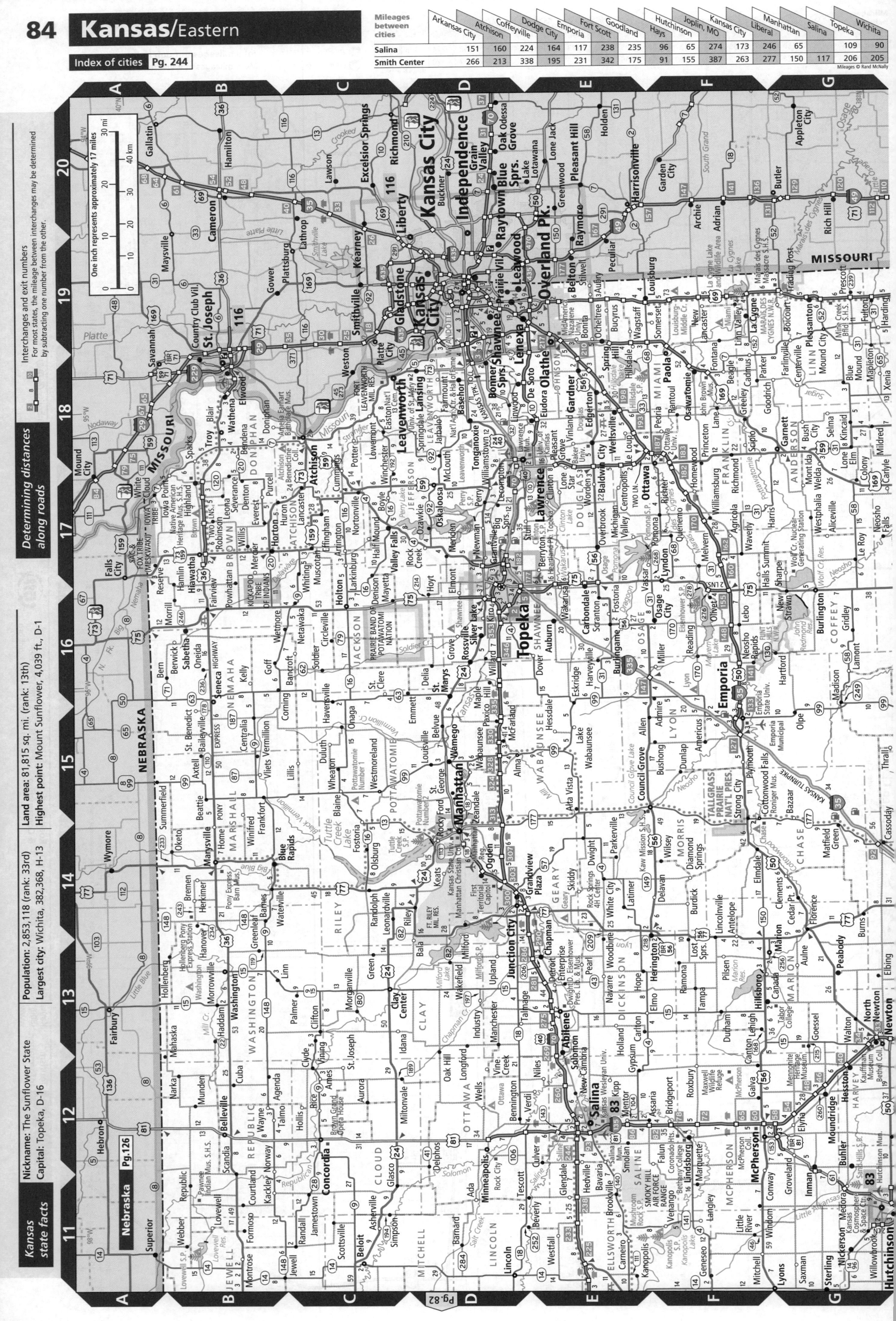

Mileages between cities	Arkansas City	Atchison	Coffeyville	Dodge City	Emporia	Fort Scott	Goodland	Hays	Hutchinson	Joplin, MO	Kansas City	Liberal	Manhattan	Salina	Topeka	Wichita
Topeka	170	55	155	273	58	136	344	204	162	196	62	349	56	109		137
Wichita	61	188	134	154	85	149	323	183	51	183	196	212	130	90	137	

Mileages © Rand McNally

Total mileages through Kansas
More mileages at www.randmcnally.com/MC

| 35 | 235 miles | 56 | 464 miles |
| 70 | 424 miles | 81 | 220 miles |

Plan a Kansas trip at www.randmcnally.com/KS

Tourism Information
Kansas Dept. of Commerce, Travel & Tourism
(800) 252-6727, (785) 296-2009
www.travelks.com

Road Conditions & Construction
511
(866) 511-5368, (785) 296-3566
511.ksdot.org, www.ksdot.org

Toll Road Information
Kansas Turnpike Authority (K-TAG)
(316) 682-4537
www.ksturnpike.com

Mileages between cities	Ashland	Bowling Green	Cave City	Covington	Elizabethtown	Frankfort	Hopkinsville	Lexington	Louisville	Mayfield	Maysville	Middlesboro	Owensboro	Paducah	Pikeville	Somerset
Ashland		269	242	138	202	140	325	117	187	383	76	227	294	372	96	175
Bowling Green	269		31	209	70	147	64	151	113	160	216	198	71	151	265	109

Mileages © Rand McNally

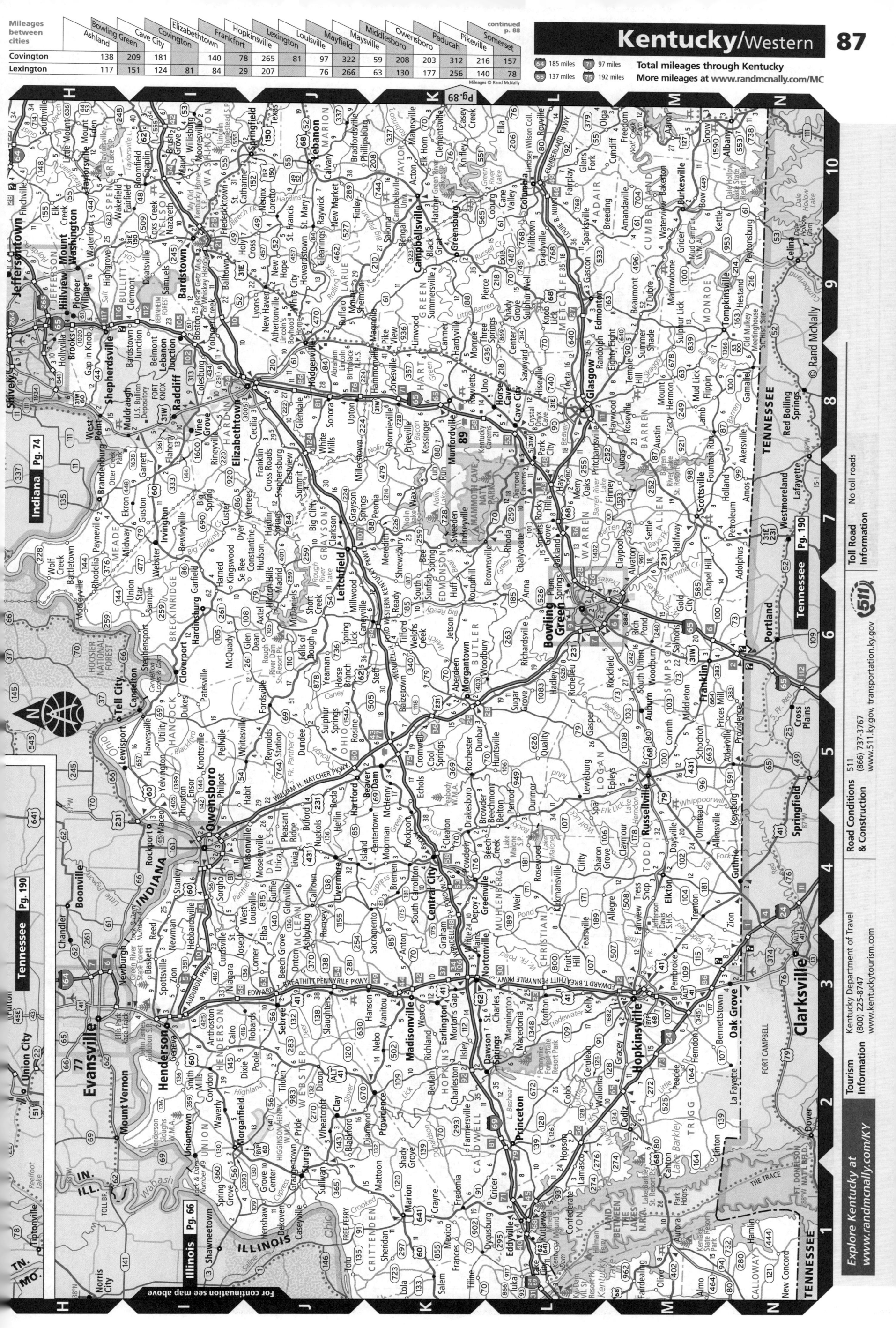

Mileages between cities	Ashland	Bowling Green	Cave City	Covington	Elizabethtown	Frankfort	Hopkinsville	Lexington	Louisville	Mayfield	Maysville	Middlesboro	Owensboro	Paducah	Pikeville	Somerset
Covington	138	209	181		140	78	265	81	97	322	59	208	203	312	216	157
Lexington	117	151	124	81	84	29	207		76	266	63	130	177	256	140	78

continued p. 88

Mileages © Rand McNally

Total mileages through Kentucky

64 185 miles	71 97 miles
65 137 miles	75 192 miles

More mileages at www.randmcnally.com/MC

Tourism Information — Kentucky Department of Travel — (800) 225-8747 — www.kentuckytourism.com

Road Conditions & Construction — 511 — (866) 737-3767 — www.511.ky.gov transportation.ky.gov

511 — www.511.ky.gov

Toll Road — No toll roads — Information

Explore Kentucky at www.randmcnally.com/KY

© Rand McNally

Mileages between cities	Ashland	Bowling Green	Cave City	Covington	Elizabethtown	Frankfort	Hopkinsville	Lexington	Louisville	Mayfield	Maysville	Middlesboro	Owensboro	Paducah	Pikeville	Somerset
Louisville	187	113	85	97	44	50	170	76		227	133	203	106	216	211	124
Middlesboro	227	198	176	208	182	157	265	130	203	363	191		275	353	125	88

Mileages © Rand McNally

Interchanges and exit numbers
For most states, the mileage between interchanges may be determined by subtracting one number from the other.

Determining distances along roads

Kentucky state facts
Nickname: The Bluegrass State
Capital: Frankfort, G-11
Population: 4,339,367 (rank: 26th)
Largest city: Louisville, 597,337, G-8
Land area: 39,728 sq. mi. (rank: 36th)
Highest point: Black Mountain, 4,145 ft., L-18

West Virginia Pg. 226

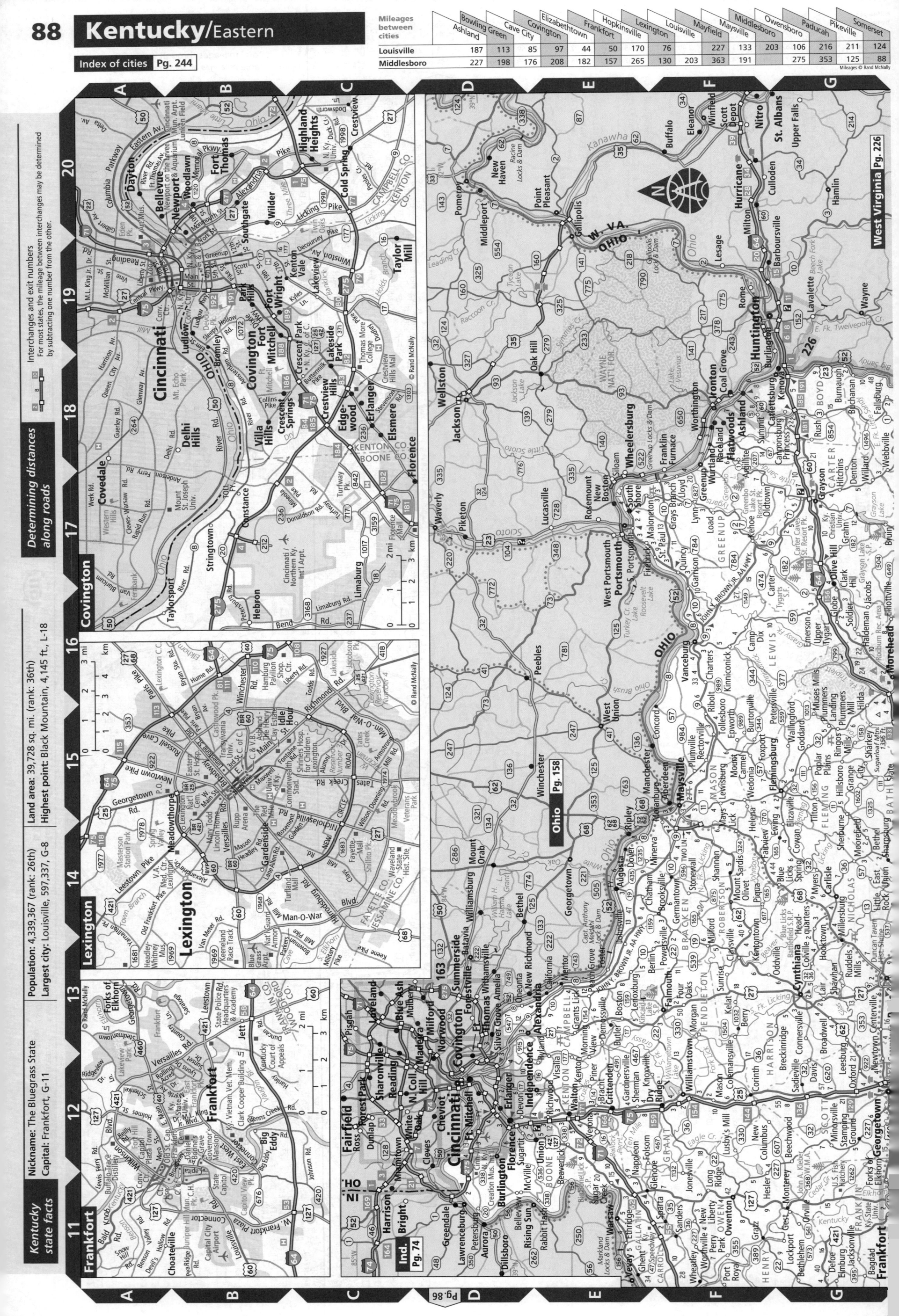

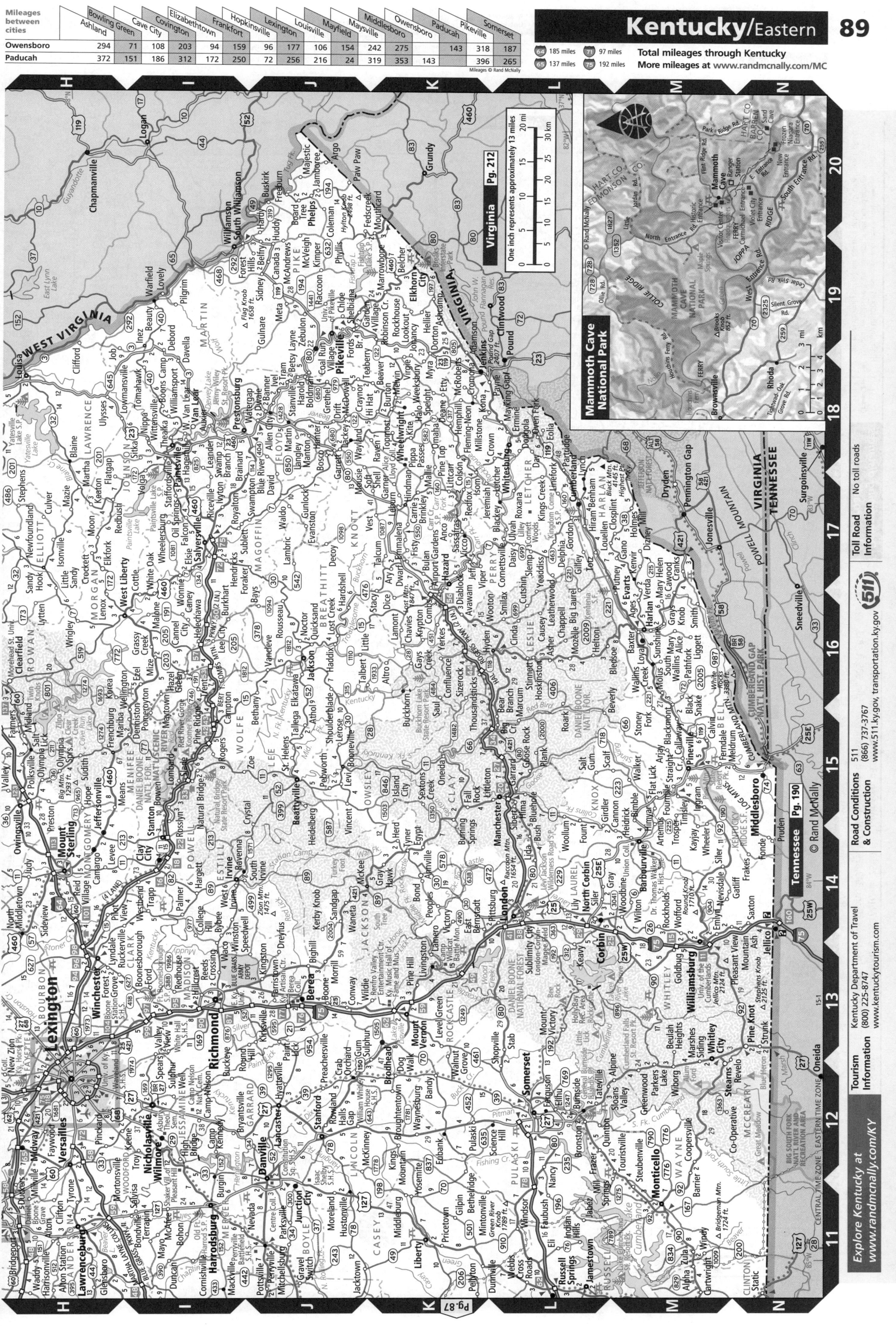

Mileages between cities	Ashland	Bowling Green	Cave City	Covington	Elizabethtown	Frankfort	Hopkinsville	Lexington	Louisville	Mayfield	Maysville	Middlesboro	Owensboro	Paducah	Pikeville	Somerset
Owensboro	294	71	108	203	94	159	96	177	106	154	242	275		143	318	187
Paducah	372	151	186	312	172	250	72	256	216	24	319	353	143		396	265

Mileages © Rand McNally

Total mileages through Kentucky

| 64 | 185 miles | 71 | 97 miles |
| 65 | 137 miles | 75 | 192 miles |

More mileages at www.randmcnally.com/MC

Mammoth Cave National Park

Virginia Pg. 212

One inch represents approximately 13 miles

Tennessee Pg. 190

© Rand McNally

| Tourism Information | Kentucky Department of Travel (800) 225-8747 www.kentuckytourism.com | Road Conditions & Construction | 511 (866) 737-3767 www.511.ky.gov, transportation.ky.gov | Toll Road Information | No toll roads |

Explore Kentucky at www.randmcnally.com/KY

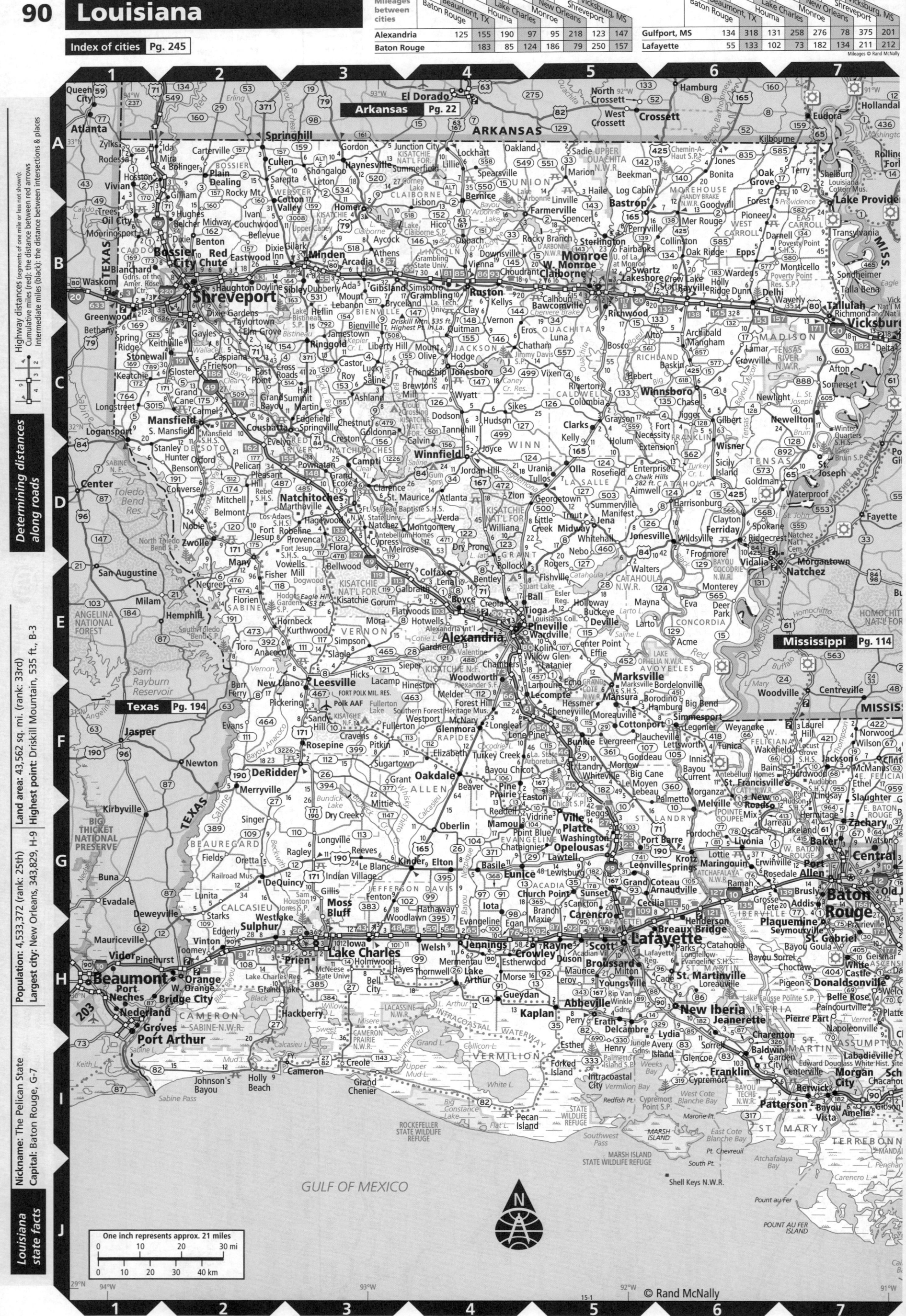

Mileages between cities

	Baton Rouge	Beaumont, TX	Houma	Lake Charles	Monroe	New Orleans	Shreveport	Vicksburg, MS
Alexandria	125	155	190	97	95	218	123	147
Baton Rouge		183	85	124	186	79	250	157

	Baton Rouge	Beaumont, TX	Houma	Lake Charles	Monroe	New Orleans	Shreveport	Vicksburg, MS
Gulfport, MS	134	318	131	258	276	78	375	201
Lafayette	55	133	102	73	182	134	211	212

Mileages © Rand McNally

Mileages between cities

	Baton Rouge	Beaumont, TX	Houma	Lake Charles	Monroe	New Orleans	Shreveport	Vicksburg, MS
Lake Charles	124	60	177		190	203	184	243
New Orleans	79	262	56	203	281		340	207
Shreveport	250	206	314	184	98	340		171
Vicksburg, MS	157	301	234	243	74	207	171	

Mileages © Rand McNally

	Total mileages through Louisiana
10 — 274 miles	49 — 208 miles
20 — 190 miles	55 — 66 miles

More mileages at www.randmcnally.com/MC

Shreveport

Baton Rouge

Central New Orleans

New Orleans

Lafayette

Monroe

Toll Bridge Information — Lake Pontchartrain Causeway (504) 835-3118, (985) 674-3641 — www.thecauseway.us

Road Conditions & Construction — 511 (877) 452-3683 — www.511la.org, www.dotd.la.gov

Tourism Information — Louisiana Office of Tourism (800) 994-8626 — www.louisianatravel.com

Get more Louisiana travel info at www.randmcnally.com/LA

© Rand McNally

Mileages between cities	Auburn	Bangor	Bar Harbor	Eastport	Houlton	Millinocket	Portland	Rangeley
Bangor	107		47	120	118	72	128	120
Eastport	226	120	118		115	125	247	242
Houlton	225	118	167	115		69	246	238
Madawaska	326	219	267	218	102	170	347	339

Mileages © Rand McNally

For continuation see map at right

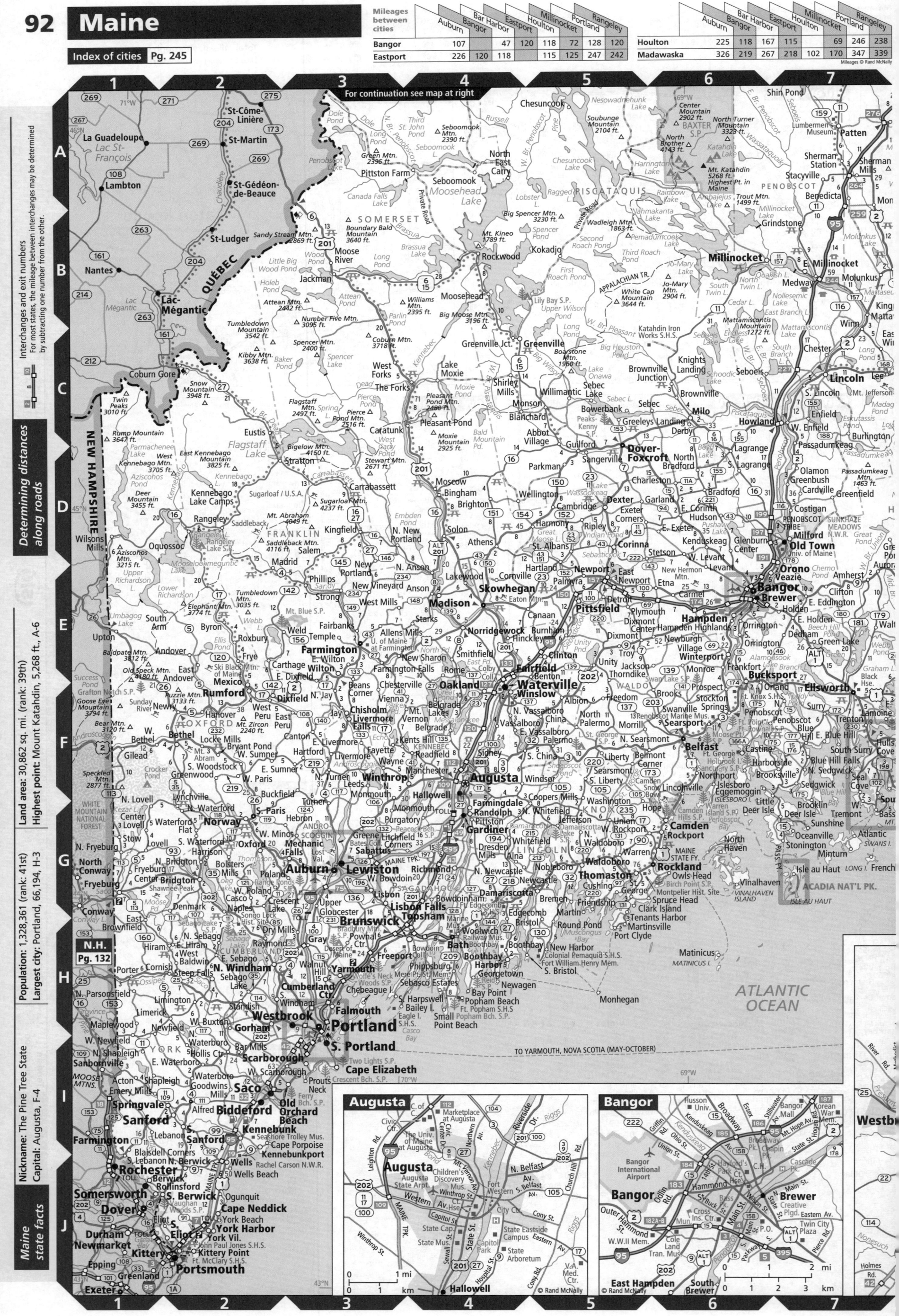

Maine state facts

Nickname: The Pine Tree State
Capital: Augusta, F-4
Population: 1,328,361 (rank: 41st)
Largest city: Portland, 66,194, H-3
Land area: 30,862 sq. mi. (rank: 39th)
Highest point: Mount Katahdin, 5,268 ft., A-6

Determining distances along roads

Interchanges and exit numbers
For most states, the mileage between interchanges may be determined by subtracting one number from the other.

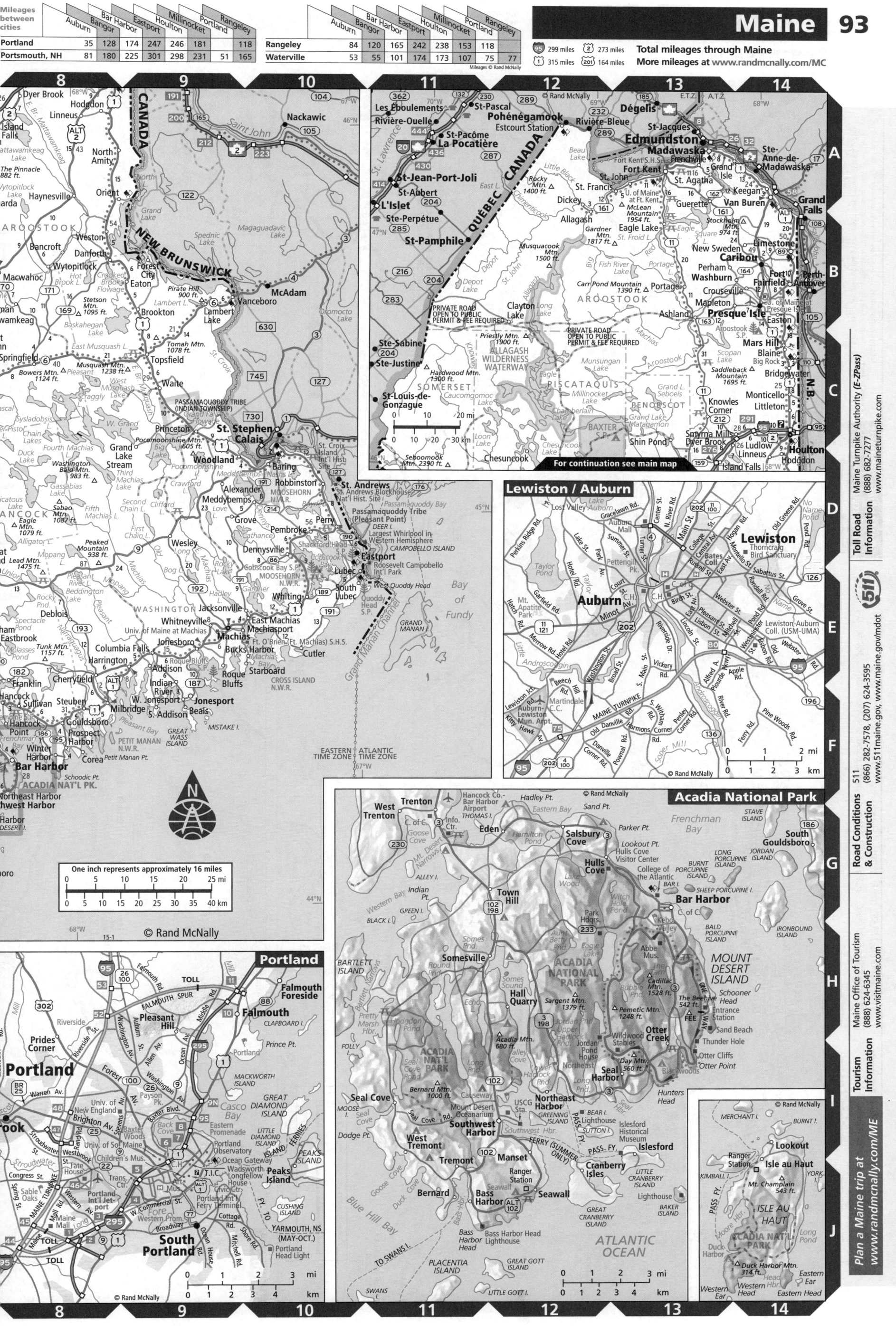

Mileages between cities

	Auburn	Bangor	Bar Harbor	Eastport	Houlton	Millinocket	Portland	Rangeley
Portland	35	128	174	247	246	181		118
Portsmouth, NH	81	180	225	301	298	231	51	165

	Auburn	Bangor	Bar Harbor	Eastport	Houlton	Millinocket	Portland	Rangeley
Rangeley	84	120	165	242	238	153	118	
Waterville	53	55	101	174	173	107	75	77

Mileages © Rand McNally

Total mileages through Maine
95 299 miles · 2 273 miles
1 315 miles · 201 164 miles
More mileages at www.randmcnally.com/MC

Lewiston / Auburn

Acadia National Park

Portland

One inch represents approximately 16 miles
0 5 10 15 20 25 mi
0 5 10 15 20 25 30 35 40 km

© Rand McNally

Toll Road Information — Maine Turnpike Authority (E-ZPass) (888) 682-7277 · www.maineturnpike.com

Road Conditions & Construction — 511 (866) 282-7578, (207) 624-3595 · www.511maine.gov, www.maine.gov/mdot

Tourism Information — Maine Office of Tourism (888) 624-6345 · www.visitmaine.com

Plan a Maine trip at www.randmcnally.com/ME

Mileages between cities	Aberdeen	Annapolis	Baltimore	Cambridge	Chestertown	Cumberland	Frederick	Hagerstown	Lexington Park	Ocean City	Pocomoke City	Rockville	St. Charles	Salisbury	Washington, DC	Wilmington, DE
Aberdeen		58	31	113	65	171	83	107	122	134	152	74	90	122	70	42
Annapolis	58		28	57	47	157	68	93	73	108	120	42	41	89	30	96

Mileages © Rand McNally

Maryland state facts

Nickname: The Old Line State
Capital: Annapolis, E-14

Population: 5,773,552 (rank: 19th)
Largest city: Baltimore, 620,961, C-13

Land area: 9,774 sq. mi. (rank: 42nd)
Highest point: Backbone Mountain, 3,360 ft., D-1

Determining distances along roads

Highway distances (segments of one mile or less not shown):
Cumulative miles (red): the distance between red arrows
Intermediate miles (black): the distance between intersections & places

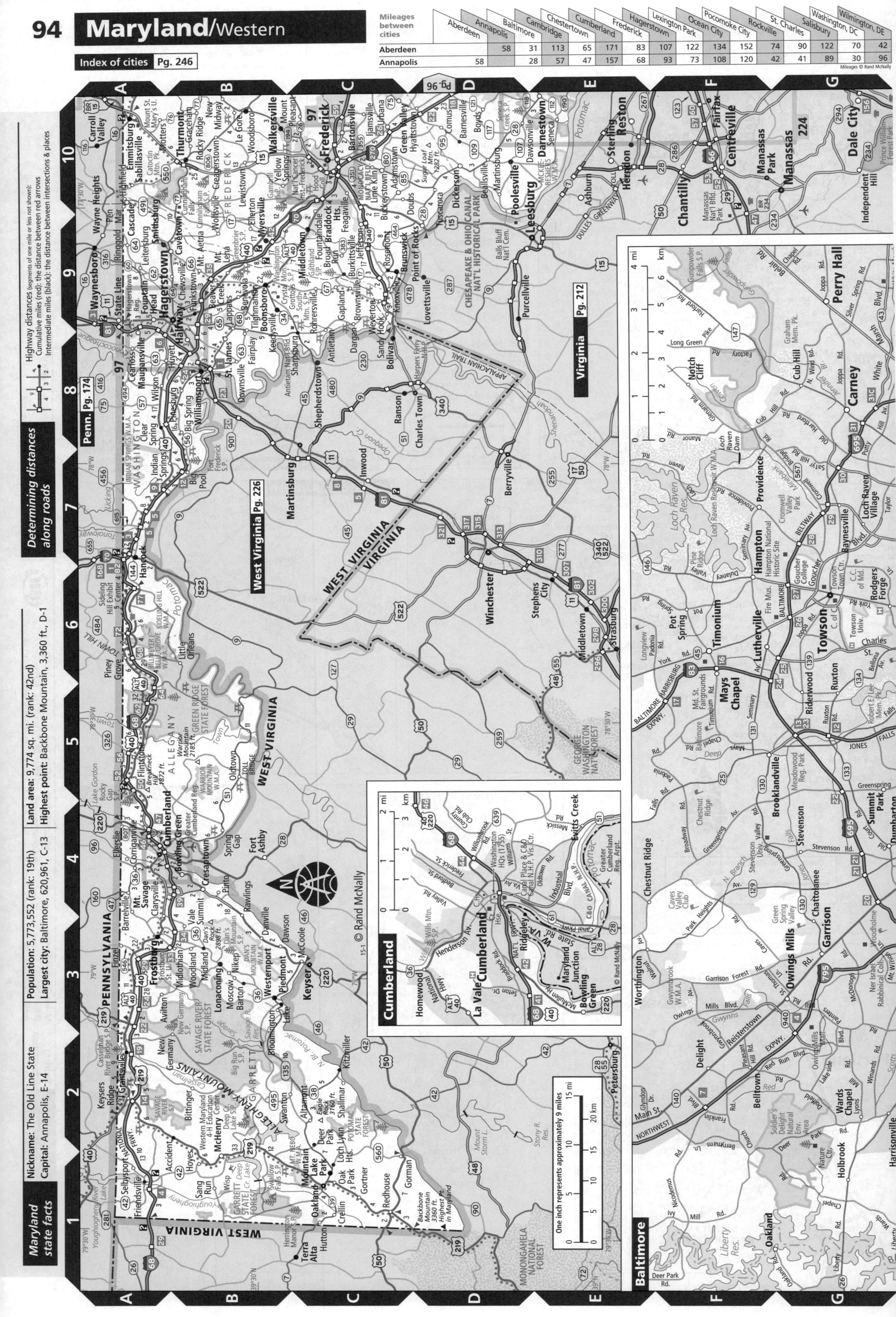

Cumberland

Baltimore

© Rand McNally

One inch represents approximately 9 miles

Mileages between cities	Aberdeen	Annapolis	Baltimore	Cambridge	Chestertown	Cumberland	Frederick	Hagerstown	Lexington Park	Ocean City	Pocomoke City	Rockville	St. Charles	Salisbury	Washington, DC	Wilmington, DE
Baltimore	31	28		84	73	136	47	72	93	136	146	42	59	116	39	70
Cumberland	171	157	136	212	203		88	67	200	263	275	116	166	244	134	209

continued p. 96

Mileages © Rand McNally

Pg.97

Total mileages through Maryland
More mileages at www.randmcnally.com/MC

68	81 miles	81	12 miles
70	94 miles	95	110 miles

Toll Road — Maryland Transportation Authority (E-ZPass) (866) 713-1596. In Maryland: (410) 537-1000 www.mdta.maryland.gov

Road Conditions & Construction — 511, (855) 466-9511, (410) 582-5650 www.roads.maryland.gov md511.org

Tourism Information — Maryland Office of Tourism (866) 639-3526 www.visitmaryland.org

Explore Maryland at www.randmcnally.com/MD

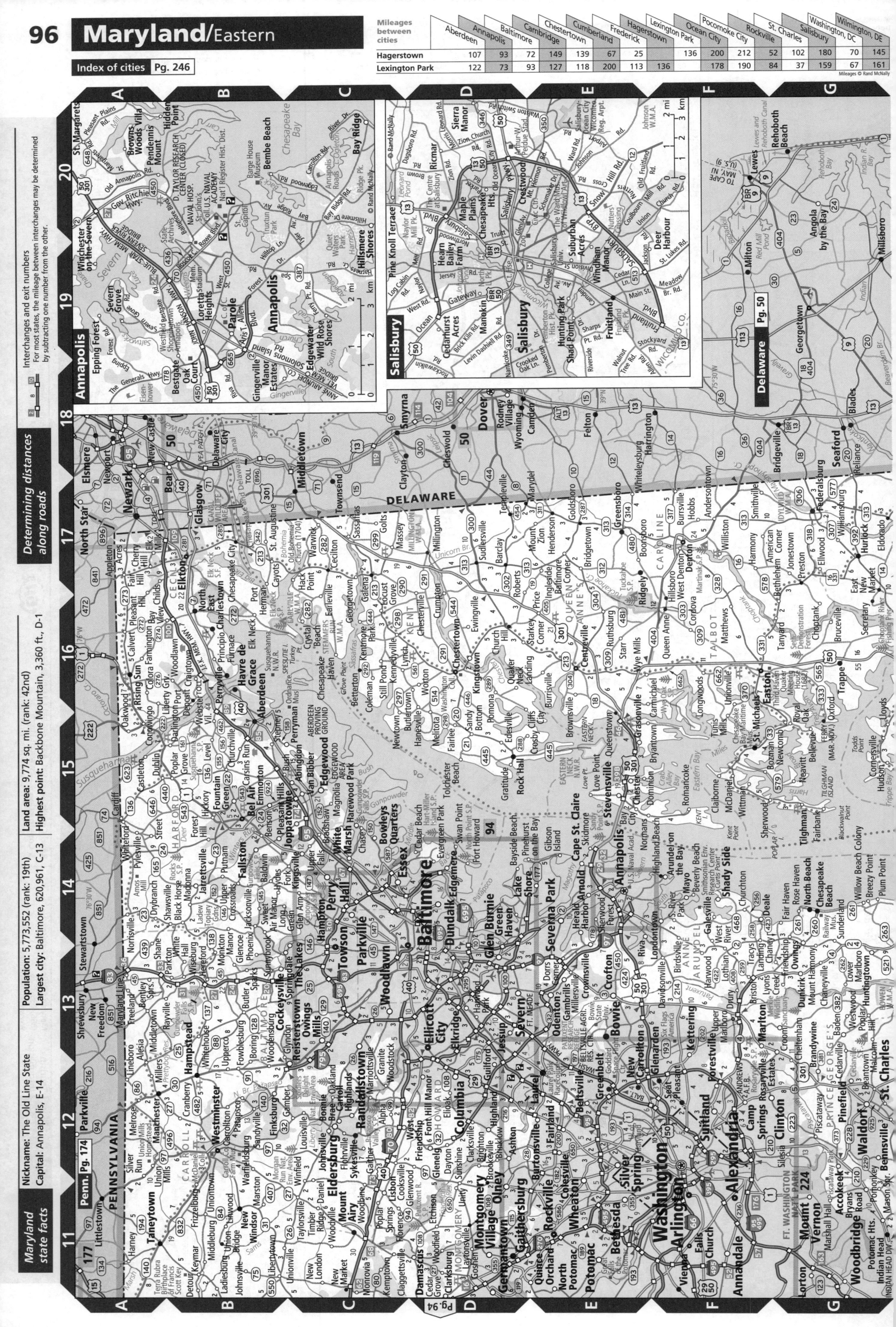

Mileages between cities	Aberdeen	Annapolis	Baltimore	Cambridge	Chestertown	Cumberland	Frederick	Hagerstown	Lexington Park	Ocean City	Pocomoke City	Rockville	St. Charles	Salisbury	Washington, DC	Wilmington, DE
Hagerstown	107	93	72	149	139	67	25		136	200	212	52	102	180	70	145
Lexington Park	122	73	93	127	118	200	113	136		178	190	84	37	159	67	161

Mileages © Rand McNally

Maryland state facts

Nickname: The Old Line State
Capital: Annapolis, E-14

Population: 5,773,552 (rank: 19th)
Largest city: Baltimore, 620,961, C-13

Land area: 9,774 sq. mi. (rank: 42nd)
Highest point: Backbone Mountain, 3,360 ft., D-1

Determining distances along roads

Interchanges and exit numbers

For most states, the mileage between interchanges may be determined by subtracting one number from the other.

Mileages between cities	Aberdeen	Annapolis	Baltimore	Cambridge	Chestertown	Cumberland	Frederick	Hagerstown	Lexington Park	Ocean City	Pocomoke City	Rockville	St. Charles	Salisbury	Washington, DC	Wilmington, DE
Salisbury	122	89	116	32	78	244	156	180	159	29	26	130	128		118	107
Washington, DC	70	30	39	86	76	134	48	70	67	139	148	19	30	118		109

Mileages © Rand McNally

Total mileages through Maryland

68	81 miles	81	12 miles
70	94 miles	95	110 miles

More mileages at www.randmcnally.com/MC

Frederick

Hagerstown

Central Baltimore

Virginia Pg. 212

Virginia Pg. 95

© Rand McNally

Tourism Information
Maryland Office of Tourism
(866) 639-3526
www.visitmaryland.org

Road Conditions & Construction
511, (855) 466-9511, (410) 582-5650
www.md511.org
www.roads.maryland.gov

Toll Road Information
Maryland Transportation Authority (E-ZPass)
(866) 713-1596, In Maryland: (410) 537-1000
www.mdta.maryland.gov

Explore Maryland at www.randmcnally.com/MD

Mileages between cities	Boston	Brockton	Falmouth	Fitchburg	Gloucester	Greenfield	Lowell	Nantucket	New Bedford	North Adams	Pittsfield	Plymouth	Providence, RI	Provincetown	Springfield	Worcester
Boston		24	76	47	39	94	29	101*	58	157	136	40	50	116	90	43
Gloucester	39	63	114	74		120	47	140*	97	157	169	78	90	154	122	75

*via ferry
Mileages © Rand McNally

Massachusetts state facts

Nickname: The Bay State
Capital: Boston, E-14

Population: 6,547,629 (rank: 14th)
Largest city: Boston, 617,594, E-14

Land area: 7,840 sq. mi. (rank: 45th)
Highest point: Mount Greylock, 3,491 ft., C-2

Determining distances along roads

Highway distances (segments of one mile or less not shown):
Cumulative miles (red): the distance between cities
Intermediate miles (black): the distance between intersections & places

One inch represents approximately 7 miles

© Rand McNally

New Hampshire Pg. 132

Vermont Pg. 210

New York Pg. 140

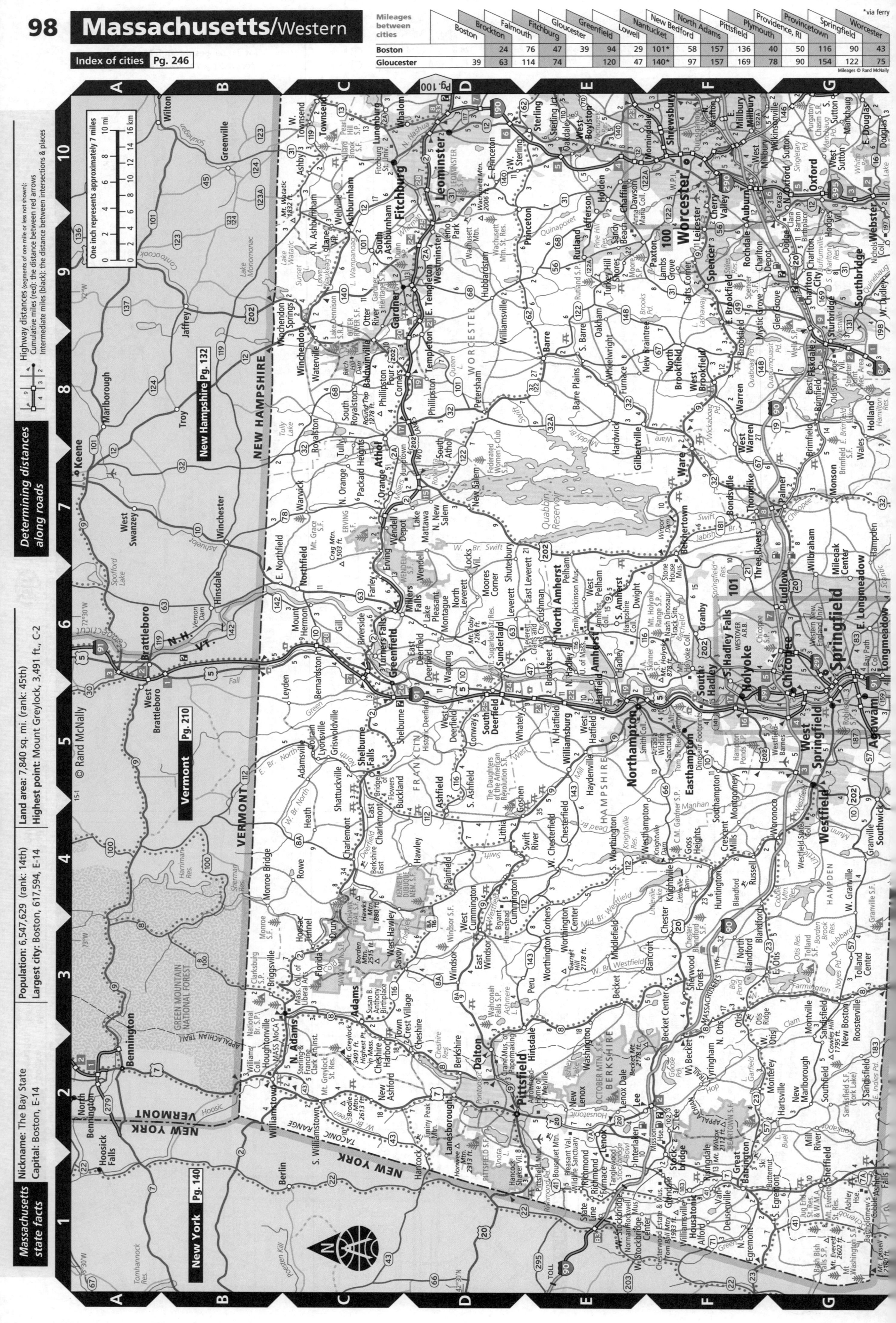

Mileages between cities	Boston	Brockton	Falmouth	Fitchburg	Gloucester	Greenfield	Lowell	Nantucket	New Bedford	North Adams	Pittsfield	Plymouth	Providence, RI	Provincetown	Springfield	Worcester continued p. 100
Lowell	29	50	102	32	47	78		130*	84	115	139	69	69	145	92	41
New Bedford	58	37	40	94	97	148	84	77*		182	161	37	31	91	114	71

Mileages © Rand McNally

Total mileages through Massachusetts
More mileages at www.randmcnally.com/MC

| 90 | 136 miles | 93 | 47 miles |
| 91 | 55 miles | 95 | 92 miles |

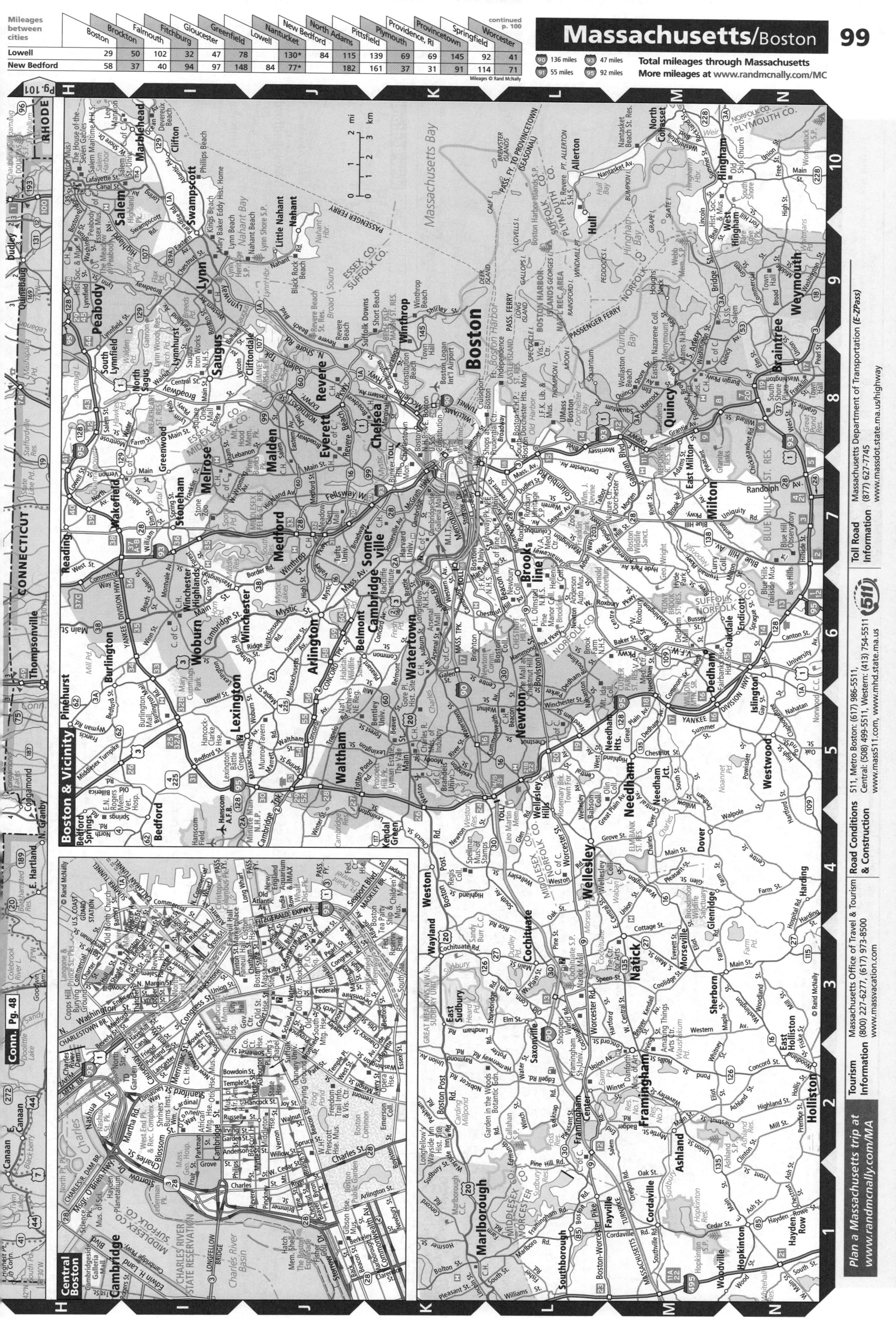

Index of cities Pg. 246

Mileages between cities

	Boston	Brockton	Falmouth	Fitchburg	Gloucester	Greenfield	Lowell	Nantucket	New Bedford	North Adams	Pittsfield	Plymouth	Providence, RI	Provincetown	Springfield	Worcester
Pittsfield	136	150	189	124	169	79	139	226*	161	22		167	130	240	51	98
Provincetown	116	106	69	162	154	208	145	78*	91	262	240	77	119		194	146

*via ferry

Mileages © Rand McNally

Determining distances along roads

Interchanges and exit numbers
For most states, the mileage between interchanges may be determined
by subtracting one number from the other.

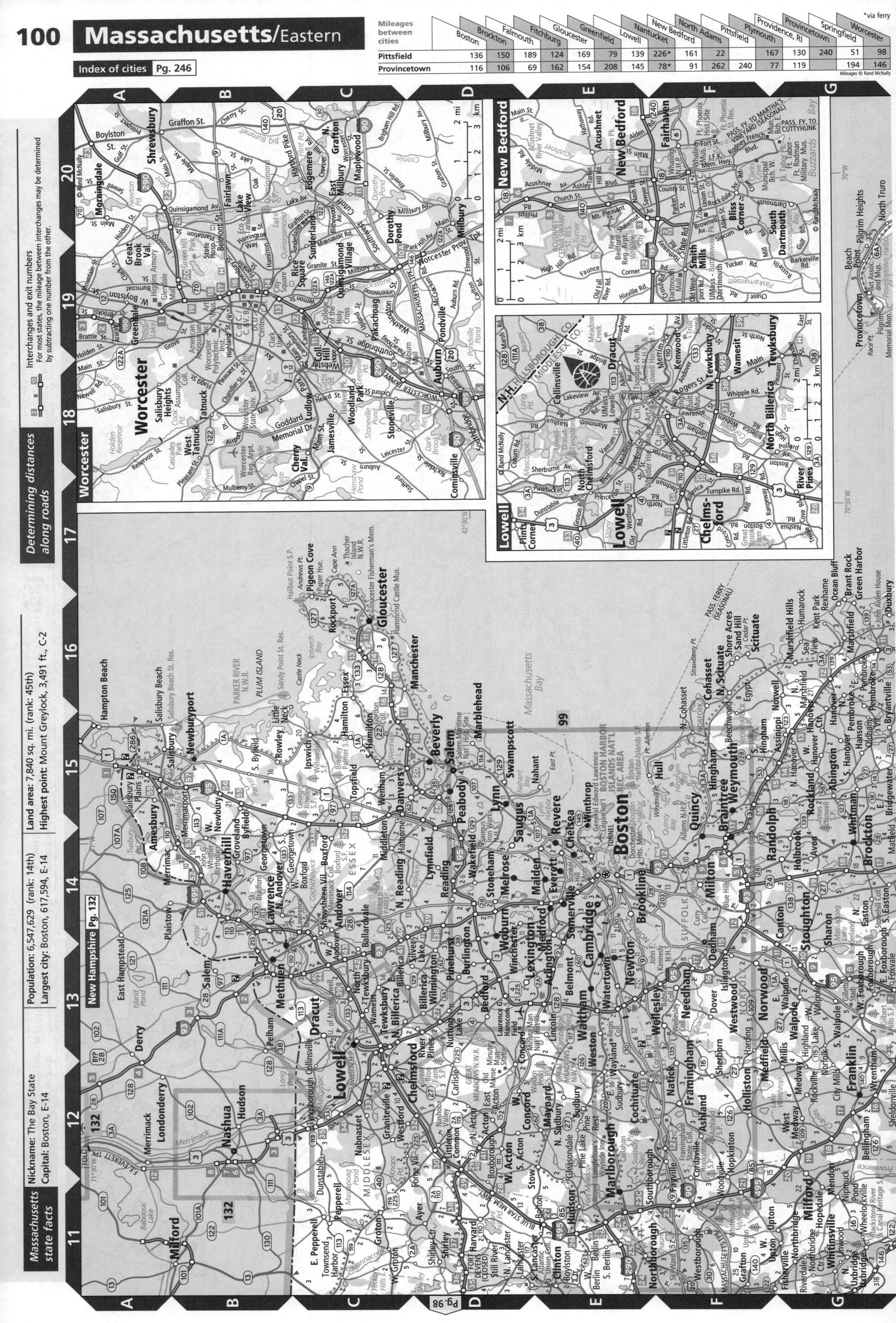

42°N

Mileages between cities

	Boston	Brockton	Falmouth	Fitchburg	Gloucester	Greenfield	Lowell	Nantucket	New Bedford	North Adams	Pittsfield	Plymouth	Providence, RI	Provincetown	Springfield	Worcester
Springfield	90	103	143	77	122	38	92	180*	114	73	51	121	83	194		51
Worcester	43	56	96	26	75	72	41	133*	71	120	98	74	40	146	51	

*via ferry

Mileages © Rand McNally

Total mileages through Massachusetts

90	136 miles	93	47 miles
91	55 miles	95	92 miles

More mileages at www.randmcnally.com/MC

© Rand McNally

One inch represents approximately 7 miles

0 2 4 6 8 10 mi
0 2 4 6 8 10 12 14 16 km

Plan a Massachusetts trip at www.randmcnally.com/MA

Tourism Information — Massachusetts Office of Travel & Tourism (800) 227-6277, (617) 973-8500 www.massvacation.com

Road Conditions & Construction — 511, Metro Boston: (617) 986-5511, Central: (508) 499-5511, Western: (413) 754-5511 www.mass511.com, www.mhd.state.ma.us

Toll Road Information — Massachusetts Department of Transportation (E-ZPass) (877) 627-7745 www.massdot.state.ma.us/highway

ATLANTIC OCEAN

NANTUCKET ISLAND

MARTHA'S VINEYARD

Nantucket Sound

Buzzards Bay

Cape Cod Bay

CAPE COD NATIONAL SEASHORE

CAPE COD

Springfield (inset map)

RHODE ISLAND

Pg. 184

Pg. 99

Mileages between cities	Alpena	Chicago, IL	Detroit	Grand Rapids	Houghton	Ironwood	Kalamazoo	Ludington	Mackinaw City	Menominee	Muskegon	Port Huron	Saginaw	Sault Ste. Marie	Toledo, OH	Traverse City
Ann Arbor	227	240	43	132	538	584	98	228	272	473	172	102	86	329	51	238
Detroit	244	280		157	553	599	140	252	290	488	197	62	102	345	59	255

Mileages © Rand McNally

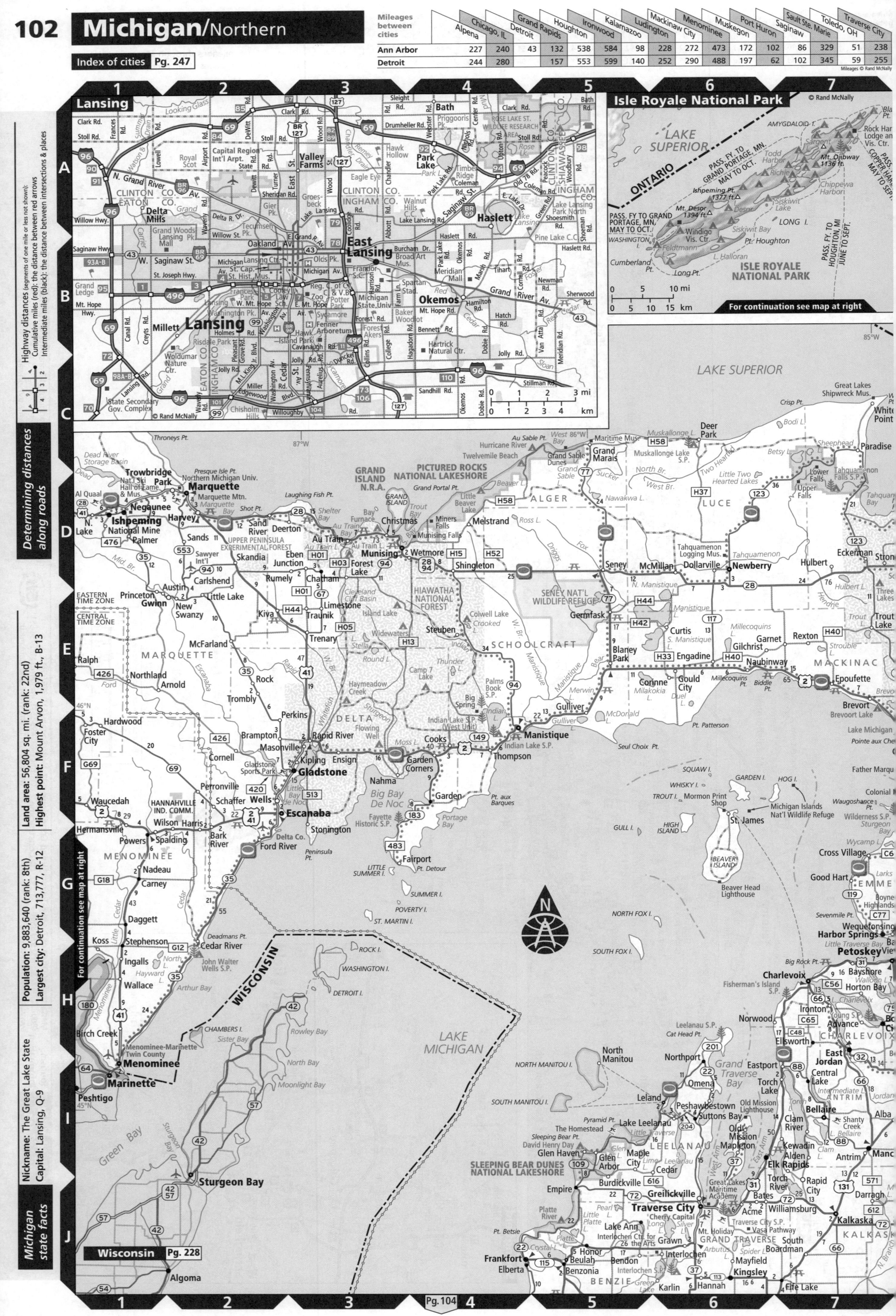

Mileages between cities

	Alpena	Chicago, IL	Detroit	Grand Rapids	Houghton	Ironwood	Kalamazoo	Ludington	Mackinaw City	Menominee	Muskegon	Port Huron	Saginaw	Sault Ste. Marie	Toledo, OH	Traverse City
Flint	178	271	68	113	489	534	130	186	224	423	152	66	37	280	107	188
Grand Rapids	249	177	157		502	552	50	97	236	438	41	180	115	292	185	140

continued p. 104

Mileages © Rand McNally

69 199 miles, 94 275 miles, 75 396 miles, 96 192 miles

Total mileages through Michigan
More mileages at www.randmcnally.com/MC

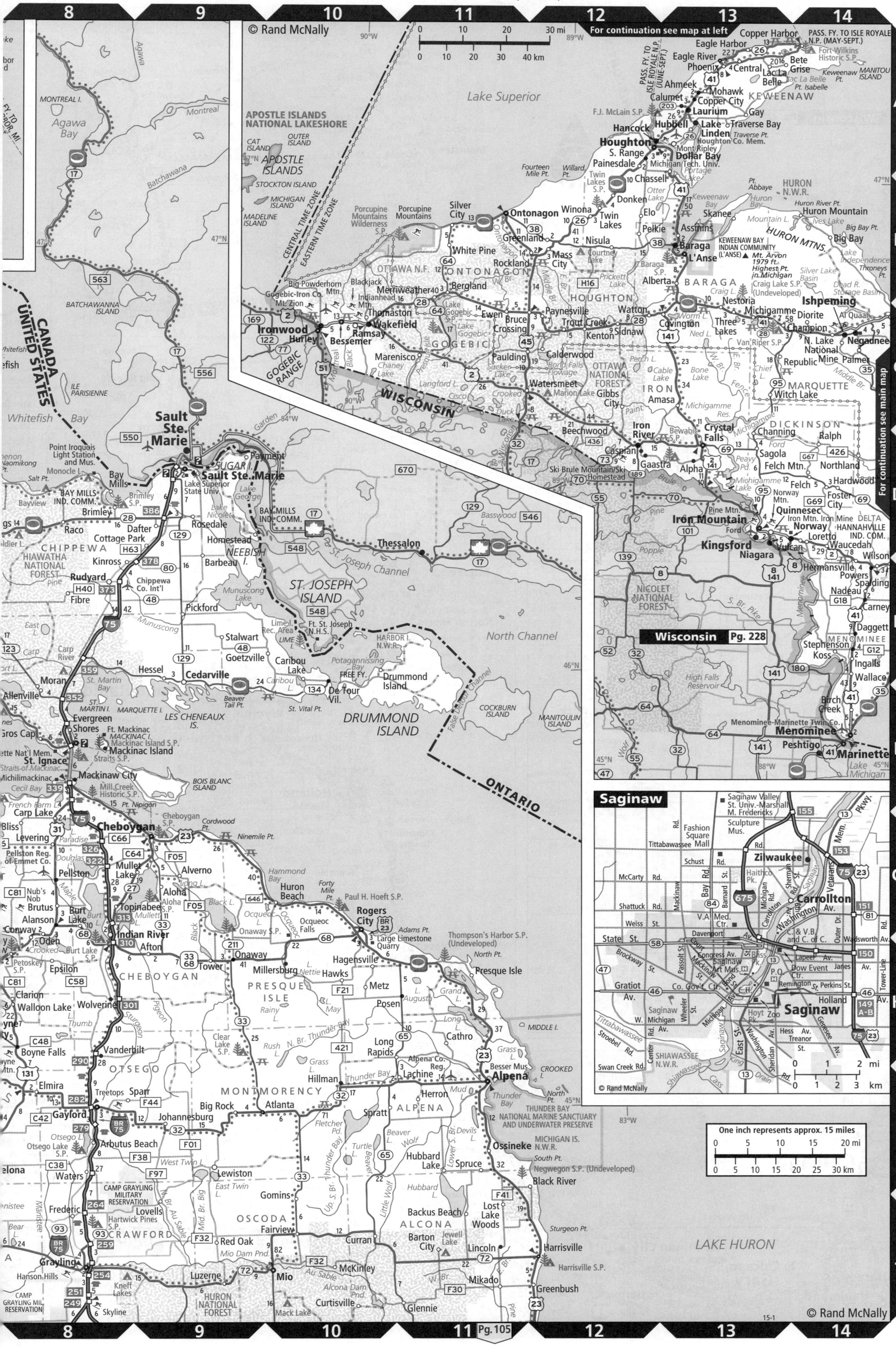

Toll Bridge Information
Michigan Department of Transportation (all other toll bridges): (517) 373-2090; www.michigan.gov/mdot, www.mackinacbridge.org

Road Conditions & Construction
(800) 381-8477 (517) 335-3084
www.michigan.gov/drive

Tourism Information
Travel Michigan
(888) 784-7328, (800) 644-2489
www.michigan.org

Get more Michigan info at www.randmcnally.com/MI

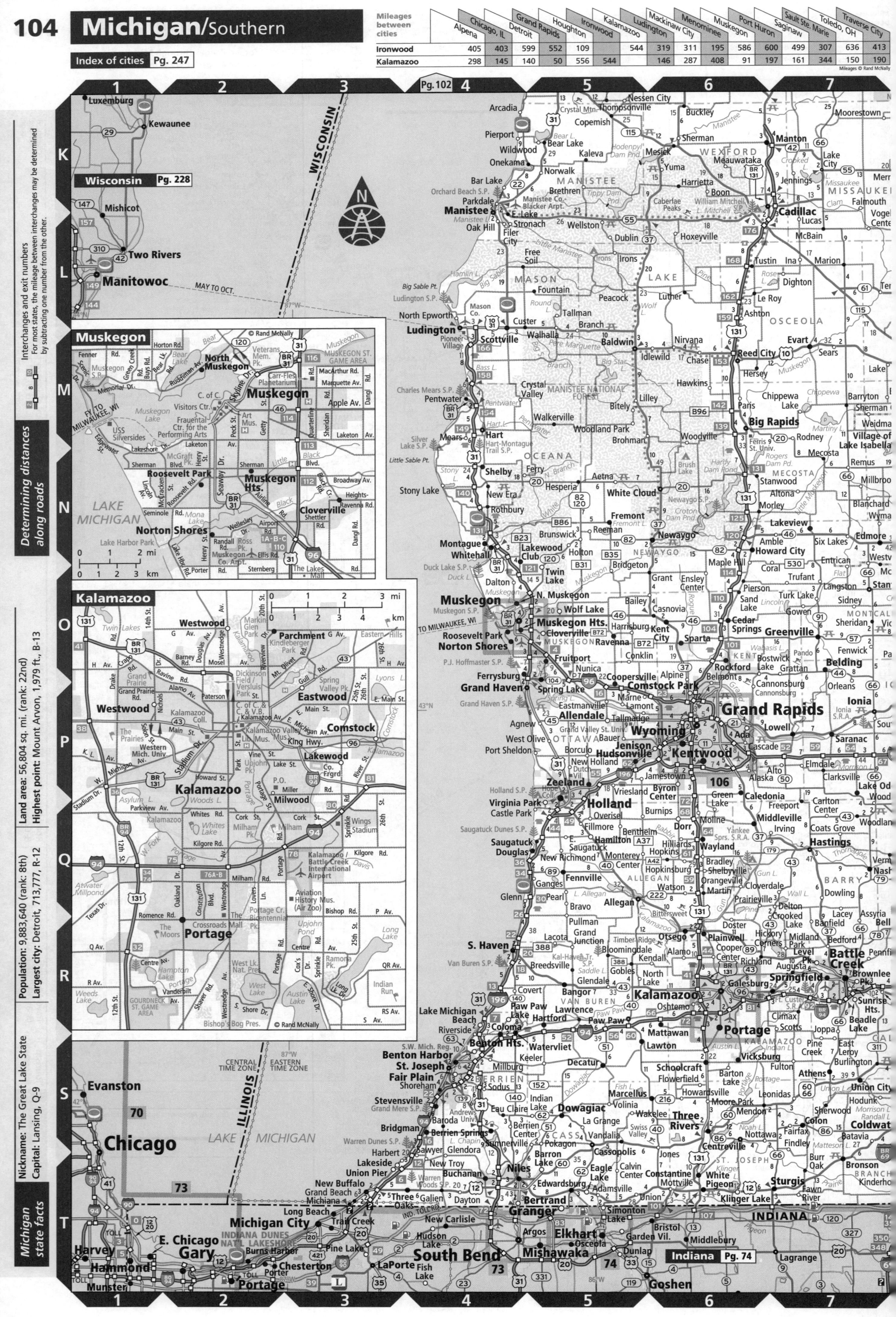

Mileages between cities	Alpena	Chicago, IL	Detroit	Grand Rapids	Houghton	Ironwood	Kalamazoo	Ludington	Mackinaw City	Menominee	Muskegon	Port Huron	Saginaw	Sault Ste. Marie	Toledo, OH	Traverse City
Ironwood	405	403	599	552	109		544	319	311	195	586	600	499	307	636	413
Kalamazoo	298	145	140	50	556	544		146	287	408	91	197	161	344	150	190

Mileages © Rand McNally

Pg. 102
Pg. 106

Mileages between cities	Alpena	Chicago, IL	Detroit	Grand Rapids	Houghton	Ironwood	Kalamazoo	Ludington	Mackinaw City	Menominee	Muskegon	Port Huron	Saginaw	Sault Ste. Marie	Toledo, OH	Traverse City
Lansing	228	216	90	68	494	539	75	162	228	429	107	122	88	284	118	180
Mackinaw City	94	412	290	236	266	311	287	218		200	251	290	188	56	327	102

Mileages ©2012 Rand McNally

Total mileages through Michigan

More mileages at www.r.com/MC

| 69 | 199 miles | 94 | 275 miles |
| 75 | 396 miles | 96 | 192 miles |

One inch represents approx. 15 miles

© Rand McNally

City sights to see
- Arab American National Museum, Dearborn, K-6
- Cranbrook Art Museum, Bloomfield Hills, G-5
- Detroit Zoo, Royal Oak, H-6
- Edsel & Eleanor Ford House, Grosse Pointe Shores, I-9
- Frederik Meijer Gardens, Grand Rapids, A-3
- Gerald R. Ford Museum, Grand Rapids, B-2

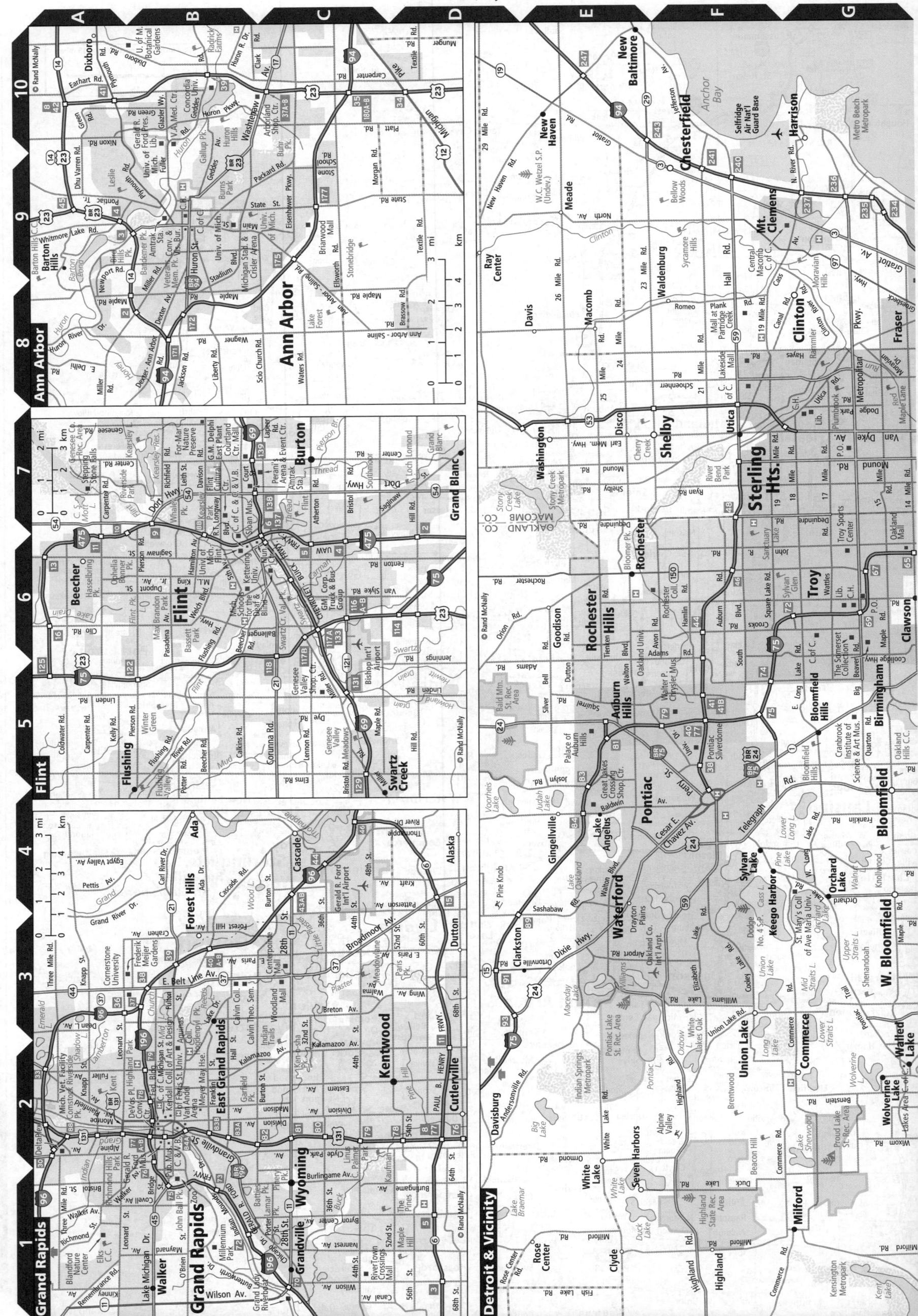

- Gerald R. Ford Presidential Library, Ann Arbor, B-10
- Henry Ford Museum, Dearborn, K-5
- Motown Historical Museum, Detroit, J-7
- New Detroit Science Center, Detroit, J-7
- Renaissance Center, Detroit, N-10
- Sloan Musuem, Flint, B-7
- University of Michigan, Ann Arbor, B-9

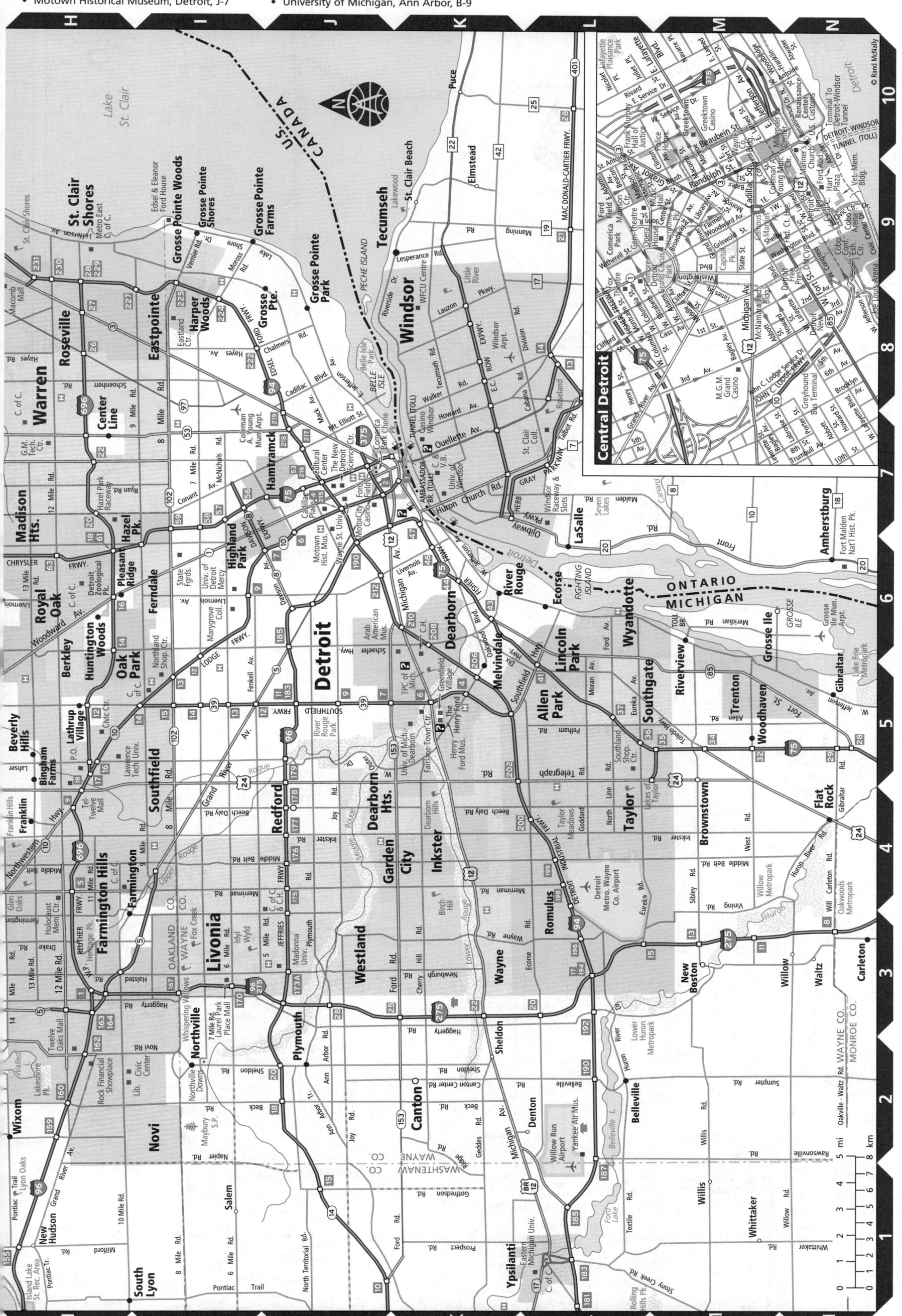

Mileages between cities	Albert Lea	Bemidji	Brainerd	Duluth	Grand Forks, ND	Grand Marais	Hibbing	Int'l Falls	Mankato	Marshall	Minneapolis	Moorhead	Rochester	St. Cloud	Sioux Falls, SD	Willmar
Bemidji	316		97	151	114	259	105	112	290	258	222	135	306	151	380	188
Duluth	247	151	113		266	110	76	162	233	273	152	250	226	141	390	204

Mileages © Rand McNally

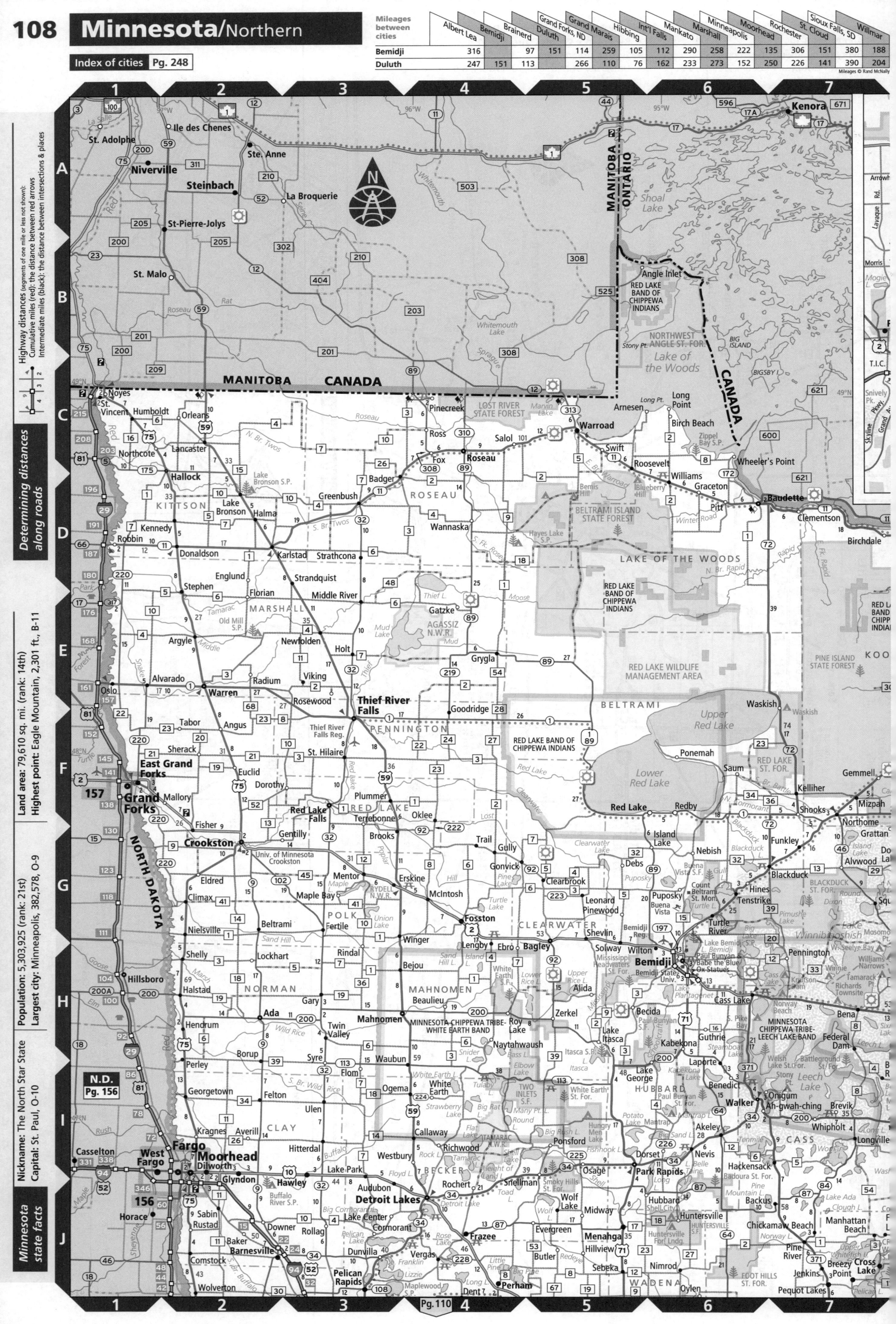

N.D. Pg. 156

Pg. 110

Mileages between cities	Albert Lea	Bemidji	Brainerd	Duluth	Grand Forks, ND	Grand Marais	Hibbing	Int'l Falls	Mankato	Marshall	Minneapolis	Moorhead	Rochester	St. Cloud	Sioux Falls, SD	Willmar
Minneapolis	96	222	130	152	314	262	208	293	80	153		233	86	65	236	93
Moorhead	328	135	136	250	82	361	212	249	303	206	233		321	170	244	172

continued p. 110

Mileages © Rand McNally

Total mileages through Minnesota
- 35 260 miles
- 90 276 miles
- 94 260 miles
- 2 255 miles

More mileages at www.randmcnally.com/MC

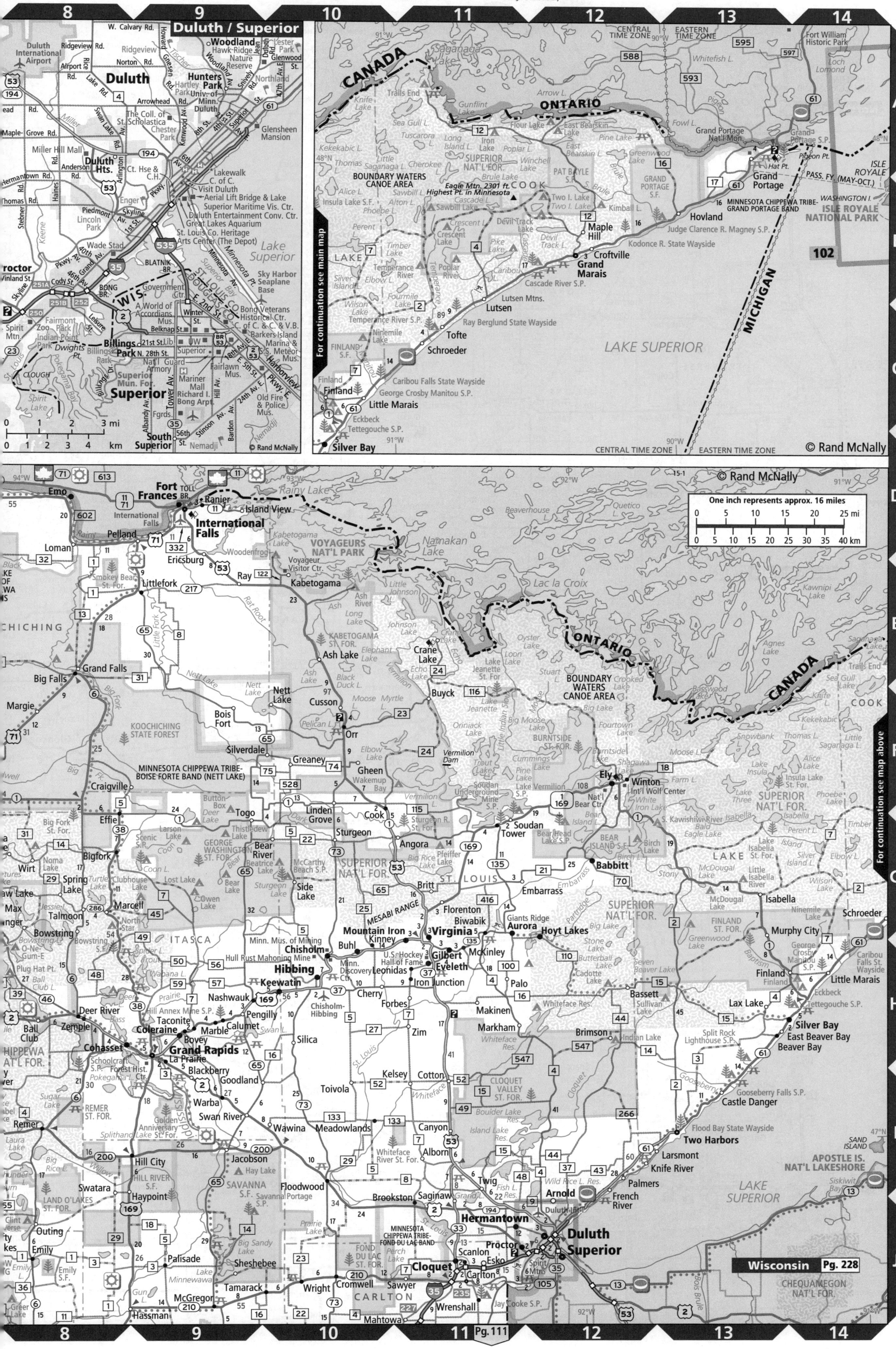

Index of cities Pg. 248

Mileages between cities	Albert Lea	Bemidji	Brainerd	Duluth	Grand Forks, ND	Grand Marais	Hibbing	Int'l Falls	Mankato	Marshall	Minneapolis	Moorhead	Rochester	St. Cloud	Sioux Falls, SD	Willmar
Rochester	62	306	213	226	401	338	280	366	86	194	86	321		153	236	178
St. Cloud	160	151	63	141	251	253	173	251	135	130	65	170	153		220	62

Mileages © Rand McNally

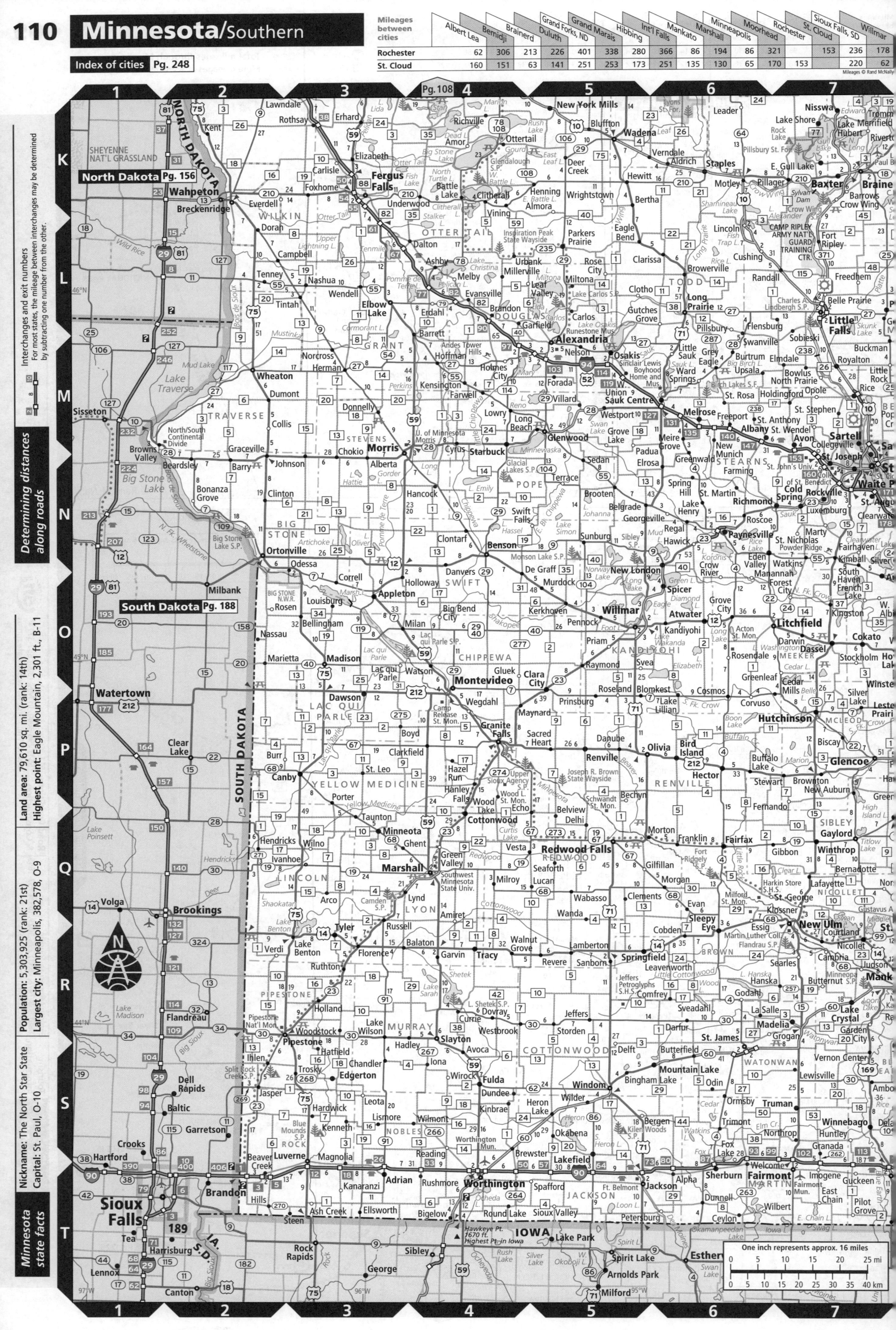

Mileages between cities	Albert Lea	Bemidji	Brainerd	Duluth	Grand Forks, ND	Grand Marais	Hibbing	Int'l Falls	Mankato	Marshall	Minneapolis	Moorhead	Rochester	St. Cloud	Sioux Falls, SD	Willmar
St. Paul	98	230	137	149	325	260	204	290	87	159	9	243	78	75	241	102
Sioux Falls, SD	176	380	281	390	319	500	456	494	155	91	236	244	236	220		158

Mileages © Rand McNally

Total mileages through Minnesota

35	260 miles	94	260 miles
90	276 miles	2	255 miles

More mileages at www.randmcnally.com/MC

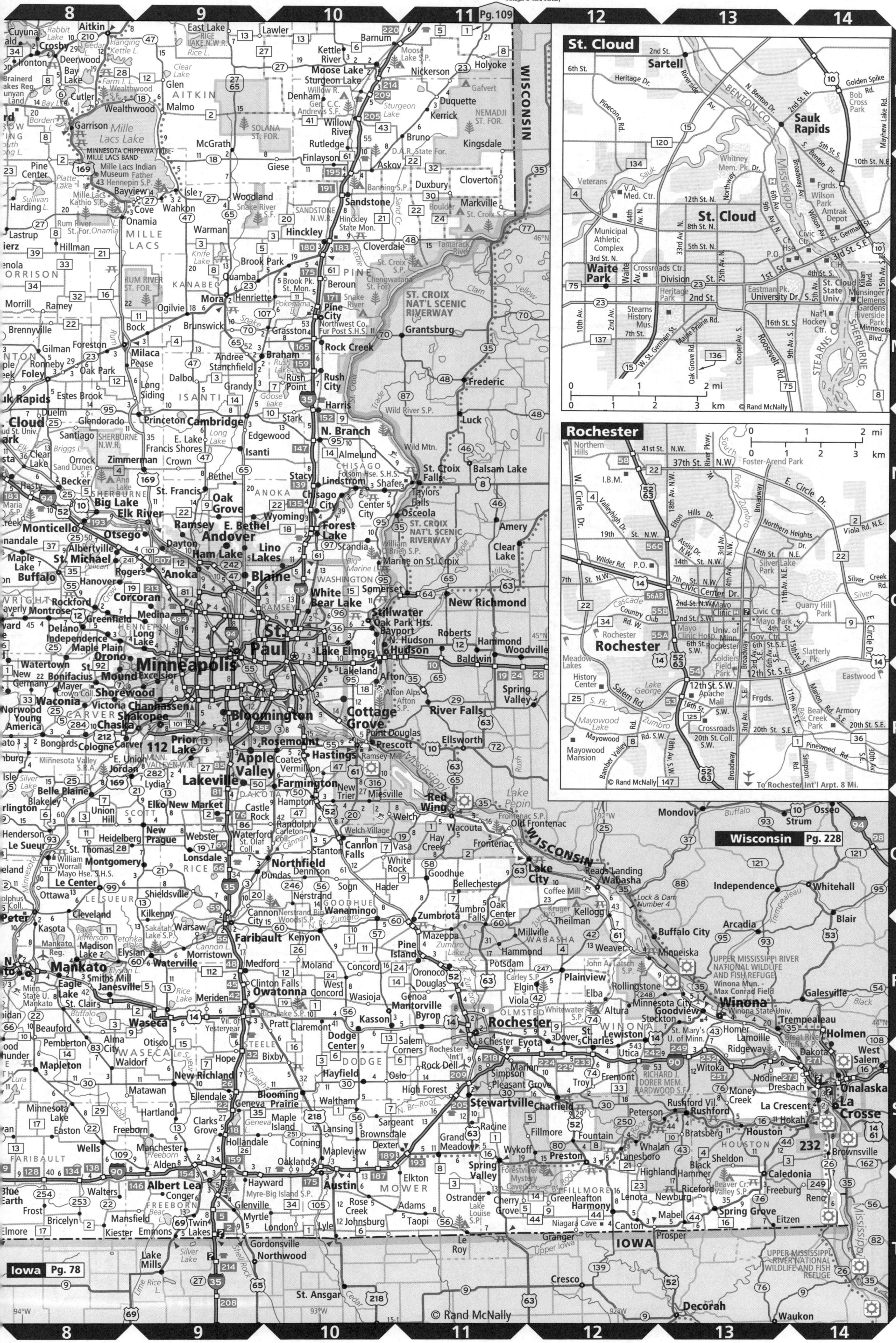

St. Cloud (inset map)

0 — 1 — 2 mi
0 — 1 — 2 km
© Rand McNally

Rochester (inset map)

0 — 1 — 2 mi
0 — 1 — 2 3 km
© Rand McNally 147

Wisconsin Pg. 228

Iowa Pg. 78

Iowa Pg. 78

© Rand McNally

City sights to see
- Bell Mus. of Natural History, Minneapolis, L-4
- Cathedral of St. Paul, St. Paul, M-7
- Frederick R. Weisman Art Museum, Minneapolis, M-4
- Mall of America, Bloomington, I-5
- Mill City Museum, Minneapolis, L-3
- Minneapolis Institute of the Arts, Minneapolis, N-2

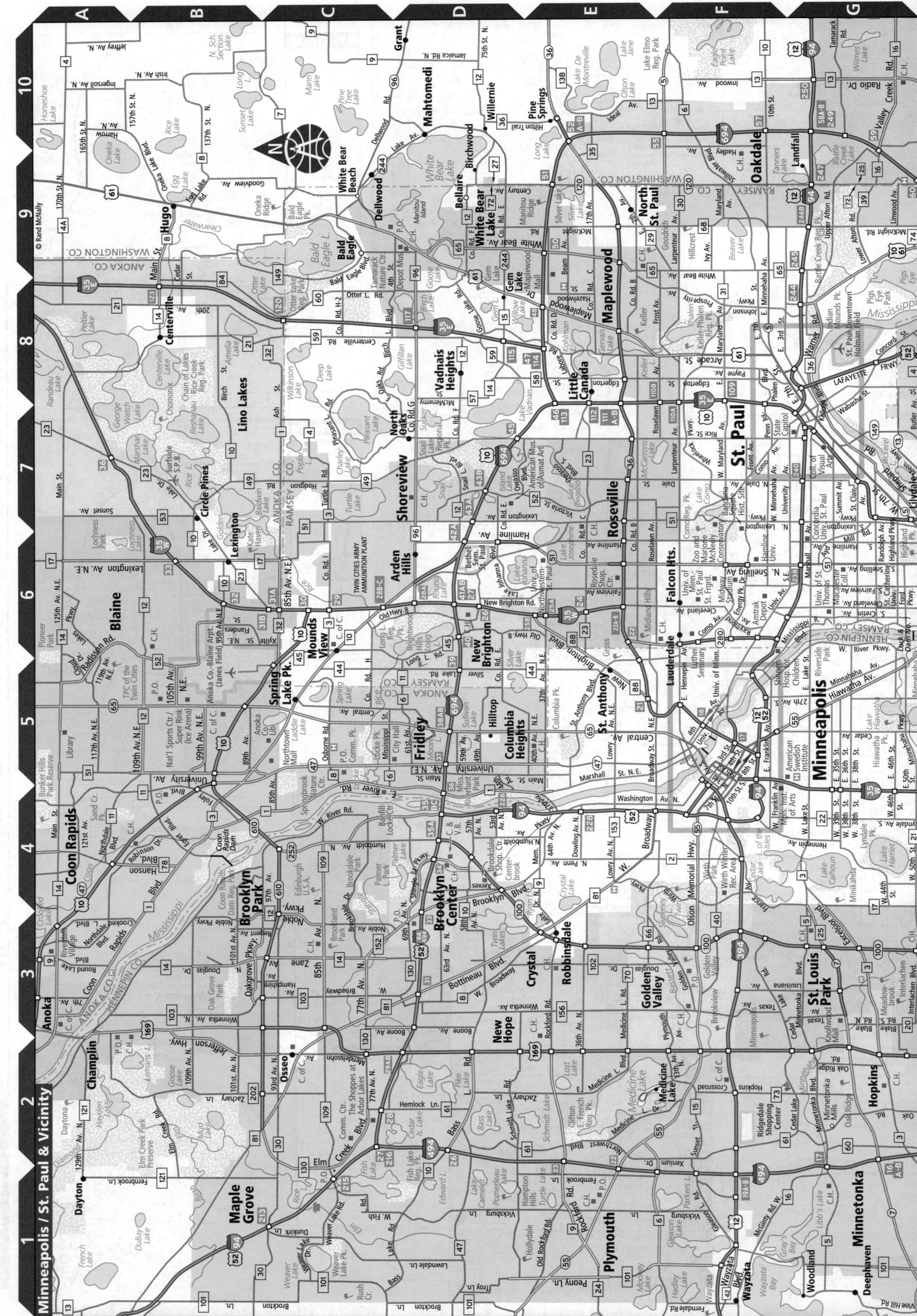

- Minneapolis Sculpture Garden, Minneapolis, M-1
- Minnesota History Center, St. Paul, M-7
- Minnesota State Capitol, St. Paul, L-7
- Ordway Center for the Performing Arts, St. Paul, M-7
- Science Museum of Minnesota, St. Paul, M-7
- Walker Art Center, Minneapolis, M-1

Mileages between cities	Batesville	Biloxi	Hattiesburg	Jackson	Memphis, TN	Natchez	Tupelo	Vicksburg
Biloxi	320		80	172	379	228	315	214
Greenville	112	293	210	121	152	152	177	91

	Batesville	Biloxi	Hattiesburg	Jackson	Memphis, TN	Natchez	Tupelo	Vicksburg
Jackson	149	172	89		209	103	190	44
Memphis, TN	61	379	297	209		304	105	245

Mileages © Rand McNally

Mississippi state facts

Nickname: The Magnolia State
Capital: Jackson, H-6

Population: 2,967,297 (rank: 31st)
Largest city: Jackson, 173,514, H-6

Land area: 46,907 sq. mi. (rank: 31st)
Highest point: Woodall Mountain, 806 ft., B-10

Determining distances along roads

Highway distances (segments of one mile or less not shown):
- Cumulative miles (red): the distance between red arrows
- Intermediate miles (black): the distance between intersections & places

Mileages between cities	Batesville	Biloxi	Hattiesburg	Jackson	Memphis, TN	Natchez	Tupelo	Vicksburg
Meridian	176	172	89	91	234	194	142	134
New Orleans, LA	335	90	109	183	394	171	340	207

	Batesville	Biloxi	Hattiesburg	Jackson	Memphis, TN	Natchez	Tupelo	Vicksburg
Tupelo	74	315	232	190	105	283		225
Vicksburg	188	214	131	44	245	70	225	

Mileages © Rand McNally

Total mileages through Mississippi
More mileages at www.randmcnally.com/MC

- 10: 77 miles
- 20: 169 miles
- 55: 290 miles
- 59: 172 miles

Mileages between cities	Branson	Cape Girardeau	Columbia	Hannibal	Hayti	Jefferson City	Joplin	Kansas City	Kirksville	Maryville	Osage Beach	Poplar Bluff	Rolla	St. Louis	Springfield	West Plains
Cape Girardeau	295		225	218	80	216	336	348	313	445	218	82	158	114	270	182
Columbia	205	225		97	301	32	236	124	91	222	76	261	93	126	168	191

Mileages © Rand McNally

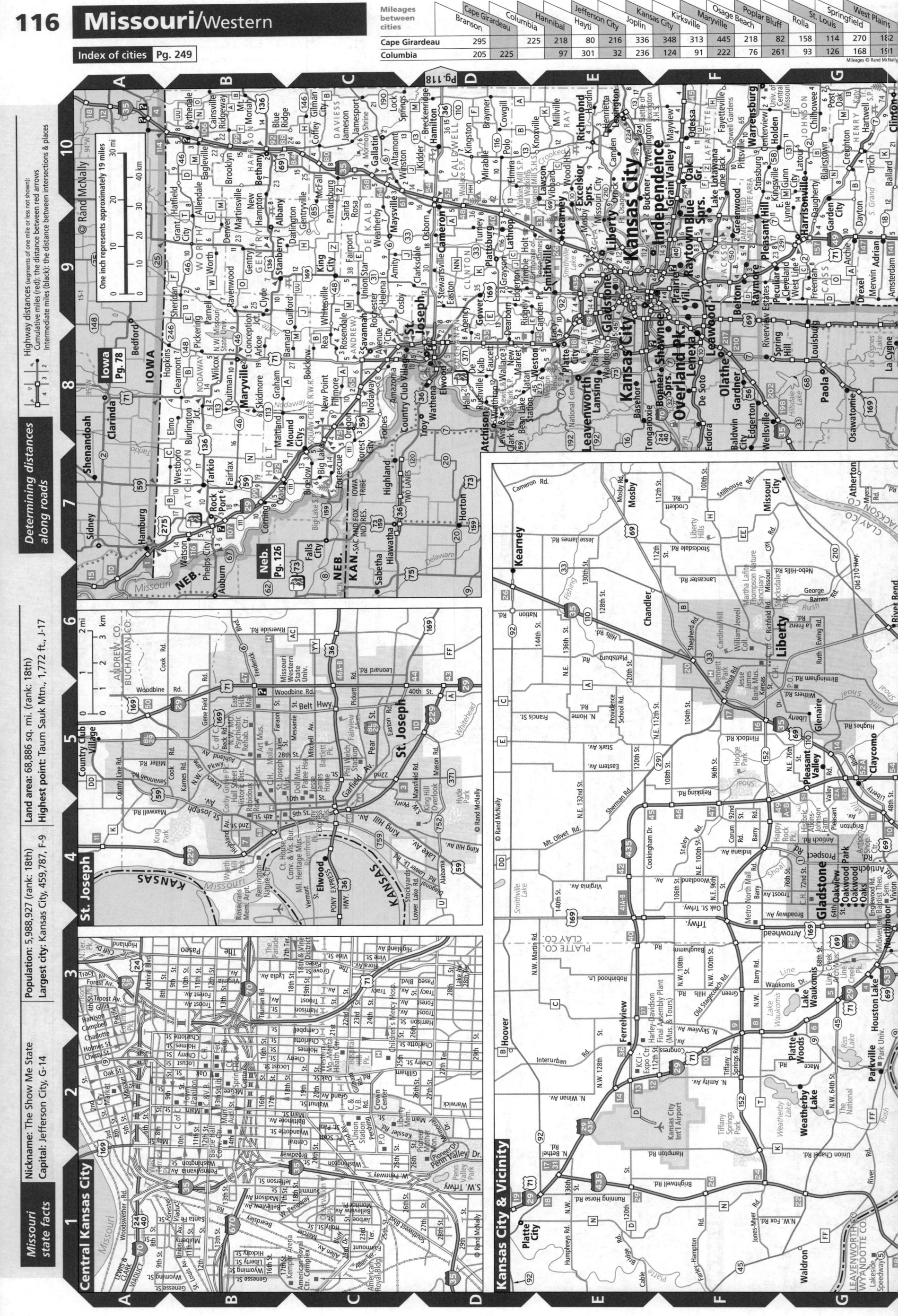

Missouri state facts

Nickname: The Show Me State
Capital: Jefferson City, G-14

Population: 5,988,927 (rank: 18th)
Largest city: Kansas City, 459,787, F-9

Land area: 68,886 sq. mi. (rank: 18th)
Highest point: Taum Sauk Mtn., 1,772 ft., J-17

Determining distances along roads

Highway distances (segments of one mile or less not shown):
Cumulative miles (red): the distance between red arrows
Intermediate miles (black): the distance between intersections & places

Central Kansas City

St. Joseph

Kansas City & Vicinity

continued p. 118

Mileages between cities	Branson	Cape Girardeau	Columbia	Hannibal	Jefferson City Hayti	Joplin	Kansas City	Kirksville	Maryville	Osage Beach	Poplar Bluff	Rolla	St. Louis	Springfield	West Plains
Joplin	109	336	236	312	319	206		157	312	243	161	256	178	282	70	176
Kansas City	209	348	124	209	424	156	157		157	93	164	356	219	250	166	275

Mileages © Rand McNally

Total mileages through Missouri
More mileages at www.randmcnally.com/MC

35 115 miles 55 210 miles
44 290 miles 70 252 miles

Explore Missouri at
www.randmcnally.com/MO

Tourism Information
Missouri Division of Tourism
(800) 519-2100, (573) 751-4133
www.visitmo.com

Road Conditions & Construction
(888) 275-6636
www.modot.mo.gov

Toll Road Information
No toll roads

Mileages between cities	Cape Girardeau	Branson	Columbia	Hannibal	Hayti	Jefferson City	Joplin	Kansas City	Kirksville	Maryville	Osage Beach	Poplar Bluff	Rolla	St. Louis	Springfield	West Plains
Poplar Bluff	215	82	261	255	62	223	256	356	350	457	224		147	151	191	98
St. Joseph	270	405	182	191	481	214	203	53	141	43	222	416	276	308	225	336

Mileages © Rand McNally

Missouri state facts

Nickname: The Show Me State
Capital: Jefferson City, G-14

Population: 5,988,927 | Land area: 68,886 sq. mi. (rank: 18th)
Largest city: Kansas City, 459,787, F-9 | Highest point: Taum Sauk Mtn., 1,772 ft., J-17

Determining distances along roads

Interchanges and exit numbers
For most states, the mileage between interchanges may be determined by subtracting one number from the other.

Mileages between cities	Branson	Cape Girardeau	Columbia	Hannibal	Hayti	Jefferson City	Joplin	Kansas City	Kirksville	Maryville	Osage Beach	Poplar Bluff	Rolla	St. Louis	Springfield	West Plains
St. Louis	249	114	126	120	192	124	282	250	217	347	164	151	104		213	202
Springfield	42	270	168	242	253	136	70	166	259	266	91	191	108	213		108

Mileages © Rand McNally

Total mileages through Missouri
More mileages at www.randmcnally.com/MC

35 115 miles	55 210 miles	
44 290 miles	70 252 miles	

Toll Road Information	No toll roads

Road Conditions & Construction
(888) 275-6636
www.modot.mo.gov

Tourism Information
Missouri Division of Tourism
(800) 519-2100, (573) 751-4133
www.visitmo.com

Arkansas Pg. 22

Explore Missouri at www.randmcnally.com/MO

One inch represents approximately 19 miles
30 mi
40 km

City sights to see

- Andy Williams Moon River Theatre, Branson, M-8
- Anheuser-Busch Brewery, St. Louis, I-7
- Bass Pro Shops® Outdoor World®, Springfield, C-3
- Dolly Parton's Dixie Stampede, Branson, M-9
- Gateway Arch, St. Louis, L-4
- Laumeier Sculpture Park, St. Louis, J-4
- Magic House, Kirkwood, I-4

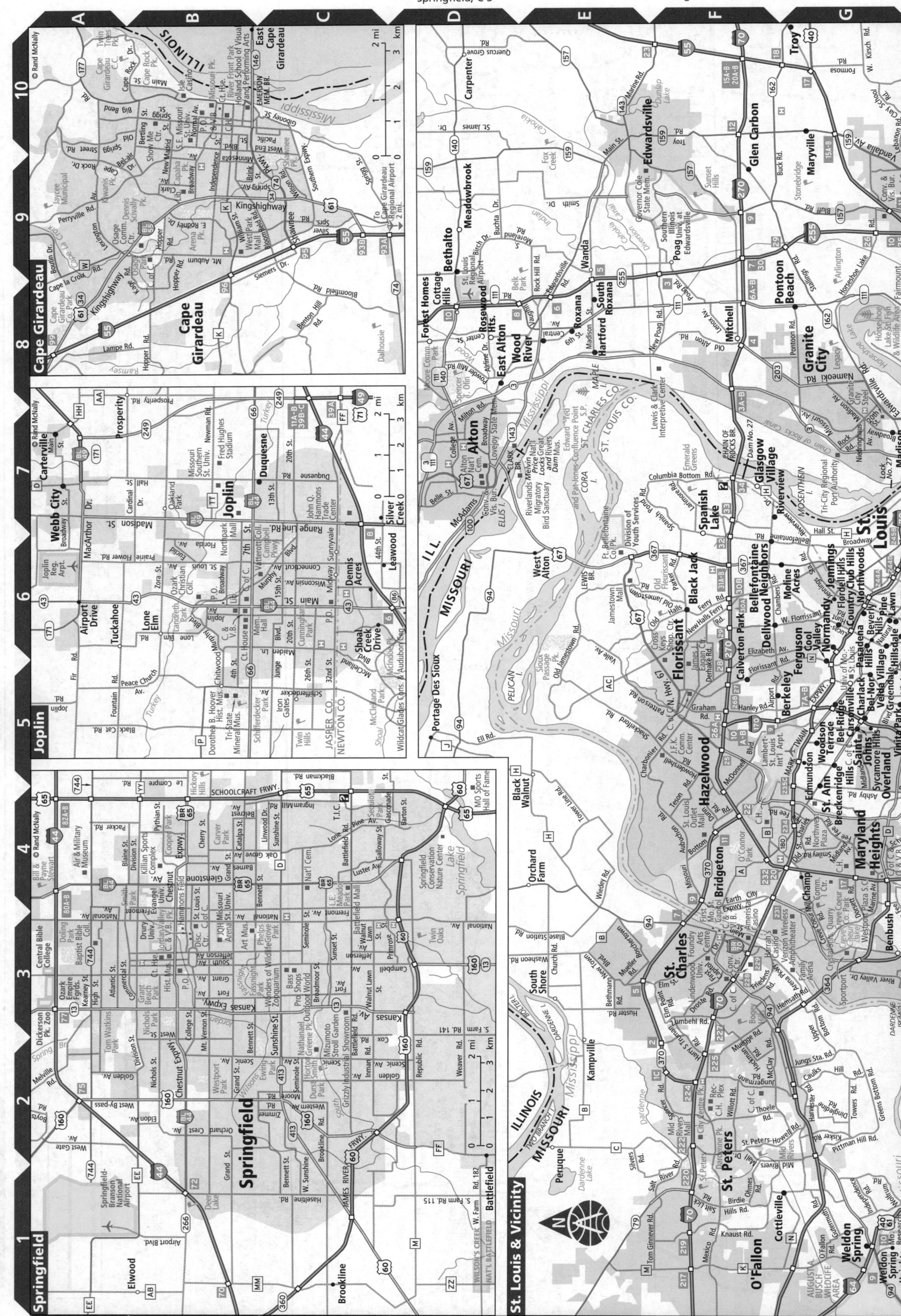

- Missouri Botanical Garden, St. Louis, I-6
- Shoji Tabuchi Theatre, Branson, L-7
- St. Louis Art Museum, St. Louis, H-6
- St. Louis Science Center, St. Louis, H-6
- St. Louis Zoo, St. Louis, H-6
- Shepherd of the Hills Homestead & Outdoor Theatre, Branson, K-6
- White Water, Branson, M-7

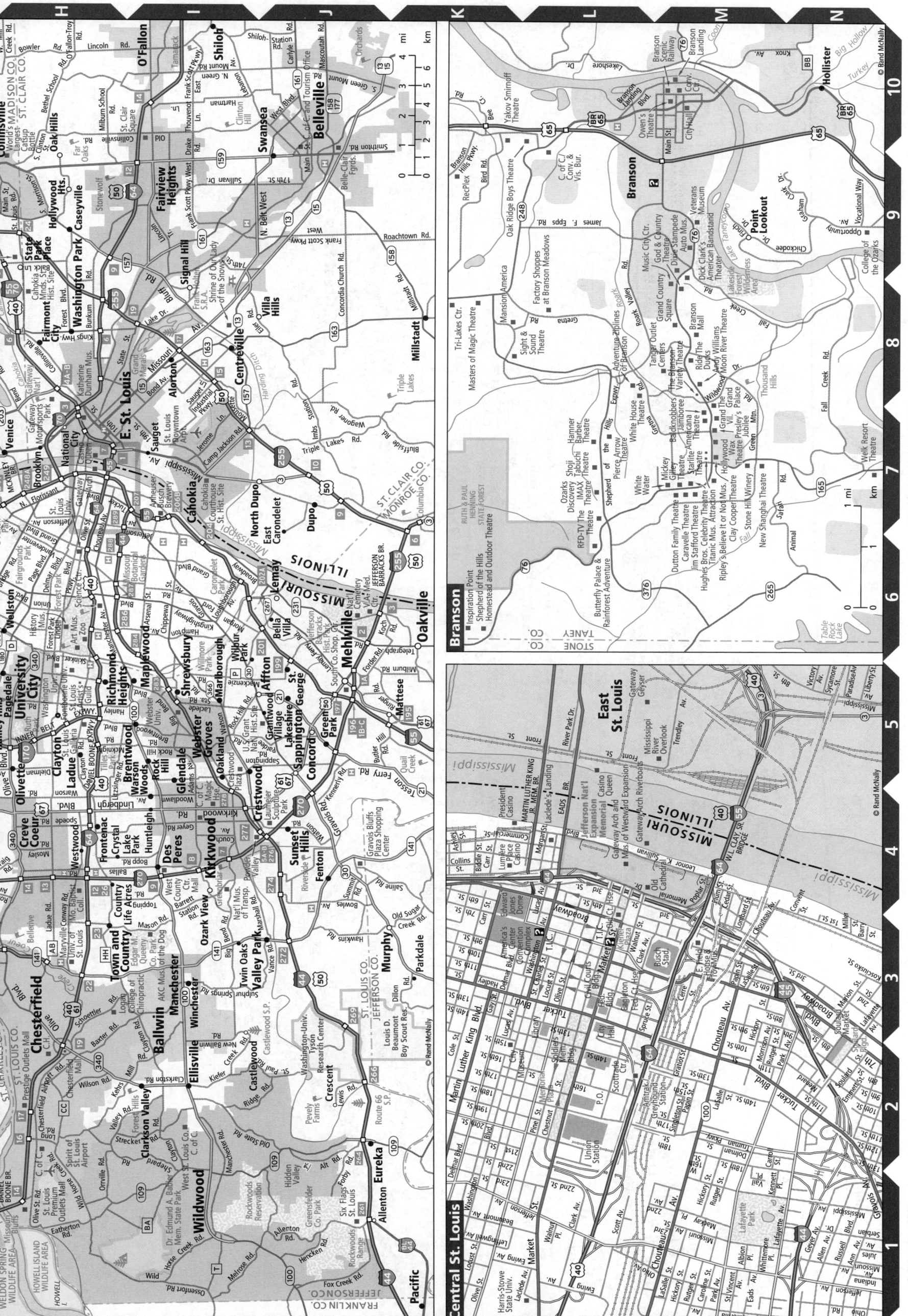

Mileages between cities	Belle Fourche, SD	Billings	Bozeman	Butte	Dillon	Glasgow	Great Falls	Havre	Kalispell	Lewistown	Libby	Miles City	Missoula	St. Mary	Sidney	W. Yellowstone
Billings	261		143	223	256	276	218	247	451	125	536	144	343	375	269	232
Butte	486	223	82		54	425	154	267	224	244	309	367	120	269	494	149

Mileages © Rand McNally

Montana state facts

Nickname: The Treasure State

Capital: Helena, G-7

Population: 989,415 (rank: 44th)

Largest city: Billings, 104,170, I-13

Land area: 145,552 sq. mi. (rank: 4th)

Highest point: Granite Peak, 12,799 ft., J-11

Determining distances along roads

Highway distances (segments of one mile or less not shown): the distance between red arrows; Cumulative miles (red); Intermediate distance between intersections & places

Mileages between cities	Belle Fourche, SD	Billings	Bozeman	Butte	Dillon	Glasgow	Great Falls	Havre	Kalispell	Lewistown	Libby	Miles City	Missoula	St. Mary	Sidney	W. Yellowstone
Great Falls	481	218	186	154	219	271		113	224	106	312	317	166	158	375	264
Helena	500	238	98	66	132	360	90	202	193	193	281	383	113	205	463	177

continued p. 124

Mileages © Rand McNally

Total mileages through Montana
More mileages at www.randmcnally.com/MC

15 396 miles 94 249 miles 90 552 miles

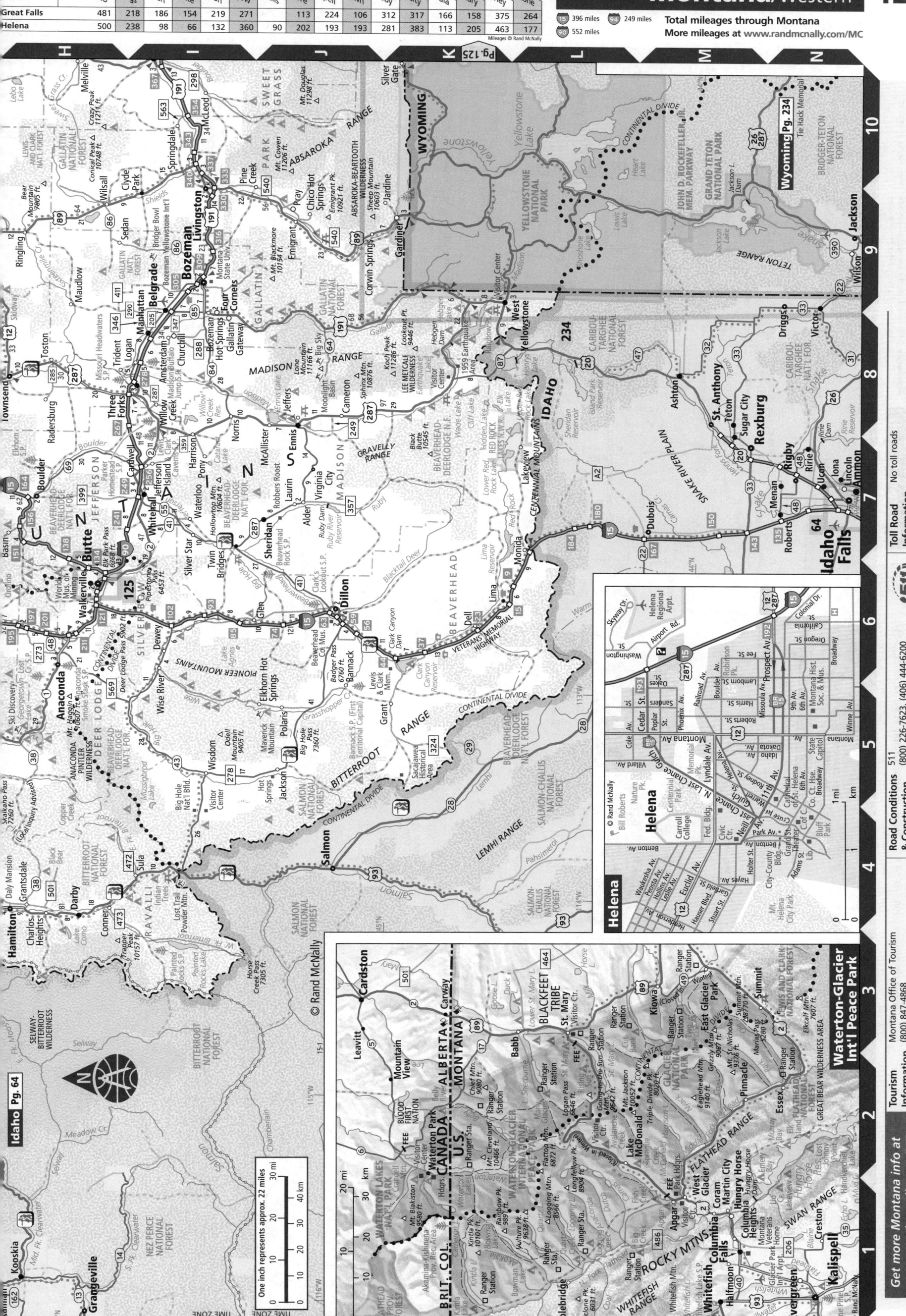

Mileages between cities	Belle Fourche, SD	Billings	Bozeman	Butte	Dillon	Glasgow	Great Falls	Havre	Kalispell	Lewistown	Libby	Miles City	Missoula	St. Mary	W. Yellowstone Sidney
Kalispell	711	451	308	224	278	419	224	261		330	88	593	121	82	558	371
Miles City	174	144	285	367	399	195	317	333	593	211	678		487	473	126	375

Mileages © Rand McNally

Montana state facts

Nickname: The Treasure State
Capital: Helena, G-7
Population: 989,415 (rank: 44th)
Largest city: Billings, G-7
Land area: 145,552 sq. mi. (rank: 4th)
Highest point: Granite Peak, 12,799 ft., J-11
Major highways: Billings, 104,170, I-13

Mileages between cities	Belle Fourche, SD	Billings	Bozeman	Butte	Dillon	Glasgow	Great Falls	Havre	Kalispell	Lewistown	Libby	Miles City	Missoula	St. Mary	Sidney	W. Yellowstone
Missoula	606	343	202	120	172	437	166	280	121	272	191	487		203	614	267
Sidney	298	269	411	494	524	140	375	298	558	270	646	126	614	490		501

Mileages © Rand McNally

Total mileages through Montana

15 · 396 miles   94 · 249 miles
90 · 552 miles

More mileages at www.randmcnally.com/MC

Index of cities Pg. 250

Mileages between cities	Beatrice	Chadron	Columbus	Falls City	Grand Island	Kearney	Lincoln	McCook	Norfolk	North Platte	Ogallala	Omaha	O'Neill	Scottsbluff	Sioux City, IA	Valentine
Grand Island	131	326	64	196		50	93	152	105	145	194	147	112	323	187	210
Lincoln	41	450	79	102	93	129		232	124	224	274	55	208	402	151	304

Mileages © Rand McNally

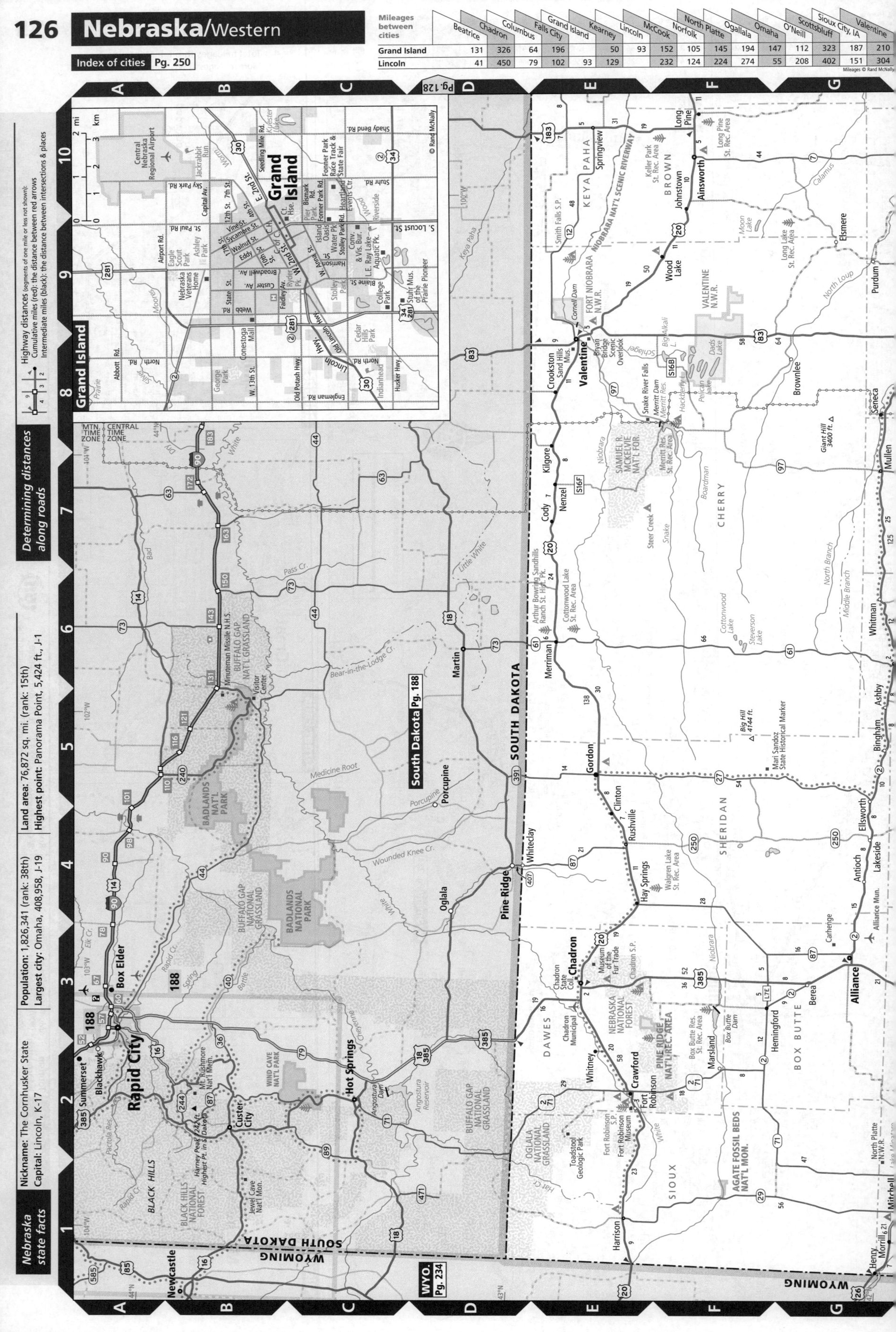

Nebraska state facts

Nickname: The Cornhusker State
Capital: Lincoln, K-17

Population: 1,826,341 (rank: 38th)
Largest city: Omaha, 408,958, J-19

Land area: 76,872 sq. mi. (rank: 15th)
Highest point: Panorama Point, 5,424 ft., J-1

Determining distances along roads

Mileages between cities	Beatrice	Chadron	Columbus	Falls City	Grand Island	Kearney	Lincoln	McCook	Norfolk	North Platte	Ogallala	Omaha	O'Neill	Scottsbluff	Sioux City, IA	Valentine
Norfolk	162	322	45	218	105	155	124	259		250	300	109	75	417	82	186
North Platte	262	229	210	327	145	99	224	67	250		53	276	189	182	373	129

Mileages © Rand McNally

continued p. 128

Total mileages through Nebraska
More mileages at www.randmcnally.com/MC

80 455 miles   83 226 miles
81 219 miles   20 436 miles

Plan a Nebraska trip at *Plan a Nebraska trip at www.randmcnally.com/NE*

Tourism Information: Nebraska Division of Travel & Tourism (877) 632-7275, (888) 444-1867 www.visitnebraska.com

Road Conditions & Construction: 511, (800) 906-9069, (402) 471-4533 www.511nebraska.org www.dor.state.ne.us

511 — Toll Road Information — No toll roads

One inch represents approximately 17 miles

© Rand McNally

Kansas Pg. 82
Colorado Pg. 42

Mileages between cities	Beatrice	Chadron	Columbus	Falls City	Grand Island	Kearney	Lincoln	McCook	Norfolk	North Platte	Ogallala	Omaha	O'Neill	Scottsbluff	Sioux City, IA	Valentine
Omaha	95	431	83	104	147	181	55	283	109	276	325		184	458	97	294
Scottsbluff	440	99	388	505	323	277	402	245	417	182	129	458	322		467	216

Mileages © Rand McNally

Nebraska state facts

Nickname: The Cornhusker State

Capital: Lincoln, K-17

Population: 1,826,341 (rank: 38th)

Largest city: Omaha, K-17

Land area: 76,872 sq. mi. (rank: 15th)

Highest point: Panorama Point, 5,424 ft., J-1

Determining distances along roads

Interchanges and exit numbers
For most states, the mileage between interchanges may be determined by subtracting one number from the other.

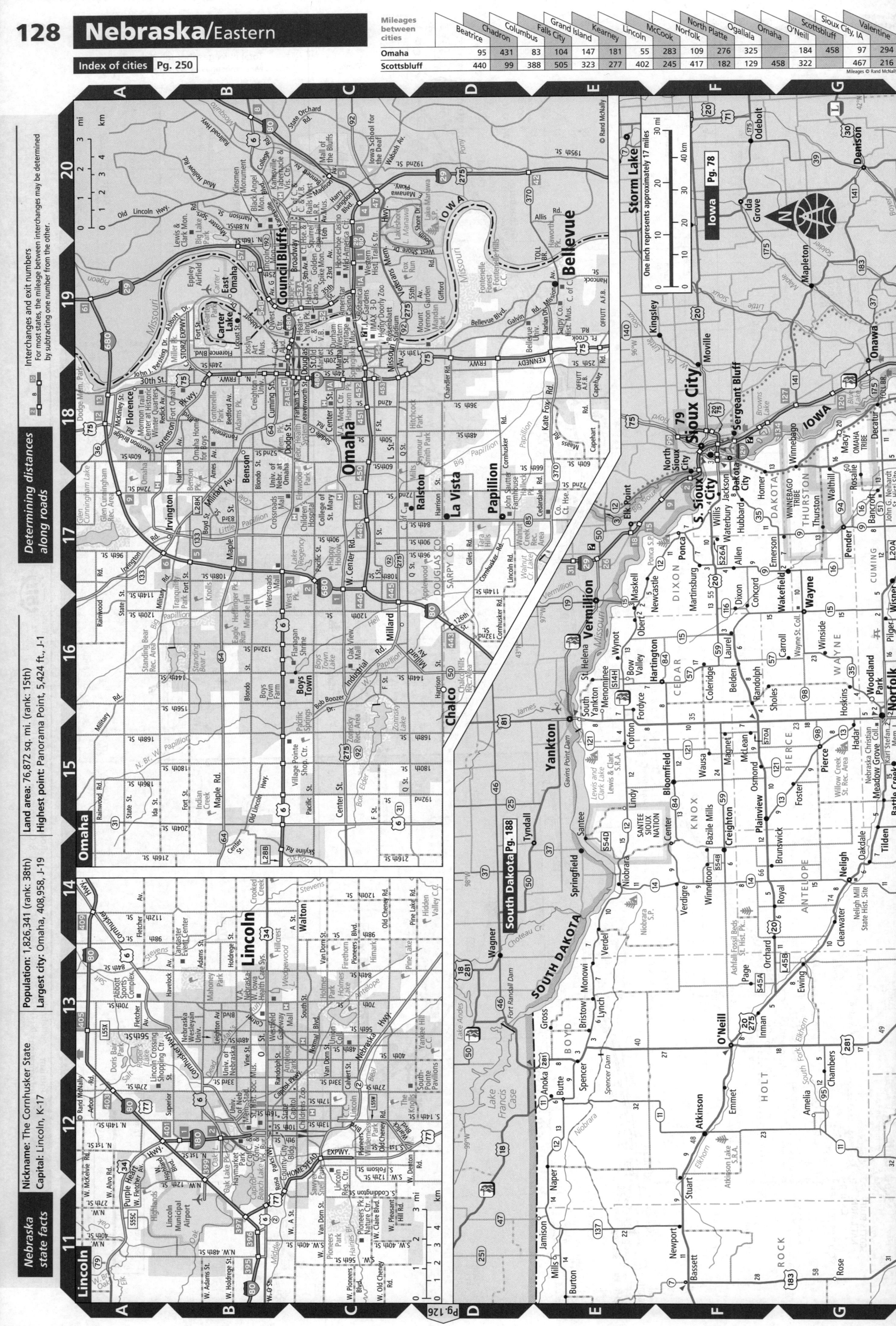

Storm Lake   Iowa Pg. 78

South Dakota Pg. 188

Pg.126

Mileages between cities	Beatrice	Chadron	Columbus	Falls City	Grand Island	Kearney	Lincoln	McCook	Norfolk	North Platte	Ogallala	Omaha	O'Neill	Scottsbluff	Sioux City, IA	Valentine
Sidney	381	131	329	445	263	218	343	186	369	122	71	394	311	77	492	251
Valentine	342	137	230	406	210	195	304	197	186	129	182	294	111	216	236	

Mileages © Rand McNally

Total mileages through Nebraska

80	455 miles	83	226 miles
81	219 miles	20	436 miles

More mileages at www.randmcnally.com/MC

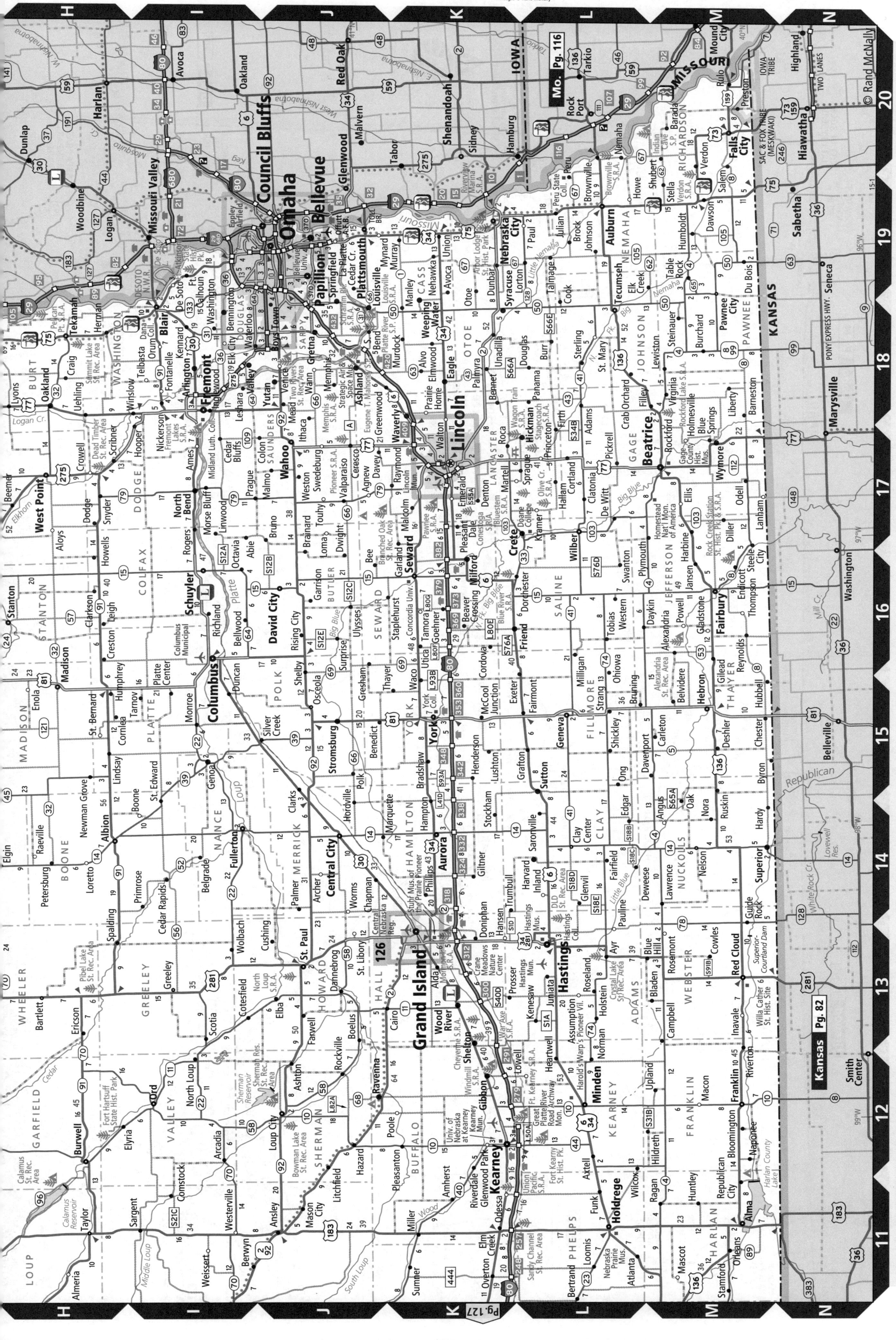

Rand McNally Nebraska Eastern highway map.

Mileages between cities	Carson City	Elko	Ely	Jackpot	Las Vegas	Reno	Tonopah	Winnemucca		Carson City	Elko	Ely	Jackpot	Las Vegas	Reno	Tonopah	Winnemucca
Elko	304		188	117	429	288	252	125	Las Vegas	435	429	241	446		447	210	472
Ely	319	188		205	241	319	167	271	Reno	32	288	319	405	447		237	163

Mileages © Rand McNally

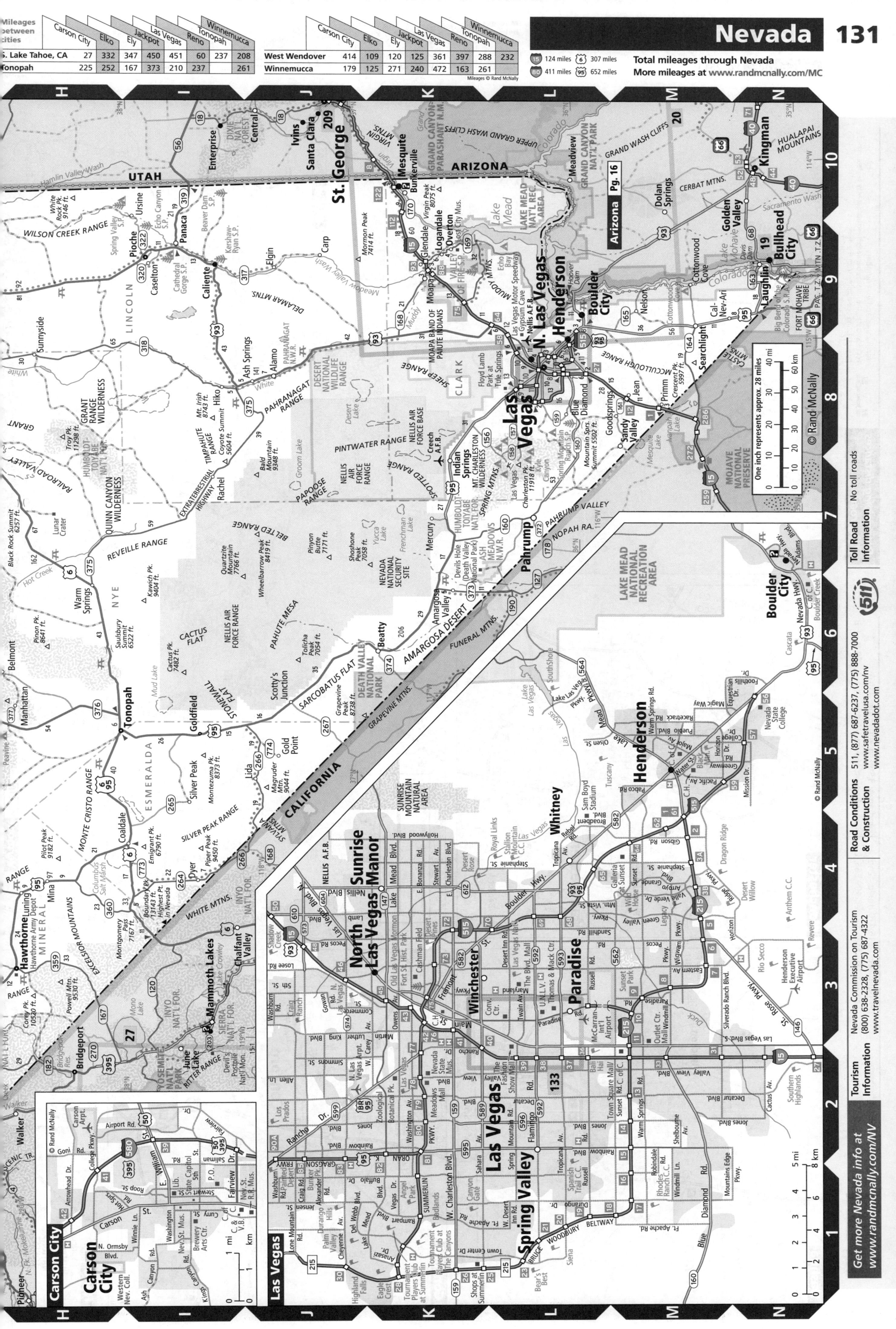

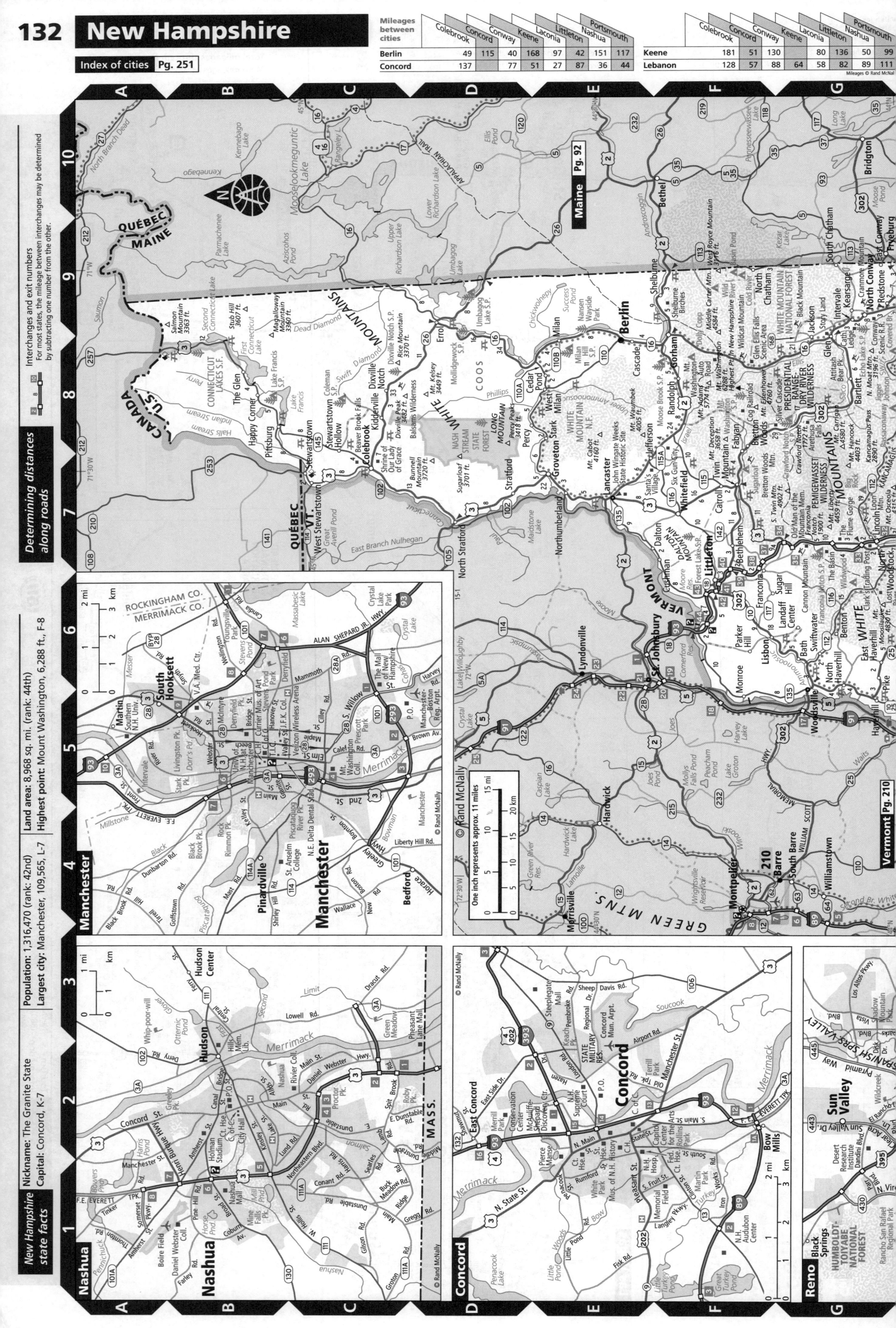

Mileages between cities

	Colebrook	Concord	Conway	Keene	Laconia	Littleton	Nashua	Portsmouth
Berlin	49	115	40	168	97	42	151	117
Concord	137		77	51	27	87	36	44

	Colebrook	Concord	Conway	Keene	Laconia	Littleton	Nashua	Portsmouth
Keene	181	51	130		80	136	50	99
Lebanon	128	57	88	64	58	82	89	111

Mileages © Rand McNally

New Hampshire state facts

Nickname: The Granite State
Capital: Concord, K-7

Population: 1,316,470 (rank: 42nd)
Largest city: Manchester, 109,565, L-7

Land area: 8,968 sq. mi. (rank: 44th)
Highest point: Mount Washington, 6,288 ft., F-8

Determining distances along roads

Interchanges and exit numbers
For most states, the mileage between interchanges may be determined by subtracting one number from the other.

Mileages between cities	Colebrook	Concord	Conway	Keene	Laconia	Littleton	Nashua	Portsmouth		Colebrook	Concord	Conway	Keene	Laconia	Littleton	Nashua	Portsmouth
Littleton	56	87	54	136	66		121	129	Nashua	172	36	113	50	63	121		54
Manchester	155	18	95	55	45	105	18	43	Portsmouth	180	44	77	99	57	129	54	

Mileages © Rand McNally

Total mileages through New Hampshire
More mileages at www.randmcnally.com/MC

89 61 miles · 95 16 miles · 93 132 miles · 2 36 miles

Plan a New Hampshire trip at www.randmcnally.com/NH

Tourism Information	New Hampshire Division of Travel & Tourism Development (800) 386-4664, (603) 271-2665 www.visitnh.com	511, (www.511.org www.nh.org
Road Conditions & Construction	511, (511.org www.nh.gov/dot	New Hampshire Department of Transportation (E-ZPass) 877) 643-9727 www.nh.gov/dot
Toll Road Information		

Sparks

Reno N.

Las Vegas Strip

© Rand McNally

Mileages between cities	Atlantic City	Camden	Cape May	Jersey City	Long Branch	Newark	New Brunswick	New York, NY	Paterson	Phillipsburg	Port Jervis, NY	Princeton	Toms River	Trenton	Vineland	Wilmington, DE
Atlantic City		58	47	120	82	115	94	126	129	138	182	99	52	90	36	82
Camden	58		88	86	76	80	61	96	94	80	143	45	55	34	36	31

Mileages © Rand McNally

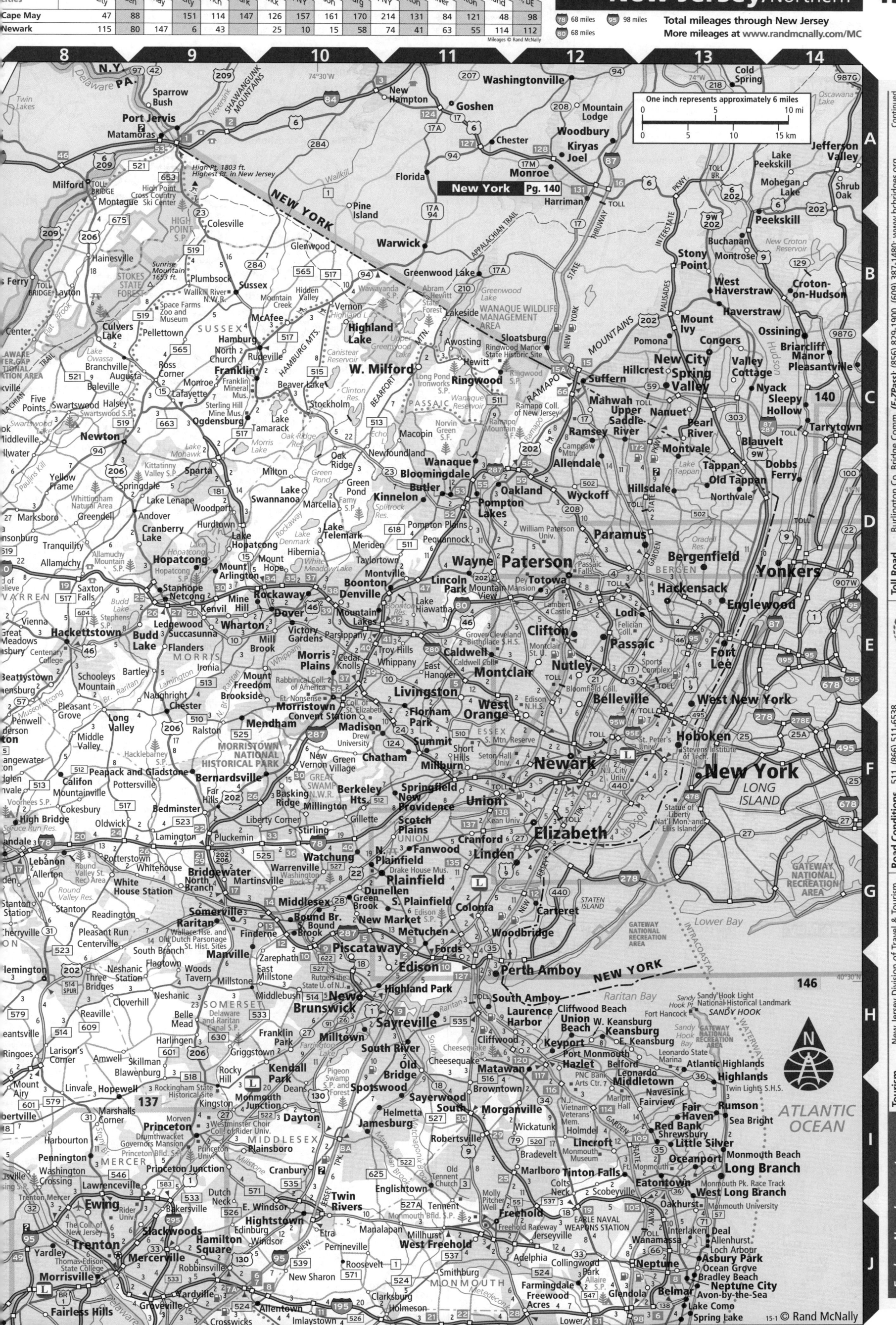

Mileages between cities	Atlantic City	Camden	Cape May	Jersey City	Long Branch	New Brunswick	New York, NY	Paterson	Phillipsburg	Port Jervis, NY	Princeton	Toms River	Trenton	Vineland	Wilmington, DE
Cape May	47	88		151	114	147	126	157	161	170	214	131	84	121	48	98
Newark	115	80	147	6	43		25	10	15	58	74	41	63	55	114	112

Mileages © Rand McNally

78 — 68 miles   95 — 98 miles   **Total mileages through New Jersey**
80 — 68 miles   More mileages at www.randmcnally.com/MC

One inch represents approximately 6 miles
0   5   10 mi
0   5   10   15 km

Pg. 137   Pg. 137

© Rand McNally   15-1

Toll Road Information Burlington Co. Bridge Comm. (E-ZPass): (856) 829-1900, (609) 387-1480; www.bcbridges.com; Del. River & Bay Authority (Del. Mem. Br., Cape May/Lewes Fy.) (E-ZPass): (302) 571-6300; www.drba.net; Delaware River Port Authority (Phila. area bridges) (E-ZPass): (877) 567-3772; www.drpa.org

Road Conditions & Construction 511, (866) 511-6538; www.511-nj.org; www.state.nj.us/transportation

Tourism Information New Jersey Division of Travel & Tourism (800) 847-4865; www.visitnj.org

Explore New Jersey at www.randmcnally.com/NJ

Continued on next page www.drba.net www.drpa.org

Mileages between cities	Atlantic City	Camden	Cape May	Jersey City	Long Branch	Newark	New Brunswick	New York, NY	Paterson	Phillipsburg	Port Jervis, NY	Princeton	Toms River	Trenton	Vineland	Wilmington, DE
New Brunswick	94	61	126	30	34	25		36	39	48	92	16	43	26	95	93
Phillipsburg	138	80	170	64	81	58	48	68	67		74	54	101	54	118	95

Mileages © Rand McNally

New Jersey state facts

Nickname: The Garden State
Capital: Trenton, J-8

Population: 8,791,894 (rank: 11th)
Largest city: Newark, 277,140, F-12

Land area: 7,417 sq. mi. (rank: 46th)
Highest point: High Point, 1,803 ft., A-9

Determining distances along roads

Interchanges and exit numbers
For most states, the mileage between interchanges may be determined by subtracting one number from the other.

Vineland (inset map)

Cape May (inset map)

Delaware Pg. 50

Maryland Pg. 94

Pennsylvania Pg. 174

© Rand McNally

Mileages between cities	Atlantic City	Camden	Cape May	Jersey City	Long Branch	New Brunswick	Newark	New York, NY	Paterson	Phillipsburg	Port Jervis, NY	Princeton	Toms River	Trenton	Vineland	Wilmington, DE
Port Jervis, NY	182	143	214	89	110	74	92	95	73	74		94	130	122	180	158
Trenton	90	34	121	61	52	55	26	66	69	54	122	11	47		69	61

Mileages © Rand McNally

| 78 68 miles | 95 98 miles | **Total mileages through New Jersey** |
| 80 68 miles | | More mileages at www.randmcnally.com/MC |

N.J. Turnpike Authority (N.J. Turnpike, Gdn. St. Pkwy.) (E-ZPass); (732) 750-5300; www.state.nj.us
Port Authority of N.Y. & N.J. (N.Y. City area bridges & tunnels) (E-ZPass); (800) 221-9903; www.panynj.gov
South Jersey Transportation Authority (Atlantic City Expressway) (E-ZPass); (609) 965-6060; www.sjta.com

Toll Road Information

511 Road Conditions & Construction — 511, (866) 511-6538; www.511-nj.org; www.state.nj.us/transportation

Tourism Information — New Jersey Division of Travel & Tourism (800) 847-4865; www.visitnj.org

Explore New Jersey at www.randmcnally.com/NJ

Continued from previous page

One inch represents approximately 6 miles

0 — 5 — 10 mi
0 — 5 — 10 — 15 km

© Rand McNally

Trenton (inset)

Levittown (inset)

© Rand McNally

Index of cities Pg. 251

New Mexico state facts

Nickname: Land of Enchantment
Capital: Santa Fe, D-6
Population: 2,059,179 (rank: 36th)
Land area: 121,356 sq. mi. (rank: 5th)
Highest point: Wheeler Peak, 13,161 ft., B-6

Determining distances along roads

Highway distances (segments of one mile or less not shown)
Cumulative miles (red); the distance between red arrows
Intermediate miles (black); the distance between intersections & places

Mileages between cities	Albuquerque	Carlsbad	Clayton	Gallup	Las Cruces	Socorro	Tucumcari	Taos		Albuquerque	Carlsbad	Clayton	Gallup	Las Cruces	Socorro	Tucumcari	Taos
Albuquerque		277	270	137	222	78	128	173	Clayton	270	374		407	415	347	163	111
Carlsbad	277		374	412	206	241	336	263	Clovis	219	180	168	356	292	248	246	83

Mileages © Rand McNally

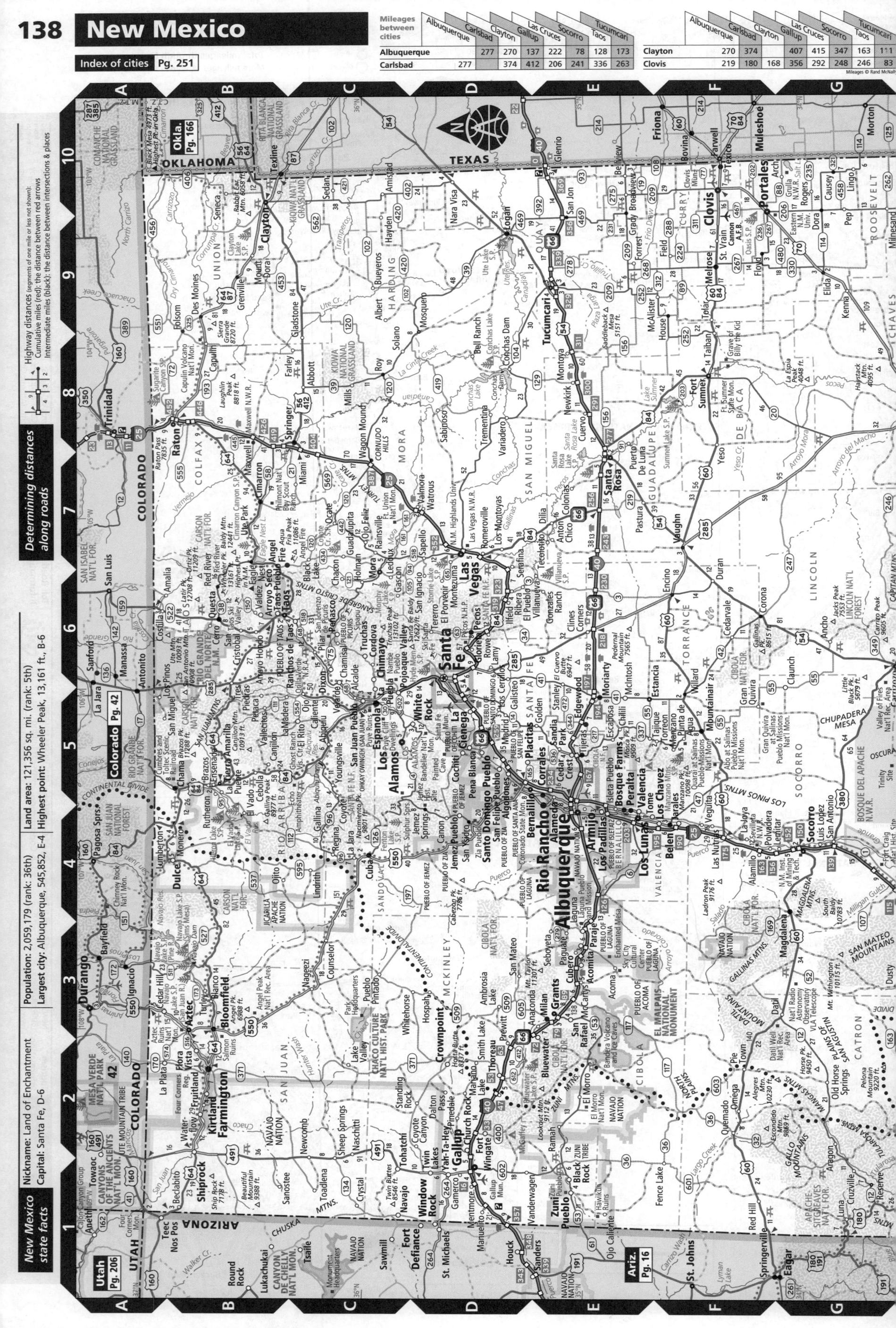

Mileages between cities	Albuquerque	Carlsbad	Clayton	Las Cruces	Gallup	Socorro	Tucumcari	Taos
Farmington	180	455	418	121	404	258	202	354
Las Cruces	222	206	415	338		146	351	303

	Albuquerque	Carlsbad	Clayton	Las Cruces	Gallup	Socorro	Tucumcari	Taos
Roswell	199	76	293	336		184	165	260	182
Santa Fe	58	268	215	197	282	136	68	166

Mileages © Rand McNally

Total mileages through New Mexico
More mileages at www.randmcnally.com/MC

10 164 miles   40 374 miles
25 462 miles

Get travel info at
www.randmcnally.com/NM

Tourism Information — New Mexico Tourism Department (505) 827-7336, (505) 827-7400 www.newmexico.org

Road Conditions & Construction — 511 (800) 432-4269, (505) 827-5100 www.nmroads.com, www.dot.state.nm.us

Toll Road — No toll roads
Information

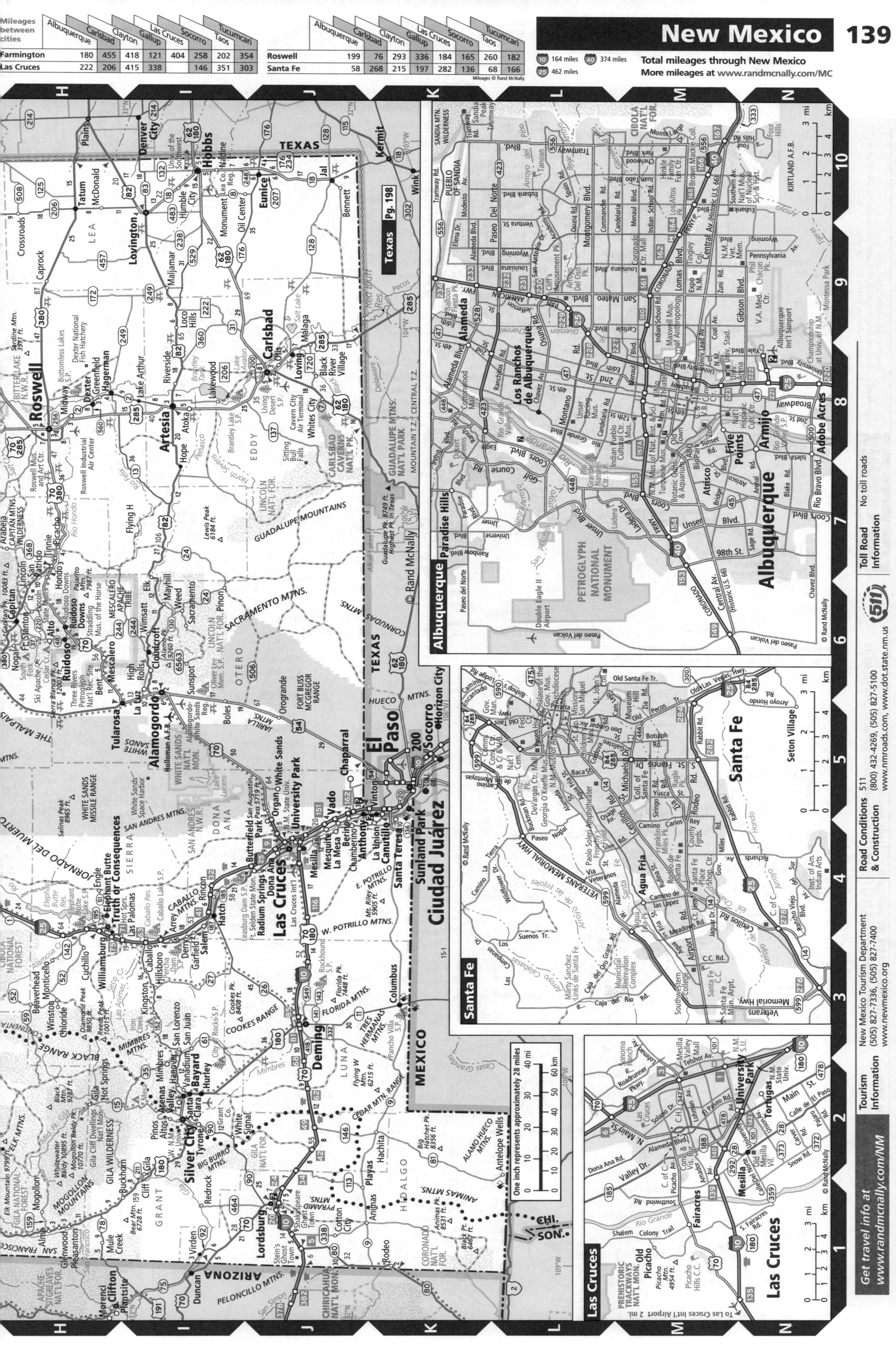

Mileages between cities	Albany	Buffalo	Hempstead	Newburgh	New York	Poughkeepsie	Riverhead	White Plains		Albany	Buffalo	Hempstead	Newburgh	New York	Poughkeepsie	Riverhead	White Plains
Albany		289	167	87	156	75	219	138	Hempstead	167	423		78	12	92	59	34
Buffalo	289		423	361	395	362	471	394	Kingston	55	339	116	37	106	19	168	87

Mileages by Rand McNally

Mileages between cities	Albany	Buffalo	Hempstead	Newburgh	New York	Poughkeepsie	Riverhead	White Plains
Montauk	260	513	97	172	107	184	42	126
Newburgh	87	361	78		72	19	130	49

	Albany	Buffalo	Hempstead	Newburgh	New York	Poughkeepsie	Riverhead	White Plains
New York	156	395	12	72		84	66	26
Poughkeepsie	75	362	92	19	84		143	60

Mileages © Rand McNally

84 72 miles   95 24 miles
87 334 miles   495 66 miles

Total mileages through New York
More mileages at www.randmcnally.com/MC

Binghamton

Utica

Central Long Island

One inch represents approximately 10 miles

0   5   10   15 mi
0   5   10   15   20 km

© Rand McNally

LONG ISLAND

Long Island Sound

ATLANTIC OCEAN

FIRE ISLAND NAT'L SEASHORE

MTA (N.Y. City in-state bridges & tunnels): 511, say "Bridges & Tunnels"; web.mta.info
N.Y. State Bridge Authority (Hudson R. bridges): (845) 691-7245; www.nysba.state.ny.us
Port Authority of N.Y. & N.J. (N.Y.C. inter-state bridges & tunnels): (800) 221-9903; www.panynj.gov

511, (888) 465-1169, (518) 457-6195
www.511ny.org, www.dot.ny.gov
Thruway: (800) 847-8929, www.thruway.ny.gov

New York State Division of Tourism
Information (800) 225-5697
www.iloveny.com

Explore New York at
www.randmcnally.com/NY

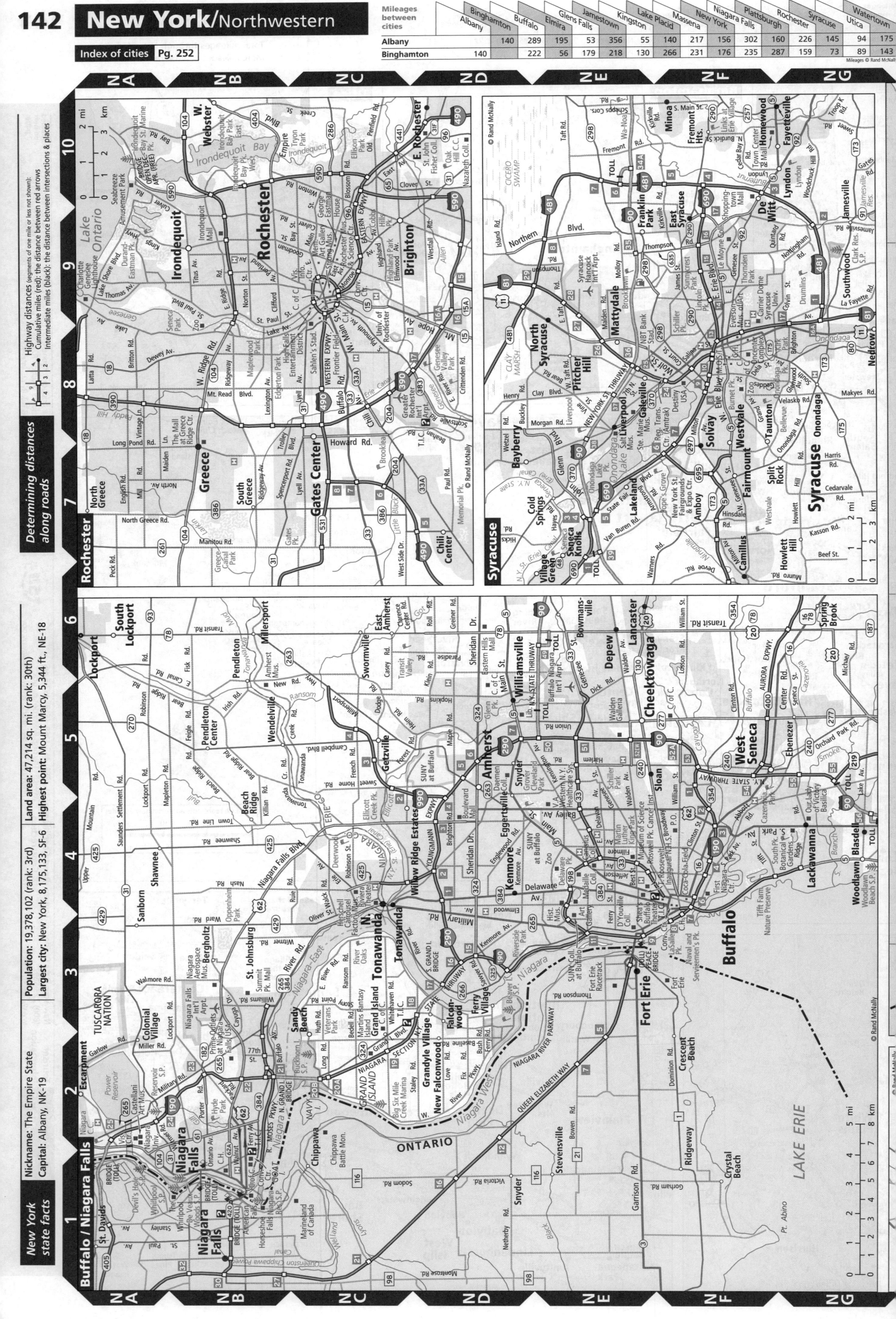

Mileages between cities	Albany	Binghamton	Buffalo	Elmira	Glens Falls	Jamestown	Kingston	Lake Placid	Massena	New York	Niagara Falls	Plattsburgh	Rochester	Syracuse	Utica	Watertown
Albany		140	289	195	53	356	55	140	217	156	302	160	226	145	94	175
Binghamton	140		222	56	179	218	130	266	231	176	235	287	159	73	89	143

Mileages © Rand McNally

New York state facts

Nickname: The Empire State
Capital: Albany, NK-19

Population: 19,378,102 (rank: 3rd)
Largest city: New York, 8,175,133, SF-6

Land area: 47,214 sq. mi. (rank: 30th)
Highest point: Mount Marcy, 5,344 ft., NE-18

Determining distances along roads

Highway distances (segments of one mile or less are not shown):
Cumulative miles (red): the distance between red arrows
Intermediate miles (black): the distance between intersections & places

Rochester

Syracuse

Buffalo / Niagara Falls

continued p. 144

Mileages between cities	Albany	Binghamton	Buffalo	Elmira	Glens Falls	Jamestown	Kingston	Lake Placid	Massena	New York	Niagara Falls	Plattsburgh	Rochester	Syracuse	Utica	Watertown
Buffalo	289	222		148	313	71	339	337	305	395	21	373	73	150	198	212
Jamestown	356	218	71	163	395		349	404	370	392	92	436	139	214	263	278

Mileages © Rand McNally

Total mileages through New York
More mileages at www.randmcnally.com/MC

81	184 miles	87	334 miles
86	176 miles	90	385 miles

One inch represents approx. 13 miles
One inch represents 20 mi / 30 km

© Rand McNally

Pennsylvania Pg. 174

Toll Road
Information New York State Thruway (E-ZPass): www.thruway.ny.gov
Buffalo & Ft. Erie Public Br. Auth. (Peace Br.) (E-ZPass): (716) 884-6744 (905) 871-1608; www.peacebridge.com
Niagara Falls Br. Comm. (ExpressPass, NEXUS): (716) 285-6322, (905) 354-5641; www.niagarafallsbridges.com

511

Road Conditions & Construction
511, (888) 465-1169, (518) 457-6195
www.511ny.org, www.dot.ny.gov
Thruway: (800) 847-8929, www.thruway.com

Tourism Information
New York State Division of Tourism
(800) 225-5697
www.iloveny.com

Explore New York at
www.randmcnally.com/NY

Continued on next page

Elmira (inset map)

LAKE ONTARIO

LAKE ERIE

PENNSYLVANIA

CANADA

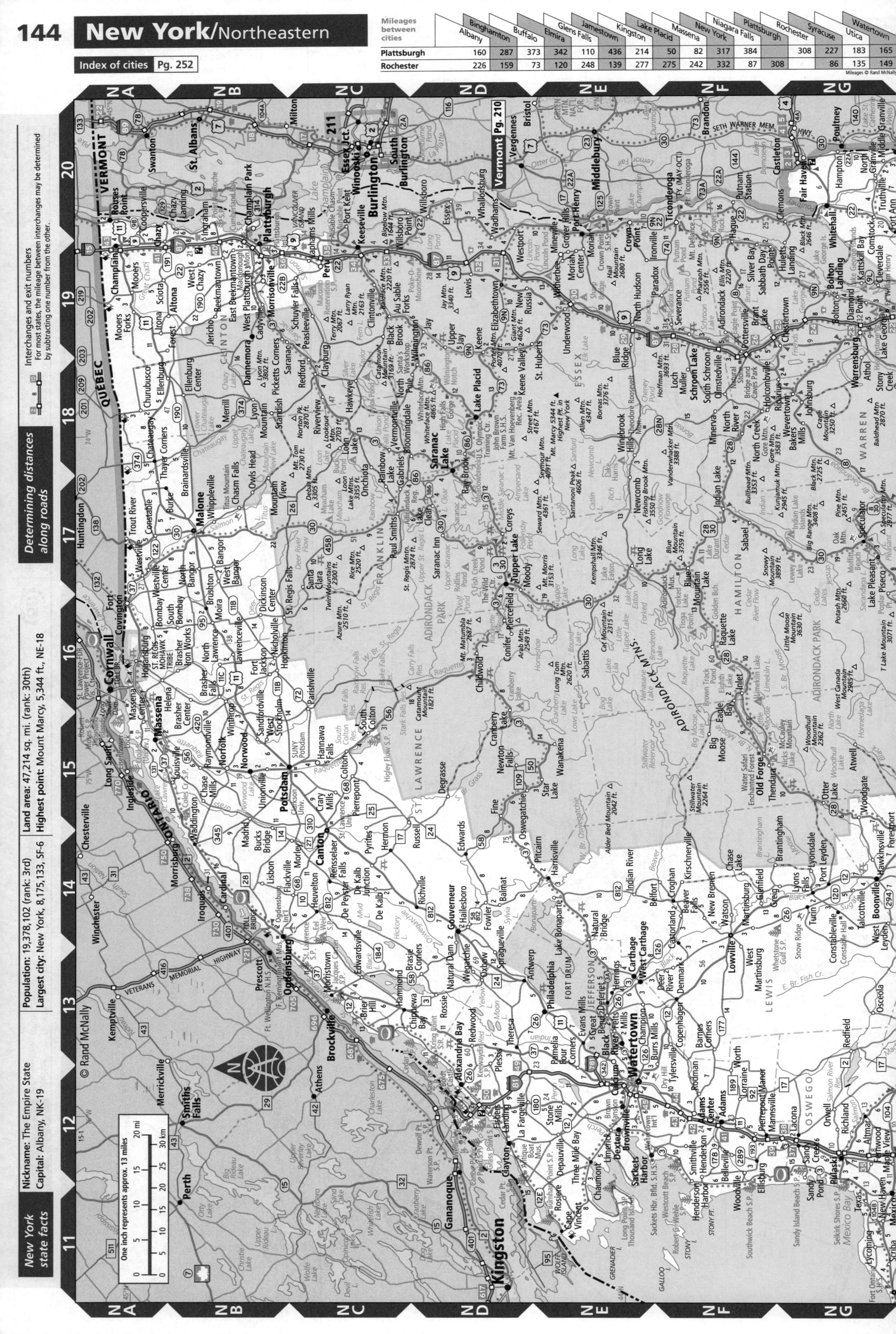

Mileages between cities	Albany	Binghamton	Buffalo	Elmira	Glens Falls	Jamestown	Kingston	Lake Placid	Massena	New York	Niagara Falls	Plattsburgh	Rochester	Syracuse	Utica	Watertown
Plattsburgh	160	287	373	342	110	436	214	50	82	317	384		308	227	183	165
Rochester	226	159	73	120	248	139	277	275	242	332	87	308		86	135	149

Mileages © Rand McNally

New York state facts

Nickname: The Empire State
Capital: Albany, NK-19

Population: 19,378,102 (rank: 3rd)
Largest city: New York, 8,175,133, SF-6

Land area: 47,214 sq. mi. (rank: 30th)
Highest point: Mount Marcy, 5,344 ft., NE-18

Determining distances along roads

Interchanges and exit numbers
For most states, the mileage between interchanges may be determined by subtracting one number from the other.

One inch represents approx. 13 miles

© Rand McNally

Mileages between cities	Albany	Binghamton	Buffalo	Elmira	Glens Falls	Jamestown	Kingston	Lake Placid	Massena	New York	Niagara Falls	Plattsburgh	Rochester	Syracuse	Utica	Watertown
Syracuse	145	73	150	90	160	214	195	195	159	246	162	227	86		53	70
Watertown	175	143	212	160	179	278	226	125	89	316	225	165	149	70	80	

Mileages © Rand McNally

Total mileages through New York

| 81 | 184 miles | 87 | 334 miles |
| 86 | 176 miles | 90 | 385 miles |

More mileages at www.randmcnally.com/MC

Explore New York at www.randmcnally.com/NY

Tourism Information
New York State Division of Tourism (800) 225-5697
www.iloveny.com

Road Conditions & Construction
511, (888) 465-1169, (518) 457-6195
511ny.org, www.dot.ny.gov
Thruway: (800) 847-8929, www.thruway.com

Toll Road Information
Ogdensburg Bridge & Port Authority: (315) 393-4080; www.ogdensport.com
Seaway International Bridge Corporation (near Massena): (613) 932-6601; www.slbc.ca
Thousand Islands Bridge Authority (Alexandria Bay): (315) 482-2501; www.tibridge.com

Continued from previous pages

Mass. Pg. 98

Conn. Pg. 48

Pg. 174

Pennsylvania Pg. 174

Pg. 143

City sights to see

- American Museum of Natural History, Manhattan, A-4
- Battery Park, Manhattan, I-1
- Belmont Park Race Track, Elmont, H-16
- Bronx Zoo, Bronx, E-12
- Brooklyn Bridge, New York, H-2
- Carnegie Hall, Manhattan, C-4
- Central Park, Manhattan, B-4

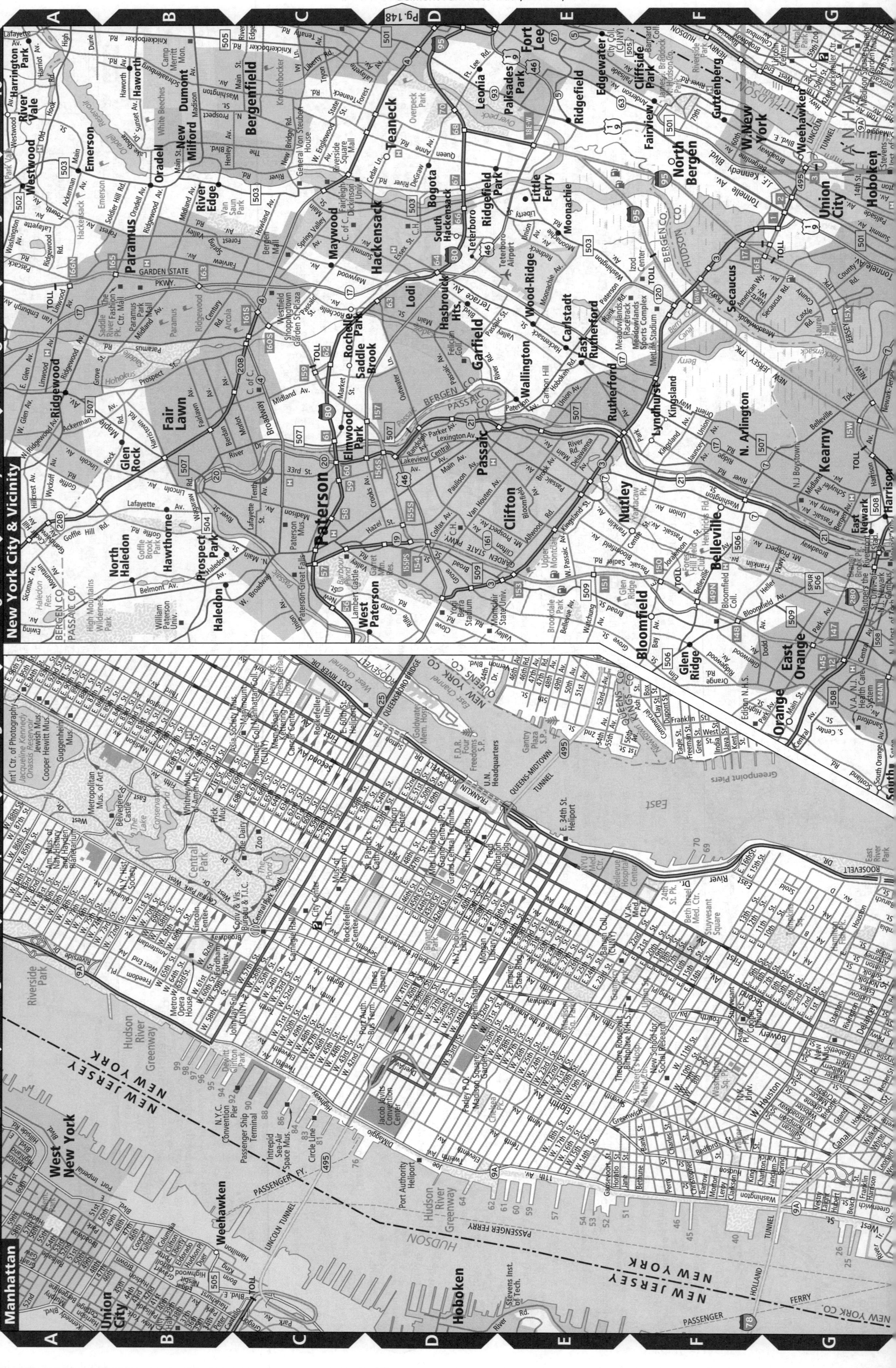

- Chrysler Building, Manhattan, D-4
- Coney Island, Brooklyn, L-10
- Edison Nat'l Historic Site, W. Orange, N.J., F-5
- Ellis Island, Jersey City, N.J./Manhattan, I-9
- Empire State Building, Manhattan, D-3
- Greenwich Village, Manhattan, H-10
- Grand Central Terminal, Manhattan, D-4

continued p.148

City sights to see—continued
- Guggenheim Museum, Manhattan, A-5
- Intrepid Sea-Air Space Mus., Manhattan, C-2
- Lincoln Center, Manhattan, B-3
- Madison Square Garden, Manhattan, D-2
- Meadowlands Sports Complex, East Rutherford, N.J., F-8
- Metropolitan Museum of Art, Manhattan, B-5

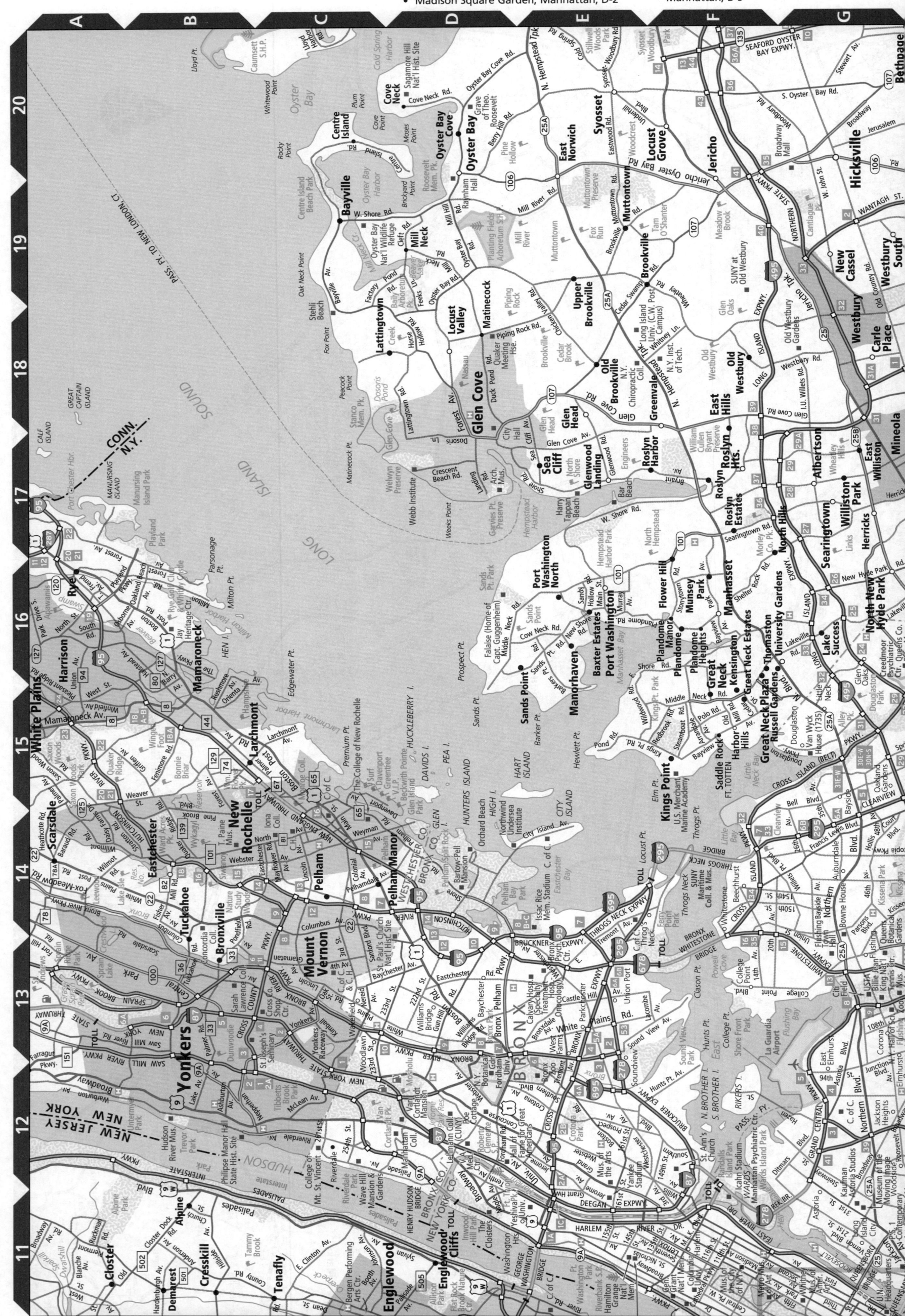

- National Sept. 11 Memorial, Manhattan, H-1
- New York Stock Exchange and Wall Street, Manhattan, H-1
- Rockefeller Center, Manhattan, C-4
- Staten Island Ferry, New York, J-9
- Statue of Liberty, Manhattan, I-9
- Times Square, Manhattan, D-3
- Yankee Stadium, Bronx, E-11

New York/New York Metro East **149**

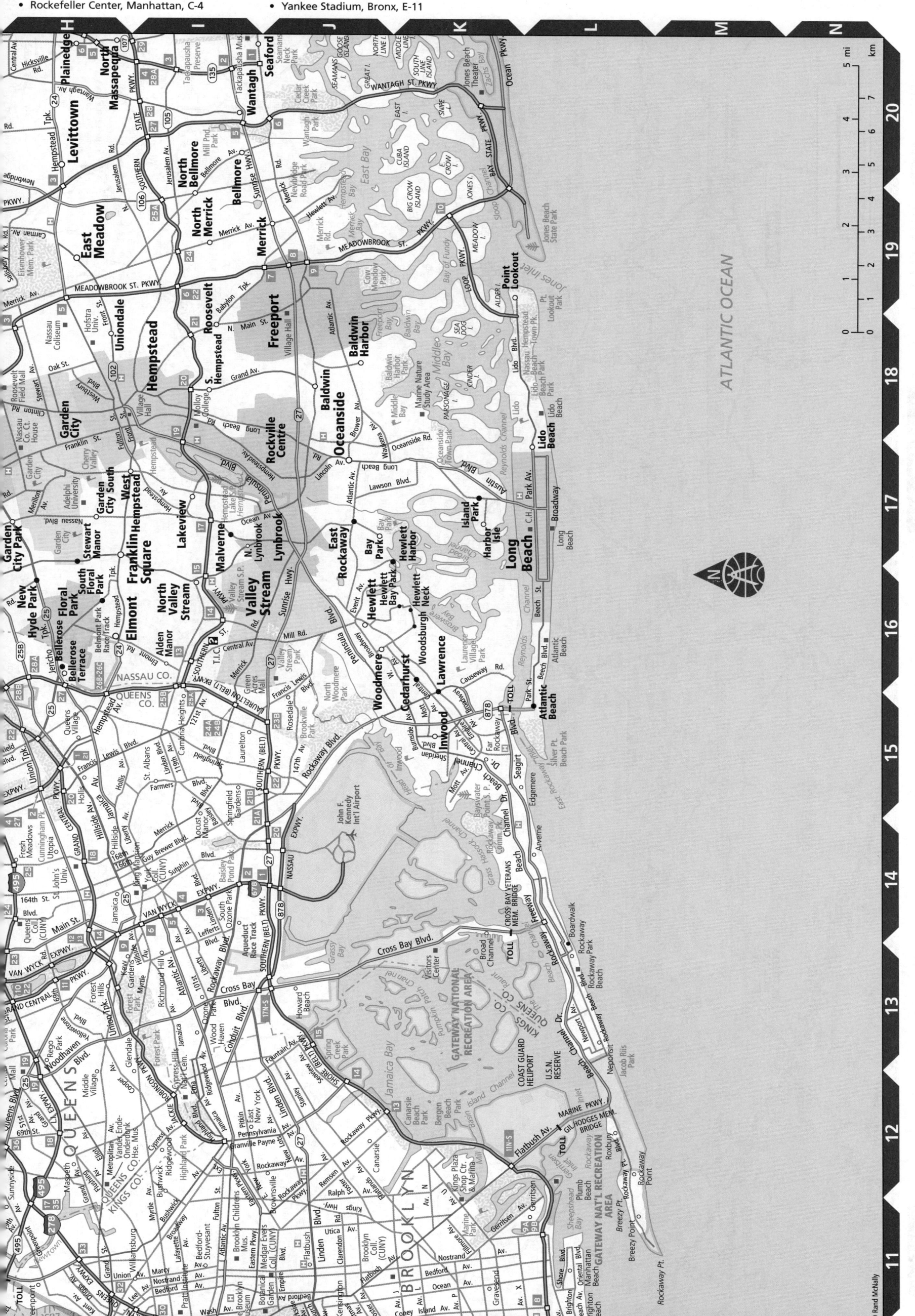

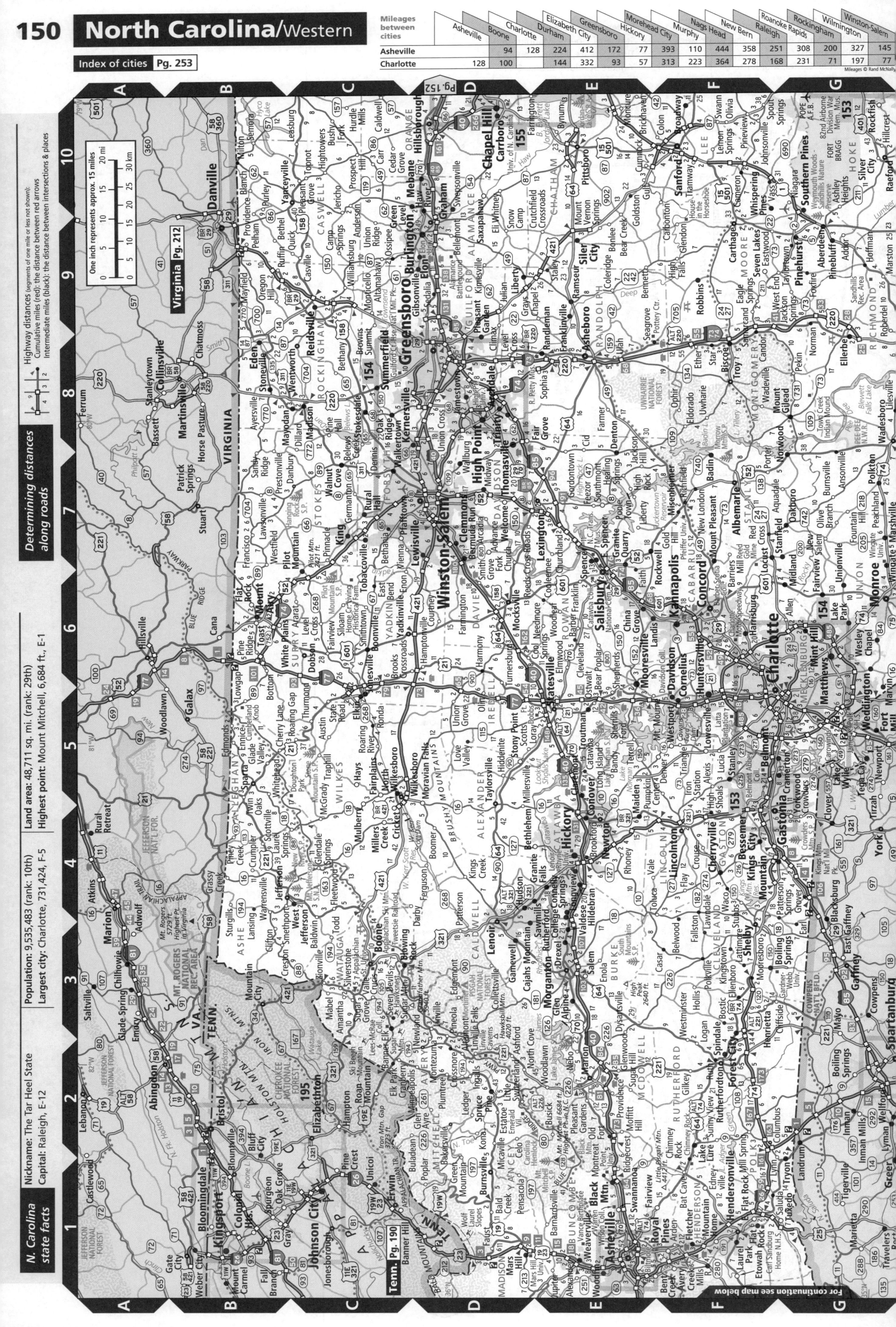

Mileages between cities	Asheville	Boone	Charlotte	Durham	Elizabeth City	Greensboro	Hickory	Morehead City	Murphy	Nags Head	New Bern	Raleigh	Roanoke Rapids	Rockingham	Wilmington	Winston-Salem
Asheville		94	128	224	412	172	77	393	110	444	358	251	308	200	327	145
Charlotte	128	100		144	332	93	57	313	223	364	278	168	231	71	231	77

Mileages © Rand McNally

N. Carolina state facts

Nickname: The Tar Heel State
Capital: Raleigh, E-12

Population: 9,535,483 (rank: 10th)
Largest city: Charlotte, 731,424, F-5

Land area: 48,711 sq. mi. (rank: 29th)
Highest point: Mount Mitchell, 6,684 ft., E-1

Determining distances along roads

Highway distances (segments of one mile or less not shown): the distance between red arrows
Cumulative miles (red); the distance between intersections & places
Intermediate miles (black); the distance between intersections & places

One inch represents approx. 15 miles

Mileages between cities	Asheville	Boone	Charlotte	Durham	Elizabeth City	Greensboro	Hickory	Morehead City	Murphy	Nags Head	New Bern	Raleigh	Roanoke Rapids	Rockingham	Wilmington	Winston-Salem
Elizabeth City	412	354	332	185		241	338	152	520	56	119	164	97	259	208	269
Fayetteville	261	202	137	89	203	94	189	138	369	234	130	63	127	64	89	119

Mileages © Rand McNally

continued p. 152

Total mileages through North Carolina

| 40 | 419 miles | 85 | 233 miles |
| 77 | 102 miles | 95 | 182 miles |

More mileages at www.randmcnally.com/MC

Plan a North Carolina trip at www.randmcnally.com/NC

Tourism Information
North Carolina Division of Tourism
(800) 847-4862, (919) 733-4171
www.visitnc.com

Road Conditions & Construction
511, (877) 511-4662
www.ncdot.gov/travel/511
www.ncdot.gov

Toll Road Information
North Carolina Turnpike Authority (NC Quick Pass)
(877) 769-7277
www.ncdot.gov/turnpike

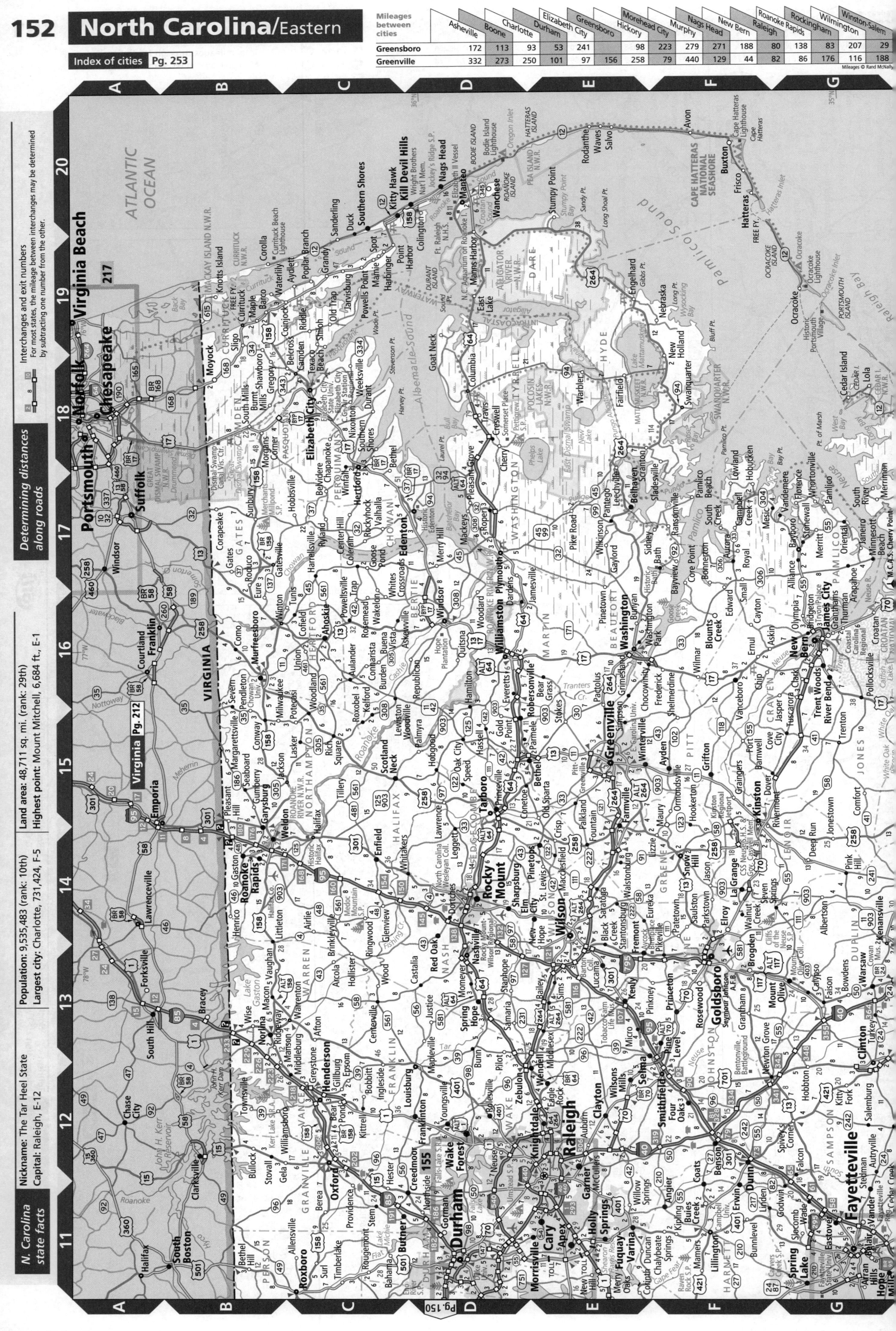

Mileages between cities	Asheville	Boone	Charlotte	Durham	Elizabeth City	Greensboro	Hickory	Morehead City	Murphy	Nags Head	New Bern	Raleigh	Roanoke Rapids	Rockingham	Wilmington	Winston-Salem
Greensboro	172	113	93	53	241		98	223	279	271	188	80	138	83	207	29
Greenville	332	273	250	101	97	156	258	79	440	129	44	82	86	176	116	188

Mileages © Rand McNally

N. Carolina state facts

Nickname: The Tar Heel State
Capital: Raleigh, E-12

Population: 9,535,483 (rank: 10th)
Largest city: Charlotte, 731,424, F-5

Land area: 48,711 sq. mi. (rank: 29th)
Highest point: Mount Mitchell, 6,684 ft., E-1

Determining distances along roads

Interchanges and exit numbers
For most states, the mileage between interchanges may be determined by subtracting one number from the other.

Mileages between cities

	Asheville	Boone	Charlotte	Durham	Elizabeth City	Greensboro	Hickory	Morehead City	Murphy	Nags Head	New Bern	Roanoke Rapids	Raleigh	Rockingham	Wilmington	Winston-Salem
Raleigh	251	192	168	22	164	80	177	146	358	195	111	89		98	130	107
Wilmington	327	319	197	156	208	207	259	91	428	230	90	130	178	127		236

Mileages © Rand McNally

North Carolina/Eastern

Total mileages through North Carolina

- 40 — 419 miles
- 85 — 233 miles
- 77 — 102 miles
- 95 — 182 miles

More mileages at www.randmcnally.com/MC

One inch represents approx. 15 miles

Plan a North Carolina trip at www.randmcnally.com/NC

Tourism Information — North Carolina Division of Tourism (800) 847-4862, (919) 733-4171 www.visitnc.com

Road Conditions & Construction — 511, (877) 511-4662 www.ncdot.org/travel/511 www.ncdot.gov

Toll Road Information — North Carolina Turnpike Authority (NC Quick Pass) (877) 769-7277 www.ncdot.gov/turnpike

© Rand McNally

City sights to see
- Discovery Place, Charlotte, H-4
- Dollywood, Pigeon Forge, Tenn., B-11
- Duke Homestead State Historic Site, Durham, F-9
- Guilford Courthouse National Military Park, Greensboro, B-6
- Historic Bethabara Park, Winston-Salem, A-1
- Mint Museum of Art, Charlotte, H-5

Greensboro / Winston-Salem / High Point

Winston-Salem • Walkertown • Oak Ridge • Summerfield • Kernersville • Colfax • Friendship • Greensboro • Sandy Ridge • Union Cross • Wallburg • Jamestown • High Point • Sedgefield • Midway • Arcadia • Enterprise • Welcome • Arnold • Thomasville • Archdale • Trinity • Glenola • Level Cross

0 1 2 3 mi
0 1 2 3 4 km

© Rand McNally

Charlotte & Vicinity

Concord • Mountain Island • Huntersville • Harrisburg • Mount Holly • Hickory Grove • Pine Ridge • McAdenville • Charlotte • Cramerton • Belmont • Paradise Point • Green Acres • Shopton • Mint Hill • Matthews • Lake Wylie • Pineville • Stallings • Hemby Bridge • Indian Trail • Lake Park

S. CAR.
N

0 1 2 3 mi
0 1 2 3 4 km

© Rand McNally

- Morehead Planetarium and Science Center, Chapel Hill, H-8
- North Carolina Museum of Life and Science, Durham, F-10
- North Carolina Museum of History, Raleigh, I-12
- North Carolina State Capitol, Raleigh, I-13
- Old Salem, Winston-Salem, B-2
- Reynolda House, Winston-Salem, B-1

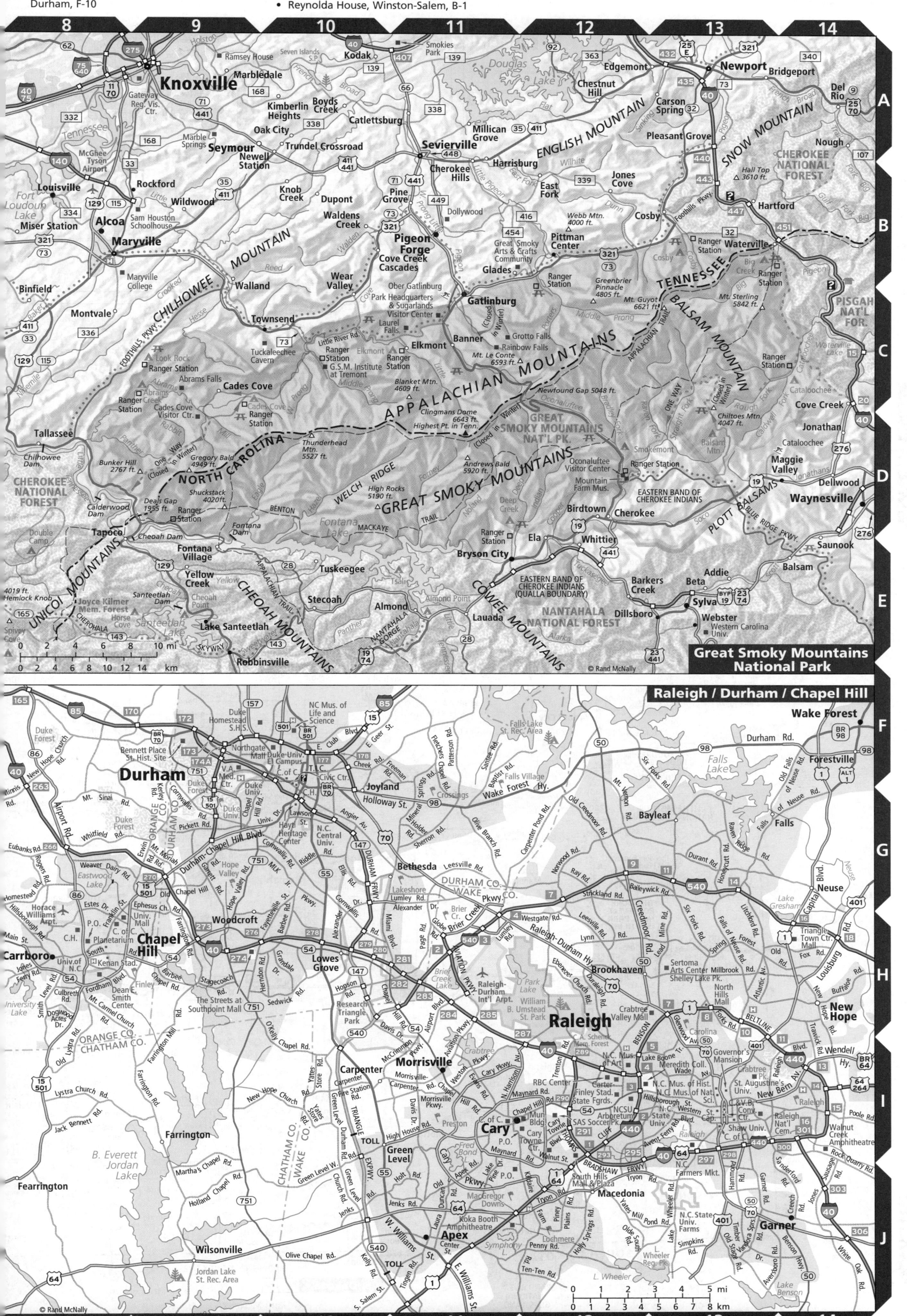

Great Smoky Mountains National Park

Raleigh / Durham / Chapel Hill

© Rand McNally

Mileages between cities	Bismarck	Bowman	Fargo	Garrison	Grand Forks	Jamestown	Williston	Winnipeg, MB		Bismarck	Bowman	Fargo	Garrison	Grand Forks	Jamestown	Williston	Winnipeg, MB
Bismarck		174	195	75	272	102	228	413	**Dickinson**	97	78	292	149	368	198	132	509
Devils Lake	180	354	165	167	89	99	245	230	**Fargo**	195	368		266	80	94	422	222

Mileages © Rand McNally

N. Dakota state facts — Nickname: The Peace Garden State — Capital: Bismarck, H-7 — Population: 672,591 (rank: 48th) — Land area: 68,976 sq. mi. (rank: 17th) — Highest point: White Butte, 3,506 ft., I-3 — Largest city: Fargo, 105,549, H-13 — Determining distances along roads: Interchanges and exit numbers — For most states, the mileage between interchanges may be determined by subtracting one number from the other.

Bismarck / Fargo / Mandan insets.

Montana Pg. 122

S. Dakota Pg. 188

Mileages between cities	Bismarck	Bowman	Fargo	Garrison	Grand Forks	Jamestown	Williston	Winnipeg, MB
Grand Forks	272	444	80	256		171	334	146
Minot	110	260	268	47	210	170	124	299
Wahpeton	243	416	54	315	131	142	470	273
Williston	228	170	422	144	334	293		424

Mileages © Rand McNally

Total mileages through North Dakota

29 218 miles	2 359 miles
94 352 miles	83 265 miles

More mileages at www.randmcnally.com/MC

Map of North Dakota, with insets of Grand Forks, Winnipeg, and Minot.

One inch represents approx. 22 miles

511, (855) 637-6237, (866) 696-3511
www.dot.nd.gov
www.dot.nd.gov/travel-info-v2/

Road Conditions & Construction

North Dakota Tourism Division
(800) 435-5663, (701) 328-2525
www.ndtourism.com

Tourism Information

Plan a North Dakota trip at www.randmcnally.com/ND

Mileages between cities	Akron	Ashtabula	Canton	Cincinnati	Cleveland	Columbus	Coshocton	Findlay	Lima	Mansfield	New Philadelphia	Pittsburgh, PA	Sandusky	Steubenville	Toledo	Youngstown
Akron		81	20	232	39	124	80	132	154	62	47	107	85	82	133	48
Cleveland	39	58	58	248		142	102	121	156	80	85	131	62	124	111	72

Mileages © Rand McN

Ohio state facts

Nickname: The Buckeye State
Capital: Columbus

Population: 11,536,504 (rank: 7th)
Largest city: Columbus, SB-9

Land area: 40,948 sq. mi. (rank: 35th)
Highest point: Campbell Hill, 1,550 ft., NL-6

Mileages between cities	Akron	Ashtabula	Canton	Cincinnati	Cleveland	Columbus	Coshocton	Findlay	Lima	Mansfield	New Philadelphia	Pittsburgh, PA	Sandusky	Steubenville	Toledo	Youngstown (continued p. 160)
Columbus	124	194	126	106	142		71	96	91	66	118	184	112	150	142	172
Defiance	180	214	185	169	157	135	177	51	44	123	190	274	98	246	57	214

Total mileages through Ohio

71 248 miles 80 237 miles
75 211 miles 90 245 miles

More mileages at www.randmcnally.com/MC

continued p. 160

Pg. 161

Pg. 162

Pg. 164

Ind. Pg. 74

INDIANA

Tourism Information
Ohio Div. of Travel & Tourism
(800) 282-5393
www.discoverohio.com

Road Conditions & Construction
(614) 466-7170, www.buckeyetraffic.org, www.dot.state.oh.us
(888) 876-7453, (440) 234-2030, (440) 234-2081
Turnpike:

Toll Road Information
J.W. Shockessny Ohio Turnpike (E-ZPass)
(888) 876-7453
www.ohioturnpike.org

Get more Ohio info at www.randmcnally.com/OH

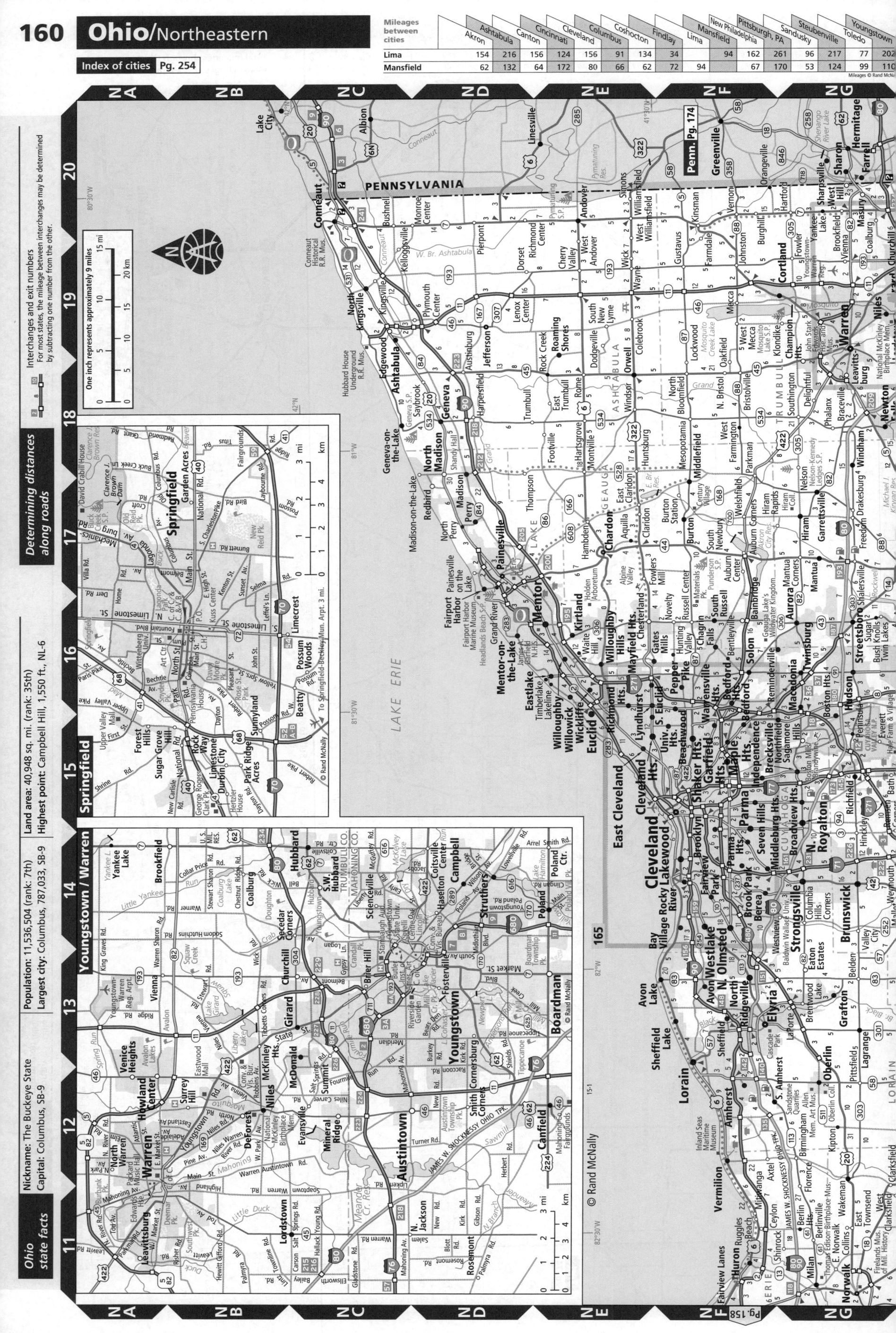

Mileages between cities	Akron	Ashtabula	Canton	Cincinnati	Cleveland	Columbus	Coshocton	Findlay	Lima	Mansfield	New Philadelphia	Pittsburgh, PA	Sandusky	Steubenville	Toledo	Youngstown
Toledo	133	171	152	200	111	142	152	44	77	99	179	228	58	221		169
Youngstown	48	57	57	279	72	172	117	180	202	110	84	67	122	66	169	

Mileages © Rand McNally

Total mileages through Ohio

| 71 | 248 miles | 80 | 237 miles |
| 75 | 211 miles | 90 | 245 miles |

More mileages at www.randmcnally.com/MC

Tourism Information
Ohio Div. of Travel & Tourism (800) 282-5393
www.discoverohio.com

Road Conditions & Construction
Ohio Div. of Travel & Tourism (614) 466-7170, www.buckeyetraffic.org, www.dot.state.oh.us
Turnpike: (888) 876-7453, (440) 234-2030, (440) 234-2081
www.ohioturnpike.org

Toll Road Information
J.W. Shocknessy Ohio Turnpike (E-ZPass)
(888) 876-7453
www.ohioturnpike.org

Get more Ohio info at
www.randmcnally.com/OH

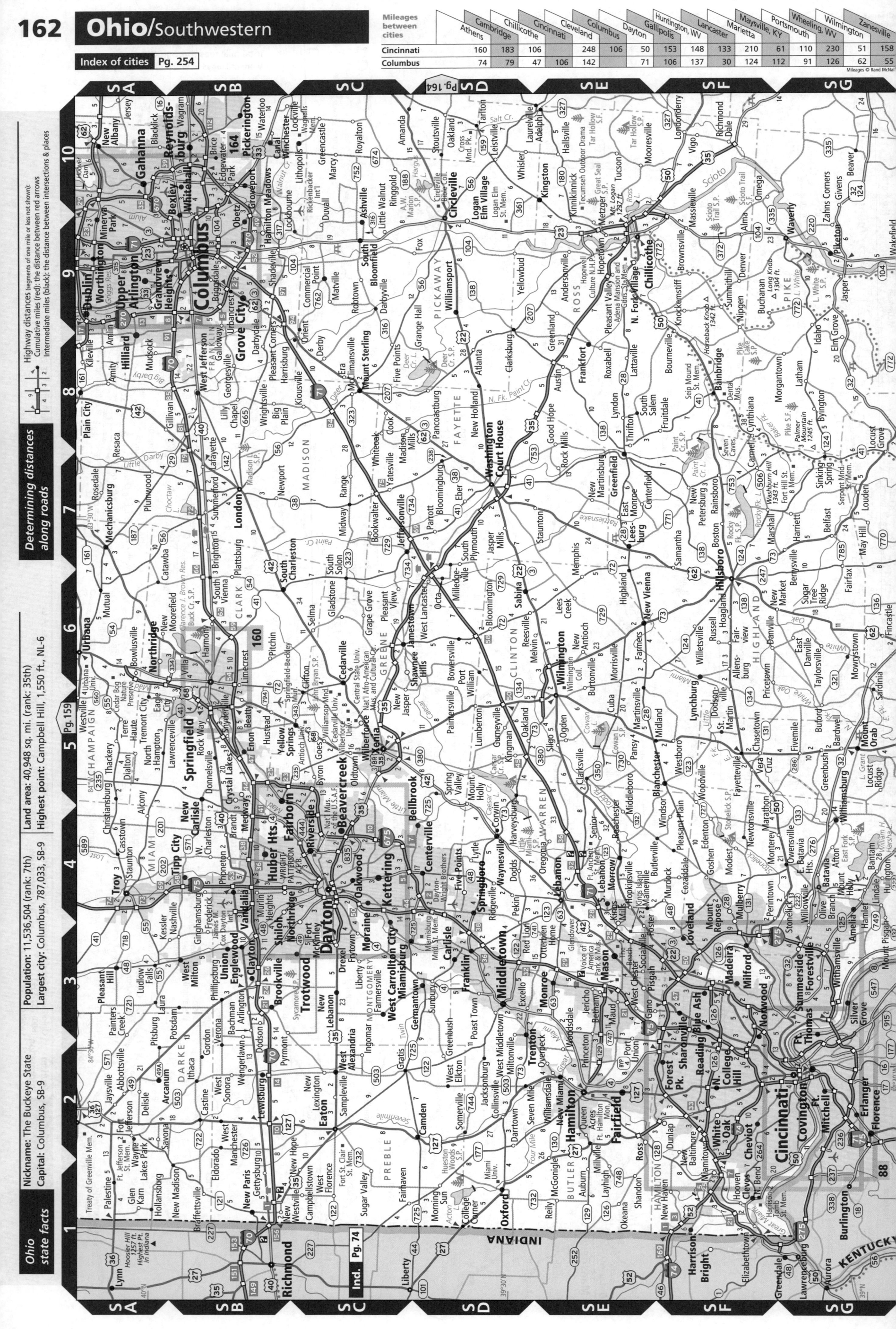

Mileages between cities	Athens	Cambridge	Chillicothe	Cincinnati	Cleveland	Columbus	Dayton	Gallipolis	Huntington, WV	Lancaster	Marietta	Maysville, KY	Portsmouth	Wheeling, WV	Wilmington	Zanesville
Cincinnati	160	183	106		248	106	50	153	148	133	210	61	110	230	51	158
Columbus	74	79	47	106	142		71	106	137	30	124	112	91	126	62	55

Mileages © Rand McNally

Ohio state facts

Nickname: The Buckeye State
Capital: Columbus, SB-9

Population: 11,536,504 (rank: 7th)
Largest city: Columbus, 787,033, SB-9

Land area: 40,948 sq. mi. (rank: 35th)
Highest point: Campbell Hill, 1,550 ft., NL-6

Determining distances along roads

Highway distances (segments of one mile or less not shown):
Cumulative miles (red): the distance between red arrows
Intermediate miles (black): the distance between intersections & places

Mileages between cities		Athens	Cambridge	Chillicothe	Cincinnati	Cleveland	Columbus	Dayton	Gallipolis	Huntington, WV	Lancaster	Marietta	Maysville, KY	Portsmouth	Wheeling, WV	Wilmington	Zanesville	continued p. 164
Dayton		134	149	77	50	212	71		137	168	101	195	108	122	197	34	126
Gallipolis		42	114	60	153	235	106	137		39	86	66	111	55	162	112	94

Mileages © Rand McNally

70 226 miles	75 211 miles	**Total mileages through Ohio**
71 248 miles	77 160 miles	**More mileages at www.randmcnally.com/MC**

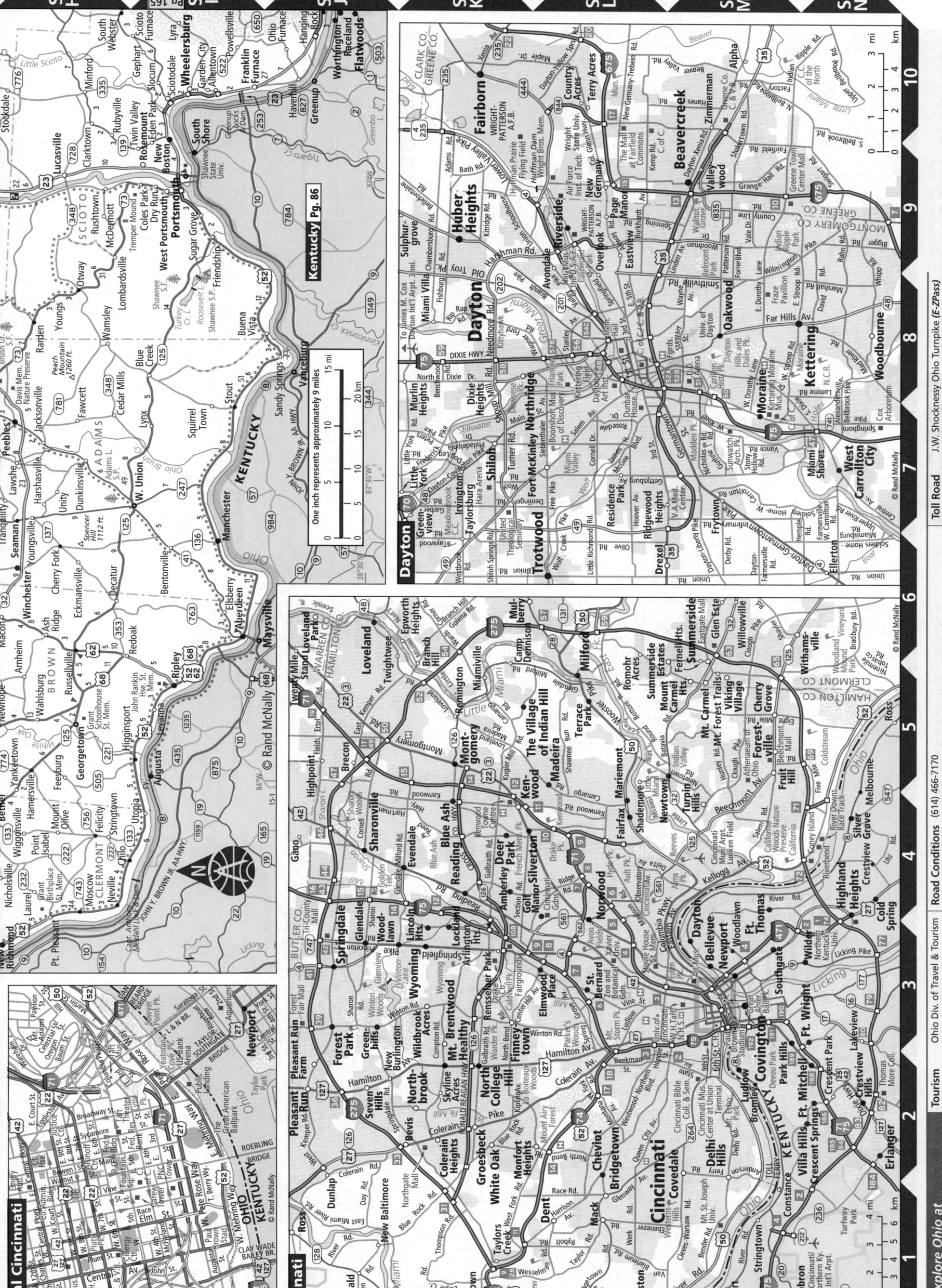

Mileages between cities	Athens	Cambridge	Chillicothe	Cincinnati	Cleveland	Columbus	Dayton	Gallipolis	Huntington, WV	Lancaster	Marietta	Maysville, KY	Portsmouth	Wheeling, WV	Wilmington	Zanesville
Marietta	44	48	104	210	164	124	195	66	106	82		165	128	90	156	69
Portsmouth	81	162	44	110	233	91	122	55	46	80	128	52		210	79	138

Mileages by Rand McNally

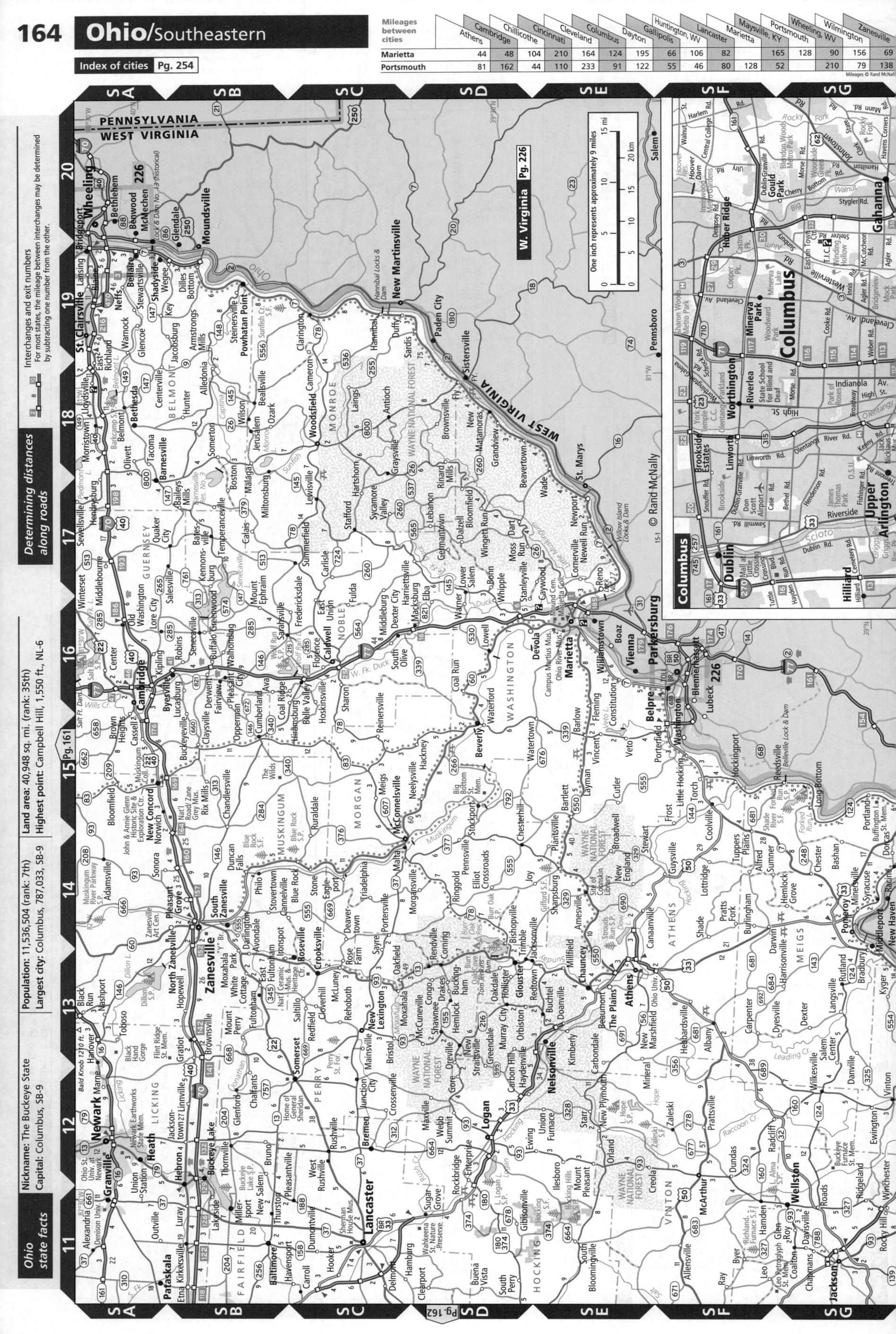

Ohio state facts

Nickname: The Buckeye State
Capital: Columbus, SB-9

Population: 11,536,504 (rank: 7th)
Largest city: Columbus, 787,033, SB-9

Land area: 40,948 sq. mi. (rank: 35th)
Highest point: Campbell Hill, 1,550 ft., NL-6

Determining distances along roads

Interchanges and exit numbers
For most states, the mileage between interchanges may be determined by subtracting one number from the other.

W. Virginia Pg. 226

One inch represents approximately 9 miles

Mileages between cities	Athens Cambridge	Chillicothe	Cincinnati	Cleveland	Columbus	Dayton	Gallipolis	Huntington, WV	Lancaster	Marietta	Maysville, KY	Portsmouth	Wheeling, WV	Wilmington	Zanesville
Springfield	118 123	69	77	185	45	27	129	160	74	168	102	114	171	38	99
Zanesville	52 24	94	158	145	55	126	94	134	45	69	164	138	72	114	

Mileages © Rand McNally

Total mileages through Ohio	
70 226 miles	75 211 miles
71 248 miles	77 160 miles

More mileages at www.randmcnally.com/MC

Cleveland & Vicinity

Central Cleveland

LAKE ERIE — 570 ft. above sea level

WEST VIRGINIA

WAYNE NATIONAL FOREST

Pg. 163

Ky. Pg. 86

Explore Ohio at www.randmcnally.com/OH

Tourism Information — Ohio Div. of Travel & Tourism (800) 282-5393 www.discoverohio.com

Road Conditions & Construction — Ohio Dept. of Transportation (614) 466-7170 www.buckeyetraffic.org, www.dot.state.oh.us Cincinnati metro area: 511, (513) 333-3333

Toll Road Information — J.W. Shocknessy Ohio Turnpike (E-ZPass) (888) 876-7453 www.ohioturnpike.org

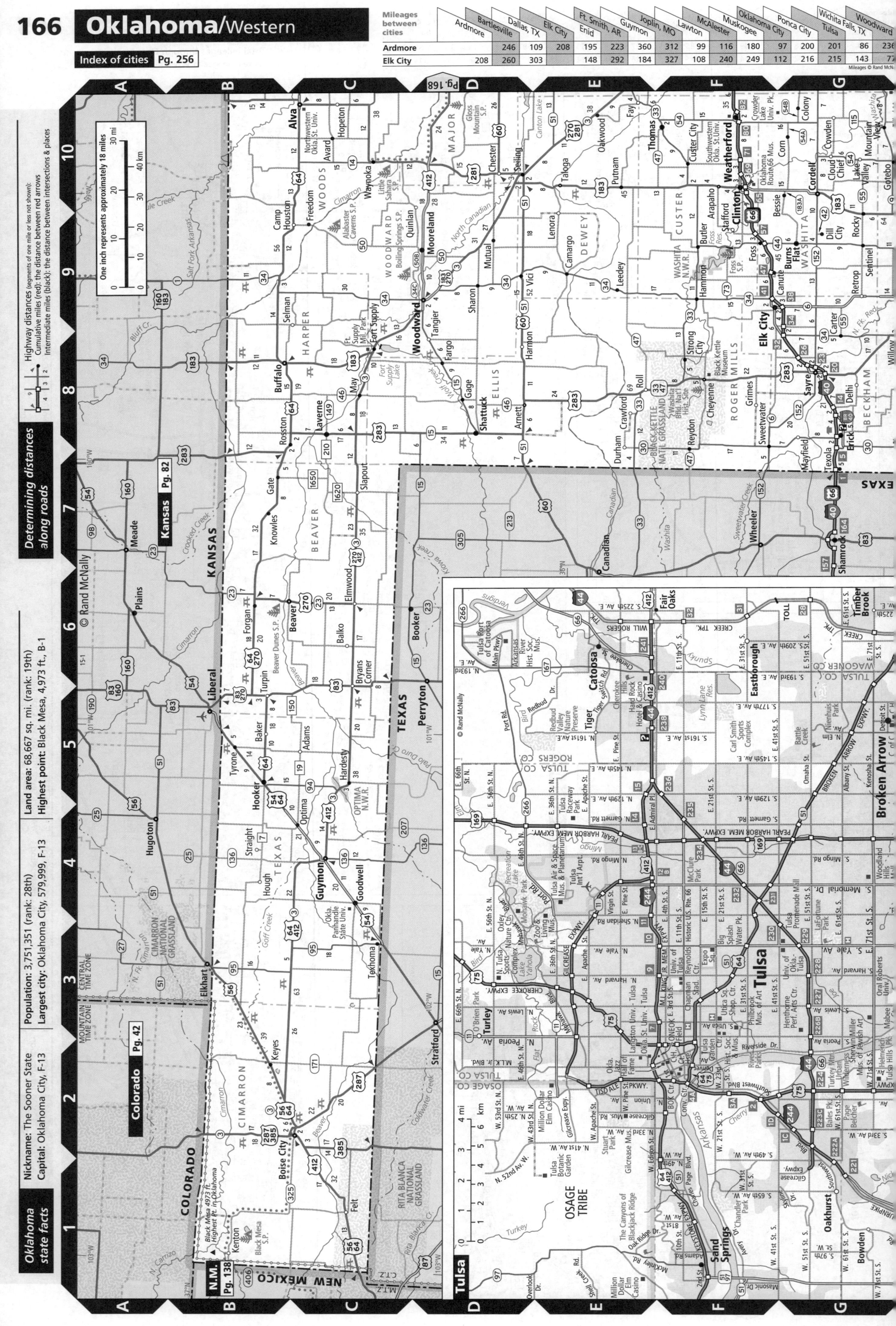

Mileages between cities

	Ardmore	Bartlesville	Dallas, TX	Elk City	Enid	Ft. Smith, AR	Guymon	Joplin, MO	Lawton	McAlester	Muskogee	Oklahoma City	Ponca City	Wichita Falls, TX	Tulsa	Woodward
Enid	195	134	302	148		232	211	227	142	204	164	99	67	114	196	87
Guymon	360	344	459	184	211	443		438	294	391	375	263	278	326	317	124

Mileages © Rand McNally

35 236 miles	44 329 miles	**Total mileages through Oklahoma**
40 331 miles	75 227 miles	More mileages at www.randmcnally.com/MC

Plan an Oklahoma trip at www.randmcnally.com/OK

Tourism Information Oklahoma Tourism & Recreation Department (800) 652-6552 www.travelok.com

Road Conditions & Construction (405) 425-2385 In OK: (888) 425-2385 www.okladot.state.ok.us

Toll Road Information Oklahoma Turnpike Authority (PIKEPASS) (405) 425-3600 www.pikepass.com

Texas Pg. 198

Pg. 169

Mileages between cities	Ardmore	Bartlesville	Dallas, TX	Elk City	Enid	Ft. Smith, AR	Guymon	Joplin, MO	Lawton	McAlester	Muskogee	Oklahoma City	Ponca City	Tulsa	Wichita Falls, TX	Woodward
Idabel	149	248	171	352	316	136	504	295	245	116	180	240	293	203	238	380
Muskogee	180	91	236	249	164	70	375	117	218	65		137	142	50	272	251

Mileages © Rand McNally

Oklahoma state facts

Nickname: The Sooner State
Capital: Oklahoma City, F-13

Population: 3,751,351 (rank: 28th)
Largest city: Oklahoma City, F-13

Land area: 68,667 sq. mi. (rank: 19th)
Highest point: Black Mesa, 4,973 ft., B-1

Determining distances along roads

Interchanges and exit numbers
For most states, the mileage between interchanges may be determined by subtracting one number from the other.

Mileages between cities	Ardmore	Bartlesville	Dallas, TX	Elk City	Enid	Ft. Smith, AR	Guymon	Joplin, MO	Lawton	McAlester	Muskogee	Oklahoma City	Ponca City	Tulsa	Wichita Falls, TX	Woodward
Oklahoma City	97	149	204	112	99	180	263	216	86	128	137		105	104	140	139
Tulsa	201	45	258	215	114	118	326	113	191	91	50	104	91		244	202

Mileages © Rand McNally

Total mileages through Oklahoma
More mileages at www.randmcnally.com/MC

35 236 miles 44 329 miles
40 331 miles 75 227 miles

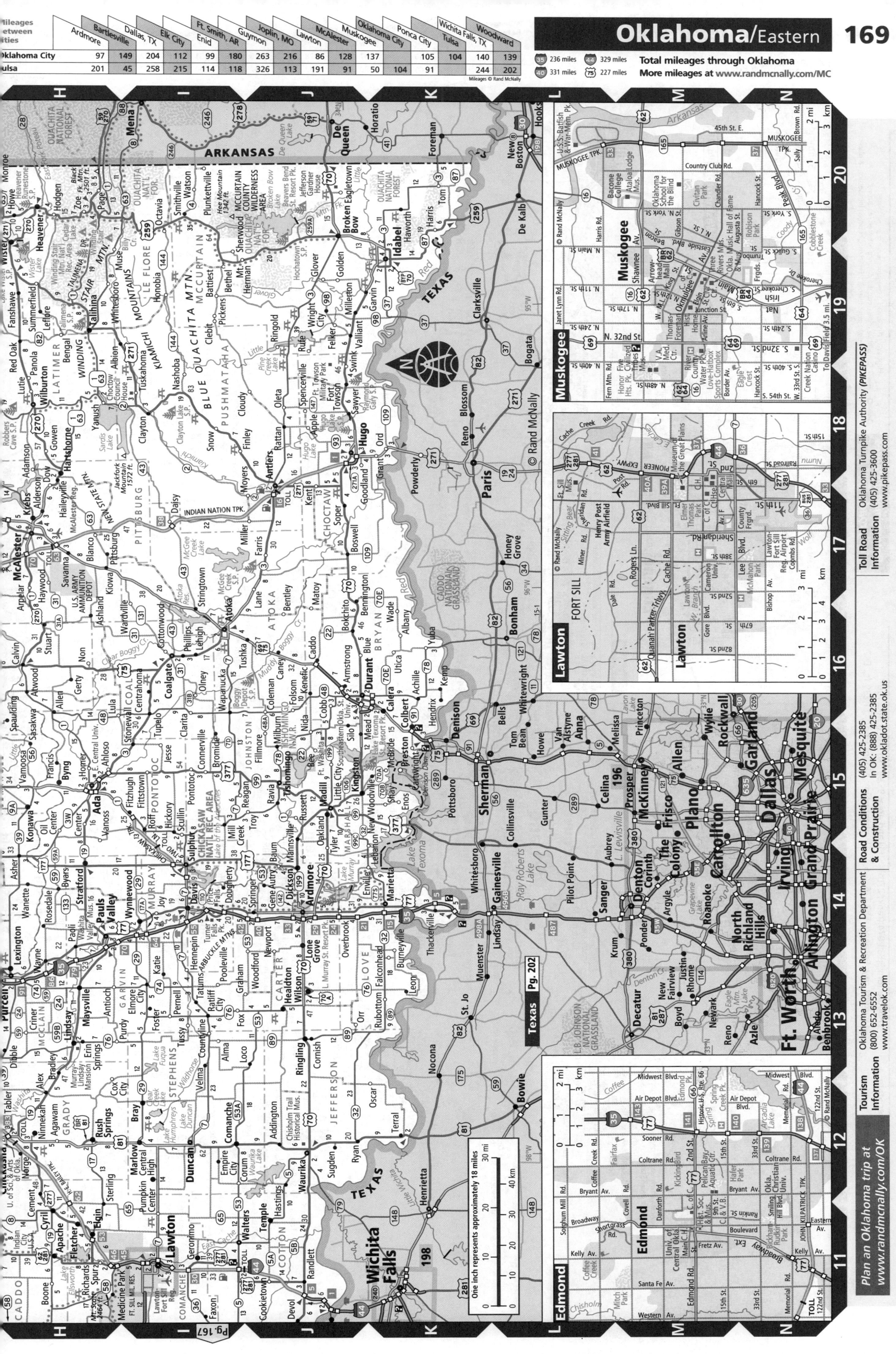

Pg.202 Texas

Muskogee

Lawton — FORT SILL

Edmond

One inch represents approximately 18 miles

Plan an Oklahoma trip at www.randmcnally.com/OK

Tourism Information — Oklahoma Tourism & Recreation Department (800) 652-6552 www.travelok.com

Road Conditions & Construction — Oklahoma Tourism & Recreation Department (405) 425-2385 In OK: (888) 425-2385 www.okladot.state.ok.us

Toll Road Information — Oklahoma Turnpike Authority (PIKEPASS) (405) 425-3600 www.pikepass.com

Index of cities **Pg. 256**

Mileages between cities

	Astoria	Bend	Brookings	Burns	Coos Bay	Crater Lake N.P.	Eugene	Gov't Camp	John Day	Lakeview	Medford	Ontario	Pendleton	Portland	Salem	The Dalles
Bend	250		287	130	228	107	115	106	151	175	172	260	242	161	131	129
Corvallis	166	127	280	257	132	187	47	126	260	284	210	387	290	82	37	165

Mileages © Rand McNally

Oregon state facts

Nickname: The Beaver State
Capital: Salem, E-4

Population: 3,831,074 (rank: 27th)
Largest city: Portland, 583,776, C-5

Land area: 95,997 sq. mi. (rank: 10th)
Highest point: Mount Hood, 11,239 ft., D-7

Determining distances along roads

Washington Pg. 218

Springfield

Eugene

© Rand McNally

Mileages between cities

	Astoria	Bend	Brookings	Burns	Coos Bay	Crater Lake N.P.	Eugene	Gov't Camp	John Day	Lakeview	Medford	Ontario	Pendleton	Portland	Salem	The Dalles
Eugene	193	115	234	245	109	142		154	249	241	166	375	318	110	66	193
McDermitt, NV	525	277	525	147	505	356	392	380	218	222	400	187	354	436	408	405

continued p. 172

Mileages © Rand McNally

Total mileages through Oregon
More mileages at www.randmcnally.com/MC

5 – 308 miles   84 – 375 miles
82 – 11 miles   101 – 348 miles

Get more Oregon info at
www.randmcnally.com/OR

Tourism Information — Travel Oregon (800) 547-7842 www.traveloregon.com

California Information — Pg. 26

Road Conditions & Construction — 511 (800) 977-6368, (503) 588-2941 www.oregon.gov/odot, www.tripcheck.com

Toll Road Information — 511 www.tripcheck.com   No toll roads

© Rand McNally

Mileages between cities	Astoria	Bend	Brookings	Burns	Coos Bay	Crater Lake N.P.	Eugene	Gov't Camp	John Day	Lakeview	Medford	Ontario	Pendleton	Portland	Salem	The Dalles
Medford	356	172	125	305	169	74	166	317	328	171		432	481	273	228	356
Ontario	464	260	547	130	488	367	375	354	131	269	432		167	374	420	291

Mileages © Rand McNally

Oregon state facts

Nickname: The Beaver State
Capital: Salem, E-4
Population: 3,831,074 (rank: 27th)
Largest city: Portland, 583,776, C-5
Land area: 95,997 sq. mi. (rank: 10th)
Highest point: Mount Hood, 11,239 ft., D-7

Interchanges and exit numbers
For most states, the mileage between interchanges may be determined by subtracting one number from the other.

Determining distances along roads

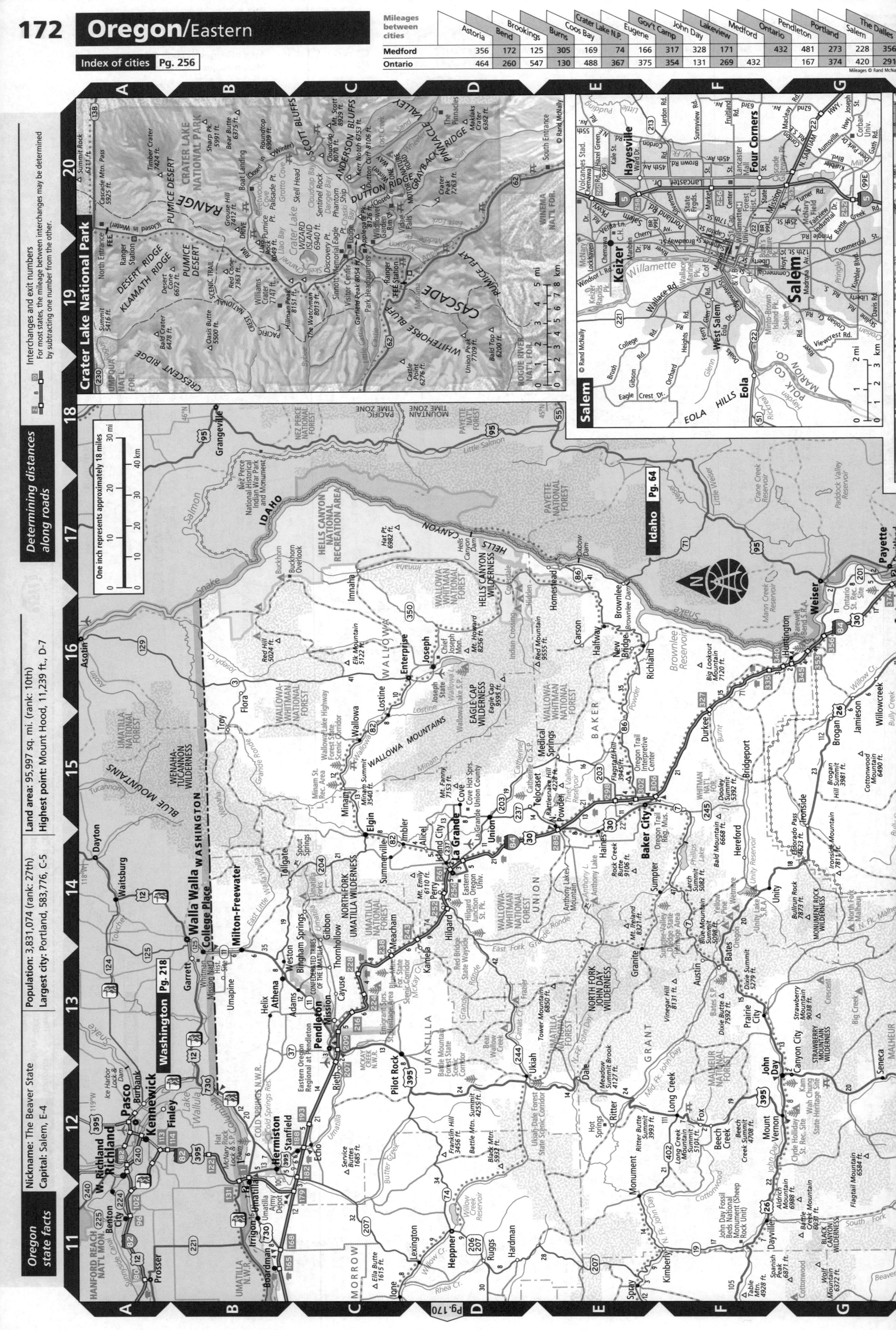

Washington Pg. 218

Idaho Pg. 64

Pg. 170

Mileages between cities

	Astoria	Bend	Brookings	Burns	Coos Bay	Crater Lake N.P.	Eugene	Gov't Camp	John Day	Lakeview	Medford	Ontario	Pendleton	Portland	Salem	The Dalles
Pendleton	298	242	550	196	428	349	318	188	126	335	481	167		208	254	125
Portland	96	161	342	281	220	250	110	55	265	336	273	374	208		47	83

Mileages © Rand McNally

5	308 miles	84	375 miles
82	11 miles	101	348 miles

Total mileages through Oregon
More mileages at www.randmcnally.com/MC

Central Portland

Portland & Vicinity

© Rand McNally

IDAHO

NEVADA

511

Get more Oregon info at www.randmcnally.com/OR

Tourism Information	Travel Oregon (800) 547-7842 www.traveloregon.com
Road Conditions & Construction	511 (800) 977-6368, (503) 588-2941 www.oregon.gov/odot, www.tripcheck.com
Toll Road Information	No toll roads

Nevada Pg. 130

Fort McDermitt Paiute and Shoshone Tribes

© Rand McNally

Pg. 171

Mileages between cities	Altoona	Chambersburg	Cumberland, MD	Du Bois	Erie	Galeton	Harrisburg	Johnstown	Kittanning	Meadville	New Castle	Philadelphia	Pittsburgh	State College	Uniontown	Warren
Altoona		90	66	71	202	135	134	46	79	165	127	234	96	41	112	130
Chambersburg	90		87	153	282	215	54	94	160	246	206	157	160	101	160	218

Mileages © Rand McN

Mileages between cities	Altoona	Chambersburg	Cumberland, MD	Du Bois	Erie	Galeton	Harrisburg	Johnstown	Kittanning	Meadville	New Castle	Philadelphia	Pittsburgh	State College	Uniontown	Warren
Erie	202	282	232	148		159	297	177	123	41	88	419	127	208	184	66
Johnstown	46	94	70	77	177	179	137		53	141	102	238	67	85	80	135

continued p. 176

Mileages © Rand McNally

70 168 miles **79** 183 miles — Total mileages through Pennsylvania
80 311 miles **90** 46 miles — More mileages at www.randmcnally.com/MC

Toll Road Information — Delaware River Port Authority (Philadelphia area bridges) (E-ZPass): (877) 567-3772; www.drpa.org — Pennsylvania Turnpike Commission (E-ZPass): (800) 331-3414; www.paturnpike.com

Road Conditions & Construction — 511 (888) 783-6783, (717) 783-5186 www.dot.state.pa.us

Tourism Information — Pennsylvania Tourism Office (800) 847-4872 www.visitpa.com

Explore Pennsylvania at www.randmcnally.com/PA

© Rand McNally

Mileages between cities	Altoona	Chambersburg, MD	Cumberland, MD	Du Bois	Erie	Galeton	Harrisburg	Johnstown	Kittanning	Meadville	New Castle	Philadelphia	Pittsburgh	State College	Uniontown	Warren
New Castle	127	206	156	110	88	197	250	102	48	52		350	52	171	108	120
Pittsburgh	96	160	111	101	127	200	203	67	42	91	52	304		135	51	148

Mileages © Rand McNally

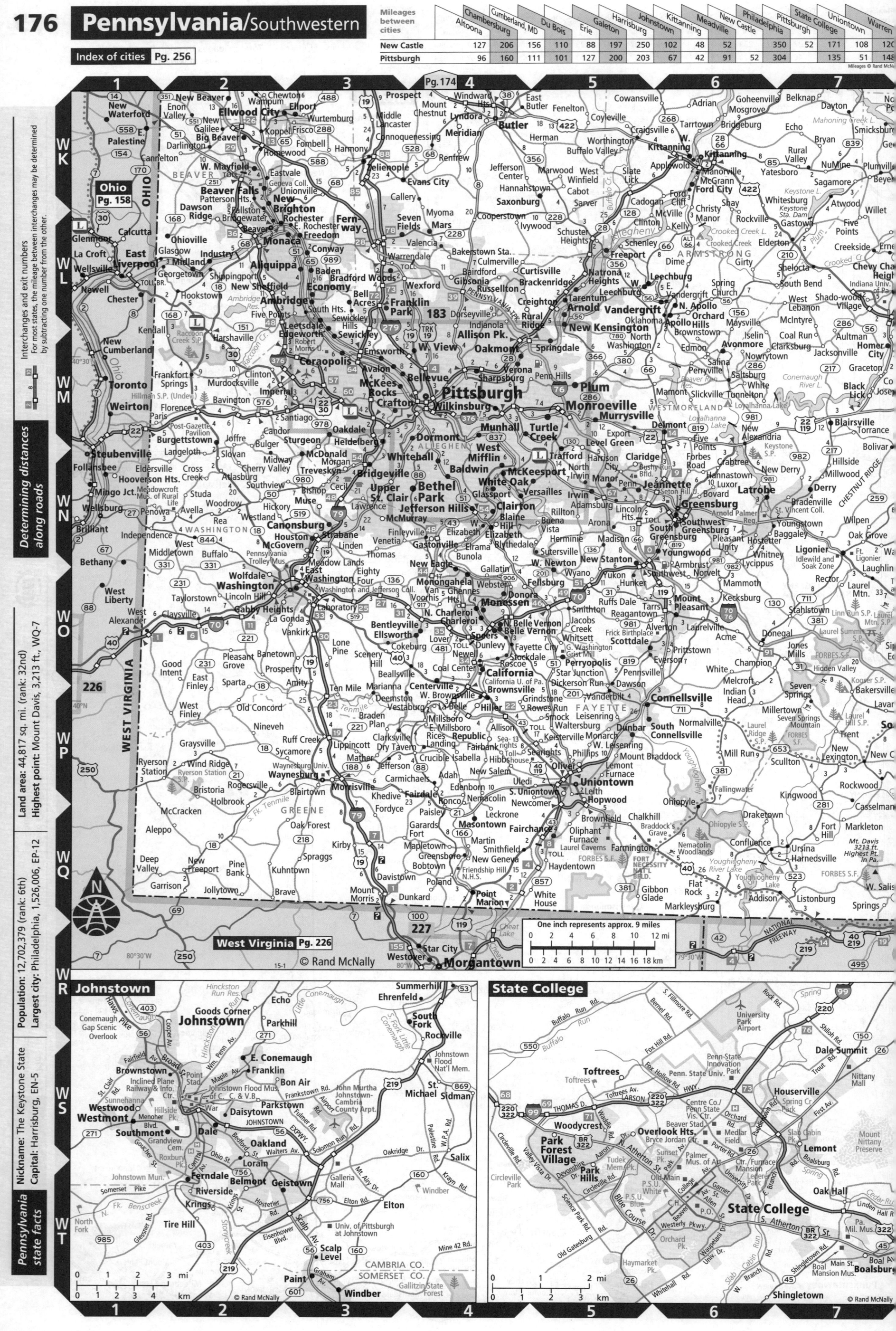

Pennsylvania state facts

Nickname: The Keystone State
Capital: Harrisburg, EN-5

Population: 12,702,379 (rank: 6th)
Largest city: Philadelphia, 1,526,006, EP-12

Land area: 44,817 sq. mi. (rank: 32nd)
Highest point: Mount Davis, 3,213 ft., WQ-7

Determining distances along roads

Interchanges and exit numbers. For most states, the mileage between interchanges may be determined by subtracting one number from the other.

Ohio Pg. 158

West Virginia Pg. 226

© Rand McNally

One inch represents approx. 9 mi.

Johnstown

State College

Mileages between Cities	Altoona	Chambersburg	Cumberland, MD	Du Bois	Erie	Galeton	Harrisburg	Johnstown	Kittanning	Meadville	New Castle	Philadelphia	Pittsburgh	State College	Uniontown	Warren
State College	41	101	106	61	208	100	87	85	120	173	171	193	135		152	119
Williamsport	100	132	166	110	257	72	83	146	168	220	219	176	196	63	212	171

Mileages by Rand McNally

Pennsylvania/Southwestern regional road map, including inset maps of "Gettysburg / Gettysburg National Military Park" and "York".

Toll Road Information: Delaware River Port Authority (Philadelphia area bridges) (E-ZPass): (877) 567-3772; www.drpa.org — Pennsylvania Turnpike Commission (E-ZPass): (800) 331-3414; www.paturnpike.com

Road Conditions & Construction: 511 (888) 783-6783, (717) 783-5186; www.dot.state.pa.us

Tourism Information: Pennsylvania Tourism Office (800) 847-4872; www.visitpa.com

Explore Pennsylvania at www.randmcnally.com/PA

© Rand McNally

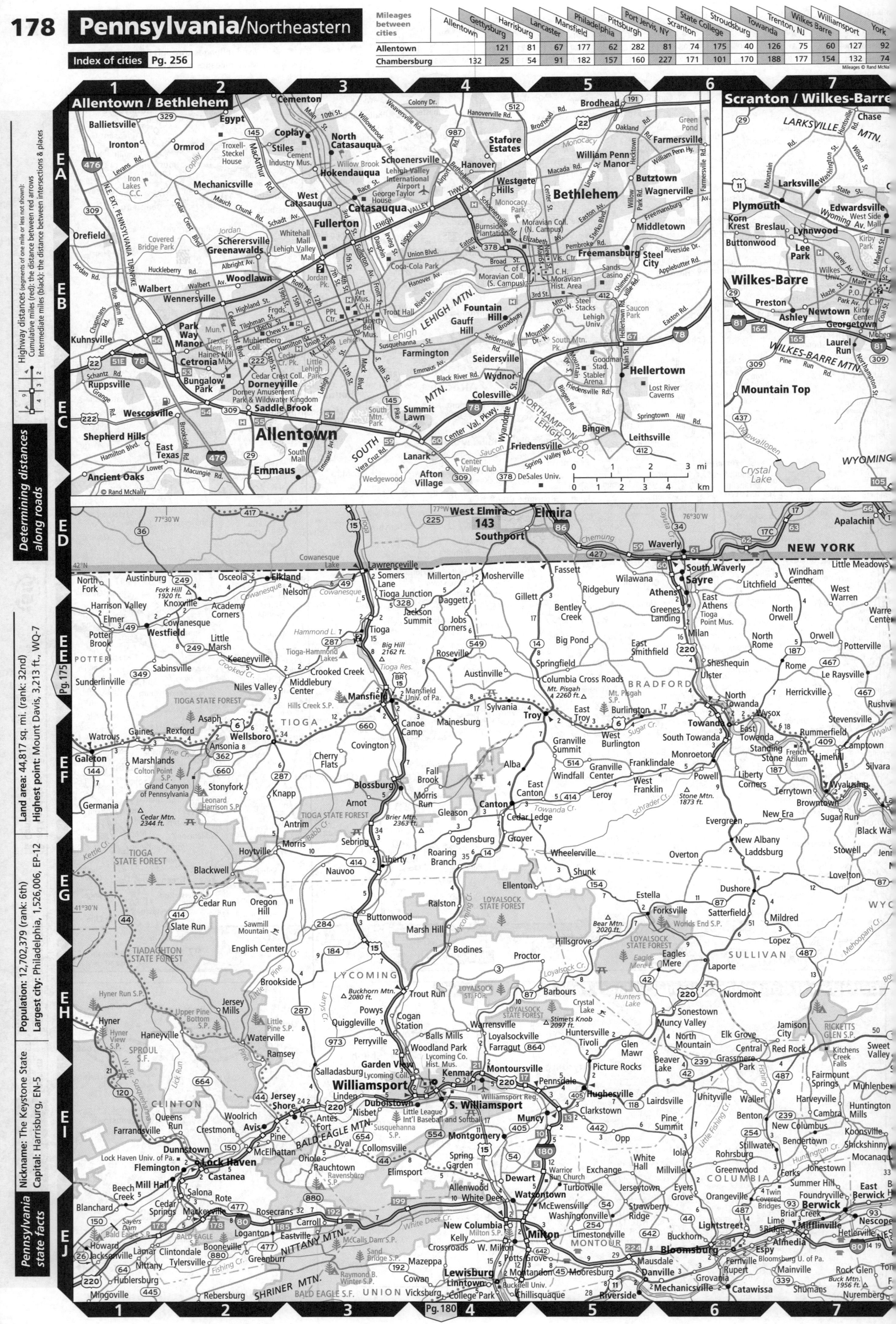

Mileages between cities	Allentown	Gettysburg	Harrisburg	Lancaster	Mansfield	Philadelphia	Pittsburgh	Port Jervis, NY	Scranton	State College	Stroudsburg	Towanda	Trenton, NJ	Wilkes Barre	Williamsport	York
Allentown		121	81	67	177	62	282	81	74	175	40	126	75	60	127	92
Chambersburg	132	25	54	91	182	157	160	227	171	101	170	188	177	154	132	74

Mileages © Rand McNa

Pennsylvania state facts

Nickname: The Keystone State
Capital: Harrisburg, EN-5
Largest city: Philadelphia, EN-5
Highest point: Mount Davis, 3,213 ft., WQ-7
Land area: 44,817 sq. mi. (rank: 32nd)
Population: 12,702,379 (rank: 6th)

Determining distances along roads

Highway distances (segments of one mile or less not shown); Cumulative miles (red); the distance between red arrows; Intermediate miles (black); the distance between intersections & places

Mileages between Cities	Allentown	Gettysburg	Harrisburg	Lancaster	Mansfield	Philadelphia	Pittsburgh	Port Jervis, NY	Scranton	State College	Stroudsburg	Towanda	Trenton, NJ	Wilkes Barre	Williamsport	continued p. 180 York
Harrisburg	81	38		39	133	107	203	176	120	87	119	139	127	104	83	26
Philadelphia	62	138	107		78	226		304	140	124	193	100	175	32	109	176	101

Mileages © Rand McNally

76 350 miles	81 232 miles
80 311 miles	95 51 miles

Total mileages through Pennsylvania
More mileages at www.randmcnally.com/MC

© Rand McNally

One inch represents approx. 9 miles

New York Pg. 140
New Jersey Pg. 134
Pg. 181

Toll Road Information — Delaware River Port Authority (Philadelphia area bridges) (E-ZPass): (877) 567-3772; www.drpa.org — Pennsylvania Turnpike Commission (E-ZPass): (800) 331-3414; www.paturnpike.com

Road Conditions & Construction — 511 (888) 783-6783, (717) 783-5186 www.dot.state.pa.us

Tourism Information — Pennsylvania Tourism Office (800) 847-4872 www.visitpa.com

Explore Pennsylvania at www.randmcnally.com/PA

Mileages between cities	Allentown	Gettysburg	Harrisburg	Lancaster	Mansfield	Philadelphia	Pittsburgh	Port Jervis, NY	Scranton	State College	Stroudsburg	Towanda	Trenton, NJ	Wilkes Barre	Williamsport	York
Reading	37	96	64	34	175	62	261	118	100	150	76	152	82	86	126	56
Scranton	74	160	120	132	102	124	279	59		150	46	64	137	16	101	146

Mileages © Rand McNally

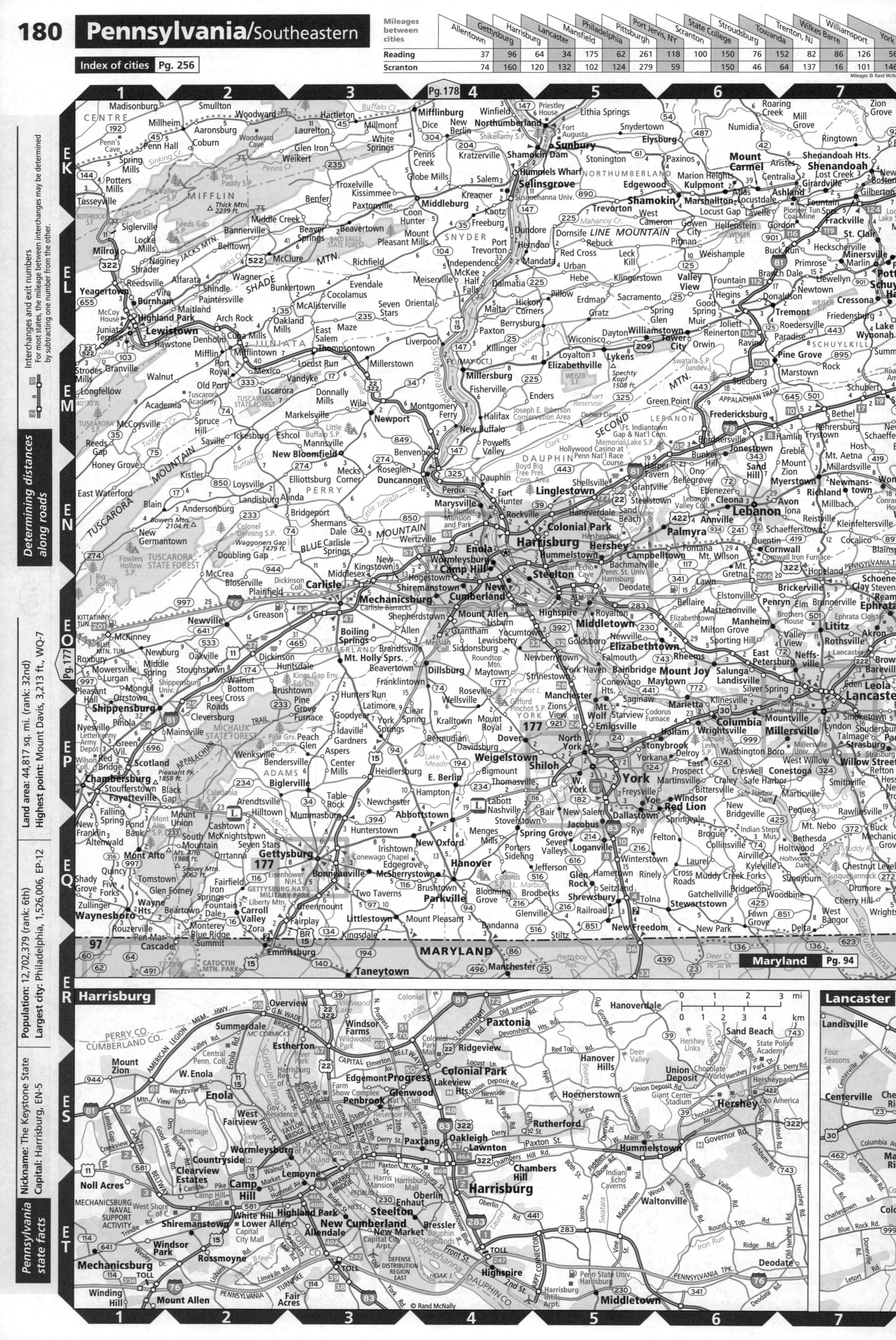

Pennsylvania state facts

Nickname: The Keystone State
Capital: Harrisburg, EN-5

Population: 12,702,379 (rank: 6th)
Largest city: Philadelphia, 1,526,006, EP-12

Land area: 44,817 sq. mi. (rank: 32nd)
Highest point: Mount Davis, 3,213 ft., WQ-7

Determining distances along roads

Interchanges and exit numbers
For most states, the mileage between interchanges may be determined by subtracting one number from the other.

Mileages between cities

	Allentown	Gettysburg	Harrisburg	Lancaster	Mansfield	Philadelphia	Pittsburgh	Port Jervis, NY	Scranton	State College	Stroudsburg	Towanda	Trenton, NJ	Wilkes Barre	Williamsport	York
State College	175	129	87	126	107	193	135	205	150		162	134	213	132	63	118
Williamsport	127	126	83	123	50	176	196	157	101	63	113	67	189	84		115

Mileages © Rand McNally

Total mileages through Pennsylvania

76	350 miles	81	232 miles
80	311 miles	95	51 miles

More mileages at www.randmcnally.com/MC

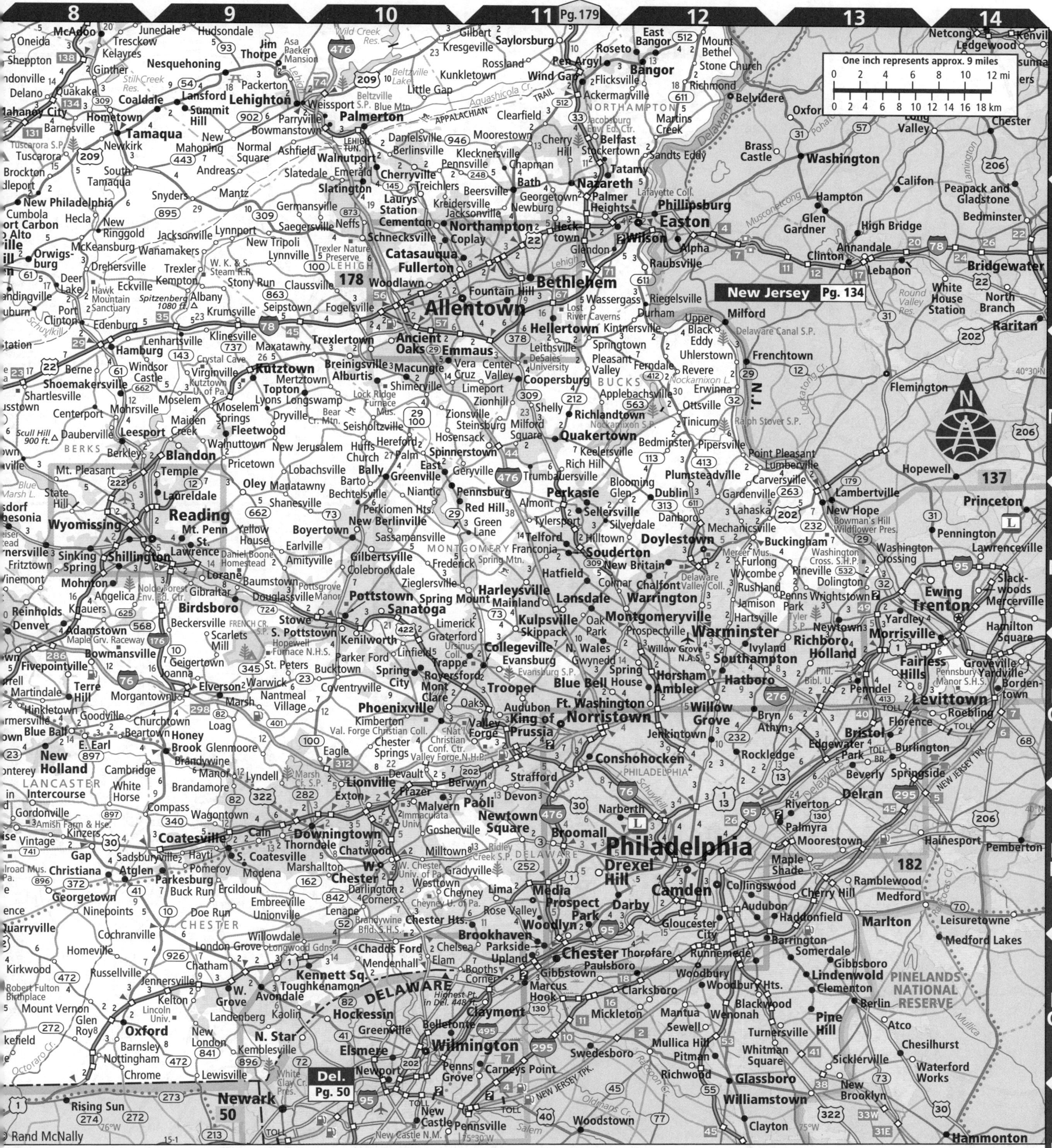

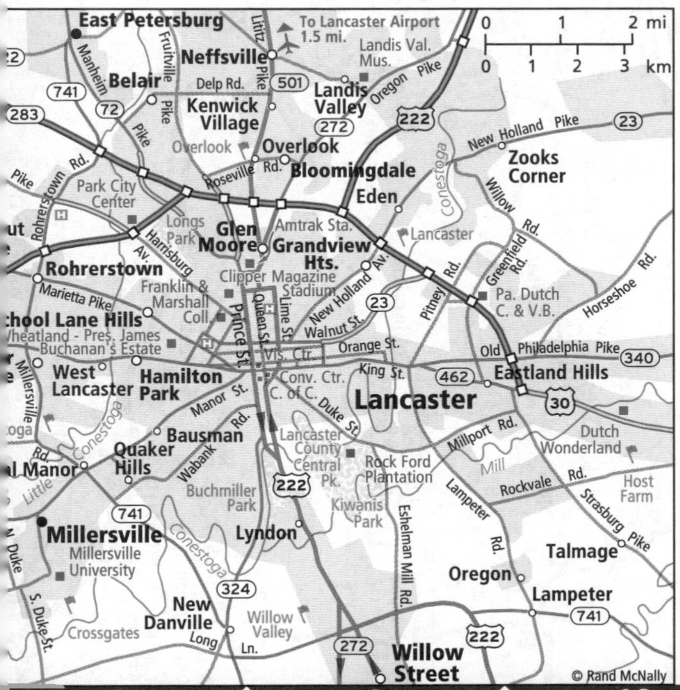

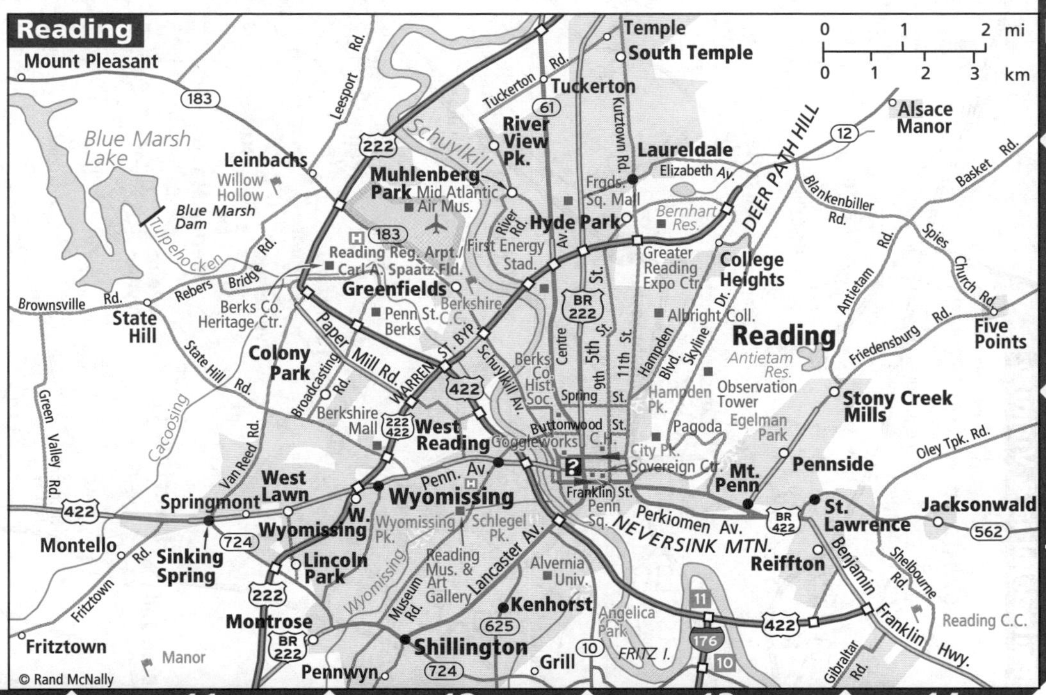

One inch represents approx. 9 miles
0 2 4 6 8 10 12 mi
0 2 4 6 8 10 12 14 16 18 km

City sights to see

- Adventure Aquarium, Camden, N.J., E-5
- The Andy Warhol Museum, Pittsburgh, L-2
- Betsy Ross House, Philadelphia, F-10
- Carnegie Science Center, Pittsburgh, L-1
- Duquesne & Monongahela Inclines, Pittsburgh, M-1 & N-2
- Franklin Institute Science Museum, Philadelphia, F-6

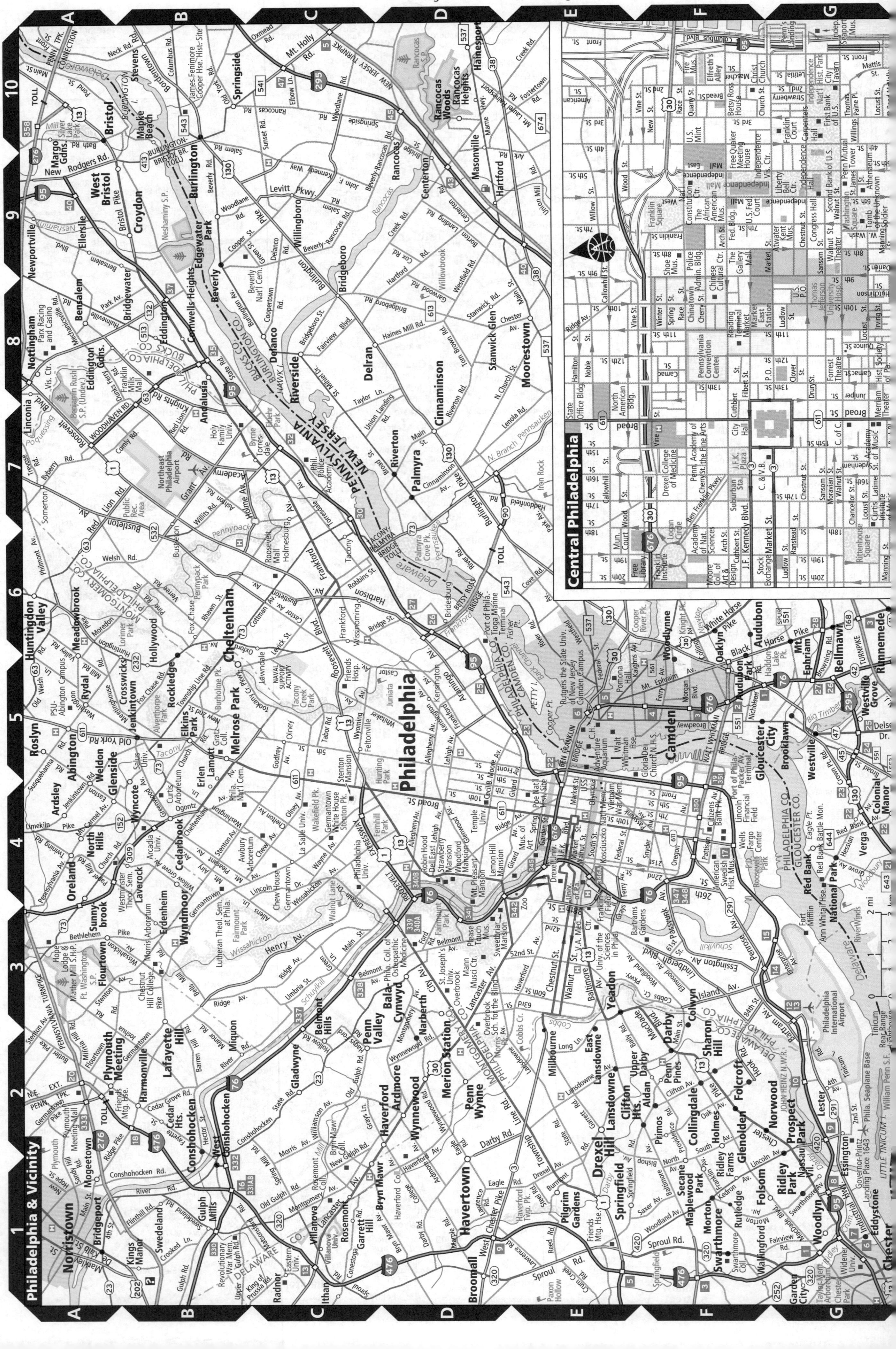

Philadelphia & Vicinity

Central Philadelphia

PENNSYLVANIA / NEW JERSEY

Philadelphia
Camden

- Independence Hall, Philadelphia, G-9
- Liberty Bell, Philadelphia, G-9
- National Constitution Center, Philadelphia, F-9
- Philadelphia Museum of Art, Philadelphia, E-4
- Point State Park, Pittsburgh, M-1
- The Strip District, Pittsburgh, L-3
- The U.S. Mint, Philadelphia, F-9
- USS *Olympia,* Philadelphia, E-5

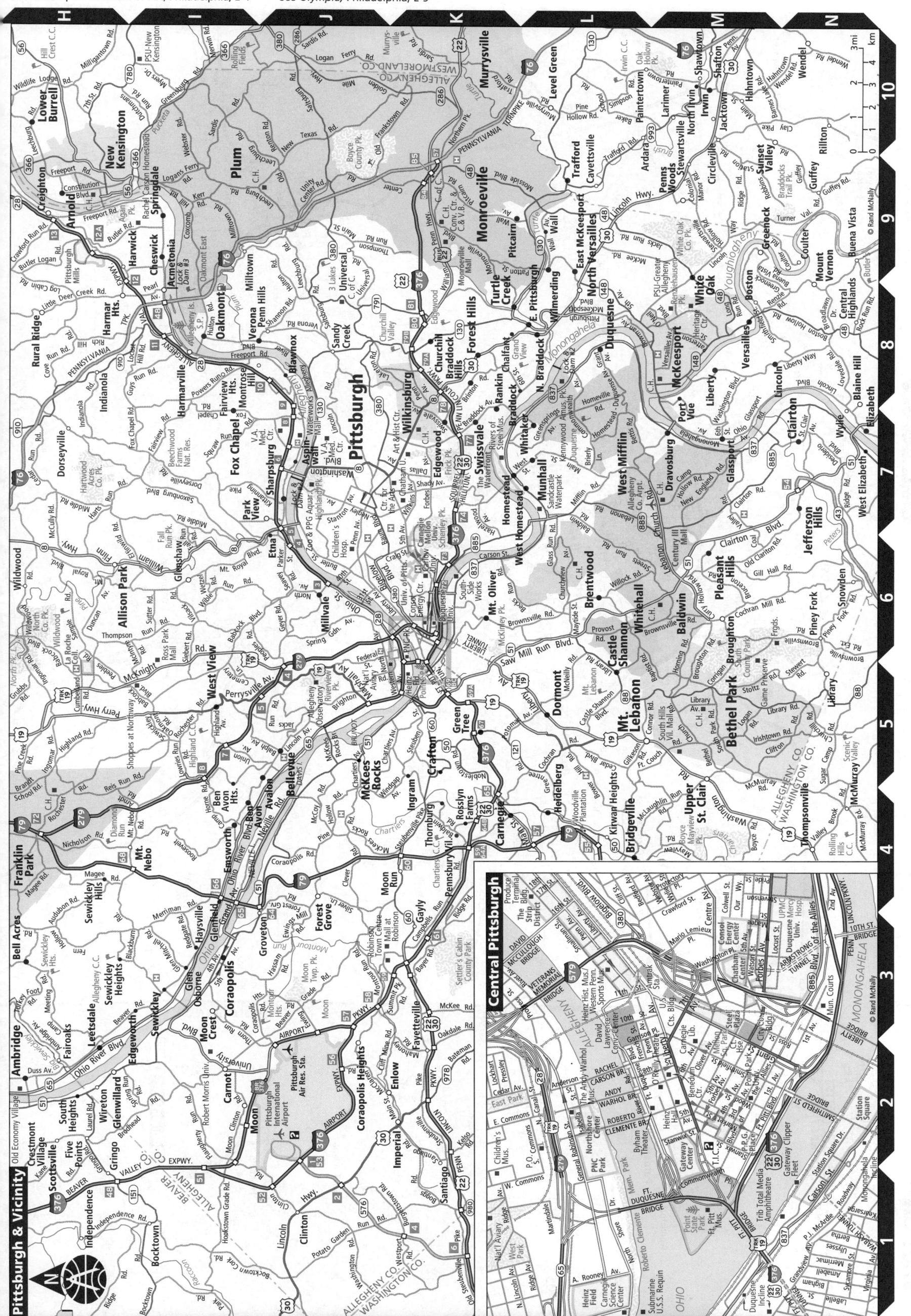

Pittsburgh & Vicinity

Central Pittsburgh

Mileages between cities	Fall River, MA	Kingston	Newport	Providence	Warwick	Westerly	Woonsocket, MA	Worcester, MA		Fall River, MA	Kingston	Newport	Providence	Warwick	Westerly	Woonsocket, MA	Worcester, MA
Chepachet	35	41	45	19	23	54	13	37	Newport	20	16		33	26	39	47	72
Fall River, MA		35	20	16	25	58	31	56	Providence	16	29	33		10	42	14	40

Mileages © Rand McNally

Rhode Island state facts

Nickname: The Ocean State
Capital: Providence, D-6

Population: 1,052,567 (rank: 43rd)
Largest city: Providence, 178,042, D-6

Land area: 1,045 sq. mi. (rank: 50th)
Highest point: Jerimoth Hill, 812 ft., C-3

Determining distances along roads

Interchanges and exit numbers
For most states, the mileage between interchanges may be determined by subtracting one number from the other.

Massachusetts Pg. 98

Connecticut Pg. 48

Total mileages through Rhode Island

95 = 42 miles   6 = 31 miles
1 = 60 miles

More mileages at www.randmcnally.com/MC

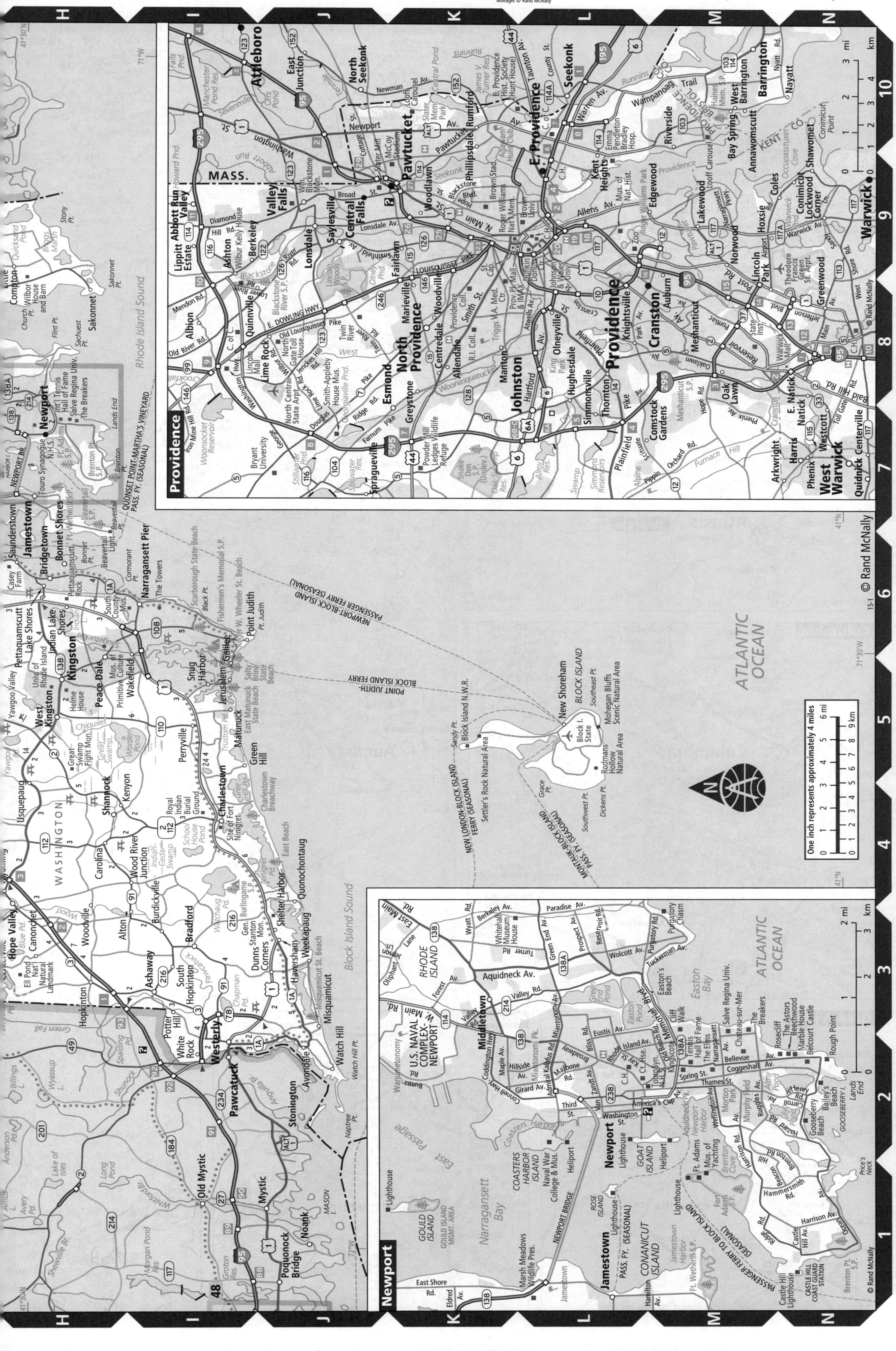

Mileages © Rand McNally

Mileages between cities	Fall River, MA	Kingston	Newport	Providence	Warwick	Westerly	Woonsocket	Worcester, MA
Warwick	25	23	26	10		37	24	50
Westerly	58	23	39	42	37		56	82
Woonsocket	31	43	47	14	24	56		27
Worcester, MA	56	68	72	40	50	82	27	

Plan a Rhode Island trip at www.randmcnally.com/RI

Tourism Information — Rhode Island Tourism Division (800) 556-2484, (401) 278-9100 — www.visitrhodeisland.com

Road Conditions 511 & Construction (888) 401-4511, (401) 222-2450 — www.tmc.state.ri.us, www.dot.state.ri.us

Toll Road Information — R.I. Turnpike & Bridge Authority (E-ZPass) (877) 743-9727 — www.ritba.org

© Rand McNally

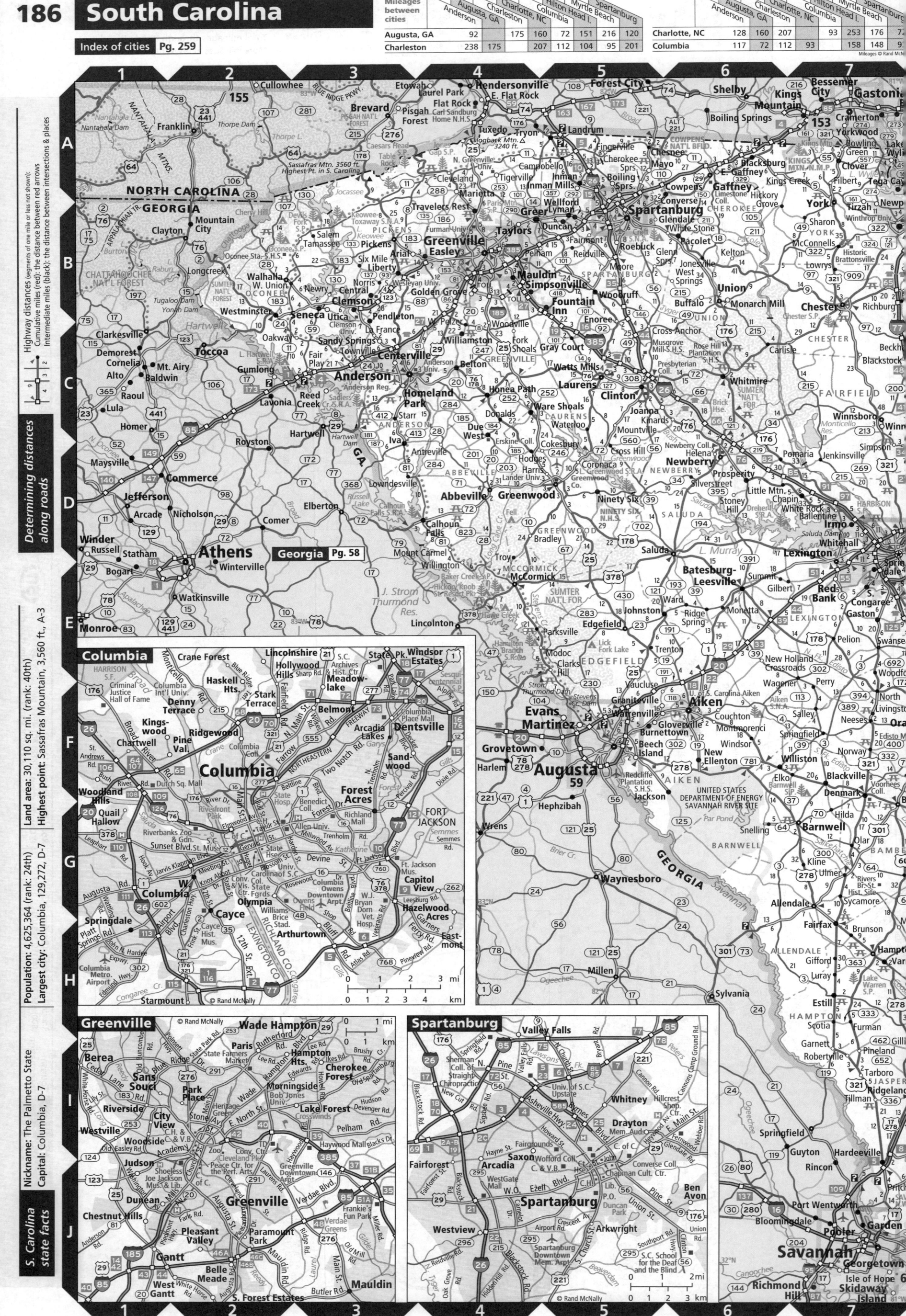

Mileages between cities	Anderson	Augusta, GA	Charleston	Charlotte, NC	Columbia	Hilton Head I.	Myrtle Beach	Spartanburg
Augusta, GA	92		175	160	72	151	216	120
Charleston	238	175		207	112	104	95	201
Charlotte, NC	128	160	207		93	253	176	74
Columbia	117	72	112	93		158	148	93

Mileages © Rand McNally

S. Carolina state facts

Nickname: The Palmetto State
Capital: Columbia, D-7
Population: 4,625,364 (rank: 24th)
Land area: 30,110 sq. mi. (rank: 40th)
Highest point: Sassafras Mountain, 3,560 ft., A-3
Largest city: Columbia, 129,272, D-7

Determining distances along roads

Highway distances (segments of one mile or less not shown):
Cumulative miles (red): the distance between red arrows
Intermediate miles (black): the distance between intersections & places

Mileages between cities

	Anderson	Augusta, GA	Charlotte, NC	Columbia	Hilton Head I.	Myrtle Beach	Spartanburg
Florence	206	148	130	104	81	177	67	169
Myrtle Beach	273	216	95	176	148	200		237

	Anderson	Augusta, GA	Charlotte, NC	Columbia	Hilton Head I.	Myrtle Beach	Spartanburg
Savannah, GA	282	134	106	251	156	34	202	246
Spartanburg	60	120	201	72	93	247	237	

Mileages © Rand McNally

Total mileages through South Carolina
More mileages at www.randmcnally.com/MC

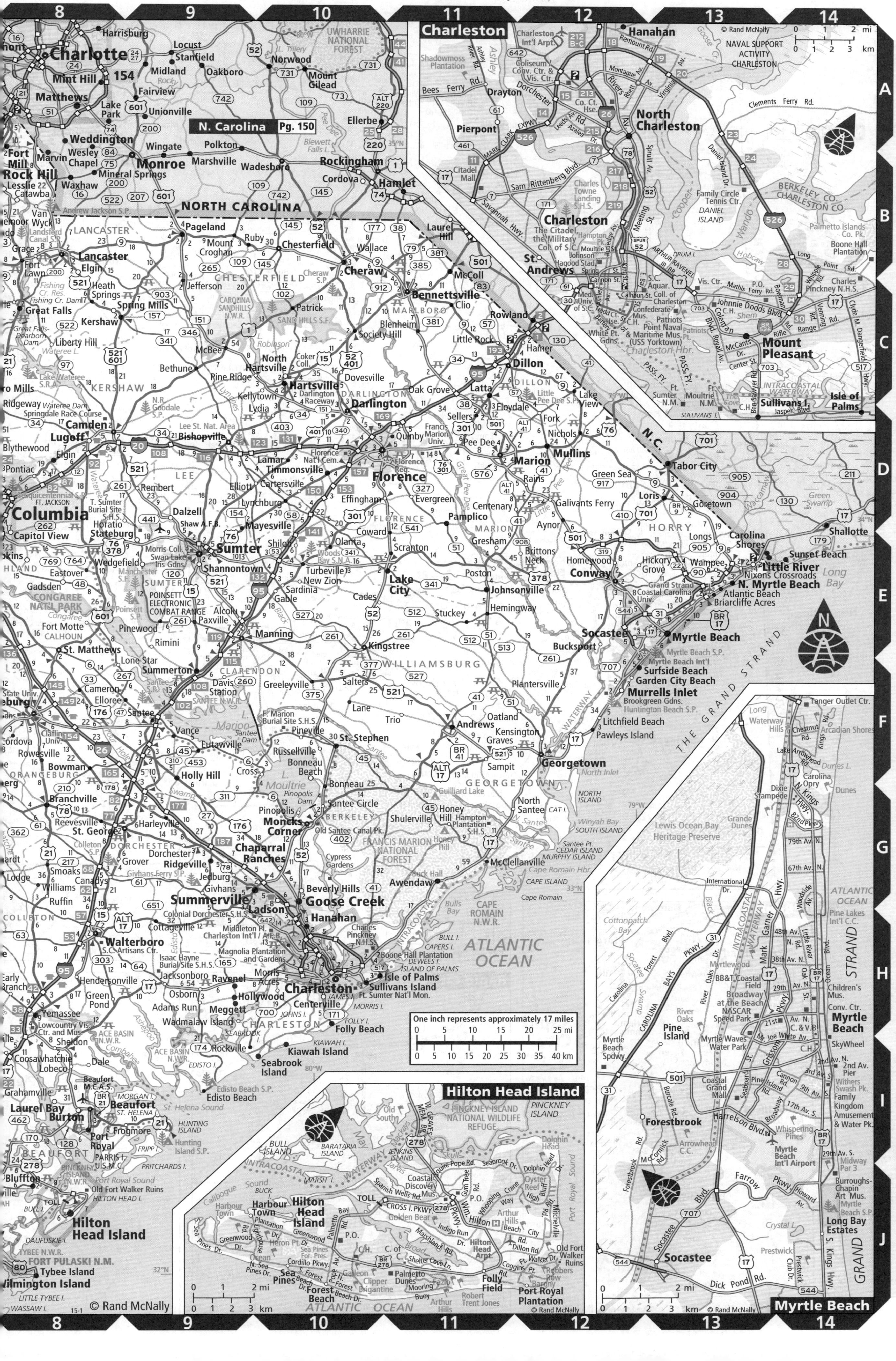

One inch represents approximately 17 miles

Hilton Head Island

Myrtle Beach

© Rand McNally

Index of cities Pg. 259

Mileages between cities	Aberdeen	Mobridge	Pierre	Pine Ridge	Rapid City	Sioux Falls	Watertown	Yankton		Aberdeen	Mobridge	Pierre	Pine Ridge	Rapid City	Sioux Falls	Watertown	Yankton
Aberdeen		100	160	360	333	203	96	236	Mobridge	100		108	308	243	303	196	33
Belle Fourche	312	212	206	172	60	403	362	421	Pierre	160	108		200	173	224	188	24

Mileages © Rand McNally

Montana Pg. 122

Wyo. Pg. 234

Nebraska Pg. 126

Black Hills Region

Rapid City

© Rand McNally

Pierre

© Rand McNally

One inch represents approx. 25 miles

S. Dakota state facts

Nickname: The Mount Rushmore State
Capital: Pierre, D-7

Population: 814,180 (rank: 46th)
Largest city: Sioux Falls, 153,888, F-13

Land area: 75,885 sq. mi. (rank: 16th)
Highest point: Harney Peak, 7,242 ft., E-2

Determining distances along roads

Interchanges and exit numbers
For most states, the mileage between interchanges may be determined by subtracting one number from the other.

Mileages between cities	Aberdeen	Mobridge	Pierre	Pine Ridge	Rapid City	Sioux Falls	Watertown	Yankton
Rapid City	333	243	173	111		347	403	365
Sioux City, IA	285	384	305	358	428	85	184	63

	Aberdeen	Mobridge	Pierre	Pine Ridge	Rapid City	Sioux Falls	Watertown	Yankton
Sioux Falls	203	303	224	356	347		103	81
Watertown	96	196	188	415	403	103		155

Mileages © Rand McNally

29 253 miles 12 317 miles
90 413 miles 83 242 miles

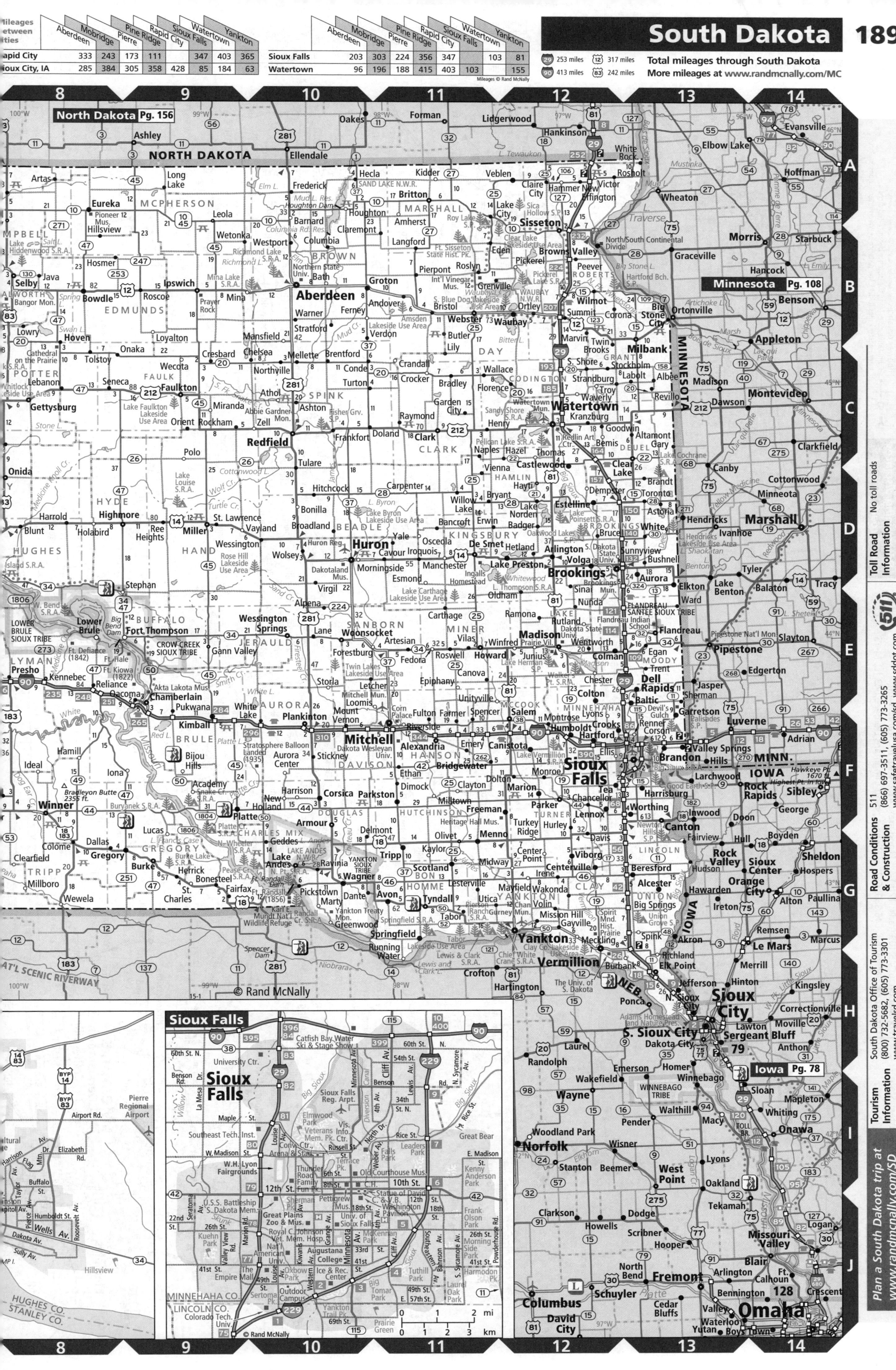

© Rand McNally

Mileages between cities	Atlanta, GA	Chattanooga	Bristol	Clarksville	Cookeville	Dyersburg	Fayetteville	Gatlinburg	Jackson	Johnson City	Knoxville	Memphis	Morristown	Nashville	Oak Ridge	Union City
Chattanooga	117		223	177	98	303	94	151	260	215	110	314	158	131	108	311
Clarksville	293	337		177	125	173	136	265	123	329	224	201	271	47	129	138

Mileages © Rand McNally

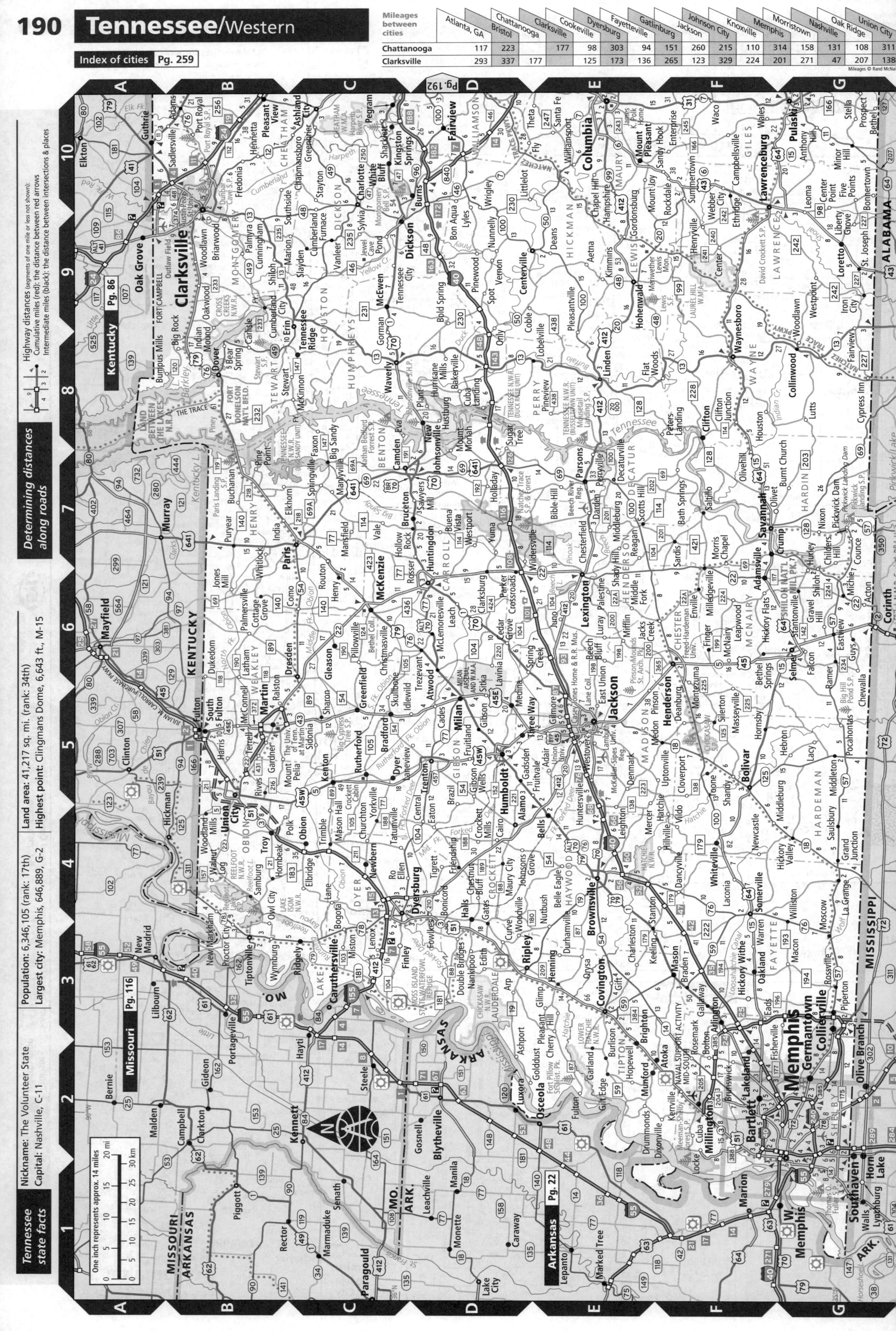

Mileages between cities	Atlanta, GA	Chattanooga Bristol	Clarksville	Cookeville	Dyersburg	Fayetteville	Gatlinburg Jackson	Johnson City	Knoxville	Memphis	Morristown	Nashville	Oak Ridge	Union City continued p. 192
Dyersburg	418	463	303	173	252		229	392	47	455	351	76	398	172	334	34
Fayetteville	211	317	94	136	109	229		246	167	308	204	243	252	90	189	224

Mileages © Rand McNally

Total mileages through Tennessee
More mileages at www.randmcnally.com/MC

| 40 455 miles | 75 161 miles |
| 65 121 miles | 81 76 miles |

Nashville

Memphis & Vicinity

Memphis

West Memphis

Bartlett

Germantown

Southaven

Olive Branch

Horn Lake

Brentwood

Belle Meade

Forest Hills

Oak Hill

Berry Hill

Hendersonville

Old Hickory

Madison

Goodlettsville

Lakewood

La Vergne

River Rest

Nolensville

Clarksville

Bordeaux

Florence

Sheffield

Tuscumbia

Muscle Shoals

Cherokee

Iuka

Holly Springs

Hernando

Coldwater

Ripley

North Tunica

Tunica

Alabama Pg. 10

Mississippi Pg. 114

© Rand McNally

Woodall Mtn. 806 ft. Highest Pt. in Mississippi

TENNESSEE

ARKANSAS

MISSISSIPPI

DAVIDSON CO.

WILLIAMSON CO.

SHELBY CO.

DESOTO CO.

CRITTENDEN CO.

SUMNER CO.

Cumberland

Explore Tennessee at
www.randmcnally.com/TN

Tourism Information — Tennessee Department of Tourist Development (615) 741-2159, www.tnvacation.com

Road Conditions & Construction — 511, (877) 244-0065, www.tn511.com, www.tdot.state.tn.us

Toll Road Information — No toll roads

Mileages between cities	Atlanta, GA	Bristol	Chattanooga	Clarksville	Cookeville	Dyersburg	Fayetteville	Gatlinburg	Jackson	Johnson City	Knoxville	Memphis	Morristown	Nashville	Oak Ridge	Union City
Johnson City	256	24	215	329	206	455	308	106	412		104	495	65	283	128	463
Knoxville	202	113	110	224	102	351	204	41	308	104		390	48	179	24	358

Mileages © Rand McNally

Tennessee state facts

Nickname: The Volunteer State
Capital: Nashville, C-11

Population: 6,346,105 (rank: 17th)
Largest city: Memphis, 646,889, G-2

Land area: 41,217 sq. mi. (rank: 34th)
Highest point: Clingmans Dome, 6,643 ft., M-15

Determining distances along roads

Interchanges and exit numbers
For most states, the mileage between interchanges may be determined by subtracting one number from the other.

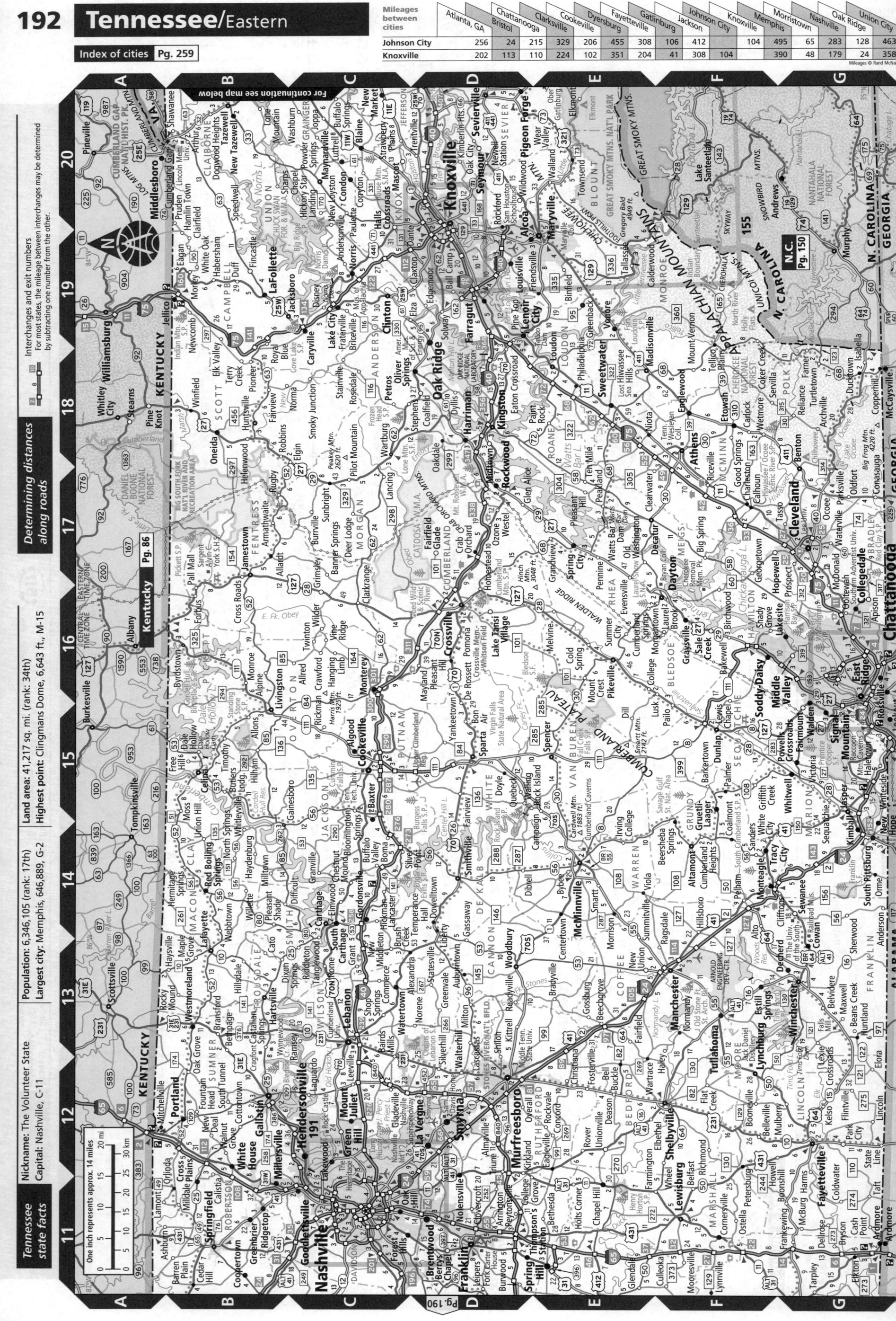

Mileages between cities	Atlanta, GA	Bristol	Chattanooga	Clarksville	Cookeville	Dyersburg	Fayetteville	Gatlinburg	Jackson	Johnson City	Knoxville	Memphis	Morristown	Nashville	Oak Ridge	Union City
Memphis	380	502	314	201	291	76	243	431	87	495	390		437	212	373	113
Nashville	249	292	131	47	80	172	90	220	129	283	179	212	226		162	168

Mileages © Rand McNally

Total mileages through Tennessee
More mileages at www.randmcnally.com/MC

| 40 | 455 miles | 75 | 161 miles |
| 65 | 121 miles | 81 | 76 miles |

Georgia Pg. 58
Alabama Pg. 10
Virginia Pg. 212
Ky. Pg. 86
North Carolina Pg. 150

Knoxville
Chattanooga

No toll roads
Toll Road Information

511
Road Conditions & Construction — 511 (877) 244-0065 www.tn511.com, www.tdot.state.tn.us
Tourism Information — Tennessee Department of Tourist Development (615) 741-2159 www.tnvacation.com
Explore Tennessee at www.randmcnally.com/TN

City sights to see

- Appalachian Caverns, Blountville, Tenn., K-3
- Battleship USS *Texas*, La Porte, D-9
- Bayou Place, Houston, K-8
- Bishop's Palace, Galveston, B-10
- Bristol Caverns, Bristol, Tenn., J-6
- Bristol Motor Speedway, Bristol, Tenn., K-4
- Contemporary Arts Museum, Houston, E-5
- Houston Fire Museum, Houston, E-5

Houston & Vicinity

Galveston

Gulf of Mexico

Texas City

Galveston Bay

Port Bolivar

Bayou Vista

Tiki Island

Cypress

Kohnville

Bammel

Westfield

Atascocita

Humble

Audobon Park

Rushwood

Fallbrook

North Houston

Jersey Vill.

Winchester Country

Concord Bridge

Cypress Meadow

Barker

Mission Bend

Four Corners

Pecan Grove

New Territory

Crabb

Sugar Land

Stafford

Missouri City

Fifth Street

Town West

Meadows Place

Oak Lake Estates

Greatwood

Aldine

Northline Terrace

Fairgreen

Greenwood Village

Beaumont Place

Houmont Park

Sheldon

Magnolia Gardens

Highlands

Channelview

Mont Belvieu

McNair

Barrett

Cloverleaf

Jacinto City

Galena Park

Pasadena

South Houston

Deer Park

La Porte

Baytown

Morgans Point

Shoreacres

Seabrook

Kemah

Nassau Bay

Webster

El Lago

Taylor Lake Village

Clear Lake Shores

Beach City

Cedar Point

Houston

West University Place

Southside Place

Bellaire

Hunters Creek Village

Hilshire Village

Spring Valley Vil.

Hedwig Village

Bunker Hill Village

Piney Point Village

Pearland

Brookside Village

Fresno

- Houston Zoo, Houston, E-5
- Minute Maid Park, L-9
- Moody Gardens, Galveston, B-9
- Museum of Natural Science, Houston, E-5
- Reliant Stadium, Houston, E-5
- Rocky Mount Museum, Piney Flats, Tenn., L-3
- Space Center Houston, Houston, G-8
- Wortham Theatre Center, Houston, K-8

City sights to see
- AT&T Stadium, Arlington, H-7
- Dallas Arts District, Dallas, B-2
- Dallas Museum of Art, Dallas, B-2
- Dallas Zoo, Dallas, H-10
- Fair Park (Cotton Bowl), Dallas, G-11
- Heard Natural Science Museum & Sanctuary, McKinney, B-13
- Old City Park, Dallas, C-3

Central Dallas

Central Fort Worth

© Rand McNally

0 1 2 3 4 5 mi
0 1 2 3 4 5 6 7 8 km

- Ripley's Believe It or Not! & Louis Tussaud's Palace of Wax, Grand Prairie, G-8
- The Sixth Floor Museum at Dealey Plaza, Dallas, B-1
- Stockyards Historic District, Fort Worth, G-4
- Sundance Square, Fort Worth, E-1
- Texas Civil War Museum, Fort Worth, G-2
- Will Rogers Memorial Center, Fort Worth, H-3

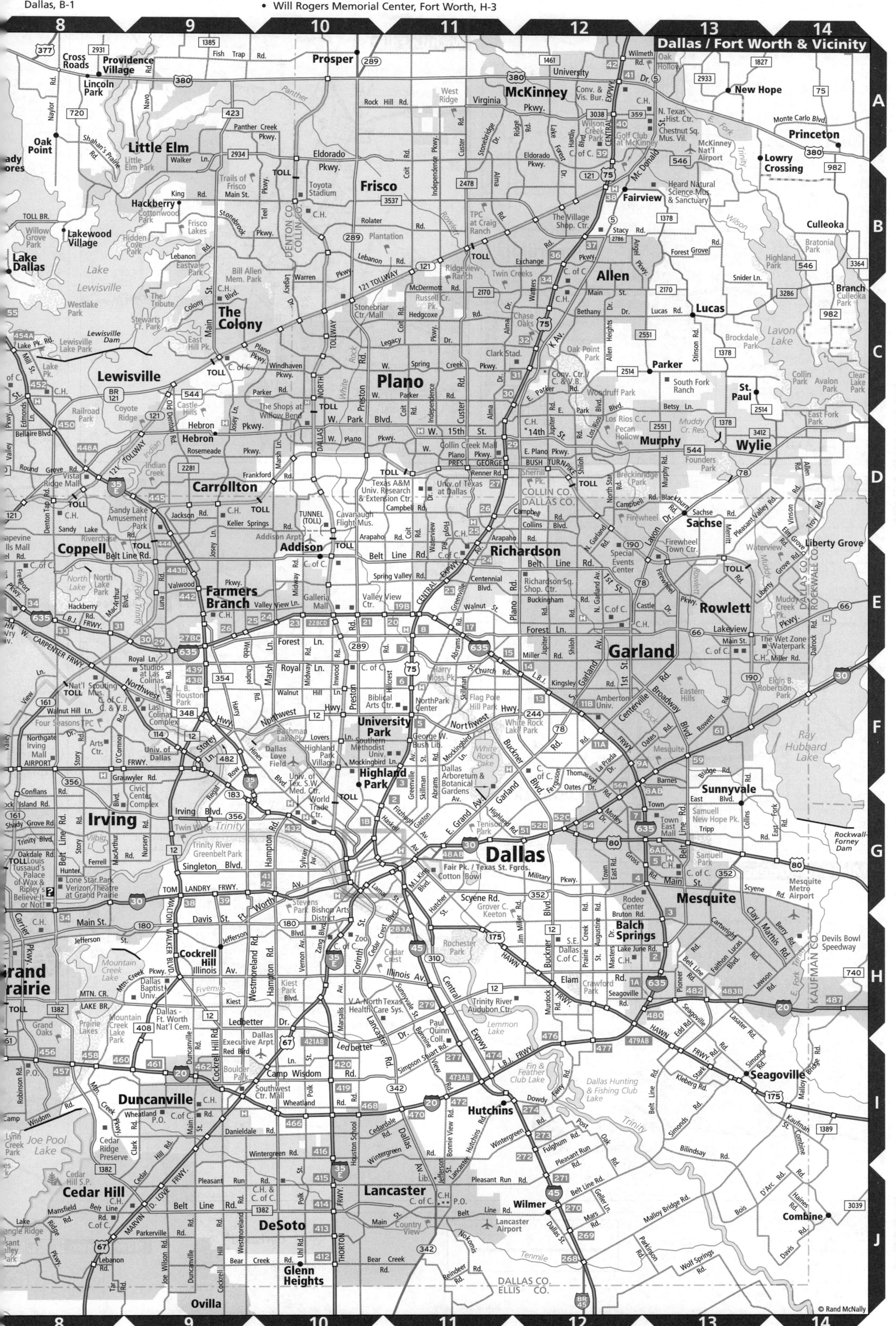

Dallas / Fort Worth & Vicinity

© Rand McNally

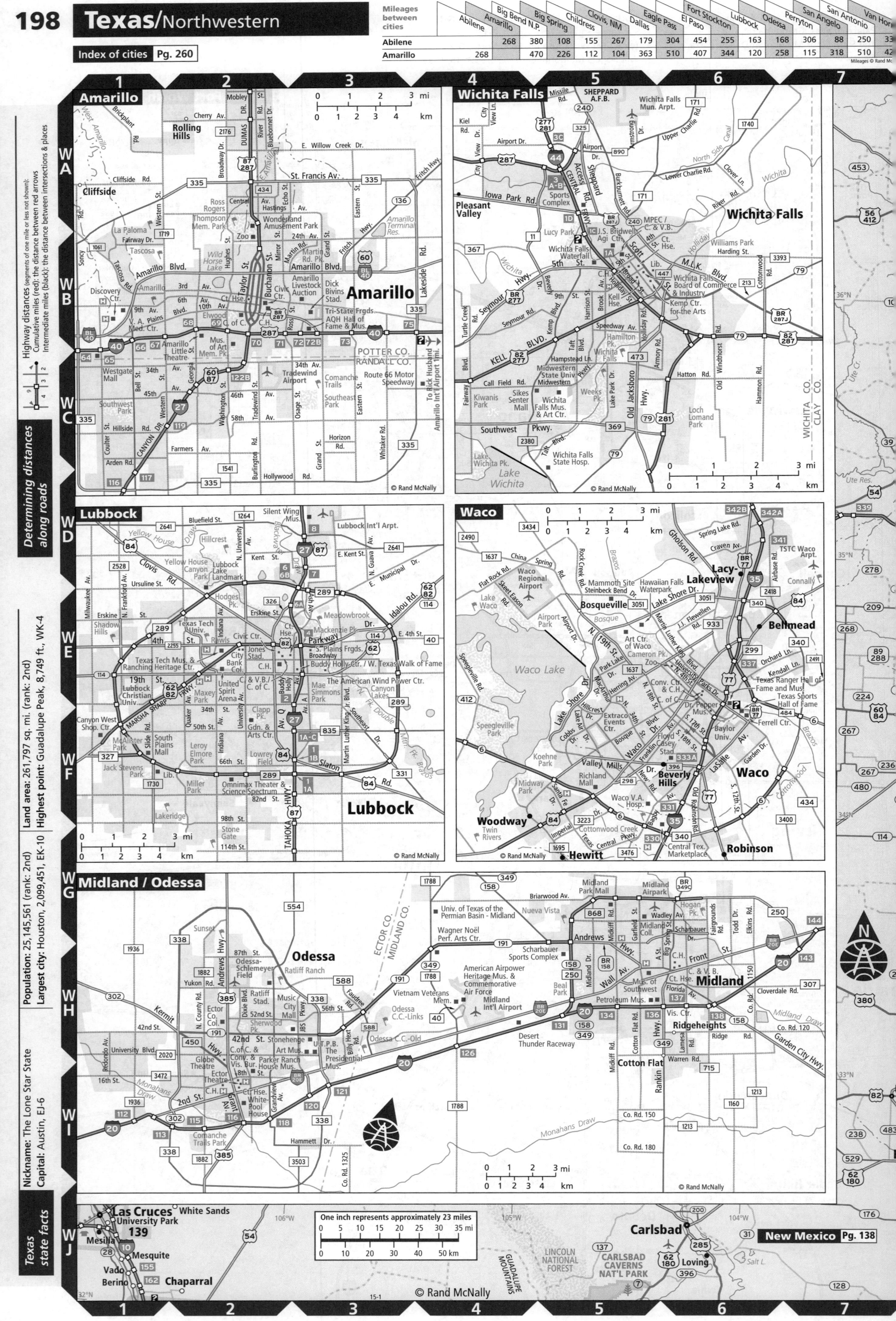

Mileages between cities	Abilene	Amarillo	Big Bend N.P.	Big Spring	Childress	Clovis, NM	Dallas	Eagle Pass	El Paso	Fort Stockton	Lubbock	Odessa	Perryton	San Angelo	San Antonio	Van Hor
Abilene		268	380	108	155	267	179	304	454	255	163	168	306	88	250	33
Amarillo	268		470	226	112	104	363	510	407	344	120	258	115	318	510	42

Mileages © Rand McN

Amarillo

Wichita Falls

Lubbock

Waco

Midland / Odessa

New Mexico Pg. 138

Texas state facts

Nickname: The Lone Star State

Capital: Austin, EJ-6

Largest city: Houston, 2,099,451, EK-10

Highest point: Guadalupe Peak, 8,749 ft., WK-4

Land area: 261,797 sq. mi. (rank: 2nd)

Population: 25,145,561 (rank: 2nd)

Determining distances along roads

Highway distances (segments of one mile or less not shown):
Cumulative miles (red): the distance between red arrows
Intermediate miles (black): the distance between intersections & places

Total mileages through Texas
10 881 miles   40 177 miles
20 636 miles
More mileages at www.randmcnally.com/MC

Mileages between cities	Abilene	Amarillo	Big Bend N.P.	Big Spring	Childress	Clovis, NM	Dallas	Eagle Pass	El Paso	Fort Stockton	Lubbock	Odessa	Perryton	San Angelo	San Antonio	Van Horn
Del Rio	241	454	242	240	383	425	426	56	428	184	333	258	534	154	151	303
El Paso	454	407	325	346	482	301	635	484		240	343	284	516	404	554	121

Mileages © Rand McNally

continued p. 200

Cameron Co. Regional Mobility Auth. (TX 550, Brownsville) (TxTag): (956) 982-5414; www.cameroncountyrma.org
Central Texas Regional Mobility Authority (TX 183A, Austin) (TxTag): (512) 996-9778; www.mobilityauthority.com

NOTE: list extends pp. 199-205

Toll Road Information

Road Conditions & Construction
(800) 452-9292, (512) 463-8588
www.txdot.gov
www.drivetexas.org/Full

Tourism Information
Texas Tourism
(800) 452-9292
www.traveltex.com

Explore Texas at www.randmcnally.com/TX

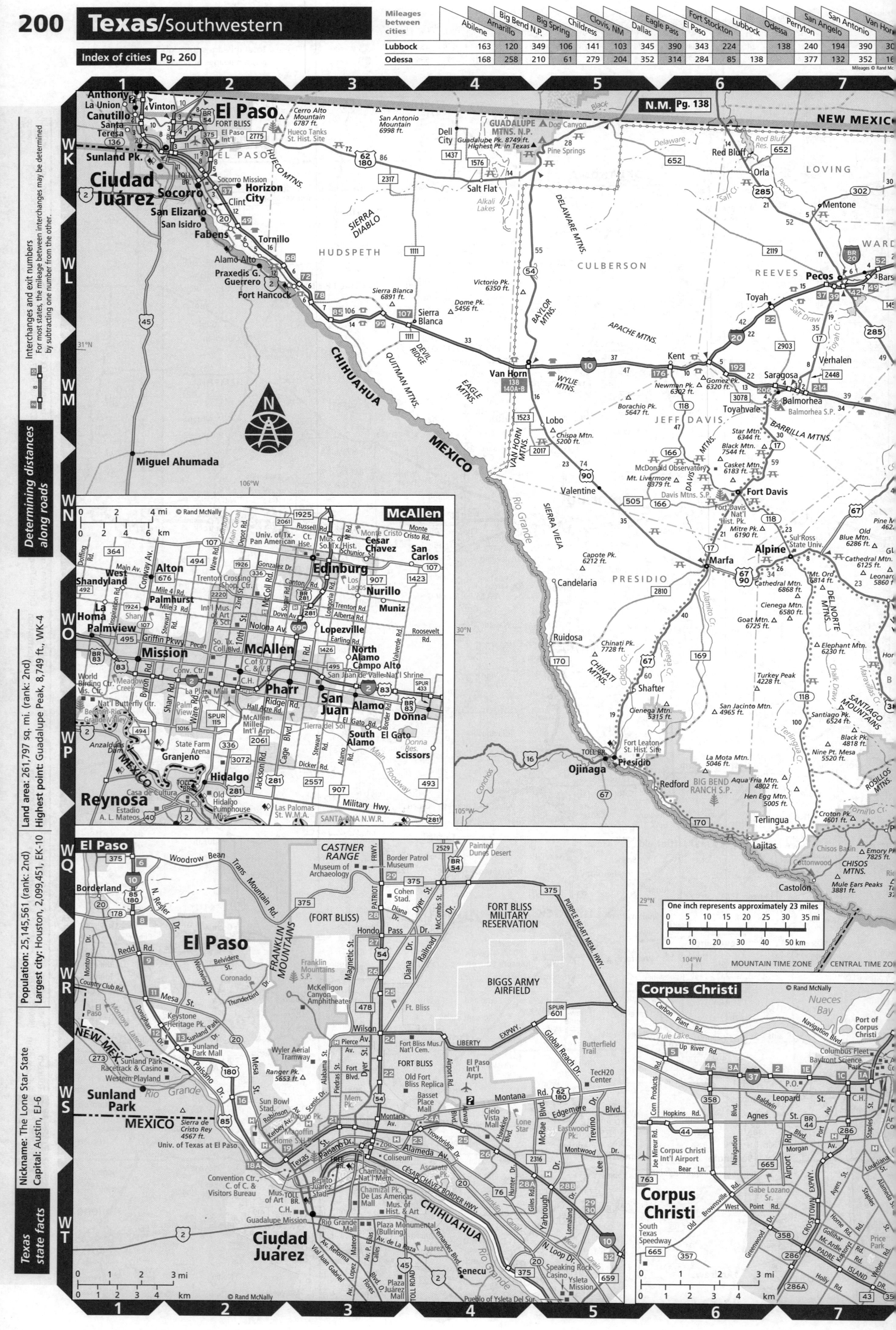

Mileages between cities

	Abilene	Amarillo	Big Bend N.P.	Big Spring	Childress	Clovis, NM	Dallas	Eagle Pass	El Paso	Fort Stockton	Lubbock	Odessa	Perryton	San Angelo	San Antonio	Van Horn
Lubbock	163	120	349	106	141	103	345	390	343	224		138	240	194	390	30
Odessa	168	258	210	61	279	204	352	314	284	85	138		377	132	352	16

Mileages © Rand Mc

Texas state facts

Nickname: The Lone Star State
Capital: Austin, EJ-6
Population: 25,145,561 (rank: 2nd)
Largest city: Houston, 2,099,451, EK-10
Land area: 261,797 sq. mi. (rank: 2nd)
Highest point: Guadalupe Peak, 8,749 ft., WK-4

Determining distances along roads

Interchanges and exit numbers
For most states, the mileage between interchanges may be determined by subtracting one number from the other.

McAllen

One inch represents approximately 23 miles
0 5 10 15 20 25 30 35 mi
0 10 20 30 40 50 km

El Paso

Corpus Christi

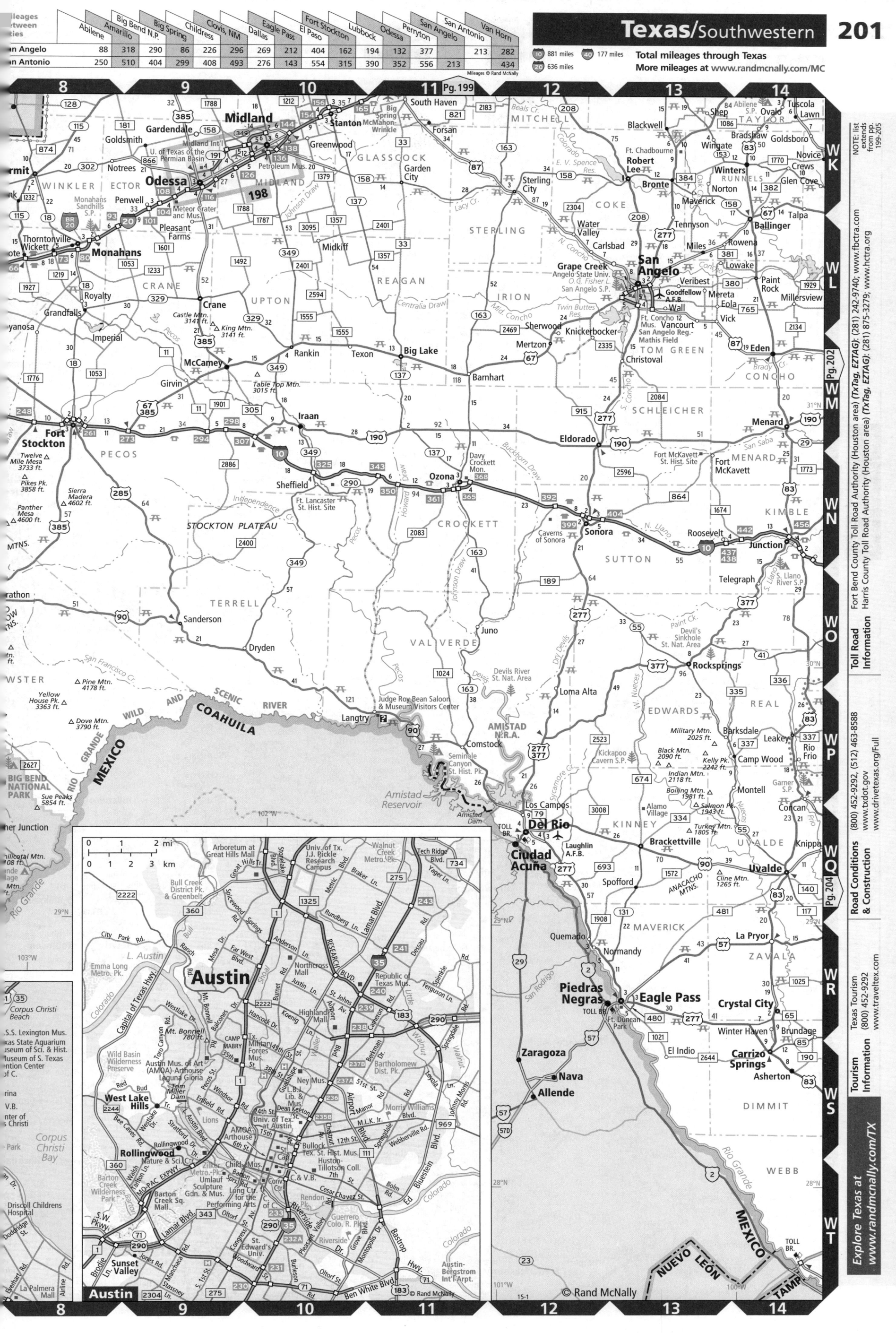

Mileages between cities	Abilene	Austin	Beaumont	Brownsville	Dallas	Houston	Laredo	Lufkin	Paris	San Angelo	San Antonio	Shreveport, LA	Texarkana	Tyler	Waco	Wichita Falls
Abilene		221	449	524	179	377	396	363	285	88	250	368	358	280	183	15
Austin	221		242	353	193	157	237	224	296	208	81	325	366	224	99	29

Mileages © Rand Mch

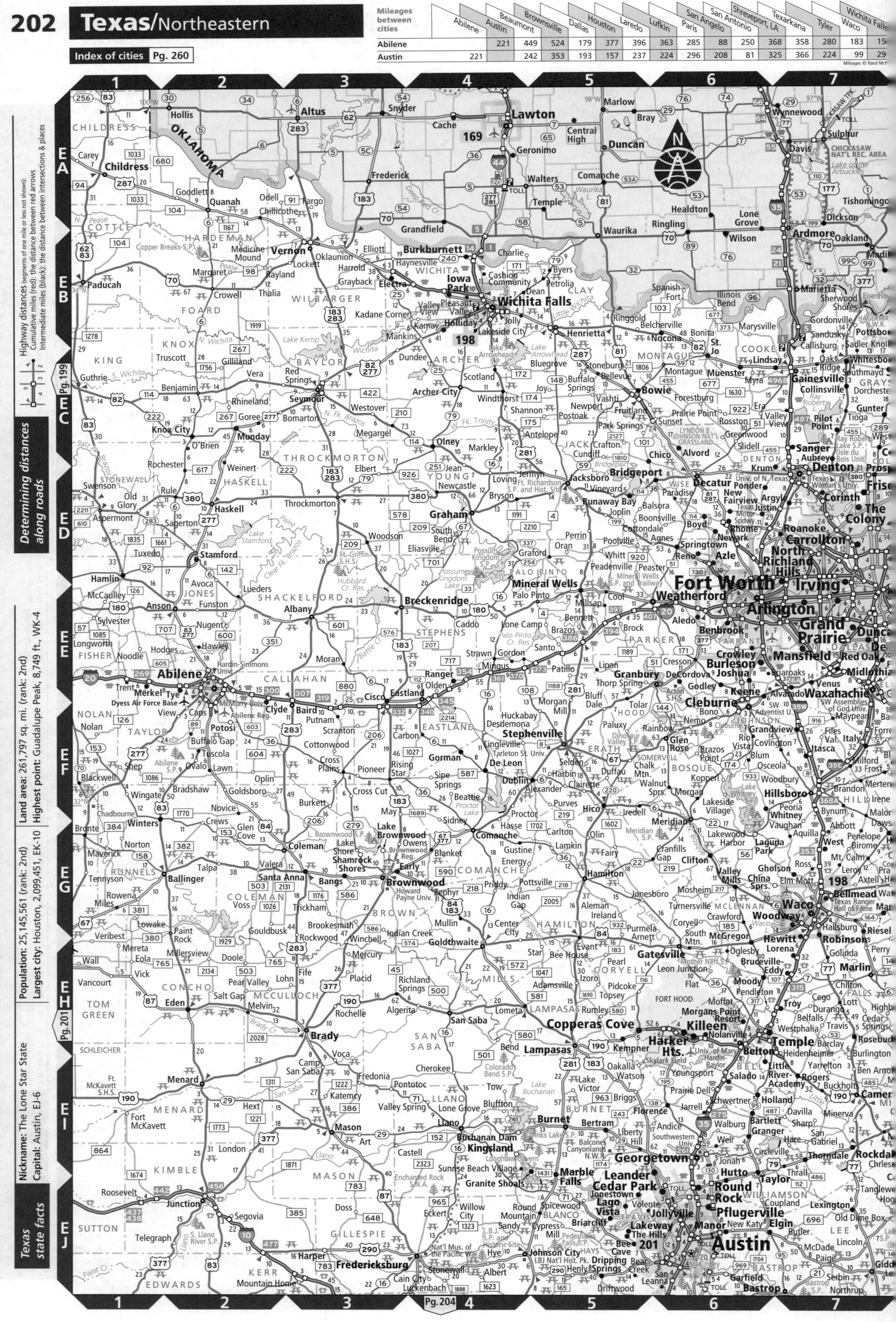

continued p. 204

Mileages between cities

	Abilene	Austin	Beaumont	Brownsville	Dallas	Houston	Laredo	Lufkin	Paris	San Angelo	San Antonio	Shreveport, LA	Texarkana	Tyler	Waco	Wichita Falls
Brownsville	524	353	439		547	354	204	473	622	491	274	596	650	530	435	614
Corpus Christi	387	217	292	156	410	207	138	328	496	355	138	449	504	392	316	477

Mileages © Rand McNally

Total mileages through Texas
10 811 miles   30 223 miles
20 636 miles   35 504 miles
More mileages at www.randmcnally.com/MC

One inch represents approximately 23 miles
0 5 10 15 20 25 30 35 mi
0 10 20 30 40 50 km

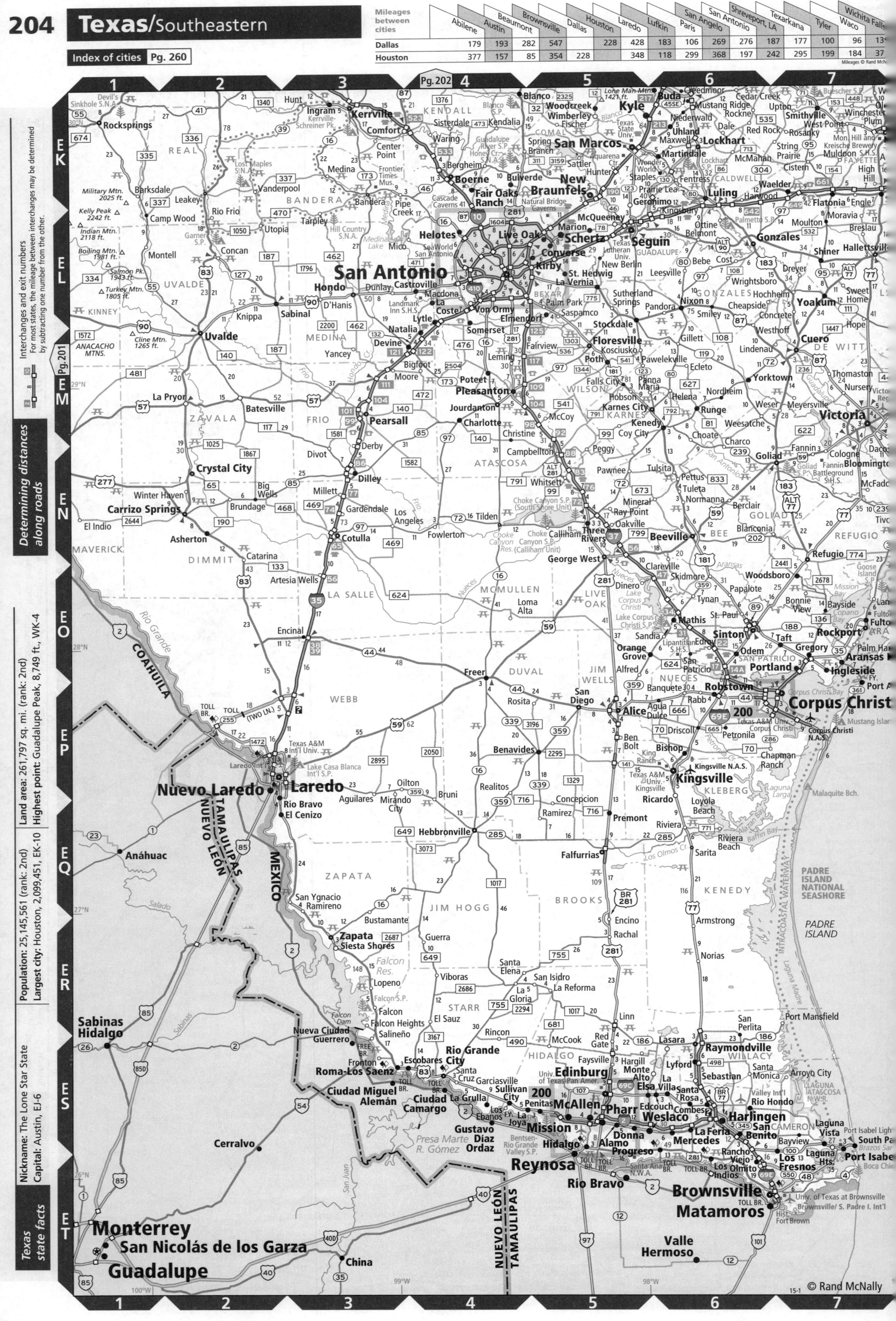

Mileages between cities	Abilene	Austin	Beaumont	Brownsville	Dallas	Houston	Laredo	Lufkin	Paris	San Angelo	San Antonio	Shreveport, LA	Texarkana	Tyler	Waco	Wichita Falls
Dallas	179	193	282	547		228	428	183	106	269	276	187	177	100	96	13°
Houston	377	157	85	354	228		348	118	299	368	197	242	295	199	184	37

Mileages © Rand McNally

© Rand McNally

15-1

Mileages between cities	Abilene	Austin	Beaumont	Brownsville	Dallas	Houston	Laredo	Lufkin	Paris	San Angelo	San Antonio	Shreveport, LA	Texarkana	Tyler	Waco	Wichita Falls
San Antonio	250	81	280	274	276	197	154	314	380	213		406	451	309	180	341
Shreveport, LA	368	325	206	596	187	242	565	120	154	455	406		72	98	226	324

Mileages © Rand McNally

Total mileages through Texas
10 = 811 miles   30 = 223 miles
20 = 636 miles   35 = 504 miles
More mileages at www.randmcnally.com/MC

Mileages between cities	Blanding	Cedar City	Grand Jct., CO	Las Vegas, NV	Logan	Moab	Ogden	Page, AZ	Park City	Price	Provo	Richfield	St. George	Salt Lake City	Vernal	Wendover
Grand Junction, CO	186	335		506	363	112	319	380	286	164	240	224	389	283	140	40
Logan	388	330	363	499		313	46	457	113	199	124	239	385	82	252	19

Mileages © Rand McNally

Utah state facts

Nickname: The Beehive State
Capital: Salt Lake City, D-8

Population: 2,763,885 (rank: 34th)
Largest city: Salt Lake City, D-8

Land area: 82,144 sq. mi. (rank: 12th)
Highest point: Kings Peak, 13,528 ft., D-11

Determining distances along roads

Highway distances (segments of one mile or less not shown):
— the distance between red arrows
Cumulative miles (red): the distance between red arrows
Intermediate miles (black): the distance between intersections & places

One inch represents approximately 20 miles

Mileages between cities	Blanding	Cedar City	Grand Jct., CO	Las Vegas, NV	Logan	Moab	Ogden	Page, AZ	Park City	Price	Provo	Richfield	St. George	Salt Lake City	Vernal	Wendover
Moab	74	287	112	456	313		269	268	238	115	190	174	341	234	207	352
Richfield	249	114	224	282	239	174	194	219	166	121	115		169	159	232	270

Mileages © Rand McNally

continued p. 208

Total mileages through Utah

15	401 miles	80	196 miles
70	232 miles	84	119 miles

More mileages at www.randmcnally.com/MC

Zion National Park

Provo

Springville

Tourism
Utah Office of Tourism
(800) 200-1160, (801) 538-1900
www.utah.com

Road Conditions & Construction
511, (866) 511-8824, (801) 887-3700
www.utahcommuterlink.com
www.udot.utah.gov

Toll Road Information
Adams Avenue Parkway, Inc. (Weber Co.)
(801) 475-1909
www.adamsavenueparkway.com

Plan a Utah trip at www.randmcnally.com/UT

© Rand McNally

Index of cities Pg. 262

Mileages between cities	Blanding	Cedar City	Grand Jct., CO	Las Vegas, NV	Logan	Moab	Ogden	Page, AZ	Park City	Price	Provo	Richfield	St. George	Salt Lake City	Vernal	Wendover
St. George	415	55	389	117	385	341	341	154	308	286	261	169		304	401	33
Salt Lake City	308	250	283	419	82	234	37	377	30	119	43	159	304		172	12

Mileages © Rand McNally

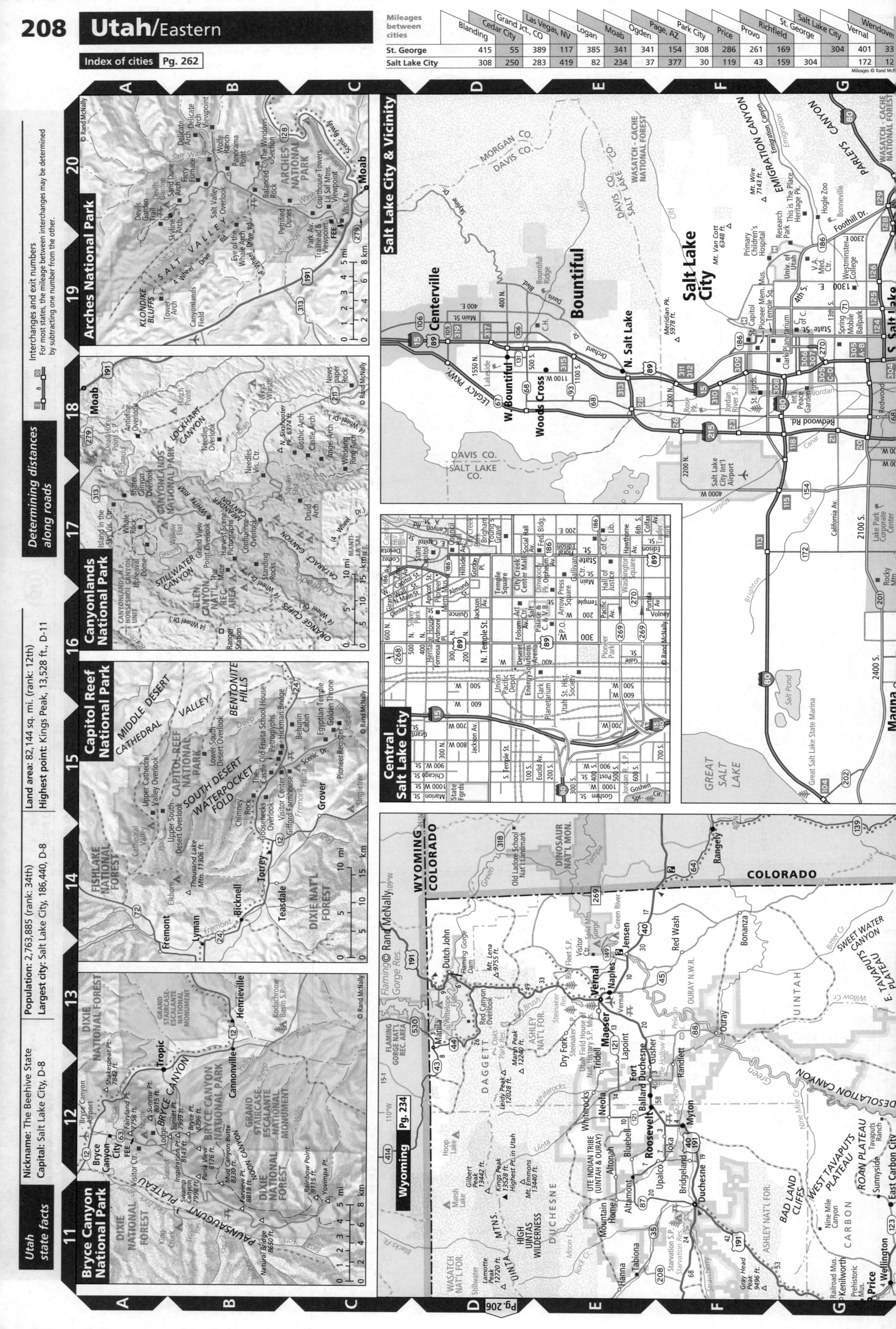

Utah state facts

Nickname: The Beehive State
Capital: Salt Lake City, D-8

Land area: 82,144 sq. mi. (rank: 12th)
Highest point: Kings Peak, 13,528 ft., D-11

Population: 2,763,885 (rank: 34th)
Largest city: Salt Lake City, D-8

Determining distances along roads

Interchanges and exit numbers
For most states, the mileage between interchanges may be determined by subtracting one number from the other.

mileages between cities	Blanding	Cedar City	Grand Jct., CO	Las Vegas, NV	Logan	Moab	Ogden	Page, AZ	Park City	Price	Provo	Richfield	St. George	Salt Lake City	Vernal	Wendover
Vernal	281	345	140	514	252	207	207	450	145	112	154	232	401	172		291
Wendover	426	317	401	361	199	352	154	503	150	237	161	270	333	121	291	

Mileages © Rand McNally

15 401 miles	80 196 miles		Total mileages through Utah
70 232 miles	84 119 miles		More mileages at www.randmcnally.com/MC

Plan a Utah trip at
www.randmcnally.com/UT

Tourism Information	Utah Office of Tourism (800) 200-1160, (801) 538-1900 www.utah.com	
Road Conditions & Construction	511, (866) 511-8824, (801) 887-3700 www.utahcommuterlink.com www.udot.utah.gov	
Toll Road Information	Adams Avenue Parkway, Inc. (Weber Co.) (801) 475-1909 www.adamsavenueparkway.com	

Mileages between cities	Albany, NY	Brattleboro	Burlington	Montpelier	Newport	Rutland	St. Johnsbury	White River Jct.
Albany, NY		78	151	156	230	90	187	128
Brattleboro	78		151	115	164	73	121	62

	Albany, NY	Brattleboro	Burlington	Montpelier	Newport	Rutland	St. Johnsbury	White River Jct.
Burlington	151	151		39	76	67	75	
Montpelier	156	115	39		78	66	37	

Mileages © Rand Mc...

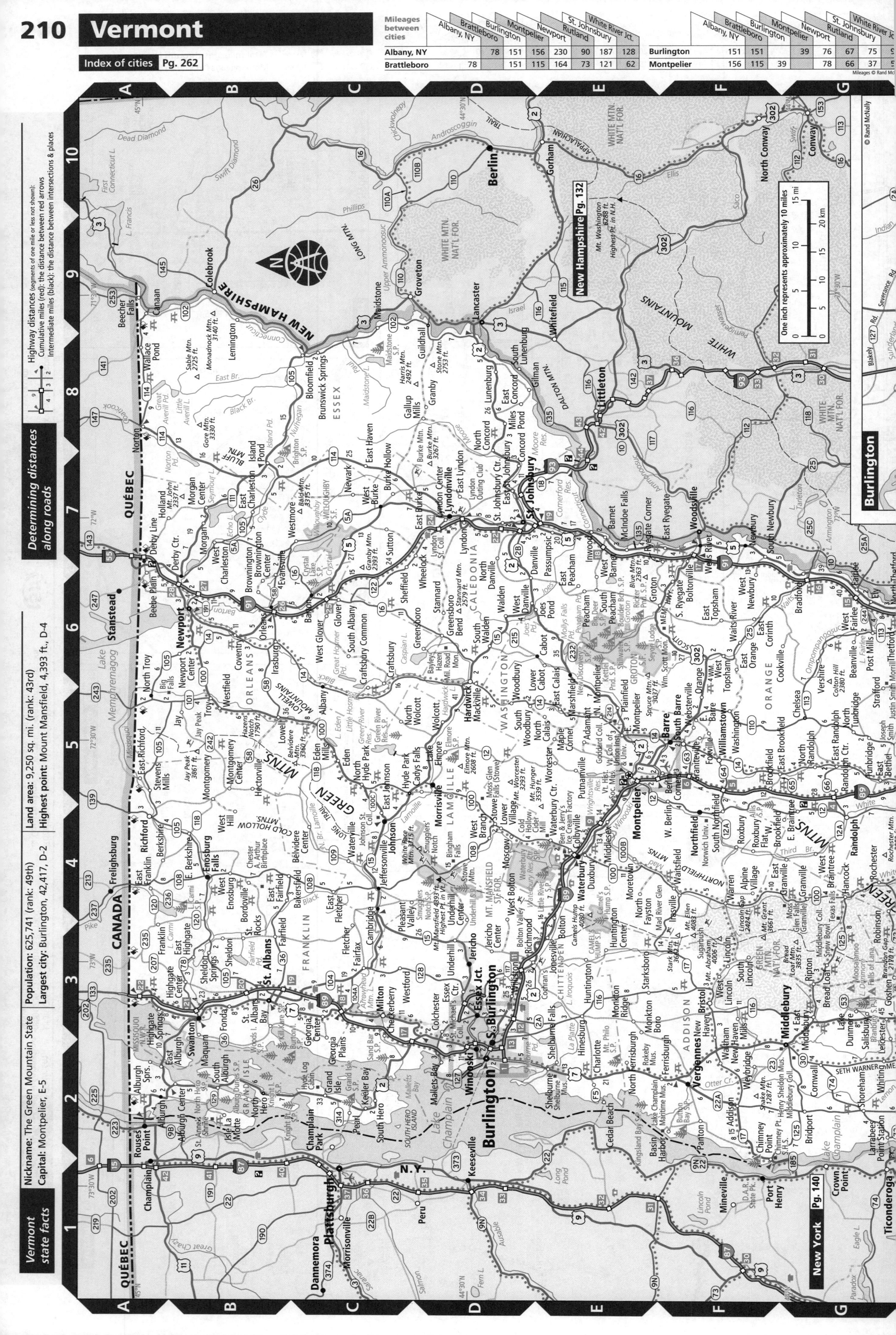

Vermont state facts

Nickname: The Green Mountain State
Capital: Montpelier
Population: 625,741 (rank: 49th)
Land area: 9,250 sq. mi. (rank: 43rd)
Highest point: Mount Mansfield, 4,393 ft., D-4
Largest city: Burlington, 42,417, D-2

Determining distances along roads

Highway distances (segments of one mile or less not shown):
- Cumulative miles (red): the distance between red arrows
- Intermediate miles (black): the distance between intersections & places

One inch represents approximately 10 miles

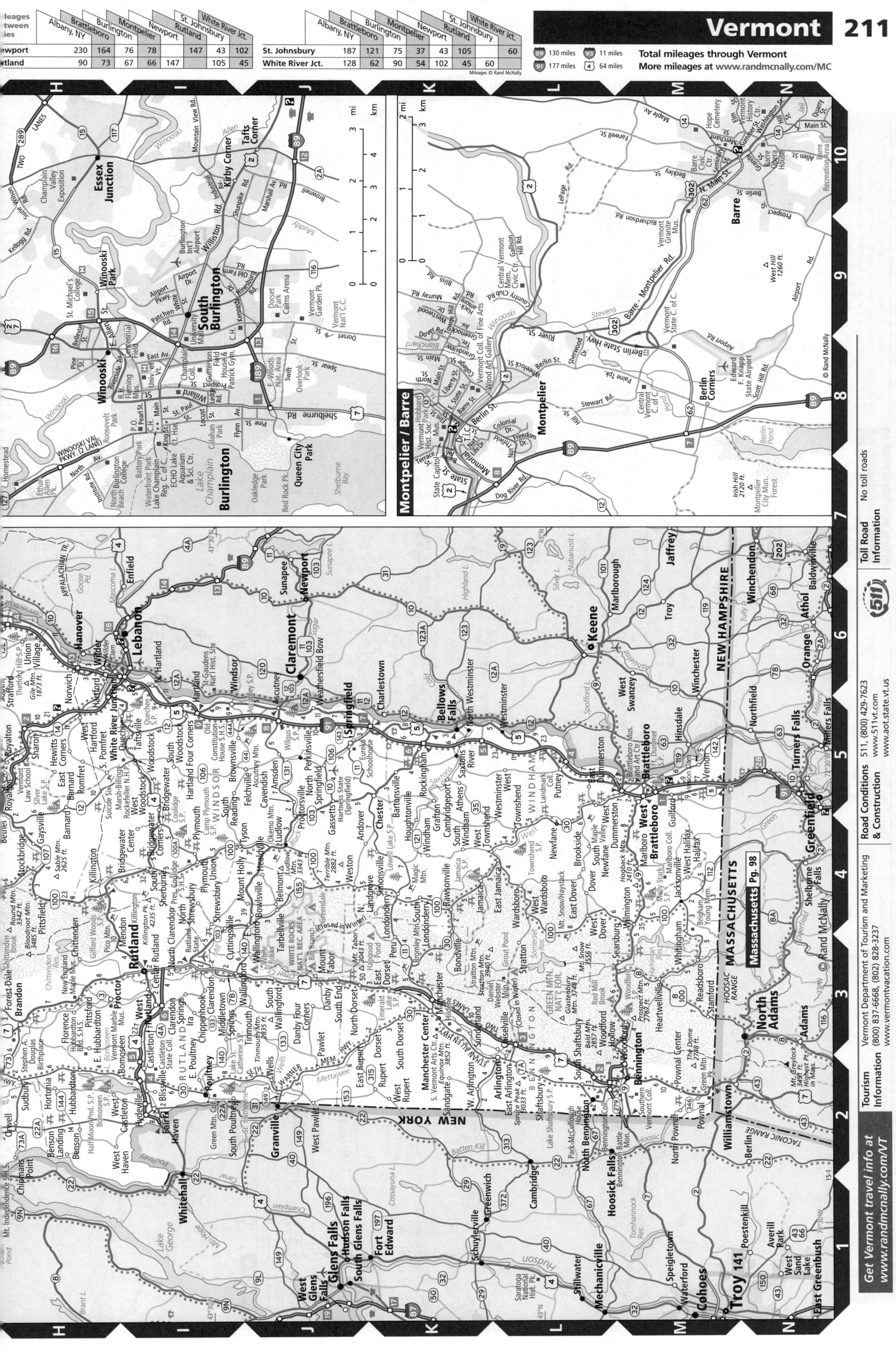

	Albany, NY	Brattleboro	Burlington	Montpelier	Newport	Rutland	St. Johnsbury	White River Jct.
Newport	230	164	76	78		147	43	102
Rutland	90	73	67	66	147		105	45

	Albany, NY	Brattleboro	Burlington	Montpelier	Newport	Rutland	St. Johnsbury	White River Jct.
St. Johnsbury	187	121	75	37	43	105		60
White River Jct.	128	62	90	54	102	45	60	

Mileages © Rand McNally

89 130 miles **93** 11 miles
91 177 miles **4** 64 miles

Total mileages through Vermont
More mileages at www.randmcnally.com/MC

Montpelier / Barre

© Rand McNally

MASSACHUSETTS Pg. 98

Index of cities Pg. 262

Index of cities Pg. 262

Mileages between cities	Chincoteague	Danville	Emporia	Fredericksburg	Harrisonburg	Lynchburg	Manassas	Norfolk	Richmond	Roanoke	Virginia Beach	Washington, DC	Williamsburg	Winchester	Wytheville
Bristol	510	192	341	323	242	200	347	407	321	145	423	377	370	310	6
Charlottesville	253	260	131	136	66	61	65	81	157	71	117	174	116	121	128	18

Mileages © Rand McNally

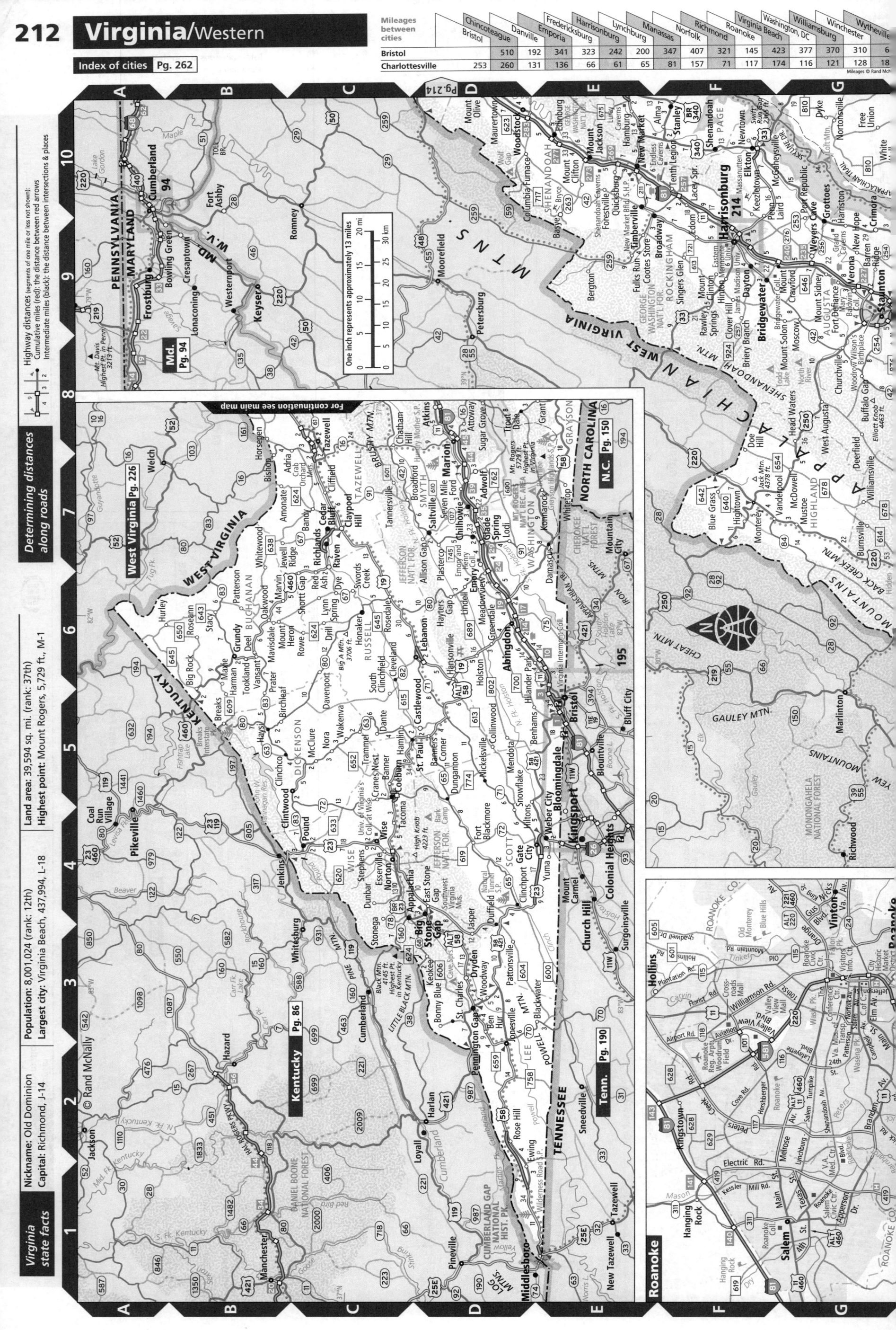

Total mileages through Virginia
More mileages at www.randmcnally.com/MC
Mileages © Rand McNally

	Chincoteague Bristol	Danville	Emporia Fredericksburg	Harrisonburg	Lynchburg	Manassas	Norfolk	Richmond	Roanoke	Virginia Beach	Washington, DC	Williamsburg	Winchester	Wytheville
...ville	192	300	115	197	163	68	215	191	144	89	206	247	199	230	124
...rfolk	407	104	191	78	139	216	189	177	91	276	17	189	41	222	340

	Total mileages through Virginia
64	298 miles
81	325 miles
69	69 miles
95	179 miles

continued p. 214

continued on next page
Pg. 215
p. 214
West Virginia Pg. 226
N. Carolina Pg. 150
For continuation see map above

Virginia

Toll Road Information (all use E-ZPass): Chesapeake Bay Bridge-Tunnel: (757) 331-2960; www.cbbt.com; Chesapeake Expressway (VA 168): (757) 204-0100; www.chesapeakeexpressway.com; Dulles Greenway: (703) 707-8870; www.dullesgreenway.com

Road Conditions & Construction: 511, (800) 578-4111, (800) 367-7623; www.511virginia.org; www.virginiadot.org/travel

Tourism Information: Virginia Tourism Corporation; (800) 847-4882; www.virginia.org

Explore Virginia www.randmcnally.com/VA

Mileages between cities	Bristol	Chincoteague	Danville	Emporia	Fredericksburg	Harrisonburg	Lynchburg	Manassas	Norfolk	Richmond	Roanoke	Virginia Beach	Washington, DC	Williamsburg	Winchester	Wytheville
Richmond	321	190	144	66	56	130	114	96	91		187	105	107	50	135	25
Roanoke	145	378	89	176	192	111	53	214	276	187		292	241	238	178	7

Mileages by Rand McNally

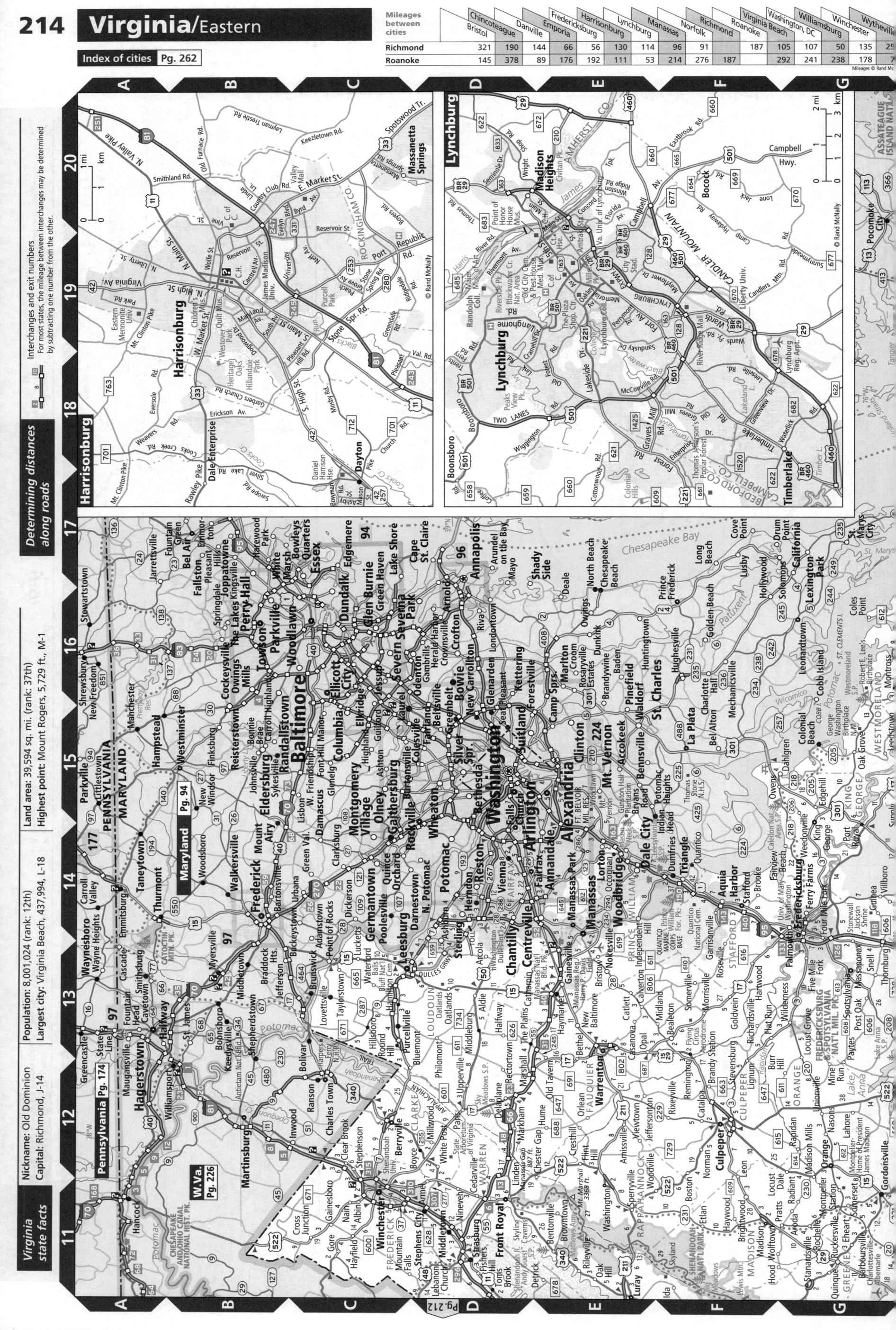

Virginia state facts

Nickname: Old Dominion
Capital: Richmond, J-14
Population: 8,001,024 (rank: 12th)
Largest city: Virginia Beach, 437,994, L-18
Land area: 39,594 sq. mi. (rank: 37th)
Highest point: Mount Rogers, 5,729 ft., M-1

Determining distances along roads

Interchanges and exit numbers
For most states, the mileage between interchanges may be determined by subtracting one number from the other.

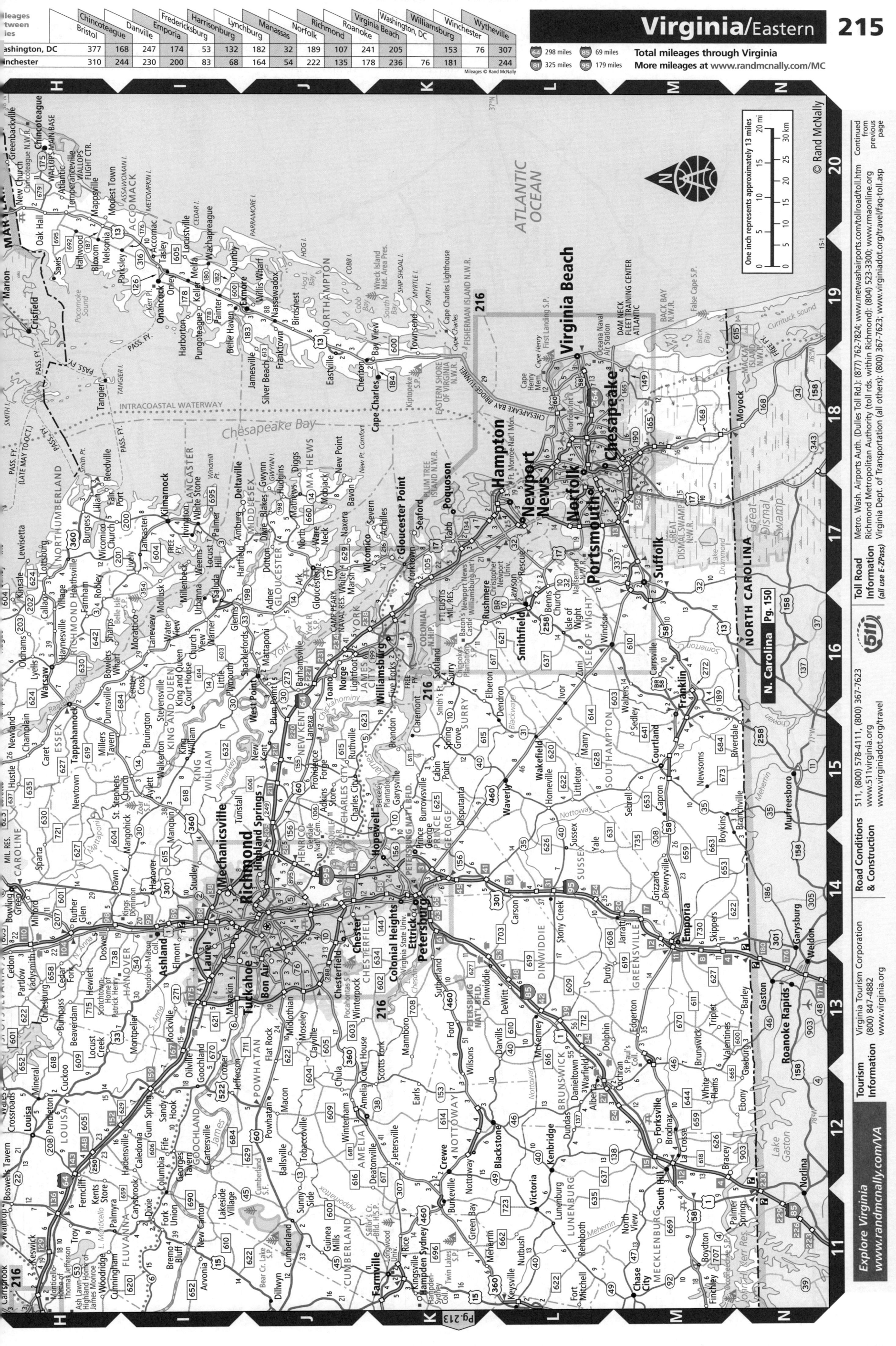

Mileages between cities	Bristol	Chincoteague	Danville	Emporia	Fredericksburg	Harrisonburg	Lynchburg	Manassas	Norfolk	Richmond	Roanoke	Virginia Beach	Washington, DC	Williamsburg	Winchester	Wytheville
Washington, DC	377	168	247	174	53	132	182	32	189	107	241	205		153	76	307
Winchester	310	244	230	200	83	68	164	54	222	135	178	236	76	181		244

Mileages © Rand McNally

Metro. Wash. Airports Auth. (Dulles Toll Rd.); (877) 762-7824; www.metwashairports.com/tollroad/toll.htm
Richmond Metropolitan Authority (toll rds. within Richmond); (804) 523-3300; www.rmaonline.org
Virginia Dept. of Transportation (all others); (800) 367-7623; www.virginiadot.org/travel/faq-toll.asp

Toll Road Information (all use E-ZPass)

511, (800) 578-4111, (800) 367-7623
www.511virginia.org
www.virginiadot.org/travel

Road Conditions & Construction

Virginia Tourism Corporation
(800) 847-4882
www.virginia.org

Tourism Information

Explore Virginia
www.randmcnally.com/VA

Continued from previous page

© Rand McNally

Pg.213
Pg.213
N. Carolina Pg. 150

City sights to see

- Agecroft Hall and Gardens, Richmond, C-7
- Children's Museum of Virginia, Portsmouth, M-6
- Chrysler Museum of Art, Norfolk, L-6
- Colonial Williamsburg, Williamsburg, F-2
- Edgar Allen Poe Museum, Richmond, C-8
- First Landing State Park, Virginia Beach, L-9
- Hermitage Foundation Museum, Norfolk, K-5

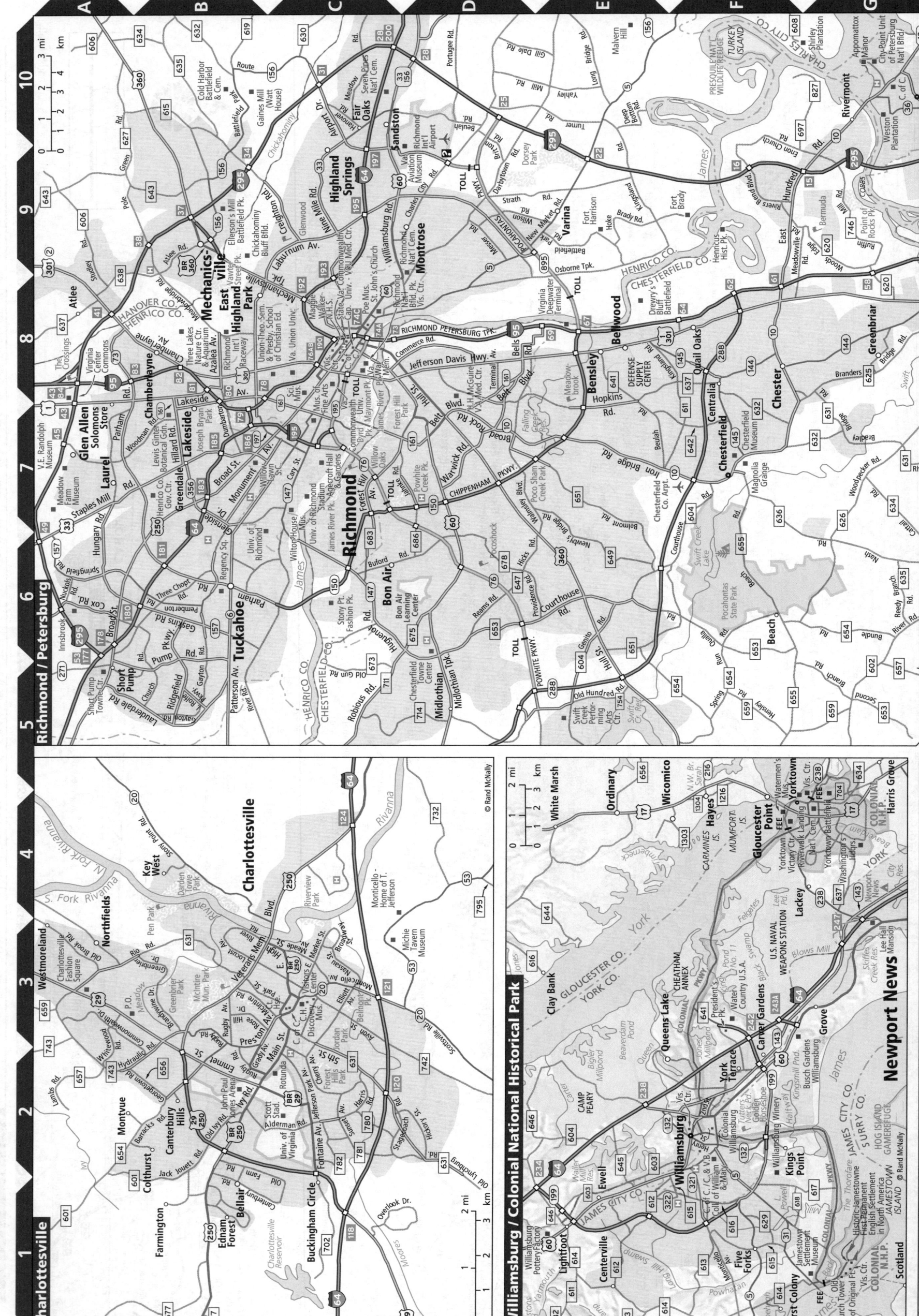

© Rand McNally

Charlottesville

Richmond / Petersburg

Williamsburg / Colonial National Historical Park

- Historic Jamestowne, Williamsburg, G-1
- Monticello, Charlottesville, D-4
- Nauticus, Norfolk, L-6
- Ocean Breeze Waterpark, Virginia Beach, M-10
- Old Cape Henry Lighthouse, Virginia Beach, K-9
- Three Lakes Nature Center and Aquarium, Richmond, B-8
- Virginia State Capitol, Richmond, C-8

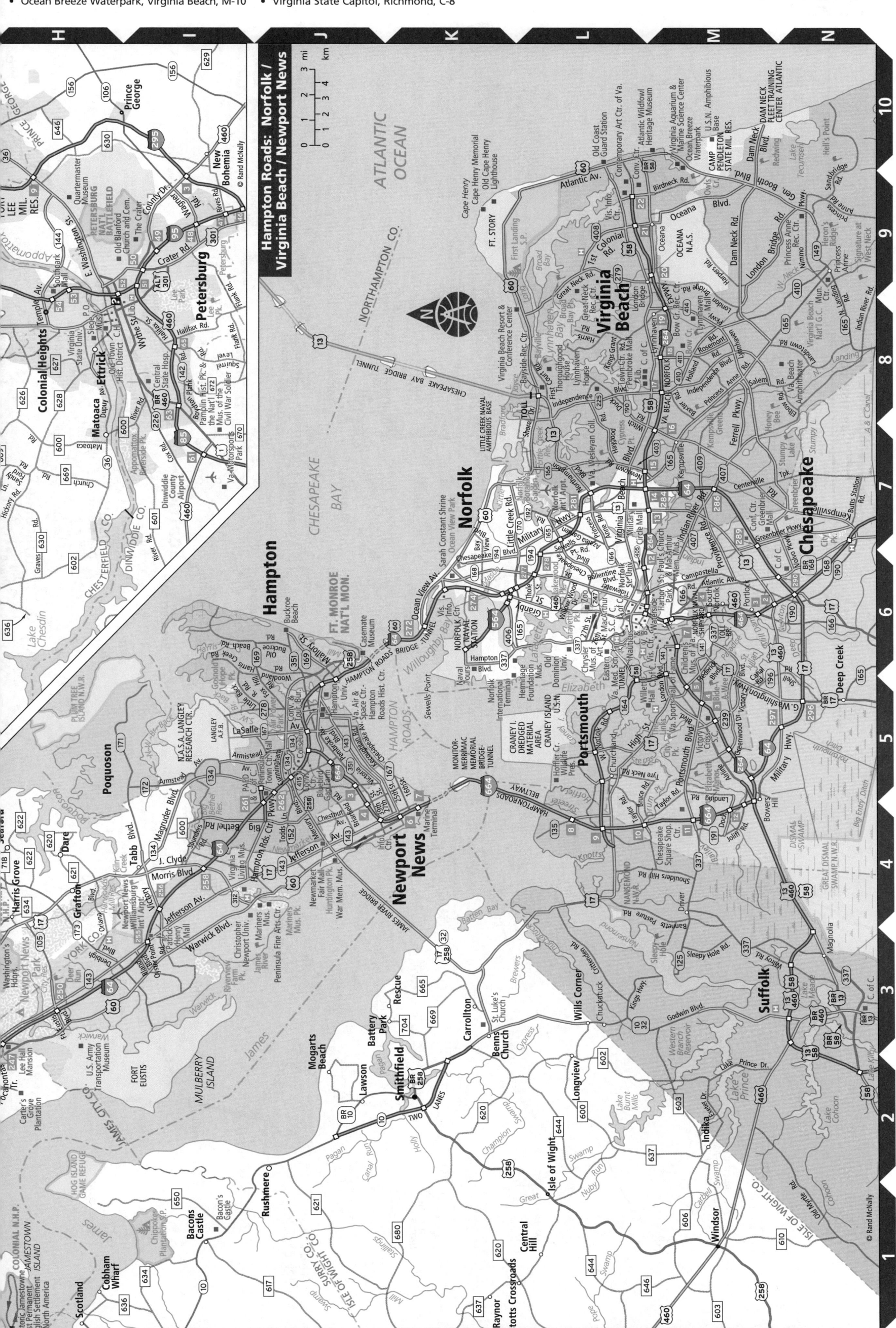

Mileages between cities	Aberdeen	Bellingham	Colville	Kennewick	Longview	Olympia	Omak	Port Angeles	Portland, OR	Seattle	Spokane	Tacoma	The Dalles, OR	Vancouver, BC	Wenatchee	Yakima
Bellingham	198		317	306	216	149	201	118	261	89	361	121	326	52	182	22
Kennewick	312	306	209		254	263	189	340	213	223	138	235	130	359	132	8

Mileages © Rand McNally

Washington state facts

Nickname: The Evergreen State
Capital: Olympia, H-6

Population: 6,724,540 (rank: 13th)
Largest city: Seattle, 608,660, F-7

Land area: 66,544 sq. mi. (rank: 20th)
Highest point: Mount Rainier, 14,411 ft., I-8

Determining distances along roads

Highway distances (segments of one mile or less not shown):
Cumulative miles (red): the distance between red arrows
Intermediate miles (black): the distance between intersections & places

continued p. 220

Mileages between cities	Aberdeen	Bellingham	Colville	Kennewick	Longview	Olympia	Omak	Port Angeles	Portland, OR	Seattle	Spokane	Tacoma	The Dalles, OR	Vancouver, BC	Wenatchee	Yakima
Lewiston, ID	402	396	173	124	381	353	237	431	339	313	102	325	256	449	228	204
Portland, OR	141	261	422	213	48	113	377	228		172	351	141	83	313	291	185

Mileages © Rand McNally

Total mileages through Washington
More mileages at www.randmcnally.com/MC

5 277 miles   90 297 miles
82 133 miles   101 373 miles

Washington State Department of Transportation (Good to Go!)
(Tacoma Narrows Bridge & SR 520 Bridge)
(866) 936-8246; www.wsdot.wa.gov/tolling

Toll Bridge Information

511
Washington State Department of Transportation
(800) 695-7623
www.wsdot.wa.gov/traffic

Road Conditions & Construction 511

Tourism Information
Washington State Tourism
(800) 544-1800, (452) 270-1962
www.experiencewa.com

Get more Washington info at www.randmcnally.com/WA

One inch represents approx. 14 miles

Olympia

Lacey

Tumwater

© Rand McNally

Mileages between cities	Aberdeen	Bellingham	Colville	Kennewick	Longview	Olympia	Omak	Port Angeles	Portland, OR	Seattle	Spokane	Tacoma	The Dalles, OR	Vancouver, BC	Wenatchee	Yakima
Seattle	108	89	350	223	127	60	236	83	172		278	32	249	141	148	14
Spokane	367	361	71	138	386	319	139	396	351	278		291	268	413	169	20

Mileages © Rand Mc

Mileages Between Cities	Aberdeen	Bellingham	Colville	Kennewick	Longview	Olympia	Omak	Port Angeles	Portland, OR	Seattle	Spokane	Tacoma	The Dalles, OR	Vancouver, BC	Wenatchee	Yakima
Tacoma	77	121	362	235	96	28	248	106	141	32	291		217	174	160	153
Yakima	230	224	272	82	166	181	192	259	185	141	201	153	102	276	106	

Mileages © Rand McNally

Total mileages through Washington
More mileages at www.randmcnally.com/MC

5: 277 miles 90: 297 miles 82: 133 miles 101: 373 miles

Washington State Department of Transportation (Good to Go!)
Toll Road Information (Tacoma Narrows Bridge & SR 520 Bridge)
(866) 936-8246; www.wsdot.wa.gov/tolling

511
Road Conditions & Construction (800) 695-7623 www.wsdot.wa.gov/traffic

Tourism Information Washington State Tourism (800) 544-1800, (452) 270-1962 www.experiencewa.com

Get more Washington info at www.randmcnally.com/WA

© Rand McNally

Yakima
Terrace Heights
Union Gap

Oregon Pg. 170

One inch represents approx. 14 miles

City sights to see
- Experience Music Project, Seattle, H-1
- Frye Art Museum, Seattle, J-3
- Klondike Gold Rush National Historical Park, Seattle, K-2
- Logmire Museum, Logmire, N-1
- Museum of Glass, Tacoma, L-6
- Nordic Heritage Museum, Seattle, C-7
- Pacific Science Center, Seattle, H-1

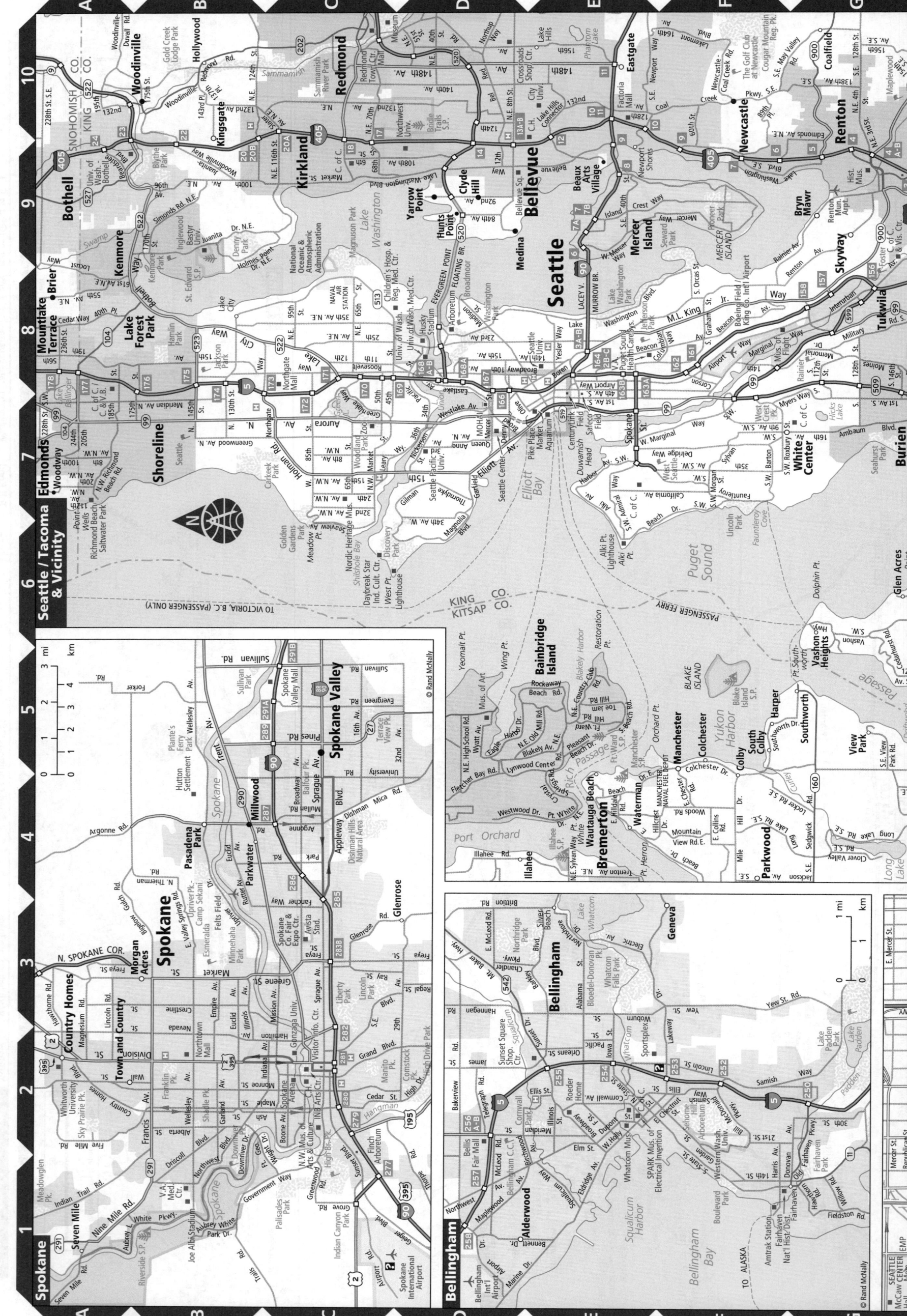

© Rand McNally

- Pike Place Market, Seattle, J-2
- Point Defiance Zoo & Aquarium, Tacoma, K-5
- Seattle Aquarium, Seattle, J-1
- Space Needle, Seattle, H-1
- Washington State History Mus., Tacoma, L-6
- Whatcom Museum of History and Art, Bellingham, E-2
- Woodland Park Zoo, Seattle, C-7

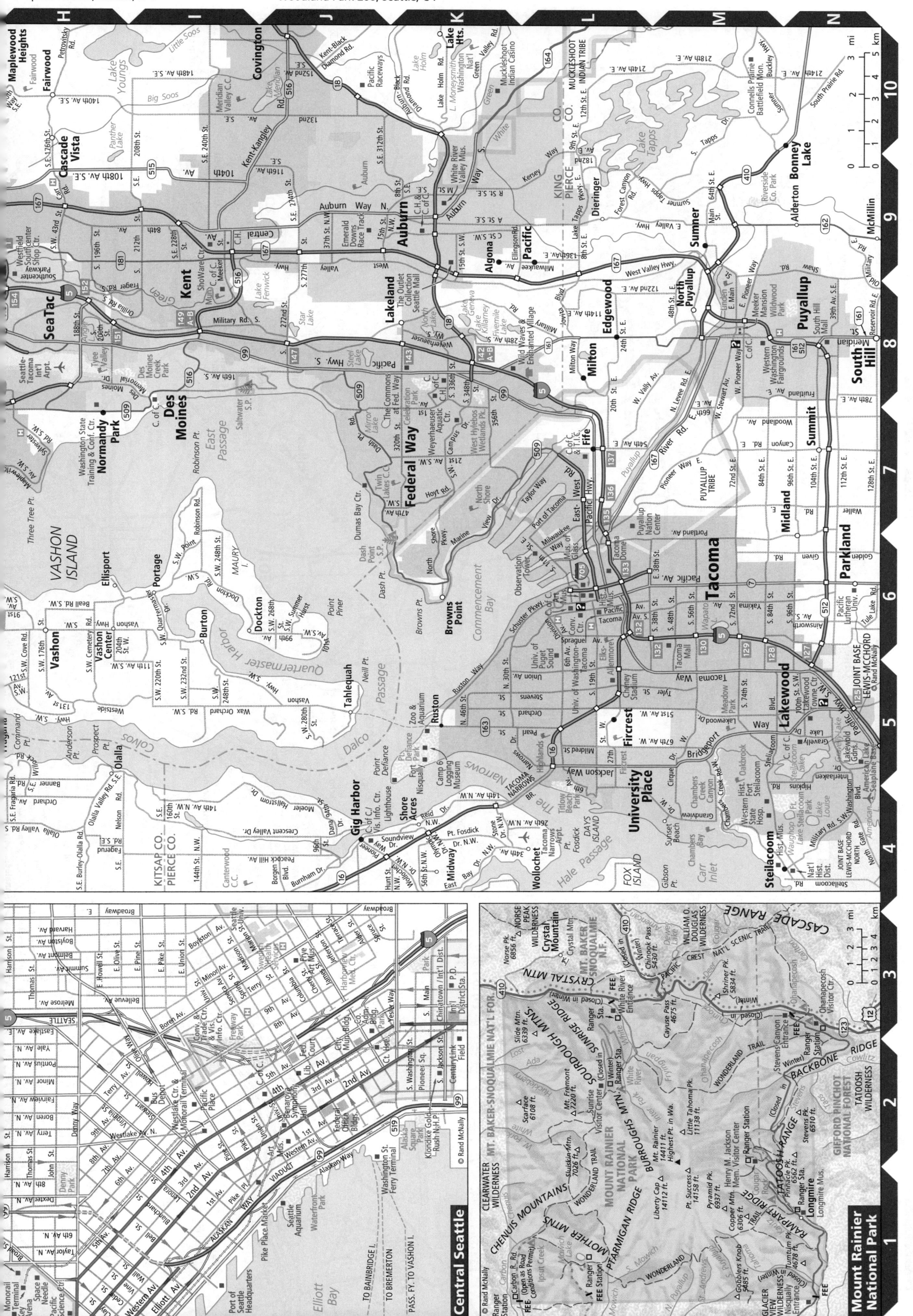

Central Seattle

Mount Rainier National Park

© Rand McNally

City sights to see

- Arlington National Cemetery, Arlington, Va., G-6
- Frederick Douglass National Historic Site, G-7
- Freedom Park, Arlington, Va., G-5
- John F. Kennedy Ctr. for the Performing Arts, K-3
- Martin Luther King Jr. Memorial, M-4
- National Arboretum, F-7
- National Mall, M-7

D.C. facts

Population: 601,723

Land area: 61 sq. mi.

Highest point: Tenleytown, 410 ft., E-5

Washington, D.C. & Vicinity

Determining distances along roads

Interchanges and exit numbers. For most states, the mileage between interchanges may be determined by subtracting one number from the other.

- National Zoological Park, F-6
- Patuxent Research Refuge National Wildlife Visitor Center, Laurel, Md., D-10
- The Pentagon, Arlington, Va., G-6
- Supreme Court of the United States, M-10
- United States Botanic Garden, M-8
- Wolf Trap National Park for the Performing Arts, Vienna, Va., E-2

Central Washington, D.C.

The following places are identified only by a letter-number key.

A-1 American Pharmaceutical Assoc.
A-2 American Red Cross
A-3 American Red Cross–D.C. Chapter
A-4 American Red Cross Nat'l Hdqtrs.
C-1 Arts and Industries Bldg.
C-2 Bureau of the Census (U.S.)
C-3 Commerce Department
C-4 Constitution Hall
C-5 Continental Hall
C-6 Corcoran Gallery of Art
D-1 Department of Agriculture
D-2 Department of Commerce
D-3 Department of the Interior
D-4 Department of the Interior South
E-1 Federal Office Bldg.
F-1 Freer Gallery of Art
G-1 General Services Admin. Bldg.
G-2 G.S.A. Regional Office Building
H-1 House Office Building
H-2 Housing & Urban Development
H-3 Hirshhorn Museum & Sculpture
J-1 Judiciary Square
L-1 Library of Congress
M-1 Metro Station Locations
N-1 National Building Museum
N-2 National Collection of Fine Arts
N-3 National Museum of African Art
N-4 National Museum of the American Indian
N-5 National Portrait Gallery
O-1 Office of Personnel Management
O-2 Old Post Office
R-1 Ripley Center
S-1 Securities & Exchange Comm.
S-2 Senate Office Building
S-3 Sewall-Belmont House
S-4 Smithsonian Discovery Theater
S-5 Sackler Gallery of Asian Art
U-1 U.S. Holocaust Memorial Museum
U-2 U.S. Navy Memorial

Get D.C. travel info at
www.randmcnally.com/DC

Tourism Information
Destination DC
(800) 422-8644, (202) 789-7000
www.washington.org

Road Conditions & Construction
311, (202) 737-4404, (202) 673-6813
www.ddot.dc.gov
geospatial.dcgis.dc.gov/dc311map

Toll Road Information
No toll roads in D.C.; see Maryland and Virginia for toll road information

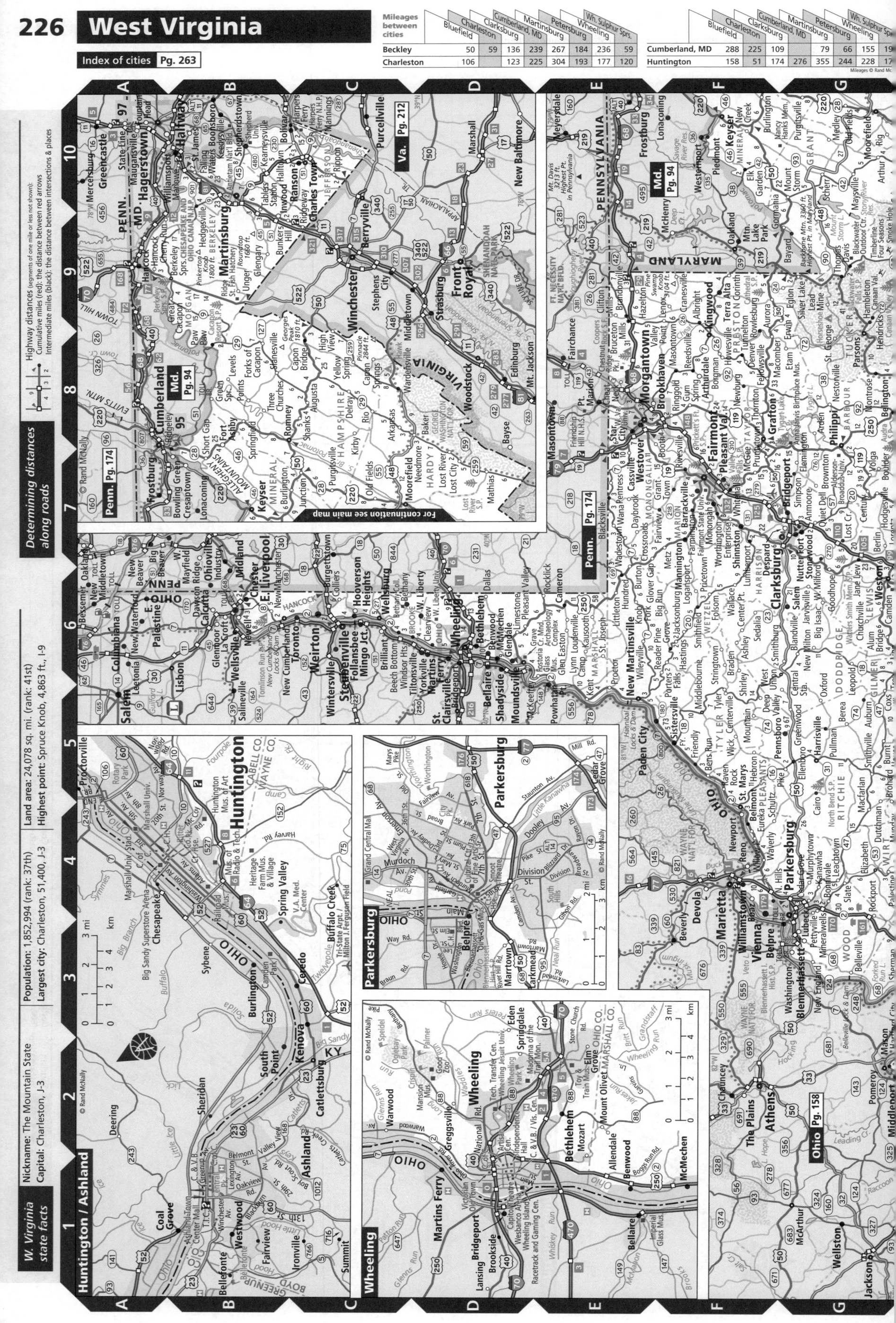

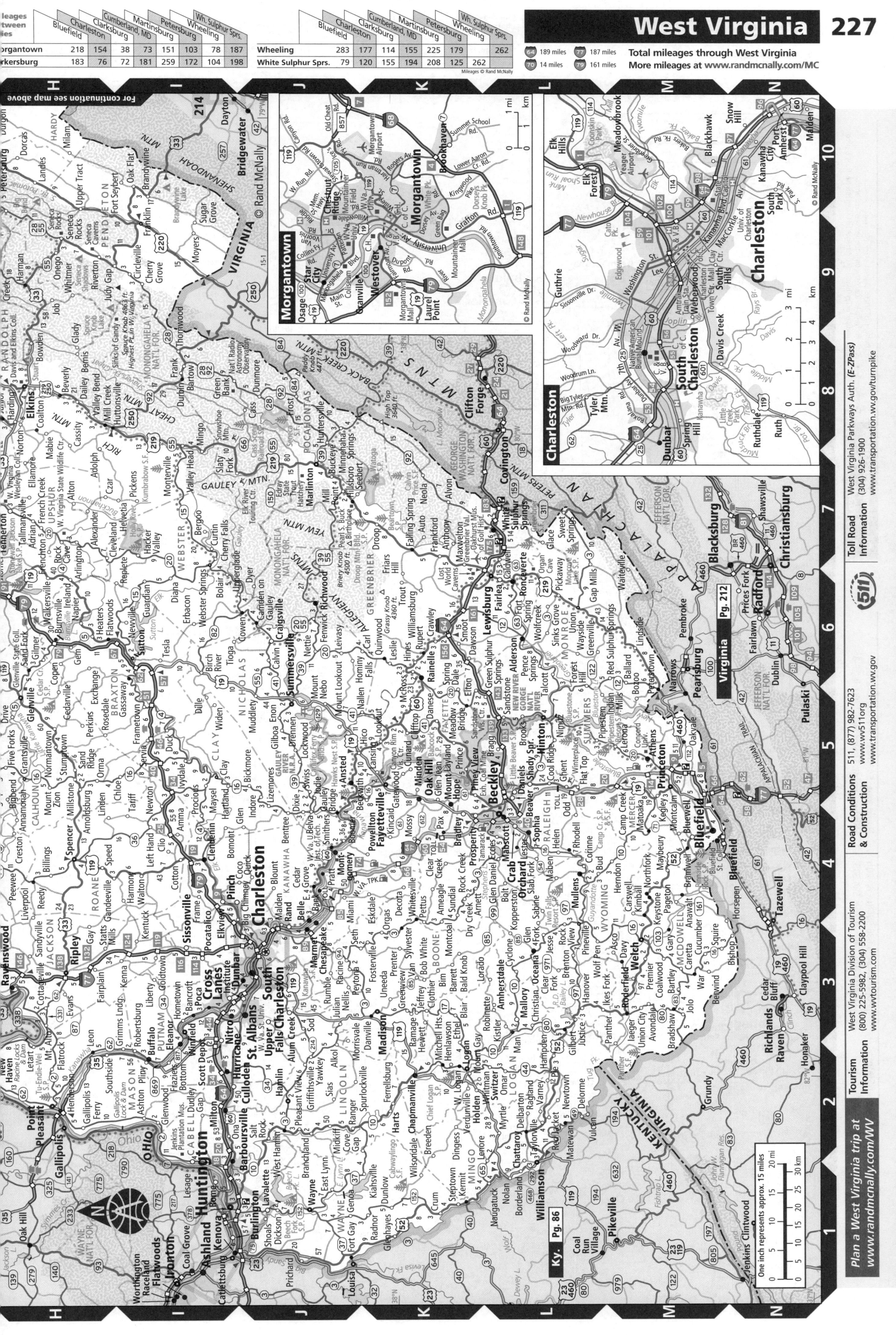

Mileages between cities	Beloit	Chicago, IL	Dubuque, IA	Eau Claire	Green Bay	Hayward	La Crosse	Madison	Milwaukee	Oshkosh	Rhinelander	Sheboygan	Sturgeon Bay	Superior	Wausau	Wisconsin Dells
Green Bay	184	206	233	192		283	203	138	116	52	136	64	44	326	96	132
La Crosse	188	281	119	86	203	190		143	209	153	214	195	248	233	170	90

Mileages © Rand McNally

continued p. 230

Total mileages through Wisconsin

| 39 | 182 miles | 90 | 189 miles |
| 43 | 192 miles | 94 | 341 miles |

More mileages at www.randmcnally.com/MC

Eau Claire

Mich. Pg. 102

Michigan Pg. 102

© Rand McNally

LAKE MICHIGAN

Green Bay

Tourism Information — Wisconsin Department of Tourism (800) 432-8747, (608) 266-2161 www.travelwisconsin.com

Road Conditions & Construction — 511 (866) 511-9472 www.511wi.gov

Toll Road Information — No toll roads

Explore Wisconsin at www.randmcnally.com/WI

Index of cities Pg. 264

Mileages between cities	Beloit	Chicago, IL	Dubuque, IA	Eau Claire	Green Bay	Hayward	La Crosse	Madison	Milwaukee	Oshkosh	Rhinelander	Sheboygan	Sturgeon Bay	Superior	Wausau	Wisconsin Dells
Madison	54	146	93	177	138	282	143		78	87	200	117	185	325	143	5
Milwaukee	74	90	171	243	116	348	209	78		86	244	54	155	390	187	12

Mileages © Rand McN

Wisconsin state facts

Nickname: The Badger State
Capital: Madison, N-9

Land area: 54,310 sq. mi. (rank: 25th)
Highest point: Timms Hill, 1,951 ft., F-8

Population: 5,686,986 (rank: 20th)
Largest city: Milwaukee, 594,833, N-13

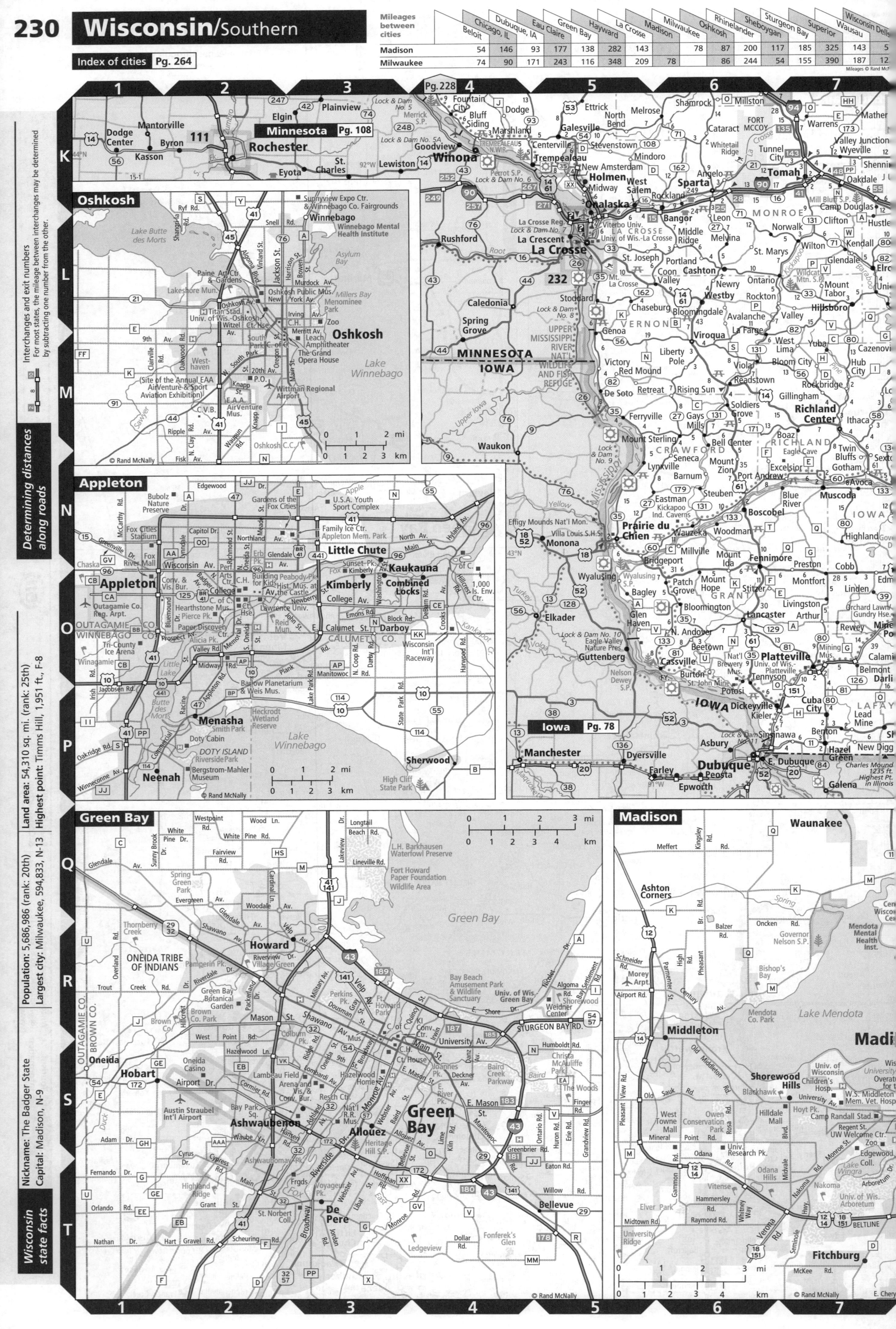

Mileages between Cities

	Beloit	Chicago, IL	Dubuque, IA	Eau Claire	Green Bay	Hayward	La Crosse	Madison	Milwaukee	Oshkosh	Rhinelander	Sheboygan	Sturgeon Bay	Superior	Wausau	Wisconsin Dells
Superior	370	462	339	149	326	70	233	325	390	332	182	388	370		232	271
Wausau	189	281	239	98	96	189	170	143	187	103	59	158	141	232		112

Mileages © Rand McNally

		Total mileages through Wisconsin
39	182 miles	90	189 miles
43	192 miles	94	341 miles

More mileages at www.randmcnally.com/MC

One inch represents approximately 15 miles

Tourism Information — Wisconsin Department of Tourism (800) 432-8747, (608) 266-2161 — www.travelwisconsin.com

Road Conditions & Construction — 511 — (866) 511-9472 — www.511wi.gov

Toll Road Information — No toll roads

Explore Wisconsin at www.randmcnally.com/WI

City sights to see
- Angel Museum, Beloit, N-6
- Betty Brinn Children's Museum, Milwaukee, L-3
- Golden Rondelle Theatre, Racine, J-10
- Harley Davidson Museum, Milwaukee, M-2
- Henry Maier Festival Park, Milwaukee, M-3
- J.M. Kohler Arts Center, Sheboygan, F-10

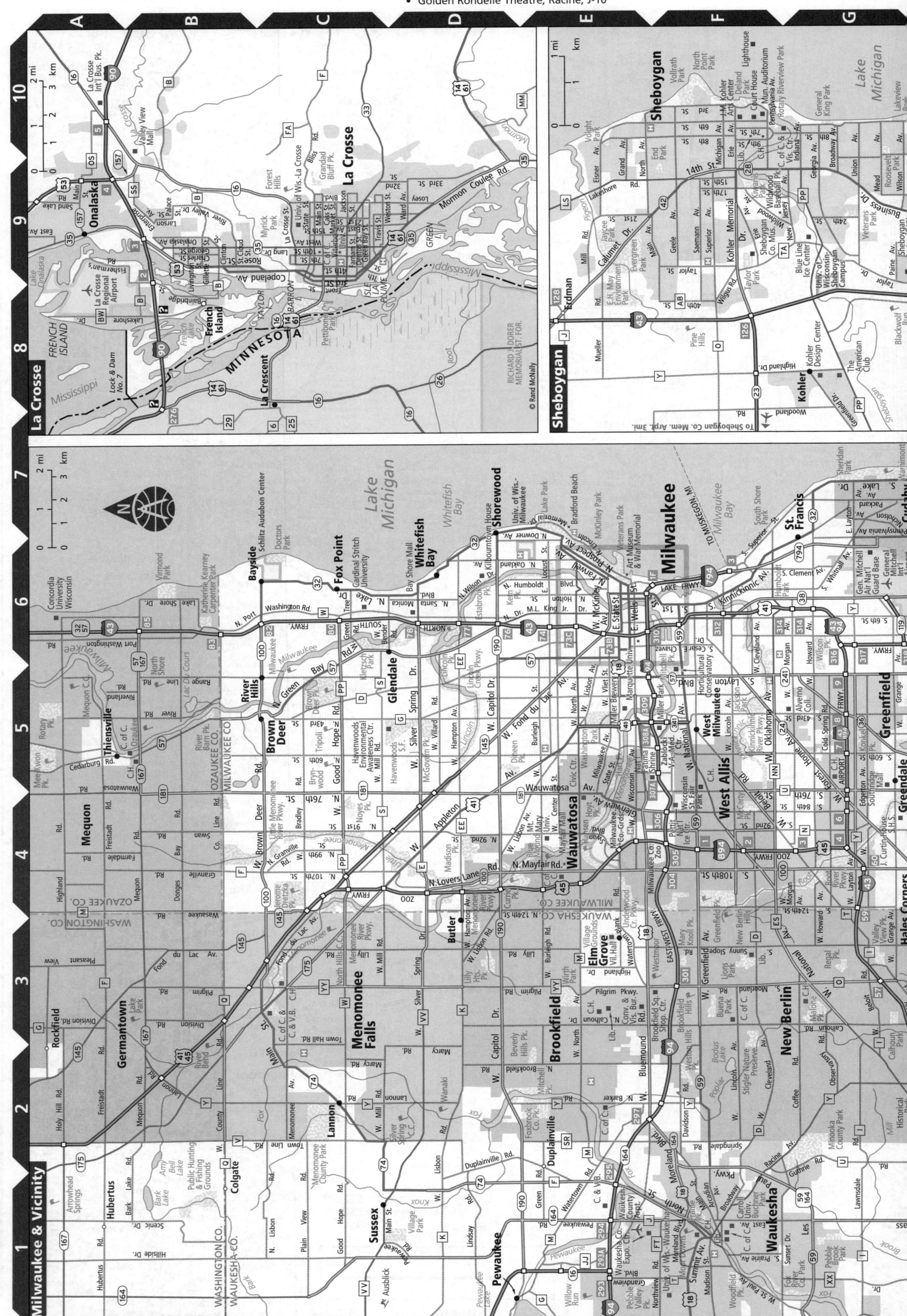

- Kenosha History Center, Kenosha, L-10
- Miller Brewery, Milwaukee, E-5
- Milwaukee Art Museum & War Memorial, Milwaukee, L-3
- Milwaukee Public Museum, Milwaukee, L-2
- Mitchell Park Horticultural Conservatory, Milwaukee, F-5
- Petit National Ice Center, Milwaukee, F-4

Index of cities Pg. 264

Mileages between cities	Casper	Cheyenne	Cody	Evanston	Gillette	Laramie	Sheridan	Spearfish, SD
Casper		178	213	325	126	147	148	219
Cheyenne	178		392	357	244	49	324	290
Cody	213	392		376	250	363	148	34
Jackson	283	432	177	190	411	383	325	50

Mileages © Rand McNally

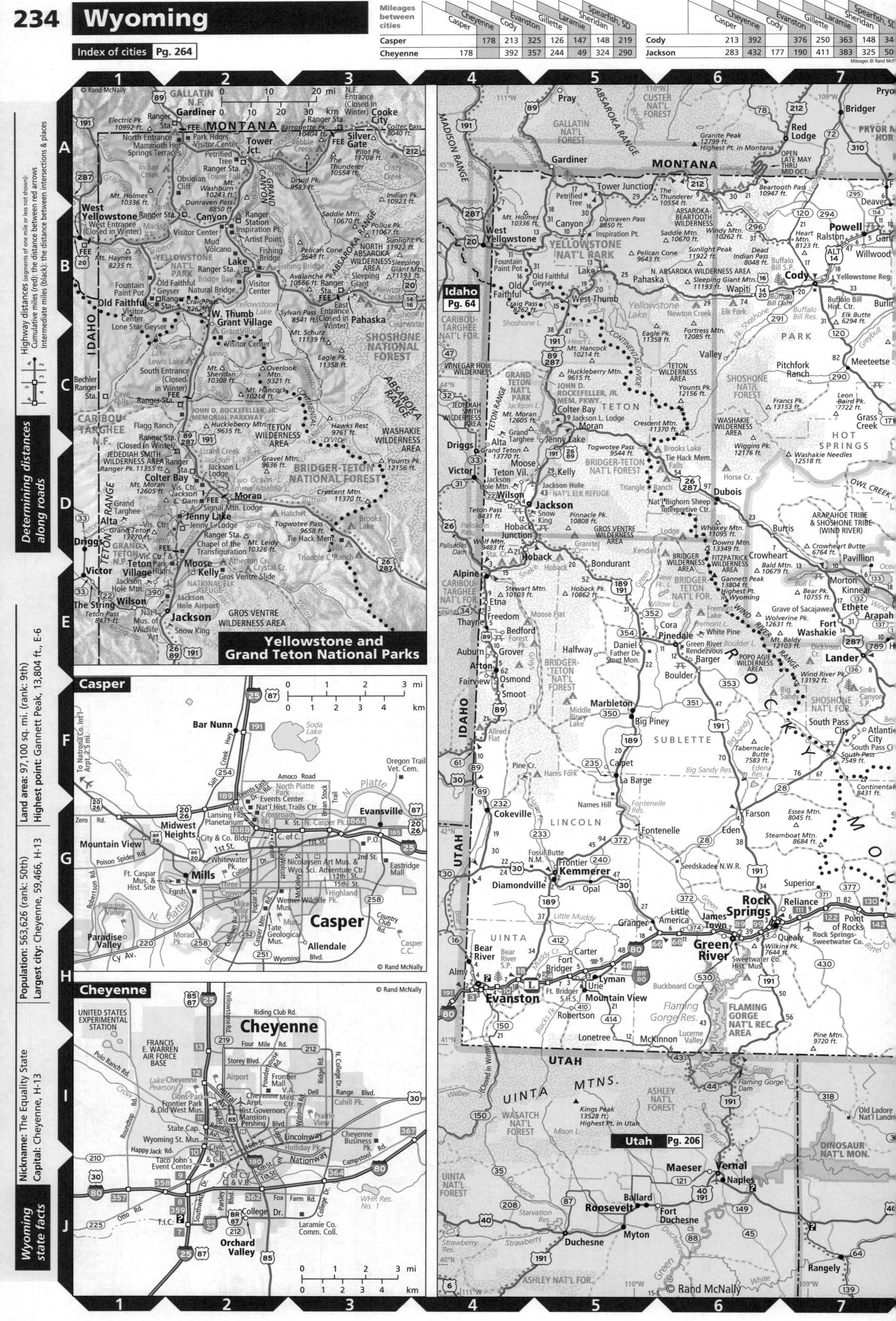

Yellowstone and Grand Teton National Parks

Casper

Cheyenne

Wyoming state facts

Nickname: The Equality State
Capital: Cheyenne, H-13
Population: 563,626 (rank: 50th)
Largest city: Cheyenne, 59,466, H-13
Land area: 97,100 sq. mi. (rank: 9th)
Highest point: Gannett Peak, 13,804 ft., E-6

Determining distances along roads

Highway distances (segments of one mile or less not shown):
Cumulative miles (red): the distance between red arrows
Intermediate miles (black): the distance between intersections & places

© Rand McNally

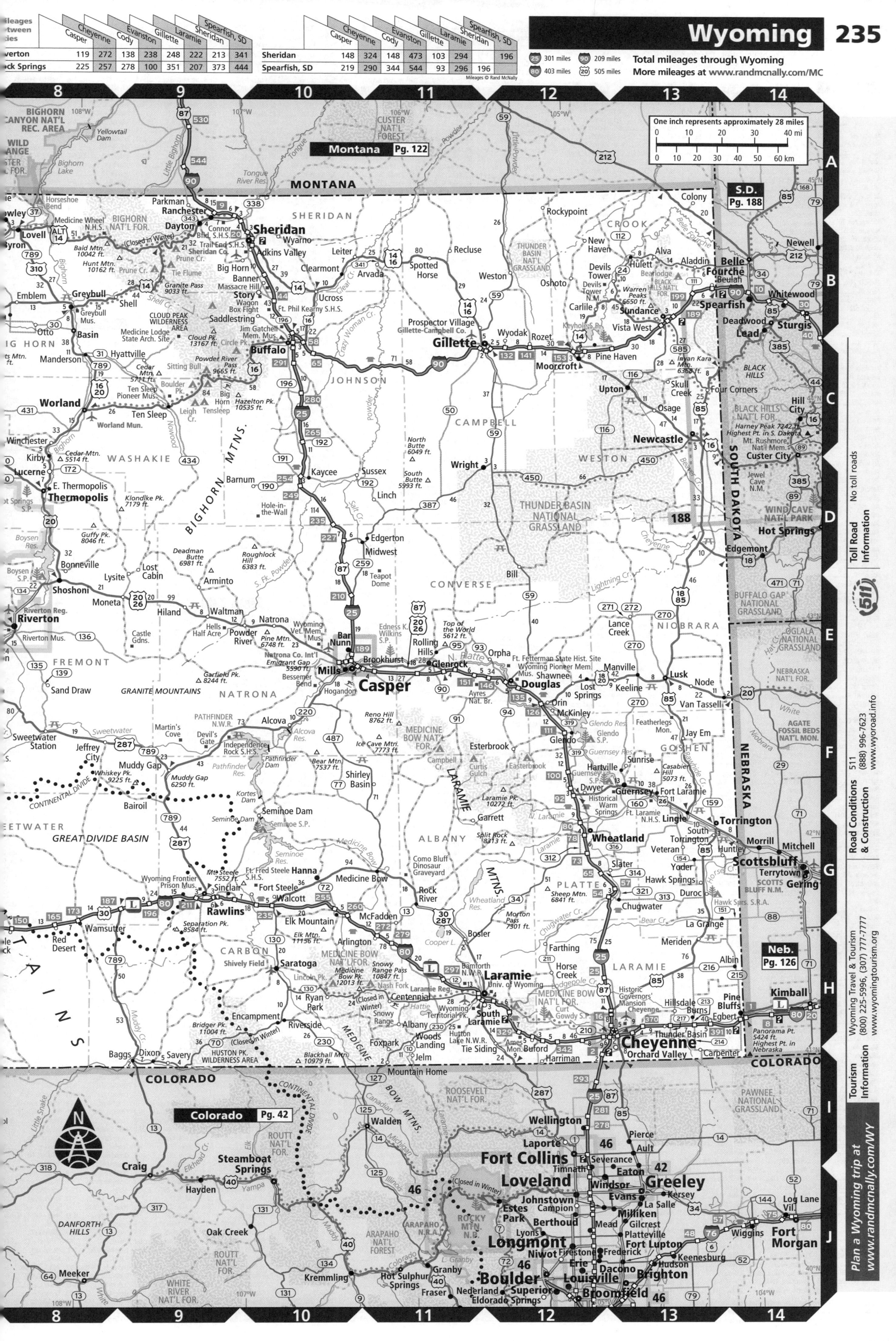

United States Counties, cities, towns & places
Populations are from the 2010 U.S. Census or are Rand McNally estimates

■ Alabama

Page locator
Map keys   Atlas pages
A–J   10–11
K–T   12–13

Abanda, 192 .... G-10
Abbeville, 2688 .. M-11
Abel, 100 .... K-10
Aberfoil, 70 .... K-10
Abernant, 500 .. F-4
Active H-6
Ada, 30 .... M-4
Adamsville, 4522 .. F-6
Addison, 758 .... D-5
Akron, 256 .... H-4
Alabama Port, 200 .. Q-3
Alabaster, 30352 .. G-6
Alberta, 200 .... K-5
Albertville, 21160 .. C-8
Alexander City,
  14875 .... H-9
Alexandria, 3917 .. E-9
Aliceville, 2486 .. G-3
Allen, 70 .... M-4
Allenton, 50 .... E-7
Allgood, 622 .... E-7
Allsboro, 85 .... B-3
Alma, 40 .... M-4
Almond, 50 .... M-8
Alpine, 300 .... G-8
Altoona, 933 .... D-8
America, 250 .... N-5
Andalusia, 9015 .. N-11
Anderson, 282 .... A-5
Anne Marie, 60 .. K-4
Anniston, 23106 .. E-9
Ansley, 50 .... M-8
Antioch, 100 .... M-8
Arab, 8050 .... C-7
Ardmore, 1194 .. A-6
Argo, 4071 .... E-7
Ariton, 764 .... M-10
Arkadelphia,
  100 .... E-6
Arley, 357 .... D-5
Armstrong, 60 .. J-10
Ashby, 100 .... H-6
Ashford, 2148 .. N-11
Ashland, 2037 .. G-9
Ashridge, 100 .. D-6
Ashville, 2212 .. E-8
Athens, 21897 .. A-6
Atkinson, 100 .. K-4
Atmore, 10194 .. O-4
Attalla, 6048 .. D-9
Atwood, 30 .... J-10
Auburn, 53380 .. I-10
Aurora, 50 .... D-8
AUTAUGA CO.,
  54571 .... J-7
Autaugaville, 870 .. J-7
Avon, 543 .... N-11
Awin I-7
Axis, 750 .... O-3
Babbie, 603 .... N-6
Baileyton, 610 .. C-7
Baker Hill, 279 .. L-11
BALDWIN CO.,
  182265 .... O-4
Ballplay, 1580 .. D-9
Bangor, 130 .... D-7
Bankhead, 90 .. E-5
Banks, 179 .... L-9
Bankston, 150 .. F-4
BARBOUR CO.,
  27457 .... K-11
Barfield, 300 .. J-10
Barnett Crossroads,
  30 .... N-5
Barney, 200 .... L-2
Barrytown, 100 .. L-2
Barton, 150 .... B-3
Bashan, 260 .... K-3
Bashi, 200 .... K-3
Batesville K-11
Bay Minette, 8044 .. O-4
Bay View Q-9
Bayou La Batre,
  2558 .... Q-2
Bear Creek, 1070 .. C-4
Beatrice, 301 .. L-5
Beaver Town, 80 .. G-2
Beaverton, 201 .. E-3
Belforest, 200 .. P-3
Belgreen, 129 .. C-3
Belk, 215 .... F-3
Bellamy, 543 .. J-3
Belle Mina, 400 .. B-6
Belleville, 170 .. M-6
Bellview K-3
Bellwood, 300 .. N-10
Belmont J-3
Beloit, 150 .... K-6
Benton, 49 .... K-6
Berlin, 60 .... D-7
Bermuda, 90 .. N-4
Berry, 1148 .. F-4
Bertha, 50 .... M-11
Bessemer, 27456 .. F-6
Beulah, 400 .. I-11
Bexar, 50 .... D-3
BIBB CO., 22915 .. H-6
Bigbee, 40 .. M-2
Billingsley, 144 .. J-7
Birmingham, 212237 .. F-7
Black, 207 .. O-10
Black Rock .. N-4
Blacksher .. N-4
Bladon Sprs., 150 .. L-2
Bleecker, 100 .. J-11
Blossburg, 190 .. P-10
BLOUNT CO.,
  57322 .... D-7
Blount Sprs., 80 .. D-7
Blountsville, 1684 .. D-7
Blue Sprs., 96 .. N-10
Bluff, 60 .. A-1
Bluff Pk. .. F-7
Bluff Spr., 300 .. G-9
Bluffton, 30 .. D-9
Boaz, 9551 .. D-8
Bodine, 328 .. I-3
Bolling, 90 .. L-6
Bomar, 30 .. D-10
Bon Air, 116 .. G-8
Bon Secour, 900 .. Q-4
Booth, 200 .. J-7
Borden Sprs., 90 .. F-10
Boykin, 275 .. K-5
Boyles .. Q-11

Boys Ranch, 140 .. O-7
Bradley, 50 .. O-7
Bradleyton, 50 .. L-7
Braggs, .. K-7
Brantley, 809 .. M-8
Brantley, 60 .. I-2
Brantleyville, 884 .. G-6
Bremen, 80 .. D-6
Brent, 4947 .. H-6
Brewton, 5408 .. N-6
Briar Hill .. K-9
Bridgeport, A-10 .. A-10
Brierfield, 20 .. H-6
Brighton, 2945 .. S-10
Brilliant, 900 .. C-4
Brookley, 120 .. N-7
Brooklyn, 60 .. D-7
Brookside, 1363 .. P-10
Brooksville, 210 .. D-7
Brookwood, 1828 .. G-5
Browns, 100 .. J-5
Brownsboro, 400 .. B-8
Brownville, 250 .. F-4
Brundidge, 2076 .. L-9
Bryant, 150 .. A-9
Bucks, 32 .. O-3
Buena Vista, 30 .. L-5
Buffalo, 40 .. H-11
Buhl, 300 .. F-3
Bullock, 70 .. M-8
BULLOCK CO.,
  10914 .... K-10
Burchfield, 30 .. C-5
Burkville, 150 .. J-7
Burnsville, 100 .. J-4
Burnt Corn, 150 .. M-5
Butler, 1894 .. K-2
BUTLER CO., 20947 .. L-6
Butler Sprs. .. L-6
Cahaba, 30 .. J-6
Cahaba Hts., 5203 .. S-13
Calcis, 230 .. F-8
Calera, 11620 .. G-7
Calhoun, 250 .. K-6
CALHOUN CO.,
  118572 .... E-9
Calvert, 277 .. N-3
Camden, 2020 .. K-5
Camp Hill, 1014 .. H-10
Campbell, 100 .. J-2
Canoe, 170 .. O-5
Capps, 30 .. M-11
Capshaw, 300 .. B-6
Carbon Hill, 2021 .. E-4
Cardiff, 55 .. P-10
Carlowville, 80 .. K-6
Carlton, 65 .. N-3
Carns, 80 .. A-9
Carolina, 297 .. N-7
Carrollton, 1019 .. G-3
Cartwright, 150 .. G-9
Casey, 30 .. L-9
Castleberry, 583 .. N-6
Catalpa .. L-9
Catherine, 82 .. K-5
Cecil, 150 .. J-8
Cedar Bluff, 1820 .. C-10
Cedar Grv., 40 .. D-4
Center Hill, 250 .. D-7
Center Pt., 16921 .. F-7
Center Star, 300 .. A-5
Centerville, 40 .. M-6
Central, 100 .. I-9
Central City .. P-10
Central Hts., 280 .. A-4
Centre, 3489 .. D-10
Centreville, 2778 .. H-6
CHAMBERS CO.,
  34215 .... H-11
Chancellor, 250 .. N-9
Chandler Sprs., 120 .. G-9
Chapel Hill .. T-12
Chapman, 380 .. L-7
Chase, 30 .. B-7
Chatom, 1288 .. M-2
Chelsea, 10183 .. G-7
Cherokee, 1048 .. B-3
CHEROKEE CO.,
  25989 .... C-10
Chesson .. O-4
Chestnut .. L-4
Chickasaw, 6106 .. P-3
Childersburg, 5175 .. G-8
Chilton .. H-6
CHILTON CO.,
  43643 .... H-7
China Grv. .. K-9
CHOCTAW CO.,
  13859 .... K-2
Chrysler, 50 .. N-4
Chunchula, 210 .. O-2
Citronelle, 3905 .. N-2
Claiborne, 150 .. M-4
Clanton, 8619 .. H-7
Clarence, 763 .. J-3
CLARKE CO., 25833 .. L-3
Claud, 50 .. J-8
Clay, 9708 .. E-7
CLAY CO., 13932 .. G-9
Clayhatchee, 589 .. N-10
Claysville, 650 .. B-8
Clayton, 1538 .. L-11
Clephane, 1498 .. Q-4
Eldridge, 130 .. E-4
Eliska, 50 .. N-4
Elkmont, 434 .. A-6
Elkwood .. A-7
Elmore, 1262 .. H-8
ELMORE CO.,
  79303 .... H-8
Elrod, 450 .. G-4
Elsanor, 60 .. P-4
Elsmede .. G-5
Emelle, 53 .. I-2
Empire, 150 .. E-6
Englewood, 350 .. O-4
Enon, 60 .. K-10
Enterprise, 26562 .. N-9
Eoda, 80 .. B-9
Epes, 192 .. I-2
Equality, 150 .. H-9

Comer, 60 .. K-11
Concord, 1837 .. O-7
CONECUH CO.,
  13228 .... M-6
Cooks Sprs., 200 .. E-8
Coopers, 200 .. J-7
COOSA CO., 11539 .. H-8
Coosada, 1224 .. I-8
Copeland .. M-2
Cordova, 2095 .. E-5
Corona, 100 .. E-5
Cotaco, 120 .. C-7
Cottage Grv. .. H-8
Cottage Hill .. S-7
Cottonton, 650 .. K-12
Cottonton, 150 .. B-4
Cottonwood, 1289 .. O-11
Country Club Estates .. S-7
Country Club Vil. .. S-6
County Line, 258 .. E-7
Courtland, 609 .. B-5
Covin, 60 .. E-3
COVINGTON CO.,
  37765 .... N-7
Cowarts, 1871 .. N-11
Coxey, 50 .. B-5
Coy, 300 .. L-5
Cragford, 150 .. G-10
Crane Hill, 250 .. D-6
Crawford .. J-11
Creek Stand .. J-10
Creeltown, 80 .. E-6
CRENSHAW CO.,
  13906 .... L-8
Creola, 1926 .. O-3
Crews, 50 .. D-3
Cromwell, 230 .. K-2
Crooked Oak, 30 .. B-4
Crossroads, 100 .. O-3
Crossville, 1862 .. C-9
Crossville, 60 .. E-3
Crumley Chapel,
  1630 .... Q-10
Cuba, 346 .. J-2
Cullman, 14775 .. D-6
CULLMAN CO.,
  80406 .... D-6
Cullomburg, 171 .. L-2
Cusseta, 123 .. I-11
Cypress, 100 .. M-5
Dadeville, 3230 .. H-10
Daleville, 5295 .. N-10
Dallas, 300 .. E-7
DALLAS CO., 43820 .. J-5
Damascus, 30 .. N-4
Dancy, 30 .. F-2
Danielsville, 580 .. F-1
Danleys Crossroads .. M-8
Danville, 300 .. C-6
Daphne, 21570 .. P-3
Darlington, 50 .. K-6
Dauphin Island,
  1238 .... Q-3
Daviston, 250 .. H-10
Davenport, 80 .. K-8
Dawson, 150 .. D-9
Dayton, 52 .. J-4
DE KALB CO.,
  71109 .... C-9
DeArmanville, 580 .. F-1
Decatur, 55683 .. B-6
Deer Pk., 188 .. N-2
Delmar, 300 .. D-4
Delta, 197 .. F-10
Demopolis, 7483 .. I-3
Deposit, 30 .. A-7
Detroit, 237 .. D-3
Dickinson, 30 .. L-4
Dixie, 60 .. N-7
Dixon Cor., 100 .. O-2
Dixons Mills, 290 .. K-4
Dixonville .. O-6
Dodge City, 593 .. D-6
Dora, 2025 .. E-6
Doster, 100 .. M-10
Dothan, 65496 .. N-11
Double Sprs., 1083 .. D-5
Douglas, 744 .. D-8
Downing .. M-7
Dozier, 389 .. M-8
Duke, 160 .. E-3
Duncanville, 150 .. H-5
Dutton, 315 .. B-9

Eva, 519 .. C-7
Evergreen, 3944 .. M-6
Ewell, 130 .. M-10
Excel, 723 .. M-5
Fabius, 50 .. A-9
Fackler, 400 .. B-9
Fadette, 100 .. O-10
Fairfield, 11117 .. R-10
Fairfield Highlands .. R-11
Fairford, 186 .. N-3
Fairhope, 15326 .. P-3
Fairview, 446 .. C-7
Fairview, 30 .. F-11
Falkville, 1279 .. C-6
Farmersville, 60 .. K-6
Faunsdale, 98 .. J-4
Fayette, 4619 .. E-3
FAYETTE CO.,
  17241 .... E-4
Fayetteville, 1284 .. G-8
Fernbank, 30 .. F-3
Fieldstown .. P-11
Fisk .. K-3
Fitzpatrick, 83 .. K-9
Five Points, 141 .. H-11
Five Points, 60 .. C-5
Flat Rock, 150 .. A-9
Flatwood, 150 .. K-4
Flomaton, 1440 .. O-5
Florala, 1980 .. O-8
Florence, 39319 .. B-4
Florette .. C-7
Floyd, 30 .. O-11
Foley, 14618 .. Q-4
Foldensville .. R-7
Hillsboro, 552 .. B-5
Hilltop .. T-7
Hissop, 658 .. H-8
Hoboken .. K-3
Hobson City, 771 .. F-9
Hodges, 288 .. C-3
Hokes Bluff, 4286 .. D-9
Hollins, 545 .. G-8
Hollis Crossroads,
  608 .... F-10
Holly Pond, 798 .. D-7
Hollywood, 1000 .. B-9
Holt, 3638 .. G-4
Holtville, 4096 .. H-8
Holy Trinity, 90 .. J-12
Homewood, 25167 .. F-7
Honoraville, 100 .. L-7
Hoover, 81619 .. F-6
Hopewell .. F-8
Horton, 250 .. D-8
Houston, 190 .. D-5
HOUSTON CO.,
  101547 .... N-11
Howard, 40 .. E-4
Hueytown, 16105 .. F-6
Huffman .. P-11
Huguley, 2540 .. H-11
Hulaco, 200 .. C-7
Huntsville, 180105 .. B-7
Hurtsboro, 553 .. K-11
Huxford, 200 .. N-5
Hybart, 100 .. L-5
Hytop, 354 .. A-9
Ider, 723 .. B-10
Independence, 40 .. G-8
Indian Sprs. .. Q-6
Indian Sprs. Vil. .. ...
  2363 .... G-7
Industry, 50 .. M-7
Inglenook .. Q-12
Ino, 30 .. N-9
Inverness, 50 .. G-7
Irondale, 12349 .. F-7
Irvington, 500 .. P-2
Isbell, 130 .. B-4
Isney, 30 .. L-1
Jachin, 30 .. J-2
Jack, 100 .. M-9
Jackson, 5228 .. M-3
JACKSON CO.,
  53227 .... A-8
Jackson Hts. .. ...
Jackson Gap, 828 .. H-9
Jacksonville, 12548 .. E-10
Jamestown, 50 .. C-5
Jasper, 14352 .. E-5
Jefferson, 20 .. J-3
JEFFERSON CO.,
  658466 .... F-5
Jemison, 2585 .. H-7
Jenifer, 180 .. E-9
Jerusalem Hts., 300 .. T-2
Johnstonville, 100 .. G-9
Jones, 130 .. J-6
Jones Chapel, 170 .. D-6
Joppa, 280 .. D-7
Jordan, 30 .. J-11
Jordan, 30 .. D-11
Josephine, 100 .. Q-4
Kansas, 226 .. E-4
Keener, 80 .. D-9
Kellerman, 130 .. G-5
Kellyton, 217 .. H-9
Kennedy, 447 .. F-3
Kent, 500 .. J-7
Killen, 1108 .. A-4
Kilpatrick, 150 .. C-9
Kimberly, 2711 .. E-6
Kimbrough, 150 .. K-4
Kinsey, 2198 .. N-11
Kinston, 540 .. N-8
Kirkland, 100 .. N-5
Knoxville, 80 .. H-4
Koenton, 30 .. M-3
Kymulga, 100 .. G-8
Laceys Chapel .. T-10
Laceys Sprs., 400 .. B-7
Lacon, 70 .. C-6
Ladonia, 3142 .. J-12
Lafayette, 3003 .. H-11
Lakeview, 143 .. C-9
Lamison, 100 .. K-4
Lamson, 300 .. ...

Hanceville, 2982 .. D-7
Hanover .. M-7
Hardaway, 110 .. J-9
Harpersville, 1637 .. G-8
Harrisburg, 160 .. H-5
Hartford, 2624 .. N-10
Hartselle, 14255 .. C-6
Harvest, 5281 .. A-7
Hatchechubbee, ...
  250 .... J-11
Hatton, 261 .. B-5
Havana, 50 .. H-4
Hawk .. F-11
Hayden, 444 .. E-7
Hayneville, 932 .. K-7
Hazel Green, 3630 .. A-7
Headland, 4510 .. N-11
Heath, 254 .. N-8
Heflin, 3480 .. F-10
Heiberger .. I-5
Helena, 16793 .. G-6
Helicon, 150 .. D-6
Henagar, 2344 .. B-10
Henderson, 50 .. M-8
HENRY CO.,
  17302 .... M-11
Heron Bay, 330 .. Q-2
Hickory Flat, 50 .. G-11
Higdon, 500 .. A-10
High Pt., 80 .. G-11
Highland Home, 300 .. K-8
Highland Lake, 412 .. E-8
Hightogy, 70 .. E-3
Hightower, 80 .. F-11
Hazel Green .. ...

... (index continues across remaining columns for Alabama, Alaska, Arizona) ...

■ Alaska

Page locator
Map keys   Atlas pages
A–J   14–15

Adak, 326 .. J-8
Akhiok, 71 .. I-5
Akiachak, 627 .. G-4
Akutan, 1027 .. J-1
Alakanuk, 677 .. E-3
Aleknagik, 219 .. H-4
Allakaket, 105 .. D-7
Ambler, 258 .. C-5
Anaktuvuk Pass, 324 .. C-7
Anchor Pt., 1930 .. H-7
Anchorage, 291826 .. G-7
Anderson, 246 .. E-7
Angoon, 459 .. I-12
Aniak, 501 .. G-4
Anvik, 85 .. F-4
Arctic Vil., 152 .. C-8
Atka, 61 .. J-8
Atmautluak, 277 .. G-4
Atqasuk, 233 .. A-6
Attu, 21 .. J-7
Barrow, 4212 .. A-6
Beaver, 84 .. D-8
Bethel, 6080 .. G-4
Bettles, 12 .. D-7
Big Delta, 591 .. E-8
Big Lake, 3350 .. G-7
Birch Creek, 33 .. D-8
Brevig Mission, 388 .. D-3
Buckland, 416 .. D-5
Candle .. D-5
Cantwell, 219 .. F-7
Cape Yakataga, 20 .. G-9
Central, 96 .. D-8
Chalkyitsik, 69 .. D-9
Chefornak, 418 .. G-3
Chevak, 938 .. F-3
Chickaloon, 272 .. G-8
Chicken, 7 .. E-8
Chignik, 91 .. I-4
Chistochina, 93 .. F-9
Chitina, 126 .. G-9
Chuathbaluk, 118 .. F-5
Circle, 104 .. D-9
Circle Hot Sprs. .. D-8
Clark's Pt., 62 .. H-4
Coffman Cove, 176 .. J-13
Cold Bay, 108 .. J-2
Coldfoot, 12 .. C-7
College, 12964 .. E-7
Cooper Ctr., 328 .. F-9
Cordova, 2239 .. G-8
Council, 2 .. D-4
Craig, 1201 .. J-13
Deadhorse .. B-7
Deering, 122 .. C-5
Delta Jct., 958 .. E-8
Dillingham, 2329 .. H-4
Dot Lake, 13 .. E-8
Eagle, 86 .. E-8
Eek, 296 .. G-4
Egegik, 109 .. H-5
Ekuk, 30 .. H-4
Ekwok, 115 .. H-4
Elfin Cove, 20 .. H-11
Elim, 330 .. D-4
Emmonak, 762 .. E-3
Eureka, 20 .. F-8
Excursion Inlet, 12 .. H-12
Fairbanks, 31535 .. E-8
False Pass, 35 .. J-2
Ferry, 33 .. E-7
Flat .. F-5
Ft. Yukon, 583 .. D-8
Gakona, 218 .. F-9
Galena, 470 .. E-5
Gambell, 681 .. D-2
Girdwood, 1800 .. G-7
Glennallen, 483 .. F-9
Golovin, 156 .. D-4
Goodnews Bay, 243 .. H-4

■ Arizona

Page locator
Map keys   Atlas pages
A–J   16–17
K–T   18–19
* City keyed to pp. 20–21

Adamana .. *M-10
Aguila, 798 .. J-5
Ahwatukee .. *K-6
Ajo, 3304 .. L-4
Alpine, 145 .. I-14
Amado, 295 .. N-10
Anegam, 151 .. M-8
Anthem, 21700 .. J-7
Apache Jct., 35840 .. J-9
Arcadia .. *I-6
Arivaca, 695 .. O-9
Arivaca Jct., 1090 .. N-10
Arizona City, 4217 .. K-8
Arizona Sun Sites .. L-12
Arizona Vil., 566 .. I-2
Arlington, 194 .. J-6
Ash Fork, 396 .. F-7
Avondale, 76238 .. J-7
Avra Valley, 6050 .. M-9
Aztec, 47 .. K-5
Bagdad, 1876 .. G-5
Bapchule, 100 .. K-8
Beaver Dam, 1962 .. *A-3
Bellemont, 200 .. E-9
Benson, 5105 .. N-11
Bisbee, 5575 .. O-12
Bisbee Jct., 30 .. O-12
Black Canyon City,
  2837 .... H-7
Blue, 30 .. I-14
Bouse, 996 .. I-3
Bowie, 449 .. M-13
Buckeye, 50876 .. J-6
Bullhead City, 39540 .. F-2
Bylas, 1962 .. K-12
Cameron, 885 .. D-9
Camp Verde, 10873 .. G-8
Cane Beds, 448 .. A-6
Carefree, 3363 .. I-8
Carmen, 400 .. O-10
Casa Blanca .. K-8
Casa Grande, 48571 .. K-8
Casas Adobes .. *A-1
Catalina, 7569 .. L-10
Catalina Foothills .. P-4
Cave Creek, 5015 .. I-8
Cedar Ridge, 40 .. C-9
Chambers, 250 .. E-13
Chandler, 236123 .. J-8
Chilchinbito, 506 .. B-12
Chino Valley, 10817 .. G-7
Chloride, 271 .. E-3
Cibecue, 1761 .. H-11
Cibola .. *H-2
Citrus Pk., 4028 .. *H-2
Clarkdale, 4097 .. G-8
Clay Sprs., 401 .. H-11
Claypool, 1538 .. I-10
Clifton, 3311 .. J-13
Cochise .. N-12
COCHISE CO.,
  131346 .... O-12
COCONINO CO.,
  134421 .... C-8
Colorado City, 4821 .. A-6
Comobabi, 80 .. M-8
Concho, 36 .. G-12
Congress, 1975 .. H-6
Continental .. N-10
Coolidge, 11825 .. K-9
Cooper Lakes, 2633 .. H-7
Cornfields, 250 .. D-12
Cornville, 3280 .. G-8
Cottonwood, 11265 .. G-8
Cowlic, 135 .. M-9
Cross Canyon, 30 .. D-13
Crown King, 40 .. H-7
Dateland, 416 .. L-4
Dennehotso, 746 .. B-13
Desert Hills, 2245 .. L-10
Dewey-Humboldt,
  3894 .... G-7
Dilkon, 184 .. E-11
Dolan Sprs., 2033 .. D-3
Dos Cabezas, 40 .. M-13
Douglas, 17378 .. O-13
Dragoon, 209 .. N-12
Dreamland Villa,
  4800 .... *J-8
Drexel Hts., 27749 .. *C-2
Dudleyville, 959 .. K-10
Duncan, 696 .. L-13
Eagar, 4885 .. H-13
E. Fork, 699 .. H-11
Ehrenberg, 1470 .. I-2
El Mirage, 31797 .. *H-3

Arkansas
Page locator
Map keys 1–10 ... Atlas pages 22–23
Map keys 11–20 ... Atlas pages 24–25

California
Page locator
Map keys NA1–NN10 ... Atlas pages 26–27
Map keys NA11–NN20 ... Atlas pages 28–29
Map keys SA1–SN10 ... Atlas pages 34–35
Map keys SA11–SN20 ... Atlas pages 36–37
* City keyed to p. 19
† City keyed to pp. 30–31
‡ City keyed to pp. 32–33
§ City keyed to pp. 38–39
◊ City keyed to pp. 40–41

Gas Pt., 30 ...NF-5
Gasquet, 661 ...NA-2
Gaviota, 70 ...SI-7
Gazelle, 70 ...NC-5
Genesee, 150 ...NG-8
Georgetown, 2367 ...NJ-8
Gerber, 1060 ...NG-6
Geyserville, 862 ...NJ-4
Glamis ...SM-18
Glen Ellen, 784 ...NK-5
Glencoe, 300 ...NK-9
Glendale, 191719 ...SJ-11
Glendora, 50073 ...†D-12
Glenhaven, 60 ...NJ-4
Glenn, 110 ...NH-6

GLENN CO.,
28122 ...NH-5
Glennville, 210 ...SE-10
Glenview, 160 ...SG-9
Goffs ...SG-18
Gold Run, 200 ...NI-8
Goleta, 29888 ...SI-7
Gonzales, 8187 ...SC-4
Goodyears Bar, 68 ...NH-8
Gorman, 50 ...SH-10
Goshen, 3006 ...SD-8
Graeagle, 737 ...NG-9
Granada Hills ...§B-4
Grand Ter., 12040 ...†E-18
Grangeville, 469 ...SD-8
Graniteville, 11 ...NH-8
Grass Valley, 12860 ...NI-8
Graton, 1707 ...NK-4
Grayson, 952 ...NM-8
Greeley Hill, 915 ...NM-10
Green Brae, 3400 ...ND-12
Greenacres, 5566 ...SL-5
Greenfield, 16330 ...SD-4
Greenview, 201 ...NB-4
Greenville, 1129 ...NF-8
Greenwood, 600 ...NJ-8
Grenada, 367 ...NG-4
Gridley, 6584 ...NH-7
Grimes, 391 ...NI-6
Grizzly Flat, 1066 ...NJ-9
Groveland, 601 ...NM-10
Grover Bch., 13156 ...SG-6
Guadalupe, 7080 ...SG-7
Gualala, 1500 ...NJ-3
Guasti ...◊E-15
Guerneville, 4534 ...NK-4
Guernsey ...SD-8
Guinda, 254 ...NJ-6
Gustine, 5520 ...SA-5
Hacienda Hts.,
54038 ...§F-10
Half Moon Bay,
11324 ...NN-4
Hamburg, 140 ...NB-4
Hamilton City,
1759 ...NG-6
Hanford, 53967 ...SD-8
Happy Camp, 1190 ...NB-3
Harbor City ...§I-7
Hardwick, 138 ...SC-8
Harmony ...SF-5
Harris ...NF-2
Harvard ...SG-15
Hat Creek, 309 ...ND-7
Hathaway Pines,
350 ...NL-9
Havasu Lake, 410 ...†L-10
Havilah ...SF-10
Hawaiian Gdns.,
14254 ...§H-9
Hawkinsville, 20 ...NB-5
Hawthorne, 84293 ...§G-6
Hayfork, 2368 ...NE-4
Hayward, 144186 ...NM-6
Healdsburg, 11254 ...NJ-4
Heber, 4275 ...SM-17
Helena ...NE-4
Helendale, 700 ...SH-13
Helm ...SC-7
Hemet, 78657 ...SK-14
Henderson Vil., 200 ...NK-8
Herald, 1184 ...NK-8
Hercules, 24060 ...NC-15
Herlong, 900 ...NF-10
Hermosa Bch.,
19506 ...§H-5
Herndon ...SD-8
Hesperia, 90173 ...SI-13
Hi Vista ...SI-12
Hickman, 441 ...NM-9
Hidden Hills, 1856 ...§b-2
Hidden Valley, 1400 ...NJ-4
Highgrove, 3988 ...◊F-18
Highland, 53104 ...SJ-13
Highway City ...SB-12
Hillsborough,
10825 ...NI-4
Hilt, 30 ...NA-5
Hinkley, 1000 ...SG-13
Hobart Mills ...NH-10
Hodge ...SH-13
Holladay, 34928 ...SB-4
Hollywood ...§C-4
Hollywood
by the Sea ...‡C-8
Holt ...NL-8
Holtville, 5939 ...SM-18
Home Gdns.,
11570 ...◊H-16
Homeland Valley,
3500 ...NI-10
Homewood, 350 ...NI-10
Honcut, 370 ...NI-7
Honeydew, 80 ...NF-2
Hooker ...NF-5
Hoopa, 1200 ...ND-3
Hope Ranch, 1600 ...*B-3
Hopeton ...NN-9
Hopland, 756 ...NJ-4
Hornbrook, 248 ...NA-5
Hornitos, 75 ...NN-10
Horse Creek ...NB-4
Hughson, 6640 ...NM-8

HUMBOLDT CO.,
134623 ...NE-2
Hume ...SB-10
Humphreys Sta. ...SB-9
Huntington Bch.,
189992 ...SK-12
Huntington Pk.,
58114 ...§F-7
Huron, 6754 ...SD-7
Hyampom, 20 ...NE-3
Hydesville, 1237 ...NE-2
Idria ...SC-6
Idyllwild, 2091 ...SK-15

Ignacio ...NB-11
Igo ...NE-5
Imperial, 14758 ...SM-17
Imperial Bch.,
26324 ...SN-14

IMPERIAL CO.,
174528 ...SM-18
Incline, 60 ...NM-1
Independence, 669 ...SB-11
Indian Wells, 4958 ...SK-16
Indio, 76036 ...SK-16
Industry, 219 ...◊F-11
Inglenook, 50 ...NH-3
Inglewood, 109673 ...SJ-11
Ingot ...NE-6
Inverness, 1304 ...NL-4

INYO CO.,
18546 ...NN-14
Inyokern, 1099 ...SF-12
Ione, 7918 ...NK-8
Iowa Hill ...NI-8
Irvine, 212375 ...SK-12
Irwin, 1050 ...NM-8
Irwindale, 1422 ...◊D-11
Isla Vista, 23096 ...SI-7
Island Mtn. ...NG-3
Isleton, 804 ...NL-7
Ivanhoe, 4495 ...SD-9
Ivanpah ...SF-18
Jackson, 4651 ...NK-8
Jacumba, 561 ...SN-16
Jamesburg ...SC-4
Jamestown, 3433 ...NL-9
Jamul, 6163 ...SN-14
Janesville, 1408 ...NF-9
Jenner, 136 ...NK-3
Jenny Lind, 730 ...NL-8
Johannesburg, 172 ...SF-12
Johnsondale ...SE-10
Johnstonville, 1024 ...NF-9
Johnsville, 20 ...NG-9
Jonesville ...NF-7
Joshua Tree, 7414 ...SJ-16
Julian, 1502 ...SM-15
Junction City, 680 ...NE-4
June Lake, 629 ...NM-12
Jupiter Valley, 1066 ...NK-9
Jurupa Valley,
94235 ...◊F-16
Keddie, 66 ...NG-8
Keeler, 66 ...SC-12
Keene, 431 ...SG-10
Kelsey, 256 ...NJ-8
Kelseyville, 3353 ...NI-4
Kelso ...SG-17
Kensington, 5077 ...ND-14
Kentfield, 6485 ...ND-11
Kenwood, 1028 ...NK-5
Kerman, 13544 ...SC-7

KERN CO.,
839631 ...SF-10
Kernville, 1395 ...SE-11
Keswick, 451 ...NE-5
Kettleman City,
1439 ...SE-7
Keyes, 5601 ...NM-8
King City, 12874 ...SD-5
Kings Bch., 3796 ...NI-10

KINGS CO.,
152982 ...SD-7
Kingsburg, 11382 ...SC-8
Kirkville ...NJ-6
Kirkwood, 100 ...NK-9
Kit Carson ...NK-9
Klamath, 779 ...NB-3
Klamath Glen, 290 ...NB-2
Klamath River ...NB-4
Kneeland, 30 ...NE-3
Knights Ferry, 700 ...NM-9
Knights, 995 ...NJ-7
Knightsen, 1568 ...NL-7
Kramer Jct., 280 ...SG-13
Kyburz, 150 ...NJ-10
La Barr Meadows,
500 ...NI-8
La Cañada Flintridge,
20246 ...§C-11
La Crescenta,
13000 ...§B-12
La Grange ...NM-9
La Habra, 60239 ...◊G-11
La Habra Hts.,
5325 ...◊G-11
La Honda, 928 ...NN-15
La Jolla ...†H-1
La Mesa, 57065 ...†I-5
La Mirada, 48527 ...§G-10
La Palma, 15568 ...SH-9
La Porte, 26 ...NH-8
La Presa, 34169 ...†I-5
La Puente, 39816 ...§D-10
La Quinta, 37467 ...SK-16
La Verne, 31063 ...§C-12
Ladera, 1426 ...NL-16
Ladera Ranch, 350 ...§L-15
Lafayette, 23893 ...NB-16
Laguna Bch.,
22733 ...SK-12
Laguna Hills,
30344 ...SK-12
Laguna Niguel,
62979 ...◊M-14
Laguna Woods,
16192 ...SK-12
L. Alpine ...NK-10
L. Arrowhead,
12424 ...SI-14
Lake City, 61 ...NB-10

LAKE CO., 64665 ...NI-4
L. Elsinore, 51821 ...SK-13
L. Forest, 77264 ...SK-12
L. Forest, 500 ...†F-8
L. Hughes, 649 ...SH-11
L. Isabella, 3466 ...SE-11
L. Los Angeles,
12328 ...SH-12
L. View Ter. ...§B-10
L. Wildwood, 4991 ...NI-8
Lakehead, 461 ...ND-5
Lakeland Vil.,
11541 ...◊K-18
Lakeport, 4753 ...NI-4
Lakeshore ...NA-5
Lakeside, 20648 ...SM-14
Lakeview, 2104 ...SJ-14
Lakewood, 80048 ...§H-9
Lamont, 15120 ...SG-10
Lanare, 189 ...SC-7
Lancaster, 156633 ...SH-11
Landers, 2300 ...SI-15
Larkspur, 11926 ...ND-11
Las Cruces, 201 ...SI-7

LASSEN CO.,
34895 ...NE-9

Lathrop, 18023 ...NM-7
Lawndale, 32769 ...§H-5
Laytonville, 1227 ...NG-3
Le Grand, 1659 ...SA-7
Leber, 1458 ...SH-10
Lee Vining, 222 ...NL-12
Leggett, 122 ...NG-2
Lemon Cove, 308 ...SC-9
Lemon Grv., 25320 ...†J-5
Lemon Hts., 2800 ...◊J-13
Lemoore, 24531 ...SD-8
Lennox, 22753 ...§G-6
Lenwood, 3543 ...SH-14
Leona Valley, 1607 ...SH-11
Lewiston, 1193 ...NE-4
Liberty Farms ...NK-7
Libfarm ...NK-7
Likely, 63 ...NB-9
Lincoln, 42819 ...NJ-7
Lincoln Acres, 1650 ...†K-4
Lincoln Vil., 4381 ...†K-9
Linda, 17773 ...NI-7
Linden, 1784 ...NL-8
Lindsay, 11768 ...SD-9
Litchfield, 195 ...NF-9
Little Lake, 50 ...SE-12
Little River, 117 ...NH-2
Little Valley ...ND-8
Loleta, 783 ...NE-2
Loma Linda, 23261 ...SJ-13
Loma Rica, 2368 ...NI-7
Monte Nido, 850 ...§E-2
Lomita, 20256 ...§J-6
Lompoc, 42434 ...SH-6
London, 1869 ...SC-8
Lone Pine, 2035 ...SC-11
Long Barn, 150 ...NL-10
Long Bch., 462257 ...SK-11
Longvale, 50 ...NH-3
Lookout, 84 ...NC-8
Loomis, 6430 ...NJ-8
Loraine ...SF-11
Los Alamitos, 11449 ...§I-9
Los Alamos, 1890 ...SH-6
Los Altos, 28976 ...NI-6
Los Altos Hills,
7922 ...NO-16
Los Angeles,
3792621 ...SI-11

LOS ANGELES CO.,
9818605 ...SI-11
Los Banos, 35972 ...SB-5
Los Gatos, 29413 ...SA-3
Los Molinos, 2037 ...NG-6
Los Nietos, 8200 ...§G-7
Los Olivos, 1132 ...SH-7
Los Ranchitos ...
425 ...NC-11
Los Serranos ...◊F-14
Lost Hills, 2412 ...SE-8
Lost Lake, 150 ...NL-8
Lotus, 700 ...NJ-8
Lower Lake, 1294 ...NJ-5
Loyalton, 769 ...NH-10
Lucas Valley, 4000 ...NC-11
Lucerne, 3067 ...NI-4
Lucerne Valley,
5811 ...SI-14
Ludlow ...SH-16
Lynwood, 69772 ...§G-7
Lytle Creek, 701 ...◊B-16
Macdoel, 133 ...NB-6
Mad River, 400 ...NE-3
Madeline ...ND-8
Madera, 61416 ...SB-7

MADERA CO.,
150865 ...NN-12
Madison, 503 ...NJ-6
Magalia, 11310 ...NG-7
Malibu, 12645 ...SJ-10
Mammoth Lakes,
8234 ...SA-11
Manchester, 195 ...NJ-3
Manhattan Bch.,
35135 ...§G-5
Manteca, 67096 ...NM-8
Manton, 347 ...NF-6
Maricopa, 1154 ...SG-8
Marin City, 2666 ...NC-12

MARIN CO.,
252409 ...NL-4
Marina, 19718 ...SC-3
Marina Del Rey, 50 ...§F-5
Mariposa, 2173 ...NN-10

MARIPOSA CO.,
18251 ...NN-10
Markleeville, 210 ...NL-11
Marshall ...NL-4
Martell, 282 ...NK-8
Martinez, 35824 ...NL-6
Marysville, 12072 ...NI-7
Massack ...NG-8
Maxwell, 1103 ...NI-6
Maywood, 27395 ...§F-7
McArthur, 338 ...ND-7
McCloud, 1101 ...NC-6
McFarland, 12707 ...SF-9
McKinleyville,
15177 ...NE-2
McKittrick, 115 ...SF-8
Mead Valley ...◊J-18
Meadow Valley ...NG-8
Meadow Vista,
464 ...NI-8
Mecca, 8577 ...SK-16
Meeks Bay ...NI-10
Meiners Oaks, 3571 ...SI-9
Mendocino, 894 ...NH-2

MENDOCINO CO.,
87841 ...NH-3
Mendota, 11014 ...SB-6
Menifee, 77519 ...SK-14
Menlo Pk., 32026 ...NN-5
Merced, 78958 ...NN-10

MERCED CO.,
255793 ...NN-9

Mesa Verde, 1023 ...SK-19
Mettler, 136 ...SG-9
Middletown, 1323 ...NJ-5
Midpines, 1204 ...NN-10
Midway City, 8485 ...§J-10
Milford, 167 ...NF-9
Mill Creek, 20 ...NF-7
Mill Valley, 13903 ...NL-5
Millbrae, 21532 ...NI-3
Millville, 727 ...NE-6
Milo ...SD-10
Milpitas, 66790 ...NN-6
Milton, 30 ...NL-8
Mineral, 123 ...NF-7
Mineral King ...SC-10
Mira Mesa ...†F-3
Mira Monte, 6854 ...SI-9
Miracle Hot Sprs., 50 ...SF-10
Mission Bch. ...†I-2
Mission Hills ...§b-4
Mission Viejo,
93305 ...SK-12
Mi-Wuk Vil., 941 ...NL-10
Moccasin ...NM-10
Modesto, 201165 ...NM-8
Mokelumne Hill,
646 ...NK-9

MODOC CO.,
9686 ...NC-9
Mojave, 4238 ...SG-11
Mokelumne Hill,
646 ...NK-9

MONO CO.,
14200 ...NL-13
Mono Hot Sprs. ...NN-12
Mono Vil. ...NL-12
Monrovia, 36590 ...§D-10
Montague, 1443 ...NB-5
Montalvin Manor,
2876 ...NC-14
Montalvo ...*B-9
Montara, 2909 ...NJ-3
Montclair, 36664 ...§S-14
Monte Nido, 850 ...§E-2
Monte Rio, 1152 ...NK-4
Monte Sereno,
3341 ...NN-18
Monte Vista,
15000 ...NM-17
Montebello, 62500 ...§F-9
Montecito, 8965 ...SI-8
Monterey, 27810 ...SC-3

MONTEREY CO.,
415057 ...SD-4
Monterey Pk.,
60269 ...§E-7
Montezuma, 163 ...NK-8
Montgomery Creek,
163 ...ND-6
Montrose, 4100 ...§C-7
Moorpark, 34441 ...SI-10
Moraga, 16016 ...NE-16
Moreno Valley,
193365 ...SJ-14
Morgan Hill, 37882 ...SA-3
Mormon Bar, 130 ...NN-10
Morongo Valley,
3552 ...SJ-15
Morro Bay, 10234 ...SF-5
Moss Bch., 3103 ...NJ-12
Mt. Baldy, 200 ...◊B-14
Mt. Bullion ...NN-10
Mt. Hebron, 95 ...NB-6
Mt. Helix, 4600 ...†J-6
Mt. Shasta, 3394 ...NC-6
Mt. View, 74066 ...NI-16
Mountain Ctr., 63 ...SK-15
Mountain Gate,
943 ...NE-5
Mountain Pass ...SF-17
Mountain Ranch,
1628 ...NL-9
Mountain View,
74066 ...NI-16
Mugginsville, 50 ...NB-4
Murphys, 2213 ...NL-9
Murrieta, 103466 ...SK-14
Murrieta Hot Sprs.,
2948 ...SK-14
Myers Flat, 146 ...NF-2
Napa, 76915 ...NK-5

NAPA CO.,
136484 ...NK-5
National City,
58582 ...SN-14
Navarro, 250 ...NI-3
Needles, 4844 ...SH-19
Nelson, 150 ...NH-6
Nevada City, 3068 ...NI-8
Nevada Sprs. ...NF-1
Newark, 42573 ...NM-6
Newberry Sprs.,
2948 ...SH-15
Newcastle, 1224 ...NJ-8
Newell, 449 ...NB-7
Newman, 10224 ...NM-8
Newport Bch.,
85186 ...SK-12
Newville ...NG-5
Nicasio, 96 ...NL-4
Nice, 2731 ...NI-4
Niland, 1006 ...SL-17
Nipomo, 16714 ...SG-6
Nipton, 58 ...SF-18
Nord, 320 ...NG-6
Norden ...NI-10
N. Bloomfield ...NH-8
N. Edwards, 1058 ...SG-12
N. Fair Oaks,
14687 ...NK-15
N. Fork, 500 ...SA-8
N. Highlands, 42694 ...†I-9
N. Hills ...§b-2
N. Hollywood ...§b-6
N. Long Bch. ...§H-8
N. Richmond,
3717 ...ND-13
N. San Juan, 269 ...NH-7
N. Shore, 3477 ...SK-16
N. Tustin, 24044 ...◊J-13
Northridge ...§C-4
Northview, 105549 ...NH-9
Norwalk, 105549 ...§H-9
Novato, 51904 ...NL-5
Noyo ...NH-2
Nuevo, 6447 ...SJ-14
Oak Grv., 100 ...SL-15
Oak Run, 200 ...NE-6
Oak View, 4066 ...SI-9

Oakdale, 20675 ...NM-8
Oakhurst, 2829 ...NN-11
Oakland, 390724 ...NM-5
Oakley, 35432 ...NL-6
Oakville, 71 ...NK-5
O'Brien, 30 ...ND-5
Occidental, 1115 ...NK-4
Ocean Bch. ...†J-1
Oceano, 7286 ...SG-6
Oceanside, 167086 ...SL-13
Ocotillo, 266 ...SM-16
Ocotillo Wells, 200 ...SL-15
Oildale, 32684 ...SF-9
Ojai, 7461 ...SI-9
Olancha, 192 ...SD-12
Old River, 200 ...SG-9
Old Sta., 51 ...NE-7
Old Town ...†I-2
Olinda ...NE-6
Olive, 150 ...◊I-12
Olive View ...§A-5
Olivehurst, 13656 ...NI-7
Olympic Valley ...*F-8
O'Neals ...SA-8
Ono, 60 ...NE-5
Ontario, 163924 ...SJ-12
Onyx, 475 ...SE-11
Orange, 136416 ...◊J-12

ORANGE CO.,
3010232 ...SK-12
Orange Cove, 9078 ...SC-9
Orange Pk. Acres ...◊I-13
Orangevale, 33960 ...†I-9
Orcutt, 28905 ...SH-6
Ordbend, 80 ...NH-6
Oregon House, 300 ...NI-7
Orick, 357 ...NC-2
Orinda, 17643 ...NL-16
Orland, 7291 ...NG-6
Orleans, 375 ...NC-3
Oro Fino, 30 ...NB-4
Oro Grande, 310 ...SH-13
Oroville, 15546 ...NH-7
Otay ...†M-4
Outingdale, 400 ...NK-9
Oxnard, 197899 ...SI-9
Pacheco, 3685 ...NC-17
Pacific ...NJ-9
Pacific Bch. ...†H-1
Pacific Grv., 15041 ...SC-3
Pacific Palisades ...§E-1
Pacifica, 37234 ...NM-5
Paicines ...SB-4
Pajaro, 3070 ...SB-3
Pala, 1050 ...SL-14
Palermo, 5382 ...NH-7
Palm City ...†M-4
Palm Desert,
48445 ...SK-15
Palm Sprs., 44552 ...SJ-15
Palmdale, 152750 ...SH-11
Palo Alto, 64403 ...NN-5
Palo Cedro, 1269 ...NE-6
Palo Verde, 171 ...SK-19
Paloma, 300 ...NL-9
Palomar Pk., 530 ...NJ-15
Palos Verdes Estates,
13438 ...§J-5
Paradise, 26218 ...NG-7
Paramount, 54098 ...§H-8
Park Vil., 100 ...SC-14
Parkfield ...SE-6
Parkway, 14670 ...†J-11
Parlier, 14494 ...SC-8
Pasadena, 137122 ...SJ-11
Paskenta, 112 ...NG-5
Paso Robles, 29793 ...SF-6
Patrick Creek ...NA-2
Patterson, 20413 ...NN-8
Pauma Valley, 800 ...SL-14
Paxton, 14 ...NG-8
Paynes Creek, 57 ...NF-6
Paynesville ...NL-11
Peanut ...NE-4
Pearblossom, 700 ...SI-12
Pearland ...§M-9
Pearsonville, 67 ...SE-12
Pebble Bch. ...SC-3
Penngrove, 2522 ...NK-4
Pennington ...NI-6
Penryn, 831 ...NJ-8
Pepperwood, 60 ...NE-2
Perris, 68386 ...SK-13
Pescadero, 643 ...NN-5
Petaluma, 57941 ...NL-4
Peters, 672 ...NL-8
Petrolia ...NF-1
Phelan, 14304 ...SI-13
Phillipsville, 140 ...NF-2
Philo, 349 ...NI-3
Pico Rivera, 62942 ...§F-7
Piedmont, 10667 ...NE-15
Piercy ...NG-2
Pilot Hill, 800 ...NJ-8
Pine Grv., 2219 ...NK-9
Pine Valley, 1510 ...SM-15
Pinecrest ...NL-10
Pinehurst, 150 ...SC-9
Pineridge, 200 ...SB-9
Pinole, 18390 ...NC-14
Piñon Hills, 7272 ...SI-12
Pinon, 1094 ...NK-9
Pioneer Pt., 1000 ...SE-13
Piru, 2063 ...SI-10
Pismo Bch., 7655 ...SG-6
Pittsburg, 63264 ...NL-6
Pittville ...ND-7
Pixley, 3310 ...SD-9
Placentia, 50533 ...§I-12

PLACER CO.,
348432 ...NI-9
Placerville, 10389 ...NJ-8
Plainview, 945 ...SD-9
Planada, 4109 ...NN-10
Plantation, 65 ...NK-3
Plaster City, 60 ...SM-17
Platina, 100 ...NE-5
Playa Del Rey ...§G-5
Pleasant Grv., 200 ...NI-7
Pleasant Hill, 33152 ...NL-6
Pleasanton, 70285 ...NM-6
Plymouth, 1005 ...NK-8
Pt. Arena, 449 ...NJ-3
Pt. Reyes Sta., 848 ...NL-4
Pollock Pines, 6871 ...NJ-9
Pomona, 149058 ...SJ-12
Pond, 200 ...SF-9
Pondosa ...NC-7
Pope Valley, 250 ...NK-5

Port Costa, 190 ...NB-15
Port Hueneme,
21723 ...SJ-9
Porter Ranch ...§B-3
Porterville, 54165 ...SD-9
Portola, 2104 ...NG-9
Portola Hills, 6391 ...◊K-15
Portola Valley,
4353 ...NL-15
Potrero, 656 ...SN-15
Potter Valley, 646 ...NH-4
Poway, 47811 ...SM-14
Pozo ...SB-8
Prather, 303 ...NH-6
Princeton, 303 ...NI-6
Proberta, 267 ...NF-6
Prunedale, 17560 ...SB-3
Pulga, 30 ...NG-7
Pumpkin Ctr., 520 ...SG-9
Quartz Hill, 10912 ...SH-11
Quincy, 1728 ...NG-8
Rackerby, 350 ...NH-7
Rail Road Flat, 475 ...NK-9
Rainbow, 1832 ...SL-14
Raisin City, 300 ...SC-7
Ramona, 20292 ...SM-14
Ranchita, 300 ...SL-15
Rancho Cordova,
64776 ...NK-7
Rancho Cucamonga,
165269 ...◊D-15
Rancho Mirage,
17218 ...SK-15
Rancho Murieta,
5488 ...NK-8
Rancho Palos Verdes,
41643 ...§J-6
Rancho
Rinconada ...NM-18
Rancho Santa Fe,
3117 ...SM-14
Rancho Santa
Margarita, 47853 ...◊K-16
Randsburg, 69 ...SF-12
Ravendale ...NE-10
Raymond, 200 ...SA-8
Red Bank ...NF-5
Red Bluff, 14076 ...NF-6
Red Hill, 2800 ...◊J-13
Red Mtn., 100 ...SF-12
Redcrest, 89 ...NE-2
Redding, 89861 ...NE-5
Redlands, 68747 ...SJ-13
Redondo Bch.,
66748 ...SJ-11
Redway, 1225 ...NF-2
Redwood City,
76815 ...NN-5
Redwood Valley,
1729 ...NI-3
Reedley, 24194 ...SC-8
Requa, 180 ...NB-2
Rescue, 1200 ...NJ-8
Reseda ...§C-4
Rialto, 99171 ...SJ-13
Rice ...SJ-19
Richardson Sprs.,
100 ...NG-6
Richfield, 300 ...NG-6
Richgrove, 2882 ...SE-9
Richmond,
103701 ...ND-13
Richvale, 244 ...NH-7
Ridgecrest, 27616 ...SF-12
Rimforest, 700 ...◊B-19
Rio del Mar, 9216 ...SB-3
Rio Dell, 3368 ...NE-2
Rio Linda, 15106 ...†F-3
Rio Oso, 366 ...NJ-7
Rio Vista, 7360 ...NL-7
Ripley, 692 ...SK-19
Ripon, 14297 ...NM-8
Ripperdan, 350 ...SB-7
River Pines, 379 ...NK-9
Riverbank, 22678 ...NM-8
Riverdale, 3153 ...SC-7
Riverside, 303871 ...SJ-13

RIVERSIDE CO.,
2189641 ...SJ-16
Robbins, 323 ...NJ-7
Robles Del Rio, 500 ...SC-3
Rocklin, 56974 ...NJ-8
Rodeo, 8679 ...NB-15
Rohnert Pk., 40971 ...NK-4
Rolinda, 200 ...SC-7
Rolling Hills, 1860 ...§J-6
Rolling Hills Estates,
8067 ...§J-6
Romoland, 980 ...◊L-20
Roosevelt Ter. ...NB-9
Rosamond, 18150 ...SH-11
Rosedale, 14058 ...SF-9
Roseland ...†L-6
Rosemead, 53764 ...§E-7
Rosemont, 22681 ...†I-4
Rosemont, 800 ...◊I-8
Roseville, 118788 ...NJ-7
Ross, 2415 ...NC-11
Rossmoor, 10244 ...§I-9
Rough & Ready,
963 ...NI-8
Round Mtn., 155 ...NE-6
Rovana ...NN-13
Rowland Hts.,
48993 ...◊F-11
Rumsey, 200 ...NJ-5
Running Sprs.,
4862 ...SI-14
Rutherford, 164 ...NK-5
Ryde, 200 ...NL-7
Sacramento,
466488 ...NK-7

SACRAMENTO CO.,
1418788 ...NK-8
Sage ...SK-14
St. Helena, 5814 ...NK-5
Salida, 13722 ...NM-8
Salinas, 150441 ...SC-3
Salmon Creek, 86 ...NL-4
Salton Sea Bch. ...SL-16
Salyer, 500 ...ND-3
Samoa, 258 ...ND-2
San Andreas, 2783 ...NL-9
San Anselmo,
12336 ...NC-11
San Antonio Hts.,
3371 ...◊D-14
San Ardo, 517 ...SD-5
San Benito ...SC-5

SAN BENITO CO.,
55269 ...SC-5
San Bernardino,
209924 ...SJ-13

SAN BERNARDINO
CO., 2035210 ...SI-15
San Bruno, 41114 ...NM-5
San Carlos, 28406 ...NN-5
San Clemente,
67116 ...SL-13
San Diego,
1307402 ...SN-14

SAN DIEGO CO.,
3095313 ...SM-15
San Dimas, 33371 ...◊D-12
San Fernando,
23645 ...SI-11
San Francisco,
805235 ...NM-5

SAN FRANCISCO CO.,
805235 ...NM-5
San Gabriel, 39718 ...§E-9
San Gregorio, 200 ...NN-5
San Jacinto, 44199 ...SK-14
San Joaquin, 4001 ...SC-7

SAN JOAQUIN CO.,
685306 ...NL-8
San Jose, 945942 ...NN-6
San Juan Bautista,
1862 ...SB-3
San Juan Capistrano,
34593 ...SK-12
San Leandro,
84950 ...NM-6
San Lorenzo,
23452 ...NM-6
San Lucas, 269 ...SD-5
San Luis Obispo,
45119 ...SG-6

SAN LUIS OBISPO
CO., 269637 ...SG-6
San Luis Rey ...†H-8
San Marcos,
83781 ...SL-14
San Marino, 13147 ...§D-9
San Martin, 7027 ...SA-3
San Mateo, 97207 ...NI-14

SAN MATEO CO.,
718451 ...NN-5
San Miguel, 2336 ...SE-6
San Pablo, 29139 ...NL-5
San Pedro ...§I-7
San Quentin, 100 ...ND-12
San Rafael, 57713 ...NL-5
San Ramon, 72148 ...NM-6
San Simeon, 462 ...SE-4
San Ysidro ...†M-2
Sand City, 334 ...SC-3
Sanger, 24770 ...SC-8
Santa Ana,
324528 ...SK-12
Santa Barbara,
88410 ...SI-8

SANTA BARBARA CO.,
423895 ...SH-8
Santa Clara,
116468 ...NL-18

SANTA CLARA CO.,
1781642 ...NN-6
Santa Clarita,
176320 ...SI-10
Santa Cruz, 59946 ...SB-3

SANTA CRUZ CO.,
262382 ...SB-3
Santa Fe Sprs.,
16223 ...§G-9
Santa Margarita,
1259 ...SG-6
Santa Maria,
99553 ...SG-6
Santa Monica,
89736 ...SJ-11
Santa Nella Vil.,
1380 ...SB-5
Santa Paula, 29321 ...SI-9
Santa Rita Pk., 170 ...SB-6
Santa Rosa,
167815 ...NK-4
Santa Venetia,
4292 ...NC-12
Santa Ynez, 4418 ...SH-7
Santa Ysabel, 100 ...SL-15
Santee, 53413 ...SM-14
Saratoga, 29926 ...NN-6
Saticoy, 1029 ...‡A-9
Sattley, 40 ...NH-10
Sausalito, 7061 ...NL-12
Sawyers Bar, 100 ...NC-4
Schellville, 200 ...NK-5
Scotia, 850 ...NE-2
Scotland, 250 ...◊B-16
Scotts Valley, 11580 ...SB-3
Seal Bch., 24168 ...§J-9
Seaside, 33025 ...SC-3
Sebastopol, 7379 ...NK-4
Sedco Hills, 3078 ...◊N-19
Seeley, 1739 ...SM-17
Seiad Valley, 270 ...NB-4
Selma, 23219 ...SC-8
Seneca ...NG-8
Shafter, 16988 ...SF-9
Shandon, 1295 ...SF-6

SHASTA CO.,
177223 ...NE-6
Shasta Lake, 10164 ...NE-5
Shaver Lake, 634 ...SB-9
Sheep Ranch, 100 ...NL-9
Shelter Cove, 693 ...NF-2
Sheridan, 1238 ...NJ-7
Sherman Oaks ...§C-4
Sherwood Forest,
2600 ...ND-14
Shingle Sprs., 4432 ...NJ-8
Shingletown, 2283 ...NE-6
Shively, 110 ...NE-2
Shore Acres, 4000 ...NB-18
Shoshone, 31 ...SD-15
Sierra City, 221 ...NH-9

SIERRA CO.,
3240 ...NH-9
Sierra Madre,
10917 ...§D-12
Sierraville, 200 ...NH-9
Signal Hill, 11016 ...§I-8
Silver City ...SM-2
Silver Strand, 1200 ...†L-8
Silverado, 800 ...◊I-15
Simi Valley, 124237 ...SI-10
Simmler ...SF-7
Siskiyou, 183 ...SH-6

SISKIYOU CO.,
44900 ...NC-5
Sisquoc, 183 ...SH-6
Sites ...NI-5
Skyforest, 750 ...◊B-20
Sleepy Hollow ...NC-11
Sloat, 100 ...NG-9
Sloughhouse, 350 ...NK-8
Smartville, 110 ...NI-7
Smith River, 866 ...NA-2
Smithflat, 250 ...NJ-8
Snelling, 231 ...NN-9
Soda Sprs., 41 ...NI-10
Solana Bch.,
12867 ...SM-14

SOLANO CO.,
413344 ...NK-6
Soledad, 25738 ...SC-4
Solvang, 4871 ...SH-7
Somerset, 600 ...NJ-9
Somes Bar, 150 ...NC-3
Somis, 1400 ...SI-9
Sonoma, 10648 ...NK-5

SONOMA CO.,
483878 ...NJ-3
Vacaville, 92428 ...NK-6
Valinda ...◊E-11
Vallejo, 115942 ...NL-5
Vallecito, 442 ...NL-9
Valley Acres, 527 ...SG-8
Valley Ford, 147 ...NL-4
Valley Home, 228 ...NM-8
Valley Sprs., 3553 ...NL-8
Valyermo, 100 ...SI-12
Venice ...§D-5
Ventucopa, 50 ...SH-8
Ventura, 106433 ...SI-9

VENTURA CO.,
823318 ...SH-9
Verdemont ...SI-13
Vernalis, 100 ...NM-8
Vernon, 112 ...§F-7
Victor, 293 ...NL-8
Victorville, 115903 ...SI-13
Vidal ...SI-20
Vidal Jct. ...SI-20
View Pk., 5500 ...§F-6
Villa Pk., 5812 ...◊J-12
Vina, 237 ...NG-6
Vincent, 15922 ...SI-11
Vine Hill, 3761 ...NC-16
Viola, 30 ...NE-7
Visalia, 124442 ...SD-9
Vista, 93834 ...SL-13
Volcano, 115 ...NK-9
Volta, 246 ...SB-5
Vorden ...NL-7
Walker, 741 ...NK-11
Wallace, 403 ...NL-8
Walnut, 29172 ...◊E-12
Walnut Creek,
64173 ...NL-6
Walnut Grove, 1542 ...NL-7
Walnut Pk., 15966 ...§F-7
Warner Sprs., 55 ...SL-15
Wasco, 25545 ...SF-9
Washington, 185 ...NI-9
Waterford, 8456 ...NM-9
Waterloo, 572 ...NL-8
Watsonville, 51199 ...SB-3
Watts ...§F-7
Wawona, 169 ...NN-11
Weaverville, 3600 ...NE-4
Weed, 2967 ...NC-5
Weimar, 850 ...NI-8
Weitchpec, 30 ...NC-3
Weldon, 2642 ...SE-11
Weott, 288 ...NF-2
W. Covina, 106098 ...§E-11
W. Hollywood,
34399 ...§E-6
W. Los Angeles ...§E-6
W. Pt., 674 ...NK-9
W. Sacramento,
48744 ...NK-7
Westhaven, 370 ...ND-2
Westlake Vil., 8270 ...SJ-10
Westley, 603 ...NM-8
Westmorland,
89701 ...SL-17
Westmorland,
2225 ...SM-17
Westport, 160 ...NH-2
Westwood, 1647 ...NE-8
Wheatland, 3456 ...NI-7
Whiskeytown, 100 ...NE-5
Whispering Pines,
100 ...NJ-4
White River ...SE-10
White Water ...SJ-15
Whitethorn, 80 ...NF-2
Whitmore, 100 ...NE-6
Whittier, 85331 ...SJ-11
Wilbur Sprs. ...NI-5
Wildomar, 32176 ...SK-13
Wildwood, 50 ...NE-4
Williams, 5123 ...NI-6
Willits, 4888 ...NH-3
Willow Creek, 1710 ...ND-3
Willow Ranch ...NB-10
Willows, 6166 ...NH-6
Wilmington ...§I-8
Wilseyville, 350 ...NK-9
Wilsona, 5 ...SK-1
Wilton, 5363 ...NK-8
Winchester, 2534 ...SK-14
Windsor, 26801 ...NK-4
Windsor Hills, 5000 ...§G-6
Winter Gdns.,
20631 ...†H-6
Winterhaven, 394 ...SM-20
Winters, 6624 ...NK-6
Winton, 10613 ...NN-9
Wofford Hts., 2200 ...SE-11
Woodacre, 14347 ...NL-18
Woodcrest, 14347 ...NL-18
Woodford, 100 ...NJ-11
Woodlake, 7279 ...SC-9
Woodland, 55468 ...NJ-6
Woodside, 5287 ...NN-15
Woodville, 1740 ...SD-9
Woody ...SE-10
Wrightwood, 4525 ...SI-12
Wyandotte, 110 ...NH-7
Wynton, 70 ...NN-9
Yermo, 1000 ...SH-14
Yettem, 211 ...SC-9
Yolo, 450 ...NJ-6

YOLO CO.,
200849 ...NJ-6
Yorba Linda,
64234 ...◊G-13
Yosemite Forks ...NN-11
Yosemite Vil.,
1035 ...NM-11
Yountville, 2933 ...NK-5
Yreka, 7765 ...NB-5
Yuba City, 64925 ...NI-7

YUBA CO., 72155 ...NI-7
Yucaipa, 51367 ...SJ-14
Yucca Valley, 20700 ...SJ-15
Zamora, 300 ...NJ-6
Zenia, 40 ...NF-3

Upper Lake, 1052 ...NI-4
Vacaville, 92428 ...NK-6

ALAMOSA CO.,
15445 ...L-11
Allenspark, 528 ...D-12
Allison, 110 ...M-5
Alma, 270 ...G-11
Almont, 70 ...H-8
Amherst, 58 ...B-20
Anton, 40 ...E-17
Antonito, 781 ...M-11
Arapahoe, 100 ...D-18
Arboles, 280 ...N-7
Arlington, 40 ...J-17
Aroya ...H-18
Arriba, 193 ...G-17
Arriola, 240 ...L-4
Arvada, 106433 ...E-13
Aspen, 6658 ...G-9
Atwood, 133 ...C-17
Ault, 1519 ...C-14
Aurora, 325078 ...F-14
Avon, 6447 ...F-10
Avondale, 674 ...J-15
Bailey, 150 ...F-12
Barnesville ...B-14
Barr Lake, 100 ...*F-9
Bartlett ...L-20
Basalt, 3857 ...F-8
Bayfield, 2333 ...M-7
Bedrock ...H-3
Beecher Island ...E-20
Bellvue, 400 ...C-13
Bennett, 2308 ...E-15
Berthoud, 5105 ...D-13
Bethune, 237 ...G-19
Beulah, 280 ...J-13
Black Forest, 13116 ...H-14
Black Hawk, 118 ...E-12
Blakeland, 700 ...J-14
Blanca, 391 ...L-12
Blanca, 385 ...L-12
Blende, 878 ...J-14
Blue Mtn., 15 ...D-4
Blue River, 849 ...F-11
Bonanza, 16 ...I-10
Boncarbo, 70 ...M-14
Bond ...E-9
Bondad ...M-6
Boone, 339 ...J-15
Boulder, 97385 ...D-13
Bow Mar, 866 ...*K-6
Bowie, 40 ...H-7
Boyero ...H-17
Brandon, 21 ...I-19
Branson, 74 ...N-16
Breckenridge, 4540 ...F-11
Breen ...M-6
Briggsdale, 140 ...C-15
Brighton, 33352 ...E-14
Bristol, 130 ...J-20
Broadmoor ...*I-1
Brookvale, 280 ...F-12
Broomfield, 55889 ...E-13
Brush, 5463 ...D-16
Buena Vista, 2617 ...H-11
Buffalo Creek ...F-12
Buford ...E-7
Burlington, 4254 ...G-20
Burns ...E-9
Byers, 1160 ...F-15
Caddoa ...J-18
Cahone, 50 ...L-4
Calhan, 780 ...H-15
Camp Bird ...K-7
Campion, 1830 ...D-13
Campo, 109 ...N-18
Cañon City, 16400 ...I-13
Capulin, 200 ...M-11
Carbondale, 6427 ...F-8
Carr, 60 ...B-13
Cascade, 500 ...H-13
Castle Pines North,
12390 ...*M-8
Castle Rock, 48231 ...F-14
Cattle Creek, 447 ...F-8
Cedaredge, 2253 ...H-6
Centennial, 100377 ...F-13
Center, 2230 ...L-11
Central City, 663 ...E-12
Chama, 245 ...M-10

CHAFFEE CO.,
17809 ...I-11
Cheraw, 252 ...J-16
Cherry Creek ...J-8
Cherry Hills Vil.,
5987 ...*J-7

CHEYENNE CO.,
1836 ...H-19
Cheyenne Wells,
846 ...H-18
Chimney Rock ...M-7
Chipita Pk., 465 ...H-13
Chivington, 40 ...I-19
Chromo ...N-8
Cimarron ...H-6
Clark ...B-9
Clarkville ...B-17

CLEAR CREEK CO.,
9088 ...F-12
Clifton, 19889 ...G-5
Coal Creek, 343 ...I-13
Coaldale, 255 ...I-11
Coalmont, 50 ...C-10
Cokedale, 129 ...M-14
Colbran, 708 ...G-6
Colona, 30 ...J-7
Colorado City, 2193 ...K-14
Colorado Spgs.,
416427 ...H-14
Columbine ...*J-6
Columbine Valley,
1256 ...*J-6
Commerce City,
45913 ...*H-7
Como, 100 ...G-11
Conejos, 58 ...M-10

CONEJOS CO.,
8256 ...M-10
Conifer, 200 ...F-12
Cope, 100 ...F-18
Cortez, 8482 ...L-5

COSTILLA CO.,
3524 ...M-12
Cotopaxi, 47 ...I-12
Cowdrey, 100 ...B-10
Craig, 9454 ...C-7
Crawford, 431 ...H-6
Creede, 290 ...K-9
Crested Butte, 1487 ...H-8
Crestone, 127 ...K-11
Cripple Creek,

Hermosa, 260 ...L-6
Hesperus ...M-6
Hiawatha, 16 ...A-5
Highland Pk., 300 ...F-12
Highlands Ranch,
96713 ...*L-7
Hillrose, 264 ...D-17
Hillside ...I-12
Holly, 802 ...J-20
Holyoke, 2313 ...C-19
Hooper, 103 ...K-11
Hot Sulphur Sprs.,
663 ...D-11
Hotchkiss, 944 ...H-7
Howard, 723 ...I-11
Hoyt, 30 ...E-15
Hudson, 2356 ...D-14

HUERFANO CO.,
6711 ...L-13
Hugo, 730 ...G-16
Idaho Sprs., 1717 ...E-12
Idalia, 88 ...E-20
Ignacio, 697 ...M-7
Indian Hills, 1280 ...*J-5
Irondale ...*G-8
Ivywild ...*H-2

JACKSON CO.,
1394 ...B-10
Jamestown, 274 ...D-12
Jansen, 112 ...M-14
Jaroso, 60 ...N-12
Jefferson, 40 ...F-11
Joes, 80 ...F-19
Johnstown, 9887 ...D-13
Julesburg, 1225 ...B-20
Karval, 65 ...H-17
Kassler ...*M-5
Keenesburg, 1127 ...D-14
Kelim, 90 ...C-13
Keota ...B-15
Kersey, 1454 ...C-14
Kim, 74 ...M-17
Kiowa, 723 ...G-14

KIOWA CO., 1398 ...I-18
Kirk, 59 ...F-19
Kit Carson, 233 ...H-18

KIT CARSON CO.,
7519 ...F-19
Knob Hill ...*H-2
Kremmling, 1444 ...D-10
La Garita ...K-10
La Jara, 818 ...M-11
La Junta, 7077 ...K-17

LA PLATA CO.,
51334 ...L-6
La Salle, 1955 ...D-14
La Valley, 160 ...M-12
La Veta, 853 ...L-13
Lafayette, 24453 ...D-13
Laird, 47 ...D-20
Lake City, 408 ...K-8
L. George, 120 ...H-12

LAKE CO., 7310 ...G-10
Lakeside, 8 ...*H-6
Lakewood, 142980 ...*I-5
Lamar, 7804 ...J-19
Laporte, 2450 ...*A-8

LARIMER CO.,
299630 ...C-12
Larkspur, 183 ...G-13
Las Animas, 2410 ...J-17

LAS ANIMAS CO.,
15507 ...M-15
Last Chance, 25 ...F-16
Lawson, 200 ...E-12
Lay ...C-7
Lazear, 140 ...H-7
Leadville, 2602 ...G-10
Lebanon, 160 ...L-5
Lewis, 212 ...L-5
Limon, 1880 ...G-16

LINCOLN CO.,
5467 ...H-17
Lincoln Pk., 3546 ...I-13
Lindon, 110 ...E-17
Littleton, 41737 ...F-13
Livermore, 80 ...B-13
Log Lane Vil., 873 ...D-16

LOGAN CO.,
22709 ...B-17
Loma, 1293 ...G-4
Lombard Vil., 600 ...I-2
Lone Tree, 10218 ...*L-8
Longmont, 86270 ...D-13
Louisville, 18376 ...D-13
Louviers, 250 ...F-13
Loveland, 66859 ...C-13
Lucerne, 160 ...C-14
Lyons, 2033 ...D-13
Lycan ...M-19
Mack, 140 ...G-4
Maher ...H-7
Malta ...G-10
Manassa, 991 ...M-11
Mancos, 1336 ...M-5
Manitou Sprs.,
4992 ...H-13
Manzanola, 434 ...J-16
Marble, 131 ...G-8
Marshall ...C-13
Marvel, 65 ...M-6
Masonville, 140 ...C-13
Matheson ...G-15
Maybell, 72 ...L-6
Maysville, 135 ...I-10
McClave, 190 ...J-18
McCoy, 24 ...E-9
Mead, 3405 ...D-13
Meeker, 2475 ...D-6
Meeker Pk., 120 ...C-12
Meredith ...F-8
Merino, 240 ...C-17

MESA CO., 146723 ...H-5
Mesita, 100 ...M-11
Milliken, 5610 ...D-14
Milner, 200 ...C-8

MINERAL CO., 712 ...L-8
Minturn, 1070 ...F-10
Model, 100 ...M-15
Moffat, 114 ...K-11

MOFFAT CO.,
13785 ...B-6
Molina, 250 ...G-6
Monte Vista, 4444 ...L-10
Montezuma, 65 ...F-11

MONTEZUMA CO.,
25535 ...M-4
Montrose, 19132 ...H-6

MORGAN CO.,
28159 ...D-15
Morrison, 428 ...*J-4
Mosca, 210 ...L-11
Mt. Crested Butte,
801 ...H-8
Mountain View,
550 ...*F-6
Mountain Vil., 1320 ...K-6
Nathrop, 200 ...I-11
Naturita, 546 ...I-3
Nederland, 1445 ...E-12
New Castle, 4518 ...F-7
Ninaview ...L-17
Niwot, 4006 ...D-13
N. Avondale, 50 ...J-15
N. Washington, 35789 ...*F-7
Norwood, 518 ...I-4
Nucla, 711 ...I-4
Nunn, 416 ...C-14
Oak Creek, 884 ...C-8
Oak Park, 144 ...H-13
Ohio, 40 ...H-9
Olathe, 1849 ...H-6
Olney Sprs., 345 ...J-15
Ophir, 159 ...K-6
Orchard, 60 ...D-15
Orchard City, 3119 ...H-6
Orchard Mesa, 6836 ...G-5
Ordway, 1080 ...J-16
Ortiz, 60 ...N-11
Otis, 475 ...D-18

OTERO CO.,
18831 ...K-16
Ouray, 1000 ...K-7

OURAY CO., 4436 ...J-7
Ovid, 318 ...B-20
Oxford, 90 ...M-6
Padroni, 36 ...B-18
Pagosa Jct., 25 ...N-8
Pagosa Sprs., 1727 ...M-8
Palisade, 2692 ...G-5
Palmer Lake, 2420 ...G-13
Paoli, 34 ...C-19
Paonia, 1451 ...H-7
Parachute, 1085 ...F-6
Paradox, 70 ...I-3
Paragon Estates,
380 ...*C-7
Parkdale ...I-13
Parlin, 50 ...H-9
Parshall, 47 ...D-10
Pearl ...B-10
Peckham, 135 ...D-14
Peetz, 238 ...B-18
Penrose, 3882 ...I-13
Peyton, 250 ...H-14

PHILLIPS CO.,
4442 ...C-19
Phippsburg, 204 ...D-8
Pierce, 834 ...C-14
Pikeview ...*F-1
Pitkin, 66 ...H-9

PITKIN CO., 17148 ...G-8
Placerville, 260 ...K-6
Platner, 35 ...D-18
Platoro, 100 ...L-10
Platteville, 2485 ...D-14
Pleasant View, 80 ...L-4
Poncha Sprs., 737 ...I-11
Poudre Pk., 100 ...C-12
Powderhorn, 50 ...J-8
Powder Wash, 70 ...A-6
Pritchett, 140 ...M-18
Proctor ...B-18
Prospect Valley, 70 ...D-15

PROWERS CO.,
12551 ...J-19
Pryor ...L-14
Pueblo, 106595 ...J-14
Pueblo West, 29637 ...J-14
Punkin Ctr. ...H-16
Purcell ...E-14

PUEBLO CO.,
159063 ...J-13
Ramah, 117 ...G-14
Rand, 40 ...C-11
Rangely, 2365 ...D-4
Raymer, 96 ...C-15
Raymond, 60 ...D-12
Red Cliff, 267 ...F-10
Red Feather Lakes,
525 ...B-12
Red Wing, 40 ...L-13
Redcliff ...F-10
Redmesa, 40 ...M-5
Redstone, 130 ...G-8
Redvale, 280 ...I-4
Rico, 265 ...K-5
Ridgway, 924 ...J-7
Rifle, 9172 ...F-6
Rio Blanco ...E-6

RIO BLANCO CO.,
6694 ...E-5

RIO GRANDE CO.,
11982 ...L-10
Rockvale, 487 ...I-13
Rocky Ford, 3957 ...K-16
Roggen, 130 ...D-15
Rollinsville, 181 ...E-12
Romeo, 404 ...M-11
Rosedale ...*L-2
Roswell ...*F-1

ROUTT CO.,
23509 ...C-8
Rush, 80 ...H-15
Rustic ...B-11
Rye, 153 ...K-13
Saguache, 485 ...J-10

SAGUACHE CO.,
6108 ...K-10
St. Petersburg ...I-11
Salida, 5236 ...I-11
Salt Creek, 587 ...J-14
San Acacio, 190 ...N-11
San Isabel, 50 ...K-13
San Luis, 629 ...N-12

SAN JUAN CO., 699 ...L-7

SAN MIGUEL CO.,
7359 ...J-4
San Pablo, 170 ...N-12
Sanford, 857 ...M-11
Sapinero ...I-8
Sargents ...J-9
Sawpit, 40 ...K-6
Security, 460 ...H-14
Sedalia, 206 ...F-13
Sedgwick, 146 ...B-19

SEDGWICK CO.,
2379 ...B-19
Segundo, 98 ...M-14
Seibert, 181 ...G-18
Severance, 3165 ...C-14
Shawnee, 100 ...F-12
Sheridan, 5664 ...*I-6
Sheridan Lake, 88 ...I-19
Silt, 2930 ...F-6

ver Cliff, 587 J-12
ver Plume, 170 F-12
verthorne, 3887 F-11
verton, 637 K-7
nla, 618 G-15
ngleton, 40 F-12
ter, 50 A-8
ck Rock J-4
owmass G-9
owmass Vil., 2826 G-9
ycer, 132 D-16
merset H-7
Fork, 386 L-9
Platte F-13
ringfield, 1451 L-19
arkville, 59 M-14
eamboat Sprs., 2388 C-9
erling, 14777 C-17
oneham, 90 C-16
orer L-5
orewall, 80 M-13
onington, 30 M-20
rasburg, 2447 E-15
ratmoor Hills, 350 *J-2
ratton, 658 G-19
ratton Meadows *J-2
ringtown, 140 G-10
gar City, 258 J-16
MMIT CO., 27994 F-11
nbeam C-6
perior, 12483 E-13
vink, 617 K-17
bernash, 417 E-11
LLER CO., 23350 H-13
luride, 2325 K-6
xas Creek I-12
atcher L-15
ornton, 118772 E-13
urman F-17
fany N-7
nnath, 625 C-13
npas K-16
ncup H-10
onerville K-18
ponas D-9
res L-11
waoc, 1087 M-4
wner, 22 I-20
nchera, 80 N-16
nidad, 9096 M-14
n Lakes, 171 G-10
o Buttes, 43 L-19
one L-15
avan I-4
il, 5305 F-10
ncorum J-5
rnon, 29 E-19
ctor, 397 I-13
ejo San Acacio M-12
gil, 40 M-13
as, 114 M-19
la Grv., 40 J-11
llegreen, 30 M-17
neland, 251 J-15
rginia Dale B-12
na, 106 G-19
alden, 608 B-10
alsenburg, 3068 L-14
alsh, 546 L-20
ard, 150 D-12
ASHINGTON CO., 4814 D-17
atkins, 653 E-14
attenberg, 330 E-14
averly, 300 B-13
elby, 14846 *G-7
ELD CO., 252825 B-15
eldona, 139 D-16
ellington, 6289 B-13
estcliffe, 568 J-12
estern Hills, 2600 *G-6
estminster, 106114 E-13
eston, 55 M-14
etmore, 60 J-13
heat Ridge, 30166 *H-5
hitepine I-10
hitewater, 200 H-5
iedfield, 4200 *J-4
iggins, 893 D-15
ild Horse, 25 H-18
iley, 405 J-19
illard, 40 C-17
illiamsburg, 662 J-13
indsor, 18644 C-13
inter Pk., 999 E-11
olcott, 15 E-9
oodland Pk., 7200 H-13
oodrow, 20 E-17
oody Creek, 263 G-9
ray, 2342 D-20
mpa, 429 D-9
ellow Jacket, 60 L-4
der H-15
ma, 3524 D-19
MA CO., 10043 D-19

Connecticut

Page locator
Map keys Atlas pages
A–J 48–49

bington, 700 B-13
ddison, 800 D-10
lingtown I-9
myville C-14
menia Union, 100 B-4
nesbury, 100 A-14
nston, 780 D-11
ndover, 600 C-11
nsonia, 19249 F-6
shford, 230 B-12
ttawan Bch., 280 G-12
atwaugan, 660 B-13
woodville, 200 C-12
very Hill, 160 E-12
von, 1800 C-8
akersville, 600 B-6
all Pond, 2400 E-3
allouville, 660 B-14
altic, 1250 D-12
antam, 759 C-5
arkhamsted B-7
eacon Falls, 1650 E-6
erkshire Estates, 220 F-5
erlin, 1230 D-8
ethany, 1280 F-7
ethel, 9549 F-4
ethlehem, 2021 D-5
irch Hill, 230 C-4
irchwood, 380 B-8
Black Pt., 20 G-12
Bloomfield, 7500 B-8
Blue Hills, 2901 H-13
Boardman Br., 100 D-4
Bolton, 230 C-10
Botsford, 490 F-5
Bozrah Street E-12
Branchville, 350 G-4
Branford, 5819 G-8
Branford Ctr., 5819 J-11
Bridgeport, 144229 H-5
Bridgewater, 500 E-4
Bristol, 60477 D-7
Broad Brook, 4069 B-9
Brookfield, 1650 E-4
Brookfield Ctr., 1550 E-4
Brooklyn, 981 C-13
Buckingham, 200 C-10
Bulls Br., 100 D-4
Bunker Hill A-2
Burlington, 500 C-7
Burnside H-14
Byram, 4146 I-3
Canaan, 1212 A-5
Candlewood Isle, 1260 E-4
Candlewood Knolls, 560 E-4
Candlewood Shores, 1800 E-4
Cannondale, 141 G-4
Canterbury, 200 C-13
Canton, 480 B-7
Canton Ctr., 380 B-7
Cedar Bch. J-7
Centerbrook, 1000 F-10
Centerville H-10
Central Vil., 1800 C-13
Chaplin, 230 C-12
Cheshire, 5786 E-7
Chester, 1558 F-10
Chesterfield F-11
Clarks Corner C-12
Clarks Falls, 170 E-14
Clinton, 3368 G-10
Cobalt, 500 E-9
Colchester, 4781 D-11
Colebrook, 400 A-6
Collinsville, 3746 C-7
Columbia, 800 C-11
Cornwall, 330 B-5
Cornwall Br., 500 B-4
Cos Cob, 6770 E-1
Coventry, 600 C-11
Cromwell, 2500 D-9
Crystal Lake, 1945 B-10
Danbury, 80893 F-4
Danielson, 4051 C-13
Darien, 20732 H-4
Dayville, 1650 B-13
Deep River, 1700 F-10
Derby, 12902 F-6
Devon J-7
Dodgingtown, 300 F-5
Double Bch., 1100 G-8
Durham, 2933 E-9
Eagleville, 460 C-11
E. Berlin, 1100 D-8
E. Bridgeport I-6
E. Brooklyn, 1638 C-13
E. Canaan, 1000 A-5
E. Farmington Hts., 450 C-8
E. Farms B-3
E. Glastonbury, 300 C-10
E. Granby, 1300 A-8
E. Haddam, 800 E-10
E. Hampton, 2691 D-10
E. Hartford, 51252 C-9
E. Hartland, 1200 A-7
E. Haven, 29257 G-7
E. Litchfield, 180 C-6
E. Morris D-6
E. Mountain B-3
E. River, 3800 G-9
E. Thompson, 640 A-14
East Vil., 100 F-6
E. Willington B-11
E. Windsor Hill, 450 B-9
E. Woodstock, 470 A-13
Eastford, 1020 B-12
Easton, 480 G-5
Ebbs Corner, 620 A-8
Ellington, 1700 B-10
Elmville, 330 B-13
Elmwood C-8
Enfield A-9
Essex, 1270 F-10
Fabyan, 530 A-13
Fair Haven I-10
Fair Haven East I-10
Fair Lawn B-3
Fairfield, 57300 H-5
FAIRFIELD CO., 916829 F-4
Fairmount A-2
Falls Vil., 538 A-4
Farmington, 3100 C-8
Fenwick, 43 G-11
Firetown, 160 B-8
Fitchville, 300 D-12
Flanders, 1330 F-11
Flanders, 170 C-4
Forest Hts. I-8
Ft. Hill, 100 G-4
Foxon I-11
Franklin, 140 D-12
Gales Ferry, 1162 F-12
Gaylordsville, 730 D-4
Georgetown, 1805 G-4
Giants Neck, 1330 G-11
Gilead, 130 D-10
Gilman, 40 D-12
Glasgo, 520 E-13
Glastonbury, 7387 C-9
Glenbrook G-3
Golden Spur, 130 F-12
Good Hill, 330 F-6
Goshen, 890 B-5
Granby, 700 A-8
Greenfield Hill H-5
Greenwich, 12942 I-3
Greystone, 160 D-6
Grosvenor Dale, 850 A-13
Groton, 10389 F-12
Groton Long Pt., 518 G-13
Grove Bch. G-10
Guilford, 2597 G-9
Gurleyville, 150 B-11
Haddam, 1300 E-10
Haddam Neck, 270 E-10
Hadlyme, 640 F-10
Hallville, 160 E-13
Hamburg, 110 F-11
Hamden, 56900 F-7
Hampton, 600 C-12
Hanover, 500 D-12
Happyland, 320 E-12
Harrisville, 90 B-13
Hartford, 124775 C-9
HARTFORD CO., 894014 B-7
Hartland A-7
Harwinton, 400 C-6
Hawleyville, 100 F-5
Hayden, 110 B-9
Hazardville, 4599 A-9
Hebron, 800 D-11
Higganum, 1698 E-9
Honeypot Glen, 1200 E-7
Hopeville D-13
Hotchkissville, 350 D-5
Huntington H-7
Hydeville, 250 A-11
Indian Neck, 2500 G-8
Ivoryton, 2600 F-10
Jewett City, 3487 D-13
Jordan Vil., 400 G-1
Kensington, 8459 D-8
Kent, 1050 C-4
Kent Furnace C-4
Killingly Ctr., 110 B-14
Killingworth, 300 F-9
Kings Cor., 270 A-9
Knollcrest, 400 E-4
Knollwood, 500 G-10
Lakeside, 1340 C-5
Lakeside, 550 D-5
Lakeview Ter., 100 A-11
Lakeville, 928 A-4
Laurel Bch. J-7
Laysville, 320 F-11
Lebanon, 440 D-11
Ledyard Ctr., 110 E-13
Leesville, 160 E-10
Leetes Island, 260 G-8
Liberty Hill, 250 D-11
Lime Rock, 160 A-4
Litchfield, 1258 C-6
LITCHFIELD CO., 189927 A-5
Long Hill, 4205 F-3
Long Hill G-5
Lords Pt., 350 F-13
Lordship J-6
Lyme Sta., 530 G-11
Lyons Plains, 350 G-5
Macedonia, 290 C-4
Madison, 2290 G-9
Manchester, 30577 C-10
Mansfield Ctr., 947 C-12
Mansfield Depot, 300 C-11
Mansfield Four Cors., 200 B-11
Marble Dale, 220 D-4
Marion, 850 E-7
Marlborough, 200 D-10
Mechanicsville, 160 A-13
Melrose, 300 A-10
Meriden, 60868 E-8
Merrow, 250 B-11
Mianus D-2
Middle Haddam, 450 E-9
Middlebury, 4200 E-6
Middlefield, 1250 E-8
MIDDLESEX CO., 165676 F-9
Middletown, 47648 E-9
Milford, 51271 G-6
Millbrook H-10
Milldale, 900 E-7
Millington, 50 E-11
Millville C-2
Milton, 120 C-5
Minortown D-6
Mixville, 1400 E-7
Mohegan, 460 E-12
Momauguin I-10
Monroe, 8500 F-5
Montowese F-8
Moodus, 1413 E-10
Moosup, 3231 C-13
Morris, 300 D-5
Morris Cove I-10
Mt. Hope, 200 B-12
Mystic, 4205 F-13
Naugatuck, 31862 E-6
Nepaug, 300 B-7
New Britain, 73206 D-8
New Canaan, 17900 H-4
New Fairfield, 5200 E-4
New Hartford, 620 B-7
New Haven, 129779 G-7
NEW HAVEN CO., 862477 E-7
New London, 27620 F-12
NEW LONDON CO., 274055 E-13
New Milford, 6523 D-4
New Preston, 1182 D-5
Newent, 230 D-13
Newington, 30562 C-8
Newtown, 1941 F-5
Niantic, 3114 F-12
Nichols I-5
Noank, 1796 F-13
Norfolk, 553 A-5
N. Ashford A-12
N. Bloomfield B-8
N. Branford, 7400 F-8
N. Canton, 270 B-7
N. Granby, 1944 A-8
N. Grosvenor Dale, 1530 A-13
N. Guilford F-9
N. Haven, 24093 F-8
N. Kent, 170 C-4
N. Madison F-9
N. Stonington, 350 F-14
N. Westchester, 300 D-10
N. Wilton, 100 G-4
N. Windham, 1000 C-12
N. Woodstock A-13
Northfield, 710 C-6
Northford, 3600 F-8
Northville, 400 D-4
Norwalk, 85603 H-4
Norwich, 40493 E-12
Oakdale, 910 E-12
Oakdale Mnr., 400 E-5
Oakland Gdns., 300 I-11
Oakville, 9047 D-6
Old Greenwich, 6611 I-3
Old Lyme, 480 G-11
Old Lyme Shores, 300 G-11
Old Mystic, 3554 F-13
Old Saybrook, 2039 G-10
Oneco, 750 C-14
Orange, 13956 G-7
Orcutts, 240 A-11
Oronoque F-6
Oswegatchie, 150 F-12
Oxford, 2100 F-6
Pachaug D-13
Palmertown, 610 E-12
Pawcatuck, 5624 F-14
Pequabuck D-7
Phoenixville B-12
Pine Br., 1000 F-6
Pine Meadow, 530 B-7
Pine Orchard, 950 G-8
Pine Rock Pk. I-7
Plainfield, 2557 D-13
Plainville, 17400 D-8
Plantsville, 6000 D-7
Platts Mills B-2
Pleasant Valley, 460 B-7
Plymouth, 1200 D-6
Pt. O'Woods, 740 G-11
Pomfret, 670 B-13
Pomfret Ctr., 390 B-13
Pomfret, 110 B-13
Ponset, 160 E-9
Poquetanuck, 220 E-13
Poquonock, 1100 B-9
Poquonock Br., 1727 F-13
Portland, 5862 D-9
Preston City, 220 E-13
Prospect, 7770 E-7
Putnam, 7214 B-13
Putnam Hts., 210 B-14
Quaddick, 540 A-14
Quaker Hill F-12
Quarryville, 410 C-10
Quinebaug, 1133 A-13
Redding, 1500 G-4
Redding Ridge, 550 F-5
Ridgebury, 220 F-3
Ridgefield, 7645 G-4
Rivercliff J-7
Riverside, 8416 I-3
Riverton, 580 A-7
Robertsville, 280 A-6
Rockfall, 980 E-9
Rockville, 7474 B-10
Rocky Hill, 16500 D-9
Rogers, 660 B-13
Roxbury, 500 E-5
Roxbury Falls, 130 E-5
Sachem Head, 500 G-8
Salem, 40 E-11
Salisbury A-4
Sandy Hook, 1200 F-5
Saybrook Manor, 1052 G-10
Saybrook Pt., 300 G-11
Scantic, 400 B-9
Scotland, 900 C-12
Seymour, 14300 F-6
Shady Rest, 270 E-5
Shailerville E-10
Sharon, 729 B-4
Sharon Valley, 300 B-4
Shelton, 39559 G-6
Sherman, 150 D-4
Short Bch., 200 G-8
Simsbury, 5836 B-8
Somers, 1789 A-10
Somersville, 1300 A-10
Sound View, 230 G-11
S. Britain, 1060 E-5
S. Canaan A-5
S. Chaplin C-12
S. End J-9
S. Glastonbury, 2000 D-9
S. Kent, 300 D-4
S. Killingly, 220 C-14
S. Lyme, 320 G-11
S. Norfolk B-5
S. Willington, 320 B-11
S. Windham, 1421 D-12
S. Windsor, 14000 B-9
S. Woodstock, 1291 A-13
Southbury, 3400 E-5
Southington D-7
Southport, 1585 H-5
Spring Glen H-10
Spring Hill, 200 C-11
Stafford Sprs., 4988 A-11
Staffordville, 720 A-11
Stamford, 122643 I-3
Stepney, 750 G-5
Sterling, 660 C-14
Sterling Hill C-14
Stevenson, 1150 F-6
Stonington, 929 F-13
Stony Creek, 830 G-8
Storrs, 15344 C-11
Straitsville F-7
Stratfield H-6
Stratford, 51384 G-6
Suffield Depot, 1325 A-9
Taconic, 350 A-4
Tariffville, 1324 B-8
Terryville, 5387 D-7
Thomaston, 1910 D-6
Thompson, 960 A-14
Thompsonville, 8577 A-9
Tolland, 1350 B-11
TOLLAND CO., 152691 B-10
Torrington, 36383 C-6
Town Plot Hill E-2
Trumbull, 36018 G-5
Twin Lakes, 380 A-5
Uncasville, 1420 F-12
Union, 60 A-12
Union City E-6
Unionville, 4400 C-7
Upper Stepney, 1000 F-5
Vernon, 28100 B-10
Voluntown, 520 D-14
Wallingford, 18209 E-8
Warehouse Pt., 2100 B-9
Warren, 240 C-5
Warrenville, 180 B-12
Washington, 700 D-5
Washington Depot, 700 D-5
Waterbury, 110366 E-6
Waterford F-12
Watertown, 3574 D-6
Waterville A-2
Wauregan, 1205 C-13
Welles Vil. I-14
Wequetequock, 850 F-14
W. Avon, 100 C-8
W. Cornwall, 330 B-4
W. Goshen, 700 B-5
W. Granby, 700 A-8
W. Hartford, 63268 C-8
W. Hartland, 400 A-7
W. Haven, 55564 G-7
W. Mystic F-13
W. Norfolk A-5
W. Redding, 200 F-4
W. Shore J-9
W. Side Hill B-2
W. Simsbury, 2447 B-8
W. Stafford, 600 A-11
W. Suffield, 860 A-9
W. Thompson, 210 A-13
W. Woodstock A-13
Westbrook, 2413 G-10
Westchester, 200 E-10
Westford, 100 B-12
Westminster C-13
Weston, 1460 G-4
Westport, 26391 H-4
Westville H-9
Wethersfield, 26668 C-9
Whigville, 450 C-7
Whitneyville I-10
Wildermere Bch. J-1
Willimantic, 17737 C-11
Willington B-11
Wilsonville, 640 A-13
Wilton, 732 G-4
Winchester Ctr., 200 B-6
Windham, 1150 C-12
WINDHAM CO., 118428 C-13
Windsor, 18800 B-9
Windsor Locks, 12498 B-9
Windsorville, 350 B-9
Winsted, 7712 B-6
Winthrop, 490 F-10
Wolcott, 6400 D-7
Woodbridge, 7860 F-7
Woodbury, 1294 E-5
Woodmont, 1488 G-7
Woodstock, 410 A-13
Woodstock Valley, 350 A-12
Woodtick, 740 D-7
Woodville C-5

Delaware

Page locator
Map keys Atlas pages
A–N 50–51

Adamsville J-2
Andrewville J-2
Anglesey, 125 C-7
Angola by the Bay, 1200 K-5
Arden, 439 C-3
Ardencroft, 231 B-3
Ardentown, 264 B-9
Argos Cor., 50 J-4
Ashland B-2
Atlanta, 65 K-2
Bay View Bch., 50 K-2
Bayard L-5
Bayville, 100 M-5
Bear, 19371 D-2
Bellefonte, 1193 C-3
Bellevue Mnr., 200 C-9
Belltown, 250 J-5
Belvidere, 800 D-7
Bethany Bch., 1060 L-5
Bethel, 171 L-2
Big Stone Bch., 15 I-4
Birchwood Pk., 400 D-6
Blackbird F-2
Blackiston G-1
Blades, 1241 K-2
Bowers Bch., 335 H-3
Brandywine, 1400 B-8
Brandywood, 800 B-9
Bridgeville, 2048 K-2
Broadkill Bch., 100 J-4
Brookside, 14353 D-6
Brownsville I-2
Bryans Store L-3
Camden, 3464 H-2
Cannon, 100 K-2
Canterbury, 150 H-2
Capitol Pk., 600 G-9
Carlisle Vil., 200 F-7
Carrcroft, 500 B-9
Carrcroft Crest, 900 B-9
Castle Hills, 2000 D-8
Centerville, 500 B-2
Chalfonte, 1400 B-9
Cheswold, 1380 G-2
Christiana, 500 D-2
Clarksville, 200 L-5
Claymont, 8253 C-3
Clayton, 2918 F-2
Cleland Hts., 900 D-8
Collins Pk., 1500 D-8
Concord, 250 K-2
Cool Spr., 50 K-4
Coventry, 1500 D-6
Coverdale Crossroads, 400 K-3
Dagsboro, 805 L-4
Darley Woods, 1300 B-9
Delaware City, 1695 D-2
Delaware Hts., 40 B-7
Delmar, 1597 M-2
Delpark Mnr., 1100 D-7
Devonshire, 2200 B-9
Dewey Bch., 341 K-5
Dover, 36047 G-2
Downs Chapel, 25 G-1
Du Ross Hts., 900 D-7
Dublin Hill, 40 L-2
Dunleith, 2400 D-8
Dupont Mnr., 300 G-2
Edgemoor, 5677 C-9
Ellendale, 381 J-3
Elsmere, 6131 C-2
Fairfax, 1600 B-8
Fairfield Farms, 700 H-8
Farmington, 110 I-2
Faulkland, 1300 C-7
Felton, 1298 H-2
Fenwick Island, 379 M-5
Fieldsboro E-2
Forest Brook Glen, 400 D-8
Forest Hills Pk., 650 C-9
Fox Hall F-7
Frankford, 847 L-4
Frederica, 774 I-3
Garfield Pk., 400 D-8
Georgetown, 6422 K-3
Glasgow, 14303 D-1
Granogue B-8
Gravel Hill, 75 K-4
Graylyn Crest, 450 B-9
Green Acres, 1100 B-9
Greenville, 2326 C-2
Greenville Pl., 1000 C-8
Greenwood, 973 J-2
Gumboro, 100 L-3
Guyencourt, 100 B-8
Gwinhurst, 400 B-10
Hamilton Pk., 200 D-8
Harbeson, 400 K-4
Harmony Hills, 800 D-6
Harrington, 3562 I-2
Hartly, 74 G-1
Hazlettville H-2
Hearns Crossroads L-2
Hearns Mill, 130 K-2
Henlopen Acres, 122 K-5
Hickman, 100 J-1
Hillcrest, 1500 C-9
Hitchens Crossroads L-3
Hockessin, 13527 C-2
Holloway Ter., 1200 D-8
Hollyville K-4
Houston, 374 I-3
Huntley, 100 H-8
Indian Bch., 10 K-5
Ivy Ridge, 1800 E-7
Jefferson Farms, 2000 D-8
Jimtown, 45 K-4
Johnson, 35 L-5
Keen-Wik, 400 M-5
Kent Acres, 1890 H-8
KENT CO., 162310 H-2
Kenton, 261 G-2
Kirkwood, 150 D-2
Kitts Hummock, 300 H-3
L. Pines, 125 L-2
Lancaster Vil. C-8
Laurel, 3708 L-2
Lebanon, 120 H-3
Leipsic, 183 G-3
Lewes, 2747 J-5
Lincoln, 500 J-3
Little Creek, 224 G-3
Little Heaven, 250 H-3
Llangollen Estates, 1400 E-7
Lynch Hts., 125 I-3
Magnolia, 225 H-3
Marshallton, 1800 C-7
Masseys, 80 K-5
Mastens Cor., 60 I-2
McClellandville, 120 C-7
Meadowood, 600 D-6
Mechanicsville D-5
Middleford, 150 K-2
Middlesex Bch., 25 L-5
Middletown, 18871 E-1
Midway, 600 K-5
Milford, 9559 I-3
Millcreek Crossroads, 100 C-1
Millsboro, 3877 L-4
Millville, 544 L-5
Milton, 2576 J-4
Minquadale, 650 D-8
Montchanin, 300 B-8
Mt. Pleasant, 100 E-1
Nassau, 125 J-4
New Castle, 5285 D-2
NEW CASTLE CO., 538479 E-3
Newark, 31454 C-1
Newport, 1055 C-2
N. Shores, 100 K-5
N. Star, 7980 C-6
Oak Lane Mnr., 950 B-9
Oak Orchard, 500 L-5
Oakley J-3
Ocean View, 1882 L-5
Odessa, 364 E-2
Ogletown, 600 C-2
Omar L-4
Pearsons Corner G-2
Penn Acres, 2000 D-8
Pennyhill, 600 C-9
Pepper L-3
Petersburg H-2
Pine Tree Cors. F-2
Pleasant Hill C-6
Pleasanton Acres, 50 E-2
Port Penn, 250 E-2
Portsville L-2
Primehook Bch., 50 J-4
Rambleton Acres, 1500 E-7
Red Lion D-2
Redden K-3
Reeves Crossing I-2
Rehoboth Bch., 1327 K-5
Richardson Pk., 500 C-8
Rising Sun, 250 H-3
Riverdale, 500 L-4
Rockland, 200 B-8
Rodney Vil., 1487 H-2
Rodric Vil., 100 H-8
Roxana, 150 L-5
St. Georges, 350 D-2
Sandtown H-1
Scottfield, 800 E-6
Scotts Corner D-2
Seaford, 6928 K-2
Sedgley Farms, 250 C-7
Selbyville, 2167 M-4
Shaft Ox Corner L-3
Sharpley, 1400 B-8
Shawnee Acres, 450 I-3
Sherwood Pk., 2000 C-7
Shortly L-3
Silverbrook, 700 C-8
Silverside Hts., 375 B-9
Silview, 1500 D-7
Slaughter Bch., 207 I-4
Smyrna, 10023 F-2
S. Bethany, 449 L-5
S. Bowers, 50 H-3
Stanton, 2000 D-7
Staytonville, 40 J-3
Stratford, 1100 E-7
Summit Br., 60 E-1
SUSSEX CO., 197145 K-3
Sussex Shores, 10 L-5
Swanwyck Estates, 800 D-8
Sycamore, 20 L-3
Talleyville, 800 C-2
The Cedars, 350 C-7
Thompsonville I-3
Townsend, 2049 F-2
Tuxedo Pk., 1300 D-7
Vernon I-2
Village of Westover G-7
Viola, 157 H-2
Ward L-3
Warwick, 100 L-4
Westover Hills, 1200 C-8
Whaleys Crossroads L-3
Whitesville, 50 M-3
Williamsville, 75 M-5
Williamsville L-5
Willow Grv., 75 H-2
Willow Run, 500 C-8
Wilmington, 70851 C-2
Wilmington Manor, 7889 D-8
Wilmington Manor Gdns., 1800 D-8
Winterthur, 100 B-8
Woodenhawk J-2
Woodland L-2
Woodland Bch., 150 F-3
Woodshade, 750 E-6
Woodside, 181 H-2
Wyoming, 1313 H-2
Yorklyn, 300 C-2

District of Columbia

Page locator
Map keys Atlas pages
A–N 224–225

Georgetown F-6
Washington, 601723 E-6

Florida

Page locator
Map keys Atlas pages
A–J 52–53
K–T 54–55

* City keyed to p. 51
† City keyed to pp. 56–57

Adamsville, 280 †D-4
Alachua, 9059 D-7
ALACHUA CO., 247336 E-7
Alafaya, 78113 H-10
Alford, 489 R-7
Allentown, 894 Q-3
Altamonte Sprs., 41496 H-10
Altha, 536 R-7
Alton, 100 C-5
Altoona, 89 G-9
Alturas, 4185 J-9
Alva, 2596 N-9
Amelia City, 730 B-10
Anclote, 260 I-6
Anglers Pk., 980 R-13
Ankona, 280 L-13
Anna Maria, 1503 K-6
Anthony, 1150 F-8
Apalachicola, 2231 T-8
Apopka, 41542 H-10
Arcadia, 7637 L-9
Archer, 1118 E-7
Aripeka, 308 H-6
Armstrong, 300 D-10
Arran C-2
Asbury Lake, 8700 C-9
Ashville B-4
Astatula, 1810 G-9
Astor, 1556 F-9
Astor Pk., 150 F-9
Athena, 60 D-4
Atlantic Bch., 12655 C-10
Atlantis, 2005 N-14
Auburndale, 13507 I-9
Aucilla, 100 B-4
Avalon Bch., 679 R-3
Ave Maria, 30 O-10
Aventura, 35762 P-14
Avon Pk., 8836 K-10
Avondale H-2
Azalea Pk., 12556 N-4
Babson Pk., 1356 J-10
Bagdad, 3761 R-3
Baker, 300 Q-4
BAKER CO., 27115 B-7
Bakers Mill B-6
Bal Harbour, 2513 †K-9
Baldwin, 1425 C-8
Balm, 1457 J-8
Barberville, 165 F-10
Barefoot Bay, 3000 J-12
Bartow, 17298 J-9
Bascom, 121 Q-7
BAY CO., 168852 S-6
Bay Hbr. Islands, 5628 †K-9
Bay Lake, 130 H-8
Bay Lake, 23 O-2
Bay Pines, 2931 *D-1
Bay Ridge, 155 K-2
Bay Sprs., 50 Q-2
Bayou George, 230 S-6
Bayport, 43 H-7
Bayshore, 300 N-9
Bayshore Gdns., 16323 †G-3
Baywood Vil., 1300 *A-1
Becker A-9
Bee Ridge, 9598 L-7
Belair, 400 *N-8
Bell, 456 D-6
Belle Glade, 17467 N-12
Belle Isle, 5988 O-4
Belleair, 3869 C-2
Belleair Bch., 1560 I-6
Belleair Bluffs, 2031 *C-1
Belleair Shores, 109 *C-1
Belleview, 4492 F-8
Bellview, 23355 R-2
Bellwood, 500 D-12
Bennett B-6
Berrydale, 441 Q-3
Beulah, 400 *H-7
Beulah, 200 R-2
Beverly Bch., 338 E-10
Beverly Hills, 8445 G-7
Big Coppitt Key, 2458 T-9
Big Pine Key, 4252 T-10
Biltmore I-1
Biscayne Pk., 3055 *K-9
Bithlo, 8268 H-11
Blackman Q-4
Bloomingdale, 22711 *C-5
Blountstown, 2514 R-7
Bloxham, 200 B-1
Bluff Sprs., 220 Q-2
Boca Del Mar, 21800 *F-9
Boca Grande, 700 N-8
Boca Pointe, 3300 *F-9
Boca Raton, 84392 O-14
Boca West, 2100 *E-9
Bokeelia, 1780 N-8
Bonifay, 2793 Q-6
Bonita Sprs., 43914 O-9
Bostwick, 300 D-9
Boulogne, 260 A-8
Bowden I-3
Bowling Green, 2930 K-9
Boyette, 5890 *D-5
Boynton Bch., 68217 N-14
Bradenton, 49546 K-7
Bradenton Bch., 1171 K-6
BRADFORD CO., 28520 D-8
Bradfordville, 470 B-2
Bradley Jct., 686 J-8
Brandon, 103483 J-7
Branford, 712 D-6
Bratt, 200 Q-2
Brent, 21804 *I-9
BREVARD CO., 543376 J-12
Briny Breezes, 601 *D-10
Bristol, 996 R-8
Broadview Pk., 7125 *I-8
Bronson, 1113 E-7
Brooker, 338 D-7
Brookridge, 4420 H-7
Brooksville, 7719 H-7
BROWARD CO., 1748066 O-12
Brownsville, 80 L-9
Bruce, 200 R-5
Bryant, 180 M-12
Bryceville, 180 B-8
Buchanan K-9
Buckhead Ridge, 1450 L-11
Buckingham, 4036 N-9
Buenaventura Lakes, 26079 I-10
Bunnell, 2676 E-10
Bushnell, 2418 H-8
CALHOUN CO., 14625 S-7
Callahan, 1123 B-9
Callaway, 14405 S-6
Cameron City, 180 K-5
Campbell, 2479 I-10
Campbellton, 230 Q-7
Campton, 125 Q-4
Campville, 200 E-8
Canal Pt., 367 M-12
Candler, 370 F-8
Canova Bch. G-14
Cantonment, 2800 R-2
Cape Canaveral, 9912 H-12
Cape Coral, 154305 N-8
Cape Haze, 400 M-8
Capitola, 165 B-3
Capps, 20 B-3
Captiva, 583 N-8
Carrabelle, 2778 D-1
Carrollwood, 33365 †B-3
Carters Cor., 250 †J-3
Caryville, 411 Q-6
Casselberry, 26241 L-4
Cassia, 90 G-10
Cedar Grv., 3397 S-6
Cedar Key, 702 F-5
Center Hill, 988 H-8
Century, 1698 Q-2
Chaires, 100 B-3
Chapman, 500 †A-4
CHARLOTTE CO., 159978 M-9
Charlotte Hbr., 3714 M-8
Chaseville G-3
Chassahowitzka, 850 G-7
Chattahoochee, 3652 R-8
Cherry Lake B-4
Chester, 370 A-9
Chiefland, 2245 E-6
Chipley, 3605 Q-6
Chipola R-7
Chokoloskee, 359 P-10
Christmas, 1146 H-11
Chuluota, 2483 H-11
Chumuckla, 850 Q-2
Citra, 950 E-8
CITRUS CO., 141236 G-7
Citrus Pk., 24252 †B-3
Citrus Ridge, 12015 P-1
Citrus Sprs., 8622 G-7
Clair-Mel City, 7500 †C-4
Clarcona, 2990 M-2
Clarksville, 150 R-7
CLAY CO., 190865 D-9
Clearwater, 107685 I-6
Clermont, 28742 H-9
Cleveland, 2990 M-8
Clewiston, 7155 M-11
Cloud Lake, 135 *B-10
Cocoa, 17140 I-12
Cocoa Bch., 11231 I-12
Coconut Creek, 52909 †F-8
Coconut Grv. †M-8
Codys Cor., 110 F-10
Coleman, 703 G-8
COLLIER CO., 321520 O-10
COLUMBIA CO., 67531 B-7
Compass Lake, 200 R-7
Conch Key, 140 S-12
Concord, 125 B-2
Conway, 13467 H-10
Cooper City, 28547 *I-8
Copeland, 30 P-10
Coral Cove, 1160 L-7
Coral Gables, 46780 O-13
Coral Sprs., 121096 O-13
Coral Ter., 24376 *M-7
Corkscrew N-10
Cornwell L-11
Cortez, 4241 G-2
Cottage Hill, 1050 R-2
Cottondale, 933 Q-7
Crawfordville, 3702 C-2
Crescent Bch., 931 D-10
Crescent City, 1577 E-10
Crestview, 20978 Q-4
Cross City, 1728 E-5
Cross Creek, 270 E-8
Crystal Bch., 1350 A-1
Crystal Lake, 135 R-6
Crystal River, 3108 G-7
Crystal Sprs., 1327 H-8
Cudjoe Key, 1763 T-10
Curlew, 780 *B-1
Cutler Bay, 40286 Q-13
Cypress, 250 R-7
Cypress Gdns., 8917 *K-5
Cypress Quarters, 1215 L-12
Dade City, 6437 I-8
Dalkeith S-7
Dania Bch., 29639 P-13
Darby, 375 I-7
Darsey, 300 A-2
Davenport, 2888 I-9
Davie, 91992 P-13
Day, 116 C-5
Daytona Bch., 61005 F-11
Daytona Bch. Shores, 4247 A-14
De Funiak Sprs., 5177 R-5
De Leon Sprs., 2614 F-10
De Soto City, 600 K-10
DE SOTO CO., 34862 L-9
DeBary, 19320 G-10
Deer Pk. I-11
Deerfield Bch., 75018 O-14
Dekle Bch., 50 D-4
DeLand, 27031 F-10
Dellwood, 75 Q-7
Delray Bch., 60522 N-14
Deltona, 85182 G-10
Denaud N-10
Destin, 12305 R-4
Dinsmore G-1
DIXIE CO., 16422 E-5
Dixie Ranch Acres, 335 I-11
Doctors Inlet, 1800 C-9
Doral, 45704 *L-7
Dorcas Q-4
Dover, 3702 J-8
Dowling Pk., 500 C-5
Drifton, 25 B-3
Duette K-8
Dukes, 200 D-7
Dundee, 3717 J-9
Dunedin, 35321 I-6
Dunnellon, 1733 F-7
Durant, 225 J-8
DUVAL CO., 864263 B-8
Eagle Lake, 2255 J-9
Earleton, 320 D-8
E. Lake Weir, 140 G-8
E. Naples, 2050 O-9
E. Palatka, 1654 E-9
E. Tampa, 750 *C-4
Eastpoint, 2337 T-8
Eaton Pk., 900 *K-2
Eatonville, 2159 M-3
Ebro, 270 R-6
Edgar, 50 E-8
Edgewater, 20750 G-11
Edgewood, 2503 N-4
Egypt Lake, 3500 *B-3
El Destinado, 550 *L-8
El Jobean, 600 M-8
El Portal, 2325 *K-8
Elfers, 13986 I-6
Elkton D-10
Ellaville B-5
Ellenton, 4275 K-7
Ellzey F-6
Eloise, 250 *K-4
Eloise Woods, 1900 *L-5
Emporia, 300 F-10
Englewood, 14863 M-7
Englewood Bch., 400 M-7
Ensley, 20602 R-2
Enterprise, 2000 G-10
Eridu, 60 C-4
ESCAMBIA CO., 297619 Q-2
Espanola, 100 E-10
Estero, 22612 N-9
Estiffanulga, 120 S-7
Esto, 364 Q-6
Eureka, 130 E-8
Eustis, 18558 G-9
Eva G-9
Everglades City, 400 P-10
Evergreen, 130 A-9
Evinston, 240 E-8
Fairbanks, 500 D-8
Fairfield, 45 F-8
Fairview Shores, 10239 M-3
Falmouth B-5
Fanning Sprs., 764 E-6
Federal Pt., 260 D-9
Fedhaven, 250 J-10
Felda, 200 N-10
Fellowship F-7
Fellsmere, 5197 J-12
Fenholloway C-4
Fern Pk., 7704 L-4
Fernandina Bch., 11487 B-10
Ferndale, 472 H-9
Ferry Pass, 28921 R-2
Fidelis, 156 Q-3
Fish Hawk *D-6
Fish Lake, 570 I-10
Fisher Island, 132 *M-9
Five Points, 1265 C-7
Flagler Bch., 4484 E-11
FLAGLER CO., 95696 E-10
Flamingo R-11
Flamingo Bay, 880 N-8
Flemington E-7
Florahome, 430 D-9
Floral City, 5217 G-7
Florida City, 11245 Q-13
Floridana Bch., 500 J-12
Florosa, 1000 R-4
Forest City, 13854 L-3
Forest Hills, 550 G-10
Ft. Drum, 140 K-12
Ft. Green, 101 K-8
Ft. Green Sprs., 231 K-8
Ft. Lauderdale, 165521 O-13
Ft. Lonesome K-8
Ft. McCoy, 300 E-8
Ft. Meade, 5626 J-9
Ft. Myers, 62298 N-9
Ft. Myers Bch., 6277 N-8
Ft. Myers Villas, 5600 †N-2
Ft. Ogden, 300 M-8
Ft. Pierce, 41590 K-13
Ft. Walton Bch., 19507 R-4
Ft. White, 567 D-6
Fountain, 450 R-6
Fountainbleau, 59764 †L-7
Fowlers Bluff, 90 E-6
Fox Town, 300 †I-2
FRANKLIN CO., 11549 D-1
Franklin Pk., 2400 †M-2
Franklintown, 500 B-10
Freeport, 1787 R-5
Frink S-7
Frontenac, 680 H-12
Frostproof, 2992 J-10
Fruit Cove, 29362 C-9
Fruitland, 500 E-9
Fruitland Pk., 4078 G-8
Fruitville, 13224 L-7
Fuller Hts., 8758 J-8
GADSDEN CO., 46389 B-1
Gainesville, 124354 E-7
Galloway, 150 *J-1
Garden City, 150 Q-4
Garden City F-1
Garden Grv., 674 I-1
Gardner, 463 L-9
Gaskin, 150 Q-5
Gateway, 8401 N-9
Geneva, 2940 G-11
Georgetown, 450 E-9
Gibsonia, 4507 *I-1
Gibsonton, 14234 J-7
Gifford, 9590 K-13
GILCHRIST CO., 16939 E-6
Gilmore H-3
GLADES CO., 12884 M-10
Gladeview, 11535 †L-8
Glen Ridge, 219 *B-10
Glen St. Mary, 437 C-8
Glendale, 110 Q-5
Glenvar Hts., 16898 †M-7
Glenwood, 600 F-10
Golden Bch., 919 *J-9
Golden Gate, 23961 O-9
Golden Gate, 2650 L-13
Golden Glades, 33145 †K-8
Goldenrod, 12039 M-4
Golf, 252 *D-9
Gonzalez, 13273 R-2
Goodbys J-3
Goodland, 267 P-9
Gordonville, 1500 †K-4
Gotha, 1915 N-2
Goulding, 4102 *J-9
Graceville, 2278 Q-6
Graham, 200 D-8
Grand Island, 1200 G-9
Grand Ridge, 892 R-7
Grandin D-8
Grant-Valkaria, 3850 J-12
Grayton Bch., 150 S-5
Grayvik, 125 R-13
Green Cove Sprs., 6908 D-9
Greenacres, 37573 N-13
Greenacres City, 37573 *B-9
Greenland J-4
Greensboro, 602 B-1
Greenville, 843 B-4
Greenwood, 686 Q-7
Gretna, 1460 B-1
Griffin *J-1
Gritney, 200 Q-6
Grove City, 1804 M-7
Grove Pk., 140 E-8
Groveland, 8729 H-9
Gulf Bch. Hts., 1600 *K-7
Gulf Breeze, 5763 R-3
Gulf City, 550 *E-3
GULF CO., 15863 T-7
Gulf Hammock, 250 F-6
Gulf Harbors, 3300 I-6
Gulf Stream, 786 *D-10
Gulfport, 12029 I-6
Hague, 400 D-7
Haines City, 20535 I-9
Hall City, 145 M-10
Hallandale Bch., 37113 P-13
HAMILTON CO., 14799 B-6
Hammond, 140 E-10
Hampton, 500 D-8
Hampton Sprs. C-4
Hamptons at Boca Raton, 11300 *E-9
Hanson B-5
Harbinwood Estates, 1900 *L-7
HARDEE CO., 27731 K-8
Harlem, 2658 M-11
Harold, 823 R-3
Hastings, 580 D-10
Havana, 1754 B-2
Haverhill, 1873 *B-9
Hawthorne, 1417 E-8
Heathrow, 5896 G-10
Hedges, 800 B-9
HENDRY CO., 39140 N-10
Hernando, 9054 G-7
HERNANDO CO., 172778 H-7
Hesperides J-10
Hialeah, 224669 P-13
Hialeah Gdns., 21744 †K-7
High Sprs., 5350 D-7
Highland Bch., 3539 N-14
Highland City, 10834 J-9
Highland Lakes, 3700 †A-2
Highland Lakes, 850 K-10
Highland View, 450 T-7
HIGHLANDS CO., 98786 L-10
Highlands Pk. Estates, 1100 L-10
Highpoint, 2300 †C-2
Hildreth D-6
Hillcrest Hts., 254 J-10
Hilliard, 3086 A-8
Hillsboro Bch., 1875 †F-10
Hillsboro Pines, 446 *F-8
HILLSBOROUGH CO., 1229226 J-8
Hinson, 150 B-2
Hobe Sound, 11521 L-13
Holder, 200 G-7
Holiday, 22403 I-6
Holiday Mnr., 100 *I-5
Holley, 1630 R-3
Hollister, 400 E-9
Holly Hill, 11659 F-11
Hollywood, 140768 P-13
Holmes Bch., 3836 K-6
HOLMES CO., 19927 Q-6
Holopaw, 240 I-11
Holt, 300 Q-4
Homeland, 366 J-9
Homestead, 60512 Q-13
Homosassa, 2578 G-7
Homosassa Sprs., 13791 G-7
Honeyville, 240 S-7
Horseshoe Bch., 169 E-5
Hosford, 650 B-1
Houston, 200 C-6
Howey-in-the-Hills, 1098 G-9
Hudson, 12158 I-6
Hull L-8
Hypoluxo, 2588 *C-10
Immokalee, 24154 N-10
Indialantic, 2720 I-12
Indian Creek, 86 *K-9
Indian Harbour Bch., 8225 I-12
Indian Lake Estates, 200 J-10
INDIAN RIVER CO., 138028 K-12
Indian River Shores, 3901 J-13
Indian Rocks Bch., 4113 I-6
Indian Shores, 1420 *C-1
Indiantown, 6083 M-12
Indrio, 330 K-13
Inglis, 1325 G-6
Inlet Bch., 400 S-5
Intercession City, 630 I-10
Interlachen, 1403 E-9
Inverness, 7210 G-7
Inwood, 6403 J-9
Islamorada, 6119 S-12
Island Grv., 100 E-8
Isleworth, 700 N-2
Istachatta, 116 H-7
Ives Estates, 19525 †J-9
JACKSON CO., 49746 Q-7
Jacksonville, 821784 C-9
Jacksonville Bch., 21362 C-10
Jacob City, 250 Q-7
Jan Phyl Vil., 5573 *K-4
Jasper, 4546 B-6
Jay, 533 Q-3
JEFFERSON CO., 14761 C-3
Jena, 200 E-5
Jennings, 878 B-5
Jensen Bch., 11707 L-13
Jerome P-10
Johnson, 300 E-8
June Pk., 4094 I-12
Juno Bch., 3176 M-14
Jupiter, 55156 M-14
Jupiter Inlet Bch. Colony, 400 M-14
Jupiter Island, 817 M-14
Kathleen, 6332 I-8
Keaton Bch., 75 D-4
Kenansville, 160 J-11
Kendale Lakes, 56148 Q-13
Kendall, 75371 Q-13
Kendrick F-8
Kenneth City, 4980 I-6
Key Biscayne, 12344 Q-13
Key Colony Bch., 797 T-11
Key Haven, 850 T-9
Key Largo, 10433 R-13
Key West, 24649 T-9
Keystone, 24039 *A-2
Keystone Hts., 1350 D-8
Keysville, 300 J-8
Killarney N-1
Kinard, 50 S-7
Kings Ferry A-9
Kings Pt., 12200 *D-9
Kissimmee, 59682 I-10
Kissimmee Pk., 160 I-10
Knights I-8
Korona, 75 E-10
Kossuthville, 400 *J-3
Kuhlman, 500 K-10
Kynesville, 120 R-7
La Crosse, 360 D-7
La Grange G-12
LaBelle, 4640 M-10
Lacoochee, 1714 H-8
Lady Lake, 13926 G-8
LAFAYETTE CO., 8870 D-5
Laguna Bch., 3932 S-5
L. Alfred, 5015 I-9
L. Bird, 50 C-4
L. Brantley, 3000 L-3
L. Buena Vista, 10 H-10
L. Butler, 1897 D-7
L. Cain Hills, 1600 N-3
Lake City, 12046 C-7
L. Clarke Shores, 3376 *B-10
LAKE CO., 297052 H-9
L. Como, 500 E-9
L. Geneva, 1200 D-8
L. Hamilton, 1231 J-9
L. Hbr., 45 N-12
L. Helen, 2624 G-10
L. Jem, 340 G-9
L. Marian Highlands, 370 J-11
L. Mary, 13822 G-10
L. Monroe, 270 G-10
L. Panasoffkee, 3551 G-8
Lake Pk., 8155 M-14
L. Placid, 2223 L-10
L. Shore I-1
L. Suzy, 1040 M-8
L. Wales, 14225 J-9
L. Worth, 34910 N-14
Lakeland, 97422 I-8
Lakeport, 300 M-11
Lakewood Pk., 11323 K-13
Lamont, 178 B-3
Lanark Vil., 600 D-1
Land O' Lakes, 31996 I-7
Lantana, 10423 N-14
Largo, 77648 I-6
Lauderdale Lakes, 32593 †H-8
Lauderdale-by-the-Sea, 6056 †G-9
Lauderhill, 66887 †H-8
Laurel, 8171 L-7
Laurel Hill, 537 Q-4
Lawtey, 730 C-8
Layton, 184 S-12
Lazy Lake, 24 *H-9
Lealman, 19879 *D-2
Lebanon Sta., 30 F-7
Lecanto, 5882 G-7
Lee, 352 B-5
LEE CO., 618754 N-9
Leesburg, 20117 G-9
Lehigh Acres, 86784 N-9
Leisure City, 22655 Q-13
Lemon Grv., 657 K-9
LEON CO., 275487 B-3
Leonia, 150 Q-5
LEVY CO., 40801 E-6
Liberty, 100 Q-5
LIBERTY CO., 8365 S-8
Lighthouse Pt., 10344 O-14
Limestone, 132 L-9
Linden, 120 H-8
Lisbon, 260 G-9
Lithia J-8
Little Havana †L-8
Live Oak, 6850 C-6
Lloyd, 215 B-3
Lochloosa, 260 E-8
Lochmoor, 1200 †M-1
Lockhart, 13060 M-3
Longboat Key, 6888 K-6
Longwood, 13657 L-4
Lorida, 340 K-10
Loughman, 2680 I-9
Lowell, 220 F-8
Loxahatchee Groves, 3180 N-13
Lulu, 100 C-7
Lumberton, 220 I-8
Luraville C-5
Lutz, 19344 I-7
Lynn Haven, 18493 S-6
Lynne, 200 F-8
Macclenny, 6374 C-8
Madeira Bch., 4263 I-6
Madison, 2843 B-4
MADISON CO., 19224 C-4
Maitland, 15751 M-4
Malabar, 2757 J-12
Malone, 2088 Q-7
Manalapan, 406 †C-10
Manasota, 540 M-7
MANATEE CO., 322833 K-7
Mandarin J-3
Mango, 11313 †B-5
Mangonia Pk., 1888 †A-10
Manhattan, 40 †F-5
Marathon, 8297 T-11
Marco Island, 16413 P-9
Margate, 53284 O-13
Marianna, 6102 Q-7
Marineland, 16 E-10
MARION CO., 331298 F-8
Marion Oaks, 4200 G-8
Martel, 200 F-8
Martin, 70 F-8
MARTIN CO., 146318 L-13
Mary Esther, 3851 R-4
Masaryktown, 1040 H-7
Mascotte, 5101 H-9
Matlacha, 677 N-8
Mayo, 1237 C-5
McAlpin, 165 C-6
McDavid, 100 Q-2
McIntosh, 452 E-8
Medart, 150 C-2
Medley, 838 †L-7
Medulla, 8892 †K-1
Melbourne, 76068 I-12
Melbourne Bch., 3101 I-12
Melbourne Shores, 600 I-12
Melbourne Vil., 662 H-13
Melrose, 1100 D-8
Memphis, 7848 †F-3
Merritt Island, 34743 I-12
Mexico Bch., 1072 T-7
Miami, 399457 P-13
Miami Bch., 87779 P-14
Miami Gdns., 107167 P-13
Miami Lakes, 29361 *K-7
Miami Shores, 10493 †K-8
Miami Sprs., 13809 †L-7
MIAMI-DADE CO., 2496435 R-12
Micanopy, 600 E-7
Micco, 9052 J-12
Miccosukee, 285 B-3
Middleburg, 13008 C-9
Midway, 3004 B-2
Midway, 1705 G-10
Mikesville, 100 D-7
Milligan, 350 Q-4
Millview, 1100 *J-7
Milton, 8826 R-3
Mims, 7058 H-11
Minneola, 9403 H-9
Miramar, 122041 *J-7
Miramar Bch., 6146 R-4
Mission Bay, 2900 *E-8
Mission City, 1700 F-11
Molino, 1277 Q-2
MONROE CO., 73090 Q-11
Montbrook F-7
Monticello, 2506 B-3
Montverde, 1463 M-1
Moore Haven, 1680 M-11
Morningside Pk., 500 O-3
Morriston, 164 F-7
Morse Shores, 3300 *L-3
Moss Bluff, 120 F-9
Mossy Head, 250 Q-5
Mt. Carmel, 227 Q-3
Mt. Dora, 12370 G-9
Mt. Pleasant, 75 B-1
Mt. Plymouth, 4011 G-9
Mulberry, 3817 J-8
Munson, 372 Q-3
Murdock M-8
Myakka City, 170 L-8
Myakka Head, 100 K-8
Myrtle Grv., 15870 R-2
Nalcrest, 500 J-10
Naples, 19537 O-9
Naples Manor, 5562 P-9
Naples Pk., 5967 O-9
Naranja, 8303 Q-13
Narcoossee, 200 I-10
NASSAU CO., 73314 B-9
Nassauville, 1900 B-9
National Gdns., 400 F-11
Navarre, 31378 R-3
Neptune Bch., 7037 C-10
New Berlin J-3
New Hope, 110 R-6
New Port Richey, 14911 I-6
New Smyrna Bch., 22464 F-11
Newberry, 4950 E-7
Newport C-2
Niceville, 12749 R-4
Nobleton, 282 H-8
Nocatee, 4524 L-9
Nokomis, 3167 L-7
Noma, 211 Q-6
N. Bay Vil., 7137 †K-9
N. Fort Myers, 39407 N-9
N. Key Largo, 1244 R-13
N. Lauderdale, 41023 †G-8
N. Miami, 58786 P-13
N. Miami Bch., 41523 P-13
N. Palm Bch., 12015 M-14
N. Port, 57357 M-8
N. Redington Bch., 1417 *D-1
N. River Shores, 3079 L-13
Northdale, 22079 I-7
Oak Grv., 300 T-7
Oak Hill, 1792 G-11
Oakdale, 50 R-7
Oakland, 2538 R-1
Oakland Pk., 41363 O-14
O'Brien, 120 D-6
Ocala, 56315 F-8
Ocean Ridge, 1786 *C-10
Ocklawaha, 860 F-8
Ocoee, 35579 M-2
Odessa, 7267 I-7
Ojus, 18036 †J-9
Okahumpka, 267 G-9
OKALOOSA CO., 180822 R-4
Okeechobee, 5621 L-11
OKEECHOBEE CO., 39996 K-11
Old Myakka, 200 *H-5
Old Town, 250 E-6
Oldsmar, 13591 I-6
Olustee, 300 C-7
Olympia Hts., 13488 †M-7
Ona, 314 K-9
Oneco, 3200 K-7
O'Neil, 455 B-9
Opa-locka, 15219 P-13
Orange, 60 S-7
Orange City, 10599 G-10
ORANGE CO., 1145956 H-11
Orange Hts., 130 D-8
Orange Lake, 700 E-8
Orange Mills, 200 E-9
Orange Pk., 8412 C-9
Orange Sprs. E-8
Orangedale, 400 D-9
Orangedale †I-2
Orangetree, 4406 O-9
Orchid, 415 J-13
Oriole Bch., 1420 *J-10
Orlando, 238300 H-10
Orlovista, 6123 N-3
Ormond Bch., 38137 F-11
Ormond-By-The-Sea, 7406 F-11
Ortega I-2
OSCEOLA CO., 268685 I-11
Osprey, 6100 L-7
Osteen, 550 G-10
Otter Creek, 134 F-6
Overstreet, 70 T-7
Oviedo, 33342 H-10
Oxford, 360 G-8
Ozona, 1900 I-6
Pace, 20039 R-3
Pahokee, 5649 M-12
Painters Hill, 50 E-10
Paisley, 818 G-9
Palatka, 10558 E-9
Palm Bay, 103190 I-12
PALM BCH. CO., 1320134 N-12
Palm Bch., 8348 N-14
Palm Bch. Gdns., 48452 M-13
Palm City, 23120 L-13
Palm Coast, 75180 E-10
Palm Hbr., 57439 I-6
Palm Shores, 900 I-12
Palm Sprs., 18928 *B-10
Palm Sprs. North, 5253 *J-7
Palm Valley, 20019 C-10
Palma Sola, 3100 *F-2
Palmdale, 100 M-10
Palmetto, 12606 K-7
Palmetto Bay, 23410 Q-13
Palmetto Estates, 13535 †N-7
Panacea, 816 C-2
Panama City, 36484 S-6
Panama City Bch., 12018 S-5
Paradise Bch., 500 *J-7
Parker, 4317 S-6
Parkland, 23962 †F-8
Parrish, 460 K-7
PASCO CO., 464697 I-7
Paxton, 644 Q-5
Pebble Creek, 7622 *A-4
Pelican Bay, 6346 O-9
Pembroke Pk., 6102 *J-9
Pembroke Pines, 154750 P-13
Penney Farms, 749 D-9
Pennsuco *K-6
Pensacola, 51923 R-2
Pensacola Bch., 1200 R-3
Perry, 7017 C-4
Picnic *D-6
Picolata D-9
Pierce, 115 J-8
Pierson, 1736 F-10
Pine Castle, 10805 N-4
Pine Forest, 2500 *I-4
Pine Hills, 60076 H-10
Pinecrest, 18223 †N-7
Pineland, 407 N-8
PINELLAS CO., 916542 J-6
Pinellas Pk., 49079 I-6
Pineola H-8
Pinetta, 300 B-5
Pinewood, 16520 *K-8

*, †, ‡, §, ◊ See explanation under state title in this index.
County and parish names are listed in capital letters & boldface type.
Independent cities (not included in a county) are listed in italics.

240 Florida–Hawaii

Pirate Hbr., 260 ... M-8
Pittman ... Q-6
Placida, 220 ... M-8
Plant City, 34721 ... J-8
Plantation, 84955 ... †H-8
Pleasant Grv., 1000 ... *J-8
Plymouth, 1250 ... L-2
Poinciana, 53193 ... I-10
Poincianna Pl., 1100 ... N-13
Pt. O'Rocks, 400 ... †H-3
Pt. Washington, 220 ... R-5
Polk City, 1562 ... I-9
POLK CO., 602095 ... J-9
Pomona Pk., 912 ... E-9
Pompano Bch., 99845 ... O-14
Ponce de Leon, 598 ... R-5
Ponce Inlet, 3032 ... F-11
Ponte Vedra Bch., 3000 ... C-10
Port Charlotte, 54392 ... M-8
Port LaBelle, 3530 ... M-10
Port Orange, 56048 ... F-11
Port Richey, 2671 ... I-6
Port St. Joe, 3445 ... T-7
Port St. John, 12267 .. E-12
Port St. Lucie, 164603 ... L-13
Port Salerno, 10091 ... L-13
Portland, 230 ... R-5
Princeton, 22038 ... Q-13
Progress Vil., 5392 ... †C-4
Prosperity, 50 ... Q-5
Providence, 250 ... D-7
Providence, 100 ... I-8
Punta Gorda, 16641 ... M-8
Punta Rassa, 1750 ... N-8
PUTNAM CO., 74364 ... E-9
Putnam Hall, 400 ... D-8
Quincy, 7972 ... B-1
Raiford, 255 ... C-8
Rainbow Lakes, 1550 ... †C-9
Rainbow Lakes Estates, 1050 ... F-7
Raleigh, 373 ... E-7
Ratliff, 2000 ... B-9
Red Head, 100 ... R-6
Red Level ... G-7
Redbay, 150 ... R-5
Reddick, 506 ... E-8
Redington Bch., 1427 ... †D-1
Redington Shores, 2121 ... J-6
Richland, 430 ... I-8
Richmond Hts., 8541 ... Q-13
Ridge Manor, 4513 ... H-8
River Pk., 5222 ... L-13
Riverview, 71050 ... J-7
Riverview ... G-2
Riviera Bch., 32488 .. M-14
Rochelle ... E-8
Rock Bluff, 90 ... R-8
Rockledge, 24926 ... I-12
Rosedale, 100 ... B-1
Roseland, 1472 ... J-12
Rosewood ... F-6
Rotonda, 8759 ... M-8
Round Lake, 50 ... R-7
Royal Palm Bch., 34140 ... N-13
Royal Palm Estates, 3025 ... †B-9
Runyon, 160 ... M-12
Ruskin, 17208 ... K-7
Russell, 500 ... C-9
Rutland ... G-8
Safety Hbr., 16884 ... J-6
St. Augustine, 12975 ... D-10
St. Augustine Bch., 6176 ... D-10
St. Augustine Shores, 7359 ... D-10
St. Catherine, 225 ... H-8
St. Cloud, 35183 ... I-10
St. James City, 3784 ... N-8
St. Joe Bch., 850 ... T-7
ST. JOHNS CO., 190039 ... D-9
St. Johns Pk., 100 ... E-10
St. Leo, 1340 ... I-8
St. Lucie, 590 ... K-13
ST. LUCIE CO., 277789 ... L-12
St. Marks, 293 ... C-2
St. Pete Bch., 9346 ... K-6
St. Petersburg, 244769 ... J-7
St. Teresa ... D-2
Salem, 100 ... D-4
Salt Sprs., 600 ... E-9
Samoset, 3854 ... K-7
Sampson City, 35 ... D-8
Samsula, 1260 ... G-11
San Antonio, 1138 ... I-8
San Carlos Pk., 16824 ... N-9
San Mateo, 1100 ... E-9
San Mateo ... F-3
Sandalfoot Cove, 16600 ... †F-8
Sanderson, 470 ... C-7
Sandy ... †H-6
Sanford, 53570 ... G-10
Sanibel, 6469 ... N-8
Sans Souci ... I-3
Santa Fe, 110 ... D-7
Santa Rosa Bch., 600 ... R-5
SANTA ROSA CO., 151372 ... Q-3
Santos, 350 ... F-8
Sarasota, 51917 ... L-7
SARASOTA CO., 379448 ... L-8
Satellite Bch., 10109 .. I-12
Satsuma, 1000 ... E-9
Schall Circle, 1117 ... †A-9
Scottsmoor, 1340 ... G-11
Sea Ranch Lakes, 670 ... †G-9
Seaglades, 900 ... *K-7
Seagrove Bch., 250 ... S-5
Seaside ... S-5
Sebastian, 21929 ... J-12
Sebring, 10491 ... K-10
Seffner, 7579 ... †B-5
Seminole, 17233 ... J-6
SEMINOLE CO., 422718 ... H-11
Seven Sprs., 2000 ... I-6
Seville, 614 ... F-10
Sewall's Pt., 1996 ... L-13
Shadeville, 200 ... C-2
Shady, 800 ... F-8
Shady Grv., 100 ... C-4
Shalimar, 717 ... R-4
Shamrock, 150 ... E-5
Sharpes, 3411 ... H-12
Shawnee ... M-11
Shell Pt., 400 ... C-2
Sherman, 175 ... L-12
Sherwood Forest, 700 ... P-2
Siesta Key, 6565 ... †H-3
Siesta Lago, 1800 ... P-3
Silver Sprs., 1050 ... F-8
Silver Sprs. Shores, 6539 ... F-8
Sink Creek, 35 ... R-7
Sky Lake, 6153 ... O-3
Slavia, 1000 ... M-5
Sneads, 1849 ... R-8
Snow Hill ... H-11
Socrum ... †I-1
Solana, 742 ... M-8
Sopchoppy, 457 ... C-2
Sorrento, 861 ... G-9
S. Apopka, 5728 ... L-2
S. Bay, 4876 ... N-12
S. Beach ... P-12
S. Daytona, 12252 ... F-11
S. Miami, 11657 ... †M-7
S. Miami Hts., 35696 ... Q-13
S. Palm Bch., 1171 ... †C-10
S. Pasadena, 4964 ... †D-1
S. Ponte Vedra Bch., 200 ... C-10
S. Punta Gorda Hts., 940 ... M-8
S. Venice, 13949 ... M-7
Southport, 1500 ... S-6
Southwest Ranches, 7345 ... †I-6
Southwood, 1700 ... N-3
Sparr, 400 ... F-8
Spring Creek, 100 ... C-2
Spring Hill, 98621 ... H-7
Spring Lake, 1100 ... K-10
Spring Lake, 458 ... H-7
Springfield, 8903 ... S-6
Spuds, 100 ... D-10
Starke, 5449 ... D-8
Steinhatchee, 1047 ... E-4
Stuart, 15593 ... L-13
Sugarloaf Shores, 700 ... T-10
Sumatra, 148 ... S-8
Summer Haven, 200 ... D-10
Summerfield, 320 ... G-8
Summerland Key, 950 ... T-10
Summerport Bch., 150 ... N-2
Sumner ... F-6
SUMTER CO., 93420 ... H-8
Sumterville, 260 ... G-8
Sun City, 150 ... K-7
Sun City Ctr., 19258 ... K-7
Sun Valley, 1300 ... †C-9
Sunland Gdns., 1600 ... K-13
Sunny Isles Bch., 20832 ... †K-9
Sunrise, 84439 ... †H-8
Sunset, 16389 ... †M-7
Sunset Pt., 600 ... S-13
Surfside, 5744 ... †K-9
Suwannee, 450 ... F-5
SUWANNEE CO., 41551 ... C-6
Suwannee Sprs. ... B-6
Svea, 75 ... Q-4
Sweet Gum Head ... Q-5
Sweetwater, 13499 ... P-13
Sweetwater Creek, 6600 ... †B-3
Sweetwater Oaks, 1100 ... L-3
Switzerland, 2900 ... C-9
Sydney, 440 ... †C-6
Taft, 2205 ... H-10
Tallahassee, 181376 ... B-2
Tallevast, 200 ... K-7
Tamarac, 60427 ... O-13
Tampa, 335709 ... J-7
Tangelo Pk., 2231 ... O-3
Tangerine, 2865 ... G-9
Tarpon Lake Villages, 1200 ... †A-2
Tarpon Sprs., 23484 ... I-6
Tarrytown, 200 ... H-8
Tatum Ridge, 200 ... †H-4
Tavares, 13951 ... G-9
Tavernier, 2136 ... S-13
Taylor, 200 ... B-7
TAYLOR CO., 22570 ... D-3
Telogia, 330 ... B-1
Temple Ter., 24541 ... J-7
Tequesta, 5629 ... M-14
Terra Ceia, 220 ... K-7
The Villages, 51442 ... G-8
Theressa, 100 ... D-8
Thomas City ... B-3
Thonotosassa, 13014 ... I-7
Three Lakes, 15047 .. †N-6
Tice, 4470 ... N-9
Tierra Verde, 3721 ... †E-2
Tiger Pt., 3090 ... R-3
Tildenville, 511 ... M-1
Titusville, 43761 ... H-11
Torrey, 650 ... K-9
Treasure Island, 6705 .. J-6
Trenton, 1999 ... E-6
Trilby, 419 ... H-8
Tropical Gulf Acres, 8200 ... M-8
Uleta, 2300 ... †J-9
Umatilla, 3456 ... G-9
UNION CO., 15535 .. C-7
Union Pk., 9765 ... M-5
University Pk., 600 ... M-5
Valkaria, 250 ... I-14
Valparaiso, 5036 ... R-4
Valrico ... †C-5
Vamo, 4727 ... L-7
Vanderbilt Bch. ... O-9
Venetia ... I-2
Venice, 20748 ... L-7
Venice Gdns., 7104 ... L-7
Venus, 50 ... L-10
Vermont Hts., 200 ... D-10
Verna ... L-8
Vernon, 687 ... R-6
Vero Bch., 15220 ... K-13
Vero Lake Estates, 1600 ... J-12
Vicksburg ... S-6
Viera, 200 ... I-12
Vilano Bch., 2678 ... D-10
Villas, 11569 ... N-9
Vineyards, 3375 ... O-9
Virginia Gdns., 2375 ... †L-7
VOLUSIA CO., 494593 ... G-11
Wabasso, 609 ... J-13
Wacissa, 386 ... B-3
Wahneta, 5091 ... †L-4
Wakulla, 135 ... C-2
WAKULLA CO., 30776 ... C-1
Waldo, 1015 ... D-8
Wallace, 1785 ... R-3
Walnut Hill, 350 ... Q-2
WALTON CO., 55043 ... R-5
Wannee, 130 ... E-6
Warm Mineral Sprs., 5061 ... M-8
Warrington, 14531 ... R-2
WASHINGTON CO., 24896 ... R-6
Waterbury, 60 ... †G-5
Watertown, 2829 ... C-7
Wauchula, 5001 ... K-9
Waukeenah, 272 ... B-3
Wausau, 383 ... R-6
Waverly, 767 ... J-9
Webster, 785 ... H-8
Weeki Wachee, 12 ... H-7
Weirsdale, 840 ... G-8
Welaka, 701 ... E-9
Wellborn, 400 ... C-6
Wellington, 56508 ... N-13
Wesley Chapel, 44092 ... I-7
W. Bay, 300 ... S-6
W. Frostproof, 200 ... J-9
W. Little River, 34699 ... †K-8
W. Melbourne, 18355 ... I-12
W. Miami, 5965 ... †L-7
W. Palm Bch., 99919 ... N-14
W. Park, 14156 ... †J-8
W. Pensacola, 21339 ... R-2
Westchester, 29862 .. †M-7
Weston, 65333 ... O-13
Westview, 9650 ... †K-8
Westville, 289 ... Q-6
Westwood Lakes, 11838 ... †M-7
Wewahitchka, 1981 ... S-7
Whisper Walk, 5100 .. †E-9
White City, 3719 ... K-13
White City, 400 ... T-7
White Sprs., 777 ... C-6
Wilbur-By-The-Sea, 1300 ... F-11
Wildwood, 6709 ... G-8
Williston, 2768 ... E-7
Williston Highlands, 2275 ... F-7
Wilton Mnrs, 11632 .. †H-9
Wimauma, 6373 ... K-7
Windermere, 2462 ... H-9
Winston, 9024 ... †J-1
Winter Bch., 2067 ... J-13
Winter Gdn., 34568 ... H-9
Winter Haven, 33874 .. J-9
Winter Pk., 27852 ... M-4
Winter Sprs., 33282 ... G-10
Woods, 130 ... S-8
Woodville, 2978 ... C-2
Worthington Sprs., 181 ... D-7
Wright, 23127 ... R-4
Yalaha, 1364 ... G-9
Yankeetown, 502 ... G-6
Yeehaw Jct., 240 ... K-11
Yniestra, 450 ... *I-10
Youmans, 600 ... †B-7
Youngstown, 150 ... S-7
Yulee, 11491 ... B-9
Zana, 220 ... L-12
Zellwood, 2817 ... G-9
Zephyrhills, 13288 ... I-8
Zolfo Sprs., 1827 ... K-9
Zuber, 125 ... F-8

Georgia

Page locator

Map keys	Atlas pages
A–J	58–59
K–T	60–61

* City keyed to pp. 62-63
† City keyed to p. 193

Abbeville, 2908 ... K-7
Acree, 130 ... L-5
Acworth, 20425 ... D-3
Adairsville, 4648 ... C-3
Adamsville ... *E-1
Adel, 5334 ... N-7
Adgateville, 25 ... G-6
Adrian, 664 ... I-9
Ailey, 432 ... J-9
Air Line, 150 ... C-8
Alamo, 2797 ... J-8
Alapaha, 668 ... M-7
Albany, 77434 ... L-5
Aldora, 103 ... H-5
Alexander, 100 ... H-11
Aline, 50 ... J-10
Allenhurst, 695 ... L-12
Allentown, 169 ... I-7
Alma, 3466 ... L-9
Almon, 500 ... F-5
Alpharetta, 57551 ... D-5
Alston, 159 ... K-9
Alta Vista ... R-3
Altman, 70 ... I-12
Alto, 1172 ... C-6
Alvaton, 100 ... G-4
Ambrose, 380 ... L-8
Americus, 17041 ... K-5
Amsterdam, 100 ... O-4
Anderson City, 30 ... M-6
Andersonville, 255 ... J-5
Apalachee, 160 ... F-7
Appling, 500 ... F-10
APPLING CO., 18236 ... K-10
Arabi, 586 ... K-6
Aragon, 1249 ... D-3
Arcade, 1786 ... D-6
Argyle, 212 ... N-9
Arlington, 1479 ... M-3
Armuchee, 200 ... C-2
Arnco Mills, 500 ... F-3
Arnoldsville, 357 ... E-7
Ashburn, 4152 ... L-6
Athens, 115452 ... E-7
Atkinson, 135 ... M-11
ATKINSON CO., 8375 ... M-8
Atlanta, 420003 ... E-4
Attapulgus, 449 ... O-4
Auburn, 6887 ... E-6
Augusta, 195844 ... F-11
Auraria, 50 ... C-5
Austell, 6581 ... E-4
Autreyville, 75 ... N-6
Avalon, 213 ... C-7
Avera, 246 ... G-9
Avondale Estates, 2960 ... *E-5
Axson, 200 ... M-9
Babcock, 40 ... N-3
BACON CO., 11096 ... L-9
Baconton, 915 ... M-5
Bainbridge, 12697 ... N-4
Bairdstown, 40 ... F-8
BAKER CO., 3451 ... M-4
Baldwin, 3279 ... C-6
BALDWIN CO., 45720 ... G-7
Ball Ground, 1433 ... D-4
BANKS CO., 18395 .. C-6
Banning, 150 ... F-3
Barnesville, 6755 ... H-5
Barnett, 45 ... F-8
Barney, 150 ... N-6
BARROW CO., 69367 ... D-6
Bartow, 286 ... H-9
BARTOW CO., 100157 ... D-3
Barwick, 386 ... N-6
Batesville ... B-6
Baxley, 4400 ... L-10
Belfast, 250 ... K-13
Bellville, 123 ... J-11
Bellville ... L-3
Belvedere Pk., 6000 .. *E-5
Bemiss, 200 ... N-7
Ben Hill ... *F-1
BEN HILL CO., 17634 ... L-7
Benevolence, 50 ... K-3
Benning Hills ... T-3
Benning Pk. ... S-3
Berlin, 551 ... N-6
BERRIEN CO., 19286 ... M-7
Berryton, 100 ... C-2
Bethlehem, 601 ... E-6
Between, 296 ... E-6
Beulah, 80 ... E-9
Beverly Hills, 1000 ... †N-12
BIBB CO., 155547 ... H-6
Bickley ... M-9
Billarp, 30 ... F-3
Bishop, 224 ... E-7
Blackshear, 3445 ... M-10
Blackshear Pl., 500 ... D-6
Blackwells, 5000 ... E-4
Blaine ... C-4
Blair Vil. ... *G-4
Blairsville, 652 ... B-5
Blakely, 5068 ... M-3
BLECKLEY CO., 13063 ... J-7
Blitchton, 250 ... J-12
Bloomingdale, 2713 .. J-12
Blue Ridge, 1290 ... B-4
Bluffton, 103 ... L-3
Blythe, 721 ... G-10
Bogart, 1034 ... E-6
Bolingbroke, 150 ... H-6
Bolton ... *D-2
Bonaire, 900 ... I-6
Bonanza, 3135 ... F-4
Boneville, 230 ... F-9
Boston, 1315 ... O-6
Bostwick, 365 ... E-7
Bowdon, 2040 ... F-2
Bowdon Jct., 400 ... F-2
Bowens Mill, 90 ... K-7
Bowersville, 465 ... C-8
Bowman, 862 ... D-8
Box Sprs., 200 ... I-3
Boykin, 143 ... N-3
Bradley, 90 ... H-6
Branchville ... N-4
BRANTLEY CO., 18411 ... N-10
Braselton, 7511 ... D-6
Braswell, 379 ... E-3
Bremen, 6227 ... E-2
Brewton, 200 ... I-8
Briar Wood Estates, 750 ... *A-1
Bridgeboro, 100 ... M-5
Bridgeman, 200 ... S-7
Brinson, 215 ... N-3
Bristol, 200 ... M-10
Bronwood, 225 ... K-4
Brookfield, 450 ... M-7
Brookhaven, 7000 ... *C-4
Brookhaven, 130 ... S-5
Brooklet, 1395 ... J-11
Brooklyn, 65 ... J-3
Brooks, 524 ... G-4
BROOKS CO., 16243 ... N-6
Broxton, 1189 ... L-8
Brunswick, 15383 ... N-12
BRYAN CO., 30233 ... K-12
Buchanan, 1104 ... E-2
Buckhead, 171 ... F-7
Buckhead ... *C-3
Buena Vista, 2173 ... J-4
Buffington ... D-4
Buford, 12225 ... D-5
Bullard, 100 ... I-7
BULLOCH CO., 70217 ... J-11
BURKE CO., 23316 ... G-10
Burroughs, 300 ... T-8
Butler, 1972 ... I-5
BUTTS CO., 23655 ... G-5
Byromville, 546 ... J-5
Byron, 4512 ... I-6
Cadley, 50 ... F-9
Cadwell, 528 ... J-8
Cairo, 9607 ... N-5
Calhoun, 15650 ... C-3
CALHOUN CO., 6694 ... L-4
Calvary, 161 ... O-4
Camak, 138 ... F-9
CAMDEN CO., 50513 ... N-12
Camilla, 5360 ... M-5
Campania, 400 ... F-10
Campton, 100 ... E-6
CANDLER CO., 10998 ... J-10
Cannonville, 100 ... H-2
Canon, 804 ... D-8
Canoochee, 71 ... I-10
Canton, 22958 ... D-4
Carbondale ... C-3
Carey Pk. ... *E-2
Carl, 255 ... E-6
Carlton, 260 ... D-8
Carnegie, 35 ... L-3
Carnesville, 577 ... C-7
Carnigan, 100 ... M-12
CARROLL CO., 110527 ... F-3
Carrollton, 24388 ... F-2
Carters, 30 ... C-3
Cartersville, 19731 ... D-3
Cary, 120 ... I-7
Cascade Hts. ... *F-2
Cassville, 650 ... D-3
Cataula, 550 ... I-3
CATOOSA CO., 63942 ... B-2
Cave Spr., 1200 ... D-2
Cecil, 286 ... N-7
Cedar Crossing, 50 ... K-10
Cedar Grv., 2000 ... *G-5
Cedar Sprs., 74 ... M-2
Cedartown, 9750 ... E-2
Center, 150 ... D-3
Center, 150 ... D-7
Center Hill ... *E-2
Center Pt., 75 ... F-2
Centerville, 7148 ... I-6
Centralhatchee, 408 ... G-2
Chalybeate Sprs., 250 ... H-4
Chamblee, 9892 ... E-4
Charing, 30 ... I-4
Charles, 90 ... J-3
Charlotteville, 35 ... K-9
CHARLTON CO., 12171 ... N-10
CHATHAM CO., 265128 ... K-13
Chatsworth, 4299 ... B-3
Chattahoochee ... *D-2
CHATTAHOOCHEE CO., 11267 ... J-3
Chattahoochee Hills, 2378 ... F-3
Chattahoochee Plantation, 150 ... *A-3
Chattanooga Valley, 3846 ... B-2
CHATTOOGA CO., 26015 ... C-1
Chattoogaville, 125 ... C-2
Chauncey, 342 ... K-8
CHEROKEE CO., 214346 ... D-4
Cherry Log, 119 ... B-4
Chester, 1596 ... J-7
Chestnut Mtn., 250 ... D-6
Chickamauga, 3101 ... B-2
Chicopee, 750 ... D-6
Chula, 250 ... L-6
Cisco, 300 ... B-3
CLARKE CO., 116714 ... E-7
Clarkesville, 1733 ... C-7
Clarkston, 7554 ... *D-6
Claxton, 2746 ... J-11
CLAY CO., 3183 ... L-3
Clayton, 2047 ... B-7
CLAYTON CO., 259424 ... F-4
Clem, 150 ... F-3
Clermont, 875 ... C-6
Cleveland, 3410 ... C-6
Climax, 280 ... N-4
CLINCH CO., 6798 ... O-9
Clinchfield, 125 ... J-6
Clinton, 80 ... H-6
Cloudland, 300 ... C-1
Clyattville, 300 ... O-7
Clyo, 370 ... I-13
Coal Mtn., 100 ... D-5
Cobb, 150 ... K-5
COBB CO., 688078 ... E-4
Cobbtown, 351 ... J-10
Cochran, 5150 ... J-7
COFFEE CO., 42356 ... M-8
Cogdell, 50 ... N-9
Cohutta, 661 ... B-3
Colbert, 592 ... E-7
Coleman, 127 ... L-3
Colemans Lake, 45 ... H-10
College Pk., 13942 ... F-4
Collins, 584 ... J-10
Colquitt, 1992 ... N-3
COLQUITT CO., 45498 ... N-6
COLUMBIA CO., 124053 ... F-10
Columbus, 189885 ... I-3
Comer, 1126 ... D-8
Commerce, 6544 ... D-7
Concord, 375 ... G-4
Coney, 45 ... K-6
Conley, 6228 ... *G-4
Constitution, 600 ... *F-4
Conyers, 15195 ... F-5
COOK CO., 17212 ... N-6
Coolidge, 525 ... N-6
Cooper Hts. ... B-2
Coopers, 300 ... H-7
Coosa, 350 ... D-2
Cordele, 11147 ... K-6
Corinth, 210 ... G-3
Cornelia, 4160 ... C-7
Cotton, 100 ... N-5
Council, 80 ... O-9
Country Club Estates, 8545 ... R-13
Covena, 50 ... I-9
Coverdale, 30 ... L-6
Covington, 13118 ... F-6
COWETA CO., 127317 ... G-3
Cox, 75 ... M-12
Crandall, 250 ... B-3
Crawford, 832 ... E-7
CRAWFORD CO., 12630 ... I-5
Crawfordville, 534 ... F-8
Crescent, 500 ... L-12
Crestwell Hts., 120 ... R-5
CRISP CO., 23439 ... K-6
Crosland, 150 ... M-6
Crystal Sprs., 1300 ... R-7
Crystal Sprs. ... C-2
Crystal Valley ... Q-4
Culloden, 175 ... H-5
Culverton, 45 ... G-8
Cumming, 5430 ... D-5
Cusseta, 11267 ... J-3
Cuthbert, 3873 ... L-3
Dacula, 4442 ... E-6
DADE CO., 16633 ... B-1
Dahlonega, 5242 ... C-5
Daisy, 129 ... J-11
Dakota, 100 ... L-6
Dallas, 11544 ... E-3
Dalton, 33128 ... B-3
Damascus, 254 ... M-3
Danburg, 130 ... E-9
Danielsville, 560 ... D-7
Danville, 238 ... I-7
Darien, 1975 ... M-12
Dasher, 912 ... O-7
Davis Crossroads ... B-2
Davisboro, 2010 ... H-9
Dawson, 4540 ... L-4
DAWSON CO., 22330 ... C-5
Dawsonville, 2536 ... C-5
DE KALB CO., 691893 ... F-5
De Soto, 195 ... K-5
De Soto Pk., 1200 ... D-2
Dearing, 549 ... F-10
Decatur, 19335 ... E-4
DECATUR CO., 27842 ... N-3
Deenwood, 2146 ... M-10
Deepstep, 131 ... H-8
Deerwood Pk., 3000 ... *E-5
Demorest, 1823 ... C-6
Denmark, 50 ... J-11
Denton, 250 ... L-9
Devereux, 70 ... G-8
Dewy Rose, 154 ... D-8
Dexter, 575 ... J-8
Diamond Hill, 75 ... D-7
Dickey ... L-3
Dillard, 339 ... B-7
Dixie, 200 ... O-6
Dixie Union, 250 ... M-9
Dock Jct., 7721 ... R-13
DODGE CO., 21796 .. J-7
Doerun, 774 ... M-5
Doles, 100 ... L-6
Donald, 75 ... K-11
Donalsonville, 2650 ... N-3
Dooling, 154 ... J-5
DOOLY CO., 14918 .. K-5
Doraville, 8330 ... E-5
DOUGHERTY CO., 94565 ... L-4
Douglas, 11589 ... L-8
DOUGLAS CO., 132403 ... F-3
Douglasville, 30961 ... E-3
Dover, 85 ... I-11
Doverel ... L-4
Draketown, 180 ... E-3
Draneville ... J-4
Druid Hills, 14568 ... *E-4
Dry Branch, 400 ... H-7
Du Pont, 120 ... N-8
Dublin, 16201 ... I-8
Ducktown ... D-5
Dudley, 571 ... I-8
Duluth, 26600 ... E-5
Dunwoody, 46267 ... *A-4
Durand, 200 ... H-3
Dutch Island, 1257 ... T-12
EARLY CO., 11008 .. M-2
E. Atlanta ... *E-4
E. Dublin, 2441 ... I-8
E. Ellijay, 546 ... B-4
E. Lake ... *E-5
E. Newnan, 1321 ... G-3
East Pt., 33712 ... F-4
Eastman, 4962 ... J-7
Eastville, 170 ... E-7
Eatonton, 6480 ... G-7
ECHOLS CO., 4034 ... O-8
Eden, 750 ... J-12
Edge Hill, 24 ... G-9
Edison, 1531 ... L-3
Edith, 50 ... O-9
EFFINGHAM CO., 52250 ... I-12
Egypt, 75 ... I-12
ELBERT CO., 20166 .. D-8
Elberta, 950 ... I-6
Elberton, 4653 ... D-8
Eldorado, 100 ... M-7
Eldorendo, 100 ... N-3
Elko, 160 ... J-6
Ellabell, 500 ... K-12
Ellaville, 1812 ... J-4
Ellenton, 281 ... N-6
Ellenwood, 400 ... *H-5
Ellerslie, 200 ... I-3
Ellijay, 1619 ... B-4
Elmodel, 75 ... M-4
EMANUEL CO., 22598 ... I-10
Embry Hills, 1600 ... *C-5
Emerson, 1470 ... D-3
Emmalane, 30 ... I-11
Empire, 393 ... J-7
Enigma, 1278 ... M-7
Enon Grv., 60 ... G-3
Enterprise, 50 ... E-8
Ephesus, 427 ... F-2
Epworth, 480 ... B-4
Esom Hill, 250 ... E-2
Etna, 60 ... D-2
Eton, 910 ... B-3
Euharlee, 4136 ... D-3
Eulonia, 100 ... L-12
Evans, 29011 ... F-10
EVANS CO., 11000 ... K-11
Everett, 350 ... M-12
Everett Sprs. ... C-2
Experiment, 2894 ... G-5
Faceville, 200 ... O-3
Fair Oaks, 8225 ... *B-1
Fairburn, 12950 ... F-4
Fairmount, 720 ... C-3
Fairplay, 200 ... F-3
Fairplay, 75 ... F-6
FANNIN CO., 23682 ... B-4
Fargo, 321 ... O-9
Farmington, 200 ... E-7
FAYETTE CO., 106567 ... F-4
Fayetteville, 15945 ... F-4
Felton, 200 ... E-2
Findlay, 70 ... J-6
Finleyson, 100 ... K-7
Fitzgerald, 9053 ... L-7
Five Points ... *E-3
Flemington, 743 ... K-12
Flintside, 50 ... K-5
Flippen, 250 ... F-5
Florence ... K-2
Flovilla, 653 ... G-6
Flowery Branch, 5679 ... D-5
FLOYD CO., 96317 ... D-2
Folkston, 2502 ... O-11
Folsom, 200 ... C-3
Forest Pk., 18468 ... F-4
Forsyth, 3788 ... H-5
FORSYTH CO., 175511 ... D-5
Ft. Gaines, 1107 ... L-2
Ft. Lamar, 85 ... D-7
Ft. McAllister, 300 ... K-13
Ft. Oglethorpe, 9263 ... B-2
Ft. Valley, 9815 ... I-6
Fortsonia, 90 ... E-8
Fowlstown, 140 ... O-4
Franklin, 993 ... G-2
FRANKLIN CO., 22084 ... C-7
Franklin Sprs., 952 ... D-8
Friendship ... J-4
Fruitland, 35 ... O-8
FULTON CO., 920581 ... D-5
Funston, 449 ... M-6
Gabbettville, 75 ... H-2
Gaillard, 30 ... I-5
Gainesville, 33804 ... D-6
Garden City, 8778 ... K-13
Garden Lakes, 4000 ... D-2
Gardi, 100 ... L-11
Garfield, 201 ... I-10
Gay, 89 ... G-4
Geneva, 105 ... I-4
Georgetown, 11823 ... T-8
Georgetown, 2513 ... K-2
Gibson, 663 ... G-9
Gillsville, 235 ... D-6
GILMER CO., 28292 ... B-4
Girard, 156 ... H-11
GLASCOCK CO., 3082 ... G-9
Glen Haven, 3000 ... *E-6
Glenn, 90 ... G-2
Glennville, 3569 ... K-11
Glenwood, 1500 ... D-2
Glenwood, 747 ... J-9
Glenwood Hills, 5200 ... *E-5
GLYNN CO., 79626 ... M-11
Glynn Haven, 450 ... R-14
Godfrey, 130 ... F-7
Good Hope, 274 ... E-6
Gordon, 2017 ... H-7
GORDON CO., 55186 ... C-3
Gordy, 50 ... M-6
Gough, 300 ... G-10
GRADY CO., 25011 .. N-4
Graham, 291 ... K-9
Grange, 30 ... H-9
Grantville, 3041 ... G-3
Gratis, 80 ... E-6
Graves, 60 ... L-4
Gray, 3276 ... H-6
Grayson, 2666 ... E-5
Graysville, 500 ... A-2
GREENE CO., 15994 ... F-7
Greensboro, 3359 ... F-7
Greenville, 876 ... H-3
Gresham Pk., 7432 ... *F-5
Gresston, 115 ... J-7
Griffin, 23643 ... G-5
Grovania, 125 ... J-6
Grove Pk. ... *E-2
Groveland, 50 ... J-11
Grovetown, 11216 ... F-10
Gumbranch, 264 ... K-11
Gumlong, 2146 ... C-8
Guyton, 1684 ... J-12
GWINNETT CO., 805321 ... E-5
Habersham, 75 ... C-6
HABERSHAM CO., 43041 ... C-6
Haddock, 750 ... H-7
Hahira, 2737 ... N-7
Halfmoon, 150 ... L-13
HALL CO., 179684 ... C-5
Halls, 50 ... D-3
Hamilton, 1016 ... H-3
Hampton, 6987 ... G-5
HANCOCK CO., 9429 ... G-8
Hannahs Mill, 3298 ... H-4
Hapeville, 6373 ... *G-3
Haralson, 166 ... G-4
HARALSON CO., 28780 ... E-2
Harlem, 2666 ... F-10
Harrietts Bluff, 100 ... N-12
Harrington, 125 ... R-14
Harris City, 85 ... H-3
HARRIS CO., 32024 ... I-3
Harrison, 489 ... H-9
Harrisonville, 120 ... G-3
HART CO., 25213 ... D-8
Hartford, 250 ... J-7
Hartsfield, 150 ... M-5
Hartwell, 4469 ... D-8
Hatley, 60 ... K-6
Hawkinsville, 4589 ... J-7
Haylow, 25 ... O-8
Hayneville, 200 ... J-6
Hazlehurst, 4226 ... K-9
HEARD CO., 11834 .. G-2
Helen, 510 ... B-6
Helena, 2883 ... K-8
Hemp ... B-5
Henderson, 220 ... J-6
HENRY CO., 203922 ... F-5
Hephzibah, 4011 ... G-10
Herndon, 75 ... H-10
Herod, 30 ... L-4
Hiawassee, 880 ... B-6
Hickox, 100 ... N-11
Higgston, 323 ... J-9
Highfalls, 300 ... G-5
Highland Mills, 700 ... G-5
Hillsboro, 200 ... G-6
Hilton, 100 ... M-2
Hiltonia, 342 ... H-11
Hinesville, 33437 ... K-12
Hinsonton, 100 ... N-5
Hiram, 3546 ... E-3
Hoboken, 528 ... N-10
Hogansville, 3060 ... G-3
Holland, 150 ... C-2
Hollingsworth ... C-7
Hollonville, 75 ... G-4
Holly Sprs., 9189 ... D-4
Holt, 50 ... L-7
Homeland, 910 ... O-11
Homer, 1141 ... D-7
Homerville, 2456 ... N-9
Honey Creek, 1060 ... F-5
Hopeful ... N-4
Horns, 75 ... I-5
Hortense, 400 ... M-11
Hoschton, 1377 ... D-6
HOUSTON CO., 139900 ... J-6
Houston Lake, 100 ... I-6
Howard, 110 ... I-4
Howell, 75 ... O-8
Hull, 198 ... E-7
Hunters, 40 ... I-12
Hutchins, 50 ... E-7
Ideal, 499 ... J-5
Ila, 337 ... D-7
Indian Sprs., 200 ... G-5
Industrial City, 800 ... C-3
Inman Pk. ... *E-4
Iron City, 310 ... N-3
IRWIN CO., 9538 ... L-7
Irwinton, 589 ... H-7
Irwinville, 200 ... L-7
Isabella, 225 ... L-6
Isle of Hope, 2402 ... K-13
Ivey, 981 ... H-7
Ivylog ... B-5
Jackson, 5045 ... G-5
JACKSON CO., 60485 ... D-7
Jacksonville, 140 ... L-8
Jacksonville, 60 ... B-6
Jake, 120 ... F-2
Jakin, 155 ... N-3
James, 100 ... H-7
Jasper, 3684 ... C-4
JASPER CO., 13900 .. G-6
Jay Bird Sprs. ... K-8
JEFF DAVIS CO., 15068 ... K-9
Jefferson, 9432 ... D-6
JEFFERSON CO., 16930 ... H-9
Jeffersonville, 1035 ... I-7
JENKINS CO., 8340 ... H-10
Jenkinsburg, 370 ... G-5
Jersey, 137 ... F-6
Jerusalem, 150 ... N-11
Jesup, 10214 ... L-11
Jewell, 100 ... G-8
Johns Creek, 76728 ... D-5
JOHNSON CO., 9980 .. I-9
Johnson Cor., 50 ... K-10
Jones, 75 ... L-12
Jones Acres, 300 ... R-8
JONES CO., 28669 ... G-6
Jonesboro, 4724 ... F-4
Jonesville, 150 ... F-2
Juliette, 300 ... G-6
Junction City, 177 ... I-4
Juniper ... I-4
Juno, 100 ... C-5
Kansas, 150 ... F-2
Kathleen, 400 ... I-6
Keller, 200 ... K-13
Kennesaw, 29783 ... D-4
Keysville, 332 ... G-10
Kibbee ... J-9
Kiker, 60 ... B-4
Kildare, 30 ... I-12
Kingsland, 15946 ... O-11
Kingston, 637 ... D-3
Kirkland, 60 ... M-8
Kirkwood ... *E-4
Kite, 241 ... I-9
Knoxville, 69 ... I-5
La Vista, 5000 ... *D-4
LaFayette, 7121 ... B-2
LaGrange, 29588 ... H-3
L. Arrowhead, 225 ... D-4
Lake City, 2612 ... *H-4
L. Lucerne, 900 ... E-5
Lake Pk., 733 ... O-7
Lakeland, 3366 ... N-8
Lakemont, 500 ... B-7
Lakeview, 4839 ... †N-13
Lakewood Hts. ... *F-3
LAMAR CO., 18317 ... H-5
Lanier, 300 ... J-12
LANIER CO., 10078 ... N-8
Lathemtown, 200 ... D-5
LAURENS CO., 48434 ... I-8
Lavonia, 2156 ... C-8
Lawrenceville, 28546 .. E-5
Lax, 120 ... M-8
Leah, 110 ... F-10
Leary, 618 ... M-4
Lebanon, 650 ... D-4
LEE CO., 28298 ... K-5
Leesburg, 2896 ... L-5
Leland ... *D-1
Lenox, 873 ... M-7
Leslie, 409 ... K-5
Lexington, 228 ... E-8
Lexsy, 50 ... I-10
LIBERTY CO., 63453 ... K-11
Lilburn, 11596 ... E-5
Lilly, 213 ... J-6
LINCOLN CO., 7996 .. E-9
Lincoln Pk., 833 ... H-4
Lincolnton, 1566 ... E-9
Lindale, 4191 ... D-2
Linton, 40 ... G-8
Lithia Sprs., 15491 ... E-4
Lithonia, 1924 ... E-5
Little Miami, 200 ... O-7
Lizella, 600 ... H-6
Locust Grv., 5402 ... G-5
Loganville, 10458 ... E-6
Lollie, 100 ... I-9
Lone Oak, 92 ... G-3
LONG CO., 14464 ... L-12
Lookout Mtn., 1602 ... A-2
Lothair ... J-9
Louise, 150 ... G-3
Louisville, 2493 ... H-9
Louvale, 300 ... J-3
Lovejoy, 6422 ... F-4
Lovett, 100 ... I-9
Lowell ... F-2
LOWNDES CO., 109233 ... O-7
Ludowici, 1703 ... L-11
Ludville, 150 ... C-4
Lula, 2758 ... C-6
Lumber City, 1328 ... K-9
Lumpkin, 2741 ... K-3
LUMPKIN CO., 29966 ... C-5
Luthersville, 874 ... G-3
Lyerly, 540 ... C-2
Lyons, 4367 ... J-10
Mableton, 37115 ... E-4
Machen, 50 ... G-6
Macon, 91351 ... H-6
MACON CO., 14740 .. J-5
Madison, 3979 ... F-7
MADISON CO., 28120 ... D-7
Madras, 50 ... F-3
Madray Sprs., 75 ... L-11
Magruder, 15 ... H-10
Manassas, 94 ... J-11
Manchester, 4230 ... H-4
Manningtown, 75 ... M-11
Manor, 400 ... N-9
Mansfield, 410 ... F-6
Marblehill, 350 ... C-4
Marietta, 56579 ... E-4
MARION CO., 8742 .. J-4
Marlborough, 1600 ... F-4
Marlow, 350 ... J-12
Marshallville, 1448 ... I-5
Martin, 381 ... C-7
Martinez, 35795 ... F-10
Matt, 90 ... D-5
Matthews, 150 ... G-10
Mauk, 60 ... I-4
Maxeys, 224 ... E-7
Mayday ... O-8
Mayfield, 150 ... G-8
Maysville, 1798 ... D-6
McCaysville, 1056 ... B-4
McDonough, 22084 ... F-5
MCDUFFIE CO., 21875 ... G-9
McIntosh, 250 ... K-12
MCINTOSH CO., 14333 ... L-12
McIntyre, 650 ... H-7
McKinnon, 75 ... M-11
McRae, 5740 ... K-8
Meansville, 182 ... H-4
Mechanicsville, 1600 ... *A-6
Meeks, 90 ... I-9
Meigs, 1035 ... N-5
Meldrim, 450 ... J-12
Melrose ... O-8
Mendes, 122 ... K-11
Menlo, 474 ... C-1
Meridian, 250 ... M-12
MERIWETHER CO., 21992 ... H-3
Merrillville, 120 ... N-6
Mershon, 200 ... M-10
Mesena, 250 ... F-9
Metasville, 80 ... E-9
Metcalf, 130 ... O-5
Metter, 4130 ... J-10
Midville, 269 ... H-10
Midway, 2121 ... L-12
Milan, 700 ... K-8
Milford, 60 ... M-4
Milledgeville, 17715 ... H-7
Millen, 3120 ... H-11
MILLER CO., 6125 .. M-3
Millwood, 180 ... M-9
Milner, 610 ... G-5
Milstead, 1500 ... F-5
Milton, 32661 ... D-5
Mineola, 150 ... N-7
Mineral Bluff, 150 ... B-5
Mitchell, 199 ... G-9
MITCHELL CO., 23498 ... M-5
Modoc, 40 ... I-10
Molena, 368 ... H-4
Moncrief ... O-5
Moniac ... P-10
Monroe, 13234 ... E-6
MONROE CO., 26424 ... H-5
Montezuma, 3460 ... J-5
MONTGOMERY CO., 9123 ... J-9
Monticello, 2657 ... G-6
Montrose, 215 ... I-7
Mora, 75 ... M-8
Moreland, 399 ... G-3
Morgan, 240 ... L-4
MORGAN CO., 17868 ... F-7
Morganton, 303 ... B-5
Morningside ... *D-4
Morris, 75 ... L-3
Morrow, 6445 ... F-4
Morven, 565 ... N-7
Moultrie, 14268 ... N-6
Mt. Airy, 1284 ... C-7
Mt. Bethel, 200 ... *A-3
Mt. Carmel, 30 ... B-2
Mt. Pleasant, 60 ... M-11
Mt. Vernon, 2451 ... J-9
Mt. Vernon, 400 ... B-3
Mt. Zion, 1696 ... F-2
Mountain City, 1088 ... B-7
Mountain View, 1100 ... *G-3
Mountville, 200 ... H-3
Mulberry Grv., 100 ... I-3
Munnerlyn, 50 ... H-11
Murphy, 100 ... N-6
MURRAY CO., 39628 ... B-3
Murrays Crossroads ... J-4
Murrayville, 800 ... C-6
MUSCOGEE CO., 189885 ... I-3
Musella, 40 ... H-5
Mystic, 300 ... L-7
Nahunta, 1053 ... M-11
Naomi, 60 ... B-2
Nashville, 4939 ... M-7
Naylor ... N-8
Needmore ... O-9
Nelson, 1314 ... C-4
Nevils, 185 ... J-11
New Branch, 60 ... K-10
New England, 175 ... B-1
New Georgia ... E-3
New Holland, 1200 ... D-6
New Hope, 150 ... E-3
New Hope ... E-9
New Town, 600 ... C-3
Newborn, 696 ... F-6
Newington, 274 ... I-12
Newnan, 33039 ... G-3
Newton, 654 ... M-4
NEWTON CO., 99958 ... F-6
Nicholls, 2798 ... L-9
Nicholson, 1696 ... D-7
Nicklesville ... I-8
Norcross, 9116 ... E-5
Norman Pk., 972 ... M-6
Normantown, 45 ... J-10
Norristown, 59 ... I-9
N. Atlanta, 40456 ... *C-4
N. Decatur, 16698 ... *D-5
N. Druid Hills, 18947 ... *D-5
N. Elberton, 150 ... D-8
N. High Shoals, 652 ... E-7
N. West Pt., 700 ... H-2
Norwood, 239 ... F-9
Nuberg, 130 ... D-8
Nunez, 147 ... I-10
Oak Grv., 2850 ... *D-5
Oak Pk., 484 ... J-10
Oakdale ... *C-1
Oakfield, 200 ... L-5
Oakhurst Siding ... *E-5
Oakland ... G-4
Oakland City ... *F-2
Oakland Hts. ... D-3
Oakman, 150 ... C-3
Oakwood, 3970 ... D-6
Ochlocknee, 676 ... N-5
Ocilla, 3414 ... L-7
Oconee, 252 ... H-8
OCONEE CO., 32808 ... E-7
Odum, 504 ... L-11
Offerman, 441 ... M-10
Oglethorpe, 1328 ... J-5
OGLETHORPE CO., 14899 ... E-7
Ohoopee, 70 ... J-10
Okefenokee ... N-10
Oliver, 239 ... I-12
Omaha, 115 ... J-2
Omega, 1221 ... M-6
Orchard Hill, 209 ... G-5
Ormewood ... *F-4
Osierfield, 100 ... L-8
Oxford, 2134 ... F-6
Pace ... F-5
Palmetto, 4488 ... F-3
Palmyra, 60 ... L-5
Pantertown, 150 ... B-4
Panthersville, 9749 ... F-5
Parkersburg, 1000 ... T-11
Parkerville ... M-5
Parrott, 158 ... K-4
Patterson, 730 ... M-10
PAULDING CO., 142324 ... E-3
Pavo, 627 ... N-6
Payne, 218 ... H-6
PEACH CO., 27695 ... I-6
Peachtree City, 34364 ... F-4
Pearson, 2117 ... M-8
Pelham, 3898 ... N-5
Pembroke, 2196 ... J-12
Pendergrass, 422 ... D-6
Penfield, 150 ... F-7
Pennville, 250 ... C-2
Perkins, 91 ... H-11
Perry, 13839 ... I-6
Petross ... J-9
Phillipsburg, 707 ... M-7
Philomath, 150 ... E-8
Phinizy, 50 ... F-10
PICKENS CO., 29431 ... C-4
PIERCE CO., 18758 ... M-10
PIKE CO., 17869 ... G-4
Pine Grv., 50 ... L-9
Pine Hbr., 125 ... L-12
Pine Log, 150 ... C-3
Pine Mtn., 1304 ... H-3
Pine Mtn. Valley, 950 ... H-3
Pine Pk., 200 ... O-5
Pinehurst, 455 ... J-6
Pineora, 300 ... J-12
Pineview, 523 ... K-7
Pitts, 320 ... K-6
Plainfield, 140 ... J-8
Plains, 776 ... K-4
Plainville, 313 ... C-3
Pleasant Hill, 50 ... H-4
Pocataligo, 100 ... D-7
Pt. Peter, 50 ... E-8
POLK CO., 41475 ... E-2
Pollards Cor. ... F-10
Pooler, 19140 ... K-13
Popes Ferry, 30 ... H-6
Port Wentworth, 5359 ... J-13
Portal, 638 ... I-11
Porterdale, 1429 ... F-6
Potterville, 170 ... I-5
Poulan, 851 ... L-6
Powder Sprs., 13940 ... E-3
Powelton, 40 ... F-8
Powersville, 110 ... I-6
Preston, 2799 ... K-4
Pretoria ... L-4
Pridgen, 50 ... L-8
Primrose, 100 ... G-3
Privette Hts., 420 ... *B-1
Prospect ... F-6
Pulaski, 266 ... J-11
PULASKI CO., 12010 ... J-7
PUTNAM CO., 21218 ... G-7
Putney, 2898 ... M-5
Queensland, 140 ... L-7
Quitman, 3850 ... O-6
QUITMAN CO., 2513 ... K-2
RABUN CO., 16276 .. B-7
Racepond, 130 ... N-10
Radium Sprs., 1400 ... L-5
Raleigh, 75 ... H-4
RANDOLPH CO., 7719 ... L-3
Ranger, 131 ... C-3
Raoul, 2558 ... C-6
Ray City, 1090 ... N-7
Raybon, 200 ... M-11
Rayle, 199 ... E-8
Raymond, 300 ... G-3
Rebecca, 187 ... L-7
Red Oak, 2800 ... *H-1
Red Rock, 85 ... L-5
Reed Creek, 2604 ... C-8
Register, 175 ... J-11
Rehoboth, 1300 ... *D-5
Reidsville, 4944 ... K-10
Remerton, 1123 ... O-7
Renfroe ... J-3
Reno, 100 ... O-4
Rentz, 295 ... J-8
Resaca, 544 ... C-3
Reynolds, 1086 ... I-5
Reynoldsville, 50 ... N-3
Rhine, 394 ... K-7
Riceboro, 809 ... L-12
Richland, 1473 ... K-3
RICHMOND CO., 200549 ... G-10
Richmond Hill, 9281 .. K-12
Riddleville, 96 ... H-9
Ridgeville, 300 ... M-12
Rincon, 8836 ... J-13
Ringgold, 3580 ... B-2
Rising Fawn, 110 ... B-1
Riverdale, 15134 ... F-4
Riverland Ter. ... S-2
Riverside, 35 ... N-6
Riverside ... *D-2
Roberta, 1007 ... I-5
Robertstown, 250 ... B-6
Rochelle, 1174 ... K-7
Rock Spr., 300 ... B-2
ROCKDALE CO., 85215 ... F-5
Rockingham, 248 ... L-9
Rockledge, 250 ... J-9
Rockmart, 4199 ... E-3
Rocky Face, 1000 ... B-3
Rocky Ford, 144 ... I-11
Rocky Mount, 55 ... G-3
Rome, 36303 ... D-2
Roopville, 218 ... F-2
Roscoe, 200 ... F-3
Rosier ... H-10
Rossville, 4105 ... A-2
Roswell, 88346 ... D-4
Round Oak, 200 ... G-6
Royston, 2582 ... D-8
Ruckersville, 75 ... D-8
Rupert, 100 ... J-4
Russell, 1203 ... E-6
Rutledge, 781 ... F-6
Rydal, 200 ... D-3
St. Clair, 150 ... G-10
St. George, 350 ... P-11
St. Marks, 45 ... G-3
St. Marys, 17121 ... O-12
St. Simons, 12743 ... N-12
Sale City, 380 ... M-5
Salem, 310 ... I-5
Sand Hill, 200 ... F-3
Sandersville, 5912 ... H-8
Sandfly, 1200 ... T-11
Sandy Cross, 260 ... D-7
Sandy Sprs., 93853 ... E-4
Santa Claus, 165 ... J-10
Sapelo Island, 150 ... M-13
Sardis, 999 ... H-11
Sargent, 900 ... F-3
Sasser, 279 ... L-4
Satolah, 30 ... B-7
Sautee Nacoochee, 363 ... B-6
Savannah, 136286 ... K-13
Scarboro, 40 ... I-11
Scarbrough Cross Roads ... *H-6
SCHLEY CO., 5010 ... J-4
Scotland, 366 ... K-8
Scott, 140 ... I-9
Scottdale, 10631 ... *D-5
Scottsboro, 100 ... H-7
Screven, 766 ... M-11
SCREVEN CO., 14593 ... H-11
Sea Island, 700 ... M-12
SEMINOLE CO., 8729 ... N-3
Senoia, 3307 ... G-4
Seville, 202 ... K-6
Shady Dale, 249 ... G-6
Shannon, 1862 ... C-2
Sharon, 140 ... F-8
Sharpsburg, 341 ... G-4
Shawnee, 70 ... I-12
Shell Bluff ... G-11
Shellman, 1083 ... L-4
Shellman Bluff, 450 ... L-12
Shiloh, 445 ... H-3
Shingler, 60 ... L-6
Sigsbee, 30 ... M-6
Siloam, 282 ... F-8
Silver Creek, 500 ... D-2
Silver Pines, 250 ... S-5
Skidaway Island, 8341 ... K-13
Sky Valley, 272 ... B-7
Smarr, 350 ... H-6
Smithville, 575 ... K-5
Smyrna, 51271 ... E-4
Snellville, 18242 ... E-5
Snipesville, 50 ... L-9
Social Circle, 4262 ... F-6
Sonoraville ... C-3
Soperton, 3115 ... J-9
S. Newport ... L-12
SPALDING CO., 64073 ... G-4
Sparks, 2052 ... N-7
Sparta, 1400 ... G-8
Spring Pl., 270 ... B-3
Springfield, 2852 ... J-12
Springvale, 60 ... K-3
Stapleton, 438 ... G-9
Stark, 100 ... G-5
Starrs Mill ... G-4
Starrsville ... F-6
Statenville, 1040 ... O-8
Statesboro, 28422 ... I-11
Statham, 2408 ... E-6
Stellaville, 50 ... G-10
Stephens, 110 ... E-7
STEPHENS CO., 26175 ... C-7
Sterling, 130 ... M-12
Stevens Pottery, 100 ... H-7
Stewart ... F-6
STEWART CO., 6058 ... J-3
Stilesboro, 150 ... D-3
Stillmore, 532 ... J-10
Stillwell, 30 ... J-13
Stilson, 150 ... J-12
Stockbridge, 25636 ... F-5
Stockton, 200 ... N-8
Stone Mtn., 5802 ... E-5
Stovall, 130 ... H-3
Subligna, 60 ... C-2
Suches, 160 ... B-5
Sugar Hill, 18522 ... D-5
Sugar Valley, 300 ... C-3
Summertown, 160 ... I-10
Summerville, 4534 ... C-2
Sumner, 427 ... L-6
Sumter, 35 ... K-5
SUMTER CO., 32819 ... K-5
Sunbury, 150 ... L-13
Sunny Side, 134 ... G-5
Sunnyside, 1303 ... M-10
Sunset Vil., 846 ... H-4
Surrency, 201 ... L-10
Suttons Cor. ... L-3
Suwanee, 15355 ... D-5
Swainsboro, 7277 ... I-10
Swords, 90 ... F-7
Sycamore, 711 ... L-6
Sylvan Hills ... *F-3
Sylvania, 2956 ... I-12
Sylvester, 6188 ... L-6
TALBOT CO., 6865 ... I-4
Talbotton, 970 ... I-4
TALIAFERRO CO., 1717 ... F-8
Talking Rock, 64 ... C-4
Tallapoosa, 3170 ... E-2
Tallulah Falls, 168 ... B-7
Talmo, 180 ... D-6
Talmo ... M-9
Tarboro, 150 ... N-11
Tarrytown, 87 ... J-9
Tate, 1000 ... C-4
TATTNALL CO., 25520 ... J-10
TAYLOR CO., 8906 ... I-5
Taylorsville, 210 ... D-3
Tazewell, 130 ... J-4
TELFAIR CO., 16500 ... K-8
Temple, 4228 ... E-3
Tennga, 400 ... A-3
Tennille, 1539 ... H-8
TERRELL CO., 9315 .. K-4
Texas ... G-2
Thalmann, 50 ... M-11
The Rock, 160 ... H-5
THOMAS CO., 44720 ... O-5
Thomaston, 9170 ... H-4
Thomasville, 18413 ... O-5
Thomasville ... *F-4
Thomson, 6778 ... F-9
Thunderbolt, 2668 ... S-11
Thyatira, 150 ... D-7
TIFT CO., 40118 ... M-6
Tifton, 16350 ... M-7
Tiger, 408 ... B-7
Tignall, 546 ... E-9
Tilton ... B-3
Toccoa, 8491 ... C-7
Toccoa Falls, 900 ... C-7
TOOMBS CO., 27223 ... K-10
Toomsboro, 472 ... H-8
Towns, 90 ... K-9
TOWNS CO., 10471 ... B-6
Townsend, 200 ... L-12
Traders Hill, 150 ... O-11
Trenton, 2301 ... B-1
TREUTLEN CO., 6885 ... J-9
Trimble, 60 ... G-3
Trion, 1827 ... C-2
TROUP CO., 67044 .. G-3
Troutman, 50 ... K-3
Tucker, 27581 ... E-5
Tunnel Hill, 856 ... B-3
Turin, 274 ... G-4
TURNER CO., 8930 ... L-6
Turnerville, 300 ... B-7
TWIGGS CO., 9023 .. H-7
Twin City, 1742 ... I-10
Twin Lakes, 950 ... O-7
Ty Ty, 725 ... M-6
Tybee Island, 2990 ... K-14
Tyrone, 6879 ... F-4
Tyus, 100 ... F-2
Unadilla, 3796 ... J-6
Union City, 19456 ... F-4
UNION CO., 21356 .. B-5
Union Pt., 1617 ... F-8
Unionville, 1845 ... M-7
UPSON CO., 27153 .. H-5
Upton ... L-8
Uvalda, 598 ... K-9
Vada, 80 ... N-4
Valdosta, 54518 ... O-7
Valona, 75 ... M-12
Van Wert, 275 ... E-3
Vanna, 150 ... D-8
Varnell, 1744 ... B-3
Veal, 90 ... F-2
Veazey, 50 ... F-8
Vernonburg, 122 ... T-10
Vesta, 60 ... E-8
Victory, 40 ... F-2
Vidalia, 10473 ... J-9
Vidette, 112 ... H-10
Vienna, 4011 ... K-6
Villa Rica, 13956 ... E-3
Villanow ... B-2
Vinings, 9734 ... *C-2
Vista Grv., 3000 ... *D-5
Waco, 516 ... E-2
Wadley, 2061 ... H-9
Walden ... I-6
Waleska, 644 ... D-4
WALKER CO., 68756 ... C-2
Walnut Grv., 1330 ... E-6
Walthourville, 4111 ... L-12
WALTON CO., 83768 ... E-6
WARE CO., 36312 ... N-9
Wares Crossroads, 50 ... G-2
Waresboro, 400 ... M-9
Waresville ... G-2
Warm Sprs., 425 ... H-3
Warner Robins, 66588 .. I-6
WARREN CO., 5834 ... G-9
Warrenton, 1937 ... F-9
Warthen, 250 ... G-8
Warwick, 423 ... K-5
Washington, 4134 ... E-9
WASHINGTON CO., 21187 ... H-8
Watkinsville, 2832 ... E-7
Waverly, 400 ... N-11
Waverly Hall, 735 ... I-3
Wax, 100 ... D-2
Waycross, 14649 ... M-10
WAYNE CO., 30099 ... L-10
Waynesboro, 5766 ... G-11
Waynesville, 450 ... M-11
Wayside, 130 ... H-6
WEBSTER CO., 2799 ... K-4
Welcome, 200 ... F-3
Wenona, 200 ... K-6
Wesley, 50 ... I-10
Wesleyan Estates, 290 ... Q-5
W. End ... *E-3
W. Green, 300 ... L-9
West Pt., 3474 ... H-2
Weston, 75 ... K-4
WHEELER CO., 7421 ... K-8
Wheeler Hts., 275 ... S-7
Whigham, 471 ... N-4
White, 670 ... D-3
WHITE CO., 27144 ... C-6
White Oak, 250 ... N-11
White Plains, 284 ... F-8
Whitesburg, 588 ... F
Whitestone, 150 ... C
Whitesville, 100 ... H
WHITFIELD CO., 102599 ... B
WILCOX CO., 9255 .. K
Wiley, 200 ... E
WILKES CO., 10593 .. E
WILKINSON CO., 9563 ...
Willacoochee, 1391 ... M
Willard ... G
Williamson, 352 ... G
Wilmington Island, 15138 ... K-
Winder, 14099 ... E
Winokur, 100 ... N-
Winston, 350 ... E
Winterville, 1122 ... E
Woodbine, 1412 ... N-
Woodbury, 961 ... H
Woodcliff, 100 ... I-
Woodland, 408 ... H
Woodlawn Estates ... R
Woodstock, 23896 ... D
Woodville, 321 ... F
Woolsey, 158 ... G
WORTH CO., 21679 ... M
Worthville, 100 ... G
Wray, 100 ... L
Wrens, 2187 ... G-
Wrightsville, 2195 ...
Yates, 30 ... F
Yatesville, 357 ... H
Yorkville, 200 ... E
Young Harris, 899 ... B
Youth, 75 ... E
Zebulon, 1174 ... G
Zenith, 50 ...

Hawaii

Page locator

Map keys	Atlas pages
F–N	62–63

'Aiea, 9019 ... M
Anahola, 2223 ... H
Captain Cook, 3429 ... M
'Ewa Bch., 14955 ... N
'Ewa Villages, 6108 ... M
Haiku, 1150 ...
Hakalau, 100 ... L
Hala'ula, 469 ... L
Hālawa Hts., 4000 ... M
Hale'iwa, 3970 ...
Hāli'imaile, 964 ...
Hāna, 1235 ... K
Hanalei, 450 ... H
Hanamā'ulu, 3835 ...
Hanapepe, 2638 ...
Hau'ula, 4148 ... K
HAWAII CO., 185079 ... L-
Hawai'i Kai, 1150 ... N
Hāwī, 1081 ... L
Hilo, 43263 ... M-
Hōlualoa, 8538 ... M
Hōnaunau ... M
Honoka'a, 2258 ... L
Honokahua, 400 ...
Honokowai, 2200 ... K
Honolulu, 337256 ... J
HONOLULU CO., 953207 ...
Honomu, 509 ... L
Honouliuli, 520 ... M
Ho'olehua, 270 ... J
Ka'a'awa, 1379 ... K
Ka'alaea ... L
Kahala, 800 ... H-
Kahalu'u, 4738 ... L
Kahana, 50 ... J
Kahuku, 2614 ...
Kahului, 26337 ... K
Kailua, 38635 ... J
Kailua, 11975 ... M
Kaimuki, 6800 ... G-
Kainaliu, 290 ... M
Kalāheo, 4595 ...
Kalapana ... M-
Kalaupapa, 120 ... J
Kalihi, 1900 ... G
Kamehameha Hts., 1100 ... G
Kāne'ohe, 34597 ... J
Kapa'a, 10699 ...
Kapolei, 15186 ... M
KAUAI CO., 67091 ...
Kaunakakai, 3425 ... J
Kaupakulua, 350 ...
Kaupō ... J-
Kawailoa ... K
Kawailoa Bch., 300 ... K
Kawela, 100 ... J
Kea'au, 2253 ... M-
Kealakekua, 2019 ... M
Ke'anae, 50 ... K
Kekaha, 3537 ...
Keokea, 1612 ... K
Kīhei, 20881 ... K
Kīlauea, 2803 ... H
Kīpahulu ... J-
Koali ... J-
Kokomo, 320 ...
Koloa, 2144 ...
Kualapu'u, 2027 ... J
Kukuihaele, 336 ... L
Kuli'ou'ou, 370 ... N
Kunia Camp, 580 ... L
Kurtistown, 1298 ... M-
Lahaina, 11704 ... K
Lā'ie, 6138 ... J
Lānai City, 3102 ... K
Laupāhoehoe, 581 ... L
Līhu'e, 6455 ...
Lower Paia, 220 ...
Mā'alaea, 352 ...
Mā'ili, 9488 ... M
Mākaha, 8278 ... L
Makakilo City, 18248 ... M
Makawao, 7184 ...
Mākena, 99 ... J
Mānā ...
MAUI CO., 154834 ... J
Maunalani Hts., 700 ... G-
Maunaloa, 376 ... J
Maunawili, 2040 ... M
Mililani Town, 27629 ... L
Miloli'i ... N
Mountain View, 3924 ... M
Nā'ālehu, 866 ... N
Nānākuli, 12666 ... J
Niu, 570 ... N
Olowalu, 80 ...
Ō'ōkala, 150 ... L
Pā'auhau, 270 ... L
Pa'auilo, 595 ... L

*, †, ‡, §, ◊ See explanation under state title in this index.
County and parish names are listed in capital letters & boldface type.
Independent cities (not included in a county) are listed in italics.

cific Hts., 650....F-8
cific Palisades,
5600....M-3
hala, 1356....N-9
hoa, 945....M-10
ia, 2668....I-9
pā....N-8
pa'aloa, 320....L-9
pa'ikou, 1314....M-10
'uwela, 500....K-7
arl City, 47698....J-5
pe'ekeo, 1789....M-10
amoho....L-3
kalani, 7574....K-7
nalu'u....K-4
'uanahulu....M-8
'uiki....J-10
'ukoli'i, 200....I-8
'unēnē....I-8
'uwai....I-1
Louis Hts., 1000....G-10
reckelsville....I-9
nset Bch., 660....J-3
lupalakua, 75....K-7
lcano, 2575....M-9
hiawā, 17821....J-5
aiakoa, 900....J-9
aialua, 3860....J-7
ai'anae, 13177....J-4
aiehu, 600....I-8
aikapu, 2965....K-7
aikīkī, 3000....H-9
ailua, 2254....I-2
ailua, 120....I-10
ailuku, 15313....K-7
aimānalo, 5451....J-5
aimānalo Bch.,
481....M-6
aimea, 9212....L-9
aimea, 1855....I-2
aimea, 650....J-2
aipahu, 38216....M-3
aipi'o Acres....L-3
hitmore Vil., 4499....L-3
odlawn, 1200....F-9

Idaho

Page locator
Map keys Atlas pages
A–N 64–65

erdeen, 1994....L-6
equia, 124....M-5
DA CO., 392365....K-2
DAMS CO., 3976....H-1
sahka, 150....F-2
bion, 267....M-5
mo....N-5
nerican Falls, 4457....L-6
nmon, 13816....K-7
bon, 35....M-7
co, 995....K-6
imo, 355....M-7
hton, 1127....J-8
hol, 692....C-1
lanta....K-3
omic City, 29....K-6
ncroft, 377....M-8
nida, 125....M-8
nks, 17....J-2
ANNOCK CO.,
82839....M-7
salt, 394....K-7
yview, 350....C-2
EAR LAKE CO.,
5986....N-9
llevue, 2287....K-4
ENEWAH CO.,
9285....E-1
nnington, 190....M-8
rn, 60....M-8
g Creek....H-3
NGHAM CO.,
45607....L-6
ackfoot, 11899....L-7
LAINE CO.,
21376....K-5
anchard, 261....C-1
ss, 318....L-4
oomington, 206....M-8
ise, 205671....K-2
OISE CO., 7028....J-2
ne....K-8
ONNER CO.,
40877....C-2
nners Ferry, 2543....B-2
ONNEVILLE CO.,
104234....K-8
OUNDARY CO.,
10972....B-2
vill, 260....E-2
wmont, 150....K-1
uneau, 100....L-2
hl, 4122....M-4
rgdorf....H-2
rley, 10345....M-5
tte City, 74....K-6
TTE CO., 2891....K-6
binet....C-2
lder....D-2
ldwell, 46237....K-1
MAS CO., 1117....K-4
mbridge, 328....I-1
NYON CO.,
188923....K-1
rey, 604....K-5
reywood....C-2
ARIBOU CO.,
6963....L-7
rmen, 25....H-5
scade, 939....I-2
ASSIA CO.,
22952....M-5
stleford, 226....M-4
taldo, 260....D-2
vendish, 30....F-2
allis, 1081....I-4
atcolet....D-1
ester, 350....J-8
ilco....C-1
ubbuck, 13922....L-7
LARK CO., 982....J-7
ark Fork, 536....C-2
arkia, 80....E-2
ayton, 7....J-4
earwater, 50....G-2
LEARWATER CO.,
8761....E-3
ifton, 259....M-7
balt....H-4
colalla, 140....C-2
eur d'Alene,
44137....D-1
lburn, 100....B-2
nda....L-8
olin, 200....B-1
rral....K-4
ttonwood, 900....G-2
uncil, 839....I-2
aigmont, 501....F-2
ouch, 162....J-2
Culdesac, 380....F-1
CUSTER CO., 4368....J-4
Dalton Gdns., 2335....C-1
Darlington, 50....K-6
Dayton, 463....N-7
Deary, 506....E-2
Declo, 343....M-5
Dietrich, 332....L-4
Dingle, 200....M-8
Dixie, 25....G-3
Donnelly, 152....I-2
Dover, 556....C-2
Downey, 625....M-7
Driggs, 1660....K-9
Drummond, 16....J-8
Dubois, 677....J-7
Eagle, 19908....K-2
E. Hope, 210....C-2
Eastport....A-2
Eden, 405....M-4
Elba....M-5
Elk City, 200....G-3
Elk River, 125....E-2
Ellis, 40....I-5
Elmira....B-2
ELMORE CO.,
27038....L-3
Emida, 100....E-2
Emmett, 6557....J-2
Fairfield, 416....K-4
Featherville....K-3
Felt....J-8
Fenn, 30....G-2
Ferdinand, 159....F-2
Fernan Lake Vil., 169....D-1
Fernwood, 425....E-2
Filer, 2508....M-4
Firth, 477....L-7
Fish Haven, 50....N-8
Franklin, 641....N-8
FRANKLIN CO.,
12786....M-8
FREMONT CO.,
13242....J-8
Fruitland, 4684....J-1
Fruitvale, 100....I-2
Gannett....K-5
Garden City, 10972....B-6
Garden Valley, 394....J-2
GEM CO., 16719....J-2
Genesee, 955....F-1
Georgetown, 476....M-8
Gibbonsville....G-5
Gifford....F-2
Givens Hot Sprs., 120....K-1
Glenns Ferry, 1319....L-3
Golden....G-3
Gooding, 3567....L-4
GOODING CO.,
15464....L-4
Grace, 915....M-8
Grand View, 452....L-2
Grangeville, 3141....G-2
Grasmere....M-2
Greencreek, 30....F-2
Greenleaf, 846....K-1
Greer....F-2
Hagerman, 872....L-4
Hailey, 7960....K-4
Hamer, 48....J-7
Hammett, 300....L-3
Hansen, 1144....M-4
Harpster, 50....G-2
Harrison, 203....D-1
Harvard, 55....E-1
Hayden, 13294....C-1
Hayden Lake, 574....C-1
Hazelton, 753....M-5
Headquarters, 35....F-3
Heise....K-8
Helmer....E-2
Henry....L-8
Heyburn, 3089....M-5
Hill City....L-3
Holbrook....N-7
Hollister, 272....M-4
Homedale, 2633....K-1
Hope, 86....C-2
Horseshoe Bend, 707....J-2
Howe, 80....K-6
Hoyt, 40....D-2
Idaho City, 485....K-2
IDAHO CO., 16267....G-2
Idaho Falls, 56813....K-7
Indian Valley, 75....I-2
Inkom, 854....L-7
Iona, 1803....K-7
Irwin, 219....K-8
Island Pk., 286....I-8
JEFFERSON CO.,
26140....K-7
Jerome, 10890....M-4
JEROME CO.,
22374....L-4
Joel, 100....E-1
Juliaetta, 579....F-1
Kamiah, 1295....F-2
Kellogg, 2120....D-2
Kendrick, 303....F-1
Ketchum, 2689....K-4
Kilgore....I-7
Kimberly, 3264....M-4
King Hill, 100....L-3
Kingston, 800....D-2
Kooskia, 607....F-2
Kootenai, 678....B-2
KOOTENAI CO.,
138494....C-1
Kuna, 15210....K-2
Laclede, 400....C-1
L. Fork, 120....I-2
Lakeview, 40....C-2
Lapwai, 1137....F-1
LATAH CO., 37244....E-2
Lava Hot Sprs., 407....M-7
Leadore, 105....I-6
Lemhi, 30....I-5
LEMHI CO., 7936....H-4
Lenore....F-2
Leslie....J-5
Letha, 240....J-1
LEWIS CO., 3821....F-2
Lewiston, 31894....F-1
Lewisville, 458....K-7
Liberty....M-8
Lincoln, 3647....K-7
LINCOLN CO., 5208....L-5
Lorenzo, 100....K-8
Lost River, 68....K-5
Lowell, 25....F-3
Lowman, 42....J-3
Lucile, 100....G-2
Mackay, 517....J-5
MADISON CO.,
37536....K-8
Magic City....L-4
Malad City, 2095....M-7
Malta, 193....M-6
Marley, 100....L-4
Marsing, 1031....K-1
Marysville, 180....J-8
May, 50....I-5
McCall, 2991....I-2
McCammon, 809....M-7
Meadows, 190....I-2
Medimont....D-2
Melba, 513....K-1
Menan, 741....K-7
Meridian, 75092....K-2
Mesa, 65....I-2
Middleton, 5524....K-1
Midvale, 171....I-1
Minidoka, 112....L-5
MINIDOKA CO.,
20069....L-5
Mink Creek....M-8
Monteview....J-7
Montpelier, 2597....M-8
Moore, 189....K-6
Moreland, 1278....L-7
Moscow, 23800....E-1
Mt. Idaho....G-2
Mountain Home,
14206....L-3
Moyie Sprs., 718....B-2
Mud Lake, 358....K-7
Mullan, 692....D-3
Murphy, 97....L-1
Murray, 75....D-2
Murtaugh, 115....M-5
Nampa, 81557....K-1
Naples, 450....B-2
New Ctr.ville....J-2
New Meadows, 496....H-2
New Plymouth, 1538....J-1
Newdale, 323....J-8
NEZ PERCE CO.,
39265....F-1
Nezperce, 466....F-2
Nordman....B-1
N. Fork....H-5
Oakley, 763....M-5
Ola....J-2
Onaway, 187....E-1
ONEIDA CO., 4286....N-6
Oreana....L-2
Orofino, 3142....F-2
Orogrande....G-3
Osburn, 1555....D-2
Ovid....M-8
OWYHEE CO.,
11526....M-2
Oxford, 48....M-7
Palisades, 100....K-8
Paris, 513....M-8
Parker, 305....J-8
Parma, 1983....K-1
Patterson, 5....I-5
Paul, 1169....M-5
Payette, 7433....J-1
PAYETTE CO.,
22623....J-1
Peck, 197....F-2
Picabo, 100....K-5
Pierce, 508....F-3
Pine....K-3
Pinehurst, 1619....D-2
Pingree, 150....L-7
Pioneerville....J-2
Placerville, 53....J-2
Pleasantview, 220....N-7
Plummer, 1044....D-1
Pocatello, 54255....L-7
Pollock, 140....H-2
Ponderay, 1137....B-2
Porthill....A-2
Post Falls, 27574....C-1
Potlatch, 804....E-1
POWER CO., 7817....M-6
Preston, 5204....N-8
Prichard....D-2
Priest River, 1751....C-1
Princeton, 148....E-1
Rathdrum, 6826....C-1
Red River Hot Sprs.....G-3
Reubens, 71....F-2
Rexburg, 25484....K-8
Reynolds....L-1
Richfield, 482....L-5
Rigby, 3945....K-7
Riggins, 419....H-2
Ririe, 656....K-8
Riverside, 838....L-7
Roberts, 580....K-7
Rockland, 295....M-6
Rocky Bar....K-3
Rogerson, 100....M-4
Rose Lake....D-2
Rupert, 5554....M-5
St. Anthony, 3542....J-8
St. Charles, 131....N-8
St. Joe....D-2
St. Maries, 2402....D-2
Salmon, 3112....H-5
Samaria, 100....N-7
Samuels, 150....B-2
Sanders....E-1
Sandpoint, 7365....C-2
Santa, 100....E-2
Shelley, 4409....K-7
Shoshone, 1461....L-4
SHOSHONE CO.,
12765....D-2
Shoup, 60....H-4
Silver City....L-1
Silverton, 300....D-2
Smelterville, 627....D-2
Smiths Ferry, 75....J-2
Soda Sprs., 3058....M-8
Southwick, 40....F-2
Spalding....F-1
Spencer, 37....J-7
Spirit Lake, 1945....C-1
Springfield, 100....L-7
Stanley, 63....J-4
Star, 5793....K-2
Sterling....L-6
Stites, 221....G-2
Stone....N-6
Sugar City, 1514....J-8
Sun Valley, 1406....K-4
Sunbeam, 40....J-4
Swan Valley, 204....K-8
Swanlake....M-7
Sweet, 200....J-2
Syringa, 30....F-3
Tendoy....I-5
Tensed, 123....E-1
Terreton....K-7
Teton, 735....J-8
TETON CO., 10170....K-8
Tetonia, 269....K-8
Thatcher....M-8
The String, 100....K-9
Thornton, 100....K-8
Triumph....K-4
Troy, 862....E-1
Twin Falls, 44125....M-4
TWIN FALLS CO.,
77230....M-4
Tyhee, 1123....L-7
Ucon, 1108....K-7
Ustick....B-5
VALLEY CO., 9862....I-3
Victor, 1928....K-9
Viola, 150....E-1
Virginia....M-7
Waha....F-1
Wallace, 784....D-2
Warm Lake....I-3
Warm River, 3....J-8
Warren, 45....H-3
WASHINGTON CO.,
10198....I-1
Wayan, 35....L-8
Weippe, 441....F-2
Weiser, 5507....J-1
Wendell, 2782....L-4
Weston, 437....N-7
White Bird, 91....G-2
Whitney, 200....N-8
Wilder, 1533....K-1
Winchester, 340....F-1
Worley, 257....D-1
Yellow Pine, 32....I-3

Illinois

Page locator
Map keys Atlas pages
A–J 66–67
K–T 68–69
* City keyed to pp. 70–71
† City keyed to pp. 72–73
‡ City keyed to pp. 120–121
§ City keyed to p. 233

Abingdon, 3319....G-6
Adair, 210....H-5
Adams, 50....J-3
ADAMS CO., 67103....J-3
Addieville, 252....O-8
Addison, 36942....*H-5
Adeline, 85....B-8
Aden....P-11
Adrian, 60....H-4
Akin, 110....Q-10
Albany, 891....C-6
Albers, 1190....O-8
Albion, 1988....P-12
Alden, 250....A-11
Aledo, 3640....E-5
Alexander, 300....K-7
ALEXANDER CO.,
8238....T-8
Alexis, 831....F-5
Algonquin, 30046....B-11
Alhambra, 681....N-7
Allendale, 475....O-13
Allenville, 148....K-11
Allerton, 291....J-12
Alma, 320....N-10
Alorton, 2002....‡I-8
Alpha, 671....E-6
Alsey, 227....K-5
Alsip, 19277....*K-8
Alta, 400....G-8
Altamont, 2319....M-10
Alto Pass, 391....R-9
Alton, 27865....N-6
Altona, 531....F-6
Alvin, 279....I-13
Amboy, 2500....D-9
Anchor, 146....H-11
Ancona, 80....F-10
Andalusia, 1178....E-5
Andover, 578....E-6
Anna, 4442....S-9
Annapolis, 55....M-13
Annawan, 878....E-7
Antioch, 14430....A-12
Apple Canyon Lake,
558....A-6
Apple River, 366....A-7
Aptakisic....*D-6
Arbury Hills, 1770....*M-7
Archer....†M-15
Arcola, 2916....K-11
Arenzville, 409....J-6
Argenta, 947....J-10
Argo Fay, 100....C-7
Argyle, 100....A-10
Arlington, 193....D-9
Arlington Hts.,
75101....B-12
Armington, 343....I-9
Armstrong, 200....I-12
Aroma Pk., 743....F-13
Arrowsmith, 294....H-10
Arthur, 2288....K-11
Ashburn....*J-8
Ashkum, 761....G-12
Ashland, 1333....J-7
Ashley, 536....P-9
Ashmore, 785....K-12
Ashton, 972....C-9
Assumption, 1168....K-9
Astoria, 1141....I-6
Athens, 1988....J-7
Athensville, 50....L-6
Atkinson, 972....E-7
Atlanta, 1692....I-9
Atlas, 50....K-4
Atterberry, 120....J-7
Atwater, 100....L-7
Atwood, 1224....J-11
Auburn, 4771....K-7
Augusta, 587....I-4
Aurora, 197899....C-11
Austin....*H-8
Ava, 654....Q-8
Aviston, 1945....O-8
Avon, 799....G-6
Avondale....*G-9
Balcom, 70....S-9
Baldwin, 373....P-7
Banner, 189....H-7
Bannockburn, 1583....*D-7
Bardolph, 251....H-5
Barnhill, 80....P-11
Barrington, 10327....B-12
Barrington Hills,
4209....*E-3
Barry, 1318....K-4
Barstow, 140....S-6
Bartelso, 595....O-8
Bartlett, 41208....*G-3
Bartonville, 6471....H-8
Basco, 98....H-3
Batavia, 26045....C-11
Batchtown, 214....M-5
Bath, 333....I-6
Bay City....T-11
Baylis, 205....K-4
Beach Pk., 13638....A-12
Beardstown, 6123....J-6
Beason, 189....I-9
Beaucoup, 80....P-9
Beaverville, 362....F-13
Bedford Pk., 580....*J-7
Beecher, 4359....E-13
Beecher City, 463....M-10
Beecreek....L-5
Belgium, 404....I-13
Belknap, 104....S-10
Bellair, 25....M-12
Belle Prairie City, 54....P-11
Belle Rive, 361....P-10
Belleview, 25....L-4
Belleville, 44478....O-7
Bellevue, 1978....G-8
Bellflower, 357....I-11
Bellmont, 276....O-12
Belltown, 40....L-6
Bellwood, 19071....*H-7
Belvidere, 25585....B-10
Bement, 1730....J-11
Benld, 1556....M-7
Bensenville, 18352....*G-6
Benson, 423....G-9
Bentley, 35....H-4
Benton, 7087....Q-10
Berdan, 50....L-6
Berkeley, 5209....*H-6
Berlin, 180....K-7
Bernadotte, 100....H-6
Berry, 70....K-8
Berryville, 30....O-12
Berwick, 160....G-5
Berwyn, 56657....*I-8
Bethalto, 9521....N-7
Bethany, 1352....K-10
Beverly, 30....J-4
Beverly....*K-9
Bible Grv., 100....N-11
Big Foot Prairie, 75....A-10
Big Rock, 1126....C-11
Biggsville, 304....G-4
Bingham, 83....M-9
Birds, 50....N-13
Bishop Hill, 128....E-6
Bismarck, 579....I-13
Bissell....†L-17
Blackstone, 100....F-10
Blandinsville, 651....H-4
Bloomfield....S-10
Bloomingdale,
22018....C-12
Bloomington, 76610....H-9
Blue Island, 23706....*K-9
Blue Mound, 1158....K-9
Blue Ridge....I-11
Bluff City, 300....M-9
Bluff Sprs., 120....J-6
Bluffs, 715....K-5
Bluford, 688....P-10
Blyton, 25....H-6
Boaz....S-10
Boden, 100....E-5
Bogota, 60....N-12
Bolingbrook,
73366....D-12
BOND CO., 17768....N-8
Bondville, 443....I-11
Bone Gap, 246....O-12
Bonfield, 382....F-12
Bonnie, 397....P-10
Boody, 276....K-9
BOONE CO.,
54165....B-10
Boos....N-12
Borton, 60....K-12
Boskydell, 30....R-9
Boulder, 100....N-9
Bourbon, 140....K-11
Bourbonnais, 18631....F-12
Bowen, 494....I-4
Braceville, 793....E-11
Bradford, 768....F-8
Bradley, 15895....F-13
Braidwood, 6191....E-12
Breese, 4442....O-8
Bremen, 50....Q-7
Bridgeport, 1886....N-13
Bridgeport....*I-9
Bridgeview, 16446....*J-7
Brighton, 2254....M-6
Brighton Pk.....*I-9
Brimfield, 868....G-7
Bristol, 500....D-11
Broadlands, 349....J-12
Broadview, 7932....*I-7
Broadwell, 145....I-8
Brocton, 322....K-12
Brookfield, 18978....*I-7
Brooklyn, 749....‡H-7
Brooklyn, 100....I-5
Brookport, 984....T-10
Brookville, 80....B-8
Broughton, 194....Q-11
BROWN CO., 6937....J-5
Brownfield, 75....S-11
Browning, 137....I-6
Browns, 134....O-12
Brownstown, 759....M-10
Brownsville, 50....Q-12
Bruce, 50....K-11
Brussels, 141....M-5
Bryant, 220....H-6
Buckingham, 300....F-12
Buckley, 600....H-12
Buckner, 462....Q-9
Buda, 538....E-8
Buffalo, 503....J-8
Buffalo Grv., 41496....B-12
Buffalo Hart, 25....J-8
Bull Valley, 1077....*B-2
Buncombe, 203....S-9
Bungay, 45....P-11
Bunker Hill, 1774....M-7
Burbank, 28925....*J-8
BUREAU CO.,
34978....E-8
Burgess, 50....F-5
Burksville, 80....P-6
Burlington, 618....B-11
Burnham, 4206....*L-10
Burnt Prairie, 52....P-11
Burr Ridge, 10559....*J-6
Burtons Br., 700....*B-3
Bushnell, 3117....H-5
Bushton, 100....K-12
Butler, 180....M-8
Butterfield, 3750....*I-5
Byron, 3753....B-9
Cabery, 266....F-12
Cable, 120....E-5
Cache, 50....T-9
Cahokia, 15241....O-6
Cairo, 2831....T-9
Caledonia, 197....A-10
Calhoun, 172....O-12
CALHOUN CO.,
5089....L-5
Calumet City,
37042....*L-10
Calumet Pk., 7835....*L-9
Calvin, 30....P-12
Camargo, 445....J-12
Cambria, 1228....R-9
Cambridge, 2160....E-6
Camden, 86....I-5
Cameron, 200....G-5
Camp Grv., 120....F-8
Camp Pt., 1132....J-4
Campbell Hill, 336....Q-8
Campton Hills,
11131....*H-1
Campus, 166....F-11
Canton, 14704....H-7
Cantrall, 139....J-8
Capron, 1376....A-10
Carbon Cliff, 2134....S-5
Carbondale, 25902....R-9
Carlinville, 5917....L-7
Carlock, 552....H-9
Carlyle, 3281....O-8
Carman, 100....G-4
Carmi, 5240....Q-12
Carol Stream,
39711....*H-4
Carpenter, 100....‡D-10
Carpentersville,
37691....B-11
Carrier Mills, 1653....R-10
CARROLL CO.,
15387....C-7
Carrollton, 2484....L-6
Carterville, 5496....R-9
Carthage, 2605....H-4
Cary, 18271....B-11
Casey, 2769....L-12
Caseyville, 4245....‡H-9
Casner, 50....J-10
CASS CO., 13642....J-6
Castleton, 130....F-7
Catlin, 2040....I-13
Cave-In-Rock, 318....S-12
Cazenovia, 100....G-9
Cedar Pt., 277....E-9
Cedarville, 741....A-8
Centerville, 50....P-12
Central City, 1172....O-9
Centralia, 13032....O-9
Centreville, 5309....‡I-8
Cerro Gordo, 1403....J-10
Chadwick, 551....C-7
Chambersburg, 100....J-5
Champaign, 81055....I-11
CHAMPAIGN CO.,
201081....J-12
Chana, 200....C-9
Chandlerville, 553....J-6
Channahon, 12560....E-11
Chapin, 512....K-6
Charleston, 21838....L-12
Charlotte, 25....G-11
Chatham, 11500....K-7
Chatham....*J-10
Chatsworth, 1205....G-11
Chauncey, 80....N-13
Chebanse, 1062....F-12
Chemung, 308....A-10
Cheneyville, 80....H-13
Chenoa, 1785....G-10
Cherry, 482....E-9
Cherry Valley, 3162....B-10
Chester, 8586....Q-7
Chesterfield, 188....L-6
Chesterville, 110....K-11
Chestnut, 246....J-9
Chicago, 2695598....C-13
Chicago Hts.,
30276....D-13
Chicago Lawn....*J-9
Chicago Ridge,
14305....*K-8
Chillicothe, 6097....F-8
Chrisman, 1343....J-13
CHRISTIAN CO.,
34800....K-8
Christopher, 2382....Q-9
Cicero, 83891....C-13
Cisco, 261....J-10
Cisne, 672....O-11
Cissna Pk., 846....H-12
Clare, 75....C-10
Claremont, 176....N-12
Clarence, 80....H-12
Clarendon Hills,
8427....*I-6
CLARK CO., 16335....L-13
Clarksburg, 50....L-10
Clarksville, 100....L-13
Clay City, 959....N-11
CLAY CO., 13815....N-11
Clayton, 709....J-4
Claytonville, 130....H-13
Clear Lake, 229....†L-17
Clearing....*J-8
Cleveland, 188....D-6
Clifton, 1468....F-12
Clinton, 7225....I-10
CLINTON CO.,
37762....N-8
Coal City, 5587....E-11
Coal Valley, 3743....E-6
Coalton, 304....L-9
Coatsburg, 147....J-4
Cobden, 1157....S-9
Coello, 608....Q-9
Coffeen, 685....M-8
Colchester, 1401....H-5
COLES CO.,
53873....K-11
Coleta, 164....C-7
Colfax, 1061....H-10
Collinsville, 25579....N-7
Collison, 100....I-13
Colmar, 70....H-4
Colona, 5099....T-6
Columbia, 9707....O-6
Columbus, 99....J-4
Compton, 303....D-9
Concord, 167....J-6
Congerville, 474....H-9
COOK CO.,
5194675....C-13
Cooks Mills, 200....K-11
Cooksville, 182....H-10
Cora, 25....Q-8
Cordova, 672....D-6
Corinth, 30....R-10
Cornell, 467....F-10
Cornland, 93....J-8
Cortland, 4270....C-10
Cottage Hills, 980....‡D-8
Coulterville, 945....P-8
Country Club Hills,
16541....*M-8
Countryside, 5895....*J-7
Cowden, 629....L-10
Cowling, 120....P-12
Crab Orchard, 333....R-10
Cragin....*H-8
CRAWFORD CO.,
19817....M-13
Creal Sprs., 543....R-10
Crescent City, 615....G-13
Crest Hill, 20837....*M-4
Creston, 662....C-10
Crestwood, 10950....*L-8
Crete, 8259....E-13
Creve Coeur, 5451....G-8
Cropsey, 120....H-11
Crossville, 745....P-12
Crystal Lake, 40743....B-11
Cuba, 1294....H-6
Cullom, 555....G-11
CUMBERLAND CO.,
11048....L-11
Curran, 212....K-7
Custer Pk., 300....E-12
Cutler, 441....Q-8
Cypress, 234....S-9
Dahinda, 150....F-6
Dahlgren, 525....P-10
Dakota, 506....A-8
Dale, 150....Q-11
Dallas City, 945....G-4
Dalton City, 544....K-10
Dalzell, 717....E-9
Dana, 159....F-10
Danforth, 604....G-12
Danvers, 1154....H-9
Danville, 33027....I-13
Darien, 22086....*J-5
Darmstadt, 68....P-7
Darwin, 60....L-13
Davis, 677....A-8
Davis Jct., 2373....B-9
Dawson Pk.....G-13
Daysville, 150....C-9
Dayton, 537....E-10
De Land, 446....I-10
De Soto, 1590....R-9
De Witt, 184....I-10
DE WITT CO., 16561....I-9
Decatur, 76122....J-10
Deer Creek, 704....G-9
Deer Grv., 48....D-8
Deer Pk., 3200....*D-4
Deer Plain, 80....N-5
Deerfield, 18225....*D-7
DeKalb, 43862....C-10
DEKALB CO.,
105160....B-10
Del Mar Woods,
120....*D-7
Delafield, 40....P-11
Delavan, 1689....H-8
Delwood....R-11
Dennison, 100....L-13
Denver, 120....I-4
Depue, 1838....E-9
Des Plaines, 58364....B-12
Deselm....E-12
Detroit, 83....K-5
Devereux Hts.....†K-17
Dewey, 150....I-11
Diamond, 2527....E-11
Diamond Lake,
1500....*C-5
Dieterich, 617....M-11
Dillon, 60....H-8
Divernon, 1172....K-8
Dix, 461....O-10
Dixmoor, 3644....*L-9
Dixon, 15733....C-8
Dixon Sprs., 50....S-10
Dolton, 23153....*L-10
Dongola, 726....S-9
Donnellson, 210....M-8
Donovan, 304....G-13
Dorsey, 200....M-7
DOUGLAS CO.,
19980....K-12
Dover, 168....E-8
Dowell, 408....Q-9
Downers Grv.,
47833....C-12
Downs, 1005....H-10
Druce Lake, 200....*A-5
Du Bois, 205....P-9
Du Quoin, 6109....Q-9
Duck Lake Woods,
400....*A-4
Duncans Mills, 60....I-6
Dundas, 250....N-12
Dunfermline, 300....H-7
Dunlap, 1386....G-8
Dunning....*G-7
DUPAGE CO.,
916924....C-12
Dupo, 4138....O-6
Durand, 1443....A-9
Dwight, 4260....F-11
Eagerville, 127....M-7
Earlville, 1701....D-10
E. Alton, 6301....N-6
E. Cape Girardeau,
385....S-8
E. Carondelet, 499....‡J-7
E. Clinton....C-6
E. Dubuque, 1704....A-5
E. Dundee, 2860....*E-2
E. Galesburg, 812....F-6
E. Hannibal, 35....K-3
E. Hardin, 30....M-5
E. Hazel Crest,
1543....*M-9
E. Lynn, 200....H-13
E. Moline, 21302....D-6
E. Peoria, 23402....G-8
E. St. Louis, 27006....O-6
Easton, 321....I-7
Eastwood Manor,
950....*A-3
Eaton, 100....M-13
Echo Lake, 550....*C-4
Eddyville, 101....S-11
Edelstein, 160....F-8
Eden, 220....P-8
Edgar, 40....K-13
EDGAR CO.,
18576....K-13
Edgewood, 440....N-10
Edgington, 450....E-5
Edinburg, 1078....K-8
Edison Pk.....*F-7
Edwards, 350....G-7
EDWARDS CO.,
6721....O-12
Edwardsville, 24293....N-7
Effingham, 12328....M-11
EFFINGHAM CO.,
34242....M-11
Egan, 50....B-8
El Dara, 78....K-4
El Paso, 2810....G-9
Elbridge, 80....K-13
Elburn, 5602....C-11
Elco, 150....S-9
Eldorado, 4122....R-11
Eldred, 201....L-5
Eleroy, 120....A-7
Elgin, 108188....B-11
Elizabeth, 761....A-6
Elizabethtown, 299....S-11
Elk Grove Vil.,
33127....*F-5
Elkhart, 405....J-8
Elkville, 928....Q-9
Ellery, 50....P-12
Elliott, 295....H-11
Ellis Grv., 363....Q-7
Ellisville, 96....G-6
Ellsworth, 195....H-10
Elmhurst, 44121....C-12
Elmira, 50....F-7
Elmwood, 2097....G-7
Elmwood Pk.,
24883....*H-7
Elsah, 673....M-6
Elvaston, 165....H-3
Elwin, 150....K-9
Elwood, 2279....E-12
Emden, 485....I-8
Emerald Pk., 400....*A-3
Emington, 117....F-11
Emma, 90....Q-12
Energy, 1146....R-9
Enfield, 596....P-11
Englewood....*J-9
Enterprise, 40....O-11
Eola, 100....*J-3
Equality, 595....R-11
Erie, 1602....D-7
Essex, 802....F-12
Etna, 60....L-11
Eureka, 5295....G-9
Evanston, 74486....B-13
Evansville, 701....Q-7
Evergreen Pk.,
19852....*K-8
Ewing, 307....Q-10
Exeter, 65....K-5
Fair Haven, 30....C-7
Fairbury, 3757....G-11
Fairdale, 200....B-10
Fairfield, 5154....P-11
Fairmont, 2459....*M-4
Fairmont City, 2635....‡H-8
Fairmount, 642....J-13
Fairview, 522....G-6
Fairview Hts., 17078....‡I-9
Fall Creek, 40....J-3
Fancher, 75....L-10
Fancy Prairie, 100....J-8
Fandon, 60....H-5
Farina, 518....N-10
Farmer City, 2037....I-10
Farmersville, 724....L-8
Farmington, 2448....G-7
FAYETTE CO.,
22140....M-9
Fayetteville, 366....P-7
Fenton, 170....D-7
Ferris, 156....H-4
Fiatt, 200....H-6
Fieldon, 239....M-5
Fillmore, 330....M-9
Findlay, 683....K-10
Fisher, 1881....I-11
Fishhook, 30....J-4
Fithian, 485....I-12
Five Islands Pk.,
220....*G-2
Flag Ctr., 100....C-9
Flanagan, 1110....G-10
Flat Rock, 331....N-13
Flatville, 60....I-12
Flora, 5070....N-11
Floraville, 53....P-6
Florence, 100....B-8
Florence, 38....K-5
Flossmoor, 9464....*M-9
Foosland, 101....H-11
FORD CO., 14081....H-12
Ford Hts., 2763....*N-10
Forest City, 246....H-7
Forest Homes, 1700....‡D-8
Forest Lake, 1659....*C-5
Forest Pk., 14167....*I-7
Forest View, 698....*I-7
Forrest, 1220....G-11
Forreston, 1446....B-8
Forsyth, 3490....J-10
Fosterburg, 250....M-6
Fountain Green, 120....H-4
Fowler, 400....J-3
Fox Lake, 10579....A-12
Fox River Grv., 4854....B-11
Frankfort, 17782....D-12
Franklin, 610....K-7
FRANKLIN CO.,
39561....Q-10
Franklin Grv., 1021....C-9
Franklin Pk., 18333....*G-7
Frederick, 100....I-5
Freeburg, 4354....O-7
Freeman Spur, 287....Q-9
Freeport, 25638....B-8
Fulton, 3481....C-6
FULTON CO.,
37069....H-6
Fults, 26....P-6
Funks Grv.....H-9
Future City, 150....T-9
Gage Pk.....*J-9
Galatia, 933....Q-11
Gale....T-8
Galena, 3429....A-6
Galesburg, 32195....F-6
GALLATIN CO.,
5589....R-12
Galt, 210....C-7
Galton, 20....K-11
Galva, 2589....F-7
Ganntown, 35....S-10
Garden of Eden,
140....F-13
Garden Plain, 80....C-6
Garden Prairie, 352....B-10
Gardner, 1463....F-11
Garrett, 162....J-11
Gays, 281....L-11
Geff, 367....O-11
Geneseo, 6586....E-6
Geneva, 21495....C-11
Genoa, 5193....B-10
Georgetown, 3474....J-13
Gerlaw, 150....F-5
German Valley, 463....B-8
Germantown, 1269....O-8
Germantown Hills,
3438....G-8
Gibson City, 3407....H-11
Gibsonia....R-12
Gifford, 975....I-12
Gila, 35....M-11
Gilberts, 6879....*E-1
Gilead, 30....M-5
Gillespie, 3319....M-7
Gilman, 1814....G-12
Gilson, 190....G-6
Girard, 2103....L-7
Gladstone, 281....G-4
Glasford, 1022....H-7
Glasgow, 141....K-5
Glen Carbon, 12934....‡F-9
Glen Ellyn, 27450....*H-5
Glenarm, 200....K-8
Glencoe, 8723....B-13
Glendale, 50....S-10
Glendale Hts.,
34208....*G-4
Glenview, 44692....*E-7
Glenwood, 8969....*M-9
Godfrey, 17982....M-6
Godley, 601....E-11
Golconda, 668....S-11
Golden, 644....I-4
Golden Eagle, 50....N-5
Golden Gate, 68....P-12
Golf, 500....*F-8
Good Hope, 396....H-5
Goodenow, 140....E-13
Goodfield, 860....G-9
Goodwine, 80....H-13
Gordon, 20....M-13
Goreville, 1049....R-9
Gorham, 236....R-8
Grafton, 674....M-5
Grand Detour, 429....C-8
Grand Ridge, 560....E-10
Grand Tower, 605....R-8
Grandview, 1441....†L-17
Grandview, 110....K-13
Granite City, 29849....N-6
Grant Pk., 1331....E-13
Grantfork, 337....N-8
Grantsburg, 150....S-10
Granville, 1427....E-9
Graymont, 130....G-10
Grayslake, 20957....*B-5
Grayville, 1666....P-12
Green Oaks, 3866....*B-6
Green Valley, 709....H-8
Greenbush, 100....G-5
GREENE CO.,
13886....L-5
Greenfield, 1071....L-6
Greenup, 1513....L-12
Greenview, 778....I-7
Greenville, 7000....N-8
Gridley, 1432....G-10
Griggsville, 1226....K-5
Grimsby....R-8
Groveland, 500....H-8
GRUNDY CO.,
50063....E-11
Gulfport, 54....G-4
Gurnee, 31295....*A-6
Hagarstown, 100....M-9
Hainesville, 3597....*A-5
Half Day....*C-6
Hallsville, 80....I-9
Hamburg, 128....L-5
Hamburg....N-9
Hamel, 816....N-7
Hamilton, 2951....H-3
HAMILTON CO.,
8457....P-11
Hammond, 509....J-10
Hampshire, 5563....B-11
Hampton, 1863....R-5
HANCOCK CO.,
19104....H-3
Hanna City, 1225....G-7
Hanover, 844....B-6
Hanover Pk., 37973....*F-4
Harco, 100....R-10
Hardin, 967....M-5
HARDIN CO.,
4320....S-11
Harding, 120....D-10
Hardinville....N-13
Harmon, 120....D-8
Harper, 30....B-8
Harrisburg, 9017....R-11
Harrison, 160....A-9
Harrisonville....P-6
Harristown, 1367....J-9
Hartford, 1429....‡E-8
Hartsburg, 314....I-8
Harvard, 9447....A-10
Harvel, 223....L-8
Harvey, 25282....D-13
Harwood Hts.,
8612....*G-7
Havana, 3301....I-7
Hawthorn Woods,
7663....*C-5
Hayes....J-11
Hazel Crest, 14100....*M-9
Hazel Dell, 100....M-12
Hebron, 1216....A-11
Hecker, 481....P-7
Hegeler, 1900....I-13
Hegewisch....*L-10
Henderson, 255....F-6
HENDERSON CO.,
7331....G-4
Hennepin, 757....E-9
Henning, 251....I-13
Henry, 2464....F-8
HENRY CO., 50486....E-6
Herald, 80....Q-12
Herbert, 100....B-10
Hermon, 50....G-6
Herod, 70....R-11
Herrick, 436....M-9
Herrin, 12501....R-9
Herscher, 1591....F-12
Hersman, 80....J-5
Hettick, 181....L-7
Hewittville, 450....K-9
Heyworth, 2841....I-9
Hickory Grv., 400....J-3
Hickory Hills, 14049....*J-7
Hidalgo, 106....M-12
Highland, 9919....N-8
Highland Hills....*I-5
Highland Lake....*A-5
Highland Pk.,
29763....B-13
Highway Vil.....†J-17
Highwood, 5405....B-13
Hillcrest, 1326....C-9
Hillerman, 35....T-10
Hillsboro, 6207....M-8
Hillsdale, 523....D-6
Hillside, 8157....*H-6
Hillview, 193....L-5
Hinckley, 2070....C-10
Hindsboro, 313....K-12
Hinsdale, 16816....*J-6
Hodgkins, 1897....*J-7
Hoffman, 508....O-9
Hoffman Estates,
51895....*F-4
Holcomb, 270....B-9
Holder, 60....H-10
Holiday Hills, 610....*B-3
Hollywood Hts.,
1060....‡H-9
Homer, 1193....J-12
Homer Glen, 24220....*L-6
Hometown, 4349....*J-8
Homewood, 19323....*M-9
Hoopeston, 5351....H-13
Hooppole, 204....D-7
Hopedale, 865....H-8
Hopewell, 410....F-8
Hopkins Pk., 603....F-13
Hord, 175....N-11
Hoyleton, 531....O-9
Hudson, 1838....H-9
Huey, 169....O-9
Hull, 461....K-3
Humboldt, 437....K-11
Hume, 380....J-13
Humm Wye, 25....S-11
Hunt City, 90....M-12
Huntley, 24291....B-11
Hurst, 795....Q-9
Hutsonville, 554....M-13
Hutton, 50....L-12
Hyde Pk.....*J-10
Illinois City, 250....E-4
Illiopolis, 891....J-9
Ina, 2338....P-10
Indian Creek, 462....*C-6
Indian Head Pk.,
3809....*J-6
Indian Oaks, 500....E-13
Indianola, 276....J-13
Industry, 478....I-5
Ingalls Pk., 3314....*N-5
Ingleside, 1700....*A-4
Ingraham, 150....N-11
Inverness, 7399....*E-5
Iola, 141....N-10
Ipava, 470....H-6
Irene....B-10
Iroquois, 154....G-13
IROQUOIS CO.,
29718....G-12
Irving, 495....M-8
Irving Pk.....*G-8
Irvington, 659....O-9
Irwin, 74....F-12
Island Lake, 8080....*B-3
Itasca, 8649....*G-5
Iuka, 489....O-10
Ivanhoe, 100....*B-5
Ivesdale, 267....J-11
JACKSON CO.,
60218....Q-8
Jacksonville, 19446....K-6
Jamestown, 120....N-8
Janesville, 150....L-11
JASPER CO.,
9698....M-12
JEFFERSON CO.,
38827....O-10
Jefferson Pk.....*G-8
Jerome, 1656....†M-16
JERSEY CO.,
22985....M-6
Jerseyville, 8465....M-6
Jewett, 223....M-12
JO DAVIESS CO.,
22678....B-6
JOHNSON CO.,
12582....S-10
Johnsonville, 77....O-11
Johnston City, 3543....R-10
Joliet, 147433....D-12
Jonesboro, 1821....S-9
Joppa, 360....T-10
Joslin, 100....D-6
Joy, 417....E-4
Junction, 129....R-12
Junction City, 482....O-9
Justice, 12926....*J-7
Kampsville, 328....L-5
Kane, 438....M-6
KANE CO.,
515269....C-11
Kaneville, 484....C-11
Kangley, 251....F-10
Kankakee, 27537....F-12
KANKAKEE CO.,
113449....F-12
Kansas, 787....K-12
Kappa, 227....G-9
Karbers Ridge, 45....R-11
Karnak, 499....S-10
Kasbeer, 85....D-8
Kaskaskia, 14....Q-7
Keenes, 83....P-10
Keeneyville, 300....*G-4
Keensburg, 210....P-13
Keithsburg, 609....F-4
Kell, 219....O-10
Kellerville, 30....J-4
Kemper, 70....M-6
Kempton, 231....F-11
KENDALL CO.,
114736....D-11
Kenilworth, 2513....*E-8
Kenney, 326....I-9
Kent, 100....A-7
Keptown, 45....M-10
Kewanee, 12916....E-7
Keyesport, 421....N-9
Kickapoo, 400....G-7
Kilbourne, 302....I-7
Kildeer, 3968....*D-5
Kincaid, 1505....K-8
Kinderhook, 216....K-3
Kings, 250....C-9
Kingston, 1164....B-10
Kingston, 30....J-4
Kingston Mines, 302....H-7
Kinmundy, 796....N-10
Kinsman, 99....E-11
Kirkland, 1744....B-10
Kirksville, 50....K-10
Kirkwood, 714....G-5
Knollwood, 1747....*B-7
KNOX CO., 52919....F-6
Knoxville, 2911....F-6
La Clede, 100....N-10
La Fox, 250....*H-1
La Grange, 15550....*I-7
La Grange Highlands,
3650....*J-6
La Grange Pk.,
13579....*I-7
La Harpe, 1235....H-4
La Hogue, 30....G-12
La Moille, 726....D-9
La Prairie, 47....I-4
La Rose, 144....F-9
La Salle, 9609....E-9
LA SALLE CO.,
113924....E-10
Lacon, 1937....F-8
Ladd, 1295....E-9
Lafayette, 223....F-7
L. Barrington, 4973....*C-4
L. Bluff, 5722....B-12
Lake City, 110....K-10
LAKE CO.,
703462....B-12
L. Forest, 19375....B-13
L. Fork, 100....J-8
L. Holiday, 4761....D-10
Lake in the Hills,
28965....*D-2
L. Killarney, 700....*C-3
L. Lawrence, 150....N-13
L. Mattoon, 1000....L-11
L. Summerset, 2048....A-8
L. Villa, 8741....A-12
L. Wildwood, 500....F-9
L. Zurich, 19631....B-12
Lakemoor, 6017....A-11
Lakeview....*G-9
Lakewood, 3811....*C-1
Lakewood, 100....L-10
Lanark, 1457....B-7
Lancaster, 150....O-13
Landes....N-13
Lane, 130....I-10
Langleyville, 432....K-8
Lansing, 28331....*M-10
LaPlace, 259....J-10
Larchland....G-5
Latham, 380....J-9
Laura, 150....F-7
Lawndale, 150....I-9
Lawndale....*I-8
Lawrence, 200....A-10
LAWRENCE CO.,
16833....N-13
Lawrenceville,
4348....N-13
Le Roy, 3560....H-10
Leaf River, 443....B-8
Lebanon, 4418....O-7
Lee, 337....C-10
Lee Ctr., 250....C-9
LEE CO., 36031....D-8
Leesville, 100....F-13
Leland, 977....D-10
Leland Grv., 1503....†M-16
Lemont, 16000....*K-5
Lena, 2912....A-7
Lenzburg, 521....P-7
Leonore, 130....E-9
Lerna, 286....L-11
Lewistown, 2384....H-6
Lexington, 2060....G-10
Liberty, 516....J-4
Libertyville, 20315....B-12
Lick Creek, 60....S-9
Lily Lake, 993....C-11
Lilymoor, 450....*A-3
Lima, 163....I-3
Lincoln, 14504....I-8
Lincolnshire, 7275....*D-6
Lincolnwood, 12590....*F-8
Lindenhurst, 14462....A-12
Lindenwood, 300....B-9
Lis....M-11
Lisbon, 285....D-11
Lisbon Ctr.....*M-1
Lisle, 22390....C-12
Litchfield, 6939....M-8
Literberry, 100....J-6
Little America, 200....H-7
Little York, 331....F-5
Littleton, 181....I-5
Lively Grv., 45....P-8
Liverpool, 129....H-7
Livingston, 858....M-7
LIVINGSTON CO.,
38950....F-11
Loami, 745....K-7
Lockport, 24839....D-12
Loda, 407....H-12
Lodge, 100....I-11
Logan, 327....Q-10
Logan....K-13
LOGAN CO., 30305....I-8
Logan Sq.....*H-9
Lomax, 454....G-4
Lombard, 43165....*H-5
London Mills, 392....G-6
Long Creek, 1328....J-10
Long Grv., 8043....*D-5
Long Lake, 3515....*A-4
Long Pt., 226....F-10
Longview, 153....J-12
Loogootee, 70....N-10
Loop....*H-9
Loraine, 313....I-3
Loran, 40....B-7
Lostant, 498....F-9
Louisville, 1139....N-11
Loves Pk., 23996....A-9
Lovington, 1130....K-10
Low Pt., 200....G-9
Lowder, 100....K-7
Lowell, 50....E-9
Ludlow, 371....H-12
Lyndon, 648....D-7
Lynn Ctr., 150....E-6
Lynnville, 117....K-6
Lynwood, 9007....*M-10
Lyons, 10729....*I-7
Macedonia, 63....Q-10
Machesney Pk.,
23499....A-9
Mackinaw, 1950....H-8
Macomb, 19288....H-5
Macon, 1138....K-9
MACON CO.,
110768....J-9
MACOUPIN CO.,
47765....L-7
Madison, 3891....‡G-7
MADISON CO.,
269282....N-7
Maeystown, 157....P-6
Magnolia, 260....F-9
Mahomet, 7258....I-11
Makanda, 561....R-9
Malta, 1164....C-10
Manchester, 292....K-6
Manhattan, 7051....E-12
Manito, 1642....H-7
Manlius, 359....E-8
Mansfield, 906....I-11
Manteno, 9204....E-13
Manville, 50....F-10
Maple Pk., 1310....C-10
Mapleton, 270....H-7
Maquon, 284....G-6
Marblehead, 100....J-3
Marcelline, 100....I-3
Marengo, 7648....B-10
Marietta, 112....H-6
Marine, 960....N-7
Marion, 17193....R-10
MARION CO.,
39437....O-10
Marissa, 1979....P-7
Markham, 12508....*L-9
Marley, 100....*M-6
Maroa, 1801....J-10
Marseilles, 5094....E-10
Marshall, 3933....L-13
MARSHALL CO.,
12640....F-9
Martinsville, 1167....L-13
Martinton, 381....F-13
Maryville, 7487....‡G-10
Mascoutah, 7483....O-7
Mason, 345....N-10
Mason City, 2343....I-8
MASON CO., 14666....I-7
MASSAC CO.,
15429....T-10
Matherville, 723....E-5
Matteson, 19009....*N-8
Mattoon, 18555....L-11
Maunie, 139....Q-12
Maywood, 24090....*H-7
Mazon, 1015....E-11
McClure, 402....S-8
McConnell, 250....A-7
McCook, 228....*J-7
McCormick....R-10
McCullom Lake,
1049....*A-2
MCDONOUGH CO.,
32612....I-5
McHenry, 26992....A-11
MCHENRY CO.,
308760....A-11
McLean, 830....I-9
MCLEAN CO.,
169572....H-10
McLeansboro, 2883....Q-11
McNabb, 285....F-9
Meadowbrook,
1000....‡D-9
Meadows, 300....G-10
Mechanicsburg, 590....J-8
Media, 107....G-4
Medinah....*G-5
Medora, 419....M-6
Melrose....L-13
Melrose Pk., 25411....*H-7
Melvin, 452....H-11
MENARD CO.,
12705....I-7
Mendon, 953....I-3
Mendota, 7372....D-9
Menominee, 248....A-5
Meppen, 60....M-5
MERCER CO.,
16434....E-5
Meredosia, 1044....J-5
Meriden, 50....D-9
Mermet....S-10
Merna, 40....H-10
Merrionette Pk.,
1900....*K-9
Metamora, 3636....G-8
Metcalf, 189....J-13
Metropolis, 6537....T-10
Mettawa, 547....*C-6
Meyer, 50....I-3
Michael, 50....L-5
Middletown, 324....I-8
Midlothian, 14819....*L-8
Midway, 330....H-8
Midway, 25....T-10
Milan, 5099....T-3
Milford, 1306....G-13
Mill Creek, 65....S-9
Mill Shoals, 215....P-11
Milledgeville, 1032....C-7
Millersburg, 100....E-5
Millersville, 65....L-9
Millington, 665....D-10
Millstadt, 4011....O-6
Milton, 271....K-5
Mineral, 237....E-7
Minier, 1252....H-9
Minonk, 2078....G-9
Minooka, 10924....E-11
Mitchell, 1356....‡F-8
Mitchellsville, 100....R-11
Modesto, 189....L-7
Modoc, 100....Q-6
Moecherville....*J-2
Mokena, 18740....*M-7
Moline, 43483....D-5
Momence, 3310....F-13
Monee, 5148....E-13
Monica, 80....F-7
Monmouth, 9444....F-5
Monroe Ctr., 471....B-9
MONROE CO.,
32957....P-6
Montgomery,
18438....D-11
MONTGOMERY CO.,
30104....L-8
Monticello, 5548....J-11
Montrose, 201....M-11
Mooseheart, 100....*I-2
MORGAN CO.,
35547....J-6
Morgan Pk.....*K-9
Morris, 13636....E-11
Morrison, 4188....C-7
Morrisonville, 1056....L-8
Morton, 16267....H-8
Morton Grv., 23270....*F-7
MOULTRIE CO.,
14846....K-10
Mound City, 588....T-9
Mounds, 810....T-9
Mt. Auburn, 480....K-9
Mt. Carmel, 7284....O-13
Mt. Carroll, 1717....B-7
Mt. Erie, 88....O-12
Mt. Greenwood....*K-8
Mt. Morris, 2998....B-8
Mt. Olive, 2099....M-7
Mt. Pleasant, 50....S-9
Mt. Prospect, 54167....*E-6
Mt. Pulaski, 1566....J-9
Mt. Sterling, 2025....J-5
Mt. Vernon, 15277....P-10
Mt. Zion, 5833....K-10
Moweaqua, 1831....K-9
Mozier, 50....L-5
Muddy, 68....R-11
Mulberry Grv., 634....N-9
Mulkeytown, 175....Q-9
Mundelein, 31064....*C-5
Murdock, 150....J-12
Murphysboro, 7970....R-8
Murrayville, 587....K-6
Nachusa, 270....C-8
Naperville, 141853....C-12
Naplate, 496....E-10
Naples, 130....K-5
Nashville, 3258....P-8
Nason, 236....P-9
National City....‡H-7
Nauvoo, 1149....H-3
Near North Side....*H-9
Nebo, 340....L-5
Nekoma, 30....F-6
Nelson, 170....C-8
Neoga, 1636....L-11
Neponset, 473....E-7
Neunert, 25....R-8
New Athens, 2054....P-7
New Baden, 3349....O-7
New Bedford, 75....D-7
New Berlin, 1346....K-7
New Boston, 683....F-4
New Burnside, 211....R-10
New Canton, 359....K-4
New Columbia, 150....S-10
New Delhi, 40....M-6
New Douglas, 319....M-8
New Grand Chain,
210....T-9
New Hanover, 60....O-6
New Haven, 433....Q-12
New Hebron, 50....M-13
New Holland, 269....I-8
New Lenox, 24394....D-12
New Liberty, 70....T-11
New Memphis, 300....O-8
New Milford, 697....B-9
New Minden, 215....O-8
New Philadelphia,
100....H-5
New Salem, 137....K-4
New Windsor, 748....E-6
Newark, 992....D-11
Newbern, 100....M-6
Newman, 865....J-12
Newton, 2849....M-12
Niantic, 707....J-9
Niles, 29803....*F-7
Nilwood, 239....L-7
Niota, 300....G-3
Noble, 677....N-12
Nokomis, 2256....L-9
Nora, 121....A-7
Normal, 52497....H-9
Normandy, 30....D-8
Norridge, 14572....*G-7
Norris, 213....G-7
Norris City, 1275....Q-11
N. Aurora, 16760....C-11
N. Barrington, 3047....*C-4
N. Chicago, 32574....A-12
N. Dupo, 1380....‡J-7
N. Glen Ellyn, 1400....*H-5
N. Henderson, 187....F-5
N. Riverside, 6672....*I-7
Northbrook, 33170....*E-7
Northfield, 5420....*E-8
Northlake, 12323....*H-6
Nortonville, 50....K-6
Norway, 300....E-10
Norwood Pk.....*G-7
Nutwood, 120....M-5
Oak Brook, 7883....*I-6
Oak Forest, 27962....*L-8
Oak Grv., 396....E-5
Oak Hill, 100....G-7
Oak Hills, 1150....‡H-9
Oak Lawn, 56690....D-13
Oak Pk., 51878....C-13
Oak Run, 547....F-6
Oakbrook Ter., 2134....*I-6
Oakdale, 221....P-8
Oakford, 286....I-7
Oakland, 880....K-12
Oakwood, 1595....I-13
Oakwood Hills,
2083....*C-3
Oblong, 1466....M-12
Oconee, 180....L-9
Odell, 1046....F-11
Odin, 1076....O-9
O'Fallon, 28281....O-7
Ogden, 810....I-12
OGLE CO., 53497....B-8
Oglesby, 3791....E-9
Ohio, 513....D-8
Ohlman, 135....L-9
Oilfield....L-12
Okawville, 1434....O-8
Old Kane....M-6
Old Ripley, 108....N-8
Old Shawneetown,
193....R-12
Olive Branch, 864....T-8
Oliver, 110....L-13
Olmsted, 333....T-9
Olney, 9115....N-12
Olympia Fields,
4988....*N-9
Omaha, 266....Q-11
Omega, 50....N-10
Onarga, 1368....G-12
Oneco, 50....A-8
Oneida, 700....F-6
Ontarioville....*G-4
Opdyke, 254....P-10
Ophiem, 170....E-6
Oquawka, 1371....F-4
Orange Prairie....†H-15
Orangeville, 793....A-8
Oraville, 100....Q-8
Orchardville, 100....O-10
Oreana, 875....J-10
Oregon, 3721....C-9
Orient, 358....Q-9
Orion, 1861....E-6
Orland Hills, 7149....*M-7
Orland Pk., 56767....D-12
Osceola, 50....E-7
Oskaloosa....N-10
Oswego, 30355....D-11
Ottawa, 18768....E-10
Otterville, 126....M-6
Owaneco, 239....L-9
Oxville, 30....K-5
Ozark, 110....S-10
Palatine, 68557....B-12
Palestine, 1369....M-13
Palmer, 229....L-8
Palmyra, 698....L-7
Palos Hts., 12515....*L-8
Palos Hills, 17484....*K-7
Palos Pk., 4847....*K-7
Pana, 5847....L-9
Panama, 343....M-8
Pankeyville, 200....R-11
Panola, 45....G-9
Papineau, 171....F-13
Paris, 8837....K-13

*, †, ‡, §, ◊ See explanation under state title in this index.
County and parish names are listed in capital letters & boldface type.
Independent cities (not included in a county) are listed in italics.

Illinois (continued)

Park City, 7570 ....*A-7
Park Forest, 21975 ......D-13
Park Ridge, 37480 .....*F-7
Parkersburg, 199 ....O-12
Passport, 30 ....N-12
Patoka, 584 ....L-11
Patterson, 142 ....L-5
Patton, 90 ....O-13
Paw Paw, 870 ....D-9
Pawnee, 2739 ....K-8
Paxton, 4473 ....H-12
Payson, 1026 ....J-3
Pearl, 138 ....L-5
Pearl City, 838 ....B-7
Pecatonica, 2195 ......A-8
Pekin, 34094 ....H-8
Penfield, 150 ....H-12
Peoria, 115007 ....G-8

PEORIA CO.,
186494 ....G-7
Peoria Hts, 6156 ......G-8
Pinckneyville, 5648 ...Q-9
Pingree Grv, 4532 .....B-11
Pinkstaff, 150 ....N-13
Piper City, 826 ....G-12
Pittsburg, 572 ....R-10
Pittsfield, 4576 ......K-4
Plainfield, 39581 .....D-12
Plainview, 150 ....M-7
Plainville, 264 ....J-3
Plano, 10856 ....D-11
Plato Ctr., 120 ....*F-1
Plattville, 242 ....D-11
Pleasant Hill, 966 ....L-4
Pleasant Mound,
  100 ....N-9
Pleasant Plains, 802 ..J-7
Plymouth, 505 ....H-4
Poag, 30 ....*F-9
Pocahontas, 784 ....N-8
Polo, 2355 ....C-8
Pontiac, 11931 ....G-10
Pontoon Bch., 5836..*G-8
Pontoosuc, 146 ....G-3
POPE CO., 4470 ....S-11
Poplar Grv., 5023 .....A-10
Port Barrington,
  1517 ....*C-3
Port Byron, 1647 ......D-6
Portage Pk. *L-9
Posen, 5987 ....*L-9
Posey, 75 ....O-8
Potomac, 750 ....I-13
Pottstown, 70 ....†I-15
Prairie City, 379 .....G-5
Prairie du Rocher,
  604 ....O-6
Prairie Grv., 1904 ...*C-3
Prairie View *D-6
Preemption, 350 ....E-5
Prentice, 30 ....J-7
Preston Hts., 2575...*N-8
Princeton, 7660 ....E-8
Princeville, 1738 .....F-7
Prophetstown, 2080 ...D-7
Prospect Hts.,
  16256 ....*E-6
Pulaski, 206 ....T-9
PULASKI CO., 6161..T-9
Pulleys Mill, 60 ......R-9
Pullman *K-10
Putnam, 200 ....F-7
PUTNAM CO., 6006..D-8
Quincy, 40633 ....J-3
Radford, 220 ....P-9
Radom, 220 ....P-9
Raleigh, 350 ....Q-11
Ramsey, 1037 ....M-9
Rankin, 561 ....H-13
Ransom, 384 ....F-10
Rantoul, 12941 ....H-11
Rapatee, 80 ....G-6
Rapids City, 959 ......D-6
Rardin, 160 ....K-12
Raritan, 138 ....G-4
Raymond, 1006 ....L-8
Red Bud, 3698 ....O-7
Reddick, 173 ....K-13
Redmon, 173 ....K-13
Reevesville, 100 ......S-10
Renault, 200 ....O-6
Reynolds, 539 ....C-5
Reynoldsville S-8
Rice, 100 ....N-12
RICHLAND CO.,
  16233 ....N-12
Richmond, 1874 ....A-11
Richton Pk., 13646..*N-8
Richview, 253 ....P-9
Ridge Farm, 882 ......I-13
Ridgefield, 120 ......*B-1
Ridgway, 869 ....R-12
Ridott, 164 ....B-8
Riggston, 40 ....K-5
Rinard, 110 ....N-11
Ringwood, 836 ....A-11
Rio, 220 ....F-6
Ripley, 86 ....J-5
Rising Sun, 35 ....Q-12
Ritchie, 60 ....E-12
River Forest, 11172..*H-7
River Grv., 10227 ....*H-7
Riverdale, 13549 .....*L-9
Riverside, 8875 ......*I-7
Riverton, 3455 ....J-8
Riverview, 200 ....J-8
Riverwoods, 3660 ....*D-7
Robbins, 5337 ....*L-9
Roberts, 362 ....H-11
Robinson, 7713 ....M-13
Roby, 80 ....P-6
Rochelle, 9574 ....C-9

Rochester, 3689 ....K-8
Rock City, 315 ....A-8
Rock Falls, 9266 ......C-8
Rock Grv., 150 ....A-8
Rock Island, 39018 ...D-5
ROCK ISLAND CO.,
  147546 ....E-4
Rock River Ter., 230..B-9
S. Elgin, 21985 ....*G-2
S. Holland, 22030..*M-10
S. Jacksonville, 3331..K-6
S. Pekin, 1146 ....H-8
S. Roxana, 2053 ......*E-8
S. Shore *J-10
S. Wilmington, 681 ...F-11
Southern View,
  1642 ....*M-16
Sparland, 406 ....F-8
Sparta, 4302 ....P-7
Spaulding, 873 ....I-8
Speer, 100 ....G-8
Spring Bay, 452 ....G-8
Spring Gdn., 90 ....P-10
Spring Grv., 5778 ....A-11
Spring Hill, 50 ....*H-6
Spring Valley, 5558 ..E-9
Springerton, 150 .....P-11
Springfield, 116250..J-8
Standard City, 152 ...L-7
Stanford, 596 ....H-9
STARK CO., 5994....F-7
State Park Pl., 2600..*H-9
Staunton, 5139 ....M-7
Steel City, 150 ....Q-10
Steeleville, 2083 .....Q-8
Steger, 9570 ....D-13
Stelle, 100 ....F-12
Sterling, 15370 ....C-8
Steward, 256 ....C-9
Stewardson, 734 ......L-10
Stillman Valley, 1120..B-9
Stillwell, 80 ....I-3
Stockland, 150 ....H-13
Stockton, 1862 ....A-7
Stone Pk., 4946 ......*H-7
Stonefort, 297 ....R-10
Stonington, 932 ......K-9
Stoy, 104 ....M-13
Strasburg, 467 ....L-10
Stratford, 50 ....A-8
Strawn, 100 ....G-11
Streamwood, 39858..*F-3
Streator, 13710 ....F-10
Stronghurst, 883 .....G-4
Sublette, 409 ....C-9
Sugar Grv., 8997 .....C-11
Sullivan, 4440 ....L-10
Summer Hill, 100 .....K-4
Summerfield, 451 .....O-7
Summit, 11054 ....*J-7
Summum, 150 ....I-6
Sumner, 3174 ....N-13
Sun River Ter., 528..F-13
Sunfield, 220 ....Q-9
Sunny Hill, 80 ....G-8
Sunnyland ....†J-18
Swan Creek, 90 ....G-5
Swansea, 13430 ....O-7
Swanwick, 100 ....P-8
Sycamore, 15170 ......C-10
Sylvan Lake, 430 .....*C-5
Symerton, 84 ....E-12
Table Grv., 416 ....H-6
Tallula, 488 ....J-7
Talmaco, 40 ....N-9
Tamaroa, 638 ....P-9
Tamms, 1056 ....T-9
Tampico, 790 ....D-7
Taylor Ridge, 200 ....E-5
Taylor Sprs., 690 ....M-8
Tazewell, 11246 .....*N-8

Sorento, 498 ....M-8
S. Barrington, 4565 ..*E-4
S. Beloit, 7892 ....A-9
S. Chicago *J-10
  4139 ....*N-9
S. Deering *N-9
Valley View, 2100 ....*G-2
Valmeyer, 1263 ....P-6
Van Burensburg, 50 ..M-9
Van Orin, 120 ....D-8
Vandalia, 7042 ....M-9
Varna, 384 ....F-8
Venedy, 138 ....O-8
Venice, 1890 ....*H-7
Vera, 100 ....M-9
Vergennes, 298 ....Q-8
Vermilion, 225 ....K-13
Vermont, 667 ....I-6
Vernon, 129 ....N-9
Vernon Hills, 25113..*C-6
Verona, 215 ....E-11
Versailles, 478 ......J-5
Victoria, 316 ....F-6
Vienna, 1434 ....S-10
Viola, 955 ....E-5
Viola Pk., 21904 ....*H-5
Villa Ridge, 500 .....T-9
Villa Grv., 2537 .....J-12
Villa Hills, 1410 ...*J-8
Violet Hill, 90 ....T-9
Virden, 3425 ....L-7
Virginia, 1611 ....J-6
Volo, 2929 ....A-12
Wacker, 50 ....G-5
Waddams Grv., 60 ....A-7
Wadsworth, 3815 ....A-12
Waggoner, 266 ....L-8
Walkville, 50 ....N-12
Walnut, 1416 ....D-8
Walnut Grv., 90 ......H-5
Walnut Hill, 108 .....O-9
Walpole, 50 ....O-11
Walsh, 140 ....O-7
Waltonville, 434 .....P-9
Wamac, 1185 ....O-9
Wanda, 80 ....*E-9
Wapella, 558 ....I-10
Ware, 260 ....S-8
Warren, 1428 ....A-7

WARREN CO.,
17707 ....G-5
Warrensburg, 1210 ...J-9
Warrenville, 13140..*I-3
Warsaw, 1607 ....H-3
Wasco, 300 ....*G-1
Washburn, 1155 ....F-9
Washington, 15134..G-8
Washington Pk.,
  14716 ....P-8
Washington Pk.,
  ....*I-9
Wasson, 200 ....R-11
Watoga, 843 ....P-6
Waterloo, 9811 ....O-6
Waterman, 1506 ......C-10
Watseka, 5255 ....G-13
Watson, 754 ....M-11
Wauconda, 13603 ....B-12
Waukegan, 89078 ....A-12
Waverly, 1307 ....K-7
Wayne, 2431 ....*G-3
Wayne City, 1032 ....P-11
Waynesville, 434 .....I-9
Wedron, 300 ....E-10
Weldon, 429 ....I-10
Wellington, 242 .....H-13
Wenona, 1056 ....F-9
Wenonah, 37 ....*I-8
W. Brooklyn, 240 .....D-8
W. Chicago, 27086...*H-3
W. City, 661 ....Q-10
W. Dundee, 7331 .....*E-2
W. End A-10
W. Frankfort, 8182 ..Q-10
W. Jersey, 50 ....F-7
W. Liberty, 180 ......N-12
W. Peoria, 4458 .....*I-15
W. Point, 178 ....I-3
W. Salem, 897 ....O-12
W. Union, 288 ....M-13
W. Vienna, 90 ....S-9
W. York, 129 ....M-13
Westchester, 16718..*I-7
Western Sprs.,
  12975 ....*I-6
Westervelt, 128 ......L-10
Westfield, 601 ....L-12
Westmont, 24685 ....*J-5
Weston, 100 ....G-11
Westville, 3202 .....I-13
Wetaug, 50 ....S-9
Wheaton, 52894 .....C-12
Wheeler, 147 ....M-12
Wheeling, 37648 ....*E-6
White Ash, 232 ......M-7
White Hall, 2629 .....K-6
White Heath, 290 ....I-11
WHITESIDE CO.,
58498 ....C-7
Whittington, 200 .....Q-10
Wildwood *A-5
Will Co., 677560..E-12
Williamsfield, 578 ...F-7

Illinois–Indiana

Wood River, 10657...N-6
Woodbine, 140 ....A-6
Woodburn, 170 ....M-7
Woodbury, 70 ....M-11
WOODFORD CO.,
38664 ....G-9
Woodhull, 811 ....F-6
Woodland, 324 ....G-13
Woodlawn, 698 ....P-9
Woodridge, 32971 ...*J-5
Woodson, 512 ....K-6
Woodstock, 24770 ...A-11
Woodworth, 500 ......*L-8
Woosung, 180 ....C-8
Worden, 1044 ....N-7
Worth, 10789 ....*K-8
Wrights, 100 ....L-6
Wyanet, 991 ....E-8
Wynoose, 40 ....O-12
Wyoming, 1429 ....F-7
Xenia, 391 ....O-10
Yale, 86 ....M-12
Yates City, 693 ......G-7
York, 100 ....M-13
Yorkfield *H-6
York Ctr. *H-6
Yorktown, 100 ....D-7
Yorkville, 16921 .....D-11
Yuton E-1
Zeigler, 1801 ....Q-9
Zion, 24413 ....A-13

Aberdeen, 90 ....O-13
Abington, 80 ....K-13
Aboite, 50 ....D-12
Abydel, 30 ....R-7
Acme, 30 ....N-9
Adams, 175 ....L-8
Adams, 150 ....L-8
ADAMS CO.,
34387 ....E-13
Adams Lake, 500 .....B-12
Adamsboro E-8
Ade, 20 ....E-4
Advance, 477 ....I-7
Aetna *M-13
Ainsworth *N-14
Akron, 1187 ....D-9
Alamo, 86 ....J-7
Albany, 2365 ....G-11
Albion, 2349 ....B-11
Alert, 90 ....M-10
Alexandria, 5145 .....H-10
Alford, 90 ....Q-5
Alfordsville, 101 ....P-6
Aigiers, 50 ....P-5
Alanthus, 843 ....P-6
Allendale, 250 ....L-4
Alpine, 40 ....K-12
Alquina, 130 ....K-13
Alta, 150 ....J-4
Alton, 55 ....R-8
Altona, 197 ....C-12
Alvarado, 30 ....B-14
Ambia, 239 ....G-4
Amboy, 384 ....F-10
Americus, 423 ....G-6
Amity, 225 ....L-9
Amo, 401 ....K-7
Anderson, 56129 .....H-10
Andersonville, 250 ..L-12
Andrews, 1149 ....E-11
Angola, 8612 ....A-13
Annapolis, 100 ....J-5
Anoka, 60 ....E-9
Antioch, 150 ....H-7
Arba, 40 ....K-14
Arcadia, 1666 ....H-9
Arcola, 180 ....D-12
Ardmore, 2200 ......*I-18
Argos, 1691 ....C-8
Arida, 150 ....L-11
Arlington, 433 ....K-11
Armstrong, 30 ....E-4
Arthur, 75 ....L-6
Ashland, 80 ....K-12
Ashley, 863 ....B-13
Athens, 130 ....D-9
Atherton, 85 ....K-6
Atlanta, 725 ....H-9
Attica, 3245 ....H-5
Atwood, 300 ....C-10
Auburn, 12731 ....C-13
Augusta, 50 ....*B-17
Aultshire K-11
Aurora, 3750 ....N-13
Austin, 4295 ....O-10
Avilla, 2401 ....C-12
Avoca, 250 ....O-7
Avon, 12446 ....I-8
Avondale, 500 ....I-8
Bainbridge, 746 ......I-6
Bakers Cor., 70 ......I-9
Banquo, 50 ....F-11
Barbee, 900 ....C-10
Bargersville, 4013 ..L-9
Barnard, 30 ....I-5
Bartonia, 120 ....J-14
Bartonia, 30 ....I-4
Bass Lake, 1195 ......C-7
Batesville, 6520 .....M-12
Bath, 100 ....L-13
Battle Ground, 1334..G-6
Beanblossom, 200 ....M-8
Beardstown, 30 ....M-7
Beaver City E-7
Beaver Dam, 250 ......D-9
Beck's Mill O-9
Bedford, 13413 ....O-7
Beech Grv., 14192 ...K-9
Beehunter, 30 ....N-5
Belle Union, 90 ......J-6
Bellefontaine, 40 ...I-10
Bellmore, 100 ....J-5
Belmont, 100 ....M-8
Ben Davis *E-16
Bendix, 3362 ....B-8
Bennetts Switch, 90 .F-9
Bennington, 80 ....O-13

Benton, 150 ....B-10
BENTON CO., 8854..F-4
Bentonville, 65 ......K-12
Berne, 3999 ....F-13
Bethany, 81 ....M-9
Bethany, 25 ....M-9
Bethel, 90 ....M-9
Bethlehem, 100 ....O-11
Beverly Shores, 613..A-6
Bicknell, 2915 ....O-4
Bippus, 200 ....E-11
Birdseye, 416 ....R-7
Blackford Co.,
  12766 ....G-12
Blackhawk, 80 ....M-4
Blaine, 10 ....M-8
Blairsville, 250 .....S-2
Blanford, 342 ....K-4
Blocher, 200 ....P-11
Bloomfield, 2405 ....N-6
Blooming Grv., 75 ...L-13
Bloomingdale, 335 ...I-5
Bloomingport, 60 ....I-13
Bloomington, 80405..M-7
Blountsville, 341 ....I-12
Blue Lake, 300 ....C-12
Blue Ridge, 250 ......L-11
Bluffton, 9897 ....E-12
Boggstown, 400 ......K-10
Bono, 25 ....O-8
BOONE CO., 56640..I-8
Boone Grv., 175 .....C-5
Boonville, 6246 ......S-4
Borden, 808 ....Q-9
Boston, 136 ....K-14
Boswell, 777 ....G-5
Boundary City, 20 ...H-13
Bourbon, 1810 ....C-9
Bowling Green, 300 ..L-5
Bowman O-8
Boxley, 100 ....H-9
Boylston, 90 ....H-8
Bradford, 150 ....Q-9
Branchville, 70 ......R-7
Brazil, 7912 ....L-5
Bremen, 4588 ....B-9
Brems, 25 ....C-7
Bretzville, 50 ....R-6
Brewersville, 50 ....N-11
Brick Chapel, 40 .....K-6
Bridgeport *E-15
Bridgeton, 150 ....L-5
Bright, 5693 ....M-14
Brighton, 125 ....B-12
Brimfield, 150 ....B-12
Bringhurst, 125 .....G-7
Bristol, 1602 ....A-10
Bristow, 120 ....R-6
Brook, 997 ....E-4
Brooklyn, 1598 ....L-8
Brooksburg, 21285 ..I-8
Brookston, 1554 .....F-6
Brookville, 2596 .....L-13
BROWN CO.,
15242 ....M-8
Browns Valley, 90 ...I-6
Brownsburg, 21285 ..I-8
Brownstown, 2947 ...O-9
Brownsville, 250 .....K-13
Bruce Lake, 100 ......D-8
Bruceville, 478 .....O-4
Brushy Prairie, 30 ..A-12
Bryant, 252 ....G-13
Bryantsburg, 50 .....O-12
Buck Creek, 207 .....G-6
Buckskin, 180 ....R-4
Bucktown, 20 ....K-12
Buddha, 400 ....O-7
Buena Vista, 80 .....R-6
Buffalo, 692 ....E-6
Buffaloville, 40 .....S-4
Bunker Hill, 888 .....F-9
Bunker Hill, 100 .....F-9
Burket, 195 ....D-9
Burlington, 603 ......G-8
Burlington Bch., 900..B-5
Burnettsville, 346 ..F-7
Burney, 130 ....M-11
Burns City, 1156 ....N-5
Burnsville, 80 ....M-9
Burr Oak, 150 ....C-8
Burrows, 240 ....F-7
Busseron, 30 ....O-4
Butler, 2684 ....B-13
Butler Ctr., 35 .....C-13
Butlerville, 282 .....N-11
Byrneville, 40 ....Q-9
Cadiz, 150 ....J-11
Cale, 35 ....R-6
Cambria, 100 ....N-7
Cambridge City,
  1870 ....K-12
Camby *G-15
Camden, 611 ....F-7
Cammack, 300 ....H-11
Canaan, 90 ....N-12
Cannelburg, 135 .....P-5
Cannelton, 1563 .....T-6
Canton, 175 ....P-9
Carbon, 397 ....K-5
Carbondale, 15 ......H-6
Cardonia, 90 ....L-5
Carefree, 25 ....R-8
Carlisle, 692 ....N-4
Carlos, 80 ....J-13
Carmel, 79191 ....I-9
Carp I-6
Carpentersville, 40 .I-6
CARROLL CO.,
20155 ....G-7
Carthage, 927 ....K-11
Cass, 150 ....I-6
CASS CO., 38966....F-8
Cassville, 120 ....G-9
Castleton *A-20
Cataract, 50 ....L-6
Cates, 125 ....I-4
Catlin, 100 ....K-5
Cato, 30 ....Q-5
Cayuga, 1162 ....J-4
Cedar Grv., 156 .....L-13
Cedar Lake, 11560 ...C-4
Celestine, 250 ......Q-6
Center, 250 ....Q-9
Center Pt., 50 ....L-6
Center Sq., 20 ....O-13
Centerton, 200 ......M-8
Centerville, 2552 ...J-13
Central, 35 ....S-9
Central Barren, 120..O-9
Ceylon, 60 ....F-13
Chalmers, 508 ....F-6
Chambersburg, 50 ....M-9
Chandler, 2867 ....S-4
Chapel Creek, 400 ...M-10
Chapel Hill *E-15
Charlestown, 7585 ...Q-11
Charlottesville, 450..K-11
Chelsea, 125 ....P-11
Chester, 50 ....J-13

Chesterfield, 2547 ...I-11
Chesterton, 13068 ...A-5
Chili, 150 ....E-9
China, ...O-12
Chrisney, 481 ....S-5
Churubusco, 1796 ...C-12
Cicero, 4812 ....H-9
Cincinnati, 50 ....N-7
Circleville, 300 .....K-11
Clark Co.,
  110232 ....Q-10
Clarks Hill, 611 .....H-7
Clarksburg, 149 .....L-12
Clarksville, 21724 ..R-10
Clarksville, 150 .....I-10
Clay City, 861 ....M-5
Claypool, 431 ....C-10
Clayton, 972 ....K-8
Clear Creek, 1200 ...N-7
Clear Lake, 339 ......A-13
Clear Spr., 75 ....O-8
Clermont, 1356 ......J-8
Clifford, 233 ....M-10
Clifton, 4893 ....N-4
Clinton, 4893 ....N-4
CLINTON CO.,
33224 ....H-7
Clinton Falls, 100 ..I-8
Clover Vil., 200 .....O-11
Cloverdale, 2172 ....L-6
Cloverland, 100 .....M-5
Clunette, 75 ....C-10
Clymers, 120 ....E-8
Coal City, 270 ....M-5
Coal Creek, 10 ......J-5
Coalmont, 402 ....M-5
Coatesville, 523 ....K-7
Coesse, 100 ....D-11
Colburn, 193 ....G-6
Cold Sprs., 180 .....B-13
Colfax, 691 ....H-7
Collamer, 50 ....D-10
Collegeville, 330 ...E-5
Collett G-13
Collins, 60 ....C-11
Coloma, 80 ....J-4
Columbia City,
  8750 ....D-11
Columbus, 44061 .....M-10
Commiskey, 150 ......O-11
Connersville, 13481..K-12
Converse, 1265 ....F-10
Cornettsville, 20 ...O-5
Cortland, 175 ....N-9
Corunna, 264 ....B-12
Cory, 135 ....L-5
Corydon, 3122 ....R-9
Country Club Hts.,
  79 ....G-2
Country Vil., 100 ...H-11
Covington, 2645 .....I-4
Cowan, 250 ....I-12
Craigville, 135 ......E-13
Crandall, 152 ....R-9
Crane, 184 ....O-6
Crawford Co.,
  10713 ....Q-7
Crawfordsville, 15915..I-6
Creston, 80 ....B-11
Cromwell, 512 ....C-11
Crooked Lake, 300 ...A-13
Cross Plains, 150 ...N-12
Crothersville, 1591..O-10
Crown Ctr., 30 ......J-13
Crown Pt., 27317 ....B-4
Crows Nest, 73 .....*C-18
Crumstown, 120 ......A-8
Crystal, 100 ....L-8
Culver, 1353 ....C-8
Cumberland, 5169 ...J-9
Cunot, 100 ....L-6
Curtisville, 150 ....H-10
Cutler, 125 ....G-7
Cuzco, 50 ....Q-7
Cyclone, 20 ....H-8
Cynthiana, 545 .....R-3
Dabney, 50 ....N-12
Dale, 1570 ....S-5
Daleville, 1647 .....I-11
Dalton, 40 ....J-13
Dana, 608 ....J-4
Danville, 9001 ......J-7
Darlington, 843 .....H-6
Darmstadt, 1407 ....S-3
Davenport, 100 ......P-6
DAVIESS CO.,
31648 ....O-5
Daylight, 200 ....S-4
Dayton, 1420 ....G-6
De Camp Gdns., 150..D-3
De Gonia, 40 ....S-5
Decatur, 9405 ....E-13
DECATUR CO.,
25740 ....M-11
Decker, 249 ....O-3
Deedsville, 150 .....E-8
Deer Creek, 160 .....F-8
Deerfield, 50 ....G-13
Delaware, 150 ....H-12
DELAWARE CO.,
117671 ....H-11
Delong, 140 ....D-8
Delphi, 2893 ....F-7
Demotte, 3814 ....C-5
Denham, 150 ....D-7
Denver, 482 ....E-9
Deputy, 86 ....O-11
Desoto, 180 ....H-11
Diamond, 150 ....K-5
Dillman, 25 ....O-6
Dillsboro, 1327 .....N-13
Disko, 80 ....D-9
Dixon, 160 ....O-11
Dodd, 150 ....P-9
Dogwood, 30 ....O-9
Dolan, 50 ....M-7
Domestic P-8
Donaldson, 90 ....B-8
Doolittle Mills, 80..R-7
Dover, 100 ....M-13
Dover, 60 ....K-11
Dover Hill, 114 ......P-6
Dublin, 790 ....K-12
Dubois, 846 ....Q-6
DUBOIS CO.,
41889 ....Q-6
Dudleytown, 30 ......O-10
Dugger, 920 ....N-5
Dune Acres, 182 .....A-5
Dunfee, 40 ....D-11
Dunkirk, 2362 ....G-12
Dunlap, 6235 ....A-10
Dunlapsville, 45 ....L-14
Dunnington, 30 ......P-4
Dunns Br., 70 ....D-5

Dunreith, 177 ....J-11
Dupont, 339 ....O-11
Dyer, 16390 ....B-4
Eagle Vil., 120 .....I-8
Eagletown, 30 ....I-9
Earl Pk., 348 ....F-4
E. Chicago, 29698 ...A-4
E. Enterprise, 148 ..O-13
E. Germantown,
  410 ....J-13
Eaton, 1805 ....H-12
Eckerty, 150 ....R-7
Economy, 187 ....I-13
Eden, 80 ....J-11
Edgerton, 100 ....D-14
Edinburgh, 4480 ....L-9
Edna Mills, 40 ......G-7
Edwardsport, 303 ...O-4
Edwardsville, 600 ...R-10
Ege, 30 ....C-12
Ekin, 60 ....H-9
Elberfeld, 625 ......R-4
Elizabeth, 162 ......R-9
Elizabethtown, 504 ..N-10
Elkhart, 51874 .....A-10
Elkhart Co.,
  197559 ....B-9
Ellettsville, 6378 ..M-7
Elnora, 640 ....O-5
Elrod, 60 ....N-12
Elston, 100 ....F-7
Elwood, 8614 ....H-10
Elwon, 30 ....N-7
Eminence, 40 ....L-7
Emison, 154 ....O-4
Emma, 150 ....A-11
Emporia, 50 ....I-11
Enchanted Hills,
  ....B-11
English, 645 ....Q-7
English Lake, 30 ....C-6
Enterprise T-5
Epsom, 30 ....O-5
Etna Green, 586 .....C-9
Eureka, 80 ....T-5
Evansville, 117429 ..S-3
Fair Oaks, 145 ......D-5
Fairbanks, 125 ......M-3
Fairland, 315 ....K-10
Fairmount, 2954 .....G-11
Fairview, 100 ....H-12
Fairview, 100 ....O-13
Fairview Pk., 1386 ..K-4
Falmouth, 125 ....K-12
Farmers Retreat, 60..N-13
Farmersburg, 1118 ..M-4
Farmersville, 150 ...S-2
Farmland, 1333 ......H-13
Fayette, 100 ....J-8
Fayetteville, 100 ...N-7
FAYETTE CO.,
24277 ....K-12
Ferdinand, 2157 .....R-6
Ferguson Hill, 160 ..L-1
Fiat, 30 ....G-13
Fillmore, 533 ....K-6
Fincastle, 30 ....J-6
Fish Lake, 1016 .....B-7
Fishers, 76794 ....J-9
Fishersburg, 120 ...I-10
Five Points, 125 ...K-8
Flat Rock, 250 ......L-11
Fletcher Lake, 40 ...E-8
Flint, 90 ....A-13
Flora, 2036 ....G-7
Florence, 80 ....O-13
Flossie, 100 ....N-8
FLOYD CO., 74578..Q-9
Floyds Knobs, 800 ...Q-10
Folsomville, 50 .....R-5
Fontanet, 423 ....K-5
Foraker, 80 ....A-9
Foresman, 25 ....E-5
Forest Hill, 100 ....M-11
Forest, 100 ....H-8
Ft. Branch, 2771 ....R-3
Ft. Ritner, 80 ......O-8
Ft. Wayne, 253691 ...D-12
Fortville, 3929 .....J-10
Foster, 15 ....J-11
Fountain, 80 ....N-11
Fountain City, 796 ..J-13
FOUNTAIN CO.,
17240 ....I-5
Fountaintown, 150 ..K-10
Fowler, 2317 ....F-5
Fowlerton, 261 ......G-11
Francesville, 879 ...E-6
Francisco, 469 ......Q-4
Frankfort, 16422 ....H-7
Franklin, 23172 .....L-9
FRANKLIN CO.,
23087 ....L-13
Franklin, 19657 .....L-9
Franks Corner, 120 ..G-9
Franklin, 1862 ......N-10
Fredericksburg, 85 ..Q-9
Fredonia, 80 ....R-8
Freedom, 160 ....M-6
Freeland Pk., 50 ....F-4
Freelandville, 643 ..O-4
Freetown, 385 ....N-9
Fremont, 2138 ....A-13
French Lick, 1807 ...P-7
Frenchtown, 30 ......R-8
Friendship, 100 .....N-12
Fritchton, 50 ....O-4
Fulda, 330 ....R-6
Fulton, 333 ....E-8
FULTON CO.,
20836 ....D-8
Gadsden, 30 ....J-11
Galena, 180 ....Q-9
Galveston, 1311 .....F-8
Garden Vil., 400 ....L-1
Garrett, 6286 ....C-12
Gary, 80294 ....A-4
Gas City, 5965 ......G-11
Gaston, 871 ....H-11
Gatchel S-7
Geneva, 1293 ....F-13
Geneva, 100 ....L-11
Genevieve, 268 ......S-5
Georgetown, 2876 ...R-9
Georgetown, 100 .....H-11
Gessie, 80 ....J-4
Gibson City, 30 .....R-4
GIBSON CO.,
33503 ....R-3
Gifford, 45 ....C-11
Gilboa, 25 ....H-11
Gilead, 25 ....E-10
Gilman, 70 ....H-8
Gimco City, 70 ......I-11
Gings, ...K-4
Glen Pk., 30 ....B-4
Glendale, 90 ....P-5
Glenn, 450 ....M-8
Glenwood, 250 ....K-12

Glezen, 100 ....Q-4
Gnaw Bone, 125 ......M-9
Goblesville, 75 .....D-11
Goldsmith, 225 ......H-9
Goodland, 1043 ......F-4
Goodman, 30 ....H-10
Goshen, 31719 ....B-10
Gosport, 826 ....L-7
Grabill, 1053 ....C-13
Grammer, 160 ....M-10
Grandview, 749 ......S-5
Granger, 30465 ......A-9
Grantsburg, 30 ......Q-7
GRANT CO.,
70061 ....G-10
Grass Creek, 80 .....E-8
Gravelton, 30 ....B-10
Grayford, 100 ....N-11
Graysville, 135 .....N-3
Green Hill, 125 .....I-4
Greencastle, 10326..K-6
Greendale, 595 ......N-13
GREENE CO.,
33165 ....N-6
Greenfield, 20602 ..J-10
Greens Fork, 423 ...J-13
Greensboro, 180 .....I-11
Greensburg, 11492 ..M-11
Greentown, 2415 .....G-9
Greenville, 595 .....Q-9
Greenwood, 49791 ...K-9
Griffin, 172 ....R-2
Griffith, 16893 .....B-4
Groveland, 75 ....J-6
Grovertown, 150 .....C-7
Guilford, 150 ....M-13
Guion, 30 ....J-5
Guthrie, 25 ....N-7
Gwynneville, 250 ...K-11
Hackleman, 40 ....G-10
Hadley, 60 ....K-7
Hagerstown, 1787 ...J-12
Halbert, 100 ....L-2
Hall, 100 ....S-7
Hamburg, 100 ....L-12
Hamilton, 1532 .....B-13
HAMILTON CO.,
274569 ....I-9
Hamlet, 800 ....C-7
Hammond, 80830 .....A-4
Hancock Chapel N-7
HANCOCK CO.,
70002 ....J-10
Handy, 125 ....N-7
Hanna, 463 ....B-6
Hanover, 3546 ....P-11
Hardinsburg, 248 ...Q-8
Harlan, 1634 ....C-13
Harmony, 656 ....L-5
Harrisburg, 50 .....K-12
HARRISON CO.,
39364 ....R-9
Harrodsburg, 691 ...N-7
Hartford, 40 ....N-13
Hartford City, 6220..G-12
Hartsville, 362 .....M-10
Hartzel, 200 ....P-8
Harveysburg, 40 .....J-5
Haskell, 25 ....B-6
Hatfield, 813 ....S-5
Haubstadt, 1577 ....R-3
Havana, 30 ....N-11
Hayden, 350 ....N-10
Hazelwood, 250 ......K-7
Hazleton, 263 ....Q-3
Headlee, 45 ....F-5
Heath Q-7
Hebron, 3724 ....C-5
Hedrick, 55 ....H-4
Heilman P-5
Helmer, 81 ....B-12
Heltonville, 500 ....O-8
Hemlock, 150 ....G-9
Henderson, 40 ....K-13
Heirdom, 100 ....R-8
HENDRICKS CO.,
145448 ....K-7
Hendricksville, 70 ..M-7
Henryville, 1905 ....P-10
Herbst, 112 ....F-12
Heritage Lake, 1300..K-7
Hessler, 150 ....S-3
Highland, 4489 ......S-2
Highland, 23727 ....*M-11
Hillham, 75 ....P-6
Hillisburg, 180 .....H-8
Hillsboro, 538 ......I-5
Hillsdale, 250 ......K-4
Hitchcock J-7
Hoagland, 821 ....E-13
Hobart, 29059 ......*M-13
Hobbieville, 100 ...N-7
Hobbs, 170 ....H-9
Holland, 626 ....R-5
Holton, 480 ....N-11
Home Pl., 1300 .....I-9
Homer, 200 ....K-11
Honey Creek, 120 ...H-11
Hoosier Highlands,
  100 ....L-6
Hope, 2102 ....M-10
Hortonville, 200 ...I-10
Houston, 60 ....O-9
Howard, 30 ....N-7
HOWARD CO.,
20836 ....G-8
Howe, 807 ....A-11
Howell T-12
Howesville, 30 ......M-5
Hudson, 518 ....B-13
Hudson Lake, 1297 ..A-7
Huntertown, 4810 ...C-12
Huntingburg, 6057 ..R-6
Huntington, 17391 ..E-11
HUNTINGTON CO.,
37124 ....E-11
Huntsville, 40 ......K-12
Huron, 300 ....O-7
Hyde Pk., 200 ....S-3
Hymera, 801 ....N-4
Idaville, 461 ....F-7
Ijamsville, 70 ......Q-6
Independence, 100 ..G-5
Indian Hts., 3011 ..G-9
Indian Spr., 60 ....O-6
Indian Vil., 30 ...*I-19
Indiana Bch., 80 ...E-7
Indianapolis, 820445..J-9
Ingalls, 2394 ....J-10
Ingersol, 30 ....I-11
Intake, 30 ....Q-9
Ireland, 450 ....Q-5
Irvington J-2

Jackson Co.,
  42376 ....O-9
Jacksonburg, 100 ...J-13
Jalapa, 100 ....F-10
Jamestown, 958 ......I-7
Jamestown, 500 ......A-13
Jamestown, 300 ......I-9
Jasonville, 2222 ....M-5
Jasper, 15038 ....Q-6
JASPER CO., 33478..D-5
JAY CO., 21253.....G-13
JEFFERSON CO.,
32428 ....O-11
Jeffersonville,
  44953 ....R-10
Jennings Co.,
  28525 ....N-10
Jerome, 100 ....G-10
Jessup, 40 ....K-5
Jewell Vil., 700 ....M-10
Johnson, 75 ....R-3
JOHNSON CO.,
139654 ....L-9
Johnstown, 60 ....I-12
Jolietville, 250 ....I-9
Jonesboro, 1756 .....G-11
Jonesville, 177 .....N-10
Jordan, 75 ....J-7
Judah, 60 ....O-7
Judyville, 60 ....H-4
Julietta J-2
Kasson, 150 ....S-3
Kempton, 335 ....H-8
Kendallville, 9862 ..B-12
Kennard, 471 ....I-11
Kent, 70 ....O-11
Kentland, 1748 ......F-4
Keowna, 613 ....D-8
Keystone, 152 ....F-12
Kilmore, 45 ....H-8
Kimball, 822 ....Q-8
Kimmell, 423 ....B-11
Kingman, 511 ....I-4
Kingsbury, 242 ......B-6
Kingsford Hts., 1435..B-7
Kingsland, 75 ......E-12
Kirklin, 788 ....H-8
Kirkpatrick H-6
Kirksville N-7
Kitchel, 25 ....K-13
Klondike F-6
Knightstown, 2182 ..J-11
Knightsville, 872 ...L-5
Kniman, 75 ....D-5
Knob Hill N-7
Knox, 3704 ....C-7
KNOX CO., 38440....P-4
Kokomo, 45468 ....G-9
Koleen, 60 ....N-6
Koontz Lake, 1557 ..B-7
KOSCIUSKO CO.,
77358 ....C-10
Kossuth P-9
Kouts, 1879 ....C-5
Kramer, 90 ....H-5
Kurtz, 125 ....N-8
Kyana, 30 ....Q-6
La Crosse, 551 ......C-6
La Fontaine, 875 ...F-10
La Paz, 561 ....B-8
Laconia, 30 ....S-9
Ladoga, 985 ....J-6
Lafayette, 67140 ...G-6
Lagrange, 2625 .....A-11
LAGRANGE CO.,
37128 ....B-11
Lagro, 415 ....E-10
L. Bruce, 150 ....D-8
L. Cicott, 100 .....F-7
LAKE CO., 496005..C-4
L. Dalecarlia, 1355..C-4
L. Eliza, 600 ....C-5
L. Holiday, 750 ....A-9
L. James, 800 ......A-13
Lake of the Woods,
  700 ....B-8
Lake on the Green, ..N-8
Lake Sta., 12572 ...*M-14
Lake Village, 765 ..D-4
Lakes of the
  Four Seasons, 7033..B-5
Laketon, 450 ....E-10
Lakeville, 786 ......B-8
Lamar, 100 ....S-6
Lancaster, 100 ......B-13
Lanesville, 564 .....R-9
Laotto, 250 ....C-12
Lapel, 2068 ....I-10
Laporte, 22053 ......A-6
LAPORTE CO.,
111467 ....B-7
Larwill, 283 ....D-11
Laud, 100 ....D-11
Laughery N-12
Lawrence, 46001 .....J-9
Lawrenceburg,
  5042 ....N-14
Lawrenceport, 100 ..O-8
Lawrenceville, 70 ...I-13
Lawton, 30 ....P-7
Leases Cor. B-6
Leavenworth, 238 ...R-8
Lebanon, 15792 ......I-7
Lee, 25 ....J-11
Leesburg, 555 ....C-10
Leesville, 60 ....O-8
Leipsic, 90 ....P-5
Leisure, 30 ....H-10
Leiters Ford, 200 ..D-8
Lena, 70 ....O-4
Leo-Cedarville,
  3603 ....C-13
Leopold, 100 ....R-7
Leota, 40 ....P-10
Leroy, 200 ....C-5
Letts, 150 ....M-10
Lewis, 175 ....M-5
Lewisburg, 100 ......J-11
Lewisville, 366 .....J-11
Lexington, 450 ......P-11
Liberty, 2133 ....L-13
Liberty, 100 ....L-11
Liberty Ctr., 220 ..E-12
Liberty Mills, 100 ..D-11
Ligonier, 4405 ......B-11
Lincoln, 90 ....R-8
Lincoln City, 100 ..S-5
Lincolnville, 150 ...E-11
Linden, 759 ....H-6
Linkville, 30 ....B-9
Linnsburg, 60 ....I-6
Linton, 5413 ....N-5
Linwood, 170 ....H-10
Lisbon, 20 ....E-12
Little York, 230 ....O-10
Livonia, 128 ....O-8
Lizton, 459 ....J-7
Locke, 80 ....B-10
Lockport, 70 ....F-7

Lodi, 85 ....J-4
Logansport, 18396 ..F-8
Lomax, 30 ....J-13
London, 100 ....K-10
Long Bch., 1179 .....A-6
Loogootee, 2751 .....P-6
Lookout R-8
Lorane P-6
Lottaville, 2387 ....A-4
Louisville R-8
Lovett, 65 ....O-11
Lowell, 8276 ....C-4
Lower Sunset Pk.,
  120 ....B-4
Lucerne, 130 ....E-8
Lyford, 400 ....K-4
Lynn, 1097 ....I-13
Lynnville, 888 ......R-4
Lyons, 742 ....N-5
Mace, 150 ....I-6
Mackey, 106 ....R-4
Macy, 209 ....E-9
Madison, 11967 ......O-12
MADISON CO.,
131636 ....H-10
Magnet, 40 ....S-7
Majenica, 25 ....E-11
Malden, 120 ....C-5
Manchester, 420 ....K-13
Manhattan, 50 ......K-6
Manilla, 267 ....K-11
Mansfield, 30 ....L-5
Manson, 35 ....H-7
Maple Lane *I-20
Maples, 100 ....D-13
Maplewood, 50 ....K-9
Marco, 100 ....N-6
Marengo, 828 ....Q-8
Mariah Hill, 300 ...R-6
Marietta, 200 ....L-10
Marion, 29948 ....G-11
Markland O-12
Markle, 1095 ....E-12
Markleville, 528 ...I-11
Mars Hill *F-17
Marshall, 324 ....J-5
MARSHALL CO.,
47051 ....C-8
Marshfield, 60 .....H-4
Martin, 463 ....J-11
Martinsburg, 150 ...P-9
Martinsville, 11828..L-8
Maryland, 800 ....M-2
Marysville, 150 .....P-11
Matthews, 596 ....G-11
Mauckport, 81 ....S-9
Max, 50 ....H-7
Maxinkuckee C-8
Maxwell, 200 ....J-10
Mays, 175 ....K-11
Maysville, 150 ......H-12
Maywood *F-17
McCordsville, 4797 ..J-10
McCoysburg, 40 .....E-5
McCutchanville, 300..S-3
McGrawsville, 70 ...G-9
McRoss, 347 ....J-11
Meadowbrook, 200 ...I-9
Medaryville, 614 ...D-6
Medford, 80 ....H-7
Medora, 693 ....O-9
Mellott, 197 ....H-5
Melody Hill, 3628 ..S-3
Mentone, 1001 ....D-9
Mentor R-7
Meridian Hills,
  1616 ....*B-18
Merom, 228 ....N-3
Merriam, 80 ....C-11
Merrillville, 35246..B-4
Metamora, 974 ....L-13
Metea, 60 ....E-8
Metz, 90 ....A-13
Mexico, 836 ....E-9
Miami, 325 ....F-9
MIAMI CO., 36903..F-9
Michiana Shores,
  313 ....A-6
Michigan City,
  31479 ....A-6
Michigantown, 467 ..H-8
Middleboro, 200 ....J-14
Middlebury, 3420 ...A-10
Middlefork H-7
Middletown, 2322 ..I-11
Middletown, 100 ....L-11
Middletown Pk., 850..J-1
Midland, 100 ....N-5
Mier, 78 ....G-10
Milan, 1899 ....N-12
Milford, 1562 ....B-10
Milford, 150 ....J-13
Milledgeville H-8
Millersburg, 949 ...B-10
Millersville J-2
Millersport *I-19
Milligan, 35 ....J-5
Millport O-10
Milltown, 843 ....Q-8
Milroy, 590 ....L-11
Milton, 490 ....J-12
Miltonville, 300 ...S-5
Mishawaka, 48252 ...A-9
Mitchell, 4350 .....P-7
Model, 196 ....J-13
Modoc, 220 ....I-13
Mongo, 200 ....A-11
Monon, 1682 ....E-6
Monroe, 777 ....F-12
Monroe City, 545 ...P-4
MONROE CO.,
137974 ....M-7
Monroeville, 1235 ..E-13
Monrovia, 1063 ......L-7
Monterey, 218 ......D-7
Montezuma, 1022 ...J-4
Montgomery, 343 ...P-5
MONTGOMERY CO.,
38124 ....J-6

Mooresville, 9326 ...K-8
Moran, 75 ....H-7
MORGAN CO.,
68894 ....L-7
Morgantown, 986 .....L-8
Morocco, 1129 ....E-4
Morris, 300 ....M-12
Morristown, 1218 ...K-10
Morton, 100 ....J-6
Moscow, 100 ....L-11
Mt. Auburn, 117 ....L-12
Mt. Auburn, 45 .....L-10
Mt. Ayr, 122 ....E-4
Mt. Carmel, 86 .....L-14
Mt. Comfort, 300 ...J-10
Mt. Etna, 94 ....F-11
Mt. Meridian, 50 ...K-6
Mt. Pleasant, 70 ..I-12
Mt. Pleasant P-7
Mt. Sterling, 25 ...O-13
Mt. Summit, 352 ....I-12
Mt. Vernon, 6687 ...T-2
Mt. Zion, 30 ....I-12
Mulberry, 1254 ......H-7
Muncie, 70085 ......H-12
Munster, 23603 .....B-4
Murray, 110 ....G-12
Nabb, 150 ....P-11
Napoleon, 234 ......M-12
Nappanee, 6648 .....B-9
Nashville, 803 ......M-8
Nebraska, 90 ....N-11
Needham, 80 ....L-9
Needmore, 150 ....N-8
Needmore, 30 ....M-8
Nevada Mills, 30 ...A-13
New Albany, 36372 ..R-10
New Alsace, 150 .....M-13
New Amsterdam, 27 ..S-8
New Boston, 45 .....J-11
New Boston, 70 .....R-7
New Brunswick, 30 ..J-7
New Carlisle, 1861 ..A-7
New Castle, 18114 ..I-12
New Chicago,
  2035 ....*M-13
New Columbus, 125..I-11
New Corydon, 100 ..G-13
New Elliott, 800 ..*N-12
New Frankfort, 20 ..N-10
New Goshen, 390 ....K-4
New Harmony, 789 ...R-2
New Lebanon, 120 ...M-3
New Lisbon, 200 ....J-12
New Marion, 120 ....N-12
New Market, 636 ....I-6
New Maysville, 60 ..J-6
New Middleton, 93 ..R-9
New Mt. Pleasant,
  20 ....H-13
New Palestine,
  2055 ....J-10
New Paris, 1494 ....B-10
New Pekin, 1401 ....Q-9
New Philadelphia, 60..P-9
New Pittsburg, 35 ..I-13
New Pt., 331 ....M-12
New Richmond, 333 ..H-6
New Ross, 347 ......I-7
New Salem, 200 .....L-12
New Salisbury, 613 ..R-9
New Trenton, 252 ...M-13
New Washington,
  566 ....P-11
New Waverly, 150 ...F-8
New Whiteland,
  5472 ....K-9
New Winchester, 70 ..J-7
Newark, 75 ....N-6
Newberry, 193 ......O-5
Newburgh, 3325 .....S-4
Newburg, 100 ....R-6
Newport, 515 ....J-4
NEWTON CO.,
14244 ....D-4
Newtonville, 90 .....S-6
Newtown, 256 ....H-5
Niblack, 120 ....O-4
Nineveh, 250 ....L-8
NOBLE CO.,
47536 ....C-12
Noblesville, 51969 ..I-9
Norman, 100 ....N-9
Norris *A-18
North, 100 ....J-6
Norristown, 40 .....L-10
N. Crows Nest, 45 ..*B-18
N. Grove, 120 ......F-9
N. Hayden N-10
N. Judson, 1772 ....C-7
N. Liberty, 1896 ...B-8
N. Manchester,
  6112 ....D-10
N. Salem, 518 ......J-7
N. Terre Haute, 4305..L-4
N. Vernon, 6728 ....N-10
N. Webster, 1146 ...C-10
Norway, 36 ....F-7
Notre Dame, 5973..*I-19
Nottingham, 30 .....S-6
Nulltown, 60 ....K-12
Nyesville, 30 ....J-5
Oak Forest, 100 ....L-12
Oaktown, 608 ....O-4
Oakville, 210 ......H-12
Oatsville, 40 ....P-4
Oceola, 2463 ....A-9
Odell, 80 ....J-7
Odon, 1424 ....O-5

Owensburg, 406 ......O-7
Owensville, 1284 ...R-3
Oxford, 1162 ....G-4
Packerton, 90 ....D-10
Palestine, 300 .....M-11
Palmyra, 930 ....Q-9
Paoli, 3677 ....P-8
Paragon, 659 ....L-7
Paris Crossing, 100..O-11
PARKE CO., 17339..J-5
Parker City, 1419 ..H-12
Parr, 150 ....E-5
Patoka, 735 ....R-3
Patricksburg, 275 ..M-6
Patriot, 209 ....O-13
Patronville, 30 ....S-5
Paxton, 300 ....N-4
Paynesville, 30 .....K-4
Pekin, 1374 ....Q-9
Pence, 85 ....H-4
Pendleton, 4253 ....I-10
Pennton, 120 ....H-7
Pennville, 701 ......G-12
Pennville, 100 .....Q-6
Peoga, 100 ....M-9
Peoria, 50 ....E-7
Peppertown, 201 ....M-12
Perkinsville, 150 ..I-10
PERRY CO., 19338..S-5
Perrysburg, 50 .....E-9
Perrysville, 454 ...J-4
Peru, 11417 ....E-9
Petersburg, 2383 ...Q-5
Petersville, 200 ...M-10
Petroleum, 150 .....F-12
Pheasant Run,
  1200 ....E-4
Philadelphia, 300 ..J-10
Philomath, 35 ....L-13
Phlox, 100 ....P-5
Pickard, 60 ....E-7
Pierceton, 1015 ....C-11
Pike P-5
PIKE CO., 12845....Q-5
Pimento, 125 ....L-4
Pine Lake, 1700 ....A-6
Pine Vil., 177 .....H-5
Pinhook, 40 ....P-8
Pinola, 50 ....B-7
Pittsboro, 2928 ....J-7
Pittsburg, 50 ......J-11
Plainfield, 27631 ..J-8
Plainville, 476 .....O-5
Plato, 20 ....M-9
Pleasant Lake, 500 ..B-13
Pleasant Mills, 156..E-13
Pleasant View, 100 ..K-9
Plevna, 70 ....G-9
Plum Tree, 25 ......F-11
Plymouth, 10033 ....C-8
Poe, 110 ....E-13
Point Isabel, 70 ...G-10
Poland, 150 ....L-6
Poneto, 369 ....F-12
Porter, 4858 ....A-5
Portage, 36608 .....A-5
Portersville, 120 ..Q-6
Portland, 6223 .....G-13
POSEY CO., 25910..S-2
Poseyville, 1045 ...R-3
Potato Creek, 250 ..M-8
Preble, 140 ....E-13
Princes Lakes, 1312..L-9
Princeton, 8644 ....Q-3
Progress, 40 ....L-7
Prospect, 100 ......P-7
Providence, 75 .....R-8
Pulaski, 150 ....E-7
PULASKI CO.,
13402 ....D-7
Putnamville, 160 ..K-6
Pyrmont, 220 ....G-6
Queensville, 100 ...N-10
Quercus Grv., 50 ...C-12
Quincy, 150 ....L-7
Raccoon, 30 ....K-5
Radioville, 40 ......D-4
Ragersville, 141 ...K-14
Ragsdale, 170 ......O-4
Rainsville, 50 .....H-5
Raleigh, 30 ....K-11
Ramsey, 200 ....R-9
RANDOLPH CO.,
26171 ....H-13
Raub, 100 ....G-4
Ravenswood J-2
Ray, 60 ....A-13
Rays Crossing, 60 ..K-10
Reddington, 200 ....N-10
Redkey, 1353 ....G-12
Reelsville, 150 .....K-6
Remington, 1185 ....E-5
Rensselaer, 5859 ...E-5
Reynolds, 533 ......F-6
Richland, 50 ....S-4
Richland City, 425 ..S-5
Richmond, 36812 ....J-14
Richvalley, 120 ....E-10
Rigdon, 60 ....G-10
Riley, 221 ....L-4
Rileysburg, 100 ....J-4
Riley, 221 ....L-4
Rising Sun, 2347 ...N-13
Rivare, 60 ....E-13
Riverside, 75 ......R-9
Riverton, 25 ....L-4
Riverview, 90 ......J-3
Roachdale, 926 .....J-6
Roann, 479 ....E-10
Roanoke, 1722 ......E-11
Rob Roy, 50 ....H-5
Robertsdale *L-11
Robinwood, 150 .....H-7
Rochester, 6218 ....D-8
Rockfield, 100 .....F-7
Rockford, 450 ......N-9
Rockland, 120 .....K-11
Rockport, 2160 .....S-5
Rockville, 2607 ....J-5
Rocky Ripple, 606 ..*C-18
Roll, 30 ....F-11
Rolling Hills, 450 ..H-10
Rolling Prairie, 582..A-7
Rome, 100 ....S-7
Rome City, 1361 ....B-11
Romney, 450 ....H-6

Ogden, 100 ....J-11
Ogden Dunes, 1313 ..A-5
Ohio Co., 6128 ....N-13
Oldenburg, 674 .....M-12
Olean, 150 ....M-13
Olin, 75 ....B-12
Ontario, 230 ....A-11
Oolitic, 1184 ......O-7
Ora, 30 ....D-7
Orange, 80 ....K-12
Orange, 40 ....H-11
ORANGE CO.,
19840 ....P-7
Orestes, 414 ....H-10
Oriole R-7
Orland, 424 ....A-12
Orleans, 2242 ......O-8
Osceola, 2483 .....A-9
Osgood, 1624 ....N-12
Ossian, 3289 ....E-12
Oswego, 100 ....C-10
Otis, 80 ....A-6
Otisco, 500 ....Q-10
Otterbein, 1262 ...G-5
Otwell, 434 ....Q-5
Overpeck, 50 ....F-13
Owen Co., 21575..M-6

seburg K-13
sedale, 725 K-4
seland, 630 A-8
selawn, 4131 D-4
ss, 47890 B-4
sston, 50 I-8
ssville, 1653 G-7
th Pk., 150 F-7
yal Ctr., 861 E-7
yalton, 50 J-8
yerton, 900 H-12
gby, 50 M-10
SH CO., 17392 K-11
sshville, 6341 K-11
ssellville, 358 J-6
ssiaville, 1094 G-8
Anthony, 400 R-6
Bernice, 646 K-4
Croix, 60 R-7
Henry, 130 R-6
Joe, 460 C-13
John, 14850 B-4
Joseph, 75 S-3
JOSEPH CO.,
66931 B-8
Leon, 678 M-13
Louis Crossing,
M-10
Marks, 100 R-6
Mary-of-the-Woods,
97 L-4
Meinrad, 706 R-6
Omer, 75 L-11
Paul, 1031 L-11
Peter, 70 M-13
Philip, 500 S-3
Wendel, 500 R-3
amonia, 157 G-14
em, 6319 P-9
em, 40 H-14
em F-14
ine City, 90 L-5
tillo, 92 P-8
maria, 75 L-9
n Jacinto N-11
n Pierre, 144 C-6
ndborn, 415 O-5
ndusky, 60 L-11
nta Claus, 2481 S-6
nta Fe, 100 F-9
ratoga, 254 H-13
rdinia, 125 M-11
chererville, 29243 B-4
aneider, 277 D-4
nellville, 250 Q-6
pio, 153 N-10
pio, 30 L-14
ircleville, 140 H-8
otland, 134 O-6
otl, 60 A-11
ott City, 15 M-4
OTT CO., 24181 P-10
ottsburg, 6747 P-10
alia, 130 G-7
elyville, 1029 L-4
ellersburg, 6128 Q-10
ma, 866 H-12
vin, 50 R-5
via, 180 E-10
vastopol, 30 D-9
ton, 60 K-11
ymour, 17503 N-10
adeland, 1610 G-6
amrock Lakes,
31 G-11
annondale, 35 I-7
arpsville, 607 G-9
elburn, 1252 M-4
elby, 539 C-4
ELBY CO.,
4436 L-10
elbyville, 19191 L-10
eridan, 2665 I-8
rdel, 160 H-12
oshewana, 658 A-11
ickville, 100 K-4
dley, 830 K-11
dals, 756 P-6
lver Lake, 915 C-10
rre Acres *B-18
eria, 50 R-6
ey, 83 D-10
ler Lake, 915 D-10
mith, 70 O-14
erwood, 50 J-4
onton Lake,
678 A-9
a, 20 E-7
uth Valley, 1800 K-8
uthfield, 30 H-12
uthville, 200 N-7
ude S-2
uth, 200 N-6
erset, 401 F-10
erville, 293 R-4
nerd, 101168 R-4
ncer, 75 N-12
enter, 150 B-7
ate, 40 M-13
lilford, 200 B-12
Washington, 220 P-5
Whitley, 1751 D-11
thport, 1712 K-9
thwest, 50 B-9
thwood, 500 M-2
rock, 50 O-8
rta, 75 N-13
tanburg, 110 I-14
arsville, 40 M-9
ed, 300 Q-10
edway, 11812 J-8
icherville, 30 E-10
itterville, 500 K-2
ncer, 2217 M-6
NCER CO.,
952 S-5
ncerville, 350 C-13
eland, 890 I-11
ytown, 50 N-9
ing Grv., 344 I-13
ing Hills, 98 *C-17
ing Lake, 218 J-10
ingport, 149 I-12
ingvalle, 300 O-7
urgeon, 207 R-4
er R-3
ford, 100 N-7
City, 344 F-7
RKE CO.,
363 C-7
e Line, 143 H-4
nton, 534 L-5
ndal, 150 R-3
UBEN CO.,
185 B-13
venson S-4
vartsville, 180 R-2
esville, 316 K-7
well, 275 B-7
esville, 198 M-7
ckdale E-9
kwell, 545 H-6
e Head N-9

Stonebluff, 120 I-5
Stones Crossing, 150 K-9
Story N-8
Straughn, 222 J-12
Stroh, 400 B-12
Sullivan, 4249 N-4
SULLIVAN CO.,
21475 N-4
Sulphur, 100 R-7
Sulphur Sprs., 399 I-11
Sumava Resorts, 300 D-4
Summitville, 967 H-11
Sunman, 1049 M-13
Sunshine Gdns. *F-17
Swan, 55 C-12
Swanington, 60 F-4
Swayzee, 981 G-10
Sweetser, 1229 G-10
Switz City, 293 N-5
SWITZERLAND CO.,
10613 O-13
Sycamore, 90 G-10
Sycamore Pk., 120 K-11
Sylvania J-4
Syracuse, 2810 B-10
Tab, 60 G-4
Talbot, 40 G-4
Talma, 130 D-9
Tampico, 60 O-9
Tangier, 30 J-4
Taswell, 130 Q-7
Taylorsville, 919 M-9
Taylorville, 104 L-1
Teegarden, 160 B-8
Tefft, 100 D-6
Tell City, 7272 S-6
Templeton, 120 G-5
Tennyson, 279 S-5
Terhune, 90 I-8
Terre Haute, 60785 L-4
Tetersburg, 50 H-9
Thayer, 400 D-4
Thomaston, 20 C-6
Thornhope, 150 E-7
Thorntown, 1520 I-7
Thurman, 40 *L-20
Tilden I-8
Tiosa, 150 D-9
Tippecanoe, 350 C-9
TIPPECANOE CO.,
172780 H-6
Tipton, 5106 H-9
TIPTON CO., 15936 H-9
Toad Hop, 108 L-1
Tobinsport T-7
Tocsin, 120 E-13
Tolleston *M-12
Topeka, 1153 B-11
Toto, 200 C-7
Town of Pines, 708 A-6
Townley D-13
Tracy, 200 B-7
Traders Pt. *B-15
Trafalgar, 1101 L-9
Trail Creek, 2052 A-6
Travisville, 30 F-12
Treaty, 30 F-10
Trenton, 35 G-12
Trevlac, 150 M-8
Tri-Lakes, 1421 C-11
Trinity Sprs., 60 O-6
Troy, 385 S-6
Tunker D-11
Tunnelton, 120 O-8
Turner, 100 L-5
Twelve Mile, 225 E-8
Twin Lakes, 200 C-8
Tyner, 250 B-8
Ulen, 117 I-8
Underwood, 200 P-10
Union, 90 Q-4
Union City, 3584 H-14
UNION CO., 7516 K-13
Union Mills, 400 B-6
Unionale, 310 E-12
Unionport I-13
Uniontown, 60 O-10
Unionville, 150 M-8
Universal, 362 K-4
Upland, 3845 G-11
Urbana, 350 E-10
Utica, 776 Q-11
Valeene, 130 Q-8
Valentine, 50 B-11
Valley City, 35 S-8
Valley Mills *F-16
Vallonia, 336 O-9
Valparaiso, 31730 B-5
Van Bibber Lake, 485 K-6
Van Buren, 864 F-11
Van Buren Pk., 700 R-12
Vandalia, 35 M-6
VANDERBURGH CO.,
179703 R-3
Veedersburg, 2180 I-5
Velpen, 150 Q-5
Vera Cruz, 80 F-13
VERMILLION CO.,
16212 J-4
Vernon, 318 N-11
Versailles, 2113 N-12
Vevay, 1683 O-13
Vicksburg, 200 N-5
Vienna, 120 P-10
Vigo M-4
VIGO CO., 107848 M-4
Vincennes, 18423 P-3
Wabash, 10666 E-10
WABASH CO.,
32888 E-10
Wadena, 35 F-5
Wadesville, 500 R-2
Wakarusa, 1758 B-9
Waldron, 804 L-10
Walesboro, 125 N-10
Walkerton, 2144 B-7
Wallace, 105 I-5
Walnut D-9
Walton, 1049 F-8
Wanamaker *F-20
Wanatah, 1048 B-6
Warren, 1239 F-11
WARREN CO.,
8508 G-4
Warren Pk., 1480 *D-20
Warrenton, 110 R-3
WARRICK CO.,
59689 R-4
Warrington, 50 I-11
Warsaw, 13559 C-10
Washington, 11509 P-5
WASHINGTON CO.,
28262 P-9
Waterford, 350 B-6
Waterford Mills,
200 B-10
Waterloo, 2242 B-13
Waterloo K-13
Watson, 500 Q-10
Waugh I-8
Waveland, 420 J-5
Waverly, 200 K-8

Wawaka, 200 B-11
Wawpecong, 70 F-9
Waymansville, 75 N-9
WAYNE CO.,
68917 J-13
Waynedale *M-18
Waynesburg, 35 M-11
Waynesville, 160 N-10
Waynetown, 958 I-5
Webster, 250 J-13
WELLS CO., 27636 F-12
W. Baden Sprs., 574 P-7
W. College Cor., 676 K-14
W. Elwood, 100 H-10
W. Fork R-7
W. Franklin, 150 S-3
W. Harrison, 289 M-14
W. Lafayette, 29596 G-6
W. Lebanon, 723 H-4
W. Middleton, 225 G-8
W. Newton *G-16
W. Terre Haute, 2236 L-4
Westfield, 30068 I-9
Westlawn, 700 D-12
Westphalia, 202 O-5
Westpoint, 594 H-5
Westport, 1379 M-11
Westville, 5853 B-6
Westwood, 150 J-11
Wheatfield, 853 C-5
Wheatland, 480 P-4
Wheeler, 443 B-5
Wheeling, 100 H-11
Wheeling, 30 G-8
Whitcomb, 60 L-13
Whitcomb Hts., 300 L-4
WHITE CO., 24643 F-6
Whitehall, 50 M-7
Whiteland, 4169 L-9
Whitestown, 2867 I-8
Whitesville, 60 J-6
Whitewater, 83 J-14
Whitfield, 100 P-5
Whiting, 4997 *K-11
WHITLEY CO.,
33292 D-11
Wilders C-6
Wildwood Lake, 70 Q-7
Wilfred, 40 M-4
Wilkinson, 449 J-11
Williams, 286 O-7
Williams, 60 E-13
Williams Creek, 407 J-9
Williamsburg, 360 J-13
Williamsport, 1898 H-4
Williamstown, 40 L-11
Willow Branch, 150 J-10
Wilmington, 150 N-13
Wilmot, 60 C-11
Winamac, 2490 D-7
Winchester, 4935 H-13
Windfall, 708 H-9
Windsor, 110 I-12
Winfield, 4383 B-5
Wingate, 263 H-5
Winona, 200 C-8
Winona Lake, 4908 C-10
Winslow, 864 Q-5
Wirt, 25 O-11
Wolcott, 1001 F-5
Wolcottville, 998 B-12
Wolflake, 250 C-11
Woodburn, 1520 D-13
Woodbury, 150 J-10
Woodland, 60 B-9
Woodland Pk., 200 I-3
Woodlawn Hts., 79 G-2
Woodridge L-2
Woodruff, 35 B-12
Wooster, 35 C-10
Worthington, 1463 N-6
Wyatt, 400 B-9
Wynnedale, 231 *C-17
Yankeetown, 250 S-4
Yeddo, 110 I-5
Yeoman, 139 F-7
Yoder, 250 E-12
Yorktown, 9405 H-11
Young America, 235 G-8
Youngstown, 100 L-4
Yountsville, 100 I-6
Zanesville, 600 E-12
Zenas, 40 N-11
Zionsville, 14160 J-8
Zulu, 40 D-13

Iowa

Page locator
Map keys	Atlas pages
1–10	78–79
11–20	80–81

* City keyed to p. 68
† City keyed to p. 128

Abingdon, 80 K-14
Ackley, 1589 E-11
Ackworth, 83 J-10
Adair, 781 J-7
ADAIR CO., 7682 J-7
ADAMS CO., 4029 L-6
Adaza G-7
Adel, 3682 I-8
Afton, 845 K-8
Agency, 638 K-13
Ainsworth, 567 J-16
Akron, 1486 D-1
Albert City, 699 D-6
Albia, 3766 K-12
Albion, 505 G-11
Alburnett, 673 G-15
Alden, 787 E-10
Alexander, 175 D-10
Algona, 5560 C-8
ALLAMAKEE CO.,
14330 B-16
Alleman, 432 H-10
Allendorf, 70 B-4
Allerton, 501 L-10
Allison, 1029 D-12
Alpha, 90 C-14
Alta, 1883 E-5
Alta Vista, 266 C-13
Alton, 1216 C-3
Altoona, 14541 I-10
Alvord, 196 B-2
Amana, 442 H-15
Amber, 100 G-17
Ames, 58965 G-10
Anamosa, 5533 G-16
Anderson, 65 L-4
Andover, 103 G-19
Andrew, 434 G-18
Anita, 972 J-6
Ankeny, 45582 H-10
Anthon, 565 F-3
Aplington, 1128 E-12
APPANOOSE CO.,
12887 M-11
Arcadia, 484 G-5
Archer, 131 C-3
Aredale, 74 D-11
Argyle, 100 M-16

Arion, 108 H-4
Arispe, 100 L-8
Arlington, 429 D-15
Armstrong, 926 B-7
Arnolds Pk., 1126 B-5
Artesian E-13
Arthur, 206 F-5
Asbury, 4170 E-18
Ashton, 458 B-3
Aspinwall, 40 H-5
Atalissa, 311 I-17
Athelstan, 19 M-7
Atkins, 1670 G-15
Atlantic, 7112 J-5
Attica, 80 J-11
Auburn, 322 F-6
Audubon, 2176 H-6
AUDUBON CO.,
6119 I-6
Augusta, 100 L-16
Aurelia, 1036 E-4
Aurora, 185 E-15
Austinville, 100 E-11
Avery, 120 K-12
Avoca, 1506 I-4
Ayrshire, 143 C-6
Badger, 561 E-8
Bagley, 303 H-7
Baldwin, 109 G-18
Balltown, 68 E-17
Bancroft, 732 B-8
Bangor, 30 G-11
Bankston, 25 E-17
Barnes City, 176 I-13
Barnum, 191 E-7
Bartlett, 50 L-3
Bassett, 66 C-13
Batavia, 499 K-14
Battle Creek, 713 F-4
Baxter, 1101 H-11
Bayard, 471 H-7
Beacon, 494 J-12
Beaconsfield, 15 L-8
Beaman, 191 G-12
Beaver, 48 G-8
Bedford, 1440 M-6
Beebeetown I-3
Beech, 80 J-10
Belknap, 75 L-13
Belle Plaine, 2534 H-13
Bellevue, 2191 F-19
Belmond, 2376 D-10
Beloit, 70 B-1
Bennett, 405 H-17
Benton, 41 L-7
BENTON CO.,
26076 G-14
Bentonsport, 40 L-15
Berkley, 32 H-8
Bernard, 112 F-18
Bertram, 294 H-16
Berwick, 600 A-20
Bethlehem L-11
Bettendorf, 33217 I-19
Bevington, 63 J-9
Big Rock, 70 H-18
Bingham L-4
Birmingham, 448 L-14
BLACK HAWK CO.,
131090 F-13
Bladensburg K-14
Blairsburg, 215 F-9
Blairstown, 692 H-14
Blakesburg, 296 K-12
Blanchard, 38 M-5
Blencoe, 224 H-3
Blockton, 192 M-7
Bloomfield, 2640 L-13
Blue Grass, 1452 I-18
Bluffton, 50 B-14
Bode, 302 D-8
Bolan, 33 B-11
Bonair B-14
Bonaparte, 433 L-15
Bondurant, 3860 I-10
Boone, 12661 G-9
BOONE CO., 26306 H-9
Booneville, 85 I-9
Botna H-5
Bouton, 129 H-8
Boxholm, 195 G-8
Boyd, 30 C-13
Boyden, 707 C-3
Boyer, 30 G-5
Braddyville, 159 M-5
Bradford, 99 E-11
Bradgate, 86 D-7
Brandon, 309 F-14
Brayton, 128 I-6
Brazil, 90 L-12
Breda, 483 G-6
Bremer, 30 D-13
BREMER CO.,
24276 D-13
Bridgewater, 182 J-6
Brighton, 652 K-15
Bristow, 160 D-12
Britt, 2069 C-9
Bronson, 322 F-2
Brooklyn, 1468 H-13
Brooks, 60 K-6
Brunsville, 151 D-2
Bryant, 35 G-19
Buchanan, 30 H-16
BUCHANAN CO.,
20958 E-15
Buck Grv., 43 H-4
Buckcreek D-14
Buckeye, 108 F-10
Buckingham, 40 F-13
BUENA VISTA CO.,
20260 E-5
Buffalo, 1270 I-18
Buffalo Ctr., 905 B-9
Burchinal, 40 C-11
Burlington, 25663 L-17
Burnside, 130 F-8
Burr Oak, 166 B-15
Burt, 533 C-8
Bussey, 422 K-12
BUTLER CO.,
14867 E-12
Cairo, 30 K-16
Calamus, 439 H-18
CALHOUN CO.,
9670 F-6
California Jct., 85 I-3
Callender, 376 F-8
Calmar, 978 C-15
Calumet, 170 D-4
Camanche, 4448 H-19
Cambria, 50 L-10
Cambridge, 827 H-10
Canby J-7
Canton, 40 G-17
Cantril, 222 M-14
Capitol Hts., 900 B-20
Carbon, 34 K-6
Carl K-6
Carlisle, 3876 I-10
Carmel, 70 C-2
Carnarvon, 60 F-5

Carpenter, 109 B-11
Carroll, 10103 G-6
CARROLL CO.,
20816 G-6
Carson, 812 J-4
Carter Lake, 3785 *B-19
Cartersville E-14
Cascade, 2159 F-17
Casey, 426 I-7
CASS CO., 13956 J-6
Castalia, 173 C-15
Castana, 147 G-3
Cedar, 120 J-13
Cedar Bluff, 60 H-16
CEDAR CO.,
18499 H-17
Cedar Falls, 39260 E-13
Cedar Rapids,
126326 G-15
Cedar Valley, 30 H-16
Cedar View, 50 C-12
Center Jct., 111 G-17
Center Pt., 2421 G-15
Centerville, 5528 L-12
Central City, 1257 G-16
Centralia, 134 E-18
CERRO GORDO CO.,
44151 C-11
Chapin, 87 D-11
Chariton, 4321 K-10
Charles City, 7652 C-12
Charleston, 50 M-16
Charlotte, 394 G-19
Charter Oak, 502 G-4
Chatsworth, 79 D-1
Chelsea, 267 H-13
Cherokee, 5253 D-4
CHEROKEE CO.,
12072 E-3
Chester, 127 B-13
Chickasaw, 40 C-13
CHICKASAW CO.,
12439 C-13
Chillicothe, 97 K-13
Church B-16
Churchville, 50 J-9
Churdan, 386 G-7
Cincinnati, 357 M-12
Clare, 146 E-7
Clarence, 974 H-17
Clarinda, 5572 L-5
Clarion, 2850 E-9
CLARKE CO., 9286 L-9
Clarksville, 1439 D-12
CLAY CO., 16667 C-5
Clayton, 43 D-17
Clayton Ctr., 30 D-16
CLAYTON CO.,
18129 D-15
Clear Lake, 7777 C-10
Clearfield, 363 L-7
Cleghorn, 240 D-4
Clemons, 148 G-11
Clermont, 632 C-15
Cleves, 20 F-11
Climbing Hill, 97 F-2
Clinton, 26885 H-20
CLINTON CO.,
49116 H-19
Clio, 80 M-10
Clive, 15447 I-9
Cloverdale B-4
Clutier, 213 G-13
Coalville, 610 F-8
Coburg, 42 L-5
Coggon, 658 F-16
Coin, 193 M-5
Colesburg, 404 E-17
Colfax, 2093 I-11
College Sprs., 214 M-5
Collins, 495 H-10
Colo, 876 G-10
Columbia, 100 K-11
Columbus City, 391 J-16
Columbus Jct., 1899 J-16
Colwell, 73 C-12
Conesville, 432 J-16
Confidence, 25 L-11
Conrad, 1108 G-12
Conroy, 259 H-14
Conway, 41 L-7
Coon Rapids, 1305 H-6
Cooper, 35 H-7
Coppock, 47 K-15
Coralville, 18907 I-15
Corley, 26 I-5
Cornelia, 80 D-9
Cornell F-5
Corning, 1635 K-6
Correctionville, 821 E-3
Corwith, 309 D-9
Corydon, 1585 L-10
Cotter, 48 J-16
Coulter, 281 E-10
Council Bluffs, 62230 J-3
Covington, 200 H-15
Craig, 89 D-2
Cranston, 40 J-16
CRAWFORD CO.,
17096 G-5
Crawfordsville, 264 J-16
Crescent, 617 J-3
Cresco, 3868 B-14
Creston, 7834 K-7
Cromwell, 107 K-7
Croton, 50 M-15
Crystal Lake, 250 C-9
Cumberland, 262 J-6
Cumming, 351 I-9
Curlew, 58 D-6
Cushing, 220 F-3
Cylinder, 88 C-7
Dakota City, 843 E-8
Dallas Ctr., 1623 H-8
DALLAS CO., 66135 I-8
Dana, 71 G-8
Danbury, 348 F-3
Danville, 934 L-16
Davenport, 99685 I-18
Davis City, 204 M-9
DAVIS CO., 8753 L-13
Dawson, 131 H-8
Dayton, 837 F-8
De Soto, 1050 I-8
De Witt, 5322 H-19
Decatur City, 197 L-9
DECATUR CO.,
8457 M-9
Decorah, 8127 B-15
Dedham, 266 H-6
Deep River, 279 I-13
Defiance, 284 H-4
Delaware, 159 E-16
DELAWARE CO.,
17764 F-16
Delhi, 460 F-16
Delmar, 525 G-18
Deloit, 264 G-5
Delphos, 25 M-7
Delta, 328 J-13
Denison, 8298 G-4
Denmark, 423 L-16

Denver, 1780 E-13
Depew C-7
Derby, 115 L-10
Des Moines, 203433 I-10
DES MOINES CO.,
40325 L-16
Dewar, 250 E-14
Dexter, 611 I-8
Diagonal, 330 L-7
Dickens, 185 C-6
DICKINSON CO.,
16667 B-5
Dike, 1209 F-12
Dillon, 30 H-12
Dinsdale, 40 F-13
Dixon, 247 H-18
Dolliver, 66 B-7
Donahue, 346 H-18
Donnan D-15
Donnellson, 912 M-16
Doon, 577 B-2
Dorchester, 70 B-16
Douds, 152 L-14
Dougherty, 58 D-11
Dow City, 510 H-4
Downey, 100 I-16
Dows, 538 E-10
Drakesville, 184 L-13
Dubuque, 57637 E-18
DUBUQUE CO.,
93653 F-17
Dumont, 637 E-11
Dunbar, 50 H-12
Duncan, 131 C-9
Duncombe, 410 F-8
Dundee, 174 E-16
Dunkerton, 852 E-14
Dunlap, 1042 H-4
Durango, 22 E-18
Durant, 1832 I-17
Dyersville, 4058 E-17
Dysart, 1379 G-13
Eagle Ctr. F-13
Eagle Grv., 3583 E-9
Earlham, 1450 I-8
Earling, 437 H-4
Earlville, 812 E-16
Early, 557 F-5
E. Amana, 56 H-15
E. Peru, 125 J-9
Eddyville, 1024 K-12
Edgewood, 864 E-16
Edna, 20 B-3
Elberon, 196 G-13
Eldon, 928 L-13
Eldora, 2732 F-11
Eldorado, 80 C-15
Eldridge, 5651 I-18
Elgin, 683 D-15
Elk Horn, 662 I-5
Elk Run Hts., 1117 F-13
Elkader, 1273 D-16
Elkhart, 683 H-10
Elkport, 37 D-16
Elliott, 350 K-5
Ellston, 43 L-8
Ellsworth, 531 F-10
Elma, 546 C-13
Elvira, 60 H-19
Elwood, 100 G-18
Ely, 1776 H-15
Emerson, 438 K-4
Emery C-11
EMMET CO.,
10302 B-6
Emmetsburg, 3904 C-7
Epworth, 1860 F-17
Essex, 798 L-5
Estherville, 6360 B-6
Evans, 30 J-12
Evansdale, 4751 F-13
Everly, 603 C-5
Ewart, 30 I-12
Exira, 840 I-6
Exline, 160 M-12
Fairbank, 1113 E-14
Fairfax, 2123 H-15
Fairfield, 9464 K-14
Fairport, 300 J-17
Fairview, 80 G-16
Farley, 1537 F-17
Farlin, 70 G-7
Farmersburg, 302 D-16
Farmington, 664 M-15
Farnhamville, 371 F-7
Farragut, 485 L-4
Farson, 40 K-14
Faulkner, 30 E-11
Fayette, 1338 D-15
FAYETTE CO.,
20880 D-14
Fenton, 279 C-7
Ferguson, 126 H-12
Fern, 30 F-12
Fernald, 90 G-10
Fertile, 370 B-10
Festina, 150 C-15
Finchford, 130 E-13
Flagler, 50 J-11
Florenceville, 40 B-14
Floris, 138 L-13
Floyd, 335 C-12
FLOYD CO.,
16303 C-12
Folletts, 100 H-19
Fonda, 631 E-6
Fontanelle, 672 J-7
Forest City, 4151 B-9
Ft. Atkinson, 349 C-14
Ft. Des Moines D-19
Ft. Dodge, 25206 E-8
Ft. Madison, 11051 M-16
Fostoria, 231 C-5
Franklin, 143 M-16
FRANKLIN CO.,
10680 E-10
Frankville, 150 C-15
Fraser, 102 G-9
Fredericksburg, 931 D-14
Frederika, 183 D-13
Fredonia, 244 J-16
Freeman I-14
Freeport, 150 B-15
Fremont, 743 K-13
FREMONT CO.,
7441 L-4
Froelich C-16
Fruitland, 977 J-17
Fulton, 30 G-18
Galesburg, 70 I-12
Galt, 32 E-10
Galva, 434 E-4
Garber, 88 D-16
Garden City, 89 F-10
Garden Grv., 211 L-10
Gardiner H-8
Garnavillo, 745 D-16
Garner, 3129 C-10
Garrison, 371 G-14
Garwin, 527 G-12
Gaza, 40 C-4
Geneva, 165 E-11

George, 1080 B-3
Georgetown K-11
German Valley B-8
Germantown, 50 D-3
Giard, 40 C-16
Gibson, 61 I-13
Gifford, 100 F-11
Gilbert, 1082 G-9
Gilbertville, 712 F-14
Gillett Grv., 49 C-5
Gilman, 509 H-12
Gilmore City, 504 E-7
Gladbrook, 945 G-12
Glasgow, 30 L-15
Glenwood, 5269 K-3
Glidden, 1146 G-6
Goldfield, 635 E-9
Goodell, 139 D-10
Goose Lake, 240 G-19
Gowrie, 1037 F-8
Graettinger, 844 C-6
Graf, 79 E-17
Grafton, 252 B-11
Grand Jct., 824 G-8
Grand Mound, 642 H-18
Grand River, 236 L-9
Grandview, 556 J-17
Granger, 1244 H-9
Granger Homesteads,
240 H-9
Granite B-1
Grant, 92 K-6
Granville, 312 C-3
Gravity, 188 L-6
Gray, 63 H-6
Greeley, 256 E-16
Green Castle, 30 H-11
Green Island, 50 G-19
Green Mtn., 126 G-12
Greene, 1130 D-12
GREENE CO., 9336 H-7
Greenfield, 1982 J-7
Greenville, 75 C-5
Grimes, 8246 I-9
Grinnell, 9218 H-12
Griswold, 1036 J-5
Grundy Ctr., 2706 F-12
GRUNDY CO.,
12453 F-12
Gruver, 94 B-6
Guernsey, 63 I-13
Gunder, 50 D-16
Guss L-6
Guthrie Ctr., 1569 I-7
GUTHRIE CO.,
10954 I-6
Guttenberg, 1919 D-17
Halbur, 246 G-6
Hale, 70 G-17
Hamburg, 1187 M-3
Hamilton, 130 K-12
HAMILTON CO.,
15673 F-9
Hamlin, 70 I-6
Hampton, 4461 E-11
Hancock, 196 J-4
HANCOCK CO.,
11341 C-9
Hanford, 30 C-11
Hanley, 60 K-9
Hanlontown, 226 B-10
Hanover E-5
Hansell, 98 D-11
Harcourt, 303 F-8
Hardin, 60 C-9
HARDIN CO.,
17534 F-11
Hardy, 47 D-8
Harlan, 5106 I-5
Harper, 114 J-14
Harpers Ferry, 328 C-17
Harris, 170 B-4
HARRISON CO.,
14928 H-3
Hartford, 771 J-10
Hartley, 1672 C-4
Hartwick, 86 H-13
Harvard, 30 M-11
Harvey, 235 J-12
Haskins, 40 J-16
Hastings, 152 K-4
Havelock, 138 D-6
Haven H-13
Haverhill, 173 H-11
Hawarden, 2546 C-1
Hawkeye, 449 D-14
Hawleyville L-6
Hawthorne, 30 K-4
Hayesville, 50 J-14
Hayfield, 43 C-9
Hazleton, 823 E-14
Hedrick, 764 K-13
Henderson, 185 K-4
HENRY CO.,
20145 K-16
Hepburn, 23 L-5
Herndon, 40 H-7
Hesper, 150 B-15
Hiawatha, 7024 G-15
Highland Ctr., 40 K-13
Highlandville, 40 B-15
Highview F-9
Hills, 703 I-15
Hillsboro, 180 L-15
Hinton, 928 E-2
Hiteman, 100 K-12
Hobarton C-8
Holbrook I-14
Holiday Lake, 433 H-13
Holland, 282 F-12
Holly Sprs., 50 F-2
Holmes E-9
Holstein, 1396 E-4
Holy Cross, 374 E-17
Homer F-9
Homestead, 148 H-15
Hopeville, 30 L-8
Hopkinton, 628 F-16
Hornick, 225 F-2
Horton, 50 D-13
Hospers, 698 C-3
Houghton, 146 L-16
HOWARD CO.,
9566 B-13
Hubbard, 845 F-10
Hudson, 2282 F-13
Hull, 2175 C-2
Humboldt, 4690 E-8
HUMBOLDT CO.,
9815 D-8
Humeston, 494 L-10
Huntington, 30 B-6
Hutchins, 28 C-9
Huxley, 3317 H-10
Iconium, 40 L-12
IDA CO., 7089 F-4
Ida Grv., 2142 F-4
Imogene, 72 L-4
Independence, 5966 F-15
Indianola, 14782 J-10
Inwood, 814 B-2
Ionia, 291 C-13
Iowa Ctr., 30 H-10

Iowa City, 67862 I-16
IOWA CO., 16355 I-14
Iowa Falls, 5238 E-11
Ira, 50 H-11
Ireton, 609 C-2
Irving, 30 H-13
Irvington, 38 C-8
Irwin, 341 H-5
JACKSON CO.,
19848 F-18
Jackson Jct., 58 C-14
Jacksonville, 30 I-5
Jamaica, 224 H-8
James, 50 E-2
Jamison, 30 K-9
Janesville, 930 E-13
JASPER CO.,
36842 H-11
Jefferson, 4345 G-7
JEFFERSON CO.,
16843 L-14
Jerico, 30 C-13
Jerome, 70 L-11
Jesup, 2520 F-14
Jewell, 1215 F-9
JOHNSON CO.,
130882 I-15
Johnston, 17278 I-9
Joice, 222 B-10
Jolley, 41 F-6
JONES CO.,
20638 G-17
Jordan G-9
Kalona, 2363 I-15
Kamrar, 199 F-9
Kanawha, 652 D-9
Kellerton, 315 L-8
Kelley, 309 H-9
Kellogg, 599 I-12
Kendallville, 40 B-14
Kensett, 266 B-11
Kent, 61 L-7
Keokuk, 10780 N-16
KEOKUK CO.,
10511 J-14
Keomah Vil., 84 J-13
Keosauqua, 1006 L-14
Keota, 1009 J-14
Kesley, 100 E-12
Keswick, 246 J-14
Keystone, 622 G-14
Killduff, 120 I-12
Kimballton, 322 I-5
King, 150 F-18
Kingsley, 1411 E-3
Kingston, 120 K-17
Kinross, 73 I-14
Kirkman, 64 H-5
Kirkville, 167 K-13
Kiron, 279 G-5
Klemme, 507 C-10
Klinger, 30 E-14
Knierim, 60 F-7
Knoke, 30 E-6
Knoxville, 7313 J-11
Kossuth, 100 K-17
KOSSUTH CO.,
15543 C-8
Koszta H-14
La Fayette, 60 G-15
La Motte, 260 F-18
La Porte City, 2285 F-14
Lacey, 40 J-12
Lacona, 361 K-10
Ladora, 283 H-14
Lake City, 1727 F-6
L. Mills, 2100 B-10
Lake Pk., 1105 B-5
L. View, 1142 F-5
Lakeside, 596 E-5
Lakota, 255 B-8
Lambs Grv., 172 I-11
Lamoille, 50 G-11
Lamoni, 2324 M-9
Lamont, 461 E-15
Lanesboro, 121 G-6
Langdon, 70 C-5
Langworthy, 50 G-16
Lansing, 999 B-16
Lanyon, 60 G-8
Larchwood, 866 B-2
Larrabee, 132 D-4
Latimer, 507 D-10
Laurel, 239 H-12
Laurens, 1258 D-6
Lawler, 439 C-14
Lawn Hill, 30 F-11
Lawton, 908 E-2
Le Claire, 3765 I-19
Le Grand, 938 G-12
Le Mars, 9826 D-2
Le Roy, 15 L-10
Leando, 115 L-14
Lebanon, 40 C-2
Lebanon L-14
Ledyard, 130 B-8
LEE CO., 35862 L-16
Lehigh, 416 F-8
Leighton, 162 J-12
Leland, 289 B-10
Lenox, 1407 L-7
Leon, 1977 L-9
Lester, 294 B-2
Letts, 384 J-17
Lewis, 433 J-5
Libertyville, 315 K-14
Liberty Ctr., 100 K-10
Libertyville, 315 K-14
Lidderdale, 180 G-6
Lime Sprs., 505 B-13
Linby, 30 K-14
Lincoln, 162 F-12
Linden, 199 I-8
Lineville, 217 M-10
LINN CO., 211226 F-16
Linn Grv., 154 D-5
Lisbon, 2152 H-16
Liscomb, 301 G-11
Little Cedar, 60 B-12
Little Rock, 459 B-3
Little Sioux, 170 H-3
Little Turkey, 30 C-14
Littleport, 20 D-16
Littleton, 220 E-14
Livermore, 384 D-8
Lockridge, 268 K-15
Logan, 1534 H-3
Logansport, 140 G-9
Lohrville, 368 F-7
Lone Rock, 146 C-8
Lone Tree, 1300 J-16
Long Grv., 808 H-18
Lorah I-6
Lorimor, 360 K-8
Lost Nation, 446 G-18
Louisa, 80 C-4
LOUISA CO.,
11387 K-16
Lourdes, 30 B-13
Loveland, 35 I-3
Lovilia, 538 K-12
Lovington, 700 B-19
Low Moor, 288 H-19

Lowden, 789 H-17
Lowell, 100 L-16
Lu Verne, 261 D-8
Luana, 269 C-16
Lucas, 216 K-10
LUCAS CO., 8898 K-10
Luther, 122 H-9
Luton F-2
Luxemburg, 240 E-17
Luzerne, 96 H-14
Lyman, 100 J-6
Lynnville, 379 I-12
LYON CO., 11581 B-2
Lytton, 315 F-6
Macedonia, 246 K-4
Macksburg, 113 J-8
MADISON CO.,
15679 J-9
Madrid, 2543 H-9
Magnolia, 183 I-3
Maharishi Vedic City,
259 K-14
MAHASKA CO.,
22381 J-12
Malcom, 287 I-13
Mallard, 274 D-7
Malone, 25 H-19
Maloy, 29 M-7
Malvern, 1142 K-4
Manchester, 5179 E-16
Manilla, 776 H-5
Manly, 1323 B-11
Manning, 1500 H-5
Manson, 1690 E-7
Maple Hill, 30 B-7
Maple River, 80 G-6
Mapleton, 1224 G-3
Maquoketa, 6141 G-18
Marathon, 237 D-6
Marble Rock, 307 D-12
Marcus, 1117 D-3
Marengo, 2528 H-14
Marietta, 50 G-11
Marion, 34768 G-15
MARION CO.,
33309 J-11
Mark, 30 M-13
Marne, 120 J-5
Marquette, 375 C-17
MARSHALL CO.,
40648 H-11
Marshalltown,
27552 G-12
Martelle, 255 G-16
Martensdale, 465 J-9
Martinsburg, 112 K-14
Marysville, 66 K-12
Mason City, 28079 C-11
Masonville, 127 E-15
Massena, 355 J-6
Massey, 120 F-18
Massillon, 50 H-17
Matlock, 87 B-3
Maurice, 275 D-2
Maxwell, 920 H-10
May City, 110 B-4
Maynard, 518 D-15
Maysville, 176 I-18
McCallsburg, 333 G-10
McCausland, 291 H-19
McClelland, 151 J-3
McGregor, 871 C-17
McIntire, 122 B-12
McNally D-2
Mechanicsville,
1146 H-16
Mederville, 30 D-16
Mediapolis, 1560 K-17
Medora, 50 K-10
Melbourne, 830 H-11
Melcher-Dallas,
1288 J-11
Melrose, 112 L-11
Melvin, 214 B-4
Menlo, 353 I-7
Meriden, 159 D-4
Merrill, 755 D-2
Meservey, 256 D-10
Meyer, 31 B-12
Middleburg, 30 C-3
Middletown, 318 L-17
Midway, 150 G-15
Miles, 445 G-19
Milford, 2898 B-5
Miller, 60 C-10
Millersburg, 159 I-14
Millerton, 45 L-10
MILLS CO., 15059 K-4
Millville, 30 E-17
Milo, 775 J-10
Milton, 443 M-14
Minburn, 365 H-8
Minden, 599 I-4
Mineola, 166 K-3
Mingo, 302 H-11
Missouri Valley, 2838 I-3
Mitchell, 138 B-12
MITCHELL CO.,
10776 B-12
Mitchellville, 2254 I-10
Modale, 283 I-3
Moingona, 100 G-9
Mona, 34 B-11
Mondamin, 402 H-3
Moneta C-4
Monmouth, 153 G-18
Monona, 1549 C-16
MONONA CO.,
9243 G-3
Monroe, 1830 I-11
MONROE CO.,
7970 K-12
Monteith, 50 I-7
Monterey, 30 M-13
Montezuma, 1462 I-13
Montgomery, 80 B-5
MONTGOMERY CO.,
10740 K-5
Monticello, 3796 F-17
Montour, 249 G-12
Montpelier, 230 I-18
Montrose, 898 M-16
Mooar, 80 M-16
Moorhead, 226 H-3
Moorland, 169 F-8
Moran, 50 H-9
Moravia, 665 L-12
Morley, 115 G-16
Morning Sun, 836 K-17
Morrison, 94 F-12
Morse, 80 H-16
Morton Mills, 25 K-6
Moscow, 300 I-17

Moulton, 605 M-12
Mt. Auburn, 150 F-14
Mt. Ayr, 1691 L-8
Mt. Carmel, 70 G-6
Mt. Etna, 30 K-6
Mt. Hamill, 30 L-16
Mt. Joy, 400 I-19
Mt. Pleasant, 8668 K-16
Mt. Sterling, 36 M-15
Mt. Union, 107 K-16
Mt. Vernon, 4506 H-16
Mt. Zion, 30 L-15
Moville, 1618 E-2
Munterville K-12
Murray, 756 K-9
Muscatine, 22886 J-17
MUSCATINE CO.,
42745 I-17
Mystic, 425 L-12
Napier, 50 G-9
Nashua, 1663 D-13
Nashville, 30 G-18
Nemaha, 85 E-5
Neola, 842 I-4
Neptune, 30 E-2
Nevada, 6798 G-10
New Albin, 522 A-16
New Boston, 60 M-16
New Hampton,
3571 C-13
New Hartford, 516 E-12
New Haven, 91 B-12
New Liberty, 137 H-18
New London, 1897 L-16
New Market, 415 L-6
New Providence,
228 F-11
New Sharon, 1293 I-12
New Vienna, 407 E-17
New Virginia, 489 K-9
Newburg, 120 H-12
Newell, 876 E-6
Newhall, 875 G-14
Newkirk, 70 C-3
Newton, 15254 I-11
Nichols, 374 I-16
Noble, 50 K-15
Nodaway, 114 L-6
Nora Sprs., 1431 C-11
N. Buena Vista, 121 E-17
N. English, 1041 I-14
N. Liberty, 13374 H-15
N. Washington, 117 C-13
Northboro, 58 M-5
Northwood, 1989 B-11
Norwalk, 8945 I-9
Norway, 545 H-14
Norwich, 30 L-5
Norwood, 30 K-10
Norwoodville, 1200 B-20
Numa, 92 M-11
Oakland, 1527 J-4
Oakland Acres, 156 I-12
Oakland Mills, 50 L-15
Oakley, 30 K-10
Oakville, 173 K-17
O'BRIEN CO.,
14398 C-3
Ocheyedan, 490 B-4
Odebolt, 1013 F-5
Oelwein, 6415 E-14
Ogden, 2044 G-8
Okoboji, 807 B-5
Olds, 229 K-16
Olin, 698 G-17
Ollie, 215 K-14
Onawa, 2998 G-2
Oneida, 40 E-16
Onslow, 197 G-17
Oran, 150 E-14
Orange City, 6004 C-3
Orchard, 71 C-12
Orient, 408 K-7
Orleans, 608 B-5
Osage, 3619 B-12
Osborne D-16
Osceola, 4929 K-9
OSCEOLA CO.,
6462 B-4
Osgood C-6
Oskaloosa, 11463 J-12
Ossian, 845 C-15
Osterdock, 59 D-17
Otho, 542 F-8
Otley, 300 J-11
Oto, 108 F-3
Otranto, 27 B-11
Otter Creek, 100 F-18
Otterville, 50 E-14
Ottosen, 55 D-7
Ottumwa, 25023 K-13
Owasa, 43 F-11
Oxford, 807 H-15
Oxford Jct., 496 G-17
Oxford Mills, 100 G-17
Oyens, 103 D-3
Pacific Jct., 471 K-3
Packard D-12
Packwood, 204 K-14
PAGE CO., 15932 L-5
Palmer, 165 E-7
Palmyra, 50 J-10
Palo, 1026 G-15
PALO ALTO CO.,
9421 D-7
Panama, 221 H-4
Panora, 1124 I-7
Panorama Pk., 129 *R-4
Paralta, 50 G-16
Paris, 60 F-15
Paris, 40 L-13
Park View, 2389 H-19
Parkersburg, 1870 E-12
Parnell, 193 I-14
Paton, 236 G-8
Patterson, 130 J-9
Paullina, 1056 D-4
Pekin, 30 K-14
Pella, 10352 J-12
Peoria, 110 J-12
Peosta, 1377 F-18
Percival, 87 L-3
Perkins, 30 C-2
Perry, 7702 H-8
Pershing, 300 J-11
Persia, 319 I-4
Petersburg, 140 E-16
Peterson, 334 D-5
Pierson, 366 E-3
Pilot Grv., 40 L-16
Pilot Mound, 173 G-8
Pioneer, 23 E-7
Piper F-7

Pisgah, 251 H-3
Pittsburg L-14
Pitzer J-8
Plainfield, 436 D-13
Plainview, 50 I-18
Plano, 70 L-11
Pleasant Grv., 40 K-16
Pleasant Hill, 8785 I-10
Pleasant Plain, 93 K-15
Pleasant Prairie I-18
Pleasant Valley, 70 I-19
Pleasanton, 49 M-9
Pleasantville, 1694 J-11
Plover, 77 D-7
Plymouth, 382 C-11
PLYMOUTH CO.,
24986 E-2
Pocahontas, 1789 E-6
POCAHONTAS CO.,
7310 E-6
Polk City, 3418 H-9
POLK CO.,
430640 H-10
Pomeroy, 662 E-6
Popejoy, 79 E-10
Portland, 35 C-11
Portsmouth, 195 I-4
Postville, 2227 C-15
POTTAWATTAMIE CO.,
93158 J-4
Powersville D-12
POWESHIEK CO.,
18914 H-13
Prairie City, 1680 I-11
Prairieburg, 178 F-16
Prescott, 257 K-7
Preston, 1012 G-19
Primghar, 909 C-4
Primrose, 30 M-15
Princeton, 886 I-19
Prole, 50 J-9
Promise City, 111 L-11
Protivin, 283 C-14
Pulaski, 260 L-14
Quarry, 60 G-12
Quasqueton, 554 F-15
Quimby, 319 E-4
Radcliffe, 545 F-10
Rake, 225 B-9
Ralston, 79 G-7
Randalia, 68 D-15
Randall, 173 G-10
Randolph, 168 L-4
Rands F-7
Rathbun, 89 L-12
Raymond, 788 F-14
Readlyn, 808 E-14
Reasnor, 152 I-11
Red Line H-5
Red Oak, 5742 K-5
Redding, 82 M-7
Redfield, 835 I-8
Reinbeck, 1664 F-13
Rembrandt, 203 D-5
Remsen, 1663 D-3
Renwick, 242 D-9
Rhodes, 305 H-11
Riceville, 785 B-13
Richard, 30 F-7
Richland, 584 K-14
Richmond, 100 J-15
Rickardsville, 182 E-17
Ricketts, 145 G-4
Ridgeport, 30 G-9
Ridgeway, 315 B-14
Rinard, 52 F-7
RINGGOLD CO.,
5131 L-7
Ringsted, 422 B-7
Rippey, 292 H-8
Ritter B-3
River Hts., 580 H-16
River Sioux, 59 H-2
Riverdale, 405 I-19
Riverside, 993 I-16
Riverton, 304 L-4
Robins, 3142 G-15
Rochester, 133 I-17
Rock Creek, 30 C-12
Rock Falls, 155 C-11
Rock Rapids, 2549 B-2
Rock Valley, 3354 C-2
Rockford, 860 C-11
Rockwell, 1039 D-11
Rockwell City, 1709 F-7
Rodney, 60 G-3
Roelyn, 30 F-7
Roland, 1284 G-10
Rolfe, 584 D-7
Rome, 117 K-15
Rose Hill, 168 J-13
Roselle, 60 G-6
Ross, 60 H-6
Rossie, 70 C-5
Rossville, 60 C-16
Rowan, 158 E-10
Rowley, 264 F-15
Royal, 446 C-5
Rubio, 60 J-15
Rudd, 369 C-12
Runnells, 507 I-10
Russell, 554 K-11
Ruthven, 737 C-6
Rutland, 126 D-8
Ryan, 361 F-16
Sabula, 576 G-20
Sac City, 2220 F-6
SAC CO., 10350 F-5
Sageville, 122 E-18
St. Ansgar, 1107 B-12
St. Anthony, 102 G-11
St. Benedict, 39 C-8
St. Charles, 653 J-9
St. Donatus, 135 F-18
St. Joseph, 61 D-8
St. Lucas, 143 C-14
St. Marys, 127 J-9
St. Olaf, 108 D-16
St. Paul, 129 L-16
Salem, 383 L-15
Salina, 25 K-15
Salix, 363 F-2
Sanborn, 1404 C-4
Sand Sprs., 40 F-17
Sandusky, 70 M-16
Sandyville, 51 J-10
Saratoga, 60 B-13
Saude C-14
Savannah, 30 M-13
Saydel, 3500 A-19
Saylorville, 3301 A-19
Scarville, 72 B-10

Schaller, 772 E-5
Schleswig, 882 G-4
Schley, 30 B-14
Scotch Grv., 60 G-17
SCOTT CO.,
165224 H-19
Scranton, 557 G-7
Searsboro, 148 I-12
Selma, 80 L-14
Seneca, 30 B-7
Seney, 80 D-2
Sergeant Bluff, 4227 F-2
Sewal, 40 M-11
Sexton, 37 C-8
Seymour, 701 M-11
Shambaugh, 191 M-5
Shannon City, 71 L-8
Sharon Ctr., 120 I-15
Sharpsburg, 89 L-7
Sheffield, 1172 D-11
Shelby, 641 I-4
SHELBY CO., 12167 I-4
Sheldahl, 319 H-9
Sheldon, 5188 C-3
Shell Rock, 1296 E-13
Shellsburg, 983 G-15
Shenandoah, 5150 L-4
Sherrill, 177 E-18
Sherwood F-6
Shipley G-10
Shueyville, 577 H-15
Siam M-6
Sibley, 2798 B-3
Sidney, 1138 L-4
Sigourney, 2059 J-14
Silver City, 245 K-4
Sinclair E-12
Sioux Ctr., 7048 C-2
Sioux City, 82684 E-2
SIOUX CO., 33704 C-2
Sioux Rapids, 775 D-5
Slater, 1489 H-9
Slifer, 30 F-7
Sloan, 973 F-2
Smithland, 224 F-3
Soldier, 174 G-3
Solon, 2037 H-16
Somers, 113 F-7
S. Amana, 159 H-14
S. English, 212 I-14
Spaulding K-7
Spencer, 11233 C-5
Sperry, 70 K-17
Spillville, 367 C-14
Spirit Lake, 4840 B-5
Spragueville, 81 G-19
Spring Grv., 100 L-17
Spring Hill, 63 J-9
Springbrook, 144 G-19
Springdale, 50 I-16
Springville, 1074 G-16
Stacyville, 494 B-12
Stanhope, 422 F-9
Stanley, 125 E-15
Stanton, 689 K-5
Stanwood, 684 H-17
Stanzel J-8
State Ctr., 1468 G-11
Steamboat Rock,
310 F-11
Stennett K-5
Stilson G-9
Stockport, 296 L-15
Stockton, 197 I-18
Stone City, 192 G-16
Storm Lake, 10600 E-5
Story City, 3431 G-10
STORY CO.,
89542 G-10
Stout, 224 E-12
Strahan, 30 K-4
Stratford, 743 F-9
Strawberry Pt.,
1279 E-16
Struble, 78 D-2
Stuart, 1648 I-7
Sully, 821 I-12
Sulphur Sprs., 40 E-5
Summerset, 150 J-10
Summitville, 50 M-16
Sumner, 2028 D-14
Sunbury, 50 I-17
Superior, 130 B-6
Sutherland, 649 D-4
Swaledale, 165 D-10
Swan, 72 J-10
Swea City, 536 B-8
Swedesburg, 130 K-16
Swisher, 879 H-15
Tabor, 1040 L-4
Taintor, 40 I-12
Tama, 2877 H-13
TAMA CO., 17767 G-13
Tara E-8
TAYLOR CO., 6317 M-6
Teeds Grv., 100 G-19
Templeton, 362 H-6
Ten Mile, 30 G-19
Tennant, 68 I-4
Tennville Jct., 20 K-5
Terril, 367 B-6
Thayer, 50 K-8
Thirty M-12
Thompson, 502 B-9
Thor, 186 E-8
Thornburg, 67 J-13
Thornton, 422 D-10
Thurman, 229 L-3
Ticonic G-3
Tiffin, 1947 I-15
Tingley, 184 L-8
Tipton, 3221 H-17
Titonka, 476 C-8
Toddville, 200 G-15
Toeterville, 48 B-12
Toledo, 2341 G-13
Toolesboro, 40 K-17
Toronto, 124 H-18
Tracy, 450 J-12
Traer, 1703 G-13
Trenton, 120 K-15
Treynor, 919 J-4
Tripoli, 1313 D-13
Troy, 70 L-14
Troy Mills, 200 F-15
Truesdale, 81 E-5
Truro, 485 K-9
Turin, 68 G-3
Turkey River E-17
Twin View Hts., 350 H-16
Udell, 47 L-12
Ulmer, 30 F-6
Underwood, 917 J-3

Union, 397 F-11
UNION CO., 12534 K-7
Unionville, 102 L-12
University Hts., 1051 I-16
University Pk., 487 J-12
Urbana, 1458 G-15
Urbandale, 39463 I-9
Ute, 374 G-3
Vail, 436 G-5
Valeria, 57 H-10
VAN BUREN CO.,
7570 L-14
Van Cleve, 50 H-11
Van Horne, 682 G-14
Van Meter, 1016 I-9
Van Wert, 230 L-9
Vandalia, 60 I-10
Varina, 71 E-6
Ventura, 717 C-10
Vernon, 40 L-15
Vernon Sprs., 40 B-14
Vernon View, 120 K-20
Victor, 893 H-13
Villisca, 1252 L-5
Vincennes, 40 M-16
Vincent, 174 E-8
Vining, 50 G-13
Vinton, 5257 G-14
Viola, 120 G-16
Volga, 208 D-16
Volney, 30 C-16
Voorhies, 60 F-13
Wadena, 262 D-15
Wahpeton, 341 B-5
Walcott, 1629 I-18
Wales, 25 K-5
Walford, 1463 H-15
Walker, 791 F-15
Wall Lake, 819 F-5
Wallingford, 197 B-6
Walnut, 785 I-5
Wapello, 2067 K-17
WAPELLO CO.,
35625 L-13
Ware D-6
WARREN CO.,
46225 J-10
Washburn, 876 F-13
Washington, 7266 J-15
WASHINGTON CO.,
21704 J-15
Washta, 248 E-3
Waterloo, 68406 E-13
Waterville, 144 C-16
Watkins, 118 H-14
Waubeek, 100 G-16
Waucoma, 257 C-14
Waukee, 13790 I-9
Waukon, 3897 B-16
Waukon Jct., 20 C-17
Waverly, 9874 E-13
Wayland, 966 K-15
WAYNE CO.,
6403 M-10
Webb, 141 D-6
Webster, 88 J-14
Webster City, 8070 F-9
WEBSTER CO.,
38013 F-8
Weldon, 125 L-9
Wellman, 1408 I-15
Wellsburg, 707 F-12
Welton, 165 H-18
Wesley, 390 C-8
W. Amana, 140 I-14
W. Bend, 785 D-7
W. Branch, 2322 I-16
W. Burlington, 2968 L-17
W. Chester, 146 J-15
W. Des Moines,
56609 I-9
W. Grove, 50 L-13
W. Lemars, 30 D-2
W. Liberty, 3736 I-16
W. Okoboji, 289 B-5
West Point, 966 L-16
W. Union, 2486 D-15
Westfield, 132 D-1
Westgate, 211 D-14
Weston, 92 J-3
Westphalia, 127 H-4
Westside, 299 G-5
Westwood, 112 K-15
Wever, 140 L-17
What Cheer, 646 J-13
Wheatland, 764 H-18
Whiting, 762 G-2
Whittemore, 504 C-7
Whitten, 149 F-11
Whittier, 130 G-16
Wick, 40 J-9
Willey, 88 G-6
Williams, 344 F-10
Williamsburg, 3068 I-14
Williamson, 152 K-11
Williamstown K-7
Williamstown, 100 I-15
Wilton, 2802 I-17
Windsor Hts., 4860 B-18
Winfield, 1134 K-16
WINNEBAGO CO.,
10866 B-9
WINNESHIEK CO.,
21056 B-14
Winterset, 5190 J-8
Winthrop, 850 F-15
Wiota, 116 J-6
Wiscotta, 40 I-8
Woden, 229 C-9
Wood C-17
Woodbine, 1459 H-3
Woodburn, 202 K-10
WOODBURY CO.,
102172 F-3
Woodland M-10
Woodward, 1024 H-9
Woolstock, 168 E-9
WORTH CO.,
7598 B-11
Worthington, 401 F-17
Wright, 50 J-13
WRIGHT CO.,
13229 E-9
Wyman, 30 K-16
Wyoming, 515 G-17
Yale, 246 H-7
Yarmouth, 120 K-16
Yetter, 34 F-6
Yorktown, 85 L-5
Zaneta F-13
Zearing, 554 G-11
Zion K-8
Zwingle, 91 F-18

*, †, ‡, §, ◊ See explanation under state title in this index.
County and parish names are listed in capital letters & boldface type.
Independent cities (not included in a county) are listed in italics.

Kansas

Page locator
Map keys 1–10: Atlas pages 82–83
Map keys 11–20: Atlas pages 84–85
* City keyed to p. 117

Abbyville, 87 ... H-11
Abilene, 6844 ... E-13
Ada, 100 ... D-11
Adams, 20 ... I-11
Admire, 156 ... F-16
Agenda, 68 ... B-12
Agra, 267 ... B-8
Agricola ... F-17
Akron ... J-13
Alamota, 25 ... F-6
Albert, 175 ... F-9
Alden, 148 ... G-10
Alexander, 65 ... F-7
Aliceville, 40 ... G-17
Allen, 177 ... E-15
ALLEN CO., 13371 ... H-17
Alma, 832 ... D-15
Almena, 408 ... B-7
Alta Vista, 444 ... E-15
Altamont, 1080 ... J-18
Alton, 103 ... C-9
Altoona, 414 ... I-17
Americus, 894 ... F-15
Ames, 40 ... C-12
Amy ... F-5
Andale, 928 ... H-12
ANDERSON CO., 8102 ... G-17
Andover, 11791 ... H-13
Angelus, 45 ... D-5
Angola, 50 ... J-17
Anson, 30 ... I-12
Antelope ... F-14
Anthony, 2269 ... J-11
Antonino, 50 ... E-8
Arcadia, 310 ... H-19
Argonia, 501 ... J-12
Arkansas City, 12415 ... J-13
Arlington, 473 ... H-11
Arma, 1481 ... I-19
Arnold, 50 ... F-6
Arrington, 40 ... C-17
Ash Grv. ... D-10
Asherville, 28 ... C-11
Ashland, 867 ... J-7
Ashton, 25 ... J-13
Assaria, 413 ... E-12
Atchison, 11021 ... C-18
ATCHISON CO., 16924 ... C-17
Athol, 44 ... B-9
Atlanta, 195 ... I-14
Attica, 626 ... J-11
Atwood, 1194 ... B-4
Aubry, 100 ... E-19
Auburn, 1227 ... E-16
Augusta, 9274 ... H-13
Aulne, 50 ... G-13
Aurora, 60 ... C-12
Axtell, 406 ... B-15
Baileyville, 181 ... B-15
Bala, 30 ... D-13
Baldwin City, 4515 ... E-18
Bancroft ... C-16
BARBER CO., 4861 ... J-9
Barnard, 70 ... D-11
Barnes, 159 ... B-14
Bartlett, 80 ... J-18
BARTON CO., 27674 ... F-9
Basehor, 4613 ... D-18
Bassett, 14 ... H-17
Bavaria, 90 ... E-12
Baxter Sprs., 4238 ... J-19
Bazaar, 25 ... G-15
Bazine, 334 ... F-7
Beagle, 70 ... F-18
Beardsley ... B-3
Beattie, 200 ... B-15
Beaumont, 200 ... I-15
Beaver, 40 ... F-9
Beeler, 45 ... F-6
Bellaire, 6769 ... H-13
Bellaire ... B-9
Belle Plaine, 1681 ... I-13
Belleville, 1991 ... B-12
Belmont, 35 ... I-11
Beloit, 3835 ... C-11
Belpre, 84 ... H-8
Belvidere, 25 ... I-8
Belvue, 205 ... D-15
Bendena, 117 ... B-18
Benedict, 73 ... I-16
Bennington, 672 ... D-12
Bentley, 530 ... H-12
Benton, 880 ... H-13
Bern, 166 ... B-16
Berryton, 400 ... E-17
Berwick ... B-16
Beulah, 60 ... I-19
Beverly, 162 ... D-11
Big Bow, 95 ... I-2
Big Sprs., 75 ... D-17
Bird City, 447 ... B-3
Bison, 255 ... F-8
Blaine, 80 ... C-15
Blair, 40 ... B-18
Blakeman ... B-4
Bloom, 75 ... I-6
Bloomington, 60 ... C-9
Blue Mound, 275 ... G-18
Blue Rapids, 1019 ... B-14
Bluff City, 65 ... J-11
Bogue, 143 ... C-7
Boicourt, 30 ... G-19
Bolton, 40 ... J-16
Bonita ... *N-1
Bonner Sprs., 7314 ... D-18
BOURBON CO., 15173 ... H-18
Boyle, 30 ... C-17
Brainerd, 70 ... H-13
Brazilton, 80 ... I-18
Bremen, 80 ... B-14
Brenham ... I-8
Brewster, 305 ... C-3
Bridgeport, 75 ... F-12
Bronson, 323 ... H-18
Brookville, 262 ... E-11
BROWN CO., 9984 ... B-17
Brownell, 29 ... F-7
Bucklin, 794 ... I-7
Bucyrus, 193 ... E-19
Buffalo, 232 ... H-17
Buhler, 1327 ... G-12
Bunker Hill, 95 ... E-9
Burden, 535 ... J-14
Burdett, 247 ... G-7
Burdick, 75 ... F-14
Burlingame, 934 ... E-16
Burlington, 2674 ... G-16
Burns, 228 ... G-14
Burr Oak, 174 ... B-10
Burrton, 901 ... G-12
Bush City ... G-18
Bushong, 34 ... F-15
Bushton, 279 ... F-10
BUTLER CO., 65880 ... H-14
Byers, 35 ... H-9
Cadmus ... F-18
Cairo, 20 ... I-10
Caldwell, 1068 ... J-12
Calista ... I-10
Calvert, 25 ... B-7
Cambridge, 82 ... J-14
Canada, 75 ... F-13
Caney, 2203 ... J-16
Canton, 748 ... F-12
Capaldo ... I-19
Carbondale, 1437 ... E-16
Carlton, 42 ... E-13
Carlyle, 100 ... G-17
Carneiro ... E-11
Cassoday, 129 ... G-14
Castleton, 25 ... H-11
Catharine, 104 ... E-8
Cawker City, 469 ... C-10
Cedar, 14 ... C-9
Cedar Bluffs, 35 ... A-5
Cedar Pt., 28 ... G-14
Cedar Vale, 579 ... J-15
Centerville, 100 ... G-18
Centralia, 512 ... B-15
Centropolis, 170 ... E-17
Chanute, 9119 ... H-17
Chapman, 1393 ... E-13
Charleston, 25 ... H-5
Chase, 477 ... F-10
CHASE CO., 2790 ... G-14
Chautauqua, 111 ... J-15
CHAUTAUQUA CO., 3669 ... J-15
Cheney, 2094 ... I-12
Cherokee, 714 ... I-19
CHEROKEE CO., 21603 ... J-18
Cherryvale, 2367 ... J-17
Chetopa, 1125 ... J-18
CHEYENNE CO., 2726 ... B-2
Cimarron, 2184 ... H-5
Circleville, 170 ... C-16
Claflin, 645 ... F-10
CLARK CO., 2215 ... J-6
Claudell ... B-9
Clay Ctr., 4334 ... C-13
CLAY CO., 8535 ... D-13
Clayton, 59 ... B-6
Clearwater, 2481 ... I-12
Clements ... G-14
Clifton, 554 ... C-13
Climax, 72 ... H-15
Clinton, 40 ... E-17
Clonmel ... I-12
CLOUD CO., 9533 ... C-11
Clyde, 716 ... C-12
Coats, 83 ... I-9
Codell, 75 ... D-8
COFFEY CO., 8601 ... G-16
Coffeyville, 10295 ... J-17
Colby, 5387 ... C-4
Coldwater, 828 ... J-8
Collyer, 109 ... D-6
Colony, 408 ... G-17
Columbus, 3312 ... J-19
Colwich, 1327 ... H-12
COMANCHE CO., 1891 ... J-8
Concordia, 5395 ... C-12
Conway ... F-12
Conway Sprs., 1272 ... I-12
Coolidge, 95 ... G-1
Copeland, 310 ... I-5
Corbin, 100 ... J-12
Corning, 157 ... B-16
Corwin, 25 ... J-10
Cottonwood Falls, 903 ... F-15
Council Grv., 2182 ... E-15
Countryside, 295 ... *J-2
Courtland, 285 ... B-11
COWLEY CO., 36311 ... J-14
Coyville, 46 ... H-16
CRAWFORD CO., 39134 ... I-18
Crestline, 110 ... J-19
Croweburg, 75 ... I-19
Cuba, 156 ... B-12
Cullison, 101 ... I-9
Culver, 121 ... E-12
Cummings, 70 ... C-17
Cunningham, 454 ... I-10
Dalton ... J-13
Damar, 132 ... D-7
Danville, 38 ... J-11
De Graff ... H-14
De Soto, 5720 ... D-18
Dearing, 431 ... J-17
DECATUR CO., 2961 ... B-5
Deerfield, 700 ... H-3
Delavan, 25 ... F-14
Delia, 169 ... D-16
Delphos, 359 ... D-12
Denison, 187 ... C-17
Denmark ... D-10
Dennis, 150 ... I-17
Densmore, 35 ... C-7
Denton, 148 ... B-17
Derby, 22158 ... I-13
Detroit, 114 ... E-13
Devon, 30 ... H-19
Dexter, 278 ... J-14
Diamond Sprs. ... F-14
DICKINSON CO., 19754 ... E-13
Dighton, 1038 ... F-5
Dodge City, 27340 ... H-6
Doniphan ... B-18
DONIPHAN CO., 7945 ... B-18
Dorrance, 185 ... E-10
DOUGLAS CO., 110826 ... E-17
Douglass, 1700 ... I-13
Dover, 140 ... E-16
Downs, 900 ... C-10
Dresden, 41 ... C-5
Duluth, 25 ... C-15
Dundee, 60 ... G-9
Dunlap, 30 ... F-15
Duquoin ... I-11
Durham, 112 ... F-13
Dwight, 272 ... E-14
Earlton, 55 ... I-17
Eastborough, 773 ... M-9
Easton, 253 ... C-18
Edgerton, 1671 ... E-18
Edmond, 49 ... C-7
Edna, 442 ... J-17
Edson, 40 ... C-3
EDWARDS CO., 3037 ... H-8
Edwardsville, 4340 ... *I-1
Effingham, 546 ... C-17
El Dorado, 13021 ... H-14
Elbing, 229 ... G-13
Elgin, 89 ... K-15
Elk City, 325 ... J-16
ELK CO., 2882 ... I-15
Elk Falls, 107 ... I-15
Elkhart, 2205 ... J-2
Ellinwood, 2131 ... F-10
Ellis, 2062 ... E-7
ELLIS CO., 28452 ... D-8
Ellsworth, 3120 ... E-10
ELLSWORTH CO., 6497 ... E-11
Elmdale, 55 ... F-14
Elmo, 30 ... E-13
Elmont, 100 ... D-16
Elsmore, 77 ... H-18
Elwood, 1224 ... B-18
Elyria, 75 ... G-12
Emmett, 191 ... C-16
Emporia, 24916 ... F-15
Englevale, 25 ... I-19
Englewood, 77 ... J-6
Ensign, 187 ... I-6
Enterprise, 855 ... E-13
Erie, 1150 ... I-18
Esbon, 99 ... B-10
Eskridge, 534 ... E-16
Eudora, 6136 ... E-18
Eureka, 2633 ... H-15
Everest, 284 ... B-17
Fairmount, 100 ... D-18
Fairview, 260 ... B-16
Fairway, 3882 ... *J-3
Fall River, 162 ... I-16
Falun, 87 ... F-12
Farlington, 75 ... I-19
Farlinville ... G-19
Faulkner, 30 ... J-18
Fellsburg, 20 ... H-8
FINNEY CO., 36776 ... G-5
Floral, 40 ... I-14
Florence, 465 ... G-14
Fontana, 224 ... F-19
Ford, 216 ... I-7
FORD CO., 33848 ... I-6
Formoso, 93 ... B-11
Ft. Dodge, 165 ... H-6
Ft. Scott, 8087 ... H-19
Fostoria, 70 ... C-14
Fostoria, 35 ... E-16
Fowler, 590 ... I-6
Frankfort, 726 ... B-15
Franklin, 375 ... I-19
FRANKLIN CO., 25992 ... F-17
Frederick, 18 ... F-10
Fredonia, 2482 ... I-16
Freeport, 5 ... J-11
Friend, 30 ... G-4
Frontenac, 3437 ... I-19
Fulton, 163 ... G-19
Furley, 100 ... H-13
Galatia, 39 ... F-9
Galena, 3085 ... J-19
Galesburg, 126 ... I-17
Galva, 870 ... F-12
Garden City, 26658 ... H-4
Garden Plain, 849 ... I-12
Gardner, 19123 ... E-18
Garfield, 190 ... G-8
Garland, 100 ... H-19
Garnett, 3415 ... G-18
Gas, 564 ... H-17
Gaylord, 114 ... C-9
GEARY CO., 34362 ... E-14
Gem, 88 ... C-4
Geneseo, 267 ... F-11
Geuda Sprs., 185 ... J-13
Girard, 2789 ... I-19
Glade, 96 ... B-8
Glasco, 498 ... C-11
Glen Elder, 445 ... C-10
Glendale, 35 ... E-11
Goddard, 4344 ... I-12
Goessel, 539 ... G-13
Goff, 126 ... B-16
Goodland, 4489 ... C-2
Goodrich, 40 ... G-18
Gorham, 334 ... E-9
Gove, 80 ... E-5
GOVE CO., 2695 ... E-5
GRAHAM CO., 2597 ... D-6
Grainfield, 277 ... D-5
Grandview Plaza, 1560 ... D-14
GRANT CO., 7829 ... I-3
Grantville, 180 ... D-17
GRAY CO., 6006 ... H-5
Great Bend, 15995 ... F-9
Greeley, 302 ... F-18
GREELEY CO., 1247 ... F-2
Green, 128 ... C-13
Greenleaf, 331 ... B-13
Greensburg, 777 ... I-8
Greenwich, 80 ... K-10
Greenwich Hts., 960 ... M-10
GREENWOOD CO., 6689 ... H-15
Grenola, 216 ... I-15
Gretna ... B-8
Gridley, 341 ... G-16
Grigston ... F-5
Grinnell, 259 ... D-5
Gross, 50 ... I-19
Grove ... D-16
Groveland ... G-12
Gypsum, 405 ... E-12
Hackney, 25 ... J-13
Haddam, 104 ... B-13
Half Mound ... C-17
Hallowell, 200 ... J-18
Halls Summit ... F-17
Halstead, 2085 ... H-12
Hamilton, 268 ... H-15
HAMILTON CO., 2690 ... G-2
Hamlin, 46 ... B-17
Hammond ... H-19
Hanover, 682 ... B-14
Hanston, 206 ... G-7
Harding ... G-19
Hardtner, 172 ... K-9
Harlan, 25 ... C-9
Harper, 1473 ... J-11
HARPER CO., 6034 ... J-11
Harris, 51 ... F-17
Hartford, 371 ... G-16
HARVEY CO., 34684 ... G-12
Harveyville, 236 ... E-16
HASKELL CO., 4256 ... I-4
Havana, 104 ... J-16
Haven, 1237 ... H-12
Havensville, 133 ... C-16
Haverhill, 50 ... H-14
Haviland, 701 ... I-8
Hays, 20510 ... E-8
Haysville, 10826 ... I-13
Hazelton, 93 ... J-10
Healy, 234 ... F-5
Hedville, 50 ... E-12
Heizer, 125 ... F-9
Hepler, 132 ... H-18
Herington, 2526 ... E-14
Herkimer, 50 ... B-14
Herndon, 129 ... B-4
Hessdale ... E-15
Hesston, 3709 ... G-12
Hewins, 40 ... J-15
Hiattville, 60 ... H-19
Hiawatha, 3172 ... B-17
Hickok, 80 ... I-3
Highland, 1012 ... B-17
Highland Pk. ... M-16
Hill City, 1474 ... C-7
Hillsboro, 2993 ... F-13
Hillsdale, 229 ... E-19
Hitschmann, 20 ... F-10
HODGEMAN CO., 1916 ... G-6
Hoisington, 2706 ... F-9
Holcomb, 2094 ... H-4
Holland ... E-13
Hollenberg, 21 ... B-13
Hollis ... C-12
Holton, 3329 ... C-16
Holyrood, 447 ... F-10
Home, 160 ... B-14
Homewood, 30 ... F-17
Hope, 368 ... E-13
Hopewell ... H-9
Horace, 70 ... F-2
Horton, 1776 ... B-17
Howard, 687 ... I-15
Hoxie, 1201 ... C-5
Hoyt, 669 ... D-16
Hudson, 129 ... G-9
Hugoton, 3904 ... J-3
Humboldt, 1953 ... H-17
Hunnewell, 67 ... K-12
Hunter, 57 ... D-10
Huron, 54 ... B-17
Hutchinson, 42080 ... G-11
Idana, 70 ... C-13
Independence, 9483 ... J-17
Industry ... D-13
Ingalls, 306 ... H-5
Inman, 1377 ... G-12
Iola, 5704 ... H-17
Ionia, 80 ... C-10
Iowa Pt., 35 ... B-17
Isabel, 90 ... I-10
Iuka, 163 ... H-9
JACKSON CO., 13462 ... C-16
Jamestown, 286 ... C-11
Jarbalo, 100 ... D-18
Jefferson, 50 ... J-17
JEFFERSON CO., 19126 ... D-17
Jennings, 96 ... B-6
Jetmore, 867 ... G-6
Jewell, 432 ... B-11
JEWELL CO., 3077 ... B-11
Johnson, 1495 ... I-2
JOHNSON CO., 544179 ... E-18
Junction City, 23353 ... D-14
Kackley, 25 ... B-11
Kalvesta, 40 ... G-6
Kanopolis, 492 ... E-11
Kanorado, 153 ... C-1
Kansas City, 145786 ... D-19
KEARNY CO., 3977 ... G-3
Keats, 170 ... D-14
Kelly, 40 ... B-16
Kendall, 250 ... H-2
Kensington, 473 ... B-9
Kimball ... H-18
Kincaid, 122 ... G-18
Kingman, 3177 ... I-11
KINGMAN CO., 7858 ... I-11
Kingsdown, 200 ... I-7
Kinsley, 1457 ... H-8
Kiowa, 1026 ... K-10
KIOWA CO., 2553 ... I-8
Kipp, 59 ... E-12
Kiro ... D-16
Kirwin, 171 ... B-8
Kismet, 459 ... J-4
La Crosse, 1342 ... F-8
La Cygne, 1149 ... F-19
La Harpe, 578 ... H-18
Labette, 78 ... J-18
LABETTE CO., 21607 ... J-18
Lafontaine, 100 ... I-16
Lake City, 50 ... J-9
L. Quivira, 906 ... *J-1
L. Wabaunsee, 250 ... E-15
Lakin, 2216 ... H-3
Lamont, 45 ... G-16
Lancaster, 298 ... C-17
Lane, 225 ... F-18
LANE CO., 1750 ... F-5
Langdon, 42 ... H-10
Langley ... F-11
Lansing, 11265 ... D-18
Larkinburg, 30 ... C-17
Larned, 4054 ... G-8
Latham, 139 ... I-14
Latimer, 20 ... E-14
Lawrence, 87643 ... D-18
Lawton, 90 ... J-19
Le Loup, 50 ... E-18
Le Roy, 561 ... G-17
Leavenworth, 35251 ... C-18
LEAVENWORTH CO., 76227 ... D-18
Leawood, 31867 ... D-19
Lebanon, 218 ... B-10
Lebo, 940 ... F-16
Lecompton, 625 ... D-17
Lehigh, 175 ... F-13
Lenexa, 48190 ... D-19
Lenora, 250 ... C-6
Leon, 704 ... H-14
Leona, 48 ... B-17
Leonardville, 449 ... C-14
Leoti, 1534 ... F-3
Leoville, 50 ... C-5
Levant, 61 ... C-3
Lewis, 451 ... H-8
Liberal, 20525 ... J-4
Liberty, 123 ... J-17
Liebenthal, 103 ... F-8
Lillis ... C-15
Lincoln, 1297 ... D-11
LINCOLN CO., 3241 ... D-11
Lincolnville, 203 ... F-13
Lindsborg, 3458 ... F-12
Linn, 410 ... B-13
LINN CO., 9656 ... G-18
Linn Valley, 804 ... F-19
Linwood, 375 ... D-18
Little River, 557 ... F-11
Logan, 589 ... B-7
LOGAN CO., 2756 ... E-3
Lone Elm, 25 ... G-18
Lone Star ... E-17
Long Island, 134 ... B-7
Longford, 79 ... D-13
Longton, 348 ... I-16
Loretta, 30 ... F-8
Lorraine, 138 ... F-10
Lost Sprs., 70 ... F-13
Louisburg, 4315 ... E-19
Louisville, 188 ... D-15
Lovewell, 25 ... B-11
Lowemont ... C-18
Lucas, 393 ... D-10
Ludell, 100 ... B-4
Luray, 194 ... D-9
Lyndon, 1052 ... F-17
LYON CO., 33690 ... F-15
Lyons, 3739 ... G-11
Macksville, 549 ... H-9
Madison, 701 ... G-15
Mahaska, 83 ... A-12
Maize, 3420 ... H-12
Manchester, 95 ... D-13
Manhattan, 52281 ... D-14
Mankato, 869 ... B-10
Manning ... F-5
Manter, 171 ... I-2
Maple City, 20 ... J-14
Maple Hill, 620 ... D-16
Mapleton, 84 ... G-19
Marienthal, 71 ... F-3
Marion, 1927 ... F-13
MARION CO., 12660 ... G-13
Marquette, 641 ... F-11
MARSHALL CO., 10117 ... B-14
Marysville, 3294 ... B-14
Matfield Green, 47 ... G-14
Mayetta, 341 ... C-16
Mayfield, 113 ... J-12
McCracken, 190 ... F-7
McCune, 405 ... I-18
McDonald, 160 ... B-3
McFarland, 256 ... D-15
McLouth, 880 ... D-18
McPherson, 13155 ... F-12
MCPHERSON CO., 29180 ... F-11
Meade, 1721 ... J-5
MEADE CO., 4575 ... J-5
Medicine Lodge, 2009 ... J-10
Medora, 50 ... G-11
Melrose, 50 ... J-18
Melvern, 385 ... F-17
Menlo, 61 ... C-5
Mentor, 100 ... E-12
Mercier, 25 ... B-17
Meriden, 813 ... D-17
Merriam, 11003 ... *J-2
MIAMI CO., 32787 ... F-18
Michigan Valley, 150 ... E-17
Midway ... I-11
Milan, 82 ... I-12
Milberger, 25 ... E-9
Mildred, 28 ... G-18
Milford, 530 ... D-14
Miller, 50 ... F-16
Milton, 155 ... I-12
Miltonvale, 539 ... C-12
Mingo, 40 ... D-4
Minneapolis, 2032 ... D-12
Minneola, 745 ... I-6
Mission, 9323 ... *J-3
Mission Hills, 3498 ... *J-3
Mission Woods, 178 ... *J-3
Mitchell ... F-11
MITCHELL CO., 6373 ... D-11
Modoc, 35 ... F-4
Moline, 371 ... I-15
Monmouth ... I-18
Mont Ida, 50 ... G-17
Montana, 55 ... J-18
Montezuma, 966 ... I-5
MONTGOMERY CO., 35471 ... I-16
Montrose ... B-11
Monument, 75 ... D-4
Moran, 558 ... H-18
Morehead, 50 ... I-17
Morganville, 192 ... C-13
Morland, 154 ... C-6
Morrill, 230 ... B-16
MORRIS CO., 5923 ... F-14
Morrowville, 155 ... B-13
MORTON CO., 3233 ... J-2
Moscow, 310 ... I-3
Mound City, 694 ... G-19
Mound Valley, 407 ... J-17
Moundridge, 1737 ... G-12
Mt. Hope, 813 ... H-12
Mulberry, 520 ... I-19
Mullinville, 255 ... I-7
Mulvane, 6111 ... I-13
Munden, 100 ... B-12
Munjor, 213 ... E-8
Murdock, 75 ... I-11
Muscotah, 176 ... C-17
Narka, 94 ... B-12
Nashville, 64 ... I-10
Natoma, 335 ... D-9
Navarre, 75 ... E-13
Neal, 65 ... H-16
Nekoma, 80 ... F-8
NEMAHA CO., 10178 ... B-16
Neodesha, 2486 ... I-17
NEOSHO CO., 16512 ... I-17
Neosho Falls, 141 ... G-17
Neosho Rapids, 265 ... F-16
Ness City, 1449 ... F-6
NESS CO., 3107 ... F-7
Netawaka, 143 ... C-16
Neutral ... J-19
New Albany, 56 ... I-16
New Almelo, 50 ... C-6
New Cambria, 126 ... E-12
New Lancaster, 25 ... F-19
New Salem, 80 ... J-14
New Strawn, 394 ... G-16
Newman, 40 ... D-17
Newton, 19132 ... G-13
Nickerson, 1070 ... G-11
Nicodemus, 60 ... C-7
Niles, 40 ... E-12
Niotaze, 82 ... J-16
Norcatur, 151 ... B-6
N. Newton, 1759 ... G-13
N. Topeka ... L-16
Northbranch, 25 ... B-10
Norton, 2928 ... B-7
NORTON CO., 5671 ... B-6
Nortonville, 637 ... C-17
Norway, 40 ... B-12
Norwich, 491 ... I-11
Oak Hill, 24 ... D-13
Oak Valley, 25 ... I-16
Oakland ... L-16
Oaklawn, 3000 ... N-9
Oakley, 2045 ... D-4
Oberlin, 1788 ... B-5
Ocheltree, 100 ... E-19
Odin, 101 ... F-10
Offerle, 199 ... H-7
Ogallah, 90 ... E-7
Ogden, 2087 ... D-14
Oketo, 66 ... B-14
Olathe, 125872 ... E-19
Olivet, 67 ... F-16
Olmitz, 114 ... F-9
Olpe, 546 ... G-15
Olsburg, 219 ... C-14
Onaga, 702 ... C-15
Oneida, 75 ... B-16
Opolis, 130 ... I-19
Osage City, 2943 ... F-16
OSAGE CO., 16295 ... E-16
Osawatomie, 4447 ... F-18
Osborne, 1431 ... C-9
OSBORNE CO., 3858 ... C-9
Oskaloosa, 1113 ... D-17
Oswego, 1829 ... J-18
Otis, 282 ... F-8
Ottawa, 12649 ... F-18
OTTAWA CO., 6091 ... D-12
Overbrook, 1058 ... E-17
Overland Pk., 173372 ... D-19
Oxford, 1049 ... J-13
Ozawkie, 645 ... D-17
Page City, 40 ... D-4
Palco, 277 ... D-7
Palmer, 111 ... C-13
Paola, 5602 ... F-18
Paradise, 49 ... D-9
Park, 126 ... D-5
Park City, 7297 ... H-13
Parker, 277 ... F-18
Parkerfield, 426 ... J-14
Parkerville, 59 ... E-14
Parsons, 10500 ... I-18
Partridge, 248 ... H-11
Pauline ... N-15
PAWNEE CO., 6973 ... G-7
Pawnee Rock, 252 ... G-9
Paxico, 221 ... D-15
Peabody, 1210 ... G-13
Pearl ... E-13
Peck, 110 ... I-13
Penalosa, 17 ... H-10
Penokee, 150 ... C-6
Peoria, 40 ... F-18
Perry, 929 ... D-17
Perth, 50 ... J-12
Peru, 139 ... J-16
Petrolia, 85 ... H-17
Pfeifer, 80 ... E-8
PHILLIPS CO., 5642 ... B-8
Phillipsburg, 2581 ... B-8
Pickrell Cor., 40 ... H-14
Piedmont, 250 ... I-15
Pierceville, 100 ... H-5
Pilsen, 200 ... F-13
Piqua, 107 ... H-17
Pittsburg, 20233 ... I-19
Plains, 1146 ... J-5
Plainville, 1903 ... D-8
Pleasant Grv. ... E-17
Pleasanton, 1216 ... G-19
Plevna, 98 ... H-10
Plymouth, 50 ... F-15
Pomona, 832 ... F-17
Portis, 103 ... C-9
POTTAWATOMIE CO., 21604 ... C-15
Potter, 100 ... C-18
Potwin, 449 ... H-13
Powhattan, 77 ... B-17
Prairie View, 134 ... B-7
Prairie Vil., 21447 ... D-19
Pratt, 6835 ... I-9
PRATT CO., 9656 ... I-9
Prescott, 264 ... G-19
Preston, 158 ... H-10
Pretty Prairie, 680 ... H-11
Princeton, 277 ... F-18
Prospect, 500 ... H-14
Protection, 514 ... J-7
Purcell ... B-17
Quenemo, 388 ... F-17
Quincy ... H-16
Quinter, 918 ... D-6
Radium, 25 ... G-9
Radley, 200 ... I-19
Rago, 30 ... I-11
Ramona, 187 ... F-13
Randall, 65 ... C-11
Randolph, 163 ... C-14
Ransom, 294 ... F-6
Rantoul, 184 ... F-18
RAWLINS CO., 2519 ... B-4
Raymond, 79 ... G-10
Reading, 231 ... F-16
Redfield, 146 ... H-19
Redwing, 20 ... F-9
Reece, 140 ... H-15
RENO CO., 64511 ... H-11
Republic, 116 ... B-11
REPUBLIC CO., 4980 ... B-12
Reserve, 84 ... A-17
Rexford, 232 ... C-5
Rice ... C-12
RICE CO., 10083 ... F-10
Richfield, 43 ... J-2
Richmond, 464 ... F-18
Richter, 20 ... F-17
Riley, 939 ... D-14
RILEY CO., 71115 ... C-14
Riverdale, 60 ... I-13
Riverton, 929 ... J-19
Robinson, 234 ... B-17
Rock, 80 ... I-13
Rock Creek, 50 ... D-17
Rocky Ford ... D-14
Roeland Pk., 6731 ... *J-3
Rolla, 442 ... J-2
Rome ... J-12
ROOKS CO., 5181 ... D-8
Roper ... H-17
Rosalia, 171 ... H-14
Rose ... H-17
Rose Hill, 3931 ... I-13
Roseland, 77 ... J-19
Rossville, 1151 ... D-16
Roxbury, 104 ... F-12
Rozel, 156 ... G-8
Ruleton, 30 ... C-2
Rush Ctr., 170 ... F-8
RUSH CO., 3307 ... F-8
Russell, 4506 ... E-9
RUSSELL CO., 6970 ... D-9
Russell Sprs., 24 ... E-3
Sabetha, 2571 ... B-16
St. Benedict, 70 ... B-15
St. Clere ... C-16
St. Francis, 1329 ... B-2
St. George, 639 ... D-15
St. John, 1295 ... H-9
St. Joseph, 55 ... C-12
St. Leo, 25 ... I-10
St. Mark, 100 ... H-12
St. Marys, 2627 ... D-16
St. Paul, 629 ... I-18
St. Peter, 30 ... D-6
Salina, 47707 ... E-12
SALINE CO., 55606 ... E-11
Sanford ... G-8
Satanta, 1133 ... I-4
Savonburg, 109 ... H-18
Sawyer, 124 ... I-9
Saxman, 25 ... G-11
Scammon, 482 ... J-19
Scandia, 372 ... B-11
Schoenchen, 207 ... E-8
Schulte, 50 ... I-12
Scipio ... F-18
Scott City, 3816 ... F-4
SCOTT CO., 4936 ... F-4
Scottsville, 25 ... C-11
Scranton, 710 ... E-16
Sedan, 1124 ... J-15
Sedgwick, 1695 ... H-12
SEDGWICK CO., 498365 ... I-12
Seguin, 25 ... C-5
Selden, 219 ... C-5
Selkirk, 35 ... F-3
Selma ... G-18
Seneca, 1991 ... B-16
Severance, 94 ... B-17
Severy, 259 ... I-15
Seward, 64 ... G-9
SEWARD CO., 22952 ... J-4
Shallow Water, 40 ... F-4
Sharon, 158 ... J-10
Sharon Sprs., 748 ... E-2
Sharpe ... G-17
Shaw ... I-18
Shawnee, 62209 ... D-19
SHAWNEE CO., 177934 ... E-16
SHERIDAN CO., 2556 ... D-5
Sherman, 50 ... J-18
SHERMAN CO., 6010 ... C-2
Sherwin, 40 ... J-18
Shields, 30 ... F-5
Silver Lake, 1439 ... D-16
Silverdale, 50 ... J-14
Simpson, 86 ... C-11
Sitka ... J-7
Skiddy ... E-14
Smith Ctr., 1665 ... B-9
SMITH CO., 3853 ... B-9
Smolan, 215 ... E-12
Soldier, 136 ... C-16
Solomon, 1095 ... E-13
Somerset, 40 ... F-19
S. Haven, 363 ... J-12
S. Hutchinson, 2457 ... G-11
S. Mound ... I-18
Sparks, 50 ... B-18
Spearville, 773 ... H-7
Speed, 37 ... B-8
Spivey, 78 ... I-11
Spring Hill, 5437 ... E-19
Springdale, 30 ... D-18
Stafford, 1042 ... H-10
STAFFORD CO., 4437 ... G-9
Stanley ... *M-2
STANTON CO., 2235 ... H-1
Stark, 72 ... H-18
Sterling, 2328 ... G-11
STEVENS CO., 5724 ... J-3
Stilwell, 250 ... E-19
Stippville, 30 ... J-19
Stockton, 1329 ... C-8
Strauss ... I-18
Strong City, 485 ... F-15
Studley, 50 ... C-6
Stull, 45 ... D-17
Stuttgart, 75 ... B-8
Sublette, 1453 ... I-4
Summerfield, 156 ... A-15
SUMNER CO., 24132 ... J-12
Sun City, 53 ... I-9
Suppesville, 75 ... I-12
Susank, 34 ... F-9
Sycamore, 200 ... J-17
Sylvan Grv., 279 ... D-10
Sylvia, 218 ... H-10
Syracuse, 1812 ... G-2
Talmage, 99 ... D-13
Talmo, 50 ... B-12
Tampa, 112 ... F-13
Tasco ... C-6
Tecumseh, 650 ... M-17
Terra Hts. ... N-15
Tescott, 319 ... D-11
Thayer, 497 ... I-17
THOMAS CO., 7900 ... C-3
Thrall ... G-15
Timken, 76 ... F-8
Tipton, 210 ... C-10
Tonganoxie, 4996 ... D-18
Topeka, 127473 ... D-16
Toronto, 281 ... H-16
Towanda, 1450 ... H-13
Trading Post ... G-19
Traer, 25 ... B-5
Trego Ctr. ... E-6
TREGO CO., 3001 ... E-6
Tribune, 741 ... F-2
Trousdale ... H-8
Troy, 1010 ... B-18
Turon, 387 ... H-10
Tyro, 220 ... J-16
Udall, 746 ... I-13
Ulysses, 6161 ... I-3
Uniontown, 272 ... H-18
Upland, 25 ... D-13
Urbana, 30 ... I-17
Utica, 158 ... F-6
Valeda, 70 ... J-17
Valley Ctr., 6822 ... H-13
Valley Falls, 1192 ... C-17
Varner ... H-11
Vassar, 530 ... E-17
Venango, 100 ... F-11
Verdi ... E-12
Vermillion, 112 ... B-15
Vernon ... H-17
Vesper, 25 ... D-10
Victoria, 1214 ... E-8
Vilas ... H-17
Vine Creek ... D-12
Vining, 45 ... C-13
Vinland, 30 ... E-18
Viola, 130 ... I-12
Virgil, 71 ... H-16
Vliets, 35 ... B-15
Voda ... D-6
Wabaunsee, 110 ... D-15
WABAUNSEE CO., 7053 ... E-15
Wagstaff, 25 ... E-19
Wakarusa, 260 ... E-16
WaKeeney, 1862 ... D-7
Wakefield, 980 ... D-13
Waldo, 30 ... D-9
Waldron, 11 ... K-11
Walker, 60 ... E-9
Wallace, 57 ... E-2
WALLACE CO., 1485 ... D-2
Walnut, 220 ... I-18
Walton, 235 ... G-13
Wamego, 4372 ... D-15
Washington, 1131 ... B-13
WASHINGTON CO., 5799 ... B-13
Waterloo, 30 ... I-11
Waterville, 680 ... B-14
Wathena, 1364 ... B-18
Wauneta ... J-15
Waverly, 592 ... F-17
Wayne ... B-12
Wayside, 65 ... J-16
Webber, 25 ... B-11
Weir, 686 ... I-19
Welda, 129 ... G-18
Wellington, 8172 ... J-12
Wells, 40 ... D-12
Wellsford, 25 ... I-9
Wellsville, 1857 ... E-18
Weskan, 161 ... E-2
W. Mineral, 185 ... J-19
Westfall, 40 ... E-11
Westmoreland, 778 ... C-15
Westphalia, 163 ... G-17
Westwood, 1506 ... *J-3
Westwood Hills, 359 ... *J-3
Wetmore, 368 ... B-16
Wheaton, 95 ... C-15
Wheeler, 50 ... B-2
White City, 618 ... E-14
White Cloud, 176 ... A-17
Whitewater, 718 ... H-13
Whiting, 187 ... C-17
Wichita, 382368 ... H-13
WICHITA CO., 2234 ... F-3
Wilburton ... J-2
Willard, 92 ... D-16
Williamsburg, 397 ... F-17
Williamstown, 75 ... D-17
Willis, 38 ... B-17
Willowbrook, 87 ... G-11
Willowdale, 20 ... I-10
Wilmore, 53 ... J-8
Wilmot, 30 ... I-14
Wilroads Gdns., 609 ... H-6
Wilsey, 153 ... F-14
Wilson, 781 ... E-10
WILSON CO., 9409 ... I-16
Winchester, 551 ... C-17
Windom, 130 ... F-11
Windthorst, 15 ... H-7
Winfield, 12301 ... J-13
Winifred, 25 ... B-15
Winona, 162 ... D-3
Womer ... B-9
Woodbine, 170 ... E-13
Woodruff, 25 ... A-8
WOODSON CO., 3309 ... H-16
Woodston, 136 ... C-8
Worden ... E-17
Wright, 163 ... H-6
WYANDOTTE CO., 157505 ... D-19
Xenia, 25 ... G-18
Yates Ctr., 1417 ... H-16
Yoder, 194 ... H-11
Zeandale, 50 ... D-15
Zenda, 90 ... I-10
Zenith ... H-10
Zook ... G-8
Zurich, 99 ... D-8

Kentucky

Page locator
Map keys 1–10: Atlas pages 86–87
Map keys 11–20: Atlas pages 88–89
* City keyed to p. 163
† City keyed to p. 226

Aaron, 70 ... M-10
Aberdeen, 200 ... K-5
Acton, 125 ... K-10
ADAIR CO., 18656 ... L-10
Adairville, 852 ... N-5
Adamson ... K-18
Adolphus, 150 ... N-7
Ages, 500 ... M-16
Airport Gdns., 700 ... K-17
Akersville ... N-8
Albany, 2033 ... M-10
Alexandria, 8477 ... D-13
Allegre, 100 ... L-4
Allen City, 193 ... J-18
ALLEN CO., 19956 ... M-7
Allensville, 157 ... M-4
Almo, 100 ... M-1
Alpha, 25 ... M-11
Alpine, 50 ... M-12
Alton, 300 ... H-11
Alton Sta., 450 ... H-11
Altro, 35 ... K-16
Alvaton, 80 ... M-6
Amandaville ... M-10
Amos, 50 ... N-7
Anchorage, 2348 ... B-10
Anco, 360 ... K-17
ANDERSON CO., 21421 ... H-11
Anna ... L-6
Annville, 1095 ... K-14
Anthoston, 250 ... I-3
Anton, 200 ... K-3
Argillite, 50 ... F-18
Argo ... J-20
Arjay, 600 ... M-15
Arlington, 324 ... F-2
Artemus, 590 ... M-15
Ary, 60 ... K-17
Ashbyburg, 40 ... J-3
Ashcamp, 150 ... K-19
Asher, 100 ... L-16
Ashland, 21684 ... F-18
Athertonville, 75 ... J-9
Athol, 75 ... J-15
Auburn, 1340 ... M-5
Audubon Pk., 1473 ... C-7
Augusta, 1190 ... E-14
Aurora, 200 ... M-1
Austin, 150 ... M-8
Auxier, 669 ... I-18
Avawam, 250 ... K-16
Axtel, 60 ... J-6
Bagdad, 220 ... G-11
Baizetown, 25 ... K-5
Bakerton, 35 ... M-10
BALLARD CO., 8249 ... E-2
Ballardsville, 200 ... G-10
Balltown, 80 ... I-9
Bandana, 203 ... E-3
Bandy ... K-12
Banner, 100 ... J-18
Barbourmeade, 1218 ... A-9
Barbourville, 3165 ... M-14
Bardstown, 11700 ... I-9
Bardstown Jct. ... I-9
Bardwell, 723 ... F-2
Barlow, 675 ... E-2
BARREN CO., 42173 ... M-8
Barrier, 75 ... M-12
Baskett, 300 ... I-3
BATH CO., 11591 ... G-15
Battletown, 150 ... H-7
Baxter, 800 ... M-16
Bays, 25 ... J-16
Bear Branch, 80 ... L-15
Beattyville, 1307 ... J-15
Beaumont, 100 ... M-9
Beauty, 600 ... I-19
Beaver, 200 ... K-18
Beaver Dam, 3409 ... K-5
Beaverlick, 75 ... E-12
Beda ... J-5
Bedford, 599 ... F-10
Bee Spr., 150 ... K-7
Beech Creek, 250 ... L-4
Beech Grv., 243 ... J-3
Beechmont, 689 ... L-4
Beechwood ... G-12
Beechwood Vil., 1324 ... B-8
Belcher, 150 ... K-19
Belfry, 600 ... J-19
BELL CO., 28691 ... M-15
Bellefonte, 888 ... †B-1
Bellemeade, 865 ... B-9
Belleview, 343 ... D-11
Bellevue, 5955 ... A-20
Belmont, 100 ... I-9
Belton, 250 ... L-4
Bengal ... K-9
Benham, 500 ... L-17
Bennettstown, 35 ... M-2
Benton, 4349 ... F-4
Berea, 13561 ... J-13
Berkley, 125 ... F-2
Berlin, 45 ... E-13
Berry, 264 ... F-13
Bethany, 65 ... J-16
Bethel, 200 ... G-14
Bethelridge, 30 ... K-12
Bethlehem, 260 ... G-11
Betsy Layne, 688 ... J-18
Beulah, 50 ... K-2
Beulah Hts., 50 ... M-13
Beverly, 30 ... L-15
Bewleyville, 100 ... I-7
Big Clifty, 300 ... J-7
Big Creek, 300 ... L-15
Big Eddy, 150 ... B-12
Big Laurel, 120 ... L-16
Big Spr., 90 ... I-7
Bighill, 200 ... J-13
Bimble, 200 ... M-15
Birdsville ... E-4
Black Gnat, 50 ... K-9
Black Snake, 200 ... M-16
Blackey, 120 ... L-17
Blackford, 100 ... J-2
Blackmont, 300 ... M-16
Blaine, 47 ... H-18
Blandville, 90 ... F-2
Bledsoe, 50 ... L-16
Bloomfield, 838 ... I-10
Blue Licks Spr. ... G-14
Blue Ridge Mnr., 767 ... B-9
Blue River, 30 ... J-18
Bluehole ... L-15
Board Tree, 50 ... J-20
Boaz, 20 ... F-4
Bohon, 30 ... I-11
Boldman, 130 ... J-18
Bond, 90 ... K-14
Bondville ... I-11
Bonnieville, 255 ... K-8
Boone ... J-13
BOONE CO., 118811 ... E-11
Boonesborough ... I-13
Booneville, 81 ... J-15
Boons Camp, 125 ... I-18
Bosco, 200 ... J-18
Boston, 266 ... I-9
Boston, 80 ... E-13
BOURBON CO., 19985 ... H-13
Bow, 25 ... M-10
Bowen, 35 ... I-15
Bowling Green, 58067 ... L-6
BOYD CO., 49542 ... G-18
BOYLE CO., 28432 ... J-11
Bracht ... E-12
BRACKEN CO., 8488 ... F-13
Bradfordsville, 294 ... J-10
Brainard ... J-17
Brandenburg, 2643 ... H-7
BREATHITT CO., 13878 ... J-16
Breckinridge ... G-13
BRECKINRIDGE CO., 20059 ... I-6
Breeding, 60 ... L-9
Bremen, 197 ... K-4
Brewers, 125 ... F-4
Briarwood, 435 ... B-9
Bridgeport, 200 ... H-11
Briensburg, 250 ... F-4
Brinkley, 125 ... K-17
Broad Fields, 250 ... B-8
Broadwell ... G-13
Brodhead, 1211 ... K-13
Bromley, 763 ... B-19
Bronston, 400 ... L-12
Brooks, 2401 ... H-9
Brooksville, 642 ... F-14
Broughtentown, 50 ... K-12
Browder, 300 ... K-4
Brownsboro Farm, 648 ... A-9
Brownsboro Vil., 319 ... B-8
Brownsville, 836 ... K-7
Bruin, 60 ... G-17
Brush Grv. ... I-10
Bryantsville, 130 ... I-12
Buchanan, 50 ... G-18
Buckeye ... I-12
Buckhorn, 162 ... K-16
Buckner, 5837 ... G-9
Buechel, 7272 ... C-8
Buffalo, 498 ... J-9
Buford, 75 ... J-5
Bulan, 600 ... K-17
BULLITT CO., 74319 ... H-9
Burgin, 965 ... I-12
Burkesville, 1521 ... M-10
Burkhart, 30 ... I-16
Burlington, 15926 ... D-12
Burna, 257 ... D-4
Burnaugh, 175 ... G-18
Burning Sprs., 100 ... K-15
Burnside, 611 ... L-12
Burton, 70 ... K-18
Burtonville, 60 ... F-15
Bush, 15 ... L-14
Buskirk, 150 ... J-20
Butler, 612 ... E-13
BUTLER CO., 12690 ... K-6
Bybee, 150 ... I-14
Cadiz, 2558 ... M-2
Cairo, 150 ... I-2
CALDWELL CO., 12984 ... K-1
Calhoun, 763 ... J-4
California, 90 ... E-13
Callaway, 300 ... M-15
CALLOWAY CO., 37191 ... N-1
Calvary, 60 ... J-10
Calvert City, 2566 ... E-4
Calvin, 150 ... M-15
Camargo, 1081 ... H-14
Cambridge, 175 ... C-9
Camp Dix, 30 ... F-16
Camp Kennedy, 30 ... I-12
Camp Nelson, 40 ... I-12
CAMPBELL CO., 90336 ... E-13
Campbellsburg, 813 ... F-10
Campbellsville, 9108 ... K-10
Campton, 441 ... I-15
Canada, 400 ... J-19
Cane Valley, 150 ... L-10
Caney, 100 ... I-16
Caneyville, 608 ... K-6
Canmer, 140 ... K-8
Cannel City, 250 ... I-16
Cannon, 150 ... M-14
Cannonsburg, 856 ... G-18
Canton, 75 ... M-1
Carlisle, 2010 ... G-14
CARLISLE CO., 5104 ... F-2
Carrie, 80 ... K-17
CARROLL CO., 10811 ... F-11
Carrollton, 3938 ... F-10
Carrsville, 50 ... D-4
Carter, 50 ... F-17
CARTER CO., 27720 ... G-17
Cartwright, 40 ... M-11
CASEY CO., 15955 ... K-11
Casey Creek, 50 ... K-10
Caseyville, 40 ... J-1
Catlettsburg, 1856 ... G-18
Causey ... L-16
Cave City, 2240 ... L-8
Cawood, 731 ... M-16
Cayce, 123 ... G-2
Cecil, 125 ... E-3
Cecilia, 572 ... J-8
Center, 125 ... L-9
Centertown, 423 ... K-4
Centerville, 120 ... G-13
Central City, 5978 ... K-4
Cerulean, 314 ... L-2
Chalybeate, 50 ... L-7
Chapel Hill, 50 ... M-7
Chaplin, 418 ... I-10
Chappell, 50 ... L-16
Charleston, 200 ... K-2
Charters ... F-16
Chatham, 40 ... E-14
Chavies, 170 ... K-16
Cherokee ... B-8
Cherrywood Vil., 327 ... B-8
Chestnut Grv., 60 ... G-10
Chloe, 150 ... J-19
Choateville, 200 ... A-11
CHRISTIAN CO., 73955 ... L-3
Cinda, 60 ... L-16
CLARK CO., 35613 ... I-13
Clark Hill, 300 ... G-16
Clarkson, 875 ... J-7
Clay, 1181 ... J-2
Clay City, 1077 ... I-14
CLAY CO., 21730 ... K-15
Claymour ... M-4
Claypool ... M-7
Claysville, 50 ... F-13
Clearfield, 1300 ... H-16
Cleaton, 500 ... K-4
Clementsville, 75 ... K-10
Clermont, 250 ... I-9
Clifford, 40 ... H-19
Clifton, 200 ... H-11
Clifty, 275 ... L-4
Clinton, 1388 ... G-2
CLINTON CO., 10272 ... N-11
Closplint, 150 ... M-17
Cloverport, 1152 ... I-6
Coal Run Vil., 1706 ... J-19
Cobb, 30 ... L-2
Coburg ... K-10
Cold Spr., 5912 ... C-20
Coldstream, 1100 ... A-10
Coldwater, 125 ... G-4
Coleman ... J-20
Colemansville, 40 ... F-13
Colesburg, 90 ... I-8
College Hill ... I-14
Colonial Ter. ... B-9
Colson ... K-18
Columbia, 4452 ... L-10
Columbus, 170 ... F-2
Colville ... G-13
Combs, 900 ... K-16
Comer ... J-3
Concord, 35 ... F-15
Confederate ... L-1
Confluence, 20 ... K-16
Connersville, 35 ... G-13
Constance, 100 ... B-17
Constantine, 40 ... J-7
Conway, 50 ... J-13
Cool Sprs., 50 ... K-5
Co-Operative, 180 ... M-12
Coopersville, 80 ... M-12
Coral Ridge ... E-7
Corbin, 7304 ... L-14
Corinth, 232 ... F-12
Corinth ... M-5
Cornettsville, 90 ... L-17
Cornishville, 90 ... I-11
Corydon, 720 ... I-2
Cottle ... I-16
Covington, 40640 ... D-12
Cowan, 150 ... G-14
Coxs Creek, 50 ... I-9
Crab Orchard, 841 ... J-12
Cranks, 120 ... M-17
Crayne, 173 ... K-1
Craynor, 85 ... J-18
Crescent Pk. ... C-18
Crescent Sprs., 3801 ... B-18
Crestview, 475 ... C-20
Crestview Hills, 3148 ... C-18
Crestwood, 4531 ... G-9
Crider, 60 ... L-1
Crittenden, 3815 ... E-12
CRITTENDEN CO., 9315 ... K-1
Crockett, 40 ... H-17
Crofton, 749 ... L-3
Cromona, 400 ... K-18
Cromwell, 240 ... K-5
Cropper, 150 ... G-10
Crossland, 50 ... G-4
Crown, 50 ... L-18
Crutchfield, 110 ... G-3
Crystal, 20 ... J-15
Cub Run, 125 ... K-7
Cuba, 125 ... G-3
Culver, 30 ... H-17
Cumberland, 2237 ... L-17
CUMBERLAND CO., 6856 ... M-9
Cundiff ... L-10
Cunningham, 400 ... F-3
Curdsville, 150 ... I-3
Custer, 125 ... I-7
Cutshin, 100 ... L-16
Cynthiana, 6402 ... G-13
Daisy, 200 ... L-17
Danville, 16218 ... J-12
Davella ... I-18
David, 300 ... J-17
DAVIESS CO., 96656 ... J-4
Davis ... G-12
Dawson Sprs., 2764 ... L-2
Day ... L-18
Daysville, 75 ... M-4
Dayton, 5338 ... A-20
Deane, 80 ... K-18
Deatsville, 80 ... I-9
Debord, 30 ... I-18
Decoy, 20 ... J-17
Defoe, 50 ... G-11
Dekoven, 125 ... J-1
Delphia, 100 ... L-17
Demossville, 60 ... E-13
Denniston, 75 ... I-15
Denton, 30 ... G-17
Depoy, 70 ... K-4
Dermont, 75 ... B-2
Devon, 50 ... D-12
Dexter, 277 ... G-5
Diablock, 453 ... K-17
Diamond, 150 ... K-2
Dice, 20 ... K-16
Dixie, 100 ... I-2
Dixon, 786 ... J-2
Dizney, 250 ... M-17
Dog Walk ... K-12
Dongola ... L-18
Dorton, 250 ... K-18
Douglass Hills, 5484 ... B-9
Dover, 252 ... E-14
Draffenville, 300 ... F-4
Drakesboro, 515 ... K-4
Dreyfus, 150 ... J-13
Drift, 300 ... J-18
Dry Ridge, 2191 ... F-12
Dublin, 50 ... G-3
Dubre, 60 ... M-9
Duckers ... H-11
Dukedom, 50 ... G-3
Dukes ... I-5
Dunbar, 75 ... K-5
Duncan ... I-11
Dundee, 150 ... J-5
Dunmor, 200 ... L-4
Dunnville, 225 ... K-11
Dwale, 329 ... J-18
Dwarf, 100 ... K-17
Dycusburg, 26 ... K-1
Dyer, 125 ... I-7
Earlington, 1413 ... K-3
E. Bernstadt, 716 ... K-14
E. Union ... G-14
Eastview, 60 ... J-7
Echols, 50 ... K-5
Eddyville, 2554 ... L-1
Edgewood, 8575 ... C-18
EDMONSON CO., 12161 ... K-6
Edmonton, 1595 ... L-9
Egypt, 30 ... K-14
Eighty Eight, 75 ... M-8
Ekron, 135 ... I-7
Elba, 30 ... J-3
Eli, 100 ... L-11
Elihu, 100 ... L-12
Elizabethtown, 28531 ... I-8
Elizaville, 181 ... G-14
Elk Creek, 20 ... H-10
Elk Horn, 50 ... K-10
Elkatawa, 50 ... J-16
Elkfork, 1539 ... H-17
Elkhorn City, 982 ... K-19
Elkton, 2062 ... M-4
Ella ... L-10
ELLIOTT CO., 7852 ... H-17
Elliottville, 40 ... G-16
Elmburg, 75 ... G-11
Elsie, 25 ... I-17
Elsmere, 8451 ... C-18
Emerson, 25 ... G-16
Eminence, 2498 ... G-10
Emlyn, 427 ... M-14
Emmalena, 100 ... K-17
English, 150 ... F-10
Ensor ... I-5
Eolia, 300 ... L-18
Epleys, 75 ... M-5
Epworth ... F-15
Erlanger, 18082 ... D-12
Ermine, 300 ... L-18
ESTILL CO., 14672 ... I-14
Ethridge ... E-11
Etty, 100 ... K-18
Eubank, 319 ... K-12
Evanston ... J-17
Evarts, 962 ... M-17
Ewing, 264 ... G-14
Exie ... L-9
Ezel, 235 ... I-16
Fairdale ... E-7
Fairdealing, 100 ... M-1
Fairfield, 113 ... I-10
Fairplay, 20 ... L-10
Fairview, 286 ... M-3
Fairview, 40 ... F-14
Fairview ... †B-1
Falcon, 120 ... I-17
Fall Rock, 90 ... K-15
Falls of Rough, 75 ... J-6
Fallsburg, 125 ... G-18
Falmouth, 2169 ... F-13
Fancy Farm, 458 ... F-3
Farmers, 284 ... H-15
Farmersville, 40 ... K-2
Farmington, 245 ... G-4
Farristown ... J-13
Faubush, 80 ... L-11
FAYETTE CO., 295803 ... H-12
Faywood, 100 ... H-12
Fearsville, 60 ... L-3
Fedscreek, 175 ... J-20
Ferguson, 924 ... L-12
Fern Creek, 17870 ... D-9
Ferndale, 200 ... M-15
Fincastle, 817 ... A-10
Finchville, 200 ... H-10
Finley, 20 ... J-10
Finney ... M-7
Firebrick, 350 ... E-17
Fisty, 125 ... K-17
Flaherty, 250 ... I-7
Flat Lick, 960 ... M-15
Flatgap, 100 ... H-17
Flatwoods, 7423 ... F-18
FLEMING CO., 14348 ... G-14
Fleming-Neon, 770 ... K-18
Flemingsburg, 2658 ... G-15
Flippin, 35 ... M-8
Florence, 29951 ... D-12
FLOYD CO., 39451 ... J-18
Folsom, 40 ... E-12
Folsomdale, 150 ... F-3
Fonde, 75 ... N-14
Foraker, 40 ... J-17
Ford, 140 ... I-13
Fords Branch, 200 ... J-19
Fordsville, 524 ... J-5
Forest Grv., 125 ... H-13
Forest Hills, 444 ... C-9
Forest Hills, 300 ... J-19
Forks of Elkhorn, 150 ... A-13
Ft. Mitchell, 8207 ... D-12
Ft. Thomas, 16325 ... D-12
Ft. Wright, 5723 ... B-19
Foster, 40 ... E-13
Fount ... L-15
Fountain Run, 217 ... M-8
Four Oaks, 140 ... F-13
Fourmile, 450 ... M-15
Foxport, 50 ... F-15
Frakes, 125 ... N-14
Frances, 50 ... K-1
Frankfort, 25527 ... G-11
Franklin, 8408 ... M-6
FRANKLIN CO., 49285 ... G-11
Franklin Cross Roads, 60 ... J-8
Frazer, 35 ... L-12
Fredericktown, 150 ... I-10
Fredonia, 401 ... K-1
Freeburn, 399 ... J-20
Freedom ... M-10
Frenchburg, 486 ... H-15
Fruit Hill ... L-3
Fulgham, 60 ... G-3
Fulton, 2445 ... G-3
FULTON CO., 6813 ... G-2
Future City, 200 ... E-3
Gage, 40 ... E-3
GALLATIN CO., 8589 ... E-11
Gamaliel, 376 ... N-8
Gano, 300 ... M-17
Gap in Knob, 180 ... H-9
Garden Vil., 100 ... J-19
Gardenside ... B-14
Gardnersville, 50 ... E-12
Garfield, 150 ... I-7
Garner, 150 ... K-17
Garrard, 65 ... L-15
GARRARD CO., 16912 ... J-12
Garrett, 500 ... J-18
Garrett, 150 ... I-
Garrison, 866 ... F-
Gascon ... L
Gasper ... L
Gatliff, 60 ... M-1
Gays Creek, 80 ... K-1
Geneva, 150 ... I
Georgetown, 29098 ... G-1
Germantown, 154 ... F-
Gest, 50 ... G-
Ghent, 323 ... E-
Gilbertsville, 458 ... E
Gilley, 50 ... L-
Gilpin, 50 ... K-1
Girdler, 250 ... L-
Glasgow, 14028 ... L
Gleanings ... J
Glen Dean, 50 ... J
Glencoe, 360 ... E-1
Glendale, 350 ... J
Glens Fork, 100 ... L-
Glensboro, 130 ... H-
Glenview, 531 ... A
Glenview Hills, 319 ... A
Glenville, 20 ... J
Globe, 250 ... G-
Goddard ... G-
Gold City ... M
Goldbug, 100 ... M-
Goose Rock, 200 ... L-
Gordon, 100 ... L-
Goshen, 909 ... G
Gracey, 138 ... M
Gradyville, 75 ... L
Graham, 700 ... K
Grahamville, 200 ... E
Grahn, 550 ... G-
Grange City, 75 ... G-
Grangertown, 100 ... J
GRANT CO., 4662 ... F-
Grants Lick, 100 ... E-
Grassy Creek ... I-
Gratz, 78 ... F-
Gravel Switch, 75 ... J-
GRAVES CO., 37121 ... F
Gray, 750 ... L-
Gray Hawk, 100 ... K-
Graymoor-Devondale, 2870 ... E
Grays Branch, 125 ... F-
Grays Knob, 300 ... M-
Grayson, 4217 ... G-
GRAYSON CO., 25746 ... J
Grayson Sprs.
GREEN CO., 11258 ... K
Green Spr., 715 ... A
Greensburg, 2163 ... K
Greenup, 1188 ... F-
GREENUP CO., 36910 ... F-
Greenville, 4312 ... K
Greenwood, 95 ... M-
Grethel, 100 ... J-
Grider, 50 ... M
Grove Ctr., 70
Guffie
Gulnare ... J-
Gum Sulphur ... K-
Gunlock, 20 ... J-
Guston, 200
Guthrie, 1419 ... M
Habit, 100
Haddix, 150 ... J-
Hadley, 25
Hagerhill, 150 ... I-
Haldeman, 250 ... G
Halfway, 35 ... M
Halls Gap, 90 ... J
Halo, 150 ... K
Hamlin, 175 ... M
Hammonville, 30
Hampton, 100
HANCOCK CO., 8565
Hanson, 742
Hardin, 615
HARDIN CO., 105543
Hardin Sprs.
Hardinsburg, 2343
Hardshell, 15 ... J
Hardy, 650 ... J
Hardyville, 156
Hargett ... I
Harlan, 1745 ... M
HARLAN CO., 29278 ... L-
Harned, 140
Harold, 400 ... J
HARRISON CO., 18846 ... F
Harrisonville, 75 ... H
Harrods Creek
Harrodsburg, 8340 ... I
HART CO., 18199
Hartford, 2672
Hatcher, 60 ... K
Hawesville, 945
Hays, 30
Haywood
Hazard, 4456 ... K
Hazel, 410
Hazel Green, 228
Headquarters ... G
Hebbardsville, 125
Hebron, 5929 ... B
Heflin
Heidelberg, 300
Heidrick, 700 ... M
Helechawa, 25
Helena, 50 ... F
Hellier, 400 ... K
Helton, 30 ... L
Hemphill, 500 ... K
Henderson, 28757
HENDERSON CO., 46250
Hendricks, 60
Hendron, 4687
HENRY CO., 15416 ... F
Henshaw, 100
Herd, 15 ... K
Heritage Creek, 1435
Herndon, 150
Hesler, 60 ... F
Hestand, 25
Hi Hat, 200 ... K
Hickman, 2395
HICKMAN CO., 4902
Hickory, 150
High Br., 242
High Pt., 100
Highgrove
Highland Hts., 6923 ... C
Highland Pk.

*, †, ‡, §, ◊ See explanation under state title in this index.
County and parish names are listed in capital letters & boldface type.
Independent cities (not included in a county) are listed in italics.

LAWRENCE CO., 15860 ... H-18
Lawrenceburg, 10505 ... H-11
Leander, 30 ... J-18
Leatherwood, 140 ... L-17
Lebanon, 5539 ... J-10
Lebanon Jct., 1813 ... I-8
Leburn, 70 ... K-17
Lecta, 80 ... L-8
Ledbetter, 1683 ... L-4
Lee City, 100 ... J-16
Leesburg, 75 ... G-13
Leitchfield, 6699 ... I-7
Lenox, 20 ... H-16
Lenoxburg, 40 ... E-13
Lerose, 100 ... J-15
Leslie, 150 ... L-17

LESLIE CO., 11310 ... L-16
Letcher, 150 ... L-17

LETCHER CO., 24519 ... L-17
Levee, 40 ... H-14
Level Green, 40 ... K-13
Levi, 40 ... L-15

LEWIS CO., 13870 ... F-16
Lewisburg, 810 ... L-5
Lewisburg, 75 ... L-5
Lewisport, 1670 ... I-5
Lexington, 295803 ... H-12
Liberty, 2168 ... K-11
Lida, 100 ... L-14
Liggett, 150 ... M-16
Lily, 500 ... L-14
Limaburg, 200 ... C-16

LINCOLN CO., 24742 ... J-12
Lindseyville, 200 ... K-7
Linefork, 150 ... L-17
Linton, 40 ... M-2
Linwood, 50 ... K-8
Littcarr, 75 ... K-17
Little, 40 ... J-16
Little Mount, 60 ... H-10
Little Rock, 75 ... H-14
Little Sandy, 50 ... H-16
Littleton, 275 ... L-15
Livermore, 1365 ... J-4
Livia, 15 ... J-4
Livingston, 226 ... K-13

LIVINGSTON CO., 9519 ... D-4
Lloyd, 900 ... F-17
Load, 100 ... F-17
Lockport, 100 ... G-11
LOGAN CO., 26835 ... L-5
Lola, 200 ... D-4
Lombard, 15 ... I-15
London, 7993 ... L-14
Lone Oak, 450 ... E-3
Long Ridge, 40 ... H-11
Lookout, 350 ... K-19
Loretto, 713 ... J-10
Lost Creek, 40 ... J-16
Louisa, 2467 ... H-18
Louisville, 597337 ... G-8
Lovelaceville, 148 ... F-3
Lovely, 700 ... J-19
Lowes, 98 ... E-4
Lowmansville, 50 ... H-18
Loyall, 1461 ... M-16
Lucas, 120 ... M-8
Ludlow, 4407 ... B-9
Lusby's Mill, 50 ... F-12
Lynch, 747 ... L-17
Lyndon, 11002 ... B-9
Lynn, 150 ... G-4
Lynn Grv., 250 ... G-4
Lynnview, 914 ... C-7
Lynnville, 120 ... G-4

LYON CO., 8314 ... L-1
Lyons, 60 ... J-1
Lytten, 40 ... L-2
Macedonia, L-2
Maceo, 413 ... I-4
Mackville, 222 ... I-11

MADISON CO., 82916 ... J-13
Madisonville, 19591 ... K-3
Madrid, 50 ... J-7
Magnolia, 524 ... J-8
MAGOFFIN CO., 13333 ... J-17
Majestic, 400 ... J-20
Mallie, 50 ... K-17
Malone, 100 ... L-14
Maloneton, 200 ... F-17
Mammoth Cave, 30 ... K-8
Manitou, 150 ... K-3
Mannington, 125 ... L-3
Mansville, 150 ... K-10
Manton, 200 ... J-18
Marcum, L-20
Mariba, 50 ... I-15
Marion, 3039 ... K-1

MARION CO., 19820 ... J-10
Marrowbone, 400 ... L-19
Marrowbone, 217 ... M-9

MARSHALL CO., 31448 ... F-4
Marshes Siding, 700 ... M-12
Martin, 634 ... J-18

MARTIN CO., 12929 ... I-19
Mary Alice, 350 ... M-16
Mary Helen, 160 ... M-16
Mason, 90 ... F-16

MASON CO., 17490 ... F-15
Maslowville, 1014 ... A-4
Massac, 4505 ... E-3
Matanzas, M-1
Maud, 40 ... A-4
Mayfield, 10024 ... F-3
Mayking, 487 ... L-18
Mayo, I-16
Mays Lick, 242 ... F-14
Maysville, 9011 ... F-15
Maytown, 243 ... I-16
Mazie, 30 ... H-17
McAfee, 50 ... I-11
McAndrews, 450 ... J-19

MCCRACKEN CO., 65565 ... E-3

MCCREARY CO., 18306 ... N-12
McDaniels, 200 ... J-6
McDowell, 400 ... J-18
McHenry, 388 ... K-5
McKee, 800 ... K-14
McKinney, 275 ... J-12
...

MEADE CO., 28602 ... H-7
Meadow Vale, 736 ... A-9
Meadowthorpe ... B-3
Meadowview Estates, 363 ... H-7
Means, 150 ... H-15
Melber, 300 ... F-3
Melbourne, 401 ... *SN-4
Meldrum, 150 ... N-15
Melvin, 250 ... K-17
Memphis Jct., 250 ... C-3

MENIFEE CO., 6306 ... I-15
Mentor, 193 ... E-13

MERCER CO., 21331 ... I-11
Meredith, K-7
Merry Oaks, 50 ... L-7
Meta, 250 ... J-19

METCALFE CO., 10099 ... L-9
Mexico, 30 ... K-1
Middleburg, 300 ... K-11
Middlesboro, M-1
10334 ... N-15
Middleton, 60 ... M-5
Middletown, 7218 ... G-9
Midland, 175 ... H-13
Midway, 1641 ... H-12
Midway, 40 ... H-7
Midway, 45 ... G-4
Milburn, 250 ... F-3
Milford, 90 ... F-13
Mill Sprs., 50 ... M-12
Millersburg, 792 ... G-13
Millerstown, 40 ... J-8
Millstone, 117 ... K-18
Milltown, 25 ... L-9
Millville, 200 ... H-12
Millwood, 75 ... J-6
Milton, 574 ... E-10
Minerva, 70 ... F-14
Minorsville, 50 ... G-12
Mintonville, K-11
Mitchellsburg, 350 ... J-11
Mize, 10 ... I-16
Molus, 130 ... M-16

MONROE CO., 10963 ... M-9
Monterey, 138 ... G-11
Monticello, 6188 ... M-11

MONTGOMERY CO., 26499 ... H-14
Mooleyville, 60 ... H-6
Moon, 10 ... H-17
Moorefield, 125 ... G-14
Mooresville, 45 ... I-10
Moorland, 431 ... B-9
Moorman, 175 ... K-4
Moranburg ... F-14
Morehead, 6845 ... G-16
Morehead, 150 ... H-11
Morgan, 30 ... F-13

MORGAN CO., 13923 ... H-16
Morganfield, 3285 ... J-2
Morgantown, 2394 ... K-5
Morning View, 100 ... E-12
Morrill, 100 ... J-13
Mortons Gap, 863 ... K-3
Morrisville, 90 ... H-12
Moscow, 45 ... G-2
Moseleyville, 200 ... I-4
Mt. Carmel, 100 ... F-15
Mt. Eden, 200 ... H-10
Mt. Hermon, 40 ... M-8
Mt. Olivet, 299 ... F-14
Mt. Sherman, 250 ... I-9
Mt. Sterling, 6895 ... H-14
Mt. Vernon, 2477 ... K-13
Mt. Victory, L-13
Mt. Washington, 9117 ... H-9
Mountain Ash, 200 ... N-14
Mousie, 400 ... J-18
Mouthcard, 150 ... K-19
Mozelle, 150 ... M-16
Mud Lick, M-8

MUHLENBERG CO., 31499 ... L-4
Muldraugh, 947 ... I-8
Munfordville, 1615 ... K-8
Murray, 17741 ... G-4
Murray Hill, 582 ... A-9
Muses Mills, 80 ... G-15
Myers, 50 ... K-14
Myra, 100 ... K-18
Nancy, 400 ... L-12
Napoleon, 50 ... J-7
Natural Br., 10 ... I-15
Nazareth, 400 ... J-10
Nebo, 236 ... K-2
Nelson, 250 ... L-8

NELSON CO., 43437 ... I-9
Nerinx, 300 ... J-10
Nevada, J-11
Nevisdale, 200 ... M-14
New Castle, 912 ... G-10
New Columbus, 75 ... F-12
New Concord, 100 ... N-1
New Haven, 855 ... I-9
New Hope, 129 ... J-9
New Liberty, 175 ... F-11
New Market, 50 ... J-10
New Zion, 120 ... H-10
Newburg ... C-7
Newfoundland, 40 ... H-17
Newman, 100 ... L-14
Newport, 15273 ... B-20
Newtown, 50 ... G-13
Nicholasville, 28015 ... I-12

NICHOLAS CO., 7135 ... G-14
Nicholasville, 28015 ... I-12
Noctor, 40 ... J-16
Norbourne Estates, 441 ... A-9
N. Corbin, 1773 ... L-14
N. Middletown, 643 ... *N-14
Northfield, 1000 ... A-9
Northville, 1204 ... A-9
Norwood, 370 ... B-9
Nuckols, 60 ... J-4
Oak Grv., 7489 ... N-3
Oakdale, 1900 ... C-4
Oakland, 200 ... L-7
Oakville, 250 ... J-4
Oddville, F-13
Ohio, M-1

OHIO CO., 23842 ... J-5
Oil Sprs., 150 ... I-17
Okolona, 17807 ... D-8
Olaton, 200 ... J-5
Oldtown, 80 ... F-17
Olga, I-16
Olive Hill, 1599 ... G-16
Olmstead, 50 ... D-11

Olympia, 125 ... H-15
Olympia Sprs. ... H-15
Omaha, K-18
Oneida, 410 ... K-15
Oneonta, D-13
Onton, 141 ... J-3
Orville ... I-18
Oscar, 50 ... E-2
Oven Fork, 170 ... L-18
Owensboro, 57265 ... I-4
Owenton, 1327 ... F-11
Owingsville, 1530 ... H-15

OWEN CO., 10841 ... F-11

OWSLEY CO., 4755 ... K-15
Oxford, G-12
Paducah, 25024 ... E-4
Paint Lick, 150 ... J-13
Paintsville, 3459 ... I-18
Palma, 100 ... F-4
Palmer, I-14
Paris, 8553 ... G-13
Park City, 537 ... L-7
Park Hills, 2970 ... B-19
Parkers Lake, 55 ... M-12
Parksville, 400 ... J-11
Parkway Vil., 650 ... C-7
Partridge, 50 ... L-18
Patesville ... I-5
Pathfork, 379 ... M-16
Paw Paw, 75 ... J-20
Payne Gap, 329 ... K-18
Peach Grv., 100 ... E-13
Pebworth, J-15
Peedee, 30 ... M-2
Pellville, 120 ... I-5
Pellyton, K-11
Pembroke, 869 ... M-3
Pendleton, 80 ... H-10

PENDLETON CO., 14877 ... F-13
Penrod, 70 ... L-4
Peonia, 40 ... K-7
Peoples, 20 ... K-16
Perry Pk., 160 ... F-11
Perryville, 751 ... I-11
Petersburg, 620 ... D-11
Petersville, 20 ... F-16
Petroleum, 50 ... M-8
Pewee Valley, 1456 ... G-9
Peytonsburg, 60 ... N-10
Phelps, 893 ... J-20
Phillipsburg, 100 ... J-11
Philpot, 400 ... I-4
Phyllis, 350 ... J-19
Pierce, I-15
Pikeview, 20 ... K-19
Pikeville, 6903 ... J-19
Pilgrim, 150 ... I-19
Pilot Oak, 100 ... G-3
Pilot View, H-14
Pinckard, 30 ... I-12
Pine Hill, 40 ... K-13
Pine Knot, 1621 ... N-13
Pine Ridge, 125 ... I-15
Pine Top, 100 ... K-18
Piner, I-12
Pineville, 1732 ... M-15
Pioneer Vil., 2030 ... H-9
Pippa Passes, 533 ... K-18
Piqua, F-14
Pittsburg, 600 ... L-14
Plank, 20 ... K-15
Plantation, 832 ... B-9
Pleasant Ridge, 200 ... J-4
Pleasant View, 50 ... H-12
Pleasure Ridge Pk., 25776 ... D-5
Pleasureville, 834 ... G-10
Plum Sprs., 453 ... L-6
Plummers, 30 ... L-5
Plummers Mill, L-5
Plumville, 150 ... I-3
Polksville, 60 ... K-16
Pomeroyton, 75 ... I-15
Poole, 400 ... J-2
Poplar Hills, 362 ... C-8
Poplar Plains, 120 ... G-15
Port Royal, 130 ... F-11
Pottsville, D-13
Powderly, 745 ... K-4

POWELL CO., 12613 ... I-14
Powersville, 60 ... F-14
Prairie Vil., A-9
Preachersville, 30 ... J-12
Preston, 150 ... H-15
Prestonsburg, 3255 ... I-18
Prestonville, 161 ... F-10
Prices Mill, 40 ... M-5
Pricetown, L-15
Priceville, 50 ... K-8
Pride, 75 ... J-2
Princess, 200 ... G-18
Princeton, 6329 ... L-2
Pritchardsville, 30 ... L-6
Prospect, 4698 ... G-9
Providence, 3193 ... K-2
Providence, 30 ... N-5
Pruden, 150 ... N-14
Pryorsburg, 311 ... G-3
Pulaski, 100 ... L-12

PULASKI CO., 63063 ... L-12
Putney, 250 ... M-16
Quality, 50 ... L-5
Quicksand, 150 ... J-16
Quincy, 350 ... F-17
Quinton, K-7
Rabbit Hash, 315 ... C-11
Raccoon, 400 ... J-19
Raceland, 2424 ... F-18
Radcliff, 21688 ... H-8
Ragland, G-2
Randolph, I-8
Raven, 75 ... K-16
Ravenna, 605 ... I-14
Raywick, 134 ... I-9
Ready, 100 ... L-13
Rectorville, 75 ... F-15
Redbush, 60 ... I-17
Redfox, 60 ... K-17
Redhouse, I-13
Reed, 100 ... I-4
Reeds Crossing, 150 ... I-13
Reid Vil., 150 ... J-8
Reidland, 4491 ... E-4
Revelo, 200 ... N-13
Reynolds Sta., 100 ... J-6
Rhoda, 100 ... L-7
Rhodelia, 20 ... H-6
Ribolt, 80 ... F-16
Riceville, K-15
Rich Pond, 300 ... L-6
Richardsville, 150 ... L-6
Richelieu, L-7
Richland, 75 ... M-17
Richlawn, 405 ... B-8

Richmond, 31364 ... I-13
Richwood, E-12
Rineyville, 400 ... I-8
Ringos Mills, 45 ... G-15
River Bluff, 403 ... G-9
Riverside Gdns. ... C-7
Riverwood, 446 ... A-8
Rock, 75 ... L-16
Robards, 515 ... J-3
Robinson Creek, 400 ... K-19
Rochester, 152 ... K-5

ROCKCASTLE CO., 17056 ... K-13
Rockfield, 70 ... M-6
Rockholds, 390 ... M-14
Rockhouse, 200 ... K-19
Rockport, 266 ... K-4
Rocky Hill, 160 ... L-7
Rogers, 100 ... I-15
Rolling Fields, 646 ... B-8
Rolling Hills, 959 ... B-9
Rome, 150 ... C-1
Roseville, M-8
Rosewood, L-2
Rosine, 113 ... J-5
Ross, 150 ... *SN-5
Rosslyn ... J-1
Round Hill, 120 ... L-7
Roundhill, K-6
Rousseau, 110 ... J-16

ROWAN CO., 23333 ... H-16
Rowland, 75 ... J-12
Rowletts, 300 ... K-8
Roxana, 150 ... L-17
Royalton, 260 ... J-17
Royville, 55 ... L-10
Ruckerville, L-14
Ruddles Mills, 200 ... G-13
Rumsey, 200 ... J-4
Rush, 200 ... G-18

RUSSELL CO., 17565 ... L-11
Russell Sprs., 2441 ... L-11
Russellville, 6960 ... M-5
Ryland, 200 ... E-12
Sacramento, 468 ... K-4
Sadieville, 303 ... G-12
St. Catharine, 500 ... I-10
St. Charles, 277 ... K-3
St. Dennis, 977 ... C-6
St. Francis, 80 ... I-9
St. Helens, 100 ... J-15
St. Joseph, 50 ... I-13
St. Mary, 150 ... I-10
St. Matthews, 17472 ... G-9
St. Paul, 80 ... F-17
St. Regis Pk., 1454 ... C-9
Salem, 752 ... K-1
Salmons, 40 ... M-6
Saloma, 40 ... K-10
Salt Gum, 20 ... L-15
Salt Lick, 303 ... H-15
Salvisa, 400 ... I-11
Salyersville, 1883 ... J-17
Sample, 70 ... J-6
Samuels, 60 ... I-9
Sanders, 238 ... F-11
Sandgap, 300 ... K-14
Sandy Hook, 675 ... H-17
Sardis, 103 ... G-14
Sassafras, 950 ... K-17
Saul, 30 ... K-16
Savoyard ... L-7
Saxton, 120 ... N-14
Scalf, 30 ... M-15
Schochoh, 60 ... M-5
Science Hill, 693 ... L-12
Scottsburg, 20 ... J-10
Scuddy, 30 ... K-17
Sebree, 1603 ... J-3
Sedalia, 295 ... G-4
Seneca Gdns., 696 ... C-8
Settle, M-7
Sextons Creek, 30 ... K-15
Shady Grv., 35 ... K-2
Shady Grv., 60 ... I-15
Shannon ... F-14
Sharkey, 60 ... H-16

SHELBY CO., 42074 ... G-10
Shelbyville, 14045 ... G-10
Shepherdsville, 11222 ... H-9
Sherburne, 60 ... G-15
Sheridan, 40 ... J-17
Sherman, 50 ... F-12
Shively, 15264 ... C-6
Shopville ... L-12
Short Creek, 45 ... J-6
Shoulderblade ... J-16
Shrewsbury, 60 ... J-6
Sibert, 150 ... L-15
Sideview, 40 ... H-14
Sidney, 200 ... J-19
Siler, 300 ... N-14
Siler, 60 ... M-14
Siloam, 175 ... G-15
Silver Grv., 1102 ... D-13

SIMPSON CO., 17327 ... M-6
Simpsonville, 2484 ... G-10
Sitka, 150 ... I-18
Sizerock, 40 ... L-16
Skylight, 90 ... G-9
Slade, 80 ... I-15
Slate Valley, 40 ... H-15
Slaughters, 216 ... J-3
Slemp, 50 ... L-17
Sligo, 60 ... G-10
Sloans Valley, 200 ... L-12
Smilax, 100 ... L-16
Smith, 150 ... M-16
Smith Mills, 450 ... J-2
Smithfield, 106 ... G-10
Smithland, 350 ... L-4
Smiths Grv., 714 ... L-7
Smyrna ... D-8
Snow, M-10
Soft Shell, 30 ... K-17
Soldier, 200 ... G-16
Somerset, 11196 ... L-12
Sonora, 513 ... I-8
Sorgho, 160 ... I-4
South, 25 ... K-8
S. Carrollton, 184 ... K-4
S. Irvine, 400 ... I-14
S. Park, M-5
S. Park View, 75 ... C-8
S. Portsmouth, 900 ... F-17
S. Shore, 1122 ... F-17

S. Union, 75 ... M-6
S. Wallins, 859 ... M-16
S. Williamson, 602 ... J-19
Southgate, 3803 ... B-20
Southville ... H-10
Spa ... L-10
Sparksville, 50 ... L-10
Sparta, 231 ... F-11
Spears ... J-13
Speedwell ... J-13
Speight, 100 ... K-18

SPENCER CO., 17061 ... H-10
Spottsville, 325 ... J-3
Spring Grv., 60 ... I-3
Spring Lick, 40 ... J-6
Spring Mill, 287 ... D-8
Spring Valley, 654 ... A-9
Springfield, 2519 ... I-10
Springlee, 426 ... B-8
Stab, 20 ... L-13
Stacy, 70 ... K-16
Staffordsville, 200 ... I-18
Stamping Ground, 643 ... G-12
Stanford, 3487 ... J-12
Stanley, 300 ... I-4
Stanton, 2733 ... I-14
Stanville, 125 ... J-18
State Line, 10 ... G-2
Static ... N-11
Stearns, 1416 ... M-12
Steff, 10 ... K-6
Stella, 240 ... G-4
Stephens, 15 ... H-17
Stephensburg, 150 ... I-8
Stephensport, 200 ... I-6
Steubenville, 150 ... M-11
Stinnett, 125 ... L-16
Stoney Fork, 125 ... M-15
Stonewall ... J-12
Stony Point, 75 ... K-18
Stopover ... J-20
Strathmoor Vil., 648 ... C-8
Stringtown, 40 ... B-17
Strunk, 70 ... N-13
Sturgis, 1898 ... J-1
Sublett ... J-11
Sublimity City, 800 ... L-14
Sugar Creek, 25 ... L-11
Sugartit ... D-12
Sullivan, 300 ... J-1
Sulphur, 220 ... F-10
Sulphur Lick, 40 ... M-8
Sulphur Sprs., 30 ... J-5
Sulphur Well, 50 ... L-8
Summer Shade, 307 ... M-9
Summersville, 568 ... K-9
Summit, 150 ... J-7
Summit, 150 ... J-7
Sunfish, 30 ... K-6
Sunrise, 45 ... F-13
Sunshine, 30 ... M-16
Swamp Branch, 10 ... I-17
Swampton ... J-17
Sweeden, 125 ... K-7
Sylvania ... D-5
Symsonia, 615 ... F-4
Talbert, 70 ... K-14
Talcum, 300 ... K-17
Tallega, 30 ... J-15
Tateville, 500 ... L-12

TAYLOR CO., 24512 ... K-10
Taylor Mill, 6604 ... C-19
Taylorsport, 100 ... A-16
Taylorsville, 763 ... H-10
Teaberry, 100 ... J-18
Temple Hill, 75 ... M-8
Terrapin ... I-11
Texas, 60 ... I-10
Thealka, 400 ... I-18
Thousandsticks, 70 ... K-16
Three Sprs., 80 ... C-4
Three Sprs., 30 ... I-8
Thruston, 500 ... I-4
Tilden, 40 ... J-2
Tilford, K-6
Tiline, 75 ... L-4
Tilton, 50 ... G-15
Timsley, 100 ... M-15

TODD CO., 12460 ... M-4
Todds Pt. ... G-10
Tolesboro, 600 ... F-16
Tolu, 88 ... L-1
Tomahawk, 150 ... I-18
Tompkinsville, 2402 ... M-9
Topmost, 200 ... K-18
Totz, 250 ... L-17
Tram, 125 ... J-18
Trapp, 30 ... I-13
Trent, 50 ... K-17
Trenton, 384 ... M-4
Tress Shop ... J-13

TRIGG CO., 14339 ... M-2

TRIMBLE CO., 8809 ... F-10
Trosper, 120 ... M-15
Troy ... N-15
Turkey, 40 ... J-17
Tyner, 100 ... K-14
Tyrone, 100 ... H-11
Ulvah, 75 ... L-17
Ulysses, 30 ... I-18

UNION CO., 15007 ... I-2
Union Star, 50 ... I-6
Uniontown, 1002 ... I-2
Uno, 25 ... L-8
Upper Tygart, 40 ... G-16
Upton, 683 ... I-8
Utica, 300 ... I-4
Utility ... L-5
Valley View, 150 ... I-13
Van Lear, 1050 ... I-18
Vanceburg, 1518 ... F-16
Vancleve, 80 ... J-16
Verda, 1455 ... M-12
Versailles, 8568 ... H-12
Vertrees ... I-7
Vest, 50 ... K-17
Vicco, 334 ... K-17
Victory, 60 ... H-8
Villa Hills, 7489 ... B-18
Vincent, 30 ... J-15
Vine Grv., 4520 ... I-8
Viola, 110 ... F-4
Viper, 150 ... L-17
Virgie, 279 ... K-18
Vivian ... I-17
Volga, 50 ... I-17
Waco, 200 ... I-13
Wade, 100 ... K-16
Wadesboro, L-3
Waketield, 100 ... F-16
Walker, 75 ... M-15
Wallingford, 100 ... G-15

Wallins Creek, 156 ... M-16
Wallonia, 60 ... L-2
Walnut Grv., 10 ... K-13
Walton, 3635 ... E-12
Waneta, 75 ... I-14
Warfield, 269 ... I-19

WARREN CO., 113792 ... L-7
Warsaw, 1615 ... E-11

WASHINGTON CO., 11717 ... I-10
Water Valley, 279 ... G-3
Waterford, 90 ... H-11
Watergap ... I-18
Waterview, 40 ... M-9
Watterson Pk., 976 ... C-8
Waverly, 308 ... J-1
Waverly Hills ... D-5
Wax ... J-7
Wayland, 426 ... J-18

WAYNE CO., 20813 ... M-12
Webbs Cross Roads, 50 ... L-11
Webbville, 80 ... H-18
Webster, 120 ... I-7

WEBSTER CO., 13621 ... J-2
Wedonia, 50 ... K-18
Weeksbury, 800 ... K-18
Weir, 70 ... L-4
Welchs Creek, 65 ... K-6
Wellington, 565 ... C-8
Wellington, 80 ... I-8
Wesco, 250 ... K-3
W. Buechel, 1230 ... C-8
W. Irvine, 500 ... I-14
W. Liberty, 3435 ... I-16
W. Louisville, 100 ... I-3
W. Paducah, 100 ... E-3
West Point, 790 ... H-8
W. Van Lear, 600 ... I-18
Westbend, 300 ... I-14
Westwood, 4746 ... TB-1
Westwood, 634 ... B-9
Wheatcroft, 162 ... J-2
Wheatley, 50 ... F-11
Wheeler ... M-15
Wheelersburg, 60 ... I-17
Wheelwright, 780 ... K-18
White City, 50 ... I-8
White Mills, 150 ... J-8
White Oak, 55 ... I-16
White Plains, 884 ... K-3
Whitesburg, 2139 ... L-18
Whitesville, 552 ... I-5
Whitley City, 1170 ... M-13

WHITLEY CO., 35637 ... M-13
Wiborg, 40 ... M-13
Wickliffe, 688 ... F-2
Wilder, 3035 ... B-20
Wildie, 150 ... K-13
Willard, 150 ... G-17
Williamsburg, 5245 ... M-14
Williamsport, 200 ... I-18
Williamstown, 3925 ... F-12
Willisburg, 282 ... I-10
Wilmore, 3686 ... I-12
Wilton ... M-14
Winchester, 18368 ... H-13
Winding Falls ... B-8
Windsor, 50 ... L-11
Windy, 75 ... M-11
Wingo, 632 ... G-3
Winston, 150 ... J-7
Wittensville, 200 ... I-18
Wolf Creek, 80 ... H-6

WOLFE CO., 7355 ... I-15
Wonnie ... J-17
Woodbine, 500 ... M-14
Woodbury, 355 ... M-6
Woodbury, 90 ... L-5

WOODFORD CO., 24939 ... I-11
Woodland Hills, 400 ... C-7
Woodlawn, 229 ... *SM-3
Woodlawn Pk., 942 ... B-8
Wooton, 200 ... L-16
Worthington, 1609 ... F-18
Worthington Hills, 1446 ... A-10
Worthville, 185 ... F-11
Wrigley, 100 ... H-16
Wurtland, 995 ... F-18
Yeaddiss, 50 ... L-16
Yeaman ... J-6
Yellowstone, 175 ... I-5
Yerkes, 140 ... K-17
Yosemite, 250 ... K-11
Zebulon, 200 ... J-19
Zion, 350 ... J-3
Zoe, 40 ... J-15
Zula ... M-11

Louisiana
Page locator
Map keys   Atlas pages
A–J   90–91

ACADIA PAR., 61773 ... G-5
Acme, 90 ... E-6
Addis, 3593 ... G-2
Afton ... C-7
Aimwell, 40 ... D-5
Akers, 150 ... H-9
Albany, 1088 ... G-8
Alda, 300 ... A-3
Alexandria, 47723 ... E-4
Algiers ... E-14
Allemands, 750 ... I-10

ALLEN PAR., 25764 ... F-4
Alto, 160 ... C-6
Alton, 380 ... G-2
Amelia, 2459 ... I-7
Amite, 4141 ... F-8
Anacoco, 869 ... E-3
Angie, 251 ... F-10
Arabi, 3635 ... H-9
Arcadia, 2919 ... B-3
Archibald, 230 ... C-6
Arnaudville, 1057 ... G-5
Ascension ... H-7

ASCENSION PAR., 107215 ... H-7

ASSUMPTION PAR., 23421 ... I-7
Athens, 245 ... B-3
Atlanta, 80 ... D-4
Avery Island, 350 ... H-5
Avondale, 4954 ... E-12

AVOYELLES PAR., 42073 ... E-5
Aycock ... B-3
Bains, 60 ... F-7
Baker, 13895 ... G-2
Baldwin, 2436 ... I-6
Ball, 4000 ... E-4
Basile, 1821 ... G-4
Baskin, 254 ... C-6
Bastrop, 11365 ... B-5
Baton Rouge, 229493 ... G-7
Bawcomville, 3588 ... B-5
Bayou Blue, 12352 ... I-8
Bayou Chicot, 150 ... F-5
Bayou Current ... F-6
Bayou Goula, 612 ... H-7
Bayou Sorrel, 420 ... H-7
Bayou Vista, 4652 ... I-7
Baywood, 180 ... G-7

BEAUREGARD PAR., 35654 ... F-3
Beaver ... B-5
Beekman, 200 ... A-6
Beggs ... B-3
Belcher, 263 ... A-2
Bell City, 350 ... H-4
Belle Chasse, 12679 ... I-9
Belle Rose, 1902 ... H-7
Bellevue, 70 ... B-3
Bellwood ... E-3
Belmont, 361 ... D-2
Benson, 130 ... C-2
Benton, 1948 ... A-2
Bernice, 1689 ... B-4
Berwick, 4946 ... I-7
Bethany, 150 ... C-1
Bienville, 218 ... C-3

BIENVILLE PAR., 14353 ... B-3
Big Bend, 60 ... F-6
Big Cane, 50 ... F-5
Blanchard, 2899 ... B-1
Bogalusa, 12232 ... F-10
Bohemia, 40 ... I-10
Bolinger, 200 ... A-2
Bolivar, 200 ... F-6
Bonita, 284 ... A-6
Bonnabel Pl. ... D-12
Boothville, 854 ... J-11
Bordelonville, 525 ... F-5
Borodino, 240 ... F-5
Bosco, 50 ... C-5

BOSSIER PAR., 116979 ... A-2
Bourg, 2579 ... I-8
Boyce, 1004 ... E-4
Branch, 388 ... G-5
Breaux Br., 8139 ... H-5
Brewtons Mill ... C-5
Bridge City, 7706 ... C-12
Broadmoor ... B-13
Broussard, 8197 ... H-5
Brusly, 2589 ... G-7
Bryceland, 50 ... B-3
Buckeye, 100 ... E-4
Bunkie, 4171 ... F-5
Burr Ferry, 120 ... E-2
Bush, 300 ... G-9

CADDO PAR., 254967 ... B-1
Cade, 1723 ... H-5
Cadeville ... C-5

CALCASIEU PAR., 192768 ... G-3

CALDWELL PAR., 10132 ... C-5
Calhoun, 679 ... B-5
Calvin, 236 ... D-3
Cameron, 406 ... I-3

CAMERON PAR., 6839 ... H-2
Campti, 1056 ... D-3
Cankton, 484 ... G-5
Carencro, 7526 ... G-5
Carlisle, 50 ... B-4
Carmel, 70 ... C-2
Carterville ... B-2
Caspiana, 60 ... C-2
Castor, 258 ... C-3
Catahoula, 1094 ... H-6

CATAHOULA PAR., 10407 ... D-6
Cecilia, 1980 ... G-6
Cedar Grv. ... B-10
Center Pt., 492 ... E-5
Centerville, 700 ... I-6
Central, 26864 ... G-7
Chacahoula, 150 ... I-8
Chackbay, 5177 ... H-8
Chalmette, 16751 ... H-10
Chambers, 200 ... A-4
Charenton, 1903 ... I-6
Chase, 170 ... C-6
Chataignier, 364 ... G-5
Chatham, 557 ... C-4
Chauvin, 2912 ... I-8
Cheneyville, 625 ... F-5
Chestnut, 40 ... C-3
Chipola ... F-9
Choctaw ... H-7
Choudrant, 845 ... B-4
Church Pt., 4560 ... G-5
Claiborne, 11507 ... B-5

CLAIBORNE PAR., 17195 ... A-3
Clarence, 430 ... D-3
Clarks, 1017 ... C-5
Clayton, 711 ... D-6
Clifton ... C-3
Clinton, 1653 ... F-7
Colfax, 1558 ... E-4
College Town ... B-5
Collinston, 327 ... B-6
Columbia, 390 ... C-5

CONCORDIA PAR., 20822 ... E-6
Convent, 711 ... H-8
Converse, 440 ... D-2
Cotton Valley, 1009 ... A-2
Cottonport, 2006 ... F-5
Couchwood, 140 ... B-2
Coushatta, 1964 ... C-3
Covington, 8765 ... G-9
Cravens, 150 ... F-4
Creola, 213 ... E-4
Creole, 250 ... I-3
Creston, 70 ... D-3
Crew Lake, 140 ... B-6
Cross Roads, 50 ... C-2
Crowley, 13265 ... G-5
Crown Pt., 980 ... I-9
Crowville, 280 ... C-6
Crozier, 1250 ... A-2
Cullen, 1163 ... A-3
Cut Off, 5976 ... I-9
Cypremort ... H-6
Cypress, 150 ... D-4
Dalcour, 140 ... I-9
Darlington ... F-8
Darnell, 100 ... B-6
Darrow, 460 ... H-7
Davant, 10 ... I-10

DE SOTO PAR., 26656 ... D-2
Deer Pk. ... E-6
Delacroix, 450 ... I-10
Delcambre, 1866 ... H-5
Delhi, 2919 ... B-6
Delmont Pl. ... A-12
Delta, 266 ... C-7
Denham Sprs., 10215 ... G-7
DeQuincy, 3235 ... G-2
DeRidder, 10578 ... F-3
Derry, 30 ... D-4
Des Allemands, 2505 ... I-8
Deville, 1463 ... E-5
Diamond, 180 ... I-10
Dixie, 100 ... B-2
Dixie Gdns., 500 ... C-4
Dixie Inn, 273 ... B-3
Dodson, 337 ... C-4
Donaldsonville, 7436 ... H-7
Donner, 260 ... I-7
Downsville, 141 ... B-4
Doyline, 818 ... B-2
Dry Creek, 300 ... G-3
Dry Prong, 436 ... D-4
Dubach, 961 ... B-4
Dubberly, 273 ... B-3
Dulac, 1463 ... J-8
Dunn, 180 ... B-6
Duplessis, 350 ... H-7
Duson, 1716 ... G-5

E. BATON ROUGE PAR., 440171 ... G-7

E. CARROLL PAR., 7759 ... A-7

E. FELICIANA PAR., 20267 ... F-7
East Point, 90 ... C-2
Easton, 170 ... C-4
Eastwood, 4093 ... B-2
Echo, 300 ... E-5
Edgard, 2441 ... H-8
Edgefield, 218 ... C-3
Edgerly, 400 ... H-2
Effie, 200 ... E-5
Egan, 631 ... H-4
Elizabeth, 532 ... F-4
Elm Grv., 230 ... C-2
Elmwood, 4635 ... C-12
Elton, 1128 ... G-4
Empire, 993 ... J-10
Enterprise, 150 ... D-6
Epps, 854 ... A-6
Erath, 2114 ... H-5
Eros, 155 ... C-4
Erwinville, 2192 ... G-7
Estelle, 16377 ... I-9
Esther ... H-5
Estherwood, 889 ... H-4
Ethel, 300 ... F-7
Eunice, 10398 ... G-4
Eros ... B-2
Bush, 300 ... G-9
Evangeline, 360 ... G-4

EVANGELINE PAR., 33984 ... G-4
Evans, 250 ... F-3
Evelyn, 50 ... C-2
Evergreen, 310 ... F-5
Extension, 100 ... B-6
Fairbanks, 280 ... B-5
Farmerville, 3860 ... B-4
Felixville, 50 ... F-8
Fenton, 379 ... G-3
Ferriday, 3511 ... D-6
Fields, 40 ... G-2
Fisher, 230 ... D-2
Fishville ... E-4
Flatwoods, 280 ... E-4
Flora, 130 ... D-3
Florien, 633 ... E-2
Fluker, 300 ... F-8
Folsom, 716 ... G-9
Fordoche, 948 ... G-6
Forest, 355 ... B-6
Forest Hill, 818 ... F-4
Forest Oaks ... B-14
Forked Island, 300 ... H-5
Ft. Jesup, 509 ... D-2
Ft. Necessity, 190 ... C-6
Franklin, 7660 ... I-6

FRANKLIN PAR., 20767 ... C-6
Franklinton, 3857 ... F-9
French Settlement, 1116 ... G-8
Friendship, 60 ... B-6
Frierson, 143 ... C-2
Frogmore, 80 ... D-6
Frost ... F-8
Fullerton, 50 ... F-3
Galbraith ... E-4
Galliano, 7676 ... I-9
Garden City, 300 ... I-6
Gardner, 150 ... E-4
Garyville, 2811 ... H-8
Gayles ... C-2
Geismar, 200 ... H-7
Georgetown, 327 ... D-4
Gibsland, 979 ... B-3
Gibson, 200 ... I-7
Gilbert, 521 ... C-6
Gilliam, 164 ... A-2
Gillis, 657 ... G-3
Glencoe, 211 ... F-8
Glenmora, 1342 ... F-4
Gloster, 94 ... C-2
Golden Meadow, 2101 ... I-9
Goldman ... D-7
Goldonna, 430 ... C-3
Gonzales, 9781 ... H-7
Goodwill, 200 ... B-6
Gordon ... A-4
Gorum, 50 ... D-4
Goudeau, 130 ... F-5
Grambling, 4949 ... B-4
Gramercy, 3613 ... H-8
Grand Bayou, 60 ... C-2
Grand Cane, 242 ... C-2
Grand Coteau, 947 ... G-5
Grand Ecore, 600 ... D-3
Grand Isle, 1296 ... J-10
Grand Lake, 300 ... I-3
Grangeville, 70 ... F-8
Grant, 70 ... F-3

GRANT PAR., 22309 ... D-4
Gray, 5584 ... I-8
Grayson, 532 ... C-5
Greensburg, 3219 ... F-8
Greenwood, 3219 ... B-1
Gretna, 17736 ... H-9
Grosse Tete, 647 ... G-6
Gueydan, 1398 ... H-4
Hackberry, 1261 ... H-2
Hackley ... A-4
Hagewood, 150 ... D-3
Hahnville, 3344 ... H-9
Haile, 130 ... A-5
Hall Summit, 300 ... C-3
Hamburg, 280 ... F-5
Hammond, 20019 ... G-8
Happy Jack, 200 ... I-10
Harahan, 9277 ... H-9
Hardwood, 500 ... F-7
Harrisonburg, 348 ... D-6
Harvey, 20348 ... F-13
Hathaway ... G-4
Haughton, 3454 ... B-2
Hayes, 780 ... H-3
Haynesville, 2327 ... A-3
Head of Island, 250 ... H-8
Hebert, 200 ... C-6
Heflin, 244 ... B-3
Henderson, 1674 ... G-6
Henry, 350 ... H-5
Hermitage, 250 ... G-7
Hessmer, 802 ... F-5
Hicks, 50 ... E-3
Hico, 100 ... B-5
Hineston, 150 ... E-4
Hodge, 470 ... C-4
Holloway, 70 ... E-5
Holly Bch., 140 ... I-2
Holly Ridge, 50 ... B-6
Holmwood ... H-3
Holum, 50 ... H-5
Homer, 3237 ... B-3
Hornbeck, 480 ... E-2
Hosston, 318 ... A-1
Hotwells, 150 ... E-4
Houma, 33727 ... I-8
Hudson ... C-4
Hughes, 110 ... B-2
Husser, 50 ... F-9
Iberia ... H-6

IBERIA PAR., 73240 ... H-6

IBERVILLE PAR., 33387 ... G-6
Ida, 221 ... A-1
Independence, 1665 ... G-8
Indian Vil., 300 ... H-2
Innis, 250 ... F-6
Inniswold, 6180 ... C-13
Intracoastal City, 180 ... I-5
Iota, 1500 ... G-5
Iowa, 2996 ... H-3
Ironton, 230 ... I-10
Ivan ... B-2
Jackson, 3842 ... F-7

JACKSON PAR., 16274 ... C-4
Jamestown, 139 ... C-3
Jarreau, 520 ... G-6
Jean Lafitte, 1903 ... I-9
Jeanerette, 5530 ... H-6
Jefferson, 11193 ... E-12

JEFFERSON DAVIS PAR., 31594 ... G-3

JEFFERSON PAR., 432552 ... I-9
Jena, 3398 ... D-5
Jennings, 10383 ... H-4
Jigger, 180 ... C-6
Johnson's Bayou, 150 ... I-2
Jones, 300 ... A-6
Jonesboro, 4704 ... C-4
Jonesville, 2265 ... D-6
Joyce, 384 ... C-4
Junction City, 582 ... A-4
Kaplan, 4600 ... H-5
Keatchie, 295 ... C-1
Keithville, 300 ... B-2
Kelly, 200 ... C-5
Kellys ... B-3
Kenner, 66702 ... H-9
Kentwood, 2198 ... F-8
Kilbourne, 416 ... A-7
Killian, 1206 ... G-8
Kinder, 2477 ... G-4
Kisatchie, 80 ... D-3
Kolin, 50 ... E-4
Kraemer, 314 ... H-8
Krotz Sprs., 1198 ... G-6
Kurthwood, 70 ... E-3

LA SALLE PAR., 14890 ... D-5
Labadieville, 1854 ... I-7
Lacamp, 100 ... E-3
Lacombe, 8679 ... G-10
Lafayette, 120623 ... H-5

LAFAYETTE PAR., 221578 ... H-5
Lafitte, 972 ... I-9

LAFOURCHE PAR., 96318 ... I-9
L. Arthur, 2738 ... H-4
L. Charles, 71993 ... H-3
L. Providence, 3991 ... B-7
Lakeland, 300 ... G-6
Lakeshore, 1930 ... B-5
Lakeview, 948 ... A-8
Lakeview ... D-13
Lamar ... C-2
Lamourie, 30 ... E-4
Laplace, 29872 ... H-8
Larose, 7400 ... I-9
Larto, 60 ... D-6
Latanier, 500 ... E-4
Laurel Hill, 30 ... F-7
Lawtell, 700 ... G-5
Le Blanc, 200 ... G-4
Le Moyen, 200 ... F-5
Lebeau, 200 ... F-5
Lecompte, 1227 ... F-4
Lees, 750 ... C-3
Leesville, 6612 ... E-3
Legonier, 200 ... F-5
Leonville, 1084 ... G-5
Leroy, 150 ... H-5
Lettsworth, 200 ... F-6
Lewisburg, 200 ... G-5
Liberty Hill, 60 ... A-3

Lillie, 118 ... A-4

LINCOLN PAR., 46735 ... B-4
Lindsay, 20 ... C-4
Linville, 150 ... A-5
Lisbon, 185 ... A-4
Lismore, 130 ... C-5
Live Oak Mnt., 1900 ... E-11
Livingston, 1769 ... G-8

LIVINGSTON PAR., 128026 ... G-8
Livonia, 1442 ... G-6
Lockport, 2578 ... I-8
Logansport, 1555 ... C-1
Lone Pine ... F-5
Longleaf, 300 ... F-4
Longstreet, 157 ... C-1
Longville, 635 ... G-3
Loranger, 670 ... G-9
Loreauville, 887 ... H-6
Lottie, 130 ... A-5
Lucky, 272 ... C-3
Luling, 1879 ... H-9
Luna, 50 ... C-5
Lutcher, 3559 ... H-8
Ragley, 100 ... G-3
Ramah ... G-7

MADISON PAR., 12093 ... C-6
Madisonville, 748 ... G-9
Mamou, 3242 ... G-4
Mandeville, 11560 ... G-9
Mangham, 672 ... C-6
Manifest, 125 ... D-6
Mansfield, 5001 ... C-2
Mansura, 1419 ... F-5
Many, 2853 ... D-2
Maringouin, 1098 ... G-6
Marion, 765 ... A-5
Marksville, 5702 ... F-5
Marrero, 33141 ... H-9
Marthaville, 330 ... D-3
Martin, 594 ... C-3
Mathews, 2209 ... I-8
Maurepas, 150 ... H-8
Maurice, 964 ... H-5
Maxie, 100 ... G-4
Mayna, 100 ... C-6
McManus, 300 ... F-7
McNary, 211 ... F-4
Melrose, 150 ... D-3
Melville, 1041 ... G-6
Mer Rouge, 645 ... B-6
Meraux, 5811 ... H-10
Mermentau, 661 ... H-4
Metairie, 138481 ... H-9
Midway, 1291 ... D-5
Midway ... B-2
Milton, 3030 ... H-5
Minden, 13082 ... B-3
Mira, 100 ... A-1
Mittie, 120 ... G-4
Mix, 200 ... G-6
Monroe, 48815 ... B-5
Montegut, 1540 ... I-8
Monterey, 439 ... E-6
Montgomery, 723 ... D-3
Monticello, 5172 ... A-14
Montpelier, 266 ... G-8
Montrose ... C-6
Mooringsport, 793 ... B-1
Mora, 150 ... D-3
Moreauville, 929 ... F-5

MOREHOUSE PAR., 27979 ... A-6
Morgan City, 12404 ... I-7
Morganza, 659 ... G-6
Morrow, 530 ... F-5
Morse, 812 ... H-4
Moss Bluff, 11557 ... G-3
Mt. Hermon, 300 ... F-9
Mt. Lebanon, 83 ... B-3
Mt. Olive ... F-7
Mt. Olivet, 100 ... F-7
Nairn, 100 ... J-10
Napoleonville, 660 ... H-7
Natchez, 550 ... D-3

NATCHITOCHES PAR., 39566 ... D-3
Nebo, 150 ... D-5
Negreet, 150 ... E-2
New Iberia, 30617 ... H-6
New Llano, 2504 ... E-3
New Orleans ... H-9
New Roads, 4831 ... G-6
Newellton, 1137 ... C-7
Noble, 252 ... D-2
Norco, 3074 ... H-9
Norwood, 322 ... F-7
Oak Grv., 1727 ... A-7
Oak Manor ... B-14
Oak Ridge, 144 ... B-6
Oakdale, 7780 ... F-4
Oakland ... A-4
Oberlin, 1896 ... G-4
Oil City, 1008 ... B-1
Old Jefferson, 6980 ... G-7
Olla, 1376 ... D-5
Opelousas, 16634 ... G-5

ORLEANS PAR., 343829 ... H-9
Oscar, 200 ... G-6

OUACHITA PAR., 153720 ... C-5

Pioneer, 156 ... B-6
Pitkin, 576 ... F-4
Plain Dealing, 1015 ... A-2
Plaquemine, 7119 ... H-7

PLAQUEMINES PAR., 23042 ... I-10
Plattenville, 390 ... H-7
Plauchville, 280 ... F-5
Pleasant Hill, 723 ... D-2

POINTE COUPEE PAR., 22802 ... G-6
Pollock, 469 ... E-4
Ponchatoula, 6559 ... G-9
Poplar Grv., 200 ... A-2
Port Allen, 5180 ... G-7
Port Barre, 2055 ... G-5
Port Fourchon, 150 ... J-9
Port Sulphur, 1760 ... I-10
Port Vincent, 741 ... G-8
Powhatan, 135 ... D-3
Prairieville, 26895 ... H-7
Prien, 7810 ... H-3
Provencal, 611 ... D-3
Quitman, 181 ... C-4
Raceland, 10193 ... I-8

RAPIDES PAR., 131613 ... F-4
Rayne, 7953 ... G-5
Rayville, 3695 ... B-6
Red Chute, 6261 ... B-2

RED RIVER PAR., 9091 ... D-3
Reddell, 733 ... G-4
Reeves, 232 ... G-3
Reggio, 160 ... I-10
Reserve, 9766 ... H-8
Rhinehart ... E-5

RICHLAND PAR., 20725 ... C-5
Richmond, 577 ... C-6
Richwood, 3392 ... B-5
Ridgecrest, 694 ... D-6
Ringgold, 1495 ... C-3
River Ridge, 13494 ... E-11
Riverton, 80 ... C-6
Robeline, 174 ... D-3
Rocky Branch, 200 ... B-5
Rocky Mount, 100 ... B-2
Rodessa, 270 ... A-1
Rogers ... C-4
Rosedale, 793 ... G-6
Rosefield, 30 ... D-5
Roseland, 1123 ... F-8
Rosepine, 1692 ... F-3
Roy, 80 ... C-2
Ruston, 21859 ... B-4

SABINE PAR., 24233 ... E-2
Sadie ... A-5
St. Amant, 300 ... H-7
St. Benedict ... G-10

ST. BERNARD PAR., 35897 ... H-10

ST. CHARLES PAR., 52780 ... I-9
St. Francisville, 1765 ... F-7
St. Gabriel, 6677 ... H-7

ST. HELENA PAR., 11203 ... F-8
St. James, 828 ... H-8

ST. JAMES PAR., 22102 ... H-8

ST. JOHN THE BAPTIST PAR., 45924 ... H-8
St. Joseph, 1176 ... D-7
St. Landry, 450 ... F-5

ST. LANDRY PAR., 83384 ... G-5

ST. MARTIN PAR., 52160 ... H-6
St. Martinville, 6114 ... H-6

ST. MARY PAR., 54650 ... I-6
St. Maurice, 323 ... D-3

ST. TAMMANY PAR., 233740 ... G-9
Saline, 277 ... C-3
Sandy Hill, 300 ... F-7
Sarepta, 891 ... A-3
Schriever, 6853 ... I-8
Scotlandville, A-13
Scott, 8614 ... H-5
Seymourville, 3000 ... H-7
Sharon Hills, 900 ... A-13
Shelburn, 110 ... A-7
Sheridan ... G-9
Shongaloo, 162 ... A-3
Shreveport, 199311 ... B-2
Sibley, 1218 ... B-3
Sicily Island, 526 ... D-6
Sieper, 100 ... E-4
Sikes, 119 ... C-4
Simmesport, 2161 ... F-6
Simpson, 638 ... E-3
Simsboro, 643 ... B-4
Slagle, 200 ... E-3
Slaughter, 997 ... F-7
Slidell, 27068 ... H-10
Somerset ... G-7
Sondheimer, 200 ... B-7
Sorrel, 150 ... H-6
Sorrento, 1401 ... H-7
Southport ... E-11
Spearsville, 137 ... A-4
Spencer, 100 ... B-6

Talla Bena, 50 ... B-7
Tallulah, 7335 ... C-7
Tangipahoa, 748 ... F-8

TANGIPAHOA PAR., 121097 ... G-8
Tannehill ... C-4
Taylortown, 252 ... C-2

TENSAS PAR., 5252 ... D-6

TERREBONNE PAR., 111860 ... I-7
Terry, 150 ... A-7
Terrytown, 23319 ... F-14
Theriot, 200 ... I-8
Thibodaux, 14566 ... I-8
Thornwell, 190 ... H-4
Tickfaw, 694 ... G-8
Tioga, 1300 ... E-4
Toomey, 50 ... H-2
Toro ... E-2
Transylvania, 180 ... B-7
Trees, 140 ... A-3
Triumph, 216 ... J-11
Trout, 200 ... D-5
Tullos, 385 ... D-5
Tunica, 230 ... F-7
Turkey Creek, 441 ... G-4

UNION PAR., 22721 ... A-4
Urania, 1313 ... D-5
Varnado, 1461 ... F-10
Venice, 202 ... J-11
Verda, 150 ... D-4

VERMILION PAR., 57999 ... I-4
Vernon, 30 ... C-3

VERNON PAR., 52334 ... E-3
Vidalia, 4299 ... D-6
Vidrine, 150 ... G-4
Vienna, 386 ... B-4
Ville Platte, 7430 ... G-5
Vinton, 3212 ... H-2
Violet, 4973 ... H-10
Vivian, 3671 ... A-1
Vixen, 30 ... C-5
Vowells Mill, 30 ... D-3

W. BATON ROUGE PAR., 23788 ... G-7

W. CARROLL PAR., 11604 ... B-6

W. FELICIANA PAR., 15625 ... F-6
Waggaman, 10015 ... E-11
Wakefield, 110 ... F-7
Walker, 6138 ... G-8
Walters, 50 ... C-5
Warden, 90 ... A-6
Wardville, 1200 ... E-4
Warnerton ... F-9
Washington, 964 ... G-5

WASHINGTON PAR., 47168 ... F-9
Waterproof, 688 ... D-7
Watson, 1047 ... G-7
Waverly ... A-6

WEBSTER PAR., 41207 ... A-2
Welcome, 800 ... H-8
Welsh, 3226 ... H-4
W. Monroe, 13065 ... B-5
Westgate ... B-13
Westlake, 4568 ... H-3
Westminster, 3008 ... C-13
Westport ... A-6
Westwego, 8534 ... H-9
Weyanoke, 150 ... F-6
White Castle, 1883 ... H-7
Whitehall, 90 ... G-7
Whitehall ... B-13
Whiteville, 30 ... G-5
Wickland Ter. ... A-14
Wildsville, 500 ... D-6
Williana, 50 ... E-4
Willow Glen, 500 ... G-7
Willowdale ... D-12
Winnboro, 595 ... C-7

WINN PAR., 15313 ... D-4
Winnfield, 4840 ... D-4
Winnsboro, 4910 ... C-6
Wisner, 964 ... C-6
Woodland, 250 ... C-3
Woodworth, 1096 ... F-4
Wyatt ... C-4
Youngsville, 8105 ... H-5
Zachary, 14960 ... G-7
Zion ... D-7
Zwolle, 1759 ... D-2
Zylks, 60 ... A-1

Maine
Page locator
Map keys   Atlas pages
A–J   92–93

Abbot Vil., 150 ... D-5
Acton, 40 ... J-1
Addison, 250 ... E-9
Albion, 230 ... F-5
Alexander, 50 ... D-9
Alfred, 600 ... J-1
Allagash, 100 ... B-12
Allens Mills, 200 ... G-4
Alna, 130 ... H-4
Amherst, 130 ... E-8
Andover, 600 ... F-2

ANDROSCOGGIN CO., 107702 ... G-3
Anson, 752 ... G-4
Appleton, 50 ... G-6
Arrowsic, 420 ... H-5
Ashland, 709 ... B-13

AROOSTOOK CO., 71870 ... B-8
Ashland, 709 ... B-13
Athens, 280 ... D-6
Atlantic, 60 ... F-8
Auburn, 23555 ... G-3
Augusta, 19136 ... G-4
Aurora, 60 ... E-7
Bailey Island, 650 ... H-3
Bancroft, 30 ... C-9
Bangor, 33039 ... E-6
Bar Hbr., 2752 ... F-8
Bar Mills, 280 ... I-2
Baring, 150 ... D-10
Bass Hbr., 500 ... F-8
Bath, 8514 ... H-4
Bay Pt. ... H-4
Beals, 500 ... E-9
Beans Cor. ... F-3
Belfast, 6668 ... F-6
Belgrade, 300 ... F-4
Belgrade Lks., 300 ... F-4
Belmont Cor., 30 ... F-6
Benedicta, 60 ... C-8

Column 1 (Maine continued)

Benton, 120 ....E-5
Bernard, 200 ....J-11
Berwick, 2187 ....J-1
Bethel, 1200 ....H-2
Biddeford, 21277 ....J-2
Bingham, 758 ....D-4
Blaine, 301 ....C-14
Blaisdell Cors., 200 ....I-1
Blanchard, ...C-4
Blue Hill, 943 ....F-7
Blue Hill Falls, 100 ....F-7
Bolsters Mills, 90 ....G-2
Boothbay, 450 ....H-4
Boothbay Hbr., 1086 ....H-4
Bowdoinham, 722 ....G-4
Bowerbank, 70 ....C-5
Bradford, 400 ....D-6
Bremen, 100 ....G-5
Brewer, 9482 ....E-6
Bridgewater, 300 ....C-14
Bridgton, 2071 ....G-2
Brighton, 40 ....H-5
Bristol, 230 ....H-5
Brooklin, 230 ....F-7
Brooks, 400 ....F-6
Brooksville, 120 ....F-7
Brookton, 170 ....B-9
Brownfield, 350 ....H-1
Brownville, 800 ....C-6
Brownville Jct., 800 ....C-6
Brunswick, 15175 ....H-4
Bryant Pond, 500 ....F-2
Buckfield, 400 ....F-2
Bucks Hbr., 120 ....E-10
Bucksport, 2885 ....F-6
Burlington, 140 ....C-7
Burnham, 200 ....E-5
Byron, 80 ....F-2
Calais, 3123 ....C-10
Cambridge, 120 ....D-5
Camden, 3570 ....G-6
Canaan, 400 ....E-5
Canton, 400 ....F-3
Cape Elizabeth, 8850 ....I-3
Cape Neddick, 2568 ....J-2
Cape Porpoise, 500 ....J-2
Caratunk, 70 ....C-4
Cardville, 150 ....D-7
Caribou, 8189 ....B-14
Carmel, 550 ....E-6
Carrabassett, 230 ....D-3
Carthage, ...F-3
Casco, 587 ....G-2
Castine, 1343 ....F-7
Center Lovell, 200 ....G-1
Charleston, 200 ....D-6
Chebeague Island, 340 ....H-3
Cherryfield, 350 ....E-8
Chester, 100 ....C-7
Chesterville, 110 ....F-3
Chesuncook, ...A-5
China, 450 ....F-5
Chisholm, 1380 ....F-3
Clark Island, 120 ....G-6
Clayton Lake, 20 ....B-12
Clifton, 150 ....E-7
Clinton, 1419 ....E-5
Coburn Gore, 10 ....C-2
Columbia Falls, 250 ....E-9
Coopers Mills, 250 ....G-5
Corea, 300 ....E-8
Corinna, 1100 ....D-5
Cornish, 600 ....H-1
Cornville, ...D-7
Costigan, 60 ....D-7
Cranberry Isles, 90 ....J-12
Crescent Lake, 200 ....H-2
Crouseville, 380 ....B-14
Cumberland Ctr., 2499 ....H-3
CUMBERLAND CO., 281674 ....H-2
Cushing, 50 ....G-6
Cutler, 500 ....E-10
Damariscotta, 1142 ....G-5
Danforth, 500 ....C-9
Deblois, 30 ....E-8
Dedham, 130 ....E-6
Deer Isle, 400 ....G-7
Denmark, 130 ....G-2
Dennysville, 150 ....D-10
Derby, ...C-6
Detroit, 150 ....E-5
Dexter, 2158 ....D-5
Dickey, ...A-12
Dixfield, 1076 ....F-2
Dixmont, 80 ....E-6
Dover-Foxcroft, 2528 ....D-5
Dresden Mills, 140 ....G-4
Dry Mills, 350 ....H-2
Dyer Brook, 60 ....A-8
Eagle Lake, 625 ....B-13
E. Andover, 150 ....F-2
E. Blue Hill, 150 ....F-7
E. Brownfield, 80 ....H-1
E. Corinth, 180 ....D-6
E. Dixfield, 120 ....F-3
E. Eddington, 250 ....E-7
E. Exeter, ...D-6
E. Hampden, 250 ....E-6
E. Hiram, 250 ....H-1
E. Holden, 180 ....E-7
E. Lamoine, 50 ....F-7
E. Livermore, 60 ....F-3
E. Machias, 500 ....E-9
E. Millinocket, 1567 ....B-7
E. Newport, 120 ....E-5
E. Peru, 100 ....F-3
E. Sebago, 320 ....H-2
E. Sumner, 100 ....F-3
E. Vassalboro, 800 ....F-5
E. Waterboro, 250 ....I-2
E. Wilton, 350 ....F-3
E. Winn, 100 ....C-7
Eastbrook, 130 ....E-7
Easton, 300 ....B-14
Eastport, 1331 ....D-10
Eaton, 40 ....D-9
Eden, 75 ....G-12
Edgecomb, 110 ....H-4
Eggemoggin, ...F-6
Eliot, 90 ....J-1
Ellsworth, 7741 ....F-7
Emery Mills, 200 ....I-2
Enfield, 350 ....C-7
Enforest Sta., 10 ....A-12
Etna, 140 ....E-6
Eustis, 80 ....C-2
Exeter Cors., 80 ....D-6
Fairbanks, 180 ....E-4
Fairfield, 2638 ....E-4
Falmouth, 1855 ....H-3

Column 2

Falmouth Foreside, 1511 ....H-10
Farmingdale, 1970 ....G-4
Farmington, 4288 ....E-3
Farmington Falls, 300 ....E-3
Fayette, 100 ....F-4
Forest City, 50 ....B-8
Ft. Fairfield, 1825 ....B-14
Ft. Kent, 2488 ....A-13
Frankfort, 180 ....E-6
Franklin, 300 ....F-8
FRANKLIN CO., 30768 ....D-2
Freedom, 400 ....F-5
Freeport, 1485 ....H-3
Frenchboro, 61 ....G-7
Frenchville, 480 ....A-13
Friendship, 600 ....G-6
Frye, 60 ....F-2
Fryeburg, 1631 ....G-1
Gardiner, 5800 ....G-4
Garland, 150 ....D-5
Georgetown, 150 ....H-4
Gilead, 50 ....G-1
Glenburn Ctr., 60 ....D-6
Goodwins Mills, 50 ....I-2
Gorham, 6882 ....H-2
Gouldsboro, 200 ....F-8
Grand Isle, 380 ....A-13
Grand Lake Stream, 140 ....C-9
Gray, 850 ....H-3
Great Pond, 50 ....D-7
Greeleys, ...C-5
Green Lake, ...E-7
Greenbush, 150 ....D-7
Greene, 500 ....G-3
Greenfield, 60 ....D-7
Greenville, 1623 ....C-4
Greenville Jct., 450 ....C-4
Greenwood, ...G-2
Grindstone, 50 ....B-7
N. Anson, 750 ....E-4
Grove, 40 ....D-3
Guerette, 50 ....A-13
Guilford, 903 ....D-5
Hall Quarry, 100 ....H-12
Hallowell, 2381 ....F-4
Hampden, 4343 ....E-6
Hampden Highlands, 800 ....E-6
Hancock, 400 ....F-8
HANCOCK CO., 54418 ....D-8
Hancock Pt., 40 ....F-8
Hanover, 180 ....F-2
Harborside, 100 ....F-7
Harmony, 280 ....D-5
Harrington, 300 ....E-8
Harrison, 600 ....G-2
Hartford, 60 ....F-3
Hartland, 813 ....E-5
Haynesville, 70 ....A-8
Hebron, 300 ....F-2
Hinckley, 120 ....E-4
Hiram, 350 ....H-2
Hodgdon, 350 ....A-8
Holden, 130 ....E-7
Hollis Ctr., 250 ....I-2
Hope, 100 ....G-5
Houlton, 4856 ....C-14
Howland, 1096 ....C-7
Hudson, 150 ....D-6
Hulls Cove, 250 ....F-8
Indian River, 60 ....E-9
Island Falls, 600 ....A-7
Isle au Haut, 70 ....G-7
Islesboro, 140 ....F-6
Islesford, 80 ....J-12
Jackman, 800 ....B-3
Jackson, 100 ....F-6
Jacksonville, 150 ....E-10
Jay, 600 ....F-3
Jefferson, 280 ....G-5
Jonesboro, 200 ....E-9
Jonesport, 1100 ....E-9
Keegan, 200 ....A-14
Kenduskeag, 350 ....D-6
Kennebago Lake Camps, ...E-2
KENNEBEC CO., 122151 ....F-4
Kennebunk, 5214 ....I-2
Kennebunkport, 1238 ....I-2
Kents Hill, 200 ....F-3
Kingfield, 850 ....D-3
Kingman, 140 ....C-8
Kittery, 4562 ....J-1
Kittery Pt., 1012 ....J-2
Knights, 200 ....C-7
Knowles Cor., ...C-13
Kokadjo, 10 ....B-5
Lagrange, 120 ....D-6
L. Moxie, ...C-3
Lakewood, 80 ....D-4
Lambert Lake, 130 ....B-9
Lebanon, 90 ....I-1
Lee, 250 ....C-7
Leeds, 80 ....F-3
Levant, 250 ....E-6
Lewiston, 36592 ....G-3
Liberty, 180 ....F-5
Limerick, 400 ....I-2
Limestone, 1075 ....B-14
Limington, 250 ....I-2
Lincoln, 2884 ....C-7
LINCOLN CO., 34457 ....G-4
Lincolnville, 300 ....F-6
Linneus, 100 ....A-8
Lisbon, 1400 ....G-3
Lisbon Falls, 4100 ....G-3
Litchfield Cors., 100 ....G-3
Little Deer Isle, 150 ....F-6
Littleton, 200 ....C-14
Livermore, 200 ....F-3
Livermore Falls, 1594 ....F-3
Locke Mills, 200 ....F-2
Lookout, ...I-14
Lovell, 220 ....G-1
Lubec, 349 ....E-10
Ludlow, 40 ....C-14
Lynchville, ...G-2
Machias, 1274 ....E-9
Machiasport, 250 ....E-10
Macwahoc, 80 ....B-8
Madawaska, 2967 ....A-13
Madison, 2613 ....E-4
Madrid, 60 ....E-3
Manchester, 650 ....F-4
Manset, 100 ....J-12
Mapleton, 1855 ....B-14

Column 3

Maplewood, 30 ....H-1
Mars Hill, 980 ....C-14
Martin, ...G-5
Martinsville, 100 ....H-6
Matinicus, 50 ....H-6
Mattawamkeag, 650 ....B-7
Mechanic Falls, 2237 ....G-3
Medfield, 300 ....D-10
Medway, 900 ....B-7
Mexico, 1743 ....F-2
Milbridge, 600 ....F-8
Milford, 2233 ....D-7
Millinocket, 4466 ....B-6
Milo, 1847 ....C-6
Minturn, 90 ....G-7
Molunkus, 40 ....B-8
Monarda, ...B-8
Monhegan, 150 ....H-5
Monmouth, 600 ....G-3
Monroe, 140 ....E-6
Monson, 500 ....C-5
Monticello, 400 ....C-14
Moose River, 200 ....B-3
Moosehead, 20 ....B-4
Morrill, 150 ....F-6
Morrow, 150 ....F-5
Mt. Vernon, 200 ....F-3
Naples, 428 ....G-2
New Canada, 350 ....A-13
New England, ...E-6
New Gloucester, 200 ....H-3
New Harbor, ...H-5
New Limerick, 500 ....C-14
New Portland, 200 ....D-3
New Sharon, 200 ....E-3
New Sweden, 60 ....B-14
New Vineyard, 220 ....E-3
Newagen, 130 ....H-4
Newburgh Vil., 120 ....E-6
Newcastle, 667 ....G-5
Newfield, 225 ....H-1
Newport, 1776 ....E-5
Newry, 150 ....F-2
Nobleboro, 100 ....G-5
Norridgewock, 1438 ....E-4
N. Amity, ...A-8
N. Anson, 750 ....E-4
N. Berwick, 1615 ....J-2
N. Bradford, 50 ....D-6
N. Bridgton, 500 ....G-2
N. E. Carry, ...A-4
N. Fryeburg, 70 ....G-1
N. Haven, 280 ....G-6
N. Jay, 200 ....F-3
N. Lovell, ...G-1
N. Monmouth, 200 ....F-3
N. New Portland, 225 ....D-3
N. Newcastle, ...G-5
N. Palermo, ...F-5
N. Parsonsfield, 50 ....H-1
N. Searsmont, ...F-5
N. Sebago, 280 ....H-2
N. Sedgwick, ...F-7
N. Shapleigh, 130 ....I-1
N. Turner, 350 ....F-3
N. Vassalboro, 900 ....F-4
N. Waldoboro, 180 ....G-5
N. Waterboro, 200 ....I-2
N. Waterford, 300 ....G-2
N. Whitefield, 60 ....G-4
N. Windham, 4904 ....H-2
N. Lovell, ...G-1
Northeast Harbor, 650 ....F-7
Northport, 90 ....F-6
Norway, 2748 ....G-2
Oakland, 2602 ....F-4
Oceanville, 70 ....G-7
Ogunquit, 892 ....J-2
Olamon, 220 ....D-7
Old Orchard Bch., 8624 ....I-3
Old Town, 7840 ....D-7
Oquossoc, 150 ....E-2
Orient, 30 ....A-8
Orland, 300 ....F-6
Orono, 9474 ....D-7
Orrington, 400 ....E-6
Otter Creek, 200 ....J-13
Owls Head, 350 ....G-6
Oxford, 1263 ....G-2
Palermo, 100 ....F-5
Palmyra, 160 ....E-5
Parkman, 80 ....D-5
Passadumkeag, 150 ....D-7
Patten, 1000 ....A-7
Peaks Island, 500 ....I-3
Pembroke, 280 ....D-10
Penobscot, 100 ....F-7
PENOBSCOT CO., 153923 ....A-7
Perham, 100 ....B-13
Perry, 90 ....D-10
Phillips, 750 ....E-3
Phippsburg, 150 ....H-4
Pittsfield, 3150 ....E-5
Pittston, 100 ....G-4
Pittston Farm, ...B-4
Pleasant Hill, 900 ....H-3
Pleasant Pond, 20 ....G-3
Plymouth, 200 ....E-5
Poland, 350 ....G-3
Popham Bch., 40 ....H-4
Port Clyde, 500 ....H-6
Portage, 350 ....B-13
Porter, 250 ....H-1
Portland, 66194 ....H-3
Presque Isle, 9692 ....B-14
Prides Corner, ...H-3
Prospect, 300 ....F-6
Prospect Hbr., 400 ....F-8
Prouts Neck, 500 ....I-3
Purgatory, ...H-4
Randolph, 1772 ....G-4
Rangeley, 700 ....E-2
Raymond, 600 ....H-2
Readfield, 600 ....F-4
Richmond, 1760 ....G-4
Ripley, 110 ....D-5
Robbinston, 200 ....D-10
Rockland, 7297 ....G-6
Rockport, 1200 ....G-6
Rockwood, 50 ....B-4
Rome, 200 ....E-4
Roque Bluffs, 100 ....E-9
Round Pond, 400 ....H-5
Roxbury, 180 ....F-2
Rumford, 4218 ....F-2
Sabattus, 1300 ....G-3
Saco, 18482 ....I-3

Column 4

SAGADAHOC CO., 35293 ....G-4
St. Agatha, 500 ....A-13
St. Albans, 250 ....D-5
St. Francis, 300 ....A-13
St. George, 280 ....G-5
St. John, 130 ....A-13
Salem, 50 ....D-3
Salsbury Cove, 250 ....G-12
Sanford, 9761 ....I-2
Sangerville, 600 ....D-5
Scarborough, 4403 ....I-3
Seal Cove, 100 ....F-7
Seal Hbr., 250 ....J-13
Searsmont, 180 ....F-5
Searsport, 992 ....F-6
Seawall, 50 ....J-12
Sebago Lake, 200 ....H-2
Sebasco Estates, 200 ....H-4
Sebec, 50 ....C-6
Sebec Lake, 5 ....C-5
Seboeis, 30 ....C-6
Seboomook, ...B-4
Sedgwick, 150 ....F-7
Shapleigh, 180 ....I-1
Sherman, Sta., 325 ....A-7
Shin Pond, ...C-13
Shirley Mills, 150 ....C-4
Sidney, ...F-4
Skowhegan, 6297 ....E-4
Small Pt. Bch., ...H-4
Smithfield, 230 ....E-4
Smyrna Mills, 250 ....C-14
Solon, 450 ....D-4
Somerville, 250 ....H-12
S. Addison, 100 ....F-8
S. Arm, 20 ....F-2
S. Berwick, 3000 ....J-1
S. Brewer, ...J-6
S. Bristol, 500 ....H-4
S. China, 500 ....F-4
S. Eliot, 3550 ....J-2
S. Gouldsboro, 175 ....G-14
S. Harpswell, 250 ....H-3
S. Lagrange, 60 ....D-6
S. Lebanon, 230 ....I-1
S. Liberty, ...F-5
S. Lincoln, 180 ....C-7
S. Lubec, 120 ....E-10
S. Orrington, 360 ....E-6
S. Paris, 2267 ....G-2
S. Portland, 25002 ....I-3
S. Sanford, 4536 ....I-2
S. Surry, ...F-7
S. Waterford, 180 ....G-2
S. Windham, 1374 ....H-2
S. Woodstock, 70 ....F-2
Southwest Harbor, 720 ....F-7
Springfield, 120 ....C-8
Springvale, 3292 ....I-1
Spruce Head, 220 ....G-5
Stacyville, 40 ....A-7
Standish, 469 ....H-2
Stardust, 50 ....E-10
Starks, 140 ....E-4
Steep Falls, 1139 ....H-2
Steuben, 150 ....F-8
Stockton Sprs., 330 ....F-6
Stonington, 800 ....G-7
Stow, ...G-1
Stratton, 400 ....D-3
Strong, 700 ....E-3
Sullivan, 180 ....F-8
Sunshine, 60 ....F-7
Surry, 230 ....F-7
Swanville, 150 ....F-6
Temple, 230 ....E-3
Tenants Hbr., 400 ....G-5
The Forks, 10 ....C-4
Thomaston, 1875 ....G-5
Thorndike, 140 ....F-5
Topsfield, 130 ....C-8
Topsham, 5931 ....H-4
Town Hill, 60 ....G-12
Tremont, 80 ....F-7
Trenton, 70 ....F-8
Troy, 80 ....E-5
Turner, 500 ....F-3
Union, 600 ....G-5
Unity, 469 ....E-5
Upper Gloucester, ...H-3
Van Buren, 1937 ....A-14
Vanceboro, 190 ....B-9
Vassalboro, 200 ....F-4
Vienna, 70 ....F-4
Vinalhaven, 800 ....G-6
Waite, 40 ....C-9
W. Baldwin, 150 ....H-2
W. Bethel, 180 ....F-1
W. Bowdoin, 10 ....G-3
W. Buxton, 300 ....H-2
W. Enfield, 300 ....C-7
W. Forks, 30 ....C-3
W. Jonesport, ...E-9
W. Levant, ...D-6
W. Mills, 100 ....E-3
W. Minot, 130 ....G-3
W. Newfield, 300 ....H-1
W. Paris, 550 ....F-2
W. Peru, 150 ....F-2
W. Poland, 350 ....G-2
W. Rockport, 250 ....G-6
W. Scarborough, 900 ....I-3
W. Sumner, 30 ....F-2
W. Tremont, 80 ....G-7
W. Trenton, ...G-12
Westbrook, 17494 ....H-3

Column 5

Weston, 90 ....B-8
Whitefield, 100 ....G-4
Whiting, 110 ....E-10
Whitneyville, 150 ....E-9
Willimantic, 400 ....D-1
Wilsons Mills, 30 ....D-1
Wilton, 2198 ....E-3
Windsor, 100 ....F-4
Winn, 200 ....C-7
Winslow, 7794 ....F-4
Winter Hbr., 426 ....F-8
Winterport, 1340 ....E-6
Winthrop, 2650 ....F-4
Woodland, 952 ....D-9
Woolwich, 800 ....H-4
Wytopitlock, 150 ....B-8
Yarmouth, 5869 ....H-3
York, 800 ....J-2
York Bch., 2033 ....J-2
York Vil., 1000 ....J-2
YORK CO., 197131 ....I-1

Maryland

Page locator
Map keys   Atlas pages
1–10   94–95
11–20   96–97
* City keyed to pp. 224–225

Abell, 160 ....J-17
Aberdeen, 14959 ....B-15
Abingdon, 240 ....C-14
Accident, 325 ....A-2
Accokeek, 10573 ....G-12
Adamstown, 2372 ....C-10
Adelina, 50 ....H-13
Adelphi, 15086 ....*D-7
Airey, 30 ....H-16
Alberth Hts., 140 ....I-1
Alesia, 230 ....A-12
S. Berwick, 3000 ....J-1
S. Brewer, ...J-6
Allen, 210 ....H-17
Allens Fresh, 100 ....H-12
Alpha, 100 ....C-12
Altamont, ...C-2
American Corner, ...*C-9
Ammendale, ...*D-7
Andersontown, 30 ....F-7
Andrews, 130 ....I-16
Annapolis, 38394 ....E-14
Annapolis Jct., 800 ....N-3
ANNE ARUNDEL CO., 537656 ....F-13
Antietam, 89 ....C-8
Appleton Acres, 200 ....A-17
Aquasco, 981 ....H-13
Arbutus, 20483 ....A-4
Ardmore, ...*F-8
Argonne Hills, ...*B-10
Arnold, 23106 ....E-14
Arundel Gdns, 1250 ....A-16
Arundel on the Bay, 1100 ....F-14
Ashton, 1500 ....D-12
Aspen Hill, 48759 ....*C-6
Athol, 50 ....I-17
Avenue, 450 ....I-13
Avilton, ...B-2
Baden, 2128 ....G-13
Baldwin, 420 ....B-13
Ballard, ...*I-9
Baltimore, 620961 ....C-17
BALTIMORE CO., 805029 ....B-13
Baltimore Corner, ...I-7
Baltimore Highlands, 7019 ....K-5
Barclay, 120 ....D-16
Barnaby Vil., 5300 ....*H-7
Barnesville, 172 ....D-10
Barrelville, 73 ....A-4
Barstow, 200 ....H-13
Barton, 457 ....B-3
Bartonsville, 1451 ....C-10
Bay City, ...E-15
Bay Ridge, 2200 ....C-20
Bay View, 300 ....B-16
Baynesville, ...B-17
Bayside Bch., 950 ....D-14
Beachville, 300 ....J-1
Beallsville, 400 ....D-10
Beantown, ...G-12
Beaver Creek, 251 ....B-9
Beaver Dam, 50 ....A-13
Bel Air, 10120 ....B-15
Bel Alton, 1000 ....H-12
Belhaven, 500 ....K-6
Bellevue, 330 ....G-15
Veazie, 1630 ....E-6
Beltsville, 16772 ....L-12
Bembe Bch., ...D-20
Benedict, 261 ....H-13
Benevola, ...B-8
Bennsville, 11923 ....G-12
Benson, ...B-14
Bentley Sprs., 130 ....A-13
Berlin, 4485 ....I-20
Berwyn Hts., 3123 ....*D-8
Bestgate, ...B-17
Bethany Manor, 500 ....I-1
Bethesda, 60858 ....I-11
Bethlehem, 50 ....G-16
Betterton, 345 ....C-16
Beverly Bch., 170 ....F-14
Big Pines, 500 ....*B-3
Big Pool, 82 ....B-7
Big Spring, 84 ....B-8
Birdsville, 250 ....G-13
Bishop, 40 ....J-20
Bishops Head, 200 ....I-16
Bishopville, 531 ....H-20
Bittinger, 70 ....B-2
Bivalve, 201 ....I-17
Black Horse, 130 ....B-14
Bladensburg, 9148 ....*F-8
Bloomington, 305 ....B-3
Bloomsbury, ...*C-9
Bonnie Brae, 1250 ....C-17
Boonsboro, 3336 ....B-9
Boonsboro, ...C-9
Boring, 300 ....A-13
Bowens, 60 ....H-13
Bowie, 54727 ....F-13
Bowleys Quarters, 6755 ....C-14
Bowling Green, 1077 ....B-4
Boxiron, 110 ....I-20
Boyds, 900 ....D-11
Bozman, 440 ....H-15
Bradshaw, 500 ....C-14

Column 6 (Maryland continued)

Brandywine, 6719 ....G-12
Breezewood Farms, 50 ....J-1
Breezy Pt., 230 ....H-13
Brentwood, 3046 ....*F-8
Bridgeport, 860 ....M-17
Bridgetown, 80 ....E-17
Brighton, 100 ....D-12
Brightwood Acres, 30 ....A-15
Brinkleigh Mnr., 2500 ....J-2
Brinklow, 30 ....C-12
Bristol, 30 ....F-13
Broad Run, ...C-9
Brookeville, 134 ....D-11
Brooklandville, 1700 ....F-5
Brooklyn Pk., 14373 ....K-6
Brookmead, 260 ....*B-2
Brookview, 60 ....H-17
Brookwood, 2200 ....*J-10
Broomes Island, 405 ....H-13
Browns Woods Villa, 400 ....B-4
Brownsville, 100 ....E-16
Brownsville, 89 ....C-9
Bruceville, 60 ....B-11
Brunswick, 5870 ....C-9
Bryans Road, 7244 ....G-11
Bryantown, 655 ....H-12
Bryantown, 30 ....H-12
Buckeystown, 1019 ....C-10
Bucktown, 30 ....H-16
Budds Creek, ...I-13
Burkittsville, 151 ....C-9
Burnsville, 100 ....I-16
Burrsville, 130 ....F-17
Burtonsville, 8323 ....L-12
Bush, ...B-15
Butler, 350 ....B-13
Butlertown, 505 ....D-16
Byrdtown, 110 ....A-17
Cabin John, 2280 ....*E-4
California, 11701 ....I-13
Callaway, 470 ....I-14
Calvert, 150 ....A-16
CALVERT CO., 88737 ....H-13
Calverton, 17724 ....*C-8
Cambridge, 12326 ....H-16
Camp Sprs., 19096 ....F-12
Canton, ...C-17
Cape Isle of Wight, 750 ....J-20
Cape St. Claire, 8747 ....E-14
Capitol Hts., 4337 ....*G-8
Cardiff, 230 ....A-15
Carmichael, 30 ....G-15
Carney, 29941 ....G-8
CAROLINE CO., 33066 ....F-17
Carroll Highlands, 2000 ....C-12
Carrollton, 30 ....C-12
Carsins Run, 100 ....B-15
Cascade, 1000 ....A-10
Castleton, 200 ....A-14
Catonsville, 41567 ....J-4
Catonsville Manor, 2600 ....J-4
Cavetown, 1473 ....B-9
Cayots, ...B-17
Cearfoss, 178 ....A-8
Cecilton, 608 ....D-17
CECIL CO., 101108 ....B-17
Cecilton, 663 ....D-17
Cedar Bch., 500 ....G-16
Cedar Grv., 500 ....D-11
Cedar Hts., 1 ....*F-8
Cedar Lawn, 400 ....M-16
Cedarhurst Acres, 300 ....D-19
Cedarville, 717 ....G-13
Centerville, 4285 ....E-16
Ceresville, 170 ....C-10
Champ, 100 ....J-17
Chance, 353 ....I-16
Chaney, ...H-13
Chaptico, 850 ....I-13
CHARLES CO., 146551 ....H-12
Charlestown, 1183 ....B-16
Charlotte Hall, 1420 ....I-12
Chase, 920 ....C-14
Chateau Valley, 1900 ....K-1
Chattolanee, ...F-4
Cheltenham, 950 ....G-13
Cherry Hill, 500 ....A-17
Chesaco Pk., 450 ....G-8
Chesapeake Bch., 5753 ....H-13
Chesapeake City, 673 ....B-17
Chesapeake Haven, 250 ....I-16
Chesapeake Hts., 550 ....G-16
Chester, 4167 ....E-15
Chestertown, 5252 ....D-16
Chesterville, 100 ....D-16
Chestnut Hill Estates, ...J-2
Chestnut Ridge, 230 ....E-4
Cheverly, 6173 ....*F-8
Chevy Chase, 9545 ....*E-5
Chevy Chase View, 920 ....*D-5
Chewsville, 238 ....B-9
Chicamuxen, 100 ....H-11
Childs, 370 ....A-17
Chillum, 33513 ....*E-7
Choptank, 129 ....G-16
Christs Rock, 100 ....H-16
Church Creek, 125 ....H-16
Church Hill, 745 ....D-16
Churchton, ...G-13
Churchville, 600 ....B-14
Claggettsville, 400 ....C-11
Claiborne, 170 ....G-15
Clarksburg, 13766 ....D-11
Clarksville, 830 ....D-12
Clarysville, 73 ....A-4
Clear Spr., 358 ....A-8
Clements, 270 ....I-12
Cliffs City, 60 ....H-13
Clinton, 35970 ....F-12
Clopper, 1000 ....*A-3
Clover Hill, 3260 ....C-10
Cloverly, 15126 ....*A-7
Cobb Island, 1166 ....I-12
Cockeysville, 20776 ....B-13
Cokesbury, 110 ....I-18
Coleman, 150 ....E-17
Colesville, 14647 ....E-12
College Pk., 30413 ....*D-8

Column 7

Colmar Mnr., 1404 ....*F-8
Colonial Pk., ...N-17
Colora, 170 ....A-16
Coltons Pt., 500 ....J-13
Columbia, 99615 ....L-1
Columbia Pk., 1000 ....*F-9
Comus, ...D-10
Conowingo, 500 ....A-15
Contee, ...*C-9
Cooksville, 500 ....C-12
Cordova, 562 ....F-16
Corinth, 100 ....C-9
Cornersville, 100 ....G-15
Corriganville, 455 ....A-4
Cottage City, 1305 ....*F-8
Cove Pt., 1200 ....I-14
Coxs Corner, ...I-12
Craigtown, 200 ....B-16
Cranberry, 200 ....B-12
Crapo, 130 ....I-16
Creagerstown, 150 ....B-10
Crellin, 264 ....C-1
Cresaptown, 4592 ....B-4
Crestwood, 200 ....I-16
Crisfield, 2726 ....K-17
Crocheron, 120 ....I-16
Crofton, 27348 ....E-13
Croom, 2631 ....G-13
Cropley, ...*E-3
Crosby, 50 ....D-15
Crownsville, 1757 ....E-13
Crumpton, 550 ....D-16
Crystal Bch., 500 ....C-16
Cub Hill, ...G-8
Cumberland, 20859 ....A-4
Damascus, 15257 ....D-11
Dameron, 350 ....J-13
Dames Quarter, 167 ....J-17
Daniel, 100 ....C-2
Danville, 271 ....B-3
Dares Bch., 500 ....H-14
Dargan, 165 ....C-9
Darlington, 409 ....A-15
Darnestown, 6802 ....E-10
Davidsonville, 780 ....F-13
Dawson, 103 ....B-3
Deal Island, 471 ....J-16
Deale, 4945 ....F-14
Deer Harbour, 250 ....F-19
Deer Pk., 399 ....C-2
Defense Hts., 2250 ....*E-9
Delight, ...F-4
Delmar, 3003 ....H-18
Denton, 4418 ....F-17
Dentsville, 50 ....H-12
Derwood, 2381 ....*M-4
Detour, 120 ....B-11
Dickerson, 1000 ....D-10
District Hts., 5837 ....*G-8
Dominion, 470 ....E-15
Doncaster, 200 ....H-11
Dorchester, 120 ....B-10
DORCHESTER CO., 32618 ....H-16
Dorrs Cor., 170 ....E-13
Dorsey, 1350 ....M-3
Doubs, 160 ....C-10
Dowell, 300 ....I-14
Downsville, 355 ....B-8
Drayden, 110 ....J-14
Drum Pt., 2731 ....I-14
Drury, 300 ....F-13
Dublin, 500 ....A-15
Dumbarton, ...G-4
Dundalk, 63597 ....D-14
Dunkirk, 2520 ....G-13
Dynard, 50 ....I-13
Eagle Hbr., 63 ....H-13
Earleville, 500 ....C-16
E. New Market, 400 ....G-17
Eastalco, 400 ....C-10
Eastern, 15945 ....I-16
Eastgate, 1250 ....*E-8
Eastpoint, ...A-18
Eastview, 300 ....M-18
Eden, 815 ....H-17
Edesville, 169 ....D-15
Edgemere, 8669 ....D-14
Edgewater, 9023 ....F-13
Edgewood, 25562 ....C-15
Edmonston, 1445 ....*E-8
Ednor, ...*A-7
Eldersburg, 30531 ....C-12
Eldorado, 59 ....H-17
Elioak, 290 ....K-1
Elk Mills, 230 ....A-17
Elk Neck, 130 ....B-16
Elkridge, 15593 ....D-13
Elkton, 15443 ....B-17
Ellerslie, 572 ....A-4
Ellicott City, 65834 ....D-13
Elliott, 52 ....I-16
Ellwood, 150 ....A-16
Elmwood, 1650 ....H-8
Emmitsburg, 2814 ....A-10
Emory Grv., 5300 ....*A-4
Epping Forest, ...A-19
Essex, 39262 ....C-14
Etchison, 200 ....D-11
Evergreen Pk., 70 ....B-17
Evitts Creek, 250 ....A-4
Ewell, 130 ....K-17
Ewingville, 120 ....D-17
Fair Haven, 500 ....G-14
Fairbank, 50 ....H-15
Fairfield, 23681 ....C-16
Fairlee, 490 ....D-15
Fairmount, 457 ....J-17
Fairmount Hts., 1494 ....*F-8
Fairplay, 580 ....B-8
Fairview, 680 ....M-18
Fallston, 8958 ....B-14
Farmington, 180 ....A-16
Faulkner, 400 ....H-12
Feagaville, 220 ....C-10
Federalsburg, 2739 ....G-17
Fells Pt., ...D-7
Ferndale, 16746 ....L-5
Fiddlersburg, 180 ....M-17
Finzel, 547 ....A-3
Fishing Creek, 163 ....I-15
Flintstone, 200 ....A-5
Florence, 100 ....C-11
Flohrville, 800 ....C-12
Foltz, 100 ....K-1
Fork, 500 ....C-14
Ft. Foote Vil., 10007 ....*I-6
Ft. Howard, 890 ....D-14
Fountain Green, 1400 ....B-15

Column 8

Fountain Head, 1350 ....A-9
Fountaindale, ...C-10
Fowblesburg, 250 ....B-12
Foxhall, ...*C-6
Frederick, 65239 ....C-10
FREDERICK CO., 233385 ....B-10
Freeland, 600 ....A-13
Friendly, 9500 ....*J-7
Friendly Farms, ...*J-7
Friendship, 447 ....G-14
Friendsville, 491 ....A-1
Frizzellburg, 28 ....B-11
Frostburg, 9002 ....A-3
Fruitland, 4866 ....E-19
Fruitland Mnr., 7 ....H-18
Fulton, 2049 ....*A-8
Funkstown, 904 ....B-9
Furnace Branch, ...M-6
Gaither, 300 ....C-12
Gaithersburg, 59933 ....D-11
Galena, 612 ....C-17
Galestown, 138 ....H-17
Gallaudet, 450 ....*J-8
Galveston, 684 ....F-14
Gamber, 250 ....C-12
Gambrills, 2800 ....E-13
Gapland, 109 ....C-9
Garland, 500 ....*J-6
GARRETT CO., 30097 ....B-2
Garrett Pk., 992 ....*D-5
Garrison, 8823 ....G-3
Georgetown, 143 ....C-17
Germantown, ...D-11
Gibson Island, 400 ....E-14
Gingerville Manor Estates, ...B-18
Girdletree, 149 ....J-19
Glen Arm, 730 ....B-14
Glen Burnie, 67639 ....D-13
Glen Echo, 255 ....*E-4
Glen Hills, 1400 ....*C-3
Glen Mar Pk., ...J-3
Glenarden, 6000 ....*F-12
Glencoe, 220 ....B-13
Glenelg, 500 ....D-12
Glenmont, 13529 ....*C-6
Glenn Dale, 13466 ....*E-10
Glenwood, 200 ....C-12
Glyndon, 900 ....B-13
Golden Bch., 3796 ....H-13
Golden Hill, 40 ....I-15
Goldsboro, 246 ....E-17
Golts, 150 ....C-17
Good Hope, ...B-7
Goodwill, 50 ....J-18
Gorman, 100 ....C-2
Gortner, 230 ....C-1
Goshen, 300 ....D-11
Governors Run, 30 ....H-14
Graceham, 120 ....B-10
Granite, 960 ....J-3
Grantsville, 766 ....A-2
Grasonville, 3425 ....E-15
Gratitude, ...E-15
Great Mills, 700 ....J-14
Green Haven, 200 ....D-14
Green Hill, 70 ....C-17
Green Valley, 3000 ....C-10
Greenbelt, 23068 ....L-12
Greenberry Hills, ...C-17
Greensboro, 1931 ....E-17
Greentree, ...N-6
Guilford, 1000 ....L-1
Gunpowder, ...B-13
Hagerstown, 39662 ....B-9
Halethorpe, 2000 ....K-4
Halfway, 10701 ....B-8
Hampden, ...C-17
Hampstead, 6323 ....B-12
Hampton, 5052 ....F-6
Hancock, 1545 ....A-7
Hanover, 210 ....L-4
Harewood Pk., ...C-15
Harford, ...C-15
Harmony, 200 ....G-17
Harney, 240 ....A-11
Harmans, 270 ....L-4
Harundale, ...M-6
Harwood, 450 ....F-13
Harwood Pk., ...C-15
Havre de Grace, 12952 ....B-16
Hebbville, 2500 ....H-3
Hebron, 1084 ....H-18
Helen, 70 ....I-13
Henderson, 146 ....E-17
Herald Hbr., 2603 ....E-14
Hereford, 700 ....B-13
Hernwood Hts., 960 ....H-2
Hickory, 610 ....B-15
Hidden Pt., 70 ....A-20
High Pt., 3900 ....H-8
High Ridge, 2500 ....N-1
Highfield, 210 ....A-10
Highland, 1034 ....D-12
Highland Bch., 90 ....C-20
Hillandale, 5937 ....*C-7
Hillcrest Hts., ...*H-7
Hillcrest Hts., 380 ....M-1
Hillsboro, 158 ....F-16
Hillsmere Shores, 2977 ....C-20
Hobbs, 60 ....F-17
Holbrook, 200 ....G-13
Hollywood, 1000 ....I-14
Homeland, ...C-17
Honga, 100 ....I-15
Hopewell, 250 ....H-17
Hopewell, 7 ....H-17
Howard, 200 ....H-12
HOWARD CO., 287085 ....D-12
Hoyes, ...B-1
Hughesville, 2197 ....H-13
Hunting Pt., 240 ....G-11
Huntingtown, 3311 ....G-13
Hurlock, 2092 ....G-17
Hutton, 190 ....C-1
Hyattstown, 500 ....D-10
Hyattsville, 17557 ....*E-8
Hydes, 250 ....B-14
Ijamsville, 400 ....C-10
Ilchester, 23476 ....K-3
Indian Head, 3844 ....G-11
Indian Sprs., 64 ....B-7
Ingleside, 190 ....E-16
Ironshire, ...J-20

Column 9

Ironsides, 180 ....H-11
Island Creek, 100 ....H-14
Island View, 200 ....I-16
Issue, 430 ....I-12
Jacksonville, 600 ....B-14
Jacobsville, ...N-8
Jarrettsville, 2916 ....B-14
Jefferson, 2111 ....C-9
Jefferson Hts., 800 ....M-17
Jessup, 7137 ....D-13
Johnsville, 1000 ....B-11
Johnsville, 491 ....A-11
Jonestown, 250 ....G-17
Joppatowne, 12616 ....C-15
Keedysville, 1152 ....B-9
Kemp Mill Estates, 3050 ....*D-6
Kemptown, ...C-11
Kennedyville, 199 ....C-16
Kensington, 2213 ....*D-5
Kent Vil., 2700 ....*F-9
Kentmore Pk., 250 ....C-16
Kenwood, 2500 ....I-8
Kettering, 12790 ....F-13
Keymar, 500 ....B-11
Keysers Ridge, 30 ....A-2
Kings Pk., 3000 ....H-17
Kingston, 50 ....J-17
Kingston, 1733 ....D-16
Kingsville, 4318 ....C-14
Kitzmiller, 321 ....C-2
Knollwood, 250 ....*D-7
Knoxville, 340 ....C-9
La Plata, 8753 ....H-12
La Vale, 3551 ....D-3
Ladiesburg, 230 ....B-11
Lake Shore, 19477 ....E-14
Lakeview, 750 ....N-1
Landover, 640 ....*E-9
Landover Hills, 1687 ....*E-9
Langley Pk., 18755 ....*E-7
Lanham, 10157 ....*E-9
Lansdowne, 8409 ....K-5
Lappans, 30 ....B-9
Largo, 10070 ....*F-10
Laurel, 25115 ....L-12
Lawsonia, ...K-17
Layhill, 5169 ....*B-6
Laytonsville, 353 ....D-11
Le Gore, 100 ....B-10
Leitersburg, 573 ....A-9
Leonardtown, 2930 ....I-13
Level, 400 ....B-15
Lewisdale, 3100 ....*E-7
Lewistown, 270 ....B-10
Lexington Pk., 11626 ....J-14
Liberty Manor, 920 ....H-3
Libertytown, 950 ....B-11
Libertytown, 1000 ....B-11
Lime Kiln, ...C-10
Lineboro, 350 ....A-12
Linhigh, 2100 ....H-8
Linkwood, 240 ....H-16
Linthicum, 10324 ....L-5
Linwood, 130 ....B-11
Lipins Cor., 80 ....I-17
Lisbon, 1150 ....C-11
Little Orleans, 42 ....B-6
Lloyds, 30 ....G-15
Loch Lynn Hts., 552 ....C-1
Loch Raven Vil., 30 ....G-7
Lochearn, 25333 ....H-4
Locust Grv., 30 ....C-16
Lonaconing, 1214 ....B-3
Londontown, 4000 ....F-14
Long Bch., 1821 ....H-14
Long Green, 500 ....B-14
Longwoods, 50 ....F-16
Loretta Hts., ...B-19
Lothian, 300 ....F-13
Louisville, 200 ....I-16
Love Pt., 290 ....E-15
Loveville, 640 ....I-13
Lower Marlboro, 170 ....G-13
Luke, 65 ....B-3
Lusby, 1835 ....H-14
Lutherville, 6504 ....F-6
Luxmanor, 500 ....*C-5
Lynch, 200 ....I-16
Lynne Acres, 6700 ....J-4
Lyons Creek, 50 ....G-13
Maddox, 200 ....I-13
Madison, 200 ....H-16
Madonna, 200 ....B-14
Magnolia, 150 ....C-14
Malcolm, 50 ....G-11
Manchester, 4808 ....A-12
Manokin, 350 ....J-17
Manor, 400 ....H-12
Manor View, ...I-9
Maple Plains, 390 ....D-19
Maplewood, 1000 ....I-18
Marbury, 770 ....H-11
Mardela Sprs., 347 ....H-17
Margate, 1500 ....M-6
Marion, 1050 ....K-17
Marley, 1500 ....M-6
Marlton, 9031 ....F-13
Marriottsville, 350 ....C-12
Marshall Hall, 250 ....F-11
Marston, 50 ....B-11
Martinsburg, ...D-10
Marydel, 141 ....D-17
Maryland City, 16093 ....E-13
Maryland Line, 400 ....A-13
Mason Sprs., 30 ....H-11
Massey, 160 ....C-17
Matthews, 30 ....I-7
Maugansville, 3071 ....A-8
Mayo, 8098 ....F-14
Mays Chapel, 11420 ....F-6
McAlpine, 400 ....M-3
McCoole, 511 ....D-3
McDaniel, 177 ....H-15
McHenry, 1000 ....B-2
Meadowcliff, ...B-18
Meadowood, 1100 ....*C-7
Mechanicsville, 1508 ....I-13
Melitota, 70 ....D-16
Melrose, 200 ....A-12
Middle River, 25191 ....C-14
Middleburg, 50 ....B-11
Middletown, 4136 ....C-9
Midland, 446 ....B-3
Midlothian, 320 ....A-3
Milford, 690 ....H-18
Millers, 180 ....A-12
Millersville, 500 ....E-13
Millington, 642 ....D-17
Monie, 100 ....J-17
Monkton, 800 ....B-13
Monrovia, 416 ....C-11

Column 10

Montevideo, 230 ....M-3
MONTGOMERY CO., 971777 ....D-11
Montgomery Vil., 32032 ....D-11
Montpelier, 3600 ....*C-5
Montrose, ...*C-5
Morganton, 200 ....I-12
Morganza, 330 ....I-13
Morningside, 2015 ....*H-9
Moscow, 240 ....C-2
Motters, ...A-10
Mt. Aetna, 561 ....B-9
Mt. Airy, 9288 ....C-11
Mt. Harmony, 250 ....G-14
Mt. Rainier, 2000 ....I-2
Mt. Lena, 515 ....B-9
Mt. Pleasant, 330 ....C-10
Mt. Rainier, 8080 ....*F-7
Mt. Savage, 873 ....A-4
Mt. Vernon, 779 ....J-17
Mt. Victoria, 150 ....H-12
Mt. Zion, 80 ....I-17
Mountain Lake Pk., 2092 ....C-1
Muirkirk, 650 ....*C-9
Myersville, 1626 ....B-9
Nanjemoy, 240 ....H-11
Nanticoke, 210 ....J-17
Neavitt, 300 ....H-15
New Carrollton, 12135 ....E-12
New Germany, 30 ....B-2
New London, 170 ....C-11
New Market, 656 ....C-11
New Midway, 380 ....B-10
New Windsor, 1396 ....B-11
Newark, 336 ....I-19
Newburg, 300 ....I-12
Newcomb, 250 ....G-15
Newport, 200 ....H-12
Newtown, 330 ....H-12
Newtown, 80 ....I-18
Nikep, 116 ....B-3
Norbeck, ...*B-5
Normans, 100 ....C-15
Norrisville, 250 ....A-14
N. Beach, 1978 ....G-14
N. East, 3572 ....B-16
North Point, ...D-14
N. Potomac, 24410 ....*D-1
Norwood, 250 ....*B-6
Notch Cliff, ...F-8
Oak Court, ...B-18
Oak Pk., 30 ....C-17
Oak Ridge, 580 ....N-16
Oak View, 3400 ....*D-7
Oakland, 250 ....C-1
Oakland, 1925 ....C-1
Oakland, ...F-1
Oaklawn, 1600 ....*D-5
Oakley, 50 ....I-13
Ocean City, 7102 ....I-20
Ocean Pines, 11710 ....I-20
Odenton, 37132 ....E-13
Oella, 850 ....J-3
Old Farm, 3450 ....*C-4
Oldtown, 86 ....A-5
Olivet, 500 ....I-13
Olney, 33844 ....D-11
Oraville, 50 ....H-17
Orchard Bch., 2000 ....M-8
Orchard Hills, 1250 ....L-16
Oriole, 100 ....J-17
Overlea, 12275 ....H-8
Owings, 1000 ....G-14
Owings Mills, 30622 ....G-4
Oxford, 651 ....G-15
Oxon Hill-Glassmanor, 35355 ....*I-7
Palmer Pk., ...*F-9
Paradise Bch., 350 ....M-9
Paramount, 1450 ....B-9
Park Hall, 700 ....J-14
Parkhurst, ...B-19
Parkton, 500 ....A-13
Parkville, 30734 ....G-8
Parole, 15922 ....E-14
Parsonsburg, 339 ....I-19
Patapsco, 250 ....A-12
Paw Paw, 50 ....G-13
Pen Mar, 210 ....A-10
Pendennis Mount, 300 ....B-18
Perry Hall, 28474 ....C-14
Perryman, 2342 ....B-15
Perryville, 4361 ....B-16
Pfeiffer Cors., 1 ....B-4
Phoenix, 600 ....B-13
Pikesville, 30764 ....G-4
Pine Knoll Ter., 350 ....C-20
Pine Orchard Meadows, 690 ....C-12
Pinefield, 8800 ....G-13
Piney Point, 949 ....J-14
Piney Glen Farms, 470 ....*C-3
Pinto, 300 ....B-4
Pioneer City, ...N-2
Piscataway, 30 ....G-12
Pisgah, 300 ....H-11
Pittsville, 1417 ....I-19
Pleasant Hill, 3379 ....A-14
Pleasant Hills, 3379 ....B-14
Plum Pt., 200 ....H-14
Pocomoke City, 4184 ....K-18
Pomfret, 517 ....H-12
Pomona, 50 ....I-18
Pomonkey, 300 ....G-12
Poolesville, 4883 ....D-10
Popes Creek, 80 ....I-12
Poplar Grv., 200 ....*C-7
Poplar Hill, ...I-13
Poplar Sprs., 200 ....C-12
Port Deposit, 653 ....A-16
Port Herman, 250 ....B-17
Port Republic, 200 ....H-14
Port Tobacco, 30 ....H-12
Potomac, 44965 ....*D-1
Potomac Hts., 1117 ....G-11
Powellville, 180 ....I-19
Preston, 719 ....G-17
Price, 180 ....F-16
Prince Frederick, 2538 ....H-14
PRINCE GEORGES CO., 863420 ....G-12

Column 11

Princess Anne, 3290 ....J-18
Principio Furnace, 100 ....B-16
Providence, 1400 ....F-7
Public, 230 ....I-19
Pumphrey, 5317 ....L-6
Putnam, 300 ....B-14
390 ....E-19
Quaker Neck, 30 ....D-16
Quantico, 133 ....I-17
Queen Anne, 222 ....F-16
QUEEN ANNES CO., 47798 ....E-16
Queenstown, 664 ....E-15
Quince Orchard, 5500 ....E-11
Randallstown, 32430 ....C-13
Randolph Hills, 6150 ....*C-5
Rawlings, 693 ....B-4
Rayville, 100 ....B-13
Redhouse, 30 ....C-1
Redland, 17242 ....*A-4
Rehobeth, 50 ....K-18
Reeds Grv., 50 ....H-17
Reisterstown, 25968 ....C-12
Relay, ...K-4
Thomas, ...H-15
Thurmont, 6170 ....A-10
Tilghman, 784 ....H-15
Tilghman, 465 ....B-8
Timber Ridge, ...A-7
Timberview, ...L-3
Timonium, 9925 ....F-6
Tobytown, 210 ....*C-2
Tolchester Bch., 329 ....D-15
Tompkinsville, 80 ....I-13
Towson, 55197 ....C-13
Tracys, 440 ....F-14
Tracys Landing, 900 ....G-14
Trappe, 1077 ....G-16
Travilah, 12159 ....*C-2
Tuckahoe, 35 ....F-16
Tuscarora, 350 ....D-10
Tuxedo, ...*F-8
University Pk., 2548 ....*E-8
Upper Crossroads, ...B-14
Upper Fairmount, 450 ....J-17
Upper Falls, 450 ....C-14
Upper Hill, 190 ....J-17
Upper Marlboro, 631 ....G-13
Upperco, 700 ....B-12
Urbana, 9175 ....C-10
Vale Summit, 136 ....B-3
Valley Lee, 500 ....J-14
Valley Mede, 4700 ....J-2
Van Bibber, 1000 ....C-15
Van Lear Manor, 1050 ....N-15
Venice on the Bay, 400 ....I-13
Venton, 150 ....J-17
Vienna, 271 ....H-17
Viers Mill Vil., ...*C-5
Villa Nova, 940 ....H-4
Waldorf, 67752 ....G-12
Walkersville, 5800 ....B-10
Wallville, ...H-14
Walston, 50 ....D-20
Wards Chapel, 270 ....G-2
Warfieldsburg, ...B-11
Warwick, 850 ....C-17
WASHINGTON CO., 147430 ....A-8
Washington Grv., 555 ....*A-4
Waterloo, ...M-3
Waterview, 40 ....I-17
Webster Vil., 380 ....B-15
Welcome, 600 ....H-11
Wellington Estates, ...B-19
Wenona, 390 ....J-16
W. Denton, 52 ....F-17
W. Edmondale, 3450 ....J-4
W. Friendship, 1200 ....C-12
W. River, ...F-14
W. Ocean City, 4375 ....I-20
Westernport, 1888 ....B-3
Westgate, ...E-17
Westminster, 18590 ....B-12
Westover, 800 ....J-17
Westphalia, 30 ....F-13
Wetipquin, 80 ....I-17
Weverton, 140 ....C-9
Whaleyville, 149 ....I-19
White Hall, 200 ....A-13
White Marsh, 9513 ....C-14
White Oak, 17403 ....*C-7
White Plains, ...G-12
White Rock Bch., 450 ....I-13
Whitehaven, 43 ....I-17
Whitehouse, ...B-17
Whiteleysburg, ...E-17
Wicomico City, 98733 ....H-18
Shipley, ...L-5
Shookstown, 550 ....M-18
Showell, 400 ....H-20
Silesia, 200 ....*I-7
Silver Hill, 5950 ....*H-8
Silver Run, 180 ....A-12
Silver Sands, 50 ....I-19
Silver Spr., 71452 ....*E-12
Skidmore, 450 ....D-14
Smithsburg, 2975 ....A-9
Smithville, 100 ....F-17
Willow Bch. Colony, 350 ....D-13
Wilson, 50 ....A-8
Wilton Farm Acres, 1900 ....C-12
Winchester on the Severn Mnr., 290 ....E-19
Winfield, 200 ....C-12
Wingate, 150 ....I-16
Wittman, 450 ....H-15
Wolfsville, 100 ....B-9
Wood Pt., ...H-16
Woodbine, 350 ....C-12
Woodensburg, 150 ....C-13
Woodfield, ...D-11
Woodland, 113 ....H-8
Woodlawn, 37879 ....C-13
Woodlawn Hts., 100 ....B-16

Column 12

Woodlawn Hts., 2400 ....*F-9
Woodmont, ...B-7
Woodmoor, 8400 ....*C-7
Woodmore, 3936 ....*F-10
Woodsboro, 1141 ....B-10
Woodstock, 850 ....C-12
Woodville, ...B-8
Woolford, 290 ....H-16
Worthington, 2350 ....H-6
Worthington, 90 ....F-4
Wooton, 249 ....B-4
Wye Mills, 400 ....F-15
Yellow Sprs., 450 ....B-10

Massachusetts

Page locator
Map keys   Atlas pages
1–10   98–99
11–20   100–101
* City keyed to map p. 185

Abington, 15985 ....G-16
Acoaxet, 220 ....L-1
Acton, 2300 ....D-5
Acushnet, 3073 ....J-2
Adams, 5515 ....A-2
Adamsville, ...L-1
Agawam, 28144 ....C-7
Alford, 160 ....B-1
Allerton, ...C-1
Amesbury, 12327 ....A-1
Amherst, 19065 ....C-4
Andover, 8762 ....C-2
Arlington, 42844 ....E-12
Ashburnham, 700 ....I-5
Ashby, 700 ....I-7
Ashfield, 1050 ....B-3
Ashland, 12100 ....F-7
Ashley Falls, 850 ....A-1
Ashley Hts., 110 ....L-1
Assinippi, 1400 ....H-16
Assonet, 1300 ....J-1
Athol, 8265 ....I-5
Attleboro, 43593 ....H-6
Auburn, 15901 ....E-7
Avon, 4300 ....G-6
Ayer, 2868 ....C-5
Back Bay, ...B-3
Baldwinville, 2028 ....I-6
Ballardvale, 1400 ....C-2
Bancroft, ...I-16
Barnstable, 211 ....I-11
BARNSTABLE CO., 215888 ....J-11
Barre, 1009 ....I-6
Barre Plains, 400 ....I-5
Bayswater, 250 ....H-1
Bass River, ...I-20
Bayview, 290 ....A-4
Beach Pt., 50 ....I-9
Beacon Hill, ...A-3
Becket, 600 ....B-4
Becket Ctr., 30 ....B-4
Bedford, 13300 ....D-5
Bedford Sprs., ...C-3
Beechwood, 500 ....G-17
Belchertown, 2899 ....C-4
Bellingham, 4854 ....G-6
Belmont, 24729 ....E-12
Berkley, 200 ....J-1
Barnstable, 118 ....I-11
BERKSHIRE CO., 131219 ....A-2
Bernardston, 900 ....B-3
Beverly, 39502 ....D-8
Billerica, 6850 ....D-7
Blackstone, 5000 ....G-6
Blandford, 393 ....C-5
Bliss Cor., 5466 ....K-2
Bolton, 500 ....D-6
Bondsville, 1850 ....D-3
Boston, 617594 ....E-8
Bourne, 1418 ....J-11
Bournedale, 150 ....I-11
Boxborough, 500 ....D-6
Boxford, 2339 ....C-1
Boylston Ctr., 950 ....E-6
Bradstreet, 200 ....A-4
Braintree, 33698 ....F-13
Braley's, 350 ....K-2
Brant Rock, 1800 ....G-17
Brewster, 2000 ....I-9
Bridgewater, 7841 ....H-1
Briggsville, ...A-3
Brighton, ...A-3
Brightwood, ...M-17
Brimfield, 800 ....D-3
Bristol, ...E-8
BRISTOL CO., 548285 ....J-1
Brockton, 93810 ....G-6
Brookfield, 853 ....E-3
Brookline, 58732 ....F-12
Bryantville, 1800 ....H-17
Buckland, 200 ....B-3
Buena Vista Shores, 700 ....B-4
Burlington, 24498 ....D-7
Buzzards Bay, 3859 ....J-11
Byfield, 1300 ....A-1
Cambridge, 105162 ....E-11
Canton, 18530 ....F-6
Carlisle, 400 ....D-6
Carver, 1500 ....I-7
Cataumet, 1500 ....J-11
Cedarville, 400 ....I-2
Central Vil., 700 ....L-1
Chaffin, 4000 ....E-6
Charlemont, 800 ....B-3
Charlton, 550 ....E-8
Charlton City, 1400 ....E-8
Charlton Depot, 400 ....E-8
Chartley, 750 ....H-6
Chatham, 1121 ....I-11
Chelmsford, 33800 ....C-7
Chelsea, 35177 ....E-12
Cherry Valley, 1200 ....F-7
Cheshire, 514 ....A-2
Chester, 627 ....C-4
Chesterfield, 700 ....B-4
Chicopee, 55298 ....C-6
Chicopee Falls, ...C-6
Chilmark, 250 ....L-11
Clifton, ...D-8
Cliftondale, ...E-12
Clinton, 7389 ....D-6
Cochesett, 400 ....G-6
Cochituate, 6569 ....E-7
College Hill, ...I-16
Collinsville, ...G-6
Colrain, 500 ....B-3
Cominsville, ...G-8
Concord, 4070 ....E-7
Congamond, 500 ....D-7
Conway, 500 ....B-3

*, †, ‡, §, ◊   See explanation under state title in this index.
County and parish names are listed in capital letters & boldface type.
Independent cities (not included in a county) are listed in italics.

daville, 2650 ... F-11
scent Mills ... F-4
nmington, 300 ... D-4
hman, 400 ... E-6
tyhunk, 70 ... L-15
ton, 6750 ... D-2
nvers, 26493 ... C-15
wson, 150 ... E-10
dham, 24729 ... F-13
erfield, 643 ... D-5
nnis, 2407 ... J-19
nnis Port, 3162 ... J-19
ghton, 1100 ... I-14
dge, 200 ... G-9
rchester Ctr. ... L-7
rothy Pond, 1700 ... C-20
uglas, 400 ... G-10
ver, 2265 ... F-13
acut, 25600 ... C-13
ury, 150 ... C-3
dley, 3700 ... G-9
KES CO., 6535 ... L-16
nstable, 900 ... C-12
xbury, 1802 ... G-16
ight, 200 ... E-6
Acton, 950 ... D-12
Billerica, 3850 ... C-13
Boston ... K-8
Brewster, 800 ... I-20
Bridgewater, 400 ... H-15
Brimfield, 150 ... G-8
Brookfield, 1323 ... F-9
Charlemont, 200 ... C-4
Deerfield ... D-6
Dennis, 2753 ... J-19
Douglas, 2557 ... G-10
Falmouth, 6038 ... K-17
Foxborough, 000 ... G-13
Freetown, 850 ... I-15
Harwich, 4872 ... J-20
Holliston ... N-2
Junction ... *J-10
Leverett, 170 ... E-6
Longmeadow, 3370 ... G-6
Mansfield, 350 ... H-13
Marion, 370 ... J-16
Millbury, 1000 ... F-10
Milton ... M-8
Northfield ... B-6
Orleans, 1200 ... I-20
Otis, 200 ... F-3
Pembroke ... G-16
Pepperell, 2059 ... C-11
Princeton, 200 ... D-10
Sandwich, 3940 ... J-18
Springfield ... L-12
Sudbury, 800 ... E-12
Sudbury Sta., 800 ... K-3
Templeton, 1350 ... D-9
Walpole, 3800 ... G-13
Wareham, 1500 ... J-16
Windsor, 100 ... D-3
stham, 1250 ... I-20
sthampton, 15994 ... F-5
ston, 530 ... H-14
stondale, 750 ... H-14
gartown, 1500 ... L-17
gemere ... C-20
ypt, 900 ... F-16
sville, 120 ... I-17
nwood, 500 ... H-15
nwood ... K-11
dicott ... N-6
ing, 420 ... C-7
sex, 1471 ... C-16
SEX CO., 743159 ... C-14
erett, 41667 ... E-14
rhaven, 15870 ... J-15
rlawn ... B-20
rview ... K-12
l River, 88857 ... J-14
mouth, 3799 ... K-17
ley, 50 ... C-6
ville, 1000 ... F-12
herville, 2750 ... F-11
kdale, 2583 ... G-8
chburg, 40318 ... C-10
e Cors., 110 ... H-14
nts Cor., 40 ... D-17
rida, 50 ... C-3
rest Pk. ... M-12
restdale, 4099 ... J-17
rge Vil., 850 ... C-12
xborough, 5625 ... G-13
xvale, 500 ... G-13
amingham, 68318 ... F-12
amingham Ctr. ... L-2
anklin, 29560 ... G-12
ANKLIN CO., 1372 ... D-5
rnace ... E-8
rdner, 20228 ... C-9
y Head, 130 ... M-16
orgetown, 2200 ... B-14
bertville, 1050 ... E-8
l, 150 ... C-6
easondale, 250 ... E-11
en Grv., 270 ... G-9
endale, 400 ... F-1
enridge, 350 ... M-4
oucester, 28789 ... C-16
shen, 600 ... D-4
ss Hts., 100 ... F-4
afton, 1650 ... F-11
anby, 1368 ... F-6
aniteville, 1200 ... C-12
anville, 450 ... G-4
ay Gables, 600 ... J-17
eat Barrington, 231 ... F-1
eat Brook Valley ... A-20
een Hbr., 1500 ... G-16
eendale ... A-19
eenfield, 13716 ... C-5
eenwood ... I-7
iswoldville, 380 ... C-5
oton, 1124 ... C-11
oveland, 3800 ... B-14
adley, 970 ... E-6
alifax, 980 ... H-15
amilton, 1000 ... C-15
ampden, 900 ... G-7
AMPDEN CO., 463490 ... G-4
AMPSHIRE CO., 58080 ... E-4
ancock, 200 ... D-1
anover, 2500 ... G-15
anover Ctr., 1000 ... G-15
anson, 2118 ... G-15
arding, 850 ... F-13
ardwick, 530 ... E-8
artsville, 125 ... G-2
arvard, 1200 ... D-11
arwich, 1798 ... J-20
arwich Port, 1644 ... J-20
atchville, 330 ... K-17
Hatfield, 1318 ... E-6
Hathorne, 230 ... C-15
Haverhill, 60879 ... B-14
Hawley, 60 ... D-4
Hayden Row, 200 ... N-1
Haydenville, 550 ... E-5
Head of Westport, 650 ... K-14
Heath, 150 ... C-4
Heaven Hts., 330 ... I-15
Highland Lake, 200 ... G-13
Highland Pk. ... K-11
Highlands ... K-11
Hingham, 5650 ... F-15
Hinsdale, 1050 ... D-3
Hixville, 150 ... J-14
Hodges Vil., 100 ... G-9
Holbrook, 10791 ... G-14
Holden, 4200 ... E-10
Holland, 1464 ... G-8
Holliston, 12920 ... F-12
Holly Woods, 70 ... J-16
Holyoke, 39880 ... F-5
Hoosac Tunnel ... C-3
Hopedale, 3753 ... G-11
Hopkinton, 2550 ... F-12
Horseneck Bch. ... L-14
Hortonville, 260 ... I-13
Houghs Neck ... M-9
Houghtonville ... B-3
Housatonic, 1109 ... F-1
Hubbardston, 800 ... D-9
Hudson, 14907 ... E-11
Hull, 10293 ... E-15
Humarock, 500 ... G-16
Huntington, 936 ... F-4
Hyannis ... J-19
Hyde Pk. ... M-7
Indian Mound Bch., 900 ... J-17
Indian Orchard ... L-13
Interlaken, 300 ... E-1
Ipswich, 4222 ... C-15
Island Creek, 160 ... H-16
Islington, 4800 ... F-13
Jamesville ... C-18
Jefferson, 1000 ... E-9
Katama, 400 ... M-17
Kendal Green ... K-4
Kent Pk., 550 ... G-16
Kenwood ... F-19
Kingston, 5591 ... H-16
Knightville ... F-4
L. Mattawa, 150 ... D-7
L. Pleasant, 300 ... D-6
L. View ... B-20
Lakeville, 150 ... I-15
Lambs Grv., 150 ... F-9
Lancaster, 900 ... D-11
Lane Vil., 130 ... C-9
Lanesborough, 1000 ... D-2
Lawrence, 76377 ... B-13
Lee, 2051 ... E-2
Leicester, 3200 ... F-9
Leino Pk., 230 ... D-9
Lenox, 1675 ... E-2
Lenox Dale, 600 ... E-2
Leominster, 40759 ... D-10
Leverett, 500 ... D-6
Lexington, 31394 ... D-13
Leyden, 700 ... C-5
Lincoln, 2850 ... E-13
Linwood, 750 ... G-11
Lithia, 100 ... D-4
Little Nahant ... J-9
Little Neck, 50 ... C-16
Littleton Common, 2789 ... D-12
Lobsterville, 50 ... M-16
Locks Vil., 200 ... D-6
Long Plain, 300 ... J-15
Longmeadow, 15784 ... G-6
Lowell, 106519 ... C-13
Ludlow, 18820 ... G-6
Ludlow ... C-18
Lunenburg, 1760 ... C-10
Lynn, 90329 ... D-15
Lynnfield, 11596 ... D-14
Lynnhurst ... I-8
Lyonsville, 650 ... C-5
Madaket, 236 ... M-19
Malden, 59450 ... E-14
Manchaug, 800 ... G-10
Manchester, 5100 ... C-16
Manomet, 1600 ... H-17
Mansfield, 7360 ... H-13
Maplewood ... C-20
Marblehead, 19808 ... D-15
Marion, 1111 ... J-16
Marlborough, 38499 ... E-11
Marshfield, 4335 ... G-16
Marshfield Hills, 2356 ... G-16
Mashpee, 800 ... J-17
Matfield, 700 ... H-14
Mattapoisett, 2915 ... J-16
Maynard, 10106 ... E-12
Medfield, 6483 ... F-13
Medford, 56173 ... E-14
Medway, 4000 ... G-12
Melrose, 26983 ... D-14
Mendon, 1000 ... G-11
Menemsha, 250 ... M-16
Merrimac, 2200 ... B-14
Merrimacport, 250 ... B-14
Methuen, 47255 ... B-13
Middleborough, 7319 ... I-15
Middlefield, 350 ... E-3
MIDDLESEX CO., 1503085 ... C-11
Middleton, 4920 ... C-14
Mileoak Ctr., 2050 ... G-6
Milford, 25055 ... G-12
Mill River, 400 ... G-2
Millbury, 5000 ... F-10
Millers Falls, 1139 ... C-6
Millis, 3800 ... G-12
Millville, 2240 ... H-11
Milton, 27003 ... F-14
Monomoy, 250 ... M-20
Monponsett, 730 ... H-15
Monroe Br., 90 ... B-4
Monson, 2107 ... G-7
Montague, 830 ... D-6
Monterey, 600 ... F-2
Montgomery, 325 ... F-4
Montville, 90 ... G-2
Monument Bch., 2790 ... J-17
Moores Cor., 100 ... D-6
Morningdale, 1150 ... E-10
Morseville ... M-3
Mt. Hermon, 650 ... C-6
Myricks, 60 ... I-14
Mystic Grv., 150 ... F-9
Nabnasset, 3600 ... C-12
Nahant, 3410 ... E-15
Nantucket, 7446 ... M-20
NANTUCKET CO., 10172 ... M-20
Nashaquitsa, 150 ... M-16
Natick, 32200 ... F-12
Needham, 28886 ... F-13
Needham Hts. ... L-5
Needham Jct. ... M-5
New Ashford, 80 ... C-2
New Bedford, 95072 ... J-15
New Boston, 110 ... G-3
New Braintree, 500 ... E-8
New Lenox, 800 ... E-2
New Marlborough, 185 ... G-2
New Salem, 450 ... D-7
New Seabury, 717 ... K-17
Newburyport, 17416 ... B-15
Newton, 85146 ... E-13
Nonquitt, 200 ... K-15
Norfolk, 550 ... G-13
NORFOLK CO., 670850 ... E-14
N. Acton, 900 ... D-12
N. Adams, 13708 ... C-3
N. Amherst, 6819 ... E-6
N. Andover, 22800 ... B-14
N. Ashburnham, 800 ... C-9
N. Attleborough, 16790 ... H-13
N. Billerica, 5500 ... C-13
N. Blandford ... F-3
N. Brookfield, 2265 ... F-8
N. Carver, 600 ... H-16
N. Chatham, 950 ... J-20
N. Chelmsford ... E-17
N. Cohasset, 500 ... F-15
N. Dighton, 1250 ... I-14
N. Eastham, 1806 ... I-20
N. Easton, 4500 ... G-14
N. Egremont, 300 ... F-1
N. Falmouth, 3084 ... J-17
N. Grafton, 3150 ... F-10
N. Hadley, 350 ... E-6
N. Hanover, 980 ... G-15
N. Harwich, 500 ... J-19
N. Hatfield, 470 ... E-5
N. Lancaster, 260 ... D-11
N. Leverett, 200 ... D-6
N. Marshfield, 450 ... G-16
N. Middleboro, 250 ... H-15
N. New Salem, 50 ... D-7
N. Orange, 80 ... C-7
N. Otis ... F-3
N. Oxford, 1200 ... G-10
N. Pembroke, 3292 ... G-16
N. Reading, 12000 ... C-14
N. Rehoboth ... I-13
N. Saugus ... I-8
N. Scituate, 5077 ... F-16
N. Seekonk, 2643 ... *J-10
N. Sudbury, 2600 ... E-12
N. Swansea, 900 ... J-13
N. Tewksbury, 1200 ... C-13
N. Tisbury, 200 ... L-16
N. Truro, 950 ... G-20
N. Uxbridge, 1800 ... G-11
N. Westport, 4571 ... J-14
Northampton, 28549 ... E-5
Northborough, 6167 ... E-11
Northbridge, 3600 ... G-11
Northbridge Ctr., 220 ... G-11
Northfield, 1089 ... C-6
Norton, 2671 ... H-13
Norton Grv., 2100 ... H-13
Norwell, 1200 ... G-16
Norwood, 28602 ... F-13
Nutting Lake, 3200 ... D-13
Oak Bluffs, 2000 ... L-17
Oakdale, 600 ... E-10
Oakdale ... M-6
Oakham, 600 ... E-9
Ocean Bluff, 2500 ... G-16
Ocean Grv., 2811 ... J-13
Ocean Hts. ... L-17
Oldham Vil., 900 ... G-15
Onset, 1573 ... J-16
Orange, 4018 ... C-7
Orleans, 1621 ... I-20
Otis, 650 ... F-3
Otter River, 630 ... C-9
Oxford, 6103 ... G-10
Packard Hts., 50 ... C-8
Pakachoag ... C-19
Palmer, 3900 ... G-7
Parkwood Bch., 250 ... J-16
Paxton, 1600 ... E-9
Peabody, 51251 ... D-15
Pelham, 500 ... E-7
Pembroke, 2100 ... G-16
Pepperell, 2504 ... C-11
Peru, 400 ... D-3
Petersham, 243 ... D-8
Phillipston, 200 ... D-8
Phillipston Four Corners, 50 ... D-8
Pigeon Cove, 1800 ... C-16
Pilgrim Hts. ... G-19
Pine Lake, 750 ... E-12
Pine Pt. ... M-12
Pine Rest, 750 ... E-12
Pinehurst, 7152 ... D-13
Pittsfield, 44737 ... D-2
Plainfield, 150 ... D-4
Plainville, 6900 ... H-13
Pleasant Lake, 450 ... J-20
Plymouth, 7494 ... H-16
PLYMOUTH CO., 494919 ... H-15
Plympton, 500 ... H-15
Pocasset, 2851 ... J-17
Pt. Independence, 870 ... J-16
Polpis, 100 ... M-20
Pondville ... D-19
Popponesset, 220 ... K-18
Princeton, 1100 ... D-10
Priscilla Bch., 450 ... H-17
Provincetown, 2642 ... G-19
Quaise, 40 ... M-20
Quidnet, 100 ... M-20
Quincy, 92271 ... F-14
Quinsigamond Vil. ... C-19
Quissett, 200 ... K-16
Randolph, 32112 ... G-14
Raynham, 2100 ... H-14
Raynham Ctr., 4100 ... H-14
Reading, 24747 ... D-14
Rehoboth, 400 ... I-13
Revere, 51755 ... E-14
Rexhame, 600 ... G-16
Rice Sq. ... C-19
Richmond, 250 ... E-1
Richmond Furnace ... E-1
Risingdale, 100 ... F-1
River Pines, 3600 ... D-13
Riverdale, 110 ... G-11
Riverside, 350 ... C-6
Rochdale, 1150 ... F-9
Rochester, 600 ... J-15
Rock, 600 ... I-15
Rock Hbr. ... I-20
Rockland, 16100 ... G-15
Rockport, 4966 ... C-16
Rockville, 300 ... G-12
Roosterville, 50 ... G-3
Rowe, 80 ... C-4
Rowley, 1416 ... B-15
Roxbury ... L-7
Royalston, 370 ... C-8
Russell, 786 ... F-4
Russells Mills, 160 ... K-14
Rutland, 2111 ... E-9
Sagamore, 3623 ... J-17
Sagamore Bch., 1100 ... I-17
Sagamore Highlands, 100 ... I-17
Salem, 41340 ... D-15
Salisbury, 4869 ... A-15
Salisbury Bch. ... A-15
Salisbury Hts. ... A-18
Salisbury Plains, 600 ... A-15
Sand Hill, 1800 ... F-16
Sandisfield, 225 ... G-2
Sandwich, 2962 ... J-17
Sandy Bch., 60 ... E-9
Saugus, 26628 ... D-14
Savoy, 150 ... D-3
Saxonville ... L-3
Scituate, 5245 ... F-16
Sea View, 100 ... G-16
Seekonk, 10400 ... I-13
Segreganset, 400 ... I-14
Sharon, 5658 ... G-13
Shattuckville, 170 ... C-5
Shawsheen Vil., 2600 ... C-14
Sheffield, 1150 ... G-1
Shelburne, 150 ... C-5
Shelburne Falls, 1731 ... C-5
Sheldonville, 450 ... H-12
Sherborn, 1400 ... F-12
Sherwood Forest, 400 ... F-3
Shirley, 1441 ... D-11
Shirley Ctr., 220 ... D-11
Shore Acres, 1200 ... F-16
Shore Acres, 50 ... K-15
Shrewsbury, 31600 ... F-10
Shutesbury, 700 ... D-7
Siasconset, 205 ... M-20
Silver Bch., 1300 ... J-16
Silver Lake, 2900 ... C-13
Silver Lake, 220 ... H-16
Sippewisset, 1500 ... K-17
Sixteen Acres ... M-13
Smith Mills, 4760 ... K-15
Somerset, 18165 ... J-14
Somerville, 75754 ... E-14
S. Acton, 3200 ... D-12
S. Amherst, 4994 ... E-6
S. Ashburnham, 1062 ... C-9
S. Ashfield, 70 ... D-5
S. Athol ... D-7
S. Barre, 550 ... E-8
S. Berlin, 300 ... E-11
S. Boston ... L-8
S. Byfield, 50 ... B-15
S. Carver ... I-16
S. Chatham, 950 ... J-20
S. Dartmouth, 9800 ... K-15
S. Deerfield, 1880 ... D-5
S. Dennis, 3643 ... J-19
S. Duxbury, 3360 ... H-16
S. Easton, 1500 ... G-14
S. Egremont, 600 ... G-1
S. Georgetown, 150 ... B-14
S. Hadley, 5500 ... F-6
S. Hadley Falls, 5100 ... F-6
S. Hamilton, 2800 ... C-15
S. Hanover, 1000 ... G-15
S. Harwich, 800 ... J-20
S. Hingham, 4000 ... F-15
S. Lancaster, 1894 ... D-11
S. Lee, 500 ... F-2
S. Lynnfield ... H-8
S. Middleboro, 480 ... I-15
S. Orleans, 750 ... J-20
S. Royalston, 450 ... C-8
S. Sandisfield ... G-2
S. Sutton, 175 ... G-10
S. Swansea, 1000 ... J-13
S. Walpole, 1300 ... G-13
S. Wellfleet, 600 ... H-20
S. Westport, 180 ... K-14
S. Williamstown ... C-2
S. Worthington ... E-4
S. Yarmouth, 11092 ... J-19
Southampton, 550 ... F-5
Southborough, 1500 ... F-11
Southbridge, 12878 ... G-9
Southfield, 200 ... G-2
Southwick, 1250 ... G-5
Spencer, 5700 ... F-9
Springdale ... K-11
Springfield, 153060 ... G-6
Squantum ... L-8
State Line, 80 ... E-1
Sterling, 1350 ... E-10
Sterling Jct., 600 ... E-10
Still River, 300 ... D-11
Stockbridge, 1100 ... F-1
Stoneham, 21437 ... D-14
Stoneville ... C-18
Stoughton, 26700 ... G-14
Stow, 1250 ... E-12
Sturbridge, 2253 ... G-8
Sudbury, 1950 ... E-12
SUFFOLK CO., 722023 ... F-14
Sunderland, 1100 ... D-6
Sunderland ... C-19
Surfside, 150 ... M-20
Sutton, 600 ... G-10
Swampscott, 13787 ... D-15
Swansea, 900 ... J-13
Swansea Ctr., 300 ... J-13
Swift River, 250 ... D-4
Tafts Cor., 50 ... F-9
Tatnuck ... B-18
Taunton, 55874 ... I-14
Teaticket, 1692 ... K-17
Templeton, 1000 ... D-8
Tewksbury, 11000 ... C-13
Texas, 430 ... G-9
Thorndike, 1150 ... F-7
Three Rivers, 2900 ... F-7
Tinkertown, 100 ... H-16
Tolland Ctr., 200 ... G-3
Tonset, 500 ... I-20
Topsfield, 2717 ... C-15
Touisset, 1500 ... J-13
Town Crest Vil., 120 ... C-2
Townsend, 1128 ... C-10
Townsend Hbr., 900 ... C-11
Truro, 550 ... H-20
Tully, 200 ... C-7
Turkey Hill Shores, 170 ... E-9
Turners Falls, 4470 ... C-6
Tyngsborough, 250 ... C-12
Tyringham, 200 ... F-2
Upton, 3013 ... G-11
Uxbridge, 3500 ... G-11
Vallersville, 150 ... I-17
Van Deusenville, 100 ... F-1
Vineyard Haven, 2114 ... L-17
Wakeby, 100 ... J-17
Wakefield, 24932 ... D-14
Wales, 800 ... G-8
Walpole, 5918 ... G-13
Waltham, 60632 ... E-13
Wamesit, 2700 ... C-13
Wapping, 110 ... D-5
Waquoit Vil., 500 ... K-17
Ware, 6170 ... F-7
Wareham Ctr., 2896 ... J-16
Warren, 1405 ... F-8
Warrentown, 370 ... H-15
Warwick, 250 ... C-7
Washington, 100 ... E-3
Watertown, 31915 ... E-13
Waterville, 800 ... C-8
Waterville, 200 ... H-15
Wauwinet, 80 ... M-20
Wayland, 2500 ... E-12
Webster, 11412 ... G-10
Wellesley, 27982 ... F-13
Wellesley Hills ... L-4
Wellfleet, 1200 ... H-20
Wellville, 110 ... C-9
Wendell, 400 ... D-7
Wendell Depot, 90 ... C-7
Wenham, 4200 ... C-15
W. Acton, 5200 ... D-12
W. Andover, 2000 ... C-13
W. Becket, 50 ... F-2
W. Berlin, 100 ... E-11
W. Boxford, 800 ... B-14
W. Boylston, 3300 ... E-10
W. Bridgewater, 2100 ... H-14
W. Brookfield, 1413 ... F-8
W. Chatham, 1410 ... J-20
W. Chesterfield, 200 ... E-4
W. Chop ... L-17
W. Concord, 6028 ... D-12
W. Cummington, 150 ... D-3
W. Deerfield ... D-5
W. Dennis, 2242 ... J-19
W. Dudley, 300 ... G-9
W. Falmouth, 1738 ... K-17
W. Foxborough, 1100 ... G-13
W. Granville, 175 ... G-4
W. Groton, 900 ... C-11
W. Hanover, 1700 ... G-15
W. Harwich, 1500 ... J-19
W. Hatfield, 350 ... E-5
W. Hawley ... C-4
W. Hingham ... M-10
W. Mansfield, 650 ... H-13
W. Medway, 2000 ... G-12
W. Millbury, 300 ... G-10
W. Newbury, 1100 ... B-14
W. Otis ... F-2
W. Pelham, 550 ... E-6
W. Roxbury ... M-6
W. Springfield, 28391 ... G-5
W. Sterling, 100 ... D-10
W. Stockbridge, 850 ... E-1
W. Stockbridge Ctr., 120 ... E-1
W. Sutton, 200 ... G-10
W. Tatnuck ... B-18
W. Tisbury, 600 ... L-16
W. Townsend, 700 ... C-10
W. Upton, 1100 ... G-11
W. Walpole, 150 ... G-13
W. Wareham, 2064 ... I-16
W. Warren, 1300 ... F-8
W. Wrentham, 150 ... H-12
W. Yarmouth, 6012 ... J-19
Westborough, 4045 ... F-11
Westfield, 41094 ... G-5
Westford, 1400 ... C-12
Westhampton, 300 ... F-5
Westminster, 1100 ... D-9
Weston, 10200 ... E-13
Westport Factory, 250 ... K-14
Westport Pt., 600 ... K-14
Westwood, 6500 ... F-13
Weymouth, 53988 ... F-15
Whalom, 1400 ... D-10
Whately, 630 ... D-5
Wheelockville, 500 ... G-11
Wheelwright, 500 ... E-8
White Horse Bch., 1250 ... H-17
White Island Shores, 2106 ... I-17
Whitinsville, 6704 ... G-11
Whitman, 13240 ... G-15
Wilbraham, 3915 ... G-6
Wilkinsonville, 900 ... F-10
Williamsburg, 1200 ... E-5
Williamstown, 4325 ... B-2
Williamsville, 220 ... F-1
Williamsville, 100 ... D-8
Willimansett ... K-11
Wilmington, 22325 ... D-13
Winchendon, 4213 ... C-9
Winchendon Sprs., 500 ... C-9
Winchester, 21374 ... D-14
Winchester Highlands ... I-7
Windsor, 200 ... D-3
Winnecunnet, 450 ... H-14
Winthrop, 18303 ... E-14
Woburn, 38120 ... D-14
Woodland Pk. ... C-18
Woods Hole, 781 ... K-16
Woodville, 250 ... F-11
Worcester, 181045 ... F-10
WORCESTER CO., 798552 ... D-8
Woronoco, 300 ... G-4
Worthington Ctr., 125 ... E-4
Worthington Cors., 550 ... E-4
Wrentham, 2250 ... G-13
Yarmouth, 1300 ... J-19
Yarmouth Port, 5320 ... J-19

Michigan

Page locator

Map keys	Atlas pages
A–J	102–103
K–T	104–105

* City keyed to pp. 106–107

Acme, 500 ... J-6
Ada, 2300 ... P-6
Adair, 130 ... P-13
Adamsville, 190 ... T-5
Addison, 605 ... S-9
Adrian, 21133 ... S-10
Advance, 328 ... H-7
Aetna ... N-5
Afton, 150 ... H-9
Agnew, 180 ... P-5
Ahmeek, 146 ... A-13
Akron, 402 ... N-11
Alabaster, 110 ... L-11
Alamo, 140 ... R-6
Alanson, 738 ... G-8
Alaska, 280 ... P-6
Alba, 295 ... I-7
Alberta, 30 ... B-13
Albion, 8616 ... R-8
Albright Shores, 150 ... M-9
ALCONA CO., 10942 ... J-11
Alden, 125 ... I-7
Alger, 180 ... L-10
ALGER CO., 9601 ... D-5
Algonac, 4110 ... Q-14
Allegan, 4998 ... Q-5
ALLEGAN CO., 111408 ... Q-5
Allen, 191 ... S-8
Allen Pk., 28210 ... *L-5
Allendale, 17579 ... P-5
Allenton, 360 ... P-13
Allenville ... F-8
Alma, 9383 ... N-8
Almont, 2674 ... P-12
Aloha, 100 ... G-9
Alpena, 10483 ... I-11
ALPENA CO., 29598 ... I-11
Alpha, 145 ... D-13
Alpine, 250 ... O-6
Alto, 300 ... P-7
Altona, 30 ... N-7
Alverno ... G-9
Amasa, 283 ... C-13
Amble, 90 ... N-7
Anchorville ... Q-13
Ann Arbor, 113934 ... R-11
Antrim, 230 ... I-7
ANTRIM CO., 23580 ... I-7
Applegate, 248 ... N-13
Arbutus Bch., 250 ... I-8
Arcadia, 291 ... K-4
ARENAC CO., 15899 ... L-10
Argentine, 2525 ... P-10
Argyle, 160 ... N-13
Armada, 1730 ... P-13
Arnold, 50 ... E-1
Ashley, 563 ... O-9
Ashton, 110 ... L-6
Assinins ... B-13
Assyria, 50 ... R-7
Athens, 1024 ... S-7
Atlanta, 827 ... I-9
Atlas, 290 ... P-11
Attica, 994 ... O-12
Au Gres, 889 ... L-11
Au Sable, 1404 ... K-12
Au Train, 490 ... D-3
Auburn, 2087 ... N-10
Auburn Hills, 21412 ... *F-5
Augusta, 885 ... R-7
Aurelius, 270 ... Q-9
Austin, 70 ... E-1
Averill, 400 ... M-9
Avoca, 270 ... O-13
Azalia, 120 ... S-11
Bach, 30 ... M-12
Backus Bch., 730 ... J-11
Bad Axe, 3129 ... M-12
Bailey, 330 ... O-6
Baldwin, 1208 ... M-5
Bancroft, 545 ... P-10
Banfield, 40 ... R-7
Bangor, 1885 ... R-5
Bannister, 250 ... O-9
Bar Lake, 280 ... K-4
Baraga, 2053 ... B-13
BARAGA CO., 8860 ... B-13
Barbeau, 100 ... D-9
Bark River, 280 ... G-2
Baroda, 873 ... S-4
Barron Lake, 1570 ... T-5
BARRY CO., 59173 ... Q-7
Barryton, 355 ... M-7
Barton City, 350 ... J-11
Barton Hills, 294 ... *A-9
Barton Lake, 420 ... S-6
Batavia, 120 ... S-7
Bates, 30 ... J-6
Bath, 2083 ... P-9
Battle Creek, 52347 ... R-7
Bauer, 190 ... P-5
Bay City, 34932 ... N-10
BAY CO., 107771 ... M-10
Bay Mills, 170 ... D-8
Bay Pk. ... M-11
Bay Port, 477 ... M-11
Bay View, 133 ... H-8
Bayshore, 260 ... H-7
Beadle Lake, 1550 ... R-7
Beal City, 357 ... M-8
Bear Lake, 286 ... K-5
Beaverton, 1071 ... M-9
Bedford ... R-7
Beecher, 10232 ... *A-6
Beechwood, 30 ... C-12
Belding, 5757 ... O-7
Bell Oak, 30 ... Q-10
Bellaire, 1086 ... I-7
Belleville, 3991 ... R-11
Bellevue, 1282 ... R-8
Belmont, 730 ... P-6
Bendon, 208 ... J-5
Bennington, 50 ... P-9
Bentheim, 100 ... Q-5
Bentley, 100 ... L-10
Benton Hbr., 10038 ... S-4
Benton Hts., 4084 ... S-4
BENZIE CO., 17525 ... J-5
Benzonia, 497 ... J-5
Bergland, 670 ... B-11
Berkley, 14970 ... *H-5
Berrien Ctr., 250 ... S-4
BERRIEN CO., 156813 ... S-4
Berrien Sprs., 1800 ... S-4
Bertrand, 5500 ... T-4
Berville, 310 ... P-13
Bessemer, 1905 ... C-10
Bete Grise ... A-13
Beulah, 342 ... J-5
Beverly Hills, 10267 ... *H-5
Big Bay, 319 ... B-14
Big Rapids, 10601 ... M-6
Big Rock ... I-9
Bingham Farms, 1111 ... *H-5
Birch Bch., 360 ... O-14
Birch Creek ... H-1
Birch Run, 1555 ... O-11
Birmingham, 20103 ... *G-5
Bitely, 200 ... M-5
Black River, 200 ... I-12
Blaine ... O-14
Blanchard, 450 ... N-7
Blaney Pk., 30 ... E-5
Bliss, 50 ... G-8
Blissfield, 3340 ... T-10
Bloomfield, 41070 ... *G-4
Bloomfield Hills, 3869 ... *G-5
Bloomingdale, 454 ... R-5
Boon, 167 ... K-6
Borculo, 400 ... P-5
Bostwick Lake, 800 ... O-6
Boyne City, 3735 ... H-7
Boyne Falls, 294 ... H-8
Bradley, 170 ... Q-6
Brampton, 260 ... F-2
Branch, 140 ... M-5
BRANCH CO., 45248 ... T-7
Brant, 80 ... O-9
Bravo, 40 ... Q-5
Breckenridge, 1328 ... N-9
Breedsville, 199 ... R-5
Brethren, 410 ... K-5
Brevort, 130 ... E-7
Bridgeport, 6950 ... N-10
Bridgeton, 30 ... O-5
Bridgewater, 140 ... R-10
Bridgman, 2291 ... S-4
Brighton, 7444 ... Q-11
Brimley, 560 ... D-8
Brinton, 70 ... M-7
Britton, 586 ... S-11
Brockway, 30 ... O-13
Brohman, 200 ... M-5
Bronson, 2349 ... T-7
Brookfield, 50 ... R-8
Brooklyn, 1206 ... S-9
Brown City, 1325 ... O-13
Brownlee Pk., 2108 ... R-7
Brownstown ... *M-5
Bruce Crossing, 300 ... C-12
Brunswick, 50 ... N-5
Brutus, 218 ... G-8
Buchanan, 4456 ... T-4
Buckley, 697 ... K-6
Bullock Creek, 750 ... N-9
Bunker Hill, 130 ... Q-9
Burdickville, 30 ... I-5
Burlington, 261 ... S-7
Burnips, 190 ... Q-5
Burnside, 50 ... O-12
Burr Oak, 828 ... T-7
Burt Lake, 120 ... G-8
Burton, 29999 ... P-11
Burton, 30 ... P-9
Butler, 30 ... S-8
Butternut, 130 ... O-8
Byron, 581 ... P-10
Byron Ctr., 5822 ... P-6
Cadillac, 10355 ... K-6
Cadmus, 100 ... S-10
Calderwood ... C-12
Caledonia, 1511 ... P-6
CALHOUN CO., 136146 ... S-7
California, 50 ... T-8
Calumet, 726 ... A-13
Calvin Ctr., 70 ... T-5
Cambria, 280 ... T-8
Camden, 512 ... T-8
Cannonsburg, 240 ... P-6
Canton, 76366 ... *K-2
Capac, 1890 ... P-13
Caribou Lake, 30 ... E-10
Carland, 80 ... O-9
Carleton, 2345 ... S-12
Carlshend, 120 ... D-2
Carlton Ctr., 70 ... Q-7
Carney, 192 ... G-1
Caro, 4229 ... N-11
Carp Lake, 357 ... G-8
Carrollton, 6602 ... N-10
Carson City, 1093 ... O-8
Carsonville, 527 ... N-13
Cascade ... P-6
Caseville, 777 ... L-12
Casnovia, 319 ... O-6
Caspian, 906 ... D-12
Cass City, 2428 ... N-12
CASS CO., 52293 ... S-5
Cassopolis, 1774 ... S-5
Castle Pk., 50 ... Q-5
Cathro, 290 ... H-11
Cedar, 93 ... I-6
Cedar Lake, 290 ... N-8
Cedar River, 40 ... G-2
Cedar Sprs., 3509 ... O-6
Cedarville, 1070 ... E-9
Cement City, 438 ... S-9
Center Line, 8257 ... *H-7
Central ... A-13
Central Lake, 952 ... I-7
Centreville, 1425 ... S-6
Ceresco, 230 ... R-7
Champion, 450 ... C-13
Channing, 550 ... D-13
Chapin, 60 ... O-9
Charlevoix, 2513 ... H-7
CHARLEVOIX CO., 25949 ... H-7
Charlotte, 9074 ... Q-8
Chase, 250 ... M-6
Chassell, 710 ... A-13
Chatham, 220 ... D-3
Cheboygan, 4867 ... G-9
CHEBOYGAN CO., 26152 ... H-9
Chelsea, 4944 ... R-10
Chesaning, 2394 ... O-10
Chester, 50 ... Q-8
Chesterfield, 480 ... *F-9
CHIPPEWA CO., 38520 ... D-8
Chippewa Lake, 160 ... M-7
Christmas, 200 ... D-3
Clam River ... I-7
Clare, 3118 ... M-8
CLARE CO., 30926 ... M-8
Clarion, 120 ... H-8
Clarkston, 882 ... Q-12
Clarksville, 394 ... P-7
Clawson, 11825 ... *G-6
Clayton, 344 ... T-10
Clear Lake, 230 ... K-9
Clifford, 324 ... O-12
Climax, 767 ... R-7
Clinton, 95648 ... *G-8
Clinton, 2336 ... S-10
CLINTON CO., 75382 ... P-8
Clio, 2646 ... O-11
Cloverdale, 250 ... Q-7
Cloverville, 1950 ... O-5
Clyde, 210 ... *E-1
Coats Grv. ... Q-7
Coe, 40 ... N-8
Cohoctah, 110 ... P-10
Cohoctah Ctr., 40 ... P-10
Coldwater, 10945 ... S-8
Coleman, 1243 ... M-9
Colling ... N-11
Coloma, 1483 ... S-4
Colon, 1173 ... S-7
Columbiaville, 787 ... O-12
Commerce, 5000 ... Q-11
Comstock, 5600 ... P-3
Comstock Pk., 10088 ... P-6
Concord, 1050 ... R-8
Conklin, 290 ... O-5
Constantine, 2076 ... T-6
Conway, 204 ... G-8
Cooks, 160 ... F-4
Cooper Ctr., 250 ... R-6
Coopersville, 4275 ... P-5
Copemish, 194 ... K-5
Copper City, 190 ... A-13
Copper Hbr., 108 ... A-14
Coral, 230 ... N-7
Corinne ... E-6
Cornell, 80 ... F-2
Corunna, 3497 ... P-10
Cottage Pk., 50 ... D-9
Covert, 640 ... R-4
Covington, 300 ... C-13
CRAWFORD CO., 14074 ... J-8
Crooked Lake, 230 ... R-6
Cross Vil., 93 ... G-7
Croswell, 2447 ... O-13
Crump, 60 ... M-10
Crystal, 680 ... O-8
Crystal Falls, 1469 ... D-13
Crystal Valley, 110 ... M-4
Cumber ... M-12
Curran, 300 ... J-10
Curtis, 620 ... E-6
Curtisville, 50 ... J-10
Custer, 284 ... M-4
Cutlerville, 14370 ... *D-2
Dafter, 160 ... D-9
Daggett, 258 ... G-1
Dalton, 320 ... O-4
Dansville, 563 ... Q-9
Darragh ... J-7
Davis, 160 ... *E-8
Davisburg, 450 ... *D-2
Davison, 5173 ... P-11
Dayton, 150 ... T-4
De Tour Vil., 325 ... E-10
Dearborn, 98153 ... R-12
Dearborn Hts., 57774 ... *J-4
Decatur, 1819 ... S-5
Decker, 100 ... N-12
Deckerville, 830 ... N-13
Deer Pk., 20 ... C-6
Deerfield, 898 ... S-11
Deerton, 230 ... D-3
Deford, 200 ... N-12
Delano ... L-11
DELTA CO., 37069 ... F-3
Delta Mills, 330 ... A-1
Delton, 872 ... Q-7
Denton, 330 ... *L-2
Detroit, 713777 ... R-12
Detroit Bch., 2087 ... S-12
Devereaux, 60 ... R-8
DeWitt, 4507 ... P-9
Dexter, 4067 ... R-10
DICKINSON CO., 26168 ... C-13
Dighton, 80 ... L-7
Dimondale, 1234 ... Q-8
Diorite, 200 ... C-14
Disco ... *E-7
Dixboro, 500 ... R-11
Dollar Bay, 1082 ... A-13
Dollarville, 90 ... D-6
Donken, 30 ... B-12
Dorr, 1600 ... Q-6
Doster, 40 ... R-6
Douglas, 1232 ... Q-5
Dowagiac, 5879 ... S-5
Dowling, 374 ... Q-7
Drayton Plains ... *E-4
Drummond Island, 300 ... E-10
Dryden, 951 ... P-12
Dublin, 50 ... L-5
Duck Lake, 500 ... R-8
Duel ... M-10
Duffield, 40 ... P-10
Dundee, 3957 ... S-11
Durand, 3446 ... P-10
Dutton, 630 ... *D-3
Eagle, 123 ... P-8
Eagle Hbr., 76 ... A-13
Eagle Lake, 1160 ... T-5
Eagle River, 71 ... A-13
E. Grand Rapids, 10694 ... *B-3
E. Jordan, 2351 ... H-7
E. Lake, 512 ... L-4
E. Lansing, 48579 ... Q-9
E. Leroy, 190 ... S-7
E. Saugatuck, 100 ... Q-5
E. Tawas, 2808 ... K-11
Eastmanville, 60 ... P-5
Easton, 30 ... O-10
Eastpointe, 32442 ... Q-13
Eastport, 218 ... I-7
Eastwood, 6340 ... P-3
EATON CO., 107759 ... Q-8
Eaton Rapids, 5214 ... Q-8
Eau Claire, 625 ... S-4
Eben Jct., 410 ... D-3
Eckerman, 250 ... D-7
Eckford, 70 ... R-8
Ecorse, 9512 ... *L-6
Eden, 300 ... Q-9
Edenville, 410 ... M-9
Edmore, 1201 ... N-7
Edwardsburg, 1259 ... T-5
Elba, 200 ... P-11
Elberta, 372 ... J-4
Elk Rapids, 1642 ... I-6
Elkton, 808 ... M-12
Ellsworth, 349 ... H-7
Elm Hall, 200 ... N-8
Elmdale, 30 ... P-7
Elmer ... N-13
Elmira, 230 ... I-8
Elo, 30 ... B-12
Elsie, 966 ... O-9
Elwell, 270 ... N-8
EMMET CO., 32694 ... G-7
Emmett, 269 ... P-13
Empire, 375 ... J-5
Engadine, 480 ... E-6
Ensign, 40 ... F-3
Ensley Ctr., 30 ... O-6
Entrican, 80 ... O-7
Epoufette, 70 ... E-7
Epsilon, 50 ... H-8
Erie, 690 ... T-11
Escanaba, 12616 ... F-2
Essexville, 3478 ... N-10
Estey, 100 ... M-9
Estral Bch., 418 ... S-12
Eureka, 210 ... O-9
Evart, 1903 ... M-7
Evergreen Shores, 180 ... F-8
Ewen, 470 ... C-11
Fair Haven ... Q-13
Fair Plain, 7631 ... S-4
Fairfax, 40 ... S-7
Fairfield, 240 ... T-10
Fairgrove, 563 ... N-11
Fairport, 100 ... G-3
Fairview, 570 ... J-10
Falmouth, 280 ... K-7
Fargo, 90 ... O-13
Farmington, 10372 ... *H-3
Farmington Hills, 79740 ... Q-12
Farrandville, 820 ... O-11
Farwell, 871 ... M-8
Fawn River, 30 ... T-7
Felch, 300 ... D-14
Felch Mtn., 40 ... D-14
Fennville, 1398 ... Q-5
Fenton, 11756 ... P-11
Fenwick, 150 ... O-7
Ferndale, 19900 ... *I-6
Ferry, 200 ... N-4
Ferrysburg, 2892 ... O-4
Fibre, 30 ... E-8
Fife Lake, 443 ... J-7
Filer City, 116 ... L-4
Filion, 200 ... M-12
Fillmore, 50 ... Q-5
Findley, 40 ... S-7
Fitchburg, 80 ... R-9
Flat Rock, 9878 ... S-12
Flint, 102434 ... P-11
Flowerfield, 130 ... S-6
Flushing, 8389 ... O-10
Ford River, 280 ... G-2
Forest Hills, 25867 ... *B-3
Forest Lake, 60 ... D-3
Forester, 80 ... N-14
Forestville, 136 ... M-13
Foster City, 350 ... F-1
Fostoria, 694 ... O-12
Fountain, 193 ... L-5
Fowler, 1208 ... P-8
Fowlerville, 2886 ... Q-10
Frankenmuth, 4944 ... O-11
Frankentrost, 50 ... N-11
Frankfort, 1286 ... J-4
Franklin, 3150 ... *H-4
Fraser, 14480 ... *G-8
Frederic, 570 ... J-8
Free Soil, 144 ... L-4
Freeland, 6969 ... N-10
Freeport, 483 ... Q-7
Fremont, 4081 ... N-5
Frontier, 210 ... T-9
Fruitport, 1093 ... O-5
Fulton, 400 ... S-7
Gaastra, 347 ... D-12
Gagetown, 388 ... M-12
Gaines, 380 ... P-10
Galesburg, 2009 ... R-7
Galien, 549 ... T-4
Ganges, 80 ... Q-5
Garden, 221 ... F-4
Garden City, 27692 ... *J-4
Garden Cors., 110 ... F-4
Garnet, 90 ... E-7
Gay, 60 ... A-13
Gaylord, 3645 ... I-8
Genesee ... O-11
GENESEE CO., 425790 ... O-10
Gera, 20 ... N-11
Germfask, 250 ... E-5
Gibbs City ... C-12
Gibraltar, 4656 ... S-12
Gilchrist, 20 ... E-6
Gilford, 230 ... N-11
Gingellville, 320 ... *E-4
Girard, 200 ... S-8
Gladstone, 4973 ... F-3
Gladwin, 2933 ... L-9
GLADWIN CO., 25692 ... L-9
Glen Arbor, 229 ... I-5
Glen Haven, 60 ... I-5
Glendale ... R-5
Glendora, 40 ... T-4
Glenn, 270 ... Q-4
Glennie, 400 ... J-11
Gobles, 829 ... R-5
Goetzville, 100 ... E-10
GOGEBIC CO., 16427 ... C-11
Gomins, 170 ... J-10
Good Hart, 60 ... G-7
Goodells, 340 ... P-13
Goodison, 190 ... *E-6
Goodrich, 1860 ... P-11
Gould City, 200 ... E-6
Gowen, 350 ... O-7
Grand Bch., 272 ... T-3
Grand Blanc, 8276 ... P-11
Grand Haven, 10412 ... P-4
Grand Jct., 230 ... R-5
Grand Ledge, 7786 ... Q-8
Grand Marais, 330 ... C-5
Grand Rapids, 188040 ... P-6
GRAND TRAVERSE CO., 86986 ... J-6
Grandville, 15378 ... *C-1
Grant, 894 ... O-6
Grass Lake, 1173 ... R-10
GRATIOT CO., 42476 ... O-8
Grattan, 130 ... O-7
Grawn, 772 ... J-6
Grayling, 1884 ... J-8
Green Lake, 400 ... Q-6
Greenbush, 250 ... J-12
Greenland, 340 ... B-12
Greenville, 8481 ... O-7
Gregory, 420 ... R-10
Greilickville, 1530 ... J-6
Gresham ... Q-8
Grind Stone City, 70 ... L-13
Gros Cap, 70 ... F-8
Grosse Ile, 10894 ... *M-6
Grosse Pointe, 5421 ... *J-8
Grosse Pointe Farms, 9479 ... *I-9
Grosse Pointe Pk., 11555 ... *J-8
Grosse Pointe Shores, 2823 ... *I-9
Grosse Pointe Woods, 16135 ... *I-9
Gulliver, 100 ... F-5
Gwinn, 1917 ... E-2
Hadley, 580 ... P-12
Hagensville ... H-10
Hale, 400 ... K-10
Hamburg, 1050 ... R-11
Hamilton, 1170 ... Q-5
Hamtramck, 22423 ... R-12
Hancock, 4634 ... A-12
Hannah ... J-6
Hanover, 441 ... S-9
Harbert, 600 ... T-3
Harbor Bch., 1703 ... M-13
Harbor Sprs., 1194 ... G-7
Hardwood, 200 ... F-1
Harper Woods, 14236 ... *I-8
Harrietta, 143 ... K-6
Harris, 30 ... G-2
Harrisburg ... O-5
Harrison, 24461 ... *G-10
Harrison, 2114 ... L-8
Harrisville, 493 ... J-12
Hart, 2126 ... M-4
Hartford, 2688 ... R-5
Hartland, 570 ... Q-11
Harvey, 1393 ... D-2
Haslett, 19220 ... Q-9
Hastings, 7350 ... Q-7
Hawkins, 20 ... M-6
Hawks, 70 ... H-10
Hazel Pk., 16422 ... *I-7
Hell, 40 ... R-10
Hemlock, 1466 ... N-9
Henderson, 399 ... O-10
Hermansville, 550 ... G-1
Herron, 100 ... I-11
Hersey, 350 ... M-6
Hesperia, 954 ... N-5
Hessel, 270 ... E-9
Hickory Cors., 322 ... R-7
Higgins Lake, 460 ... K-8
Highland, 800 ... Q-11
Highland Pk., 11776 ... *I-6
Hilliards, 30 ... Q-6
Hillman, 701 ... I-10
Hillsdale, 8305 ... S-9
HILLSDALE CO., 46688 ... T-8
Hodunk ... S-7
Holland, 33051 ... P-5
Holly, 6086 ... P-11
Holt, 23973 ... Q-9
Holton, 580 ... N-5
Homer, 1668 ... S-8
Homestead, 60 ... D-9
Honor, 328 ... J-5
Hope, 100 ... M-9
Hopkins, 610 ... Q-6
Hopkinsburg, 50 ... Q-6
Horton, 380 ... S-9
Horton Bay, 512 ... H-7
Houghton, 7708 ... A-12
HOUGHTON CO., 36628 ... B-12
Houghton Lake, 3427 ... K-8
Houghton Pt., 120 ... K-8
Howard City, 1808 ... N-6
Howardsville, 40 ... S-6
Howell, 9489 ... Q-10
Hoxeyville, 60 ... L-6
Hubbard Lake, 210 ... I-11
Hubbardston, 395 ... O-8
Hubbell, 946 ... A-13
Hudson, 2307 ... T-9
Hudsonville, 7116 ... P-5
Hulbert, 350 ... D-7
Huntington Woods, 6238 ... *H-6
Huron Bch., 200 ... G-10
HURON CO., 33118 ... M-12
Huron Mtn., 30 ... B-14
Huronia Hts., 460 ... O-14
Ida, 1020 ... S-11
Idlewild, 270 ... M-6
Imlay City, 3597 ... P-12
Ina ... L-7
Indian Lake, 640 ... S-5
Indian River, 1959 ... G-8
Ingalls, 160 ... H-1
INGHAM CO., 280895 ... Q-9
Inkster, 25369 ... *K-4
Interlochen, 583 ... J-6
Ionia, 11394 ... P-7
IONIA CO., 63905 ... P-7
IOSCO CO., 25887 ... K-11
IRON CO., 11817 ... C-12
Iron Mtn., 7624 ... D-13
Iron River, 3029 ... D-12
Irons, 50 ... L-5
Ironton, 140 ... H-7
Ironwood, 5387 ... C-10
Irving, 120 ... Q-7
ISABELLA CO., 70311 ... N-8
Ishpeming, 6470 ... D-1
Ithaca, 2910 ... O-8
Jackson, 33534 ... R-9
JACKSON CO., 160248 ... R-9
Jamestown ... P-5
Jasper, 412 ... T-10
Jeddo, 110 ... O-14
Jenison, 16538 ... P-6
Jennings, 264 ... K-7
Jerome, 150 ... S-9
Johannesburg, 250 ... I-9
Jones, 290 ... S-6
Jonesville, 2258 ... S-8
Joppa ... R-7
Juddville, 30 ... O-10
Juniata, 100 ... N-11
Kalamazoo, 74262 ... R-6
KALAMAZOO CO., 250331 ... S-6
Kalamo, 80 ... Q-8
Kaleva, 470 ... K-5
Kalkaska, 2020 ... J-7
KALKASKA CO., 17153 ... J-7
Karlin, 100 ... J-6
Kawkawlin, 450 ... M-10
Keego Hbr., 2970 ... *F-4
Keeler, 180 ... S-5
Kendall, 250 ... R-6
Kent City, 1057 ... O-6
KENT CO., 602622 ... O-6
Kenton, 250 ... C-12
Kentwood, 48707 ... P-6
Kewadin, 570 ... I-7
KEWEENAW CO., 2156 ... A-13
Kilmanagh, 30 ... M-12
Kinde, 448 ... L-12
Kinderhook, 150 ... T-8
Kings Mill, 50 ... O-12
Kingsford, 5133 ... D-13
Kingsley, 1480 ... J-6
Kingston, 440 ... N-12
Kinneville, 30 ... R-9
Kinross ... E-8
Kipling, 310 ... F-3
Kiva ... E-2
Klinger Lake, 1000 ... T-6
Koss, 30 ... H-1
La Grange, 120 ... S-5
La Salle, 250 ... S-12
Lac La Belle, 30 ... A-13
Lacey, 80 ... Q-7
Lachine, 200 ... I-11
Lacota, 250 ... R-5
Laingsburg, 1283 ... P-9
Lake, 550 ... M-7
L. Angelus, 290 ... *E-4
L. Ann, 268 ... J-5
Lake City, 836 ... K-7
LAKE CO., 11539 ... L-6
L. George, 430 ... L-8
L. Leelanau, 253 ... I-6
L. Linden, 1007 ... A-13
L. Michigan Bch., 1216 ... R-4
L. Nepessing, 690 ... P-12
L. Odessa, 2018 ... P-7
L. Orion, 2973 ... P-12
Lakeland, 1050 ... Q-10
Lakeport, 350 ... O-14
Lakeside, 1100 ... T-3
Lakeview, 1007 ... N-7
Lakeville, 340 ... P-12
Lakewood, 1560 ... P-3
Lakewood Club, 1291 ... N-4
Lamb, 140 ... P-13
Lambertville, 9953 ... T-11
Lamont, 300 ... P-5
Langston, 150 ... O-7
L'Anse, 2011 ... B-13
Lansing, 114297 ... Q-9
Lapeer, 8841 ... O-12
LAPEER CO., 88319 ... O-12
Laporte, 150 ... N-10
Lathrup Vil., 4075 ... *H-5
Laurium, 1977 ... A-13
Lawrence, 996 ... R-5
Lawton, 1900 ... S-5
Layton Cors., 30 ... O-10
Le Roy, 256 ... L-6
Leaton, 30 ... M-8
LEELANAU CO., 21708 ... I-6
Leland, 377 ... I-6
LENAWEE CO., 99892 ... S-10
Lennon, 511 ... P-10
Leonard, 403 ... P-12
Leoni, 90 ... R-9
Leonidas, 220 ... S-7
Leslie, 1851 ... R-9
Level Pk., 3490 ... R-7
Levering, 215 ... G-8
Lewiston, 1392 ... I-9
Lexington, 1178 ... O-14
Lexington Hts., 520 ... O-14
Liberty, 110 ... S-9
Lilley ... M-5
Limestone, 60 ... E-3
Lincoln, 337 ... J-11
Lincoln Pk., 38144 ... *L-5
Linden, 3991 ... P-11
Linwood, 500 ... M-10
Litchfield, 1369 ... S-8
Little Lake, 800 ... E-2
LIVINGSTON CO., 180967 ... Q-10
Livonia, 96942 ... R-12
Long Lake, 170 ... K-10
Long Rapids, 50 ... H-10
Loomis, 213 ... M-8
Loretto, 400 ... D-14
Lost Lake Woods, 312 ... J-11
Lovells, 130 ... J-9
Lowell, 3783 ... P-7
Lucas, 150 ... L-7
LUCE CO., 6631 ... D-6
Ludington, 8076 ... M-4
Lum, 270 ... O-12
Luna Pier, 1436 ... T-12
Lupton, 348 ... K-10
Luther, 318 ... L-6
Luzerne, 610 ... J-9
Lyons, 789 ... P-8
MACKINAC CO., 11113 ... E-7
Mackinac Island, 492 ... F-8
Mackinaw City, 806 ... F-8
Macomb, 160 ... *E-8
MACOMB CO., 840978 ... P-13
Macon, 100 ... S-10
Madison Hts., 29694 ... *H-6
Mancelona, 1390 ... I-7
Manchester, 2091 ... S-10
Manistee, 6226 ... L-4
MANISTEE CO., 24733 ... K-5
Manistique, 3097 ... F-4
Manitou Bch., 1400 ... S-9
Manton, 1287 ... K-6
Maple City, 207 ... I-5
Maple Hill ... N-6
Maple Rapids, 672 ... O-8
Maple Ridge, 30 ... L-10
Mapleton, 100 ... I-6
Marcellus, 1198 ... S-6
Marenisco, 254 ... C-11
Marine City, 4248 ... P-14
Marion, 872 ... L-7
Marlette, 1875 ... N-12
Marne, 490 ... P-5
Marquette, 21355 ... D-2
MARQUETTE CO., 67077 ... E-1
Marshall, 7088 ... R-8
Martin, 410 ... Q-6
Marysville, 9959 ... P-14
Mason, 8252 ... Q-9
MASON CO., 28705 ... L-4
Masonville ... F-3
Mass City, 430 ... B-12
Matherton, 140 ... O-8
Mattawan, 1997 ... R-6
Maybee, 562 ... S-11
Mayfield, 170 ... J-6
Mayville, 950 ... N-12
McBain, 656 ... L-7
McBride, 205 ... O-7
McFarland, 70 ... E-2
McGregor, 60 ... N-13
McKinley, 220 ... J-10
McMillan, 200 ... D-6
Meade, 160 ... *E-9
Mears, 360 ... M-4
Meauwataka ... K-6
Mecosta, 457 ... N-7
MECOSTA CO., 42798 ... N-7
Medina, 70 ... T-9
Melita, 30 ... L-10
Melstrand, 60 ... D-4
Melvin, 180 ... O-13
Melvindale, 10715 ... *K-5
Memphis, 1183 ... P-13
Mendon, 870 ... S-6
Menominee, 8599 ... I-1
MENOMINEE CO., 24029 ... G-1
Meredith, 200 ... L-8
Merrill, 778 ... N-9
Merritt, 120 ... K-8
Merriweather, 130 ... B-11
Mesick, 394 ... K-6
Metamora, 565 ... P-12
Metz, 90 ... H-10
Michiana, 182 ... T-3
Michigamme, 271 ... C-13
Michigan Ctr., 4672 ... R-9
Middleton, 500 ... O-8
Middleville, 3319 ... Q-6
Midland, 41863 ... N-9
MIDLAND CO., 83629 ... N-9
Midland Pk., 450 ... R-7
Mikado, 150 ... J-11
Milan, 5836 ... S-11
Milford, 6175 ... Q-11
Millbrook, 110 ... N-7
Millburg, 180 ... S-4
Millersburg, 206 ... H-10
Millett, 770 ... Q-8
Millington, 1072 ... O-11
Millville ... Q-10
Milwood ... P-2
Minden City, 197 ... M-13
Mio, 1826 ... J-10
MISSAUKEE CO., 14849 ... K-7
Mohawk, 600 ... A-13
Moline, 750 ... Q-6
Monroe, 20733 ... S-12
MONROE CO., 152021 ... S-11
Montague, 2361 ... N-4
MONTCALM CO., 63342 ... O-7
Monterey Ctr. ... Q-5
Montgomery, 342 ... T-8
MONTMORENCY CO., 9765 ... I-9
Montrose, 1657 ... O-10
Moore Pk., 130 ... S-6
Moorestown, 100 ... K-7
Mooreville, 70 ... S-11
Moran, 200 ... F-8
Morenci, 2220 ... T-10
Morley, 493 ... N-6
Morrice, 927 ... P-10
Morseville, 30 ... O-10
Moscow, 190 ... S-9
Mottville, 200 ... T-6
Mt. Clemens, 16314 ... Q-13
Mt. Forest, 30 ... M-10
Mt. Morris, 3086 ... O-11
Mt. Pleasant, 26016 ... N-8
Muir, 604 ... P-8
Mullet Lake, 250 ... G-9
Mulliken, 553 ... Q-8
Munger, 200 ... N-11
Munising, 2355 ... D-3
Munith, 350 ... R-9
Munson, 50 ... T-9
Muskegon, 38401 ... O-4
MUSKEGON CO., 172188 ... O-5
Muskegon Hts., 10856 ... O-4
Nadeau, 260 ... G-1
Nahma, 210 ... F-3
Napoleon, 1258 ... S-9
Nashville, 1628 ... Q-7
National City, 80 ... K-11
National Mine, 490 ... D-1
Naubinway, 350 ... E-6
Needmore ... Q-8
Negaunee, 4568 ... D-1
Nelson ... O-9
Nessen City, 97 ... K-5
Nestoria ... C-13
New Baltimore, 12084 ... Q-13
New Boston, 1300 ... R-12
New Buffalo, 1883 ... T-3
New Era, 451 ... N-4
New Greenleaf, 30 ... M-12
New Haven, 4642 ... P-13
New Holland, 130 ... P-5
New Hudson, 110 ... *H-1
New Lothrop, 581 ... O-10
New Richmond, 180 ... Q-5
New Swanzy, 570 ... E-2
New Troy, 497 ... T-4
Newaygo, 1976 ... N-6
NEWAYGO CO., 48460 ... N-5
Newberry, 1519 ... D-6
Newport, 1070 ... S-12
Niles, 11600 ... T-4
Nirvana, 50 ... M-6
Nisula, 100 ... B-12
N. Adams, 477 ... S-9
N. Bradley, 70 ... M-9
N. Branch, 1033 ... O-12
N. Epworth ... L-4
N. Lake, 380 ... O-11
N. Lake, 270 ... R-5
N. Lake, 120 ... D-1
N. Lakeport, 300 ... O-14
N. Manitou, 170 ... I-5
N. Morenci, 90 ... T-10
N. Muskegon, 3786 ... O-4
N. Star, 300 ... O-9
N. Street, 80 ... O-14
Northland, 60 ... E-1
Northport, 526 ... I-6
Northville, 5970 ... *I-2
Northwood, 1100 ... O-2
Norton Shores, 23994 ... O-4
Norwalk ... K-5
Norway, 2845 ... D-13
Norwood, 142 ... H-7
Nottawa, 270 ... S-6
Novi, 55224 ... Q-11
Nunica, 360 ... O-5
Oak Grv., 150 ... Q-10
Oak Hill, 569 ... L-4
Oak Pk., 29319 ... *H-5
Oakhurst, 50 ... M-11
OAKLAND CO., 1202362 ... P-12
Oakley, 290 ... O-10
Oakville, 50 ... S-11
OCEANA CO., 26570 ... N-5
Oden, 363 ... G-8
Ogden Ctr., 90 ... T-10
OGEMAW CO., 21699 ... K-9
Oil City ... N-9
Okemos, 21369 ... Q-9
Old Mission, 300 ... I-6
Olivet, 1605 ... R-8
Omena, 267 ... I-6
Omer, 313 ... L-10
Onaway, 880 ... H-9
Onekama, 411 ... K-5
Onondaga, 250 ... R-9
Onsted, 917 ... S-10
Ontonagon, 1494 ... B-11
ONTONAGON CO., 6780 ... B-11
Orangeville, 250 ... Q-6
Orchard Lake, 2375 ... *G-4
Orleans, 230 ... P-7
Ortonville, 1442 ... P-11
OSCEOLA CO., 23528 ... L-7
Oscoda, 903 ... K-12
OSCODA CO., 8640 ... J-9
Oshtemo ... R-6
Osseo, 320 ... S-9
Ossineke, 938 ... I-11
Otisville, 864 ... O-11
Otsego, 3956 ... R-6
OTSEGO CO., 24164 ... I-8
OTTAWA CO., 263801 ... P-5
Ottawa Lake, 190 ... T-11
Otter Lake, 389 ... O-11
Overisel, 160 ... Q-5
Ovid, 1603 ... P-9
Owendale, 241 ... M-12
Owosso, 15194 ... P-10
Oxford, 3436 ... P-12
Painesdale, 450 ... A-12
Palmer, 418 ... D-1
Palms, 30 ... M-13
Palmyra, 370 ... T-10
Palo, 250 ... O-8
Paradise, 340 ... C-7
Parchment, 1804 ... O-2
Paris, 230 ... M-6
Parisville, 50 ... M-13
Park Lake, 390 ... P-9
Parkdale, 704 ... K-4
Parkers Cors., 40 ... Q-10
Parma, 769 ... R-9
Parshallville, 80 ... Q-11
Partello ... R-8
Paulding, 100 ... C-11
Paw Paw, 3534 ... R-5
Paw Paw Lake, 3511 ... R-4
Payment, 110 ... D-9
Paynesville, 30 ... C-12
Peacock, 60 ... L-5
Pearl, 60 ... Q-5
Pearl Bch., 2829 ... Q-14
Peck, 632 ... O-13
Pelkie, 160 ... B-12
Pellston, 822 ... G-8
Pennfield, 100 ... R-7
Pentwater, 857 ... M-4
Perkins, 400 ... F-2
Perrinton, 406 ... O-8
Perronville, 60 ... F-2
Perry, 2188 ... P-9
Peshawbestown, 90 ... I-6
Petersburg, 1146 ... S-11
Petoskey, 5670 ... H-7
Pewamo, 469 ... P-8
Phoenix, 20 ... A-13
Pickford, 450 ... E-9
Pierport, 40 ... K-4
Pierson, 172 ... O-6
Pigeon, 1208 ... M-12
Pinckney, 2427 ... Q-10
Pinconning, 1307 ... M-10
Pine Creek ... S-7
Pine Run, 660 ... O-11
Piney Woods, 500 ... L-8
Pinnebog, 60 ... L-12
Pittsburg ... P-9
Pittsford, 530 ... T-9
Plainfield, 40 ... Q-10
Plainwell, 3804 ... R-6
Pleasant Ridge, 2526 ... *H-6
Pleasant Valley ... N-9
Plymouth, 9132 ... *J-2
Pokagon, 140 ... S-5
Pompeii, 200 ... O-9
Pontiac, 59515 ... Q-12
Port Austin, 664 ... L-12
Port Hope, 267 ... L-13
Port Huron, 30184 ... P-14
Port Sanilac, 623 ... N-14
Port Sheldon, 180 ... P-5
Portage, 46292 ... R-6
Portland, 3883 ... P-8
Posen, 234 ... H-11
Poseyville, 100 ... N-9
Potterville, 2617 ... Q-8
Powers, 422 ... G-1
Prairieville, 180 ... Q-6
Prattville, 200 ... T-9
Prescott, 266 ... L-10
Presque Isle, 120 ... H-11
PRESQUE ISLE CO., 13376 ... H-9
Princeton, 180 ... E-1
Prudenville, 1682 ... K-8

*, †, ‡, §, ◊ See explanation under state title in this index.
County and parish names are listed in capital letters & boldface type.
Independent cities (not included in a county) are listed in italics.

Pulaski, 130 S-8
Pullman, 600 Q-5
Quanicassee, 130 N-11
Quincy, 1652 S-8
Quinnesec, 1191 D-13
Raco, 50 D-8
Ralph, 60 E-1
Ramsay, 1080 C-10
Rankin, 220 P-11
Ransom, 130 T-9
Rapid City, 1352 J-7
Rapid River, 800 F-3
Ravenna, 1219 O-5
Ray, 60 T-8
Ray Ctr. *D-9
Reading, 1078 T-8
Red Oak J-9
Redford, 51622 *J-4
Reed City, 2425 M-6
Reeman, 110 N-5
Reese, 1454 N-11
Remus, 480 N-7
Republic, 570 C-13
Rexton, 160 E-7
Rhodes, 130 M-9
Richland, 751 R-6
Richmond, 5735 P-13
Richmondville, 30 N-13
Richville, 370 N-11
Ridgeway, 200 S-10
Riga, 400 T-11
Riley Ctr., 60 P-13
River Rouge, 7903 *K-6
Riverdale, 400 N-8
Riverside, 290 S-4
Riverview, 12486 *M-6
Rives Jct., 450 R-9
Roberts, 50 Q-14
Rochester, 12711 Q-12
Rochester Hills, 70995 Q-12
Rock, 440 E-2
Rockford, 5719 O-6
Rockland, 270 B-12
Rockwood, 3289 S-12
Rodney, 160 M-7
Rogers City, 2827 G-10
Rollin, 110 S-9
Romeo, 3596 P-12
Romulus, 23989 R-12
Roosevelt Pk., 3831 O-4
Roscommon, 1075 K-8
ROSCOMMON CO., 24449 K-8
Rose Ctr., 170 *E-1
Rose City, 653 K-10
Roseburg, 30 O-13
Rosebush, 368 M-8
Rosedale D-9
Roseville, 47299 Q-13
Rothbury, 432 N-4
Royal Oak, 57236 *H-6
Rudyard, 1100 E-8
Rumely, 90 D-3
Russellville, 220 O-11
Ruth, 230 M-13
Saginaw, 51508 N-10
SAGINAW CO., 200169 O-10
Sagola, 180 D-13
St. Charles, 2054 O-10
St. Clair, 5485 P-14
ST. CLAIR CO., 163040 P-13
St. Clair Shores, 59715 Q-13
St. Helen, 2668 K-9
St. Ignace, 2452 F-8
St. James, 205 F-6
St. Johns, 7865 P-9
St. Joseph, 8365 S-4
ST. JOSEPH CO., 61295 T-6
St. Louis, 7482 N-8
Salem, 350 *I-1
Saline, 8810 R-11
Samaria, 480 T-11
Sand Creek, 110 T-10
Sand Lake, 500 O-6
Sand River, 80 D-2
Sands, 60 D-2
Sandusky, 2679 N-13
Sanford, 859 M-9
SANILAC CO., 43114 N-13
Saranac, 1325 P-7
Saugatuck, 925 Q-5
Sault Ste. Marie, 14144 D-9
Sawyer, 500 T-4
Schaffer, 150 F-2
Schoolcraft, 1525 S-6
SCHOOLCRAFT CO., 8485 E-4
Scofield S-11
Scotts, 350 R-7
Scottville, 1214 M-4
Sears, 90 M-7
Sebewaing, 1759 M-11
Selkirk, 40 K-10
Seney, 200 D-5
Seven Harbors, 4700 *E-1
Shabbona, 90 N-12
Shady Shores, 350 K-10
Shaftsburg, 270 P-9
Shelby, 65159 *E-7
Shelby, 2065 N-4
Shelbyville, 160 Q-6
Sheldon, 590 *K-2
Shepardsville, 70 P-9
Shepherd, 1515 N-8
Sheridan, 649 O-7
Sherman, 30 K-6
Sherman City, 30 M-7
Sherwood, 309 S-7
SHIAWASSEE CO., 70648 P-10
Shiawasseetown, 80 P-10
Shields, 6587 N-10
Shingleton, 320 D-4
Shoreham, 862 S-4
Sidnaw, 300 C-12
Sidney, 120 O-7
Silver City, 60 B-11
Silverwood, 170 N-12
Six Lakes, 420 N-7
Skandia, 300 D-2
Skanee, 100 B-13
Skeels L-8
Skidway Lake, 3392 L-10
Snover, 448 N-13
Sodus, 180 S-4
Somerset, 140 S-9
Somerset Ctr., 440 S-9
S. Boardman, 536 J-7
S. Branch, 150 K-10
S. Haven, 4403 R-4
S. Ionia, 100 P-7
S. Lyon, 11327 Q-11
S. Range, 758 A-12
S. Rockwood, 1675 S-12
Southfield, 71739 Q-12
Southgate, 30047 *M-5
Spalding, 590 G-1
Sparlingville P-14
Sparr, 30 I-8
Sparta, 4140 O-6
Spratt I-10
Spring Arbor, 2881 R-9
Spring Lake, 2323 O-5
Springfield, 5260 R-7
Springport, 800 R-8
Springville, 60 S-10
Spruce, 120 I-11
Stalwart, 60 E-9
Standish, 1509 L-10
Stanton, 1417 O-7
Stanwood, 211 N-6
Stephenson, 862 H-1
Sterling, 530 L-10
Sterling Hts., 129699 Q-12
Steuben, 70 E-4
Stevensville, 1142 S-4
Stockbridge, 1218 R-10
Stonington F-3
Stony Lake, 50 N-4
Stronach, 162 L-4
Strongs, 380 D-7
Sturgis, 10994 T-7
Sumner, 170 O-8
Sumnerville, 180 S-5
Sunfield, 578 Q-8
Sunrise Hts., 1350 R-7
Suttons Bay, 618 I-6
Swartz Creek, 5758 P-10
Sylvan Lake, 1720 *F-4
Tallmadge P-5
Tallman, 70 L-5
Tawas City, 1827 K-11
Taylor, 63131 R-12
Tecumseh, 8521 S-10
Tekonsha, 717 S-8
Temperance, 8517 T-11
Temple, 300 L-7
Thomaston, 80 C-10
Thompson, 200 F-4
Thompsonville, 441 K-5
Thornville, 60 P-12
Three Lakes, 150 C-13
Three Oaks, 1622 T-4
Three Rivers, 7811 S-6
Tipton, 200 S-10
Topinabee, 400 G-8
Torch Lake, 80 I-7
Torch River, 410 I-7
Tower, 300 H-9
Traunik, 100 E-3
Traverse Bay, 40 A-13
Traverse City, 14674 J-6
Trenary, 300 E-3
Trenton, 18853 S-12
Trombly, 40 E-2
Trout Creek, 230 C-12
Trout Lake, 370 E-7
Trowbridge Pk., 2176 D-2
Troy, 80980 Q-12
Trufant, 500 O-7
Turk Lake, 350 O-7
Turner, 114 L-10
Tuscola, 100 O-11
TUSCOLA CO., 55729 N-11
Tustin, 230 L-6
Twin Lake, 1720 O-5
Twin Lakes, 150 B-12
Twining, 181 L-10
Tyre, 40 M-13
Ubly, 858 M-13
Unadilla, 100 R-10
Union, 200 T-5
Union City, 1599 S-7
Union Lake, 8500 *F-3
Union Pier, 1100 T-3
Unionville, 508 M-11
Utica, 4757 *F-7
Valley Ctr. O-13
Valley Farms, 950 A-3
VAN BUREN CO., 76258 R-5
Vandalia, 301 S-5
Vanderbilt, 562 H-8
Vandercook Lake, 4721 R-9
Vassar, 2697 N-11
Vermontville, 759 Q-7
Vernon, 783 P-10
Verona, 80 M-13
Vestaburg, 420 N-8
Vickeryville, 100 O-8
Vicksburg, 2906 S-6
Village of Lake Isabella, 1681 N-8
Virginia Pk., 1800 Q-5
Vogel Ctr., 110 L-7
Volinia, 40 S-5
Vriesland, 150 P-5
Vulcan, 100 D-14
Wacousta, 1440 P-8
Wadhams, 150 P-14
Wakefield, 1851 C-10
Wakelee, 80 S-5
Waldenburg, 110 *F-8
Waldron, 538 T-9
Walhalla, 380 M-5
Walker, 23537 *B-1
Walkerville, 247 M-5
Wallace, 150 H-1
Walled Lake, 6999 *G-2
Walloon Lake, 290 H-8
Waltz, 500 *N-3
Warren, 134056 Q-13
Washington, 1850 Q-12
WASHTENAW CO., 344791 R-10
Waterford, 71981 Q-12
Waterloo, 190 R-10
Waters, 150 I-8
Watersmeet, 428 C-11
Watertown, 100 N-13
Watervliet, 1735 R-4
Watrousville, 200 N-11
Watson, 30 Q-6
Watton, 150 C-12
Waucedah, 50 F-1
Wayland, 4079 Q-6
Wayne, 17593 *K-3
WAYNE CO., 1820584 R-12
Webberville, 1272 Q-10
Weidman, 959 M-8
Wells, 1000 F-2
Wellston, 311 L-5
Wequetonsing G-7
W. Bloomfield *G-4
W. Branch, 2139 K-9
W. Olive, 200 P-5
W. Windsor Q-8
Westland, 84094 R-12
Weston, 300 T-10
Westphalia, 923 P-8
Westville, 50 O-7
Westwood, 8653 P-1
Wetmore, 480 D-4
WEXFORD CO., 32735 K-6
Wheeler, 320 N-9
White Cloud, 1408 N-6
White Lake, 3200 *E-2
White Pigeon, 1522 T-6
White Pine, 474 B-11
Whitefish Pt., 50 C-7
Whitehall, 2706 N-4
Whitmore Lake, 6423 R-11
Whittaker, 240 S-11
Whittemore, 384 K-10
Wildwood, 80 K-5
Willard M-10
Williamsburg, 400 J-6
Williamston, 3854 Q-9
Willis, 300 *M-1
Willow, 430 *N-3
Wilmot, 140 N-12
Wilson, 150 G-2
Winegars L-9
Winn, 450 N-8
Winona, 40 B-12
Wisner, 110 N-11
Witch Lake, 80 C-13
Wixom, 13498 Q-11
Wolf Lake, 4104 O-5
Wolverine, 244 H-8
Wolverine Lake, 4312 *G-2
Woodbury, 80 Q-7
Wooden Shoe Vil., 330 L-9
Woodhaven, 12875 *M-5
Woodland, 425 Q-7
Woodland Bch., 2049 S-12
Woodland Pk., 200 M-5
Woodville, 50 M-6
Wyandotte, 25883 R-12
Wyman, 50 N-7
Wyoming, 72125 P-6
Yale, 1955 O-13
Ypsilanti, 19435 R-11
Yuma, 80 K-6
Zeeland, 5504 P-5
Zilwaukee, 1658 N-10

Minnesota

Page locator

Map keys	Atlas pages
A–J	108–109
K–T	110–111

* City keyed to pp. 112–113

Ada, 1707 H-2
Adams, 787 T-10
Adrian, 1209 T-3
Afton, 2886 P-10
Ah-gwah-ching, 50 I-6
Aitkin, 2165 K-8
AITKIN CO., 16202 K-9
Akeley, 432 I-6
Albany, 2561 M-6
Albert Lea, 18016 T-9
Alberta, 103 N-3
Albertville, 7044 O-8
Alborn, 200 I-11
Alden, 661 S-9
Aldrich, 48 K-6
Alexandria, 11070 M-5
Alida, 20 H-5
Alma City, 40 R-8
Almelund, 150 N-10
Almora, 50 K-5
Alpha, 116 T-6
Altura, 493 R-12
Alvarado, 363 E-1
Alvwood G-7
Amboy, 534 S-7
Amiret, 60 Q-4
Amor K-4
Andover, 30598 O-9
Andree, 30 M-9
Angle Inlet, 60 B-5
Angora, 100 G-11
Angus, 50 F-2
Annandale, 3228 O-7
Anoka, 17142 O-9
ANOKA CO., 330844 N-9
Apple Valley, 49084 P-9
Appleton, 1412 O-3
Arco, 75 Q-3
Arden Hills, 9552 *D-6
Argyle, 639 E-2
Arlington, 2233 Q-7
Arnesen C-5
Arnold, 2960 J-12
Ash Creek, 25 T-3
Ash Lake, 30 E-10
Ashby, 446 L-4
Askov, 364 L-10
Atwater, 1133 O-6
Audubon, 519 J-3
Aurora, 1682 G-11
Austin, 24718 T-10
Averill, 40 I-2
Avoca, 147 S-4
Avon, 1396 M-7
Babbitt, 1475 G-12
Backus, 250 J-7
Badger, 375 D-3
Bagley, 1392 G-5
Baker, 55 J-2
Balaton, 643 R-3
Bald Eagle, 1800 *C-9
Ball Club, 342 H-8
Barnesville, 2563 J-2
Barnum, 613 K-10
Barrett, 415 M-4
Barrows, 75 K-7
Barry, 16 N-2
Bassett, 50 H-12
Battle Lake, 875 K-4
Baudette, 1106 D-6
Baxter, 7610 K-7
Bay Lake, 80 K-8
Bayport, 3471 O-10
Bayview, 40 L-9
Bear River G-10
Beardsley, 233 N-2
Beauford, 60 R-8
Beaulieu, 48 H-4
Beaver Bay, 181 H-13
Beaver Creek, 297 T-2
Bechyn, 30 P-5
Becida H-5
Becker, 4538 N-8
BECKER CO., 32504 I-4
Bejou, 89 H-3
Belgrade, 740 N-5
Bellaire, 1900 *D-9
Belle Plaine, 6661 Q-8
Belle Prairie, 500 L-7
Bellechester, 175 Q-11
Bellingham, 168 O-3
Beltrami, 107 G-2
BELTRAMI CO., 44442 E-5
Belview, 384 Q-5
Bemidji, 13431 H-6
Bena, 116 H-7
Benedict, 90 I-6
Benson, 3240 N-4
BENTON CO., 38451 M-7
Bergen, 35 S-5
Bernadotte, 25 Q-7
Beroun, 100 M-10
Bertha, 497 K-5
Bethel, 466 N-9
Big Bend City, 60 O-4
Big Falls, 236 E-8
Big Lake, 10060 N-8
BIG STONE CO., 5269 N-2
Bigelow, 235 T-4
Bigfork, 446 G-8
Bingham Lake, 126 S-5
Birch Bch. C-6
Birchdale, 30 D-7
Birchwood, 870 *D-9
Bird Island, 1042 P-6
Biscay, 113 P-7
Biwabik, 969 G-11
Bixby, 100 S-10
Black Hammer, 50 T-13
Blackberry, 50 I-9
Blackduck, 785 G-6
Blaine, 57186 O-9
Blakeley, 100 Q-8
Blomkest, 157 P-5
Blooming Prairie, 1996 S-10
Bloomington, 82893 P-9
Blue Earth, 3353 T-7
BLUE EARTH CO., 64013 S-7
Bluffton, 207 K-5
Bock, 106 M-9
Bois Fort, 350 F-9
Bonanza Grv. N-2
Bongards P-8
Borup, 110 I-2
Bovey, 804 H-9
Bowlus, 290 M-7
Bowstring, 25 G-8
Boy River, 47 I-7
Boyd, 175 P-3
Braham, 1793 M-9
Brainerd, 13590 K-7
Brandon, 489 L-4
Bratsberg S-13
Breckenridge, 3386 K-2
Breezy Pt., 2346 J-7
Brennyville, 35 M-8
Brevik, 30 I-7
Brewster, 473 S-4
Bricelyn, 365 T-8
Brimson, 40 H-12
Britt, 80 G-11
Brook Pk., 139 L-10
Brooklyn Ctr., 30104 *D-3
Brooklyn Pk., 75781 *B-3
Brooks, 141 G-3
Brookston, 141 J-11
Brooten, 743 N-5
Browerville, 790 L-6
BROWN CO., 25893 R-6
Browns Valley, 589 M-1
Brownsdale, 676 S-10
Brownsville, 466 S-14
Brownton, 762 P-7
Bruno, 102 K-11
Brunswick, 80 M-9
Buckman, 270 M-7
Buffalo, 15453 O-8
Buffalo Lake, 733 P-6
Buhl, 1000 H-10
Burnsville, 60306 *J-4
Burr, 20 P-2
Burtrum, 144 M-6
Butler J-5
Butterfield, 586 S-6
Butternut, 30 R-7
Buyck, 25 F-11
Byron, 4914 R-11
Caledonia, 2868 T-13
Callaway, 234 I-4
Calumet, 367 H-9
Cambria, 80 R-7
Cambridge, 8111 N-9
Campbell, 158 L-2
Canby, 1795 P-3
Cannon City, 60 Q-9
Cannon Falls, 4083 Q-10
Canton, 346 T-12
Canyon, 70 I-11
Carlisle, 30 K-3
Carlos, 502 L-5
Carlton, 862 J-11
CARLTON CO., 35386 J-10
Carver, 3724 P-8
CARVER CO., 91042 P-8
CASS CO., 28567 I-7
Cass Lake, 770 H-6
Castle Danger, 35 I-13
Castle Rock, 150 Q-10
Cedar Mills, 45 P-7
Center City, 628 N-10
Centerville, 3792 *B-8
Ceylon, 369 T-6
Champlin, 23089 *A-2
Chandler, 270 S-3
Chanhassen, 22952 P-9
Chaska, 23770 P-9
Chatfield, 2779 S-12
Cherry, 100 H-10
Cherry Grv., 70 T-11
Chester, 200 R-11
Chickamaw Bch., 114 J-7
CHIPPEWA CO., 12441 O-4
Chisago City, 4967 N-10
CHISAGO CO., 53887 N-10
Chisholm, 4976 H-10
Chokio, 400 N-3
Circle Pines, 4918 *B-7
Clara City, 1360 P-5
Claremont, 548 R-10
Clarissa, 681 L-6
Clarkfield, 863 P-4
Clarks Grv., 706 S-9
CLAY CO., 58999 I-2
Clear Lake, 545 N-8
Clearbrook, 518 G-5
Clearwater, 1735 N-8
CLEARWATER CO., 8695 G-5
Clements, 153 Q-5
Clementson, 20 D-7
Cleveland, 719 Q-8
Climax, 267 G-2
Clinton, 449 N-2
Clinton Falls, 40 R-9
Clitherall, 112 K-4
Clontarf, 164 N-4
Cloquet, 12124 J-11
Clotho, 25 L-5
Cloverdale, 40 L-10
Cloverton, 35 L-11
Coates, 161 P-10
Cobden, 36 R-6
Cohasset, 2698 H-8
Cokato, 2694 O-7
Cold Spr., 4025 N-7
Coleraine, 1970 H-9
Collegeville, 200 N-7
Collis, 20 M-2
Cologne, 1519 P-8
Columbia Hts., 19496 *D-5
Comfrey, 382 R-6
Comstock, 93 J-2
Concord, 60 R-10
Conger, 146 T-9
Cook, 574 F-10
COOK CO., 5176 F-14
Coon Rapids, 61476 *A-4
Corcoran, 5379 O-9
Cormorant J-3
Corning S-10
Correll, 34 O-3
Corvuso, 25 P-6
Cosmos, 473 P-6
Cottage Grv., 34589 P-10
Cotton, 200 I-11
Cottonwood, 1212 Q-4
COTTONWOOD CO., 11687 S-5
Courtland, 611 R-7
Cove, 75 L-8
Craigville F-8
Crane Lake, 300 E-11
Croftville, 40 B-12
Cromwell, 234 J-10
Crookston, 7891 G-2
Crosby, 2386 K-8
Cross Lake, 2141 J-7
Crow River, 20 O-6
Crow Wing, 25 K-7
CROW WING CO., 62500 K-7
Crown, 50 N-9
Crystal, 22151 *E-3
Currie, 233 R-4
Cushing, 70 L-6
Cusson, 40 F-10
Cutler, 100 K-8
Cuyuna, 332 K-8
Cyrus, 288 M-4
Dakota, 323 S-14
DAKOTA CO., 398552 Q-9
Dalbo, 100 M-9
Dalton, 253 L-4
Danube, 505 P-5
Danvers, 97 N-4
Darfur, 108 R-6
Darwin, 350 O-7
Dassel, 1469 O-7
Dawson, 1540 P-3
Dayton, 4671 O-9
De Graff, 115 O-4
Debs, 25 G-5
Deephaven, 3642 *G-1
Deer Creek, 322 K-5
Deer River, 930 H-8
Deerwood, 532 K-8
Delano, 5464 O-8
Delavan, 179 S-8
Delft, 100 S-5
Delhi, 70 Q-5
Dellwood, 1063 *C-9
Denham, 35 K-10
Dennison, 212 Q-10
Dent, 192 J-4
Detroit Lakes, 8569 J-4
Dexter, 341 S-11
Dilworth, 4024 I-2
Dodge Ctr., 2670 R-10
DODGE CO., 20087 S-10
Donaldson, 42 D-2
Donnelly, 241 M-3
Dora Lake, 40 G-8
Doran, 55 L-2
Dorothy, 25 F-3
Dorset, 80 I-6
Douglas, 150 R-11
DOUGLAS CO., 36009 L-4
Dover, 735 R-12
Dovray, 57 R-4
Downer, 90 J-2
Dresbach, 150 S-14
Duelm, 70 N-8
Duluth, 86265 J-12
Duluth Hts. A-8
Dumont, 100 M-2
Dundas, 1367 Q-9
Dundee, 68 S-4
Dunnell, 167 T-6
Dunvilla, 100 J-3
Duquette, 70 K-11
Duxbury, 20 L-11
Eagan, 64206 *J-7
Eagle Bend, 535 L-5
Eagle Lake, 2422 R-8
E. Beaver Bay, 20 H-13
E. Bethel, 11626 N-9
E. Chain, 200 T-7
E. Grand Forks, 8601 F-1
E. Gull Lake, 1004 K-7
E. Lake, 30 K-9
E. Lake Francis Shores, 170 N-9
E. Union, 60 P-8
Easton, 199 S-8
Ebro, 64 H-4
Echo, 278 Q-5
Eden Prairie, 60797 *I-1
Eden Valley, 1042 N-6
Edgerton, 1189 S-3
Edgewood, 120 N-9
Edina, 47941 *H-3
Effie, 123 G-8
Eitzen, 243 T-13
Elba, 152 R-12
Elbow Lake, 1176 L-3
Eldred, 50 G-2
Elgin, 1089 R-12
Elizabeth, 173 K-3
Elk River, 22974 N-9
Elko New Market, 4110 Q-9
Elkton, 141 T-11
Ellendale, 691 S-9
Ellsworth, 463 T-3
Elmdale, 116 M-7
Elmore, 663 T-7
Elrosa, 211 N-6
Ely, 3460 F-12
Elysian, 652 R-8
Embarrass, 100 G-11
Emily, 813 J-8
Emmons, 391 T-9
Englund D-2
Erdahl, 50 L-4
Erhard, 148 K-3
Ericsburg, 90 D-9
Erskine, 503 G-3
Esko, 1869 J-11
Essig, 50 Q-6
Estes Brook, 35 M-8
Euclid, 150 F-2
Evan, 86 Q-6
Evansville, 612 L-4
Eveleth, 3718 H-11
Everdell K-2
Evergreen J-5
Excelsior, 2188 P-9
Eyota, 1977 R-12
Fairfax, 1235 Q-6
Fairhaven, 358 N-7
Fairmont, 10666 T-7
Falcon Hts., 5321 *F-6
Faribault, 23352 R-9
FARIBAULT CO., 14553 S-8
Farming, 50 N-6
Farmington, 21086 P-10
Farwell, 51 M-4
Federal Dam, 110 H-7
Felton, 177 I-2
Fergus Falls, 13138 K-3
Fernando, 25 P-7
Fertile, 842 G-3
Fifty Lakes, 387 J-7
Fillmore, 100 S-11
FILLMORE CO., 20866 T-12
Finland, 195 H-14
Finlayson, 315 L-10
Fisher, 435 G-2
Flensburg, 225 L-7
Flom, 90 I-3
Floodwood, 528 I-10
Florence, 39 R-3
Florenton, 100 G-11
Florian E-2
Foley, 2603 M-8
Forada, 185 M-5
Forbes, 110 H-11
Forest City, 80 O-7
Forest Lake, 18375 O-10
Foreston, 533 M-8
Ft. Ripley, 69 L-7
Fosston, 1527 G-4
Fountain, 410 S-12
Fox C-4
Fox Lake, 100 S-6
Foxhome, 116 K-3
Franklin, 510 Q-6
Frazee, 1350 J-4
Freeborn, 297 S-9
FREEBORN CO., 31255 T-9
Freeburg, 60 T-14
Freedhem, 50 L-7
Freeport, 632 M-6
Fremont S-12
French Lake, 30 O-7
French River, 400 I-12
Fridley, 27208 *D-5
Frontenac, 282 Q-11
Frost, 198 T-8
Fulda, 1318 S-4
Funkley, 5 G-7
Garden City, 255 R-7
Garfield, 354 L-4
Garrison, 210 K-8
Garvin, 135 R-4
Gary, 214 H-3
Gatzke, 50 E-4
Gaylord, 2305 Q-7
Gem Lake, 393 *D-8
Gemmell F-7
Geneva, 555 S-9
Genoa, 60 R-11
Genola, 75 L-7
Gentilly, 100 G-2
Georgetown, 129 I-2
Georgeville, 30 N-6
Gheen, 60 F-10
Ghent, 370 Q-3
Gibbon, 772 Q-6
Giese L-10
Gilbert, 1799 H-11
Gilfillan Q-5
Gilman, 224 M-8
Glen, 100 K-9
Glencoe, 5631 P-7
Glendorado, 20 N-8
Glenville, 643 T-9
Glenwood, 2564 M-5
Gluek O-4
Glyndon, 1394 I-2
Godahl, 20 R-6
Golden Valley, 20371 *E-3
Gonvick, 282 G-4
Good Thunder, 583 R-8
Goodhue, 1176 Q-11
GOODHUE CO., 46183 Q-10
Goodland, 150 I-9
Goodridge, 132 F-4
Goodview, 4036 R-13
Gordonsville, 100 T-9
Graceton, 30 D-6
Graceville, 577 N-2
Granada, 303 S-7
Grand Falls E-8
Grand Marais, 1351 B-12
Grand Meadow, 1139 S-11
Grand Portage, 200 A-13
Grand Rapids, 10869 H-9
Grandy, 150 M-9
Granger, 100 T-12
Granite Falls, 2897 P-4
Grant, 4096 *D-10
GRANT CO., 6018 M-3
Grasston, 158 M-10
Grattan, 40 G-7
Greaney, 25 F-10
Green Isle, 559 P-8
Green Valley, 100 Q-4
Greenbush, 719 D-3
Greenfield, 2777 O-8
Greenleaf, 40 O-7
Greenleafton, 80 T-12
Greenwald, 222 N-6
Grey Eagle, 348 M-6
Grogan, 30 R-6
Grove City, 635 O-6
Grove Lake, 30 M-5
Grygla, 221 E-4
Guckeen, 100 T-7
Gully, 66 G-4
Gutches Grv. L-6
Guthrie, 60 H-6
Hackensack, 313 I-7
Hader, 30 Q-10
Hadley, 61 R-4
Hallock, 981 C-2
Halma, 61 D-2
Halstad, 597 H-2
Ham Lake, 15296 O-9
Hamburg, 513 P-8
Hammond, 132 R-11
Hampton, 689 Q-10
Hancock, 765 N-4
Hanley Falls, 304 P-4
Hanover, 2938 O-8
Hanska, 402 R-7
Harding, 125 L-8
Hardwick, 198 S-3
Harmony, 1020 T-12
Harris, 1132 N-10
Hartland, 315 S-9
Hassman J-8
Hastings, 22172 P-10
Hasty, 40 N-8
Hatfield, 54 S-3
Hawick, 120 N-6
Hawley, 2067 I-3
Hay Creek, 60 Q-11
Hayfield, 1340 S-10
Haypoint I-8
Hayward, 250 T-9
Hazel Run, 63 P-4
Hector, 1151 P-6
Heidelberg, 122 Q-8
Henderson, 886 Q-8
Hendricks, 713 Q-2
Hendrum, 307 H-2
HENNEPIN CO., 1152425 O-8
Henning, 802 K-5
Henriette, 71 M-10
Herman, 437 M-3
Hermantown, 9414 J-11
Heron Lake, 698 S-5
Hewitt, 266 K-5
Hibbing, 16361 H-10
High Forest, 100 S-11
Highland S-12
Hill City, 633 I-9
Hillman, 38 L-8
Hills, 686 T-2
Hilltop, 744 *D-5
Hillview, 20 J-5
Hinckley, 1800 L-10
Hines, 60 G-6
Hitterdal, 201 I-3
Hoffman, 681 M-4
Hokah, 580 S-14
Holdingford, 708 M-7
Holland, 187 R-3
Hollandale, 303 S-9
Holloway, 92 O-3
Holmes City, 90 M-4
Holt, 88 E-3
Holyoke, 60 K-11
Homer, 181 R-13
Hope, 120 S-9
Hopkins, 17591 *G-2
Houston, 979 S-13
HOUSTON CO., 19027 S-13
Hovland, 250 B-13
Howard Lake, 1962 O-7
Hoyt Lakes, 2017 G-12
Hubbard, 150 J-5
HUBBARD CO., 20428 I-5
Hugo, 13332 *B-9
Humboldt, 45 C-1
Hunters Pk. A-9
Huntersville, 20 J-6
Huntley, 150 S-7
Hutchinson, 14178 P-7
Ihlen, 63 S-2
Imogene, 70 T-7
Independence, 3504 O-8
Inger, 212 G-8
International Falls, 6424 D-9
Inver Grv. Hts., 33880 *J-8
Iona, 137 S-4
Iron Jct., 86 H-11
Ironton, 572 K-8
Isabella, 100 G-13
Isanti, 5251 N-9
ISANTI CO., 37816 M-9
Island Lake G-6
Island View, 150 D-9
Isle, 751 L-9
ITASCA CO., 45058 G-9
Ivanhoe, 559 Q-3
Jackson, 3299 T-5
JACKSON CO., 10266 T-5
Jacobson, 150 I-9
Janesville, 2256 R-8
Jasper, 633 S-2
Jeffers, 369 R-5
Jenkins, 430 J-7
Johnsburg, 25 T-10
Johnson, 29 N-3
Jordan, 5470 P-8
Judson, 150 R-7
Kabekona, 60 H-6
Kabetogama, 100 E-10
KANABEC CO., 16239 M-9
Kanaranzi, 60 T-3
Kandiyohi, 491 O-6
KANDIYOHI CO., 42239 O-5
Karlstad, 760 D-2
Kasota, 675 R-8
Kasson, 5931 R-10
Keewatin, 1068 H-10
Kelliher, 262 F-7
Kellogg, 456 Q-12
Kelsey, 30 I-11
Kennedy, 193 D-2
Kenneth, 68 S-3
Kensington, 292 M-4
Kent, 81 K-2
Kenyon, 1815 R-10
Kerkhoven, 759 O-5
Kerrick, 65 K-11
Kettle River, 180 K-10
Kiester, 501 T-8
Kilkenny, 134 R-9
Kimball, 762 N-7
Kinbrae, 12 S-4
Kingsdale L-11
Kingston, 161 O-7
Kinney, 169 H-10
KITTSON CO., 4552 D-2
Klossner, 50 Q-7
Knife River, 300 I-12
KOOCHICHING CO., 13311 E-7
Kragnes, 60 I-2
La Crescent, 4830 S-14
La Prairie, 665 H-9
La Salle, 87 R-6
Lac qui Parle, 50 O-3
LAC QUI PARLE CO., 7259 P-3
Lafayette, 504 Q-7
L. Benton, 683 R-3
L. Bronson, 229 D-2
Lake Center, 25 J-3
Lake City, 5063 Q-12
LAKE CO., 10866 G-13
L. Crystal, 2549 R-7
L. Elmo, 8069 O-10
L. George, 230 I-6
L. Henry, 103 N-6
L. Hubert, 300 K-7
L. Itasca, 50 H-5
L. Lillian, 238 P-6
LAKE OF THE WOODS CO., 4045 D-5
Lake Pk., 783 I-3
L. Shore, 1004 K-7
L. Wilson, 251 R-3
Lakefield, 1694 S-5
Lakeland, 1796 P-10
Lakeville, 55954 P-9
Lamberton, 824 R-5
Lamoille, 50 R-13
Lancaster, 340 C-2
Landfall, 686 *G-9
Lanesboro, 754 S-12
Lansing, 181 S-10
Laporte, 111 I-6
Larsmont, 50 I-12
Lastrup, 104 L-8
Lauderdale, 2379 *F-6
Lawler, 60 K-9
Lawndale J-3
Lax Lake H-13
Le Center, 2499 Q-8
Le Roy, 929 T-11
Le Sueur, 4058 Q-8
LE SUEUR CO., 27703 Q-8
Leader, 50 K-6
Leaf Valley L-4
Leavenworth, 40 R-6
Lengby, 86 H-4
Lenora, 35 T-12
Leonard, 41 G-5
Leonidas, 52 H-11
Leota, 209 S-3
Lester Prairie, 1730 P-8
Lewiston, 1620 R-12
Lewisville, 250 S-7
Lexington, 2049 *B-6
Lilydale, 623 *G-7
Lincoln, 70 L-6
LINCOLN CO., 5896 Q-3
Linden Grv. F-10
Lindstrom, 4442 N-10
Lino Lakes, 20216 O-10
Lismore, 227 S-3
Litchfield, 6726 O-6
Little Canada, 9773 *E-8
Little Falls, 8343 L-7
Little Marais, 50 H-14
Little Rock, 30 M-7
Little Sauk, 70 M-6
Littlefork, 647 E-9
Lockhart, 30 H-2
Loman, 100 D-8
London, 50 T-10
Long Bch., 335 M-5
Long Lake, 1768 O-9
Long Pt., 43 C-6
Long Prairie, 3458 L-6
Long Siding, 100 M-9
Longville, 156 I-7
Lonsdale, 3674 Q-9
Louisburg, 47 O-3
Lowry, 299 M-4
Lucan, 191 Q-5
Lutsen, 190 B-11
Luverne, 4745 S-3
Luxemburg, 150 N-7
Lydia, 80 P-9
Lyle, 551 T-10
Lynd, 448 Q-3
LYON CO., 25857 Q-4
Mabel, 780 T-13
Madelia, 2308 R-7
Madison, 1551 O-3
Madison Lake, 1017 R-8
Magnolia, 222 T-3
Mahnomen, 1214 H-3
MAHNOMEN CO., 5413 H-4
Mahtomedi, 7676 *D-10
Mahtowa, 370 J-11
Makinen, 50 H-11
Mallory, 25 F-2
Malmo, 50 K-9
Manannah, 50 O-6
Manchester, 57 S-9
Manhattan Bch., 57 J-7
Mankato, 39309 R-8
Mansfield, 25 T-9
Mantorville, 1197 R-10
Maple Bay, 60 G-3
Maple Grv., 61567 *B-1
Maple Hill, 50 B-12
Maple Island, 150 S-10
Maple Lake, 2059 O-8
Maple Plain, 1768 O-8
Mapleton, 1756 S-8
Mapleview, 176 S-10
Maplewood, 38018 *E-8
Marble, 701 H-9
Marcell, 100 G-8
Margie, 40 F-8
Marietta, 162 O-2
Marine on St. Croix, 689 O-10
Marion, 100 S-11
Markham, 50 H-11
Markville, 80 L-11
Marshall, 13680 Q-4
MARSHALL CO., 9439 E-2
MARTIN CO., 20840 T-6
Marty, 50 N-7
Matawan, 50 S-8
Max, 25 G-8
Mayer, 1749 P-8
Maynard, 366 P-4
Mazeppa, 842 R-11
McGrath, 80 L-9
McGregor, 391 J-9
McIntosh, 625 G-4
McKinley, 128 H-11
MCLEOD CO., 36651 P-7
Meadowlands, 134 I-10
Medford, 1239 R-9
Medicine Lake, 371 *E-2
Medina, 4892 O-9
MEEKER CO., 23300 O-7
Meire Grv., 179 M-6
Melby, 40 L-4
Melrose, 3598 M-6
Menahga, 1306 J-5
Mendota, 198 *H-6
Mendota Hts., 11071 *H-7
Mentor, 153 G-3
Meriden, 150 R-9
Merrifield, 140 K-7
Middle River, 303 E-3
Midway, 25 J-5
Miesville, 125 Q-10
Milaca, 2946 M-8
Milan, 369 O-3
MILLE LACS CO., 26097 L-8
Millerville, 106 L-4
Millville, 182 R-11
Milroy, 252 Q-4
Miltona, 424 L-5
Minneapolis, 382578 O-9
Minneiska, 111 R-12
Minneota, 1392 Q-3
Minnesota City, 204 R-13
Minnesota Lake, 687 S-8
Minnetonka, 49734 *G-1
Minnetonka Mills *G-2
Mizpah, 56 F-7
Moland R-10
Money Creek, 80 S-13
Montevideo, 5383 O-4
Montgomery, 2956 Q-9
Monticello, 12759 N-8
Montrose, 2847 O-8
Moorhead, 38065 I-2
Moose Lake, 2751 K-10
Mora, 3571 M-9
Morgan, 896 Q-6
Morrill, 70 M-8
Morris, 5286 N-3
MORRISON CO., 33198 L-8
Morristown, 987 R-9
Morton, 411 Q-5
Motley, 671 K-6
Mound, 9052 P-8
Mounds View, 12155 *C-6
Mountain Iron, 2869 H-11
Mountain Lake, 2104 S-6
MOWER CO., 39163 T-10
Murdock, 278 O-5
Murphy City, 30 G-13
MURRAY CO., 8725 R-3
Myrtle, 48 T-10
Nashua, 68 L-3
Nashwauk, 983 H-9
Nassau, 72 O-2
Naytahwaush, 578 H-4
Nebish, 30 G-6
Nelson, 187 M-5
Nerstrand, 295 Q-10
Nett Lake, 284 F-10
Nevis, 390 I-6
New Auburn, 456 P-7
New Brighton, 21456 *D-6
New Germany, 372 P-8
New Hope, 20339 *D-3
New London, 1251 N-6
New Munich, 320 M-6
New Prague, 7321 Q-9
New Richland, 1203 S-9
New Trier, 112 Q-10
New Ulm, 13522 Q-7
New York Mills, 1199 K-5
Newburg, 40 T-13
Newfolden, 368 E-3
Newport, 3435 *I-9
Nickerson, 40 K-11
Nicollet, 1093 R-7
NICOLLET CO., 32727 Q-7
Nicols *J-5
Nielsville, 90 G-2
Nimrod, 69 J-6
Nisswa, 1971 K-7
NOBLES CO., 21378 S-3
Nodine, 50 S-13
Norcross, 70 M-3
NORMAN CO., 6852 H-2
Norseland, 30 Q-7
N. Branch, 10125 N-10
N. Mankato, 13394 R-8
N. Oaks, 4469 *D-7
N. Prairie, 50 M-7
N. St. Paul, 11460 *E-9
Northcote C-1
Northfield, 20007 Q-10
Northome, 200 F-7
Northrop, 227 S-7
Norwood Young America, 3549 P-8
Noyes, 25 C-1
Oak Ctr., 40 Q-11
Oak Grv., 8031 N-9
Oak Pk., 130 M-8
Oak Pk. Hts., 4339 O-10
Oakdale, 27378 *F-9
Oakland, 130 S-10
Odessa, 135 N-3
Odin, 106 S-6
Ogema, 184 I-4
Ogilvie, 369 M-9
Okabena, 188 S-5
Oklee, 435 F-4
Old Frontenac, 250 Q-11
Olivia, 2484 P-5
OLMSTED CO., 144248 R-11
Onamia, 878 L-8
Onigum, 60 I-6
Opole, 90 M-7
Orleans, 10 C-2
Ormsby, 131 S-6
Orono, 7437 O-8
Oronoco, 1300 R-11
Orr, 267 F-10
Orrock, 50 N-8
Ortonville, 1916 N-2
Osage, 323 I-5
Osakis, 1740 M-5
Oslo, 330 E-1
Oslo S-10
Osseo, 2430 *C-2
Ostrander, 254 T-11
Otisco, 100 S-9
Otsego, 13571 O-9
Ottawa, 100 Q-8
OTTER TAIL CO., 57303 L-4
Ottertail, 572 K-4
Outing, 250 J-8
Owatonna, 25599 R-9
Oylen, 25 J-6
Padua, 25 M-5
Palisade, 167 J-9
Palmers I-12
Palo H-11
Park Rapids, 3709 I-5
Parkers Prairie, 1011 L-5
Paynesville, 2432 N-6
Pease, 242 M-8
Pelican Rapids, 2464 J-3
Pelland D-9
Pemberton, 247 R-8
Pengilly, 850 H-9
Pennington, 90 H-7
PENNINGTON CO., 13930 F-3
Pennock, 508 O-5
Pequot Lakes, 2162 J-7
Perham, 2985 J-4
Perley, 92 H-2
Petersburg, 35 T-6
Peterson, 199 S-13
Pierz, 1393 L-7
Pillager, 469 K-7
Pillsbury, 45 L-6
Pilot Grv., 25 T-7
Pine Ctr., 80 L-8
Pine City, 3123 M-10
PINE CO., 29750 L-10
Pine Island, 3263 R-11
Pine River, 944 J-7
Pine Sprs., 408 *E-10
Pinecreek C-4
Pinewood, 60 G-5
Pipestone, 4317 R-2
PIPESTONE CO., 9596 R-2
Pitt, 25 D-6
Plainview, 3340 R-12
Plato, 320 P-8
Pleasant Grv., 70 S-11
Plummer, 292 F-3
Plymouth, 70576 *E-1
Pt. Douglas, 65 P-10
POLK CO., 31600 G-3
Ponemah, 724 F-6
Ponsford, 200 I-5
POPE CO., 10995 N-4
Popple Creek M-8
Porter, 183 F-3
Potsdam, 30 R-11
Pratt, 40 R-10
Preston, 1325 S-12
Priam, 30 O-5
Princeton, 4698 N-9
Prinsburg, 497 P-5
Prior Lake, 22796 P-9
Proctor, 3057 J-11
Prosper, 50 T-12
Puposky, 35 G-6
Quamba, 123 M-9
Racine, 442 S-11
Radium, 30 E-2
Ramey, 50 M-8
Ramsey, 23668 O-9
RAMSEY CO., 508640 O-10
Randall, 650 L-7
Randolph, 436 Q-10
Ranier, 145 D-9
Rapidan, 150 R-8
Ray, 80 E-9
Raymond, 764 O-5
Reading, 150 S-4
Reads, 250 Q-12
Red Lake, 1731 F-6
RED LAKE CO., 4089 F-3
Red Lake Falls, 1427 F-3
Red Wing, 16459 Q-11
Redby, 1334 F-6
REDWOOD CO., 16059 Q-5
Redwood Falls, 5254 Q-5
Regal, 34 N-6
Remer, 370 I-8
Reno, 40 T-14
Renville, 1287 P-5
RENVILLE CO., 15730 P-6
Revere, 95 R-5
Rice, 1275 M-7
RICE CO., 64142 Q-9
Riceford, 20 T-13
Richfield, 35228 *H-4
Richmond, 1422 N-7
Richville, 96 K-4
Richwood, 100 I-4
Ridgeway, 40 S-13
Rindal, 25 H-3
Riverton, 117 K-8
Robbin, 30 D-1
Robbinsdale, 13953 *E-3
Rochert, 100 J-4
Rochester, 106769 R-11
ROCK CO., 9687 S-3
Rock Creek, 1628 M-10
Rock Dell, 40 S-11
Rockford, 4316 O-8
Rockville, 2448 N-7
Rogers, 8597 O-9
Rollag, 30 J-3
Rollingstone, 664 R-13
Ronneby, 67 M-8
Roosevelt, 151 C-5
Roscoe, 102 N-6
Rose City, 40 L-5
Rose Creek, 394 T-10
Roseau, 2633 C-4
ROSEAU CO., 15629 D-4
Roseland, 250 P-5
Rosemount, 21874 P-10
Rosen, 40 O-2
Rosendale O-6
Roseville, 33660 *E-7
Rosewood, 25 E-3
Ross, 20 C-4
Rothsay, 493 K-3
Round Lake, 376 T-4
Roy Lake, 12 H-4
Royalton, 1242 M-7
Rush City, 3079 M-10
Rush Pt., 60 M-10
Rushford, 1731 S-13
Rushford Vil., 807 S-13
Rushmore, 342 T-4
Russell, 338 Q-3
Rustad, 40 J-2
Ruthton, 241 R-3
Rutledge, 229 K-10
Sabin, 522 J-2
Sacred Heart, 548 P-5
Saginaw, 100 J-11
St. Anthony, 8226 *E-5
St. Anthony, 86 M-6
St. Augusta, 3317 N-7
St. Bonifacius, 2283 P-8
St. Charles, 3735 S-12
St. Clair, 868 R-8
St. Cloud, 65842 N-7
St. Francis, 7218 N-9
St. George, 60 Q-6
St. Hilaire, 279 F-3
St. James, 4605 S-6
St. Joseph, 6534 N-7
St. Leo, 100 P-3
ST. LOUIS CO., 200226 G-11
St. Louis Pk., 45250 *G-3
St. Martin, 308 N-6
St. Michael, 16399 O-8
St. Nicholas, 50 N-7
St. Paul, 285068 O-10
St. Paul Pk., 5279 *I-9
St. Peter, 11196 Q-8
St. Rosa, 68 M-6
St. Stephen, 851 M-7
St. Thomas, 40 Q-8
St. Vincent, 64 C-1
St. Wendel, 50 M-7
Salem Cors., 30 S-11
Salol, 80 C-4
Sanborn, 339 R-5
Sandstone, 2849 L-10
Santiago, 75 N-8
Sargeant, 61 S-10
Sartell, 15876 M-7
Sauk Centre, 4317 M-6
Sauk Rapids, 12773 N-7
Saum, 40 F-6
Savage, 26911 *J-3
Sawyer, 200 J-11
Scandia, 3936 O-10
Scanlon, 991 J-11
Schroeder, 350 G-14
SCOTT CO., 129928 Q-8
Seaforth, 86 Q-5
Searles, 171 R-7
Sebeka, 711 J-5
Sedan, 45 N-5
Shafer, 1045 N-10
Shakopee, 37076 P-9
Sheldon, 50 S-13
Shelly, 191 H-2
Sherack F-2
Sherburn, 1137 T-6
SHERBURNE CO., 88499 N-8
Sheshebee, 100 J-9
Shevlin, 176 G-5
Shieldsville Q-9
Shooks, 30 F-7
Shoreview, 25043 *D-7
Shorewood, 7307 P-9
SIBLEY CO., 15226 Q-7
Side Lake, 180 G-10
Silica, 50 H-10
Silver Bay, 1887 H-13
Silver Creek, 256 N-8
Silver Lake, 837 P-7
Silverdale F-10
Simpson, 90 S-11
Sioux Valley, 30 T-5
Slayton, 2153 R-4
Sleepy Eye, 3599 R-6
Smiths Mill, 50 R-8
Snellman, 20 I-5
Sobieski, 195 L-7
Sogn, 30 Q-10
Solway, 96 H-5
Soudan, 446 G-11
S. Haven, 187 N-7
S. St. Paul, 20160 *H-8
Spafford T-5
Spicer, 1167 O-6
Spring Grv., 1330 T-13
Spring Hill, 85 N-6
Spring Lake, 50 G-8
Spring Lake Pk., 6412 *C-5
Spring Valley, 2479 S-11
Springfield, 2152 R-5
Squaw Lake, 107 G-7
Stacy, 1456 N-10
Stanchfield, 118 M-9
Stanton, 50 Q-10
Staples, 2981 K-6
Starbuck, 1302 M-4
Stark, 75 N-10
STEARNS CO., 150642 N-6
STEELE CO., 36576 S-9
Steen, 180 T-3
Stephen, 658 E-2
STEVENS CO., 9726 M-3
Stewart, 571 P-7
Stewartville, 5916 S-11
Stillwater, 18225 O-10
Stockholm, 25 O-7
Stockton, 697 R-13
Storden, 219 R-5
Strandquist, 69 D-3
Strathcona, 44 D-3
Sturgeon, 30 G-10
Sturgeon Lake, 439 K-10
Sunburg, 100 N-5
Sunfish Lake, 521 *H-7
Svea, 100 O-5
Sveadahl R-6
Swan River, 50 I-9
Swanville, 350 M-6
Swatara, 50 I-8
Swift, 30 C-5
SWIFT CO., 9783 O-4
Swift Falls, 70 N-5
Syre I-3
Tabor, 40 F-2
Taconite, 360 H-9
Talmoon, 60 G-8
Tamarack, 94 J-10
Taopi, 58 T-11
Taunton, 139 Q-3
Taylors Falls, 976 N-11
Tenney, 5 L-2
Tenstrike, 201 G-6
Terrace, 40 N-5
Terrebonne, 25 F-3
Theilman, 70 R-12
Thief River Falls, 8573 F-3
Tintah, 63 L-3
TODD CO., 24895 L-6
Tofte, 250 C-11
Togo G-9
Toivola, 30 I-10
Tower, 500 G-11
Tracy, 2163 R-4
Trail, 46 G-4
TRAVERSE CO., 3558 M-2
Trimont, 747 S-6
Trommald, 98 K-8
Trosky, 86 S-3
Troy S-12
Truman, 1115 S-7
Turtle River, 77 G-6
Twig, 200 I-11
Twin Lakes, 151 T-9
Twin Valley, 821 H-3
Two Harbors, 3745 I-13
Tyler, 1143 R-3
Ulen, 547 I-3
Underwood, 341 K-4
Union Hill Q-8
Upsala, 427 M-6
Urbank, 54 L-4
Utica, 291 S-12
Vadnais Hts., 12302 *D-8
Vasa, 70 Q-10
Verdi, 70 R-2
Vergas, 331 J-4
Vermillion, 419 P-10
Verndale, 602 K-5
Vernon Ctr., 332 S-7
Vesta, 319 Q-4
Victoria, 7345 P-8
Viking, 104 E-3
Villard, 254 M-5
Vining, 78 K-4
Viola, 90 R-12
Virginia, 8712 G-11
Wabasha, 2521 Q-12
WABASHA CO., 21676 R-12
Wabasso, 696 Q-5
Waconia, 10697 P-8
Wacouta, 80 Q-11
Wadena, 4088 K-5
WADENA CO., 13843 J-5
Wahkon, 206 L-9
Waite Pk., 6715 N-7
Waldorf, 229 S-8
Walker, 941 I-6
Walnut Grv., 871 R-4
Walters, 73 T-8
Waltham, 151 S-10
Wanamingo, 1086 R-10
Wanda, 84 Q-5
Wannaska, 90 D-4
Warba, 181 I-9
Ward Sprs., 60 M-6
Warman, 30 L-9
Warren, 1563 E-2
Warroad, 1781 C-5
Warsaw, 627 R-9
Waseca, 9410 R-9
WASECA CO., 19136 S-8
WASHINGTON CO., 238136 O-10
Wasioja, 70 R-10
Waskish, 75 F-7
Waterford, 75 Q-10
Watertown, 4205 O-8
Waterville, 1868 R-9
Watkins, 962 N-7
WATONWAN CO., 11211 S-6
Watson, 205 O-4
Waubun, 400 I-4
Waverly, 1357 O-8
Wawina, 25 I-10
Wayzata, 3688 *F-1
Wealthwood, 30 K-8
Weaver, 50 R-12
Webster, 150 Q-9
Wegdahl, 100 P-4
Welch, 80 Q-10
Welcome, 686 T-6
Wells, 2343 S-8
Wendell, 167 L-3
W. Albion O-7
W. Concord, 782 R-10
W. St. Paul, 19540 *H-7
W. Union, 111 M-5
Westbrook, 739 R-4
Westbury I-4
Westport, 57 M-5
Whalan, 63 S-12
Wheaton, 1424 M-2
Wheeler's Pt., 220 C-6
Whipholt, 99 I-7
White Bear Bch., 500 *C-9
White Bear Lake, 23797 O-10
White Earth, 580 I-4
White Rock, 50 Q-10
Wilbert, 40 T-6
Wilder, 60 S-5
WILKIN CO., 6576 K-2
Willernie, 507 *D-10
Williams, 191 D-6
Willmar, 19610 O-5
Willow River, 415 K-10
Wilmont, 339 S-4
Wilno, 35 Q-3
Wilton, 204 H-6
Windom, 4646 S-5
Winger, 220 G-3
Winnebago, 1437 S-7
Winona, 27592 R-13
WINONA CO., 51461 R-12
Winsted, 2355 P-8
Winthrop, 1399 Q-7
Winton, 172 F-12
Wirock, 25 S-
Wirt, 30 G-
Witoka, 90 S-
Wolf Lake, 57
Wolverton, 142
Wood Lake, 439 P-
Woodbury, 61961 *H-
Woodland, 437 *C-
Woodland
Woodstock, 124 F-
Worthington, 12764 T-
Wrenshall, 399 J-
Wright, 127 J-
WRIGHT CO., 124700 O-
Wrightstown, 30 K-
Wykoff, 444 S-
Wyoming, 7791 N-
YELLOW MEDICINE CO., 10438 P-
Zemple, 93 H-
Zerkel H-
Zim, 100 H-
Zimmerman, 5228 N-
Zumbro Falls, 207 R-
Zumbrota, 3252 R-

Mississippi

Page locator

Map keys	Atlas pages
A–N	114–115

Abbeville, 419 C
Aberdeen, 5612 D
Ackerman, 1510 F
Acona, 50 F
ADAMS CO., 32297 J
Agricola, 200
Alcorn, 200
ALCORN CO., 37057 B
Algoma, 590 C
Alligator, 208 D
AMITE CO., 13131 K
Amory, 7316 D
Anding, 60 G
Anguilla, 726 F
Ansley, 270 M
Arcola, 361 F
Arkabutla, 380 B
Arm, 80 J
Arnold Line, 1719 E
Artesia, 440 E
Ashland, 569 B
Askew, 150 B
ATTALA CO., 19564 F
Auburn
Austin, 70 B
Avalon, 100 E
Avera, 60 K
Avon, 150 F
Bailey, 150 H
Baldwyn, 3297 B
Banner, 100 D
Barton, 60 A
Bassfield, 254 J
Batesville, 7463 C
Battles J
Baxterville, 320 K
Bay St. Louis, 9260 M
Bay Sprs., 1786
Beatty F
Beaumont, 951 K
Beauregard, 326 J
Beauvoir M
Becker, 260 D
Belen, 250 C
Bellefontaine, 250 E
Belmont, 2021 B-
Belzoni, 2235 F
Benoit, 477 E
Benton, 400 G
BENTON CO., 8729 B
Bentonia, 440 G
Benwood, 60 D
Berclair E
Bethany, 30 C
Bethlehem, 120 B
Beulah, 348 D
Bexley K
Big Creek, 154 D
Big Pt., 611 L
Bigbee Valley, 80 F-
Biggersville, 300 B
Biloxi, 44054 M
Black Hawk, 100 E
Blackwater, 80 G
Blaine, 50 E
Blair, 60 C
Blue Mtn., 920 B
Blue Sprs., 228 C
Bobo, 100 C
Bogue Chitto, 887 G
Bogue Chitto, 522 J
Boice I
BOLIVAR CO., 34145 D
Bolton, 567 H
Bond, 500 L
Bonita H
Booneville, 8743 B
Bourbon F
Bovina, 140 H
Boyle, 650 E
Bradley E
Brandon, 21705 H
Braxton, 183 I
Brazil D
Brookhaven, 12513 J
Brooklyn, 900 K
Brooksville, 1223 F
Brown Town, 50 K-
Brownfield, 250 A
Brownsville, 40 H
Bruce, 1939 D
Buckatunna, 516 J
Bude, 1063 J
Buena Vista, 70 D
Buena Vista B
Bunker Hill, 150 J
Burnsville, 936 B-
Byhalia, 1302 B
Byram, 11489 H
Caesar, 250 L
Caledonia, 1041 E-
Calhoun J
Calhoun City, 1774 D
CALHOUN CO., 14962 D
Camden, 700 G
Canaan, 40 A
Cannonsburg, 130 J
Canton, 13189 G
Carlisle, 90 I
Carnes, 150 K
Carpenter, 110 I
Carriere, 880 L
CARROLL CO., 10597 E
Carrollton, 190 E
Carson, 500 J

*, †, ‡, §, ◊ See explanation under state title in this index.
County and parish names are listed in capital letters & boldface type.
Independent cities (not included in a county) are listed in italics.

ter, 80 F-5
rterville F-3
rthage, 5075 G-7
y, 313 G-4
cilla, 100 D-6
yuga, 40 H-5
dar Bluff, 450 E-9
nter Ridge I-7
ntreville, 1684 K-4
alybeate, 320 A-8
arleston, 2193 D-6
atawa, 160 K-5
atham, 40 F-4
eraw K-6
ester, 220 E-8
ICKASAW CO., 7392 D-8
icora J-9
octaw, 250 E-4
OCTAW CO., 547 F-8
unky, 326 H-8
urch Hill, 40 J-3
AIBORNE CO., 604 I-4
ra, 410 J-9
ARKE CO., 6732 H-9
arksdale, 17962 C-5
AY CO., 20634 E-8
ary, 1150 H-6
m, 50 J-7
eveland, 12334 D-5
ftonville, 90 F-9
nton, 25216 H-5
overdale, 645 J-3
ahoma, 377 C-5
AHOMA CO., 151 D-5
ffeeville, 905 D-7
la, 50 E-6
dwater, 1677 B-6
es, 60 K-4
llins, 2586 J-7
llinsville, 1948 H-9
lumbia, 6582 K-6
lumbus, 23640 E-9
mmerce B-5
mo, 1279 C-6
nehatta, 1342 H-8
PIAH CO., 29449 I-5
rinth, 14573 A-9
tton Plant, 40 B-8
urtland, 511 C-6
VINGTON CO., 9568 J-7
wart D-6
kburg, 30 F-6
anfield, 140 J-4
awford, 641 F-9
enshaw, 885 C-6
osby, 318 K-4
ossroads L-7
owder, 712 C-6
uger, 386 E-6
upp, 80 G-5
ystal Sprs., 5044 I-5
evas, 170 M-8
rtis Sta., 140 C-6
nthia A-1
leville, 150 G-9
rbun K-6
rling, 226 C-6
rlove F-5
Kalb, 1164 G-9
Lisle, 1147 M-8
Soto, 200 I-9
SOTO CO., 61252 B-6
catur, 1841 H-8
emer, 90 G-8
eson, 30 D-4
lta City, 250 F-4
nham J-9
nmark, 70 C-7
nnis, 280 B-10
ntville, 100 I-5
rby, 50 L-7
rma, 1025 D-8
amondhead, 8425 M-8
berville, 9486 M-9
o, 452 I-6
ddsville, 98 E-5
loroso, 45 K-3
rsey, 100 C-9
w, 1927 D-5
bbs B-5
blin, 160 D-5
ck Hill, 732 E-7
ffee, 110 H-8
mas, 470 B-9
ncan, 423 D-5
ndee, 200 B-5
rant, 2673 F-6
gle Lake, 200 H-4
stabuchie, 210 J-8
stport, 300 B-10
enezer, 60 F-6
u, 895 C-8
diceton, 150 J-4
en, 103 F-5
inburg, 110 G-8
wards, 1034 H-5
ypt, 80 D-9
ctric Mills, 50 G-9
zabeth, 140 E-4
ott, 990 E-7
stown, 120 C-9
sville, 4448 J-8
sville Jct., 30 J-8
d, 140 D-6
on, 40 K-6
ondale, 50 G-9
terprise, 526 H-9
terprise, 200 C-8
zor, 150 H-9
catawpa, 3722 M-9
ill F-4
hel, 418 F-7
a C-8
cutta I-9
dora, 200 B-6
pora, 2197 E-8
ansville, 75 B-5
ergreen, 80 C-9
rfield, 90 C-9
rview, 200 C-10
con, 167 C-6
kner, 514 B-8
nnin H-6
rmington, 2186 A-9
rrell, 218 C-5
yette, 1614 J-4
ntress, 90 F-8
rnwood, 400 K-5
ler, 30 G-4
ra, 1886 G-5
rence, 4141 H-6
wood, 7823 C-3
rest, 5684 H-7
rest Hill D-1
kville, 150 H-7
FORREST CO., 74934 K-8
Ft. Adams, 80 K-3
Foxworth, 603 K-6
FRANKLIN CO., 8118 J-4
French Camp, 174 F-7
Friars Pt., 1200 C-5
Friendship, 200 C-8
Fruitland Pk. L-8
Fulton, 3961 C-9
Furrs, 150 C-9
Gallman, 400 I-5
Garden City J-4
Garlandville H-8
Gatesville, 80 I-6
Gattman, 90 D-10
Gautier, 18572 M-9
Geeville B-9
GEORGE CO., 22578 L-9
Georgetown, 286 I-6
Gholson F-9
Gibson, 100 D-9
Gillsburg K-5
Gitano I-8
Glade, 140 J-8
Glen Allan, 500 F-4
Glendale, 1657 J-8
Glendora, 151 D-6
Glens, 412 B-9
Gloster, 960 K-4
Glover, 50 A-6
Gluckstadt, 210 H-6
Golden, 191 C-10
Good Hope, 110 G-7
Goodman, 1386 F-6
Gore Sprs., 110 D-7
Goss, 100 J-6
Grace, 270 F-4
Grand Gulf, 60 I-4
Gravestown, 200 B-8
GREENE CO., 14400 K-9
Greenville, 34400 E-4
Greenwood, 15205 E-6
Greenwood Sprs., 260 D-10
Grenada, 13092 D-7
GRENADA CO., 21906 D-7
Gulf Hills, 7144 M-5
Gulfport, 67793 M-8
Gunnison, 452 D-4
Guntown, 2083 C-9
Hamburg, 120 J-4
Hamilton, 457 D-9
HANCOCK CO., 43929 M-7
Handsboro M-2
Hardy, 80 D-6
Harmontown, 200 B-7
Harperville, 170 H-7
HARRISON CO., 187105 L-8
Harriston, 340 I-4
Harrisville, 380 I-6
Hatley, 482 D-9
Hattiesburg, 45989 K-8
Hazlehurst, 4009 I-5
Heads E-4
Hebron, 80 J-6
Hebron, 50 J-7
Heidelberg, 718 I-8
Helena, 1184 M-9
Hermanville, 400 I-4
Hernando, 14090 B-6
Hickory, 530 H-8
Hickory Flat, 601 B-8
Highpoint F-8
Hightown, 150 B-9
Hillman, 40 K-9
Hillsboro, 1130 H-7
HINDS CO., 245285 I-5
Hinkle, 160 B-9
Hintonville, 340 K-8
Hiwannee I-9
Hohenlinden D-8
Holcomb, 600 D-6
Hollandale, 2702 F-4
Holly Bluff, 300 G-5
Holly Ridge, 100 E-5
Holly Sprs., 7699 B-7
Hollywood, 80 B-5
HOLMES CO., 19198 F-6
Homewood, 75 H-7
Homochitto K-4
Hopewell, 30 I-6
Horn Lake, 26066 A-6
Hot Coffee I-7
Houlka, 626 D-8
House, 100 G-8
Houston, 3623 D-8
Howard, 30 F-6
Hub K-7
HUMPHREYS CO., 9375 F-5
Hurley, 1551 L-9
Hurricane, 200 C-8
Hushpuckena, 60 D-5
Improve J-7
Independence, 350 B-7
Indianola, 10683 E-5
Ingomar, 250 C-8
Ingrams Mill, 50 B-7
Inverness, 1019 E-5
Isola, 713 F-5
ISSAQUENA CO., 1406 G-4
ITAWAMBA CO., 23401 C-9
Itta Bena, 2049 E-5
Iuka, 3028 B-10
Jacinto, 220 B-9
Jackson, 173514 H-6
JACKSON CO., 139668 L-9
James F-4
JASPER CO., 17062 I-8
Jayess, 110 J-6
JEFFERSON CO., 7726 I-4
JEFFERSON DAVIS CO., 12487 J-6
Johns H-6
Johnson, 30 J-8
JONES CO., 67761 J-8
Jonestown, 1298 C-5
Jumpertown, 480 B-9
KEMPER CO., 10456 G-9
Kendrick, 270 A-9
Kewanee, 60 H-9
Kilmichael, 699 E-7
Kiln, 2238 M-7
Kingston, 390 J-3
Kirby J-4
Knoxville, 100 J-4
Kokomo, 210 K-6
Kosciusko, 7402 F-7
Kossuth, 209 B-9
LAFAYETTE CO., 47351 C-7
Lake, 324 H-8
L. Cormorant, 270 B-6
Lake of Hills, 200 B-6
L. View, 200 A-6
Lakeshore, 1200 M-7
Lamar, 150 A-8
LAMAR CO., 55658 K-7
Lamar Pk. F-1
Lambert, 1638 C-6
Lamont, 70 E-4
Lampton, 130 K-7
Landon M-1
Latimer, 6079 M-9
Lauderdale, 442 G-9
LAUDERDALE CO., 80261 H-9
Laurel, 18540 J-8
Lawrence, 200 H-8
LAWRENCE CO., 12929 J-6
Laws Hill, 170 B-7
Le Tourneau, 200 H-4
Leaf, 120 K-9
LEAKE CO., 23805 G-7
Leakesville, 898 K-9
Learned, 94 H-5
LEE CO., 82910 C-9
Leedy, 100 B-10
Leesburg H-7
Leflore, 50 E-6
LEFLORE CO., 32317 E-6
Leland, 4481 E-4
Lena, 148 G-7
Lewisburg, 120 B-6
Lexington, 1731 F-6
Liberty, 728 K-4
LINCOLN CO., 34869 J-5
Little Rock, 230 G-8
Little Yazoo, 110 G-5
Litton E-4
Lodi, 50 E-7
Long Bch., 14792 M-8
Long Lake, 100 H-4
Longtown, 250 C-6
Longview, 390 E-8
Looxahoma, 110 B-7
Lorman, 560 I-4
Louin, 277 I-8
Louise, 199 F-5
Louisville, 6631 F-8
LOWNDES CO., 59779 E-9
Loyd Star, 30 J-5
Lucas, 30 J-6
Lucedale, 2923 L-9
Lucien, 50 J-5
Ludlow, 240 G-7
Lula, 298 C-5
Lumberton, 2086 K-7
Lyman, 1277 M-8
Lynchburg, 2437 A-6
Lyon, 350 C-5
Maben, 871 E-8
Macon, 2768 F-9
Madden, 320 G-8
Madison, 24149 H-6
MADISON CO., 95203 G-6
Magee, 4408 I-7
Magnolia, 2420 K-5
Mahned, 150 K-8
Malvina, 30 D-4
Mantachie, 1144 C-9
Mantee, 232 D-8
Marietta, 256 C-9
Marion, 1479 H-9
MARION CO., 27088 K-7
Marks, 1735 C-6
MARSHALL CO., 37144 B-7
Martin, 110 G-9
Martinsville I-5
Mashulaville, 60 F-9
Matherville, 50 I-9
Mathiston, 698 E-8
Mattson, 150 D-5
Maybank, 30 J-7
Mayersville, 547 G-4
Mayhew, 110 E-9
McAdams, 250 F-7
McCall Creek, 140 J-5
McCarley, 150 E-6
McComb, 12790 K-5
McCondy, 120 D-9
McCool, 135 F-8
McDonald, 50 G-8
McHenry, 160 L-8
McLain, 441 K-9
McLaurin, 530 K-8
McLeod F-9
McNeill, 1050 L-7
Meadville, 449 J-4
Mendenhall, 2504 I-6
Meridian, 41148 H-9
Merigold, 439 D-5
Merrill, 100 K-9
Mesa K-6
Metcalfe, 1067 E-4
Michigan City, 250 A-8
Midnight, 230 F-5
Mill Creek J-8
Miller, 80 A-7
Minter City, 200 D-6
Mississippi City N-2
Mize, 340 I-7
Money, 120 E-6
MONROE CO., 36989 E-9
MONTGOMERY CO., 10925 E-7
Monticello, 1571 J-6
Montpelier, 160 D-8
Montrose, 140 I-8
Mooreville, 650 C-9
Moorhead, 2405 E-5
Morgan City, 255 E-5
Morgantown, 1412 J-3
Morgantown, 300 K-6
Morton, 3462 H-7
Moscow, 110 G-9
Moselle, 700 J-8
Moss, 250 I-8
Moss Pt., 13704 M-9
Mound Bayou, 1533 D-5
Mt. Olive, 982 I-7
Mt. Pleasant, 400 A-7
Murphy F-5
Myrick, 110 J-8
Myrtle, 490 B-8
Natchez, 15792 J-3
Necaise L-7
Neely, 200 K-9
Nellieburg, 1414 H-9
Neshoba, 150 G-8
NESHOBA CO., 29676 G-8
Nettleton, 1992 D-9
New Albany, 8034 C-8
New Augusta, 644 K-8
New Byram, 500 H-6
New Harmony, 100 C-8
New Hebron, 447 J-6
New Hope, 3193 E-10
New Site, 250 B-9
New Town B-6
New Wren, 210 D-9
Newton, 3373 H-8
NEWTON CO., 21720 H-8
Nicholson, 3092 M-7
Nitta Yuma, 80 F-4
Nola, 130 J-6
N. Carrollton, 473 E-6
N. Crossroads, 50 A-10
N. Gulfport M-1
N. Tunica, 1035 B-5
Noxapater, 472 F-8
NOXUBEE CO., 11545 F-9
Oak Grv., 640 K-7
Oak Vale, 160 J-6
Oakland, 527 D-6
Oakley, 250 H-5
Obadiah, 170 H-9
Ocean Sprs., 17442 M-9
Ofahoma, 220 G-7
Oil City, 75 G-5
Okolona, 2692 D-9
OKTIBBEHA CO., 47671 E-9
Old Hamilton, 60 D-9
Old Houlka, 30 D-8
Oldham, 60 B-10
Olive Branch, 33484 A-7
Oloh, 100 K-7
Oma, 30 J-6
Orange Grv., 570 M-10
Orange Grv. L-1
Osborn, 80 E-9
Osyka, 440 K-5
Ovett, 630 J-8
Oxford, 18916 C-7
Ozona L-7
Pace, 274 D-4
Pachuta, 261 I-9
Paden, 116 B-10
Palmers Crossing F-2
Palmetto, 50 C-9
PANOLA CO., 34707 C-6
Panther Burn, 90 F-4
Parham, 290 D-10
Paris, 160 C-7
Pascagoula, 22392 M-9
Pass Christian, 4613 M-8
Pattison, 330 I-4
Paulding, 150 I-8
Paulette, 30 F-9
Paynes D-6
Pearl, 25092 H-6
Pearl River, 3601 G-8
PEARL RIVER CO., 55834 L-7
Pearlington, 1332 M-7
Pearson D-3
Pecan, 80 M-10
Pelahatchie, 1334 H-7
Peoples B-9
Percy F-4
Perkinston, 100 L-8
PERRY CO., 12250 K-8
Perthshire, 50 D-4
Petal, 10454 J-8
Pheba, 700 E-8
Philadelphia, 7477 G-8
Philipp, 350 D-6
Picayune, 10878 M-7
Pickens, 1157 G-6
PIKE CO., 40404 K-5
Pine Ridge J-3
Pinebur, 70 K-7
Piney Woods, 100 I-6
Pinola, 130 I-6
Pittsboro, 202 D-8
Plantersville, 1155 C-9
Plattsburg F-8
Pleasant Grv., 110 C-6
Pleasant Hill, 100 B-6
Pocahontas, 100 H-6
Polkville, 833 H-7
Pontotoc, 5625 C-8
PONTOTOC CO., 29957 D-8
Pope, 215 C-6
Poplar Creek, 70 E-7
Poplarville, 2894 L-7
Port Gibson, 1567 I-4
Porterville, 100 G-9
Post, 30 G-8
Potts Camp, 523 B-8
Prairie, 210 D-9
Prairie Pt., 50 F-10
Prentiss, 1081 J-6
PRENTISS CO., 25276 B-9
Preston, 100 G-9
Pricedale, 100 K-5
Prichard, 30 B-6
Progress, 210 K-5
Puckett, 316 I-7
Pulaski, 140 H-7
Purvis, 2175 K-7
Pyland, 130 D-8
Quentin, 50 J-5
Quincy, 160 D-10
Quitman, 2323 I-9
QUITMAN CO., 8223 C-5
Quito, 60 E-6
Raleigh, 1462 I-7
Randolph, 400 C-8
RANKIN CO., 141617 H-6
Ratliff, 120 C-9
Rawls Sprs., 1254 J-7
Raymond, 1933 H-5
Raytown, 140 G-7
Red Banks, 580 B-7
Red Lick, 150 I-4
Redwater, 633 G-7
Redwood, 200 H-4
Reform, 110 E-8
Refuge F-4
Rena Lara, 270 C-5
Renova, 668 D-5
Rich, 100 C-5
Richland, 6912 H-6
Richland, 30 F-6
Richton, 1068 J-8
Ridgeland, 24047 H-6
Rienzi, 317 B-9
Ripley, 5395 B-8
Robinsonville, 260 B-5
Rodney, 90 I-4
Rolling Fork, 2143 G-4
Rome, 180 D-5
Rose Hill, 250 H-8
Rosedale, 1873 D-4
Rosetta, 40 K-4
Roundlake, 100 D-4
Roxie, 497 J-4
Ruleville, 3007 D-5
Runnelstown J-8
Russell, 110 H-9
Russum, 90 I-4
Ruth, 230 J-5
Sallis, 134 F-7
Saltillo, 4752 C-9
Sanatorium, 500 I-7
Sand Hill, 250 H-6
Sand Hill, 150 J-9
Sandersville, 731 I-8
Sandy Hook, 210 K-7
Sanford, 150 J-7
Sarah, 230 B-6
Sardis, 1703 C-6
Sarepta, 50 C-8
Satartia, 55 G-5
Saucier, 1342 L-8
Savage, 160 B-6
Schlater, 310 E-5
Scobey, 90 D-6
Scooba, 732 G-9
Scott, 300 E-4
SCOTT CO., 28264 H-7
Sebastopol, 272 G-8
Seminary, 314 J-7
Senatobia, 8165 B-6
Sessums, 170 E-9
Shady Grv., 420 I-8
Shady Grv., 30 I-5
Shannon, 1753 C-9
SHARKEY CO., 4916 G-4
Sharon, 1406 I-8
Sharon, 420 G-6
Shaw, 1952 E-5
Shelby, 2229 D-5
Sherard, 150 C-5
Sherman, 650 C-9
Sherwood, 30 E-8
Shivers I-6
Shubuta, 441 I-9
Shuqualak, 501 F-9
Sibley, 290 J-3
Sidon, 509 E-6
Silver City, 337 F-5
Silver Creek, 210 J-6
SIMPSON CO., 27503 I-6
Singleton G-7
Skene, 200 E-4
Slate Spr., 110 D-7
Slayden, 120 A-7
Sledge, 545 C-6
SMITH CO., 16491 I-7
Smithdale, 100 J-5
Smithville, 942 D-10
Snow Lake Shores, 319 B-8
Sontag, 220 J-6
Soso, 408 I-8
Southaven, 48982 A-6
Splunge, 210 D-10
Springdale C-7
Springville, 80 C-8
St. Martin, 7730 M-5
Stallo G-8
Star, 550 I-6
Starkville, 23888 E-9
State Line, 565 J-9
Steens, 210 E-10
Stewart, 280 E-7
STONE CO., 17786 L-8
Stoneville, 250 E-4
Stonewall, 1088 H-9
Stovall, 30 C-5
Stratton, 1250 H-8
Strayhorn, 250 B-6
Stringer, 430 I-8
Stringtown E-4
Sturgis, 254 E-8
Summit, 1705 K-5
Sumner, 316 D-5
Sumrall, 1421 J-7
Sunflower, 1159 E-5
SUNFLOWER CO., 29450 E-5
Sunnyside E-5
Swan Lake, 80 D-6
Sweatman E-7
Swiftown, 110 F-5
Sylvarena, 112 I-7
Symonds, 100 D-4
TALLAHATCHIE CO., 15378 D-6
Tallula, 60 G-4
Talowah, 150 K-7
TATE CO., 28886 B-6
Taylor, 322 C-7
Taylorsville, 1353 I-7
Tchula, 2096 F-6
Ten Mile L-8
Terry, 1063 I-6
Thaxton, 643 C-8
Thomastown, 200 G-7
Thompson, 30 K-5
Thorn, 50 D-8
Thornton, 200 F-5
Thrashers, 250 B-9
Threadville, 30 I-9
Three Rivers, 200 L-9
Tillatoba, 91 D-6
Tinsley, 260 G-5
Tiplersville, 120 B-8
TIPPAH CO., 22232 B-8
Tippo, 120 D-6
Tishomingo, 339 B-10
TISHOMINGO CO., 19593 B-10
Toccopola, 246 C-8
Tomnolen, 120 E-7
Toomsuba, 773 H-9
Topeka, 60 J-6
Tralake, 50 F-4
Trebloc, 100 D-9
Tremont, 465 C-10
Tribbett, 35 E-4
Troy, 180 C-8
Tucker, 662 G-8
Tula, 120 C-7
Tunica, 1030 B-5
TUNICA CO., 10778 C-5
Tupelo, 34546 C-9
Tuscola, 60 G-7
Tutwiler, 3550 D-5
Twin, 80 K-7
Tylertown, 1609 K-6
Tyro, 100 B-7
Union, 1988 G-8
Union Church, 200 J-4
UNION CO., 27134 C-8
Utica, 820 I-5
Vaiden, 734 E-7
Valley, 30 G-5
Valley Pk., 230 G-4
Van Vleet, 200 D-8
Vance, 250 D-5
Vancleave, 5886 L-9
Vardaman, 1316 D-8
Vaughan, 260 G-6
Verona, 3006 C-9
Vicksburg, 23856 H-4
Victoria, 570 B-7
Vossburg, 250 I-8
Wade, 1074 L-9
Walls, 1162 A-6
Walnut, 771 A-8
Walnut Grv., 1911 G-7
Walthall, 144 E-8
WALTHALL CO., 15443 K-6
Wanilla, 80 J-6
WARREN CO., 48773 H-5
Warsaw, 60 B-7
Washington, 750 J-3
WASHINGTON CO., 51137 F-4
Water Valley, 3392 C-7
Waterford, 350 B-7
Watson, 120 B-7
Waveland, 6435 M-7
Way G-6
WAYNE CO., 20747 J-9
Waynesboro, 5043 J-9
Wayside, 300 F-4
Webb, 565 D-5
WEBSTER CO., 10253 E-7
Weir, 459 F-8
Wenasoga, 220 A-9
Wesson, 1925 J-5
West, 185 F-7
West Point, 11307 E-9
Wheeler, 600 B-9
Whistler, 150 J-9
White Apple J-4
White Oak, 100 I-7
Whites, 120 E-9
Whitfield, 120 J-8
Whitney D-5
Whynot, 50 H-9
Wiggins, 4390 L-8
Wilkinson K-3
WILKINSON CO., 9878 K-3
Williamsburg, 135 J-7
Williamsville, 320 F-7
Winborn, 60 B-8
Winchester, 100 J-9
Winona, 5043 E-7
WINSTON CO., 19198 F-8
Winstonville, 191 D-5
Woodland, 125 D-8
Woodville, 1096 K-3
Wool Market L-3
Wyatte B-7
YALOBUSHA CO., 12678 D-7
Yazoo City, 11403 G-5
YAZOO CO., 28065 G-5
Zama, 100 F-7
Zion C-8

Missouri

Page locator

Map keys	Atlas pages
1–10	116–117
11–20	118–119

* City keyed to pp. 120–121

Abesville, 100 L-11
Acorn Ridge, 30 K-18
Adair B-13
ADAIR CO., 25607 B-13
Adrian, 1677 G-9
Advance, 1347 K-19
Affton, 20307 *J-5
Agency, 684 D-8
Airport Drive, 698 *A-6
Alba, 555 J-9
Albany, 1730 B-9
Aldrich, 80 J-11
Alexandria, 159 B-15
Allendale, 53 B-9
Allenton *J-1
Alma, 402 F-11
Almartha L-13
Altamont, 204 C-10
Altenburg, 352 I-19
Alton, 871 L-16
Amazonia, 312 C-8
Americus, 60 F-15
Amity, 54 C-9
Amoret, 190 H-9
Amsterdam, 242 G-9
Anabel, 30 D-13
Anderson, 1961 L-9
ANDREW CO., 17291 C-8
Annada, 29 E-17
Annapolis, 345 J-17
Anniston, 232 L-20
Anutt, 60 I-15
Appleton City, 1127 H-10
Aquilla K-19
Arab, 130 K-18
Arbela, 41 B-14
Arbyrd, 509 N-18
Arcadia, 608 J-17
Archie, 1170 G-9
Arcola, 55 J-10
Argyle, 162 H-14
Arkoe, 68 B-8
Armstrong, 284 E-13
Arnold, 20808 G-18
Arrow Rock, 56 F-12
Asbury, 207 J-9
Ash Grv., 1472 J-11
Ash Hill, 30 L-18
Ashburn, 52 D-16
Asherville, 40 K-18
Ashland, 3707 F-14
Ashley, 90 E-16
Ashton, 40 B-15
ATCHISON CO., 5685 B-7
Atherton, 200 G-7
Atlanta, 385 C-13
Auburn E-16
AUDRAIN CO., 25529 E-14
Augusta, 253 G-17
Aullville, 100 F-11
Aurora, 7508 K-10
Auxvasse, 983 F-14
Ava, 2993 K-13
Avalon, 70 D-11
Avenue City, 90 C-8
Avilla, 125 K-10
Avondale, 440 H-4
Bahner G-12
Bakersfield, 246 L-14
Ballard, 80 G-10
Ballwin, 30404 G-17
Baring, 132 B-14
Barnard, 221 C-8
Barnett, 203 G-13
Barnhart, 5682 G-18
BARRY CO., 35597 L-10
BARTON CO., 12402 J-9
BATES CO., 17049 H-9
Battlefield, 5590 K-11
Beaman F-12
Bean Lake Sta., 100 D-8
Bearcreek I-11
Beaufort, 260 G-16
Bedford, 40 D-11
Belgique I-19
Belgrade, 250 I-17
Bell City, 448 K-19
Bella Villa, 729 *J-6
Belle, 1545 H-15
Bellefontaine Neighbors, 10860 *F-6
Belleview, 200 I-17
Bellflower, 393 F-16
Bel-Nor, 1499 *G-5
Bel-Ridge, 2737 *G-5
Belton, 23116 F-9
Bem H-15
Benbush, 2000 *G-3
Benton, 863 K-19
Benton City, 104 E-15
BENTON CO., 19056 H-12
Berkeley, 8978 *F-5
Bernie, 1958 L-19
Berryman I-16
Bertrand, 821 K-20
Bethany, 3292 B-10
Bethel, 122 C-14
Beverly Hills, 574 *G-6
Bevier, 718 D-13
Bible Grv., 40 B-14
Biehle, 48 I-19
Big Lake, 159 C-7
Big Piney I-14
Big Spr., 167 F-15
Bigelow, 27 C-7
Billings, 1035 K-11
Birch Tree, 679 K-15
Birmingham, 183 H-5
Bismarck, 1546 I-17
Bixby, 100 I-16
Black, 210 J-16
Black Jack, 6929 *F-6
Black Walnut *E-5
Blackburn, 249 E-11
Blackwater, 162 F-12
Blackwell, 80 H-17
Blairstown, 97 G-10
Bland, 539 H-15
Blodgett, 213 K-20
Bloomfield, 1933 K-19
Bloomsdale, 521 H-18
Blue Eye, 167 M-11
Blue Ridge, 30 C-10
Blue Sprs., 52575 F-9
Blue Summit, 1200 I-5
Blythedale, 193 B-10
Bogard, 164 E-11
Bois D'Arc, 500 J-11
Bolckow, 187 C-8
Bolivar, 10325 J-11
BOLLINGER CO., 12363 K-18
Bona, 30 J-11
Bonne Terre, 6864 I-17
BOONE CO., 162642 E-13
Boonesboro, 60 F-12
Boonville, 8319 F-13
Boss, 100 I-16
Bosworth, 305 D-11
Bourbon, 1632 H-16
Bowen G-11
Bowling Green, 5334 E-16
Boynton B-12
Bradleyville, 100 L-12
Bragg City, 149 M-19
Braggadocio, 200 M-19
Branch, 200 I-12
Brandsville, 161 L-15
Branson, 10520 L-12
Brashear, 273 C-13
Braymer, 878 D-10
Brazeau, 90 I-19
Brazito, 80 G-14
Breckenridge, 383 D-10
Breckenridge Hills, 4746 *G-5
Brentwood, 8055 *I-5
Brewer, 374 I-19
Briar L-16
Bridgeton, 11550 *F-4
Brighton, 220 J-11
Brimson, 63 C-11
Brinktown, 100 H-14
Bronaugh, 249 I-9
Brookfield, 4542 D-12
Brookline, 326 K-11
Brooklyn B-10
Broseley, 200 L-18
Browning, 265 C-12
Brownington, 107 H-11
Browns, 100 F-14
Brumley, 91 H-13
Bruner, 100 K-12
Brunswick, 858 E-12
BUCHANAN CO., 89201 D-8
Bucklin, 467 D-12
Buckner, 3076 E-10
Bucyrus, 50 J-14
Buell, 70 F-15
Buffalo, 3084 I-12
Bunceton, 354 F-12
Bunker, 407 J-16
Burfordville, 80 J-19
Burlington Jct., 537 B-8
Butler, 4219 H-9
BUTLER CO., 42794 L-18
Butterfield, 470 L-10
Bynumville, 50 D-13
Cabool, 2146 K-14
Cadet, 150 H-17
Cainsville, 290 B-10
Cairo, 292 D-13
CALDWELL CO., 9424 D-10
Caledonia, 130 I-17
Calhoun, 469 G-11
California, 4278 G-13
Callao, 292 D-13
CALLAWAY CO., 44332 F-14
Calverton Pk., 1293 *F-5
Calwood, 100 F-14
Camden, 191 E-10
CAMDEN CO., 44002 I-13
Camden Pt., 474 D-8
Camdenton, 3718 H-13
Cameron, 9933 D-9
Campbell, 1992 L-18
Canaan, 110 H-15
Canalou, 338 L-19
Canton, 2377 C-15
Cape Fair, 600 L-11
Cape Girardeau, 37941 J-20
CAPE GIRARDEAU CO., 75674 J-19
Caplinger Mills I-10
Capps H-14
Cardwell, 713 N-18
Carl Jct., 7445 K-9
CARROLL CO., 9295 E-11
Carrollton, 3784 E-11
Carsonville, 2000 *G-5
CARTER CO., 6265 K-16
Carterville, 1891 *A-7
Carthage, 14378 K-9
Caruth, 100 M-18
Caruthersville, 6168 M-19
Carytown, 271 J-9
Cascade J-18
CASS CO., 99478 G-9
Cassville, 3266 L-10
Castlewood, 400 *I-3
Catron, 67 L-19
Caulfield, 110 L-14
CEDAR CO., 13982 I-10
Cedar Hill, 1721 G-17
Cedar Sprs., 85 I-10
Cedarcreek, 100 L-12
Center, 508 D-15
Centertown, 278 G-13
Centerview, 267 F-10
Centerville, 191 J-16
Centralia, 4027 E-14
Chadwick, 190 K-12
Chaffee, 2955 K-19
Chamois, 396 G-15
Champ, 13 *G-4
Chandler E-6
CHARITON CO., 7831 E-12
Charity, 120 J-12
Charlack, 1363 *G-5
Charleston, 5947 K-20
Cherryville, 135 I-16
Chesapeake, 49 K-11
Chesterfield, 47484 G-17
Chicopee, 60 K-16
Chilhowee, 325 G-10
Chillicothe, 9515 D-11
Chitwood *B-5
CHRISTIAN CO., 77422 K-12
Chula, 210 C-11
Clarence, 813 D-14
Clark, 298 E-13
CLARK CO., 7139 B-14
Clarksburg, 334 G-13
Clarksdale, 271 D-9
Clarkson Valley, 2632 *I-2
Clarksville, 442 E-16
Clarkton, 1288 M-19
CLAY CO., 221939 E-9
Claycomo, 1430 G-5
Clayton, 15939 *H-5
Clearmont, 170 B-8
Cleveland, 661 G-9
Clever, 2139 K-11
Clifton City F-12
Clifton Hill, 114 E-13
Climax Sprs., 124 H-12
Clinton, 9008 G-10
CLINTON CO., 20743 D-9
Clyde, 82 B-9
Coal H-11
Coatsville A-13
Cobalt Vil., 226 J-18
Coffey, 166 C-10
Coffman, 80 I-18
Coldwater J-18
Cole Camp, 1121 G-12
COLE CO., 75990 G-13
College Mound, 50 D-13
Collins, 159 I-11
Coloma, 30 D-11
Colony, 30 B-14
Columbia, 108500 F-13
Commerce, 67 K-20
Competition J-13
Conception Jct., 198 B-9
Concord, 16421 *J-5
Concordia, 2450 F-11
Connelsville, 120 B-13
Conway, 788 J-12
Cook Sta. I-15
Cool Valley, 1196 *G-5
COOPER CO., 17601 F-13
Cooter, 469 N-19
Corder, 404 E-11
Cornelia G-11
Corning, 15 B-7
Corridon, 50 J-16
Cosby, 124 C-9
Cottleville, 3075 *G-1
Couch, 80 L-16
Country Club Hills, 1274 *G-6
Country Club Vil., 2449 C-8
Country Life Acres, 74 *H-4
Cowgill, 188 D-10
Craig, 248 B-7
Crane, 1462 K-11
CRAWFORD CO., 24696 I-16
Creighton, 349 G-10
Crescent, 200 *J-2
Crestwood, 11912 *I-5
Creve Coeur, 17833 *H-4
Crocker, 1110 I-14
Cross Timbers, 216 H-12
Crystal City, 4855 H-18
Crystal Lake Pk., 470 *H-4
Cuba, 3356 H-15
Current View, 85 M-17
Curryville, 225 E-16
Cyrene, 90 E-16
DADE CO., 7883 J-10
Dadeville, 234 J-11
Daisy J-19
DALLAS CO., 16777 J-12
Dalton, 17 E-12
Danby, 60 H-18
Danville, 34 F-15
Darksville D-13
Darlington, 121 B-9
Daugherty, 130 G-9
DAVIESS CO., 8433 C-10
Davis, 100 F-16
Dawn, 128 D-11
Dawson, 40 J-14
Dayton, 120 G-10
De Kalb, 220 D-8
DE KALB CO., 12892 C-9
De Soto, 6400 H-17
De Witt, 124 E-12
Dearborn, 496 D-8
Decaturville I-13
Dederick, 30 I-10
Deepwater, 433 H-10
Deerfield, 81 I-9
Deering, 100 M-19
Defiance, 155 G-17
Dellwood, 5025 *F-6
Delta, 438 K-19
Dennis Acres, 76 *C-6
DENT CO., 15657 J-15
Denton, 120 N-19
Denver, 39 B-9
Des Arc, 177 J-17
Des Peres, 8373 *I-4
Desloge, 5054 I-17
Devils Elbow, 200 I-14
Dexter, 7864 L-19
Diamond, 902 K-9
Diehlstadt, 161 K-20
Diggins, 299 K-12
Dillard I-16
Dittmer, 600 H-17
Dixon, 1549 I-14
Doe Run, 915 I-17
Dogwood K-12
Dongola, 80 K-19
Doniphan, 1997 L-17
Doolittle, 630 I-14
Dora, 80 L-14
DOUGLAS CO., 13684 K-13
Dover, 103 E-11
Downing, 335 B-13
Drake G-15
Dresden, 300 F-11
Drexel, 965 G-9
Dudley, 232 L-18
Duenweg, 1121 K-9
Duncans Br., 30 D-14
DUNKLIN CO., 31953 M-18
Dunlap, 50 C-11
Dunnegan, 200 I-11
Duquesne, 1763 *C-7
Durham, 190 C-15
Dutchtown, 94 J-19
Dutzow, 250 G-16
Eagle Rock, 199 L-10
Eagleville, 316 B-10
Easley F-13
E. Lynne, 303 G-9
E. Prairie, 3176 L-20
Easton, 234 D-9
Eastwood, 40 K-16
Edgar Sprs., 208 I-14
Edgehill J-16
Edgerton, 546 D-9
Edina, 1176 C-14
Edinburg, 92 C-11
Edmundson, 834 *G-5
Edwards, 40 H-12
Egypt Mills, 120 J-20
El Dorado Sprs., 3593 I-10
Eldon, 4567 H-13
Eldridge I-13
Elk Creek, 85 K-14
Elkland, 200 J-12
Elkton I-11
Ellington, 987 K-16
Ellisville, 9133 *I-2
Ellsinore, 446 K-17
Elmer, 80 C-13
Elmira, 50 D-10
Elmo, 168 B-8
Elsberry, 1934 E-17
Elsey, 200 L-11
Elwood, 150 *B-1
Emden, 40 D-14
Emerson, 70 C-15
Eminence, 600 K-16
Emma, 233 F-11
Enon, 80 G-13
Eolia, 522 E-16
Essex, 472 L-19
Ethel, 62 C-13
Etterville, 150 G-13
Eudora, 200 J-11
Eugene, 150 H-13
Eunice, 40 K-15
Eureka, 10189 G-17
Evening Shade, 350 J-14
Evergreen, 28 J-13
Everton, 319 J-11
Ewing, 456 C-15
Excello, 49 D-13
Excelsior Sprs., 11084 E-9
Exeter, 772 L-10
Fagus, 100 L-18
Fair Grv., 1393 J-12
Fair Play, 475 I-11
Fairdealing, 676 L-17
Fairfax, 638 B-7
Fairmont, 30 B-14
Fairport, 90 C-9
Fairview, 383 L-10
Fairview, 30 J-14
Farber, 322 E-15
Farley, 269 E-8
Farmer E-16
Farmersville, 30 C-11
Farmington, 16240 I-18
Farrar, 60 I-19
Faucett, 350 D-8
Fayette, 2688 E-13
Fayetteville, 100 F-10
Fenton, 4022 *J-4
Ferguson, 21203 *G-5
Ferrelview, 451 E-2
Fertile, 90 H-17
Festus, 11602 H-18
Fidelity, 257 K-9
Filley, 80 I-10
Fillmore, 184 C-8
Fisk, 342 L-18
Flag Spr., 120 H-15
Flat, 80 I-14
Flemington, 148 I-11
Fletcher, 320 H-17
Flint Hill, 525 F-17
Flordell Hills, 822 *G-6
Florence, 140 G-12
Florissant, 52158 F-18
Foley, 161 F-17
Foose, 110 J-12
Forbes, 70 C-8
Fordland, 800 K-12
Forest City, 268 C-8
Forest Green, 40 E-12
Foristell, 505 F-16
Forsyth, 2255 L-12
Fortescue, 32 C-7
Fortuna, 165 G-12
Foster, 117 H-9
Four Seasons, 2217 H-13
Frankclay, 221 I-17
Frankford, 323 D-16
FRANKLIN CO., 101492 G-16
Fredericktown, 3985 J-18
Freeburg, 437 H-14
Freeman, 482 G-9
Freistatt, 163 K-10
Fremont, 129 K-16
Fremont Hills, 826 K-12
French Vil., 300 I-18
Friedheim, 135 J-19
Frisbee, 50 M-19
Fristoe, 120 H-11
Frohna, 254 I-19
Frontenac, 3482 *H-4
Fruitland, 200 J-19
Fulton, 12790 F-14
Furner, 200 C-18
Gainesville, 773 L-13
Galena, 440 L-11
Gallatin, 1786 C-10
Galt, 253 C-11
Garden City, 1642 G-10
Garrison L-12
Gasconade, 223 G-15
GASCONADE CO., 15222 G-15
Gentry, 72 B-9
GENTRY CO., 6738 B-9
Gentryville, 30 C-9
Gentryville L-13
Georgetown, 130 F-12
Gerald, 1345 G-16
Gerster, 25 I-11
Gibbs, 107 C-13
Gideon, 1093 M-19
Gifford, 50 C-13
Gilliam, 197 E-12
Gilman City, 383 C-10
Gladstone, 25410 E-9
Glasgow, 1103 E-12
Glasgow Vil., 5429 *F-7
Glenaire, 545 G-5
Glenallen, 85 J-18
Glendale, 5925 *I-5
Glennonville, 140 L-18
Glensted, 100 G-12
Glenwood, 196 B-13
Glidewell, 70 J-11
Golden, 280 L-11
Golden City, 765 J-10
Goldman, 150 H-17
Goldsberry C-13
Goodman, 1248 L-9
Goodson, 85 I-12
Gordonville, 391 J-19
Gorin, 91 B-14
Goshen B-11
Gower, 1526 D-9
Graff, 50 J-14
Graham, 171 B-8
Grain Valley, 12854 F-10
Granby, 2134 K-9
Grand Pass, 66 E-11
Grandin, 243 L-17
Grandview, 24475 M-4
Granger, 34 B-14
Graniteville, 30 I-17
Grant City, 859 B-9
Grantwood Vil., 863 *J-5
Grassy J-18
Gravois Mills, 144 H-12
Gray Summit, 2701 G-17
Grayson, 125 D-9
Green Castle, 275 B-12
Green City, 657 B-12
Green Pk., 2622 *J-5
Green Ridge, 475 G-11
Greendale, 651 *G-5
GREENE CO., 275174 J-11
Greenfield, 1371 J-10
Greensburg, 30 B-14
Greentop, 442 B-13
Greenville, 511 K-18
Greenwood, 5221 F-9
Greer L-16
Grovespring J-13
Grubville, 200 H-17
GRUNDY CO., 10261 B-11
Guilford, 85 C-8
Gunn City, 118 G-10
Guthrie, 150 F-14
Hagers Grv. D-14
Hale, 419 D-11
Halfway, 173 J-12
Halls, 50 D-8
Hallsville, 1491 E-14
Halltown, 173 K-11
Hamilton, 1809 D-10
Hams Prairie, 100 F-14
Hancock, 50 I-14
Hanley Hills, 2101 *H-5
Hannibal, 17916 D-15
Hardin, 569 E-10
Harper H-11
Harris, 61 B-11
Harrisburg, 266 E-13
HARRISON CO., 8957 B-10
Harrisonville, 10019 G-9
Hartford, 30 B-12
Hartsburg, 103 G-14
Hartville, 613 K-13
Hartwell, 16 G-10
Harwood, 47 I-10
Hatfield, 50 B-10
Hatton, 110 F-14
Hawk Pt., 669 F-16
Hayti, 2939 M-19
Haywood City, 206 K-19
Hazelwood, 25703 *F-4
Helena, 200 C-9
Hematite, 250 H-17
Hendrickson, 50 K-18
Henley, 100 H-13
Henrietta, 369 E-10
HENRY CO., 22272 G-10
Herculaneum, 3468 H-18
Hermann, 2431 G-15
Hermitage, 467 I-11
HICKORY CO., 9627 H-11
Hickory Hill G-13
Higbee, 568 E-13
Higginsville, 4797 F-11
High Gate H-15
High Hill, 195 F-16
High Pt., 100 G-13
High Ridge, 4305 G-17
Highlandville, 911 K-11
Hilda L-12
Hill Top, 110 L-17
Hillsboro, 2821 H-17
Hillsdale, 1478 *G-6
Hinton, 150 F-13
Holcomb, 635 M-19
Holden, 2252 G-10
Holland, 229 N-19
Holliday, 137 D-14
Hollister, 4426 L-12
Holt, 447 E-9
HOLT CO., 4912 B-7
Holts Summit, 3247 G-14
Homestown, 151 M-19
Hoover, 150 D-2
Hopewell, 120 G-16
Hopkins, 532 B-8
Horine, 821 H-18
Hornersville, 663 N-18
Horton, 50 H-9
Houston, 2081 J-14
Houston Lake, 235 G-3
Houstonia, 220 F-11
HOWARD CO., 10144 E-13
Howardville, 383 L-19
HOWELL CO., 40400 K-14
Hughesville, 183 F-11
Humansville, 1048 I-11
Hume, 336 H-9
Humphreys, 118 C-11
Hunnewell, 184 D-14
Hunter, 168 K-17
Huntleigh, 334 *I-4
Huntsdale, 31 F-13
Huntsville, 1564 E-13
Hurdland, 163 C-14
Hurley, 178 K-11
Iatan, 45 D-8
Iberia, 736 H-14
Ilasco, 80 D-16
Independence, 116830 E-9
Indian Grv., 40 D-12
IRON CO., 10630 J-17
Iron Gates *C-5
Iron Mtn. Lake, 737 I-17
Irondale, 445 I-17
Ironton, 1460 J-17
Irwin, 69 J-9
Isabella L-13
Jackson, 13758 J-19
JACKSON CO., 674158 F-9
Jacksonville, 151 D-13
Jadwin, 60 J-15
Jameson, 133 C-10
Jamesport, 524 C-10
Jamestown, 386 F-13
Jane, 120 L-9
Japan, 90 H-16
Jasper, 931 J-9
JASPER CO., 117404 J-9
Jefferson City, 43079 G-14
JEFFERSON CO., 218733 H-17
Jenkins, 90 L-11
Jennings, 14712 *G-6
Jerico Sprs., 228 I-10
Jerome, 250 I-14
JOHNSON CO., 52595 G-10
Jonesburg, 768 F-16
Joplin, 50150 K-9
Junction City, 327 J-18
Kahoka, 2078 B-15
Kampville, 100 F-17
Kansas City, 459787 F-9
Kaseyville D-13
Kearney, 8381 E-9
Kelso, 586 K-19
Kendricktown, 200 K-9
Kennett, 10932 M-18
Kenoma, 110 J-9
Kewanee, 220 L-19
Keytesville, 471 E-12
Kidder, 323 D-10
Kimberling City, 2400 L-11
King City, 1013 C-9
Kingdom City, 128 F-14
Kingston, 348 D-10
Kingsville, 269 F-10
Kirbyville, 207 L-12
Kirksville, 17505 C-13
Kirkwood, 27540 *I-4
Kliever, 100 G-13
Knob Lick, 110 I-18
Knob Noster, 2709 F-11
Knox City, 216 C-14
KNOX CO., 4131 C-14
Knoxville, 85 E-10
Koeltztown, 130 H-14
Koshkonong, 212 L-15
Krakow, 100 G-16
La Belle, 660 C-14
La Grange, 931 C-15
La Monte, 1140 F-11
La Plata, 1366 C-13
Labadie, 600 G-17
Laclede, 345 D-12
LACLEDE CO., 35571 J-13
Laddonia, 513 E-15
Ladue, 8521 *H-5
LAFAYETTE CO., 33381 F-10
L. Lotawana, 1939 F-9
L. Ozark, 1586 H-13
L. St. Louis, 14545 F-17
L. Tapawingo, 730 J-7
L. Waukomis, 870 G-3
L. Winnebago, 1131 M-7
Lakenan, 70 D-14
Lakeshire, 1432 *J-5
Lakeview Hts., 100 H-12
Lamar, 4532 J-9
Lamine F-12
Lampe, 400 L-11
Lanagan, 419 L-9
Lancaster, 728 B-13
Lanton, 40 L-15
Laquey, 300 I-14
Laredo, 198 C-11
Latham, 140 G-13
Lathrop, 2086 D-9
Latour, 62 G-10
LAWRENCE CO., 38634 J-10
Lawrenceton, 80 I-18
Lawson, 2473 E-10
Leadington, 422 I-17
Leadmine I-12
Leadwood, 1282 I-17
Leasburg, 338 H-16
Leawood, 682 *C-6
Lebanon, 14474 I-13
Lecoma, 60 I-15
Leeper, 160 K-17
Lees Summit, 91364 L-6
Leesville, 100 H-11
Leeton, 566 G-11
Lemay, 16645 *J-6
Lemons, 100 B-12
Lenox I-15
Lentner D-14
Leonard, 61 C-14
Leora, 30 K-19
Leslie, 171 G-16
Lesterville, 180 J-17
Lewis, 80 G-11
Lewis & Clark Vil., 132 D-8
LEWIS CO., 10211 C-15
Lewistown, 534 C-15
Lexington, 4726 E-10
Liberal, 759 J-9
Liberty, 29149 E-9
Libertyville, 120 I-18
Licking, 3124 J-15
Lilbourn, 1190 L-19
Lincoln, 1190 G-11
LINCOLN CO., 52566 F-16
Linden, 125 K-12
Linn, 1459 G-15
LINN CO., 12761 C-12
Linn Creek, 244 H-13
Linneus, 278 C-12
LIVINGSTON CO., 15195 C-11
Livonia, 74 B-13
Lock Sprs., 57 C-10
Lockwood, 936 J-10
Lodi J-18
Lone Elm, 140 *B-6
Lone Elm, 80 F-13
Lone Jack, 1050 F-10
Lonedell, 400 H-17
Long Lane, 125 J-12
Longtown, 102 I-19
Loose Creek G-14
Louisburg, 122 I-12
Louisiana, 3364 E-16
Louisville E-16
Lowndes K-18
Lowry City, 640 H-11
Lucerne, 85 B-11
Ludlow, 137 D-11
Luray, 99 B-14
Lynchburg J-14
Macks Creek, 244 I-12
Macon, 5471 D-13
MACON CO., 15566 C-13
Madison, 554 D-14
MADISON CO., 12226 J-18
Maitland, 343 B-8
Malden, 4275 L-19
Malta Bend, 250 E-11
Manchester, 18094 *I-3
Manes, 50 J-13
Mansfield, 1296 K-13
Many Sprs. L-16
Maplewood, 8046 *I-5
Marble Hill, 1477 J-19
Marceline, 2233 D-12
MARIES CO., 9176 H-14
MARION CO., 28781 D-15
Marionville, 2225 K-11
Marlborough, 2179 *I-5
Marquand, 203 J-18
Marshall, 13065 E-12
Marshfield, 6633 J-12
Marston, 503 L-19
Marthasville, 1136 G-16
Martinsburg, 304 E-15
Martinstown, 30 B-13
Martinsville, 30 B-10
Maryknoll, 220 F-17
Maryland Hts., 27472 *G-4
Marys Home H-13
Maryville, 11972 B-8
Mattese, 2500 *K-5
Matthews, 628 L-19
Maysville, 1114 C-9
Mayview, 212 F-10
McBride I-19
MCDONALD CO., 23083 L-9
McDowell, 80 L-10
McFall, 93 C-10
McGee, 80 K-18
Meadville, 462 D-11
Medill, 150 B-15
Mehlville, 28380 *J-5
Meinert J-10
Memphis, 1822 B-14
Mendon, 171 D-12
Menfro, 30 I-19
Mercer, 318 B-11
MERCER CO., 3785 B-11
Merwin, 58 G-9
Meta, 229 H-14
Metz, 49 H-9
Mexico, 11543 E-14
Miami, 175 E-12
Middle Grv., 30 E-14
Middletown, 167 E-15
Midway, 200 F-13
Midway *C-6
Mike, 30 D-12
Milan, 1960 C-12
Milford, 26 J-10
Mill Grv. B-11
Mill Spr., 189 K-17
Millard, 89 C-13
Miller, 699 K-10
MILLER CO., 24748 H-13
Millersburg, 235 F-14
Millersville, 250 J-19
Millville E-10
Millwood E-16
Milo, 90 I-9
Mindenmines, 365 J-9
Miner, 984 K-20
Mirabile, 50 D-10
MISSISSIPPI CO., 14358 L-20
Missouri City, 267 E-9
Moberly, 13974 E-13
Modena, 60 B-11
Mokane, 185 G-14
Moline Acres, 2442 *G-6
Molino, 80 E-14
Monegaw Sprs. H-10
Monett, 8873 K-10
MONITEAU CO., 15607 G-13
Monroe City, 2531 D-15
MONROE CO., 8840 D-14
Montevallo, 50 I-10
Montgomery City, 2834 F-15
MONTGOMERY CO., 12236 F-15
Monticello, 98 C-15
Montreal, 150 I-13
Montrose, 384 H-10
Montserrat, 80 F-11
Moody, 80 L-14
Mooresville, 91 D-11
Mora, 80 G-12
Morehouse, 973 L-19
Morgan, 100 J-13
MORGAN CO., 20565 G-12
Morley, 697 K-19
Morrison, 139 G-15
Morrisville, 388 J-11
Mosby, 190 E-9
Moscow Mills, 2509 F-16
Moselle, 160 G-17
Mound City, 1159 C-7
Moundville, 124 I-9
Mt. Airy, 30 E-13
Mt. Leonard, 87 E-11
Mt. Moriah, 87 B-10
Mt. Sterling G-15
Mt. Vernon, 4575 K-10
Mt. Zion H-11
Mountain Grv., 4789 K-14
Mountain View, 2719 K-15
Murphy, 8690 *K-3
Murry, 80 F-14
Myrtle, 120 M-16
Mystic C-12
Napton, 50 F-12
Nashville, 100 J-9
Naylor, 632 L-17
Nebo J-13
Neelys J-20
Neelyville, 483 L-17
Nelson, 192 F-12
Neosho, 11835 L-9
Nevada, 8386 I-9
New Bloomfield, 669 G-14
New Boston, 60 C-12
New Cambria, 195 D-13
New Florence, 769 F-15
New Franklin, 1089 F-13
New Hamburg, 250 K-19
New Hampton, 291 B-10
New Hartford E-16
New Haven, 2089 G-16
New Hope, 90 E-17
New London, 974 D-15
New Madrid, 3116 L-20
NEW MADRID CO., 18956 M-19
New Market, 80 D-8
New Melle, 475 G-17
New Pt., 50 C-8
New Wells, 90 J-19
Newark, 94 C-14
Newburg, 470 I-14
NEWTON CO., 58114 L-9
Newtonia, 199 K-9
Newtown, 183 B-11
Niangua, 405 J-12
Nixa, 19022 K-11
Nodaway, 125 C-8
NODAWAY CO., 23370 B-8
Noel, 1832 L-9
Norborne, 708 E-11
Normandy, 5008 *G-6
N. Kansas City, 4208 H-4
Northmoor, 325 G-3
Northview, 150 J-12
Northwoods, 4227 *G-6
Northwye, 200 I-15
Norwood, 665 K-13
Novelty, 139 C-14
Novinger, 456 B-13
Oak Grv., 7795 F-10
Oak Grove Vil., 509 H-16
Oak Ridge, 243 J-19
Oakland, 1381 *I-5
Oakland Pk. *B-7
Oaks, 129 G-4
Oakview, 375 G-4
Oakville, 36143 *K-6
Oakwood, 185 G-4
Oakwood Pk., 188 G-4
Oates J-16
Odessa, 5300 F-10
Odin J-13
O'Fallon, 79329 F-17
Old Appleton, 85 J-19
Old Mines, 200 H-17
Old Monroe, 265 F-17
Olden, 80 L-14
Olivette, 7737 *H-5
Olney F-16
Olympian Vil., 774 H-17
Oran, 1294 K-19
Orchard Farm, 300 *E-4

*, †, ‡, §, ◊ See explanation under state title in this index.
County and parish names are listed in capital letters & boldface type.
Independent cities (not included in a county) are listed in italics.

Oregon, 857 C-8
OREGON CO., 10881 L-16
Orrick, 837 E-10
Osage Bch., 4351 H-13
OSAGE CO., 13878 G-14
Osborn, 423 D-9
Osceola, 947 H-11
Osgood, 48 C-11
Oskaloosa I-9
Otterville, 454 G-12
Otto, 500 G-17
Overland, 16062 *G-4
Owensville, 2676 H-15
Oxly, 200 L-17
Ozark, 17820 K-12
OZARK CO., 9723 L-13
Ozark View, 1000 *I-4
Pacific, 7002 G-17
Pagedale, 3304 *H-5
Painton, 50 K-19
Palmyra, 3595 D-15
Paris, 1220 D-14
Park Hills, 8759 I-17
Parkdale, 170 *K-3
Parkville, 5554 G-2
Parma, 713 L-19
Parnell, 191 B-9
Pasadena Hills, 930 *G-6
Pascola, 108 M-19
Passaic, 34 H-9
Patterson, 250 K-17
Patton, 120 J-18
Patton Jct., 90 J-18
Pattonsburg, 348 C-10
Paynesville, 77 E-16
Peace Valley L-15
Peach Orchard M-19
Peaksville, 30 B-15
Peculiar, 4608 F-9
PEMISCOT CO., 18296 M-19
Pennsboro, 30 J-10
Perry, 693 E-15
PERRY CO., 18971 I-19
Perryville, 8225 I-19
Pershing G-15
Peruque, 80 *E-2
PETTIS CO., 42201 G-11
Pevely, 5484 H-18
Phelps, 80 K-10
Phelps City, 24 B-7
PHELPS CO., 45156 J-14
Philadelphia, 265 D-15
Phillipsburg, 202 J-13
Pickering, 160 B-8
Piedmont, 1977 K-17
Pierce City, 1292 K-10
PIKE CO., 18516 E-16
Pilot Grv., 768 F-12
Pilot Knob, 746 I-17
Pine Crest, 40 K-15
Pine Lawn, 3275 *G-6
Pineville, 791 L-9
Pittsburg, 200 I-11
Pittsville, 80 F-10
Plad I-12
Plato, 109 J-14
Platte City, 4691 E-8
PLATTE CO., 89322 E-8
Platte Woods, 385 G-2
Plattsburg, 2319 D-9
Pleasant Hill, 8113 F-9
Pleasant Hope, 614 J-11
Pleasant Valley, 2961 G-5
Plevna, 21 C-14
Pocahontas, 114 J-19
Pt. Lookout, 1200 *M-9
Pt. Pleasant M-20
POLK CO., 31137 I-11
Pollock, 89 B-12
Polo, 575 D-10
Pomona, 511 L-14
Pontiac, 175 L-13
Poplar Bluff, 17023 L-18
Portage Des Sioux, 328 *D-5
Portageville, 3228 M-19
Portland, 130 G-15
Post Oak G-10
Potosi, 2660 I-17
Pottersville L-14
Powe, 110 L-18
Powell, 85 L-9
Powersville, 60 B-11
Poynor, 100 L-17
Prairie City H-10
Prairie Hill, 90 D-13
Prairie Home, 280 F-13
Preston, 223 I-12
Princeton, 1166 B-11
Prosperity, 120 *A-8
PULASKI CO., 52274 I-14
Purdin, 190 C-12
Purdy, 1098 L-10
PUTNAM CO., 4979 B-12
Puxico, 881 K-18
Queen City, 598 B-13
Quincy H-11
Quitman, 45 B-8
Qulin, 458 L-18
Racine, 200 K-9
RALLS CO., 10167 E-15
Randles, 130 K-19
Randolph, 52 H-5
RANDOLPH CO., 25414 D-13
Ravanna, 98 B-11
Ravenwood, 440 B-9
RAY CO., 23494 E-10
Raymondville, 363 J-15
Raymore, 19206 F-9
Raytown, 29526 F-9
Rea, 50 C-8
Readsville F-15
Redford, 100 J-17
Reeds, 95 K-10
Reeds Spr., 913 L-11
Reger, 80 C-12
Renick, 172 E-13
Rensselaer, 228 D-15
Republic, 14751 K-11
Revere, 79 B-15
Reynolds, 100 J-16
REYNOLDS CO., 6696 J-16
Rhineland, 142 G-15
Rhyse J-15
Rich Fountain, 220 G-14
Rich Hill, 1396 H-9
Richards, 96 I-9
Richland, 1863 I-13
Richmond, 5797 E-10
Richmond Hts., 8603 *H-5
Richwoods, 300 H-17
Ridgedale, 450 M-12
Ridgely, 104 D-9
Ridgeway, 464 B-10
Ridgley, 120 L-10
RIPLEY CO., 14100 L-17
Risco, 346 L-19
Ritchey, 82 K-9
River Aux Vases, 110 I-18
River Bend, 10 G-6
Riverside, 2937 H-3
Riverview, 2856 *F-7
Riverview Estates, 82 F-9
Rives, 63 N-19
Roach, 200 I-12
Roads D-11
Roanoke, 30 E-13
Robertsville, 250 G-17
Roby, 150 J-14
Rocheport, 239 F-13
Rochester, 200 C-9
Rock Hill, 4635 *I-5
Rock Port, 1318 B-7
Rockbridge L-13
Rockville, 166 H-10
Rocky Comfort, 190 L-10
Rocky Mount, 130 H-13
Rogersville, 3073 K-12
Rolla, 19559 I-15
Roscoe, 124 I-10
Rosebud, 409 G-15
Roselle, 60 J-17
Rosendale, 143 C-8
Rothville, 99 D-12
Round Spr. J-15
Rover L-15
Rush Hill, 151 E-15
Rushville, 303 D-8
Russellville, 807 G-13
Rutledge, 109 B-14
Sabula, 50 J-17
Saginaw, 297 K-9
St. Ann, 13020 *G-4
St. Anthony, 130 H-14
St. Catharine, 90 D-12
St. Charles, 65794 F-17
ST. CHARLES CO., 360485 G-16
St. Clair, 4724 H-16
ST. CLAIR CO., 9805 H-10
St. Clement, 78 E-16
St. Elizabeth, 336 H-14
ST. FRANCOIS CO., 65359 I-18
St. Francisville, 179 B-15
St. George, 1337 *J-5
St. James, 4216 H-15
St. Johns, 6517 *G-5
St. Joseph, 76780 D-8
St. Louis, 319294 G-18
ST. LOUIS CO., 998954 G-17
St. Martins, 1140 G-13
St. Mary, 360 I-19
St. Patrick, 30 B-15
St. Paul, 1829 F-17
St. Peters, 52575 F-17
St. Robert, 4340 I-14
St. Thomas, 263 G-14
Ste. Genevieve, 4410 H-18
STE. GENEVIEVE CO., 18145 I-18
Salcedo, 90 K-19
Salem, 4950 I-15
SALINE CO., 23370 F-11
Salisbury, 1618 E-12
Sandy Hook F-13
Santa Fe, 100 E-15
Santa Rosa C-10
Sappington, 7580 *J-5
Sarcoxie, 1330 K-10
Savannah, 5057 C-8
Saverton, 80 D-16
Schell City, 249 H-10
SCHUYLER CO., 4431 B-13
Scopus, 160 J-19
SCOTLAND CO., 4843 B-14
Scott City, 4565 J-20
SCOTT CO., 39191 K-20
Sedalia, 21387 G-12
Sedgewickville, 173 J-19
Seligman, 851 L-10
Senath, 1767 M-18
Seneca, 2336 L-9
Seymour, 1921 K-13
SHANNON CO., 8441 K-15
Shaw, 80 F-14
Shelbina, 1704 D-14
SHELBY CO., 6373 D-14
Shelbyville, 552 D-14
Sheldon, 543 I-9
Shell Knob, 1379 L-11
Sheridan, 195 B-9
Shirley, 120 I-17
Shoal Creek Drive, 337 *C-6
Shrewsbury, 6254 *I-5
Sikeston, 16318 K-19
Silex, 187 E-16
Silva, 300 K-18
Silver Creek, 623 *C-7
Silver Lake, 30 I-19
Simmons, 30 K-14
Skidmore, 284 B-8
Slater, 1856 E-12
Sleeper, 100 I-13
Smithton, 570 G-12
Smithville, 8425 E-9
S. Fork, 241 L-14
S. Lineville, 28 B-11
S. Shore, 200 F-17
South West City, 970 L-9
Spanish Lake, 19650 *F-6
Sparta, 1756 K-12
Spencerburg E-15
Spickard, 254 B-11
Spokane, 177 L-11
Springfield, 159498 K-11
Springhill C-11
Spruce, 80 H-10
Squires, 110 L-13
Stanberry, 1185 B-9
Stanton, 200 H-16
Stark E-16
Stark City, 139 L-9
Steedman, 135 G-15
Steele, 2172 N-19
Steelville, 1642 I-16
Steffenville, 30 C-14
Stella, 158 L-9
Stephens, 140 F-14
Stet, 30 E-11
Stewartsville, 750 D-9
Stockton, 1819 I-10
STODDARD CO., 29968 L-19
STONE CO., 32202 L-11
Stony Hill, 90 G-16
Stotesbury, 18 I-9
Stotts City, 220 K-10
Stoutland, 192 I-13
Stoutsville, 36 D-14
Stover, 1094 G-12
Strafford, 2358 J-12
Strain H-16
Strasburg, 141 F-10
Sturdivant, 100 K-18
Sturgeon, 872 E-14
Sublette, 30 B-13
Success J-14
Sugar Creek, 3345 I-5
Sullivan, 7081 H-16
SULLIVAN CO., 6714 B-12
Summersville, 502 K-15
Sumner, 102 D-12
Sunnyvale *C-6
Sunrise Bch., 431 H-13
Sunset Hills, 8496 *J-4
Swedeborg, 200 I-13
Sweet Sprs., 1484 F-11
Swiss G-15
Sycamore Hills, 668 *G-5
Syracuse, 172 G-12
Tallapoosa, 168 L-19
TANEY CO., 51675 L-12
Taneyville, 396 L-12
Taos, 878 G-14
Tarkio, 1583 B-7
Taylor, 150 C-15
Tebbetts, 170 G-14
Tecumseh, 100 L-14
Teresita, 100 K-15
TEXAS CO., 26008 K-14
Thayer, 2243 L-15
Theodosia, 243 L-13
Thomasville, 68 L-15
Thompson, 200 E-14
Thornfield, 80 L-13
Tiff City, 120 L-9
Tiffin, 80 I-10
Tightwad, 69 H-11
Tina, 157 D-11
Tindall, 77 C-11
Tipton, 3262 G-13
Town & Country, 10815 *H-3
Tracy, 208 E-8
Treloar, 130 G-16
Trenton, 6001 C-11
Trimble, 646 D-9
Triplett, 41 D-12
Troy, 10540 F-16
Truxton, 91 F-16
Tuckahoe, 90 *A-6
Tunas I-12
Turney, 148 D-9
Tuscumbia, 203 H-13
Twin Oaks, 392 *I-3
Udall, 120 L-14
Union, 10204 G-16
Union City K-11
Union Star, 437 C-9
Unionville, 1865 B-12
Unity Vil., 99 K-6
University City, 35371 *H-5
Urbana, 417 I-12
Urich, 505 G-10
Utica, 269 D-11
Valles Mines, 500 H-17
Valley Pk., 6942 *J-3
Valley View, 300 H-18
Van Buren, 819 K-16
Vandalia, 3899 E-15
Vandiver, 71 E-15
Vanduser, 267 K-19
Vanzant, 80 K-14
Velda Vil., 1420 *G-6
Velda Vil. Hills, 1055 *G-6
Verdella J-9
VERNON CO., 21159 I-9
Verona, 619 K-10
Versailles, 2482 G-12
Vibbard, 210 E-10
Viburnum, 693 I-16
Vichy, 220 H-15
Vienna, 610 H-14
Villa Ridge, 2636 G-17
Vineland, 120 H-17
Vinita Pk., 1880 *G-5
Vinita Ter., 277 *G-5
Viola L-11
Virginia H-9
Vista, 54 H-11
Wainwright, 85 G-14
Wakenda E-11
Waldron, 200 E-8
Walker, 270 I-9
Wallace, 115 D-8
Walnut Grv., 665 J-11
Walnut Shade, 300 L-12
Wappapello, 150 K-18
Wardell, 427 M-19
Wardsville, 1506 G-14
Warren D-15
WARREN CO., 32513 F-16
Warrensburg, 18838 F-10
Warrenton, 7880 F-16
Warsaw, 2127 H-11
Warson Woods, 1962 *I-4
Washburn, 435 L-10
Washington, 13982 G-16
WASHINGTON CO., 25195 H-16
Wasola, 113 L-13
Watson, 100 B-7
Waverly, 849 E-11
Wayland, 533 B-15
WAYNE CO., 13521 K-18
Waynesville, 4830 I-14
Weatherby, 107 C-9
Weatherby Lake, 1723 G-2
Weaubleau, 418 I-11
Webb City, 10996 K-9
WEBSTER CO., 36202 J-12
Webster Groves, 22995 *I-5
Weingarten, 133 I-18
Weldon Spr., 5443 F-17
Weldon Spr. Hts., 91 *G-1
Wellington, 812 E-10
Wellston, 2313 *H-6
Wellsville, 1217 F-15
Wentworth, 147 K-10
Wentzville, 29070 F-17
Wesco I-15
W. Alton, 522 F-18
W. Line, 97 G-9
W. Plains, 11986 L-15
W. Quincy, 30 C-15
Westboro, 141 B-7
Weston, 1641 E-8
Westphalia, 389 G-14
Westview, 110 L-9
Westwood, 278 *H-4
Wheatland, 371 I-11
Wheaton, 696 L-10
Wheeling, 271 D-11
Whitakerville, 100 H-11
White Church L-15
White Oak, 50 M-19
Whiteside, 75 E-16
Whitesville, 80 C-9
Whitewater, 125 J-19
Whiting, 150 L-20
Wilbur Pk., 471 *I-6
Wilcox, 70 B-8
Wilderness L-16
Wildwood, 35517 G-17
Willard, 5288 J-11
Williamsburg, 100 F-15
Williamstown B-15
Williamsville, 342 K-17
Willmathsville B-13
Willow Sprs., 2184 K-14
Wilson City, 115 K-20
Wilton, 80 F-13
Winchester, 1547 *I-3
Winchester, 110 B-15
Windsor, 2901 G-11
Windyville I-12
Winfield, 1404 F-17
Winigan, 44 C-12
Winona, 1335 K-16
Winston, 259 C-10
Winthrop, 60 D-8
Wishart J-11
Wittenberg, 60 I-20
Wolf Island, 30 L-20
Wood Hts., 717 E-10
Woodlawn D-14
Woodson Ter., 4063 *G-5
Wooldridge, 61 F-13
Worth, 63 B-9
WORTH CO., 2171 B-9
Worthington, 81 B-13
Wright City, 3119 F-16
WRIGHT CO., 18815 J-13
Wyaconda, 227 B-14
Wyatt, 319 K-20
Yukon, 60 J-15
Zalma, 122 K-18

Montana

Page locator

Map keys	Atlas pages
1–10	122–123
11–20	124–125

Absarokee, 1150 I-11
Acton, 60 H-13
Agawam D-7
Agency, 100 E-4
Alberton, 420 F-3
Alder, 103 J-7
Alhambra G-7
Alpine J-11
Alzada, 29 J-20
Amsterdam, 180 I-8
Anaconda, 9298 H-6
Angela, 10 G-16
Antelope, 51 B-19
Apgar B-4
Arlee, 636 E-4
Armington, 75 E-9
Ashland, 824 I-17
Ashuelot, 40 E-8
Augusta, 309 E-7
Avon, 111 G-6
Babb, 174 B-5
Bainville, 208 C-20
Baker, 1741 G-20
Ballantine, 320 H-13
Bannack, 25 J-5
Basin, 212 H-7
Bearcreek, 79 J-12
BEAVERHEAD CO., 9246 K-6
Belfry, 218 J-12
Belgrade, 7389 I-8
Belknap, 158 D-2
Belle Creek, 20 J-18
Belt, 597 E-9
Benchland, 10 F-10
Benteen, 30 J-15
Biddle, 41 J-18
Big Arm, 177 D-4
BIG HORN CO., 12865 I-15
Big Sandy, 598 C-10
Big Timber, 1641 I-10
Bigfork, 4270 C-4
Bighorn, 15 H-15
Billings, 104170 I-13
Billings Hts., 6000 M-19
Birney, 137 J-16
Black Eagle, 904 E-8
Blackfoot, 80 B-6
BLAINE CO., 6491 B-12
Bloomfield, 15 E-18
Bonner, 200 F-4
Boulder, 1183 H-7
Box Elder, 87 C-10
Boyd, 35 J-12
Boyes, 25 J-19
Bozeman, 37280 I-9
Bozeman Hot Sprs., 75 I-8
Brady, 140 D-7
Bridger, 708 J-12
Broadus, 468 I-18
Broadview, 192 H-12
BROADWATER CO., 5612 G-8
Brockton, 255 C-18
Brockway, 35 E-17
Brooks F-11
Browning, 1016 B-6
Brusett, 5 E-15
Buffalo, 10 F-11
Busby, 745 I-15
Butte, 33525 H-6
Bynum, 31 D-7
Camas, 58 D-3
Cameron, 10 J-8
Canyon Creek, 250 F-7
Canyon Ferry G-8
Capitol, 5 I-20
CARBON CO., 10078 J-12
Cardwell, 50 I-7
Carlyle F-20
Carter, 58 D-9
CARTER CO., 1160 I-19
Cartersville H-16
Cascade, 685 E-8
CASCADE CO., 81327 F-8
Cat Creek F-14
Centerville, 25 E-9
Charlo, 379 E-4
Charlos Hts., 120 H-4
Checkerboard, 20 G-10
Chester, 847 B-9
Chico Hot Sprs. J-9
Chinook, 1203 B-12
Choteau, 1684 D-7
CHOUTEAU CO., 5813 D-10
Christina, 20 E-11
Churchill, 902 I-8
Circle, 615 E-17
Clancy, 1661 G-7
Clinton, 1052 F-4
Clyde Pk., 288 I-9
Coalridge B-19
Coalwood I-18
Coffee Creek, 65 E-10
Cohagen, 15 F-16
Collins D-8
Colstrip, 2214 H-16
Columbia Falls, 4688 C-4
Columbia Hts., 110 C-4
Columbus, 1893 I-12
Condon, 343 E-5
Conner, 216 H-4
Conrad, 2570 C-7
Cooke City, 75 K-11
Coram, 539 C-4
Corbin G-7
Corvallis, 976 G-4
Corwin Sprs., 109 J-9
Craig, 43 F-7
Crane, 102 D-20
Creston, 70 C-4
Crow Agency, 1616 I-15
Culbertson, 714 C-19
Cushman H-12
Custer, 159 H-14
CUSTER CO., 11699 H-18
Cut Bank, 2869 B-7
Dagmar, 50 B-19
DANIELS CO., 1751 A-17
Darby, 720 H-4
DAWSON CO., 8966 E-18
Dayton, 84 D-4
De Borgia, 78 E-2
Decker, 20 K-16
Deer Lodge, 3111 G-6
DEER LODGE CO., 9298 H-5
Dell, 25 K-6
Delphia, 20 G-13
Denton, 255 E-10
Devon, 5 C-8
Dewey, 50 I-6
Dillon, 4134 J-6
Dixon, 203 E-4
Dodson, 124 C-13
Drummond, 309 G-5
Dunkirk, 10 C-8
Dupuyer, 86 C-6
Dutton, 316 D-8
E. Glacier Pk. Vil., 363 C-5
E. Helena, 1984 G-7
E. Missoula M-13
Edgar, 114 J-12
Ekalaka, 332 H-19
Elkhorn Hot Sprs., 60 J-5
Elliston, 219 G-6
Elmo, 180 D-4
Emigrant, 488 J-9
Ennis, 838 J-8
Essex, 30 C-5
Ethridge, 15 B-7
Eureka, 1037 A-3
Evaro, 322 F-4
Evergreen, 7616 C-4
Fairfield, 708 E-7
Fairview, 840 D-20
Fallon, 164 F-18
FALLON CO., 2890 G-19
Farmington D-7
Ferdig B-8
FERGUS CO., 11586 E-12
Fishtail, 85 J-11
FLATHEAD CO., 90928 D-5
Flaxville, 71 B-18
Florence, 765 G-4
Floweree, 25 D-9
Forest Pk., 1000 F-19
Forestgrove, 60 F-12
Forsyth, 1777 H-16
Ft. Belknap Agency, 1293 C-12
Ft. Benton, 1464 D-9
Ft. Kipp, 40 C-19
Ft. Peck, 233 C-16
Ft. Shaw, 280 E-8
Ft. Smith, 161 J-14
Fortine, 325 B-3
Four Buttes, 20 B-17
Four Corners, 3146 I-8
Frazer, 362 C-17
Frenchtown, 1825 F-4
Froid, 185 C-19
Fromberg, 438 J-12
Galata, 25 C-8
GALLATIN CO., 89513 J-8
Gallatin Gateway, 856 I-8
Gardiner, 875 K-9
GARFIELD CO., 1206 F-15
Garneill, 10 G-11
Garrison, 96 G-6
Garryowen, 60 I-15
Geraldine, 261 E-10
Geyser, 87 E-10
Gibson Flats, 100 N-17
Gildford, 179 B-10
GLACIER CO., 13399 B-6
Glasgow, 3250 C-16
Glen, 30 J-6
Glendive, 4935 F-19
Glentana, 10 B-16
Goldcreek, 10 G-6
GOLDEN VALLEY CO., 884 G-12
GRANITE CO., 3079 G-5
Grant, 25 K-5
Grantsdale, 175 H-4
Grass Range, 110 F-12
Great Falls, 58505 E-8
Greenough F-5
Greycliff, 112 I-11
Halfmoon, 100 M-1
Hall, 100 G-5
Hamilton, 4348 H-4
Hammond, 15 J-19
Happys Inn, 164 C-2
Hardin, 3505 I-14
Hardy F-8
Harlem, 808 B-12
Harlowton, 997 G-11
Harrison, 137 I-7
Hathaway, 30 H-17
Haugan, 90 E-2
Havre, 9310 B-11
Hays, 843 D-12
Heart Butte, 582 C-6
Helena, 28190 G-7
Helmville, 80 F-6
Heron, 282 C-1
Highwood, 176 E-9
Hilger, 40 E-11
HILL CO., 16096 B-10
Hingham, 118 B-10
Hinsdale, 217 C-15
Hobson, 215 F-11
Hogeland, 60 B-12
Holter Dam F-7
Homestead, 50 B-19
Hot Sprs., 544 D-3
Howard H-16
Hungry Horse, 826 C-4
Huntley, 446 I-13
Huson, 210 F-3
Hysham, 312 H-15
Ingomar, 20 G-15
Inverness, 55 B-9
Ismay, 19 G-19
Jackson, 50 J-5
Jardine, 57 K-9
Jeffers, 80 J-8
Jefferson City, 472 G-7
JEFFERSON CO., 11406 H-7
Jefferson Island I-7
Joliet, 595 J-12
Joplin, 157 B-9
Jordan, 343 E-15
JUDITH BASIN CO., 2072 F-10
Judith Gap, 126 G-11
Kalispell, 19927 C-4
Kevin, 154 B-7
Kila, 392 C-3
Kinsey, 25 G-17
Kiowa B-5
Klein, 168 G-13
Kremlin, 98 B-10
LAKE CO., 28746 D-3
L. McDonald, 5 B-4
Lakeside, 2669 C-4
Lakeview, 10 L-7
Lambert, 160 D-19
Lame Deer, 2052 I-16
Landusky D-13
Larslan, 25 B-16
Laurel, 6718 I-12
Laurin, 60 J-7
Lavina, 187 H-12
Ledger, 25 C-8
LEWIS & CLARK CO., 63395 E-6
Lewistown, 5901 F-11
Libby, 2628 B-2
LIBERTY CO., 2339 B-9
Lima, 221 K-6
Lincoln, 1013 F-6
LINCOLN CO., 19687 B-2
Lindsay, 50 E-18
Livingston, 7044 I-9
Lloyd, 10 C-11
Lockwood, 6797 M-20
Lodge Grass, 428 J-15
Lodge Pole, 265 D-13
Logan, 99 I-8
Lohman B-11
Lolo, 3892 F-4
Lolo Hot Sprs., 10 F-3
Loma, 85 D-10
Lonepine, 162 D-3
Loring, 10 B-14
Lothair, 15 C-8
Lustre, 25 C-17
Luther J-11
MADISON CO., 7691 J-7
Madoc, 15 B-18
Maiden F-12
Malta, 1997 C-14
Manhattan, 1520 I-8
Marion, 886 C-3
Marsh F-19
Martin City, 500 C-4
Martinsdale, 64 G-10
Marysville, 80 G-7
Maudlow, 5 H-9
Maxville, 130 G-5
McAllister, 100 J-8
McCabe, 20 C-19
MCCONE CO., 1734 D-17
McLeod, 10 I-10
MEAGHER CO., 1891 F-8
Medicine Lake, 225 B-19
Melstone, 96 G-14
Melville, 20 H-10
Mildred, 30 G-19
Miles City, 8410 G-17
Milford Colony, 130 E-7
Miller Colony, 70 D-7
MINERAL CO., 4223 F-3
Missoula, 66788 F-4
MISSOULA CO., 109299 F-3
Moccasin, 35 F-11
Moiese, 5 E-4
Molt, 20 I-12
Monarch, 80 F-9
Monida, 10 L-7
Montague, 15 D-10
Montana City, 2715 G-7
Moore, 193 F-11
Mosby, 15 F-14
Muddy, 617 I-16
Musselshell, 60 G-13
MUSSELSHELL CO., 4538 G-13
Myers H-15
Nashua, 290 C-16
Neihart, 51 F-9
Niarada, 27 D-3
Norris, 60 I-8
Noxon, 218 C-1
Nye, 30 J-11
Oilmont, 35 B-8
Olive, 5 I-18
Olney, 191 B-3
Opheim, 85 B-16
Orchard Homes, 5197 M-11
Oswego, 30 C-17
Otter, 5 J-17
Outlook, 47 A-19
Ovando, 81 F-5
Pablo, 2254 D-4
Paradise, 163 E-3
Park City, 983 I-12
PARK CO., 15636 J-10
Peerless, 70 B-17
Pendroy, 35 C-7
Perma E-3
PETROLEUM CO., 494 E-13
Philipsburg, 820 G-5
PHILLIPS CO., 4253 C-13
Piltzville, 395 F-4
Pine Creek J-9
Pinesdale, 917 G-4
Pinnacle, 15 C-5
Plains, 1048 E-3
Plentywood, 1734 B-19
Plevna, 162 G-19
Polaris, 10 J-5
Polebridge, 30 B-4
Polson, 4488 D-4
Pompeys Pillar, 70 H-14
PONDERA CO., 6153 C-8
Pony, 118 I-7
Poplar, 810 C-18
Portage D-9
Potomac, 30 F-5
POWDER RIVER CO., 1743 J-17
Powderville, 10 I-18
POWELL CO., 7027 G-6
Power, 179 D-8
PRAIRIE CO., 1179 F-17
Pray, 681 J-9
Proctor, 75 D-4
Pryor, 618 J-13
Radersburg, 66 H-8
Rapelje, 225 H-12
Ravalli, 76 E-4
RAVALLI CO., 40212 I-4
Raymond, 10 A-19
Raynesford, 50 E-9
Red Lodge, 2125 J-12
Redstone, 50 B-18
Reed Pt., 193 I-11
Regina, 10 D-14
Reserve, 23 B-19
Rexford, 105 A-2
Richey, 177 D-18
Richland, 60 B-17
RICHLAND CO., 9746 D-19
Rimini G-7
Ringling, 60 H-9
Roberts, 361 J-12
Rock Sprs., 20 F-16
Rockvale I-12
Rocky Boy, 170 C-11
Rollins, 209 D-4
Ronan, 1871 E-4
ROOSEVELT CO., 10425 C-19
Roscoe, 15 J-11
Rosebud, 111 H-16
ROSEBUD CO., 9233 G-16
Roundup, 1788 G-13
Roy, 108 E-12
Rudyard, 258 B-10
Ryegate, 245 H-12
Saco, 197 C-15
St. Ignatius, 842 E-4
St. Labre Mission, 400 I-16
St. Marie, 264 C-16
St. Mary, 20 B-5
St. Regis, 319 E-2
St. Xavier, 83 J-14
Saltese, 40 E-2
Sand Coulee, 212 E-8
Sand Sprs., 20 F-14
Sanders, 20 H-15
SANDERS CO., 11413 D-2
Santa Rita, 113 B-7
Sapphire Vil., 50 F-10
Savage, 300 E-19
Scobey, 1017 B-18
Sedan, 99 H-9
Seeley Lake, 1659 E-5
Shawmut, 42 H-11
Shelby, 3376 B-8
Shepherd, 516 H-13
Sheridan, 642 J-7
SHERIDAN CO., 3384 B-19
Sidney, 5191 D-20
Silesia, 96 I-12
SILVER BOW CO., 34200 I-6
Silver Gate, 20 K-10
Silver Star, 100 I-7
Simms, 354 E-7
Simpson A-10
Somers, 1109 C-4
Sonnette, 5 J-17
Springdale, 42 I-10
Square Butte, 25 E-10
Stanford, 401 F-10
Starr School, 252 B-6
Stevensville, 1809 G-4
STILLWATER CO., 9117 H-12
Stockett, 169 E-9
Stryker, 26 B-3
Suffolk, 15 E-11
Sula, 37 I-4
Sumatra G-14
Summit M-3
Sun Prairie D-14
Sun River, 124 E-8
Sunburst, 375 B-7
Superior, 812 E-3
Swan Lake, 113 D-4
Sweet Grass, 58 A-7
SWEET GRASS CO., 3651 J-10
Tampico, 15 C-15
Teigen, 10 F-13
Terry, 605 F-18
TETON CO., 6073 D-6
Thompson Falls, 1313 D-2
Three Forks, 1869 I-8
TOOLE CO., 5324 B-8
Toston, 108 H-8
Townsend, 1878 H-8
Tracy, 225 E-9
TREASURE CO., 718 H-15
Trego, 541 B-3
Trident, 15 H-8
Trout Creek, 242 D-2
Troy, 938 B-1
Turner, 61 B-13
Twin Bridges, 375 I-7
Twodot, 35 G-10
Ulm, 738 E-8
Utica, 20 F-10
Valier, 509 C-7
VALLEY CO., 7369 B-15
Vananda G-15
Vandalia, 20 C-15
Vaughn, 658 E-8
Victor, 745 G-4
Vida, 50 D-18
Virgelle D-10
Virginia City, 190 J-7
Volborg, 5 H-17
Wagner C-13
Walkerville, 675 H-6
Washoe J-12
Waterloo, 50 I-7
W. Glacier, 227 B-4
W. Riverside, 800 F-4
W. Yellowstone, 1271 K-9
Westby, 168 A-20
WHEATLAND CO., 2168 G-11
White Haven, 140 C-2
White Pine D-2
White Sulphur Sprs., 939 G-9
Whitefish, 6357 C-4
Whitehall, 1038 I-7
Whitetail, 110 A-18
Whitewater, 64 B-14
Whitlash, 35 B-8
Wibaux, 589 F-20
WIBAUX CO., 1017 E-20
Wickes, 30 G-7
Willard, 5 H-20
Willow Creek, 210 I-8
Wilsall, 178 H-9
Windham, 35 F-10
Winifred, 208 E-11
Winnett, 182 F-13
Winston, 147 G-8
Wisdom, 98 I-5
Wise River, 60 I-6
Wolf Creek, 150 F-7
Wolf Pt., 2621 C-17
Woods Bay, 661 D-4
Woodside G-4
Worden, 577 H-13
Wyola, 215 J-15
Yaak, 248 A-2
YELLOWSTONE CO., 147972 H-13
York G-8
Zortman, 69 D-13
Zurich, 50 B-12

Nebraska

Page locator

Map keys	Atlas pages
1–10	126–127
11–20	128–129

Abie, 69 I-17
Adams, 573 L-18
ADAMS CO., 31364 L-13
Agnew, 60 J-17
Ainsworth, 1728 F-10
Albion, 1650 H-14
Alda, 642 K-13
Alexandria, 177 M-16
Allen, 377 F-17
Alliance, 8491 G-3
Alma, 1133 M-11
Almeria H-11
Aloys H-17
Alvo, 132 K-18
Amelia, 30 G-12
Ames, 24 I-17
Amherst, 248 K-11
Angora, 20 H-3
Angus, 40 M-14
Anoka, 6 E-12
Anselmo, 145 I-10
Ansley, 441 J-11
ANTELOPE CO., 6685 G-14
Antioch G-4
Arapahoe, 1026 M-10
Arcadia, 311 I-12
Archer, 81 J-14
Arlington, 1243 I-18
Arnold, 597 I-9
Arthur, 117 I-6
ARTHUR CO., 460 I-5
Ashby, 100 G-5
Ashland, 2453 J-18
Ashton, 194 J-12
Assumption, 30 L-13
Atkinson, 1245 F-12
Atlanta, 131 L-11
Auburn, 3460 L-19
Aurora, 4479 K-14
Avoca, 242 K-19
Axtell, 726 L-12
Ayr, 94 L-13
Bancroft, 495 G-17
BANNER CO., 690 I-1
Barada, 24 M-20
Barneston, 116 M-18
Bartlett, 117 H-13
Bartley, 283 M-9
Bassett, 619 F-11
Battle Creek, 1207 G-15
Bayard, 1209 H-2
Bazile Mills, 29 F-14
Beatrice, 12459 M-17
Beaver City, 609 M-10
Beaver Crossing, 403 K-16
Bee, 191 J-16
Beemer, 678 H-17
Belden, 115 F-16
Belgrade, 126 I-14
Bellevue, 50137 J-19
Bellwood, 435 I-16
Belvidere, 48 M-15
Benedict, 234 J-15
Benkelman, 953 M-6
Bennet, 719 K-18
Bennington, 1458 I-18
Benson B-18
Berea, 41 G-3
Bertrand, 750 L-11
Berwyn, 83 I-11
Big Sprs., 400 J-5
Bingham, 40 G-5
Bladen, 237 M-13
BLAINE CO., 478 H-9
Blair, 7990 I-18
Bloomfield, 1028 F-15
Bloomington, 103 M-12
Blue Hill, 936 M-13
Blue Sprs., 331 M-17
Boelus, 189 J-13
Boone, 20 I-14
BOONE CO., 5505 H-14
Bow Valley, 116 E-16
BOX BUTTE CO., 11308 G-2
BOYD CO., 2099 E-13
Boys Town, 745 J-18
Bradshaw, 273 K-15
Brady, 428 J-9
Brainard, 330 J-16
Brandon, 10 K-5
Brewster, 17 H-10
Bridgeport, 1545 H-3
Bristow, 65 E-13
Broadwater, 128 I-3
Brock, 112 L-19
Broken Bow, 3559 I-10
BROWN CO., 3145 F-10
Brownlee, 15 G-8
Brownson, 20 J-3
Brownville, 132 L-20
Brule, 326 J-5
Bruning, 279 L-15
Bruno, 99 J-17
Brunswick, 138 F-14
BUFFALO CO., 46102 K-12
Burchard, 82 M-18
Burr, 57 L-18
BURT CO., 6858 H-18
Burton, 10 E-11
Burwell, 1210 H-12
Bushnell, 124 J-1
BUTLER CO., 8395 J-16
Butte, 326 E-12
Byron, 83 M-15
Cairo, 785 K-13
Callaway, 539 J-10
Cambridge, 1063 M-9
Campbell, 347 M-13
Carleton, 91 M-15
Carroll, 229 G-16
CASS CO., 25241 K-19
Cedar Bluffs, 610 I-17
CEDAR CO., 8852 F-16
Cedar Creek, 390 J-19
Cedar Rapids, 382 I-14
Center, 94 F-14
Central City, 2934 J-14
Ceresco, 889 J-17
Chadron, 5851 E-3
Chalco, 10994 D-16
Chambers, 268 G-12
Champion, 103 L-6
Chapman, 287 J-14
Chappell, 929 J-4
CHASE CO., 3966 L-5
CHERRY CO., 5713 F-7
Chester, 232 M-15
CHEYENNE CO., 9998 J-3
Clarks, 369 J-15
Clarkson, 658 H-16
Clatonia, 231 L-17
Clay Ctr., 760 L-14
CLAY CO., 6542 L-14
Clearwater, 419 G-14
Clinton, 41 E-4
Cody, 154 E-7
Coleridge, 473 F-16
COLFAX CO., 10515 I-16
Colon, 110 J-17
Colton J-3
Columbus, 22111 I-16
Comstock, 93 I-11
Concord, 166 F-16
Cook, 321 L-18
Cordova, 137 K-16
Cornlea, 36 H-15
Cortland, 482 L-17
Cotesfield, 46 I-13
Cowles, 30 M-13
Cozad, 3977 K-10
Crab Orchard, 38 L-18
Craig, 199 H-18
Crawford, 997 E-2
Creighton, 1154 F-14
Creston, 203 H-16
Crete, 6960 L-17
Crofton, 726 E-15
Crookston, 69 E-8
Crowell H-17
Culbertson, 595 M-8
CUMING CO., 9139 G-17
Curtis, 939 L-8
Cushing, 32 J-13
CUSTER CO., 10939 J-10
Dakota City, 1919 F-18
DAKOTA CO., 21006 F-17
Dalton, 315 I-3
Danbury, 101 M-9
Dannebrog, 303 J-13
Darr K-10
Davenport, 294 M-15
Davey, 154 J-17
David City, 2906 J-16
DAWES CO., 9182 E-2
Dawson, 146 M-19
DAWSON CO., 24326 K-10
Daykin, 166 L-16
De Soto, 30 I-19
De Witt, 513 L-17
Decatur, 481 G-18
Denton, 190 K-17
Deshler, 747 M-15
DEUEL CO., 1941 J-4
Deweese, 67 L-14
Dickens K-7
Diller, 260 M-17
Dix, 255 J-2
Dixon, 87 F-16
DIXON CO., 6000 F-16
Dodge, 612 H-17
DODGE CO., 36691 I-17
Doniphan, 829 K-13
Dorchester, 586 K-16
Douglas, 173 L-18
DOUGLAS CO., 517110 I-18
Du Bois, 147 M-19
Dunbar, 187 K-19
Duncan, 351 I-15
DUNDY CO., 2008 M-6
Dunning, 103 H-9
Dwight, 204 J-16
Eagle, 1024 K-18
E. Omaha B-19
Eddyville, 97 K-10
Edgar, 498 L-14
Edison, 133 M-10
Elba, 215 J-13
Elgin, 661 H-14
Elk City, 50 I-18
Elk Creek, 98 M-19
Ellis, 70 M-17
Ellsworth, 30 G-5
Elm Creek, 901 K-11
Elmwood, 634 K-18
Elsie, 106 K-6
Elsmere, 30 G-9
Elwood, 707 L-10
Elyria, 51 H-12
Emerald, 170 K-17
Emerson, 840 G-17
Emmet, 48 F-12
Enders, 42 L-6
Endicott, 132 M-16
Enola, 40 H-15
Ericson, 92 H-13
Eustis, 401 L-10
Ewing, 387 G-13
Exeter, 591 L-15
Fairbury, 3942 M-16
Fairfield, 387 L-14
Fairmont, 560 L-15
Falls City, 4325 M-20
Farnam, 171 K-9
Farwell, 122 J-13
Filley, 132 M-18
FILLMORE CO., 5890 L-15
Firth, 590 L-17
Florence A-18
Fontanelle, 54 I-18
Fordyce, 139 E-16
Ft. Calhoun, 908 I-19
Ft. Robinson, 60 E-2
Foster, 51 G-15
Franklin, 1000 M-12
FRANKLIN CO., 3225 M-12
Fremont, 26397 I-18
Friend, 1027 K-16
FRONTIER CO., 2756 L-8
Fullerton, 1307 I-14
Funk, 194 L-11
FURNAS CO., 4959 M-9
GAGE CO., 22311 L-17
Gandy, 32 I-9
GARDEN CO., 2057 I-4
GARFIELD CO., 2049 H-12
Garland, 216 K-17
Garrison, 54 J-16
Gates I-10
Geneva, 2217 L-15
Genoa, 1003 I-15
Gering, 8500 H-1
Gibbon, 1833 K-12
Gilead, 39 M-16
Giltner, 352 K-14
Gladstone, 30 M-16
Glenvil, 310 L-14
Glenwood Pk., 250 K-12
Goehner, 154 K-16
Gordon, 1612 E-5
GOSPER CO., 2044 L-10
Gothenburg, 3574 K-9
Grafton, 126 L-15
Grainton, 25 K-7
Grand Island, 48520 K-13
Grant, 1165 K-6
GRANT CO., 614 H-5
Greeley, 466 I-13
GREELEY CO., 2538 I-13
Greenwood, 568 J-18
Gresham, 223 J-16
Gretna, 4441 J-18
Gross, 2 E-13
Guide Rock, 225 M-14
Gurley, 214 I-3
Hadar, 293 G-15
Haigler, 158 M-5
HALL CO., 58607 J-13
Hallam, 213 L-17
Halsey, 76 H-9
HAMILTON CO., 9124 K-14
Hamlet, 57 L-7
Hampton, 423 K-14
Hansen, 50 K-13
Harbine, 49 M-17
Hardy, 159 M-14
HARLAN CO., 3423 M-11
Harrisburg, 100 I-1
Harrison, 251 E-1
Hartington, 1554 F-16
Harvard, 1013 L-14
Hastings, 24907 L-13
Hay Sprs., 570 E-4
Hayes Ctr., 214 L-7
HAYES CO., 967 L-7
Hazard, 70 J-12
Heartwell, 71 L-12
Hebron, 1579 M-15
Hemingford, 803 F-3
Henderson, 991 K-15
Hendley, 24 M-10
Henry, 106 G-1
Herman, 268 H-18
Hershey, 665 J-7
Hickman, 1657 L-17
Hildreth, 378 M-12
HITCHCOCK CO., 2908 M-7
Holbrook, 207 M-10
Holdrege, 5495 L-11
Holmesville, 51 M-17
Holstein, 214 L-13
HOLT CO., 10435 F-12
Homer, 549 F-18
HOOKER CO., 736 H-7
Hooper, 830 I-17
Hordville, 144 J-14
Hoskins, 285 G-16
HOWARD CO., 6274 J-13
Howe, 30 L-19
Howells, 561 H-16
Hubbard, 236 F-17
Hubbell, 68 M-15
Humboldt, 877 M-19
Humphrey, 760 H-15
Huntley, 44 M-11
Hyannis, 182 G-6
Imperial, 2071 L-6
Inavale, 117 M-13
Indianola, 584 M-9
Inglewood, 325 I-18
Inland, 62 L-14
Inman, 129 F-13
Irvington, 150 B-17
Ithaca, 148 J-18
Jackson, 223 F-17
Jamison E-11
Jansen, 118 M-16
JEFFERSON CO., 7547 M-16
Johnson, 328 L-19
JOHNSON CO., 5217 L-18
Johnstown, 64 F-10
Julian, 59 L-19
Juniata, 755 L-13
Kearney, 30787 K-12
KEARNEY CO., 6489 L-12
KEITH CO., 8368 J-6
Kenesaw, 880 L-13
Kennard, 361 I-18
KEYA PAHA CO., 824 E-10
Keystone, 59 J-6
Kilgore, 77 E-8
Kimball, 2496 J-1
KIMBALL CO., 3821 J-1
KNOX CO., 8701 F-15
Kramer, 60 L-17
La Platte, 114 J-19
La Vista, 15758 D-17
Lakeside, 30 G-4
Lamar, 23 L-5
LANCASTER CO., 285407 K-17
Lanham, 30 M-17
Laurel, 964 F-16
Lawrence, 304 M-14
Lebanon, 80 M-9
Leigh, 405 H-16
Lemoyne, 82 J-6
Leshara, 112 I-18
Lewellen, 224 I-5
Lewiston, 68 M-18
Lexington, 10230 K-10
Liberty, 76 M-18
Lincoln, 258379 K-17
LINCOLN CO., 36288 K-8
Lindsay, 255 H-15
Lindy, 13 E-15
Linwood, 88 I-17
Lisco, 64 I-4
Litchfield, 262 J-12
Lodgepole, 318 J-4
LOGAN CO., 763 I-8
Loma, 30 J-17
Long Pine, 305 F-10
Loomis, 382 L-11
Lorenzo, 58 J-3
Loretto, 42 H-14
Lorton, 41 L-19
Louisville, 1106 J-18
Loup City, 1029 J-12
LOUP CO., 632 H-11
Lowell, 30 L-12
Lushton, 30 K-15
Lyman, 341 H-1
Lynch, 245 E-13
Lyons, 851 H-18
Macon, 30 M-12
Macy, 1023 G-18
Madison, 2438 H-15
MADISON CO., 34876 H-15
Madrid, 231 K-6
Magnet, 57 F-15
Malcolm, 382 K-17
Malmo, 120 J-17
Manley, 178 K-18
Marion, 40 M-9
Marquette, 229 J-14
Marsland, 10 F-2
Martell, 100 K-17
Martinsburg, 94 F-17
Mascot M-11
Maskell, 76 E-16
Mason City, 171 J-11
Max, 57 M-6
Maxwell, 312 J-8
Maywood, 261 L-8
McCook, 7698 M-8
McCool Jct., 409 K-15
McGrew, 105 H-2
McLean, 36 F-15
MCPHERSON CO., 539 I-7
Mead, 569 J-18
Meadow Grv., 301 G-15
Melbeta, 112 H-2
Memphis, 114 J-18
Menominee, 30 E-15
Merna, 363 I-10
MERRICK CO., 7845 J-14
Merriman, 128 E-6
Milburn H-10
Milford, 2090 K-16
Millard C-16
Miller, 136 K-11
Milligan, 285 L-16
Mills E-11
Minatare, 816 H-2
Minden, 2923 L-12
Mitchell, 1702 H-1
Monowi, 1 E-13
Monroe, 284 I-15
Moorefield, 32 K-9
Morrill, 921 G-1
MORRILL CO., 5042 H-3
Morse Bluff, 135 I-17
Mullen, 509 G-7
Murdock, 236 K-18
Murray, 463 K-19
Mynard, 60 J-19
NANCE CO., 3735 I-14
Naper, 84 E-12
Naponee, 106 M-12
Nebraska City, 7289 K-19
Nehawka, 204 K-19
Neligh, 1599 G-14
Nelson, 488 M-14
Nemaha, 149 L-20
NEMAHA CO., 7248 L-19
Nenzel, 20 E-7
Newcastle, 325 E-17
Newman Grv., 721 H-15
Newport, 97 F-11
Nickerson, 369 I-18
Niobrara, 370 E-14
Nora, 21 M-14
Norfolk, 24210 G-15
Norman, 43 L-12
N. Bend, 1177 I-17
N. Loup, 297 I-12
N. Platte, 24733 J-8
Northport, 80 H-3
NUCKOLLS CO., 4500 M-14
Oak, 66 M-14
Oakdale, 322 G-14
Oakland, 1244 H-18
Obert, 23 E-16
Oconto, 151 J-10
Octavia, 127 I-16
Odell, 307 M-17
Odessa, 130 K-11
Ogallala, 4737 J-6
Ohiowa, 115 L-16
Omaha, 408958 J-19
O'Neill, 3705 F-13
Ong, 63 L-15
Orchard, 379 F-14
Ord, 2112 I-12
Orleans, 386 M-11
Orum, 30 I-18
Osceola, 880 J-15
Oshkosh, 884 I-4
Osmond, 783 F-15
Otoe, 171 K-19
OTOE CO., 15740 K-18
Overton, 594 K-11
Oxford, 779 M-10
Page, 166 F-13
Palisade, 351 L-7
Palmer, 472 J-14
Palmyra, 545 K-18
Panama, 256 L-18
Papillion, 18894 J-19
Parks, 23 M-6
Paul L-19
Pauline, 60 L-13
Pawnee City, 878 M-19
PAWNEE CO., 2773 M-18
Paxton, 523 J-7
Pender, 1002 G-17
PERKINS CO., 2970 K-6
Peru, 865 L-19
Petersburg, 333 H-14
PHELPS CO., 9188 L-11
Phillips, 287 K-14
Pickrell, 199 L-17
Pierce, 1767 G-15
PIERCE CO., 7266 G-15
Pilger, 352 G-16
Plainview, 1246 F-15
Platte Ctr., 336 I-15
PLATTE CO., 32237 I-15
Plattsmouth, 6502 J-19
Pleasant Dale, 205 K-17
Pleasanton, 341 K-12
Plymouth, 409 M-17
Polk, 322 J-15
POLK CO., 5406 J-15
Ponca, 961 F-17
Poole, 19 K-12
Potter, 337 J-2
Powell, 20 M-16
Prague, 303 I-17
Prairie Home, 70 K-18
Preston, 28 M-20
Primrose, 61 I-14
Princeton, 50 L-17
Prosser, 66 K-13
Purdum, 20 G-9
Raeville, 22 H-14
Ragan, 38 M-11
Ralston, 5943 C-17
Randolph, 944 F-16
Ravenna, 1360 J-12
Raymond, 167 K-17
Red Cloud, 1020 M-13
RED WILLOW CO., 11055 M-8
Redington, 30 I-2
Republican City, 150 M-11
Reynolds, 69 M-16
RICHARDSON CO., 8363 M-20
Richland, 73 I-16
Ringgold I-8
Rising City, 374 J-16
Riverdale, 182 K-12
Riverton, 89 M-13
Roca, 220 K-17
ROCK CO., 1526 G-11
Rockford M-17
Rockville, 106 J-12
Rogers, 95 I-17
Rosalie, 160 G-17
Roscoe, 63 J-6
Rose, 10 G-11
Roseland, 235 L-13
Rosemont, 20 M-13
Royal, 63 F-14
Rulo, 172 M-20
Rushville, 890 E-4
Ruskin, 123 M-15
St. Bernard, 30 H-15
St. Edward, 705 I-14
St. Helena, 96 E-16
St. Libory, 264 J-13
St. Mary, 50 L-18
St. Paul, 2290 J-13
Salem, 112 M-20
SALINE CO., 14200 L-16
Santee, 346 E-14
Sarben, 31 J-7
Sargent, 525 I-11
Saronville, 47 L-14
SARPY CO., 158840 J-18
SAUNDERS CO., 20780 J-17
Schuyler, 6211 I-
Scotia, 318 I-
SCOTTS BLUFF CO., 36970 H
Scottsbluff, 15039 H
Scribner, 857 H-
Seneca, 33 G
Seward, 6964 K-
SEWARD CO., 16750 J-
Shelby, 714 J-
Shelton, 1059 K-
SHERIDAN CO., 5469 F
SHERMAN CO., 3152 J-
Shickley, 341 L-
Sholes, 21 F-
Shubert, 150 M-
Sidney, 6757
Silver Creek, 362 J-
SIOUX CO., 1311 F
Smithfield, 54 L-
Snyder, 300 H-
S. Bend, 99 J-
S. Sioux City, 13353 F-
S. Yankton, 50 E-
Spalding, 487 H
Spencer, 455 E-
Sprague, 142 L-
Springfield, 1529 J-
Springview, 242 E-
Stamford, 183 M
Stanton, 1577 H-
STANTON CO., 6129 H-
Staplehurst, 242 K-
Stapleton, 305
Steele City, 61 M-
Steinauer, 75 M-
Stella, 152 M-
Sterling, 476 L-
Stockham, 44 K-
Stockville, 25
Strang, 29 L-
Stratton, 343 M
Stromsburg, 1171 J-
Stuart, 590 F-
Sumner, 236 K-
Sunol, 73
Superior, 1957 M-
Surprise, 43 J-
Sutherland, 1286
Sutton, 1502 L-
Swanton, 94 L-
Swedeburg, 40 J-
Syracuse, 1942 K-
Table Rock, 269 M-
Talmage, 233 L-
Tamora, 58 K-
Tarnov, 46 I-
Taylor, 190 H-
Tecumseh, 1677 L-
Tekamah, 1736 H-
Telbasta I-
Terrytown, 1198 H
Thayer, 62 K-
THAYER CO., 5228 M-
Thedford, 188 H
THOMAS CO., 647 H
Thompson M-
Thurston, 132 G-
THURSTON CO., 6940 G-
Tilden, 953 G
Tobias, 106 L-
Touhy, 30 J-
Trenton, 560 M
Trumbull, 205 K-
Tryon, 157
Uehling, 230 H-
Ulysses, 171 J-
Unadilla, 311 K-
Union, 233 K-
Upland, 143 M-
Utica, 861 K-
Valentine, 2737 E
Valley, 1875 I-
VALLEY CO., 4260 I-
Valparaiso, 570 J-
Venango, 164 K
Venice, 75 J-
Verdel, 30 E-
Verdigre, 575 F-
Verdon, 172 M-
Virginia, 60 M-
Waco, 236 K-
Wahoo, 4508 J-
Wakefield, 1451 G-
Wallace, 366 K
Walthill, 780 G-
Walton, 306 K-
Wann, 86 J-
Washington, 150 I-
WASHINGTON CO., 20234 H-
Waterbury, 73 F-
Waterloo, 848 I-
Wauneta, 577 L
Wausa, 634 F-
Waverly, 3277 K-
Wayne, 5660 G-
WAYNE CO., 9595 G-
WEBSTER CO., 3812 M-
Weeping Water, 1050 K-
Weissert, 30 I-
Wellfleet, 78 K
West Pt., 3364 H-
Western, 235 L-
Westerville, 39 I-
Weston, 324 J-
WHEELER CO., 818 H-
Whiteclay, 10 D
Whitman, 140 G
Whitney, 77 E
Wilber, 1855 L-
Wilcox, 358 L-
Willis F-
Willow Island, 26 K
Wilsonville, 93 M
Winnebago, 774 G-
Winnetoon, 68 F-
Winside, 427 G-
Winslow, 103 I-
Wisner, 1170 G-
Wolbach, 283 I-
Wood Lake, 63 F
Wood River, 1325 K-
Woodland Pk., 1866 G-
Worms, 30 J-
Wymore, 1457 M-
Wynot, 166 E-
York, 7766 K-
YORK CO., 13665 K-
Yutan, 1174 J-

***, †, ‡, §, ◊ See explanation under state title in this index.**
County and parish names are listed in capital letters & boldface type.
Independent cities (not included in a county) are listed in italics.

Nevada

Page locator
Map keys ... Atlas pages
A–N ... 130–131
...ty keyed to p. 20
...ty keyed to pp. 132–133

...mo, 1080 .... J-8
...analza Valley, 380 ... K-6
...in, 595 .... F-2
...stin, 197 .... F-2
...cer, 68 .... G-10
...tty, 1010 .... K-6
...mont, 25 .... H-6
...owawe, 280 .... D-7
...lck Sprs., 230 .... †G-1
...le Diamond, 290 .... L-8
...ulder City, 15023 ...... L-9
...kerville, 1303 .... K-10
...iente, 1130 .... M-9
...-Nev-Ari, 244 .... M-9
...lin, 2368 .... D-7
...80 .... M-9
...scent Valley, 392 ...... †L-6
...stal Bay, 305 .... †F-9
...rant D-9
...rie D-9
...ron, 8964 .... F-2
...eth, 100 .... G-2
...rio, 47 .... A-3
DOUGLAS CO.,
  45997 .... G-2
...ckwater, 20 .... G-7
...ohy, 25 .... D-6
...rer, 259 ....
...h Pt., 250 .... †G-9
...la, 18297 .... C-7
ELKO CO., 48818 .... L-7
...4255 .... F-8
...pire, 217 .... D-2
ESMERALDA CO.,
  783 .... J-5
...eka, 610 .... F-8
EUREKA CO., 1987 .... E-6
...on, 8606 .... F-3
...nley, 19368 .... F-2
...obs, 269 .... G-4
...ndnerville, 5656 .... G-2
...acoa, 939 .... †G-10
...lach, 206 .... D-2
...nbrook, 215 .... G-1
...ndale, 50 .... K-9
...conda, 214 .... G-5
...pt, 20 .... J-5
...den Valley, 1556 .... F-2
...dfield, 268 .... J-5
...odsprings, 229 .... M-8
...lley J-2
...eck, 40 .... C-8
...hthorne, 3269 .... H-3
...derson, 257729 .... L-8
...iden Valley, 1000 ...... †J-3
...3 .... J-5
HUMBOLDT CO.,
  16528 .... B-4
...ay, 171 .... J-2
...ine Vil., 8777 .... F-1
...ngn Sprs., 991 .... K-7
...kpot, 1195 .... A-9
...s Valley, 250 .... †G-10
...idge, 80 .... D-8
...n, 200 .... M-8
...es, 30 .... J-7
...sburg, 2152 .... †G-1
...ison, 113 .... F-5
...eridge, 371 .... †G-3
...3 .... J-5
LINCOLN CO., 5345 .... L-9
...andale K-9
...rlock, 1894 .... E-3
...d, 282 .... G-8
...ning, 60 .... H-4
LYON CO., 51980 .... G-2
...ors Pl. ....
...nhattan, 200 .... H-6
...son, 400 .... G-2
...ermitt, 172 .... A-5
...DIll, 1148 .... K-7
...cury, 50 .... K-7
...squite, 15276 .... K-10
...na, 50 .... J-5
...City H-8
...na, 155 .... H-4
...den, 3001 .... G-2
MINERAL CO.,
  ...72 .... H-3
...pa, 1025 .... H-3
...ntain City, 100 .... B-7
...nt Jo D-7
...n Washoe City, ... F-2
...on, 374 .... G-2
...as Vegas, 216961 .... L-8
...CO, 43946 .... H-5
...ana, 100 .... A-8
...anka, 155 .... A-8
...hee, 953 .... D-4
...rump, 36441 .... L-7
...ca, 963 .... H-9
...dise, 223207 .... L-8
...adise Valley, 109 ...... B-5
FLUSHING CO.,
  ...53 .... D-3
...ne, 1002 .... H-3
...el Valley, 5765 .... G-1
...ichton, 100 ....
...hel, 54 .... H-3
...o, 225221 .... F-2
...nd Hill, 400 .... †J-3
...y Valley, 100 .... H-8
...ay Valley, 2051 .... M-9
...ry's Jct., 100 .... F-2
...tlight, 539 .... M-9

Silver City, 150 .... F-2
Silver Peak, 107 .... I-5
Silver Sprs., 5296 .... F-2
Skyland, 376 .... †G-9
Smith, 160 .... G-2
S. Hills, 1100 .... †J-2
Sparks, 90264 .... F-2
Spring Creek, 12361 ...... D-7
Spring Valley, 178395 .... L-2
Stagecoach, 1874 .... F-2
Stateline, 897 .... G-1
Steamboat, 300 .... F-2
Stillwater, 200 .... F-3
Sun Valley, 19299 .... F-2
Sunnyside, 30 .... H-8
Sunrise Mnr., 189372 ..... K-4
Sutcliffe, 253 .... F-2
Tonopah, 2478 .... H-5
Topaz Lake, 157 .... G-2
Tuscarora, 100 ....
Ursine, 91 ....
Valmy, 37 .... C-5
Verdi, 1415 .... F-2
Virginia City, 855 .... F-2
Vya B-2
Wabuska, 500 .... F-2
Wadsworth, 834 .... F-2
Walker Lake, 275 .... G-3
Warm Sprs. H-6
Washoe City, 500 .... F-2

WASHOE CO.,
  ...951269 .... K-8
Weed Hts., 240 .... G-2
Wellington, 300 .... G-2
Wells, 1292 .... C-8
W. Wendover, 4410 .... D-10

WHITE PINE CO.,
  10030 .... L-4
Whitney, 38585 .... L-4
Willow Bch., 25 .... *E-1
Winchester, 27978 .... L-3
Winnemucca, 7396 .... C-4
Yerington, 3048 .... G-2
Zephyr Cove, 565 .... G-1

New Hampshire

Page locator
Map keys ... Atlas pages
A–N ... 132–133

Acworth, 230 .... K-5
Albany H-9
Alexandria, 150 .... H-6
Allenstown, 450 .... L-8
Alstead, 544 .... L-4
Alstead Ctr., 70 .... L-4
Alton, 501 .... J-8
Alton Bay, 900 .... J-8
Amherst, 613 .... M-7
Andover, 500 .... J-6
Antrim, 1397 .... L-6
Ashland, 1244 .... H-7
Ashuelot, 350 .... M-4
Atkinson, 900 .... L-8
Auburn, 450 .... L-8
Barnstead, 380 .... K-8
Barrington, 600 .... K-9
Bartlett, 373 .... G-8
Bath, 250 .... G-6
Bedford, 1800 .... M-7
Beebe River, 60 .... H-7

BELKNAP CO.,
  60088 .... J-8
Belmont, 1301 .... J-7
Bennington, 381 .... L-6
Benton, 80 .... G-6
Berlin, 10051 .... E-8
Bethlehem, 972 .... F-7
Boscawen, 400 .... K-7
Bow Mills, 700 .... K-7
Bowkerville, 70 .... M-5
Bradford, 356 .... K-6
Brentwood, 400 .... L-9
Bretton Woods, 30 .... F-8
Bridgewater, 130 .... I-7
Bristol, 1688 .... I-7
Brookfield, 40 .... J-9
Brookline, 700 .... N-7
Campton, 700 .... H-7
Canaan, 524 .... I-6
Canaan Ctr., 250 .... I-5
Canaan Street, 300 .... I-5
Candia, 1285 .... L-8
Candia Four Corners,
  150 .... L-8
Canobie Lake, 700 .... M-8
Canterbury, 300 .... K-7
Carroll F-7

CARROLL CO.,
  47818 .... I-8
Cascade, 180 .... E-8
Cedar Pond, 60 .... E-8
Center Barnstead,
  350 .... K-8
Center Conway, 400 .... H-9
Center Effingham,
  150 .... I-9
Center Harbor, 650 .... I-7
Center Ossipee, 561 ...... I-9
Center Sandwich,
  123 .... H-8
Center Strafford, 250 .... K-9
Center Tuftonboro,
  450 .... I-8
Charlestown, 1152 .... K-4
Chase Vil., 150 .... L-6
Chesham, 120 .... M-5

CHESHIRE CO.,
  77117 .... L-5
Chester, 600 .... M-8
Chesterfield, 450 .... M-4
Chichester, 250 .... K-8
Chocorua, 400 .... H-8
Christian Hollow, 70 ..... L-4
Claremont, 13355 .... I-4
Clinton Vil., 400 .... L-6
Cold River, 70 .... L-4
Colebrook, 1394 .... C-7
Concord, 42695 .... K-7
Contoocook, 1444 .... K-7
Conway, 1823 .... H-9
Cornish, 200 .... I-5
Cornish Ctr., 350 .... I-5
Cornish Flat, 350 .... I-5
Cornish Mills, 100 .... I-5
Croydon, 130 .... J-5
Croydon Flat, 100 .... I-5
Cushman, 90 .... F-7
Danbury, 500 .... J-6
Danville, 900 .... M-8
Davisville, ...
Deerfield, 200 .... L-8
Deerfield Parade, 200 .... L-8
Deering, 300 .... L-6
Derry, 22015 .... L-8
Dixville Notch, 10 .... D-7
Dorchester, 60 .... H-6
Dover, 29987 .... K-10
Drewsville, 150 .... L-4

Dublin, 650 .... M-5
Dunbarton Ctr., 230 ...... L-7
Durham, 10345 .... L-9
E. Alstead, 200 .... L-4
E. Andover, 350 .... J-6
E. Candia, 120 .... L-8
E. Concord, ... D-2
E. Conway, 130 .... Q-9
E. Derry, 850 .... M-8
E. Grafton, ...
E. Hampstead, 1400 .... M-9
E. Haverhill, 110 .... G-6
E. Hebron, 150 .... H-7
E. Lempster, 300 .... K-5
E. Rindge, 250 .... N-6
E. Sullivan, 170 .... L-5
E. Sutton, ... K-6
E. Swanzey, 350 .... M-5
E. Unity, 130 .... K-5
E. Wakefield, 90 .... I-9
E. Washington, 60 .... K-6
Eaton Ctr., 100 .... H-9
Effingham, 80 .... I-9
Effingham Falls, 100 ..... H-9
Elkins, 120 .... J-6
Ellsworth, ...
Elmwood, 80 .... L-6
Epping, 1681 .... L-9
Epsom, 250 .... K-8
Errol, 170 .... D-9
Etna, 350 .... I-5
Exeter, 9242 .... L-9
Fabyan, ... F-8
Farmington, 3885 .... J-9
Fitzwilliam, 900 .... M-5
Fitzwilliam Depot,
  500 .... M-5
Francestown, 300 .... L-6
Franconia, 600 .... F-6
Franklin, 8477 .... J-7
Freedom, 400 .... H-9
Fremont, 900 .... L-8
Georges Mills, 400 .... J-5
Gilford, 650 .... I-8
Gilmanton, 700 .... J-8
Gilmanton Ironworks,
  600 .... J-8
Gilsum, 400 .... L-5
Glen, 250 .... G-8
Glencliff, 90 .... H-6
Glendale, 400 .... I-8
Goffstown, 3196 .... L-7
Gorham, 1600 .... E-8
Goshen, 350 .... K-5
Gossville, 350 .... K-8
Grafton, 230 .... I-6
Grafton Ctr., 50 .... I-6
Grantham, 300 .... J-5
Greenfield, 900 .... M-6
Greenland, 1400 .... L-10
Greenville, 1108 .... M-6
Groton, 140 .... H-6
Grovetown, 1118 .... E-7
Guild, 325 .... J-5
Hampstead, 900 .... M-8
Hampton, 9656 .... M-10
Hampton Bch.,
  2275 .... M-10
Hampton Falls, 550 .... M-10
Hancock, 204 .... L-6
Hanover, 8636 .... I-5
Hanover Ctr., 150 .... I-5
Happy Corner, ... B-8
Haverhill, 400 .... G-6
Hebron, 150 .... H-7
Henniker, 1747 .... K-6
High Br., 100 .... N-6
Hill, 280 .... J-7
Hillsboro, 1976 .... L-6
Hillsborough, ...

HILLSBOROUGH CO.,
  400721 .... L-6
Hillsborough Lower Vil.,
  .... L-6
Hillsborough Upper Vil.,
  340 .... L-6
Hinsdale, 1548 .... M-4
Holderness, 400 .... H-7
Hollis, 600 .... N-7
Hooksett, 4147 .... L-8
Hopkinton, 400 .... K-7
Hudson, 7336 .... M-8
Intervale, 400 .... H-8
Jackson, 350 .... G-8
Jaffrey, 2757 .... M-6
Jaffrey Ctr., 400 .... M-6
Jefferson, 230 .... E-7
Kearsarge, 100 .... H-8
Keene, 23409 .... M-5
Kelleys Corner, ... K-8
Kensington, 240 .... M-9
Kidderville, ... C-7
Kingston, 700 .... M-9
Laconia, 15951 .... J-7
Lancaster, 1725 .... E-7
Landaff Ctr., 30 .... G-6
Langdon, 200 .... K-4
Lebanon, 13151 .... I-5
Lee, 150 .... L-9
Lempster, 70 .... K-5
Lincoln, 993 .... G-7
Lisbon, 980 .... G-6
Little Boars Head,
  120 .... L-10
Littleton, 4412 .... F-6
Lochmere, 400 .... J-7
Londonderry, 11037 .... M-8
Loudon, 559 .... K-7
Lower Gilmanton, ... J-8
Lyme, 450 .... H-5
Lyme Ctr., 120 .... H-5
Lyndeborough, 100 .... M-6
Madbury, 150 .... K-9
Madison, 250 .... H-9
Manchester, 109565 .... L-7
Marlborough, 1094 .... M-5
Marlow, 450 .... L-5
Marshall Cor., 80 .... L-8
Mason, 200 .... N-6
Melvin Vil., 241 .... I-8
Meredith Ctr., 120 .... I-7
Meriden, 500 .... I-5
Merrimack, 25494 .... M-7

MERRIMACK CO.,
  146445 .... K-6
Middleton Cors., 150 ..... J-9
Milan, 400 .... E-8
Milford, 8835 .... M-7
Milton, 500 .... J-9
Milton Mills, 299 .... J-9
Monroe, 280 .... F-5
Mont Vernon, 600 .... M-7

Moultonborough, 350 ...... I-8
Mt. Sunapee, 250 .... K-5
Munsonville, 230 .... L-5
Nashua, 86494 .... M-7
Nelson, 130 .... L-5
New Boston, 850 .... L-7
New Castle, 840 .... L-10
New Durham, 350 .... J-9
New Hampton, 351 .... I-7
New Ipswich, 800 .... M-6
New London, 1415 .... J-6
Newbury, 200 .... K-5
Newfields, 301 .... L-9
Newmarket, 5297 .... L-9
Newport, 4769 .... K-5
Newton, 650 .... M-9
Noone, 80 .... M-6
N. Branch, 150 .... L-6
N. Charlestown, 150 ...... K-4
N. Chatham, 80 .... G-9
N. Chichester, 250 .... K-8
N. Conway, 2349 .... G-9
N. Hampton, 500 .... L-10
N. Haverhill, 450 .... G-6
N. Newport, 200 .... J-5
N. Pelham, 400 .... M-8
N. Salem, 300 .... M-8
N. Sanbornton, 300 .... J-7
N. Sandwich, 100 .... H-8
N. Stratford, 400 .... D-7
N. Sutton, 270 .... K-6
North Village, 160 .... J-9
N. Walpole, 828 .... L-4
N. Woodstock, 528 .... G-7
Northfield, 1500 .... J-7
Northumberland, 100 ...... E-7
Northwood, 650 .... K-9
Northwood Ridge,
  250 .... K-8
Nottingham, 280 .... L-9
Orange, 120 .... I-6
Orford, 400 .... H-5
Orfordville, 120 .... H-5
Ossipee, 250 .... I-9
Pages Cor., 90 .... I-7
Parker Hill, ...
Passaconaway, 40 .... H-8
Pelham, 1200 .... N-8
Pembroke, 400 .... L-7
Percy, 60 .... D-7
Peterborough, 3103 .... M-6
Piermont, 210 .... H-5
Pike, 220 .... G-6
Pinardville, 4780 .... B-4
Pittsburg, 400 .... B-7
Pittsfield, 1576 .... K-8
Plainfield, 225 .... I-5
Plaistow, 220 .... M-9
Plymouth, 4456 .... I-7
Portsmouth, 20779 .... L-10
Potter Pl., 60 .... J-6
Randolph, 200 .... E-8
Raymond, 2855 .... L-8
Redstone, 150 .... G-9
Richmond, 150 .... M-5
Rindge, 400 .... M-6
Riverdale, 56 .... L-7
Rochester, 29752 .... K-9
Rollinsford, 1560 .... K-10
Rumney, 430 .... H-6
Rumney Depot, 320 .... H-6
Rye, 850 .... L-10
Rye Bch., 450 .... L-10
Salem, 12000 .... M-8
Salisbury, 330 .... J-7
Salisbury Hts., 100 ...... J-7
Sanbornton, 320 .... J-7
Sanbornville, 1056 .... I-9
Sandown, 600 .... M-8
Sandwich, 60 .... H-8
Scotland, 70 .... L-4
Seabrook, 900 .... M-10
Sharon, 80 .... M-6
Shelburne, ... F-9
Short Falls, 90 .... K-8
Silver Lake, 300 .... H-9
Snowville, 50 .... H-9
Somersworth, ...
11766 .... K-10
S. Acworth, 200 .... K-5
S. Barnstead, 70 .... J-8
S. Charlestown, ... K-4
S. Chatham, 90 .... G-9
S. Danville, 250 .... M-9
S. Deerfield, ...
S. Effingham, 120 .... I-9
S. Hooksett, 5418 .... L-8
S. Lyndeboro, 250 .... M-7
S. Merrimack, 200 .... M-7
S. Newbury, 150 .... K-6
S. Newbury, 150 ....
S. Stoddard, ... L-5
S. Sutton, 170 .... K-6
S. Tamworth, 200 .... H-8
S. Weare, 250 .... L-7
S. Wolfeboro, 600 .... I-8
Spofford, 500 .... M-4
Springfield, 80 .... J-6
Squantum, 120 .... M-7
Stark, 130 .... D-7
Stewartstown, 180 .... C-7
Stewartstown Hollow,
  100 .... C-8
Stinson Lake, 60 .... H-6
Stoddard, 300 .... L-5
Strafford, 400 .... K-9

STRAFFORD CO.,
  123143 .... K-9
Stratford, 150 .... D-7
Sugar Hill, 200 .... F-6
Suissevale, 800 .... I-8
Summit, ...
Sunapee, 1000 .... J-5
Suncook, 5379 .... L-8
Surry, 150 .... L-4
Swanzey, 300 .... M-5
Swiftwater, 120 .... G-6
Tamworth, 400 .... H-8
Temple, 600 .... M-6
The Glen, ...
Thornton, 150 .... H-7
Tilton, 1300 .... J-7
Troy, 1221 .... M-5
Twin Mtn., 800 .... F-7
Union, 204 .... J-9
Unity, 150 .... K-5
Wakefield, 140 .... I-9
Walpole, 605 .... L-4
Warner, 550 .... K-6
Warren, 550 .... H-6
Washington, 150 .... K-5
Waterville Valley, ...
120 .... H-7
Weare, 300 .... L-7

New Jersey

Page locator
Map keys ... Atlas pages
A–J ... 134–135
K–T ... 136–137
* City keyed to p. 50
† City keyed to pp. 146–147
‡ City keyed to p. 148
§ City keyed to p. 182

Absecon, 8411 .... P-10
Adamston, ... K-12
Adelphia, 150 .... J-12
Aldene, ... †J-4
Aldine, 50 .... O-5
Allamuchy, 78 .... D-8
Allendale, 6505 .... C-12
Allenhurst, 496 .... I-13
Allenton, 400 .... N-4
Allerton, 100 .... G-8
Alloway, 3467 .... O-5
Almonesson, 800 .... M-6
Alpha, 2369 .... F-7
Alpine, 1849 .... †B-11
Amwell, 100 .... F-9
Anderson, 342 .... F-7
Andover, 600 .... D-8
Annandale, 1695 .... G-8
Asbury, 273 .... F-7
Asbury Pk., 16116 .... J-13
Atco, 3500 .... M-8
Atlantic City,
  39558 .... Q-10

ATLANTIC CO.,
  274549 .... P-9
Atlantic Highlands,
  4385 .... H-13
Auburn, 150 .... N-5
Audubon, 8819 .... M-7
Audubon Pk., 1023 .... §F-5
Augusta, 100 .... C-9
Avalon, 1334 .... S-9
Avenel, 17011 .... †L-4
Avon-by-the-Sea,
  1901 .... J-13
Awosting, 500 .... C-11
Bakersville, 200 .... J-9
Baleville, 90 .... C-9
Bamber Lake, 250 .... M-11
Baptistown, 200 .... F-7
Bargaintown, 1600 .... Q-10
Barnegat, 2817 .... N-12
Barnegat Bch., 300 .... M-12
Barnegat Light,
  574 .... N-12
Barnegat Pines,
  400 .... M-12
Bartley, ... E-8
Basking Ridge,
  4000 .... G-10
Batsto, 10 .... O-9
Bay Head, 968 .... K-13
Bay Shore, ...
Bayonne, 63024 .... F-7
Bayville, 900 .... L-12
Beach Haven, 1170 .... O-12
Beach Haven Crest,
  100 .... O-12
Beach Haven Hts.,
  300 .... O-12
Beach Haven Ter.,
  .... O-12
Beach Haven West,
  3896 .... N-12
Beachwood, 11045 .... L-12
Beattystown, 4642 .... E-8
Beaver Lake, 250 .... C-9
Bedminster, 3000 .... F-9
Beesleys Pt., 850 .... Q-9
Belcoville, 200 .... P-9
Belford, 1785 .... H-13
Belle Mead, 216 .... H-9
Belleplain, 597 .... Q-9
Belleville, 35928 .... E-12
Bellmawr, 11262 .... §G-5
Belmar, 5794 .... J-13
Belvidere, 2681 .... E-7
Berkeley Hts.,
  13407 .... †E-2
Berlin, 7588 .... M-7
Bernardsville, 7707 ...... F-10
Beverly, 2577 .... K-5
Bivalve, 50 .... O-6
Blackwood, 4545 .... M-7
Blairstown, 515 .... D-7
Blawenburg, 200 .... H-9
Bloomfield, 47683 .... C-2
Bloomingdale,
  7656 .... B-11
Bloomsbury, 870 .... F-7
Blue Anchor, 500 .... N-8
Bogota, 8187 .... A-5

Webster, 120 .... K-7
Wendell, 120 .... K-5
Wentworth, 280 .... H-6
W. Alton J-8
W. Campton, 140 .... H-7
W. Canaan, 120 .... I-5
W. Chesterfield, 550 ..... M-4
W. Epping, 350 .... L-8
W. Hampstead, 200 .... M-8
W. Henniker, 300 .... K-6
W. Hopkinton, 30 .... K-6
W. Milan, 100 .... D-8
W. Nottingham, 170 .... K-9
W. Ossipee, 150 .... H-8
W. Peterborough,
  500 .... M-6
W. Plymouth, ...
W. Rindge, 330 .... M-5
W. Rumney, 150 .... H-6
W. Rye, 300 .... L-10
W. Springfield, 90 .... J-5
W. Stewartstown,
  386 .... C-7
W. Swanzey, 1308 .... M-4
W. Thornton, 160 .... H-7
W. Wilton, 200 .... M-6
Westmoreland, 300 .... L-4
Westport, 500 .... M-4
Westville, 400 .... M-9
Whitefield, 1142 .... F-7
Whittier, 50 .... H-8
Wilmot, 120 .... J-6
Wilmot Flat, 350 .... J-6
Wilton, 1163 .... M-7
Winchester, 1733 .... M-4
Windham, 300 .... M-8
Winnisquam, 650 .... J-7
Wolfeboro, 2838 .... I-8
Wolfeboro Ctr., ...
Wolfeboro Falls, 900 ..... I-8
Wonalancet, 60 .... H-8
Woodman, 80 .... J-4
Woodstock, 280 .... H-7
Woodsville, 1126 .... G-5

New Jersey (cont.)

Bonhamtown .... †M-2
Boonton, 8347 .... E-11
Bordentown, 3924 .... K-9
Bound Brook,
  10402 .... G-10
Bradevelt, 150 .... I-12
Bradley Bch., 4298 .... J-13
Brainards, 202 .... E-7
Branchville, 841 .... C-8
Breton Woods, ... K-12
Bricksboro, 40 .... Q-7
Bridgeboro, ...
Bridgeport, ... M-5
Bridgeton, 25448 .... P-6
Bridgeville, 106 .... F-7
Brielle, 4774 .... K-13
Brigantine, 9450 .... P-11
Brighton Bch., 150 .... O-12
Broadway, 244 .... F-7
Brooklawn, 1955 .... §G-5
Brookside, 1800 .... G-10
Brookville, ... M-11
Brotmanville, 150 .... O-6
Browns Mills,
  11223 .... L-10
Browntown, 2400 .... L-11
Buckshutem, 100 .... Q-7
Budd Lake, 8968 .... E-9
Buddtown, 70 .... L-9
Buena, 4603 .... P-7
Bunnvale, 400 .... F-8
Burleigh, 725 .... S-8
Burlington, 9920 .... K-8

BURLINGTON CO.,
  448734 .... L-9
Butler, 7539 .... D-11
Buttzville, 146 .... E-7
Caldwell, 7822 .... E-11
Califon, 1076 .... F-8
Camden, 77344 .... L-6

CAMDEN CO.,
  513657 .... N-8
Candlewood, 4000 .... K-12
Canton, 350 .... P-6
Cape May, 3607 .... T-7

CAPE MAY CO.,
  97265 .... R-8
Cape May Court House,
  5338 .... S-8
Cape May Pt., 291 .... T-7
Cardiff, 400 .... Q-10
Carlls Cor., 900 .... P-6
Carlstadt, 6127 .... A-4
Carlton Hill, ... B-4
Carmel, 150 .... P-6
Carneys Pt., 7382 .... N-4
Carpenterville, 90 .... E-7
Cecil O-7
Cedar Brook, 800 .... N-8
Cedar Crest Manor,
  150 .... N-4
Cedar Grv., 12300 .... B-1
Center Sq., 150 .... N-5
Centerton, 30 .... §O-9
Centerton, 500 .... O-8
Centre Grv., ... O-8
Chadwick, 250 .... L-13
Chambers Corners, ... L-9
Changewater, 250 .... F-7
Chatham, 8962 .... F-11
Chatsworth, 500 .... M-10
Cheesequake, 300 .... H-11
Cherry Hill, 2100 .... L-7
Cherryville, 50 .... F-8
Chesilhurst, 1634 .... N-8
Chester, 1649 .... F-9
Chesterfield, 200 .... K-9
Chrome, ... †L-5
Cinnaminson, ... L-7
Clark, 14597 .... †J-3
Clarksboro, 1700 .... M-6
Clarksburg, 400 .... J-10
Clarkstown, 200 .... P-9
Clayton, 8179 .... N-6
Clementon, 5000 .... M-7
Clermont, 100 .... R-8
Cliffside Pk., 23594 ..... C-6
Cliffwood, 1500 .... H-12
Cliffwood Bch.,
  3194 .... H-12
Clinton, 2719 .... G-8
Closter, 8373 .... †A-11
Clover Leaf Lakes,
  .... P-9
Cloverhill, 150 .... H-8
Cohansey, 50 .... P-7
Cold Spr., 600 .... T-7
Colesville, 120 .... B-9
Collings Lakes, 1706 ..... O-8
Collingswood, 13926 ...... L-7
Collingwood Pk.,
  .... J-12
Cologne, 1100 .... P-9
Colonia, 17795 .... G-11
Colonial Manor, ... §G-4
Columbia, 300 .... D-6
Columbus, 700 .... K-9
Conc,onvertown, 250 ...... P-10
Convent Sta., 1800 .... F-10
Cookstown, 300 .... K-9
Corbin City, 492 .... Q-8
Cornish, ...
Country Lake Estates,
  .... N-9
Cranberry Lake,
  .... D-8
Cranbury, 2181 .... I-10
Cranford, 22578 .... †H-3
Cream Ridge, 150 .... K-10
Cresskill, 8573 .... †B-7
Crestwood Vil.,
  7907 .... L-11
Croton, 60 .... H-9
Culvers Lake, 1100 .... C-8
Cumberland, 500 .... P-7

CUMBERLAND CO.,
  156898 .... Q-6
Daretown, 25 .... O-5
Dayton, 7063 .... I-10
Deal, 750 .... J-13
Deans, 600 .... I-10
Deepwater, 500 .... N-4
Deerfield, 350 .... O-6
Del Haven, 1200 .... S-7
Delanco, ...
Delaware, 150 .... D-6
Delmont, 650 .... R-7
Delran, 13200 .... L-7

Haworth, 3382 .... †B-10
Hawthorne, 18791 .... †B-7
Hazen, 30 .... E-7
Hazlet, 12000 .... H-12
Hedding, 150 .... K-9
Heislerville, 500 .... R-7
Helmetta, 2178 .... I-10
Hewitt, 200 .... C-11
Hibernia, 200 .... D-10
High Br., 3648 .... F-9
Highland Lake,
  4933 .... B-10
Highland Pk., ... H-10
E. Keansburg, 3000 .... H-12
E. Millstone, 579 .... H-10
E. Newark, 2406 .... D-3
E. Orange, 64270 .... D-2
E. Rutherford, 8913 ...... B-4
E. Vineland, 300 .... P-7
E. Windsor, 4000 .... J-10
Eatontown, 12709 .... I-13
Edgewater, 11513 .... B-6
Edgewater Pk., 2000 ...... K-8
Edinburg J-9
Edison, 97597 .... H-11
Egg Hbr. City, 4243 ...... O-9
Eldora, 120 .... R-7
Eldridge Pk., 3000 .... R-13
Elizabeth, 124969 .... F-12
Elm, 200 .... N-8
Elmer, 1395 .... O-6
Elmwood Pk., 19403 .... A-3
Elwood, 1437 .... O-9
Emerson, 7401 .... †A-9
Englewood, 27147 .... E-13
Englewood Cliffs,
  5281 .... A-7
Englishtown, 1847 .... I-11
Erma, 2134 .... T-8
Essex Fells, ...
783969 .... F-11
Estell Manor, 1735 .... Q-8
Etra, 30 .... J-10
Everittstown, 50 .... F-7
Ewan, 250 .... N-6
Ewing, 35707 .... J-8
Fair Haven, 6121 .... I-13
Fair Lawn, 32457 .... †B-7
Fairfield, 7300 .... D-1
Fairton, 400 .... P-6
Fairview, 13835 .... C-6
Fairview, 3806 .... I-13
Fanwood, 7318 .... G-11
Far Hills, 919 .... F-9
Farmingdale, 1329 .... J-12
Farmington, 450 .... H-1
Ferrell, 80 .... N-6
Fieldsboro, 560 .... K-9
Finderne, 5600 .... G-10
Fiveville, 175 .... G-6
Five Points, ... C-8
Flagtown, 600 .... H-9
Flanders, 2200 .... E-9
Flemington, 4581 .... H-8
Florence, 5500 .... K-8
Florham Pk., 11696 .... E-11
Folsom, 1885 .... O-8
Fords, 15187 .... H-11
Forked River, 5244 .... M-12
Ft. Lee, 35345 .... E-13
Fortescue, 500 .... R-6
Foul Rift, 40 .... E-7
Franklin, 5045 .... C-10
Franklin Pk., 13295 ...... H-10
Franklinville, 1500 ...... O-7
Freehold, 12052 .... I-11
Freewood Acres,
  1900 .... I-12
Frenchtown, 1373 .... H-7
Fries Mill, 200 .... N-7
Gandys Bch., 60 .... Q-6
Garfield, 30487 .... A-4
Garwood, 4226 .... †J-3
Georgetown, 60 .... K-9
Germania, 200 .... P-9
Gibbsboro, 2274 .... M-7
Gibbstown, 3739 .... M-5
Gifford Pk., ... L-12
Gillette, 900 .... F-10
Gillwood, 1500 .... H-12
Glassboro, 18579 .... N-6
Glen Gardner, 1704 .... F-7
Glen Ridge, 7527 .... C-2
Glen Rock, 11601 .... †B-7
Glendola, 2400 .... J-13
Glenwood, 200 .... B-10
Gloucester City,
  11456 .... M-6

GLOUCESTER CO.,
  288288 .... O-7
Golf Mnr., 200 .... *D-9
Golf View, 500 .... §D-9
Linvale, 30 .... J-8
Linwood, 7092 .... Q-10
Little Egg Harbor, ...
Little Falls, 11193 ...... A-1
Little Ferry, 10626 ...... B-5
Little York, 500 .... G-7
Livingston, 27391 .... E-11
Loch Arbour, 194 .... J-13
Lodi, 24136 .... C-13
Long Branch, 30719 .... I-13
Long Valley, 1879 .... F-8
Longport, 895 .... Q-10
Greenbank, 700 .... O-9
Greendell, 200 .... D-8
Greenwich, 700 .... P-5
Grenloch, 450 .... M-7
Griggstown, 819 .... H-9
Grouseland, 900 .... M-8
Guttenberg, 11176 .... C-5
Hackensack, 43010 .... E-13
Hacketstown, 9724 .... E-8
Haddonfield, 11593 .... M-7
Hainesburg, 400 .... D-6
Hainesport, 1200 .... L-8
Haledon, 8318 .... A-2
Halsey, 60 ....
Hamburg, 3277 .... C-10
Hamilton Sq., 12784 ...... J-9
Hampton, 1401 .... F-7
Hancocks Br., 254 .... N-4
Hanover, 600 .... E-11
Harding Lakes, 1000 ...... P-8
Harlingen, 297 .... H-9
Harmersville, ... P-5
Harrington, 40 ....
Harrington Pk., ...
4664 .... †A-10
Harrison, 27472 .... D-3
Harrisonville, 200 .... N-5
Harvey Cedars, 337 .... N-12
Hasbrouck Hts.,
  11842 .... A-5
Haven Bch., 200 .... O-12

McAfee...–New Mexico

McAfee, 1400 .... B-10
McKee City, 1200 .... P-9
Meadford Farms,
  100 .... B-10
Meadowbrook Vil.,
  150 .... O-11
Medford, 2400 .... L-8
Medford Lakes,
  4146 .... M-8
Mendham, 4981 .... F-9
Menlo Pk. Ter., ... †M-3

MERCER CO.,
  366513 .... D-10
Mercerville, 13230 .... J-9
Meriden, 80 .... D-10
Metedeconk, ... K-12
Metuchen, 13574 .... G-11
Mickleton, 1200 .... M-6
Middle Valley, 150 .... F-8
Middlebush, 250 .... H-10
Middlesex, 13635 .... G-10

MIDDLESEX CO.,
  809858 .... I-10
Middletown, 24000 .... I-12
Midland Pk., 7000 .... †A-8
Milford, 1233 .... G-6
Millbrook, 100 .... C-7
Millbrook, 1700 .... E-10
Millburn, 19765 .... F-11
Millstone, 2585 .... I-8
Millstone, 2500 .... F-10
Millstone, 418 .... H-9
Millton, 6893 .... H-10
Millville, 28400 .... P-7
Milmay, 350 .... O-8
Milton, 400 .... O-4
Mine Hill, 2800 .... E-9
Mizpah, 1000 .... P-8
Monmouth Bch.,
  3279 .... I-13

MONMOUTH CO.,
  630380 .... J-11
Monmouth Jct., ...
2887 .... I-10
Monroe, 75 .... O-8
Monroeville, 200 .... O-6
Montague, 40 .... A-9
Montclair, 38658 .... C-2
Montvale, 7844 .... C-13
Montville, 2600 .... D-11
Moonachie, 2708 .... B-5
Moorestown, 19000 .... L-7
Morganville, 5040 .... I-12

MORRIS CO.,
  492276 .... E-9
Morris Plains, 5532 ...... E-10
Morristown, 18411 .... E-10
Mt. Airy, 80 .... H-8
Mt. Arlington, 5050 ...... D-9
Mt. Ephraim, 4676 .... §G-6
Mt. Freedom, 1700 .... M-2
Mt. Hermon, 141 .... D-7
Mt. Holly, ...
Mt. Hope, 375 .... D-10
Mt. Laurel, 800 .... L-8
Mt. Royal, 900 .... M-6
Mountain Lakes,
  4160 .... D-11
Mountain View, ... D-11
Mountainville, 78 .... F-8
Mullica Hill, 3882 .... N-6
Mystic Island, 8493 ...... O-11
National Pk., 3036 .... §G-4
Naughright, 100 .... E-8
Navesink, 2020 .... I-13
Neptune, 19000 .... J-13
Neptune City, 4869 .... J-13
Nesco, ... O-9
Neshanic, 150 .... H-9
Neshanic Sta., 500 .... H-9
Netcong, 3232 .... E-9
New Brunswick,
  55181 .... H-11
New Egypt, 2512 .... K-10
New Gretna, 600 .... O-10
New Hampton, 200 .... F-7
New Lisbon, 350 .... L-9
New Market, 20000 .... †L-1
New Milford,
  16341 .... †B-10
New Providence,
  12171 .... F-11
New Sharon, ...
New Vernon, 600 .... F-10
New Vil., 421 .... F-6
Newark, 277140 .... F-12
Newfield, 1553 .... O-7
Newfoundland, 400 .... C-10
Newport, 700 .... Q-6
Newton, 7997 .... C-9
Newtonville, 200 .... O-8
Norma, 400 .... P-7
Normandy Bch., ... K-13
N. Beach, 200 .... M-12
N. Beach Haven,
  2235 .... O-12
N. Bergen, ... C-5
N. Branch, 1300 .... G-9
N. Caldwell, 6183 .... B-1
N. Cape May, 3226 .... T-7
N. Church, 100 .... C-9
N. Haledon, 8417 .... †B-6
N. Plainfield, 21936 ..... G-10
N. Tappan, 5750 .... B-13
Oldwick, 200 .... F-8
Olivet, 1408 .... O-6

Oradell, 7978 .... †B-9
Orange, 32868 .... D-2
Ortley Bch., 1500 .... L-13
Osbornsville, ... K-12
Othello, ... O-5
Oxford, 1090 .... E-7
Oyster Creek, ... P-11
Palermo, 1200 .... R-9
Palisades Pk., 19622 ..... B-6
Paramus, 26342 .... D-13
Parkertown, 800 .... O-11
Parkway Pines,
  .... K-12
Parsippany, ... E-10
Passaic, 69781 .... C-13

PASSAIC CO.,
  501226 .... C-11
Paterson, 146199 .... D-12
Paulins, 200 .... E-8
Paulsboro, 6097 .... M-6
Peapack & Gladstone,
  2582 .... F-9
Pedricktown, 524 .... N-4
Pellettown, 50 .... C-9
Pemberton, 1409 .... L-9
Pennington, 2585 .... I-8
Penns Grv., 5147 .... N-4
Pennsville, 11888 .... N-4
Penton, 70 .... O-4
Pennwell, 50 .... F-8
Pequannock, 200 .... D-11
Perrineville, 400 .... J-10
Perth Amboy,
  50814 .... H-11
Petersburg, 900 .... R-9
Phillipsburg, 1495 ...... C-6
Pierces Pt., 40 .... S-8
Pine Bch., 217 .... L-12
Pine Hill, 10233 .... M-7
Pine Lake Pk., 8707 ...... L-12
Pinewald, 1700 .... M-12
Piscataway, 56044 .... H-10
Pitman, 9011 .... N-6
Pittstown, 600 .... G-7
Plainfield, 49808 .... G-10
Plainsboro, 2000 .... I-10
Pleasant Grv., ... F-9
Pleasant Mills, ... O-9
Pleasant Plains, ... L-12
Pleasant Run, ... G-9
Pleasant Valley, 200 .... F-7
Pleasantville, ...
20249 .... Q-10
Pluckemin, 300 .... G-9
Plumbsock, ... B-9
Pt. Pleasant, 18392 ...... K-13
Pt. Pleasant Bch.,
  4665 .... K-13
Pointers, 200 .... O-4
Polkville, ... D-10
Pomona, 7124 .... P-10
Pompton Lakes,
  11097 .... D-11
Pompton Plains, ... D-11
Port Colden, 122 .... F-7
Port Elizabeth, 650 ...... Q-7
Port Monmouth,
  3818 .... H-12
Port Murray, 129 .... E-8
Port Norris, 1377 .... R-7
Port Reading, 3782 ...... †L-5
Port Republic, 1115 ...... O-10
Potterstown, 100 .... G-8
Pottersville, 600 .... F-9
Princeton, 12307 .... I-9
Princeton Jct., 2465 ..... I-9
Prospect Pk., 5865 ...... †B-6
Pumptown, 2000 .... †L-2
Quakertown, 200 .... G-7
Quinton, 588 .... O-4
Rahway, 27346 .... †K-4
Ralston, 150 .... F-9
Ramblewood, 5907 .... L-7
Ramsey, 14473 .... C-12
Ramtown, 6242 .... K-12
Rancocas, 600 .... K-8
Rancocas Hts., 750 ...... §D-10
Rancocas Woods,
  1400 .... L-8
Raritan, 6881 .... G-9
Raven Rock, ... H-7
Readington, 500 .... G-8
Red Bank, 12206 .... I-13
Red Lion, ... L-9
Reds Bch., 70 .... S-8
Repaupo, 100 .... M-5
Richland, 600 .... P-7
Richwood, 3450 .... N-6
Ridgefield, 11032 ...... †B-5
Ridgefield Pk., 12729 ... B-5
Ridgeway, ... L-11
Ridgewood, 24958 .... †A-7
Riegel Ridge, 250 .... G-6
Riegelsville, 500 .... G-6
Ringoes, 600 .... H-8
Ringwood, 12228 .... C-11
Rio Grande, 2670 .... S-8

Waretown, 1569 .... M-12
WARREN CO.,
  108692 .... E-8
Warren Glen, 300 .... G-6
Warrenville, 1000 .... G-10
Washington, 6461 .... †J-7
Washington Crossing,
  500 .... I-8
Watchung, 5801 .... G-10
Waterford Works,
  1000 .... M-8
Wayne, 54069 .... D-11
Weehawken D-5
Weekstown, 140 .... O-9
Wenonah, 2278 .... M-6
W. Atlantic City,
  900 .... Q-10
W. Cape May, 1024 .... †T-7
W. Collingswood Hts.,
  .... §G-5
W. Creek, 800 .... O-11
W. Freehold, 13613 .... J-11
W. Keansburg,
  1500 .... H-12
W. Long Branch,
  8097 .... I-13
W. Milford, 26410 .... C-11
W. New York,
  49708 .... C-5
W. Orange, 44943 .... F-12
W. Paterson, 10987 ...... A-2
W. Portal, 100 .... G-7
W. Tuckerton, 700 .... O-11
W. Wildwood, 603 .... T-8
Westfield, 30316 .... †J-3
Westville, 4500 .... M-6
Westville Grv.,
  1500 .... §G-5
W. Creek, 800 ....
Weymouth, 200 .... P-8
Wharton, 6522 .... E-10
Whippany F-10
White Horse, 9494 .... T-13
White House Sta.,
  2089 .... G-8
Whitehouse, 800 .... G-9
Whitesbog, 1100 .... L-10
Whitesville, 120 .... K-11
Whiting, 950 .... L-11
Whitman Sq., 3500 .... N-7
Wickatunk, 300 .... I-12
Wildwood, 5325 .... T-8
Wildwood Crest,
  3270 .... T-8
Williamstown,
  15567 .... N-7
Willingboro K-8
Willow Grv., ...
Windsor, 250 .... J-9
Winslow, 800 .... N-8
Woodbine, 2472 .... R-8
Woodbridge, 19265 ...... G-11
Woodbury, 10174 .... M-6
Woodbury Hts., ...
3055 .... M-6
Wood-Lynne, 2978 .... §F-5
Woodport, 200 .... D-9
Wood-Ridge, 7626 .... B-4
Woodruff, 70 .... P-8
Woods Tavern, 200 .... H-12
Woodstown, 3505 .... N-5
Wrightstown, 802 .... K-9
Wyckoff, 16508 .... D-12
Yardville, 7186 .... J-9
Yellow Frame, ... F-8
Yorketown, 50 .... D-13
Zarephath, 37 .... G-10

New Mexico

Page locator
Map keys ... Atlas pages
A–N ... 138–139

Abbott, ... C-8
Abiquiu, 231 .... C-5
Acoma, 400 .... E-3
Acomita, 800 .... E-3
Adobe Acres, 2500 .... N-8
Agua Fria, 2800 .... M-4
Alameda, ...
Alamillo, 102 .... F-4
Alamogordo, 30403 .... J-6
Albuquerque, 545852 ...... E-4
Alcalde, 285 .... C-5
Algodones, 814 .... D-5
Alma, 100 .... H-1
Alto, 800 .... K-6
Amalia, 200 .... B-6
Ambrosia Lake, 250 ...... D-2
Amistad, 30 .... C-10
Ancho, 200 .... J-6
Angel Fire, 1216 .... B-7
Animas, 237 .... J-1
Antelope Wells, ...
Anthony, 9360 .... J-5
Anton Chico, 188 .... E-7
Arabela, 200 .... J-7
Aragon, 10 .... G-2
Arch, ... K-10
Arenas Valley, 1522 ..... I-2
Arrey, 232 .... I-4
Arroyo Hondo, 474 .... B-6
Arroyo Seco, 1785 .... B-6
Artesia, 10692 .... I-8
Atoka, 1077 .... I-8
Aztec, 6763 .... B-3
Bard, ... F-10
Bayard, 2328 .... I-2
Beaverhead, 30 .... H-2
Belen, 7269 .... F-4
Bell Ranch, 20 .... D-8
Belling, ...
Bent, 600 .... K-6
Bernal, 100 .... D-7
Berino, 1441 .... J-5
Black Lake, ... C-7

BERNALILLO CO.,
  662564 .... E-4
Black Lake, ... C-7
Black River Vil., ... J-8
Black Rock, 1323 .... D-1
Blanco, 388 .... B-3
Bloomfield, 8112 .... B-3
Bluewater, 628 .... D-2
Boles, 450 .... I-5
Bosque Farms, 3904 ..... E-4

Brazos, 44 .... B-5
Broadview, 30 .... E-10
Buckhorn, 200 .... I-1
Bueyeros, 30 .... C-9
Butterfield Pk., 500 ... J-4
Caballo, 117 .... I-4
Canjilon, 256 .... B-5
Canon, 327 .... D-4
Capitan, 1489 .... J-6
Caprock, 30 .... H-9
Capulin, 66 .... B-8
Carlsbad, 26138 .... J-8
Carrizozo, 996 .... J-6

CATRON CO., 3725 .... G-2
Causey, 110 .... G-9
Cebolla, 100 .... B-5
Cedar Crest, 958 .... E-5
Cedar Hill, 847 .... A-3
Cedarvale, 20 .... F-6
Cerro, 250 .... B-6
Chacon, 250 .... C-6
Chama, 1022 .... B-5
Chamberino, 919 .... J-5
Chamisal, 310 .... C-6
Chaparral, 14631 .... J-5

CHAVES CO.,
  65645 .... G-9
Chilili, 137 .... E-5
Chimayo, 3177 .... C-6
Chloride, 50 .... H-3
Church Rock, 1128 ...... D-2

CIBOLA CO., 27213 ...... E-2
Cimarron, 1021 .... B-7
Claunch, 3025 .... G-5
Clayton, 2980 .... B-10
Cliff, 293 .... I-2
Clines Corners, 90 ..... E-6
Cloudcroft, 674 .... J-6
Clovis, 37775 .... F-10
Cochiti, 528 .... D-4

COLFAX CO.,
  13750 .... B-7
Colonias, 30 .... E-7
Columbus, 1664 .... K-3
Conchas Dam, 186 ...... D-8
Continental Divide,
  250 .... D-2
Cordova, 414 .... C-6
Corona, 172 .... G-6
Corrales, 8329 .... E-4
Costilla, 205 .... A-6
Cotton City, 388 ...... J-1
Counselor, 40 .... C-4
Coyote, 128 .... C-5
Coyote Canyon, 200 .... D-2
Crossroads, 90 .... H-10
Crownpoint, 2278 ...... D-2
Cruzville, 2 .... G-1
Crystal, 311 .... C-1
Cuba, 731 .... C-4
Cubero, 289 .... E-3
Cuchillo, 70 .... H-3
Cuervo, 90 .... E-7

CURRY CO., 48376 ...... F-9
Dalton Pass, 100 ...... D-2
Datil, 54 .... G-3

DE BACA CO., 2022 ..... F-8
Deming, 14855 .... J-3
Derry, 120 .... I-4
Des Moines, 143 .... B-9
Dexter, 1266 .... H-8
Dilia, 80 .... D-7
Dixon, 926 .... C-6
Dona Ana, 1211 .... J-4

DONA ANA CO.,
  209233 .... J-4
Dora, 133 .... G-10
Dulce, 2743 .... B-4
Duran, 35 .... F-6
Dusty, 30 .... H-3
Eagle Nest, 290 .... B-7

EDDY CO., 53829 .... J-8
Edgewood, 3735 .... E-5
El Morro, 100 ....
El Porvenir, 100 ...... D-6
El Rito, 808 .... C-5
El Pueblo, 50 .... D-6
El Rito, 808 .... C-5
El Vado, 20 .... B-4
Elephant Butte,
  1431 .... I-4
Elida, 197 .... G-9
Elk, ... K-7
Encino, 82 .... F-6
Engle, ... I-4
Ensenada, 107 .... B-5
Escabosa, 150 .... E-5
Espanola, 10224 ..... C-5
Estancia, 1655 ...... E-5
Eunice, 2922 .... I-10
Fairacres, 824 ...... J-4
Farley, ... C-8
Farmington, 45877 ... B-3
Fence Lake, 42 ...... F-1
Field, ...
Five Points, 4200 ... M-8
Flora Vista, 2191 ... B-3
Floyd, 133 .... G-9
Flying H, 50 .... H-7
Folsom, 56 .... B-9
Forrest, 60 .... F-9
Ft. Stanton, 100 ... J-6
Ft. Sumner, 1031 ... F-8
Ft. Wingate, 950 ... D-2
Fruitland, ...
Tucumcari, 3347 .... D-11
Galisteo, 253 ...... D-5
Gallina, 286 .... C-4
Gamerco, 400 .... D-1
Garfield, 137 ...... I-4
Gascon, ... C-6
Gila, 314 .... I-2
Gila Hot Sprs., 40 . H-2
Gladstone, 20 ..... C-9
Glenrio, 30 .... E-11
Glenwood, 143 ..... H-1
Glorieta, 430 ..... D-6
Golden, 37 .... E-5
Gonzales Ranch, 40 . E-6
Grady, 107 .... E-9
Gran Quivira, 150 .. F-5

GRANT CO., 29514 ... I-1
Grants, 9182 .... E-3
Grenville, 38 ..... B-9

GUADALUPE CO.,
  4687 .... E-7
Guadalupita, 250 ... C-7
Hachita, 49 .... J-2
Hagerman, 1257 .... H-8
Hanover, 167 ...... I-2

HARDING CO., 695 ... C-9
Hatch, 1648 .... I-4
Hayden, ...

HIDALGO CO.,
4894 ....K-1
High Rolls, 834 ....I-6
Hillsboro, 124 ....I-5
Hobbs, 34122 ....I-10
Holman, 250 ....C-6
Hondo, 250 ....H-7
Hope, 105 ....I-7
Hospah, 160 ....D-3
House, 68 ....F-9
Humble City, 160 ....I-9
Hurley, 1297 ....I-2
Ilfeld, 100 ....C-6
Isleta Pueblo E-4
Jal, 2047 ....I-10
Jarales, 2475 ....E-4
Jemez Pueblo, 1788 ......D-4
Jemez Sprs., 250 ....D-4
Kenna, 30 ....G-9
Kingston, 32 ....I-3
Kirtland, 7875 ....B-2
La Cienega, 3819 ....D-5
La Jara, 207 ....C-4
La Joya, 82 ....D-4
La Luz, 1697 ....I-6
La Mesa, 728 ....I-4
La Plata, 612 ....A-2
La Puebla, 1186 ....C-5
La Puente, 80 ....B-5
La Union, 1106 ....K-4
Laguna, 1241 ....E-3
L. Arthur, 436 ....I-8
L. Valley, 64 ....C-2
Lakewood, 100 ....I-8
LaMadera, 154 ....B-5
Lamy, 218 ....D-6
Las Cruces, 97618 ....I-4
Las Nutrias, 149 ....F-4
Las Palomas, 173 ....I-4
Las Vegas, 13753 ....D-7
LEA CO., 64727 ....H-9
Ledoux, 180 ....C-6
Lemitar, 330 ....C-4
Lincoln, 100 ....H-6
LINCOLN CO.,
20497 ....G-6
Lindrith, 50 ....C-4
Lingo, 20 ....G-10
Loco Hills, 129 ....I-9
Logan, 1042 ....G-9
Lordsburg, 2797 ....I-1
Los Alamos, 12019 ....C-5
LOS ALAMOS CO.,
17950 ....C-5
Los Cerrillos, 321 ....D-5
Los Chavez, 5446 ....F-4
Los Lunas, 14835 ....E-4
Los Montoyas D-7
Los Padillas, 2500 ....E-4
Los Pinos, 30 ....D-7
Los Ranchos de
  Albuquerque, 6024 ...I-8
Loving, 1413 ....I-8
Lovington, 11009 ....I-10
Luis Lopez, 107 ....G-4
Lumberton, 73 ....B-4
Luna, 158 ....C-2
LUNA CO., 25095 ...J-2
Madrid, 204 ....D-5
Magdalena, 938 ....G-4
Malaga, 147 ....J-8
Maljamar, 200 ....I-9
Manuelito, 203 ....D-1
Manzano, 29 ....E-5
Mariano Lake D-2
Maxwell, 254 ....B-8
Mayhill, 75 ....I-6
McAlister, 60 ....F-9
McCartys, 48 ....E-3
McDonald, 50 ....G-10
McIntosh, 184 ....E-5
MCKINLEY CO.,
71492 ....D-3
Melrose, 651 ....E-9
Mentmore, 200 ....D-1
Mescalero, 1338 ....H-6
Mesilla, 2196 ....I-4
Mesquite, 1112 ....I-4
Miami, 100 ....C-7
Midway, 971 ....H-9
Milan, 3245 ....D-3
Mills, 50 ....D-7
Milnesand, 30 ....G-10
Mimbres, 667 ....I-2
Mogollon, 30 ....B-4
Monero B-4
Montezuma, 200 ....D-7
Monticello, 80 ....H-3
Montoya, 30 ....F-8
Mora, 656 ....C-6
MORA CO., 4881 ....C-7
Moriarty, 1910 ....E-5
Mosquero, 93 ....D-9
Mt. Dora, 100 ....C-8
Mountainair, 928 ....F-5
Mule Creek, 30 ....H-1
Nadine, 76 ....I-9
Nageezi, 286 ....C-3
Nara Visa, 95 ....D-10
Naschitti, 301 ....C-2
Navajo, 1645 ....C-1
Newcomb, 339 ....C-2
Newkirk, 71 ....E-8
Nogal, 96 ....H-6
Ocate, 50 ....C-7
Oil City H-9
Ojito B-4
Ojo Caliente, 350 ....C-5
Ojo Caliente E-1
Ojo Feliz, 80 ....C-7
Old Albuquerque M-8
Old Horse Sprs. G-2
Old Picacho, 200 ....M-1
Omega, 30 ....H-2
Organ, 323 ....J-5
Orogrande, 52 ....J-6
Otis, 150 ....I-8
OTERO CO., 63797 ..I-6
Paguate, 420 ....E-4
Paradise Hills, 4256 ......K-7
Parajel, 777 ....E-3
Pastura, 23 ....E-7
Pecos, 1392 ....D-6
Pena Blanca, 709 ....D-5
Penasco, 589 ....C-6
Pep, 30 ....G-10
Peralta, 3660 ....E-4
Petaca, 90 ....B-5
Picacho, 100 ....H-7
Pie Town, 186 ....F-2
Pilar, 80 ....C-6
Pinedale, 30 ....D-2
Pinon, 25 ....I-6
Pinos Altos, 198 ....I-2
Placitas, 4977 ....D-5
Playas, 74 ....J-1
Pleasanton, 106 ....H-1
Pojoaque Valley,
  1907 ....C-5
Polvadera, 269 ....F-4
Portales, 12280 ....F-10
Prewitt, 460 ....D-2
Pueblo Pintado, 192 .....C-3
Puerto De Luna, 141 .....E-8
Punta de Agua, 30 ....E-5
QUAY CO., 9041 ....E-9
Quemado, 228 ....F-2
Questa, 1770 ....B-6
Radium Sprs., 1699 ......I-4
Rainsville, 50 ....C-7
Ramah, 370 ....D-2
Ranchos de Taos,
  2518 ....C-6
Raton, 6885 ....B-8
Red Hill, 80 ....F-1
Red River, 477 ....B-6
Redrock, 50 ....I-1
Regina, 105 ....C-4
Reserve, 289 ....G-1
Ribera, 416 ....D-6
Rincon, 271 ....I-4
RIO ARRIBA CO.,
40246 ....B-4
Rio Rancho, 87521 ....C-4
Riverside, 80 ....I-8
Rodeo, 101 ....K-1
Rogers, 50 ....G-10
Romeroville C-7
ROOSEVELT CO.,
19846 ....G-9
Roswell, 48366 ....H-8
Rowe, 415 ....D-6
Roy, 234 ....C-8
Ruidoso, 8029 ....H-6
Ruidoso Downs,
  2815 ....H-6
Rutherton, 100 ....B-5
ALBANY CO.,
304204 ....NK-8
Albertson, 5182 ....†G-17
Albia SI-6
Albion, 6056 ....NH-6
Alcove, 200 ....NK-18
Alden, 2605 ....NJ-5
Alden Manor ....†F-16
Alder Creek, 450 ....NH-14
Alexander, 509 ....NJ-5
Alexandria Bay,
  1078 ....ND-12
Alfred, 4174 ....NL-7
Alfred Sta., 590 ....NL-7
Allegany, 1816 ....NM-5
Allentown, 350 ....NM-4
Alligerville, 135 ....NN-18
Alloway, 100 ....N-5
Alma, 225 ....NM-6
Almond, 466 ....NL-7
Alpine, 250 ....NL-10
Altamont, 1720 ....NJ-18
Altay, 400 ....NL-9
Altmar, 407 ....NG-12
Alton, 550 ....NH-8
Altona, 730 ....NB-19
Amagansett, 1165 ....SE-13
Amawalk, 1390 ....SD-7
Amber, 350 ....NJ-11
Amboy Ctr. NH-12
Amboy Cty. NF-12
Amenia, 955 ....NN-20
Ames, 145 ....NJ-16
Amherst, 45800 ....NJ-4
Amity, 60 ....SD-5
Amityville, 9523 ....SJ-10
Amsterdam,
  18929 ....NJ-17
Ancram, 450 ....NM-19
Ancramdale, 500 ....NM-19
Andes, 252 ....NM-16
Andover, 1042 ....NM-7
Angelica, 869 ....NL-6
Angola, 2127 ....NK-3
Angola-on-the-Lake,
  1675 ....NK-3
Annadale *M-6
Annandale-on-Hudson,
  100 ....NM-18
Antwerp, 686 ....ND-13
Apalachin, 1131 ....NM-12
Appleton, 200 ....NH-4
Apulia Sta., 300 ....NJ-12
Arcade, 2071 ....NK-5
Arden, 100 ....SD-6
Argyle, 306 ....NH-20
Arkport, 844 ....NL-7
Arlington, 4061 ....SB-7
Armonk, 4330 ....SD-7
Armor, 1550 ....NK-4
Arthursburg, 215 ....SB-7
Arverne ....†T-14
Asharoken, 654 ....SE-9
Ashford, 70 ....NK-5
Ashville, 800 ....NM-3
Athens, 1668 ....NL-19
Athol, 250 ....NG-18
Atlanta, 150 ....NL-8
Atlantic Bch., 1891 ......SG-7
Attica, 2547 ....NJ-5
Atwell, 20 ....NH-15
Au Sable Forks,
  623 ....NC-19
Auburn, 27687 ....NJ-10
Auburndale ....†G-14
Augusta, 100 ....NJ-14
Austerlitz, 400 ....NL-19
Ava, 300 ....NG-13
Averill Pk., 1693 ....NK-19
Avoca, 946 ....NL-8
Avon, 3394 ....NJ-7
Babylon, 12166 ....SJ-11
Bainbridge, 1355 ....NL-14
Baiting Hollow SH-12
Bakers Mills, 280 ....NG-18
Baldwin, 24033 ....†J-8
Baldwin Hbr., 8102 .....†J-18
Baldwinsville,
  7378 ....NJ-11
Ballston Spa, 5409 ......NI-19
Balmat, 100 ....ND-14
Balmville, 3178 ....SB-6
Bangor, 300 ....NB-17
Barker, 533 ....NH-5
Barnes Cors., 150 ....NF-13
Barneveld, 244 ....NH-14
Barryville, 600 ....SC-3
Barton, 300 ....NM-11
Basom, 200 ....NI-5
Batavia, 15465 ....NI-6
Batchellerville, 70 ....NH-18
Bath, 5786 ....NL-8
Bath Bch. *K-10
Bayberry ....†H-14
Bay Pk., 2212 ....†J-17
Bay Ridge *K-9
Bay Shore, 26337 ....SF-9
Bayberry, 6200 ....ND-7
Baychester ....†D-13
Bayport, 8896 ....SJ-14
Bayside ....†G-15
Bayville, 6669 ....SE-8
Beach Ridge NI-4
Beacon, 15541 ....SC-6
Bearsville, 300 ....NM-18
Beaver Dams, 600 ......NL-9
Beaver Falls, 700 ....NF-14
Beaver Meadow,
  100 ....NK-5
Bedford, 1834 ....SD-8
Bedford Hills, 3001 .....SD-7
Bedford-Stuyvesant ...†J-11
Beechhurst ....†F-14
Beekmantown,
  300 ....NB-19
Belfast, 837 ....NL-6
Belfort, 50 ....NF-14
Belle Terre, 792 ....SE-10
Bellerose, 1193 ....†H-16
Bellerose Ter. ....
Belleville, 226 ....NF-12
Bellmore, 16218 ....†J-20
Bellport, 2084 ....SF-10
Bellvale, 200 ....SD-5
Belmont, 969 ....NL-6
Bemus Pt., 364 ....NM-3
Benedict, 110 ....NL-10
Bennington, 200 ....NJ-5
Benson, 100 ....NH-17
Benton Ctr., 200 ....NJ-9
Bergholtz, 700 ....NI-4
Bergen, 1176 ....NI-6
Berkshire, 350 ....NL-12
Berlin, 1200 ....NJ-20
Berne, 600 ....NK-18
Bernhards Bay,
  400 ....NH-12
Bethany Ctr., 200 ....NJ-6
Bethel, 350 ....SB-3
Bethpage, 16429 ....†G-20
Big Flats, 5277 ....NM-9
Big Indian, 350 ....NM-17
Big Moose, 75 ....NF-15
Billings, 450 ....SB-7
Binghamton,
  47376 ....NM-12
Birdsall, 50 ....NL-6
Black Brook, 200 ....NC-19
Black Creek, 250 ....NL-5
Black River, 1348 ....NE-13
Bladsell, 2553 ....NJ-4
Blauvelt, 5689 ....SE-7
Bleecker, 115 ....NH-17
Bliss, 527 ....NK-5
Blodgett Mills,
  303 ....NK-12
Bloomfield, 1361 ....NJ-8
Bloomingburg, 420 .....SB-5
Bloomingdale,
  800 ....NB-18
Bloomville, 213 ....NL-16
Blossvale, 500 ....NH-13
Blue Mtn. Lake,
  100 ....NF-17
Blue Pt., 4773 ....SJ-14
Blue Ridge ....†L-13
Boardwalk ....†L-13
Bolton, 2200 ....NG-19
Bolton Landing,
  600 ....NG-18
Bombay, 300 ....NA-16
Boonville, 2072 ....NG-14
Borden, 40 ....NM-8
Border City, 500 ....NJ-9
Bordolino, 100 ....NJ-11
Boston, 500 ....NK-4
Bouckville, 450 ....NJ-13
Bovina Ctr., 200 ....NL-16
Bowmansville, 600 .....NI-4
Braddock Hts., 700 .....ND-7
Bradford, 200 ....NL-9
Brainardsville,
  200 ....NB-20
Branchport, 400 ....NK-9
Brant, 600 ....NK-3
Brant Lake, 850 ....NF-19
Brantingham, 300 ......NF-14
Brasher Ctr., 85 ....NB-16
Brasher Falls, 669 ......NB-16
Brasher Iron Works,
  175 ....NB-16
Brasie Cors., 30 ....ND-13
Breakabeen, 80 ....NK-17
Breesport, 626 ....NM-10
Breezy Pt. ....†L-11
Brentwood, 60664 ......SF-9
Brewerton, 4000 ....NH-11
Brewster, 2390 ....SC-8
Briarcliff Mnr., 7867 ...SD-7
Bridgehampton,
  1756 ....SE-13
Bridgeport, 1490 ....NI-12
Bridgewater, 470 ....NJ-14
Brier Hill, 400 ....NC-13
Brighton, 36609 ....NI-7
Brightwaters, 3103 .....SJ-12
Bristol, 100 ....NJ-8
Bristol Sprs., 120 ....NJ-8
Broad Channel ....†K-14
Broadalbin, 1327 ....NI-17
Brockport, 8366 ....NI-7
Brockton, 1486 ....NL-3
Bronxville, 6323 ....†B-13
Brookfield, 600 ....NJ-14
Brooktondale, 500 .....NL-11
Brookville, 3465 ....†E-19
BROOME CO.,
200600 ....NM-12
Brownsville ....†J-12
Brownville, 1119 ....NE-12
Brunswick, 800 ....NJ-20
Brushton, 474 ....NB-16
Buchanan, 2230 ....SD-6
Bucks Br., 40 ....NB-15
Buffalo, 261310 ....NJ-4
Bullville, 900 ....SB-5
Burdett, 340 ....NL-10
Burke, 211 ....NB-17
Burlingham, 500 ....SB-5
Burlington Flats,
  100 ....NJ-15
Burns, 150 ....NL-7
Burnt Hills, 1620 ....NI-18
Burnville, 100 ....NH-13
Burt, 400 ....NH-4
Burtonsville, 100 ....NJ-17
Bushnellsville,
  200 ....NM-17
Bushwick ....†J-12
Busti, 350 ....NM-2
Byron, 400 ....NI-6
Cadosia, 300 ....NM-14
Cadyville, 900 ....NB-19
Cairo, 1402 ....NL-18
Calcium, 3491 ....NE-13
Caledonia, 2261 ....NJ-7
Callicoon, 167 ....SA-2
Callicoon Ctr., 430 .....NN-15
Calverton, 6510 ....SE-11
Cambria Hts. ....†I-15
Cambridge, 1870 ....NI-20
Camden, 2231 ....NH-13
Cameron, 200 ....NM-8
Cameron Mills,
  125 ....NM-8
Camillus, 1213 ....NI-11
Campbell, 713 ....NL-9
Campbell Hall, 650 .....SC-5
Campville, 350 ....NM-12
Canaan, 450 ....NL-20
Canajoharie, 2229 .....NJ-16
Canandaigua,
  10545 ....NJ-8
Canaseraga, 500 ....NK-7
Canastota, 4804 ....NI-13
Candor, 851 ....NL-11
Caneadea, 900 ....NL-6
Canisteo, 2270 ....NL-7
Canton, 6314 ....NC-14
Cape Vincent, 726 .....NE-11
Cardiff, 150 ....NJ-11
Carle Pl., 4981 ....†G-18
Carlisle, 700 ....NJ-17
Carmel, 3600 ....SC-7
Caroga Lake, 518 ....NI-17
Caroline, 70 ....NL-11
Carrollton, 100 ....NM-4
Carthage, 3747 ....NE-13
Cassadaga, 634 ....NL-2
Cassville, 250 ....NJ-14
Castile, 1015 ....NK-6
Castle Creek, 400 ......NL-12
Castleton Corners *K-7
Castleton-on-Hudson,
  1473 ....NK-19
Castorland, 351 ....NF-14
Catharine, 100 ....NL-10
Cato, 532 ....NI-10
Caton, 150 ....NM-9
Catskill, 4081 ....NL-19
Cattaraugus, 1002 ....NL-4
Caughdenoy, 150 ......NH-12
Cayuga, 549 ....NJ-10
Cayuga Hts., 3729 .....NK-11
Cayuta, 200 ....NL-10
Cazenovia, 2835 ....NJ-13
Cedar Hill, 300 ....NK-19
Cedarhurst, 6592 ......†K-16
Cedarville, 200 ....NJ-15
Celoron, 1112 ....NM-2
Center Moriches,
  7580 ....SF-11
Centereach, 31578 ....SF-10
Centerport, 5508 ......SE-9
Centerville, 250 ....NK-5
Central Br., 593 ....NJ-17
Central Islip, 34450 ...SF-9
Central Sq., 1848 ......NH-12
Central Valley, 200 ....SD-6
Ceres, 400 ....NM-5
Chadwicks, 1506 ......NI-14
Chaffee, 350 ....NK-4
Chambers, 500 ....NM-9
Champion, 110 ....NE-13
Champlain, 1101 ....NA-19
Champlain Pk. ....
Chapin, 180 ....NJ-8
Chappaqua, 1436 .....SD-7
Charleston *M-5
Charleston Four Cors. ...
Charlotte, 320 ....NI-16
Charlton, 320 ....NI-18
Chase Lake, 75 ....NF-15
Chase Mills, 250 ....NB-15
Chasm Falls NB-17
Chateaugay, 834 ....NA-17
Chatham, 1770 ....NL-19
Chaumont, 624 ....NE-12
Chautauqua, 191 ......NL-2
CHAUTAUQUA CO.,
134905 ....NL-2
Chazy, 565 ....NB-19
Chazy, 100 ....NB-20
Cheektowaga,
  75178 ....NI-5
Chemung, 600 ....NM-10
Chemung Ctr., 250 .....NM-10
Chenango Br.,
  2883 ....NM-12
CHENANGO CO.,
50477 ....NK-13
Chenango Forks,
  500 ....NL-13
Cheneys Pt., 300 ....NJ-11
Cherry Creek, 461 ......NL-3
Cherry Valley, 520 .....NJ-16
Cherryplain, 300 ....NK-20
Cheshire, 250 ....NJ-8
Chester, 3969 ....SC-5
Chestertown, 677 ......NG-19
Childwold, 100 ....ND-16
Chili Ctr., 4350 ....NI-7
Chippewa Bay,
  350 ....ND-13
Chittenango, 5081 ....NI-13
Choconut Ctr., 250 ....SB-11
Churchtown, 300 ....NM-19
Churchville, 1961 ......NI-7
Churubusco, 200 ....NA-18
Cicero, 1100 ....NI-12
Cincinnatus, 400 ....NK-13
Circleville, 1350 ....SC-5
Clarence, 2646 ....NI-4
Clarence Ctr., 2257 ...NI-4
Clarendon, 350 ....NH-6
Clark Mills, 1905 ....NI-14
Clarks Mills, 130 ....NI-19
Clarkson, 4358 ....NH-6
Clarksville, 800 ....NK-18
Claryville, 100 ....NN-16
Claverack, 1000 ....NL-19
Clay, 700 ....NI-11
Clayburg, 100 ....NB-18
Clayton, 1978 ....ND-12
Clayville, 350 ....NI-14
Clemons, 100 ....NG-20
Clermont, 500 ....NM-19
Cleveland, 750 ....NH-12
Cleverdale, 500 ....NG-19
Clifton, 150 ....NL-3
Clifton *K-8
Clifton Pk., 1200 ....NI-16
Clifton Sprs., 2127 .....NI-9
Climax, 165 ....NL-18
Clinton, 1942 ....NI-14
CLINTON CO.,
82128 ....NB-19
Clinton Cors., 450 ......NN-19
Clinton Pk., 880 ....SJ-5
Clintondale, 1452 ......SB-6
Clintonville, 200 ....NC-19
Clyde, 2093 ....NI-9
Clymer, 600 ....NM-1
Cobleskill, 4678 ....NK-17
Cochecton, 200 ....SA-2
Coeymans Hollow,
  500 ....NK-18
Cohocton, 838 ....NK-8
Cohoes, 15066 ....NJ-19
Cold Brook, 329 ....NH-15
Cold Spr., 2013 ....SC-6
Cold Spr. Hbr.,
  5070 ....SH-10
Cold Sprs., 650 ....NE-7
Colden, 550 ....NK-4
College Pt. ....†F-13
Colliersville, 150 ....NK-15
Collins, 500 ....NK-3
Collins Ctr., 480 ....NK-4
Colonial Vil. NA-2
Colonie, 7793 ....NI-19
Colosse, 120 ....NH-12
Colton, 345 ....NC-15
Columbus, 150 ....NK-14
Commack, 36124 ......SF-9
Comstock, 350 ....NG-20
Conesus, 400 ....NJ-7
Conesville, 150 ....NL-17
Conewango, 50 ....NL-3
Conewango Valley,
  400 ....NL-3
Coney Island *L-10
Congers, 8363 ....SD-7
Conifer, 70 ....ND-16
Conklin, 300 ....NM-13
Connelly Pk., 100 ......NM-2
Conquest, 75 ....NI-10
Constable, 350 ....NA-17
Constableville,
  242 ....NG-14
Constantia, 1182 ....NH-12
Cooks Falls, 200 ....NN-15
Coopers Plains,
  598 ....NM-9
Cooperstown,
  1852 ....NK-15
Coopersville, 210 ......NA-20
Copake, 1200 ....NM-20
Copake Falls, 500 ......NM-20
Copenhagen, 801 ......NF-13
Coram, 39113 ....SF-10
Corbett, 150 ....NM-15
Corbettsville, 460 .....NM-13
Coreys, 130 ....ND-17
Corfu, 709 ....NI-5
Corinth, 2559 ....NH-19
Corning, 11183 ....NM-9
Cornwall-on-Hudson,
  3018 ....SC-6
Cornwallville, 130 .....NL-18
Corona ....†G-13
Cortland, 19204 ....NK-12
CORTLAND CO.,
49336 ....NK-12
Cossayuna, 350 ....NH-20
Cottage, 110 ....NL-3
Cove Neck, 286 ....†D-20
Coventry, 250 ....NL-13
Coventryville, 85 ....NL-13
Covington, 180 ....NJ-6
Cowlesville, 50 ....NJ-5
Coxsackie, 2813 ....NL-19
Cragsmoor, 449 ....SB-5
Cranberry Creek,
  225 ....NH-17
Cranberry Lake,
  200 ....ND-16
Crary Mills, 120 ....NC-15
Craryville, 600 ....NM-19
Crescent, 500 ....NI-19
Crittenden, 250 ....NI-5
Croghan, 618 ....NF-14
Cropseyville, 200 ......NJ-20
Cross River, 980 ....SD-8
Croton Falls, 200 ......SC-7
Croton-on-Hudson,
  8070 ....SD-7
Crown Pt., 1000 ....NE-20
Cuba, 1575 ....NM-5
Cuddebackville,
  1100 ....SC-4
Curriers, 110 ....NK-5
Cutchogue, 3349 ......SE-12
Cutting, 90 ....NM-2
Cuyler, 150 ....NK-13
Cuylerville, 97 ....NJ-7
Dalton, 362 ....NK-6
Damascus, 200 ....NM-14
Danby, 250 ....NL-11
Dannemora, 3936 .....NB-19
Dansville, 4719 ....NK-7
Darien, 300 ....NJ-5
Darien Ctr., 700 ....NJ-5
Davenport, 450 ....NK-16
Davenport Ctr.,
  349 ....NK-16
Davis Pk. SJ-14
Dayton, 350 ....NL-3
De Kalb, 100 ....NC-14
De Kalb Jct., 519 ......NC-14
De Lancey, 110 ....NL-15
De Peyster, 300 ....NC-14
De Witt NI-12
Deansboro, 500 ....NI-14
Deer Pk., 27745 ....SF-9
Deer River, 300 ....NF-13
Deferiet, 294 ....NE-13
Defreestville, 960 .....NK-19
Degrasse, 140 ....NC-15
Delanson, 377 ....NJ-18
Delevan, 1089 ....NK-5
Delhi, 3087 ....NL-15
Delmar, 8300 ....NK-19
Delphi Falls, 500 ....NJ-12
Denmark, 150 ....NF-13
Depauville, 577 ....NE-12
Depew, 15303 ....NJ-4
Deposit, 1663 ....NM-14
Derby, 1200 ....NK-3
DeRuyter, 558 ....NJ-12
Dewittville, 350 ....NL-2
Dexter, 1052 ....NE-12
Diamond Pt., 400 ......NG-19
Dickinson Ctr.,
  200 ....NB-16
Dix Hills, 26892 ....SI-10
Dobbs Ferry, 10578 ...SE-7
Dolgeville, 2206 ....NI-16
Dorloo, 450 ....NK-17
Dormansville, 100 .....NK-18
Douglaston ....†G-15
Dover Furnace SB-8
Dover Plains, 1323 ....SA-8
Downsville, 617 ....NM-15
Dresden, 308 ....NK-9
Dryden, 1890 ....NK-11
Duanesburg, 391 ......NJ-18
Dundee, 1725 ....NK-9
Dunkirk, 12563 ....NK-2
Dunsbach Ferry,
  650 ....NI-19
Dunsburn SH-11
Durham, 150 ....NL-18
Durhamville, 841 ......NI-13
Durlandville, 160 ......NC-5
Eagle, 150 ....NK-5
Eagle Bay, 200 ....NF-16
Eagle Br., 450 ....NI-20
Eagle Hbr., 250 ....NH-5
Eagleville, 60 ....NI-20
Earlton, 255 ....NL-18
Earlville, 872 ....NJ-13
East Amherst, 700 .....NI-4
E. Aurora, 6236 ....NJ-4
E. Avon, 500 ....NJ-7
E. Beekmantown,
  125 ....NB-19
E. Berne, 200 ....NK-18
E. Bethany, 150 ....NJ-6
E. Branch, 400 ....NM-15
E. Chatham, 500 ....NL-19
E. Corning, 650 ....NM-9
E. Durham, 600 ....NL-18
E. Eden, 300 ....NK-4
E. Elmhurst ....†G-12
E. Glenville, 6616 .....NI-18
E. Greenbush,
  4487 ....NK-19
E. Greenwich, 220 .....NI-20
E. Hampton, 1083 .....SE-13
E. Hills, 6955 ....†F-8
E. Homer, 200 ....NK-13
E. Islip, 14475 ....SJ-12
E. Marion, 926 ....SD-12
E. Meadow, 38132 ....SF-8
E. Meredith, 200 ....NL-15
E. Nassau, 587 ....NK-20
E. New York ....†J-12
E. Northport, 20217 ..SF-9
E. Norwich, 2709 .....†E-19
E. Otto, 300 ....NK-4
E. Palmyra, 135 ....NI-9
E. Pembroke, 600 .....NI-5
E. Penfield, 200 ....NI-8
E. Pharsalia, 160 ......NK-13
E. Quogue, 4757 ......SF-12
E. Randolph, 200 ......NL-3
E. Rochester, 6587 ...ND-10
E. Rockaway, 9818 ...†J-17
E. Schodack, 500 .....NK-19
E. Springfield, 220 ...NJ-16
E. Syracuse, 3084 ....NI-9
E. Williamson, 500 ...NH-9
E. Williston, 2556 ....†G-17
E. Windsor, 50 ....NM-13
E. Worcester, 300 ....NK-16
Eastchester, 19554 ...†B-14
Eastport, 1831 ....SF-11
Eaton, 500 ....NJ-13
Ebenezer NG-5
Eddyville, 3516 ....NL-18
Eden, 3516 ....NK-3
Edgemere ....†K-15
Edinburg, 300 ....NH-18
Edmeston, 657 ....NK-14
Edwards, 439 ....NP-14
Edwardsville, 15019 ..ND-5
Eggertsville, 150 ....NL-15
Elba, 676 ....NI-6
Elbridge, 1058 ....NI-11
Eldred, 500 ....SB-3
Elizabethtown,
  754 ....NC-19
Elizaville, 600 ....NM-19
Ellenburg, 500 ....NA-18
Ellenburg Ctr. NA-18
Ellenville, 6079 ....NN-16
Ellery NL-2
Ellicott, 550 ....NL-3
Ellicottville, 4135 .....NL-5
Ellington, 500 ....NL-3
Elma, 300 ....NJ-4
Elmira, 29200 ....NM-10
Elm Valley, 75 ....NM-7
Elmira Ctr., 2571 ......NM-10
Elmira Hts., 4097 .....NM-10
Elmont, 33198 ....SH-7
Elmsford, 4664 ....SH-7
Elmwood, 200 ....NJ-5
Eltingville *M-6
Emmons, 150 ....NK-15
Endicott, 13392 ....NM-12
Endwell, 11446 ....NM-12
Enfield, 200 ....NL-10
Enfield Falls, 350 ......NL-10
Englewood ....
Ephratah, 400 ....NI-16
Erieville, 400 ....NJ-13
Erin, 483 ....NM-10
Escarpment, 120 ....NA-2
Esopus, 650 ....NM-18
Esperance, 345 ....NJ-17
Essex, 400 ....ND-20
ESSEX CO.,
39370 ....NE-18
Etna, 550 ....NK-11
Euclid, 180 ....NI-11
Evans Mills, 621 ....NE-13
Fabius, 352 ....NJ-12
Fair Haven, 745 ....NH-10
Fairfield, 150 ....NI-15
Fairmount, 10224 .....NI-11
Fairport, 5353 ....NI-8
Fairview, 3099 ....SI-7
Falconer, 2420 ....NM-3
Falcowood, 1500 .....ND-3
Fallsburg, 800 ....SB-4
Fancher, 300 ....NH-6
Far Rockaway ....†K-15
Farmersville Sta.,
  ....NL-5
Farmersville,
  ....NL-5
Farmingdale, 8189 ...SJ-10
Farmington, 100 ....NI-8
Farmingville,
  15481 ....SF-10
Farnham, 382 ....NK-3
Fayette, 430 ....NJ-10
Fayetteville, 4373 ....NI-12
Fernchurch, 372 ....NL-13
Ferndale, 850 ....SA-4
Ferndale, 1580 ....NL-13
Ferry Vil., 200 ....ND-3
Fillmore, 603 ....NK-6
Findley Lake, 800 .....NM-1
Fine, 300 ....ND-15
Fire Island Pines,
  900 ....SG-10
Fishers, 400 ....NI-8
Fishers Island, 236 ...SD-14
Fishers, 89 ....ND-12
Fishkill, 2117 ....SB-7
Fishs Eddy, 350 ....NN-15
Flackville, 110 ....NC-14
Flanders, 4472 ....SE-11
Flatbush ....†J-11
Fleischmanns,
  351 ....NM-17
Fleming, 220 ....NJ-10
Floral Pk., 15863 ......†H-16
Florida, 2833 ....SC-5
Flower Hill, 4665 ......†F-16
Floyd, 300 ....NH-14
Flushing ....†G-13
Fluvanna, 900 ....NM-2
Fly Creek, 350 ....NK-15
Fonda, 795 ....NI-17
Forest, 400 ....NB-19
Forest Hills ....†H-13
Forestburg, 100 ....SB-4
Forestport, 900 ....NH-14
Forestville, 697 ....NL-3
Ft. Ann, 484 ....NG-20
Ft. Covington,
  1200 ....NA-16
Ft. Edward, 3375 .....NH-19
Ft. Hunter, 1250 ......NJ-17
Ft. Jackson, 135 ....NB-16
Ft. Johnson, 490 ......NI-17
Ft. Plain, 2322 ....NJ-16
Ft. Salonga,
  10008 ....SE-9
Fosterdale, 150 ....SB-3
Fourth Lake, 300 ......NH-19
Fowler, 300 ....ND-14
Franklin, 500 ....NL-14
Franklinville, 1740 ....NL-5
Fraser, 30 ....NL-15
Fredonia, 11230 ....NL-2
Freedom, 200 ....NK-5
Freehold, 500 ....NL-18
Freeport, 500 ....SG-8
Freeville, 520 ....NK-11
Fresh Meadows ....†H-14
Frewsburg, 1906 ......NM-3
Friendship, 1218 ......NL-6
Fruit Valley, 50 ....NH-10
Fulton, 11896 ....NH-11
FULTON CO.,
55531 ....NI-17
Fultonham, 400 ....NK-17
Fultonville, 784 ....NJ-17
Hartfield, 100 ....NL-2
Hartford, 500 ....NH-20
Gabriels, 250 ....NC-17
Gainesville, 229 ....NK-6
Gaines, 200 ....NH-6
Galeville, 4617 ....NI-12
Gallupville, 325 ....NK-17
Galway, 200 ....NI-18
Gang Mills, 4185 ......NM-9
Gansevoort, 800 ......NH-19
Garden City,
  22371 ....†H-18
Garden City Pk.,
  7806 ....†G-17
Garden City South,
  4024 ....†H-17
Gardiner, 950 ....SB-6
Gardnertown, 4373 ...SB-6
Garrattsville, 150 ......NK-15
Garrison, 800 ....SC-6
Gasport, 1248 ....NH-4
Gates Ctr., 4910 ......NI-7
Genegantslet ....
GENESEE CO.,
60079 ....NI-6
Geneseo, 8031 ....NJ-7
Geneva, 13261 ....NJ-9
Genoa, 400 ....NJ-10
Georgetown, 500 .....NJ-13
German, 80 ....NL-13
Gernman, 250 ....NL-9
Germantown,
  845 ....NM-18
Gilbert, 244 ....NM-12
Gerry, 800 ....NL-3
Getzville, 2300 ....NI-4
Ghent, 564 ....NL-19
Gilbertsville, 399 ......NK-14
Gilboa, 150 ....NL-17
Girard, 4664 ....NM-1
Glasco, 2099 ....NM-18
Glen Aubrey, 485 .....NL-12
Glen Cove, 26964 .....SF-8
Glen Head, 4697 ......†E-18
Glen Oaks ....†G-16
Glen Spey, 500 ....SC-3
Glendale ....†H-13
Glenfield, 430 ....NF-14
Glenham, 1900 ....SC-6
Glenford, 550 ....NM-18
Glenmont, 2000 ....NK-19
Glens Falls, 14700 ....NH-19
Glenwood, 500 ....NK-4
Glenwood, 3779 ......†E-17
Gloversville, 15665 ...NH-17
Godeffroy, 550 ....SC-4
Golden's Br., 1630 ...SC-7
Gorham, 617 ....NJ-9
Goshen, 5454 ....SC-5
Gouverneur, 3949 ....ND-14
Gowanda, 2709 ....NK-3
Grafton, 500 ....NJ-20
Grahamsville, 700 ....NN-17
Granby Ctr., 100 ......NH-11
Grand Gorge,
  1000 ....NL-17
Grand Island, 800 ....NI-3
Grandyle Vil., 4629 ...ND-3
Graniteville *L-6
Granville, 2543 ....NG-20
Gravesend *K-11
Gravesville, 100 ....NH-15
Gray, 75 ....NH-14
Great Bend, 843 ....NE-13
Great Neck, 9989 .....SF-7
Great Neck Estates,
  2761 ....†F-15
Great Neck Plaza,
  6707 ....†F-16
Great Valley, 250 .....NL-4
Greece, 65000 ....NH-7
Green Island, 2620 ...SH-5
Green River, 200 ....NL-20
Greene, 1580 ....NL-13
GREENE CO.,
49221 ....NL-18
Greenfield Ctr.,
  700 ....NH-18
Greenfield Pk., 500 ...SI-4
Greenlawn, 13742 ....SH-11
Greenport, 2197 ....SD-12
Greenvale, 1094 ......†E-18
Greenville, 7116 ....SI-7
Greenville, 688 ....NL-18
Greenwich, 1777 .....NI-20
Greenwood, 520 ......NM-7
Greenwood Lake,
  3154 ....SD-5
Greig, 300 ....NG-14
Groom Cors., 370 .....SF-3
Groton, 2363 ....NK-11
Groveland, 300 ....NK-7
Grover Hills, 300 ......NI-20
Grymes Hill *K-8
Guilderland, 1900 ....NJ-18
Guilderland Ctr.,
  ....NJ-18
Guilford, 362 ....NL-14
Gurn Spr., 145 ....NH-19
Hadley, 1009 ....NH-18
Hagaman, 1292 ....NI-18
Hague, 450 ....NF-19
Hailesboro, 624 ....ND-14
Haines Falls, 700 ......NL-18
Halcottsville, 240 .....NL-16
Halesite, 2948 ....SH-11
Halfmoon, 150 ....NI-19
Hall Hollow Hills,
  1200 ....SI-10
Hallsport, 150 ....NM-7
Hamburg, 9409 ....NJ-4
Hamden, 250 ....NM-15
Hamilton, 4239 ....NJ-13
HAMILTON CO.,
4836 ....NF-16
Hamlet, 80 ....NL-3
Hamlin, 5521 ....NH-6
Hammond, 280 ....NC-13
Hammondsport,
  661 ....NL-8
Hampton, 400 ....NG-20
Hampton Bays,
  13603 ....SE-12
Hampton Mnr., 2417 ..SI-5
Hancock, 1031 ....NN-14
Hankins, 400 ....NN-15
Hannawa Falls,
  1042 ....NC-15
Hannibal, 555 ....NH-10
Hannibal Ctr., 115 ....NH-10
Harford, 200 ....NL-11
Harford Mills, 180 ....NL-12
Harlem ....†F-11
Harpersfield, 110 .....NL-16
Harpursville, 500 .....NM-13
Harriman, 2424 ....SD-6
Harris, 600 ....SB-4
Harris Hill, 1500 ....NI-4
Harrison, 13620 ....†A-18
Harrisville, 628 ....NC-14
Hartfield, 100 ....NL-2
Hartford, 500 ....NH-20
Hartman Cors., 100 ..SI-2
Hartsdale, 5293 ....SI-7
Hartsville, 200 ....NL-7
Hartwick, 629 ....NK-15
Hartwick Seminary,
  100 ....NK-15
Hartwood, 50 ....SB-4
Hasbrouck, 200 ....NM-16
Haskinville, 100 ....NL-7
Hastings, 350 ....NH-12
Hauppauge, 20882 ..SH-12
Haven, 70 ....SB-8
Haverstraw, 11910 ...SD-6
Hawleyton ....
Hawkinsville, 100 .....NH-14
Head of the Harbor,
  1472 ....SH-11
Hector, 300 ....NK-10
Helena, 150 ....NA-15
Hemlock, 557 ....NJ-7
Hempstead, 53891 ..SF-8
Henderson, 224 ....NF-12
Henderson Hbr.,
  350 ....NF-12
Henrietta, 1200 ....NI-7
Hensonville, 600 ......NL-18
Herbertsville, 376 .....NL-4
Herkimer, 7743 ....NI-15
HERKIMER CO.,
64519 ....NH-15
Hermon, 422 ....NC-14
Herricks, 4295 ....†G-17
Herrings, 90 ....NE-13
Heuvelton, 714 ....NC-14
Hewitt, 300 ....NK-8
Hewlett, 6829 ....†J-16
Hewlett Bay Pk.,
  404 ....†J-16
Hewlett Hbr., 1263 ..†K-17
Hewlett Neck, 445 ...†K-16
Hicksville, 41547 ......SF-8
Higgins Bay, 50 ....NH-16
High Falls, 627 ....NN-17
High Mkt. NG-14
Highland, 5647 ....SB-6
Highland Falls, 3900 ..SC-6
Highland Lake,
  1800 ....SA-2
Highland-on-the-Lake,
  ....
Highmount, 300 ....NM-17
Hillburn, 900 ....SD-6
Hillcrest, 7558 ....SH-6
Hillside SI-6
Hilton, 5886 ....NH-7
Himrod, 300 ....NK-9
Hinckley, 250 ....NH-15
Hinsdale, 900 ....NM-5
Hobart, 441 ....NL-16
Hoffmeister, 45 ....NH-15
Hogansburg, 100 .....NA-16
Holbrook, 27195 ......SI-13
Holcombville, 200 ....NF-18
Holland, 1206 ....NK-5
Holland Patent,
  458 ....NH-14
Holley, 1811 ....NH-6
Hollis ....†H-15
Holmes, 460 ....SB-8
Holmesville, 150 ......NK-14
Holtsville, 19914 ......SI-14
Homer, 3291 ....NK-13
Homewood, 1450 .....NG-10
Honeoye, 575 ....NJ-8
Honeoye Falls, 2674 ..NJ-7
Hoosick, 400 ....NJ-20
Hoosick Falls,
  3501 ....NI-20
Hope Falls, 80 ....NH-17
Hope Farm, 300 ....SI-2
Hopewell Jct., 376 ...SB-7
Hopkinton, 200 ....NB-16
Hornby, 300 ....NM-9
Hornell, 8563 ....NL-7
Horseheads,
  6461 ....NM-10
Houghton, 1693 ......NL-6
Howard, 200 ....NL-7
Howard Bch. ....†J-13
Howells, 350 ....SC-5
Howlett Hill, 650 .....NG-7
Hubbardsville, 250 ...NJ-14
Hudson, 6713 ....NL-19
Hudson Falls,
  7281 ....NH-19
Hughsonville, 1400 ..SB-7
Huguenot, 800 ....SC-4
Huguenot *M-6
Hulberton, 100 ....NH-6
Huletts Lndg., 90 .....NG-19
Hume, 400 ....NK-6
Hunter, 500 ....NL-18
Huntington, 18046 ...SH-10
Huntington Bay,
  1425 ....SH-10
Huntington Sta.,
  29300 ....SF-9
Hurley, 3458 ....NN-18
Hurleyville, 750 ....SA-4
Hyde Pk., 1908 ....NN-18
Hyde Pk., 100 ....NJ-9
Hyndsville, 200 ....NK-16
Hyndsville Sprs.,
  ....NK-16
Ilion, 8053 ....NI-15
Indian Falls, 170 ......NI-5
Indian Lake, 600 ......NF-17
Indian River, 45 ....NE-14
Ingleside, 90 ....NK-8
Ingraham, 110 ....NB-19
Inlet, 400 ....NH-16
Interlaken, 800 ....NK-10
Inwood, 9792 ....SG-7
Ionia, 300 ....NJ-8
Irona, 300 ....NA-19
Irondequoit, 51692 ..NH-7
Ironville, 100 ....NE-19
Irving, 600 ....NL-3
Irvington, 6420 ....SE-7
Ischua, 200 ....NL-5
Island Pk., 4655 ....†K-17
Islandia, 3335 ....SI-13
Islip, 18689 ....SF-9
Islip Ter., 5389 ....SI-12
Italy, 100 ....NK-8
Ithaca, 30014 ....NK-11
Jacks Reef, 500 ....NI-11
Jackson Hts. ....†G-12
Jacksonville, 670 .....NK-10
Jamaica ....†H-14
Jamesport, 1710 ......SE-12
Jamestown, 31146 ...NM-2
Jamesville, 900 ....NJ-12
Jasper, 500 ....NM-8
Java Ctr., 200 ....NK-5
Java Vil., 350 ....NK-5
Jay, 500 ....NC-19
Jefferson, 500 ....NK-16
JEFFERSON CO.,
116229 ....NE-13
Jefferson Valley,
  6700 ....SC-7
Jeffersonville, 359 ...NN-15
Jericho, 13567 ....SF-8
Jewell, 100 ....NK-5
Jewettville, 150 ....NJ-4
Johnsburg, 300 ....NG-18
Johnson, 450 ....SC-5
Johnson City,
  15174 ....NM-12
Johnson Creek, 280 ..NH-5
Johnsonburg, 120 ....NJ-5
Johnsonville, 380 .....NJ-20
Johnstown, 8743 .....NI-17
Jordan, 1368 ....NI-11
Jordanville, 210 ....NJ-15
Kanona, 450 ....NL-8
Katonah, 1679 ....SD-7
Kattskill Bay, 500 .....NG-19
Keene, 400 ....NC-18
Keene Valley, 200 ....NC-18
Keeseville, 1815 ......NC-19
Kelsey, 70 ....NL-14
Kendall, 100 ....NH-6
Kenmore, 15423 .....ND-4
Kennedy, 465 ....NM-3
Kenoza Lake, 400 ....SB-3
Kensington, 1161 .....†F-15
Kent, 200 ....SC-7
Kent Cliffs, 110 ....SC-7
Kenyonville, 110 ......NH-6
Kerhonkson, 1684 ....NN-17
Keuka, 150 ....NK-9
Keuka Pk., 1137 ......NK-9
Kew Gdns. ....†H-14
Kiamesha Lake, 850 ...SA-4
Kiantone, 500 ....NM-3
Kill Buck, 650 ....NL-4
Killawog, 300 ....NL-12
Kinderhook, 1211 ....NL-19
King Ferry, 300 ....NK-10
Kingsbury, 100 ....NH-20
Kingston, 23893 ......NN-18
Kirkland, 400 ....NI-14
Kirkville, 450 ....NI-12
Kiryas Joel, 20175 ...SC-5
Knapp Creek, 150 ....NM-4
Knowlesville, 300 .....NH-6
Knox, 400 ....NJ-18
Knoxboro, 150 ....NI-14
Kossuth, 60 ....NM-6
Krumville, 150 ....NN-17
La Fargeville, 608 ....ND-12
Lackawanna,
  18141 ....NG-4
Lacona, 582 ....NG-12
LaFayette, 1000 ....NI-12
Lagrangeville, 500 ...SB-7
L. Bluff, 50 ....NH-9
L. Bonaparte, 50 ......NF-14
L. Carmel, 8282 ......SC-7
L. Clear, 400 ....NC-17
L. Delta, 2020 ....NH-14
L. Erie Bch., 3872 ....NK-3
L. George, 906 ....NG-19
L. Grove, 11163 ......SH-13
L. Hill, 400 ....NM-18
L. Huntington, 600 ..SB-3
L. Katrine, 2397 ......NM-18
L. Luzerne, 1150 ......NH-19
L. Peekskill, 2150 ....SC-7
L. Placid, 2521 ....NC-18
L. Pleasant, 350 ......NG-17
L. Ronkonkoma,
  20155 ....SI-13
L. Success, 2934 .....†G-16
Lakeland, 2786 ....NI-7
Lakemont, 250 ....NK-9
Lakeport, 500 ....NI-12
Lakeview, 5615 ....†J-17
Lakeville, 756 ....NJ-7
Lakewood, 3002 ......NM-2
Lamberton, 130 ....NL-2
Lancaster, 10352 .....NI-4
Lanesville, 350 ....NM-17
Langford, 230 ....NK-4
Lansing, 3529 ....NK-11
Lansing, 230 ....SF-11
Laphams Mills,
  ....NB-19
Larchmont, 5864 .....†B-15
Lassellsville, 300 .....NI-16
Latham, 4200 ....SH-5
Lattingtown, 1739 ...†D-18
Laurel, 1394 ....SE-12
Laurel Hollow,
  1952 ....SH-10
Laurelton ....†I-15
Laurens, 263 ....NK-15
Lava, 50 ....SB-3
Lawrence, 6483 ....†K-16
Lawrenceville,
  ....NA-16
Lawtons, 460 ....NK-3
Lawyersville, 200 .....NJ-17
Le Roy, 4391 ....NI-6
Lebanon, 350 ....NJ-13
Lebanon Sprs.,
  ....NK-20
Lee, 200 ....NH-14
Lee Ctr., 620 ....NH-14
Leeds, 377 ....NL-18
Leicester, 468 ....NJ-6
Leon, 350 ....NL-3
Leonardsville, 500 ...NJ-14
Levanna, 50 ....NJ-10
Levittown, 51881 ....SF-8
Lewbeach, 250 ....NN-16
Lewis, 450 ....ND-19
Lewis, 263 ....NL-5
Lewiston, 2781 ....NI-3
Lexington, 500 ....NL-17
Liberty, 4392 ....NN-16
Lido Bch., 2897 ....SG-8
Lily Dale, 500 ....NL-2
Lima, 2139 ....NJ-7
Lime Lake, 867 ....NL-5
Limerick, 170 ....NE-12
Limestone, 389 ....NM-4
Lincoln, 140 ....NI-13
Lincolndale, 1800 ...SC-7
Lindenhurst, 27253 ..SF-9
Lindley, 500 ....NM-8
Linwood, 74 ....NJ-6
Lisbon, 500 ....NB-14
Lisle, 320 ....NL-12
Littauer Cos. SG-5
Little Falls, 4946 ......NI-16
Little Genesee,
  270 ....NM-5
Little Neck ....†G-16
Little Valley, 1143 ....NL-4
Liverpool, 2347 ....NI-8
Livingston Mnr.,
  1221 ....NN-16
Livingstonville,
  ....NK-17
Livonia, 1409 ....NJ-7
Livonia Ctr., 421 .....NJ-7
Lloyd Hbr., 3660 .....SG-9
Lockport, 21165 ......NH-4
Locke, 291 ....NK-10
Lodi, 291 ....NK-10
Loch Muller, 100 .....NF-18
Loch Sheldrake,
  ....SA-4
Lockwood, 280 ....NM-11
Locke, 291 ....NK-10
Locust Grv., 9700 ....†F-20
Locust Mnr. ....†I-15
Locust Valley, 3406 ..SF-8
Lodi, 291 ....NK-10
Long Bch., 33275 ....SG-8
Long Eddy, 400 ....NN-14
Long Island City ....†G-11
Long Lake, 547 ....NE-17
Loon Lake, 200 ....NB-18
Lordville, 174 ....NN-14
Lorraine, 250 ....NG-12
Louisville, 1350 ......NA-15
Lowville, 3470 ....NF-14
Lounsberry, 200 ......NL-11
Ludlowville, 440 ....NK-11
Lycoming, 650 ....NH-11
Lyndon, 19427 ....†F-17
Lyndonville, 838 ......NH-5
Lyon Mtn., 423 ....NB-18
Lyons, 3619 ....NI-9
Lyons Falls, 566 ......NG-14
Lysander, 100 ....NI-11
Macedon, 1528 ......NI-8
Machias, 471 ....NL-5
Madison, 322 ....NJ-14
MADISON CO.,
72454 ....NJ-13
Madrid, 1545 ....NB-15
Mahopac, 8369 ....SC-7
Maine, 1110 ....NL-12
Malden, 600 ....NM-18
Mallory, 100 ....NH-12
Malone, 5911 ....NB-17
Malta, 1110 ....NI-19
Malta Ridge, 130 .....NI-19
Malverne, 8514 ....†J-16
Mamaroneck,
  18929 ....SE-8
Manchester, 1709 ...NI-8
Manhasset, 8080 .....†E-16
Manhattan Bch. *L-11
Manitou Bch., 250 ...NH-7
Manlius, 4704 ....NI-12
Mannsville, 354 ....NF-12
Manorhaven, 6556 ..†E-16
Manorville, 14314 ...SE-11
Maple Sprs., 400 .....NL-2
Maple View, 280 ......NG-12
Maplecrest, 150 ......NL-18
Maplehurst, 200 ......NM-5
Maplewood, 800 .....SH-5
Marathon, 919 ....NL-12
Marcellus, 1813 ......NI-11
Margaretville,
  596 ....NM-16
Marietta, 80 ....NJ-11
Marion, 1511 ....NI-9
Marlboro, 3669 ....SB-6
Martindale, 400 ......NM-14
Martville, 150 ....NH-10
Maryland, 165 ....NK-16
Masonville, 600 ......NL-14
Maspeth ....†H-12
Massapequa,
  21685 ....SG-8
Massapequa Pk.,
  17008 ....SJ-10
Massena, 10936 ......NA-15
Massena Ctr., 50 ....NA-15
Mastic, 15481 ....SF-11
Mastic Bch.,
  11543 ....SF-11
Matinecock, 810 .....†D-18
Mattituck, 4219 ......SE-12
Mattydale, 6446 .....NI-8
Maybrook, 2958 .....SC-5
Mayfield, 830 ....NI-17
Maywood, 3400 .....SH-3
McConnellsville,
  ....NH-13
McDonough, 300 ....NK-13
McGraw, 1052 ....NK-12
McKownville, 4850 ...SI-3
McLean, 600 ....NK-11
Meadowdale SI-1
Mechanicstown,
  ....SC-5
Mechanicville,
  ....NI-19
Mecklenburg, 280 ...NL-10
Meco, 500 ....NI-17
Medford, 24142 ......SF-10
Medina, 6065 ....NH-5
Medusa, 350 ....NL-18
Medway, 285 ....NL-18
Melrose, 350 ....NJ-19
Melville, 18985 ....SI-10
Menands, 3990 ....NJ-19
Mendon, 300 ....NI-8
Meredith, 256 ....NL-15
Meridian, 350 ....NI-11
Merrill, 200 ....NB-19
Merrick, 22097 ....†J-19
Merrifield, 2209 ......SC-5
Mexico, 1624 ....NG-11
Middle Falls, 270 .....NI-20
Middle Granville,
  ....NG-20
Middle Grv., 620 ......NI-18
Middle Hope, 3000 ..SB-6
Middle Island, 10483 ..SF-10
Middleburgh,
  ....NK-17
Middlefield, 350 ......NK-16
Middleport, 1840 ....NH-5
Middlesex, 400 ....NK-8
Middletown, 28086 ..SC-5
Middleville, 512 ......NI-15
Midland Bch. *L-8
Milan, 150 ....NM-19
Milford, 415 ....NK-15
Mill Neck, 997 ....†D-19
Millbrook, 1452 ......NN-19
Miller Pl., 12339 .....SE-10
Millersport NB-4
Millerton, 958 ....NM-20
Millport, 312 ....NL-10
Millwood, 300 ....SD-7
Milo Ctr. NK-9
Milton, 1403 ....SB-6
Minaville, 220 ....NI-17
Mineola, 18799 ......SF-8
Minerva, 300 ....NF-18
Minetto, 1069 ....NH-11
Mineville, 1269 ....NE-19
Minisink Ford, 150 ...NN-14
Minoa, 3449 ....NI-12
Model City, 300 ....NH-3
Modena, 800 ....SB-6
Mohawk, 2731 ....NI-15
Mohawk Hill NG-14
Mohawk View, 100 ..SG-3
Mohegan Lake,
  3600 ....SC-7
Mohonk Lake SB-5
Moira, 500 ....NB-16
Mombaccus, 150 .....NN-17
Mongaup Valley,
  ....SB-3
Monroe, 8364 ....SC-6
Montague NF-13
Montauk, 3326 ....SE-14
Montezuma, 450 ....NI-10
Montgomery, 3814 ..SB-5
Monticello, 6726 .....SB-4
Montour Falls,
  1815 ....NL-10
Montrose, 2731 ......SD-7
Mooers, 442 ....NA-19
Mooers Forks, 600 ..NA-19
Moravia, 1282 ....NK-11
Moreland, 100 ....NI-8
Moriah, 400 ....NE-19
Moriah Ctr., 400 .....NE-19
Morley, 400 ....NB-15
Mormos, 583 ....NN-15
Morris, 583 ....NK-15
Morrisonville,
  ....NB-19
Morristown, 394 .....NC-13
Morrisville, 2199 ....NJ-13
Moscow, 100 ....NJ-7
Mott Haven ....†F-12
Mottville, 200 ....NI-11
Mt. Ivy, 6878 ....SD-6
Mt. Kisco, 10877 .....SD-7
Mt. Morris, 2986 .....NJ-7
Mt. Sinai, 9941 ....SE-10
Mt. Tremper, 650 ....NM-17
Mt. Upton, 570 ....NL-14
Mt. Vernon, 2800 ....SE-7
Mt. Vision, 225 ....NK-15
Mountain Dale, 200 ..SA-4
Mountain Lodge,
  1000 ....SC-6
Mountain View,
  150 ....NA-17
Mountainville, 600 ...SC-6
Mumford, 800 ....NI-7
Munnsville, 414 ....NI-13
Munsey Pk., 2693 ...†F-16
Munsons Corners,
  2728 ....NK-12
Murray, 100 ....NH-6
Muttontown, 3497 ...†E-19
Myers Corner, 6790 ..SB-7
Nanuet, 17882 ....SH-4
Napanoch, 1174 .....SA-4
Naples, 1041 ....NK-8
Narrowsburg, 431 ...SA-2
NASSAU CO.,
1339532 ....SF-8
Nassau, 1133 ....NK-20
Natural Bridge, 365 ..NE-13
Natural Dam, 60 ......NC-13
Nedrow, 2244 ....NI-12
Nelliston, 596 ....NJ-16
Nelson, 300 ....NJ-13
Nelsonville, 628 ......SC-6
Neponsit ....
Nesconset, 13387 ...SH-13
Neversink, 350 ....NN-16
New Albion, 200 ......NL-4
New Baltimore,
  960 ....NL-19
New Berlin, 1028 .....NK-14
New Bremen, 200 ....NF-14
New Brighton *K-8
New Cassel,
  14059 ....†G-18
New City, 33559 .....SI-7
New Dorp *L-7
New Dorp Bch. *L-7
New Falconwood,
  1200 ....ND-3
New Hampton,
  1847 ....SC-5
New Hartford,
  1847 ....NI-14
New Haven, 400 .....NG-11
New Hyde Pk.,
  9712 ....†G-16
New Kingston,
  150 ....NM-16
New Lebanon,
  950 ....NK-20
New Lisbon, 100 .....NK-15
New Milford, 400 ....SC-4
New Paltz, 6818 .....SA-6
New Rochelle,
  77062 ....SE-7
New Russia, 160 .....ND-19
New Salem, 450 .....NK-18
New Scotland, 300 ..NK-18
New Suffolk, 349 .....SE-12
New Utrecht *K-10
New Windsor, 8922 ...SC-6
New Woodstock,
  500 ....NJ-12
New York Mills,
  3327 ....NI-14
Newark, 9145 ....NI-9
Newark Valley,
  997 ....NL-12
Newburgh, 28866 ...SC-6
Newcomb, 300 ....NE-18
Newfane, 3822 ....NH-4
Newfield Hamlet,
  759 ....NL-10
Newport, 640 ....NI-15
Newton Falls, 400 ...ND-15
Newtonville, 4000 ...NI-19
NIAGARA CO.,
216469 ....NH-4
Niagara Falls,
  50193 ....NH-3
Nichols, 512 ....NM-11
Nicholville, 370 ....NB-16
Nile, 250 ....NM-6
Nimmonsburg,
  900 ....NM-12
Nineveh, 400 ....NM-13
Niobe, 150 ....NM-2
Niskayuna, 4859 .....NI-18
Nissequogue,
  1749 ....SH-12
Niverville, 1663 ......NL-19
Norfolk, 1327 ....NB-15
Normansville,
  ....NK-18
N. Argyle, 250 ....NH-20
N. Babylon, 800 ......SI-11
N. Bellmore, 19941 ..†K-19
N. Bethlehem, 400 ..NK-18
N. Blenheim, 200 ....NK-17
N. Boston, 2521 ......NK-4
N. Branch, 500 ....NN-15
N. Broadalbin, 65 ....NH-17
N. Brookfield, 250 ...NJ-14
N. Chemung, 200 ....NM-10
N. Chili, 2300 ....NI-7
N. Clymer, 250 ....NM-1
N. Collins, 1232 ......NK-3
N. Creek, 616 ....NF-18
N. Cuba, 80 ....NM-5
N. Granville, 500 .....NG-20
N. Greece, 300 ....NH-7
N. Harpersfield,
  ....NL-16
N. Hills, 5074 ....†F-16
N. Hoosick, 350 ......NI-20
N. Hornell, 778 ....NL-7
N. Hudson, 100 ......NE-19
N. Java, 250 ....NK-5
N. Lawrence, 400 ...NB-16
N. Lynbrook, 793 ....†J-16
N. Massapequa,
  17886 ....†K-20
N. Merrick, 12013 ...†J-19
N. New Hyde Pk.,
  14899 ....†G-16
N. Norwich, 500 .....NK-13
N. Petersburg, 250 ..NJ-20
N. Pharsalia, 130 ....NL-13
N. Pitcher, 170 ....NK-13
N. Pole, 70 ....NC-18
N. Rose, 600 ....NI-9
N. Salem, 200 ....SC-8
N. Sea, 1438 ....SE-12
N. Syracuse, 6800 ...NI-12
N. Tarrytown SD-7
N. Tonawanda,
  31568 ....NI-3
N. Valley Stream,
  16628 ....†I-16
N. Western, 500 ......NH-14

*, †, ‡, § See explanation under state title in this index.
County and parish names are listed in capital letters & boldface type.
Independent cities (not included in a county) are listed in *italics*.

Column 1

rthport, 7401 ......SE-9
rthumberland,
,50 ....NM-9
rthville, 1099 ......NH-17
rton Hill, 385 ....NL-18
rwich, 7190 ....NK-14
rwood, 1657 ......NB-15
wyack, 3568 ....SE-12
ack, 6765 ....SD-7
k Bch., 100 ....SL-9
kdale, 7974 ....SJ-13
akfield, 1813 ......NI-5
akland Gdns. .....†G-15
kwood *L-7
kwood Bch. *L-7
kburg, 200 ....NN-15
i, 45 ....NM-5
ean Bch., 79 ....SG-10
essa, 591 ....NL-10
ldensburg,
1128 ....NB-14
io, 70 ....NH-15
ioville, 250 ....SA-6
cott, 1241 ....NH-4
d Brookville,
134 ....†E-18
fried, 918 ....SE-10
d Forge, 756 .....NF-15
d Westbury,
671 ....†F-18
ean, 14452 ......NM-5
vebridge, 400 ...NN-18
verea, 150 ....NM-9
nstedville, 400 ...NF-18
chiota, 85 ....NC-18
eida, 11393 .....NI-13
NEIDA CO.,
34878 ....NH-13
eonta, 13901 ...NK-15
NONDAGA CO.,
67026 ....NI-12
ondaga Hill,
000 ....NG-8
tario, 2160 ....NH-8
tario Ctr., 600 ...NH-8
NTARIO CO.,
07931 ....NJ-8
penheim, 500 ...NI-16
amel, 150 ....NL-6
RANGE CO.,
72813 ....SC-4
ange Lake, 6982 ..SB-5
chard Knoll, 250 ...NH-1
chard Pk., 3246 ...NJ-4
ent, 743 ....SD-13
skany, 1400 ......NI-14
skany Falls, 282 ...NJ-14
RLEANS CO.,
2883 ....NH-6
well, 400 ....NG-12
sceola, 200 ......NG-13
sining, 25060 ....SD-7
wegatchie, 300 ...NL-15
wego, 18142 .....NG-11
WEGO CO.,
122109 ....NG-12
ego, 100 ....NL-15
sco, 250 ....NJ-11
sville, 1068 ....SC-4
SEGO CO.,
2259 ....NK-15
selic, 400 ....NJ-13
ter Lake, 400 .....NI-13
co, 550 ....NL-4
aquaga, 400 .....NM-13
d, 602 ....NN-11
vasco, 400 ....NJ-11
wego, 3896 ......NM-11
ls Head, 350 ....NB-17
bow, 108 ....NI-13
ford, 1450 ....NL-13
ster Bay, 6707 ...SF-8
ster Bay Cove,
197 ....†D-20
one Pk. ....†J-13
nted Post, 1809 ..NM-9
atine Br., 737 .....NJ-16
enville, 1037 ......NM-18
ermo, 20 ....NH-11
myra, 3536 ....NH-8
melia Four Cors.,
.......................NE-12
name, 479 ....NM-7
ther Lake, 30 ....NM-13
adox, 100 ....NF-19
ris, 200 ....NI-14
fish, 450 ....NM-4
shville, 647 ....NC-16
k Ter., 200 ....†E-13
ksville, 200 ......NN-16
kville ....†F-18
ichogue, 11798 ...SF-10
ttersonville, 600 ...NJ-18
ul Smiths, 671 ....NC-17
wling, 2347 ....SB-8
arl Creek, 150 ....NL-6
sleeville, 400 ....NN-19
conic, 683 ....SE-12
ekskill, 23583 ....SD-7
kin, 250 ....NI-4
ham, 6910 ....*C-14
iham Mnr., 5486 ...†C-14
mbroke, 200 ......NI-5
dleton, Ctr.,120 ...NB-5
dleton Ctr., 120 ...NB-5
nfield, 6300 ....NI-10
nn Yan, 5159 .....NK-9
nkinsville, 400 ...NN-17
rry, 3673 ....NJ-6
rry Ctr., 100 ......NJ-6
rrysburg, 401 ....NL-3
rryville, 96 ....NM-13
ru, 1591 ....NC-19
teboro, 600 ......NJ-20
rolla, 70 ....NM-16
elps, 1989 ....NH-8
iiladelphia,
250 ....NC-16
illips Creek, 70 ...NL-6
ilmont, 1379 .....NM-16
oenicia, 309 ......NM-17
oenix, 2382 ......NH-11
ercefield, 200 ....ND-16
rrepont Manor,
250 ....NF-12
ard, 220 ....NJ-7
ne Bush, 1780 ...SB-5
ine City, 420 .....NM-10

Column 2

Pine Island, 1500 ...SD-5
Pine Lake, 25 ....NH-16
Pine Plains, 1353 ...NM-19
Pine Valley, 813 .....NL-10
Pinehurst, 1850 .....NJ-3
Piseco, 200 ....NG-16
Pitcairn, 125 ....NE-14
Pitcher, 500 ....†L-12
Pitcher Hill, 5000 ...NE-8
Pittsfield, 100 ....NI-14
Pittsford, 1355 ......NI-8
Pittstown, 100 ....NJ-17
Plainedge, 8817 ....SJ-10
Plainview, 26217 ...SF-8
Plandome, 1349 ....†F-16
Plandome Hts.,
1005 ....†F-16
Plandome Manor,
872 ....†E-18
Plattekill, 1260 ......SB-6
Plattsburgh,
19989 ....NB-19
Pleasant Plains *M-5
Pleasant Valley,
1145 ....SA-7
Pleasantville, 7019 ..SD-7
Plessis, 164 ....ND-13
Plymouth, 400 ......NJ-14
Poestenkill, 1061 ...NJ-19
Pt. Lookout, 1219 ...*K-19
Poland, 508 ....NH-15
Pomona, 3103 ......SD-6
Pompey, 500 ....NJ-12
Pond Eddy, 350 .....SC-3
Poolville, 250 ....NJ-14
Poquott, 953 ....NE-9
Port Byron, 1290 ...NI-10
Port Chester, 28967 ..SE-8
Port Dickinson,
1641 ....NM-12
Port Ewen, 3546 ...NN-18
Port Gibson, 453 ...NI-9
Port Henry, 1194 ...NC-20
Port Jefferson,
7750 ....SE-10
Port Jervis, 8828 ...SC-4
Port Kent, 250 ....NC-20
Port Leyden, 672 ...NG-14
Port Richmond *J-7
Port Washington,
15846 ....SF-7
Port Washington
North, 3154 ....†E-16
Portageville, 500 ...NK-6
Porter Cors., 350 ...NI-18
Portland, 950 ....NL-2
Portlandville, 400 ...NK-15
Portville, 1014 ....NM-5
Potsdam, 9428 .....NC-15
Potter, 135 ....NK-9
Pottersville, 424 ....NF-19
Poughkeepsie,
32736 ....SB-6
Poughquag, 450 ...SB-7
Pratts Hollow, 70 ...NJ-13
Prattsburg, 950 .....NK-8
Prattsville, 355 ......NL-17
Preble, 550 ....NJ-12
Presho, 150 ....NM-9
Preston, 125 ....NK-13
Preston Hollow,
220 ....NK-17
Princes Bay *M-6
Prospect, 240 ....NH-15
Pulaski, 2365 ....NG-12
Pultney, 400 ....NK-9
Pultneyville, 698 ...NH-9
Purdys, 970 ....SC-8
PUTNAM CO.,
99710 ....SC-7
Putnam Lake, 3844 ...SC-8
Putnam Sta., 300 ...NF-20
Pyrites, 200 ....NC-15
Quaker Hill, 150 ....SC-8
Quarry Hts., 600 ...SH-8
QUEENS CO.,
2230722 ....SG-7
Queens Vil. ....†H-15
Queensbury, 830 ...NH-19
Quogue, 967 ....SF-11
Rainbow Lake,
200 ....NC-17
Randall, 250 ....NJ-17
Randolph, 1286 ....NM-3
Ransomville, 1419 ...NH-4
Rapids, 1636 ....NI-4
Raquette Lake,
... .NF-16
Rathbone, 100 ......NM-8
Ravena, 3268 ....NK-18
Ray Brook, 400 .....ND-18
Raymertown, 500 ...NJ-19
Raymondville, 500 ..NB-15
Reading Ctr., 175 ...NL-9
Red Creek, 532 ....NH-10
Red Hook, 1961 ....NM-19
Red Oaks Mill, 3613 ..SB-7
Redfield, 250 ....NG-12
Redford, 477 ....NC-18
Redwood, 605 ......ND-13
Rego Pk. ....†H-13
Remsen, 508 ....NH-15
Rensselaer, 9392 ...SJ-5
RENSSELAER CO.,
159429 ....NJ-20
Rensselaer Falls,
332 ....NC-14
Rensselaerville,
... .NK-18
Retsof, 340 ....NJ-7
Rexford, 500 ....NJ-18
Rexville, 90 ....NM-7
Rhinebeck, 2657 ...NN-18
Rhinecliff, 426 ......NN-18
Richfield Sprs.,
1264 ....NJ-15
Richford, 650 ....NL-12
Richland, 650 ......NG-12
RICHMOND CO.,
468730 ....SG-6
Richmond Hill ....†I-14
Richmond Valley ...*N-5
Richmondville,
918 ....NK-16
Richville, 323 ....ND-14
Ridge, 13336 ....SE-10
Ridgeway, 100 .....NH-4
Ridgewood, 210 ...NH-4
Ridgewood ....†I-12
Rifton, 456 ....NN-18
Rigney Bluff, 1090 ..NH-7
Rio, 180 ....SC-4
Ripley, 872 ....NM-1
Riparius, 200 ....NG-18
Riverhead, 13290 ...SE-11
Riverside, 497 ......NM-3
Riverside Sta., 400 ..NL-9
Riverview, 200 ......NC-12
Rochdale, 1800 ....SB-7
Rochester, 210565 ..NI-7

Column 3

Rock City Falls,
700 ....NI-18
Rock Glen, 120 .....NK-6
Rock Hill, 1742 ......SB-4
Rock Stream, 100 ...NK-9
Rockaway Pt. *L-12
Rockaway Pt. *L-12
Rockdale, 150 ......NL-14
Rockland, 300 ......NN-15
ROCKLAND CO.,
311687 ....SD-6
Rockville Centre,
24023 ....SG-8
Rockwood, 300 .....NI-17
Rocky Pt., 14014 ...SE-10
Rodman, 153 ....NF-12
Roessleville SI-4
Rome, 33725 ....NH-14
Romulus, 800 ......NJ-9
Ronkonkoma,
19082 ....SH-13
Roosevelt, 16258 ...†I-18
Roosevelt Bch.,
... .NH-4
Roscoe, 541 ....NN-15
Rose, 400 ....ND-13
Rosebank *K-8
Roseboom, 200 ....NJ-15
Rosedale, 2911 ....NJ-15
Rosedale Vil. ....†J-15
1349 ....NM-14
Rosiere, 60 ....NE-11
Roslyn, 2770 ....†F-17
Roslyn Estates,
1251 ....†F-17
Roslyn Hbr., 1051 ...†F-17
Roslyn Hts., 6577 ...†F-17
Ross Cors., 800 ...NM-12
Rossburg, 80 ....NK-6
Rossie, 150 ....ND-13
Rossville *M-5
Rotterdam, 20652 ...NJ-18
Rotterdam Jct., ...NI-18
Round Lake, 623 ...NI-19
Round Top, 600 ....NL-18
Rouses Pt., 2209 ...NA-20
Roxbury, 900 ....NL-16
Roxbury *L-12
Rural Grv., 200 .....NJ-17
Rush, 500 ....NI-7
Rushford, 363 ......NL-5
Rushville, 677 ......NJ-8
Russell, 300 ....NC-14
Russell Gdns., 945 ...†F-16
Rye, 15720 ....SE-7
Rye Brook, 9347 ...SD-8
Sabael, 200 ....NF-17
Sabattis, 30 ....NE-16
Sabbath Day Pt.,
160 ....NF-19
Sackets Harbor,
1450 ....NE-12
Saddle Rock, 830 ...†T-15
Sag Hbr., 2169 ....SE-13
Sagaponack, 313 ...SE-13
St. Albans ....†I-15
St. George *J-8
St. Huberts, 35 .....NE-19
St. James, 13268 ...SH-13
St. Johnsburg, 525 ...NB-3
St. Johnsville,
1732 ....NI-16
St. Brooklyn *I-11
St. Butler, 250 ......NI-10
S. Byron, 300 ......NI-6
S. Cairo, 950 ....NL-18
S. Colton, 400 .....NC-15
S. Columbia, 100 ...NI-14
S. Corinth, 250 ....NH-18
S. Corning, 1145 ...NM-9
S. Dansville, 125 ...NK-7
S. Dayton, 620 .....NL-3
S. Edmeston, 120 ...NJ-14
S. Floral Pk., 1764 ...†I-16
S. Glens Falls,
3518 ....NH-18
S. Granville, 500 ...NG-20
S. Greece, 100 ....NB-7
S. Hannibal, 35 ...NH-11
S. Hartford, 100 ...NG-20
S. Hempstead,
3243 ....†I-18
S. Huntington,
9422 ....SI-10
S. Jamesport, 600 ...SE-12
S. Kortright, 180 ...NL-16
S. Livonia, 200 ....NJ-7
S. Lockport, 8324 ...NI-4
S. New Berlin, 350 ...NK-14
S. Onondaga, 650 ...NJ-11
S. Otselic, 500 .....NK-13
S. Ozone Pk. ....†I-14
S. Ripley NL-1
S. Salem, 12300 ...SD-8
S. Schroon, 200 ...NF-19
S. Sodus, 130 ......NH-9
S. Stockton NL-2
S. Wales, 450 ......NJ-4
S. Warsaw, 200 ...NK-5
S. Worcester, 150 ...NK-16
Southampton,
3109 ....SE-12
Southeast Owasco,
... .NJ-11
66135 ....NK-17
Southfields, 600 ...SD-5
Southold, 5748 ....SD-12
Southport, 7238 ...NM-10
Southwood, 900 ...NJ-12
Spafford, 910 ....NJ-11
Sparrow Bush, 1200 ...SC-4
Speculator, 324 ....NG-17
Speedsville, 400 ...NL-12
Speigletown, 1200 ...NJ-19
Spencer, 759 ....NL-11
Spencerport, 3601 ...NI-7
Spencertown, 500 ...NL-19
Split Rock, 350 ....NJ-12
Spragueville, 135 ...ND-13
Spring Brook, 350 ...NJ-4
Spring Glen, 600 ...SB-5
Spring Valley, 31347 ...SD-6
Springfield Ctr.,
400 ....NK-16
Springfield Gdns. ...†I-15
Springs, 6592 ......SE-13
Springville, 4296 ...NK-4
Springwater, 670 ...NJ-7
Staatsburg, 377 ...NN-18
Stafford, 500 ....NI-6
Stamford, 1119 ....NL-16
Standish, 190 ......NB-18
Stanford Hts. SI-3
1050 ....NH-15
Stanfordville, 630 ...NN-19
Stanley, 300 ....NJ-8
Stannards, 360 ....NM-6
Star Lake, 809 .....NC-15
Starkville, 120 .....NJ-16
Slate Line, 100 ....NM-1
Steamburg, 900 ...NM-3

Column 4

Shandaken, 500 ....NM-17
Sharon Sprs., 558 ...NJ-16
Shawnee NA-4
Sheds, 70 ....NJ-13
Shelby, 300 ....NH-5
Sheldrake, 110 .....NK-10
Sheldrake Sprs.,
100 ....NK-10
Shelter Island,
1333 ....SD-12
Shelter Island Hts.,
1048 ....SD-12
Sherburne, 1367 ...NK-14
Sheridan, 400 ......NK-2
Sherman, 730 .....NM-1
Sherrill, 3071 ....NI-13
Shinnecock Hills,
2188 ....SE-12
Shirley, 27854 ......SF-11
Shokan, 1183 ......NM-18
Shongo, 125 ....NM-6
Shoreham, 531 ....SE-10
Short Tract, 500 ...NL-6
Shortsville, 1439 ...NI-8
Shrub Oak, 2011 ...SC-7
Shushan, 350 ......NI-20
Sidney, 3900 ....NL-14
Sidney Ctr., 800 ...NL-14
Silver Bay, 250 .....NF-19
Silver Creek, 2656 ...NL-3
Silver Lake, 100 ...NK-5
Silver Sprs., 782 ...NK-6
Sinclairville, 588 ...NL-2
Skaneateles, 2450 ...NJ-11
Skaneateles Falls,
850 ....NI-11
Slate Hill, 800 ......SC-5
Slaterville Sprs.,
300 ....NL-11
Sleepy Hollow, 9870 ..SE-7
Slingerlands, 2100 ...NJ-3
Sloan, 3661 ....NK-5
Sloansville, 200 ...NJ-17
Sloatsburg, 3039 ...SD-6
Smallwood, 580 ...NN-14
Smithboro, 200 ...NM-12
Smithtown, 26470 ...SH-12
Smithville, 500 ....NM-12
Smithville Flats,
351 ....NL-13
Smyrna, 213 ....NK-13
Snyder ND-5
Sodus, 1819 ....NH-9
Sodus Ctr., 200 ...NH-9
Sodus Pt., 900 ....NH-9
Solon, 50 ....NK-12
Solvay, 6584 ....NI-11
Somerset, 70 ....NH-4
Sonora, 70 ....NL-9
Sonyea, 350 ....NK-7
Sound Bch., 7612 ...SE-10
Soundview ....†E-13
S. Alabama, 100 ...NI-5
S. Amenia, 100 ....NN-20
S. Apalachin, 120 ...NM-12
S. Argyle, 230 ......NH-20
S. Beach *L-8
S. Berne NK-18
S. Bethlehem, 350 ...NJ-18
S. Bolivar, 75 ......NM-6
S. Bombay NB-16
S. Bristol, 100 .....NJ-8
S. Brooklyn *I-11
S. Butler, 250 ......NI-10
S. Cairo, 950 ....NL-18
Wales Ctr., 400 (actually column 5)

Column 5

Stephentown, 750 ...NK-20
Sterling, 300 ....NH-10
Stewart Manor,
1896 ....†H-14
Stilesville, 85 ....NM-14
Stillwater, 1738 ...NI-19
Stittville, 700 ....NH-14
Stockbridge, 100 ...NI-13
Stockport, 400 .....NL-19
Stockton, 450 .....NL-2
Stone Mills, 45 ....NE-12
Stone Ridge, 1173 ...NN-18
Stony Brook,
13740 ....SH-12
Stony Creek, 250 ...NG-18
Stony Pt., 12147 ...SD-6
Stormville, 700 ....SB-7
Stottville, 1375 ....NL-19
Stow, 300 ....NM-2
Stratford, 300 .....NH-16
Strykersville, 647 ...NJ-5
Studley Mills, 70 ...ND-19
Stuyvesant Falls,
... .NL-19
Suffern, 10723 ....SD-6
Sugar Loaf, 400 ...SC-5
SULLIVAN CO.,
77547 ....NN-15
Sullivanville, 120 ...NM-10
Summer Hill, 110 ...NK-11
Summit, 300 ....NK-16
Summitville, 700 ...SB-5
Sundown, 200 .....NN-17
Sunnyside ....†H-11
Surprise, 200 ......NL-18
Swain, 200 ....NK-6
Swan Lake, 1200 ...SA-3
Swormville, 50 ....NI-4
Sycaway, 1950 ...SH-6
Sylvan Bch., 897 ...NH-13
Syicaville, 2450 ...NJ-11
Syosset, 18829 ...SF-8
Syracuse, 145170 ...NI-12
Taberg, 550 ....NH-14
Taborton, 200 .....NK-20
Taghkanic, 120 ....NL-19
Talcottville, 120 ...NG-14
Tannersville, 539 ...NL-18
Tappan, 6613 .....SE-7
Tarrytown, 11277 ...SE-7
Taylor, 200 ....NK-12
Terryville, 11849 ...SG-14
Texas, 175 ....NG-11
Texas Valley, 75 ...NK-12
Thayer Corners, 100 ...NA-17
Thendara, 280 ....NF-15
Theresa, 863 ......ND-13
Thomaston, 2617 ...†F-16
Thompson Ridge,
450 ....SB-5
Thompsonville, 400 ...SB-4
Three Mile Bay,
... .NE-11
Three Rivers, 200 ...NI-11
Throg's Neck ....†E-14
Thurston, 100 .....NL-8
Ticonderoga,
3382 ....NF-19
Tillson, 1586 ....NN-18
Tioga Ctr., 300 ...NM-11
TIOGA CO.,
51125 ....NM-11
Tivoli, 1118 ....NM-18
Todt Hill *K-7
Tomkins Cove, 850 ...SD-6
Tonawanda, 15130 ...NC-4
Tottenville *N-5
Town Line, 2367 ...NJ-4
Towners, 150 ......SC-8
Travis *L-6
Treadwell, 200 ....NL-15
Triangle, 350 ......NL-12
Tribes Hill, 1003 ...NI-17
Troupsburg, 300 ...NM-8
Trout Creek, 250 ...NM-14
Trout River, 150 ...NA-17
Troy, 50129 ....NJ-19
Trumansburg,
1797 ....NK-10
Trumbulls Corners,
110 ....NL-11
Truthville, 380 .....NG-20
Truxton, 500 ....NJ-12
Tuckahoe, 6486 ...*B-13
Tuckahoe, 1873 ...SE-12
Tully, 873 ....NJ-12
Tunnel, 200 ....NL-13
Tupper Lake, 3667 ...ND-17
Turin, 232 ....NG-14
Tuscarora, 74 .....NM-8
Tuxedo Pk., 623 ...SD-6
Twin Orchards,
1600 ....NC-10
Tylersville, 110 ....NH-6
Tyre, 180 ....NI-10
Tyrone, 500 ....NL-9
ULSTER CO.,
182493 ....NN-17
Unadilla, 1128 ....NL-14
Unadilla Forks,
150 ....NJ-14
Underwood, 55 ...NE-19
Union Ctr., 1500 ...NM-12
Union Hill, 800 ....NH-8
Union Port ....†E-13
Union Sprs., 1197 ...NJ-10
Uniondale, 24759 ...†I-18
Unionville, 612 ....SC-20
W. Lebanon, 450 ...NK-20
W. Leyden, 500 ...NG-14
W. Martinsburg,
... .NG-14
W. Milton, 350 ....NI-18
W. Monroe, 400 ...NH-11
W. New Brighton ...*J-8
W. Nyack, 6663 ...SC-3
W. Park, 800 ......NN-18
W. Plattsburgh,
150 ....NB-19
W. Point, 6763 ...SC-6
W. Sand Lake,
2660 ....NK-19
W. Sayville, 5011 ...SJ-13
W. Schuyler, 240 ...NI-14
W. Seneca, 44711 ...NJ-4
W. Shokan, 350 ...NM-17
W. Stephentown,
330 ....NK-20
W. Stockholm,
150 ....NB-15
W. Taghkanic,
300 ....NM-19
W. Valley, 518 .....NL-4
W. Walworth, 350 ...NI-8
W. Webster, 8700 ...NH-8
W. Windsor, 350 ...NM-13
W. Winfield, 826 ...NJ-15

Column 6

Vernon Ctr., 400 ...NI-14
Verona, 852 ....NI-13
Versailles, 280 ....NK-3
Vesper, 180 ....NJ-12
Vestal, 5000 ....NM-12
Veteran, 250 ....NM-18
Victor, 2696 ....NI-8
Victory, 140 ....NI-10
Victory Mills, 605 ...NI-19
Vienna, 4000 ......NH-13
Village Green,
3891 ....NE-6
Village of the Branch,
1807 ....SH-12
Vine Valley, 200 ...NJ-8
Virgil, 300 ....NK-12
Vista, 750 ....SD-8
Volney, 150 ....NH-11
Voorheesville,
2789 ....NK-18
Waddington, 972 ...NB-14
Wading River,
7709 ....SE-11
Wainscott, 650 ...SE-13
Wakefield ....†C-13
Walden, 6978 .....SB-6
Wales Ctr., 400 ...NJ-5
Walker Valley, 853 ...SB-5
Wallace, 200 ......NL-8
Wallington, 110 ...NH-9
Wallkill, 2288 .....SB-6
Walton, 3088 ......NM-15
Walworth, 650 ....NI-8
Wampsville, 543 ...NI-13
Wanakah, 3199 ...NJ-3
Wanakena, 250 ...NE-15
Wantagh, 18871 ...†I-20
Wappingers Falls,
5522 ....SB-7
Warners, 500 ......NI-11
Warnerville, 1000 ...NK-17
Warren, 1000 .....NJ-15
WARREN CO.,
65707 ....NG-18
Warrensburg,
4273 ....NG-19
3103 ....NG-19
Warsaw, 3473 ....NK-6
Warwick, 6731 ...SD-5
WASHINGTON CO.,
63216 ....NH-20
Washington Mills,
1183 ....SC-12
Washingtonville,
5899 ....SC-6
Wassaic, 700 .....NN-20
Water Island SJ-14
Waterford, 1990 ...NJ-19
Waterloo, 5171 ...NJ-10
Waterport, 400 ...NH-5
Watertown,
27023 ....NE-12
Waterville, 1583 ...NJ-14
Watervliet, 10254 ...NH-5
Watkins Glen,
1859 ....NL-10
Watson, 100 ....NF-14
Watts Flats, 100 ...NM-2
Waverly, 4444 ....NM-11
Wawarsing, 800 ...SA-5
Wayland, 1865 ...NK-7
Wayne, 550 ....NK-9
Wayne Ctr., 100 ...NI-9
WAYNE CO.,
93772 ....NI-9
Webbs Mills, 300 ...NM-9
Webster, 5399 ....NH-8
Websters Crossing,
69 ....NK-7
Weedsport, 1815 ...NI-10
Wegatchie, 65 ....ND-13
Wells Br., 300 ....NL-14
Wellsburg, 580 ...NM-10
Wellsville, 4679 ...NM-6
Wendelville, 150 ...NI-4
W. Amboy, 125 ...NH-12
W. Babylon, 43213 ...SF-9
W. Bangor, 250 ...NB-17
W. Bloomfield, 600 ...NJ-8
W. Branch, 100 ...NJ-15
W. Burlington, 100 ...NJ-15
W. Camp, 400 ...NM-18
W. Carthage,
2012 ....NE-13
W. Chazy, 529 ...NB-19
W. Chenango SA-4
W. Clarksville, 300 ...NM-5
W. Corners, 1800 ...SB-9
W. Danby, 200 ...NL-11
W. Davenport, 250 ...NL-15
W. Eaton, 500 ...NJ-13
W. Edmeston, 125 ...NJ-14
W. Elmira, 4967 ...NM-10
W. Exeter, 100 ...NJ-15
W. Farms ....†E-13
W. Fulton, 200 ...NK-17
W. Galway, 150 ...NI-18
W. Glens Falls,
7071 ....NH-19
W. Groton, 60 ....NK-11
W. Haverstraw,
10165 ....SD-6
W. Hebron, 175 ...NH-20
W. Hempstead ....†H-17
W. Hills, 5592 ....SI-10
W. Hurley, 990 ...NM-18
W. Islip, 28335 ...SJ-11
W. Kill, 200 ....NL-17
W. Laurens, 450 ...NK-15

Column 7 — WESTCHESTER CO. etc.

Westbrookville, 500 ...SC-4
Verona, 852 (dup)
WESTCHESTER CO.,
949113 ....SD-8
Westdale, 400 ......NH-13
Westerleigh *K-7
Westerlo, 680 ......NK-18
Westernville, 400 ...NH-14
Westfield, 3224 ...NL-1
Westford, 250 .....NK-16
Westhampton,
3079 ....SF-11
Westhampton Bch.,
1721 ....SF-11
Westmere, 7284 ...NJ-18
Westmoreland,
427 ....NI-14
Weston, 90 ....NL-3
Weston Mills,
1472 ....NM-5
Westport, 518 .....ND-20
Westtown, 700 ...SC-4
Westvale, 4963 ...NI-7
Westville, 100 .....NA-17
Westville Ctr., 120 ...NA-17
Wevertown, 220 ...NF-19
Whallonsburg,
600 ....NN-20
Wheatley Hts.,
5130 ....SI-10
Wheatville, 150 ...NI-5
Wheeler, 130 .....NL-8
Whippleville, 200 ...NB-17
White Creek, 200 ...NI-20
White Lake, 2400 ...NN-14
White Plains, 56853 ...SE-7
White Sulphur Sprs.,
600 ....NN-16
Whitehall, 2614 ...NG-20
Whitesboro, 3772 ...SA-12
Whitestone ....†E-14
Whitesville, 800 ...NM-7
Whitney Pt., 964 ...NL-12
Willard, 600 ....NK-10
Willet, 400 ....NK-13
Williams Br. ....†D-13
Williamsburg *I-11
Williamson, 2495 ...NH-9
Williamstown,
600 ....NH-12
Willing, 800 ....NM-6
Willow Pt., 1700 ...SB-10
Willow Ridge Estates,
4800 ....NC-4
Willowemoc, 70 ...NN-16
Willsboro, 753 ...ND-20
Willsboro Pt., 500 ...NC-20
Willseyville, 300 ...NL-11
Wilmington, 937 ...ND-18
Wilson, 1264 .....NH-4
Wilton, 600 ....NH-19
Windham, 367 ...NL-17
Windsor, 916 .....NM-13
Winebrook Hills,
200 ....NE-18
Wingdale, 650 ...SB-8
Winthrop, 500 ....NB-16
Wiscoy, 165 ....NK-6
Witherbee, 347 ...NE-19
Wolcott, 1701 ...NH-10
Wolcottsville, 600 ...NI-5
Wood Haven ....†I-13
Woodbourne, 1200 ...SA-4
Woodbury, 10686 ...SC-6
Woodbury, 8907 ...SH-10
Woodgate, 450 ...NG-15
Woodhull, 350 ...NM-8
Woodland, 125 ...NM-17
Woodlawn, 1000 ...NG-4
Woodmere, 17121 ...†J-16
Woodridge, 847 ...SB-4
Woodrow *L-6
Woodsburgh, 778 ...*K-16
Woodside ....†I-11
Woodstock, 2088 ...NM-18
Woodville J-11
Worcester, 1113 ...NK-16
Worth, 25 ....NF-12
Wrights Cors., 200 ...NH-4
Wurtsboro, 1244 ...SB-4
Wyandanch, 11647 ...SI-11
Wynantskill, 3276 ...SI-6
Wyoming, 434 .....NJ-6
WYOMING CO.,
42155 ....NJ-5
Yaphank, 5945 ...SF-10
Yates Ctr., 200 ....NH-8
Yates, 650 ....NH-5
YATES CO., 25348.NK-9
Yonkers, 195976 ...SE-7
York, 650 ....NJ-6
Yorkshire, 1180 ...NK-5
Yorktown Hts., 1781 ...SD-7
Yorkville, 2689 ...NI-14
Youngstown, 1935 ...NH-3
Youngsville, 850 ...NN-16
Yulan, 750 ....SC-3

North Carolina

Page locator

Map keys	Atlas pages
1–10	150–151
11–20	154–155

* City keyed to pp. 154–155

Abbottsburg, 190 ...H-11
Aberdeen, 6350 ...G-9
Addie *E-13
Addor G-9
Advance, 1138 ....C-9
Afton, 60 ....C-13
Ahoskie, 5039 ....C-16
Airlie, 50 ....C-14
W. Milton, 350 ...
W. Monroe, 400 ...NH-11
W. New Brighton ...*J-8
W. Nyack, 6663 ...
ALAMANCE CO.,
151131 ....D-9
Albemarle, 15903 ...F-7
Albertson, 180 ...G-13
Alarka *E-13
Alamance, 250 ...E-1
ALEXANDER CO.,
37198 ....D-4
Alexis, 600 ....F-3
Alert C-13
Alexander, 200 ...E-4
ALLEGHANY CO.,
11155 ....B-4
Allen B-6
Allensville, 80 ....C-11
Alliance, 776 .....G-17
Alma, 50 ....H-10
Almond, 150 .....*E-13
Almont *B-18
Altamahaw, 347 ...C-9
Altamont D-2
W. Stockholm ...
ANSON CO.,
26948 ....H-7

Column — WAYNE CO. area / North Carolina continued

Ansonville, 631 ...G-7
Apex, 37476 ....E-11
Aquadale, 397 ...G-7
Aquone, 220 ......M-2
Arabia, 110 ....H-10
Arapahoe, 556 ...G-17
Ararat, 50 ....C-6
Arcadia, 130 ......D-7
Archdale, 11415 ...D-8
Arcola, 60 ....C-13
Arden, 800 ....*E-1
Arnold *E-1
Arran Hills, 2240 ...M-15
Ash, 250 ....J-12
Asheboro, 25012 ...E-8
Asheville, 83393 ...E-1
Ashford C-4
Ashley Hts., 380 ...G-10
Askewville, 241 ...C-16
Askin, 200 ....H-11
Atkinson, 299 .....I-13
Atlantic, 543 ......H-18
Atlantic Bch., 1495 ...H-17
Auburn, 350 ......E-12
Aulander, 895 ...C-16
Aurora, 520 ....F-17
Austin E-1
Autryville, 196 ...G-12
Avery Creek, 1950 ...F-1
Avon, 770 ....E-20
Ayden, 4932 ......F-15
Aydlett, 240 ......C-19
Ayersville, 150 ...N-3
Azalea M-9
Badin, 1974 ......F-7
Bahama, 500 .....C-11
Bailey, 569 ....E-13
Bakersville, 464 ...D-2
Bald Creek, 110 ...D-1
Bald Head Island,
158 ....K-13
Balsam, 400 .....L-4
Balsam Grv., 120 ...M-4
Banner Elk, 1028 ...C-3
Banner Mill, 30 ...F-2
Bat Cave, 600 ...F-1
Bath, 249 ....F-17
Bayboro, 1263 ...G-17
Bayleaf, 800 ......*G-13
Bayview, 346 .....F-17
Bear Creek, 130 ...E-9
Bear Grass, 73 ...E-16
Beard, 170 ....L-1
Bear Poplar E-6
Beargrass, 73 ...E-16
Beaufort, 4039 ...H-17

Final columns — North Carolina counties

Burlington, 49963 ...D-9
Burney, 70 ....H-11
Burnsville, 1693 ...D-1
Burnsville, 50 ....G-7
Burnt Mills, 50 ...C-10
Bushy Fork, 150 ...C-10
Busick D-2
Butner, 7591 .....C-11
Butters, 294 ......I-11
Buxton, 1273 ....E-20
Bynum, 490 ......E-10
Cajahs Mtn., 2823 ...D-3
Calabash, 1967 ...K-12
Calypso, 589 .....G-13
Camden, 599 ...C-18
Cameron, 285 ...F-10
Camp Sprs., 40 ...C-9
Campbell Creek,
... .F-17
Candler, 600 .....F-17
Candor, 840 ......F-8
Canton, 4227 ....L-5
Cape Carteret,
1917 ....H-16
Carbonton, 60 ...E-9
Carolina Bch., 5706 ...K-14
Carolina Shores,
3048 ....K-12
Carpenter, 300 ...*I-10
Carr, 50 ....C-10
Carrboro, 19582 ...D-10
CARTERET CO.,
66449 ....H-16
Carthage, 2205 ...F-9
Carvers, 70 ....J-12
Cary, 135234 ....E-11
Casar, 297 ....F-3
Cashiers, 50 .....M-4
Castalia, 268 .....D-13
Castle Hayne, 1202 ...I-14
Casville, 150 .....C-9
Caswell Bch., 398 ...K-13
CASWELL CO.,
23719 ....C-9
Catawba, 603 ...E-5
CATAWBA CO.,
154358 ....E-4
Catherine Lake,
200 ....H-15
Cayton, 70 ....F-16
Cedar Creek, 210 ...G-11
Cedar Grv., 150 ...C-10
Cedar Island, 300 ...G-18
Cedar Mtn., 300 ...G-1
Cedar Pt., 1279 ...H-16
Celo D-2
Center Hill, 350 ...C-17
Centerville, 89 ...C-13
Cerro Gordo, 207 ...J-11
Chadbourn, 1856 ...J-11
Chalybeate Sprs.,
... .F-10
Chapanoke C-18
Chapel Hill, 57233 ...D-10
Charlotte, 731424 ...F-5
CHATHAM CO.,
63505 ....E-10
Cherokee, 2138 ...L-3
CHEROKEE CO.,
27444 ....M-1
Cherry, 50 ....F-17
Cherry Lane, 60 ...B-5
Cherryville, 5760 ...F-4
Chimney Rock, 113 ...F-1
China Grv., 3563 ...E-6
Chinquapin, 30 ...H-14
Chip, 180 ....F-18
Chocowinity, 820 ...E-16
CHOWAN CO.,
14793 ....C-17
Churchland, 180 ...C-7
Cid E-7
Claremont, 1352 ...E-5
Clark, 80 ....G-15
Clarkton, 837 ...I-12
Clayton, 16116 ...E-12
Clemmons, 18627 ...D-7
Cliffdale G-11
Cliffside, 611 ......F-3
Clifton, 100 ....N-3
Climax, 450 ......D-8
Clinton, 8639 ...G-12
Clyde, 1278 ....L-4
Coats, 2112 ......F-11
Cofield, 413 ......C-16
Coinjock, 335 ...C-19
Colerain, 204 ....C-17
Coleridge, 200 ...E-8
Colfax, 1050 .....*B-13
Colington D-20
Collettsville, 200 ...D-3
Colon, 100 ....E-10
Columbia, 891 ...D-18
Columbus, 992 ...F-2

HERTFORD CO. column

HERTFORD CO.,
24669 ....C-16
Hester C-11
Hickory, 40010 ...E-4
Hickory Grv., 80 ...*G-1
Hiddenite, 536 ...D-5
High Falls, 220 ...E-9
High Hampton, 50 ...M-4
High Pt., 104371 ...D-8
High Rock, 696 ...F-4
High Shoals, 696 ...F-4
Highlands, 924 ...M-4
Hightowers C-10
Hightsville, 739 ...L-19
Hildebran, 2023 ...E-4
Hillcrest, 440 .....G-10
Hillsborough, 6087 ...D-10
Hiwassee Dam, 300 ...M-1
Hobbsville, 170 ...C-17
Hobbton, 40 ....G-12
Hobgood, 348 ...D-15
Hobucken, 129 ...F-17
Hoffman, 588 .....G-9
HOKE CO., 46952 ...G-10
Holden Bch., 575 ...K-13
Hollister, 674 ....C-13
Holly Ridge, 1268 ...I-15
Holly Sprs., 24661 ...E-11
Hookerton, 409 ...F-14
Hope Mills, 15176 ...G-11
Hot Sprs., 560 ...J-5
Hubert, 350 ....H-16
Hudson, 3776 ...D-4
Huntersville, 46773 ...F-5
Hurdle Mills, 60 ...C-10
HYDE CO., 5810 ...E-18
Indian Trail, 33518 ...J-7
Ingalls, 200 ....D-2
Ingleside, 70 .....C-13
Ingold, 471 ....H-12
IREDELL CO.,
159437 ....D-5
Iron Sta., 755 ...F-5
Ivanhoe, 264 ....I-13
Jackson, 513 ...C-15
JACKSON CO.,
40271 ....M-4
Jackson Hill E-7
Jackson Sprs., 300 ...G-9
Jacksonville, 70145 ...H-15
James City, 5899 ...G-16
Jamestown, 3382 ...D-8
Jamesville, 491 ...D-16
Janeiro, 40 ....G-17
Jarvisburg, 450 ...C-19
Jason, 100 ....F-14
Jasper, 130 ....C-19
Jefferson, 1611 ...B-4
Jericho, 30 ....C-17
Jerome, 80 ....H-11
Johns, 50 ....H-9
Johnsonville, 260 ...F-10
JOHNSTON CO.,
168878 ....F-12
Jonathan, 590 ...*J-4
JONES CO.,
10153 ....G-15
Jonestown, 30 ...C-8
Jonesville, 2225 ...C-6
Joyland *G-10
Julian, 400 ....D-9
Jupiter, 80 ....E-1
Justice, 30 ....D-13
Kannapolis, 42625 ...F-6
Kelford, 251 ......C-15
Kellum, 30 ....H-15
Kellumtown, 400 ...H-15
Kelly, 544 ....I-12
Kenansville, 855 ...G-13
Kenly, 1339 ....E-13
Kernersville, 23123 ...D-8
Kerr, 30 ....H-13
Kill Devil Hills,
6683 ....D-20
Kimesville, 140 ...D-9
King, 6904 ....C-7
Kings Creek, 180 ...D-3
Kings Grant, 8113 ...L-20
Kings Mtn., 10296 ...G-4
Kingstown, 681 ...F-3
Kinston, 21677 ...F-15
Kipling, 200 ....F-11
Kittrell, 467 ....C-12
Kitty Fork, 50 .....D-8
Kitty Hawk, 3272 ...C-20
Knightdale, 11401 ...E-12
Knotts Island, 620 ...B-19
Kona, 70 ....D-2
Kure Bch., 2012 ...K-14
Kyle M-2
La Grange, 2873 ...F-14
L. Junaluska, 2734 ...L-4
L. Lure, 1192 .....F-2
Lake Park, 3422 ...G-6
L. Santeetlah, 45 ...L-2
L. Toxaway, 470 ...M-4
L. Waccamaw, 1480 ...J-12
Landis, 3109 .....E-6
Lansing, 158 .....B-4
Lasker, 122 ....C-15
Lattimore, 488 ...F-3
Laurada C-7
Laurel Hill, 1254 ...H-9
Laurel Pk., 2103 ...F-1
Laurel Sprs., 60 ...B-4
Laurinburg, 15962 ...H-9
Lawndale, 606 ...F-3
Lawrence, 80 ...C-15
Lawsonville, 130 ...C-7
Leasburg, 250 ...C-10
Ledger, 280 ......D-2
Leechville, 30 ...E-18
Leggett, 60 ....D-14
Leicester, 600 ...E-1
Leland, 13527 ...I-13
Lemon Sprs., 600 ...F-10
Lenoir, 18228 ...D-3
LENOIR CO.,
59495 ....G-14
Level Cross, 380 ...D-8
Level Cross F-6
Lewisville, 12639 ...D-7
Lexington, 18931 ...E-7
Liberty, 2656 .....D-9
Lillesville, 536 ...G-8
Lillington, 3194 ...F-11

LINCOLN CO. column

LINCOLN CO.,
78265 ....F-4
Lincolnton, 10486 ...F-4
Linden, 130 ....F-11
Linville, 300 ......D-3
Linville Falls, 350 ...D-2
Lisbon, 100 ....J-12
Little River F-18
Little Switzerland,
300 ....D-2
Littleton, 674 .....B-14
Lizzie, 50 ....F-14
Locust, 2930 ....F-7
Logan F-2
Lola, 40 ....G-18
Long Island, 200 ...E-5
Longcreek, 230 ...J-13
Longview, 4871 ...E-4
Longwood, 430 ...K-12
Loray, 190 ....E-5
Louisburg, 3359 ...D-12
Love Valley, 90 ...D-5
Lowell, 3526 .....M-14
Lowes Grv. *H-10
Lowesville, 2945 ...F-5
Lowgap, 324 .....B-5
Lowland, 450 ...F-17
Lucama, 1108 ...E-13
Lucia, 160 ....F-5
Lumber Br., 94 ...H-10
Lumberton, 21542 ...I-11
Lyman, 100 ......N-3
Lynn, 530 ....F-1
Mabel, 90 ....C-3
Macclesfield, 471 ...E-14
Macedonia *J-12
Mackeys, 130 ...D-17
Macon, 119 ......B-13
MACON CO.,
33922 ....M-3
Madison, 2246 ...C-8
MADISON CO.,
20764 ....D-1
Maggie Valley, 1150 ...L-4
Magnolia, 939 ...G-13
Maiden, 3310 ...E-4
Mamers, 826 ....F-11
Mamie, 60 ....C-19
Manns Hbr., 821 ...D-20
Manson, 150 .....B-12
Manteo, 1434 ...D-20
Maple, 250 ....B-19
Maple Hill, 390 ...H-14
Mapleville, 30 ...D-13
Marble, 321 ......M-2
Margarettsville, 240 ...B-15
Marietta, 175 ....J-10
Marion, 7838 ....E-2
Mars Hill, 1869 ...D-1
Marshall, 872 ...K-5
Marshallberg, 403 ...H-18
Marshville, 2402 ...G-7
Marston, 260 ...G-9
Martin, 260 ....G-9
MARTIN CO.,
24505 ....E-16
Marvin, 5579 ...G-5
Matthews, 27198 ...G-6
Maury, 1685 .....F-14
Maxton, 2426 ...H-10
Mayfield, 130 ...A-5
Mayodan, 2478 ...C-8
Maysville, 1019 ...H-16
McAdenville, 651 ...*G-1
McCullers E-11
McDowell Co.,
44996 ....E-2
McFarlan, 117 ...H-8
McGrady, 220 ...C-4
Mebane, 11393 ...D-10
MECKLENBURG CO.,
919628 ....G-5
Merrimon, 130 ...G-17
Merritt, 190 ....G-17
Merry Hill, 80 .....D-17
Merry Oaks, 150 ...E-10
Mesic, 220 ....F-17
Micaville, 250 ...D-2
Micro, 441 ....E-13
Middleburg, 133 ...C-12
Middlesex, 822 ...E-13
Midland, 3073 ...G-6
Midway, 4679 ...*D-2
Mill Spr., Spur ...F-1
Millers Creek, 2112 ...C-4
Millersville, 220 ...J-3
Mills River, 6802 ...F-1
Milltown, 150 .....L-2
Milton, 166 ....B-10
Milwaukee, 280 ...B-15
Mineral Sprs., 2639 ...H-6
Minneapolis, 250 ...D-3
Minnesott Bch.,
440 ....G-17
Mint Hill, 22722 ...G-6
Misenheimer, 728 ...F-7
MITCHELL CO.,
15579 ....D-1
Mocksville, 5051 ...D-6
Moffitt Hill, 30 ...D-1
Mollie, 30 ....J-12
Momeyer, 224 ...D-13
Moncure, 711 ...E-10
Monroe, 32797 ...G-6
Montezuma, 250 ...D-2
MONTGOMERY CO.,
27798 ....F-8
Monticello, 100 ...J-2
Montreat, 723 ...E-1
MOORE CO., 88247.F-9
Mooresboro, 311 ...F-3
Mooresville, 31714 ...E-5
Moravian Falls, 1901 ...D-5
Morehead City,
8661 ....H-17
Morgans Cor., 30 ...B-18
Morganton, 16918 ...E-3
Morrisville, 18576 ...E-11
Morven, 511 .....H-8
Mt. Airy, 10388 ...B-6
Mt. Gilead, 1181 ...G-8
Mt. Holly, 13656 ...*G-1
Mt. Mourne, 580 ...E-5
Mt. Olive, 4589 ...G-13
Mt. Pleasant, 1652 ...F-7
Mt. Vernon Sprs., 30 ...E-9
Mountain Home,
... .M-1
Moyock, 3759 ...B-18
Mulberry, 2332 ...C-4
Murfreesboro, 2835 ...B-16
Murphy, 1627 ...M-1

Murraysville, 7279...K-20
Myrtle Grv., 8875...J-14
Nags Head, 2757...D-20
Nakina, 150...J-12
NASH CO., 95840...D-13
Nashville, 5352...D-13
Navassa, 1505...J-13
Nebo, 840...E-2
Nebraska, 110...F-19
Needmore, 110...E-6
Neuse, 380...D-12
New Bern, 29524...G-16
NEW HANOVER CO., 202667...J-14
New Hill, 360...E-11
New Holland, 40...F-18
New Hope, 370...E-13
New Hope...*H-14
New London, 600...F-7
New Salem, 120...G-7
Newland, 698...D-2
Newport, 4150...H-17
Newton, 12968...E-4
Newton Grv., 569...F-12
Niagara, 180...G-10
Nixonton, 120...C-18
Norlina, 1118...B-13
Norman, 138...G-9
N. Cove, 100...D-2
N. Harlowe, 100...H-17
N. Topsail Bch., 743...I-15
N. Wilkesboro, 4245...C-5
NORTHAMPTON CO., 22099...C-15
Northside, 70...D-11
Northwest, 735...J-13
Norwood, 2379...G-7
Oak City, 317...D-15
Oak Island, 6783...K-13
Oak Ridge, 6185...C-8
Oakboro, 1859...G-7
Ocean Isle Bch., 550...K-12
Ocracoke, 948...G-19
Ogden, 6766...L-20
Old Dock, 70...J-12
Old Fort, 908...E-2
Old Hundred, 287...H-9
Old Sparta, 50...E-15
Old Trap, 150...C-19
Olin, 120...D-5
Olive Branch, 100...G-7
Olivia, 600...F-10
Olympia, 100...G-16
ONSLOW CO., 177772...H-14
Ophir, 30...F-8
ORANGE CO., 133801...C-10
Oregon Hill, 130...B-9
Oriental, 900...G-17
Ormondsville, 50...F-15
Orrum, 91...I-11
Ossipee, 543...C-9
Ostwalt...E-5
Oteen...M-9
Otto, 200...M-3
Otway, 260...H-17
Oxford, 8461...C-12
Pactolus, 230...E-16
Pala Alto, 130...H-16
Palmyra, 30...D-15
Pamlico, 200...G-17
Pamlico Bch., 400...F-17
PAMLICO CO., 13144...G-17
Pantego, 179...E-17
Paradise Pt., 350...*I-1
Parkersburg, 150...H-12
Parkstown, 50...F-14
Parkton, 436...H-11
Parmele, 278...D-15
PASQUOTANK CO., 40661...C-18
Patetown...F-14
Patterson, 530...D-3
Patterson Sprs., 622...G-4
Peachland, 437...G-7
Pekin, 50...G-8
Peletier, 644...H-16
Pelham, 340...B-9
Pembroke, 2973...H-10
PENDER CO., 52217...I-14
Penderlea, 220...H-13
Pendleton, 220...B-15
Penrose, 400...F-1
Pensacola, 60...D-1
PERQUIMANS CO., 13453...C-17
PERSON CO., 39464...B-11
Peru, 250...I-15
Petersburg...H-15
Pfafftown, 1050...C-7
Phoenix, 100...J-13
Pike Road, 100...E-17
Pikeville, 678...F-13
Pilot, 350...D-13
Pilot Mtn., 1477...C-6
Pine Hall, 310...C-8
Pine Knoll Shores, 1339...H-17
Pine Level, 1700...F-13
Pine Ridge...B-6
Pinebluff, 1337...G-9
Pinehurst, 13124...G-9
Pineola, 200...D-3
Pinetops, 1374...E-14
Pinetown, 155...E-17
Pineview...F-10
Pineville, 7479...*J-4
Piney Creek, 60...B-4
Piney Green, 13293...H-15
Pink Hill, 552...G-14
Pinkney, 110...F-13
Pinnacle, 894...C-7
Pireway, 30...K-12
Pisgah Forest, 2150...M-5
PITT CO., 168148...F-15
Pittsboro, 3743...E-10
Pleasant Gdn., 4489...D-8
Pleasant Gdns., 450...E-2
Pleasant Grv....C-10
Pleasant Grv....D-17
Pleasant Hill, 130...B-15
Plumtree, 160...D-2
Plymouth, 3878...D-17
Point Hbr., 370...C-19
POLK CO., 20510...F-1
Polkton, 3375...G-7
Polkville, 545...F-3
Pollocksville, 311...G-16
Poole Town, 130...E-7
Poplar, 160...D-1
Poplar Branch, 550...C-19
Porter, 30...F-7
Potecasi, 300...C-15
Powells Pt., 470...C-19
Powellsville, 276...C-16
Prestonville, 30...B-7
Princeton, 1194...F-13
Princeville, 2082...D-15
Proctorville, 117...I-10
Prospect, 50...K-13
Prospect Hill, 170...C-10
Providence, 430...B-10
Providence, 180...E-2
Providence, 160...C-11
Pumpkin Ctr., 2222...H-15
Pumpkin Ctr....F-5
Purley, 70...B-10
Quick, 50...C-9
Quitsna...D-16
Raeford, 4611...G-10
Raemon, 282...I-10
Raleigh, 403892...E-12
Ramseur, 1692...E-9
Randleman, 4113...E-8
RANDOLPH CO., 141752...E-8
Ranger...M-1
Ranlo, 3434...M-14
Ransomville, 70...F-17
Raynham, 72...I-10
Red Cross, 742...F-7
Red Oak, 3430...D-14
Red Sprs., 3428...H-10
Reeds Cross Roads, 140...D-7
Reidsville, 14520...C-9
Rennert, 383...H-10
Republican, 30...D-16
Rex, 55...H-10
Rhoney, 200...E-4
Rich Sq., 958...C-15
Richardson, 110...I-11
Richfield, 613...F-7
Richlands, 1520...H-15
RICHMOND CO., 46639...G-8
Riddle, 180...C-19
Ridgecrest, 500...E-1
Ridgeway, 350...B-13
Riegelwood, 579...J-13
Ringwood, 40...C-14
River Bend, 3119...G-16
Rivermont, 350...F-14
Roanoke Rapids, 15754...B-14
Roaring Gap, 480...C-5
Roaring River, 600...C-5
Robbins, 1097...F-9
Robbinsville, 620...L-2
Roberdel, 240...G-8
Robersonville, 1488...D-15
ROBESON CO., 134168...H-10
Rockfish, 3298...G-10
Rockingham, 9558...H-8
ROCKINGHAM CO., 93643...C-8
Rockwell, 2108...E-7
Rocky Mount, 57477...D-14
Rocky Pt., 1602...I-14
Rockyhock...C-17
Rodanthe, 261...E-20
Roduco, 200...B-17
Rolesville, 3786...D-12
Ronda, 417...C-5
Roper, 611...D-17
Rose Hill, 1626...H-13
Roseboro, 1191...G-12
Rosemead, 30...C-16
Rosewood, 4300...F-13
Rosman, 576...M-5
Rougemont, 978...C-11
ROWAN CO., 138428...E-6
Rowland, 1037...I-10
Roxboro, 8362...C-11
Roxobel, 240...C-15
Royal, 70...F-17
Royal Pines, 4272...F-1
Ruffin, 368...B-9
Rural Hall, 2937...C-7
Ruth, 440...F-2
RUTHERFORD CO., 67810...F-2
Rutherford College, 1341...E-4
Rutherfordton, 4213...F-2
Ryland, 40...C-17
St. Helena, 389...I-14
St. James, 3165...K-13
St. Lewis, 70...E-14
St. Pauls, 2035...H-11
Salem, 2218...E-3
Salemburg, 435...G-12
Salisbury, 33662...E-6
Salter Path, 800...H-17
Saluda, 713...F-1
Salvo, 229...E-20
Samarcand, 150...F-9
Samaria, 80...D-13
SAMPSON CO., 63431...G-12
Sand Hill...M-7
Sanderling, 340...C-19
Sandy Creek, 260...J-13
Sandy Ridge, 400...*C-4
Sandy Ridge, 230...B-7
Sandyfield, 447...I-13
Sanford, 28094...F-10
Sapphire, 150...M-4
Saratoga, 408...E-14
Saulston, 110...F-14
Saunook, 120...L-4
Sawmills, 5240...E-4
Saxapahaw, 1648...D-10
Scaly Mtn., 480...M-3
SCOTLAND CO., 36157...H-9
Scotland Neck, 2059...C-15
Scotts, 190...D-5
Scotts Hill, 140...J-14
Scottville, 50...B-4
Scranton, 120...E-18
Seaboard, 632...B-15
Seabreeze, 1969...J-14
Seagrove, 228...F-8
Sealevel, 380...H-18
Seaside, 50...K-12
Sedalia, 623...D-9
Sedgefield, 1000...*C-6
Selma, 6073...E-13
Semora, 250...B-10
Seven Devils, 192...C-3
Seven Lakes, 4888...F-9
Seven Sprs., 110...G-14
Severn, 276...B-16
Shallotte, 3675...K-12
Shannon, 263...H-10
Sharpsburg, 2024...D-14
Shawboro, 520...B-19
Shelby, 20323...F-3
Shelmerdine...F-15
Shepherds, 250...E-5
Sherrills Ford, 900...E-5
Shiloh, 150...C-19
Shooting Creek, 100...M-2
Shopton...*I-3
Sidney, 100...F-17
Sidney, 70...J-11
Siler City, 7887...E-9
Siloam, 60...C-6
Silver City, 882...G-10
Silver Lake, 5598...J-14
Silverstone, 120...C-3
Simpson, 416...E-15
Sims, 282...E-13
Skibo...M-15
Skippers Cor., 2785...J-14
Sladesville...F-18
Sligo, 90...B-19
Slocomb, 60...G-11
Small, 50...F-17
Smethport, 200...B-4
Smith Grv., 40...D-6
Smithfield, 10966...F-12
Smithtown, 200...C-6
Sneads Ferry, 2646...I-15
Snow Camp, 100...D-9
Snow Hill, 1595...F-14
Sophia, 400...E-8
S. Creek, 130...F-17
S. Gastonia, 5433...N-13
S. Mills, 454...B-18
S. River, 170...G-17
S. Wadesboro, 160...H-8
Southern Pines, 12334...G-9
Southern Shores, 2714...C-20
Southern Shores, 60...C-18
Southmont, 1470...E-7
Southport, 2833...K-13
Sparta, 1770...B-5
Speed, 80...D-15
Spencer, 3267...E-7
Spencer Mtn., 37...L-14
Spindale, 4321...F-2
Spivey's Cor., 506...G-12
Spot...C-19
Spout Sprs....F-10
Spring Creek...K-5
Spring Hope, 1320...D-13
Spring Lake, 11964...G-11
Spruce Pine, 2175...D-2
Stacy, 280...H-18
Staley, 393...E-9
Stallings, 13831...*J-6
Stanfield, 1486...G-7
Stanhope, 130...D-13
Stanley, 3556...F-5
Stanleyville...*A-1
STANLY CO., 60585...F-7
Stantonsburg, 784...E-14
Star, 876...F-8
State Road, 480...C-5
Statesville, 24532...E-5
Stecoah, 150...L-2
Stedman, 1028...G-11
Stella, 130...H-16
Stem, 463...C-11
Stokes, 376...E-15
STOKES CO., 47401...C-7
Stokesdale, 5047...C-8
Stoneville, 1056...B-8
Stonewall, 281...G-17
Stony Pt., 1317...D-5
Stovall, 418...B-12
Stubbs, 50...F-4
Stumpy Pt., 260...E-20
Sturgills...B-4
Sugar Grv., 450...C-3
Sugar Hill, 70...E-2
Sugar Mtn., 198...C-3
Summerfield, 10232...C-8
Sunbury, 289...B-17
Sunny View, 130...F-2
Sunset Bch., 3572...K-12
Supply, 550...K-13
Surf City, 1853...I-15
Surl...C-11
SURRY CO., 73673...C-6
SWAIN CO., 13981...L-3
Swann...F-10
Swannanoa, 4576...E-1
Swanquarter, 324...F-18
Swansboro, 2663...H-16
Swepsonville, 1154...D-10
Sylva, 2588...L-4
Tabor City, 2511...J-11
Tapoco, 200...L-2
Tar Heel, 117...H-11
Tarboro, 11415...D-15
Taylorsville, 2098...D-4
Taylortown, 722...G-9
Teachey, 376...H-13
Terrell, 650...E-5
Texaco Bch., 170...C-19
Texana, 400...M-1
Thomasboro...K-12
Thomasville, 26757...D-8
Thurman, 80...G-16
Thurmond, 220...C-5
Tillery, 240...C-15
Timberlake, 280...C-11
Toast, 1450...B-6
Tobaccoville, 2441...C-7
Todd, 180...C-3
Toluca, 100...F-4
Tomahawk, 30...H-12
Tomotla, 130...M-1
Topnot, 50...C-10
Topsail Bch., 368...I-14
Topton, 230...M-2
Townsville, 350...B-12
Tramway, 250...F-10
TRANSYLVANIA CO., 33090...M-5
Trap, 30...C-16
Traphill, 220...C-5
Travis, 30...D-18
Trent Woods, 4155...G-16
Trenton, 287...G-15
Triangle, 850...F-5
Trinity, 6614...D-8
Troutman, 2383...E-5
Troy, 3189...F-8
Trust...K-5
Tryon, 1646...G-1
Tuckasegee, 420...M-4
Tunis, 250...C-16
Turkey, 292...G-13
Turnersburg, 50...D-6
Tuscarora, 50...G-16
Tuskeegee, 50...L-2
Tusquitee, 30...M-2
Tuxedo, 1100...G-1
Twin Oaks...B-5
TYRRELL CO., 4407...D-18
Ulah, 200...E-8
Unaka...M-1
Union, 300...C-16
UNION CO., 201292...G-6
Union Cross, 330...D-7
Union Grv., 400...D-5
Union Ridge, 60...C-9
Unionville, 5929...G-6
Uwharie, 150...F-8
Valdese, 4490...E-3
Vale, 100...E-4
Valhalla, 30...C-17
Valle Crucis, 412...C-3
VANCE CO., 45422...C-12
Vanceboro, 1005...F-16
Vandemere, 254...G-17
Vander, 1146...G-11
Varnamtown, 541...K-13
Vass, 720...F-10
Vaughan, 170...B-13
Venable, 330...N-7
Verona, 870...H-15
Vienna, 710...C-7
Vinton Woods, 380...L-14
Vista...I-14
Waco, 321...F-4
Wade, 556...G-11
Wadesboro, 5813...G-8
Wadeville, 150...F-8
Wagram, 840...H-10
WAKE CO., 900993...D-12
Wake Forest, 30117...D-12
Wakelon, 30...C-16
Wakulla, 105...H-10
Walkertown, 4675...C-7
Wallace, 3880...H-13
Wallburg, 3047...D-7
Walnut, 600...K-5
Walnut Cove, 1425...C-7
Walnut Creek, 835...F-14
Walstonburg, 219...E-14
Wanchese, 1642...D-20
Warbler, 100...E-18
Wards, 50...J-11
Warne, 80...M-2
WARREN CO., 20972...C-13
Warrensville, 300...B-4
Warrenton, 862...C-13
Warsaw, 3054...G-13
Washington, 9744...E-16
WASHINGTON CO., 13228...D-17
Washington Pk., 451...E-16
WATAUGA CO., 51079...C-3
Waterlily, 250...B-19
Waterville...*B-13
Watha, 190...H-14
Waves, 134...E-20
Waxhaw, 9859...H-6
WAYNE CO., 122623...F-13
Waynesville, 9869...L-4
Weaverville, 3120...E-1
Webster, 363...L-4
Weddington, 9459...G-6
Weeksville, 50...C-18
Welcome, 4162...D-7
Weldon, 1655...B-14
Wendell, 5845...E-12
Wentworth, 2807...C-8
Wesley Chapel, 7463...G-6
W. End, 600...G-9
W. Jefferson, 1299...C-4
Westfield, 260...B-7
Westminster...F-2
Westport, 4026...F-5
Wests Mill, 30...M-3
Whispering Pines, 2928...F-10
Whitakers, 744...C-14
White Lake, 802...H-12
White Oak, 338...H-11
White Plains, 1074...B-6
Whitehead, 100...B-5
Whites Crossroads, 30...C-16
Whiteville, 5394...J-11
Whittier, 350...*E-12
Whortonville, 110...G-17
Wildwood, 100...H-17
WILKES CO., 69340...C-5
Wilkesboro, 3413...C-5
Wilkinson, 30...E-17
Willard, 350...H-13
Williamsboro, 60...B-12
Williamsburg, 120...C-9
Williamston, 5511...D-16
Williston, 350...H-18
Willow Sprs., 450...E-11
Wilmar, 50...F-16
Wilmington, 106476...J-14
Wilson, 49167...E-14
WILSON CO., 81234...E-14
Wilsons Mill, 2277...E-12
Wilsonville...*J-9
Windsor, 3630...D-16
Winfall, 594...C-18
Wingate, 3491...G-6
Winnabow, 150...J-13
Winston-Salem, 229617...D-7
Winterville, 9269...E-15
Winton, 769...B-16
Wise, 550...B-13
Wood, 90...C-13
Woodard, 40...D-16
Woodcroft...*H-9
Woodfin, 6123...E-1
Woodland, 809...C-15
Woodlawn...E-2
Woodleaf, 380...E-6
Woodrow, 100...L-5
Wrightsboro, 4496...K-19
Wrightsville...M-20
Wrightsville Bch., 2477...J-14
YADKIN CO., 38406...C-6
Yadkinville, 2959...C-6
YANCEY CO., 17818...D-1
Yanceyville, 2039...C-10
Yellow Creek, 30...*E-9
Yorick, 50...H-12
Yorkwood, 1150...N-13
Youngsville, 1157...D-12
Zebulon, 4433...E-12
Zionville, 230...C-3

North Dakota

Page locator

Map keys	Atlas pages
A–J	156–157

Abercrombie, 263...I-13
Absaraka, 35...H-12
Adams, 127...E-11
ADAMS CO., 2343...J-4
Adrian, 50...I-10
Agate, 20...D-9
Akra, 20...D-11
Alamo, 57...D-3
Alexander, 223...F-2
Alfred, 20...I-9
Alice, 40...H-12
Alkabo...C-2
Almont, 122...H-6
Alsen, 35...D-10
Ambrose, 26...C-3
Amenia, 94...H-12
Amidon, 20...I-3
Anamoose, 227...F-8
Aneta, 222...F-11
Anselm...I-12
Antler, 27...C-6
Appam, 25...D-2
Ardoch, 67...E-12
Arena...H-8
Argusville, 475...H-13
Arnegard, 115...F-3
Arthur, 337...H-12
Arvilla, 200...F-12
Ashley, 749...J-9
Auburn, 48...D-12
Ayr, 17...H-12
Backoo, 30...D-11
Baker, 20...E-8
Baldwin, 60...H-7
Balfour, 26...F-7
Balta, 65...E-8
Bantry, 14...D-7
Barlow, 40...F-9
BARNES CO., 11066...H-11
Barney, 52...I-13
Bartlett...E-10
Barton, 20...D-8
Bathgate, 43...C-12
Battleview, 40...D-4
Beach, 1019...H-2
Belcourt, 2078...D-8
Belden...E-4
Belfield, 800...H-3
Benedict, 66...F-6
BENSON CO., 6660...E-9
Bentley...I-5
Bergen, 7...F-7
Berlin, 34...I-10
Berthold, 454...E-5
Berwick...E-8
Beulah, 3121...G-5
BILLINGS CO., 783...G-2
Binford, 183...F-10
Bisbee, 126...D-9
Bismarck, 61272...H-7
Blabon...G-11
Blaisdell, 75...E-5
Blanchard, 26...G-12
Bordulac, 50...G-10
Bottineau, 2211...D-7
BOTTINEAU CO., 6429...D-7
Bowbells, 336...D-5
Bowdon, 131...G-8
Bowesmont, 40...D-12
Bowman, 1650...J-3
BOWMAN CO., 3151...J-2
Braddock, 21...I-8
Brampton, 20...J-11
Brantford...F-10
Breien, 20...I-6
Bremen, 40...F-9
Briarwood, 73...H-13
Brinsmade, 35...E-9
Brocket, 57...E-10
Buchanan, 90...H-10
Bucyrus, 27...J-4
Buffalo, 188...H-12
BURKE CO., 1968...D-4
BURLEIGH CO., 81308...H-7
Burlington, 1060...E-6
Burnstad...I-8
Burt...I-5
Butte, 68...F-7
Buxton, 323...F-12
Caledonia, 39...G-13
Calio, 22...D-10
Calvin, 20...D-10
Cando, 1115...D-9
Cannon Ball, 875...I-7
Carbury...C-7
Carolville, 30...E-2
Carpio, 157...D-5
Carrington, 2065...G-9
Carson, 293...I-5
Cartwright, 30...F-2
CASS CO., 149778...H-12
Casselton, 2329...H-12
Cathay, 43...G-9
Cavalier, 1302...D-12
CAVALIER CO., 3993...D-10
Cayuga, 27...J-12
Center, 571...H-6
Chaffee, 100...H-12
Charlson...E-4
Chaseley, 40...G-8
Christine, 150...I-13
Churchs Ferry, 12...E-9
Cleveland, 83...H-9
Clifford, 44...G-12
Clyde, 60...D-10
Cogswell, 99...J-11
Coleharbor, 79...G-6
Colfax, 121...I-13
Colgate, 25...G-12
Columbus, 133...C-4
Concrete...D-11
Conway, 23...E-12
Cooperstown, 984...G-11
Corinth...D-3
Coteau, 30...D-4
Coulee, 30...D-5
Courtenay, 45...G-10
Crary, 142...E-10
Crete, 40...J-11
Crosby, 1070...C-3
Crystal, 138...D-11
Crystal Sprs....H-9
Cummings, 75...G-12
Dahlen, 18...E-11
Davenport, 252...H-13
Dawson, 61...H-8
Dazey, 104...G-11
De Lamere, 30...I-12
Deering, 98...E-6
Denbigh, 15...E-7
Denhoff, 20...G-8
Des Lacs, 204...E-6
Devils Lake, 7141...E-10
Dickey, 42...I-10
DICKEY CO., 5289...J-10
Dickinson, 17787...H-4
DIVIDE CO., 2071...D-3
Dodge, 87...G-5
Donnybrook, 59...D-5
Douglas, 64...F-6
Doyon, 40...E-10
Drake, 275...F-7
Drayton, 824...D-12
Dresden...D-10
Driscoll, 82...H-8
Dunn Ctr., 146...G-4
DUNN CO., 3536...G-4
Dunseith, 773...D-8
Dwight, 82...I-13
E. Fairview, 76...F-2
Eckelson, 40...H-11
Eckman...D-6
EDDY CO., 2385...F-9
Edgeley, 563...I-10
Edinburg, 196...D-11
Edmore, 182...E-10
Edmunds...G-10
Egeland, 28...D-9
Eldridge, 50...H-10
Elgin, 642...I-5
Ellendale, 1394...J-10
Elliott, 25...I-11
Embden, 59...H-12
Emerado, 414...F-12
EMMONS CO., 3550...I-8
Enderlin, 886...I-12
Englevale, 40...I-11
Epping, 100...E-3
Erie, 50...G-12
Esmond, 100...E-8
Fairdale, 38...D-11
Fairfield, 140...G-3
Fairmount, 367...J-13
Falkirk, 20...G-6
Fargo, 105549...H-13
Fessenden, 479...F-9
Fillmore, 30...E-8
Fingal, 97...H-11
Finley, 445...G-11
Flasher, 232...I-6
Flaxton, 66...C-4
Flora, 20...F-9
Fonda...D-8
Forbes, 53...J-10
Fordville, 212...E-11
Forest River, 125...E-12
Forman, 504...J-12
Ft. Clark...G-6
Ft. Ransom, 77...I-11
Ft. Rice, 30...I-7
Ft. Totten, 1243...F-9
Ft. Yates, 184...J-7
Fortuna, 22...C-2
FOSTER CO., 3343...G-9
Foxholm, 75...E-6
Fredonia, 46...I-9
Frison, 220...E-10
Frontier, 214...H-13
Fryburg, 50...H-3
Fullerton, 54...J-10
Gackle, 310...I-9
Galchutt, 65...I-13
Galesburg, 108...G-12
Gardar, 30...D-11
Gardena, 29...D-7
Gardner, 74...G-13
Garrison, 1453...F-6
Garske, 30...E-10
Gascoyne, 16...J-3
Geneseo, 60...J-12
Gilby, 237...E-12
Gladstone, 239...H-4
Glasston, 30...D-12
Glen Ullin, 807...H-5
Glenburn, 380...D-6
Glenfield, 91...G-10
Glover...J-11
Golden Valley, 182...G-5
GOLDEN VALLEY CO., 1680...G-2
Golva, 61...H-2
Goodrich, 98...G-8
Grace City, 63...G-10
Grafton, 4284...E-12
Grand Forks, 52838...F-12
GRAND FORKS CO., 66861...F-12
Grand Rapids, 25...I-10
Grandin, 173...G-13
Grano, 7...D-6
GRANT CO., 2394...I-5
Granville, 241...E-7
Grassy Butte, 50...G-3
Great Bend, 60...J-13
Grenora, 244...D-2
GRIGGS CO., 2420...G-11
Guelph, 25...J-11
Guthrie...F-7
Gwinner, 753...J-12
Hague, 71...J-8
Halliday, 188...G-4
Hamar, 20...F-10
Hamberg, 21...F-9
Hamilton, 61...D-12
Hamlet...D-3
Hampden, 48...D-10
Hankinson, 919...J-13
Hanks, 10...D-2
Hannaford, 131...G-11
Hannah, 15...C-10
Hannover, 30...H-6
Hansboro, 12...C-9
Harlow, 50...E-9
Harvey, 1783...F-8
Harwood, 718...H-13
Hastings, 40...H-11
Hatton, 777...F-12
Havana, 71...J-12
Haynes, 23...J-4
Hazelton, 235...I-7
Hazen, 2411...G-5
Heaton, 30...G-9
Hebron, 747...H-5
Heil, 15...I-5
Heimdal, 27...F-8
Hensel, 45...D-11
Hensler, 30...G-6
Hettinger, 1226...J-4
HETTINGER CO., 2477...I-4
Hillsboro, 1603...G-13
Honeyford...E-12
Hoople, 242...D-12
Hope, 258...G-11
Horace, 2430...H-13
Huff, 30...I-7
Hull...J-8
Hunter, 261...G-12
Hurdsfield, 84...G-8
Inkster, 50...E-12
Jamestown, 15427...H-10
Jessie, 25...G-11
Johnstown, 40...E-12
Joliette, 25...D-12
Juanita...G-10
Jud, 72...I-10
Judson, 50...H-6
Karlsruhe, 82...E-7
Kathryn, 52...H-11
Keene, 60...F-3
Kelso...G-13
Kempton, 25...F-12
Kenmare, 1096...D-5
Kensal, 163...G-10
KIDDER CO., 2435...G-8
Kief, 13...F-7
Killdeer, 751...G-4
Kindred, 692...I-13
Kintyre, 50...I-8
Kloten, 40...F-11
Knox, 25...E-8
Kramer, 29...D-7
Kulm, 354...I-10
LA MOURE CO., 4139...I-10
L. Williams, 25...G-9
Lakewood Pk., 220...E-10
Lakota, 672...E-10
Lamoure, 889...I-11
Landa, 38...C-7
Langdon, 1878...D-10
Lankin, 98...E-11
Lansford, 245...D-6
Larimore, 1346...F-12
Lark...I-6
Larson, 12...C-4
Lawton, 30...E-10
Leal, 20...H-11
Leeds, 427...E-9
Lefor, 50...H-4
Lehr, 80...I-9
Leith, 16...I-5
Leonard, 223...I-12
Leroy, 50...C-11
Lidgerwood, 652...J-12
Lignite, 155...C-4
Lincoln, 2406...H-7
Linton, 1097...I-8
Lisbon, 2154...I-12
Litchville, 172...I-11
Logan, 194...E-6
LOGAN CO., 1990...I-9
Loma, 16...D-10
Loraine, 9...D-6
Lostwood...D-4
Ludden, 23...J-11
Luverne, 31...G-11
Lynchburg, 30...H-12
Maddock, 382...F-9
Maida, 35...C-10
Makoti, 154...F-5
Mandan, 18331...H-7
Mandaree, 596...F-4
Manfred, 35...F-8
Manning, 74...G-4
Mantador, 64...J-13
Manvel, 360...E-12
Mapes, 20...E-11
Mapleton, 762...H-13
Marion, 133...I-11
Marmarth, 136...I-2
Marshall, 10...G-4
Martin, 78...F-8
Max, 334...F-6
Maxbass, 84...D-6
Mayville, 1858...G-12
Maza...E-9
McCanna, 35...E-11
McClusky, 380...G-7
McGregor, 80...D-3
McHenry, 56...F-10
MCHENRY CO., 5395...E-7
MCINTOSH CO., 2809...J-9
McKenzie, 50...H-7
MCKENZIE CO., 6360...F-2
MCLEAN CO., 8962...F-6
McLeod, 27...I-12
McVille, 349...F-11
Medina, 308...H-9
Medora, 112...H-2
Mekinock, 150...E-12
Melville...G-9
Menoken, 70...H-7
Mercer, 94...G-7
MERCER CO., 8424...G-5
Merricourt, 10...J-10
Michigan, 294...E-11
Millarton...I-10
Milnor, 653...I-12
Milton, 58...D-11
Minnewaukan, 224...E-9
Minot, 40888...E-6
Minto, 604...E-12
Moffit, 75...I-7
Mohall, 783...D-6
Monango, 36...J-10
Montpelier, 87...H-10
Mooreton, 197...I-13
MORTON CO., 27471...I-5
Mott, 721...I-4
Mt. Carmel...C-10
Mountain, 92...D-11
MOUNTRAIL CO., 7673...E-4
Munich, 210...D-10
Mylo, 20...D-8
Napoleon, 792...I-8
Nash, 32...D-12
Neche, 371...C-12
Nekoma, 50...D-10
NELSON CO., 3126...F-11
New England, 600...I-3
New Hradec, 130...H-3
New Leipzig, 221...I-5
New Rockford, 1391...F-9
New Salem, 946...H-6
New Town, 1925...F-4
Newburg, 110...D-7
Niagara, 53...E-11
Niobe, 30...D-5
Nome, 62...I-11
Noonan, 121...C-3
Norma...D-5
N. Lemmon, 40...J-5
Northgate, 25...C-5
Northwood, 945...F-12
Nortonville, 50...I-10
Norwich, 60...E-6
Oakes, 1856...J-11
Oakwood, 80...D-12
Oberon, 105...F-9
Olga...D-11
OLIVER CO., 1846...G-5
Oriska, 118...H-11
Orr, 30...E-11
Orrin, 22...E-8
Osnabrock, 134...D-11
Overly, 18...D-8
Oxbow, 305...H-13
Page, 232...G-12
Palermo, 74...E-5
Park River, 1403...E-11
Parshall, 903...F-5
Pekin, 70...F-11
Pembina, 592...C-12
PEMBINA CO., 7413...D-11
Penn, 60...E-9
Perth, 9...D-9
Petersburg, 192...E-11
Pettibone, 70...H-9
Picardville...G-7
Pick City, 123...G-6
PIERCE CO., 4357...D-8
Pillsbury, 12...G-11
Pingree, 60...G-10
Pisek, 106...E-11
Plaza, 171...E-5
Pleasant Lake...E-8
Porcupine, 146...J-6
Portal, 126...C-4
Portland, 606...G-12
Powers Lake, 280...D-4
Price...H-6
Raleigh, 12...I-6
RAMSEY CO., 11451...E-10
RANSOM CO., 5457...I-11
Raub...F-5
Rawson...F-2
Ray, 592...E-3
Red Willow Lake, 50...F-11
Reeder, 162...J-3
Regan, 43...G-7
Regent, 160...I-4
Reile's Acres, 513...H-13
RENVILLE CO., 2470...C-5
Reynolds, 301...F-12
Rhame, 169...I-2
Richardton, 529...H-4
RICHLAND CO., 16321...I-12
Riverdale, 205...G-6
Robinson, 37...G-8
Rock Lake, 101...D-9
Rogers, 46...H-11
Rolette, 594...D-8
ROLETTE CO., 13937...D-8
Rolla, 1280...D-9
Roseglen, 20...F-5
Ross, 97...E-4
Rugby, 2876...E-8
Ruso, 4...F-6
Russell...D-7
Ruthville, 191...E-6
Rutland, 163...J-12
Ryder, 85...F-5
St. Anthony, 50...I-6
St. Gertrude, 50...I-6
St. John, 341...C-8
St. Michael, 30...F-10
St. Thomas, 331...D-12
Sanborn, 192...H-11
Sanish...F-4
SARGENT CO., 3829...J-12
Sarles, 28...C-9
Sawyer, 357...E-6
Scenic East, 75...E-2
Scranton, 281...J-3
Selfridge, 160...J-6
Selz, 46...F-8
Sentinel Butte, 56...H-2
Sharon, 96...F-11
Sheldon, 116...I-12
SHERIDAN CO., 1321...F-7
Sherwood, 242...C-5
Sheyenne, 204...F-9
Shields, 30...J-6
Sibley, 30...G-11
Silva...E-8
SIOUX CO., 4153...J-6
SLOPE CO., 727...I-2
Solen, 83...I-7
Souris, 58...C-7
S. Heart, 301...H-3
Southam, 20...E-10
Spiritwood, 18...H-10
Spiritwood Lake, 90...H-10
Spring Brook, 27...E-3
Stanley, 1458...E-4
Stanton, 366...G-6
STARK CO., 24199...H-4
Starkweather, 117...D-10
Steele, 715...H-8
STEELE CO., 1975...F-11
Sterling, 80...H-7
Stirum, 50...J-11
Strasburg, 409...J-8
Streeter, 170...I-9
STUTSMAN CO., 21100...H-9
Surrey, 934...E-6
Sutton, 17...G-10
Sykeston, 117...G-9
Tagus...E-5
Tappen, 197...H-8
Taylor, 148...H-4
Temvik...I-8
Thompson, 986...F-12
Tioga, 1230...E-3
Tokio, 100...F-10
Tolley, 47...D-5
Tolna, 166...F-10
Tower City, 253...H-12
Towner, 533...E-7
TOWNER CO., 2246...D-9
TRAILL CO., 8121...F-12
Trenton, 250...E-2
Turtle Lake, 581...G-7
Tuttle, 80...G-8
Twin Buttes, 80...G-4
Underwood, 778...G-6
Upham, 130...D-7
Valley City, 6585...H-11
Velva, 1084...E-7
Venlo, 100...I-12
Venturia, 10...J-9
Verona, 85...I-11
Veseleyville, 75...E-12
Voltaire, 40...E-7
Voss, 30...E-12
Wahpeton, 7766...I-13
Walcott, 235...I-13
Wales, 31...C-10
Walhalla, 996...C-11
WALSH CO., 11119...E-11
Walum, 25...G-11
WARD CO., 61675...E-5
Warsaw, 80...E-12
Warwick, 65...F-10
Washburn, 1246...G-6
Watford City, 1744...F-3
Webster, 75...E-10
WELLS CO., 4207...G-8
Wellsburg...F-8
W. Fargo, 25830...H-13
Westfield, 20...J-8
Westhope, 429...C-6
Wheatland, 68...H-12
Wheelock, 30...E-3
White Earth, 80...E-4
Whitman, 30...E-11
Wildrose, 110...D-3
WILLIAMS CO., 22398...D-3
Williston, 14716...E-2
Willow City, 163...D-7
Wilton, 711...G-7
Wimbledon, 216...G-10
Windsor, 25...H-9
Wing, 152...G-7
Wishek, 1002...J-9
Wolford, 36...D-8
Woodworth, 50...G-9
Wyndmere, 429...I-12
York, 23...E-9
Ypsilanti, 104...H-10
Zahl, 40...D-2
Zap, 237...G-5
Zeeland, 86...J-8

Ohio

Page locator

Map keys	Atlas pages
NA1–NN10	158–159
NA11–NN20	160–161
SA1–SN10	162–163
SA11–SN20	164–165

* City keyed to p. 226

Abbottsville...NN-2
Aberdeen, 1638...SI-6
Academia, 100...NL-11
Ada, 5952...NJ-5
ADAMS CO., 28550...SH-7
Adams Mills, 160...NN-14
Adamsville, 114...NN-14
Adamsville...SH-12
Adario, 120...NI-11
Addison, 250...SH-13
Addyston, 938...SL-1
Adelphi, 380...SE-10
Adena, 759...NM-19
Adrian, 100...NI-7
Africa, 50...NM-9
Afton, 200...SG-4
Aid, 150...SJ-12
Akron, 199110...NH-16
Albany, 828...SF-13
Albion, 70...NI-13
Alcony, 150...SA-4
Alexandria, 517...NN-11
Alexis...NA-2
Alfred...SF-14
Alger, 860...NJ-5
Alledonia, 60...SB-18
Allen Ctr....NM-7
ALLEN CO., 106331...NJ-4
Allensburg, 100...SF-6
Allensville, 65...SF-11
Allentown, 300...SI-10
Allentown, 160...NJ-4
Alliance, 22322...NI-17
Alma, 35...SF-9
Alpha...SM-10
Alvada, 100...NH-7
Alvordton, 217...NE-3
Amanda, 737...SD-10
Amberley, 3585...SK-4
Amberly...SI-20
Amelia, 4801...SG-4
Amesville, 154...SE-14
Amherst, 12021...NF-12
Amity, 200...NL-12
Amity, 60...NN-8
Amlin, 500...NN-8
Amsden, 180...NG-7
Amsterdam, 511...NL-18
Andersonville, 779...SE-9
Andis...SJ-11
Andover, 1145...NE-20
Ankenytown, 60...NK-11
Anna, 1567...NL-4
Annapolis, 90...NL-19
Ansonia, 1174...NM-1
Antioch, 86...SC-18
Antiquity, 100...SH-14
Antrim, 100...NN-16
Antwerp, 1736...NG-1
Apple Creek, 1173...NJ-14
Apple Grv., 90...SH-14
Aquilla, 340...NE-17
Arabia, 50...SI-12
Arcadia, 590...NH-7
Arcanum, 2129...SA-2
Archbold, 4346...NE-3
Arlington, 1455...NI-6
Arlington, 120...SB-3
Arlington Hts., 745...SK-3
Armstrongs Mills, 100...SB-19
Arnheim, 120...SH-5
Arnold, 50...NN-8
Arthur...NG-3
Ash Ridge, 50...SH-6
Ashland, 20362...NI-12
ASHLAND CO., 53139...NI-12
Ashley, 1330...NL-9
Ashtabula, 19124...NC-19
ASHTABULA CO., 101497...NE-18
Ashville, 4097...SC-9
Assumption, 80...NE-5
Athalia, 373...SJ-12
Athens, 23832...SE-13
ATHENS CO., 64757...SF-14
Atlanta, 160...SD-8
Attica, 899...NH-9
Attica Jct., 100...NH-9
Atwater, 758...NH-17
Auburn, 200...SE-1
Auburn Ctr., 100...NF-17
Auburn Cors., 260...NF-17
AUGLAIZE CO., 45949...NK-4
Augusta, 270...NJ-18
Aurora, 15548...NG-16
Austin, 40...SE-8
Austinburg, 516...ND-18
Austintown, 29677...NH-19
Ava, 200...SB-16
Avon, 21193...NF-13
Avon Lake, 22581...NF-13
Avondale, 3050...NJ-16
Avondale, 400...SB-13
Avondale...SL-9
Axtel...NF-12
Ayersville, 350...NG-3
Bachman, 35...SB-3
Bailey Lake, 371...NI-12
Baileys Mills...SB-17
Bainbridge, 3267...NF-16
Bainbridge, 860...SF-8
Bairdstown, 130...NH-6
Bakersville, 150...NL-15
Ballville, 2976...NG-8
Baltic, 795...NL-15
Baltimore, 2966...SB-11
Bangs, 200...NL-11
Bannock, 211...NN-18
Bantam, 150...SG-4
Barberton, 26550...NH-15
Bardwell, 100...SG-5
Barlow, 200...SE-15
Barnesville, 4193...SA-17
Barnhill, 396...NL-16
Barrs Mills, 100...NK-15
Bartles...SI-11
Bartlett, 200...SE-15
Barton, 465...NN-19
Bascom, 390...NH-8
Bashan, 35...SG-14
Batavia, 1509...SG-4
Batesville, 71...SB-17
Bath, 500...NG-15
Bay Br., 100...NF-10
Bay View, 632...NF-10
Bay Vil., 15651...NF-14
Bayard, 90...NJ-18
Beach City, 1033...NK-15
Beachwood, 11953...NF-16
Beallsville, 409...SB-18
Beamsville, 140...NM-2
Beatty, 90...SB-5
Beaumont, 30...SE-13
Beaver, 449...SG-10
Beavercreek, 45193...SC-4
Beaverdam, 382...NJ-5
Beavertown, 80...SD-18
Bedford, 13074...NF-15
Bedford Hts., 10751...NF-16
Belden, 50...NG-13
Belfast, 120...SG-7
Bellaire, 4278...SA-19
Bellaire Gdns., 100...NK-8
Bellbrook, 6943...SD-4
Belle Ctr., 813...NK-6
Belle Valley, 223...SC-16
Belle Vernon, 40...NI-8
Bellefontaine, 13370...NL-5
Bellepoint, 100...NM-8
Bellevue, 8202...NG-10
Bellville, 1918...NK-11
Belmont, 453...NN-18
BELMONT CO., 70400...NN-17
Belmore, 143...NH-5
Beloit, 978...NI-18
Belpre, 6441...SF-16
Bentleyville, 864...NF-16
Benton, 100...NI-8
Benton...NK-14
Benton Ridge, 299...NI-5
Bentonville, 287...SI-6
Berea, 19093...NF-14
Bergholz, 664...NK-18
Berkey, 237...ND-5
Berkshire, 100...NM-9
Berlin, 898...NK-14
Berlin Ctr., 250...NH-18
Berlin Hts., 714...NG-11
Berlinville, 70...NG-11
Berrysville, 100...SG-7
Berwick, 100...NH-8
Bethany, 260...SE-3
Bethel, 2711...SH-4
Bethesda, 1256...SA-18
Bettsville, 661...NG-8
Beverly, 1313...SD-15
Bevis, 1100...SK-2
Bexley, 13057...SB-9
Bidwell, 350...SH-12
Big Island, 200...NK-8
Big Plain, 150...SB-8
Big Prairie, 300...NK-13
Big Sprs., 130...NL-6
Birmingham, 500...NG-12
Birmingham, 45...NM-16
Bishopville...SD-14
Blachleyville, 120...NJ-13
Black Horse, 500...NH-17
Black Run...NN-13
Blackfork, 250...SH-11
Blacklick, 300...SA-10
Blacklick Estates, 8682...SI-20
Bladen, 50...SI-13
Bladensburg, 191...NM-12
Blaine, 500...NN-19
Blairmont...NM-18
Blakeslee, 96...NE-1
Blanchard...NJ-6
Blanchester, 4243...SF-5
Blissfield, 100...NL-14
Bloom Ctr., 30...NL-5
Bloomdale, 678...NH-6
Bloomer, 50...NM-2
Bloomfield, 60...NN-15
Bloomfield, 25...SD-17
Bloomfield...NL-10
Blooming Grv., 80...NJ-10
Bloomingburg, 938...SD-7
Bloomingdale, 202...NL-19
Bloomington, 50...SD-6
Bloomingville...NF-10
Bloomville, 956...NH-9
Blue Ash, 12114...SF-3
Blue Creek, 25...SI-8
Blue Rock, 125...SC-14
Bluffton, 4125...NI-5
Boardman, 35376...NH-19
Bogart, 120...NF-10
Bolivar, 994...NK-16
Bonn, 70...SD-17
Bono, 200...NE-8
Bookwalter, 120...SC-7
Boston, 120...SF-7
Boston, 30...SB-17
Boston Hts., 1300...NG-15
Botkins, 1155...NL-4
Bourneville, 199...SF-8
Bowerston, 398...NL-17
Bowersville, 312...SD-6
Bowling Green, 30028...NF-6
Bowlusville, 30...SA-6
Braceville, 250...NG-18
Bradbury, 200...SG-13
Bradford, 1842...NN-2
Bradley, 90...NM-19
Bradner, 985...NG-7
Bradrick, 110...SK-12
Brady Lake, 464...NH-16
Braffettsville, 70...SB-1
Branch Hill, 370...SK-5
Brandon, 200...NM-11
Brandt, 320...SB-4
Bratenahl, 1197...SK-18
Brecksville, 13656...NG-15
Brecon, 244...SJ-5
Bremen, 1425...SC-12
Brentwood, 5500...SK-3
Brentwood Lake, 650...NG-13
Brewster, 2112...NJ-15
Brice, 114...SB-10
Briceton, 150...NH-2
Bridgeport, 1831...NN-19
Bridgetown North, 12569...SL-1
Bridgewater Ctr., 70...NE-2
Brier Hill...NC-13
Briggsdale, 180...SB-9
Brighton, 130...NH-12
Brighton, 50...SB-7
Brilliant, 1482...NM-20
Brimfield, 3343...NH-16
Brinkhaven, 125...NL-13
Bristol, 70...SC-13
Bristolville, 500...NF-18
Brittain...NC-6
Broadview Hts., 19400...NG-15
Broadway, 500...NL-7
Broadwell...SE-14
Brock, 50...NM-2
Brokensword, 30...NI-9
Brook Pk., 19212...NF-14
Brookfield, 300...NG-20
Brookfield Ctr., 1207...NB-14
Brooklyn, 11169...NF-15
Brooklyn Hts., 1543...SM-17
Brookside, 632...*D-1
Brookside Estates, 670...SF-18
Brookville, 5884...SB-3
Broughton, 120...NH-2
BROWN CO., 44846...SH-5
Brown Hts., 200...SA-16
Brownsville, 220...SB-13
Brownsville, 200...SF-9
Brownsville, 70...SD-18
Brunersburg, 140...NG-3
Bruno...SB-12
Brunswick, 34255...NG-14
Bryan, 8545...NF-2
Buchanan, 50...SF-9
Buchtel, 558...SE-13
Buckeye Lake, 2746...SB-12
Buckeyeville, 80...SB-15
Buckingham, 25...SD-13
Buckland, 233...NK-3
Bucyrus, 12362...NJ-9
Buena Vista, 150...SJ-8
Buena Vista...SD-11
Buffalo, 401...SB-16
Buford, 352...SG-5
Burbank, 207...NI-13
Burghill, 250...NF-20
Burgoon, 172...NG-8
Burkettsville, 244...NL-1
Burlingham, 50...SF-14
Burlington, 2676...SK-11
Burlington, 130...NE-3
Burton, 1455...NF-17
Burton City...NI-15
Burton Sta., 40...NF-17
Burtonville, 100...SE-5
Bushnell...NC-20
Butler, 933...NK-11
BUTLER CO., 368130...SE-1
Butlerville, 163...SF-4
Byer, 45...SF-11
Byesville, 2438...SB-16
Byhalia, 130...NL-7
Byington, 50...SG-8
Byron, 50...SC-5
Cable, 200...NM-6
Cadiz, 3353...NM-18
Cadmus, 60...SI-12
Cairo, 524...NJ-4
Cairo, 120...NI-16
Calais, 25...SB-17
Calcutta, 3742...NJ-20
Caldwell, 1748...SC-16
Caledonia, 577...NK-9
Calla...NI-19
Cambridge, 10635...SA-16
Camden, 2046...SD-2
Cameron, 180...SC-19
Camp Dennison, 375...SK-5
Campbell, 8235...NH-20
Campbellsport...NH-17
Campbellstown, 120...SC-1
Canaanville...SE-14
Canal Fulton, 5479...NI-15
Canal Lewisville, 320...NM-14
Canal Winchester, 7101...SB-10
Canfield, 7515...NH-19
Cannelville, 250...SC-14
Cannons Creek...SI-11
Canton, 73007...NJ-16
Carbon Hill, 233...SD-13
Carbondale, 120...SE-13
Cardington, 2047...NL-9
Carey, 3674...NI-7
Carlisle, 4915...SD-3
Carlisle, 50...SC-17
Carmel, 30...SF-7
Caroline, 80...NH-9
Carpenter, 25...SF-13
Carroll, 524...SC-11
CARROLL CO., 28836...NK-17
Carrollton, 3241...NK-18
Carrothers, 60...NI-9
Carthagena, 40...NL-2
Carysville, 100...NM-4
Cassell, 100...SA-15
Cassella, 125...NL-2
Casstown, 267...NN-4
Castalia, 852...NF-10
Castine, 130...SB-2
Catawba, 272...SA-6
Catawba Island, 200...NE-10
Cavett...NI-2
Caywood...SE-17
Cecil, 188...NG-2
Cedar Mills, 20...SH-7
Cedarville, 4019...SC-6
Celeryville, 210...NH-10
Celina, 10400...NK-2
Center, 150...NN-16
Center Sta., 30...SI-11
Center Vil., 280...NN-10
Centerburg, 1773...NM-10
Centerfield, 60...SE-7
Centerton, 200...NH-10
Centerville, 23999...SD-4
Centerville, 150...SA-18
Ceylon, 90...NF-11
Chagrin Falls, 4113...NF-16
Chalfants...SB-12
CHAMPAIGN CO., 40097...NN-5
Champion Hts., 6498...NG-18
Chandlersville, 220...SB-15
Chapmans, 50...SG-11
Chardon, 5148...NE-17
Charity Rotch...NB-8
Charlestown, 150...NH-17
Charloe, 60...NH-3
Charm, 160...NK-14
Chasetown, 40...SF-5
Chatfield, 189...NI-9
Chatham, 220...NH-13
Chattanooga, 120...NK-1
Chauncey, 1049...SE-13
Cherry Fork, 155...SH-6
Cherry Grv., 4378...SM-5
Cherry Valley, 120...NE-19
Chesapeake, 745...SK-12
Cheshire, 132...SH-13
Cheshire, 100...NM-9
Chester, 260...SG-14
Chesterhill, 289...SD-14
Chesterland, 2521...NE-16
Chesterville, 228...NL-10
Cheviot, 8375...SF-2
Chickasaw, 290...NL-2
Chili...NL-15
Chillicothe, 21901...SE-9
Chilo, 63...SI-4
Chippewa Lake, 711...NH-14
Christiansburg, 526...NN-4
Churchill, 2149...NH-19
Cincinnati, 296943...SG-2
Circleville, 13314...SD-9
Claiborne, 180...NL-7
Claridon, 170...NE-17
Claridon, 120...NK-9
Clarington, 384...SC-19
Clark, 170...NL-14
CLARK CO., 138333...SB-6
Clarksburg, 455...SD-9
Clarksfield, 200...NG-12
Clarkson, 80...NJ-20
Clarksville, 548...SE-5
Clarktown, 958...SH-10
Clay, 20...SH-11
Clay Ctr., 276...NE-7
Claysville, 140...SB-15
Clayton, 13209...SB-3
Clearport...SD-11
CLERMONT CO., 197363...SH-4
Cleveland, 396815...NF-15
Cleveland Hts., 46121...NE-15
Cleves, 3234...SF-1
Clifton, 152...SC-5
Clinton, 1214...NI-15
CLINTON CO., 42040...SD-6
Cloverdale, 168...NH-3
Cloverhill, 40...SC-13
Clyde, 6325...NG-9
Coal Grv., 2165...SJ-11
Coal Ridge, 100...SC-16
Coal Run, 200...SD-16
Coalburg, 240...NG-20
Coalton, 479...SG-11
Coitsville Ctr....ND-14
Colby...NG-9
Coldwater, 4427...NL-2
Colebrook, 150...NE-19
Colerain, 450...NN-19
Colerain Hts., 2600...SK-2
Coles Pk., 300...SI-9
Coletown, 90...NN-1
College Cor., 407...SD-1
Collins, 631...NG-11
Collinsville, 230...SD-2
Colton, 180...NF-5
Columbia, 220...NK-16
Columbia, 100...NE-1
Columbia...NC-7
Columbia Hills Cors....NG-14
Columbiana, 6384...NI-19
COLUMBIANA CO., 107841...NJ-19
Columbus, 787033...SB-9
Columbus Grv., 2137...NI-4
Commercial Pt., 1582...SC-9
Conant, 50...NJ-3
Condit, 70...NM-10
Conesville, 347...NM-14
Congo, 110...SD-13
Congress, 185...NI-13
Conneaut, 12841...NC-20
Conotton, 70...NL-17
Conover, 130...NN-4
Constitution, 50...SE-16
Continental, 1153...NH-3
Converse, 25...NJ-3
Convoy, 1085...NI-1
Cook...SC-8
Coolville, 496...SF-15
Cooperdale, 100...NM-13
Copley, 750...NH-
Cornersburg...ND-
Cornerville, 70...SE-
Corning, 583...SD-
Cortland, 7104...NG-
Corwin, 421...SD
Coshocton, 11216...NM-
COSHOCTON CO., 36901...NM-
Country Acres...SL-
Covedale, 6447...SM
Covington, 2584...NN
Cozaddale, 250...SF
Craig Bch., 1180...NH-
Craigton, 25...NJ-
Cranberry Prairie, 100...NL
Crawford, 100...N
CRAWFORD CO., 43784...N
Creola, 90...SE-
Crestline, 4630...NJ-
Creston, 2171...NI-
Cridersville, 1852...NK
Crissey, 220...NE
Crooksville, 2534...SC-
Crossenville, 40...SC-
Croton, 397...NM-
Crown City, 413...SJ-
Crystal Lakes, 1483...SB
Crystal Rock Pk., 300...NF-
Crystal Sprs., 250...NI-
Cuba, 160...SE
Cumberland, 367...SB-
Curtice, 1526...NE
Custar, 179...NG
Cutler, 130...SE-
CUYAHOGA CO., 1280122...NG-
Cuyahoga Falls, 49652...NH-
Cuyahoga Hts., 638...SM-
Cygnet, 597...NG
Cynthiana, 68...SH
Dalton, 1830...NJ-
Dalzell...SD-
Damascus, 443...NI-
Danville, 1044...NL-
Danville, 120...SH
Danville...SG-
Darbydale, 793...SE
Darbyville, 222...SC
DARKE CO., 52959...NM
Darlington, 35...SB-
Darrtown, 516...SD
Dart, 30...SD-
Darwin...SF-
Davisville, 45...SG-
Dawn, 170...NM
Dayton, 141527...SC
De Graff, 1285...NM
Deavertown, 200...SC-
Decatur, 250...SH
Deer Pk., 5736...SK
Deerfield, 520...NH-
Deering, 90...SJ-
Deersville, 79...NM-
Defiance, 16494...NG
DEFIANCE CO., 39037...NG
DeForest, 1150...NB-
Delaware, 34753...NM
DELAWARE CO., 174214...NM
Delhi Hills, 20000...SM
Delightful, 40...NG-
Delisle, 50...SA
Dellroy, 356...NK-
Delmont...SC-
Delphi, 100...NH-
Delphos, 7101...N
Delta, 3103...NE
Denmark...NK
Dennison, 2655...NL-
Dent, 10497...SI
Denver, 25...SF
Derby, 408...SC
Derwent, 250...SB-
Deshler, 1799...NG
Deunquat, 50...N
Devola, 2652...SD-
Deweyville, 30...NH
Dexter, 70...SG-
Dexter City, 129...SC-
Dialton, 60...SA
Diamond, 200...NH-
Dilles Bottom, 130...SB-
Dillonvale, 665...NM-
Dixie Hts....SK
Dixon, 70...N
Doanville, 160...SE-
Dobbston...SJ-
Dodds, 80...SD
Dodgeville, 110...NE-
Dodson, 25...SB
Dodsonville, 70...SF
Dola, 140...NJ
Donnelsville, 304...SB
Dorcas...SG-
Dorset, 200...ND-
Dover, 12826...NK-
Doylestown, 3051...NI-
Drakes, 70...SD-
Drakesburg, 55...NG-
Dresden, 1529...NN-
Drexel, 2076...SC
Dry Run, 750...S
Dublin, 41751...NN
Duffy, 230...SC-
Dumontville...SC-
Dunbridge, 250...NF
Duncan Falls, 880...SB-
Dundas, 220...SF-
Dundee, 297...NK-
Dunkinsville, 50...SH
Dunkirk, 875...NJ
Dunlap, 1719...SF
Dupont, 318...NH
Durbin, 25...NB-
Duvall, 50...SC
Dyesville...SG-
Eagle City, 70...SB
Eagleport, 35...SC-
Eagleville, 35...NG
E. Akron...NC
E. Alliance, 1175...NI-
E. Batavia Hts., 150...SG
E. Cadiz...NM-
E. Canton, 1591...NJ-
E. Claridon, 260...NE-
E. Cleveland, 17843...NE-
E. Danville, 100...SG
E. Fairfield, 100...NJ-
E. Fultonham, 335...SB-
E. Greenville, 180...NJ-
E. Liberty, 366...NM

*, †, ‡, §, ◊ See explanation under state title in this index.
County and parish names are listed in capital letters & boldface type.
Independent cities (not included in a county) are listed in *italics*.

Liverpool, 1195...NK-20
Monroe, 120...SE-7
Norwalk, 80...NG-11
Palestine, 4721...NI-20
Richland, 300...NN-18
Rochester, 231...NJ-18
Sparta, 819...NJ-16
Springfield, 350...NL-19
Townsend, 80...NG-11
Trumbull, 80...NE-18
Union, 30...SC-16
stlake, 18577...NE-16
ston, 200...NI-15
stview...SL-9
ton, 8407...SC-2
ton Estates, 222...NG-13
er, 300...SD-7
kmansville...SH-6
en Pk., 430...SI-9
enton, 300...SF-4
gerton, 2012...NF-1
gewater Pk., 00...SB-10
gewood, 4432...NC-19
inburg, 250...NH-17
ison, 437...NK-10
on, 834...NE-1
a, 70...SD-16
lorado, 509...SB-2
ery, 25...NG-4
gin, 57...NJ-2
da, 1905...NJ-4
zabethtown, 350...SF-1
ton, 80...NJ-19
erton...SN-6
iot Crossroads...SD-14
isonville, 50...SJ-11
sberry, 60...SI-6
sworth, 260...NH-18
n Grv., 35...SG-8
more, 1410...NF-8
nwood Pl., 2188...SL-3
oy, 35...NM-1
ria, 54533...NF-13
pire, 299...NK-20
glewood, 13465...SB-3
on, 2415...SB-5
terprise, 170...SD-12
worth...NI-11
worth Hts., 150...SK-6
, 130...SC-8
IE CO., 77079...NF-11
s, 25...NN-5
in, 80...NF-9
yville, 80...NK-8
ex, 90...NL-7
a, 1215...SB-11
clid, 48920...NE-15
reka, 100...SI-13
ansport, 300...NF-3
ansville, 200...NC-12
endale, 2767...SK-4
erett, 25...NG-15
ving, 30...SE-12
vington, 65...SG-12
cello, 50...SD-3
rborn, 32352...SB-5
rfax, 1699...SL-4
rfax, 40...SG-7
rfield, 42510...SE-2
rfield, 50...NL-19
IRFIELD CO., 46156...SB-11
rhaven, 200...SC-1
rhope, 1720...NJ-17
rlawn, 7437...NH-15
rpoint, 500...NN-18
rport Hbr., 109...ND-17
rview, 83...SB-16
rview, 50...SF-6
rview Lanes, 000...NF-10
rview Pk., 6826...NF-14
lsburg, 80...NM-12
mdale, 200...NF-20
mer, 120...NF-2
mers, 45...SE-6
merstown, 330...NL-15
mersville, 1009...SC-3
wcett...SH-7
yette, 1283...NE-3
YETTE CO., 9030...SD-8
yetteville, 330...SF-5
esburg, 500...SH-5
icity, 818...SH-4
nald, 25...SJ-1
nell Hts., 330...SM-6
castle, 85...SG-6
dlay, 41202...NH-6
neytown, 12741...SK-3
estone Pk...NC-5
chville, 350...NH-11
e Points, 1824...SD-4
e Points, 120...SC-8
emile...SG-5
t Rock, 233...NG-9
ming, 40...SE-16
tcher, 473...NN-4
rence, 200...NG-12
rence, 150...NN-19
rence, 100...SC-16
rida, 232...NG-4
shing, 879...NN-18
, 80...SD-18
otville...NE-18
raker, 130...NJ-6
est, 1461...NJ-7
est Hill...NB-6
est Hills, 200...NA-15
est Pk., 18720...SF-2
estville, 10532...SG-3
Jefferson, 80...SA-2
Jennings, 485...NI-3
Loramie, 1478...NL-3
McKinley, 3989...SL-7
Recovery, 1430...NL-1
Seneca, 254...NG-8
Shawnee, 3726...NJ-4
ster...SE-3
sterville...ND-13
storia, 13441...NH-7
wler, 250...NG-19
wlers Mill, 320...NE-17
x, 25...SD-9
ankfort, 1064...SE-8
anklin, 11771...SD-3
ANKLIN CO., 163414...NN-10
anklin Furnace, 660...SI-10
anklin Sq., 240...NI-19
azeysburg, 1326...NN-13
ederick, 150...SB-3
edericksburg, 23...NJ-14
edericksdale...SC-16
Fredericktown, 2493...NL-11
Fredericktown, 200...NJ-20
Freeburg, 90...NI-17
Freedom, 90...NG-17
Freeport, 369...NM-17
Fremont, 16734...NG-8
Frenchtown, 60...NM-2
Fresno, 140...NL-15
Friendship, 351...SI-9
Frost, 25...SF-15
Fruit Hill, 3755...SM-5
Fruitdale, 50...SF-8
Fryburg, 150...NK-4
Frytown, 45...SC-3
Fulda, 40...SC-16
Fulton, 258...NL-10
FULTON CO., 42698...NE-3
Fultonham, 176...SB-13
Funk, 110...NJ-13
Gahanna, 33248...SA-10
Galena, 653...NM-9
Galion, 10512...NJ-10
Gallia...SH-11
GALLIA CO., 30934...SH-12
Gallipolis, 3641...SH-13
Galloway, 250...SB-9
Gambier, 2391...NL-12
Ganges, 120...NI-11
Gano, 200...SF-3
Garden Acres, 250...NB-17
Garden City, 300...SI-10
Garfield, 120...NI-18
Garfield Hts., 28849...NF-15
Garrettsville, 2325...NG-17
Gates Mills, 2270...NE-16
GEAUGA CO., 93389...NE-17
Geneva, 6215...ND-18
Geneva-on-the-Lake, 1288...NC-18
Genoa, 2336...NF-7
Georges Run, 400...NM-20
Georgesville, 160...SB-8
Georgetown, 4331...SH-5
Georgetown, 150...NM-18
Gephart...SI-10
Gerald, 50...NF-4
Germano, 200...NL-18
Germantown, 5547...SD-3
Germantown, 35...SD-17
Getaway, 100...SJ-12
Gettysburg, 513...NN-2
Gettysburg, 80...SB-1
Geyer, 50...NK-4
Ghent, 1600...NH-15
Gibisonville, 130...SD-11
Gibsonburg, 2581...NF-7
Gilboa, 184...NH-5
Gillivan...SB-8
Gilmore, 85...NM-16
Ginghamsburg, 250...SB-4
Girard, 9958...NH-19
Girton, 50...NG-7
Givens, 75...SG-10
Gladstone, 30...SC-6
Glandorf, 1001...NH-4
Glasgow, 40...NJ-19
Glasgow...NM-15
Glen Este, 350...SM-6
Glen Karn, 40...SA-1
Glen Roy, 100...SG-11
Glencoe, 310...SA-19
Glendale, 2155...SJ-3
Glenford, 173...SB-12
Glenmont, 272...NK-13
Glenmoor, 1987...NJ-20
Glenmore, 50...NJ-1
Glouster, 1791...SD-13
Gnadenhutten, 1288...NL-16
Goes, 100...SC-5
Golf Manor, 3611...SL-4
Gomer, 350...NI-4
Good Hope, 234...SE-8
Goodyear Hts...NB-6
Gordon, 212...SB-2
Gore, 240...SD-12
Goshen, 730...SF-4
Goshen, 200...NL-16
Gould Pk...SG-20
Grafton, 6636...NG-13
Grand Rapids, 965...NF-5
Grand River, 399...ND-17
Grandview, 60...SD-18
Grandview Hts., 6536...SB-9
Grandview Hts., 170...NM-4
Grange Hall, 20...SD-8
Granger, 90...NH-15
Grant, 60...NJ-6
Granville, 5646...NN-11
Grape Grv., 35...SC-6
Gratiot, 221...SB-13
Gratis, 881...SC-2
Graysville, 76...SC-18
Graytown, 180...NE-8
Green, 25699...NI-16
Green Camp, 374...NK-8
Green Sprs., 1368...NG-9
Greenbush...SD-2
Greenbush...SG-5
Greencastle...SC-10
Greendale, 30...SD-13
GREENE CO., 161573...SC-6
Greenfield, 4639...SE-7
Greenford, 700...NI-19
Greenhills, 3615...SJ-3
Greenland...SE-9
Greensburg, 600...NI-16
Greentown, 3804...NI-16
Greenview...SK-7
Greenville, 13227...NN-2
Greenwich, 1476...NH-11
Greenwood, 40...SB-16
Greer, 50...NK-13
Grelton, 110...NG-4
Groesbeck, 6788...SK-2
Grove City, 35575...SB-9
Groveport, 5363...SJ-20
Grover Hill, 402...NH-2
Guerne, 250...NJ-14
Guernsey, 50...NM-15
GUERNSEY CO., 40087...NM-16
Guilford, 320...NJ-18
Gurneyville...SD-5
Gustavus...NF-19
Gutman, 35...NK-4
Guysville, 250...SF-14
Gypsum, 200...NF-9
Hackney, 40...SD-15
Hallock, 100...NE-2
Hallsville, 230...SE-10
Hambden, 180...NE-17
Hamburg...SC-11
Hamden, 879...SF-11
Hamersville, 546...SH-5
Hamilton, 62477...SE-2
HAMILTON CO., 802374...SF-1
Hamilton Meadows, 2100...SB-9
Hamler, 576...NG-4
Hamlet, 160...SG-4
Hammansburg, 100...NG-6
Hammondsville, 400...NK-19
HANCOCK CO., 74782...NI-5
Hanging Rock, 221...SJ-10
Hanley Vil...NJ-11
Hannibal, 411...SC-19
Hanover, 921...NN-12
Hanover...NL-18
Hanoverton, 408...NJ-18
Harbor View, 123...ND-7
Hardin, 80...NM-3
HARDIN CO., 32058...NJ-6
Harlem, 150...NN-10
Harlem Sprs., 300...NK-18
Harmon, 50...NJ-15
Harmony, 250...SB-6
Harper, 70...NL-6
Harpersfield...ND-18
Harpster, 204...NJ-8
Harriett, 30...SG-7
Harriettsville, 60...SD-17
Harrisburg, 320...SC-8
Harrisburg, 100...NI-17
Harrison, 9897...SF-1
HARRISON CO., 15864...NM-17
Harrisonville, 150...SG-13
Harrisville, 235...NM-18
Harrod, 417...NJ-5
Harshasville...SH-7
Hartford, 350...NG-20
Hartland...NH-11
Hartsgrove, 300...NE-18
Hartshorn...SC-17
Hartville, 2944...NI-16
Harveysburg, 546...SD-5
Haselton...ND-14
Haskins, 1188...NF-6
Hatton, 50...NG-7
Havana, 110...NH-10
Havensport, 60...SC-11
Haverhill, 120...SJ-10
Haviland, 215...NH-2
Haydenville, 381...SD-12
Hayesville, 448...NJ-12
Heath, 10310...SA-12
Hebbardsville, 50...SF-13
Hebron, 2336...SB-12
Hecla, 200...SJ-11
Helena, 224...NG-8
Hemlock, 155...SD-13
Hemlock Grv., 70...SG-14
Hendrysburg, 150...NN-17
HENRY CO., 28215...NG-4
Hepburn, 100...NK-7
Hessville, 214...NF-8
Hicksville, 3581...NG-1
Higginsport, 251...SI-5
Highland, 254...SE-6
HIGHLAND CO., 43589...SF-6
Highland Hts., 8345...SK-20
Highland Hills, 1130...SM-19
Highland Pk., 700...NJ-15
Highlandtown, 100...NK-19
Highpoint, 1503...SJ-5
Hill Grv., 100...NM-1
Hilliard, 28435...SA-8
Hills & Dales, 221...NB-9
Hillsboro, 6605...SF-6
Hinckley, 500...NG-14
Hiram, 1406...NG-17
Hiram Rapids, 250...NF-17
Hiramsburg...SC-16
Hitchcock...SH-11
Hoagland, 50...SF-6
HOCKING CO., 29380...SE-11
Hockingport, 212...SF-15
Holgate, 1109...NG-4
Holiday City, 52...NE-2
Holland, 1764...NB-1
Hollansburg, 227...SA-1
Hollister, 300...SD-13
Holloway, 338...NM-17
HOLMES CO., 42366...NK-13
Holmesville, 372...NK-14
Homer, 250...NM-11
Homerville, 80...NH-13
Homeworth, 481...NI-18
Honeytown, 40...NJ-14
Hooker...SC-11
Hooven, 534...SF-1
Hopedale, 950...NM-18
Hopetown, 50...SE-9
Hopewell, 250...SB-13
Hopkinsville...SE-4
Hoskinsville...SC-16
Houcktown, 180...NI-6
Houston, 220...NM-3
Howard, 242...NL-12
Howenstein, 160...NJ-16
Howland Ctr., 6351...NA-12
Hoytville, 303...NG-5
Hubbard, 7874...NH-20
Huber Hts., 38101...SB-4
Huber Ridge, 4604...SF-19
Hudson, 22262...NG-16
Hulington, 100...SG-4
Hume, 135...NK-3
Hunter...SB-18
Hunting Valley, 705...NF-16
Huntington, 220...NH-12
Huntsburg, 300...NE-18
Huntsville, 431...NL-5
Huron, 7149...NF-11
HURON CO., 59626...NH-11
Hustead, 120...SB-5
Hyatts, 50...NM-8
Iberia, 452...NK-10
Idaho, 50...SG-9
Iler...NG-8
Ilesboro...SE-12
Independence, 7133...NF-15
Independence, 100...NG-3
Ingomar, 60...SC-2
Irondale, 387...NK-19
Ironspot, 150...SB-13
Ironton, 11129...SJ-11
Irvington...SK-7
Irwin, 150...NN-7
Island View, 300...NK-5
Isle St. George, 50...ND-10
Isleta...NM-15
Ithaca, 136...SB-2
Jackson, 6397...SG-11
Jackson Ctr., 1462...NL-4
JACKSON CO., 33225...SH-11
Jacksonburg, 63...SD-2
Jacksontown, 350...SB-12
Jacksonville, 481...SE-13
Jacksonville, 75...SH-7
Jacobsburg, 200...SB-19
Jamestown, 1993...SC-6
Jasper, 250...SG-9
Jasper Mills, 40...SD-7
Jaysville, 30...NN-2
Jefferson, 3120...ND-19
Jefferson, 200...NJ-13
JEFFERSON CO., 69709...NK-19
Jeffersonville, 1203...SC-7
Jelloway, 90...NK-12
Jenera, 221...NI-6
Jericho, 200...SE-3
Jerome, 200...NN-8
Jeromesville, 562...NJ-13
Jerry City, 427...NG-6
Jersey, 250...NN-10
Jerusalem, 161...SB-18
Jewell, 160...NG-3
Jewett, 692...NL-18
Johnston, 250...NF-19
Johnstown, 4632...NN-10
Jonestown, 80...NJ-2
Joy...SE-14
Junction, 100...NG-2
Junction City, 819...SC-12
Justus, 100...NJ-15
Kalida, 1542...NI-4
Kanauga, 175...SH-13
Kansas, 179...NG-8
Keene, 100...NL-14
Kelleys Island, 312...NE-10
Kelloggsville, 200...NC-19
Kemp, 70...NJ-3
Kendall Hts., 850...NB-8
Kennard, 40...NM-6
Kennonsburg, 50...SB-17
Kensington, 320...NJ-18
Kent, 28904...NH-16
Kenton, 8262...NK-6
Kenwood, 6981...SK-4
Kerr, 90...SH-13
Kessler, 100...SB-3
Kettering, 56163...SC-4
Kettlersville, 179...NL-3
Key...SA-19
Kidron, 944...NJ-15
Kieferville, 40...NH-4
Kilbourne, 139...NM-9
Kileville, 25...NN-8
Kilgore, 100...NL-18
Killbuck, 817...NL-13
Kimball, 110...NG-10
Kimberly, 40...SE-13
Kimbolton, 144...NN-15
Kingman...SD-5
Kings Creek, 300...NN-6
Kings Mills, 1319...SE-3
Kingston, 1032...SE-10
Kingsville, 650...NC-19
Kingsway...NF-8
Kinnikinnick, 65...SE-9
Kinsman, 600...NF-20
Kiousville...SC-8
Kipling, 180...SA-16
Kipton, 243...NG-12
Kirby, 118...NJ-7
Kirkersville, 525...SB-11
Kirkpatrick, 80...NJ-9
Kirkwood, 60...NM-4
Kirtland, 6866...NE-16
Kitts Hill, 200...SJ-11
Klondike, 250...NG-19
Knockemstiff...SF-9
KNOX CO., 60921...NM-12
Knoxville, 180...NK-19
Kossuth, 80...NK-3
Kunkle, 246...NE-2
Kyger, 60...SG-13
La Croft, 1144...NK-20
La Grange, 70...SJ-11
La Rue, 747...NK-7
Lacarne, 200...NF-9
Lafayette, 445...NJ-5
Lafayette, 202...SB-7
Lafayette, 120...NH-14
Lafferty, 304...NN-18
Lagrange, 2103...NG-13
Laings, 30...SC-18
L. Cable, 2500...NB-9
LAKE CO., 230041...ND-17
L. Fork...NJ-13
L. Milton, 1100...NH-18
L. O'Springs, 600...NB-8
Lakeline, 226...NE-16
Lakemore, 3068...NH-16
Lakeside, 694...NE-10
Lakeside, 200...SB-11
Lakeview, 1072...NL-5
Lakeville, 130...NK-13
Lakewood, 52131...NF-14
Lancaster, 38780...SC-11
Landeck, 100...NJ-3
Langsville, 80...SG-13
Lansing, 634...NN-19
LaPorte, 400...NG-13
Latham, 230...SG-8
Lattasburg, 100...NI-13
Lattaville, 60...SE-8
Latty, 193...NH-2
Laura, 474...SA-3
Laurel, 150...SH-4
Laurel Ridge, 2350...NI-16
Laurelville, 527...SE-10
LAWRENCE CO., 62450...SI-11
Lawrenceville, 300...SA-5
Lawshe, 60...SH-7
Layhigh, 60...SE-1
Layland, 50...NL-14
Layman...SE-15
Leavittsburg, 1973...NG-18
Leavittsville, 100...NK-17
Lebanon, 20033...SE-4
Lebanon, 50...SD-17
Lees Creek, 160...SE-6
Leesburg, 1314...SE-7
Leesville, 200...NJ-10
Leesville, 158...NL-17
Leetonia, 1959...NI-19
Leipsic, 2093...NH-5
Leistville, 40...SD-10
Lemert, 30...NI-8
Lemoyne, 300...NF-7
Lena, 100...NN-4
Lenox Ctr., 60...ND-19
Leo...SF-11
Leonardsburg...NL-9
Letart Falls, 180...SH-14
Levanna, 80...SI-5
Lewis Ctr., 350...NM-9
Lewisburg, 1820...SB-2
Lewistown, 222...NL-5
Lewisville, 176...SC-17
Lexington, 4822...NJ-11
Liberty, 240...SC-3
Liberty Ctr., 1180...NF-4
LICKING CO., 166492...NN-11
Lightsville, 30...NM-1
Lilly Chapel, 200...SB-8
Lima, 38771...NJ-4
Limaville, 151...NI-17
Lime City, 120...ND-2
Limecrest, 400...SB-6
Limestone, 50...NE-8
Limestone City, 40...NB-15
Lincoln Hts., 3286...SK-3
Lincoln Vil., 9032...SI-17
Lindale, 200...SG-4
Lindsey, 446...NF-8
Linndale, 179...SM-16
Linnville, 90...SJ-12
Linnville, 60...SB-12
Linworth...SF-18
Lisbon, 2821...NJ-19
Litchfield, 400...NH-13
Lithopolis, 1106...SC-10
Little Hocking, 263...SF-15
Little Sandusky, 50...NJ-8
Little Walnut, 80...SC-9
Little Washington...NJ-11
Little York, 400...SK-7
Lloydsville, 150...NN-18
Lock...NM-11
Lockbourne, 237...SC-9
Lockington, 141...NM-3
Lockland, 3449...SK-3
Lockville, 90...SC-10
Lockwood, 30...NF-18
Locust Grv., 220...SG-7
Locust Ridge...SG-5
Lodi, 2746...NH-13
Logan, 7152...SD-12
LOGAN CO., 45858...NL-5
Logan Elm Vil., 1118...SD-9
Logansville, 55...NL-5
Lombardsville, 40...SH-9
London, 9904...SB-7
Londonderry, 400...SF-10
Londonderry, 40...NN-17
Long Bottom, 70...SG-15
Lorain, 64097...NF-13
LORAIN CO., 301356...NG-12
Lordstown, 3417...NH-18
Lore City, 325...SA-16
Lottridge...SF-14
Louden...SG-7
Loudonville, 2641...NK-12
Louisville, 9186...NI-17
Loveland, 12081...SF-3
Loveland Pk., 1523...SJ-6
Lowell, 549...SD-16
Lowellville, 1155...NH-20
Lower Salem, 86...SD-17
Lucas, 615...NJ-12
LUCAS CO., 441815...NE-5
Lucasburg...SB-16
Lucasville, 2757...SH-9
Luckey, 1012...NF-7
Ludlow Falls, 208...SA-3
Lumberton, 150...SD-5
Luray, 110...SB-11
Lykens, 70...NI-9
Lynchburg, 1499...SF-6
Lyndhurst, 14001...NE-16
Lyndon, 200...SE-8
Lynx, 220...SI-7
Lyons, 562...ND-4
Lyra, 40...SI-10
Lytle, 200...SD-4
Macedon, 70...NL-1
Macedonia, 11188...NG-16
Mack, 11585...SL-1
Macksburg, 186...SD-16
Macon, 140...SH-6
Madeira, 8726...SF-3
Madison, 3184...ND-18
MADISON CO., 43435...NN-7
Madison Mills, 60...SC-8
Madison-on-the-Lake, 950...ND-18
Magnetic Sprs., 268...NL-8
Magnolia, 978...NK-17
MAHONING CO., 238823...NI-18
Maineville, 975...SE-4
Mainsville, 30...SC-13
Malaga, 180...SB-18
Malinta, 265...NG-4
Mallet Creek, 300...NH-14
Malta, 671...SC-14
Malvern, 1189...NJ-17
Manchester, 4000...NI-15
Manchester, 2023...SI-6
Mandale, 50...NH-3
Mansfield, 47821...NJ-11
Mantua, 1043...NG-17
Mantua Cors., 80...NG-17
Maple Hts., 23138...NF-15
Maple Valley...NB-5
Mapleton, 90...NJ-17
Maplewood, 230...NL-4
Marathon, 300...SF-5
Marble Cliff, 573...SH-18
Marblehead, 903...NE-10
Marchand...NA-9
Marcy...SC-10
Marengo, 342...NL-10
Maria Stein, 300...NL-2
Mariemont, 3403...SL-4
Marietta, 14085...SE-16
Marion, 36837...NK-8
MARION CO., 66501...NK-7
Mark Ctr., 200...NG-2
Marlboro, 500...NI-17
Marne, 783...NN-12
Marseilles, 112...NJ-7
Marshall, 110...SF-7
Marshallville, 756...NI-15
Martel, 250...NK-9
Martins Ferry, 6915...NN-19
Martinsburg, 237...NM-12
Martinsville, 463...SE-5
Marysville, 22094...NM-7
Mason, 30712...SE-3
Massieville, 400...SF-9
Massillon, 32149...NJ-16
Masury, 2064...NG-20
Matville...SC-9
Maud, 500...SE-3
Maumee, 14286...NC-1
Maximo, 200...NI-17
Maxville, 100...SD-12
May Hill, 50...SG-7
Mayfield, 3460...SK-20
Mayfield Hts., 19155...NE-16
Mayflower Vil...NC-7
Maynard, 400...NN-19
Maysville, 100...NJ-14
Maysville, 50...NJ-5
McArthur, 1701...SF-12
McCartyville, 160...NL-3
McClimansville, 60...SC-8
McClure, 725...NF-5
McComb, 1648...NH-5
McConnelsville, 1784...SC-14
McCuneville, 90...SD-13
McCutchenville, 400...NI-8
McDermott, 434...SH-9
McDonald, 3263...NH-19
McDonaldsville, 180...NI-16
McGill, 20...NH-1
McGonigle, 130...SE-2
McGuffey, 501...NJ-5
McKinley Hts., 1060...NB-13
McLuney, 75...SC-13
McZena, 40...NJ-13
Mecca, 60...NF-19
Mechanicsburg, 1644...NN-6
Mechanicstown, 280...NK-18
Medina, 26678...NH-14
MEDINA CO., 172332...NH-13
Medway, 2000...SB-5
Meeker, 150...NK-8
Meigs, 40...SC-15
MEIGS CO., 23770...SG-13
Melbern, 200...NF-2
Melmore, 153...NH-8
Melrose, 275...NH-3
Melvin, 90...SE-6
Memphis...SE-6
Mendon, 662...NJ-2
Mentor, 47159...NE-16
Mentor-on-the-Lake, 7443...ND-16
Mercer, 50...NK-2
MERCER CO., 40814...NK-1
Mercerville, 100...SI-13
Mermill...NG-6
Mesopotamia, 300...NF-18
Metamora, 627...ND-5
Metzger, 200...SE-9
Mexico, 60...NI-8
Meyers Lake, 569...NC-9
MIAMI CO., 102506...NN-3
Miami Shores...SN-7
Miami Villa...SK-8
Miamisburg, 20181...SD-3
Miamitown, 1259...SF-1
Miamiville, 242...SK-5
Middle Bass, 100...NE-10
Middle Pt., 576...NI-2
Middleboro, 50...SE-4
Middlebourne, 80...NN-16
Middlebranch, 220...NI-16
Middleburg, 220...NM-6
Middleburg, 50...SC-17
Middleburg Hts., 15946...NF-14
Middlebury, 30...NI-1
Middlefield, 2694...NF-17
Middleport, 2530...SG-14
Middleton, 80...NI-19
Middletown, 48694...SD-3
Middletown, 25...NM-6
Midland, 315...SF-5
Midvale, 754...NL-16
Midway, 322...SC-7
Mifflin, 137...NJ-12
Milan, 1367...NG-11
Milford, 6709...SF-3
Milford Ctr., 792...NM-7
Millbrook, 60...NJ-13
Millbury, 1200...NE-7
Milledgeville, 112...SD-7
Miller, 200...SJ-12
Miller City, 137...NH-4
Millersburg, 3025...NK-14
Millersport, 1044...SB-11
Millerstown, 90...NN-5
Millersville, 150...NG-8
Millfield, 341...SE-13
Millport, 110...NJ-18
Millville, 708...SE-2
Millwood, 200...NL-12
Milton Ctr., 144...NG-5
Miltonsburg, 43...SB-18
Miltonville, 170...SD-3
Mineral...SE-13
Mineral City, 727...NK-16
Mineral Ridge, 3892...NH-19
Minersville, 70...SG-14
Minerva, 3720...NJ-17
Minerva Pk., 1272...NN-9
Minford, 693...SH-10
Mingo, 100...NM-6
Mingo Jct., 3454...NL-20
Minster, 2805...NL-3
Mitiwanga, 130...NF-11
Modest...SF-4
Mogadore, 3853...NH-16
Mohicanville, 100...NJ-13
Moline, 470...NC-2
Monclova, 120...NE-6
Monfort Hts., 11948...SL-2
Monnett, 60...NJ-9
Monroe, 12442...SE-3
Monroe Ctr., 100...ND-20
MONROE CO., 14642...SC-18
Monroeville, 1400...NG-10
Monroeville, 50...NK-19
Monterey, 120...SG-4
Montezuma, 165...NL-2
Montgomery, 10251...SK-5
MONTGOMERY CO., 535153...SC-3
Monticello, 40...NJ-2
Montpelier, 4072...NE-2
Montra, 100...NL-4
Montrose, 350...NH-15
Montville, 330...NE-18
Moorefield, 100...NM-17
Mooresville...SE-10
Moraine, 6307...SC-4
Moreland, 100...NJ-14
Moreland Hills, 3320...SM-20
MORGAN CO., 15054...SC-15
Morgansville, 25...SD-14
Morgantown, 50...SG-8
Morning Sun, 200...SD-1
Morral, 399...NJ-8
Morristown, 303...NN-18
Morrisville, 70...SE-6
Morrow, 1188...SE-4
MORROW CO., 34827...NK-9
Moscow, 185...SH-4
Moss Run...SD-17
Moulton, 130...NK-3
Mt. Air, 300...NN-9
Mt. Blanchard, 492...NI-6
Mt. Carmel, 4741...SM-5
Mt. Carmel Hts., 1200...SM-5
Mt. Cory, 204...NI-5
Mt. Eaton, 241...NJ-15
Mt. Ephraim, 80...SB-16
Mt. Forest Trails, 450...SM-5
Mt. Gilead, 3660...NK-10
Mt. Healthy, 6098...SK-2
Mt. Holly, 250...SG-4
Mt. Holly...SD-5
Mt. Hope, 200...NK-14
Mt. Jefferson, 100...NM-3
Mt. Liberty, 250...NL-11
Mt. Olive...SH-4
Mt. Orab, 3664...SG-5
Mt. Perry, 220...SB-13
Mt. Pisgah, 100...SG-4
Mt. Pleasant, 478...NM-19
Mt. Pleasant, 70...SE-12
Mt. Pleasant...NA-9
Mt. Repose, 4672...SF-4
Mt. Sterling, 1782...SC-8
Mt. Vernon, 16990...NL-11
Mt. Victory, 627...NK-7
Mowrystown, 360...SG-6
Moxahala, 300...SC-13
Moxahala Pk., 200...SB-13
Mudsock, 25...SA-8
Mulberry, 3323...SF-4
Munroe Falls, 5012...NA-6
Murdock...SF-4
Murlin Hts., 550...SB-4
Murray City, 449...SD-13
MUSKINGUM CO., 86074...NN-14
Mutual, 104...NN-6
Nankin, 400...NI-12
Napoleon, 8749...NF-4
Nashport, 260...NN-13
Nashville, 197...NK-13
Nashville, 100...SB-3
Navarre, 1957...NJ-16
Neapolis, 423...NF-5
Neelysville, 40...SD-15
Neffs, 993...NN-19
Negley, 281...NJ-20
Nellie, 131...NL-13
Nelson, 80...NG-18
Nelsonville, 5392...SE-13
Neptune, 130...NK-2
Nettle Lake, 200...ND-1
Nevada, 760...NJ-8
Neville, 100...SH-4
New Albany, 7724...NN-10
New Albany, 75...NI-19
New Alexander, 50...NJ-18
New Alexandria, 272...NM-19
New Antioch, 220...SE-6
New Athens, 320...NM-18
New Baltimore, 661...SF-2
New Baltimore, 250...NI-17
New Bavaria, 99...NG-4
New Bedford, 220...NL-14
New Bloomington, 515...NK-7
New Boston, 2272...SI-9
New Bremen, 2978...NL-3
New Burlington, 5069...SJ-2
New California, 1411...NN-8
New Carlisle, 5785...SB-5
New Concord, 2491...SA-15
New Cumberland, 150...NK-17
New Dover, 130...NM-8
New England, 50...SE-14
New Franklin, 230...NJ-17
New Gdn., 100...NJ-18
New Germany...SL-9
New Guilford, 30...NM-13
New Hagerstown, 40...NL-17
New Hampshire, 174...NK-5
New Harrisburg, 100...NK-17
New Harrison, 50...NN-2
New Haven, 583...SF-1
New Haven, 399...NH-10
New Holland, 801...SD-8
New Hope, 150...SC-1
New Jasper, 100...SC-5
New Knoxville, 879...NL-3
New Lebanon, 3995...SC-3
New Lexington, 4731...SC-13
New Lexington, 100...SC-2
New London, 2461...NH-12
New Madison, 892...SB-1
New Market, 50...SG-6
New Marshfield, 326...SE-13
New Martinsburg, 150...SE-7
New Matamoras, 896...SD-18
New Miami, 2249...SE-2
New Middletown, 1621...NI-20
New Moorefield, 300...SA-6
New Moscow, 35...NM-14
New Paris, 1629...SB-1
New Petersburg, 150...SF-7
New Philadelphia, 17288...NL-16
New Pittsburg, 388...NJ-13
New Plymouth, 120...SE-12
New Richland, 100...NL-5
New Richmond, 2582...SH-3
New Riegel, 249...NH-7
New Rochester, 75...NF-7
New Rumley, 140...NL-18
New Salem, 130...SB-12
New Somerset, 150...NK-19
New Springfield, 600...NI-20
New Stark, 70...NJ-6
New Straitsville, 722...SD-13
New Vienna, 1224...SE-6
New Washington, 967...NI-10
New Waterford, 1238...NI-20
New Weston, 136...NL-1
New Westville, 90...SB-1
New Winchester, 40...NJ-9
Newark, 47573...NN-12
Newburgh Hts., 2167...SM-18
Newcastle, 100...NL-13
Newcomerstown, 3822...NM-15
Newell Run...SE-17
Newhope, 150...SH-5
Newman, 300...NJ-15
Newport, 1003...SE-17
Newport, 200...NL-16
Newport, 198...NM-3
Newport, 180...SB-7
Newton Falls, 4795...NG-18
Newtonsville, 392...SF-4
Newtown, 2672...SM-5
Ney, 354...NF-2
Nicholsville, 200...SH-4
Niles, 19266...NG-19
Nipgen, 100...SF-9
NOBLE CO., 14645...SC-16
N. Auburn, 40...NI-10
N. Baltimore, 3432...NH-6
N. Bend, 857...SF-1
N. Benton, 280...NI-18
N. Bloomfield, 500...NF-18
N. Bristol, 160...NF-18
N. Canton, 17488...NI-16
N. College Hill, 9397...SF-2
N. Creek, 80...NH-3
N. Fairfield, 560...NH-11
N. Fork Vil., 1700...SE-9
N. Georgetown, 150...NI-18
N. Hampton, 478...SA-5
N. Industry, 2700...NJ-16
N. Jackson, 900...NH-18
N. Kingsville, 2923...NC-19
N. Lawrence, 268...NI-15
N. Lewisburg, 1490...NM-6
N. Liberty, 80...NK-12
N. Lima, 900...NI-19
N. Madison, 8547...ND-18
N. Monroeville, 40...NG-10
N. Olmsted, 32718...NF-14
N. Perry, 893...ND-17
N. Randall, 1027...SM-19
N. Ridgeville, 29465...NF-13
N. Robinson, 205...NJ-10
N. Royalton, 30444...NG-15
N. Salem, 100...NN-15
N. Star, 236...NM-2
N. Warren...NA-12
N. Woodbury, 90...NK-10
N. Zanesville, 2816...SB-14
Northbrook, 10668...SK-2
Northfield, 3677...NG-15
Northridge, 8500...SB-4
Northridge, 7572...SA-6
Northup, 100...SI-13
Northwood, 5265...NE-7
Northwood, 80...NL-6
Norton, 12085...NH-15
Norton, 50...NL-9
Norwalk, 17012...NG-11
Norwich, 102...SA-15
Norwood, 19207...SF-3
Nova, 430...NH-12
Novelty, 500...NF-16
Oak Hbr., 2759...NF-8
Oak Hill, 1551...SH-11
Oakdale, 570...NB-8
Oakdale...SD-13
Oakfield, 100...SC-13
Oakfield, 40...NF-18
Oakland, 120...SD-10
Oakland...SD-5
Oakshade, 100...NE-4
Oakwood, 9202...SC-4
Oakwood, 3667...SN-20
Oakwood, 608...NH-3
Oberlin, 8286...NG-12
Obetz, 4532...SB-9
Oceola, 190...NJ-8
Octa, 59...SD-6
Ogden, 100...SE-5
Ohio City, 705...NJ-2
Ohio Furnace, 150...SJ-10
Okeana, 240...SE-1
Okolona, 140...NF-4
Old Fort, 186...NG-8
Old Washington, 279...NN-16
Oldtown, 80...SC-5
Olena, 350...NH-11
Olive Branch, 200...SG-4
Olive Green, 65...NM-10
Olivesburg, 80...NI-11
Olivett, 80...SA-18
Olmsted Falls, 9024...SN-14
Omega, 130...SF-10
Oneida, 150...NJ-17
Ontario, 6225...NJ-11
Opperman, 30...SB-16
Oran, 50...NM-3
Orange, 3323...SM-20
Orange, 35...NM-15
Orangeville, 197...NF-20
Orbiston, 40...SD-13
Orchard Island, 300...NL-5
Oregon, 20291...NE-7
Oregonia, 300...SE-4
Oreville, 150...SD-13
Orient, 270...SC-9
Orland, 50...SE-12
Orrville, 8380...NI-14
Orwell, 1660...NE-18
Osgood, 302...NL-2
Ostrander, 643...NM-8
Otsego, 50...NN-14
Ottawa, 4460...NH-4
OTTAWA CO., 41428...NE-7
Ottawa Hills, 4517...NB-1
Otterbien Home, 700...SE-3
Ottokee, 35...NE-4
Ottoville, 976...NI-3
Otway, 87...SH-8
Outville, 110...SA-11
Overlook...SL-8
Overpeck, 300...SE-2
Overton, 140...NI-13
Owensville, 794...SG-4
Oxford, 21371...SD-1
Ozark, 40...SB-18
Padua, 70...NK-1
Page Manor...SL-9
Pagetown, 40...NL-10
Painesville, 19563...ND-17
Painesville on the Lake, 850...ND-17
Painters Creek, 150...NN-2
Paintersville, 70...SD-5
Palestine, 200...NN-1
Palmyra, 240...NH-18
Pancoastburg, 87...SD-8
Pandora, 1153...NI-5
Pansy...SE-5
Paris, 220...NJ-17
Park Ridge Acres, 300...NB-15
Parkertown, 25...NG-10
Parkman, 600...NF-18
Parma, 81601...NF-15
Parma Hts., 20718...NF-14
Parral, 218...NK-16
Parrott...SD-7
Pasco, 50...NM-4
Pataskala, 14962...SA-11
Patmos...NI-18
Patriot, 140...SI-12
Patterson, 139...NJ-7
Pattersonville, 30...NJ-18
Paulding, 3605...NH-2
PAULDING CO., 19614...NH-1
Pavonia, 100...NJ-11
Payne, 1194...NH-1
Pedro, 110...SJ-11
Peebles, 1782...SH-7
Pekin, 250...SD-4
Pekin, 100...NJ-17
Pemberton, 350...NM-4
Pemberville, 1371...NF-7
Penfield, 100...NH-13
Peninsula, 565...NG-15
Pennsville, 150...SD-14
Peoli, 30...NM-16
Peoria, 230...NM-7
Pepper Pike, 5979...NF-16
Perintown, 150...SF-4
Perry, 1663...ND-17
PERRY CO., 36058...SC-12
Perry Hts., 8441...NC-8
Perrysburg, 20623...NE-6
Perrysville, 735...NK-12
Perrysville, 60...NL-17
Perryton, 100...NN-12
Peru, 70...NH-10
Petersburg, 950...NI-20
Pettisville, 498...NE-3
Pfeiffer Sta., 30...NK-7
Phalanx...NG-18
Pharisburg, 50...NL-8
Phillipsburg, 557...SB-3
Philo, 733...SB-14
Philothea, 120...NL-1
Phoneton, 220...SB-4
PICKAWAY CO., 55698...SD-9
Pickerington, 18291...SB-10
Pickrelltown, 60...NM-6
Piedmont, 200...NM-17
Pierpont, 420...ND-20
Pigeon Run, 250...NJ-15
PIKE CO., 28709...SG-9
Piketon, 2181...SG-9
Pikeville, 40...NM-2
Pine Grv., 50...SJ-11
Piney Fork, 350...NM-19
Pioneer, 1380...ND-2
Piqua, 20522...NN-3
Pisgah, 1000...SE-3
Pitchin, 150...SB-6
Pitsburg, 388...SA-2
Pittsfield, 200...NG-12
Plain City, 4225...NN-8
Plainfield, 157...NM-15
Plants, 150...SH-14
Plantsville, 25...SE-14
Plattsburg, 160...SB-6
Plattsville, 100...NM-4
Pleasant Bend, 50...NG-4
Pleasant City, 447...SB-16
Pleasant Cors., 80...SB-9
Pleasant Grv., 1742...SB-14
Pleasant Grv., 130...NM-19
Pleasant Hill, 1200...NN-3
Pleasant Home, 200...NI-13
Pleasant Plain, 154...SF-4
Pleasant Run, 4953...SJ-2
Pleasant Run Farm, 4654...SJ-2
Pleasant Valley, 500...SE-9
Pleasant View, 35...SC-6
Pleasantville, 960...SC-11
Plumwood, 319...SA-7
Plymouth, 1857...NI-10
Plymouth Ctr., 50...ND-19
Poast Town, 150...SD-3
Pt. Isabel, 45...SH-4
Point Pl...NA-3
Pt. Pleasant, 35...SH-4
Poland, 2555...NH-20
Poland Ctr., 250...NE-14
Polk, 336...NI-12
Pomeroy, 1852...SG-14
Port Clinton, 6056...NF-9
Port Jefferson, 371...NM-4
Port Union, 100...SE-3
Port Washington, 569...NM-16
Port William, 254...SD-6
Portage, 438...NG-6
PORTAGE CO., 161419...NH-17
Portage Lakes, 6968...NI-15
Porter, 150...SH-13
Porterfield, 130...SF-15
Portersville, 85...SC-14
Portland, 120...SG-15
Portsmouth, 20226...SI-9
Possum Woods, 200...NC-16
Potsdam, 288...SB-3
Powell, 11500...NN-9
Powellsville, 50...SI-10
Powhatan Pt., 1592...SB-19
Pratts Fork...SF-14
Prattsville, 30...SF-12
PREBLE CO., 42270...SC-1
Pricetown, 60...SF-6
Princeton, 120...SE-3
Proctorville, 574...SK-12
Prospect, 1112...NL-8
Pulaski, 132...NF-2
Pulaskiville, 50...NK-10
Put-in-Bay, 138...NE-10
PUTNAM CO., 34499...NI-4
Pyrmont, 120...SB-3
Pyro, 150...SH-11
Quaker City, 502...SB-17
Queen Acres, 650...SE-2
Quincy, 706...NM-5
Raccoon Island...SI-13
Racine, 675...SG-14
Radcliff, 150...SF-12
Radnor, 201...NL-8
Ragersville, 150...NL-15
Rainsboro, 280...SF-7
Randolph, 750...NH-17
Range, 40...SC-7
Rarden, 159...SH-8
Ravenna, 11724...NH-17
Rawson, 570...NI-5
Ray, 100...SF-11
Rayland, 417...NM-19
Raymond, 257...NM-7
Reading, 10385...SF-3
Red Lion, 200...SD-3
Redbird, 2000...ND-17
Redfield, 50...SC-13
Redhaw, 50...NI-13
Redoak...SH-6
Redtown...SE-13
Reedsburg, 150...NJ-13
Reedsville, 300...SG-15
Reedtown, 50...NH-10
Reedurban, 4400...NJ-16
Reese, 400...SJ-19
Reesville, 250...SD-6
Rehoboth, 100...SC-13
Reily, 200...SE-1
Reinersville, 100...SC-15
Reminderville, 3404...NF-16
Remington, 328...SK-5
Remsen Cors., 75...NG-15
Rendville, 36...SD-13
Reno, 1293...SE-17
Reno Bch., 430...NE-8
Rensselaer Pk., 850...SK-3
Republic, 549...NH-9
Resaca, 40...NN-7
Residence Pk...SL-7
Reynoldsburg, 35893...SB-10
Rice...NH-3
Riceland, 200...NJ-14
Rich Hill, 75...NM-10
Richfield, 3648...NG-15
Richfield Ctr., 110...NE-5
RICHLAND CO., 124475...NI-11
Richmond, 481...NL-19
Richmond Ctr., 100...ND-20
Richmond Dale, 377...SF-10
Richmond Hts., 10546...NE-16
Richville, 3324...NJ-16
Richwood, 2229...NL-8
Ridgeland, 50...SG-11
Ridgeton, 20...NI-9
Ridgeville, 200...SD-4
Ridgeville Corners, 435...NF-3
Ridgeway, 338...NK-6
Ridgewood Hts...SM-7
Rimer, 50...NI-3
Rinard Mills, 30...SD-18
Ringgold, 200...SC-10
Ringgold, 25...SD-14
Rio Grande, 830...SH-12
Ripley, 1750...SI-5
Risingsun, 606...NG-7
Rittman, 6491...NI-14
River Cors., 60...NH-13
Riverlea, 545...SF-18
Riverside, 25201...SC-4
Rix Mills, 40...SB-15
Roachester, 500...SE-4
Roads, 160...SG-11
Roaming Shores, 1508...NE-19
Robertsville, 331...NJ-17
Robins, 90...SB-16
Robtown...SC-9
Rochester, 182...NH-12
Rock Camp, 80...SJ-11
Rock Creek, 529...NE-18
Rock Mills, 30...SE-7
Rock Way, 160...SB-5
Rockbridge, 182...SD-11
Rockford, 1120...NJ-2
Rockport, 90...NI-4
Rocky Hill...SG-11
Rocky Ridge, 417...NE-8
Rocky River, 20213...NF-14
Rodney, 250...SH-12
Rogers, 237...NJ-20
Rollersville, 40...NG-7
Rome, 1450...SK-12
Rome, 200...NE-18
Rome, 90...NI-11
Romohr Acres, 300...SL-6
Rootstown, 650...NH-17
Rose Farm, 200...SC-13
Rosedale, 180...NN-7
Roseland, 2150...NJ-11
Rosemont, 90...ND-11
Rosemount, 2112...SI-9
Roseville, 1852...SC-13
Rosewood, 257...NM-5
Ross, 3417...SE-2
ROSS CO., 78064...SE-9
Rossburg, 201...NM-2
Rossford, 6293...NE-6
Roswell, 219...NL-16
Roundhead, 300...NK-5
Rowsburg, 90...NI-13
Roxabell, 200...SE-8
Royalton, 260...SC-10
Rubyville...SH-10
Rudolph, 458...NG-6
Ruggles, 40...NH-12
Ruggles Bch., 50...NF-11
Ruraldale, 60...SC-14
Rush Run, 250...NM-19
Rushmore, 50...NI-3
Rushsylvania, 516...NL-6
Rushtown...SH-9
Rushville, 302...SC-12
Russell, 50...SF-6
Russell Ctr., 200...NF-16
Russells Pt., 1391...NL-5
Russellville, 561...SH-6
Russia, 640...NM-3
Rutland, 393...SG-13
Sabina, 2564...SD-6
Sagamore Hills, 1930...NG-15
Sahara Sands, 650...NB-8
St. Bernard, 4368...SL-3
St. Clairsville, 5184...NN-18
St. Henry, 2427...NL-2
St. Johns, 185...NK-4
St. Louisville, 373...NM-12
St. Martin, 129...SF-5
St. Marys, 8332...NK-3
St. Paris, 2089...NN-5
Salem, 12303...NI-18
Salem Ctr., 80...SG-13
Salesville, 129...SB-17
Salineville, 1311...NK-19
Saltillo, 110...SC-13
Samantha, 130...SF-6
Sampleville, 200...SC-2
San Margherita, 300...SH-17
Sandusky, 25793...NF-10
SANDUSKY CO., 60944...NF-8
Sandy Sprs...SJ-8
Sandyville, 368...NK-16
Santa Fe, 100...NL-4
Sarahsville, 166...SB-16
Sardinia, 980...SG-5
Sardis, 559...SD-19
Savannah, 413...NI-12
Savona, 50...SA-2
Sawyerwood, 1540...NC-6
Saybrook...ND-18
Sayre...SC-13
Schoenbrunn, 700...NL-16
Schumm, 25...NJ-1
Scienceville...NC-14
Scio, 763...NL-18
SCIOTO CO., 79499...SH-9
Scioto Furnace, 250...SI-10
Sciotodale, 1081...SI-10
Scotch Ridge, 90...NF-7
Scott, 286...NI-2
Scottown, 100...SJ-12
Seal, 25...NI-8
Seaman, 944...SH-7
Sebring, 4420...NI-18
Secedar Corners, 300...NC-14
Selma, 130...SC-6
SENECA CO., 56745...NH-8
Senecaville, 457...SB-16
Senior...SE-4
Seven Hills, 11804...NF-15
Seven Hills, 2000...SJ-2
Seven Mile, 751...SD-2
Seventeen, 120...NL-16
Seville, 2296...NH-14
Sewellsville, 35...NN-17
Shade, 120...SF-14
Shademore, 40...SL-5
Shadeville, 100...SB-9
Shadyside, 3785...SA-19
Shaker Hts., 28448...NF-15
Shalersville, 220...NG-17
Shandon, 400...SE-1
Sharon, 90...SC-16
Sharon Ctr., 350...NH-15
Sharonville, 13560...SF-3
Sharpsburg, 50...SE-14
Shauck, 200...NK-10
Shawnee, 655...SD-13
Shawnee Hills, 2171...SC-6
Shawnee Hills, 681...NN-8
Sheffield, 3982...NF-13
Sheffield Lake, 9137...NF-13
Shelby, 9317...NI-10
SHELBY CO., 49423...NM-3
Shenandoah, 100...NI-11
Sheridan, 500...SJ-11
Sherrodsville, 304...NK-17
Sherwood, 827...NG-2
Shiloh, 11000...SB-4
Shiloh, 649...NI-11
Shinrock...NG-11
Shreve, 1514...NJ-13
Sidney, 21229...NM-4
Signal, 40...NJ-19
Silver Lake, 2519...NH-16
Silverton, 4788...SK-4
Simons, 70...NE-20
Sinking Spr., 133...SG-7
Skyline Acres, 1717...SK-2
Sligo, 300...SE-5
Slocum...SI-10
Smith Corners...ND-12
Smithfield, 869...NM-19
Smithville, 1252...NI-14
Smyrna, 40...NM-17
Snyderville, 200...SB-5
Socialville...SE-3
Solon, 23348...NF-16
Somerdale, 320...NK-16
Somerset, 1481...SC-12
Somerton, 180...SB-18
Somerville, 281...SD-2
Sonora, 250...SA-14
S. Amherst, 1688...NF-12
S. Bloomfield, 1744...SC-9
S. Bloomingville, 40...SE-11
S. Charleston, 1693...SB-6
S. Condit, 110...NM-10
S. Euclid, 22295...NE-15
S. Hill Pk., 1040...NB-1
S. Lebanon, 4115...SE-4
S. New Lyme, 120...NE-19
S. Newbury, 70...NF-17
S. Olive, 40...SC-16
S. Perry, 140...SD-11
S. Plymouth, 20...SD-7
South Point, 3958...*B-2
S. Russell, 3810...NF-16
S. Salem, 204...SE-8
S. Solon, 355...SC-6
S. Vienna, 384...SB-6
S. Webster, 866...SH-10
S. West Hubbard...NC-14
S. Woodbury, 30...NL-10
S. Zanesville, 1989...SB-14
Southington, 400...NG-18
Sparta, 161...NL-10
Spencer, 753...NH-13
Spencerville, 2223...NJ-3
Spring Mill, 150...NJ-11
Spring Mtn., 80...NL-13
Spring Valley, 479...SD-5
Springboro, 17409...SD-4
Springdale, 11223...SJ-3
Springfield, 60608...SB-6
Springhills, 150...NM-5
Springville, 40...NJ-13
Squirrel Town...SI-7
Stafford, 81...SC-17
Standley...NG-3
Stanleyville, 40...SD-16
Stanwood, 30...NJ-15
STARK CO., 375586...NJ-17
Starr, 25...SE-12
Staunton, 120...NN-4
Staunton, 100...SE-7
Steam Cors...NJ-10
Steinersville, 200...SB-19
Stelvideo, 90...NN-2
Sterling, 457...NI-14
Steuben, 60...NH-10
Steubenville, 18659...NL-20
Stewart, 247...SE-14
Stewartsville, 200...SA-19
Stillwater, 150...NM-17
Stockdale, 135...SH-10
Stockport, 503...SD-15
Stone...SC-14
Stone Creek, 177...NL-15
Stonelick, 100...SG-4
Stony Ridge, 411...NF-7
Stout, 94...SI-7
Stoutsville, 560...SD-10
Stovertown, 35...SB-14
Stow, 34837...NH-16
Strasburg, 2608...NK-16
Stratford, 80...NM-9
Stratton, 294...NK-20
Streetsboro, 16028...NG-16
Stringtown, 50...SH-4
Strongsville, 44750...NG-14
Struthers, 10713...NH-20
Stryker, 1335...NF-3
Suffield, 500...NH-16
Sugar Bush Knolls, 177...NG-16
Sugar Grv., 426...SD-11
Sugar Grv., 160...NK-19
Sugar Grv., 150...SI-9
Sugar Grv. Hill, 300...NB-15
Sugar Ridge, 130...NF-6
Sugar Tree Ridge, 110...SG-6
Sugar Valley, 25...SC-1
Sugarcreek, 2220...NK-15
Sullivan, 450...NH-12
Sulphur Sprs., 194...NI-9
Sulphurgrove...SK-9
Summerfield, 254...SC-17
Summerford, 250...SB-7
Summerside, 5083...SG-3
Summerside Estates, 1700...SM-6
Summersville, 80...NL-7
Summit, 700...NC-13
SUMMIT CO., 541781...NH-15
Summithill, 20...SF-9
Summitville, 135...NJ-18
Sumner...SF-14
Sun Valley...SJ-20
Sunbury, 4389...NM-10
Sunbury, 110...SD-3
Sunnyland, 250...NB-15
Surrey Hill, 700...NB-12
Swanders, 80...NL-4
Swanton, 3690...NE-5
Sybene, 200...SK-12
Sycamore, 861...NI-8
Sycamore Valley, 25...SC-17
Sylvania, 18965...ND-6
Syracuse, 826...SG-14
Tacoma, 100...SA-18
Tallmadge, 17537...NH-16
Tarlton, 282...SD-10
Tawawa, 100...NM-4
Taylors Creek, 660...SK-1
Taylorsburg...SK-6
Taylorsville...SG-6
Tedrow, 173...NE-4
Temperanceville, 80...SB-17
Terrace Pk., 2251...SL-5
Terre Haute, 180...NN-5
Terry Acres, 165...SL-10
Texas, 130...NF-5
Thackery, 120...NN-5
The Bend, 100...NG-2
The Plains, 3080...SE-13
The Vil. of Indian Hill, 5785...SK-5
Thomastown...NC-6
Thompson, 370...ND-18
Thornville, 991...SB-12
Thrifton, 40...SE-8
Thurman, 103...SH-12
Thurston, 604...SB-11
Tiffin, 17963...NH-8
Tiltonsville, 1372...NM-19
Timberlake, 675...NE-16
Tipp City, 9689...SB-4
Tippecanoe, 121...NM-17
Tipton, 25...NH-1
Tiro, 280...NI-10
Tiverton, 80...NL-13
Toboso, 200...NN-12
Toledo, 287208...NE-7
Tontogany, 367...NF-6
Torch, 300...SF-15
Toronto, 5091...NL-20
Townwood, 25...NH-5
Trail...NK-15
Tranquility, 30...SH-7
Tremont City, 375...SA-5
Trenton, 11869...SD-3
Triadelphia, 40...SC-14
Trimble, 390...SD-13
Trinway, 365...NN-13
Trotwood, 24431...SC-3
Trowbridge, 50...NE-8
Troy, 25058...NN-3
Trumbull, 200...ND-18
TRUMBULL CO., 210312...NG-18
Tucson...SE-10
Tuppers Plains, 465...SF-14
Turpin Hills, 5099...SM-4
Tuscarawas, 1056...NL-16
TUSCARAWAS CO., 92582...NM-16
Twenty Mile Stand, 300...SJ-6
Twightwee...SJ-6
Twin Lakes, 300...NG-16
Twin Valley, 300...SI-9
Twinsburg, 18795...NG-16
Tymochtee, 25...NI-8
Tyndall, 150...NM-14
Uhrichsville, 5413...NL-16
Union, 6419...SB-3
Union City, 1666...NM-1
UNION CO., 52300...NL-7
Union Furnace, 430...SE-12
Union Sta...SA-11
Unionport, 150...NL-19
Uniontown, 3309...NI-16
Uniontown, 230...NN-18
Unionvale, 90...NM-18
Unionville Ctr., 233...NN-7
Uniopolis, 222...NK-4
Unity, 100...NI-20
Unity, 30...SH-7
University Hts., 13539...NF-15
University View, 500...SH-18
Upper Arlington, 33771...SA-9
Upper Sandusky, 6596...NJ-8
Urbana, 11793...NN-5
Urbancrest, 960...SB-9
Utica, 2132...NM-11
Utopia, 70...SI-4
Valley City, 400...NG-14
Valley Hi, 212...NM-6
Valley View, 2034...SN-18
Valley View, 620...SH-17
Valleywood...SM-9
Van Buren, 328...NH-6
Van Wert, 10846...NI-2
VAN WERT CO., 28744...NJ-2
Vanatta, 130...NN-11
Vandalia, 15246...SB-4
Vanlue, 359...NI-7
Vaughnsville, 262...NI-4
Venedocia, 124...NJ-2
Venice Hts., 1300...NA-12
Vera Cruz...SF-5
Vermilion, 10594...NF-12
Vernon, 100...NF-20
Vernon...SI-11
Verona, 494...SB-2
Versailles, 2687...NM-2
Veto, 110...SE-15
Vickery, 121...NF-9
Vienna, 600...NG-19
Vigo, 120...SF-10
Viking Vil., 1230...SM-5
Villa, 120...SB-6
Villa Nova, 800...NK-3
Vincent, 339...SE-15
Vinton, 222...SG-12
VINTON CO., 13435...SF-11
Wabash, 70...NK-1
Waco, 380...NJ-16
Wade...SE-18
Wadsworth, 21567...NH-15
Wagram, 125...SB-10
Wahlsburg, 30...SH-5
Wainwright, 250...NL-16
Waite Hill, 471...NE-16
Wakatomika, 40...NM-13
Wakefield, 140...SH-9
Wakeman, 1047...NG-12
Walbridge, 3019...NC-3
Waldo, 338...NL-9
Walhonding, 100...SB-16
Walhonding, 90...NL-13
Walnut Creek, 878...NK-15
Walton Hills, 2281...SN-19
Wamsley, 90...SH-8
Wapakoneta, 9867...NK-4
Warner, 130...SD-16
Warnock, 200...SA-19
Warren, 41557...NG-19
WARREN CO., 212693...SE-4
Warrensburg...NM-8
Warrensville Hts., 13542...NF-15
Warrenton, 50...NM-19
Warsaw, 682...NL-13
WASHINGTON CO., 61778...SD-16
Washington Court House, 14192...SD-7
Washingtonville, 801...NI-19
Waterford, 450...SD-15
Waterford, 70...NK-11
Waterloo, 170...SB-10
Waterloo, 150...SI-12
Watertown, 220...SE-15
Waterville, 5523...NF-6
Watkins, 130...NM-8
Wauseon, 7332...NE-4
Waverly, 4408...SG-9
Wayland, 200...NH-18
Wayne, 887...NG-7
Wayne, 100...NE-19
WAYNE CO., 114520...NI-14
Wayne Lakes Pk., 718...SA-2

***, †, ‡, §, ◊ See explanation under state title in this index.**
County and parish names are listed in capital letters & boldface type.
Independent cities (not included in a county) are listed in italics.

Waynesburg, 923 ... NJ-17
Waynesfield, 847 ... NK-5
Waynesville, 2834 ... SD-4
Webb Summit ... SD-12
Webster, 100 ... NM-2
Wegee, 160 ... SB-19
Wellington, 4802 ... NH-12
Wellston, 5663 ... SG-11
Wellsville, 3541 ... NK-19
Welshfield, 150 ... NF-17
Wengerlawn, 85 ... SB-3
W. Akron ... NC-5
W. Alexandria, 1340 .. SC-2
W. Andover, 100 ... NE-19
W. Bedford, 60 ... NM-13
W. Carlisle, 30 ... NM-13
W. Carrollton City, 13818 ... SC-3
W. Charleston, 100 ... SB-4
W. Chester, 800 ... SE-3
W. Chester, 100 ... NM-16
W. Clarksfield, 100 ... NG-11
W. Elkton, 197 ... SD-2
W. Farmington, 499 ... NF-18
W. Florence, 40 ... SC-1
W. Hill, 2273 ... NG-20
W. Independence, 40 ... NH-7
W. Jefferson, 4222 ... SB-8
W. Jefferson, 120 ... NE-2
W. Lafayette, 2321 ... NM-15
W. Lancaster, 75 ... SD-6
W. Lebanon, 120 ... NJ-15
W. Leipsic, 206 ... NH-4
W. Liberty, 1805 ... NM-5
W. Liberty, 50 ... NI-10
W. Liberty, 40 ... NL-9
W. Lodi, 80 ... NH-9
W. Manchester, 474 .. SB-2
W. Mansfield, 682 ... NL-6
W. Mecca, 120 ... NF-19
W. Middletown, 550 ... SD-3
W. Millgrove, 174 ... NG-7
W. Milton, 4630 ... SB-3
W. Newton ... NK-5
West Point, 220 ... NJ-19
W. Portsmouth, 3149 ... SI-9
W. Rushville, 134 ... SC-12
W. Salem, 1464 ... NI-13
W. Sonora, 100 ... SB-2
W. Union, 3241 ... SI-7
W. Unity, 1671 ... NE-3
W. Williamsfield, 110 ... NE-20
Westboro, 270 ... SF-5
Westerville, 36120 ... NN-9
Westfield, 110 ... NL-9
Westfield Ctr., 1115 ... NH-14
Westhope, 80 ... NG-5
Westlake, 32729 ... NF-14
Westminster, 100 ... NJ-4
Weston, 1590 ... NG-5
Westview, 530 ... NG-14
Westville, 250 ... NI-18
Westville, 200 ... NN-5
Wetsel ... NI-2
Weymouth, 180 ... NG-14
Wharton, 358 ... NI-7
Wheelersburg, 6437 ... SI-10
Whipple, 130 ... SD-16
Whisler, 120 ... SD-10
White Cottage, 300 ... SB-13
White Oak, 19167 ... SF-2
White Sulphur ... NM-8
Whitehall, 18062 ... SB-10
Whitehouse, 4149 ... NF-5
Whiteoak, 40 ... SC-8
White's, 375 ... NF-9
Wick, 90 ... NE-19
Wickliffe, 12750 ... NE-16
Wiggonsville, 80 ... SH-4
Wilberforce, 2271 ... SC-5
Wildbrook Acres, 1500 ... SK-3
Wilgus, 30 ... SJ-12
Wilkesville, 149 ... SG-12
Willard, 6236 ... NH-10
Willetsville, 50 ... SF-6
Williams Ctr., 300 ... NF-2
WILLIAMS CO., 37642 ... NE-2
Williamsburg, 2490 .. SG-4
Williamsdale, 581 ... SE-2
Williamsfield, 400 .. NE-20
Williamsport, 1023 ... SD-9
Williamsport, 70 ... NK-10
Williamstown, 100 ... NJ-6
Williston, 487 ... NE-7
Willoughby, 22268 ... NE-16
Willoughby Hills, 9485 ... NE-16
Willow Wood, 20 ... SJ-12
Willowdale Lake, 600 ... NA-8
Willowdell, 75 ... NM-2
Willowick, 14171 ... NE-16
Willowville, 500 ... SG-3
Willshire, 397 ... NJ-1
Wilmington, 12520 ... SE-5
Wilmot, 304 ... NK-15
Wilson, 125 ... SB-18
Winchester, 1051 ... SH-6
Winchester, 50 ... SG-11
Windham, 2209 ... NG-18
Windsor, 400 ... NE-18
Windsor, 120 ... NJ-11
Windsor ... SF-4
Winesburg, 352 ... NK-15
Winfield, 200 ... NK-15
Wingett Run, 40 ... SD-17
Winona, 250 ... NI-18
Winterset, 150 ... NN-16
Wintersville, 3924 ... NL-19
Withamsville, 7021 .. SG-3
Wolf Run, 120 ... NL-18
WOOD CO., 125488 ... NG-6
Woodbourne, 6050 .. SN-8
Woodington, 100 ... NM-1
Woodlawn, 3294 ... SK-3
Woodmere, 884 ... SL-20
Woodsdale, 200 ... SE-2
Woodsfield, 2384 ... SC-18
Woodstock, 305 ... NM-7
Woodville, 2135 ... NF-7
Woodville ... SF-5
Woodworth, 700 ... NI-19
Wooster, 26119 ... NJ-14
Wooster Hts., 850 ... NJ-11
Worstville, 25 ... NH-1
Worthington, 13575 ... NN-9
Wren, 194 ... NJ-1
Wrightsville ... SB-8
Wyandot, 50 ... NJ-8
WYANDOT CO., 22615 ... NJ-7
Wyoming, 8428 ... SK-3
Xenia, 25719 ... SC-5
Yankee Lake, 79 ... NG-20
Yankeetown, 250 ... SH-5
Yatesville, 20 ... SC-7
Yellow Sprs., 3487 ... SC-5
Yellowbud, 120 ... SD-9
York, 90 ... NM-19
York Ctr., 100 ... NL-7
Yorkshire, 96 ... NM-2
Yorkville, 1079 ... NM-19
Youngs, 110 ... SH-8
Youngstown, 66982 ... NH-19
Youngsville, 50 ... SH-7
Zahns Corners ... SG-9
Zaleski, 278 ... SF-12
Zanesfield, 197 ... NL-6
Zanesville, 25487 ... SB-14
Zimmerman ... SM-10
Zoar, 169 ... NK-16
Zoarville, 230 ... NK-16
Zone, 30 ... NE-3

Oklahoma

Page locator

Map keys	Atlas pages
1–10	166–167
11–20	168–169

Achille, 492 ... K-16
Ada, 16810 ... H-15
Adair, 790 ... D-18
ADAIR CO., 22683 .. E-19
Adams, 200 ... C-5
Adamson, 150 ... H-18
Addington, 114 ... J-12
Afton, 1049 ... C-19
Agawam, 50 ... H-12
Agra, 339 ... E-14
Ahloso, 90 ... H-15
Akins, 493 ... F-20
Albany, 143 ... K-16
Albert, 120 ... G-11
Albion, 106 ... H-19
Alderson, 304 ... H-17
Alex, 550 ... H-12
Alfalfa, 100 ... G-11
ALFALFA CO., 5642 ... C-11
Aline, 207 ... C-11
Allen, 932 ... H-16
Alluwe, 90 ... C-18
Alma, 80 ... I-13
Altus, 19813 ... I-9
Alva, 4945 ... C-10
Amber, 419 ... G-12
Ames, 239 ... D-11
Amorita, 37 ... B-11
Anadarko, 6762 ... G-11
Antioch, 80 ... H-13
Antlers, 2453 ... J-17
Apache, 1444 ... H-11
Apple, 40 ... J-18
Arapaho, 796 ... F-10
Arcadia, 247 ... F-13
Ardmore, 24283 ... J-14
Arkoma, 1989 ... G-20
Arlington, 25 ... F-15
Armstrong, 105 ... J-16
Arnett, 524 ... D-8
Arpelar, 272 ... H-17
Asher, 393 ... H-14
Ashland, 66 ... H-16
Atoka, 3107 ... I-16
ATOKA CO., 14182 ... J-16
Atwood, 74 ... H-16
Avant, 320 ... C-16
Avard, 30 ... C-10
Avery, 60 ... E-15
Aydelotte ... F-14
Baker, 50 ... B-5
Bald Hill ... F-17
Balko, 100 ... C-6
Ballard, 120 ... D-20
Barnsdall, 1243 ... C-16
Baron, 140 ... E-20
Bartlesville, 35750 ... C-16
Battiest, 250 ... I-19
Baum ... J-14
Bearden, 133 ... G-16
Beaver, 1515 ... B-6
BEAVER CO., 5636 ... C-7
BECKHAM CO., 22119 ... G-8
Bee, 140 ... J-15
Beggs, 1321 ... F-16
Bengal, 100 ... H-19
Bennington, 334 ... J-17
Bentley, 100 ... J-16
Bernice, 562 ... C-19
Bessie, 181 ... G-10
Bethany, 19051 ... F-13
Bethel, 260 ... I-19
Bethel Acres, 2895 ... G-14
Big Cabin, 265 ... C-18
Billings, 509 ... C-13
Binger, 672 ... G-11
Bison, 65 ... D-12
Bixby, 20884 ... E-17
Blackburn, 108 ... D-15
Blackwell, 7092 ... C-14
BLAINE CO., 11943 ... E-11
Blair, 818 ... H-9
Blanchard, 7670 ... G-13
Blanco, 200 ... H-17
Blocker, 200 ... G-18
Blue, 195 ... J-16
Bluejacket, 339 ... B-19
Boatman, 100 ... D-18
Boise City, 1266 ... C-2
Bokchito, 632 ... J-16
Bokoshe, 512 ... G-19
Boley, 1184 ... F-15
Boone, 25 ... H-11
Boswell, 709 ... J-17
Bowden ... G-1
Bowlegs, 405 ... G-15
Bowring, 100 ... B-16
Boynton, 248 ... F-17
Braden ... G-20
Bradley, 130 ... H-13
Braggs, 259 ... F-18
Braman, 217 ... B-13
Bray, 1209 ... I-12
Breckinridge, 245 ... D-13
Briartown, 150 ... G-18
Bridge Creek, 336 ... G-13
Bridgeport, 116 ... F-11
Bristow, 4222 ... E-16
Britton ... J-4
Broken Arrow, 98850 ... E-17
Broken Bow, 4120 ... J-20
Bromide, 165 ... I-15
Brooksville, 63 ... G-14
Brushy, 900 ... F-19
BRYAN CO., 42416 ... K-16
Bryans Cor., 100 ... C-5
Buffalo, 1299 ... B-8
Bunch, 80 ... F-19
Burbank, 141 ... C-15
Burlington, 152 ... B-11
Burneyville, 60 ... K-14
Burns Flat, 2057 ... G-9
Bushyhead, 1314 ... C-18
Butler, 287 ... F-9
Butner, 100 ... G-15
Byars, 255 ... H-14
Byng, 1175 ... H-15
Byron, 35 ... B-11
Cache, 2796 ... I-10
Caddo, 997 ... J-16
CADDO CO., 29600 ... H-11
Calera, 2164 ... K-16
Calhoun, 50 ... G-19
Calumet, 507 ... F-12
Calvin, 294 ... H-16
Camargo, 178 ... E-9
Cameron, 302 ... G-20
Camp Houston ... C-9
Canadian, 220 ... G-17
CANADIAN CO., 115541 ... F-12
Caney, 205 ... J-16
Caney Ridge, 130 ... E-19
Canton, 625 ... E-11
Canute, 541 ... F-9
Capron, 23 ... B-11
Carmen, 355 ... C-11
Carnegie, 1723 ... G-11
Carney, 647 ... E-14
Carrier, 85 ... C-12
Carter, 256 ... G-8
CARTER CO., 47557 ... J-13
Cartwright, 609 ... K-15
Cashion, 802 ... E-13
Castle, 106 ... F-16
Catoosa, 7151 ... D-17
Cedar Crest, 312 ... D-18
Cedar Valley, 288 ... E-13
Cement, 501 ... H-12
Center, 120 ... H-15
Centerview ... F-15
Centrahoma, 97 ... I-16
Central High, 1199 ... I-12
Centralia, 35 ... C-18
Ceres ... C-14
Chandler, 3100 ... F-14
Chattanooga, 461 ... I-10
Checotah, 3335 ... F-18
Chelsea, 1964 ... C-18
Cherokee, 1498 ... C-11
CHEROKEE CO., 46987 ... E-19
Cherry Tree, 883 ... E-20
Chester, 117 ... D-10
Chewey, 135 ... D-19
Cheyenne, 801 ... F-8
Chickasha, 16036 ... H-12
Childers, 40 ... C-17
Chilocco, 30 ... B-14
Choctaw, 11146 ... F-14
CHOCTAW CO., 15205 ... J-17
Chouteau, 2097 ... D-18
Christie, 218 ... E-19
Cimarron City, 150 ... E-13
CIMARRON CO., 2475 ... B-2
Claremore, 18581 ... D-17
Clarita, 150 ... I-16
Clayton, 821 ... I-18
Clearview, 48 ... G-16
Clebit ... I-19
Cleo Sprs., 338 ... D-11
Cleora, 1463 ... C-19
Cleveland, 3251 ... D-15
CLEVELAND CO., 255755 ... G-13
Clinton, 9033 ... F-10
Cloud Chief, 50 ... G-10
Cloudy, 50 ... J-18
COAL CO., 5925 ... I-16
Coalgate, 1967 ... I-16
Cobb ... J-16
Cogar, 25 ... G-12
Colbert, 1140 ... K-15
Colcord, 815 ... D-19
Cole, 555 ... G-13
Coleman, 180 ... J-16
Collinsville, 5606 ... D-17
Colony, 136 ... G-10
Comanche, 1663 ... I-12
COMANCHE CO., 124098 ... I-11
Commerce, 2473 ... B-19
Connerville, 250 ... I-15
Cookietown ... J-11
Cookson, 900 ... F-19
Cooperton, 16 ... H-10
Copan, 733 ... B-17
Copeland, 1629 ... C-19
Cordell, 2915 ... G-10
Corn, 503 ... G-10
Cornish, 163 ... J-13
Corum, 30 ... I-12
COTTON CO., 6193 ... J-11
Cottonwood, 160 ... I-16
Council Hill, 158 ... F-17
Countyline, 300 ... I-13
Covington, 527 ... D-13
Cowden ... G-10
Coweta, 9943 ... E-17
Cowlington, 155 ... G-19
Cox City, 100 ... H-13
Coyle, 325 ... E-14
CRAIG CO., 15029 ... C-18
Crawford, 50 ... E-8
CREEK CO., 69967 .. E-15
Crescent, 1411 ... E-13
Criner, 50 ... H-13
Cromwell, 286 ... G-15
Crowder, 430 ... G-17
Cushing, 7826 ... E-15
Custer City, 375 ... F-10
CUSTER CO., 27469 .. F-9
Cyril, 1059 ... H-11
Dacoma, 107 ... C-11
Daisy, 50 ... I-17
Dale, 181 ... G-14
Davenport, 814 ... F-15
Davidson, 315 ... J-9
Davis, 2683 ... I-14
Deer Creek, 130 ... C-13
Del City, 21332 ... F-13
Delaware, 417 ... C-17
DELAWARE CO., 41487 ... C-19
Delhi, 60 ... G-8
Depew, 476 ... E-15
Devol, 151 ... J-11
Dewar, 888 ... F-17
Dewey, 3432 ... C-17
DEWEY CO., 4810 ... E-9
Dibble, 878 ... H-13
Dickson, 1207 ... J-14
Dill City, 562 ... G-9
Disney, 311 ... C-19
Dixon, 250 ... G-15
Dotyville, 101 ... B-19
Dougherty, 215 ... I-14
Douglas, 32 ... D-13
Dover, 464 ... E-12
Dow, 100 ... H-17
Driftwood, 25 ... B-11
Drummond, 455 ... D-12
Drumright, 2907 ... E-15
Duke, 424 ... I-8
Duncan, 23431 ... I-12
Dunjee Pk. ... K-7
Durant, 15856 ... J-16
Durham, 120 ... E-7
Dustin, 395 ... G-16
Eagle City, 50 ... E-11
Eagletown, 528 ... J-20
Eakly, 338 ... G-11
Earlsboro, 628 ... G-15
Eastborough, 1000 ... F-6
Edmond, 81405 ... F-13
El Reno, 16749 ... F-12
Eldon, 368 ... E-19
Eldorado, 446 ... I-8
Elgin, 2156 ... H-11
Elk City, 11693 ... F-9
ELLIS CO., 4151 ... D-8
Elmer, 96 ... I-9
Elmore City, 697 ... I-13
Elmwood, 25 ... C-6
Empire City, 955 ... I-12
Enid, 49379 ... D-12
Enos ... K-15
Enterprise, 200 ... G-18
Enville ... K-14
Eram ... F-17
Erick, 1052 ... G-8
Erin Sprs., 87 ... H-13
Etowah, 92 ... G-14
Eufaula, 2813 ... G-18
Fair Oaks, 103 ... D-17
Fairfax, 1380 ... C-15
Fairland, 1057 ... C-19
Fairmont, 134 ... D-13
Fairview, 2579 ... D-11
Falconhead, 300 ... K-14
Fallis, 27 ... F-14
Fame ... G-17
Fanshawe, 419 ... H-19
Fargo, 364 ... D-8
Farris, 150 ... J-17
Faxon, 136 ... I-11
Fay, 150 ... E-10
Felker, 100 ... J-19
Felt, 93 ... C-1
Fillmore, 45 ... J-15
Finley, 150 ... I-18
Fittstown, 500 ... I-15
Fitzhugh, 230 ... I-15
Fletcher, 1177 ... H-11
Folsom, 50 ... J-16
Foraker, 19 ... B-15
Forest Pk., 998 ... K-5
Forgan, 547 ... B-6
Ft. Cobb, 634 ... G-11
Ft. Coffee, 424 ... G-20
Ft. Gibson, 4154 ... E-18
Ft. Supply, 330 ... C-8
Ft. Towson, 519 ... J-18
Foss, 151 ... F-9
Foster, 161 ... I-13
Fox, 300 ... I-13
Foyil, 344 ... D-18
Francis, 315 ... H-15
Frederick, 3940 ... I-10
Freedom, 289 ... C-9
Friendship, 24 ... H-9
Gage, 442 ... D-8
Gans, 312 ... F-20
Garber, 822 ... D-13
GARFIELD CO., 60580 ... C-12
Garvin, 256 ... J-19
GARVIN CO., 27576 ... I-13
Gate, 93 ... B-7
Geary, 1280 ... F-11
Gene Autry, 158 ... J-14
Geronimo, 1268 ... I-11
Gerty, 118 ... H-16
Glencoe, 601 ... D-14
Glenpool, 10808 ... E-16
Glover, 150 ... J-19
Golden, 200 ... J-19
Goldsby, 1801 ... G-13
Goltry, 249 ... C-12
Goodland, 50 ... J-18
Goodwell, 1293 ... C-4
Gore, 977 ... F-19
Gotebo, 226 ... G-10
Gould, 141 ... I-8
Gowen, 250 ... H-18
Gracemont, 318 ... G-11
GRADY CO., 52431 ... H-12
Graham, 250 ... J-13
Grainola, 31 ... B-15
Grandfield, 1038 ... J-10
Granite, 2065 ... H-9
Grant, 289 ... K-18
GRANT CO., 4527 .. B-12
Gray Horse, 60 ... C-15
Grayson, 159 ... F-17
Green Pastures ... J-7
Greenfield, 93 ... F-11
GREER CO., 6239 ... H-8
Grimes ... F-8
Grove, 6623 ... C-19
Guthrie, 10191 ... E-13
Guymon, 11442 ... C-4
Haileyville, 813 ... H-18
Hallett, 125 ... D-15
Hammon, 568 ... F-9
Hanna, 138 ... G-17
Hanson, 150 ... F-20
Hardesty, 212 ... C-5
Harjo ... G-15
Harmon, 25 ... D-8
HARMON CO., 2922 ... H-7
HARPER CO., 3685 .. C-8
Harrah, 5095 ... F-14
Harris, 150 ... K-20
Hartshorne, 2125 ... H-18
Haskell, 2007 ... E-17
HASKELL CO., 12769 ... G-18
Hastings, 143 ... J-12
Haworth, 297 ... K-20
Hayward, 30 ... D-13
Haywood, 300 ... H-17
Headrick, 94 ... I-9
Healdton, 2788 ... J-13
Heavener, 3414 ... H-20
Helena, 1403 ... C-11
Hendrix, 79 ... K-16
Hennepin, 250 ... I-13
Hennessey, 2131 ... E-12
Henryetta, 5927 ... F-17
Hess, 50 ... I-9
Hester ... H-9
Hickory, 71 ... I-15
Hillsdale, 121 ... C-12
Hinton, 3196 ... F-11
Hitchcock, 121 ... E-11
Hitchita, 88 ... F-17
Hobart, 3756 ... H-9
Hodgen, 260 ... H-20
Hoffman, 127 ... F-17
Holdenville, 5771 ... G-16
Hollis, 2060 ... I-7
Hollister, 50 ... J-10
Homer, 100 ... H-15
Homestead, 70 ... D-11
Hominy, 3565 ... D-16
Honobia, 150 ... I-19
Hooker, 1918 ... B-5
Hopeton, 40 ... C-10
Horntown, 97 ... G-16
Hough, 100 ... B-4
Howe, 802 ... H-20
HUGHES CO., 14003 ... G-16
Hugo, 5310 ... J-18
Hulbert, 590 ... E-18
Humphreys, 150 ... I-9
Hunter, 165 ... C-13
Hydro, 969 ... F-11
Idabel, 7010 ... K-19
Indiahoma, 344 ... I-10
Indianola, 162 ... G-17
Ingalls, 60 ... E-14
Ingersoll, 20 ... C-11
Inola, 1788 ... D-18
Isabella, 136 ... D-11
JACKSON CO., 26446 ... I-8
Jacktown, 30 ... F-14
Jay, 2448 ... D-19
Jefferson, 12 ... C-12
JEFFERSON CO., 6472 ... J-12
Jenks, 16924 ... E-17
Jennings, 363 ... D-15
Jesse ... I-15
Jet, 213 ... C-11
Johnson, 247 ... F-15
JOHNSTON CO., 10957 ... J-15
Jones, 2692 ... F-14
Joy ... I-14
Kansas, 802 ... D-19
Katie, 348 ... I-13
Kaw City, 375 ... C-15
KAY CO., 46562 ... B-14
Keefton, 100 ... F-18
Kellyville, 1150 ... E-16
Kemp, 133 ... K-16
Kendrick, 139 ... E-15
Kenefic, 196 ... J-16
Kent ... J-17
Kenton, 17 ... B-1
Kenwood, 1224 ... D-19
Keota, 564 ... G-19
Ketchum, 442 ... C-19
Keyes, 324 ... B-2
Keys, 565 ... E-19
Kiefer, 1685 ... E-16
Kildare, 100 ... C-14
Kingfisher, 4633 ... E-12
KINGFISHER CO., 15034 ... E-12
Kingston, 1601 ... J-15
Kinta, 297 ... G-18
Kiowa, 731 ... H-17
KIOWA CO., 9446 .. H-10
Knowles, 11 ... B-7
Konawa, 1298 ... H-15
Krebs, 2053 ... H-17
Kremlin, 255 ... C-12
Lacey ... E-12
Lahoma, 611 ... D-12
L. Aluma, 88 ... J-5
L. Valley ... G-10
Lamar, 158 ... G-16
Lambert, 6 ... C-11
Lamont, 417 ... C-13
Lane, 414 ... J-17
Langley, 819 ... C-19
Langston, 1724 ... E-14
LATIMER CO., 11154 ... H-18
Laverne, 1344 ... C-8
Lawrence Creek, 149 ... E-16
Lawton, 96867 ... I-11
LE FLORE CO., 50384 ... I-19
Leach, 237 ... D-19
Lebanon, 303 ... K-14
Leedey, 435 ... E-9
Leflore, 190 ... H-19
Lehigh, 356 ... I-16
Lenapah, 293 ... B-17
Lenna, 40 ... G-17
Lenora ... E-9
Leon, 91 ... K-13
Leonard, 550 ... E-17
Lequire, 250 ... G-19
Lewisville ... G-18
Lexington, 2152 ... H-13
Liberty, 220 ... E-17
Liberty, 220 ... F-20
Lillard Pk. ... L-3
Lima, 53 ... G-15
LINCOLN CO., 34273 ... E-14
Lindsay, 2840 ... H-13
Little City, 150 ... J-15
Loco, 122 ... J-13
Locust Grv., 1423 ... D-18
LOGAN CO., 41848 ... E-13
Lone Grv., 5054 ... J-14
Lone Wolf, 438 ... H-9
Longdale, 262 ... D-11
Longtown, 2739 ... G-18
Lookeba, 166 ... G-11
LOVE CO., 9423 ... J-13
Loveland, 13 ... J-10
Lovell, 60 ... E-13
Loyal, 79 ... E-12
Lucien, 88 ... D-13
Lula, 30 ... H-16
Luther, 1221 ... F-14
Lutie ... H-18
Macomb, 32 ... G-14
Madill, 3770 ... J-15
MAJOR CO., 7527 .. D-10
Manchester, 103 ... B-12
Mangum, 3010 ... H-8
Manitou, 181 ... I-10
Mannford, 3076 ... D-16
Mannsville, 863 ... J-15
Maramec, 91 ... D-15
Marble City, 263 ... F-19
Marietta, 2626 ... K-14
Marland, 225 ... C-14
Marlow, 4662 ... I-12
Marshall, 272 ... D-13
MARSHALL CO., 15840 ... J-14
Martha, 162 ... H-9
Martin ... F-18
Mason, 100 ... F-16
Matoy ... J-16
Maud, 1048 ... G-15
May, 39 ... C-8
MAYES CO., 41259 ... D-18
Mayfield, 10 ... G-8
Maysville, 1232 ... H-13
Mazie, 91 ... D-18
McAlester, 18383 ... H-17
McBride, 80 ... K-15
MCCLAIN CO., 34506 ... H-13
McCurtain, 516 ... G-19
MCCURTAIN CO., 33151 ... I-19
MCINTOSH CO., 20252 ... G-17
McLain ... F-18
McLoud, 4044 ... F-14
Mead, 122 ... J-15
Medford, 996 ... C-13
Medicine Pk., 382 ... H-11
Meeker, 1144 ... F-14
Meno, 235 ... D-12
Meridian, 38 ... E-14
Miami, 13570 ... B-19
Midwest City, 54371 ... F-13
Milburn, 317 ... J-15
Milfay, 170 ... F-15
Mill Creek, 319 ... I-15
Miller ... J-17
Millerton, 320 ... J-19
Minco, 1632 ... G-12
Moffett, 128 ... F-20
Monroe, 200 ... H-20
Moore, 55081 ... G-13
Mooreland, 1190 ... D-9
Morris, 1479 ... F-17
Morrison, 733 ... D-14
Mounds, 1168 ... E-16
Mt. Herman, 150 ... I-19
Mountain Pk., 409 ... I-10
Mountain View, 795 ... G-10
Moyers, 100 ... J-17
Muldrow, 3466 ... F-20
Mulhall, 225 ... E-13
MURRAY CO., 13488 ... I-14
Muse, 200 ... H-19
Muskogee, 39223 ... E-18
MUSKOGEE CO., 70990 ... F-17
Mustang, 17395 ... G-13
Mutual, 61 ... D-9
Narcissa, 99 ... B-19
Nardin, 52 ... C-13
Nash, 204 ... C-12
Nashoba, 150 ... I-18
Nelagoney, 120 ... C-16
New Woodville, 132 .. K-15
Newcastle, 7685 ... G-13
Newkirk, 2317 ... B-14
Newport, 50 ... J-14
Nichols Hills, 3710 ... J-4
Nicoma Pk., 2393 ... K-7
Nida, 30 ... J-15
Ninnekah, 1002 ... H-12
Noble, 6481 ... G-13
NOBLE CO., 11561 ... C-14
Non, 40 ... H-16
Norge, 145 ... H-12
Norman, 110925 ... G-13
N. Enid, 860 ... D-12
Notchietown, 373 ... F-19
Nowata, 3731 ... C-17
NOWATA CO., 10536 ... B-17
Oakhurst, 2185 ... E-16
Oakland, 1057 ... J-15
Oaks, 288 ... D-19
Oakwood, 65 ... E-10
Ochelata, 424 ... C-16
Octavia, 50 ... I-20
Oglesby, 100 ... C-17
Oil Ctr. ... H-15
Oilton, 1013 ... E-15
Okarche, 1215 ... F-12
Okay, 620 ... E-18
Okeene, 1204 ... E-11
Okemah, 3223 ... F-16
Okesa, 120 ... C-16
OKFUSKEE CO., 12191 ... F-15
Oklahoma City, 579999 ... F-13
OKLAHOMA CO., 718633 ... F-13
Okmulgee, 12321 ... F-17
OKMULGEE CO., 40069 ... E-17
Oktaha, 390 ... F-18
Oleta, 50 ... J-18
Olive, 200 ... E-15
Olney, 130 ... I-16
Olustee, 607 ... I-9
Onapa ... F-18
Oologah, 1146 ... D-17
Optima, 356 ... C-4
Ord ... K-18
Orienta, 25 ... D-11
Orlando, 148 ... D-13
Orr, 30 ... J-13
Osage, 156 ... D-16
OSAGE CO., 47472 ... C-15
Oscar, 20 ... K-12
OTTAWA CO., 31848 ... B-19
Overbrook, 100 ... J-14
Owasso, 28915 ... D-17
Paden, 461 ... F-15
Page, 25 ... H-20
Panama, 1413 ... G-20
Panola, 300 ... H-18
Paoli, 610 ... H-14
Paradise Hill, 85 ... F-19
Park Hill, 3909 ... E-19
Parkland, 50 ... E-15
Pauls Valley, 6187 ... H-14
Pawhuska, 3584 ... C-16
Pawnee, 2196 ... D-15
PAWNEE CO., 16577 ... D-14
PAYNE CO., 77350 .. E-14
Pearson, 25 ... G-14
Peckham, 75 ... B-14
Peggs, 813 ... E-19
Pensacola, 125 ... C-18
Perkins, 2831 ... E-14
Pernell, 200 ... I-13
Perry, 5126 ... D-14
Pershing, 50 ... C-16
Phillips, 135 ... I-16
Pickens, 170 ... I-19
Piedmont, 5720 ... F-12
Pink, 2058 ... G-14
Pittsburg, 207 ... H-17
PITTSBURG CO., 45837 ... I-17
Plunkettville, 80 ... I-20
Pocasset, 156 ... G-12
Pocola, 4056 ... G-20
Ponca City, 25387 ... C-14
Pond Creek, 856 ... C-12
Pontotoc, 200 ... I-15
PONTOTOC CO., 37492 ... I-15
Pooleville, 100 ... I-13
Porter, 566 ... E-18
Porum, 727 ... G-18
Poteau, 8520 ... G-20
POTTAWATOMIE CO., 69442 ... G-14
Prague, 2386 ... F-15
Preston, 500 ... F-17
Proctor, 231 ... E-19
Prue, 465 ... D-16
Pryor, 9539 ... D-18
Pumpkin Ctr. ... I-11
Purcell, 5884 ... H-13
Purdy, 45 ... H-13
PUSHMATAHA CO., 11572 ... I-18
Putnam, 29 ... E-10
Pyramid Cors., 45 ... B-18
Quapaw, 906 ... B-19
Quinlan ... D-10
Quinton, 1051 ... G-18
Ralston, 330 ... C-15
Ramona, 535 ... C-17
Randlett, 438 ... J-11
Ratliff City, 120 ... I-13
Rattan, 310 ... J-18
Ravia, 528 ... J-15
Reagan, 50 ... I-15
Red Bird, 137 ... E-17
Red Oak, 549 ... H-19
Red Rock, 283 ... D-14
Reed, 40 ... H-8
Renfrow, 12 ... B-13
Rentiesville, 128 ... F-18
Retrop ... G-9
Reydon, 210 ... F-7
Richards Spur ... H-11
Richland, 400 ... F-12
Ringling, 1037 ... J-13
Ringold, 100 ... J-19
Ringwood, 497 ... D-11
Ripley, 403 ... E-14
Rock Island, 646 ... G-20
Rocky, 162 ... G-9
Rocky Pt., 370 ... E-18
Roff, 725 ... I-15
ROGER MILLS CO., 3647 ... F-8
ROGERS CO., 86905 ... D-17
Roland, 3169 ... F-20
Roll, 25 ... E-8
Roosevelt, 248 ... H-10
Rose, 285 ... D-19
Rosedale, 68 ... H-14
Rosston, 31 ... C-8
Rubottom, 70 ... K-13
Rufe, 200 ... J-19
Rush Sprs., 1231 ... H-12
Russell, 25 ... H-8
Russett ... J-15
Ryan, 816 ... J-12
St. Louis, 158 ... G-15
Salina, 1396 ... D-18
Sallisaw, 8880 ... F-19
Salt Fork ... C-13
Sand Sprs., 18906 ... D-16
Sapulpa, 20544 ... E-16
Sasakwa, 150 ... H-15
Savanna, 686 ... H-17
Sawyer, 321 ... J-18
Sayre, 4375 ... G-8
Schulter, 509 ... F-17
Scipio, 50 ... G-17
Scraper, 191 ... D-19
Scullin ... I-15
Seiling, 860 ... D-10
Selman, 25 ... C-9
Seminole, 7488 ... G-15
SEMINOLE CO., 25482 ... H-15
Sentinel, 901 ... G-9
Sequoyah, 698 ... D-17
SEQUOYAH CO., 42391 ... F-20
Seward, 50 ... E-13
Shady Pt., 1026 ... G-20
Shamrock, 101 ... E-15
Sharon, 135 ... D-9
Shattuck, 1356 ... D-8
Shawnee, 29857 ... G-14
Shay ... K-15
Sherwood, 80 ... I-19
Shidler, 441 ... C-15
Sickles, 110 ... G-11
Silo, 331 ... J-15
Silver City ... E-15
Skedee, 51 ... D-15
Skiatook, 7397 ... D-16
Slapout, 20 ... C-7
Slaughterville, 4137 ... G-13
Slick, 131 ... E-16
Smith Vil., 66 ... L-5
Smithville, 113 ... I-20
Snow, 130 ... I-18
Snyder, 1394 ... I-10
Soper, 261 ... J-17
S. Coffeyville, 785 ... B-17
Southard, 80 ... E-11
Sparks, 169 ... F-15
Spaulding, 178 ... H-16
Spavinaw, 437 ... D-19
Spencer, 3912 ... J-6
Spencerville, 200 ... J-18
Sperry, 1206 ... D-16
Spiro, 2164 ... G-20
Springer, 700 ... J-14
Stafford, 25 ... F-9
STEPHENS CO., 45048 ... I-12
Sterling, 793 ... H-11
Stidham, 18 ... G-17
Stigler, 2685 ... G-19
Stillwater, 45688 ... E-14
Stilwell, 3949 ... E-20
Stonewall, 470 ... I-15
Straight ... B-4
Stratford, 1525 ... H-14
Stringtown, 410 ... I-16
Strong City, 47 ... F-8
Stroud, 2690 ... F-15
Stuart, 180 ... H-16
Sugden, 43 ... J-12
Sulphur, 4929 ... I-14
Summerfield, 150 ... H-19
Summit, 139 ... F-18
Surrey Hills ... I-1
Sweetwater, 87 ... F-7
Swink, 66 ... J-18
Tabler ... H-12
Taft, 250 ... E-18
Tahlequah, 15753 ... E-19
Taiwah, 189 ... D-17
Talala, 273 ... C-17
Talihina, 1114 ... H-19
Taloga, 299 ... E-10
Tamaha, 176 ... F-19
Tangier ... D-8
Tatums, 151 ... I-13
Tecumseh, 6457 ... G-14
Temple, 1002 ... J-11
Terlton, 106 ... D-15
Terral, 382 ... K-12
Texanna, 2261 ... G-18
TEXAS CO., 20640 ... B-4
Texhoma, 926 ... C-3
Texola, 36 ... G-7
Thackerville, 445 ... K-14
The Village, 8929 ... J-4
Thomas, 1181 ... F-10
TILLMAN CO., 7992 ... I-10
Timber Brook, 1000 ... E-17
Tipton, 847 ... I-9
Tishomingo, 3034 ... J-15
Tom, 150 ... K-20
Tonkawa, 3216 ... C-13
Tribbey, 391 ... G-14
Troy, 40 ... J-15
Tryon, 491 ... E-14
Tullahassee, 106 ... E-18
Tulsa, 391906 ... D-17
TULSA CO., 603403 ... D-17
Tupelo, 329 ... I-16
Turley, 2756 ... D-17
Turpin, 467 ... B-5
Tushka, 312 ... J-16
Tuskahoma, 151 ... I-18
Tussy, 80 ... I-13
Tuttle, 6019 ... G-12
Twin Oaks, 198 ... D-19
Tyler ... J-14
Tyrone, 762 ... B-5
Union City, 1645 ... G-12
Utica, 50 ... K-16
Valley Brook, 765 ... L-5
Valliant, 754 ... J-19
Vamoosa, 80 ... H-15
Vanoss, 100 ... H-15
Velma, 620 ... I-13
Vera, 241 ... D-17
Verden, 530 ... G-12
Verdigris, 3993 ... D-17
Vernon, 60 ... G-17
Vian, 1466 ... F-19
Vici, 699 ... D-9
Victory, 25 ... I-9
Vinita, 5743 ... C-18
Vinson, 50 ... H-8
Vivian ... G-17
Wade, 70 ... K-16
Wagoner, 8323 ... E-18
WAGONER CO., 73085 ... E-18
Wainwright, 165 ... F-17
Wakita, 344 ... B-12
Walters, 2551 ... I-11
Wanette, 350 ... H-14
Wann, 125 ... B-17
Wapanucka, 438 ... I-16
Wardville ... I-16
Warner, 1641 ... F-18
Warr Acres, 10043 ... J-3
Warren, 80 ... H-9
Warwick, 148 ... F-14
Washington, 618 ... G-13
WASHINGTON CO., 50976 ... C-17
Washita, 130 ... G-11
WASHITA CO., 11629 ... G-9
Watonga, 5111 ... E-11
Watova, 150 ... C-17
Watson, 300 ... I-20
Watts, 324 ... D-20
Waukomis, 1286 ... D-12
Waurika, 2064 ... J-12
Wayne, 688 ... H-14
Waynoka, 927 ... C-10
Weatherford, 10833 .. F-10
Webb City, 62 ... C-15
Webbers Falls, 616 ... F-18
Welch, 619 ... B-18
Weleetka, 998 ... G-16
Welling, 771 ... E-19
Wellston, 788 ... F-14
Welty, 120 ... F-16
W. Siloam Sprs., 846 ... D-20
Westport, 298 ... D-16
Westville, 1639 ... E-20
Wetumka, 1282 ... G-16
Wewoka, 3430 ... G-15
Wheatland ... M-2
Whippoorwill, 100 ... B-16
White Eagle, 100 ... C-14
White Oak, 263 ... C-18
Whitefield, 391 ... G-18
Whitesboro, 250 ... H-19
Wilburton, 2843 ... H-18
Williams, 120 ... G-20
Willow, 149 ... G-8
Wilson, 1724 ... J-13
Winchester, 516 ... E-16
Wister, 1102 ... H-19
Wolco, 30 ... C-16
Wolf, 100 ... G-15
Woodford, 50 ... J-14
Woodlawn Pk., 153 ... K-2
WOODS CO., 8878 ... C-10
Woodward, 12051 ... D-9
WOODWARD CO., 20081 ... C-9
Wright City, 762 ... J-19
Wyandotte, 333 ... B-19
Wynnewood, 2212 ... I-14
Wynona, 437 ... C-16
Yale, 1227 ... D-15
Yanush, 60 ... H-18
Yeager, 75 ... G-16
Yuba, 60 ... K-16
Yukon, 22709 ... F-12
Zoe ... H-20

Oregon

Page locator

Map keys	Atlas pages
1–10	170–171
11–20	172–173

Adair Vil., 840 ... F-4
Adams, 350 ... C-13
Adel, 80 ... M-11
Adrian, 177 ... H-16
Agness, 120 ... L-2
Airlie, 100 ... F-3
Albany, 50158 ... F-4
Alfalfa ... H-8
Alicel ... D-14
Alkali Lake Sta. ... K-10
Allegany, 120 ... I-2
Alma, 30 ... H-3
Aloha, 49425 ... C-4
Alpine, 171 ... G-3
Alsea, 164 ... G-3
Alston, 270 ... B-4
Amity, 1614 ... D-4
Antelope, 46 ... E-9
Applegate, 100 ... M-3
Arago, 110 ... J-1
Arch Cape, 200 ... B-2
Arlington, 586 ... C-10
Arock, 60 ... K-16
Ashland, 20078 ... M-4
Ashwood, 30 ... F-9
Astoria, 9477 ... A-2
Athena, 1126 ... B-13
Aumsville, 3584 ... E-4
Aurora, 918 ... D-5
Austin ... F-13
Azalea, 430 ... K-3
Baker City, 9828 ... E-15
BAKER CO., 16134 .. E-15
Ballston, 80 ... E-3
Bandon, 3066 ... J-1
Banks, 1777 ... C-4
Barview, 1844 ... J-1
Barview, 170 ... C-2
Bates, 100 ... F-13
Bay City, 1286 ... C-2
Bayshore, 350 ... F-2
Beatty, 280 ... L-8
Beaver, 122 ... D-2
Beaver Marsh, 110 ... J-6
Beaverton, 89803 ... C-4
Beech Creek ... F-12
Bellfountain, 75 ... G-3
Bend, 76639 ... H-7
BENTON CO., 85579 ... G-3
Biggs Jct., 22 ... C-8
Bingham Sprs., 30 ... C-14
Birkenfeld, 60 ... B-3
Blachly, 100 ... G-3
Blodgett, 58 ... F-3
Blue River, 400 ... G-5
Bly, 700 ... L-8
Boardman, 3220 ... B-11
Bonanza, 415 ... M-7
Bonneville, 30 ... C-6
Boring, 730 ... D-5
Boyd ... C-8
Breitenbush, 40 ... E-6
Brickerville, 90 ... G-2
Bridgeport, 50 ... F-15
Brightwood, 240 ... D-6
Broadbent, 350 ... K-1
Brogan, 90 ... G-15
Brookings, 6336 ... M-1
Brothers, 150 ... H-9
Brownlee, 60 ... E-17
Brownsmead ... A-3
Brownsville, 1668 ... G-4
Buchanan, 30 ... I-13
Bunker Hill, 1444 ... J-1
Burlington, 100 ... J-17
Burns, 2806 ... I-12
Burns Jct. ... K-15
Burnt Woods ... F-3
Butte Falls, 423 ... L-5
Buxton, 100 ... C-4
Camas Valley, 380 ... J-2
Camp Sherman, 233 ... F-7
Canby, 15829 ... D-5
Cannon Bch., 1690 ... B-2
Canyon City, 703 ... G-12
Canyonville, 1884 ... K-3
Cape Meares, 99 ... C-2
Capitol Hill ... L-18
Carlton, 2007 ... D-4
Carson, 30 ... E-16
Carver, 480 ... M-20
Cascade Locks, 1144 ... C-6
Cascade Summit, 100 .. I-6
Cascadia, 147 ... G-5
Cave Jct., 1883 ... M-2
Cayuse, 68 ... C-13
Cecil ... C-10
Cedar Hills, 8300 ... L-17
Cedar Mill, 14546 ... L-17
Celilo, 80 ... C-8
Central Pt., 17169 ... L-4
Charleston, 700 ... J-1
Chemult, 270 ... J-6
Chenoweth, 1855 ... C-8
Cherry Grv., 300 ... D-4
Cheshire, 350 ... G-3
Chiloquin, 734 ... L-6
Christmas Valley, 300 .. J-9
Clackamas, 5177 ... M-19
CLACKAMAS CO., 375992 ... E-5
Clatskanie, 1737 ... B-4
CLATSOP CO., 37039 ... B-3
Cloverdale, 250 ... D-2
Coburg, 1035 ... G-4
Colton, 600 ... D-5
Columbia City, 1946 ... B-4
COLUMBIA CO., 49351 ... B-4
Condon, 682 ... D-10
Coos Bay, 15967 ... J-1
COOS CO., 63043 ... J-2
Coquille, 3866 ... J-1
Cornelius, 11869 ... C-4
Corvallis, 54462 ... F-3
Cottage Grv., 9686 ... H-4
Cove, 552 ... D-15
Crabtree, 391 ... F-4
Crane, 129 ... I-13
Crawfordsville, 332 ... G-4
Crescent, 770 ... I-7
Crescent Lake, 150 ... I-6
Creswell, 5031 ... H-4
CROOK CO., 20978 ... H-10
Crow, 100 ... H-3
Culp Creek, 220 ... I-4
Culver, 1357 ... F-8
CURRY CO., 22364 ... L-1
Curtin, 270 ... I-3
Dairy, 70 ... M-7
Dale, 80 ... E-12
Dallas, 14583 ... E-3
Damascus, 10539 ... M-20
Days Creek, 272 ... K-3
Dayton, 2534 ... D-4
Dayville, 149 ... F-11
Deadwood, 200 ... G-2
Dee, 200 ... C-7
Deer Island, 294 ... B-4
Dellwood, 50 ... I-2
Depoe Bay, 1398 ... E-2
DESCHUTES CO., 157733 ... H-8
Detroit, 202 ... F-6
Dexter, 300 ... H-4
Diamond, 70 ... K-13
Diamond Lake, 110 ... J-6
Diamond Lake Jct., 40 ... J-6
Dillard, 478 ... J-3
Dilley, 200 ... C-4
Donald, 979 ... D-4
Dorena, 350 ... H-4
DOUGLAS CO., 107667 ... J-4
Drain, 1151 ... I-3
Drew ... K-4
Drewsey, 100 ... H-14
Dufur, 604 ... D-8
Dundee, 3152 ... D-4
Dunes City, 1303 ... H-2
Durham, 1351 ... M-18
Durkee, 160 ... F-15
Eagle Creek, 430 ... D-5
Eagle Pt., 8469 ... L-4
Echo, 699 ... C-12
Eddyville, 240 ... F-2
Elgin, 1711 ... C-14
Elk City, 50 ... F-2
Elk Lake ... H-6
Elkhorn ... E-5
Elkton, 195 ... I-3
Elmira, 600 ... H-3
Elsie, 50 ... B-3
Enterprise, 1940 ... C-16
Eola, 45 ... F-18
Errol Hts. ... L-19
Estacada, 2695 ... D-5
Eugene, 156185 ... H-4
Fairview, 8920 ... C-5
Fairview, 100 ... J-2
Falcon Hts., 800 ... M-7
Fall Creek, 110 ... H-4
Falls City, 947 ... E-3
Fields, 30 ... M-13
Finn Rock, 80 ... G-5
Five Corners ... M-9
Flora ... B-16
Florence, 8466 ... H-2
Forest Grv., 21083 ... C-4
Ft. Klamath, 250 ... L-6
Ft. Rock, 50 ... J-8
Fossil, 473 ... E-10
Four Cors., 15947 ... F-20
Fox, 50 ... F-12
Frenchglen, 30 ... K-13
Fruitdale, 1177 ... L-3
Gales Creek, 100 ... C-4
Galice ... L-3
Garden Home ... L-18
Gardiner, 248 ... H-2
Garibaldi, 779 ... C-2
Gaston, 637 ... C-4
Gates, 471 ... F-5
Gateway, 40 ... F-8
Gaylord, 40 ... K-2
Gearhart, 1462 ... B-2
Gervais, 2464 ... E-4
Gibbon ... C-14
Gilbert ... L-20
Gilchrist, 500 ... I-7
GILLIAM CO., 1871 ... D-10
Gladstone, 11497 ... M-19
Glasgow, 763 ... I-1
Glenada, 270 ... H-2
Glendale, 874 ... K-3
Gleneden Bch., 900 ... E-2
Glengary, 300 ... J-3
Glenwood, 80 ... C-3
Glenwood ... B-8
Glide, 1795 ... J-4
Goble, 200 ... B-4
Gold Bch., 2253 ... L-1
Gold Hill, 1220 ... L-4
Goshen, 170 ... H-4
Government Camp, 193 ... D-7
Grand Ronde, 1661 ... E-3
Granite, 38 ... E-13
GRANT CO., 7445 ... E-13
Grants Pass, 34533 ... L-3
Grass Valley, 164 ... D-9
Green, 7515 ... J-3
Green Acres, 230 ... J-1
Greenberry, 50 ... F-3
Greenleaf, 100 ... G-3
Gresham, 105594 ... C-5
Haines, 416 ... E-14
Halfway, 288 ... E-16
Halsey, 904 ... G-4
Hampton ... I-10
Happy Valley, 13903 ... M-20
Harbor, 2391 ... M-1
Hardman, 30 ... D-11
Harlan, 130 ... F-3
HARNEY CO., 7422 ... J-12
Harper, 109 ... H-15
Harrisburg, 3567 ... G-4
Hauser, 700 ... I-1
Hayesville, 19936 ... E-20
Hebo, 232 ... D-2
Heceta Bch., 340 ... H-2
Helix, 184 ... B-13
Heppner, 1291 ... D-11
Hereford, 60 ... F-14
Hermiston, 16745 ... B-12
Hilgard ... D-14
Hillsboro, 91611 ... C-4
Hines, 1563 ... I-12
Homestead ... E-17
Hood River, 7167 ... C-7
HOOD RIVER CO., 22346 ... C-7
Horton, 50 ... G-3
Hoskins, 90 ... F-3
Hot Sprs., 50 ... M-8
Hubbard, 3173 ... D-4
Huntington, 440 ... G-16
Idanha, 134 ... F-6
Idleyld Pk., 320 ... J-4
Illinois Valley, 250 ... M-2
Imbler, 306 ... C-14
Imnaha, 90 ... C-17
Independence, 8590 ... E-4
Ione, 329 ... C-11
Ironside, 50 ... G-15
Irrigon, 1826 ... B-11
Irving, 450 ... G-4
Island City, 989 ... D-14
JACKSON CO., 203206 ... L-4
Jacksonville, 2785 ... M-4
Jamieson, 90 ... G-16
Jasper, 90 ... H-4
Jeffers Gdn., 368 ... A-2
Jefferson, 3098 ... F-4
JEFFERSON CO., 21720 ... F-8
Jewell, 50 ... B-3
John Day, 1744 ... G-12
Johnson City, 566 ... M-19
Jordan Valley, 181 ... K-17
Joseph, 1081 ... D-16
JOSEPHINE CO., 82713 ... L-3
Junction City, 5392 ... G-4
Juntura, 57 ... H-14
Kamela, 30 ... D-13
Keizer, 36478 ... E-4
Keno, 1100 ... M-6
Kent, 40 ... D-9
Kenton ... K-18
Kerby, 595 ... M-2
Kernville, 50 ... E-2
Kimberly, 50 ... F-11
King City, 3111 ... M-17
Kings Valley, 65 ... F-3
KLAMATH CO., 66380 ... L-7
Klamath Falls, 20840 .. M-6
Knappa, 400 ... A-3
La Grande, 13082 ... D-14
La Pine, 1653 ... I-7
Lacomb, 546 ... F-5
Lafayette, 3742 ... D-4
LAKE CO., 7895 ... K-9
L. Oswego, 36619 ... D-5
Lakeside, 1699 ... I-1
Lakeview, 2294 ... M-10
LANE CO., 351715 ... H-4
Langell Valley, 400 ... M-8
Langlois, 177 ... K-1
Lawen, 60 ... I-13
Leaburg, 250 ... G-5
Lebanon, 15518 ... F-4
Lee's Camp, 60 ... C-3
Lewisburg, 250 ... F-3
Lexington, 238 ... D-11
Lincoln Bch., 2045 ... E-2
Lincoln City, 7930 ... E-2
LINCOLN CO., 46034 ... F-2
LINN CO., 116672 ... F-5
Logsden, 300 ... F-2
London ... I-4
Lonerock, 21 ... E-10
Long Creek, 197 ... F-12
Lorane, 220 ... H-3
Lorella ... M-8
Lostine, 213 ... C-15
Lowell, 1045 ... H-4
Lyons, 1161 ... E-5
Madras, 6046 ... F-8
MALHEUR CO., 31313 ... J-15
Malin, 805 ... N-7
Manning, 110 ... C-4
Manzanita, 598 ... C-2
Mapleton, 900 ... H-2
Marcola, 560 ... G-4
Marion, 313 ... F-4
MARION CO., 315335 ... E-6
Marion Forks, 100 ... F-6
Marquam, 60 ... E-5
Maupin, 418 ... D-8
Mayger, 120 ... A-4
Mayville, 30 ... E-10
Maywood Pk., 752 ... K-19
McCoy, 50 ... E-4
McDermitt, 200 ... M-15
McKee Br., 50 ... M-4
McKenzie Br., 400 ... G-6
McMinnville, 32187 ... D-4
McNulty, 800 ... B-4
Meacham, 50 ... C-13
Medford, 74907 ... M-4
Medical Sprs., 30 ... E-15
Mehama, 292 ... E-5
Melrose, 735 ... J-3
Merlin, 1615 ... L-3
Merrill, 844 ... N-7
Metolius, 710 ... F-8
Metzger, 3765 ... M-18
Midland, 300 ... M-6
Mill City, 1855 ... F-5
Millington, 100 ... J-1
Milo, 320 ... K-4
Milton-Freewater, 7050 ... B-13
Milwaukie, 20291 ... M-19
Minam ... C-15
Mission, 1037 ... C-13
Mist, 60 ... B-4
Mitchell, 130 ... F-10
Modoc Pt., 30 ... L-6
Mohler, 60 ... C-2
Molalla, 8108 ... D-5
Monmouth, 9534 ... E-3
Monroe, 617 ... G-3
Monument, 128 ... E-11
Moro, 324 ... C-9
MORROW CO., 11173 ... C-11
Mosier, 433 ... C-7
Mt. Angel, 3286 ... E-4
Mt. Hood, 286 ... C-7
Mt. Vernon, 527 ... G-12
Mulino, 2103 ... D-5
MULTNOMAH CO., 735334 ... C-6
Murphy, 420 ... M-3
Myrtle Creek, 3439 ... K-3
Myrtle Pt., 2514 ... J-1
Nedonna, 450 ... C-2
Nehalem, 271 ... C-2
Neotsu, 350 ... E-2
Nesika Bch., 463 ... L-1
Neskowin, 134 ... D-2
Netarts, 748 ... C-2
New Br., 30 ... E-16
New Hope, 1515 ... L-3
New Pine Creek, 120 ... N-10
New Princeton, 150 .. J-13
Newberg, 22068 ... D-4
Newport, 9989 ... F-2
Nonpareil, 70 ... I-4
N. Bend, 9695 ... I-1
N. Plains, 1947 ... C-4
N. Powder, 439 ... E-15
Norway, 150 ... J-1
Noti, 200 ... H-3
Nyssa, 3267 ... H-17
Oak Grv., 16629 ... M-19
Oakland, 927 ... I-3
Oakridge, 3205 ... H-5
O'Brien, 504 ... M-2
Oceanside, 361 ... C-2
Odell, 2255 ... C-7
Odessa, 40 ... L-8
Olene, 30 ... M-7
Olex ... C-10
Olney, 210 ... B-3
Ontario, 11366 ... H-17
Ophir, 220 ... L-1
Oregon City, 31859 ... D-5
Otis, 230 ... E-2
Otter Rock, 200 ... E-2
Outlook, 100 ... M-20
Owyhee ... H-16
Pacific City, 1035 ... D-2
Paisley, 243 ... L-9
Parkdale, 311 ... C-7
Parkrose ... K-20
Paulina, 40 ... G-10
Pedee, 100 ... F-3
Pendleton, 16612 ... C-13
Peoria, 94 ... F-4
Perry, 90 ... D-14
Philomath, 4584 ... F-3
Phoenix, 4538 ... M-4
Pilot Rock, 1502 ... C-13
Pine Grv., 148 ... E-7
Pinehurst, 40 ... M-5
Pistol River, 84 ... M-1
Pittsburg, 40 ... B-4
Pleasant Hill, 110 ... H-4
Plush, 57 ... L-10
POLK CO., 75403 ... E-3
Port Orford, 1133 ... K-1
Portland, 583776 ... C-5
Post, 40 ... G-9
Powell Butte, 770 ... G-8
Powers, 689 ... K-2
Prairie City, 909 ... F-13
Prescott, 55 ... B-4
Prineville, 9253 ... G-8
Prospect, 455 ... K-5
Rainier, 1895 ... B-4
Raleigh Hills, 5896 ... L-18
Redmond, 26215 ... G-8
Reedsport, 4154 ... I-2
Remote, 30 ... K-2
Rhododendron, 800 ... D-6
Richland, 156 ... E-16
Rickreall, 77 ... E-4
Riddle, 1185 ... K-3
Rieth, 70 ... C-12
Riley, 50 ... I-11
Ritter, 50 ... E-12
Rivergrove, 289 ... M-18
Riverside, 10 ... I-14
Riverton, 100 ... J-1
Rockaway Bch., 1312 .. C-2
Rockville, 30 ... J-16
Rockwood ... L-20
Rocky Pt., 110 ... L-6
Rogue River, 2131 ... L-3
Rome ... K-15
Rose Lodge, 1894 ... E-2
Roseburg, 21181 ... J-3
Ruch, 840 ... M-4
Rufus, 249 ... C-9
Ruggs ... D-11
Russellville ... L-20
Saginaw, 100 ... H-4
St. Helens, 12883 ... B-4
St. Paul, 421 ... D-4
Salem, 154637 ... E-4
Sandy, 9570 ... D-6
Santa Clara ... A-7
Scappoose, 6592 ... C-4
Scio, 838 ... F-4
Scotts Mills, 357 ... E-5
Scottsburg, 210 ... I-2
Seal Rock, 600 ... F-2
Seaside, 6457 ... B-2
Selma, 695 ... M-2
Seneca, 199 ... G-12
Shady Cove, 2904 ... L-4
Shaniko, 36 ... E-9
Shaw, 80 ... E-4
Shedd, 204 ... F-4
Sheridan, 6127 ... D-3
SHERMAN CO., 1765 ... D-9
Sherwood, 18194 ... D-4
Siletz, 1212 ... F-2
Siltcoos, 30 ... H-2
Silver Lake, 149 ... J-8
Silverton, 9222 ... E-4
Simnasho ... E-7
Sisters, 2038 ... G-7
Sitkum ... J-2
Sixes, 220 ... K-1
Sodaville, 308 ... F-4
Sprague River, 350 ... L-7
Spray, 160 ... E-11
Springfield, 59403 ... H-4
Stanfield, 2043 ... C-12
Stayton, 7644 ... E-4
Steamboat, 60 ... J-4
Sublimity, 2681 ... E-4
Summer Lake, 70 ... K-9
Summerville, 135 ... C-14
Sumner, 50 ... J-1
Sumpter, 204 ... F-14
Sunny Valley, 180 ... L-3
Sunnyside, 6791 ... M-20
Sunriver, 1393 ... H-7
Sunset Bch., 320 ... B-2
Sutherlin, 7810 ... I-3
Suver, 50 ... F-4
Svensen, 550 ... A-3
Sweet Home, 8925 ... G-5
Swisshome, 300 ... H-2
Sylvan ... L-18
Takilma, 378 ... M-3
Talent, 6066 ... M-4
Tangent, 1164 ... F-4
Telocaset ... D-15
Tenmile, 260 ... J-3
Terrebonne, 1257 ... G
The Dalles, 13620 ... C
Thornhollow ... C-
Three Lynx, 70 ... D
Tidewater, 300 ... F
Tiernan ... H
Tierra Del Mar, 220 ... D
Tigard, 48035 ... D
Tillamook, 4935 ... C
TILLAMOOK CO., 25250 ... C
Tiller, 210 ... K
Timber, 260 ... C
Toketee Falls, 300 ... J
Toledo, 3465 ... F
Tollgate ... B-
Trail, 702 ... L
Triangle Lake, 70 ... G
Tri-City, 3931 ... K
Troutdale, 15962 ... C
Troy, 30 ... B-
Tualatin, 26054 ... D
Tumalo, 488 ... G
Turner, 1854 ... E
Twin Rocks, 510 ... C
Tygh Valley, 206 ... D
Ukiah, 186 ... D-
Umapine, 315 ... B-
Umatilla, 6906 ... B-
UMATILLA CO., 75889 ... D-
Umpqua, 240 ... J
Union, 2121 ... D-
UNION CO., 25748 ... D-
Union Creek, 30 ... K
Unionvale ... D
Unity, 71 ... F-
Vale, 1874 ... H-
Valley Falls ... L-
Vaughn, 60 ... H
Veneta, 4561 ... H
Vernonia, 2151 ... B
Vida, 450 ... G
Wagontire ... J-
Waldport, 2033 ... F
Wallowa, 808 ... C-
WALLOWA CO., 7008 ... C-
Walterville, 250 ... H
Walton, 200 ... H
Wamic, 85 ... D
Wapato ... D
Wapinitia ... E
Warm Sprs., 2945 ... F
Warren, 1787 ... B
Warrenton, 4989 ... A
Wasco, 410 ... C
WASCO CO., 25213 .. E
WASHINGTON CO., 529710 ... C
Waterloo, 229 ... F
Wedderburn, 330 ... L
W. Linn, 25109 ... N-
W. Portland ... M-
W. Salem ... F-
W. Slope, 6554 ... L-
Westfall, 80 ... H-
Westfir, 253 ... H
Weston, 667 ... B-
Westport, 321 ... A
Wheeler, 414 ... C
WHEELER CO., 1441 ... F-
White City, 7975 ... L
Whiteson, 100 ... D
Wilbur, 200 ... J
Wilderville, 380 ... L
Willamina, 2025 ... E
Williams, 1072 ... M
Willowcreek ... G-
Willowdale ... E
Wilsonville, 19509 ... D
Winchester, 2700 ... J
Winchester Bay, 382 ... I
Winston, 5379 ... J
Wolf Creek, 550 ... K
Woodburn, 24080 ... D
Woods, 80 ... D
Woodson, 60 ... B
Worden, 30 ... M
Wren, 110 ... F
Yachats, 690 ... G
Yamhill, 1024 ... D
YAMHILL CO., 99193 ... D
Yoncalla, 1047 ...
Zigzag, 300 ... D

Pennsylvania

Page locator

Map keys	Atlas pages
WA1–WJ14	174–175
WK1–WT14	176–177
EA1–EJ14	178–179
EK1–ET14	180–181

* City keyed to p. 50
† City keyed to p. 137
‡ City keyed to pp. 182–18

Aaronsburg, 613 ... EK
Abbottstown, 1011 .. EQ
Abington, 10000 ... ‡A
Academia, 30 ... EM
Academy Cors., 60 ... EE
Ackermanville, 610 .. EK-
Acme, 180 ... WO
Acmetonia, 1500 ... ‡
Acosta, 400 ... WO
Adah, 450 ... WF
ADAMS CO., 101407 ... EP
Adamsburg, 172 ... WN
Adamstown, 1789 ... EN
Adamsville, 67 ... WG
Addison, 207 ... WQ
Adrian, 200 ... WK
Afton Vil., 700 ... EC
Aiken ... WE-
Airville, 100 ... EQ
Akeley ... WD
Akron, 3876 ... EC
Alba, 157 ... EF
Albany, 20 ... EL
Albert, 60 ... EI
Albion, 1516 ... WE
Albrightsville, 202 ... EJ-
Alburtis, 2361 ... EM-
Aldan, 4152 ... ‡F
Alden, 200 ... EI
Aldenville, 170 ... EF-
Aleppo, 60 ... WQ
Alexandria, 346 ... WM-
Alfarata, 149 ... EL
Alford, 25 ... EE
Alinda ... EN
Aliquippa, 9438 ... WL
Allandale, 1000 ... ET
ALLEGHENY CO., 1223348 ... WM
Allemans, 60 ... WL-
Allen, 375 ... EO

*, †, ‡, §, ◊ See explanation under state title in this index.
County and parish names are listed in capital letters & boldface type.
Independent cities (not included in a county) are listed in italics.

enport, 648 WN-13
ens Mills WI-9
ensville, 503 WM-13
entown, 18032 EL-10
enwood, 321 EI-4
ison, 625 WP-4
ison Pk., 21552 WL-4
port, 264 WJ-12
media, 1078 EJ-6
nont, 75 EN-11
sace Mnr., 478 ER-14
renwald, 40 EQ-1
oona, 46320 WM-11
um Bank, 198 WO-10
verda, 400 WL-9
verton, 350 WO-5
nbler, 6417 EO-12
nbridge, 7050 WL-3
nity, 400 WO-3
nityville, 250 EN-9
nsbry, 65 WM-10
alomink, 200 EJ-12
cient Oaks, 661 EM-10
dalusia, 3500 ‡B-8
dersonburg, 50 EN-2
dreas, 200 EK-9
drews Settlement, 0 WE-13
gelica, 100 EN-8
gels EH-11
ita, 600 WJ-8
nandale, 275 WI-4
nisville, 35 WI-5
nville, 4767 EN-6
sonia, 50 EF-2
sonville, 100 WK-10
tes Fort, 400 EI-3
trim, 400 EF-2
ollo, 1647 WL-6
penzell, 150 EJ-11
plebachsville, 20 EM-11
plewold, 310 WK-6
arat EE-10
buckle, 50 WD-4
cadia, 220 WK-9
ch Rock, 100 EL-2
chbald, 6984 EG-10
dara, 300 ‡L-10
denheim, 25 WM-13
dmore, 12455 ‡D-2
dsley, 4500 ‡A-4
endtsville, 952 EP-2
gentine, 60 WI-5
istes, 311 EK-7
magh, 122 WM-8
mbrust, 230 WN-6
RMSTRONG CO., 8941 WL-6
nold, 5157 WL-5
not, 332 EF-3
ona, 370 WN-5
aph, 100 EF-2
bury WB-9
hfield, 300 EK-9
hland, 2817 EK-7
hland, 60 WK-11
hley, 2790 EI-9
htola, 150 WO-9
hville, 227 WM-10
pers, 350 EP-3
pinwall, 2801 ‡J-7
co, 200 EF-12
glen, 1406 EP-8
hens, 3367 EE-6
lantic, 77 WG-2
lantic WK-11
las, 809 EK-6
lasburg, 401 WN-2
wood, 107 WK-7
uburn, 741 EL-8
uburn Ctr., 50 EF-8
uburn Four Corners, 50 EF-8
udubon, 8433 EO-11
ultman, 225 WM-7
ustin, 562 WF-12
ustinburg, 60 ED-2
ustinville, 150 EE-4
valon, 4705 WM-3
vella, 804 WN-2
vis, 1484 EI-2
voca, 2661 EB-10
von, 1667 EN-6
vondale, 1265 EQ-9
vonia, 1205 WD-3
vonmore, 1011 WM-6
xemann, 150 WK-14
achmanville, 200 EN-6
aden, 4135 WL-3
aggaley, 600 WN-6
ainbridge, 1355 EO-5
air, 400 EP-5
airdford, 698 WL-4
akers Summit, 110 WN-11
akerstown Sta., 400 WL-4
akersville, 200 WP-7
akerton, 900 WL-9
ala-Cynwyd, 8000 ‡D-3
ald Eagle, 250 WL-12
aldwin, 19767 WN-4
allietsville, 250 EA-1
alls Mills, 60 EH-4
ally, 1090 EM-10
andanna, 225 EQ-4
anetown, 100 WO-3
angor, 5273 EK-12
annerville, 110 EL-2
arbours, 120 EH-5
ard, 50 WP-10
areville, 1250 EO-8
arkeyville, 207 WI-4
arnes, 200 WF-8
arnesville, 300 EK-8
arnsley, 100 EQ-8
arree, 70 WL-12
arto, 180 EN-10
ath, 2693 EL-11
aumstown, 422 EN-9
ausman, 300 ET-8
avington, 50 WM-2
axter WI-8
each Haven, 500 EJ-7
each Lake, 320 EG-12
eallsville, 466 WO-4
ear Creek Vil., 257 EI-9
ear Lake, 164 WD-6
eartown, 200 EQ-2
eartown EO-8
eaumont, 200 EH-8
eaver, 4531 WL-2
eaver Brook, 400 EJ-8
eaver Ctr., 40 WE-2
EAVER CO., 170539 WK-2
eaver Dam, 130 WE-5
eaver Falls, 8987 WK-2
eaver Lake EH-6
Beaver Meadows, 869 EJ-9
Beaver Sprs., 674 EL-3
Beaverdale, 1035 WN-9
Beavertown, 965 EL-3
Beavertown, 90 EO-4
Beavertown, 40 WN-11
Beccaria, 175 WK-11
Bechtelsville, 942 EN-10
Beckersville, 200 EO-9
Bedford, 2841 WP-10
BEDFORD CO., 49762 WO-10
Bedminster, 500 EM-12
Beech Creek, 701 EJ-1
Beechwood WG-11
Beersville, 250 EK-10
Belair, 1310 ER-8
Belden WO-10
Belfast, 1257 EK-11
Belknap, 40 WK-7
Bell Acres, 1388 WL-3
Bellaire EO-6
Belle Vernon, 1093 WO-4
Bellefonte, 6187 WK-14
Bellegrove, 300 EN-6
Belleville, 1827 WL-14
Bellevue, 8370 WM-3
Bells, 75 WK-10
Belltown, 60 EL-2
Bellwood, 1828 WL-11
Belmont, 2784 WT-2
Belmont Hills, 1500 ‡C-2
Belsano, 400 WM-9
Ben Avon, 1781 ‡I-4
Ben Avon Hts., 371 ‡I-5
Bendersville, 641 EP-3
Bendertown, 50 EI-7
Benezette, 200 WH-11
Benfer, 100 EK-3
Bensalem, 3000 ‡A-8
Benson, 191 WO-8
Bentley Creek, 160 EE-5
Bentleyville, 2581 WO-4
Benton, 824 EI-6
Benvenue, 25 EN-4
Berkley, 200 EM-8
Berkleys Mill, 60 WQ-8
BERKS CO., 411442 EM-8
Berlin, 2104 WP-8
Berlinsville, 200 EK-10
Bermudian, 40 EP-4
Berne, 130 EM-8
Bernville, 955 EM-8
Berrysburg, 368 EL-5
Berwick, 10477 EJ-7
Berwyn, 3631 EP-11
Bessemer, 1111 WJ-2
Bethany, 246 EF-11
Bethel, 499 EM-7
Bethel Pk., 32313 WN-4
Bethesda, 45 EQ-7
Bethlehem, 74982 EL-11
Bethlehem, 25 WK-9
Betula WF-11
Beyer, 100 WK-7
Big Beaver, 1970 WK-2
Big Cove Tannery, 200 WQ-12
Big Pond, 100 EE-5
Big Run, 624 WJ-9
Bigler, 398 WJ-11
Biglerville, 1200 EP-3
Bigmount, 100 EP-4
Bingen, 350 EC-5
Bingham, 40 WE-10
Bingham Ctr. WE-14
Birchardville, 40 EE-8
Bird in Hand, 402 EP-7
Birdsboro, 5163 EN-9
Birmingham, 90 WL-12
Bishop, 800 WN-3
Bittersville, 150 EP-6
Black Gap EP-1
Black Lick, 1462 WM-7
Black Walnut, 150 EF-8
Blacktown, 50 WI-3
Blackwell, 80 EG-2
Blain, 263 EN-1
Blain City, 250 WK-10
Blaine Hill, 1100 WN-4
Blainsport, 110 EN-8
BLAIR CO., 127089 WN-11
Blairs Mills, 100 WN-14
Blairsville, 3412 WM-7
Blairtown, 60 WP-3
Blakely, 6564 EG-10
Blakeslee, 300 EI-10
Blanchard, 740 EJ-1
Blandburg, 402 WL-11
Blandon, 7152 EM-9
Blawnox, 1432 ‡J-8
Blooming Glen, 650 EN-12
Blooming Grv., 200 EH-12
Blooming Grv., 100 EQ-4
Blooming Valley, 337 WF-4
Bloomingdale, 2100 ES-9
Bloomington, 80 WJ-10
Bloomsburg, 14855 EJ-6
Bloserville, 200 EO-2
Blossburg, 1538 EF-3
Blough, 80 WO-8
Blue Ball, 1031 EO-8
Blue Bell, 6067 EO-11
Blue Knob WN-10
Blue Ridge Summit, 891 ER-2
Blythedale, 250 WN-5
Boalsburg, 3722 WK-13
Boardman, 35 WK-11
Bobtown, 757 WQ-4
Bocktown ‡I-1
Bodines, 50 EG-4
Boiling Sprs., 3225 EO-3
Bolivar, 465 WN-7
Bolivar Run, 350 WD-10
Boltz, 160 WM-8
Bon Air, 600 WS-2
Bonneauville, 1800 EQ-3
Booneville, 75 EJ-2
Booths Cor., 200 EQ-10
Boothwyn, 4933 *B-10
Bordnersville EM-6
Bossardsville EJ-11
Boston, 545 ‡M-8
Boswell, 1277 WO-8
Bovard, 700 WN-6
Bovard, 40 WJ-4
Bowmanstown, 937 EK-10
Bowmansville, 2077 EO-8
Boyds Mills, 85 EF-12
Boydstown, 50 WJ-4
Boyertown, 4055 EN-10
Boynton, 200 WQ-8
Brackenridge, 3260 WL-5
Brackney, 200 ED-8
Braddock, 2159 ‡L-8
Braddock Hills, 1880 ‡K-8
Braden Plan, 250 WP-3
Bradenville, 545 WN-7
Bradford, 8770 WD-10
BRADFORD CO., 62622 EE-5
Bradford Woods, 1171 WL-3
Bradleytown, 50 WG-4
Bradys Bend, 150 WJ-5
Branch Dale, 388 EL-7
Branchton, 80 WJ-4
Branchville WD-3
Brandamore, 300 EP-9
Brandonville, 197 EK-7
Brandtsville EO-3
Brandy Camp, 200 WH-10
Brandywine Manor, 200 EO-9
Brave, 201 WQ-2
Breezewood, 300 WP-11
Breinigsville, 4138 EM-10
Brent, 90 WI-3
Brentwood, 9643 ‡L-6
Breslau, 500 EA-7
Bressler, 1437 ET-4
Briar Creek, 660 EJ-7
Brickerville, 1309 EO-7
Bridesburg ‡D-6
Bridgeburg WK-6
Bridgeport, 4554 ‡A-1
Bridgeport, 40 EN-2
Bridgeton EQ-6
Bridgeville, 5148 WN-3
Bridgewater, 704 WL-2
Bridgewater, 250 ‡B-9
Brisbin, 411 WK-11
Bristol, 9726 EO-13
Bristoria, 40 WP-2
Britton Run WE-5
Broad Top City, 452 WO-12
Brockport, 300 WI-9
Brockton, 500 EL-8
Brockway, 2072 WI-9
Brodbecks EQ-5
Brodhead, 100 EA-5
Brodheadsville, 1800 EJ-11
Brogue, 200 EQ-6
Brookdale, 60 ED-9
Brookhaven, 8006 EQ-11
Brookland, 15 WE-13
Brooklyn, 250 EF-9
Brookside, 2200 WC-4
Brookside EH-3
Brookston, 90 WF-8
Brookville, 3924 WI-8
Broomall, 10789 EP-11
Brotherton, 60 WP-8
Broughton, 3000 ‡M-6
Browndale, 525 EF-10
Brownfield, 400 WQ-5
Brownstown, 2816 EO-7
Brownstown, 744 WN-8
Brownstown, 30 WM-6
Brownsville, 2331 WP-4
Browntown, 1418 EB-9
Browntown, 90 EF-7
Bruin, 524 WJ-5
Brunnerville, 250 EO-7
Brush Valley, 300 WM-8
Brushtown, 340 EQ-4
Brushtown EO-2
Bryan, 30 WK-7
Bryn Athyn, 1375 EO-12
Bryn Mawr, 3779 ‡C-1
Buck, 120 EQ-7
Buck Hill Falls, 950 EI-11
Buck Mtn., 70 EJ-9
Buck Run, 176 EL-7
Buck Run, 150 EP-9
Buck Valley WQ-11
Buckhorn, 318 EJ-6
Buckhorn, 130 WM-10
Buckingham, 2000 EN-12
BUCKS CO., 625249 EM-11
Bucktown, 60 EO-10
Buena Vista, 600 WN-5
Buena Vista, 60 WJ-5
Buffalo, 120 WN-2
Buffalo Mills, 100 WP-10
Buffalo Run, 75 WK-13
Buffalo Valley, 120 WK-5
Bulger, 407 WM-2
Bullion, 40 WI-4
Bullis Mills WD-11
Bully Hill, 150 WH-5
Bungalow Pk., 200 EC-2
Bunker Hill, 170 EN-6
Bunkertown, 60 EL-3
Bunola, 300 WN-4
Burgettstown, 1388 WM-2
Burlington, 156 EF-5
Burnham, 2054 EL-1
Burning Well WF-10
Burnside, 234 WK-9
Burnt Cabins, 125 WO-13
Burtville WF-12
Bushkill, 1200 EI-12
Bustleton ‡B-7
Butler, 13757 WK-4
BUTLER CO., 183862 WJ-4
Buttonwood, 620 EB-6
Buttonwood EG-3
Butztown, 1500 EA-5
Byrnedale, 427 WH-10
Byromtown WG-8
Cabot, 400 WK-5
Cadogan, 400 WK-6
Cairnbrook, 520 WO-9
Caledonia, 200 WH-11
California, 6795 WO-4
Callensburg, 207 WI-6
Callery, 394 WK-4
Caln, 1519 EP-9
Calvin, 90 WN-12
Cambra, 70 EI-7
CAMBRIA CO., 143679 WL-10
Cambridge, 140 EO-8
Cambridge Sprs., 2595 WE-4
Cameron, 50 WG-12
CAMERON CO., 5085 WG-11
Camp Hill, 7888 EN-4
Campbelltown, 3616 EN-6
Camptown, 180 EF-7
Canadensis, 1200 EI-11
Canan, 140 WB-12
Candor, 60 WM-2
Cannelton, 100 WK-2
Canoe Camp, 150 EF-3
Canoe Creek, 250 WM-11
Canonsburg, 8992 WN-3
Canton, 1976 EF-4
CARBON CO., 65249 EJ-9
Carbondale, 8891 EG-10
Carlisle, 18682 EO-3
Carlisle Sprs. EN-3
Carlton, 80 WG-4
Carmichaels, 483 WP-4
Carnegie, 7972 ‡K-4
Carnot, 4500 ‡I-2
Carroll EJ-3
Carroll Valley, 3876 EQ-2
Carrolltown, 853 WL-9
Carter Camp, 20 WF-14
Carversville, 400 EN-12
Carverton, 500 EA-9
Casanova, 90 WJ-12
Cashtown, 459 EQ-2
Cassandra, 147 WM-10
Casselman, 94 WP-7
Cassville, 143 WN-12
Castanea, 1125 EI-2
Castle Gdn., 45 WH-12
Castle Shannon, 8316 ‡L-5
Catasauqua, 6436 EL-11
Catawissa, 1552 EJ-6
Cavettsville, 120 ‡L-9
Cecil, 900 WN-3
Cedar Hts., 800 ‡B-2
Cedar Ledge, 25 EF-4
Cedar Run, 100 EG-2
Cedar Sprs., 90 EJ-2
Cedarbrook, 2800 ‡B-4
Cementon, 1538 EL-10
Center Mills, 80 EP-3
Center Moreland EH-8
Center Road WF-2
Center Valley, 900 EM-11
Centerport, 387 EM-8
Centerville, 3263 WO-4
Centerville, 1700 ES-7
Centerville, 218 WF-5
Centerville, 125 WQ-10
Central, 100 EH-6
Central City, 1124 WO-9
Central Highlands, 700 ‡N-8
Centralia, 10 EK-7
CENTRE CO., 153990 EK-1
Centre Hall, 1265 WK-14
Cessna, 60 WO-10
Cetronia EC-2
Chadds Ford, 1200 EQ-10
Chalfant, 800 ‡K-8
Chalfont, 4009 EN-12
Chalkhill, 141 WQ-5
Challenge WH-10
Chambers Hill, 1500 ES-4
Chambersburg, 20268 EP-1
Chambersville, 100 WL-7
Champion, 300 WO-6
Chandlers Valley, 250 WE-7
Chaneysville, 80 WQ-10
Chapman, 199 EK-11
Chapmanville, 90 WG-5
Charleroi, 4120 WO-4
Charleston, 100 WI-2
Charlesville WP-10
Chase, 978 EA-7
Chatham, 300 EQ-9
Chatwood, 1000 EP-10
Chelsea, 160 EQ-11
Cheltenham ‡B-5
Cherry Flats, 250 EF-3
Cherry Grv. WF-8
Cherry Hill, 300 EK-11
Cherry Hill, 60 WE-2
Cherry Hill, 35 EQ-7
Cherry Tree, 364 WL-9
Cherry Valley, 200 WN-2
Cherry Valley, 66 WI-5
Cherrytown, 120 WN-11
Cherrytree WG-5
Cherryville, 1580 EK-10
Chest Sprs., 149 WL-10
Chester, 33972 EQ-11
CHESTER CO., 498886 EP-9
Chester Hts., 2531 EP-11
Chester Hill, 883 WK-12
Chester Sprs., 450 EO-10
Chestnut Grv., 100 WJ-10
Chestnut Level, 200 EQ-7
Chestnut Ridge, 100 ES-7
Cheswick, 1746 ‡I-9
Chevy Chase Hts., 1502 WL-8
Chewton, 488 WK-2
Cheyney, 150 EP-10
Chicora, 1043 WJ-5
Childs, 450 EG-10
Chillisquaque, 400 EJ-4
Chinchilla, 2098 EA-13
Choconut, 50 ED-8
Christiana, 1168 EP-8
Christmans, 100 EJ-10
Christy Mnr., 75 WK-6
Chrome EQ-8
Churchill, 3011 ‡K-8
Churchtown, 470 EO-8
Churchville, 60 WO-10
Circleville, 450 ‡M-10
Cito, 20 WQ-13
Clairton, 6796 WN-4
Clappertown, 110 WN-11
Clarence, 626 WJ-13
Clarendon, 450 WF-8
Claridge, 1200 WN-5
Clarington, 125 WH-8
Clarion, 5276 WI-6
CLARION CO., 39988 WJ-6
Clark, 640 WH-2
Clarks Green, 1476 EA-13
Clarks Mills, 120 WH-3
Clarks Summit, 5116 EG-9
Clarksburg, 180 WM-6
Clarkstown, 200 EI-5
Clarksville, 230 WP-3
Claussville, 40 EL-10
Clay, 1559 EO-7
Claylick WQ-13
Claysburg, 1625 WN-10
Claysville, 829 WO-2
Clear Ridge, 30 WO-13
Clear Run, 350 WI-9
Clear Spr., 40 EP-3
Clearfield, 6215 WJ-11
Clearfield, 200 EK-11
CLEARFIELD CO., 81642 WI-11
Clearview Estates, 2500 ET-2
Clearville, 200 WP-11
Cleona, 2080 EN-6
Clermont, 100 WF-10
Cleversburg, 100 EP-2
Clifford, 500 EF-10
Clifton, 300 EI-10
Clifton Hts., 6652 ‡F-2
Climax, 40 WJ-6
Clinton, 434 WM-2
Clinton, 75 WL-6
CLINTON CO., 39238 EI-1
Clintondale, 100 EJ-1
Clintonville, 508 WI-4
Cloe, 250 WJ-8
Clover Creek, 170 WN-11
Clyde, 50 WM-8
Clymer, 1357 WL-8
Coal Ctr., 139 WO-4
Coal City, 25 WH-5
Coal Glen, 25 WI-9
Coal Hill, 120 WH-6
Coal Run, 310 WM-7
Coaldale, 2281 EK-9
Coaldale, 161 WO-12
Coalmont, 106 WO-12
Coalport, 523 WL-10
Coaltown, 1200 WJ-2
Coatesville, 13100 EP-9
Cobham WF-7
Coburn, 236 EK-2
Cocalico EN-7
Cochranton, 1136 WG-4
Cochranville, 668 EP-9
Cocolamus, 50 EL-3
Cogan Sta., 600 EH-3
Cokeburg, 630 WO-3
Colebrookdale, 130 EN-10
Colegrove WF-11
Colesburg WE-13
Colesville, 150 EC-4
Coleville, 250 WK-13
College Hts., 550 ES-13
College Pk., 160 EJ-4
Collegeville, 5089 EO-11
Collingdale, 8786 ‡F-2
Collinsville, 150 EQ-6
Collomsville, 200 EI-3
Colmar, 800 EN-12
Colonial Mnr., 550 ET-8
Colonial Pk., 13229 EN-5
Colony Pk., 1076 ET-11
Columbia, 10400 EP-6
COLUMBIA CO., 67295 EI-6
Columbia Cross Roads, 220 EE-5
Columbus, 824 WE-6
Colver, 959 WM-9
Colwyn, 2546 ‡F-3
Commodore, 331 WL-8
Compass, 140 EP-8
Concord, 135 WN-14
Conestoga, 1258 EP-7
Coneville WE-12
Conewago Hts., 900 EO-5
Confluence, 780 WQ-6
Conneaut Lake, 653 WF-3
Conneaut Lake Pk., 200 WF-2
Conneautville, 774 WE-2
Connellsville, 7637 WP-5
Connoquenessing, 528 WK-4
Conrad WG-13
Conshohocken, 7833 EO-11
Conway, 2176 WL-3
Conyngham, 1914 EJ-8
Cookport, 75 WL-9
Cooksburg, 20 WH-7
Coolspring, 180 WJ-8
Coon Hunter, 40 EK-3
Coopersburg, 2386 EM-11
Cooperstown, 460 WG-4
Cooperstown, 200 WL-4
Coplay, 3192 EL-10
Coral, 325 WM-7
Coraopolis, 5677 WM-3
Coraopolis Hts., 1400 ‡J-2
Cork Lane, 700 EB-10
Cornwall, 4112 EN-6
Cornwells Hts., 1391 ‡B-8
Corry, 6605 WE-5
Corsica, 357 WI-7
Cortez, 350 EG-10
Coryville, 70 WE-11
Costello, 50 WG-12
Coudersport, 2546 WF-12
Coulter, 300 ‡N-9
Countryside, 2500 ES-2
Coupon, 275 WM-10
Courtdale, 732 EA-8
Cove Gap, 60 WQ-13
Coventryville, 350 EO-10
Covington, 650 EF-3
Covode, 75 WK-8
Cowan EJ-4
Cowanesque, 150 EE-2
Cowansville, 140 WK-6
Coyleville WK-5
Crabtree, 277 WN-6
Crafton, 5951 WM-3
Craigsville, 150 WK-5
Craley, 300 EP-6
Cramer, 100 WM-8
Cranberry, 300 WH-5
Cranesville, 638 WE-2
Crates WI-7
CRAWFORD CO., 88765 WF-4
Creekside, 309 WL-7
Creighton, 1500 WL-5
Crenshaw, 468 WI-9
Cresco, 500 EI-11
Cresson, 1711 WM-10
Cressona, 1651 EL-7
Crestmont, 90 EI-2
Crestmont Vil., 700 ‡H-1
Creswell EP-6
Croft, 60 WJ-11
Crooked Creek, 50 EE-3
Crosby, 225 WF-11
Cross Creek, 137 WN-2
Cross Fork, 60 WG-13
Cross Keys, 200 WM-11
Cross Keys, 70 WN-14
Cross Roads, 512 EQ-6
Crossingville, 60 WE-3
Crosswicks, 540 ‡B-5
Crown, 183 WH-7
Croydon, 9950 ‡B-9
Crucible, 725 WP-4
Crystal Spr., 100 WP-11
Cuba Mills, 90 EL-2
Culmerville, 600 WL-4
CUMBERLAND CO., 235406 EO-3
Cumbola, 443 EL-8
Curllsville, 110 WI-6
Curry Run, 45 WK-10
Curryville, 200 WN-11
Curtisville, 1064 WL-4
Curwensville, 2542 WJ-10
Custards, 30 WG-3
Custer City, 300 WE-10
Cyclone, 450 WE-10
Daggett, 50 EE-4
Dagus Mines, 400 WH-10
Daguscahonda, 120 WH-10
Daisytown, 326 WS-2
Dale, 1234 WN-8
Dale Summit, 180 WS-7
Daleville, 420 EH-10
Dallas, 2804 EH-8
Dallastown, 4049 EP-5
Dalmatia, 488 EL-4
Dalton, 1234 EG-9
Damascus, 365 EF-12
Danboro, 500 EN-12
Danielsville, 750 EK-10
Danville, 4699 EJ-5
Darby, 10687 EP-12
Darlington, 254 WK-2
Darlington Cors. EP-10
Dauberville, 848 EM-8
Dauphin, 791 EN-4
DAUPHIN CO., 268100 EN-4
Davidsburg, 25 EP-4
Davidsville, 1130 WO-8
Davistown, 60 WQ-3
Dawson, 367 WO-5
Dawson Ridge, 1200 WL-2
Day, 40 WI-7
Dayton, 553 WK-7
Dayton, 100 EM-5
Dean, 90 WL-10
Deanville, 65 WJ-6
Deckers Pt., 50 WK-8
Deemston, 722 WP-3
Deep Valley, 75 WQ-1
Deer Lake, 687 EL-8
Defiance, 239 WO-12
Degolia WE-10
Delano, 342 EK-8
DELAWARE CO., 558979 EP-11
Delaware Grv., 25 WH-3
Delaware Water Gap, 746 EJ-12
Delmont, 2686 WM-6
Delroy, 200 EP-6
Delta, 728 EQ-7
Dempseytown, 200 WG-5
Denholm, 75 EL-2
Dents Run WH-11
Denver, 3861 EO-8
Deodate, 80 EO-5
Derrick City, 1000 WD-10
Derry, 2688 WN-7
Desire, 90 WJ-9
Devault, 100 EO-10
Devon, 1515 EP-11
Dewart, 1471 EI-4
Diamond, 50 WF-5
Diamondville, 100 WL-8
Dice EK-4
Dickerson Run, 400 WP-5
Dickinson, 100 EO-2
Dickson City, 6070 EG-10
Dicksonburg WF-2
Dillsburg, 2563 EO-4
Dilltown, 250 WM-8
Dime WL-6
Dimock, 300 EF-8
Dingmans Ferry, 1000 EI-13
Distant, 750 WJ-7
Dixonville, 600 WL-8
Doe Run, 100 EP-9
Dolington, 250 EN-13
Donaldson, 328 EL-6
Donegal, 120 WO-6
Donnally Mills, 80 EM-3
Donora, 4781 WO-4
Dora, 50 WJ-7
Dormont, 8593 WM-4
Dorneyville, 4406 EC-2
Dornsife, 100 EL-5
Dorrance, 50 EI-8
Dorseyville, 650 WL-4
Dott, 40 WQ-12
Doubling Gap EN-2
Douglassville, 448 EN-9
Dover, 2007 EP-4
Downingtown, 7891 EP-10
Doylesburg, 150 WO-14
Doylestown, 8380 EN-12
Drakes Mills, 40 WE-4
Draketown, 60 WQ-6
Dravosburg, 1792 ‡M-7
Drehersville, 40 EL-8
Drexel Hill, 28043 EP-11
Drifting, 150 WJ-12
Drifton, 800 EJ-9
Driftwood, 67 WH-12
Drumore, 115 EQ-7
Drums, 600 EJ-8
Drury Run, 100 WH-14
Dry Run, 200 WO-14
Dry Tavern, 697 WP-4
Dryville, 398 EM-9
Dublin, 2158 EN-12
DuBois, 7794 WI-9
Duboistown, 1205 EI-4
Dudley, 184 WO-12
Duke Ctr., 850 WE-11
Dunbar, 1042 WP-5
Duncannon, 1522 EN-4
Duncansville, 1233 WM-11
Dundaff, 175 EF-10
Dundore, 30 EL-4
Dunkard, 150 WQ-4
Dunlevy, 381 WO-4
Dunlo, 342 WN-9
Dunmore, 14057 EH-10
Dunnstown, 1360 EI-2
Dupont, 2711 EC-10
Duquesne, 5565 ‡L-8
Durham, 200 EL-12
Duryea, 4917 EB-10
Dushore, 608 EG-6
Dutch Hill, 110 WJ-5
Dysart, 120 WL-10
Eagle, 130 EO-10
Eagle Rock, 60 WG-6
Eagles Mere, 120 EH-6
Earlston, 1122 WP-11
Earlville, 500 EN-9
E. Altoona, 200 WM-11
E. Athens, 400 EE-6
E. Bangor, 1172 EK-12
E. Benton, 175 EG-10
E. Berlin, 1521 EP-4
E. Berwick, 2007 EJ-7
E. Brady, 942 WJ-5
E. Brook, 300 WJ-3
E. Butler, 732 WK-4
E. Canton, 25 EF-5
E. Conemaugh, 1220 WN-9
E. Earl, 1144 EO-8
E. Finley WP-2
E. Freedom, 972 WN-11
E. Greenville, 2951 EM-10
E. Hickory, 150 WG-6
E. Kane, 135 WF-9
E. Lansdowne, 2668 ‡E-2
E. Lemon, 400 EG-9
E. McKeesport, 2126 ‡L-9
E. Millsboro, 400 WP-4
E. New Castle, 250 WJ-2
E. Petersburg, 4506 EO-7
E. Pittsburgh, 1822 ‡L-8
E. Prospect, 905 EP-6
E. Rochester, 567 WL-3
E. Salem, 186 EL-3
E. Sharpsburg, 110 WN-11
E. Side, 317 EJ-9
E. Smethport, 500 WE-11
E. Smithfield, 500 EE-5
E. Springfield, 400 WD-2
E. Stroudsburg, 9840 EJ-12
E. Texas, 450 EC-2
E. Titusville, 60 WF-5
E. Towanda, 400 EF-6
E. Troy, 140 EF-5
E. Vandergrift, 674 WL-6
E. Washington, 2234 WO-3
E. Waterford, 190 EN-1
E. York, 8777 WS-14
Eastland Hills, 550 ES-9
Easton, 26800 EL-12
Eastvale, 225 WK-2
Eastville, 80 EJ-3
Eatonville, 200 EG-8
Eau Claire, 316 WI-5
Ebenezer, 200 EN-6
Ebensburg, 3351 WM-9
Echo, 150 WR-3
Echo, 30 WK-7
Echo Lake, 80 EJ-12
Eckley, 30 EJ-9
Eckville EL-8
Economy, 8970 WL-3
Eddington, 1906 ‡B-8
Eddington Gdns., 800 ‡A-8
Eddystone, 2410 ‡G-1
Eden, 700 EO-7
Edenborn, 294 WP-4
Edenburg, 681 EM-8
Edendale, 100 WK-11
Edenville, 150 WP-13
Edgegrove, 500 EQ-4
Edgemont, 900 ES-3
Edgewood, 3118 ‡K-7
Edgewood, 2384 EK-6
Edgeworth, 1680 WM-3
Edie, 83 WO-8
Edinboro, 6438 WE-3
Edinburg, 200 WJ-2
Edmon, 120 WM-6
Edwardsville, 4816 EA-7
Effort, 2269 EJ-11
Egypt, 2391 EA-2
Ehrenfeld, 228 WN-9
Eighty Four, 657 WO-3
Elam, 200 EQ-10
Elberta, 180 WM-11
Elbon WH-10
Eldersville, 200 WN-2
Elderton, 356 WL-7
Eldred, 825 WE-11
Elgin, 218 WE-5
Elimsport, 65 EI-4
Elizabeth, 1493 WN-4
Elizabethtown, 11545 EO-6
Elizabethville, 1510 EM-5
Elk City, 80 WI-6
ELK CO., 31946 WG-10
Elk Grv., 45 EH-6
Elk Lake, 100 EF-8
Elkins Pk., 4700 ‡B-5
Elkland, 1821 ED-2
Ellenton, 25 EG-5
Ellerslie, 550 ‡A-9
Elliott Mills WJ-3
Elliottsburg, 220 EN-2
Ellisburg, 55 WE-13
Ellport, 1180 WK-3
Ellsworth, 1027 WO-4
Ellwood City, 7921 WK-2
Elm, 150 EO-7
Elmer EE-1
Elmhurst, 830 EH-10
Elrama, 307 WN-4
Elstonville, 60 EO-6
Elton, 600 WN-9
Elverson, 1225 EO-9
Elysburg, 2194 EK-6
Embreeville, 90 EP-9
Emeigh, 400 WL-9
Emerald, 240 EL-10
Emerickville, 150 WI-8
Emigsville, 2672 EP-5
Emlenton, 625 WI-5
Emmaus, 11211 EM-10
Emmaville, 40 WP-11
Emporium, 2073 WG-12
Emsworth, 2449 WM-3
Endeavor, 200 WG-7
Enders, 65 EM-4
Energy, 50 WJ-3
English Ctr., 60 EH-2
Enhaut, 1007 ET-4
Enid WO-12
Enlow, 1013 ‡K-2
Ennisville WL-13
Enola, 6111 EN-4
Enon Valley, 306 WK-2
Enterprise, 50 WF-6
Entriken, 125 WN-12
Ephrata, 13394 EO-7
Equinunk, 130 EE-11
Ercildoun, 100 EP-9
Erdenheim ‡B-3
Erdman, 200 EL-5
Erie, 101786 WC-4
ERIE CO., 280566 WD-4
Erlen, 800 ‡B-4
Ernest, 462 WL-7
Erwinna, 140 EM-12
Eshcol EM-2
Espy, 1642 EJ-6
Espyville, 300 WF-2
Essington ‡G-2
Estella, 50 EG-5
Estherton, 1200 ER-3
Etna, 3451 ‡J-6
Euclid, 90 WJ-4
Evans City, 1833 WK-3
Evans Falls, 270 EG-8
Evansburg, 2129 EO-11
Evendale, 165 EL-3
Everett, 1834 WP-11
Evergreen, 70 EF-6
Everson, 793 WO-5
Ewingsville, 400 ‡L-4
Exchange, 100 EI-5
Exeter, 5652 EH-9
Export, 917 WM-5
Exton, 4842 EP-10
Eyers Grv., 105 EJ-6
Factoryville, 1158 EG-9
Fair Acres, 500 ET-3
Fairbank, 600 WP-4
Fairbrook, 225 WL-13
Fairchance, 1975 WQ-5
Fairdale, 2059 WP-4
Fairdale, 40 EE-8
Fairfield, 1100 WC-4
Fairfield, 507 EQ-2
Fairhope, 50 WQ-9
Fairless Hills, 8466 EO-13
Fairmont City, 300 WJ-7
Fairmount Sprs., 40 EI-7
Fairoaks, 800 ‡H-2
Fairplay EQ-2
Fairview, 2348 WD-3
Fairview, 250 WJ-8
Fairview, 198 WJ-5
Fairview, 50 WH-3
Fairview Hts., 600 ‡I-8
Fairville, 150 *A-7
Fall Brook, 200 EF-4
Fallentimber, 150 WL-10
Falling Spr., 200 EP-1
Falls, 230 EG-9
Falls Creek, 1037 WI-9
Fallsington, 1300 †T-12
Fallston, 266 WK-2
Falmouth, 420 EO-5
Fannettsburg, 950 WO-13
Farmers Valley, 120 WE-11
Farmersville, 991 EO-7
Farmersville, 50 EA-6
Farmington, 800 EB-4
Farmington, 767 WQ-6
Farragut, 60 EH-4
Farrandsville, 120 EI-2
Farrell, 5111 WI-2
Farwell, 350 WH-14
Fassett, 175 ED-5
Fawn Grv., 452 EQ-6
Fayette City, 596 WO-4
FAYETTE CO., 136606 WP-5
Fayetteville, 3128 EP-1
Fayetteville, 300 ‡K-2
Fellsburg, 1180 WO-4
Felton, 506 EQ-6
Feltonville ‡C-5
Fenelton, 110 WK-5
Fern Brook, 550 EH-8
Fern Glen, 350 EJ-7
Ferndale, 1636 WN-8
Ferndale, 400 EM-12
Fernridge EJ-10
Fernville, 556 EJ-6
Fernway, 12414 WL-3
Fertigs, 65 WH-6
Finleyville, 461 WN-4
Fisher, 130 WH-7
Fishertown, 400 WO-10
Fisherville, 60 EM-4
Five Forks, 50 EQ-1
Five Points, 600 WL-3
Five Points, 100 ES-14
Five Points, 20 WL-7
Five Points WM-6
Fivepointville, 1156 EO-8
Flat Rock, 140 WQ-6
Fleetville, 350 EG-9
Fleetwood, 4085 EM-9
Flemington, 1330 EI-2
Flicksville, 100 EK-12
Flinton, 250 WL-10
Florence, 250 WM-2
Flourtown, 4538 ‡A-3
Fogelsville, 950 EL-10
Folcroft, 6606 ‡F-2
Folsom, 8323 ‡F-1
Fombell, 100 WK-3
Fontana, 150 EN-6
Foot of Ten, 672 WC-12
Forbes Road, 650 WN-6
Force, 253 WI-10
Ford City, 2991 WK-6
Ford Cliff, 371 WK-6
Fordyce, 20 WQ-3
Forest City, 1911 EF-10
FOREST CO., 7716 WG-7
Forest Grv., 2600 ‡J-4
Forest Hills, 6518 ‡K-8
Forest Lake, 100 EE-8
Forest Pk., 300 EI-9
Forestville, 100 WI-4
Forks EI-7
Forkston, 70 EG-8
Forksville, 145 EG-5
Ft. Hill, 35 WQ-7
Ft. Hunter, 150 EN-4
Ft. Littleton, 100 WP-13
Ft. Loudon, 886 WP-13
Ft. Washington, 5446 EO-12
Forty Fort, 4214 EH-9
Foster Brook, 1251 WD-10
Fostoria, 40 WL-11
Foundryville, 256 EJ-7
Fountain, 250 EL-6
Fountain Dale, 150 EQ-2
Fountain Hill, 4597 EL-11
Fountain Sprs., 278 EK-7
Foustown, 200 WR-12
Fox Chapel, 5388 ‡I-7
Fox Chase ‡B-6
Fox Hill, 125 EC-8
Foxburg, 183 WI-5
Frackville, 3805 EK-7
Franconia, 430 EN-11
Frankford ‡C-6
Frankfort Sprs., 130 WM-2
Franklin, 6545 WH-5
Franklin, 323 WN-9
Franklin Ctr., 30 WD-3
FRANKLIN CO., 149618 WP-13
Franklin Forks, 110 EE-9
Franklin Pk., 13470 WL-3
Franklindale, 100 EF-6
Franklintown, 489 EO-4
Franklinville, 75 WL-12
Frankstown, 200 WM-11
Frazer, 2000 EP-10
Frederick, 120 EN-10
Fredericksburg, 1357 EM-6
Fredericksburg, 733 WF-3
Fredonia, 502 WH-3
Freeburg, 575 EK-4
Freedom, 1569 WL-3
Freeland, 3531 EJ-9
Freemansburg, 2636 EB-5
Freeport, 1813 WL-5
Frenchtown, 60 WF-4
Frenchville, 200 WI-12
Freysville, 400 EP-6
Friedens, 1523 WP-8
Friedensburg, 858 EL-7
Friedensville, 800 EC-4
Friendsville, 111 EE-8
Frisco, 850 WK-3
Fritztown, 200 EN-8
Frogtown, 70 WJ-5
Frogtown, 40 WI-7
Frostburg, 120 WJ-8
Fryburg, 375 WH-6
Frystown, 380 EM-7
Fullerton, 14925 EL-10
FULTON CO., 14845 WP-12
Furlong, 700 EN-12
Gabby Hts., 1200 WO-2
Gaines, 120 EF-1
Galeton, 1149 EF-1
Galilee, 180 EF-12
Gallatin, 250 WO-4
Gallitzin, 1668 WM-10
Ganister, 85 WM-12
Gap, 1931 EP-8
Gapsville WP-11
Garards Fort, 100 WQ-3
Garden City ‡G-1
Garden View, 2503 EI-4
Gardenville, 250 EN-12
Gardners, 150 EP-3
Garland, 300 WE-6
Garrett, 456 WQ-8
Garrett Hill ‡C-1
Garrison, 50 WQ-2
Gastonville, 2818 WN-4
Gastown, 150 WL-7
Gatchellville, 60 EQ-6
Gatesburg, 100 WL-13
Gauff Hill, 350 EB-4
Gayly, 300 ‡K-3
Geeseytown, 100 WM-11
Geiger, 90 WP-8
Geigertown, 500 EO-9
Geistown, 2467 WN-9
Gelatt, 50 EE-10
Genesee, 300 WD-13
Geneva, 109 WG-3
Georgetown, 1640 EB-7
Georgetown, 1022 EP-8
Georgetown, 200 EL-11
Georgetown, 174 WL-2
Georgeville, 30 WK-8
Germania, 130 EF-1
Germansville, 250 EL-9
Germantown ‡C-4
Geryville EM-11
Gettysburg, 7620 EQ-3
Ghennes Hts., 900 WO-4
Gibbon Glade, 65 WQ-5
Gibraltar, 680 EN-9
Gibson, 200 EE-10
Gibsonia, 2733 WL-4
Gifford, 500 WE-10
Gilbert, 700 EK-11
Gilberton, 769 EK-7
Gilbertsville, 4832 EN-10
Gilfoyle, 20 WG-7
Gillett, 300 EE-5
Ginter, 120 WK-11
Ginther, 75 EK-8
Gipsy, 125 WK-9
Girard, 3104 WD-3
Girardville, 1519 EK-7
Girty, 30 WL-6
Glade City, 130 WQ-8
Gladwyne, 4000 ‡C-2
Glasgow, 250 WL-11
Glasgow, 60 WL-1
Glassport, 4483 WN-4
Gleason EF-4
Gleasonton WH-14
Glen Campbell, 245 WK-9
Glen Forney, 120 EQ-2
Glen Hazel WG-10
Glen Hope, 142 WK-10
Glen Iron, 150 EK-3
Glen Lyon, 1873 EI-8
Glen Mawr, 100 EH-5
Glen Moore, 1000 ES-9
Glen Osborne, 547 ‡I-3
Glen Richey, 270 WJ-10
Glen Rock, 2025 EQ-5
Glen Roy EQ-8
Glen Savage, 15 WP-9
Glen Summit, 250 EI-9
Glenburn, 953 EG-9
Glencoe, 15 WQ-9
Glendale, 75 EC-10
Glendon, 440 EL-11
Glenfield, 205 ‡I-4
Glenmar Gdns., 200 WD-4
Glenmoore, 900 EO-9
Glenolden, 7153 ‡F-2
Glenshaw, 8981 ‡I-6
Glenside, 8384 ‡A-4
Glenville, 100 EQ-5
Glenwillard, 1100 ‡H-2
Glenwood, 3000 ES-3
Glenwood, 50 EF-9
Globe Mills, 45 EK-4
Goheenville, 50 WK-7
Gold, 50 WE-13
Goldsboro, 952 EO-5
Good Intent, 25 WO-2
Good Spr., 90 EL-6
Goods Cor., 500 WR-2
Goodtown, 20 WP-8
Goodville, 482 EO-8
Goodyear, 100 EP-3
Gordon, 763 EL-7
Gordonville, 508 EP-8
Goshenville, 150 EP-10
Gouldsboro, 890 EI-11
Gowen City, 220 EL-6
Graceton, 257 WM-7
Graceville, 50 WP-11
Gradyville, 500 EP-11
Grampian, 356 WJ-10
Grand Valley, 175 WF-6
Grandview Hts., 2050 ES-9
Grantham, 500 EO-4
Grantville, 230 EN-5
Granville, 440 EM-1
Granville Ctr., 110 EF-5
Granville Summit, 85 EF-5
Grassflat, 511 WJ-12
Grassmere Pk., 50 EH-6
Graterford, 900 EO-11
Gratz, 765 EL-5
Gray, 275 WO-8
Graysville, 160 WP-2
Grazierville, 665 WL-11
Greason, 150 EO-2
Great Bend, 734 ED-9
Greble, 100 EM-7
Greece City, 40 WJ-5
Greeley, 1000 EH-12
Green Lane, 508 EN-11
Green Pt., 75 EM-6
Green Tree, 4432 ‡K-5
Green Vil., 400 EP-1
Greenawalds, 1200 EB-2
Greenburr, 130 EJ-2
Greencastle, 3996 WQ-14
Greendale WF-9
GREENE CO., 38686 WQ-3
Greenes, 894 EE-6
Greenfield, 40 WI-2
Greenfields, 1170 ES-12
Greenmount, 70 EQ-3
Greenock, 2195 ‡M-9
Greensboro, 260 WQ-4
Greensburg, 14892 WN-6
Greentown, 1000 EH-11
Greenville, 5919 WH-2
Greenwood, 2458 WM-11
Greenwood, 30 EI-6
Gresham, 75 WF-5
Grill, 1468 ET-12
Grindstone, 498 WP-4
Gringo, 600 ‡H-1
Grovania EJ-6
Grove City, 8322 WI-3
Grover, 200 EG-4
Groveton, 500 ‡J-3
Guffey, 100 ‡N-9
Guitonville, 50 WG-7
Gulph Mills, 450 ‡B-1
Guys Mills, 124 WF-4
Gwynedd, 600 EO-11
Hadley, 180 WH-3
Hahntown, 400 ‡M-10
Halifax, 841 EM-4
Hallam, 2673 EP-6
Hallstead, 1303 ED-9
Hallton, 30 WH-8
Hamburg, 4289 EM-8
Hametown, 80 EQ-5
Hamilton, 125 WJ-8
Hamilton Pk., 3500 ES-8
Hamlin, 1100 EH-11
Hamlin, 85 EM-6
Hammett WD-4
Hamorton, 100 *A-7
Hampton, 632 EP-4
Haneyville EH-2
Hannahstown, 80 WK-5
Hannastown, 350 WN-6
Hannaville, 176 WG-4
Hanover, 15289 EQ-4
Hanover, 800 EA-4
Hanover Hills, 160 ES-5
Hanoverdale EN-5
Harborcreek, 1500 WC-4
Harding, 400 EA-10
Harford, 250 EF-9
Harlansburg, 300 WJ-3
Harleigh, 1104 EJ-8
Harleysville, 9286 EN-11
Harmar Hts., 1050 ‡H-8
Harmarville, 1100 ‡I-8
Harmonsburg, 401 WF-3
Harmonville, 1500 ‡B-2
Harmony, 890 WK-3
Harnedsville, 90 WQ-7
Harper Tavern, 50 EN-6
Harrisburg, 49528 EN-4
Harrison City, 134 WN-5
Harrison Valley, 250 EE-1
Harrisonville, 50 WP-12
Harrisville, 897 WI-4
Harshaville WM-2
Hartleton, 283 EK-3
Hartstown, 201 WG-2
Hartsville, 700 EN-12
Harveys Lake, 2791 EH-8
Harveyville, 50 EI-7
Harwick, 899 ‡H-9
Harwood, 420 EJ-8
Hastings, 1278 WL-9
Hatboro, 7360 EO-12
Hatfield, 3290 EN-11
Haverford, 6000 ‡D-2
Havertown, 30000 ‡D-1
Hawk Run, 534 WK-12
Hawley, 1211 EG-12
Hawstone, 60 EM-2
Hawthorn, 494 WJ-7
Haydentown, 120 WQ-5
Haysville, 70 ‡I-3
Hayti, 950 EP-9
Hazel Hurst, 300 WF-10
Hazen, 125 WI-8
Hazleton, 25340 EJ-8
Heart Lake, 130 EE-9
Heathville, 15 WI-7
Hebe, 70 EL-5
Hebron Ctr. WE-13
Heckscherville, 220 EL-7
Hecktown, 1200 EL-11
Hecla, 100 EL-8
Hegins, 812 EL-6
Heidelberg, 1244 WM-3
Heidlersburg, 707 EP-3
Heilwood, 711 WL-9
Helfenstein, 100 EL-6
Helixville WO-9
Hellertown, 5898 EL-11
Helvetia, 90 WJ-9
Hemlock WE-8
Hendersonville WH-4
Henrietta, 100 WN-11
Henrys Bend, 60 WG-6
Henryville, 300 EI-11
Hepburnia, 140 WJ-10
Hereford, 930 EM-10
Herman, 400 WK-5
Herminie, 789 WN-5
Hermitage, 16220 WI-2
Herndon, 324 EL-4
Herrick Ctr., 125 EF-10
Herrickville, 75 EE-7
Hershey, 14257 EN-5
Heshbon, 50 WM-8
Hessdale, 100 EP-7
Hesston, 175 WM-12
Hetlerville EJ-7
Hibbs, 200 WP-4
Hickernell, 50 WE-3
Hickory, 740 WN-2
Hickory Cors., 60 EL-4
Hickory Grv., 30 ED-9
Highland Pk., 1900 ET-2
Highland Pk., 1380 EL-1
Highspire, 2399 EO-5
Hilldale, 1246 EB-9
Hiller, 1155 WP-4
Hilliards, 120 WI-5
Hillsdale, 250 WK-9
Hillsgrove, 200 EH-5
Hillside, 200 WN-7
Hillsville, 600 WJ-2
Hilltown, 800 EN-12
Hilltown, 60 EE-12
Hilltown EQ-2
Hinkletown, 175 EO-8
Hoadleys, 110 EG-11
Hobbie, 350 EJ-8
Hoernerstown, 50 ES-5
Hogestown, 300 EN-4
Hokendauqua, 3378 EA-3
Holbrook, 40 WQ-2
Holland, 5300 EO-13
Hollidaysburg, 5791 WM-11
Hollisterville EH-11
Hollsopple, 500 WO-8
Hollywood, 800 ‡B-5
Holmes, 2800 ‡F-2
Holmesburg ‡C-7
Holtwood, 200 EQ-7
Home, 400 WL-8
Home Camp WI-10
Homer City, 1707 WM-7
Homestead, 3165 ‡K-7
Hometown, 1349 EK-8
Homeville, 50 EQ-8
Homewood, 109 WK-2
Honeoye, 20 WD-12
Honesdale, 4480 EG-11
Honey Brook, 1713 EO-9
Honey Grv., 200 EN-1
Hooker, 100 WJ-5
Hookstown, 147 WL-2
Hooversville, 645 WO-8
Hop Bottom, 337 EF-9
Hopeland, 738 EO-7
Hopewell, 230 WO-11
Hopwood, 2090 WP-5
Horsham, 14842 EO-12
Hosensack EM-10
Host, 25 EM-7
Hostetter, 740 WN-6
Houserville, 1814 WK-13
Houston, 1296 WN-3
Houtzdale, 797 WK-11
Howard, 720 EJ-1
Hoytville, 40 EG-2
Hublersburg, 104 EJ-1
Hudson, 1443 EB-8
Hudsondale, 100 EK-9
Huey, 125 WJ-6
Huffs Church, 150 EM-10
Hughestown, 1392 EB-10
Hughesville, 2128 EI-5
Humboldt, 120 EJ-8
Hummels Wharf, 1353 EK-4
Hummelstown, 4538 EN-5
Hunker, 291 WO-5
Hunlock Creek, 300 EI-8
Hunters Run, 60 EO-3
Hunterstown, 547 EQ-3
Huntersville, 50 EH-5
Huntingdon, 7093 WM-12
HUNTINGDON CO., 45913 WN-12
Huntingdon Valley, 10000 ‡A-6
Huntington Mills, 175 EI-7
Huntsdale, 300 EO-2
Huntsville, 100 EH-8
Husband WP-8
Hustontown, 450 WP-12
Hyde, 1399 WJ-11
Hyde Pk., 2528 ES-13
Hydetown, 526 WF-5
Hyndman, 910 WQ-9
Hyner, 150 EH-1
Ickesburg, 280 EM-2
Idamar, 30 WL-8
Idaville, 177 EP-3
Imler, 150 WO-10
Imperial, 2541 WM-3
Independence, 110 WN-1
Independence, 100 ‡H-1
Independence, 70 EL-4
Indian Crossing, 20 WD-11
Indian Head, 175 WP-6
Indian Head WE-4
Indian Lake, 394 WP-9
Indian Orchard, 300 EG-11
Indiana, 13975 WL-7
INDIANA CO., 88880 WK-8
Indianola, 900 WL-4
Industry, 1835 WL-2
Ingram, 3330 ‡K-5
Inkerman, 1819 EB-9
Intercourse, 1274 EP-8
Iola, 144 EI-6
Iona, 800 EN-7
Irishtown, 430 EQ-4
Iron Sprs., 200 EQ-2
Ironton, 300 EA-1
Irvine, 200 WE-7
Irvona, 647 WK-10
Irwin, 3973 WN-5
Isabella, 275 WP-4
Iselin, 275 WM-6
Ithan ‡C-1
Ivyland, 1041 EO-12
Ivywood, 40 WL-4
Jackson, 90 EE-10
Jackson Ctr., 224 WH-3
Jackson Summit EE-4
Jacksonville, 637 WM-7
Jacksonville, 100 EL-11
Jacksonville, 95 EJ-1
Jacksonwald, 3393 ET-14
Jacktown, 200 ‡M-10
Jacobs Creek, 275 WO-5
Jacobus, 1841 EQ-5
James City, 287 WF-9
Jamestown, 617 WG-2
Jamestown, 400 WN-10
Jamison, 850 EN-12
Jamison City, 134 EH-7
Janesville, 600 WK-11
Jeannette, 9654 WN-5
Jeddo, 98 EJ-9
Jefferson, 733 EQ-4
Jefferson, 270 WP-3
Jefferson Ctr., 80 WK-4
JEFFERSON CO., 45200 WH-8
Jefferson Hills, 10619 WN-4
Jenkintown, 4422 EO-12
Jenners, 250 WO-8
Jennerstown, 695 WO-8
Jennersville, 45 EQ-9
Jenningsville, 100 EG-7
Jericho, 20 WH-12
Jermyn, 2169 EG-10
Jerome, 1017 WO-8
Jersey Mills, 55 EH-2
Jersey Shore, 4361 EI-3
Jerseytown, 184 EJ-6
Jessup, 4676 EG-10
Jim Thorpe, 4781 EK-9
Joanna, 80 EO-9
Jobs Corners EE-4
Joffre, 536 WM-2
Johnsonburg, 2483 WG-10
Johnstown, 20978 WN-8
Joliett, 275 EL-6
Jollytown, 25 WQ-2
Jonas, 60 EJ-10
Jones Mills, 300 WO-7
Jonestown, 1905 EM-6
Jonestown, 64 EI-7
Josephine, 300 WM-7
Julian, 152 WK-13
Juneau, 30 WK-8
Junedale, 200 EK-8
JUNIATA CO., 24636 EM-2
Juniata Gap, 1100 WA-12
Juniata Ter., 542 EM-1
Justus EB-14
Kane, 3730 WF-9
Kanesholm WF-9
Kaneville WG-5
Kantner, 80 WO-8
Kantz, 35 EK-4
Kaolin, 150 EQ-9
Karns City, 209 WJ-5
Karthaus, 250 WI-12
Kasiesville, 30 WQ-13
Kauffman, 150 WQ-14
Kaylor, 200 WJ-5
Kearney WO-12
Kearsarge WB-10
Keating WI-13
Keating Summit, 100 WF-12
Kecksburg, 140 WO-6
Keelersville, 100 EM-11
Keeneyville, 100 EE-2
Keewaydin WI-12
Keisterville, 300 WP-5
Kelayres, 533 EK-8
Kellersburg, 100 WJ-6
Kellettville, 100 WG-7
Kelly, 70 WL-6
Kelly Crossroads, 70 EJ-4
Kelton, 140 EQ-9
Kemblesville, 125 EQ-9
Kempton, 169 EL-9
Kendall WM-2
Kenhorst, 2877 ET-12
Kenilworth, 1907 EO-10
Kenmar, 4124 EI-4
Kennard, 20 WG-2
Kennerdell, 247 WH-5
Kennett Sq., 6072 EQ-10
Kensington ‡D-5
Kenwick Vil., 200 ER-9
Kenwood, 25 WL-8
Kerr, 250 WJ-11
Kerrmoor, 25 WK-10
Kerrtown, 305 WF-3
Kersey, 937 WH-10
Khedive, 40 WP-3
Killinger, 75 EM-4
Kimberton, 450 EO-10
Kimmelton, 80 WO-8
King WN-10
King of Prussia, 19936 EO-11
Kings Manor, 650 ‡B-1
Kingsdale, 200 ER-3
Kingsley, 200 EF-9
Kingston, 13182 EI-9
Kingwood, 120 WP-7
Kintnersville, 100 EM-12
Kinzers, 450 EP-8
Kirby, 35 WQ-3
Kirkwood, 396 EQ-8
Kirwan Hts., 500 ‡L-4
Kissimmee, 100 EK-3
Kistler, 320 WN-13
Kistler, 40 EN-2
Kittanning, 4044 WK-6
Klecknersville, 300 EK-11
Kleinfeltersville, 250 EN-7
Klinesville, 100 EM-9
Klinesville, 60 EP-6
Klingerstown, 127 EL-5
Knapp EF-2
Knauers EN-8
Knobsville, 100 WP-13
Knox, 1146 WI-6
Knox Dale, 300 WJ-8
Knoxville, 629 EE-2
Koonsville, 200 EI-7
Koppel, 762 WK-2
Korn Krest, 850 EB-6
Kossuth, 150 WH-6
Kralltown, 75 EP-4
Kratzerville, 383 EK-4
Kreamer, 822 EK-4
Kreidersville, 270 EL-10
Kremis, 20 WH-2
Kresgeville, 400 EK-10
Krings, 150 WT-2
Krumsville, 140 EL-9
Kuhnsville, 500 EB-1
Kuhntown, 30 WQ-2
Kulpmont, 2924 EK-6
Kulpsville, 8194 EN-11
Kunkle, 150 EH-8
Kunkletown, 200 EK-11
Kushequa, 60 WF-10
Kutztown, 5012 EM-9
Kylertown, 340 WJ-12
Kyleville, 25 EQ-7
La Anna EI-11
La Belle, 350 WP-4
La Gonda, 70 WO-2
La Plume, 400 EG-9
Laboratory, 850 WO-3
Labott, 50 EP-4
Laceyville, 379 EF-7
LACKAWANNA CO., 214437 EH-10
Lackawaxen, 600 EG-12
Laddsburg, 60 EG-6
Lafayette, 40 WE-10
Lafayette Hill, 6700 ‡B-3
Laflin, 1487 EB-9
Lahaska, 200 EN-12
Lairdsville, 120 EI-5
L. Ariel, 1250 EG-11
L. Carey, 400 EG-8
Lake City, 3031 WD-2
L. Como, 280 EE-11
L. Harmony, 850 EJ-10
L. Winola, 748 EG-9
L. Wynonah, 2640 EL-7
Lakemont, 1868 WM-11
Lakeside, 200 EE-10
Lakeview Hts., 600 ES-4
Lakeville, 500 EG-11
Lakewood, 300 EE-11
Lamar, 562 EJ-1
Lamartine, 200 WI-5
Lambertsville, 70 WO-8
Lamott, 800 ‡B-5
Lampeter, 1669 ET-10
Lanark, 400 EC-4
Lancaster, 59322 EP-7
LANCASTER CO., 519445 EP-8
Landenberg, 100 EQ-9
Lander, 150 WD-7
Landingville, 159 EL-8
Landis Valley, 800 ER-9
Landisburg, 218 EN-2
Landisville, 1893 EO-6
Lanes Mills, 30 WI-9
Lanesboro, 506 ED-10
Langdondale, 100 WO-11
Langeloth, 717 WN-2
Lansdale, 16269 EN-11
Lansdowne, 10620 ‡E-2
Lanse, 450 WJ-12
Lansford, 3941 EK-9
Lantz Cors., 40 WF-10
Laporte, 316 EH-6
Larabee WE-11
Larimer, 750 ‡M-10
Larksville, 4480 EI-8
Latimore, 60 EP-3
Latrobe, 8338 WN-6
Latta Grv. WN-13
Lattimer, 600 EJ-8
Laughlintown, 950 WO-7
Laurel, 25 EQ-6
Laurel Lake, 300 EE-8
Laurel Mtn., 167 WO-7
Laurel Run, 500 EI-9
Laureldale, 3911 EN-9
Laurelton, 221 EK-3
Laurelville, 150 WO-6
Laurys Sta., 1243 EL-10
Lavansville, 150 WP-7
Lavelle, 742 EK-6
Laverock, 1100 ‡B-4
Lawn, 300 EO-6
Lawndale ‡C-6
Lawnton, 3813 ES-4
Lawrence, 540 WN-3
LAWRENCE CO., 91108 WI-2
Lawrence Pk., 3982 WC-4
Lawrenceville, 581 ED-3
Lawsonham, 50 WJ-6
Lawsville Ctr., 75 EE-9
Lawton, 85 EF-8
Le Raysville, 290 EE-7
Leaders Hts., 1200 WT-13
Leamersville, 80 WN-11
Lebanon, 25477 EN-6
LEBANON CO., 133568 EM-6
Leck Kill, 200 EL-5
Leckrone, 250 WQ-4
Lecontes Mills, 125 WJ-11
Lee Pk., 3600 EI-8
Leechburg, 2156 WL-5
Leeper, 200 WH-7
Lees Cross Roads, 200 EP-2
Leesburg, 100 WI-3
Leesport, 1918 EM-8
Leetsdale, 1218 WL-3
Lehigh, 100 EH-10
LEHIGH CO., 349497 EL-10
Lehighton, 5500 EK-9
Lehman, 250 EH-8
Leinbachs, 150 ES-11

*, †, ‡, §, ◊ See explanation under state title in this index.
County and parish names are listed in capital letters & boldface type.
Independent cities (not included in a county) are listed in italics.

Leisenring, 600......WP-5
Leith, 900......WP-5
Leithsville, 300......EM-11
Lemasters, 250......WQ-13
Lemon......EF-8
Lemont, 2270......WK-13
Lemont Furnace, 827......WP-5
Lemoyne, 4553......ET-3
Lenape, 200......EP-10
Lenhartsville, 165......EM-9
Lenoxville, 130......EF-10
Leola, 7214......EO-7
Leroy, 90......EF-5
Lester......‡G-2
Level Green, 4020......WN-5
Levittown, 52983......EO-13
Lewis Run, 617......WE-10
Lewisberry, 362......EO-4
Lewisburg, 5792......EJ-4
Lewistown, 8338......EL-1
Lewisville, 225......EQ-9
Liberty, 2551......‡M-8
Liberty, 249......EG-3
Liberty Cors., 100......EF-6
Library, 6000......‡N-5
Lickingville, 60......WH-7
Lightner, 1400......WR-13
Lightstreet, 1093......EJ-6
Ligonier, 1573......WN-7
Lilly, 968......WM-10
Lima, 2735......EP-11
Lime Ridge, 890......EJ-7
Limehill......EF-7
Limeport, 250......EM-11
Limerick, 800......EN-10
Limestone, 150......WI-7
Limestoneville, 70......EJ-5
Lincoln, 1072......‡M-8
Lincoln Hts., 300......WN-5
Lincoln Hill, 500......WO-2
Lincoln Pk., 1615......ET-11
Lincolnville, 96......WE-5
Lincolnway, 1900......WS-12
Linconia, 950......‡A-8
Linden, 270......EI-3
Linden, 100......WN-3
Linesville, 1040......WF-2
Linfield, 650......EO-10
Linglestown, 6334......EN-5
Linntown, 1489......EJ-4
Linwood, 3281......*B-10
Lionville, 6189......EP-10
Lippincott, 40......WP-3
Lisburn, 400......EO-4
Listie, 700......WP-8
Listonburg......WQ-7
Litchfield, 80......ED-6
Lithia Sprs., 90......EK-5
Lititz, 9369......EO-7
Little Cooley, 50......WF-4
Little Cors., 45......WF-3
Little Gap, 300......EK-10
Little Hope, 60......WD-5
Little Marsh, 80......EE-2
Little Meadows, 273......ED-7
Littlestown, 4434......EQ-3
Liverpool, 955......EM-4
Llewellyn, 800......EL-7
Llewellyn Cors......EC-8
Loag, 200......EO-9
Lobachsville......EM-9
Lock Haven, 9772......EI-2
Locke Mills......EL-1
Locust......WK-8
Locust Gap, 450......EK-6
Locust Run, 100......EM-3
Locustdale, 177......EK-7
Loganton, 468......EJ-2
Loganville, 1240......EQ-5
London......WI-3
London Grv., 250......EQ-9
Lone Pine, 50......WO-3
Long Pond, 900......EJ-10
Longfellow, 215......EM-1
Longstown, 100......WS-14
Longswamp, 300......EM-10
Loop, 60......WC-13
Lopez, 180......EG-7
Lorain, 759......WS-2
Lorane, 4236......EN-9
Lords Valley, 70......EH-12
Loretto, 1302......WM-10
Lost Creek, 500......EK-7
Lottsville, 100......WD-6
Lovejoy, 50......WL-8
Lovelton, 100......EG-7
Lover......WO-4
Lower Allen, 6694......ET-3
Lower Burrell, 11761......‡H-10
Lowville, 130......WD-5
Loyalsockville, 400......EH-4
Loyalton, 450......EM-5
Loysburg, 330......WO-11
Loysville, 200......EN-2
Lucerne Mines, 937......WM-7
Lucinda, 300......WH-7
Luciusboro, 100......WM-8
Ludlow, 500......WF-8
Lumber City, 76......WJ-10
Lumberville, 200......EM-12
Lundys Lane, 180......WE-2
Lurgan, 90......EO-1
Luthersburg, 325......WJ-9
Luxor, 750......WN-6
Luzerne, 2845......EH-9
LUZERNE CO., 320918......EH-8
Lycippus, 90......WN-6
LYCOMING CO., 116111......EH-3
Lykens, 1779......EM-5
Lyleville, 135......WL-10
Lynch......WG-8
Lyndell, 400......EP-9
Lyndon, 750......EP-7
Lyndora, 1300......WK-4
Lynn, 130......EF-8
Lynnport, 200......EL-9
Lynnville, 55......EL-9
Lynnwood, 1300......EB-7
Lyons, 478......EM-9
Macdonaldton, 130......WP-8
Mackeyville, 250......EJ-2
Macungie, 3074......EM-10
Maddensville......WO-13
Madera, 1000......WK-11
Madison, 397......WN-5
Madisonburg, 168......EK-1
Madisonville, 150......EH-10
Madley......WP-10
Mahaffey, 368......WK-9
Mahanoy City, 4162......EK-8
Maiden Creek, 200......EM-9
Mainesburg, 200......EF-4
Mainland, 2000......EN-11
Mainsville, 300......EP-1
Mainville, 132......EJ-6
Maitland, 357......EL-2
Malta......EL-4
Malvern, 2998......EP-10
Mammoth, 525......WO-6
Mamont......WM-6
Manatawny, 200......EN-9
Manchester, 2763......EP-5
Mandata, 60......EL-5
Manheim, 4858......EO-6
Manns Choice, 300......WP-10
Mannsville, 25......EM-3
Manor, 3239......WN-5
Manor Ridge, 1000......ES-8
Manorville, 410......WK-6
Mansfield, 3625......EE-3
Mantz, 300......EL-9
Maple Bch., 100......‡B-10
Maple Grv., 135......WJ-6
Maple Lake......EH-10
Mapledale, 200......WH-4
Mapleton, 441......WN-13
Mapletown, 130......WQ-4
Maplewood......EH-11
Maplewood Pk., 1700......‡F-1
Marble, 130......WH-6
Marchand, 90......WK-8
Marcus Hook, 2397......EQ-11
Margo Gdns., 300......‡A-10
Marianna, 494......WP-3
Mariasville......WI-5
Marienville, 3137......WG-8
Marietta, 2588......EP-6
Marion, 953......WQ-14
Marion Ctr., 451......WK-8
Marion Hts., 611......EK-6
Markelsville, 25......EM-3
Markes, 100......WQ-13
Marklesburg, 204......WN-12
Markleton, 40......WQ-7
Markleysburg, 284......WQ-6
Markton......WJ-8
Marlin, 661......EL-7
Mars, 1699......WL-4
Marsh......EO-9
Marsh Hill......EG-4
Marshallton, 1441......EK-6
Marshallton, 600......EP-10
Marshburg, 50......WE-9
Marshlands, 50......EF-1
Marstown, 150......EM-6
Martha Furnace, 25......WK-13
Marticville, 400......EP-7
Martin, 110......WQ-4
Martindale, 180......EO-8
Martindale, 140......WN-10
Martins Creek, 631......EK-12
Martinsburg, 1958......WN-11
Martinsville, 100......EP-6
Marwood, 60......WK-5
Marysville, 2534......EN-4
Masontown, 3450......WQ-4
Mastersonville, 185......EO-6
Masthope, 685......EG-12
Matamoras, 2469......EH-14
Mather, 737......WP-3
Mattawana, 276......WM-14
Mausdale, 75......EJ-5
Maxatawny, 250......EM-10
Mayburg......WG-7
Mayfield, 1807......EG-10
Mayport, 80......WJ-7
Maysville, 60......WM-6
Maysville......WH-2
Maytown, 3824......EO-6
Maytown......EO-4
Maze......EL-3
Mazeppa, 225......EJ-4
McAdoo, 2300......EK-8
McAlevys Fort, 70......WL-13
McAlisterville, 971......EL-3
McCartney, 70......WK-10
McClure, 941......EL-2
McConnellsburg, 1220......WP-13
McConnellstown, 1194......WM-12
McCoysville......EM-1
McCracken, 60......WQ-1
McCrea......EN-2
McDonald, 2149......WN-3
McElhattan, 598......EI-2
McEwensville, 279......EJ-5
McGees Mills, 100......WK-9
McGovern, 2742......WN-3
McGrann, 700......WK-6
McIntyre, 220......WL-7
McKean, 388......WD-3
MCKEAN CO., 43450......WF-10
McKeansburg, 163......EL-8
McKee, 200......WN-11
McKee Half Falls, 130......EL-4
McKees Rocks, 6104......WM-3
McKeesport, 19731......WN-4
McKinney......EO-1
McKnightstown, 226......EQ-2
McLane, 75......WD-3
McMichael, 50......EJ-11
McMurray, 4647......WN-3
McSherrystown, 3038......EQ-4
McVeytown, 342......WM-14
McVille......WL-5
Meadow Lands, 822......WN-3
Meadowbrook, 1000......‡A-5
Meadville, 13388......WF-3
Mechanics Grv., 120......EQ-8
Mechanicsburg, 8981......EO-4
Mechanicsville, 3100......EJ-6
Mechanicsville, 500......EN-12
Mechanicsville, 120......EA-2
Mechanicsville, 35......WI-7
Meckesville, 25......EJ-10
Mecks Corner......EN-3
Media, 5327......EP-11
Mehoopany, 350......EG-8
Meiserville, 100......EL-4
Melcroft, 250......WO-6
Melrose Pk., 6500......‡B-5
Mendenhall, 600......EQ-10
Menges Mills, 200......EQ-4
Menno, 80......WM-14
Mentcle, 100......WL-9
Mercer, 2002......WI-3
MERCER CO., 116638......WH-2
Mercersburg, 1561......WQ-13
Meridian, 3881......WK-4
Merion Sta., 700......‡D-3
Mertztown, 664......EM-10
Meshoppen, 563......EG-8
Metal, 100......WP-13
Mexico, 472......EM-2
Meyersdale, 2184......WQ-8
Middle Creek......EK-3
Middle Lancaster, 100......WK-3
Middle Spr., 80......EO-1
Middleburg, 1309......EK-4
Middleburg, 90......EJ-9
Middlebury Ctr., 200......EE-3
Middleport, 405......EL-8
Middlesex, 250......EO-3
Middletown, 8901......EO-5
Middletown, 7378......EA-5
Midland, 2635......WL-2
Midvale......EB-8
Midway, 913......WN-2
Mifflin, 642......EM-2
MIFFLIN CO., 46682......EK-2
Mifflinburg, 3540......EK-4
Mifflintown, 936......EM-2
Mifflinville, 1253......EJ-7
Milan, 300......EE-6
Milanville, 175......EF-12
Mildred, 200......EG-6
Milesburg, 1123......WJ-13
Milford, 1021......EH-13
Milford Sq., 897......EM-11
Mill City, 450......EG-9
Mill Creek, 328......WM-13
Mill Grv., 40......EK-7
Mill Hall, 1613......EI-2
Mill Run, 400......WP-6
Mill Run, 250......WM-11
Mill Vil., 412......WE-4
Millardsville, 100......EN-7
Millbach......EN-7
Millbourne, 1159......‡E-2
Milledgeville, 60......WG-4
Millersburg, 2557......EM-4
Millerstown, 673......EM-3
Millerstown......WH-6
Millersville, 8168......EP-7
Millerton, 316......ED-4
Millertown, 200......WP-6
Millheim, 904......EK-2
Millmont, 150......EK-3
Millport, 80......WE-12
Millrift, 170......EH-14
Mills, 125......WE-14
Millsboro, 666......WP-4
Milltown, 170......EP-10
Milltown......‡I-9
Millvale, 3744......‡J-6
Millville, 948......EI-6
Millwood, 566......WN-7
Milroy, 1498......EL-1
Milton, 7042......EJ-4
Milton Grv., 100......EO-6
Milwaukee......EA-11
Mineral Sprs., 300......WJ-11
Minersville, 4397......EL-7
Mingoville, 503......EJ-1
Minisink Hills, 350......EJ-12
Miquon, 300......‡B-2
Mocanaqua, 646......EI-8
Modena, 535......EP-9
Mogeetown, 1400......‡A-1
Mohnton, 3043......EN-8
Mohrsville, 383......EM-8
Monaca, 5737......WL-3
Monarch, 200......WP-5
Monessen, 7720......WO-4
Mongul, 60......EO-1
Monongahela, 4300......WO-4
Monroe, 90......WI-6
MONROE CO., 169842......EJ-11
Monroeton, 554......EF-6
Monroeville, 28386......WM-5
Mont Alto, 1705......EQ-1
Mont Clare, 1800......EO-10
Montandon, 903......EJ-4
Montdale, 400......EG-10
Montello, 50......ET-11
Monterey, 100......EO-7
Monterey......EQ-2
Montgomery, 1579......EI-4
MONTGOMERY CO., 799874......EN-10
Montgomery Ferry, 50......EM-4
Montgomeryville, 12624......EN-12
MONTOUR CO., 18267......EJ-5
Montoursville, 4615......EI-4
Montrose, 1617......EE-9
Montrose Hill, 1600......‡J-8
Monument, 150......WI-14
Moon, 1000......‡I-2
Moon Crest, 2100......‡I-3
Moon Run, 400......‡K-4
Mooresburg, 80......EJ-5
Moorestown, 250......EK-11
Moorheadville......WC-4
Moosic, 5719......EH-9
Morann, 400......WK-11
Moravia......WJ-2
Morgan, 800......WN-3
Morgantown, 826......EO-9
Morris, 250......EG-2
Morris Run, 400......EF-4
Morrisdale, 754......WJ-12
Morrisville, 8728......EO-14
Morrisville, 1265......WP-3
Morton, 2669......‡F-1
Moscow, 2026......EH-10
Moselem, 150......EM-9
Moselem Sprs., 70......EM-9
Mosgrove......WK-6
Moshannon, 281......WJ-13
Mosherville, 200......ED-4
Mosiertown, 35......WE-3
Mostoller, 30......WO-8
Mt. Aetna, 354......EM-7
Mt. Allen, 2000......EO-4
Mt. Alton......WE-10
Mt. Bethel, 650......EK-12
Mt. Braddock, 650......WP-5
Mt. Carmel, 5893......EK-6
Mt. Chestnut, 100......WK-4
Mt. Cobb, 1799......EH-10
Mt. Eagle, 103......WJ-14
Mt. Gretna, 196......EN-6
Mt. Holly Sprs., 2030......EO-3
Mt. Jackson, 300......WJ-2
Mt. Jewett, 919......WF-10
Mt. Joy, 7410......EO-6
Mt. Lebanon, 33100......‡L-5
Mt. Morris, 737......WQ-3
Mt. Nebo, 1500......‡I-4
Mt. Nebo, 300......EQ-7
Mt. Oliver, 3403......‡K-6
Mt. Penn, 3106......EN-9
Mt. Pleasant, 4454......WO-6
Mt. Pleasant, 200......EN-8
Mt. Pleasant, 65......EQ-3
Mt. Pleasant Mills, 464......EL-4
Mt. Pocono, 3170......EI-11
Mt. Royal, 150......EP-4
Mt. Union, 2447......WN-13
Mt. Union, 100......EP-2
Mt. Vernon, 2200......‡N-8
Mt. Vernon......EQ-8
Mt. Wilson, 200......EN-6
Mt. Wolf, 1393......EP-5
Mt. Zion, 350......EN-6
Mt. Zion, 100......ES-1
Mt. Zion......EA-10
Mountain Top, 10982......EI-9
Mountainhome, 1182......EI-11
Mountville, 2802......EP-6
Mowersville, 40......EO-1
Muddy Creek Forks, 20......EQ-6
Muhlenberg, 200......EI-7
Muhlenberg Pk., 1420......ES-12
Muir, 451......EL-6
Mummasburg, 200......EQ-2
Muncy, 2477......EI-5
Muncy Valley, 270......EH-6
Munderf, 30......WH-8
Mundys Corner, 1651......WM-9
Munhall, 11406......WM-4
Munson, 275......WJ-12
Munster, 300......WM-10
Murdocksville, 100......WM-2
Murrell......EO-7
Murrysville, 20079......WM-5
Muse, 2504......WN-3
Myerstown, 3062......EN-7
Myobeach, 65......EG-8
Myoma, 100......WK-4
Myrtle......WD-12
Naginey, 120......EL-1
Nanticoke, 10465......EI-8
Nantmeal Vil., 250......EO-10
Nanty Glo, 2734......WM-9
Narberth, 4282......EP-12
Nashville, 200......EP-4
Nassau Vil., 1500......‡G-1
Natrona Hts., 2800......WL-5
Nauvoo, 40......EG-3
Nazareth, 5746......EL-11
Nectarine......WI-4
Needmore, 170......WQ-12
Neelyton, 80......WO-13
Neffs, 650......EL-10
Neffsville, 1000......EO-7
Neiltown, 25......WF-6
Nelson, 300......ED-3
Nemacolin, 937......WP-4
Nescopeck, 1583......EJ-7
Nesquehoning, 3349......EK-9
New Albany, 356......EG-6
New Alexandria, 560......WM-6
New Baltimore, 180......WP-9
New Beaver, 1502......WK-2
New Bedford, 925......WI-2
New Berlin, 873......EK-4
New Berlinville, 1368......EN-10
New Bethlehem, 989......WJ-7
New Bloomfield, 1247......EM-3
New Boston, 230......EK-7
New Br.ville, 320......EP-6
New Brighton, 6025......WK-2
New Britain, 3152......EN-12
New Buena Vista, 80......WP-9
New Buffalo, 129......EM-4
New Castle, 23273......WJ-2
New Centerville, 133......WP-7
New Columbia, 1013......EJ-4
New Columbus, 227......EI-7
New Cumberland, 7277......EO-4
New Danville, 500......ET-8
New Derry, 800......WN-7
New Eagle, 2184......WO-4
New Enterprise, 300......WO-11
New Era, 35......EF-7
New Florence, 689......WN-8
New Franklin, 275......EQ-1
New Freedom, 4464......EQ-5
New Freeport, 112......WQ-2
New Galilee, 379......WK-2
New Gdn., 300......*B-6
New Geneva, 150......WQ-4
New Germantown, 150......EN-1
New Grenada, 90......WO-12
New Hamburg, 75......WH-2
New Holland, 5378......EO-8
New Hope, 2528......EN-13
New Jerusalem, 649......EM-9
New Kensington, 13116......WL-5
New Kingstown, 495......EO-3
New Lebanon, 188......WH-4
New Lexington, 50......WP-7
New London, 350......EQ-9
New Mahoning, 170......EK-9
New Market, 816......ET-3
New Milford, 868......EE-9
New Millport, 130......WK-10
New Oxford, 1783......EQ-4
New Paris, 186......WO-10
New Pk., 300......EQ-6
New Philadelphia, 1085......EL-8
New Providence, 300......EP-7
New Richmond......WF-4
New Ringgold, 276......EL-8
New Salem, 724......EP-5
New Salem, 579......WP-4
New Schaefferstown, 223......EM-7
New Sheffield, 2000......WL-2
New Stanton, 2173......WN-5
New Tripoli, 898......EL-9
New Vernon, 25......WH-3
New Washington, 59......WK-9
New Wilmington, 2466......WI-2
Newberrytown, 150......EO-5
Newburg, 350......WM-11
Newburg, 336......EO-1
Newburg, 250......EL-11
Newburg, 92......WK-10
Newchester, 225......EP-3
Newcomer......WP-5
Newell, 541......WO-4
Newfoundland, 650......EH-11
Newkirk......EK-8
Newmanstown, 2478......EN-7
Newmansville, 40......WH-7
Newport, 1574......EM-3
Newportville, 750......‡A-9
Newry, 270......WN-11
Newton Hamilton, 205......WN-13
Newtown, 2248......EN-13
Newtown, 1400......EB-7
Newtown, 243......EL-7
Newtown Sq., 11300......EP-11
Newville, 1326......EO-2
Newville, 350......EO-5
Niantic, 100......EN-10
Nicholson, 767......EF-9
Nickleville......WH-5
Nicktown, 200......WL-9
Niles......WH-4
Niles Valley, 50......EE-2
Ninepoints, 120......EP-8
Nineveh, 125......WP-2
Nineveh, 100......WH-6
Nisbet, 550......EI-3
Nittany, 658......EJ-1
Noll Acres, 1050......ET-1
Nolo, 40......WM-8
Nordmont, 35......EH-6
Normal Sq., 600......EK-9
Normalville, 700......WP-6
Norristown, 34324......EO-11
Norrisville, 50......WF-3
N. Apollo, 1297......WL-6
N. Belle Vernon, 1971......WO-4
N. Bend, 800......WH-14
N. Bingham, 50......WD-14
N. Braddock, 4857......‡L-8
N. Catasauqua, 2849......EA-3
N. Charleroi, 1313......WO-4
North East, 4294......WC-5
N. Fork, 30......ED-1
N. Hills, 3000......‡A-4
N. Irwin, 846......WN-5
N. Liberty, 100......WI-3
N. Mountain, 500......EH-6
N. Oakland......WJ-5
N. Orwell, 100......EE-7
North Point, 75......WK-8
N. Rome, 65......EE-6
N. Springfield, 130......WD-2
N. Towanda, 400......EF-6
N. Versailles, 10200......‡L-8
N. Wales, 3229......EO-11
N. Warren, 1934......WE-8
N. Washington, 500......WM-5
N. Washington, 200......WJ-5
N. York, 1914......EP-5
Northampton, 9926......EL-10
NORTHAMPTON CO., 297735......EK-11
Northern Cambria, 3835......WL-9
Northumberland, 3804......EK-5
NORTHUMBERLAND CO., 94528......EK-5
Northvue, 700......WJ-4
Northwood, 296......WL-12
Norvelt, 948......WO-6
Norwood, 5890......‡F-2
Nottingham, 3000......‡A-8
Nottingham, 200......EQ-8
Nowrytown, 150......WM-6
Noxen, 633......EH-8
Nuangola, 679......EI-8
Numidia, 244......EK-6
NuMine, 300......WK-7
Nuremberg, 434......EJ-7
Nyesville, 75......EP-1
Oak Forest, 60......WQ-3
Oak Grv., 200......WN-7
Oak Hall......WT-7
Oak Pk., 700......EN-11
Oakdale, 1459......WM-3
Oakland, 1600......WS-2
Oakland, 1569......WJ-2
Oakland, 616......EE-10
Oakland Mills, 110......EL-2
Oakleigh, 1000......ES-4
Oakmont, 6303......WM-4
Oaks, 850......EO-11
Oakville, 150......EO-2
Oberlin, 588......ET-4
Ogdensburg, 75......EG-4
Ogletown, 150......WO-9
Ohiopyle, 59......WQ-6
Ohioville, 3533......WL-2
Ohl, 75......WJ-7
Oil City, 10557......WG-5
Oklahoma, 809......WL-6
Oklahoma, 782......WI-9
Olanta, 100......WK-10
Old Boston, 200......EC-9
Old Concord, 30......WP-2
Old Forge, 8313......EH-9
Old Port, 90......EM-2
Oley, 1282......EN-9
Oliphant Furnace, 250......WQ-5
Oliveburg, 150......WJ-8
Oliver, 2535......WP-5
Olney......‡C-5
Olyphant, 5151......EG-10
Oneida, 200......EK-8
Oneida, 100......WJ-4
Ono, 300......EN-6
Opp......EI-5
Orange, 300......EH-9
Orangeville, 508......EJ-6
Orbisonia, 428......WN-13
Orchard Bch., 125......WC-5
Orchard Hills, 1952......WL-6
Ore Hill, 95......WN-11
Ore Valley, 200......WT-14
Orefield, 750......EB-1
Oregon, 250......ET-10
Oregon Hill, 100......EG-2
Oreland, 5678......‡A-4
Oriental, 100......EL-4
Oriole, 100......EI-3
Ormrod, 300......EA-2
Ormsby, 100......WE-10
Orrstown, 262......EP-1
Orrtanna, 173......EQ-2
Orson, 125......EE-10
Orviston, 95......WI-14
Orwell, 100......EE-7
Orwigsburg, 3099......EL-8
Orwin, 314......EM-6
Osceola, 400......ED-2
Osceola Mills, 1141......WK-11
Osgood, 40......WG-2
Osterburg, 250......WO-10
Osterhout, 30......EG-9
Oswayo, 139......WE-13
Ottsville, 250......EM-12
Oval, 361......EI-3
Overbrook......‡D-3
Overlook, 200......ES-9
Overlook Hts., 1200......WS-5
Overton, 85......EG-6
Overview, 50......ER-2
Oxford, 5077......EQ-8
Packerton, 200......EK-9
Paint, 1023......WN-9
Paintersville......EL-2
Paintertown, 120......‡L-10
Paisley, 100......WQ-4
Palm, 370......EM-10
Palmer Hts., 3762......EL-11
Palmerton, 5414......EK-10
Palmyra, 7320......EN-6
Palo Alto, 1032......EL-7
Panic, 80......WJ-8
Paoli, 5575......EP-11
Paradise, 1129......EP-8
Paradise, 250......EM-6
Paradise Valley......EI-11
Pardoe, 50......WI-3
Paris, 732......WM-1
Park Forest Vil., 9660......WS-5
Park Hills, 2500......WT-5
Park View, 1300......‡J-7
Park Way Manor, 2000......EB-2
Parker, 840......WI-5
Parker Ford, 800......EO-10
Parkesburg, 3593......EP-9
Parkhill, 300......WR-2
Parkside, 2328......EQ-11
Parkstown, 175......WS-2
Parkville, 6706......EQ-4
Parryville, 525......EK-10
Patchinville, 30......WK-9
Patterson Hts., 636......WK-2
Patton, 1769......WL-10
Paupack, 600......EH-11
Pavia, 90......WN-10
Paxinos, 500......EK-6
Paxtang, 1561......ES-4
Paxton, 100......EL-4
Paxtonia, 5412......ER-4
Paxtonville, 265......EK-3
Peach Glen, 100......EP-3
Pearl, 50......WH-4
Pecks Pond......EH-12
Pen Argyl, 3595......EK-11
Pen Mar, 929......ER-2
Penbrook, 3008......ES-3
Penfield, 650......WI-10
Penn, 475......WN-5
Penn Hall, 60......EK-1
Penn Hills......WM-4
Penn Lake Pk., 308......EI-9
Penn Pines, 650......‡F-2
Penn Run, 250......WL-8
Penn Valley, 6000......‡C-2
Penn Wynne, 5697......‡D-2
Penndel, 2328......EO-13
Pennline, 40......WF-2
Penns Creek, 715......EK-3
Penns Pk., 500......EN-13
Penns Woods, 2600......‡M-9
Pennsburg, 3843......EN-10
Pennsbury Vil., 661......‡K-4
Pennsdale, 110......EI-5
Pennside, 4215......ET-13
Pennside, 35......WE-2
Pennsville, 350......EK-10
Pennsville, 200......WO-6
Pennsylvania Furnace, 150......WL-13
Pennwyn, 780......ET-12
Penowa, 20......WN-1
Penryn, 1024......EO-7
Pequea, 300......EQ-7
Perdix, 90......EN-4
Perkasie, 8511......EN-11
Perkiomen Hts., 70......EN-10
Perrine Cors......WH-4
PERRY CO., 45969......EN-3
Perryopolis, 1784......WO-5
Perryville, 180......WI-5
Perryville, 70......WM-6
Perryville, 25......EH-3
Petersburg, 480......WM-12
Petrolia, 212......WJ-5
Philadelphia, 1526006......EP-12
PHILADELPHIA CO., 1526006......EO-12
Philipsburg, 2770......WK-12
Phillips, 225......WP-5
Phillipston, 45......WJ-6
Phillipsville......WD-4
Phoenixville, 16440......EO-10
Picture Rocks, 678......EH-5
Pigeon, 20......WG-8
PIKE CO., 57369......EH-12
Pilgrim Gdns., 1650......‡E-1
Pillow, 298......EL-5
Pine, 80......EI-2
Pine Bank, 20......WQ-2
Pine Flats, 30......WL-8
Pine Glen, 190......WJ-12
Pine Grv., 2186......EM-6
Pine Grv. Furnace......EP-3
Pine Grv. Mills, 1502......WL-13
Pine Summit, 55......EI-6
Pinecroft, 100......WM-11
Pineville, 950......EN-13
Piney Fork, 400......‡N-6
Pinola, 20......EP-1
Pipersville, 600......EM-12
Pitcairn, 3294......‡K-9
Pitman, 300......EL-6
Pittsburgh, 305704......WM-4
Pittsfield, 500......WE-7
Pittston, 7739......EH-9
Pittsville, 35......WH-5
Plainfield, 399......EO-2
Plains, 4335......EB-8
Plainsville, 350......EB-8
Platea, 430......WD-3
Pleasant Gap, 2879......WK-14
Pleasant Grv., 50......WO-2
Pleasant Hall, 150......EP-1
Pleasant Hills, 8268......‡M-6
Pleasant Mount, 125......EF-11
Pleasant Union......WQ-9
Pleasant Unity, 600......WN-6
Pleasant Valley, 200......EM-11
Pleasantville, 892......WG-6
Pleasureville, 1200......WR-13
Plum, 27126......WM-5
Plumer, 150......WG-5
Plumsteadville, 2637......EN-12
Plumville, 307......WK-7
Plymouth, 5951......EI-8
Plymouth Meeting, 6177......‡A-2
Pocahontas, 125......WQ-8
Pocono Lake, 750......EI-10
Pocono Mnr., 300......EI-11
Pocono Pines, 1409......EI-11
Pocono Summit, 1500......EI-11
Point......WO-10
Pt. Marion, 1159......WQ-4
Pt. Pleasant, 800......EM-12
Poland, 75......WQ-4
Polk, 816......WH-4
Pomeroy, 401......EP-9
Pond Bank, 200......EQ-1
Pond Eddy, 50......EG-13
Pond Hill, 200......EI-8
Port Allegany, 2157......WE-11
Port Carbon, 1889......EL-7
Port Clinton, 326......EL-8
Port Griffith, 1350......EB-9
Port Matilda, 606......WK-12
Port Royal, 925......EM-2
Port Trevorton, 769......EL-4
Port Vue, 3798......‡M-8
Portage, 2638......WN-10
Porter, 25......WJ-7
Porters Sideling, 100......EQ-4
Portersville, 235......WJ-3
Portland, 519......EJ-12
Portland Mills, 40......WH-9
Potter Brook, 200......EE-1
POTTER CO., 17457......EE-1
Potters Mills, 180......EK-1
Pottersdale, 20......WI-12
Potterville, 75......EE-7
Potts Grv., 140......EJ-5
Pottstown, 22377......EN-10
Pottsville, 14324......EL-7
Powell, 150......EF-6
Powells Valley, 600......EM-4
Powys, 100......EH-3
Prescottville, 100......WJ-9
President, 100......WG-6
Preston, 240......EB-6
Preston Pk., 200......EE-11
Pricetown, 180......EM-9
Primos, 900......‡F-2
Primrose, 600......EL-7
Princeton, 150......WJ-3
Pringle, 979......EA-8
Prittstown......WO-6
Proctor, 50......EH-5
Progress, 9765......ES-3
Prompton, 250......EG-11
Prospect, 1169......WJ-4
Prospect Pk., 6454......EP-11
Prospect Pk., 327......WG-12
Prospectville, 550......EO-12
Prosperity, 175......WO-2
Pulaski, 300......WI-2
Punxsutawney, 5962......WJ-8
Purcell, 25......WQ-11
Purchase Line, 40......WL-8
Putneyville, 140......WJ-7
Puzzletown......WN-10
Quakake, 300......EK-8
Quaker Hills......ET-8
Quaker Lake, 70......ED-8
Quakertown, 8979......EM-11
Quarryville, 2576......EP-7
Quecreek, 150......WO-8
Queen, 100......WN-10
Queens Run, 50......EI-2
Quentin, 594......EN-6
Quicktown, 50......EH-10
Quiggleville, 50......EH-3
Quincy, 400......EQ-1
Radnor......‡C-1
Railroad, 278......EQ-5
Rainsburg, 133......WP-10
Ralston, 400......EG-4
Ramey, 451......WK-11
Ramsey, 45......EH-2
Rankin, 2122......‡K-7
Ransom, 250......EH-9
Rathmel, 150......WI-9
Raubsville, 1088......EL-12
Rauchtown, 726......EI-3
Ravine, 662......EM-6
Rawlinsville, 150......EQ-7
Raymilton......WH-4
Raymond......WE-13
Rea, 50......WN-2
Reading, 88082......EN-9
Reagantown, 70......WO-5
Reamstown, 3361......EO-8
Rebersburg, 494......EJ-2
Rebuck, 150......EL-5
Rector, 400......WO-7
Red Br., 200......EP-1
Red Cross, 70......EL-5
Red Hill, 2383......EN-10
Red Hill, 100......WA-12
Red Lion, 6373......EP-6
Red Rock, 30......EH-7
Redclyffe, 20......WH-8
Reeders, 350......EJ-11
Reeds Gap, 30......EM-1
Reedsville, 641......EL-1
Reels Cors., 25......WO-9
Reese, 80......WM-11
Reesedale, 50......WJ-6
Refton, 298......EP-7
Rehrersburg, 319......EM-7
Reidsburg, 40......WI-6
Reiffton, 4178......ET-13
Reinerton, 424......EL-6
Reinholds, 1803......EN-8
Reistville, 100......EN-7
Renfrew, 350......WK-4
Renovo, 1228......WH-14
Republic, 1096......WP-4
Revere, 500......EM-12
Revloc, 570......WM-9
Rew, 199......WE-10
Rexford, 100......EF-2
Rexis, 45......WM-8
Reynoldsville, 2759......WI-9
Rheems, 1598......EO-6
Rices, 463......WP-4
Riceville, 68......WE-5
Rich Hill, 50......EM-11
Richardsville, 40......WI-8
Richboro, 6563......EO-13
Richfield, 549......EL-3
Richland, 1519......EN-7
Richlandtown, 1327......EM-11
Richmond, 100......EK-12
Richmond Furnace, 50......WP-13
Richvale, 35......WN-14
Riddlesburg, 300......WO-11
Ridgebury, 170......ED-5
Ridgeview, 800......ER-4
Ridgewood, 300......EB-9
Ridgway, 4078......WH-9
Ridley Farms, 1500......‡F-1
Ridley Pk., 7002......‡G-1
Riegelsville, 868......EL-12
Rillton, 900......WN-5
Rimer, 40......WJ-6
Rimersburg, 951......WJ-6
Rinely......EQ-6
Ringgold, 225......WJ-7
Ringtown, 818......EK-7
River View Pk., 3380......ES-12
Riverside, 1932......EJ-5
Riverside, 381......WT-2
Rixford, 400......WE-10
Roaring Branch, 100......EG-4
Roaring Creek, 156......EK-6
Roaring Spr., 2585......WN-11
Robertsdale, 240......WO-12
Robesonia, 2061......EN-8
Robinson, 614......WM-7
Rochester, 3657......WL-2
Rochester Mills, 2802......WK-8
Rock, 60......EM-7
Rock Glen, 300......EJ-7
Rockhill, 371......WO-13
Rockingham, 60......WO-9
Rockland, 30......WH-5
Rockledge, 2543......EO-12
Rockport, 85......EJ-9
Rockspring......WL-13
Rockton, 200......WJ-10
Rockville, 170......WR-4
Rockville, 85......EN-4
Rockville......WL-6
Rockwood, 890......WP-7
Roedersville, 200......EL-7
Rogersville, 249......WP-2
Rogertown, 140......WE-8
Rohrerstown, 1200......ES-8
Rohrsburg, 145......EI-6
Rome, 441......EE-7
Ronco, 256......WP-4
Roscoe, 812......WO-4
Rose Pt., 90......WJ-3
Rose Valley, 913......EP-11
Rosebud, 450......WK-10
Rosecrans......EJ-2
Roseglen, 110......EN-3
Rosemont......‡C-1
Roses, 140......WG-8
Roseto, 1567......EK-12
Roseville, 189......EE-4
Roseville, 150......WI-8
Roseville, 100......EP-4
Roslyn, 10000......‡A-5
Rossiter, 646......WK-8
Rossland, 60......EK-11
Rosslyn Farms, 427......‡K-4
Rossmoyne, 1100......ET-2
Rote, 507......EJ-2
Rothsville, 3044......EO-7
Roulette, 779......WF-12
Round Top, 115......WT-9
Rouseville, 523......WG-5
Rouzerville, 917......EQ-1
Rowes Run, 564......WP-4
Rowland, 200......EG-12
Roxbury, 275......EO-1
Roxbury, 50......WP-8
Royal, 100......EF-10
Royalton, 907......EO-5
Royer, 45......WM-11
Royersford, 4752......EO-10
Ruff Creek......WP-3
Ruffs Dale, 800......WO-5
Rummel, 600......WO-9
Rummerfield, 35......EF-7
Runville, 250......WJ-13
Rupert, 183......EJ-6
Ruppsville, 400......EC-1
Rural Ridge, 1000......WL-4
Rural Valley, 876......WK-7
Rush, 100......EF-8
Rushland, 350......EN-13
Rushville, 45......EF-8
Russell, 1408......WE-8
Russell City, 60......WG-9
Russell Hill......EG-8
Russellton, 1440......WL-4
Russellville, 125......EQ-8
Russellville......WN-11
Rutherford, 4303......ES-4
Rutledge, 784......‡F-1
Rydal, 1800......‡A-5
Ryde, 70......WM-14
Rye......EQ-5
Ryerson Sta., 80......WP-2
Ryot, 30......WO-10
Sabinsville, 300......EE-1
Sabula, 200......WI-10
Sackett......WG-9
Sacramento, 300......EL-6
Saddle Brook, 1160......EC-2
Sadsburyville, 700......EP-9
Saegersville, 120......EL-10
Saegertown, 997......WF-3
Safe Hbr., 150......EP-7
Sagamore, 450......WK-7
Saginaw, 200......EP-5
St. Augustine, 20......WL-10
St. Benedict, 450......WL-9
St. Boniface, 120......WL-10
St. Clair, 3004......EL-7
St. Clairsville, 78......WO-10
St. George, 50......WI-5
St. Johns, 300......EJ-8
St. Joseph, 150......EE-8
St. Lawrence, 1809......EN-9
St. Lawrence, 40......WL-10
St. Marys, 13070......WH-10
St. Michael, 408......WN-9
St. Paul, 75......WQ-8
St. Peters, 400......EO-9
St. Petersburg, 400......WI-5
St. Thomas, 900......WP-13
Salem, 150......EK-4
Salem, 30......WG-2
Salemville, 50......WO-11
Salina, 500......WM-6
Salisbury, 727......WQ-8
Salix, 1149......WN-9
Salladasburg, 238......EI-3
Salona, 250......EJ-2
Saltillo, 346......WO-12
Saltsburg, 873......WM-6
Salunga, 2695......EO-6
Saluvia......WP-12
Sanatoga, 8378......EN-10
Sand Bch., 300......EN-5
Sand Hill, 2496......EN-6
Sandts Eddy......EK-12
Sandy, 1429......WI-9
Sandy Creek......‡J-8
Sandy Hollow, 55......WJ-6
Sandy Lake, 659......WH-3
Sandy Ridge, 407......WK-12
Sandy Run, 60......EJ-9
Sandy Valley, 40......WI-9
Sandyville, 25......EI-12
Sankertown, 675......WM-10
Santiago, 400......WM-2
Sarver, 300......WL-5
Sassamansville, 350......EN-10
Satterfield......EG-6
Saulsburg......WL-13
Saville, 20......EM-2
Saxonburg, 1525......WK-5
Saxton, 736......WO-11
Saybrook......WF-8
Saylorsburg, 1126......EK-11
Sayre, 5587......ED-6
Scalp Level, 778......WN-9
Scandia, 25......WE-8
Scarlets Mill, 100......EO-9
Scenery Hill, 600......WO-3
Schaefferstown, 941......EN-7
Schellsburg, 338......WP-10
Schenley, 55......WL-5
Scherersville, 100......EB-2
Schnecksville, 2935......EL-10
Schoeneck, 1056......EN-7
Schoenersville, 400......EA-4
School Lane Hills, 1840......ES-8
Schubert, 249......EM-7
Schuster Hts., 75......WL-5
SCHUYLKILL CO., 148289......EM-7
Schuylkill Haven, 5437......EL-7
Sciota, 700......EJ-11
Scotch Hill......WH-7
Scotland, 1395......EP-1
Scotrun, 650......EJ-11
Scottdale, 4384......WO-5
Scottsville, 2400......‡H-2
Scranton, 76089......EH-10
Scullton......WP-7
Seanor, 130......WO-9
Searights, 250......WP-4
Sebring, 30......EG-3
Secane, 1700......‡F-1
Seelyville, 300......EG-11
Seidersville, 250......EB-4
Seipstown, 30......EL-10
Seisholtzville, 100......EM-10
Seitzland, 70......EQ-5
Selinsgrove, 5654......EK-4
Sellersville, 4249......EN-11
Seminole, 250......WJ-7
Seneca, 1065......WH-5
Sergeant, 40......WF-9
Seven Fields, 2887......WL-3
Seven Sprs., 26......WP-7
Seven Stars......EL-3
Seven Stars......EQ-2
Seven Valleys, 517......EQ-5
Seward, 495......WM-8
Sewickley, 3827......WM-3
Sewickley Hts., 810......‡H-3
Sewickley Hills, 639......WL-3
Shade Gap, 105......WO-13
Shado-wood Vil., 350......WL-7
Shady Grv., 280......EQ-1
Shaffer, 120......WI-9
Shafton, 250......‡M-10
Shamokin, 7374......EK-6
Shamokin Dam, 1686......EK-5
Shanesville, 70......EN-10
Shanksville, 237......WP-8
Shannondale, 75......WJ-7
Sharon, 14038......WI-2
Sharon Ctr., 30......WE-12
Sharon Hill, 5697......‡F-2
Sharpsburg, 3446......WM-4
Sharpsville, 4415......WH-2
Shartlesville, 455......EM-8
Shavertown, 2019......EA-8
Shawmut......WH-9
Shawnee on Delaware, 400......EJ-12
Shawtown, 600......‡M-10
Shawville, 100......WJ-11
Shay......WL-6
Sheakleyville, 142......WG-3
Sheffield, 1132......WF-8
Shehawken, 40......EE-11
Shellsville, 200......EN-5
Shelly, 125......EM-11
Shelocta, 130......WL-7
Shenandoah, 5071......EK-7
Shenandoah Hts., 1233......EK-7
Shenango, 80......WH-2
Shepherd Hills, 2030......EC-1
Shepherdstown, 200......EO-4
Sheppton, 239......EK-8
Sherman, 100......ED-11
Shermans Dale, 120......EN-3
Shermansville, 50......WF-2
Sherrett, 125......WJ-6
Sheshequin, 150......EE-6
Shickshinny, 838......EI-7
Shillington, 5273......EN-8
Shiloh, 11218......EP-5
Shimerville, 130......EM-10
Shimpstown, 80......WQ-13
Shindle, 70......EL-2
Shinglehouse, 1127......WD-12
Shingletown, 150......WK-13
Shintown, 75......WH-13
Shippensburg, 5492......EP-1
Shippenville, 480......WI-6
Shippingport, 214......WL-2
Shiremanstown, 1569......EO-4
Shirleysburg, 150......WN-13
Shoemakers......EJ-12
Shoemakersville, 1378......EM-8
Shohola, 160......EG-13
Shrader, 100......EL-1
Shrewsbury, 3823......EQ-5
Shumans, 140......EJ-7
Shunk, 45......EG-5
Siddonsburg, 110......EO-4
Sidman, 431......WN-9
Sigel, 250......WH-8
Siglerville, 106......EL-1
Silkworth, 820......EH-8
Silvara, 80......EF-7
Silver Lake, 150......EE-8
Silver Spr., 300......EP-6
Silverdale, 871......EN-11
Simpson, 1275......EG-10
Sinking Spr., 4008......EN-8
Sinnemahoning, 350......WH-12
Sipesville, 350......WO-8
Sizerville, 35......WG-12
Skelp, 60......WL-11
Skinners Eddy, 40......EF-7
Skippack, 3758......EN-11
Skytop, 200......EI-11
Slate Lick, 150......WK-5
Slate Run, 60......EG-2
Slatedale, 455......EL-10
Slateford, 250......EJ-12
Slatington, 4232......EL-10
Slickville, 388......WM-6
Sligo, 720......WI-6
Slippery Rock, 3625......WJ-4
Slocum Cors., 150......EI-8
Slovan, 555......WN-2
Smethport, 1655......WE-11
Smicksburg, 46......WK-7
Smithfield, 4180......WM-12
Smithfield, 875......WQ-4
Smithport, 100......WK-9
Smithton, 399......WO-5
Smithville......EP-7
Smock, 583......WP-5
Smoke Run, 150......WK-11
Smoketown, 357......EP-7
Smullton, 125......EJ-2
Snow Shoe, 765......WJ-13
Snowden, 200......‡N-6
SNYDER CO., 39702......EL-4
Snyders, 90......EL-9
Snydersburg, 100......WH-7
Snydersville, 150......EJ-11
Snydertown, 339......EK-5
Somers Lane, 300......ED-3
Somerset, 6277......WP-8
SOMERSET CO., 77742......WP-8
Somerton......‡A-7
Sonestown, 200......EH-6
Soudersburg, 540......EP-8
Souderton, 6618......EN-11
S. Altoona......WB-13
S. Bend, 40......WL-6
S. Bethlehem, 481......WJ-7
S. Bradford, 150......WE-10
S. Canaan, 250......EG-11
S. Coatesville, 1303......EP-9
S. Connellsville, 1970......WP-5
S. Fork, 928......WN-9
S. Gibson, 175......EF-10
S. Greensburg, 2117......WN-6
S. Heights, 475......WL-3
S. Lakemont, 1100......WB-13
S. Montrose, 400......EE-9
S. Mountain, 600......EQ-2
S. New Castle, 709......WJ-2
S. Philipsburg, 410......WK-12
S. Pottstown, 2081......EN-10
S. Renovo, 439......WH-14
S. Sterling, 150......EH-11
S. Tamaqua, 200......EK-8
S. Temple, 1424......ER-13
S. Towanda, 250......EF-6
S. Uniontown, 1360......WP-5
S. Waverly, 1027......ED-6
S. Williamsport, 6379......EI-4
Southampton, 11500......EO-12
Southmont, 2284......WN-8
Southview, 276......WN-3
Southwest, 600......WO-6
Southwest Greensburg, 2155......WN-6
Sparta......WP-2
Spartansburg, 305......WE-5
Speers, 1154......WO-4
Spinnerstown, 1826......EM-11
Sporting Hill, 300......EO-6
Spraggs, 30......WQ-3
Sprankle Mills, 60......WJ-8
Spring Church, 450......WL-6
Spring City, 3323......EO-10
Spring Creek, 100......WE-6
Spring Gdn., 45......EI-4
Spring Glen, 300......EL-5
Spring Grv., 2167......EQ-4
Spring Hill, 839......WN-10
Spring House, 3804......EO-12
Spring Mills, 268......EK-1
Spring Mount, 2259......EN-11
Spring Mount, 75......WL-12
Spring Run, 350......WO-14
Springboro, 477......WE-2
Springdale, 3405......WM-5
Springfield, 23677......‡E-1
Springfield......EE-5
Springhope, 50......WO-10
Springmont, 724......ET-11
Springs, 300......WQ-7
Springtown, 750......EM-11
Springvale, 120......EQ-6
Springville, 400......EF-8
Sproul, 250......WN-10
Spruce Creek, 90......WL-12
Spruce Hill, 40......EM-2
Spry, 4891......WT-14
Stafore Estates, 1200......EA-4
Stahlstown, 300......WO-7
Standing Stone, 60......EF-7
Stanton, 70......WJ-8
Star Jct., 616......WO-5
Starbrick, 522......WE-7
Starford, 250......WL-8
Starkville......EG-9
Starlight, 135......EE-11
Starr......WG-7
Starrucca, 173......EE-10
Starview, 100......EP-5
State College, 42034......WK-13
State Hill, 40......EN-8
State Line, 2709......WQ-14
Stateline, 20......WC-5
Steamburg......WF-2
Steel City, 650......EB-5
Steelstown, 100......EN-6
Steelton, 5990......EO-4
Steinsburg, 100......EM-11
Sterling, 150......EH-11
Sterling Run, 120......WH-12
Sterrettania......WD-3
Stevens, 612......EO-8
Stevensville, 250......EF-7
Stewartstown, 2089......EQ-6
Stewartsville, 700......‡M-9
Stickney......WD-9
Stifflertown, 120......WL-9
Stiles, 1113......EA-2
Stillwater, 209......EI-7
Stiltz, 50......ER-5
Stockdale, 502......WO-4
Stockertown, 927......EK-11
Stoddartsville, 130......EI-10
Stone Church, 150......EK-12
Stoneboro, 1051......WH-3
Stoneham, 250......WE-8
Stonerstown, 376......WO-11
Stonington, 100......EK-5
Stony Creek Mills, 1045......ET-13
Stony Run, 225......EL-9
Stonybrook, 2384......EP-5
Stonyfork, 150......EF-2
Stormstown, 2366......WK-12
Stormville......EJ-11
Stoufferstown, 400......EP-1
Stoughstown, 75......EO-2
Stoverstown, 250......EQ-5
Stowe, 3695......EN-10
Stowell, 60......EG-7
Stoystown, 355......WO-8
Strabane, 1100......WN-3
Strafford, 4500......EP-11
Strasburg, 2809......EP-7
Strattanville, 550......WI-7
Strausstown, 342......EM-7
Strawberry Ridge, 30......EJ-5
Strinestown, 250......EO-5
Strodes Mills, 757......EM-1
Strongstown, 400......WM-8
Stroudsburg, 5567......EJ-12
Studa, 100......WN-2
Stump Creek, 300......WJ-9
Sturgeon, 1710......WM-3
Suedberg, 200......EM-6
Sugar Grv., 614......WD-7
Sugar Hill, 60......WI-9
Sugar Notch, 989......EI-8
Sugar Run, 100......EF-7
Sugarcreek, 5294......WH-4
SULLIVAN CO., 6428......EH-6
Summer Hill, 350......EJ-7
Summerdale, 800......ER-2
Summerhill, 490......WN-9
Summerville, 528......WI-7
Summit, 250......WM-10
Summit Hill, 3034......EK-9
Summit Lawn, 420......EC-3
Summit Mills, 175......WQ-8
Summit Sta., 174......EM-7
Sunbrook, 300......WC-12
Sunbury, 9905......EK-5
Sunderlinville, 50......EE-1
Sunnybrook, 1300......‡A-4
Sunnyburn, 80......EQ-7
Sunset Valley, 2700......‡M-10
Sunville, 30......WG-5
Surveyor, 35......WJ-11
Suscon, 700......EH-9
SUSQUEHANNA CO., 43356......EF-9
Susquehanna Depot, 1643......EE-10
Sutersville, 605......WN-5
Swanville, 150......WB-8
Swarthmore, 6194......‡F-1
Swedeland, 500......‡B-1
Sweden Valley, 223......WF-13
Sweet Valley, 500......EH-7
Swiftwater, 600......EI-11
Swissvale, 8983......‡K-7
Swoyersville, 5062......EH-9
Sybertsville, 300......EJ-8
Sycamore, 60......WP-3
Sykesville, 1157......WJ-9
Sylvan, 20......WQ-12
Sylvan Hills, 1000......WB-13
Sylvania, 219......EE-4
Table Rock, 62......EP-3
Tacony......‡C-6
Tafton, 600......EH-12
Talmage, 325......ET-10
Tamaqua, 7107......EK-8
Tamiment, 125......EI-12
Tannersville, 1200......EJ-11
Tannery, 70......EJ-9
Tarentum, 4530......WL-5
Tarrs, 600......WO-5
Tarrtown, 150......WK-6
Tatamy, 1203......EK-11
Tatesville, 175......WP-11
Taylor, 6263......EH-9
Taylorstown, 217......WO-2
Teepleville, 20......WF-4
Telford, 4872......EN-11
Temple, 1877......EM-9
Templeton, 325......WJ-6
Ten Mile, 60......WP-3
Terre Hill, 1295......EO-8
Terrytown, 100......EF-7
Thomas......WN-3
Thomas Mills, 50......WO-8
Thomasville, 450......EP-4
Thompson, 299......EE-10
Thompsontown, 697......EM-3
Thompsontown, 30......WK-10
Thompsonville, 3520......‡N-4
Thornburg, 455......‡K-4
Thorndale, 3407......EP-9
Thornhurst, 250......EI-10
Three Sprs., 444......WO-13
Throop, 4088......EC-13
Tidal, 75......WJ-6
Tidioute, 688......WF-6
Tillotson, 20......WE-5
Timberly Hts., 400......WJ-4
Timblin, 157......WJ-7
Tingley, 80......EE-9
Tinicum, 100......EM-12
Tioga, 666......EE-3
TIOGA CO., 41981......EF-3
Tioga Jct., 100......EE-3
Tiona, 400......WF-8
Tionesta, 483......WG-6
Tipton, 1083......WL-11
Tire Hill, 900......WN-8
Titusville, 5601......WF-5
Tivoli, 25......EH-5
Toby, 100......WH-10
Tobyhanna, 1200......EI-11
Todd, 952......WN-12
Toftrees, 2053......WS-5
Tolna, 40......EQ-5
Tomhicken, 160......EJ-8
Tompkinsville, 200......EG-10
Tomstown, 180......EQ-1
Topton, 2069......EM-9
Torpedo, 30......WE-6
Torrance, 250......WM-7
Torresdale......‡C-7
Toughkenamon, 1492......EQ-9
Towanda, 2919......EF-6
Tower City, 1346......EL-6
Townville, 323......WF-4
Trade City, 60......WK-8
Trafford, 3174......WN-5
Trainer, 1828......*B-10
Transfer, 500......WH-2
Trappe, 3509......EO-11
Treichlers, 600......EL-10
Tremont, 1752......EL-6
Trent......WP-7
Tresckow, 880......EK-8
Treveskyn, 1200......WN-3
Trevorton, 1834......EK-5
Trexler......EL-9
Trexlertown, 1988......EM-10
Trooper, 5744......EO-11
Trout Run, 350......EH-3
Troutville, 243......WJ-9
Troxelville, 221......EK-3
Troy, 1354......EF-5
Troy Ctr......WF-5
Trucksville, 2152......EA-8
Truittsburg, 15......WJ-7
Truman, 75......WG-11
Trumbauersville, 974......EM-11
Tryonville, 50......WF-5
Tuckerton, 300......ER-12
Tullytown, 1872......‡T-12
Tunkhannock, 1836......EG-8
Tunnelhill, 363......WM-10
Tunnelton, 110......WM-6
Turbotville, 705......EJ-5
Turkey City, 100......WI-5
Turnersville, 35......WG-2
Turnip Hole, 20......WI-6
Turtle Creek, 5349......WM-4
Turtlepoint, 90......WE-11
Tuscarora, 980......EK-8
Tuscarora, 60......EM-2
Tusseyville, 30......EK-1
Twin Lakes, 125......EH-13
Twin Rocks, 600......WM-9
Two Taverns, 50......EQ-3
Tyler, 40......WI-10
Tyler Hill, 450......EF-12
Tylersburg, 200......WH-7
Tylersport, 320......EN-11
Tylersville, 225......EJ-2
Tyrone, 5477......WL-11
Uhlerstown, 100......EM-12
Uledi, 250......WP-5
Ulster, 300......EE-6
Ulysses, 621......WE-14
Union City, 3320......WE-5
UNION CO., 44947......EJ-3
Union Dale, 267......EF-10
Union Deposit, 407......ES-6
Uniontown, 10372......WP-5
Uniontown, 100......WL-9
Unionville, 962......WJ-4
Unionville, 900......EP-9
Unionville, 350......WK-3
Unionville, 291......WK-13
Unityville, 60......EI-6
Universal......‡J-9
Upland, 3239......EQ-11
Upper Black Eddy, 550......EM-12
Upper Darby......‡F-2
Upper Exeter, 707......EH-9
Upper St. Clair, 19200......WN-3
Upper Strasburg, 225......WP-14
Upton, 100......WQ-13
Urban, 45......EL-5
Urey......WK-9
Ursina, 225......WQ-7
Utahville, 160......WL-
Utica, 189......WG
Vail......WL-
Valencia, 551......WL
Valier, 275......WK
Valley Forge, 1500......EO-
Valley View, 1683......EL
Valley View, 600......EO
Valley View, 150......WK-
Van, 60......WH
Van Ormer, 180......WL-
Van Voorhis, 166......WO
Vanderbilt, 476......WP
Vandergrift, 5205......WL
Vandling, 751......EF-
Vandyke, 80......EM
Vankirk......WO
Varden, 150......EG-
Venango, 239......WE
VENANGO CO., 54984......WG
Venetia, 450......WN
Venus, 150......WH
Vera Cruz, 250......EM-
Verona, 2474......WM
Versailles, 1515......WN
Vestaburg, 975......WP
Vicksburg, 261......EJ
Victory Hts., 250......WH
Villa Maria, 150......WI
Villanova......‡C
Vinco, 1305......WM
Vinemont, 100......EN
Vintage, 200......EP
Vintondale, 414......WM
Vira, 150......EL
Virginville, 309......EM
Volant, 168......WI
Vosburg......EG
Vowinckel, 139......WH
Wagner, 128......EL
Wagnerville......EA
Wagontown, 500......EP
Wakefield, 609......EQ
Walbert, 200......EB
Wall, 580......‡L
Wallaceton, 313......WJ-
Waller, 48......EI
Wallingford......‡F
Walls Cors., 30......EG
Wallsville, 50......EG
Walmo, 900......WJ
Walnut, 115......EM
Walnut Bottom, 300......EO
Walnutport, 2070......EK-
Walnuttown, 484......EM
Walston, 275......WJ
Waltersburg, 275......WP
Waltonville, 125......ET
Wampum, 717......WK
Wanamakers, 55......EL
Wanamie, 612......EI
Wapwallopen, 150......EJ
Warfordsburg, 135......WQ-1
Warminster, 31400......EO-1
Warren, 9710......WE
Warren Ctr., 200......EE
WARREN CO., 41815......WE-
Warrendale, 500......WL-
Warrensville, 300......EH-
Warrington, 7000......EN-1
Warrior Run, 584......EI
Warriors Mark, 350......WL-1
Warwick, 200......EO-
Washington, 13663......WO-
Washington Boro, 729......EP-
WASHINGTON CO., 207820......WN-
Washington Crossing, 850......EN-1
Washingtonville, 273......EJ-
Wassergass, 200......EL-1
Water Street, 15......WM-1
Waterfall, 100......WO-1
Waterford, 1517......WD-
Waterford, 300......WN-
Waterloo, 50......WN-1
Waterman, 140......WM-
Waterside, 50......WO-1
Waterville, 150......EH-
Watrous, 150......EF-
Watsontown, 2351......EJ-
Wattersonville, 150......WJ-
Wattsburg, 403......WD-
Waverly, 604......EG-
Waymart, 1341......EG-1
WAYNE CO., 52822......EF-1
Wayne Hts., 2545......EQ-
Waynesboro, 10568......EQ-
Waynesburg, 4176......WP-
Weatherly, 2525......EJ-
Webster, 255......WO-
Webster Mills, 25......WQ-1
Weedville, 542......WH-1
Weigelstown, 12875......EP-
Weikert, 215......EK-
Weishample, 100......EL-
Weissport, 412......EK-
Weldbank, 100......WF-
Weldon, 4300......‡A-
Wellersburg, 181......WQ-
Wells Tannery, 175......WO-1
Wellsboro, 3263......EF-
Wellsville, 242......EP-
Welsh Run......WQ-1
Wendel, 1500......‡N-1
Wenksville, 120......EP-
Wennersville, 750......EB-
Wernersville, 2494......EN-
Wertzville, 30......EN-
Wescosville, 5872......EC-
Wesley, 50......WI-
Wesleyville, 3341......WC-
W. Alexander, 604......WO-1
W. Auburn, 100......EF-
W. Bangor, 30......EQ-
W. Bingham, 50......WE-1
W. Bristol, 5000......‡B-
W. Brownsville, 992......WP-
W. Burlington, 90......EF-
W. Cameron, 165......EL-
W. Catasauqua, 700......EA-
W. Chester, 18461......EP-1
W. Clifford, 50......EF-1
W. Conshohocken, 1320......‡B-
W. Decatur, 533......WJ-1
W. Elizabeth, 518......WN-
W. Enola, 800......ES-

*, †, ‡, §, ◊ See explanation under state title in this index.
County and parish names are listed in capital letters & boldface type.
Independent cities (not included in a county) are listed in italics.

Fairfield, 60 ... WN-8
Fairview, 1282 ... ES-2
Finley, 100 ... WP-2
Franklin, 40 ... EF-5
Freedom, 240 ... WI-5
Grove, 2854 ... EQ-9
Hazleton, 4594 ... EJ-8
Hickory, 300 ... WG-6
Homestead, 929 ... ‡L-7
Kittanning, 175 ... WK-6
Lancaster, 800 ... ES-8
Lawn, 1715 ... ET-11
Lebanon, 125 ... WL-7
Leechburg, 294 ... WL-5
Leisenring, 600 ... WP-5
Liberty, 343 ... WJ-4
Liberty, 70 ... WJ-9
Mayfield, 1239 ... WK-2
Middlesex, 863 ... WI-2
Middletown, 39 ... WN-2
Mifflin, 20313 ... WN-4
Milton, 900 ... EJ-4
Monterey, 75 ... WJ-5
Nanticoke, 749 ... EI-8
Newton, 2633 ... WO-5
Pike, 20 ... WF-14
Pittsburg, 808 ... WJ-2
Pittston, 4868 ... EB-9
Reading, 4212 ... ET-12
Renovo ... WH-14
Salisbury, 85 ... WQ-8
Springfield, 300 ... WD-2
Sunbury, 192 ... WJ-4
View, 6771 ... WM-4
Warren, 50 ... EE-7
Willow, 300 ... EP-7
Winfield, 30 ... WK-5
Wyoming, 2725 ... EA-9
Wyomissing, 407 ... ET-12
York, 4617 ... EP-5
stfield, 1064 ... EE-1
stford, 150 ... WG-2
stgate Hills ... EA-4
stland, 167 ... WN-2
stline, 75 ... WF-9
stminster, 100 ... EC-9
stmont, 5181 ... WN-8
STMORELAND CO., 55169 ... WM-6
ston, 321 ... EJ-8
stover, 390 ... WK-10
stport, 80 ... WH-13
sttown, 500 ... EP-10
stville, 40 ... WI-9
stwood, 1000 ... WS-1
more ... WF-9
ford, 1100 ... WL-3
arton, 25 ... WG-12
eatland, 632 ... WI-2
eelerville ... EG-5
iskerville, 110 ... WJ-4
itaker, 1271 ... ‡L-7
ite, 400 ... WO-6
ite, 40 ... WM-6
ite Deer, 500 ... EJ-4
ite Hall ... EI-5
ite Haven, 1097 ... EJ-9
ite Hill, 580 ... ET-2
ite Horse, 130 ... EP-8
ite House, 80 ... WQ-4
ite Mills, 659 ... EG-12
ite Oak, 7862 ... WN-5
te Sprs., 550 ... EK-3
itehall, 13944 ... WN-4
ites Valley, 60 ... EF-11
tesburg, 90 ... WK-6
tney, 400 ... WN-6
tsett, 200 ... WO-5
onisco, 921 ... EM-5
noon, 90 ... WJ-6
gletown, 100 ... WJ-3
, 75 ... EM-3
awana, 50 ... ED-5
our, 140 ... WO-8
cox, 383 ... WG-10
dwood, 600 ... ‡H-6
kes-Barre, 41498 ... EI-9
kinsburg, 930 ... WM-4
et, 30 ... WL-7
iam Penn Manor, 0 ... EA-5
iamsburg, 54 ... WM-12
iamson, 200 ... WQ-13
iamsport, 29381 ... EI-4
iamstown, 87 ... EM-5
ow Grv., 726 ... EO-12
ow Hill, 100 ... WO-13
ow Street, 7578 ... EP-7
owdale ... EQ-9
merding, 2190 ... ‡L-9
more, 225 ... WN-9
en, 320 ... WN-7
on, 7896 ... EL-11
mers, 250 ... EH-10
burne, 550 ... WJ-12
d Gap, 2720 ... EK-11
d Ridge, 215 ... WP-2
dber, 4138 ... WO-9
dfall, 90 ... EF-5
dham Ctr. ... ED-7
ding Hill, 370 ... ET-1
dsor, 1319 ... EP-6
dsor Castle, 0 ... EM-8
dsor Farms, 500 ... ER-3
dsor Pk., 1100 ... ET-1
dward Hts., 0 ... WJ-4
field, 900 ... EK-4
gate, 100 ... WJ-13
terdale, 250 ... ED-11
terstown, 632 ... EQ-5
ton, 600 ... ‡H-2
inoming ... ‡C-6
enberg, 15 ... WQ-8
dale, 2888 ... WO-2
fsburg, 220 ... WP-10
nelsdorf, 2810 ... EN-7
d, 265 ... WO-12
dbine, 50 ... EQ-6
dbury, 284 ... WO-11
dcock, 157 ... WF-4
dland, 400 ... WJ-11
dland Hts., 61 ... WH-5
dland Pk., 950 ... EH-3
dlawn, 1850 ... EL-10
dlyn, 9485 ... EQ-11
drow ... WN-2
dside, 2425 ... †S-11
dward, 110 ... EK-2
dycrest, 500 ... WS-5
lrich, 800 ... EI-2
Worleytown ... WQ-14
Wormleysburg, 3070 ... EN-4
Worthington, 639 ... WK-5
Worthville, 67 ... WJ-8
Wrights ... WF-12
Wrights Corners ... WE-10
Wrightsdale, 25 ... EQ-8
Wrightstown, 400 ... EN-13
Wrightsville, 2310 ... EP-6
Wrightsville, 70 ... WE-6
Wurtemburg, 400 ... WK-3
Wyalusing, 596 ... EF-7
Wyano, 484 ... WO-5
Wycombe, 600 ... EN-13
Wydnor, 630 ... EC-4
Wylie, 100 ... ‡N-7
Wyncote, 3044 ... ‡B-4
Wyndmoor, 5498 ... ‡B-4
Wynnewood, 7800 ... ‡D-2
Wyoming, 3073 ... EB-9
WYOMING CO., 28276 ... EG-7
Wyomissing, 10461 ... EN-8
Wysox, 400 ... EF-6
Yardley, 2434 ... EN-13
Yarnell ... WJ-13
Yatesboro, 450 ... WK-7
Yatesville, 607 ... EB-9
Yeadon, 11762 ... ‡E-3
Yeagertown, 1050 ... EL-1
Yellow Creek, 60 ... WO-11
Yellow House, 200 ... EN-9
Yocumtown, 200 ... EO-5
Yoe, 1018 ... EP-5
York, 43718 ... EP-5
YORK CO., 434972 ... EP-4
York Haven, 709 ... EO-5
York Sprs., 833 ... EP-3
Yorkana, 229 ... EP-6
Yorkshire, 1700 ... WS-14
Yostville ... EH-10
Youngstown, 326 ... WN-6
Youngsville, 1729 ... WE-7
Youngwood, 3050 ... WN-6
Yukon, 677 ... WO-5
Zelienople, 3812 ... WK-3
Zieglersville, 900 ... EN-11
Zion, 2030 ... WK-14
Zion Grv., 200 ... EK-7
Zionhill, 100 ... EM-11
Zions View, 250 ... EP-5
Zionsville, 300 ... EM-10
Zooks Corner, 700 ... ES-9
Zora ... EQ-2
Zullinger, 250 ... EQ-1

Rhode Island

Page locator
Map keys A–N, Atlas pages 184–185

Abbott Run Valley, 1800 ... B-7
Adamsville, 600 ... G-9
Albion, 170 ... B-6
Allendale ... K-8
Allenton, 650 ... G-6
Alton, 400 ... I-3
Annawomscutt ... M-10
Anthony, 3400 ... E-5
Arcadia, 120 ... G-4
Arkwright, 220 ... E-5
Arnold Mills, 640 ... B-7
Ashaway, 1485 ... I-3
Ashton, 910 ... B-6
Auburn ... M-9
Austin, 150 ... G-4
Avondale, 230 ... J-2
Barrington, 16300 ... E-7
Bay Spr. ... M-10
Berkeley, 910 ... B-6
Bonnet Shores, 1500 ... H-6
Bradford, 1406 ... I-3
Bridgetown, 2200 ... H-6
Bristol, 22400 ... F-8
BRISTOL CO., 49875 ... E-7
Bristol Ferry, 180 ... F-8
Burdickville, 500 ... I-3
Canonchet, 210 ... H-3
Carolina, 970 ... H-4
Centerville, 80 ... G-3
Centerville ... N-7
Central Falls, 19376 ... C-7
Centredale ... K-8
Charlestown, 2000 ... I-4
Chepachet, 1675 ... C-4
Clayville, 300 ... D-4
Coles ... N-9
Common Fence Pt., 900 ... F-8
Comstock Gdns. ... L-7
Conimicut ... N-9
Coventry, 8600 ... E-4
Cranston, 80387 ... D-6
Cumberland Hill, 7934 ... B-6
Davisville, 550 ... F-6
Diamond Hill, 910 ... B-6
Dunns Cors., 170 ... J-3
E. Greenwich, 11800 ... F-6
E. Natick ... N-8
E. Providence, 47037 ... D-7
Edgewood ... M-9
Escoheag, 120 ... F-3
Esmond, 5000 ... C-6
Exeter, 310 ... G-5
Fairlawn ... K-9
Forestdale, 550 ... B-5
Foster, 190 ... C-3
Galilee, 560 ... I-5
Glendale, 860 ... B-4
Grants Mills ... A-6
Green Hill, 300 ... I-5
Greene, 888 ... E-3
Greenville, 8658 ... C-5
Greenwood ... N-8
Greystone ... K-8
Hamilton, 270 ... G-6
Harmony, 985 ... C-5
Harris, 1250 ... E-5
Harrisville, 1605 ... B-4
Haversham, 170 ... J-3
Hope, 350 ... E-5
Hope Valley, 1612 ... H-4
Hopkins Hollow ... F-3
Hopkinton, 590 ... H-3
Hoxsie ... M-9
Hughesdale ... L-8
Indian Lake Shores, 250 ... H-6
Island Pk., 1550 ... F-8
Jackson, 200 ... E-5
Jamestown, 5000 ... H-7
Jerusalem, 100 ... I-5
Johnston ... D-6
KENT CO., 166158 ... F-4
Kent Hts. ... L-9
Kenyon, 550 ... H-4
Kingston, 6974 ... H-5
Knightsville ... L-8
La Fayette, 760 ... G-6
Lakewood ... M-9
Lime Rock, 300 ... B-6
Lincoln Pk. ... M-8
Lippitt Estate, 380 ... I-9
Little Compton, 550 ... H-9
Lockwood Corner ... N-9
Lonsdale, 4200 ... C-6
Manton ... K-8
Manville, 3200 ... B-6
Mapleville, 1600 ... B-4
Marieville ... K-8
Matunuck, 580 ... I-5
Melville, 1320 ... G-8
Meshanticut ... M-8
Middletown, 3800 ... G-7
Misquamicut, 390 ... J-3
Mohegan, 310 ... B-4
Moosup Valley, 220 ... E-3
Moscow, 30 ... G-3
Mt. View, 700 ... F-6
Narragansett Pier, 3409 ... I-6
Nasonville, 430 ... B-4
Natick ... N-8
Nayatt ... N-10
New Shoreham, 830 ... L-5
Newport, 24672 ... H-7
NEWPORT CO., 82888 ... G-8
Nooseneck ... F-4
N. Foster ... D-3
N. Kingstown, 3000 ... G-6
N. Providence, 32000 ... C-6
N. Quidnessett, 330 ... F-6
N. Scituate, 410 ... D-5
N. Tiverton ... F-8
Norwood ... M-9
Oak Lawn ... M-8
Oakland, 600 ... B-4
Olneyville ... L-8
Pascoag, 4577 ... B-4
Pawtucket, 71148 ... C-7
Peace Dale, 3400 ... H-5
Perryville, 50 ... I-5
Pettaquamscutt Lake Shores, 750 ... H-6
Phenix ... N-7
Phillipsdale ... K-10
Plum Pt., 380 ... G-6
Pt. Judith, 430 ... I-6
Portsmouth, 4200 ... F-8
Potter Hill, 300 ... I-3
Primrose, 530 ... B-5
Providence, 178042 ... D-6
PROVIDENCE CO., 626667 ... C-4
Prudence Pk. ... F-7
Quidnessett, 2000 ... F-6
Quidnick, 2700 ... E-5
Quinnville, 370 ... B-6
Quonochontaug, 333 ... J-4
Riverside ... M-10
Rockville, 320 ... G-3
Rumford ... K-10
Sakonnet, 200 ... H-8
Saunderstown, 430 ... H-6
Saundersville, 170 ... D-5
Saylesville, 3800 ... C-6
Shannock, 1100 ... H-4
Shawomet ... N-9
Shelter Hbr., 120 ... J-3
Shores Acres, 490 ... G-6
Simmonsville ... L-7
Slatersville, 2400 ... A-5
Slocum, 110 ... G-5
Snug Hbr., 600 ... I-5
S. Foster, 130 ... D-4
S. Hopkinton, 500 ... I-3
Spragueville ... C-5
Summit, 100 ... E-4
Tarkiln, 370 ... B-5
The Hummocks, 220 ... F-8
Thornton ... L-8
Tiverton, 7557 ... F-8
Tiverton Four Corners, 160 ... G-8
Union Vil., 2300 ... B-5
Usquepaug, 530 ... H-4
Valley Falls, 11547 ... C-7
Wakefield, 300 ... I-6
Warren, 10600 ... E-8
Warwick, 82672 ... E-7
WASHINGTON CO., 126979 ... H-4
Watch Hill, 154 ... J-2
Waterman Four Cors., 120 ... D-5
Weekapaug, 425 ... J-3
W. Barrington ... M-10
W. Glocester, 200 ... C-3
W. Greenville ... C-5
W. Greenwich Ctr. ... F-3
W. Kingston, 1400 ... H-5
W. Warwick, 29100 ... E-5
Westcott ... N-7
Westerly, 17936 ... I-2
White Rock, 410 ... I-2
Wickford Jct., 100 ... G-6
Wood River Jct., 270 ... I-4
Woodlawn ... K-9
Woodville, 60 ... H-4
Woodville ... K-8
Woonsocket, 41186 ... A-5
Wyoming, 270 ... H-4

South Carolina

Page locator
Map keys A–J, Atlas pages 186–187
* City keyed to p. 59

Abbeville, 5237 ... D-4
ABBEVILLE CO., 25417 ... D-4
Adams Run, 600 ... H-9
Aiken, 29524 ... F-6
AIKEN CO., 160099 ... F-6
Alcolu, 429 ... E-9
Allendale, 3482 ... G-7
ALLENDALE CO., 10419 ... H-6
Anderson, 26686 ... C-3
ANDERSON CO., 187126 ... C-3
Andrews, 2861 ... F-11
Antreville, 140 ... D-4
Arcadia, 2634 ... I-4
Arcadia Lakes, 861 ... F-3
Arial, 2543 ... B-3
Arkwright ... J-5
Arthurtown, 1450 ... H-3
Atlantic Bch., 334 ... E-13
Awendaw, 1294 ... G-11
Aynor, 560 ... D-12
Ballentine, 730 ... D-7
Bamberg, 3607 ... G-7
BAMBERG CO., 15987 ... G-7
Barnwell, 4750 ... G-7
BARNWELL CO., 22621 ... G-6
Batesburg-Leesville, 5362 ... E-6
Beaufort, 12361 ... I-8
BEAUFORT CO., 162233 ... I-8
Beckhamville, 360 ... C-8
Beech Island, 1500 ... F-5
Belle Meade, 1900 ... J-2
Belmont, 2400 ... F-3
Belton, 4134 ... C-4
Belvedere, 5792 ... *A-13
Ben Avon, 1700 ... J-6
Bennettsville, 9069 ... C-11
Berea, 14295 ... I-1
BERKELEY CO., 177843 ... G-10
Bethune, 334 ... C-9
Beverly Hills, 1500 ... G-10
Bishopville, 3471 ... D-9
Blacksburg, 1848 ... A-6
Blackstock, 200 ... C-7
Blackville, 2406 ... F-7
Blenheim, 154 ... C-11
Bluff Estates, 600 ... H-3
Bluffton, 12530 ... J-8
Blythewood, 2034 ... D-8
Boiling Sprs., 8219 ... A-5
Bonneau, 487 ... G-10
Bonneau Bch., 1929 ... F-10
Bowling Green, 500 ... A-7
Bowman, 968 ... F-8
Bradley, 170 ... D-4
Bradleyville ... *B-13
Branchville, 1024 ... G-8
Briarcliffe Acres, 457 ... E-13
Brittons Neck, 600 ... E-12
Brunson, 554 ... H-7
Bucksport, 876 ... E-12
Buffalo, 1266 ... B-6
Burnettown, 2673 ... F-5
Burton, 6976 ... I-8
Cades, 300 ... E-10
CALHOUN CO., 15175 ... E-8
Calhoun Falls, 2004 ... D-4
Camden, 6838 ... D-8
Cameron, 424 ... F-8
Campobello, 502 ... A-5
Canadys, 200 ... G-8
Capitol View, 4000 ... E-8
Carlisle, 436 ... C-6
Cartersville, 110 ... D-10
Catawba, 1343 ... B-8
Cayce, 12528 ... G-2
Centenary, 500 ... D-12
Centerville, 6586 ... C-3
Centerville, 4400 ... H-10
Central, 5159 ... B-3
Chaparral Ranches, 5000 ... G-10
Chapin, 1445 ... D-7
Charleston, 120083 ... H-10
CHARLESTON CO., 350209 ... H-10
Chartwell, 500 ... F-1
Cheraw, 5851 ... B-10
CHEROKEE CO., 55342 ... B-6
Cherokee Forest, 2100 ... I-3
Cherokee Sprs., 110 ... A-5
Chesnee, 868 ... A-5
Chester, 5607 ... B-7
CHESTER CO., 33140 ... C-7
Chesterfield, 1472 ... B-10
CHESTERFIELD CO., 46734 ... C-9
Chestnut Hills, 1400 ... J-1
City View, 1345 ... I-1
CLARENDON CO., 34971 ... F-9
Clarks Hill, 381 ... E-5
Clearwater, 4370 ... *B-14
Clemson, 13905 ... B-3
Cleveland, 220 ... A-4
Clinton, 8490 ... C-5
Clio, 726 ... C-11
Clover, 5094 ... A-7
Cokesbury, 215 ... D-5
COLLETON CO., 38892 ... H-8
Columbia, 129272 ... D-7
Converse, 608 ... B-5
Conway, 17103 ... E-12
Coosawhatchie, 300 ... I-8
Cope, 77 ... F-7
Cordova, 169 ... F-8
Coronaca, 191 ... D-5
Cottageville, 762 ... H-9
Couchton, 500 ... F-6
Coward, 752 ... E-11
Cowpens, 2162 ... A-6
Crane Forest, 700 ... E-2
Cross, 300 ... F-10
Cross Anchor, 126 ... C-5
Cross Hill, 507 ... D-5
Dale, 150 ... I-8
Dalzell, 3059 ... D-9
Darlington, 6289 ... D-10
DARLINGTON CO., 68681 ... C-10
Davis Sta., 150 ... F-9
Denmark, 3538 ... F-7
Denny Ter., 1750 ... F-2
Dentsville, 14062 ... F-3
Dillon, 6788 ... C-11
DILLON CO., 32062 ... C-12
Donalds, 348 ... C-4
Dorchester, 450 ... G-9
DORCHESTER CO., 136555 ... G-9
Dovesville, 200 ... C-10
Drayton, 1400 ... I-5
Drayton, 700 ... A-11
Due West, 1247 ... C-4
Duncan, 3181 ... B-5
Dunean, 3671 ... J-1
Early Branch, 150 ... H-8
Easley, 19993 ... B-4
E. Gaffney, 3085 ... A-6
Eastmont, 500 ... H-4
Eastover, 813 ... E-8
Edgefield, 4750 ... E-5
EDGEFIELD CO., 26985 ... E-5
Edgemoor, 350 ... B-7
Edisto Bch., 414 ... I-9
Effingham, 230 ... D-11
Ehrhardt, 545 ... G-7
Elgin, 2607 ... B-8
Elgin, 1311 ... D-8
Elko, 193 ... F-7
Elliott, 650 ... D-10
Elloree, 692 ... F-9
Enoree, 665 ... C-5
Estill, 2040 ... H-7
Eutawville, 315 ... F-9
Evergreen, 120 ... D-11
Fair Play, 687 ... C-3
Fairfax, 2025 ... H-7
FAIRFIELD CO., 23956 ... C-7
Fairforest, 1693 ... J-4
Fairmont, 250 ... B-5
Filbert, 300 ... A-7
Fingerville, 134 ... A-5
Florence, 37056 ... D-10
FLORENCE CO., 136885 ... D-10
Floydale, 250 ... C-12
Folly Bch., 2617 ... H-10
Folly Field ... J-11
Forest Acres, 10361 ... G-3
Forest Bch. ... J-10
Forestbrook, 4612 ... I-12
Fork, 280 ... D-12
Fork Shoals, 180 ... C-4
Ft. Lawn, 895 ... B-8
Ft. Mill, 10811 ... B-8
Ft. Motte, 150 ... E-8
Fountain Inn, 7799 ... B-5
Frogmore, 300 ... I-9
Furman, 239 ... H-7
Gable, 200 ... E-10
Gadsden, 1632 ... E-8
Gaffney, 12414 ... A-6
Galivants Ferry, 180 ... D-12
Gantt, 14229 ... J-1
Garden City Bch. ... F-12
Garnett, 110 ... I-7
Gaston, 1645 ... E-7
Georgetown, 9163 ... F-12
GEORGETOWN CO., 60158 ... F-11
Gifford, 288 ... H-7
Gilbert, 565 ... E-6
Gillisonville, 200 ... I-7
Givhans, 200 ... G-9
Glendale, 307 ... B-5
Glenn Sprs., 110 ... B-5
Gloverville, 2831 ... F-5
Golden Grv., 2467 ... B-4
Goose Creek, 35938 ... G-10
Goretown, 110 ... D-13
Grace, 300 ... B-8
Grahamville, 250 ... I-8
Graniteville, 2614 ... F-5
Graves, 200 ... F-11
Gray Court, 795 ... C-5
Great Falls, 1979 ... C-8
Greeleyville, 438 ... F-10
Green Pond, 200 ... H-8
Green Sea, 200 ... D-12
Greenville, 58409 ... B-4
GREENVILLE CO., 451225 ... C-4
Greenwood, 23222 ... D-5
GREENWOOD CO., 69661 ... D-5
Greer, 25515 ... B-4
Gresham, 200 ... E-11
Grover, 180 ... G-8
Hamer, 500 ... C-12
Hampton, 2808 ... H-7
HAMPTON CO., 21090 ... H-7
Hampton Hts., 1600 ... I-2
Hanahan, 17997 ... H-10
Harbour Town ... J-9
Hardeeville, 2952 ... J-7
Harleyville, 677 ... G-9
Harris, 350 ... D-5
Hartsville, 7764 ... C-10
Haskell Hts., 1000 ... E-2
Hazelwood Acres, 1000 ... G-4
Heath Sprs., 790 ... C-8
Helena, 300 ... D-6
Hemingway, 459 ... E-11
Hendersonville, 240 ... H-8
Hickory Grv., 440 ... B-6
Hickory Grv., 250 ... E-12
Hilda, 447 ... G-7
Hilton Head Island, 37099 ... J-8
Hodges, 155 ... D-4
Holly Hill, 1277 ... F-9
Hollywood, 4714 ... H-9
Hollywood Hills, 950 ... F-2
Homeland Pk., 6296 ... C-3
Homewood, 300 ... E-12
Honea Path, 3597 ... C-4
Honey Hill, 110 ... G-11
Hopkins, 2882 ... E-8
Horatio, 300 ... D-9
HORRY CO., 269291 ... D-13
Inman, 2321 ... A-5
Inman Mills, 1050 ... A-5
Irmo, 11097 ... D-7
Isle of Palms, 4133 ... H-10
Iva, 1218 ... D-3
Jackson, 1700 ... F-6
Jacksonboro, 478 ... H-9
JASPER CO., 24777 ... I-7
Jedburg, 200 ... G-9
Jefferson, 753 ... C-9
Jenkinsville, 46 ... D-7
Joanna, 1539 ... C-5
Johnsonville, 1480 ... E-11
Johnston, 2362 ... E-5
Jonesville, 911 ... B-6
Judson, 2050 ... J-1
Kellytown, 200 ... C-10
Kelton, 150 ... B-6
Kensington, 600 ... F-12
Kershaw, 1803 ... C-8
KERSHAW CO., 61697 ... C-8
Kiawah Island, 1626 ... I-10
Kinards, 250 ... C-6
Kings Creek, 200 ... A-6
Kingstree, 3328 ... E-10
Kingswood, 2100 ... F-1
Kline, 197 ... G-7
La France, 900 ... C-3
Ladson, 13790 ... G-10
Lake City, 6675 ... E-11
L. Forest, 1000 ... I-3
L. View, 807 ... C-12
L. Wylie, 8841 ... A-7
Lamar, 989 ... D-10
Lancaster, 8526 ... B-8
LANCASTER CO., 76652 ... C-5
Lando, 300 ... B-7
Landrum, 2376 ... A-5
Lane, 508 ... F-10
Latta, 1379 ... C-11
Laurel Bay, 5891 ... I-8
Laurens, 9139 ... C-5
LAURENS CO., 66537 ... B-8
LEE CO., 19220 ... D-9
Lesslie, 3112 ... B-8
Lexington, 17870 ... E-7
LEXINGTON CO., 262391 ... E-7
Liberty, 3269 ... B-3
Liberty Hill, 160 ... C-8
Lincoln Shire, 1400 ... E-2
Litchfield Bch., 500 ... F-12
Little Mtn., 291 ... D-6
Little River, 8960 ... E-13
Little Rock, 500 ... C-11
Livingston, 136 ... F-7
Lobeco, 400 ... I-8
Lodge, 120 ... G-8
Lone Star, 200 ... F-8
Long Bay Estates, 200 ... J-14
Longcreek, 200 ... B-2
Longs, 300 ... E-13
Loris, 2396 ... D-13
Lowndesville, 128 ... D-3
Lowrys, 200 ... B-7
Lugoff, 7434 ... D-8
Luray, 127 ... H-7
Lydia, 642 ... D-10
Lyman, 3243 ... B-5
Lynchburg, 373 ... D-10
Manning, 4108 ... E-9
Marietta, 1200 ... A-4
Marion, 6939 ... D-11
MARION CO., 33062 ... D-11
MARLBORO CO., 28933 ... C-11
Mauldin, 22889 ... B-4
Mayesville, 731 ... D-9
Mayo, 1592 ... A-5
McBee, 867 ... C-9
McClellanville, 499 ... G-11
McColl, 2174 ... B-11
McConnells, 255 ... B-7
McCormick, 2783 ... E-4
MCCORMICK CO., 10233 ... E-4
Meadowlake, 2700 ... F-3
Meggett, 1226 ... H-9
Miley, 120 ... H-7
Modoc, 218 ... E-4
Monarch Mill, 1811 ... B-6
Moncks Cor., 7885 ... G-10
Monetta, 236 ... E-6
Montmorenci, 900 ... F-6
Moore, 200 ... B-5
Morningside, 750 ... I-2
Morris Acres, 450 ... H-10
Mt. Carmel, 216 ... D-4
Mt. Croghan, 195 ... B-9
Mt. Pleasant, 67843 ... C-13
Mountville, 108 ... C-5
Mullins, 4663 ... D-12
Murrells Inlet, 7547 ... F-12
Myrtle Bch., 27109 ... E-13
Neeses, 374 ... F-7
New Ellenton, 2052 ... F-6
New Holland Crossroads, 200 ... E-6
New Zion, 140 ... E-10
Newberry, 10277 ... D-6
NEWBERRY CO., 37508 ... D-5
Newport, 4136 ... B-7
Newry, 172 ... B-3
Nichols, 368 ... D-12
Ninety Six, 1998 ... D-5
Nixons Crossroads, 250 ... E-13
Norris, 813 ... B-3
North, 754 ... F-7
N. Augusta, 21348 ... *B-13
N. Charleston, 97471 ... A-12
N. Hartsville, 3251 ... C-10
N. Myrtle Bch., 13752 ... E-13
N. Santee, 300 ... G-11
Norway, 337 ... F-7
Oak Grv., 150 ... C-11
Oakway, 200 ... C-3
Oatland, 150 ... F-12
OCONEE CO., 74273 ... B-2
Olanta, 563 ... E-10
Olar, 257 ... G-7
Olympia, 1200 ... G-2
Orangeburg, 13964 ... F-8
ORANGEBURG CO., 92501 ... F-8
Osborn, 150 ... H-9
Pacolet, 2235 ... B-6
Pageland, 2760 ... B-9
Pamplico, 1226 ... D-11
Paramount Pk., 700 ... J-2
Paris, 1950 ... I-2
Park Pl., 1500 ... I-2
Parksville, 117 ... E-4
Patrick, 351 ... C-10
Pawleys Island, 103 ... F-12
Paxville, 185 ... E-9
Pee Dee, 250 ... D-11
Pelham, 500 ... B-5
Pelion, 674 ... E-7
Pendleton, 2964 ... C-3
Perry, 233 ... F-7
Pickens, 3126 ... B-3
PICKENS CO., 119224 ... B-3
Pierpont, 2700 ... A-11
Pine Island, 30 ... I-13
Pine Ridge, 400 ... C-10
Pine Valley, 1400 ... F-1
Pineland, 200 ... I-7
Pineville, 500 ... F-10
Pinewood, 538 ... E-9
Pinopolis, 948 ... G-10
Plantersville, 150 ... F-12
Pleasant Valley, 1200 ... J-2
Pomaria, 179 ... D-6
Pontiac, 250 ... D-8
Port Royal, 10678 ... I-8
Port Royal Plantation ... J-12
Poston, 150 ... E-11
Pritchardville, 150 ... J-8
Prosperity, 1180 ... D-6
Quail Hollow, 600 ... G-1
Quinby, 932 ... D-11
Rains, 500 ... D-12
Ravenel, 2465 ... H-9
Red Bank, 9617 ... E-7
Reevesville, 196 ... G-8
Reidville, 601 ... B-5
Rembert, 306 ... D-9
Richburg, 275 ... B-7
RICHLAND CO., 384504 ... E-8
Ridge Spr., 737 ... E-6
Ridgeland, 4036 ... I-7
Ridgeville, 1979 ... G-9
Ridgeway, 319 ... D-8
Ridgewood, 1600 ... F-2
Rimini, 200 ... E-9
Riverside, 2350 ... I-1
Robertville, 120 ... I-7
Rock Hill, 66154 ... B-7
Rockville, 134 ... I-9
Roebuck, 2200 ... B-5
Rowesville, 304 ... F-8
Ruby, 360 ... B-9
Ruffin, 300 ... G-8
Russellville, 488 ... F-10
St. Andrews ... B-12
St. George, 2084 ... G-9
St. Matthews, 2021 ... E-8
St. Stephen, 1697 ... F-10
Salem, 135 ... B-3
Salley, 398 ... F-7
Salters, 270 ... F-10
Saluda, 3565 ... D-6
SALUDA CO., 19875 ... D-6
Sampit, 150 ... F-11
Sandwood, 2400 ... F-3
Sandy Sprs., 1200 ... C-3
Sans Souci, 7869 ... I-1
Santee, 961 ... F-9
Santee Circle, 350 ... G-10
Sardinia, 250 ... E-10
Saxon, 3424 ... I-4
Schultz Hill ... *B-13
Scotia, 215 ... H-7
Scranton, 932 ... E-11
Sea Pines ... J-10
Seabrook Island, 1714 ... I-10
Sellers, 219 ... D-11
Seneca, 8102 ... B-3
Shannontown, 1500 ... E-9
Sharon, 494 ... B-7
Sheldon, 200 ... I-8
Shiloh, 214 ... E-10
Shulerville, 350 ... G-11
Silverstreet, 162 ... D-6
Simpson, 150 ... D-7
Simpsonville, 18238 ... B-4
Six Mile, 675 ... B-3
Smoaks, 126 ... G-8
Snelling, 274 ... G-6
Socastee, 19952 ... E-12
Society Hill, 563 ... C-10
S. Congaree, 2306 ... E-7
S. Forest Estates, 1000 ... J-2
Spartanburg, 37013 ... B-5
SPARTANBURG CO., 284307 ... B-5
Spring Mills, 1400 ... C-8
Springdale, 2636 ... E-7
Springfield, 524 ... F-7
Stark Ter., 370 ... F-2
Starmount, 600 ... H-2
Starr, 173 ... C-3
State Pk., 50 ... E-3
Stateburg, 1380 ... E-9
Stoney Hill, 150 ... D-6
Stuckey, 245 ... E-11
Sullivans Island, 1791 ... H-10
Summer Hill ... *B-13
Summerton, 1000 ... F-9
Summerville, 43392 ... G-10
Summit, 402 ... E-6
Sumter, 40524 ... E-9
SUMTER CO., 107456 ... E-9
Surfside Bch., 3837 ... F-12
Swansea, 827 ... E-7
Sycamore, 180 ... G-7
Tamassee, 200 ... B-3
Tarboro, 180 ... I-7
Taylors, 21617 ... B-4
Tega Cay, 7620 ... A-7
Tigerville, 1312 ... A-4
Tillman, 300 ... I-7
Timmonsville, 2320 ... D-10
Tirzah, 2150 ... B-7
Townville, 500 ... C-3
Travelers Rest, 4576 ... B-4
Trenton, 196 ... E-5
Trio, 250 ... F-11
Troy, 93 ... D-4
Turbeville, 766 ... E-10
Ulmer, 88 ... G-7
Union, 8393 ... B-6
UNION CO., 28961 ... B-6
Utica, 1489 ... B-3
Valley Falls, 6299 ... H-4
Van Wyck, 350 ... B-8
Vance, 170 ... F-9
Varnville, 2162 ... H-7
Vaucluse, 500 ... F-5
Wade Hampton, 20461 ... H-3
Wadmalaw Island, 300 ... H-9
Wagener, 797 ... E-7
Walhalla, 4263 ... B-2
Wallace, 892 ... B-10
Walterboro, 5398 ... H-8
Wampee, 200 ... E-13
Ward, 91 ... E-6
Ware Shoals, 2170 ... C-4
Warrenville, 1233 ... F-5
Waterloo, 166 ... C-5
Watts Mills, 1635 ... C-5
Wedgefield, 1615 ... E-9
Wellford, 2378 ... B-5
W. Columbia, 14988 ... G-2
W. Gantt, 3050 ... J-2
W. Pelzer, 880 ... C-4
W. Springs, 160 ... B-6
W. Union, 291 ... B-2
Westminster, 2418 ... B-2
Westview, 2000 ... J-4
Westville, 2200 ... I-1
White Rock, 440 ... D-7
White Stone, 200 ... B-6
Whitehall ... D-7
Whitmire, 1441 ... C-6
Whitney, 1500 ... I-5
Williams, 117 ... G-8
WILLIAMSBURG CO., 34423 ... F-11
Williamston, 3934 ... C-4
Willington, 142 ... E-4
Williston, 3139 ... F-6
Windsor, 121 ... F-6
Windsor Estates, 2200 ... E-4
Winnsboro, 3550 ... C-7
Winnsboro Mills, 1898 ... C-7
Woodford, 185 ... E-7
Woodland Hills, 2700 ... F-1
Woodruff, 4090 ... B-5
Woodside, 180 ... I-1
Woodville, 160 ... C-4
Yemassee, 1027 ... H-8
York, 7736 ... B-7
YORK CO., 226073 ... B-7

South Dakota

Page locator
Map keys A–J, Atlas pages 188–189

Aberdeen, 26091 ... B-10
Academy, 10 ... F-9
Agar, 76 ... C-8
Akaska, 42 ... B-8
Albee, 16 ... C-13
Alcester, 807 ... G-13
Alexandria, 615 ... F-11
Allen, 420 ... G-5
Alpena, 286 ... E-10
Altamont, 34 ... C-13
Amherst, 70 ... A-11
Andover, 91 ... B-11
Antelope, 826 ... G-7
Ardmore ... G-2
Arlington, 915 ... D-12
Armour, 699 ... F-10
Artas, 9 ... A-8
Artesian, 138 ... E-11
Ashton, 122 ... C-10
Astoria, 139 ... D-13
Athol, 50 ... C-10
Aurora, 532 ... D-13
Aurora Ctr., 12 ... F-10
AURORA CO., 2710 ... E-10
Avon, 590 ... G-11
Badger, 107 ... D-12
Baltic, 1089 ... E-13
Bancroft, 19 ... D-11
Barnard, 60 ... A-10
Batesland, 108 ... G-4
Bath, 172 ... B-10
BEADLE CO., 17398 ... D-10
Belle Fourche, 5594 ... D-2
Belvidere, 49 ... E-6
Bemis, 40 ... C-12
BENNETT CO., 3431 ... G-5
Beresford, 2005 ... G-13
Bethlehem, 10 ... H-3
Big Sprs., 10 ... G-13
Big Stone City, 467 ... B-13
Bijou Hills, 6 ... F-9
Bison, 333 ... B-4
Blackhawk, 2892 ... E-3
Blunt, 354 ... D-8
BON HOMME CO., 7070 ... G-11
Bonesteel, 275 ... G-9
Bonilla, 30 ... D-10
Bowdle, 502 ... B-8
Box Elder, 7800 ... E-3
Bradley, 72 ... C-11
Brandon, 8785 ... F-13
Brandt, 107 ... D-13
Brentford, 77 ... C-10
Bridger, 50 ... D-5
Bridgewater, 492 ... F-11
Bristol, 341 ... B-11
Britton, 1241 ... A-11
Broadland, 31 ... D-10
Brookings, 22056 ... D-12
BROOKINGS CO., 31965 ... D-12
BROWN CO., 36531 ... B-10
Bruce, 204 ... D-12
BRULE CO., 5255 ... F-9
Bryant, 456 ... D-11
Buffalo, 330 ... B-3
BUFFALO CO., 1912 ... E-9
Buffalo Gap, 126 ... F-3
Bullhead, 348 ... A-6
Burbank, 90 ... H-13
Burke, 604 ... G-9
Bushnell, 65 ... D-13
Butler, 17 ... B-11
BUTTE CO., 10110 ... C-3
Camp Crook, 63 ... B-2
CAMPBELL CO., 1466 ... B-8
Canistota, 656 ... F-12
Canova, 105 ... E-11
Canton, 3057 ... F-13
Caputa, 40 ... E-3
Carpenter, 30 ... D-11
Carter, 10 ... F-7
Carthage, 144 ... E-11
Castle Rock ... C-3
Castlewood, 627 ... C-12
Cavour, 114 ... D-11
Cedar Butte ... F-6
Center Pt., 20 ... G-12
Centerville, 882 ... G-12
Central City, 134 ... D-2
Chamberlain, 2387 ... E-9
Chancellor, 264 ... F-12
CHARLES MIX CO., 9129 ... G-10
Chelsea, 27 ... C-10
Cherry Creek, 300 ... D-5
Chester, 261 ... E-12
Cheyenne Crossing ... H-2
Claire City, 76 ... A-12
Claremont, 127 ... B-11
Clark, 1139 ... C-11
CLARK CO., 3691 ... C-11
CLAY CO., 13864 ... G-12
Clayton ... F-11
Clear Lake, 1273 ... C-13
Clearfield, 10 ... G-8
CODINGTON CO., 27227 ... C-12
Colman, 594 ... E-12
Colome, 296 ... G-8
Colton, 687 ... E-12
Columbia, 136 ... B-10
Conde, 140 ... C-10
Corn Creek, 105 ... F-6
Corona, 109 ... B-12
Corsica, 592 ... F-10
Corson, 70 ... F-13
CORSON CO., 4050 ... B-6
Cottonwood, 9 ... E-5
Crandall ... C-11
Creighton, 10 ... E-4
Cresbard, 104 ... C-9
Crocker, 19 ... C-11
Crooks, 1269 ... F-12
Custer, 2067 ... E-2
CUSTER CO., 8216 ... F-2
Dallas, 120 ... G-8
Dante, 84 ... G-10
Davis, 85 ... G-12
DAVISON CO., 19504 ... F-10
DAY CO., 5710 ... C-11
De Smet, 1089 ... D-11
Deadwood, 1270 ... D-2
Dell Rapids, 3633 ... E-13
Delmont, 234 ... G-10
Dempster, 70 ... D-12
DEUEL CO., 4364 ... C-13
DEWEY CO., 5301 ... C-6
Dimock, 125 ... F-11
Doland, 180 ... C-10
Dolton, 37 ... F-12
DOUGLAS CO., 3002 ... F-10
Draper, 82 ... E-7
Dupree, 525 ... C-5
Eagle Butte, 1318 ... C-6
Eden, 89 ... B-11
Edgemont, 774 ... F-2
EDMUNDS CO., 4071 ... B-8
Egan, 278 ... E-13
Elk Pt., 1963 ... H-13
Elkton, 736 ... D-13
Ellis, 90 ... F-12
Elm Sprs., 20 ... D-4
Emery, 447 ... F-11
Enning, 30 ... D-4
Epiphany, 50 ... E-11
Erwin, 45 ... D-11
Esmond ... D-11
Estelline, 768 ... D-12
Ethan, 331 ... F-11
Eureka, 868 ... A-8
Fairburn, 85 ... F-3
Fairfax, 115 ... G-9
Fairpoint ... C-4
Fairview, 60 ... G-13
Faith, 421 ... C-5
FALL RIVER CO., 7094 ... G-2
Farmer, 10 ... F-11
Farmingdale ... E-3
FAULK CO., 2364 ... C-9
Faulkton, 736 ... C-9
Fedora, 37 ... E-11
Ferney, 43 ... B-10
Firesteel, 20 ... B-6
Flandreau, 2341 ... E-13
Florence, 374 ... C-12
Forestburg, 73 ... E-11
Ft. Pierre, 2078 ... D-7
Ft. Thompson, 1282 ... E-9
Frankfort, 149 ... C-10
Frederick, 199 ... A-10
Freeman, 1306 ... F-12
Fruitdale, 64 ... D-2
Fulton, 91 ... F-11
Gann Valley, 14 ... E-9
Garden City, 53 ... C-11
Garretson, 1166 ... F-13
Gary, 227 ... C-13
Gayville, 407 ... G-12
Geddes, 208 ... G-10
Gettysburg, 1162 ... C-8
Glad Valley, 10 ... B-5
Glencross, 40 ... B-6
Glenham, 105 ... B-7
Goodwin, 146 ... C-12
GRANT CO., 7356 ... C-12
Green Grass, 35 ... C-6
Greenwood, 100 ... G-10
Gregory, 1295 ... G-9
GREGORY CO., 4271 ... G-9
Grenville, 54 ... B-11
Groton, 1458 ... B-10
HAAKON CO., 1937 ... D-5
Hamill, 11 ... F-8
HAMLIN CO., 5903 ... D-12
Hammer ... A-12
HAND CO., 3431 ... D-9
HANSON CO., 3331 ... F-11
HARDING CO., 1255 ... B-3
Harrisburg, 4089 ... F-13
Harrison, 52 ... F-10
Harrold, 124 ... D-8
Hartford, 2534 ... F-12
Hayes, 40 ... D-6
Hayti, 381 ... D-12
Hazel, 91 ... C-12
Hecla, 227 ... A-10
Henry, 267 ... C-11
Hermosa, 398 ... E-3
Herreid, 438 ... A-8
Herrick, 105 ... G-9
Hetland, 46 ... D-12
Highmore, 795 ... D-9
Hill City, 948 ... E-2
Hillsview, 3 ... B-8
Hisega ... I-3
Hitchcock, 91 ... D-10
Holabird, 20 ... D-8
Hosmer, 208 ... B-8
Hot Sprs., 3711 ... F-2
Houghton, 60 ... A-10
Hoven, 406 ... B-8
Howard, 858 ... E-11
Howes, 20 ... D-5
Hudson, 296 ... G-13
HUGHES CO., 17022 ... D-8
Humboldt, 589 ... F-12
Hurley, 415 ... F-12
Huron, 12592 ... D-10
HUTCHINSON CO., 7343 ... F-11
HYDE CO., 1420 ... D-8
Ideal, 60 ... F-8
Interior, 94 ... F-5
Iona, 10 ... F-9
Ipswich, 954 ... B-9
Irene, 420 ... G-12
Iron Lightning, 40 ... C-5
Iroquois, 266 ... D-11
Isabel, 135 ... B-6
JACKSON CO., 3031 ... F-5
Java, 129 ... B-8
Jefferson, 547 ... H-13
JERAULD CO., 2071 ... E-10
JONES CO., 1006 ... E-6
Junius, 50 ... E-12
Kadoka, 654 ... E-5
Kaylor, 47 ... G-11
Keldron, 10 ... A-5
Kenel, 50 ... A-7
Kennebec, 240 ... E-8
Keystone, 337 ... E-3
Kidder, 57 ... A-11
Kimball, 703 ... F-9
KINGSBURY CO., 5148 ... D-11
Kranzburg, 172 ... C-12
Kyle, 846 ... F-4
La Plant, 171 ... C-7
Labolt, 68 ... C-13
L. Andes, 879 ... G-10
Lake City, 51 ... A-11
LAKE CO., 11200 ... E-12
L. Norden, 467 ... D-12
L. Preston, 599 ... D-12
Lane, 59 ... E-10
Langford, 313 ... B-11
Lantry, 40 ... C-6
LAWRENCE CO., 24097 ... E-2
Lead, 3124 ... D-2
Lebanon, 47 ... C-8
Lemmon, 1227 ... A-5
Lennox, 2111 ... F-12
Leola, 457 ... A-9
Lesterville, 127 ... G-11
Letcher, 173 ... E-10
Lily, 4 ... C-11
LINCOLN CO., 44828 ... G-13
Little Eagle, 319 ... B-7
Lodgepole, 60 ... A-4
Long Lake, 31 ... A-9
Long Valley, 20 ... F-5
Loomis, 34 ... E-11
Lower Brule, 613 ... E-8
Lowry, 6 ... B-8
Loyalton ... B-9
Lucas ... G-9
Ludlow, 10 ... A-3
LYMAN CO., 3755 ... E-8
Lyons, 100 ... F-12
Madison, 6474 ... E-12
Mahto, 20 ... A-7
Manchester, 10 ... D-11
Manderson, 180 ... G-4
Mansfield, 93 ... B-10
Marion, 784 ... F-12
MARSHALL CO., 4656 ... A-11
Martin, 1071 ... G-5
Marty, 402 ... G-10
Marvin, 34 ... B-12
Mayfield, 20 ... G-12
MCCOOK CO., 5618 ... E-12
McIntosh, 173 ... A-6
McLaughlin, 663 ... A-6
MCPHERSON CO., 2459 ... A-9
MEADE CO., 25434 ... D-3
Meadow, 30 ... B-4
Meckling, 90 ... G-12
Mellette, 210 ... C-10
MELLETTE CO., 2048 ... F-6
Menno, 608 ... G-11
Midland, 129 ... E-6
Midway, 30 ... G-12
Milbank, 3353 ... B-13
Milesville, 30 ... D-5
Millboro, 10 ... G-8
Miller, 1489 ... D-9
Milltown, 10 ... F-11
Mina, 30 ... B-9
MINER CO., 2389 ... E-11
MINNEHAHA CO., 169468 ... E-12
Miranda, 20 ... C-9
Mission, 1182 ... G-7
Mission Hill, 177 ... G-12
Mission Ridge ... D-7
Mitchell, 15254 ... F-11
Mobridge, 3465 ... B-7
Monroe, 160 ... F-12
Montrose, 472 ... F-12
MOODY CO., 6486 ... E-13
Morningside, 105 ... D-10
Morristown, 67 ... A-5
Mound City, 71 ... A-8
Mt. Vernon, 462 ... F-10
Mud Butte, 10 ... C-3
Murdo, 488 ... E-7
Mystic ... I-2
Naples, 41 ... C-11
Nemo, 50 ... E-2
New Effington, 256 ... A-12
New Holland, 76 ... F-10
New Underwood, 660 ... E-3
Newell, 603 ... C-3
Nisland, 232 ... D-2
Norris, 152 ... F-6
N. Sioux City, 2530 ... H-13
Northville, 143 ... C-10
Nunda, 43 ... E-12
Oacoma, 451 ... E-9
Oelrichs, 126 ... G-3
Oglala, 1290 ... G-4
Okaton, 36 ... E-6
Okreek, 269 ... F-7
Oldham, 133 ... E-12
Olivet, 74 ... G-11
Onaka, 15 ... C-8
Onida, 658 ... D-8
Opal, 30 ... C-4
Oral, 60 ... F-3
Orient, 63 ... C-9
Ortley, 65 ... B-12
Osceola, 30 ... D-11
Owanka, 20 ... E-4
Parade, 20 ... C-6
Parker, 1022 ... F-12
Parkston, 1508 ... F-11
Parmelee, 562 ... F-6
Peever, 168 ... B-12
PENNINGTON CO., 100948 ... E-4
PERKINS CO., 2982 ... B-4
Philip, 779 ... E-5
Pickerel, 30 ... B-12
Pickstown, 201 ... G-10
Piedmont, 222 ... D-3
Pierpont, 135 ... B-11
Pierre, 13646 ... D-7
Pine Ridge, 3308 ... G-4
Plainview, 20 ... D-4
Plankinton, 707 ... F-10
Platte, 1230 ... F-9
Pollock, 241 ... A-7
Polo, 40 ... C-9
Porcupine, 1062 ... G-4
Potato Creek, 50 ... F-5
POTTER CO., 2329 ... C-8
Prairie City, 23 ... B-4
Presho, 497 ... E-8
Pringle, 112 ... F-2
Provo, 80 ... G-2
Pukwana, 285 ... F-9
Quinn, 54 ... E-4
Ralph, 10 ... A-3
Ramona, 174 ... E-12
Rapid City, 67956 ... E-3
Ravinia, 61 ... G-10
Raymond, 50 ... C-11
Red Scaffold, 100 ... C-5
Red Shirt, 40 ... F-3
Redfield, 2333 ... C-10
Redig, 10 ... B-2
Redowl, 10 ... D-4
Ree Hts., 62 ... D-9
Reliance, 191 ... E-8
Renner, 305 ... F-13
Reva, 10 ... B-3
Revillo, 119 ... C-13
Richland, 89 ... H-13
Ridgeview, 90 ... C-7
Riverside, 30 ... F-11
ROBERTS CO., 10149 ... B-12
Rochford, 50 ... E-2
Rockerville ... I-3
Rockham, 33 ... C-9
Roscoe, 329 ... B-9
Rosebud, 1587 ... G-6
Rosholt, 423 ... A-12
Roslyn, 183 ... B-11
Roswell, 15 ... E-11
Running Water, 36 ... H-11
Rutland, 80 ... E-12
St. Charles, 11 ... G-9
St. Francis, 709 ... G-6
St. Lawrence, 198 ... D-9
St. Onge, 191 ... D-2
Salem, 1347 ... F-12
Sanator ... J-2
SANBORN CO., 2355 ... E-10
Savoy ... H-2
Scenic, 80 ... E-4
Scotland, 841 ... G-11
Selby, 642 ... B-8
Seneca, 38 ... C-8
Shadehill, 20 ... A-5
SHANNON CO., 13586 ... F-4
Sharps Corner, 60 ... F-4
Sherman, 78 ... E-13
Silver City, 60 ... E-2
Sinai, 120 ... D-12
Sioux Falls, 153888 ... F-13
Sisseton, 2470 ... B-12
Smithwick, 30 ... F-3
Soldier Creek, 227 ... F-6
Sorum ... B-3
S. Shore, 225 ... C-12
Spearfish, 10494 ... D-2
Spencer, 154 ... F-11
Spink, 40 ... G-13
SPINK CO., 6415 ... C-10
Spring Creek, 268 ... G-6
Springfield, 1989 ... G-11
STANLEY CO., 2966 ... D-6
Stephan, 30 ... E-9
Stickney, 284 ... F-10
Stockholm, 108 ... C-12
Stoneville, 20 ... D-4
Storla, 6 ... E-10
Strandburg, 72 ... C-12
Stratford, 72 ... B-10
Sturgis, 6627 ... D-2
SULLY CO., 1373 ... D-7
Summerset, 1814 ... E-3
Summit, 288 ... B-12
Sunnyview, 50 ... D-12
Tabor, 423 ... G-11
Tea, 3806 ... F-12
Thomas ... C-12
Thunder Butte, 70 ... C-5
Thunder Hawk, 30 ... A-5
Tilford, 40 ... D-3
Timber Lake, 443 ... B-6
TODD CO., 9612 ... G-6
Tolstoy, 36 ... C-8
Toronto, 212 ... D-13
Trail City, 130 ... B-7
Trent, 232 ... E-13
Tripp, 647 ... G-11
TRIPP CO., 5644 ... G-8
Troy, 10 ... C-12
Tulare, 207 ... D-10
Turkey Ridge, 10 ... G-12
TURNER CO., 8347 ... F-12
Turton, 48 ... C-10
Tuthill, 30 ... G-5
Twin Brooks, 69 ... B-12
Tyndall, 1067 ... G-11
Union Ctr., 80 ... D-4
UNION CO., 14399 ... G-13
Unityville, 20 ... E-11
Utica, 65 ... G-11
Vale, 136 ... D-3
Valley Sprs., 759 ... F-13
Vayland ... D-9
Veblen, 531 ... A-12
Verdon, 5 ... B-10
Vermillion, 10571 ... G-12
Vetal ... G-6
Viborg, 782 ... G-12
Victor, 20 ... A-12
Vienna, 45 ... D-11
Vilas, 20 ... E-11
Virgil, 16 ... D-10
Vivian, 119 ... E-7
Volga, 1768 ... D-12
Volin, 161 ... G-12
Wagner, 1566 ... G-10
Wakonda, 321 ... G-12
Wakpala, 200 ... B-7
Wakpamani, 30 ... G-4
Walker, 10 ... A-6
Wall, 766 ... E-4
Wallace, 85 ... C-11
WALWORTH CO., 5438 ... B-8
Wanblee, 725 ... F-5
Ward, 48 ... E-13
Warner, 457 ... B-10
Wasta, 80 ... E-4
Watauga, 30 ... A-5
Watertown, 21482 ... C-12
Waubay, 576 ... B-12
Waverly, 37 ... C-12
Webster, 1886 ... B-11
Wecota, 20 ... C-9
Wentworth, 171 ... E-12
Wessington, 170 ... D-10
Wessington Sprs., 956 ... E-10
Westport, 133 ... B-10
Wetonka, 8 ... B-9
Wewela, 20 ... G-8
White, 485 ... D-13
White Butte, 20 ... A-4
White Lake, 372 ... F-10
White Owl, 30 ... D-4
White River, 581 ... F-7
White Rock, 3 ... A-13
Whitehorse, 141 ... B-6
Whitewood, 927 ... D-2
Willow Lake, 263 ... D-11
Wilmot, 492 ... B-12
Winfred, 52 ... E-12
Winner, 2897 ... F-8
Witten, 79 ... F-8
Wolsey, 376 ... D-10
Wood, 62 ... F-7
Woonsocket, 655 ... E-10
Worthing, 877 ... F-13
Wounded Knee, 382 ... G-4
Yale, 108 ... D-11
Yankton, 14454 ... G-12
YANKTON CO., 22438 ... G-12
Zell, 30 ... C-10
ZIEBACH CO., 2801 ... C-5

Tennessee

Page locator
Map keys 1–10, Atlas pages 190–191
Map keys 11–20, Atlas pages 192–193
* City keyed to p. 155
† City keyed to p. 195

Acton, 100 ... G-6
Adair, 70 ... E-5
Adams, 633 ... B-10
Adamsville, 2207 ... F-6
Aetna, 100 ... E-9
Afton, 250 ... K-17
Alamo, 2461 ... D-4
Alcoa, 8449 ... D-19
Alexandria, 966 ... C-13
Algood, 3495 ... C-15
Allardt, 634 ... B-17
Allons, 190 ... B-15
Allred, 100 ... C-16
Almaville, 170 ... D-12
Alpine, 200 ... B-16
Altamont, 1045 ... F-14
Alto, 50 ... F-14
Anderson, 150 ... G-14
ANDERSON CO., 75129 ... C-18
Andersonville, 472 ... C-19
Anthony Hill, 200 ... G-10
Apison, 2469 ... G-16
Arcadia, 30 ... †J-2
Archville, 120 ... G-18
Ardmore, 1213 ... G-11
Arlington, 11517 ... F-3
Armathwaite, 140 ... B-17
Arp, 290 ... D-3
Arrington, 150 ... D-11
Arthur, 400 ... B-20
Asbury, 300 ... J-14
Ashburn, 100 ... A-11
Ashland City, 4541 ... C-10
Ashport, 200 ... D-2
Athens, 13458 ... F-18
Atoka, 8387 ... F-2
Atwood, 938 ... D-6
Auburntown, 269 ... D-13
Austin Sprs., 250 ... †M-3
Baileyton, 431 ... J-17
Bairds Mills, 40 ... C-12
Bakerville, 30 ... D-8
Bakewell, 250 ... F-16
Ball Camp, 240 ... D-19
Baneberry, 482 ... K-16
Banner, 200 ... M-15
Banner Hill, 1497 ... K-18
Banner Sprs., 180 ... C-17
Barkertown, 240 ... F-15
Barren Plain, 100 ... B-11
Bartlett, 54613 ... F-2
Bath Sprs., 70 ... F-7
Baxter, 1365 ... C-15
Beans Creek ... G-13
Bear Spr., 70 ... B-8
Bearden ... K-12
BEDFORD CO., 45058 ... E-12
Beech Bluff, 250 ... E-6
Beechgrove, 190 ... E-13
Beersheba Sprs., 477 ... F-14
Belfast, 230 ... F-11
Bell Buckle, 500 ... E-12
Belle Eagle ... E-4
Belle Meade, 2912 ... L-7
Belleville, 60 ... F-12
Bells, 2437 ... E-4
Belvidere, 180 ... G-13
Benton, 1385 ... G-17
BENTON CO., 16489 ... C-7
Berry Hill, 537 ... L-8
Berrys Chapel, 3000 ... D-11
Bethel, 150 ... G-10
Bethel Sprs., 718 ... F-6
Bethesda, 50 ... E-11
Bethpage, 288 ... B-13
Bible Hill, 30 ... E-7
Big Rock, 350 ... B-8
Big Sandy, 557 ... C-7
Big Spr., 270 ... †N-4
Big Spr., 100 ... F-17
Biltmore, 1800 ... †M-5
Binfield, 140 ... E-19
Birchwood, 480 ... F-16
Blaine, 1856 ... C-20
BLEDSOE CO., 12876 ... F-16
Bloomingdale, 9888 ... I-18
Bloomington Sprs., 270 ... C-15
BLOUNT CO., 123010 ... E-20
Blountville, 3074 ... I-18
Blue Spr., 200 ... †M-6
Bluff City, 1733 ... J-19
Bogota, 200 ... C-3
Bold Spr., 30 ... D-9
Bolivar, 5417 ... F-5
Bolton, 350 ... F-2
Boma, 30 ... C-14
Bon Air, 200 ... D-15
Bon Aqua, 200 ... D-10
Bonicord ... D-4
Bonnertown, 100 ... G-10
Boone, 80 ... †M-2
Boones Creek ... †L-2
Booneville, 60 ... F-12
Boonshill, 50 ... G-11
Bordeaux ... J-7
Bowmantown, 60 ... †N-1
Boyds Creek, 120 ... *A-10
Braden, 282 ... F-3
Bradford, 1048 ... C-5
BRADLEY CO., 98963 ... G-17
Bradyville, 200 ... E-13
Bransford, 170 ... B-13
Brazil, 200 ... D-5
Brentwood, 37060 ... D-11
Briarwood, 590 ... B-9
Briceville, 800 ... C-19
Bridgeport, 30 ... *A-13
Brighton, 2735 ... E-2
Bristol, 26702 ... I-19
Brownsville, 10292 ... E-4
Bruceton, 1478 ... D-7
Brunswick, 240 ... F-2
Brush Creek, 300 ... C-13
Bryson, 30 ... G-11
Buchanan, 300 ... B-7
Buena Vista, 150 ... D-7
Buffalo Sprs., 30 ... K-15
Buffalo Valley, 100 ... C-14
Bulls Gap, 738 ... K-16
Bumpus Mills, 300 ... A-8
Burlison, 425 ... E-2
Burns, 1468 ... D-10
Burnt Church, 100 ... G-7
Burrville ... C-17
Burwood, 60 ... D-11
Butler, 500 ... J-19
Butlers, 30 ... B-15
Bybee, 450 ... K-16
Bybee, 300 ... E-14
Byrdstown, 803 ... B-16
Cades, 50 ... D-5
Cades Cove, 30 ... *C-9
Cairo, 60 ... D-4
Calderwood, 820 ... E-19
Calhoun, 490 ... F-17
Calistia, 70 ... B-12
Camden, 3582 ... C-7
Campaign, 500 ... E-15
CAMPBELL CO., 40716 ... B-19
Campbellsville, 100 ... F-10
Caney Branch ... K-16
CANNON CO., 13801 ... D-13
Carlisle, 150 ... B-8
Carlock, 200 ... F-18
CARROLL CO., 28522 ... D-6
Carson Spr., 700 ... *A-13
Carter, 500 ... J-19
CARTER CO., 57424 ... J-19
Carthage, 2306 ... C-14
Caryville, 2297 ... C-19
Cash Pt., 100 ... G-11
Castalian Sprs., 556 ... B-13
Catlettsburg ... *A-11
Cato, 50 ... B-13
Cedar Creek, 300 ... K-17
Cedar Grv., 115 ... D-6
Cedar Grv. ... †K-5
Cedar Hill, 314 ... B-11
Celina, 1495 ... B-15
Center ... F-9
Center Point ... G-10
Centertown, 243 ... E-14
Centerville, 3644 ... D-9
Central, 2279 ... †M-4
Central, 50 ... D-4
Chapel Hill, 1445 ... E-11
Chapel Hill, 120 ... E-10
Chapmansboro, 220 ... C-10
Charleston, 651 ... F-17
Charleston, 150 ... E-3
Charlotte, 1235 ... C-10
Chattanooga, 167674 ... G-16
CHEATHAM CO., 39105 ... B-10
Cherokee Hills, 600 ... L-15
Cherry, 40 ... E-3
CHESTER CO., 17131 ... F-6
Chesterfield, 469 ... E-7
Chestnut Bluff, 80 ... D-4
Chestnut Hill, 400 ... L-15
Chestnut Mound, 150 ... C-14
Chewalla, 200 ... G-6
Childers Hill ... G-7
Chinquapin Grv., 300 ... †L-5
Christiana, 350 ... E-12
Christmasville, 100 ... C-6
Chuckey, 360 ... K-17
Church Hill, 6737 ... J-17
Churchton, 100 ... C-4
CLAIBORNE CO., 32213 ... J-15
Clairfield, 200 ... B-19
Clarkrange, 575 ... C-16
Clarksburg, 393 ... D-6
Clarksville, 132929 ... B-10
Claxton, 250 ... D-19
CLAY CO., 7861 ... B-14
Clearwater, 30 ... E-17
Cleveland, 41285 ... G-17
Clifftops, 200 ... G-14
Clifton, 2694 ... F-8
Clifton Jct., 220 ... F-8
Clinton, 9841 ... C-19
Clovercroft, 30 ... D-11
Cloverport, 80 ... F-5
Coalfield, 2463 ... D-18
Coalmont, 841 ... F-14
Coble, 100 ... D-9
COCKE CO., 35662 ... K-16
COFFEE CO., 52796 ... E-13
Coker Creek, 130 ... F-19
Cold Spr., 200 ... E-16
Coldwater, 30 ... G-11
College, 100 ... E-16
College Grv., 650 ... D-11
Collegedale, 8282 ... G-16
Collierville, 43965 ... G-3
Collinwood, 982 ... G-8
Colonial Hts., 6934 ... J-18
Columbia, 34681 ... E-10
Commerce, 60 ... C-13
Como, 200 ... C-6
Conasauga, 250 ... G-17

*, †, ‡, §, ◊ See explanation under state title in this index.
County and parish names are listed in capital letters & boldface type.
Independent cities (not included in a county) are listed in italics.

Concord, 100............E-12
Condon, 2125............C-20
Cookeville, 30435......C-15
Coopertown, 4278.....B-11
Copperhill, 354...........E-8
Cornersville, 1194.....F-11
Corryton, 100............L-16
Cosby, 400................L-16
Cottage Grv., 88.........B-6
Cottontown, 367........B-12
Counce, 700...............G-7
Cove Creek Cascades,
90.......................*B-10
Covington, 9038.........E-3
Cowan, 1737...............G-13
Crab Orchard, 752......D-17
Crawford, 100............C-16
Crestwood Hills,
1600....................D-17
CROCKETT CO.,
14586...................E-3
Crockett Mills, 400......D-4
Cross Anchor, 100.......J-17
Cross Plains, 1714......B-11
Cross Roads, 180........B-17
Crossville, 10795........D-16
Crump, 1428...............F-7
Cuba, 100..................D-4
Cuba, 100..................D-8
Culleoka, 360.............F-11
Cumberland City, 311..B-9
CUMBERLAND CO.,
56053...................D-17
Cumberland Furnace,
300......................C-10
Cumberland Gap,
494......................C-19
Cumberland Hts.,
210.....................F-14
Cumberland Sprs.,
60.......................B-9
Cunningham, 60........B-9
Curve, 350.................D-3
Cypress Inn, 350........G-8
Dale Hollow, 200.......B-15
Dancyville, 50.............F-4
Dandridge, 2812........K-15
Dante, 260.................A-3
Darden, 399...............F-6
DAVIDSON CO.,
626681..................C-11
Dayton, 7191.............F-16
DE KALB CO.,
18723...................D-14
De Rossett, 200........D-15
Deanburg, 30.............F-5
Deans, 30..................E-12
Deason, 110...............E-12
Decatur, 1598............E-17
DECATUR CO.,
11757....................E-7
Decaturville, 867.........E-7
Dechard, 2361...........G-13
Deer Lodge, 300........C-17
Del Rio, 100...............L-16
Dellrose, 100..............G-11
Dibrell, 150................D-14
Dickson, 14538...........C-9
DICKSON CO.,
49666....................C-9
Difficult, 120...............B-14
Dill, 150....................E-15
Disney, 150...............B-13
Dixon Sprs., 150.........B-13
Dixonville, 170............F-9
Doelle, 130...............K-15
Dogwood Hts., 300....J-15
Donelson.....................K-9
Double Bridges, 230...D-3
Dover, 1417.................B-9
Dowelltown, 355........D-14
Doyle, 575.................D-15
Dresden, 3005............C-6
Drummonds, 500.......E-2
Ducktown, 475...........E-18
Duff, 180...................B-19
Dukedom, 80.............B-6
Dunlap, 4815............E-15
Dupont, 100..............*B-10
Durhamville, 80...........F-4
Dyer, 2341.................C-5
DYER CO., 38335......C-4
Dyersburg, 17145.......C-4
Dyllis, 80...................D-17
Eads, 310...................G-3
Eagan, 200.................B-19
Eagleville, 604............E-12
E. Fork.....................*B-12
E. Ridge, 20979.........G-16
E. Union, 150............G-15
Eastview, 705..............G-6
Eaton, 130.................D-4
Eaton Crossroad,
350.....................D-4
Edgemont, 500.........*A-13
Edgemoor, 230..........D-19
Edith, 170...................D-3
Elbethel, 200..............E-12
Elbridge, 140.............B-17
Elgin, 282..................B-18
Elizabethton, 14176...J-19
Elk Mills, 30................J-19
Elkhorn, 30...............J-15
Elkmont, 100.............M-15
Elkton, 578...............G-11
Elmwood, 100...........C-14
Elora, 400..................G-12
Elza, 200...................K-18
Embreeville, 200.......K-18
Emmett, 30................*K-6
Englewood, 1532......K-18
Enterprise, 70............F-10
Enville, 189..................F-6
Erin, 1324..................B-9
Erwin, 6097...............K-18
Estill Sprs., 2055........F-13
Ethridge, 465............F-10
Etowah, 3490...........K-18
Eva, 200.....................D-4
Evensville, 350.........E-16
Fairfield, 400...............G-4
Fairfield Glade,
6989...................D-17
Fairmount, 2825........G-15
Fairview, 7720...........D-10
Fairview, 400..............G-9
Fairview, 100..............K-16
Fairview, 30...............*N-1
Falcon...........................
Fall Branch, 1291.......J-17

Farmington, 50..........E-11
Farner, 200................G-18
Farragut, 20676.........D-19
Faxon, 60...................C-8
FAYETTE CO.,
38413....................F-3
Fayetteville, 6827.......G-12
FENTRESS CO.,
17959....................B-17
Fincastle, 1618..........B-19
Finger, 298.................F-6
Finley, 100..................C-3
Fisherville, 80..............G-3
Fishery, 100...............K-18
Five Points, 170..........G-10
Flat Creek, 200..........E-12
Flat Woods, 420..........F-8
Flintville, 627.............G-12
Flourville..................†L-3
Fly, 50.......................D-10
Forbus, 100...............B-16
Fordtown, 1900.........J-16
Forest Hills, 4812.......L-11
Fosterville, 220..........E-12
Fountain City............L-13
Fountain Head, 380...B-12
Fowlkes, 400...............D-4
Frankewing, 100........G-11
Franklin, 62487..........D-11
FRANKLIN CO.,
41052...................G-13
Fraterville, 200..........C-18
Fredonia, 50..............B-10
Free Hill, 120............B-15
Friendship, 680..........D-4
Friendsville, 913........E-19
Fruitland, 180............D-5
Fruitvale, 110.............D-5
Fulton.........................D-5
Gadsden, 470.............D-5
Gainesboro, 962.........B-14
Gallatin, 30278..........B-12
Gallaway, 680.............F-3
Gardner, 200..............B-5
Garland, 310..............E-2
Gassaway, 70.............D-13
Gates, 647.................D-3
Gatlinburg, 3944.......M-15
Georgetown, 200.....F-17
Germantown, 38844..G-2
Gibson, 396................D-5
GIBSON CO.,
49683....................D-5
Gibson Wells, 150......D-5
Gift, 100....................D-3
Giles Co., 29485.....F-10
Gilmore.......................E-2
Gladeville, 410...........C-12
Gleason, 1445............C-6
Glen Alice, 110..........D-17
Gladeville, 30.............E-11
Glimp.........................E-3
Goldust, 30................D-2
Good Sprs., 60..........F-18
Goodlettsville,
15921..................C-12
Gordonsburg,............E-9
Gordonsville, 1213....C-14
Gorman, 80................C-4
Goshen, 80...............C-13
Jonesborough, 5051..J-18
Joppa, 30...................K-15
Juno, 50.....................K-18
Keeling........................
Kelso, 130.................G-12
Kenton, 1281.............C-5
Kerrville, 210..............F-2
Kimball, 1395...........G-14
Kimberlin Hts., 680....D-20
Kimmins, 130.............D-8
Kingsport, 48205.......J-18
Kingston, 5934...........D-18
Kingston Sprs.,
2756....................C-11
Kingston Woods,
840.......................K-11
Kirkland, 30...............D-12
Kiser, 130...................K-17
Knob Creek, 70.........*B-10

Henrietta, 150............B-10
Henry, 464.................C-6
HENRY CO., 32330...B-7
Hermanville, 70..........F-7
Hermitage Sprs.,........
Hickman, 250.............C-14
HICKMAN CO.,
24690....................E-9
Hickory Flats, 100......C-13
Hickory Star, 130........C-20
Hickory Tree, 80.......*K-5
Hickory Valley, 99.......G-4
Hickory Withe, 2600...F-3
Hilham, 110...............B-15
Hicksboro, 450...........F-14
Hillsdale, 80...............B-13
Hillville, 50.................D-4
Hiwassee Mills, 150....L-18
Hohenwald, 3757......E-9
Holladay, 30...............D-7
Hollow Rock, 718........D-7
Holts Cor., 200...........F-11
Homestead, 350........D-16
Hopewell, 1874.........F-17
Hopewell, 130...........D-5
Hornbeak, 424............B-4
Hornsby, 303.............G-5
Houston, 110............B-19
Huffman, 130.............C-9
Hurley.........................D-4
Hurricane Mills, 50.....D-8
Idlewild, 150..............C-5
India, 100...................K-18
Indian Mound, 400....B-9
Indian Sprs., 2200......*J-2
Inglewood...................K-9
Inskip.........................I-12
Iron City, 328..............D-9
Irving College, 40......D-14
Isabella, 180...............G-18
Jacks Creek, 300.........F-5
Jacksboro, 2020.........B-19
Jackson, 65211...........E-5
JACKSON CO.,
11638....................C-14
Jamestown, 1959......B-17
Jasper, 3279...............G-15
Jefferson City, 8047...K-15
JEFFERSON CO.,
51407...................K-15
Jellico, 2355...............B-19
John Sevier, 800........L-14
Johnson City, 63152...J-18
JOHNSON CO.,
18244....................J-20
Johnsons Grv., 60......D-4
Jones Cove, 50..........*B-12

Limestone, 550..........K-18
Lincoln, 160...............G-12
LINCOLN CO.,
33361...................G-12
Linden, 908................E-8
Littlelot, 120...............E-10
Lobelville, 897............D-8
Locke, 110.................F-2
Lonewood, 30.............D-3
Long Mtn., 220..........J-15
Lookout Mtn...............C-13
1832.........................N-11
LOUDON CO.,
48556...................E-18
Louisville, 2439..........D-19
Loudon, 130..............K-16
Lowland, 130.............K-16
Luray, 140..................F-6
Lusk, 150...................F-16
MACON CO.,
22248...................B-14
Madison........................I-9
MADISON CO.,
98294....................E-5
Madisonville, 4577.....E-18
Manchester, 10102...F-13
Manleyville, 30............C-7
Mansfield, 30..............C-9
Maple Grv., 30...........B-13
Maple Hill, 410...........F-3
Marbledale, 500.......*A-9
Marion, 130................C-9
MARION CO.,
28237...................G-14
MARSHALL CO.,
30617....................F-11
Martin, 11473............B-5
Maryville, 27465........E-19
Mascot, 2411.............C-20
Mason, 1609..............F-3
Mason Hall, 270.........C-4
Masseyville, 100.........F-5
Maury City, 674..........D-4
Maxwell, 150............G-13
Mayland, 440.............D-16
Maynardville, 2413....C-20
McBurg, 100...............F-11
McCloud, 30...............J-16
McConnell, 100...........B-5
McDonald, 350...........G-16
McDonald Hill, 120....J-16
McEwen, 1750............C-9
McKenzie, 5310..........C-6
McKinnon, 200...........C-8
McLemoresville, 352...D-6

Nankipoo, 30..............D-3
Nashville, 601222......C-11
Neva, 30...................J-20
New Deal, 368............A-3
New Hope, 1082........G-14
New Johnsonville,
1951....................D-8
New Loyston, 30.........C-19
New Market, 1334......K-15
New Markham, 40........M-4
New Middleton,..........C-13
New Tazewell, 3037...J-15
New Union, 1431.......C-13
Newbern, 3313...........C-4
Newcastle, 30.............F-4
Newcomb, 350...........B-19
Newell Sta., 360.........D-20
Newport, 6945..........L-16
Niota, 719.................L-18
Nixon, 240.................G-7
Nolensville, 5861........D-12
Norene, 100................D-13
Norma, 120................B-18
Normandy, 141...........F-13
Oakdale, 212..............D-18
Oakland, 6623............F-3
Oakwood, 30.............C-9
Obion, 1119...............C-4
Old Hickory................I-9
Old Washington,
180.....................E-17
Oldfort, 150...............F-17
Olivehill, 160..............F-7
Oliver Sprs., 3231......D-18
Olivet, 1350...............D-13
Oneida, 3752.............B-18
Only, 120...................D-9
Ooltewah, 680...........G-16
Orebank, 1300...........†J-2
Orlinda, 859...............B-11
Orme, 126..................G-14
Orysa............................
Ostella, 400................F-11
Overall, 60.................D-12
OVERTON CO.,
22083...................C-15
Owl City, 30................D-13
Ozone, 150................D-17
Pailo.............................
Paint Rock, 300...........E-18
Palestine......................
Pall Mall, 140.............B-16
Palmer, 672................F-15
Palmersville, 100.........B-6
Palmyra, 160..............B-9
Paris, 10156................C-7
Park City, 2442...........G-3

Summitville, 450.........E-14
Sunbright, 552...........C-17
Surgoinsville, 1801.....J-17
Sutherland, 30...........J-20
Sweetwater, 5764......E-18
Sylvia, 100..................C-9
Taft, 200...................G-11
Talbott, 550...............K-15
Tallassee, 130.............E-19
Tanglewood, 170........C-14
Tarpley.......................G-11
Tasso, 660..................G-17
Tatumville, 50..............C-4
Tazewell, 2218............J-15
Teuka........................G-11
Telford, 921..............J-18
Tellico Plains, 880.......F-18
Temperance Hall,
80.......................C-14
Temple Hill, 200.........C-8
Ten Mile, 120.............E-17
Tennessee City...........C-9
Tennessee Ridge,
1368....................B-8
Terrell, 140.................D-3
Terry Creek, 80..........B-18
Theta, 190..................C-9
Thompson's Sta.,
2194....................D-11
Three Way, 1709........D-5
Tigrett, 200.................D-4
Timothy, 30................B-15
Tiptonville, 4464.........B-3
Tobaccoport................B-9
Townsend, 448...........E-19
Tracy City, 1481.........F-14
Trade, 180.................J-20
Trenton, 4264............D-5
Trenton, 20................D-20
Trentville, 420............D-20
Trezevant, 859............D-6
Trimble, 637................C-4
Triune, 120................D-12
TROUSDALE CO.,
7870.....................B-13
Troy, 1373..................C-4
Trundel Crossroad,
90.......................*A-10
Tullahoma, 18655......F-13
Turtletown, 300.........G-18
Tusculum, 2663..........K-17
Twinton, 100...............C-16
Unicoi, 3632................K-18
UNICOI CO.,
18313...................K-18
Union City, 10895.......B-5
Union Hill, 200............B-14
UNION CO.,
19109....................B-20
Uniontville, 1368........E-12
Uptonville..................F-5
Valley Forge, 2200.....*N-5
Vanleer, 395................C-9
Vernon, 50..................D-9
Victoria, 200...............G-15
Vildo..........................F-4
Vine Ridge, 120..........C-16
Viola, 131...................E-14
Vonore, 1474.............E-19
Waco, 340.................B-20
Walden, 1898.............G-15
Waldens Creek, 80....*B-10
Walker, 50..................J-17
Walkertown, 30..........J-17
Walland, 259.............E-20
Walnut Grv., 864........B-20
Walnut Hill, 2394......*J-4
Walnut Log, 50...........B-4
Walterhill, 401............D-12
Warren, 30..................F-3
WARREN CO.,
39839....................E-14
Warrensburg, 50.........K-18
Wartburg, 918............C-18
Wartrace, 651.............E-13
Washburn, 340............J-15
Waterloo, 30..............G-9
Watertown, 1477.......C-13
Waterville, 60.............L-16
Watts Bar Dam, 60......E-17
Waverly, 4105.............C-8
Slayden, 178..............C-9
Smartt, 350...............D-14
SMITH CO.,
19166....................B-13
Smithville, 4530..........D-14
Smoky Jct., 100..........C-18
Smyrna, 39974..........D-12
Sneedville, 1387.........J-16
Soddy-Daisy, 12714...F-16
Solway, 200................D-19
Somerville, 3094.........F-4
S. Carthage, 1322......C-14
S. Fulton, 2354............B-5
S. Pittsburg, 2992......G-14
S. Tunnel, 260............B-12
Southside, 170............B-10
Westpoint, 30.............G-9
Westport, 160.............D-7
Wetmore, 150............L-18
White Bluff, 3206........C-10
White City, 210...........F-14
WHITE CO.,
8062.....................D-15
White House, 10255...B-12
White Oak, 250..........B-16
White Pine, 2196........K-16
Whitesburg, 400.........K-16
Whiteside, 600...........G-15
Whiteville, 4638..........F-4
Whitleyville, 150..........B-15
Whitlock, 140.............D-7
Whitwell, 1699...........G-15
Wilder, 230...............C-16
Wildersville, 250.........E-6
Wildwood, 1098.........D-20
Wilkinsville, 100..........B-9

Texas
Map locator
Map keys Atlas pages
WA1-WT14 198–199
WK1-WT14 200–201
EA1-EJ14 202–203
EK1-ET14 204–205
* City keyed to pp. 194–195
† City keyed to pp. 196–197

Abbott, 356................EG-7
Abernathy, 2805.......WG-10
Abilene, 117063........EE-3
Abbott Cor., 400........WI-10
Ackerly, 200..............WJ-10
Adamsville, 70............EH-5
Addison, 13056.........*E-10
Adrian, 166...............WD-9
Afton, 100..................WG-12
Agnes, 20...................EG-4
Agua Dulce, 812........EP-6
Aguilares, 21..............EP-3
Aiken, 60....................WG-11
Aiken, 35...................WF-11
Alamo, 18353............ES-5
Alamo Alto, 25..........WL-2
Alamo Bch., 250........EN-6
Alamo Hts., 7031.......ER-12
Alanreed, 60.............WD-12
Alba, 504...................ED-10
Albany, 2034..............EE-3
Aldine, 15869............EK-10
Aledo, 2716...............EE-6
Aleman........................EG-5
Alexander, 50.............EF-5
Alfred, 91.................EO-5
Algerita, 40................EH-4
Algoa, 400................*I-7
Alice, 19104..............EP-5
Allen, 84246..............ED-8
Alleyton, 250..............EK-8
Allison, 200...............WC-13
Alma, 331..................EF-8
Alpine, 5905.............WN-7
Alto, 1225.................EG-11
Altair, 20..................EK-8
Alto Bonito, 15..........*H-2
Alton, 12341.............WO-1
Alvarado, 3785..........EE-7
Alvin, 24236..............EL-11
Alvord, 1334..............EC-6
Amarillo, 190695......WD-10
Ambrose..........................
Ames, 1003...............EJ-12
Amherst, 721............WF-9
Ammannsville, 80......EK-8
Anahuac, 2243..........EK-12
Anderson, 222...........EJ-9
ANDERSON CO.,
58458....................EF-9
Andrews, 11088.......WJ-9
ANDREWS CO.,
14786...................WJ-8
Angelina, 50..............EG-7
Angleton, 18862.......EL-10
Anna, 8249...............ED-8
Anna Bch., 200..........*B-9
Annona, 315.............EC-11
Anson, 2430..............EE-2
Antelope, 75..............EC-5
Anthony, 5011..........WK-1
Anton, 1126..............WG-10
Apple Sprs., 225........EH-11
Appleby, 474.............EG-12
Aquilla, 139...............EF-7
Aransas Pass, 8204....EO-7
Archer City, 1834.......EC-5
Arcola, 1642...............EL-10
Argo, 120.................EC-11
Argyle, 3282.............EC-7
Arlington, 365438.....EE-7
Armstrong, 20............EO-8
ARMSTRONG CO.,
1901....................WE-11
Arnett, 45.................EH-5
Arp, 970...................EF-11
Arroyo City, 500.........ES-5
Art, 50......................EI-3
Artesia Wells, 50........EO-3
Arvana......................WI-10
Asherton, 1084..........EN-3
Aspermont, 919........ED-1
Atascocita, 65844......*A-7
Atascosa, 890............EM-4
ATASCOSA CO.,
44911....................EN-4
Athens, 12710...........EF-9
Atlanta, 5675............ED-12
Aubrey, 2595..............EC-7
Audubon Pk., 1200...*B-9
Augusta, 25...............EG-10
Austin, 790390..........EJ-7
AUSTIN CO.,
28417...................EK-8
Austonio, 70.............EG-10
Austwell, 147............EN-6
Avalon, 150...............EF-7
Avery, 462................EC-11
Avinger, 444.............ED-12
Avoca, 120................ED-2
Axtell, 300.................EG-7
Azle, 10947..............ED-6
Baclliff, 8619.............*H-8
Bagwell, 175..............EB-11
Bailey, 289...............EE-8
BAILEY CO., 7165..WF-8
Baird, 1496................EE-3
Balch Sprs., 23728....*H-12
Balcones Hts.,
2941....................ER-11
Ballinger, 3767..........EH-2
Balmorhea, 479........WM-6
Balsora.......................EC-6
Bammel, 200.............*A-4
Bandera, 857............EK-5
BANDERA CO.,
20485...................EK-3
Bangs, 1603..............EG-3
Banquete, 726...........EP-5
Barclay, 40................EH-6
Barbilla........................
Bardwell, 649............EF-8
Barksdale, 90............EL-2
Barnhart, 200............WK-13
Barrett, 3199............*C-8
Barry, 242................EF-8

Woodlawn, 300.........B-9
Woodville, 30............D-3
Wrigley, 281.............D-10
Wright Vil., 300.........J-16
Wyknneetown, 30.....D-7
Yorkville, 180.............C-4
Yuma, 180................D-7

Texas

Barstow, 349............WL-7
Bartlett, 1623............EI-6
Bartonville, 1469.......*C-6
Barwise....................WG-11
Bassett, 100..............EC-11
Bastrop, 7218...........EJ-7
BASTROP CO.,
74171...................EJ-7
Brock, 90...................EE-6
Bronson, 275............EG-13
Bronte, 999..............EG-1
Brookeland, 100........EH-13
Brookesmith, 100.......EG-4
Brookside Vil.,
1523.....................*G-5
Brookston, 250..........EC-9
Bear Creek, 100........EH-6
Beasley, 641..............EL-9
Beattie, 25.................EF-4
Beaumont, 118296...EI-13
Beaumont Pl.,
8000......................*C-7
Beaverdam, 85...........EB-11
Bebe, 30....................EL-6
Beckville, 847.............EF-12
Bedford, 46979........*F-6
Bedias, 443...............EI-9
Bee Cave, 3925..........EJ-5
BEE CO., 31861......EN-6
Bee House.................EH-5
Beeville, 12863..........EN-6
Belcherville, 35..........EB-5
Belfalls, 75.................EH-7
Belgrade....................EI-4
Belk...........................EH-7
Bellaire, 16855...........EK-10
Bellevue, 362............WH-10
Bellmead, 9901..........EG-7
Bells, 1392................EC-8
Bellville, 4097...........EK-9
Belmont, 30...............EL-6
Belton, 18216...........EH-6
Ben Arnold, 150.........EH-6
Ben Bolt, 250.............EP-5
Ben Franklin, 130......EC-9
Ben Hur, 80...............EG-8
Ben Wheeler, 500.......EE-10
Benavides, 1362.........EP-5
Benbrook, 21234......EE-6
Bend, 100..................EH-4
Benjamin, 258...........EC-2
Bennett, 100..............EE-5
Berclair, 250...............EN-6
Bergheim, 20.............EK-4
Bernardo, 35.............EK-8
Berryville, 975............EF-10
Bertram, 1353............EI-5
Bethany, 50...............ED-12
Bethel........................EI-7
Bettie, 125................ED-11
Beverly Hills, 1995.....W-6
Bevil Oaks, 1274........EJ-12
Big Lake, 2936..........WM-11
Big Sandy, 1343.........EE-11
Big Spr., 27282..........WJ-11
Big Wells, 697...........EN-2
Bigfoot, 450...............EM-4
Birome, 30.................EG-7
Birthright..................ED-9
Bishop, 3134............EP-6
Bishop Hills, 193.......WD-10
Bivins, 200................ED-12
Black, 50...................WF-8
Blackwell, 311............EF-1
Blanco, 1739.............EK-4
BLANCO CO.,
10497...................EJ-5
Blanconia, 80.............EN-6
Blanket, 390...............EG-4
Bleakwood, 100.........EI-13
Bledsoe, 200.............WG-8
Bleiblerville, 80..........EK-8
Blessing, 927.............EM-9
Bloomburg, 404........ED-12
Bloomington, 2459....EN-8
Blossom, 1494...........EB-10
Blue Ridge, 822.........ED-8
Bluegrove, 110...........EC-5
Bluff Dale, 220...........EF-5
Bluffton, 100..............EI-4
Blum, 444..................EF-7
Boerne, 10471...........EK-4
Bogata, 1153.............EC-10
Boling, 1122..............EL-9
Bomarton, 15...........EC-3
Bon Wier, 500............EH-13
Bonham, 10127.........EC-8
Bonita, 30................EB-6
Bonney, 310.............EL-11
Bonnie View, 100.......EO-7
Bonus, 30................EL-9
Booker, 1516............WA-13
Boonsville, 40............EC-6
Borden, 50................EE-10
Bordeville, 80............EC-8
BORDEN CO.,
641......................WI-11
Borderland................WK-1
Borger, 13251...........WC-11
Bosque, 25...............EG-6
BOSQUE CO.,
18212...................EF-6
Bosqueville................EG-6
Bovina, 1868..............WE-8
Bowie, 5218..............EC-6
BOWIE CO.,
92565....................EC-12
Boxelder, 125.............EC-11
Boyd, 1207...............EC-6
Boys Ranch, 282.......WC-10
Bracken, 30...............EK-4
Brackettville,............
1688....................WQ-13
Bradshaw, 50............EF-2
Brady, 5528..............EH-3
Brandon, 30..............EF-7
Brandt, 1496.............EE-7
Brashear, 200............EC-9
Brazoria, 3019...........EL-10
BRAZORIA CO.,
313166.................EM-10
BRAZOS CO.,
194851.................EI-8
Brazos Pt., 25............EF-6
Breckenridge, 5780...EE-3
Bremond, 929............EH-8
Brenham, 15716.......EK-8
Breslau, 50...............EL-7
BREWSTER CO.,
9232...................WO-7
Briarcliff, 1438...........EI-5
Briaroaks, 640...........*H-5
Briarwood, 492..........EC-12
Briar, 5773................EE-6
Brice........................WE-12
Bridge City, 7840.......EJ-13

Column 1

., Hancock, 1750 ....WL-3
. McKavett, 50....EI-1
.. Stockton, 8283...WM-8
.. Worth, 741206....EE-6
ur Cors., 12382 ....*F-1
.wlerton, 55 .....EH-4
.ancitas, 1564 ....EH-8
ranklin, 1229 ....EC-10
.ed, 300 ....EI-13
.edericksburg,
.0530 ....EJ-4
.eeport, 12049...EM-10
.eer, 2818 ......EO-4
.ene, 35 ....EE-8
BEND CO.,
.85375 ....EL-10
.bright, 100 ....EC-10
.shear, 1134 ....EK-9
.ston, 1358 .....EO-2
.day............EH-10
endship, 50 ....ED-11
.nodwood,
.5805 ....EL-11
IO CO., 17217...EM-8
.sco, 4123 .....WE-9
.co, 116989 ....ED-12
.ton, 180 ......ES-3
.ort, 643 ......EF-7
.itvale, 408 ...EC-5
.dek, 100 ......EE-8
BEND CO.,
.80 ....EL-11
.elsburg, 68 ...EK-8
.*G-4
.day............EH-10
.ndowood, 19069...*G-4
.co, 4123 ......WE-9

Column 2

Gregory, 1907 ....EO-7
Grey Forest, 483 ..EP-9
GRIMES CO.,
26604 ....EI-9
Groesbeck, 4328 ...EG-8
Groom, 574 ......WD-12
Groves, 16144 ....EK-13
Groveton, 1057 ...EH-11
Gruver, 1194 .....WB-11
Guadalupe, 90 ...EM-7
GUADALUPE CO.,
131533 ....EJ-6
Guerra, 80 ......EO-4
Gun Barrel City,
5672 ....EE-9
Gunter, 1498 ....EC-7
Gustine, 160 ....EG-4
Guthrie, 160 ....EC-1
Guy, 75 ....EL-10
Hackberry, 968 ..†B-9
Hagansport, 70 ...EC-10
Hainesville, 100 ..EE-10
Hale Ctr., 2252 ...WF-10
HALE CO.,
36273 ....WG-10
Halfway, 60 .....WG-10
Hallettsville, 2550 ..EL-7
Hallsburg, 507 ...EG-7
Hallsville, 3577 ...EE-12
Haltom City, 40401 ..*G-4
Hamilton, 3095 ...EG-5
HAMILTON CO.,
8517 ....EG-5
Hamlin, 2124 ....EB-1
Hamshire, 656 ...EK-12
Hankamer, 600 ...EK-12

Column 3

Hub, 25 ....WE-9
Hubbard, 1423 ...EG-7
Huckaby, 150 ....EF-5
Hudson, 4731 ...EH-11
HUDSPETH CO.,
3476 ....WK-2
Huffman, 3000 ..EJ-11
Hughes Sprs.,
1760 ....ED-11
Hull, 650 ......EJ-12
Humble, 15133 ..EK-11
Hungerford, 347 ..EL-8
Hunt, 650 ......EK-3
HUNT CO., 86129..EC-9
Hunter, 40 .....EK-5
Hunters Creek Vil.,
4367 ....*D-3
Huntington, 2118...EH-12
Huntsville, 38548 ..EI-10
Hurlwood, 130 ...WG-10
Hurst, 37337 ....*G-5
Hutchins, 5338 ..†I-11
HUTCHINSON CO.,
22150 ....WB-11
Hutto, 14698 ....EJ-4
Huxley, 385 ....EG-13
Iago, 161 ......EL-9
Ida, 60 ....EC-7
Idalou, 2250 ...WG-10
Illinois Bend ..EB-6
Imperial, 278 ...WL-8
Independence, 125 ..EJ-8
Indian Creek EG-3
Indian Gap, 40 ...EG-4
Indianola, 50 ...EM-8
Industry, 304 ...EK-8
Inez, 2098 .....EM-8
Ingleside, 9387 ...EO-7
Ingram, 1804 ....EK-3
Iola, 401 ......EI-9
Iowa Colony,
Iowa Pk., 6355 ..EB-4
Ira, 300 ....WJ-12
Iraan, 1229 ....WM-10
Ireland, 30 ....EG-5
Irene, 150 .....EF-7
IRION CO., 1599..WL-12
Irving, 216290 ...ED-7
Italy, 1863 .....EF-7
Itasca, 1644 ....EF-7
Ivanhoe, 538 ....EB-11
Ivanhoe, 538 ....EI-11
Ivanhoe Vista, 3117..ES-7
Izoro, 25 ......EH-5
Jacinto City, 10553..†I-6

Column 4

Kingsbury, 782 ...EL-6
Kingsland, 6030 ..EI-4
Kingston, 140 ...EC-8
Kingsville, 26213..EP-6
KINNEY CO., 3598..EL-1
Kirby, 8000 .....EL-5
Kirbyville, 2142 ...EI-13
Kirvin, 129 .....EF-8
KLEBERG CO.,
32061 ....EP-6
Klondike, 175 ....EC-9
Knickerbocker,
170 ....WM-12
Knippa, 689 ....EL-2
Knollwood, 226 ...EC-8
Knott, 550 ......WJ-10
Knox City, 1130 ..EC-2
Kohrville, 400 ...*A-2
Kopperl, 250 ....EF-6
Kosciusko, 100 ..EM-5
Kosse, 464 .....EH-8
Kountze, 2123 ...EJ-12
Kress, 711 .....WF-10
Krum, 4157 .....ED-7
Kurten, 398 ....EI-9
Kyle, 28016 ....EK-5
La Coste, 1119 ...EL-4
La Feria, 7302 ...ES-6
La Gloria EO-5
La Grange, 4641 ..EK-7
La Grulla, 1622 ...ES-4
La Homa, 11985 ..WO-1
La Joya, 3985 ...ES-4
La Marque, 14509..EL-11
La Porte, 33800 ...EM-2
La Pryor, 1643 ...EM-2
La Reforma EO-4
La Salle, 200 ...EM-8
LA SALLE CO.,
6886 ....EO-3
La Vernia, 1034 ...EL-5
La Villa, 1957 ...ES-6
La Ward, 213 ...EM-8
Lacy-Lakeview,
6489 ....WD-6
Ladonia, 612 ....EC-9
LaFayette, 80 ...EC-13
Lago Vista, 6041 ..EJ-3
Laguna Hts., 3488..ES-7
Laguna Park, 1716..EF-6
Laguna Vista, 3117..ES-7
Laird Hill, 400 ...EE-11
L. Brownwood,
1532 ....WQ-6
L. Creek, 75 ...EC-10
L. Dallas, 7105 ...EJ-5
L. Jackson, 26849..EM-10
L. Shore, 300 ...EG-3
L. Tanglewood,
796 ....WD-10
L. Victor, 50 ...EJ-4
L. Worth, 4584 ...†G-3
Lakehills, 400 ...EL-3
Lakeport, 974 ...EE-11
Lakeside, 1307 ...†G-2
Lakeside Vil., 997..EB-4
Lakeside Vil., 600..EF-6
Laketon WE-12
Lakeview, 107 ...WE-12
Lakeview, 35 ...WH-10
Lakeway, 11391 ...EK-4
Lakewood Hbr., 40..EG-6
Lakewood Vil., 545..*B-8
Lamar, 636 .....EO-7
LAMAR CO.,
49793 ....EC-9
Lamasco, 35 ....EB-9
LAMB CO.,
13977 ....WG-9
Lamesa, 9422 ...WI-10
Lamkin, 50 .....EG-5
Lampasas, 6681 ...EH-5
LAMPASAS CO.,
19677 ....EH-5
Lancaster, 36361 ..†J-10
Lane City, 300 ...EL-9
Langtry, 30 ....WM-11
Lannius, 90 .....EC-9
Lantana, 6874 ...†C-6
Laredo, 236091 ...EP-2
Lariat, 60 ......WF-8
LaRue, 160 .....EF-9
Lasara, 1039 ...ES-6
Lassater, 50 ...EC-12
Latexo, 322 ....EG-10
Laughlin, 5910 ...EC-6
Laureles, 80 ...EP-6
Lavaca, 322 ....EB-10
LAVACA CO.,
19263 ....EL-7
Lawn, 314 ......EF-2
Lawrence, 300 ...ED-8
Lazbuddie, 250 ...WF-9
League City,
83560 ....EL-11
Leakey, 425 ....EK-2
Leander, 26521 ...EJ-4
Ledbetter, 80 ...EJ-7
Leesburg, 120 ...ED-11
Leesville, 130 ...EL-6
Lefors, 497 ....WC-12
Leggett, 450 ...EI-11
Leigh, 75 ......EE-12
Lela, 80 ....WD-13
Lelia Lake, 130 ...WE-12
Leming, 946 ....EM-4
Lenorah, 80 ....WJ-10
Leon Jct., 50 ...EH-6
Leona, 175 .....EH-9
Leonard, 1990 ...EC-8
Leroy, 337 .....EG-7
Leroy, 337 .....WC-6
Lesley, 10 .....WE-12
Levelland, 13542 ..WG-9
Lewisville, 95290 ..†C-8
Lexington, 1178 ...EJ-7
Liberty, 8397 ...EJ-11
LIBERTY CO.,
75643 ....EJ-11
Liberty Grv., 50 ...†A-9
Liberty Hill, 967 ...EJ-4
Libert Sprs., 50 ...†I-5
Lillax, 8900 ....WD-10
Lincoln, 80 ....EK-7
Lincoln Pk., 308 ..†A-8
Linden, 1988 ...ED-12
Lindenau, 50 ...EM-7
Lindsay, 1018 ...EC-7
Lingleville, 100 ...EF-5
Linn, 801 ......EP-5
Linwood, 80 ...EG-4
Lipan, 430 .....EE-5
LIPSCOMB CO.,
3302 ....WB-13
Lissie, 150 .....EL-9

Column 5

Little River-Academy,
1961 ....EH-6
Littlefield, 6372 ...WG-9
Live Oak, 13131 ...EL-5
LIVE OAK CO.,
11531 ....EO-5
Liverpool, 482 ...EL-11
Livingston, 5335 ..EI-11
Llano, 3232 .....EI-4
LLANO CO.,
19301 ....EI-4
Lobo, 50 ....WM-5
Lockett, 500 ....EB-3
Lockettville, 25 ..WH-9
Lockhart, 12698 ..EK-6
Lockney, 1842 ...WF-11
Log Cabin, 200 ...EE-9
Lohn, 150 ....EH-3
Lolita, 555 .....EM-8
Loma Alta, 100 ...EO-4
Loma Alta, 25 ...WP-12
Lometa, 856 ....EH-4
London, 200 ....EJ-3
Lone Camp, 100 ..EE-5
Lone Grv. EB-6
Lone Oak, 598 ...ED-9
Lone Star, 1581 ...ED-11
Long Branch, 120..EF-12
Long Lake, 50 ...EG-3
Long Mott, 125 ...EN-8
Longview, 80455..EE-11
Longworth EE-1
Loop, 225 ....WI-9
Lopeno, 174 ....EP-3
Lopezville, 4333 ..WO-3
Loraine, 602 ....WJ-12
Lorena, 1691 ....EH-7
Lorenzo, 1147 ...WG-11
Los Campos, 100..WQ-12
Los Ebanos, 335 ..ES-4
Los Fresnos, 5542..ES-7
Los Indios, 1083 ..ET-6
Los Ybanez, 19 ...WI-10
Lott, 759 ....EH-7
Louise, 995 ....EM-8
Lovelady, 649 ...EH-10
Loving, 250 .....EF-8
LOVING CO., 82..WK-7
Lowake, 25 .....EH-2
Lowry Crossing,
1711 ....EK-10
Loyola Bch., 130 ..EQ-6
Lozano, 229573 ..WH-10
Lubbock, 278831..WG-10
LUBBOCK CO.,
278831 ....WG-10
Lucas, 5166 .....†C-13
Luckenbach EK-3
Lueders, 346 ...EE-2
Lufkin, 35067 ...EH-11
Luling, 5411 ....EK-6
Lumberton, 11943..EJ-13
Lutie, 30 ....WD-13
Lydia, 75 ....EC-11
Lyford, 2611 ...ES-6
LYNN CO., 5915..WH-10
Lyons, 300 .....EJ-8
Lytle, 2492 ....EL-4
Mabank, 3035 ...EE-9
Macdona, 559 ...EL-4
MADISON CO.,
13664 ....EH-9
Madisonville, 4396..EI-9
Magasco, 50 ...EH-13
Magnet, 80 .....EM-8
Magnolia, 1393 ..EJ-9
Magnolia Bch., 200..EN-8
Magnolia Sprs. ..*C-8
Magnolia Sprs.,
120 ....EI-13
Malakoff, 2324 ...EF-9
Malone, 269 ....EF-7
Malta, 150 .....EC-11
Manchester, 100 ..EB-10
Mankins, 20 ....EB-4
Manor, 5037 ....EJ-6
Mansfield, 56368 ..EE-7
Manvel, 5179 ...EL-10
Maple, 100 .....WG-8
Mapleton, 30 ...WI-9
Marathon, 430 ...WO-7
Marble Falls, 6077..EI-5
Marfa, 1981 ....WN-6
Margaret, 40 ...EB-3
Marietta, 134 ...ED-11
Marion, 1066 ...EL-5
MARION CO.,
10546 ....ED-12
Markham, 1082 ...EM-9
Markley, 30 ....EE-4
Marlin, 5967 ...EH-7
Marquez, 263 ...EH-9
Marshall, 23523 ..EE-12
Marshall Creek, 431..†D-5
Mart, 2209 .....EG-7
MARTIN CO.,
4799 ....WJ-10
Martindale, 1116 ..EK-6
Martinez EL-5
Martinsville, 130 ..EG-12
Maryneal, 120 ...EB-1
Marysville EB-6
Mason, 2114 ....EI-3
MASON CO., 4012..EI-3
Massey Lake, 75 ..EG-12
Masterson, 40 ...WC-10
Matador, 607 ...WF-11
Matagorda, 503 ..EN-9
MATAGORDA CO.,
36702 ....EM-9
Mathis, 4945 ...EO-6
Maud, 1056 .....EC-12
Maurecevile, 3252..EJ-13
Maverick, 80 ...EG-1
MAVERICK CO.,
54258 ....EN-1
Maxwell, 350 ...EK-6
May, 300 ....EF-3
Maydelle, 200 ...EG-11
Maypearl, 934 ...EF-7
Maysfield, 150 ...EH-7
McAdoo, 100 ...WF-11
McAllen, 129877..ES-5
McCamey, 1887 ..WM-9
McCaulley, 200 ...EA-1
McCoy, 20 .....EN-5
McDade, 685 ...EJ-7
McFaddin, 170 ...EN-7
McGregor, 4987 ..EG-6
McKinney, 131117..EC-8
McLean, 778 ....WD-12
McLendon-Chisholm,
1917 ....†G-11
McLeod, 250 ...ED-12
McMahan, 60 ...EK-6
McNair, 1400 ...*D-7

Column 6

McQueeney, 2545 ..EL-5
Meadow, 593 ....WH-10
Meadowood Acres,
Medicine Mound, ..EB-2
Medina, 450 ....EK-3
MEDINA CO.,
46006 ....EM-3
Megargel, 203 ...EC-3
Melissa, 4695 ...EC-8
Melrose EG-12
Melvin, 178 ....EH-2
Memphis, 2290 ...WE-13
Menard, 1471 ...EI-2
MENARD CO.,
2242 ....EI-1
Mentone, 19 ....WK-7
Mercedes, 15570..ES-6
Mercury, 50 ....EH-3
Mereta, 200 ....WL-13
Meridian, 1493 ...EF-6
Merkel, 2590 ...EE-1
Mertens, 125 ...EF-7
Mertzon, 781 ...WM-12
Mesquite, 139824..EE-8
Mexia, 7459 ...EG-8
Meyersville, 120 ..EM-7
Miami, 597 .....WC-12
Mico, 100 ......EL-4
Middleton EH-8
Midfield, 150 ...EM-9
Midkiff, 180 ...WL-10
Midland, 111147..WK-10
MIDLAND CO.,
136872 ....WK-10
Midlothian, 18037..EE-7
Midway, 228 ...EH-9
Milam, 1480 ...EG-13
MILAM CO., 24757..EI-7
Milano, 428 ....EI-7
Mildred, 368 ...EF-8
Miles, 829 .....EH-1
Milford, 728 ...EF-7
Miller Grv., 125 ..ED-9
Millersview, 100 ..EH-2
Millett, 40 .....EN-3
Millican, 240 ...EI-9
MILLS CO., 4936..EH-4
Millsap, 403 ...EE-6
Mineola, 4515 ...EE-10
Mineral, 60 ....EN-6
Mineral Wells,
16788 ....EE-5
Minerva, 60 ....EI-7
Mingus, 235 ....EE-4
Minter WC-10
Mirando City, 375..EP-3
Mission, 77058 ...ES-5
Mission Bend,
36501 ....*E-1
Missouri City,
67358 ....EK-10
Mitchell, 60 ...WK-12
MITCHELL CO.,
9403 ....WK-12
Mobeetie, 101 ...WC-13
Moffat, 200 ....EH-6
Monahans, 6953..WL-8
Monkstown, 35 ..EB-9
Monroe City, 90 ..EK-12
Mont Belvieu,
3835 ....EK-11
Montague, 304 ...EC-6
MONTAGUE CO.,
19719 ....EC-5
Montalba, 150 ...EF-9
Monte Alto, 1924..ES-5
Montell EL-1
Montgomery, 621..EJ-10
MONTGOMERY CO.,
455746 ....EJ-10
Moody, 1371 ...EH-6
Moore, 475 ....EM-3
MOORE CO.,
21904 ....WC-10
Moore Sta., 201 ..EF-10
Mooring EI-8
Moran, 270 ....EE-3
Moravia EL-7
Morgan, 490 ...EF-6
Morgan Mill, 200..EF-5
Morgans Pt., 339..*F-9
Morgan's Pt. Resort,
4170 ....EG-6
Morgan City EK-11
Morgan, 500 ....EH-8
Morton, 2006 ...WG-9
Moscow, 300 ...EI-11
Mosheim, 100 ...EG-6
Moss Hill, 150 ...EJ-12
MOTLEY CO.,
1210 ....WF-12
Moulton, 886 ...EL-7
Mt. Calm, 310 ...EG-7
Mt. Enterprise, 447..EF-11
Mt. Pleasant,
15564 ....ED-11
Mt. Selman, 200 ..EF-11
Mt. Vernon, 2662..ED-10
Mountain Home, 70..EJ-3
Muenster, 1544 ..EC-6
Muldoon, 80 ...EK-7
Muleshoe, 5158 ..WF-9
Mullin, 179 ....EG-4
Mumford, 200 ...EH-8
Munday, 1300 ...EC-2
Muniz, 1370 ...WO-3
Murchison, 594 ..EF-9
Murphy, 17708 ...*D-13
Mustang Ridge, 861..EK-6
Myra, 205 .....EC-6
Myrtle Sprs., 828..EE-9
Nacogdoches,
32996 ....EG-12
NACOGDOCHES CO.,
64524 ....EG-12
Nada, 200 ......EL-9
Naples, 1378 ...ED-11
Nash, 2960 ....EC-12
Nassau Bay, 4002..*G-8
Natalia, 1431 ...EM-4
NAVARRO CO.,
47735 ....EF-8
Navasota, 7049 ..EI-9
Nazareth, 311 ...WE-10
Neches, 300 ...EF-10
Nederland, 17547..EL-13
Needmore, 40 ...WG-8
Needville, 2823 ..EL-10
Nelsonville, 96 ..EK-9
Nemo, 60 ......EF-6
Nesbitt, 281 ...EE-12
Neuville, 250 ...EH-12
Nevada, 822 ...EC-8
New Baden, 120..EH-8
New Berlin, 151 ..EL-5
New Boston, 4550..EC-12

Column 7

New Braunfels,
57740 ....EL-5
New Canaan, 3000..EJ-11
New Chapel Hill,
594 ....EE-10
New Deal, 794 ...WG-10
New Fairview, 1258..EC-6
New Home, 334 ...WH-10
New Hope, 614 ...*A-13
New Katy, 60 ...EK-10
New London, 998..EF-11
New Salem, 50 ...EF-11
New Summerfield,
1111 ....EG-11
New Taiton WJ-10
New Territory,
15186 ....*G-1
New Ulm, 350 ...EK-8
New Waverly, 1032..EI-10
New Willard, 100 ..EI-11
Newark, 1005 ...EC-6
Newcastle, 585 ..ED-4
Newgulf, 460 ...EL-9
Newport, 40 ...EC-5
Newton, 2478 ...EI-13
NEWTON CO.,
14445 ....EH-13
Niederwald, 565 ..EK-6
Niland, 1493 ...EF-8
Nixon, 2385 ....EL-6
Nobility EC-9
Nocona, 3033 ...EB-6
Nogalus, 100 ...EH-11
Nolan, 60 ......EF-1
NOLAN CO.,
15216 ....EF-1
Nolanville, 4259 ..EH-6
Nome, 588 .....EJ-12
Noodle, 50 ....EE-1
Noonday, 777 ...EF-10
Nordheim, 307 ...EM-6
Norias, 50 .....EQ-6
Normandy, 70 ...WR-12
Normangee, 685 ..EH-9
Normanna, 113 ...EN-6
N. Alamo, 3235 ...WO-3
N. Houston, 2000..*B-3
N. Richland Hills,
63343 ....ED-7
N. San Antonio Hills,
100 ....EI-10
N. Zulch, 550 ...EI-9
Nordheim, 307 ...WF-12
Northlake, 1724 ...*C-5
Northline Ter., 2700..*C-4
Norwalk EI-9
Norton, 75 .....WK-9
Norwood, 100 ...EG-12
Nortex, 125 ....WK-8
Novice, 139 ....EF-2
Novohrad EB-10
Nueces, 67 .....EO-6
NUECES CO.,
340223 ....EO-6
Nugent, 50 .....EE-2
Nuroillo, 7344 ...WO-3
Nursery, 350 ...EM-7
Oak Lake Estates,
2000 ....*F-1
Oak Pt., 2786 ...*A-8
Oak Ridge, 141 ...EC-7
Oak Ridge North,
3049 ....EJ-10
Oak Valley, 368 ..EF-8
Oakalla, 80 ....EI-5
Oakhurst, 233 ...EI-10
Oakland, 85 ....EL-7
Oakville, 100 ...EN-5
Oakwood, 510 ...EG-9
O'Brien, 106 ...EC-2
Ochiltree WB-12
OCHILTREE CO.,
10223 ....WB-12
Odell, 95 ......EA-2
Odem, 2389 ....EO-6
Odessa, 99940 ..WK-9
O'Donnell, 831 ...WI-10
Oenaville EH-6
Oglesby, 484 ...EH-6
Oilton, 353 ....EP-3
Oklahoma Ln., 57..WF-8
Oklahoma Lane ..WF-8
Oklaunion, 150 ...EB-3
Old Boston, 170 ..EC-12
Old Dime Box, 200..EJ-7
Old Glory, 70 ...EC-1
Old Ocean, 950 ..EM-9
Old River-Winfree,
1245 ....EK-11
Olden, 500 ....EF-4
Oldenburg, 100 ..EK-8
OLDHAM CO.,
2052 ....WC-9
Olmito, 1210 ...ET-6
Olmos Pk., 2237..EP-11
Olney, 3285 ....EC-4
Olton, 2215 ...WF-10
Omaha, 1021 ...EC-11
Onalaska, 1920 ..EI-10
Opdyke West, 174..WG-9
Orange, 18595 ...EJ-13
ORANGE CO.,
81837 ....EJ-13
Orange Grv., 1318..EO-5
Orchard, 50 ....EL-9
Ore City, 1144 ...ED-11
Orla, 50 ....WK-6
Osceola, 100 ...EF-7
Ottine, 130 ....EL-6
Otto EG-7
Ovalo, 250 ....EF-2
Overton, 2554 ...EF-11
Ovilla, 3492 ...†J-9
Owens, 30 .....EF-4
Owentown, 120 ...EE-10
Oyster Creek,
1111 ....EM-11
Ozona, 3225 ...WN-11
Paducah, 1186 ...EA-1
Paige, 200 .....EJ-7
Paint Rock, 273 ..EG-2
Palacios, 4718 ..EN-9
Palestine, 18712..EG-10
Palm Valley, 1304..ET-6
Palmer, 2000 ...†J-13
Palmhurst, 2607..WO-1
Palmview, 5460 ..WO-1
Palmview South,
5461 ....WO-1
Paloduro, 50 ...WE-11
PALO PINTO CO.,
28111 ....ED-4
Paluxy, 175 ...EF-5
Pampa, 17994 ...WC-12
Pandora, 100 ...EL-6
Panhandle, 2452..WD-11
Panna Maria, 96 ..EM-6
Panola, 225 ...EF-12

Column 8

PANOLA CO.,
23796 ....EF-12
Pantego, 2394 ...*H-6
Panther Jct., 110 ..WQ-7
Papalote, 70 ...EN-6
Paradise, 441 ...EC-6
Paris, 25171 ....EC-9
Park Sprs., 80 ...EC-5
Parker, 3811 ...†C-13
PARKER CO.,
116927 ....EE-5
Pasadena, 149043..EL-11
Patillo, 20 .....EF-5
Patricia, 60 ....WJ-10
Patroon, 60 ....EG-13
Pattison, 556 ...EK-10
Pattonville, 220 ...EC-10
Pawelekville, 50 ..EM-5
Pawnee, 166 ...EN-5
Paxton, 120 ....EG-13
Payne Sprs., 767..EF-9
Peacock, 50 ...WH-13
Peaster, 80 ...EE-5
Pear Valley, 40 ...EH-2
Pearl EH-4
Pearland, 91252..EL-11
Pearsall, 9146 ...EM-3
Pecan Gap, 201 ..EC-9
Pecan Grv., 15963..*F-1
PECOS CO.,
15507 ....WN-8
Peerless, 75 ...EC-10
Peggy, 10 .....EN-5
Pendleton, 100 ..EH-6
Penelope, 198 ...EG-7
Penitas, 4403 ...ES-5
Pennell, 75 ....WK-9
Peoria, 100 ....EF-7
Pep, 50 ....WG-9
Perico WB-8
Perrin, 398 ....ED-5
Perry, 60 .....EH-7
Perryton, 8802 ..WA-12
Peters EF-7
Petersburg, 1202..WG-11
Petrolia, 686 ...EB-5
Petronila, 113 ...EP-6
Pettit, 80 .....WG-9
Pettus, 558 ...EN-6
Petty, 100 .....EC-9
Pflugerville, 46936..EJ-5
Pharr, 70400 ...ES-5
Phelps, 200 ....EI-10
Phillips, 900 ...WC-11
Pickton, 150 ...ED-10
Pidcoke EH-5
Pierce, 25 .....EM-9
Pierce, 57 .....EM-9
Pilot Pt., 3856 ...EC-7
Pine Forest, 487..EJ-13
Pine Island, 988 ..EK-9
Pinehill, 40 ....EF-12
Pinehurst, 4624..EJ-10
Pinehurst, 2097..EJ-13
Pineland, 850 ...EH-13
Piney Point Vil.,
3125 ....*D-3
Pioneer, 40 ....EF-3
Pipe Creek, 500..EK-3
Pittsburg, 4497 ..ED-11
Placedo, 200 ...EN-8
Placid, 30 .....EH-3
Plains, 1481 ...WH-8
Plainview, 22194..WF-10
Plano, 259841 ...ED-8
Pleak, 1200 ...EL-10
Pleasanton, 8934..EM-4
Pleasant Farms,
110 ....WL-9
Pleasant Grv. EE-10
Pleasant Valley, 336..EB-4
Pleasant Valley, 200..WH-1
Pledger, 200 ....EL-9
Plum, 100 .....EK-7
Plum Grv., 600 ...EJ-11
Point, 820 .....ED-9
Pt. Comfort, 737..EN-8
Pointblank, 688 ..EI-11
Polar EF-3
POLK CO.,
45413 ....EH-11
Ponder, 1395 ...EC-6
Ponta, 50 .....EG-11
Pontotoc, 130 ...EI-3
Poolville, 380 ...EE-6
Port Alto, 50 ...EN-8
Port Aransas, 3480..EP-7
Port Arthur, 53818..EK-13
Port Bolivar, 1130..EL-12
Port Isabel, 5006..ES-7
Port Lavaca, 12248..EN-8
Port Mansfield, 226..EP-7
Port Neches, 13040..EL-13
Port O'Connor,
1253 ....EN-8
Porter, 7000 ...EJ-11
Porter Sprs., 100..EH-10
Portland, 15099..EO-7
Posey, 100 ....WH-10
Post, 5376 ....WH-11
Postoak, 50 ...EF-5
Poteet, 3260 ...EM-4
Poth, 1908 ....EM-5
Potosi, 2991 ...EF-2
POTTER CO.,
121073 ....WD-10
Pottsboro, 2160..EB-8
Poolville, 1178 ...EE-6
Powell, 136 ....EF-8
Poynor, 305 ...EF-9
Ozona, 2554 ...EP-11
Prairie Dell, 35 ...EJ-6
Prairie Hill, 200 ..EG-7
Prairie Lea, 200 ..EK-6
Prairie View, 5576..EJ-9
Premont, 2653 ...EO-5
Presidio, 4426 ...WP-5
PRESIDIO CO.,
7818 ....WO-5
Preston, 2096 ...EB-8
Price, 650 .....EF-11
Priddy, 180 ...EG-4
Princeton, 6807..EC-8
Pringle, 30 ....WB-11
Pritchett, 250 ...EE-11
Progreso, 5507..ES-6
Progreso Lakes,
275 ....ES-6
Prosper, 9423 ...EC-7
Providence Vil.,
4786 ....*A-8
Pryor WD-7
Purdon, 130 ...EF-8
Purley, 50 .....ED-10
Purmela, 60 ...EH-5
Putnam, 94 ....EF-3

Column 9

Pyote, 114 .....WL-8
Quail, 19 .....WE-13
Quanah, 2641 ...EA-2
Quarry WL-13
Queen City, 1476..EC-12
Quinlan, 1394 ...ED-9
Quintana, 56 ...EM-11
Quitaque, 411 ...WF-12
Quitman, 1809 ...ED-10
Rabb, 20 ......EP-6
Rachal, 35 .....EP-5
Rainbow, 80 ...EF-6
RAINS CO.,
10914 ....ED-9
Ralls, 1944 ...WG-11
Ramireno, 35 ...EP-3
Ramirez, 50 ...EO-5
Rancho Viejo, 2437..ET-6
RANDALL CO.,
120725 ....WE-10
Randolph, 200 ...EC-8
Ranger, 2468 ...EE-4
Rankin, 778 ...WM-9
Ransom Canyon,
1096 ....WG-10
Ratcliff, 200 ...EG-11
Ravenna, 209 ...EC-8
Ray Pt. EN-5
Rayburn, 50 ....EB-9
Rayland EB-2
Raymondville,
11284 ....ES-6
Raywood, 300 ...EJ-12
Reagan, 220 ...EH-8
REAGAN CO.,
3367 ....WL-11
REAL CO., 3309..EK-2
Realitos, 184 ...EP-4
Red Bluff, 40 ...WK-6
Red Gate, 50 ...EP-5
Red Oak, 10769..EE-7
RED RIVER CO.,
12860 ....EB-10
Red Rock, 80 ...EK-6
Red Sprs., 40 ...EC-2
Redbank, 150 ...EC-12
Redford, 90 ...WP-5
Redland, 1047 ..EG-11
Redwater, 1057..EC-12
Reeves, 300 ...WK-6
REEVES CO.,
13783 ....WL-6
Refugio, 2890 ...EN-6
REFUGIO CO.,
7383 ....EN-7
Reilly Sprs., 75 ...ED-10
Reklaw, 379 ...EF-11
Rendon, 12552 ...†J-5
Reno, 3166 ....EC-10
Reno, 2494 ....ED-6
Retreat, 377 ...EF-8
Rhea, 50 ......WE-8
Rhineland, 300 ...EC-2
Rhome, 1522 ...EC-6
Rhonesboro, 80 ..EE-11
Ricardo, 1048 ...EP-6
Rice, 923 ......EF-8
Richards, 300 ...EI-9
Richardson, 99223..†E-11
Richland, 264 ...EF-8
Richland Hills,
7801 ....†G-5
Richmond, 11679..EL-10
Richwood, 3510 ..EM-10
Riesel, 1007 ...EG-7
Rincon EO-5
Ringgold, 200 ...EC-5
Rio Bravo, 4794..EP-2
Rio Frio, 60 ....EK-2
Rio Grande City,
13834 ....EP-4
Rio Hondo, 2356..ES-6
Rio Vista, 873 ...EF-6
Rising Star, 835..EF-3
River Bend EH-14
River Oaks, 7427..†G-3
Riverside, 500 ...EI-10
Riviera, 689 ...EP-6
Riviera Bch., 125..EQ-6
Roane Prairie, 60..EH-9
Roans Prairie ...EI-9
Roaring Sprs.,
234 ....WG-12
Robert Lee, 1049..WK-13
ROBERTS CO.,
929 ....WC-12
ROBERTSON CO.,
16622 ....EH-8
Robinson, 10509..EG-7
Robstown, 11487..EO-6
Roby, 643 .....EE-1
Rochelle, 200 ...EH-3
Rochester, 324 ..ED-2
Rock Island, 200..EL-8
Rockdale, 5595 ..EI-7
Rockland, 120 ...EH-12
Rockne, 60 ....EK-6
Rockport, 8766..EO-7
Rocksprings, 1182..EK-1
Rockwall, 37490..ED-8
ROCKWALL CO.,
78337 ....ED-8
Rockwood, 50 ...EH-3
Rocky Mound, 75..ED-11
Roganville, 100 ...EI-13
Rogers, 1218 ...EH-7
Rolling Hills, 50 ..WA-2
Rolling Hills, 200..WD-4
Roma-Los Saenz,
9765 ....EP-4
Romayor, 150 ...EJ-11
Roosevelt, 20 ...EJ-1
Roosevelt, 56 ...WE-13
Ropesville, 434 ..WH-10
Rosalie, 80 ....EC-10
Rosanky, 180 ...EK-6
Roscoe, 1322 ...WJ-12
Rose City, 550 ...EE-2
Rose Hill Acres,
441 ....EJ-13
Rosebud, 1421 ..EH-7
Rosenberg, 30618..EL-10
Rosevine, 100 ...EH-13
Rosewood EG-9
Rosita EP-3

Column 10

Ross, 283 ......EG-7
Rosser, 332 ....EF-8
Rosston, 60 ....EC-6
Round Mtn., 181..EJ-3
Round Rock, 99887..EJ-6
Round Top, 90 ...EK-8
Rowena, 450 ...EG-1
Rowlett, 56199 ..†E-13
Roxton, 650 ...EC-9
Royal City, 9349..ED-8
Royalty, 80 ....WL-8
Royse City, 9349..ED-8
Rugby, 10 .....EC-10
Ruidosa, 80 ...WO-5
Rule, 636 ......EC-2
Rumley EH-5
Runaway Bay, 1286..ED-5
Runge, 1031 ...EM-6
RUNNELS CO.,
10501 ....EG-1
Rushwood, 3600..*B-4
Rusk, 5551 .....EG-11
RUSK CO., 53330..EF-11
Rutersville, 50 ...EK-8
Rye, 100 ......EJ-11
Sabinal, 1695 ...EL-2
SABINE CO.,
10834 ....EG-13
Sachse, 20329 ...†D-13
Sadler, 343 ...EB-7
Sagerton, 75 ...ED-2
St. Francis Vil., 500..†J-2
St. Hedwig, 2094..EL-5
St. Jo, 1043 ...EC-6
St. Paul, 1066 ...†C-13
St. Paul, 584 ...EC-6
Salado, 2074 ...EH-6
Salineño, 216 ...ES-3
Salmon EG-10
Salt Flat, 30 ...WK-4
Salt Gap EH-2
Saltillo, 200 ...ED-10
Samnorwood, 51..WD-13
San Angelo,
93200 ....WL-13
San Antonio,
1327407 ....EL-4
San Augustine,
2108 ....EG-13
SAN AUGUSTINE CO.,
8865 ....EG-13
San Benito, 24250..ES-6
San Carlos, 3130 ..WN-3
San Diego, 4488..EP-5
San Elizario,
13603 ....WK-2
San Felipe, 747 ..EK-9
San Gabriel, 75 ...EI-7
San Jacinto, 240..ER-5
SAN JACINTO CO.,
26384 ....EI-11
S. Haven, 100 ...WR-13
S. Houston, 16983..*F-6
S. Mountain, 184..EK-3
S. Padre Island,
2816 ....ES-7
S. Plains, 100 ...WF-11
Southlake, 26575..†E-5
Southland, 150 ...WH-11
Southmayd, 992..EC-7
Southside PI., 1715..*E-4
Southton, 100 ...EL-4
Spade, 70 .....WG-9
Spanish Camp ...EL-9
Spanish Fort, 50 ..EB-6
Spearman, 3368..WB-11
Speaks, 60 ....EL-8
Spofford, 75 ...WR-13
Spicewood, 200 ..EJ-4
Splendora, 1615..EJ-11
Spofford, 45 ...EL-2
Spring, 54298 ...EJ-10
Spring Branch, 100..EK-4
Spring Hill, 60 ...EE-11
Spring Valley, 3611..*D-3
Springlake, 104 ..WF-9
Springtown, 2658..ED-6
Spur, 1318 ....WH-12
Spurger, 600 ...EI-13
Stafford, 17693 ..*F-3
Stamford, 3124..ED-2
Stanton, 2492 ...WK-10
Staples, 267 ...EK-6
Star EG-4
Starr, 60936 ...ER-4
Steden WG-6
Steele EK-7
Stephenville, 17123..EF-5
Sterling City, 888..WK-12
STERLING CO.,
1143 ....WL-11
Stewart, 1881 ...WO-11
Stockdale, 1442 ..EL-5
Stonewall, 505 ...EJ-3
STONEWALL CO.,
1490 ....ED-1
Stony, 50 .....EC-7
Stowell, 1756 ...EK-12
Strawn, 653 ....EE-4
Streetman, 247 ..EG-8
Stringtown EF-8
Sublime, 170 ...EL-7
Sudan, 958 ....WF-9
Sugar Land, 78817..EK-10
Sugarland, 14835..EK-8
Seagraves, 2417..WI-9
Sulphur Bluff, 280..EC-10
Sulphur Sprs.,
15449 ....ED-10
Summerfield, 70 ..WE-9
Sumner, 30 ....EC-9
Sunnyside, 75 ...WE-10
Sunnyvale, 5130..†G-13
Sunray, 1910 ...WB-10
Sunset, 497 ...EC-5
Sunset Valley, 749..WT-8
Sunrise Bch. Vil., 713..EI-4
Swan EE-10
Sweeny, 3684 ...EM-10
Sweet Home, 60 ..EL-7
Sweetwater,
10906 ....WJ-13
Swinney Switch ..EN-5
Swisher, 40 ....WE-10
SWISHER CO.,
7854 ....WE-10
Sylvester, 200 ...EE-1

Column 11

Tahoka, 2673 ...WH-10
Talco, 516 .....EC-10
Talpa, 150 ....EG-2
Tanglewood, 80 ..*G-1
Tara, 110 ......*G-1
Tarpley, 40 ....EK-3
TARRANT CO.,
1809034 ....EE-6
Tarzan, 250 ...WJ-10
Tatum, 1385 ...EE-12
Taylor, 15191 ...EI-6
TAYLOR CO.,
131506 ....EF-1
Taylor Lake Vil.,
3544 ....*G-8
Taylor, 228 ...WK-4
Teague, 3560 ...EG-8
Tehuacana, 283..EG-8
Telegraph, 15 ...EJ-2
Telephone, 210 ..EB-9
Telferner, 700 ...EM-7
Tell, 75 ....WE-13
Temple, 66102..EH-6
Tenaha, 1160 ...EF-12
Tennessee Colony,
300 ....EG-9
Tennyson, 40 ...EG-1
Terlingua, 30 ...WQ-7
Terrell, 15816 ...ED-8
TERRELL CO.,
984 ....WO-9
Terrell Hills, 4878..EP-12
Texas City, 45099..EL-11
Texhoma, 935 ...WA-10
Texline, 507 ...WA-8
Texon, 25 ....WM-10
Thalia, 80 ....EB-2
The Colony, 36328..ED-7
The Hills, 2472 ..EJ-5
Thicket, 300 ...EJ-12
Thomas EI-11
Thomaston, 85 ..EM-7
Thompsons, 246..EL-10
Thorndale, 1336..EI-7
Thornton, 526 ...EH-8
Thorntonville, 476..WL-8
Thorp Spr., 200 ..EF-5
Three Rivers, 1848..EN-5
Throckmorton, 828..ED-3
Thrall, 839 ....EI-6
Tiki Island, 968 ..EL-11
Tilden, 261 ....EN-4
Timpson, 1155 ...EF-12
Tioga, 803 .....EC-7
Tira, 297 ......EC-10
Tivoli, 479 .....EN-8
Toco, 70 ......EC-9
Tolar, 681 .....EF-5
Tom Bean, 1045..EC-8
TOM GREEN CO.,
110224 ....EH-1
Tool, 2240 ....EF-9
Topsey, 35 ....EH-5
Tornillo, 1568 ...WL-2
Town Bluff EI-12
Town East EI-12
Town West *F-2
Toyah, 90 .....WL-7
Toyahvale, 60 ..WM-6
Travis, 50 .....EH-7
TRAVIS CO.,
1024266 ....EJ-5
Trent, 337 ....EE-1
Trenton, 635 ...EC-8
Trickham, 30 ...EG-3
Trinidad, 886 ...EF-9
Trinity, 2697 ...EH-10
TRINITY CO.,
14585 ....EH-10
Trophy Club, 8024..†D-5
Troup, 1869 ...EF-11
Trout Creek EH-13
Troy, 1645 ....EH-7
Truscott, 60 ...EC-2
Tucker, 150 ...EG-10
Tulia, 4967 ...WE-10
Tuleta, 150 ...EN-6
Turkey, 421 ...WF-12
Turnersville, 150..EH-6
Tuscola, 742 ...EF-2
Twitty WD-13
Tye, 1242 .....EE-1
TYLER CO.,
21766 ....EH-12
Tynan, 278 ....EO-6
Tyler, 96900 ...EE-10
Uhland, 1014 ...EK-6
Umbarger, 150..WE-10
Uncertain, 94 ...EE-12

Column 12

Vanderbilt, 395 ...EM-8
Vanderpool, 20 ...EK-2
Vashti, 70 .....EB-5
Vaughan, 20 ...W-11
Vealmoor, 100 ...WK-10
Vega, 884 .....WD-9
Venus, 2960 ...EE-7
Vera, 90 ......EC-2
Verhalen, 50 ...WM-7
Veribest, 40 ...EH-1
Vernon, 11002..EB-3
Viboras, 20 ...ER-4
Vick, 40 ......EH-1
Victoria, 62592..EM-7
VICTORIA CO.,
86793 ....EM-8
Vidor, 10579 ...EJ-13
View, 50 ......EE-2
Vigo Pk., 50 ...EP-6
Village Mills, 300..EI-12
Village of Tiki Island,
968 ....*B-8
Vincent, 100 ...WJ-11
Vineyard, 80 ...ED-5
Vinton, 1971 ...WK-1
Voca, 60 ......EI-3
Volente, 520 ...EJ-5
Von Ormy, 1085..EL-4
Voss, 20 ......EH-2
Votaw, 200 ....EJ-12
Waco, 124805 ...EG-7
Wadsworth, 300..EM-9
Waelder, 1065 ...EK-7
Waka, 100 ....W3-12
Wake Vil., 5492..EC-12
Wakefield EH-11
Walburg, 300 ...EI-6
WALKER CO.,
67861 ....EI-10
Walls, 1252 ...WK-9
Walnut Sprs., 827..EF-6
Walton, 90 ...EC-8
Wamba EC-12
Ward, 10658 ...WL-7
Warda, 100 ....EK-7
Waring, 100 ...EK-4
Warren, 757 ...EI-12
Warrenton, 30 ...EK-8
Washburn, 160..WD-11
Washington, 300..EI-9
WASHINGTON CO.,
33718 ....EJ-8
Waskom, 2160..EE-12
Wastella WJ-12
Watauga, 23497..†F-5
Water Valley, 100..WL-13
Watt EG-7
Waxahachie, 29621..EE-7
Wayside, 30 ...WE-11
Weatherford, 25250..EE-6
Weaver, 50 ....EH-8
WEBB CO.,
250304 ....EP-3
Webster, 10400..*G-7
Weches, 30 ...EG-10
Weesatche, 170..EM-6
Weimar, 2151 ...EK-8
Weinert, 177 ...ED-2
Weir, 450 .....EI-6
Welch, 222 ...WI-10
Weldon, 200 ...EH-10
Wellborn, 150 ...EI-8
Wellington, 2189..WE-13
Wellman, 203 ...WH-9
Wells, 790 ....EG-11
Wesner EM-7
Weslaco, 35670..ES-5
Wesley EK-9
West, 2807 ....EG-7
W. Columbia,
3905 ....EM-10
W. Lake Hills, 3063..WS-9
W. Orange, 3443..EJ-13
West Point EK-8
W. Sharyland,
2309 ....WO-1
W. Tawakoni, 1576..ED-9
W. University PI.,
14787 ....*E-4
Westbrook, 253 ..WJ-12
Westdale EG-10
Westfield, 800 ..*A-4
Westhoff, 300 ...EM-6
Westlake, 992 ...†D-5
Westminster, 861..EC-8
Westover Hills, 682..†H-3
Westphalia, 150 ..EH-7
Westworth, 2472..†H-3
Wharton, 8857..EL-9
WHARTON CO.,
41280 ....EL-9
Wheeler, 1592 ..WC-13
WHEELER CO.,
5410 ....WD-13
White Deer, 1000..WC-11
White Settlement,
16116 ....†G-2
Whiteface, 449 ..WG-8
Whiteflat, 50 ...WF-12
Whitehouse, 7660..EF-10
Whitesboro, 3793..EC-7
Whiteright, 1604..EC-8
Whitharral, 200..WG-9
Whitney, 2087 ...EF-6
Whitsett, 150 ...EN-5
WICHITA CO.,
131500 ....EB-4
Wichita Falls,
104553 ....EB-4
Wickett, 498 ...WL-8
WILBARGER CO.,
13535 ....EB-3
Wildorado, 179 ..WD-9
Wildwood, 1235..EI-12

Column 13

Vanderbilt, 395 ...EM-8

...

Willow City, 75 ... EJ-4
Wills Pt., 3524 ... EE-9
Wilmer, 3682 ... †J-12
Wilson, 489 ... WH-10
WILSON CO., 42918 ... EM-5
Wimberley, 2626 ... EK-5
Winchell, 40 ... EH-3
Winchester, 70 ... EK-7
Winchester Country, 2000 ... *B-2
Windcrest, 5364 ... ER-13
Windom, 199 ... EC-9
Windthorst, 409 ... EC-4
Winfield, 524 ... ED-10
Wingate, 150 ... EF-1
Wink, 940 ... WK-8
WINKLER CO., 7110 ... WK-8
Winnie, 3254 ... EK-12
Winnsboro, 3434 ... ED-10
Winona, 576 ... EE-10
Winter Haven, 25 ... EN-2
Winters, 2562 ... EF-1
WISE CO., 59127 ... ED-6
Wixon Valley, 254 ... EI-8
Woden, 250 ... EG-12
Wolfe City, 1412 ... EC-9
Wolfforth, 3670 ... WH-10
WOOD CO., 41964 ... ED-10
Woodbury, 40 ... EF-7
Woodcreek, 1457 ... EK-5
Woodlake, 800 ... ER-13
Woodlake, 120 ... EH-11
Woodland, 60 ... EB-10
Woodlawn, 250 ... EE-12
Woodrow, 120 ... WH-10
Woods, 100 ... EF-12
Woodsboro, 1512 ... EO-7
Woodson, 264 ... ED-3
Woodville, 2586 ... EI-12
Woodway, 8452 ... EG-7
Wortham, 1073 ... EG-8
Wrightsboro, 50 ... EL-6
Wylie, 41427 ... ED-8
Yancey, 200 ... EM-3
Yantis, 388 ... ED-10
Yarrelton, 30 ... EI-7
Yellowpine, 60 ... EH-13
Yoakum, 5815 ... EL-7
YOAKUM CO., 7879 ... WH-8
Yorktown, 2092 ... EM-6
YOUNG CO., 18550 ... ED-4
Youngsport, 90 ... EI-6
Zapata, 5089 ... ER-3
ZAPATA CO., 14018 ... EQ-3
ZAVALA CO., 11677 ... EM-2
Zavalla, 713 ... EH-12
Zephyr, 300 ... EG-4

Utah

Page locator
Map keys Atlas pages
1–10 206–207
11–20 208–209

Adamsville, 50 ... K-6
Alta, 383 ... E-9
Altamont, 225 ... E-12
Alton, 119 ... M-7
Altonah, 40 ... E-12
American Fork, 26263 ... E-9
Aneth, 501 ... M-14
Annabella, 795 ... J-8
Antimony, 122 ... K-8
Apple Valley, 701 ... N-6
Aurora, 1016 ... I-8
Avon, 367 ... B-9
Axtell, 70 ... I-8
Ballard, 801 ... E-12
Bear River City, 853 ... B-8
Beaver, 3112 ... K-7
BEAVER CO., 6629 ... J-6
Beryl, 120 ... L-5
Beryl Jct., 197 ... L-5
Bicknell, 327 ... K-9
Big Water, 475 ... N-9
Birdseye, 50 ... F-9
Blanding, 3375 ... L-13
Bluebell, 293 ... E-12
Bluff, 258 ... M-13
Bluffdale, 7598 ... E-8
Bonanza, 1 ... F-14
Boulder Town, 226 ... L-9
Bountiful, 42552 ... D-8
BOX ELDER CO., 49975 ... B-5
Brian Head, 83 ... L-6
Bridgeland, 80 ... F-12
Brigham City, 17899 ... B-8
Bryce Canyon City, 198 ... L-8
Bullfrog, 200 ... M-11
Burrville, 40 ... J-8
CACHE CO., 112656 ... B-9
Caineville ... K-10
Callao ... F-5
Cannonville, 167 ... M-8
CARBON CO., 21403 ... G-11
Carbonville, 1567 ... G-10
Castle Dale, 1630 ... H-10
Castle Valley, 319 ... J-13
Cedar City, 28857 ... L-6
Cedar Fort, 368 ... E-8
Centerfield, 1367 ... H-8
Centerville, 15335 ... D-8
Central, 613 ... M-5
Central Valley, 528 ... J-8
Charleston, 415 ... E-9
Circleville, 547 ... K-8
Cisco ... I-14
Clarkston, 666 ... A-8
Clawson, 163 ... H-10
Clear Creek, 4 ... G-10
Clearfield, 30112 ... C-8
Cleveland, 464 ... H-10
Clinton, 20426 ... C-8
Coalville, 1363 ... D-9
Copperton, 826 ... E-8
Corinne, 685 ... B-8
Cornish, 288 ... A-8
Cottonwood ... H-19
Cottonwood Hts., 33433 ... I-19
Cove Fort ... J-7
Croydon, 50 ... C-9
DAGGETT CO., 1059 ... D-12
Daniel, 938 ... E-9
DAVIS CO., 306479 ... D-7
Delta, 3436 ... H-7
Deseret, 353 ... H-7
Devils Slide ... C-9
Draper, 42274 ... E-8
Dry Fork, 30 ... E-13
Duchesne, 1690 ... F-11
DUCHESNE CO., 18607 ... E-11
Duck Creek Vil., 400 ... M-7
Dugway, 795 ... F-7
Dutch John, 145 ... D-13
Eagle Mtn., 21415 ... E-8
E. Carbon City, 1301 ... G-11
Eastland, 90 ... L-14
Echo, 56 ... D-9
Eden, 600 ... C-9
Elberta, 256 ... F-8
Elk Ridge, 2436 ... F-9
Elmo, 418 ... H-10
Elsinore, 847 ... J-8
Elwood, 1034 ... B-8
Emery, 288 ... I-10
EMERY CO., 10976 ... H-11
Enoch, 5803 ... L-6
Enterprise, 1711 ... L-5
Ephraim, 6135 ... H-9
Erda, 4642 ... E-8
Escalante, 797 ... L-9
Esk Dale, 100 ... H-4
Eureka, 669 ... F-8
Fairfield, 119 ... F-8
Fairview, 1247 ... G-9
Farmington, 18275 ... D-8
Farr West, 5928 ... A-2
Faust ... F-7
Fayette, 242 ... H-8
Ferron, 1626 ... I-10
Fielding, 455 ... B-8
Fillmore, 2435 ... I-7
Flowell, 100 ... I-7
Ft. Duchesne, 714 ... E-12
Fountain Green, 1071 ... G-9
Francis, 1077 ... E-10
Fremont, 145 ... J-9
Fruit Hts., 4987 ... F-3
Fruitland, 40 ... F-10
Gandy ... H-4
Garden City, 562 ... A-9
GARFIELD CO., 5172 ... L-10
Garland, 2400 ... B-8
Garrison, 50 ... I-4
Genola, 1370 ... F-8
Glendale, 381 ... M-7
Glenwood, 464 ... I-8
Goshen, 921 ... F-8
GRAND CO., 9225 ... I-13
Granite, 1932 ... J-20
Grantsville, 8893 ... E-7
Green River, 952 ... I-12
Greenville, 110 ... K-7
Greenwich, 30 ... J-8
Grouse Creek, 80 ... B-5
Grover ... K-9
Gunlock, 150 ... M-4
Gunnison, 3285 ... H-8
Gusher, 160 ... E-12
Halchita, 266 ... N-12
Halls Crossing, 6 ... M-11
Hamiltons Fort, 100 ... L-6
Hanksville, 219 ... J-11
Hanna, 70 ... E-11
Harrisville, 5567 ... A-2
Hatch, 133 ... L-7
Heber City, 11362 ... E-9
Helper, 2201 ... G-10
Henefer, 766 ... D-9
Henrieville, 230 ... M-8
Herriman, 21785 ... K-17
Hiawatha, 50 ... H-10
Hideout, 656 ... E-9
Hildale, 2726 ... N-6
Hinckley, 696 ... H-7
Holden, 378 ... I-8
Holladay, 26472 ... E-8
Honeyville, 1441 ... B-8
Hooper, 7218 ... C-8
Howell, 245 ... B-7
Huntington, 2129 ... H-10
Huntsville, 608 ... C-9
Hurricane, 13748 ... N-5
Hyde Pk., 3833 ... L-20
Hyrum, 7609 ... B-8
Ibapah, 60 ... F-4
Independence, 164 ... E-10
Indianola, 30 ... G-9
Ioka, 50 ... F-12
IRON CO., 46163 ... L-5
Ivins, 6753 ... M-5
Jensen, 412 ... E-13
Joseph, 344 ... J-8
JUAB CO., 10246 ... G-6
Junction, 191 ... K-8
Kamas, 1811 ... E-10
Kanab, 4312 ... N-7
Kanarraville, 355 ... M-6
KANE CO., 7125 ... M-9
Kanosh, 474 ... I-7
Kaysville, 27300 ... D-8
Kearns, 35731 ... H-17
Kenilworth, 180 ... G-11
Kingston, 173 ... K-8
Koosharem, 327 ... J-8
La Sal, 395 ... K-14
La Sal Jct. ... K-13
La Verkin, 4060 ... M-5
Laketown, 248 ... B-9
Lakeview, 100 ... H-2
Lapoint, 350 ... E-12
Layton, 67311 ... C-8
Leamington, 226 ... G-8
Leeds, 820 ... M-5
Lehi, 47407 ... E-8
Levan, 841 ... G-8
Lewiston, 1766 ... A-8
Lindon, 10070 ... F-1
Loa, 572 ... J-9
Logan, 48174 ... B-8
Long Valley Jct. ... M-7
Lund ... K-5
Lyman, 258 ... J-9
Lynndyl, 106 ... G-7
Maeser, 3601 ... E-13
Magna, 26505 ... G-16
Manderfield ... K-7
Manila, 310 ... D-13
Manti, 3276 ... H-9
Mantua, 687 ... B-8
Mapleton, 7979 ... F-9
Marriott-Slaterville, 1701 ... B-2
Marysvale, 408 ... J-8
Mayfield, 496 ... I-9
Meadow, 310 ... I-7
Meadowville ... A-9
Mendon, 1282 ... B-8
Mexican Hat, 31 ... N-12
Midvale, 27964 ... I-19
Midway, 3845 ... E-9
Milford, 1409 ... J-6
MILLARD CO., 12503 ... H-6
Millcreek, 62139 ... H-19
Minersville, 907 ... K-6
Moab, 5046 ... J-13
Modena, 100 ... L-4
Mona, 1547 ... G-8
Monroe, 2256 ... J-8
Montezuma Creek, 335 ... M-14
Monticello, 1972 ... L-14
Moore ... I-10
Morgan, 3687 ... D-9
MORGAN CO., 9469 ... C-9
Moroni, 1423 ... G-9
Mt. Pleasant, 3260 ... G-9
Mountain Home, 120 ... E-11
Murray, 46746 ... H-19
Myton, 569 ... F-12
Naples, 1755 ... E-13
Navajo Mtn., 354 ... N-11
Neola, 461 ... E-12
Nephi, 5389 ... G-8
New Harmony, 207 ... M-5
Newcastle, 247 ... L-5
Newton, 789 ... A-8
N. Logan, 8269 ... M-20
N. Ogden, 17357 ... C-8
N. Salt Lake, 16322 ... E-18
Oak City, 578 ... H-7
Oakley, 1470 ... D-10
Ogden, 82825 ... C-8
Ophir, 38 ... E-8
Orangeville, 1470 ... H-10
Orderville, 577 ... M-7
Orem, 88328 ... E-9
Ouray, 40 ... F-13
Panguitch, 1520 ... L-7
Paradise, 904 ... B-8
Paragonah, 488 ... L-7
Park City, 7558 ... E-9
Park Valley, 60 ... B-6
Parowan, 2790 ... L-6
Payson, 18294 ... F-9
Peoa, 253 ... D-9
Perry, 4512 ... B-8
Peterson, 150 ... C-9
Pine Valley, 186 ... M-5
Pintura, 50 ... M-6
PIUTE CO., 1556 ... J-8
Plain City, 5476 ... C-8
Pleasant Grv., 33509 ... E-9
Plymouth, 414 ... A-8
Portage, 245 ... A-8
Porterville, 90 ... D-9
Price, 8715 ... G-11
Promontory ... B-7
Providence, 7075 ... B-9
Provo, 112488 ... F-9
Randlett, 220 ... F-12
Randolph, 464 ... B-10
Red Wash, 30 ... F-13
Redmond, 730 ... I-8
Redwood ... G-18
RICH CO., 2264 ... B-9
Richfield, 7551 ... I-8
Richmond, 2470 ... A-9
River Hts., 1734 ... N-20
Riverdale, 8426 ... C-2
Riverside, 760 ... B-8
Riverton, 38753 ... E-8
Rockville, 245 ... N-6
Roosevelt, 6046 ... E-12
Rosette ... B-5
Roy, 36884 ... C-8
Rush Valley, 447 ... E-7
Sage Creek Jct., 50 ... B-10
St. George, 72897 ... N-5
Salem, 6423 ... F-9
Salina, 2489 ... I-8
Salt Lake City 186440 ... D-8
SAN JUAN CO., 14746 ... K-13
Sandy, 87461 ... E-8
SANPETE CO., 27822 ... H-9
Santa Clara, 6003 ... N-5
Santaquin, 9128 ... F-9
Scipio, 327 ... H-8
Scofield, 24 ... G-10
SEVIER CO., 20802 ... I-9
Shivwits, 30 ... M-4
Sigurd, 429 ... I-8
Smithfield, 9495 ... B-8
Snowville, 167 ... A-7
Soldier Summit ... F-10
S. Jordan, 50418 ... J-17
S. Ogden, 16532 ... C-2
S. Salt Lake, 23617 ... G-19
S. Weber, 6051 ... D-3
Spanish Fork, 34691 ... F-9
Spring City, 988 ... H-9
Spring Glen, 1126 ... G-10
Springdale, 529 ... M-6
Springdell, 120 ... G-3
Springville, 29466 ... F-9
Standrod ... A-5
Stansbury Pk., 5145 ... E-8
Sterling, 262 ... H-9
Stockton, 616 ... E-7
Sugarville, 30 ... H-7
Summit, 160 ... L-6
SUMMIT CO., 36324 ... D-10
Sunnyside, 377 ... G-11
Sunset, 5122 ... D-2
Sutherland, 165 ... H-7
Syracuse, 24331 ... E-1
Tabiona, 171 ... E-11
Taylor, 50 ... B-1
Taylorsville, 58652 ... H-17
Teasdale, 191 ... K-9
Terra, 50 ... E-7
Thompson Sprs., 39 ... I-13
Ticaboo, 50 ... L-11
Tooele, 31605 ... E-8
TOOELE CO., 58218 ... D-6
Toquerville, 1370 ... M-5
Torrey, 182 ... K-9
Tremonton, 7647 ... B-8
Trenton, 464 ... A-8
Tridell, 110 ... E-12
Tropic, 530 ... L-8
Trout Creek ... G-5
Ucolo ... L-14
Uintah, 1322 ... C-8
UINTAH CO., 32588 ... G-13
Union ... I-19
Upalco, 70 ... F-12
Upton ... D-10
UTAH CO., 516564 ... F-8
Vernal, 9089 ... E-13
Vernon, 243 ... F-7
Veyo, 483 ... M-5
Vineyard, 139 ... G-1
Virgin, 596 ... M-6
Wales, 302 ... H-9
Wallsburg, 250 ... E-9
Wanship, 400 ... D-9
Warren, 50 ... A-1
WASATCH CO., 23530 ... F-10
Washington, 18761 ... N-5
WASHINGTON CO., 138115 ... M-5
Washington Terrace, 9067 ... C-2
WAYNE CO., 2778 ... J-10
WEBER CO., 231236 ... C-9
Wellington, 1676 ... G-11
Wellsville, 3432 ... B-8
Wendover, 1400 ... D-4
W. Bountiful, 5265 ... D-18
W. Haven, 10272 ... B-2
W. Jordan, 103712 ... E-8
West Point, 9511 ... D-1
W. Valley City, 129480 ... D-8
W. Weber, 50 ... B-1
Whiterocks, 289 ... E-12
Willard, 1772 ... C-8
Woodruff, 180 ... B-10
Woods Cross, 9761 ... D-8
Yost ... A-5

Vermont

Page locator
Map keys Atlas pages
A–N 210–211

Adamant, 60 ... E-5
Addison, 110 ... F-2
ADDISON CO., 36821 ... F-3
Albany, 193 ... C-5
Alburgh, 497 ... A-2
Alburgh Ctr., 120 ... B-2
Alburgh Sprs., 110 ... A-2
Alpine Vil., 70 ... F-4
Amsden, 60 ... J-5
Andover, 130 ... J-4
Arlington, 1213 ... L-2
Ascutney, 540 ... J-5
Athens, 120 ... K-5
Bakersfield, 370 ... B-4
Barnard, 220 ... H-5
Barnet, 129 ... E-7
Barre, 9052 ... F-5
Barton, 737 ... C-6
Bartonsville, 200 ... K-5
Basin Hbr., 50 ... F-2
Beanville, 30 ... G-6
Beebe Plain, 200 ... A-6
Beecher Falls, 177 ... A-9
Bellows Falls, 3148 ... K-5
Belmont, 300 ... J-4
Belvidere Ctr., 60 ... C-4
Bennington, 9074 ... M-2
BENNINGTON CO., 37125 ... L-2
Benson, 308 ... H-2
Benson ... H-2
Berkshire, 130 ... A-4
Berlin Cors., 360 ... F-5
Bethel, 569 ... H-4
Blissville, 110 ... I-2
Bloomfield, 120 ... C-8
Bolton, 100 ... E-4
Boltonville ... F-7
Bomoseen, 250 ... I-2
Bondville, 150 ... K-4
Bordoville, 20 ... B-4
Bowlsville, 50 ... J-4
Bradford, 788 ... G-6
Brandon, 1648 ... H-3
Brattleboro, 7414 ... M-5
Bread Loaf ... G-3
Bridgewater, 300 ... I-5
Bridgewater Ctr., 60 ... I-4
Bridgewater Corners, 150 ... I-4
Bridport, 180 ... G-2
Bristol, 2030 ... F-3
Brookfield, 130 ... F-5
Brookside, 70 ... L-4
Brownington, 60 ... B-6
Brownington Ctr., 60 ... B-6
Brownsville, 100 ... I-5
Brunswick Sprs. ... C-8
Burke Hollow, 140 ... C-7
Burlington, 42417 ... D-2
Cabot, 233 ... D-6
Cadys Falls, 200 ... D-5
CALEDONIA CO., 31227 ... D-6
Cambridge, 236 ... C-4
Cambridgeport, 100 ... K-5
Canaan, 392 ... A-9
Castleton, 1485 ... I-2
Cavendish, 179 ... J-5
Cedar Bch. ... E-2
Center Rutland, 500 ... I-3
Charlotte, 350 ... E-2
Checkerberry, 120 ... C-3
Chelsea, 500 ... G-5
Chester, 1005 ... K-5
Chimney Pt. ... F-2
Chipmans Pt. ... H-2
Chippenhook, 190 ... I-3
Chiselville, 140 ... L-3
Chittenden, 270 ... H-3
CHITTENDEN CO., 156545 ... E-3
Clarendon, 270 ... I-3
Clarendon Sprs., 200 ... I-3
Colbyville ... E-4
Colchester, 450 ... D-3
Concord, 271 ... D-7
Cookville, 140 ... G-6
Cornwall, 100 ... G-2
Coventry, 97 ... B-6
Craftsbury, 160 ... C-6
Craftsbury Common, 180 ... C-5
Cuttingsville, 120 ... I-4
Danby, 350 ... J-3
Danby Four Cors., 80 ... J-3
Danville, 383 ... D-6
Derby Ctr., 597 ... B-6
Derby Line, 673 ... A-7
Dorset, 249 ... K-3
Dover, 100 ... L-4
Duxbury, 190 ... E-4
E. Alburgh, 70 ... A-2
E. Arlington, 620 ... L-3
E. Barnard, 30 ... H-5
E. Barre, 826 ... F-5
E. Berkshire, 100 ... B-4
E. Bethel, 200 ... G-5
E. Braintree, 50 ... G-4
E. Brookfield, 50 ... F-5
E. Burke, 132 ... C-7
E. Calais, 230 ... E-5
E. Charleston, 140 ... B-7
E. Concord, 150 ... D-8
E. Corinth, 150 ... F-6
E. Dorset, 350 ... K-3
E. Dover, 250 ... L-4
E. Dummerston, 200 ... L-5
E. Fairfield, 160 ... B-4
E. Fletcher, 20 ... C-4
E. Franklin, 80 ... A-4
E. Granville, 70 ... G-4
E. Haven, 80 ... C-7
E. Highgate, 130 ... B-3
E. Hubbardton, 70 ... H-3
E. Jamaica, 150 ... L-4
E. Johnson, 60 ... C-4
E. Lyndon, 120 ... D-7
E. Middlebury, 425 ... G-3
E. Montpelier, 80 ... E-5
E. Orange, 70 ... F-6
E. Peacham, 60 ... E-6
E. Poultney, 500 ... I-2
E. Randolph, 140 ... G-5
E. Richford, 100 ... A-5
E. Rupert, 30 ... J-3
E. Ryegate, 120 ... F-7
E. St. Johnsbury, 180 ... D-7
E. Topsham, 190 ... F-6
E. Wallingford, 280 ... J-4
Eden, 100 ... C-5
Eden Mills, 130 ... C-5
Ely, 50 ... G-6
Enosburg Falls, 1329 ... B-4
Essex Ctr., 850 ... D-3
ESSEX CO., 6306 ... C-8
Essex Jct., 9271 ... D-3
Evansville, 80 ... B-6
Fair Haven, 2269 ... I-2
Fairfax, 350 ... C-3
Fairfield, 130 ... B-3
Fairlee, 189 ... G-6
Felchville, 180 ... J-5
Ferrisburgh, 200 ... F-2
Fletcher, 60 ... C-3
Florence, 120 ... H-3
Fonda, 80 ... B-3
Forest Dale, 350 ... H-3
Foxville, 250 ... F-5
Franklin, 220 ... A-3
FRANKLIN CO., 47746 ... C-3
Gallup Mills, 20 ... D-8
Gassetts, 60 ... J-5
Gaysville, 250 ... H-4
Georgia Ctr., 150 ... C-3
Georgia Plains, 100 ... C-3
Gilman, 500 ... D-8
Glover, 303 ... C-6
Goshen, 50 ... G-3
Grafton, 300 ... K-5
Granby, 40 ... D-8
Grand Isle, 250 ... C-2
GRAND ISLE CO., 6970 ... B-2
Graniteville, 784 ... F-5
Granville, 200 ... G-4
Greensboro, 109 ... D-6
Greensboro Bend, 232 ... D-6
Groton, 437 ... F-6
Guildhall, 100 ... D-9
Guilford, 200 ... M-5
Halifax, 110 ... M-4
Hancock, 150 ... G-4
Hardwick, 1345 ... D-6
Hartford, 500 ... H-6
Hartland, 380 ... I-5
Hartland Four Corners, 200 ... I-5
Healdville ... J-4
Heartwellville, 60 ... M-3
Hectorville ... B-5
Hewitts Corners ... H-5
Highgate Ctr., 350 ... B-3
Highgate Sprs., 200 ... A-3
Hinesburg, 658 ... E-3
Holland, 100 ... A-7
Hortonia, 40 ... H-2
Houghtonville, 40 ... K-4
Hubbardton, 60 ... H-2
Huntington, 280 ... E-3
Huntington Ctr., 150 ... E-3
Hyde Pk., 462 ... C-5
Hydeville, 450 ... I-2
Inwood ... E-7
Ira, 100 ... I-3
Irasburg, 163 ... B-6
Irasville, 130 ... F-4
Island Pond, 821 ... B-7
Isle La Motte, 130 ... B-2
Jacksonville, 223 ... M-4
Jamaica, 230 ... K-4
Jay, 100 ... B-5
Jeffersonville, 729 ... C-4
Jericho, 1329 ... D-3
Jericho Ctr., 120 ... D-3
Joes Pond, 100 ... D-6
Johnson, 1443 ... C-4
Jonesville, 330 ... E-3
Keeler Bay ... C-2
Killington, 100 ... H-4
Kirby Corner, 50 ... I-10
L. Dunmore, 50 ... G-3
L. Elmore, 140 ... D-5
LAMOILLE CO., 24475 ... D-4
Larrabees Pt. Sta. ... G-2
Leicester, 50 ... G-3
Leicester Jct., 50 ... G-3
Lemington ... B-9
Lincoln, 150 ... F-3
Londonderry, 250 ... K-4
Lowell, 228 ... B-5
Lower Cabot, 60 ... E-6
Lower Vil., 300 ... D-4
Ludlow, 811 ... J-4
Lunenburg, 260 ... D-8
Lyndon, 450 ... D-7
Lyndon Ctr., 300 ... D-7
Lyndonville, 1207 ... D-7
Mackville, 100 ... D-6
Maidstone ... C-9
Mallets Bay ... D-2
Manchester, 749 ... K-3
Manchester Ctr., 2120 ... K-3
Maple Cor., 40 ... E-5
Maquam, 200 ... B-3
Marlboro, 230 ... M-4
Marshfield, 273 ... E-6
McIndoe Falls, 200 ... E-7
Mendon, 60 ... H-3
Middlebury, 6588 ... G-2
Middlesex, 200 ... E-4
Middletown Sprs., 200 ... I-3
Miles Pond, 30 ... D-8
Milton, 1861 ... C-3
Monkton Boro, 180 ... E-3
Monkton Ridge, 50 ... E-3
Montgomery, 220 ... B-5
Montgomery Ctr., 380 ... B-5
Montpelier, 7855 ... E-5
Moretown, 220 ... E-4
Morgan, 80 ... B-7
Morgan Ctr., 150 ... B-7
Morrisville, 1958 ... D-5
Moscow, 260 ... D-4
Mt. Holly, 200 ... J-4
Mt. Tabor, 100 ... J-3
New Haven, 140 ... F-3
New Haven Mills, 100 ... F-3
Newark, 70 ... C-7
Newbury, 365 ... F-7
Newfane, 118 ... L-4
Newport, 4589 ... B-6
Newport Ctr., 274 ... B-6
N. Bennington, 1643 ... L-2
N. Calais, 80 ... E-5
N. Clarendon, 550 ... I-3
N. Concord, 140 ... D-8
N. Danville, 110 ... D-7
N. Dorset ... J-3
N. Fayston ... E-4
N. Ferrisburgh, 150 ... E-2
N. Hartland, 302 ... I-6
N. Hero, 190 ... B-2
N. Hyde Pk., 380 ... C-5
N. Landgrove, 50 ... K-4
N. Montpelier, 150 ... E-5
N. Pownal, 350 ... M-2
N. Randolph, 50 ... G-5
N. Shrewsbury, 80 ... I-4
N. Springfield, 573 ... J-5
N. Thetford, 110 ... G-6
N. Troy, 620 ... A-5
N. Tunbridge, 70 ... G-5
N. Westminster, 247 ... K-5
N. Wolcott, 140 ... C-5
Northfield, 2101 ... F-4
Norton, 80 ... A-8
Norwich, 878 ... H-6
Orange, 70 ... F-5
ORANGE CO., 28936 ... F-5
Orleans, 818 ... B-6
ORLEANS CO., 27231 ... B-5
Orwell, 170 ... H-2
Panton, 50 ... F-2
Passumpsic, 200 ... E-7
Pawlet, 230 ... J-2
Peacham, 220 ... E-6
Pearl, 60 ... C-2
Perkinsville, 130 ... J-5
Peru, 150 ... K-3
Pittsfield, 140 ... H-4
Pittsford, 740 ... H-3
Plainfield, 401 ... E-5
Pleasant Valley ... C-4
Plymouth, 100 ... I-4
Plymouth Union ... I-4
Pomfret, 50 ... H-5
Post Mills, 220 ... G-6
Poultney, 1612 ... I-2
Pownal, 320 ... M-2
Pownal Ctr., 280 ... M-2
Proctor, 1740 ... H-3
Proctorsville, 454 ... J-5
Putnamville, 40 ... E-5
Putney, 523 ... L-5
Quechee, 656 ... I-5
Queen City Pk. ... J-8
Randolph, 1974 ... G-4
Randolph Ctr., 250 ... G-5
Rawsonville, 140 ... K-4
Readsboro, 321 ... M-3
Richford, 1361 ... A-4
Richmond, 723 ... D-3
Ripton, 130 ... G-3
Robinson ... G-4
Rochester, 299 ... G-4
Rockingham, 120 ... K-5
Roxbury, 300 ... F-4
Roxbury Flat, 40 ... F-4
Royalton, 100 ... H-5
Rupert, 140 ... K-2
Rutland, 16495 ... I-3
RUTLAND CO., 61642 ... I-2
Ryegate Corner, 90 ... F-7
St. Albans, 6918 ... B-3
St. Albans Bay, 500 ... B-3
St. Johnsbury, 6193 ... D-7
St. Johnsbury Ctr., 450 ... D-7
St. Rocks, 20 ... B-3
Salisbury, 200 ... G-3
Sandgate, 80 ... K-2
Saxtons River, 565 ... K-5
Searsburg, 50 ... M-3
Shaftsbury ... L-2
Sharon, 250 ... H-5
Sheffield, 230 ... C-7
Shelburne, 592 ... E-2
Shelburne Falls, 120 ... E-2
Sheldon, 320 ... B-3
Sheldon Sprs., 260 ... B-3
Shoreham, 100 ... G-2
Shrewsbury, 60 ... I-4
Simonsville, 80 ... K-4
S. Albany ... C-6
S. Alburgh, 100 ... B-2
S. Barre, 1219 ... F-5
S. Burlington, 17904 ... D-2
S. Dorset, 220 ... K-3
S. End, 40 ... J-3
S. Hero, 350 ... C-2
S. Lincoln, 70 ... F-3
S. Londonderry, 400 ... K-4
S. Lunenburg, 100 ... D-8
S. Newbury, 70 ... F-7
S. Newfane, 150 ... L-4
S. Northfield, 80 ... F-4
S. Peacham, 90 ... E-6
S. Pomfret, 160 ... H-5
S. Poultney, 110 ... I-2
S. Reading, 130 ... I-5
S. Royalton, 694 ... H-5
S. Ryegate, 450 ... F-6
S. Shaftsbury, 683 ... L-2
S. Sherburne, 80 ... I-4
S. Strafford, 150 ... H-6
S. Walden ... D-6
S. Wallingford, 230 ... J-3
S. Windham, 100 ... K-4
S. Woodbury, 70 ... D-5
S. Woodstock, 100 ... I-5
Springfield, 3979 ... J-5
Stamford, 400 ... M-3
Stannard, 30 ... D-6
Starksboro, 130 ... E-3
Stevens Mills, 30 ... A-5
Stockbridge, 100 ... H-4
Stowe, 495 ... D-4
Strafford, 70 ... G-5
Stratton ... L-3
Sudbury, 60 ... H-2
Sunderland, 220 ... K-3
Sutton, 130 ... C-7
Swanton, 2386 ... B-3
Tafts Corner, 50 ... J-10
Taftsville, 150 ... I-5
Tarbellville, 50 ... J-4
Thetford Ctr., 190 ... H-6
Thetford Hill, 130 ... H-6
Tinmouth, 80 ... J-3
Townshend, 180 ... L-4
Troy, 243 ... B-5
Tunbridge, 110 ... G-5
Tyson ... I-4
Underhill, 400 ... D-3
Underhill Ctr., 300 ... D-4
Union Vil., 50 ... H-6
Vergennes, 2588 ... F-2
Vernon, 250 ... M-5
Vershire, 120 ... G-6
Waits River, 70 ... F-6
Waitsfield, 164 ... F-4
Walden, 120 ... D-6
Wallace Pond, 100 ... A-8
Wallingford, 830 ... I-3
Waltham ... F-2
Wardsboro, 200 ... L-4
Warren, 370 ... F-4
Washington, 320 ... F-5
WASHINGTON CO., 59534 ... D-5
Waterbury, 1763 ... E-4
Waterbury Ctr., 500 ... E-4
Waterville, 110 ... C-4
Weathersfield Bow, 150 ... J-5
Websterville, 550 ... F-5
Wells, 397 ... J-2
Wells River, 399 ... F-7
W. Arlington, 50 ... K-2
W. Barnet, 80 ... E-6
W. Berlin, 150 ... F-5
W. Bolton ... D-4
W. Braintree, 110 ... G-4
W. Branch, 250 ... D-4
W. Brattleboro, 2740 ... M-5
W. Brookfield ... G-4
W. Burke, 343 ... C-7
W. Castleton ... H-2
W. Charleston, 220 ... B-7
W. Danville, 200 ... D-6
W. Dover, 350 ... L-4
W. Dummerston, 160 ... L-5
W. Enosburg, 60 ... B-4
W. Fairlee, 170 ... G-6
W. Glover, 50 ... C-6
W. Halifax, 160 ... M-4
W. Hartford, 340 ... H-5
W. Haven, 40 ... H-2
W. Hill, 30 ... B-4
W. Lincoln, 80 ... F-3
W. Newbury, 160 ... F-6
W. Pawlet, 300 ... J-2
W. Rupert, 180 ... K-2
W. Rutland, 2024 ... I-3
W. Topsham, 120 ... F-6
W. Townshend, 200 ... L-4
W. Wardsboro, 150 ... L-4
W. Woodstock, 150 ... I-5
Westfield, 100 ... B-5
Westford, 150 ... C-3
Westminster, 291 ... L-5
Westminster West, 80 ... L-5
Westmore, 100 ... C-7
Weston, 300 ... J-4
Weybridge, 140 ... F-2
Wheelock, 100 ... D-7
White River Jct., 2286 ... H-6
Whiting, 100 ... G-2
Whitingham, 330 ... M-4
Wilder, 1690 ... H-6
Williamstown, 1162 ... F-5
Williston, 450 ... D-3
Wilmington, 463 ... M-4
Windham, 70 ... K-4
WINDHAM CO., 44513 ... L-5
Windsor, 2066 ... I-5
WINDSOR CO., 56670 ... I-5
Winooski, 7267 ... D-2
Winooski Pk., 400 ... H-9
Wolcott, 180 ... D-5
Woodbury, 160 ... D-5
Woodford, 60 ... M-3
Woodford Hollow, 60 ... M-3
Woodstock, 900 ... I-5
Worcester, 112 ... E-5

Virginia

Page locator
Map keys Atlas pages
1–10 212–213
11–20 214–215
* City keyed to p. 195
† City keyed to pp. 216–217
‡ City keyed to pp. 224–225

Abbott ... J-5
Abingdon, 8191 ... D-6
Accomac, 519 ... I-19
ACCOMACK CO., 33164 ... I-20
Achilles, 650 ... K-17
Adkins Store ... J-15
Adner ... J-16
Adria, 260 ... K-1
Adwolf, 1530 ... M-1
Afton, 120 ... H-9
Aiken Summit, 60 ... M-7
ALBEMARLE CO., 98970 ... H-10
Alberta, 298 ... L-12
Albin, 300 ... C-11
Aldie, 330 ... D-13
Alexandria, 139966 ... E-15
Alleghany, 110 ... I-5
ALLEGHANY CO., 16250 ... I-5
Alleghany Spr., 140 ... K-5
Allison Gap, 700 ... D-7
Allisonia, 117 ... L-3
Alma, 130 ... F-10
Altavista, 3450 ... K-8
Alum Ridge, 80 ... L-4
Amburg, 280 ... J-17
AMELIA CO., 12690 ... J-12
Amelia Court House, 1099 ... K-12
Amherst, 2231 ... J-9
AMHERST CO., 32353 ... I-8
Amissville, 200 ... E-12
Amonate, 400 ... K-1
Andersonville, 70 ... J-10
Annalee Hts., 1800 ... ‡G-4
Annandale, 41008 ... E-14
Appalachia, 1754 ... C-4
Appomattox, 1733 ... K-9
APPOMATTOX CO., 14973 ... J-9
Aquia Hbr., 6727 ... F-14
Ararat, 350 ... M-4
Arcola, 233 ... D-13
Arcturus ... ‡J-6
Ark, 200 ... J-17
Arlington, 207627 ... D-15
Armel, 130 ... D-11
Aroda, 100 ... G-11
Arrington, 708 ... I-9
Arvonia, 750 ... I-11
Ashburn, 43511 ... D-14
Ashland, 7225 ... I-14
Ashwood, 200 ... H-6
Atkins, 1143 ... L-1
Atlantic, 862 ... H-20
Atlee, 40 ... †A-8
Attoway, 250 ... M-1
AUGUSTA CO., 73750 ... G-9
Augusta Sprs., 257 ... H-8
Austinville, 850 ... L-3
Avon, 80 ... H-9
Axton, 300 ... M-7
Aylett, 200 ... I-15
Bacons Castle, 70 ... †I-1
Bacova, 70 ... H-6
Bailey's Crossroads, 23643 ... ‡H-5
Bakers Crossroads ... ‡J-3
Ballsville, 60 ... J-12
Bandy, 100 ... K-1
Banner, 250 ... C-5
Banners Cor., 300 ... D-5
Barbours Creek ... J-6
Barboursville, 150 ... G-11
Barhamsville, 150 ... J-16
Barley, 30 ... N-13
Barren Ridge, 110 ... G-9
Barren Sprs., 100 ... L-3
Bassett, 1100 ... M-6
Bastian, 420 ... K-2
Basye, 1253 ... E-9
Batesville, 200 ... H-10
BATH CO., 4731 ... H-7
Battery Pk. ... †K-3
Bavon, 150 ... J-17
Bay View, 180 ... K-18
Baywood ... M-2
Beach ... †F-6
Bealeton, 4435 ... F-13
Beaverdam, 170 ... H-13
Bedford, 6222 ... K-7
BEDFORD CO., 68676 ... K-7
Bel Air, 1500 ... ‡G-4
Bellair, 1400 ... †B-1
Belle Haven, 6518 ... ‡I-6
Belle Haven, 532 ... I-19
Belleview, 2300 ... ‡E-3
Bells Valley, 40 ... H-7
Bellwood, 6352 ... †E-8
Belspring, 256 ... K-4
Belvedere, 2200 ... ‡H-4
Ben Hur, 390 ... D-3
Benhams ... D-5
Benns Church, 872 ... L-17
Bensley, 5819 ... †E-8
Bent Creek, 50 ... J-9
Bent Mtn., 40 ... K-5
Bentonville, 380 ... E-11
Bergton, 100 ... E-9
Berryville, 4185 ... C-12
Bethel, 250 ... E-13
Big Island, 303 ... J-8
Big Rock, 650 ... B-6
Big Stone Gap, 5614 ... D-4
Birchleaf, 260 ... B-5
Birdsnest, 80 ... J-19
Bishop, 250 ... K-1
Blacksburg, 42620 ... K-4
Blackstone, 3621 ... L-12
Blackwater, 90 ... E-3
Blairs, 916 ... M-8
Blakes, 100 ... J-17
Bland, 409 ... K-2
BLAND CO., 6824 ... K-2
Blevinstown, 800 ... ‡H-1
Bloxom, 387 ... H-19
Blue Grass, 120 ... F-7
Blue Ridge, 3084 ... J-6
Bluefield, 5444 ... K-2
Bluemont, 200 ... C-12
Bocock, 80 ... G-20
Boissevain, 900 ... K-1
Bon Air, 16366 ... J-13
Bonny Blue, 100 ... D-3
Boones Mill, 239 ... K-6
Boonsboro ... E-17
Boston, 60 ... F-12
Boswells Tavern ... H-11
BOTETOURT CO., 33148 ... I-6
Bowers Hill ... †M-5
Bowlers Wharf, 120 ... I-16
Bowling Green, 1111 ... H-14
Boyce, 589 ... D-12
Boydton, 431 ... M-11
Boykins, 564 ... M-15
Bracey, 1554 ... M-12
Branchville, 114 ... M-14
Brandon ... K-15
Brandy Sta., 360 ... F-12
Breaks, 150 ... B-5
Bremo Bluff, 190 ... I-11
Bridgewater, 5644 ... F-9
Bridle Creek, 30 ... M-2
Briery Branch, 160 ... F-9
Brightwood, 1001 ... F-11
Bristol, 17835 ... E-5
Bristow, 200 ... E-13
Broadford, 300 ... L-1
Broadway, 3691 ... E-9
Brodnax, 298 ... M-12
Brooke, 170 ... F-14
Brookneal, 1112 ... L-9
Brownsburg, 130 ... H-8
Browntown, 200 ... E-11
Broyhill Pk., 3700 ... ‡G-3
Bruington, 70 ... I-15
Brunswick ... M-13
BRUNSWICK CO., 17434 ... L-12
Buchanan, 1178 ... J-7
BUCHANAN CO., 24098 ... B-6
Buckingham, 350 ... J-10
Buckingham Circle, 900 ... †C-1
BUCKINGHAM CO., 17146 ... I-10
Bucknell Mnr., 2350 ... ‡I-6
Buena Vista, 6650 ... I-8
Buffalo Gap, 100 ... G-8
Buffalo Sprs., 50 ... M-10
Bumpass, 80 ... H-13
Burgess, 80 ... H-17
Burke, 41055 ... ‡I-2
Burkes Gdn., 50 ... K-1
Burkeville, 432 ... K-11
Burnsville, 50 ... G-7
Burnt Chimney, 100 ... K-6
Burr Hill, 90 ... G-12
Burrowsville, 70 ... K-15
Butts Corner ... ‡I-1
Cabin Pt., 40 ... K-15
Caledonia ... I-12
Callaghan, 348 ... I-5
Callands, 150 ... M-7
Callao, 550 ... H-17
Callaway, 130 ... L-6
Calverton, 239 ... E-13
CAMPBELL CO., 54842 ... K-9
Cana, 1254 ... M-4
Canterbury Hills, 300 ... †B-2
Cape Charles, 1009 ... K-18
Capron, 166 ... M-15
Caret, 60 ... H-15
Carloover, 70 ... H-6
CAROLINE CO., 28545 ... H-14
CARROLL CO., 30042 ... M-4
Carrollton, 4574 ... †K-3
Carrsbrook, 950 ... H-11
Carrsville, 359 ... M-16
Carson, 200 ... L-14
Cartersville, 380 ... I-12
Carver Gdns., 500 ... †F-2
Carysbrook, 30 ... I-11
Casanova, 190 ... E-13
Cascade, 170 ... N-7
Castlewood, 2045 ... D-5
Catalpa, 120 ... F-12
Catawba, 100 ... J-5
Catharpin, 670 ... D-13
Catlett, 296 ... E-13
Cave Spr., 24922 ... K-6
Cedar Bluff, 1137 ... C-7
Cedar Fork ... H-13
Cedarville, 450 ... D-11
Cedon, 150 ... H-13
Centenary, 30 ... I-10
Center Cross, 150 ... I-16
Centerville, 550 ... †E-1
Central Hill, 180 ... †L-1
Centralia, 200 ... †F-8
Centreville, 71135 ... E-14
Ceres, 50 ... L-1
Chamberlayne, 5456 ... †B-8
Chamblissburg, 80 ... K-7
Champlain, 150 ... H-15
Chantilly, 23039 ... D-14
Chapel ... K-3
Chapel Acres, 1200 ... ‡J-3
Charity, 50 ... M-5
Charles City, 133 ... J-15
CHARLES CITY CO., 7256 ... J-15
CHARLOTTE CO., 12586 ... L-10
Charlotte Court House, 543 ... L-10
Charlottesville, 43475 ... H-10
Chase City, 2351 ... M-11
Chatham, 1269 ... M-8
Chatham Hill, 30 ... C-8
Chatmoss, 1698 ... M-6
Check, 80 ... L-5
Cheriton, 487 ... K-18
Chesapeake, 222209 ... L-18
Chester, 20987 ... J-14
Chester Gap, 839 ... E-12
Chesterbrook, 1600 ... ‡F-4
Chesterfield, 3560 ... J-14
CHESTERFIELD CO., 316236 ... K-13
Chilesburg ... H-13
Chilhowie, 1781 ... M-1
Chincoteague, 2941 ... H-20
Christiansburg, 21041 ... K-4
Chuckatuck ... †L-3
Chula, 130 ... J-12
Church View, 70 ... I-16
Churchland ... †L-5
Churchville, 194 ... G-8
Claremont, 378 ... K-15
CLARKE CO., 14034 ... D-12
Clarksville, 1139 ... M-10
Claudville, 150 ... M-4
Clay Bank, 200 ... †E-3
Claypool Hill, 1776 ... C-7
Clayville, 80 ... J-13
Clear Brook, 190 ... C-12
Clearbrook, 550 ... K-6
Clearwater Pk., 140 ... I-6
Cleveland, 202 ... C-6
Cliffield, 150 ... K-1
Clifford, 180 ... I-9
Clifton Forge, 3884 ... I-6
Clinchco, 337 ... B-5
Clinchport, 70 ... D-4
Clintwood, 1414 ... C-5
Clover, 438 ... M-10
Clover Hill, 100 ... F-9
Cloverdale, 3119 ... J-6
Cluster Sprs., 811 ... M-9
Cobham Wharf, 80 ... †H-1
Cochran, 30 ... M-12
Cody ... L-9
Coeburn, 2139 ... C-5
Coleman Falls, 100 ... J-8
Coles Pt., 300 ... G-16
Colleen, 180 ... I-9
Collierstown, 70 ... I-7
Collingwood ... ‡J-6
Collinsville, 7335 ... M-6
Collinwood ... D-5
Colonial Bch., 3542 ... G-15
Colonial Hts., 17411 ... K-14
Colthurst, 470 ... †B-2
Columbia, 83 ... I-12
Columbia Furnace, 50 ... D-10
Comers Rock, 50 ... M-2
Concord, 1458 ... K-9
Cootes Store ... E-9
Copper Hill, 100 ... L-5
Copper Valley, 30 ... L-4
Courtland, 1284 ... M-15
Cove Creek ... K-2
Covesville, 240 ... H-10
Covington, 5961 ... I-6
CRAIG CO., 5190 ... J-5
Craigsville, 923 ... H-8
Crandon, 80 ... K-3
Cranes Nest, 200 ... C-5
Cresthill ... E-12
Crewe, 2326 ... K-12
Crimora, 2209 ... G-9
Critz, 160 ... M-5
Crockett, 330 ... L-2
Cross Jct., 50 ... C-11
Crows ... I-5
Crozet, 5565 ... H-10
Crozier, 140 ... I-13
Crystal Hill, 220 ... L-9
Cuckoo, 30 ... H-12
Cullen, 100 ... K-10
Culmore, 5200 ... ‡G-4
Culpeper, 16379 ... F-12
CULPEPER CO., 46689 ... F-12
Cumberland, 393 ... J-11
CUMBERLAND CO., 10052 ... J-11
Cunningham, 100 ... H-11
Dahlgren, 2653 ... F-15
Dale City, 65969 ... E-14
Daleville, 2557 ... J-6
Damascus, 814 ... E-7
Danieltown, 50 ... L-12
Dante, 649 ... C-5
Danville, 43055 ... N-8
Dare, 1500 ... †H-4
Darlington Hts., 30 ... K-10
Darvills, 80 ... L-13
Davenport, 100 ... C-6
Dawn ... I-14
Dayton, 1530 ... F-9
Deatonville, 50 ... K-12
Deel, 200 ... B-6
Deep Creek, 115 ... †N-5
Deerfield, 132 ... G-8
Delaplane, 200 ... D-12
Deltaville, 1119 ... J-17
Dendron, 272 ... L-15
Detrick, 40 ... E-11
DeWitt, 100 ... L-13
DICKENSON CO., 15903 ... C-5
Diggs, 80 ... J-17
Dillwyn, 447 ... J-11
Dinwiddie, 200 ... L-13
DINWIDDIE CO., 28001 ... L-13
Disputanta, 550 ... K-15
Dixie, 30 ... I-11
Dixie, 30 ... J-17
Doe Hill, 50 ... F-8
Dolphin, 80 ... M-13
Dooms, 1327 ... G-9
Doswell, 200 ... H-14
Drakes Branch, 530 ... L-10
Dranesville, 11921 ... ‡D-1
Draper, 320 ... L-3
Drewryville, 310 ... M-14
Drill ... C-6
Driver ... †M-4
Dry Fork, 150 ... M-8
Dryden, 1208 ... D-3
Dublin, 2534 ... K-4
Duffield, 91 ... D-3
Dugspur, 70 ... M-4
Dumfries, 4961 ... F-14
Dunbar, 130 ... C-4
Dundas, 150 ... L-12
Dungannon, 332 ... D-5
Dunn Loring, 8803 ... ‡F-3
Dunnsville, 150 ... H-16
Dutton, 270 ... J-17
Dye ... C-6
Dyke, 50 ... G-10
Eagle Rock, 350 ... I-6
Earls, 30 ... K-12
E. Highland Pk., 14796 ... †B-8
E. Lexington, 1463 ... I-8
E. Stone Gap, 500 ... D-4
Eastville, 305 ... J-19
Ebony, 161 ... N-12
Edgehill, 240 ... G-15
Edgerton ... M-13
Edinburg, 1041 ... E-10
Ednam Forest, 700 ... †B-1
Edom ... F-9
Eggleston, 270 ... K-4
Eheart, 90 ... G-11
Elberon, 50 ... K-16
Elk Creek, 150 ... M-2
Elkton, 2726 ... F-10
Elliston, 902 ... K-5
Elmo, 30 ... M-9
Elmont, 300 ... I-14
Elon, 200 ... J-8
Emory, 1251 ... D-7
Emporia, 5927 ... M-14
Esmont, 528 ... I-10
Esserville ... C-4
ESSEX CO., 11151 ... H-15
Etlan, 100 ... F-11
Ettrick, 6682 ... K-14
Evergreen, 170 ... K-10
Evington, 200 ... K-8
Ewell, 40 ... †E-1
Ewing, 439 ... D-1
Exmore, 1460 ... J-19
Faber, 150 ... I-10
Fair Oaks, 200 ... †C-10
Fair Port, 450 ... H-17
Fairfax, 22565 ... D-14
FAIRFAX CO., 22565 ... D-14
Fairfax Sta., 12030 ... ‡I-1
Fairfield, 600 ... H-8
Fairlawn, 2367 ... K-4
Fairview Bch., 391 ... G-14
Falling Spr., 150 ... H-6
Falls Church, 12332 ... D-14
Falls Mills, 450 ... K-2
Falmouth, 4274 ... G-14
Fancy Gap, 237 ... M-4
Farmington, 250 ... †B-1
Farmville, 8216 ... K-11
Farnham, 320 ... H-16
FAUQUIER CO., 65203 ... E-12
Favonia, 130 ... L-2
Ferncliff, 50 ... H-12
Ferrum, 2043 ... L-6
Ferry Farms, 4000 ... G-14
Fieldale, 879 ... M-6
Fife, 60 ... I-12
Figsboro ... M-6
Fincastle, 353 ... J-6
Finchley, 80 ... M-11
First Colony, 900 ... †F-1
Fishers Hill, 200 ... D-11
Fishersville, 7462 ... H-9
Five Forks, 200 ... K-16
Five Forks, 150 ... J-9
Five Mile Fork, 700 ... G-13
Flat Rock ... J-13
Flat Run, 30 ... F-13
Flint Hill, 209 ... E-12
Floyd, 425 ... L-5
FLOYD CO., 15279 ... L-5
FLUVANNA CO., 25691 ... I-11
Ford, 80 ... K-13
Forest, 9106 ... J-8
Forestville, 160 ... E-10
Fork Union, 400 ... I-11
Forksville, 1000 ... M-12
Ft. Blackmore, 250 ... D-4
Ft. Defiance, 120 ... G-9
Ft. Mitchell, 100 ... L-11
Four Corners ... ‡F-2
Four Mile Fork, 420 ... G-14
Franconia, 18245 ... ‡I-4
Franklin, 8582 ... M-15
FRANKLIN CO., 56159 ... L-6
Franklin Pk., 1800 ... ‡F-4
Franktown, 100 ... J-19
FREDERICK CO., 78305 ... C-11
Fredericksburg, 24286 ... G-14
Free Union, 193 ... G-10
Fries, 484 ... M-3
Front Royal, 14440 ... D-11
Fulks Run, 150 ... E-9
Gainesboro, 80 ... C-11
Gainesville, 11481 ... E-13
Gala, 30 ... I-6
Galax, 7042 ... M-3
Garrisonville, 300 ... F-14
Garysville, 60 ... K-15
Gasburg, 481 ... N-12
Gate City, 2034 ... E-4
Georges Tavern, 50 ... I-12
GILES CO., 17286 ... K-3
Glade Spr., 1456 ... D-7
Gladehill, 80 ... L-6
Gladstone, 50 ... J-9
Gladys, 250 ... K-9
Glasgow, 1133 ... I-7
Glen Allen, 14774 ... †A-7
Glen Lyn, 115 ... J-3
Glen Wilton, 200 ... I-6
Glenmore ... I-10
Glenns ... J-16
Glenvar, 976 ... K-5
Gloucester, 2951 ... J-17
GLOUCESTER CO., 36858 ... J-16
Gloucester Pt., 9402 ... K-17
Goldbond, 160 ... J-4
Goldvein, 200 ... F-13
Goochland, 861 ... I-12
GOOCHLAND CO., 21717 ... I-12
Goode, 170 ... K-8
Goodview, 70 ... K-7
Gordonsville, 1496 ... G-11
Gore, 160 ... C-11
Goshen, 361 ... H-7
Grafton, 1050 ... †H-4
Grant, 30 ... M-1
Gratton, 937 ... K-1
GRAYSON CO., 15533 ... M-2
Graysontown, 100 ... L-4
Great Falls, 15427 ... ‡D-2
Green Bay, 140 ... K-11
Greenbackville, 192 ... H-20
Greenbriar, 650 ... †G-8
Greendale, 100 ... D-6
Greendale ... †B-7
GREENE CO., 18403 ... G-11
Greenfield, 60 ... H-9
GREENSVILLE CO., 12243 ... M-13
Greenville, 832 ... H-8
Gretna, 1267 ... L-8
Grizzard ... M-14
Grottoes, 2668 ... G-9
Grove, 680 ... †G-3
Groveton, 14598 ... ‡I-5
Grundy, 1021 ... B-6
Guinea, 80 ... G-14
Guinea Mills ... J-11
Gum Spr., 100 ... I-12
Gunton Pk., 30 ... L-3
Gwynn, 602 ... J-17
Hadensville, 80 ... I-12
Hague, 80 ... H-16
Halfway, 60 ... D-13
Halifax, 1309 ... M-9
HALIFAX CO., 36241 ... M-9
Hallwood, 206 ... H-20
Hamburg, 30 ... E-10
Hamilton, 506 ... C-13
Hamlin, 300 ... C-5
Hampden Sydney, 1450 ... K-11
Hampton, 137436 ... L-17
Hanging Rock ... F-1
Hanover, 252 ... I-14
HANOVER CO., 99863 ... I-13
Hansonville, 200 ... D-6
Harborton, 131 ... I-19
Harman, 600 ... B-5
Harmony, 60 ... N-9
Harris Grv., 170 ... †H-4
Harrisonburg, 48914 ... F-9
Harriston, 909 ... G-9
Hartfield, 150 ... J-17
Hartwood, 50 ... F-13
Hayes, 1000 ... †F-4
Hayfield, 3909 ... ‡J-4
Hayfield, 130 ... C-11
Haymarket, 1782 ... E-13
Haynesville, 210 ... H-16
Haysi, 498 ... B-5
Hayters Gap ... D-6
Haywood, 100 ... F-11
Head Waters, 30 ... G-8
Healing Sprs., 100 ... H-6
Heathsville, 142 ... H-17
HENRICO CO., 306935 ... J-14
Henry, 220 ... M-6
HENRY CO., 54151 ... N-6
Herndon, 23292 ... D-14
Hewlett ... H-13
HIGHLAND CO., 2321 ... G-7
Highland Sprs., 15711 ... J-14
Hightown, 50 ... F-7
Hilander Pk., 400 ... E-6
Hillsboro, 80 ... C-13
Hillsville, 2681 ... M-3
Hillwood, 1650 ... ‡G-4
Hiltons, 100 ... D-5
Hinton, 250 ... F-9
Hiwassee, 264 ... L-3
Hodges, 100 ... K-8
Hollin Hall, 3200 ... ‡J-6
Hollins, 14673 ... K-6
Holly Brook ... K-3
Holmes Run Acres, 1400 ... ‡G-3
Holston, 50 ... D-6
Homeville ... L-15
Honaker, 1449 ... C-6
Hood, 90 ... G-11
Hopewell, 22591 ... K-14
Horse Pasture, 2227 ... M-6
Horsepen, 230 ... K-1
Hot Sprs., 738 ... H-6
Howardsville, 120 ... I-10
Huddleston, 100 ... K-7
Hudgins, 230 ... J-17
Hume, 160 ... E-12
Huntington, 11267 ... ‡I-6
Hurley, 600 ... A-6
Hurt, 1304 ... L-8
Hustle, 100 ... H-15
Hybla Valley, 15801 ... ‡J-5
Ida, 220 ... F-11
Idylwood, 17288 ... ‡G-3
Independence, 947 ... M-2
Independent Hill, 7419 ... E-14
Indian Sprs. ... ‡I-4
Indian Valley, 120 ... L-4
Indika ... †M-2
Ingram, 40 ... M-8
Iron Gate, 388 ... I-6
Ironto, 90 ... K-5
Irvington, 432 ... I-17
Isle of Wight, 70 ... L-16
ISLE OF WIGHT CO., 35270 ... L-16
Ivanhoe, 551 ... L-3
Ivor, 339 ... L-16
JAMES CITY CO., 67009 ... K-16
Jamesville, 80 ... J-19
Jarratt, 638 ... M-14
Jasper, 50 ... D-3
Java, 30 ... M-8
Jefferson ... I-12
Jefferson Vil., 2500 ... ‡G-4
Jeffersonton, 180 ... E-12
Jetersville, 200 ... K-12
Jewell Ridge, 350 ... B-7
Jolivue, 1129 ... G-9
Jonesville, 1034 ... D-2
Jordan Mines, 30 ... I-5
Keeling, 50 ... M-8
Keene, 200 ... H-10
Keezletown, 400 ... F-9
Keller, 178 ... I-19
Kempsville ... †M-7
Kenbridge, 1257 ... L-12
Kents Store, 50 ... H-12
Keokee, 416 ... D-3
Keswick, 200 ... H-11
Key West, 300 ... †B-4
Keysville, 832 ... L-11
Kilmarnock, 1487 ... I-17
KING & QUEEN CO., 6945 ... I-15
King & Queen Court House, 85 ... I-16
King George, 4457 ... G-15
KING GEORGE CO., 23584 ... G-15
King William, 252 ... I-15
KING WILLIAM CO., 15935 ... I-15
Kings Pk., 4333 ... ‡H-3
Kings Pt., 500 ... †F-2
Kingstown, 120 ... F-2
Kingsville, 50 ... K-11
Kinsale, 300 ... H-16
Konnarock, 200 ... E-7
La Crosse, 604 ... M-12
Lacey Spr., 150 ... F-10
Lackey, 500 ... †G-4
Ladd, 410 ... H-9
Ladysmith, 200 ... H-14
Lafayette, 449 ... K-5
Lahore ... G-12
Lakeside, 11849 ... †B-7
Lakeside Vil., 80 ... I-11
Lambsburg, 190 ... N-3
Lancaster, 80 ... I-17
LANCASTER CO., 11391 ... I-17
Laneview, 30 ... I-16
Lanexa, 250 ... J-16
Langley, 1450 ... ‡E-4
Laurel, 16713 ... I-14
Laurel Fork, 80 ... M-4
Lawrenceville, 1438 ... M-13
Lawson, 150 ... L-16
Lebanon, 3424 ... D-6
Lebanon Church, 150 ... D-11
LEE CO., 25587 ... D-2
Leedstown, 50 ... G-15
Leesburg, 42616 ... C-13
Leesville, 50 ... K-8
Leon, 40 ... F-12
Lewinsville ... ‡F-3
Lewisetta, 250 ... H-17
Lexington, 7042 ... I-7
Lightfoot, 400 ... J-16
Lignum, 180 ... F-13
Lilian, 100 ... H-17
Lincolnia, 22855 ... ‡H-4
Lincolnia Hts., 1800 ... ‡H-4
Lindell ... D-6
Linden, 200 ... D-12
Little Plymouth, 50 ... I-16
Littleton ... L-15
Lively, 300 ... I-17
Locust Creek, 50 ... H-13
Locust Dale, 40 ... G-12
Locust Grv., 60 ... G-13
Locust Hill, 150 ... I-17
Locustville, 100 ... I-19
Lodi ... D-7
London Br. ... †M-9
Long Island, 70 ... L-9
Longdale Furnace, 150 ... I-
Longview, 50 ... †L-
Loretto, 30 ... H-1
Lorton, 18610 ... E-1
Lottsburg, 450 ... H-1
LOUDOUN CO., 312311 ... D-1
Louisa, 1555 ... H-1
LOUISA CO., 33153 ... H-1
Lovettsville, 1613 ... C-1
Lovingston, 520 ... I
Low Moor, 258 ... I
Lowesville, 120 ... I
Lucketts, 50 ... C-1
Lunenburg, 165 ... L-1
LUNENBURG CO., 12914 ... L-1
Luray, 4895 ... E-1
Lyells ... H-1
Lynch Sta., 500 ... K
Lynchburg, 75568 ...
Lyndhurst, 1490 ... H
Lynn Spr. ... C
Lynnhaven ... †M
Macon, 40 ... J-
Madison, 229 ... F-
MADISON CO., 13308 ... F-
Madison Hts., 11285 ...
Madison Mills, 70 ... G-
Madisonville, 50 ... K-
Magnolia ... †N
Manakin, 300 ... I-
Manassas, 37821 ... E-
Manassas Pk., 14273 ... E-
Mangohick, 90 ... I-
Mannboro, 50 ... K-
Manquin, 100 ... I-
Manry ... L-
Mantua, 7135 ... ‡C
Mappsville, 440 ... H-
Marion, 5968 ...
Markham, 190 ... D-
Marshall, 1480 ... D-
Martinsville, 13821 ...
Marvin, 130 ...
Masonville ... ‡C
Massaponax, 210 ... G-
Massies Mill, 120 ...
Mathews, 555 ... J-
MATHEWS CO., 8978 ... J-
Matoaca, 2403 ... †
Mattaponi, 350 ... J
Maurertown, 770 ... D
Mavisdale, 450 ...
Max Meadows, 562 ...
Maxie, 400 ...
Mayo, 30 ...
McClure, 350 ...
McCoy, 250 ...
McDonalds Mill ...
McDowell, 170 ...
McGaheysville, 550 ... F
McKenney, 483 ... L
McLean, 48115 ... ‡
Meadowview, 967 ...
Meadville, 30 ...
Mechanicsburg, 170 ...
Mechanicsville, 36348 ...
MECKLENBURG CO., 32727 ... M
Meherrin, 190 ... K
Melfa, 408 ...
Mendota, 160 ...
Merrifield, 15212 ... ‡
Middlebrook, 213 ...
Middleburg, 673 ... D
MIDDLESEX CO., 10959 ... J
Middletown, 1265 ... D
Midland, 218 ... F
Midlothian, 450 ...
Mike ...
Milford, 500 ... H
Millboro, 450 ...
Millboro Sprs., 80 ...
Millenbeck ...
Millers Tavern, 50 ... H
Millwood, 250 ... D
Mine Run, 30 ... G
Mineral, 467 ... H
Mint Spr., 150 ...
Mitchelltown, 200 ...
Mobjack, 250 ...
Modest Town, 149 ... H
Mogarts Bch., 60 ...
Mollusk, 120 ...
Moneta, 220 ...
Monroe, 400 ...
Montebello, 130 ...
Monterey, 147 ...
MONTGOMERY CO., 94392 ...
Montpelier, 150 ...
Montpelier Sta., 120 ... C
Montrose, 7993 ...
Montross, 384 ... C
Montvale, 698 ...
Montvue, 150 ...
Morattico, 270 ...
Morrisville, 190 ...
Moscow ...
Moseley, 120 ...
Motley, 1015 ...
Mt. Airy, 30 ...
Mt. Clifton, 70 ...
Mt. Clinton, 80 ...
Mt. Crawford, 433 ...
Mt. Heron, 180 ...
Mt. Jackson, 1994 ...
Mt. Laurel, 50 ...
Mt. Olive, 90 ...
Mt. Sidney, 663 ...
Mt. Solon, 200 ...
Mt. Vernon, 12416 ...
Mountain Falls, 100 ...
Mountain Grv. ...
Mountain Lake, 30 ...
Mountain Valley ...
Mouth of Wilson, 150 ...
Mustoe, 30 ...
Nain ...
Narrows, 2029 ...
Naruna, 200 ...
Nasons, 30 ...
Nassawadox, 499 ...
Nathalie, 183 ...
Natural Br., 1500 ...
Natural Well, 30 ...
Naxera, 400 ...
Nellysford, 1076 ...
NELSON CO., 15020
Nelsonia, 523 ...
New Alexandria, 950 ...

*, †, ‡, §, ◊ See explanation under state title in this index.
County and parish names are listed in capital letters & boldface type.
Independent cities (not included in a county) are listed in italics.

ew Baltimore, 8119 E-13
ew Bohemia, 40 †I-10
ew Canton, 70 I-11
ew Castle, 153 J-5
ew Church, 205 H-20
ew Glasgow, 50 I-9
ew Hope, 797 G-9
ew Kent, 239 J-15
EW KENT CO., 18429 J-15
ew London K-8
ew Market, 2146 E-10
ew Pt., 300 J-17
ewbern, 300 L-4
ewington, 12943 ‡J-4
ewland H-15
ewport, 200 K-4
ewport, 100 H-8
ewport News, 180719 L-17
ewsoms, 321 M-15
ewtown, 200 F-10
ewtown, 100 H-15
celytown, 160 I-7
ckelsville, 383 D-5
neveh D-11
kesville, 1354 E-13
ra, 150 C-5
rfolk, 242803 L-18
rge, 1000 J-16
rman, 70 F-12
rth, 200 J-17
Garden, 900 H-10
Springfield, 7274 ‡H-3
View M-11
RTHAMPTON CO., 2389 J-19
rthfields, 1400 †A-3
RTHUMBERLAND O., 12330 H-17
rton, 3958 C-4
rtonsville G-10
rwood, 60 I-9
ttoway, 84 K-12
TTOWAY CO., 5853 K-12
bush L-11
k Grv., 150 G-15
k Hall, 255 H-20
k Hill E-11
kton, 34166 ‡G-2
kville, 50 J-9
kwood, 500 B-6
lands D-13
oquan, 934 E-14
ana †M-9
ville, 100 I-13
Tavern, 60 E-13
hams, 100 H-16
town, 50 M-3
ncock, 1263 I-19
ey, 516 I-19
l, 691 E-13
nge, 4721 G-12
ANGE CO., 481 G-12
inary, 1000 †E-4
kany, 80 I-6
an, 60 E-12
noco I-8
ens, 60 F-15
es, 70 M-9
E CO., 24042 F-10
t Bank, 80 J-5
ter, 229 I-19
ner, 50 I-17
ner Sprs., 100 N-11
nyra, 104 H-11
plin, 219 K-10
s, 150 D-12
lawn, 2400 ‡H-4
sley, 842 I-19
ott, 435 K-4
ow, 100 H-13
RICK CO., 490 M-4
ick Sprs., 1845 M-5
erson, 200 B-6
onsville, 100 D-3
es, 170 G-13
isburg, 2786 K-3
ar Mills J-8
broke, 1128 K-4
der, 500 ‡G-1
dleton, 60 H-12
hook, 801 L-7
Laird, 200 F-9
ington Gap, 81 D-3
ersburg, 32420 K-14
nix, 226 L-10
mont, 270 D-13
120 L-5
nit Hills, 6094 ‡F-3
y River, 250 I-9
s Gap M-3
ville, 100 L-7
SYLVANIA CO., 506 L-8
erco, 300 D-7
ant Ridge ‡H-3
Pt., 150 J-16
hontas, 389 K-1
ar Camp, 100 L-3
oson, 12150 K-17
Republic, 250 G-9
Royal, 126 G-15
ock †M-6
mouth, 95535 L-17
Oak G-13
d, 1037 C-4
atan, 700 J-12
HATAN CO., 46 J-12
r, 100 B-5
s, 120 G-11
s Fork, 1066 K-4
CE EDWARD CO., 68 K-10
e George, 2066 K-14
CE GEORGE CO., 25 K-14
CE WILLIAM CO., 002 E-13
ess Anne †N-9
ect, 400 K-10
dence Forge, J-15
ki, 9086 L-3
SKI CO., 72 K-3
oteague, 347 I-19
lville, 7727 C-13
50 M-13
Oaks, 1400 †F-8
tico, 480 F-14
s Lake, 1400 †E-2
sburg, 200 E-10
y, 282 I-19
ue, 60 G-11
rd, 16408 K-4
Radiant, 100 G-11
Randolph, 60 L-10
Raphine, 250 H-8
Rapidan, 140 G-12
RAPPAHANNOCK CO., 7373 E-11
Raven, 2270 C-7
Ravensworth, 2466 ‡H-3
Ravenwood, 2550 ‡G-4
Rawley Sprs., 150 F-9
Raynor †K-1
Rectortown, 300 D-12
Red Ash, 250 C-6
Red House, 80 K-9
Red Oak, 50 M-10
Redwood, 220 L-6
Reedville, 400 H-17
Rehoboth, 60 L-11
Remington, 598 F-13
Rescue, 400 L-17
Reston, 58404 D-14
Rice, 230 K-11
Rich Creek, 774 J-3
Richardsville, 120 F-13
Richlands, 5823 C-7
Richmond, 204214 J-14
RICHMOND CO., 9254 H-16
Ridgeway, 742 N-6
Rileyville, 150 E-11
Riner, 859 L-4
Ringgold, 350 M-8
Ripplemead, 550 K-4
Riverdale N-15
Rivermont, 500 †G-10
Rixeyville, 120 F-12
Roanoke, 97032 K-6
ROANOKE CO., 92376 J-5
Robley H-16
Rochelle, 130 G-11
Rockbridge Baths, 150 H-8
ROCKBRIDGE CO., 22307 H-8
ROCKINGHAM CO., 76314 F-9
Rockville, 200 I-13
Rocky Gap, 250 K-2
Rocky Mount, 4799 L-6
Rose Hill, 799 D-2
Roseann, 50 B-6
Rosedale, 100 C-6
Roseland, 100 I-9
Roseville, 260 F-13
Round Hill, 539 C-13
Rowe, 250 C-6
Ruckersville, 1141 G-11
Rural Retreat, 1483 L-2
Rushmere, 1018 K-16
RUSSELL CO., 28897 C-6
Rustburg, 1431 K-9
Ruther Glen, 170 H-14
Ruthville, 100 J-15
Sago, 30 L-7
St. Charles, 128 D-3
St. Paul, 970 C-5
St. Stephens Church, 120 I-15
Salem, 24802 K-6
Saltpetre Cave I-7
Saltville, 2077 D-7
Saluda, 769 I-16
Sandston, 7571 †C-10
Sandy Hook, 100 I-12
Sandy Level, 150 L-7
Sandy Pt., 130 H-16
Saxe, 100 L-10
Saxis, 241 H-19
Schuyler, 298 I-10
Scotland, 203 K-16
SCOTT CO., 23177 D-4
Scotts Fork K-12
Scottsburg, 119 M-10
Scottsville, 566 I-10
Seaford, 2700 K-17
Sebrell, 150 M-15
Sedley, 470 M-15
Selma, 529 I-6
Seven Cors., 9255 ‡G-4
Seven Mile Ford, 783 M-1
Severn, 170 K-17
Shacklefords, 250 J-16
Shady Oak, 180 ‡D-2
Sharps, 210 H-16
Shawsville, 1310 K-5
Shenandoah, 2373 F-10
SHENANDOAH CO., 41993 E-10
Sherando, 688 H-9
Sherwill K-9
Shipman, 507 I-9
Short Pump, 24729 †A-5
Shortt Gap, 50 C-6
Silver Bch., 200 J-18
Singers Glen, 250 F-9
Skippers, 300 M-14
Smithfield, 8089 L-16
SMYTH CO., 32208 M-1
Snell, 250 G-13
Snowflake, 70 D-4
Solomons Store, 100 †A-7
Somerset, 210 G-11
Somerville, 80 F-13
S. Boston, 8142 M-9
S. Clinchfield, 150 C-5
S. Hill, 4650 M-12
S. Norfolk †M-6
SOUTHAMPTON CO., 18570 L-15
Sparta, 30 H-14
Speedwell, 300 M-2
Spencer, 180 M-6
Sperryville, 342 E-11
Spotsylvania, 4239 G-13
SPOTSYLVANIA CO., 122397 H-13
Spout Spr., 240 J-9
Spring Grv., 80 K-15
Springfield, 30484 ‡I-4
Springwood, 170 J-7
Sprouses Cor., 100 J-10
Stacy, 100 B-6
Stafford, 1600 F-14
STAFFORD CO., 128961 F-13
Stanardsville, 367 G-11
Stanley, 1689 F-10
Stanleytown, 1422 M-6
Staunton, 23746 G-9
Steeles Tavern, 150 H-8
Stephens, 400 C-4
Stephens City, 1829 D-11
Stephenson, 560 C-12
Sterling, 27822 D-14
Stevens Creek, 300 M-2
Stevensburg, 140 F-12
Stevensville, 140 I-15
Stewartsville, 100 K-6
Stonega, 300 C-4
Stony Creek, 198 L-14
Stotts Crossroads †K-1
Strasburg, 6398 D-11
Stuart, 1408 M-5
Stuarts Draft, 9235 H-9
Studley, 200 I-14
Suffolk, 84585 M-17
Sugar Grv., 758 M-1
Sugar Loaf, 2500 H-1
Sugarland Run, 11799 ‡C-1
Sunny Side J-12
Supply, 60 G-15
Surry, 244 K-16
SURRY CO., 7058 K-15
Sussex, 256 L-14
SUSSEX CO., 12087 L-14
Sutherland, 100 K-13
Swansonville M-7
Swords Creek, 400 C-6
Sydnorsville L-6
Sylvatus, 80 L-3
Tabb, 950 K-17
Tacoma, 170 C-4
Tangier, 727 H-18
Tannersville, 100 C-7
Tappahannock, 2375 H-16
Tasley, 300 I-19
Taylorstown C-13
Tazewell, 4627 K-1
TAZEWELL CO., 45078 L-1
Temperanceville, 358 H-20
Templeman, 40 H-16
Tenth Legion, 80 F-10
Terrys Fork L-5
Thaxton, 250 J-7
The Hollow N-4
The Plains, 217 D-13
Thornburg, 420 G-13
Three Sprs., 120 *I-4
Timberlake, 12183 K-8
Timberville, 2522 E-10
Tiptop, 200 B-8
Toano, 1200 J-16
Tobaccoville J-12
Toms Brook, 258 D-11
Tookland, 500 B-6
Townsend, 250 K-19
Trammel, 400 C-5
Triangle, 8188 F-14
Triplet, 40 M-13
Trout Dale, 178 M-1
Troutville, 431 J-6
Troy, 70 H-11
Tuckahoe, 44990 †B-6
Tunstall I-15
Turbeville, 80 M-9
Tyler Pk., 1250 ‡G-4
Tysons Cor., 19627 ‡F-3
Unionville, 90 G-12
Upperville, 400 D-12
Urbanna, 476 I-16
Vale ‡G-1
Valentines, 60 M-13
Vanderpool F-7
Vansant, 470 B-6
Varina, 3000 †E-9
Vera, 60 J-10
Vernon Hill, 60 M-9
Verona, 4239 G-9
Vesta, 150 M-5
Vesuvius, 230 H-8
Victoria, 1725 L-11
Vienna, 15687 D-14
Viewtown, 50 E-12
Village, 130 H-16
Villamont, 200 J-6
Villboro G-14
Vinton, 8098 K-6
Virgilina, 154 N-10
Virginia Beach, 437994 L-18
Virginia Hills, 2840 ‡I-5
Volens, 40 L-9
Volney, 30 M-1
Wachapreague, 232 I-19
Wakefield, 927 L-15
Wakenva, 70 C-5
Waldrop, 60 H-11
Walkerton, 200 I-15
Walters, 180 M-16
Ware Neck, 270 J-17
Wares Crossroads H-12
Warfield, 115 L-13
Warm Sprs., 123 H-6
Warner, 40 I-16
WARREN CO., 37575 D-12
Warrenton, 9611 E-13
Warsaw, 1512 H-16
Washington, 135 E-11
WASHINGTON CO., 54876 D-7
Water View, 180 I-16
Waterford, 400 C-13
Waverly, 2149 L-15
Waynesboro, 21006 H-9
Waynewood, 3450 ‡J-6
Weber City, 1327 E-4
Weedonville, 180 G-15
Weems, 220 I-17
Wellington, 1750 ‡J-6
W. Augusta, 200 G-8
West Point, 3306 J-16
W. Springfield, 22460 ‡I-3
Westmoreland, 900 †A-3
WESTMORELAND CO., 17454 G-15
Weyanoke, 1500 ‡H-4
Weyers Cave, 2473 G-9
White Hall, 90 G-10
White Marsh, 400 J-17
White Plains, 80 M-12
White Post, 200 D-12
White Stone, 352 I-17
Whitetop, 150 M-1
Whitewood, 150 B-7
Wicomico, 1350 K-17
Wicomico Church, 450 H-17
Wilderness, 30 G-13
Williamsburg, 14068 K-16
Williamsville, 40 G-7
Willis, 130 L-4
Willis Wharf, 250 J-19
Wills Cor., 50 †L-3
Wilsons, 100 K-12
Wilton Woods, 1400 ‡I-5
Winchester, 26203 C-11
Windsor, 2626 M-16
Winfall, 60 K-9
Wingina, 80 I-10
Winterham, 40 J-12
Winterpock, 40 J-13
Wirtz, 150 L-6
Wise, 3286 C-4
WISE CO., 41452 C-4
Wolftown, 200 F-11
Woodbridge, 4055 E-14
Woodford, 100 G-14
Woodlawn, 2343 M-3
Woodridge, 30 H-11
Woodstock, 5097 D-10
Woodville, 100 E-11
Woodway, 200 D-3
Woolwine, 350 M-5
Wylliesburg, 280 L-10
WYTHE CO., 29235 L-2
Wytheville, 8211 L-2
Yale, 50 L-14
Yancey Mills, 200 H-10
YORK CO., 65464 J-16
York Ter., 800 †F-2
Yorktown, 195 K-17
Yuma, 100 E-4
Zuni, 300 L-16

Washington

Page locator

Map keys	Atlas pages
1–10	218–219
11–20	220–221

* City keyed to pp. 222–223

Aberdeen, 16896 H-3
Aberdeen Gdns., 279 H-4
Acme, 246 B-7
ADAMS CO., 18728 I-16
Addy, 268 C-18
Adna, 150 I-5
Ahtanum, 3601 J-11
Airway Hts., 6114 F-18
Albion, 579 I-19
Alder, 227 I-7
Alderton, 2893 *N-9
Alderwood, 1760 †D-1
Alger, 403 B-7
Algona, 3014 *K-9
Allen, 180 C-7
Allyn, 1963 G-6
Almira, 284 F-15
Aloha, 50 G-3
Altoona, 39 K-4
Amanda Pk., 252 F-3
Amboy, 1608 L-7
Anacortes, 15778 C-6
Anatone, 100 K-20
Arden, 60 C-18
Ardenvoir, 130 F-12
Ariel, 100 L-6
Arlington, 17926 D-8
Ashford, 217 I-8
Asotin, 1251 J-20
ASOTIN CO., 21623 K-19
Auburn, 70180 G-7
Ayer, 50 J-17
Bainbridge Island †D-5
Baring, 220 E-9
Barstow, 59 B-17
Basin City, 1092 J-15
Battle Ground, 17571 M-6
Bay Ctr., 276 I-3
Bay View, 150 E-7
Bayview, 696 C-7
Beaux Arts Vil., 299 *E-9
Beaver, 600 D-2
Belfair, 3931 G-6
Bellevue, 122363 *E-9
Bellingham, 80885 B-7
Belmont, 20 H-20
Belvidere, 60 D-15
Benge, 50 H-17
Benton City, 3038 K-14
BENTON CO., 175177 J-13
Beverly, 300 I-13
Bickleton, 88 L-12
Big Lake, 1835 C-7
Bingen, 712 M-9
Birch Bay, 8413 A-6
Black Diamond, 4151 G-8
Blaine, 4684 A-6
Blanchard, 180 B-7
Blue Lake, 130 F-14
Bluecreek, 70 C-18
Blueslide C-19
Blyn, 101 E-5
Bonney Lake, 17374 H-7
Bothell, 33505 †A-9
Bow, 180 C-7
Boyds, 34 B-17
Bremerton, 37729 F-6
Brewster, 2370 D-13
Bridgeport, 2409 E-13
Brier, 6087 †A-8
Brinnon, 797 F-6
Browns Pt., 1950 *K-6
Brownstown, 50 J-11
Bryant, 1870 D-7
Bryn Mawr, 1500 *G-9
Buckley, 4354 H-8
Bucoda, 562 I-6
Buena, 990 J-12
Burbank, 3291 K-15
Burien, 33313 G-7
Burlington, 8388 C-7
Burton, 280 G-7
BZ Cor., 80 L-9
Camano, 13347 D-7
Camas, 19355 M-7
Carbonado, 610 H-8
Carlisle, 60 H-3
Carlsborg, 995 D-5
Carlton, 70 D-12
Carnation, 1786 F-8
Carrolls, 100 K-6
Carson, 2279 M-8
Cascade Valley, 2246 H-14
Cascade Vista, 7800 *H-10
Cashmere, 3063 F-11
Castle Rock, 1982 K-5
Cathlamet, 532 K-4
Cedar Falls G-8
Cedonia D-17
Centerville, 112 M-10
Central Pk., 2685 H-4
Centralia, 16336 I-5
Chattaroy, 450 E-19
Chehalis, 7259 I-5
Chelan, 3890 E-13
CHELAN CO., 72453 E-11
Chelan Falls, 329 E-13
Cheney, 10590 F-19
Chesaw, 50 A-15
Chewelah, 2607 D-18
Chimacum, 800 E-6
Chinook, 466 K-3
Cinebar, 80 J-6
Clallam Bay, 363 D-2
CLALLAM CO., 71404 E-4
CLARK CO., 425363 M-7
Clarkston, 7229 J-20
Clayton, 443 E-18
Cle Elum, 1872 G-10
Clear Lake, 1419 H-7
Clear Lake, 1002 C-7
Clearview, 3324 E-8
Clearwater, 200 F-2
Cliffdell, 104 H-10
Clinton, 928 E-7
Clyde Hill, 2984 †D-9
Coalfield, 400 *G-10
Colbert, 130 E-19
Colby, 200 *F-5
Colchester, 200 *F-5
Coles Cor., 40 F-11
Colfax, 2805 I-19
College Pl., 8765 L-17
Colton, 418 J-20
COLUMBIA CO., 4078 K-18
Colville, 4673 C-18
Colville Indian Agency, 200 D-15
Conconully, 210 C-13
Concrete, 705 C-8
Connell, 4209 I-15
Conway, 91 C-7
Cook, 70 M-9
Copalis Bch., 415 H-3
Copalis Crossing, 200 H-3
Cosmopolis, 1649 H-3
Cougar, 100 L-7
Coulee City, 562 F-14
Coulee Dam, 1098 E-15
Country Homes, 5841 †A-2
Coupeville, 1831 D-6
Covington, 17575 G-8
Cowiche, 428 I-11
COWLITZ CO., 102410 K-6
Crescent Bar, 140 G-13
Creston, 236 E-16
Crystal Mtn., 30 H-9
Cunningham, 25 I-16
Curlew, 118 A-16
Curtis, 50 J-5
Cusick, 207 C-19
Custer, 366 A-6
Dallesport, 1202 M-10
Danville, 34 A-16
Darrington, 1347 D-9
Davenport, 1734 F-17
Dayton, 2526 K-18
Deep Creek, 40 F-18
Deer Hbr., 100 B-6
Deer Pk., 3652 E-19
Deming, 353 B-7
Des Moines, 29673 G-7
Desert Aire, 1626 I-13
Diablo, 50 B-10
Diamond, 50 H-19
Diamond Lake, 220 D-19
Dieringer *L-9
Disautel, 78 C-14
Dixie, 197 K-17
Dockton, 300 *I-6
Dodge J-18
Doe Bay, 40 B-6
Donald, 91 J-12
Doty, 300 I-5
Douglas, 40 F-13
DOUGLAS CO., 38431 F-13
Dryden, 500 F-11
Dungeness, 250 D-5
DuPont, 8199 H-6
Dusty, 30 I-18
Duvall, 6695 F-8
E. Wenatchee, 13190 G-12
Eastgate, 4958 †E-10
Easton, 478 G-10
Eastsound, 1100 B-6
Eatonville, 2758 I-7
Edgewood, 9387 *L-8
Edison, 133 C-7
Edmonds, 39709 †A-7
Edwall, 100 F-18
Elbe, 29 I-7
Electric City, 968 E-15
Elk, 70 D-19
Elk Plain, 14205 H-7
Ellensburg, 18174 H-11
Ellisforde, 30 B-14
Ellisport, 150 *H-6
Elma, 3107 H-4
Elmer City, 238 E-15
Eltopia, 250 J-15
Endicott, 289 H-18
Entiat, 1112 F-12
Enumclaw, 10669 G-8
Ephrata, 7664 G-14
Eschbach, 415 I-11
Ethel, 200 J-6
Eureka, 50 K-16
Evans, 70 B-17
Everett, 103019 E-7
Everson, 2481 A-7
Ewan, 50 H-18
Fairfield, 612 G-19
Fairhaven *G-1
Fairwood, 19102 *H-10
Farmington, 146 H-20
Federal Way, 89306 G-7
Ferndale, 11415 B-6
FERRY CO., 7551 C-16
Fife, 9173 *L-7
Finley, 6012 K-15
Fircrest, 6497 *L-5
Ford, 50 E-18
Fords Prairie, 1959 I-5
Forks, 3532 E-2
Fragaria, 100 *H-5
Frances J-4
FRANKLIN CO., 78163 J-15
Freeland, 2045 E-7
Freeman, 70 F-19
Friday Hbr., 2162 C-5
Fruitland, 50 D-17
Gardiner, 300 D-6
Garfield, 597 H-20
GARFIELD CO., 2266 J-18
Garrett, 1419 K-17
Geneva, 2321 *F-3
George, 501 H-13
Gifford, 100 C-17
Gig Hbr., 7126 G-6
Glacier, 211 A-8
Gleed, 2906 I-11
Glen Acres, 100 *G-6
Glenoma, 340 J-7
Glenrose, 100 †D-3
Glenwood, 320 L-10
Gold Bar, 2075 E-9
Goldendale, 3407 L-11
Goose Prairie, 40 I-10
Graham, 23491 H-7
Grand Coulee, 988 E-15
Grand Mound, 2981 I-5
Grandview, 10862 K-13
Granger, 3246 K-12
Granite Falls, 3364 D-8
GRANT CO., 89120 G-15
Grapeview, 954 G-6
Grayland, 953 I-3
GRAYS HBR. CO., 72797 G-3
Grays River, 263 J-4
Greenwater, 67 H-9
Grisdale, 50 G-4
Hamilton, 301 C-8
Hansville, 3091 E-7
Harper, 150 *F-5
Harrah, 625 J-11
Harrington, 424 F-17
Hartline, 151 F-15
Hatton, 101 I-16
Havillah, 30 B-14
Hay, 50 I-18
Hobart, 6221 G-8
Holly F-5
Hollywood, 800 †B-10
Home Valley, 80 M-8
Hoodsport, 376 G-5
Hooper, 75 I-17
Hoquiam, 8726 H-3
Humptulips, 255 G-3
Hunters, 180 D-17
Hunts Pt., 394 †D-9
Husum, 130 L-9
Illahee, 400 †D-4
Ilwaco, 936 K-3
Inchelium, 409 D-17
Index, 178 E-9
Ione, 447 B-19
Irby, 30 G-15
ISLAND CO., 78506 D-6
Issaquah, 30434 F-8
JEFFERSON CO., 29872 F-4
Johnson, 100 I-20
Joyce, 150 D-4
Kahlotus, 193 I-16
Kalama, 2344 L-6
Kapowsin, 333 H-7
Keller, 234 D-16
Kelso, 11925 K-5
Kendall, 191 A-8
Kenmore, 20460 †A-8
Kennewick, 73917 K-15
Kent, 92411 G-7
Kettle Falls, 1595 B-17
Keyport, 554 F-6
KING CO., 1931249 F-9
Kingsgate, 13065 †B-10
Kingston, 2099 E-7
Kiona, 60 K-14
Kirkland, 48787 †C-9
KITSAP CO., 251133 F-6
Kittitas, 1381 H-12
KITTITAS CO., 40915 H-11
Klickitat, 362 L-10
KLICKITAT CO., 20318 L-12
Kooskooskie, 80 L-17
La Center, 2800 L-6
La Conner, 891 C-7
La Grande, 109 I-7
La Push, 500 E-2
Lacey, 42393 H-6
LaCrosse, 313 I-18
Lake City †B-8
L. Forest Pk., 12598 †A-8
Lake Hts. *K-10
L. Hills †E-10
L. Stevens, 28069 E-8
Lakebay, 600 G-6
Lakedale, 500 G-10
Lakeland, 12000 †K-8
Lakeview Pk., 915 G-14
Lakewood, 58163 H-7
Lamona, 40 G-16
Lamont, 70 G-18
Latah, 183 G-20
Laurier, 1 A-17
Lawrence, 30 B-7
Leavenworth, 1965 F-11
Lebam, 160 J-4
Leland, 50 E-6
LEWIS CO., 75455 I-6
Lexington, 800 K-6
Liberty, 100 G-11
Lilliwaup, 150 G-5
Lincoln, 150 E-16
LINCOLN CO., 10570 F-16
Lind, 564 H-16
Littlerock, 420 I-5
Lofall, 2289 E-6
Long Bch., 1392 J-3
Longbranch, 3784 G-6
Longmire, 50 I-8
Longview, 36648 K-5
Longview Hts., 3851 K-5
Loomis, 159 B-13
Loon Lake, 783 D-18
Lopez, 600 C-6
Lowden, 60 L-16
Lucerne, 20 D-11
Lyle, 499 M-10
Lyman, 438 C-8
Lynden, 11951 A-7
Lynnwood, 35836 E-7
Mabana, 50 D-7
Mabton, 2286 K-13
Malaga, 450 G-12
Malden, 203 G-19
Malo, 28 B-16
Malone, 475 H-5
Malott, 487 D-13
Manchester, 5413 *F-5
Mansfield, 320 E-13
Manson, 1468 E-12
Maple Falls, 324 A-8
Maple Valley, 22684 G-8
Maplewood Hts., 3300 *H-10
Marblemount, 203 C-9
Marcus, 183 B-17
Markham, 111 H-3
Marlin, 48 G-15
Marshall, 100 F-19
Maryhill, 58 M-11
Marysville, 60020 D-7
MASON CO., 60699 H-5
Matlock, 130 G-4
Mattawa, 4437 I-13
Maytown, 70 I-6
Mazama, 90 C-12
McCleary, 1653 H-5
McKenna, 716 H-6
McMillin, 1547 H-7
Mead, 7275 E-19
Medical Lake, 5060 F-18
Medina, 2969 †D-9
Melbourne, 50 H-4
Menlo, 250 I-4
Mercer Island, 22699 *E-9
Mesa, 489 J-15
Metaline, 173 A-19
Metaline Falls, 238 A-19
Methow, 68 D-13
Mica, 130 F-19
Midland, 8962 *N-6
Midway *K-4
Milan, 80 E-19
Miles, 30 E-17
Mill Creek, 18244 E-7
Millwood, 1786 †B-4
Milton, 6968 *L-8
Mineral, 202 I-7
Moclips, 207 G-2
Mohler, 25 G-17
Molson A-14
Monroe, 17304 E-8
Monse D-13
Montesano, 3976 H-4
Morgan Acres, 1500 †B-3
Morton, 1126 J-7
Moses Lake, 20366 H-14
Mossyrock, 759 J-7
Mt. Pleasant, 1200 D-5
Mt. Vernon, 31743 C-7
Mountlake Ter., 19909 †A-8
Moxee City, 3308 J-12
Mukilteo, 20254 E-7
Naches, 795 I-11
Nahcotta, 200 J-3
Napavine, 1766 J-6
Naselle, 419 J-3
Neah Bay, 865 C-2
Neilton, 315 G-3
Nespelem, 236 D-15
Newcastle, 10380 *F-10
Newhalem, 350 B-10
Newport, 2126 D-20
Newport Shores *E-9
Nighthawk, 25 A-13
Nooksack, 1338 A-7
Normandy Pk., 6335 *H-7
N. Bend, 5731 F-8
N. Bonneville, 956 M-8
N. Cove, 70 I-3
N. Puyallup, 1743 *M-8
Northport, 295 A-18
Oak Hbr., 22075 D-6
Oakesdale, 422 H-19
Oakville, 684 I-5
Ocean City, 200 H-3
Ocean Pk., 1573 J-3
Ocean Shores, 5569 H-3
Odessa, 910 G-16
Okanogan, 2552 C-14
OKANOGAN CO., 41120 B-13
Olalla, 600 *H-5
Olga, 150 B-6
Olympia, 46478 H-6
Omak, 4845 C-14
Onalaska, 621 J-6
Orcas, 300 B-6
Orchards, 19556 M-6
Orient, 115 B-17
Orin, 35 C-18
Orondo, 400 F-12
Oroville, 1686 A-14
Orting, 6746 H-7
Oso, 180 D-8
Othello, 7364 I-15
Outlook, 292 K-12
Oysterville, 50 J-3
Ozette, 50 D-1
Pacific, 6606 *L-9
Pacific Bch., 291 G-2
PACIFIC CO., 20920 J-4
Packwood, 342 J-9
Palisades, 180 G-13
Palmer, 300 G-8
Palouse, 998 H-20
Parker, 154 J-12
Parkland, 35803 H-7
Parkwater †B-4
Parkwood, 7126 *F-4
Pasadena Pk., 1700 †B-4
Pasco, 59781 K-15
Pataha City, 70 J-19
Pateros, 667 D-13
Paterson, 150 L-14
Pe Ell, 632 J-5
PEND OREILLE CO., 13001 B-19
Peshastin, 900 F-11
PIERCE CO., 795225 I-7
Pine City, 50 G-19
Pinecliff, 75 I-10
Plain F-11
Plaza, 20 G-19
Plymouth, 200 L-14
Pt. Roberts, 1314 A-5
Pomeroy, 1425 J-19
Port Angeles, 19038 D-4
Port Gamble, 400 E-6
Port Orchard, 11144 F-6
Port Stanley C-6
Port Townsend, 9113 D-6
Portage, 60 †I-6
Porter, 207 H-5
Poulsbo, 9200 F-6
Prairie, 50 C-7
Prescott, 318 K-17
Prosser, 5714 K-13
Pullman, 29799 I-20
Purdy, 1544 G-6
Puyallup, 37022 H-7
Queets, 174 F-2
Quilcene, 596 E-6
Quinault, 250 F-3
Quincy, 6750 G-13
Rainier, 1794 I-6
Ralston H-17
Randle, 850 J-8
Ravensdale, 1101 G-8
Raymond, 2882 I-4
Reardan, 571 F-18
Redmond, 54144 †C-10
Renton, 90927 G-7
Republic, 1073 B-16
Rice, 40 C-17
Richland, 48058 K-14
Ridgefield, 4763 L-6
Rimrock, 50 I-10
Ritzville, 1673 H-17
Riverside, 280 C-14
Robe, 230 D-8
Roche Hbr., 350 B-5
Rochester, 2388 I-5
Rock Island, 788 G-12
Rockford, 470 F-20
Rockport, 109 C-9
Ronald, 308 G-10
Roosevelt, 156 M-12
Rosalia, 550 G-19
Rosburg, 317 K-4
Roslyn, 893 G-10
Roy, 793 H-6
Royal City, 2140 I-13
Ruff H-15
Ruston, 749 *K-5
Ryderwood, 395 J-5
St. John, 537 H-19
Salkum, 350 J-6
Salmon Creek, 19686 M-6
Sammamish, 45780 F-8
SAN JUAN CO., 15769 C-5
Sappho D-2
Satsop, 675 H-4
Satus, 750 K-12
Sawyer J-12
Schawana, 200 I-13
SeaTac, 26909 G-7
Seattle, 608660 F-7
Seaview, 650 J-3
Sedro-Woolley, 10540 C-7
Sekiu, 27 D-2
Selah, 7147 I-11
Selleck, 200 G-8
Sequim, 6606 D-5
Seven Bays, 270 E-17
Seven Mile, 170 †A-1
Shaw Island, 200 C-6
Shelton, 9834 G-5
Shore Acres, 250 *K-4
Shoreline, 53007 †B-7
Shrine Bch., 200 E-12
Silvana, 90 D-7
Silver Bch. †E-3
Silver Brook, 520 J-8
Silver Lake, 200 K-6
Silverdale, 19204 F-6
Silverton, 40 D-9
Similk Bch., 270 C-7
SKAGIT CO., 116901 C-8
Skamania, 180 M-8
SKAMANIA CO., 11066 L-8
Skamokawa, 401 K-4
Skokomish, 617 G-5
Skykomish, 198 F-9
Skyway, 8500 *G-9
Smokey Pt., 1556 D-7
Snohomish, 9098 E-8
SNOHOMISH CO., 713335 E-9
Snoqualmie, 10670 F-8
Snoqualmie Pass, 311 G-9
Soap Lake, 1514 G-14
S. Bend, 1637 I-3
S. Cle Elum, 532 H-10
S. Colby, 300 *F-5
S. Hill, 52431 *N-8
South Point, 130 E-6
S. Prairie, 434 H-8
S. Wenatchee, 1553 G-12
Southworth, 2185 *G-5
Spanaway, 27227 H-7
Spangle, 278 G-19
Spokane, 208916 F-19
SPOKANE CO., 471221 F-19
Spokane Valley, 89755 F-19
Sprague, 446 G-18
Springdale, 285 D-18
Stanwood, 6231 D-7
Starbuck, 129 J-17
Stehekin, 80 D-11
Steilacoom, 5985 H-6
Steptoe, 180 H-19
STEVENS CO., 43531 D-18
Stevenson, 1465 M-8
Sudden Valley, 6441 B-7
Sultan, 4651 E-8
Sumas, 1307 A-7
Summit, 7985 *N-7
Sumner, 9451 G-7
Suncrest, 1500 E-18
Sunnyside, 15858 K-13
Sunnyslope, 3252 G-12
Sunset Bch., 100 *M-4
Tacoma, 198397 G-7
Tahlequah, 100 *J-5
Taholah, 840 G-2
Tahuya, 450 G-5
Tampico, 312 J-11
Tanglewilde, 5892 L-4
Tanner, 1018 G-8
Teanaway H-11
Tekoa, 778 G-20
Telma, 50 E-11
Tenino, 1695 I-6
Terrace Hts., 6937 M-20
Thornton, 120 H-19
Thorp, 240 H-11
THURSTON CO., 252264 I-6
Tieton, 1191 I-11
Tiger B-19
Tokeland, 151 I-3
Toledo, 725 J-6
Tonasket, 1032 B-14
Toppenish, 8949 J-12
Torboy, 49 B-16
Touchet, 421 L-16
Toutle, 350 K-6
Town & Country, 4857 †A-2
Trout Lake, 557 L-9
Tukwila, 19107 *G-8
Tulalip, 350 D-7
Tumtum, 400 E-18
Tumwater, 17371 H-6
Twisp, 919 C-12
Tyler, 50 G-18
Underwood, 500 M-9
Union, 631 G-5
Union Gap, 6047 J-11
Uniontown, 294 J-20
University Pl., 31144 G-7
Usk, 200 C-19
Utsalady, 230 D-7
Vader, 621 J-5
Valley, 146 D-18
Valleyford, 200 F-19
Vancouver, 161791 M-6
Vantage, 74 H-13
Vashon, 10624 G-7
Vashon Ctr., 80 *H-6
Vashon Hts., 700 *G-6
Vaughn, 544 G-6
Verlot, 285 D-8
View Pk. *G-5
Wahkiacus, 60 L-10
WAHKIAKUM CO., 3978 J-4
Waitsburg, 1217 K-17
Waldron, 100 B-5
Walla Walla, 31731 K-17
WALLA WALLA CO., 58781 J-16
Wallula, 179 K-15
Wapato, 4997 J-12
Warden, 2692 H-15
Warm Bch., 2437 D-7
Washougal, 14095 M-7
Washtucna, 208 I-17
Waterman †E-4
Waterville, 1138 F-12
Wauconda, 35 B-15
Wautauga Bch., 150 *E-5
Waverly, 106 G-19
Wellpinit, 500 E-17
Wenatchee, 31925 G-12
W. Richland, 11811 K-14
W. Sound, 100 B-6
Westport, 2099 H-3
WHATCOM CO., 201140 B-8
Wheeler, 220 H-15
White Ctr., 13495 *F-7
White Salmon, 2224 M-9
White Swan, 793 J-11
Whites, 50 H-5
WHITMAN CO., 44776 H-18
Wickersham, 150 B-7
Wilbur, 884 E-16
Wiley City, 300 J-11
Wilkeson, 477 H-8
Willapa, 210 I-4
Willard, 100 M-9
Wilson Creek, 205 G-15
Winchester, 30 G-13
Winlock, 1339 J-5
Winona, 50 H-18
Winthrop, 394 C-12
Wishram, 342 M-10
Withrow, 60 F-13
Wollochet, 6651 *L-4
Woodinville, 10938 †B-10
Woodland, 5509 L-6
Woodway, 1307 †A-7
Yacolt, 1566 L-7
Yakima, 91067 J-11
YAKIMA CO., 243231 J-12
Yale L-7
Yarrow Pt., 1001 †D-9
Yelm, 6848 H-6
Zillah, 2964 J-12

West Virginia

Page locator

Map keys	Atlas pages
A–J	226–227

* City keyed to p. 95

Adolph H-8
Adrian, 300 H-7
Albright, 299 F-9
Alderson, 1184 L-6
Alexander H-7
Alkol, 200 J-2
Allendale, 150 E-2
Alton, 50 H-7
Alum Br., 100 G-6
Alum Creek, 1749 J-3
Alvon, 80 K-7
Ameagle, 80 K-4
Amherstdale, 350 L-3
Amma, 125 I-4
Anawalt, 226 M-4
Anmoore, 770 G-7
Annamoriah, 40 H-4
Ansted, 1404 J-5
Anthony, 60 K-7
Arden, 75 G-8
Arkansas, 100 C-8
Arlington, 140 H-7
Arnett, 400 K-4
Arnoldsburg, 140 H-5
Arthur, 25 G-10
Arthurdale, 1500 F-8
Asco M-3
Ashley, 30 F-6
Ashton, 30 I-2
Athens, 1048 M-5
Auburn, 97 G-5
Augusta, 400 C-8
Aurora, 201 F-9
Auto, 10 K-7
Avondale, 200 M-3
Baker, 80 D-8
Bald Knob, 150 K-3
Ballard, 180 M-6
Bancroft, 587 I-3
BARBOUR CO., 16589 G-8
Barboursville, 3964 I-2
Barrackville, 1302 F-7
Barrett, 200 K-3
Bartley, 224 M-3
Bartow, 111 I-8
Bayard, 290 G-9
Beaver, 1308 L-5
Beckley, 17614 L-4
Beckwith, 175 K-5
Beech Bottom, 523 C-6
Belington, 1921 G-8
Belle, 1260 J-4
Belleville, 35 G-3
Belmont, 903 F-4
Belva, 95 J-4
Bemis, 30 H-8
Bens Run, 150 F-5
Bentree, 300 J-4
Benwood, 1420 D-6
Berea, 30 G-5
Bergoo, 94 I-7
BERKELEY CO., 104169 B-9
Berkeley Sprs., 624 B-9
Berlin, 125 G-7
Berwind, 278 M-3
Bethany, 1036 C-6
Bethlehem, 2499 D-6
Beverly, 702 H-8
Bickmore, 80 J-5
Big Chimney, 627 J-4
Big Isaac, 40 G-6
Big Run, 15 F-6
Big Sprs., 40 H-5
Bigbend, 150 H-5
Billings, 40 H-4
Bim, 400 K-3
Birch River, 107 I-6
Bishop, 200 N-3
Blackhawk M-10
Blacksville, 171 E-7
Blair, 500 K-3
Blandville, 25 G-6
Blennerhassett, 3089 G-3
Blount, 260 J-4
Bluefield, 10447 M-4
Bluewell, 2184 M-4
Boaz, 1297 F-4
Bob White, 400 K-3
Bolair, 150 I-6
Bolivar, 1045 C-10
Bolt, 548 L-4
Bomont, 90 I-4
Bonnivale, 150 G-4
Boomer, 615 J-4
BOONE CO., 24629 K-3
Booth, 220 E-8
Borderland, 300 L-1
Borgman, 40 F-8
Boulder, 50 G-7
Bowden, 9 H-8
Bozoo, 40 M-5
Braden, 60 F-6
Bradley, 2040 K-4
Bradshaw, 337 M-3
Bragg L-5
Bramwell, 364 M-4
Branchland, 400 J-2
Brandonville, 101 E-9
Brandywine, 218 I-10
BRAXTON CO., 14523 H-5
Breeden, 150 K-2
Brenton, 249 L-3
Bridgeport, 8149 G-7
Brohard, 50 G-5
BROOKE CO., 24069 C-6
Brookhaven, 5171 K-10
Brooks L-5
Brownton, 350 G-7
Bruceton Mills, 85 E-9
Buckeye, 200 J-7
Buckhannon, 5639 H-7
Bud, 487 L-4
Buffalo, 1236 I-2
Buffalo Creek, 900 C-4
Bunker Hill, 700 B-9
Burlington, 182 C-7
Burnsville, 510 H-6
Burnt House, 60 G-5
Burton, 100 E-6
CABELL CO., 96319 I-2
Cabins, 225 H-10
Cairo, 281 G-5
Caldwell, 400 L-7
CALHOUN CO., 7627 H-4
Calvin, 40 J-6
Camden, 80 G-6
Camden on Gauley, 169 J-6
Cameron, 946 E-6
Camp Creek, 60 M-5
Capon Br., 355 C-8
Capon Sprs., 165 C-8
Caretta, 600 M-3
Carl K-6
Carswell, 450 M-4
Cass, 52 J-8
Cassity, 75 H-8
Cassville, 701 E-7
Cedar Grv., 997 J-4
Cedar Grv., 350 G-4
Cedarville, 100 H-5
Center Pt., 50 F-6
Centerville, 130 F-5
Central Sta., 60 G-5
Century, 115 G-7
Ceredo, 1450 C-3
Chapmanville, 1256 K-2
Charles Town, 5259 C-10
Charleston, 51400 J-3
Chattaroy, 756 L-2
Cheat Neck, 500 E-8
Cherry Falls, 200 I-7
Cherry Grv., 40 I-9
Cherry Run, 25 A-9
Chesapeake, 1554 J-4
Chester, 2585 B-6
Chestnut Ridge, 800 J-10
Chloe, 75 I-5
Christian, 100 L-3
Churchville, 40 G-6
Circleville, 125 I-9
Clarksburg, 16578 G-7
Clay, 491 I-5
CLAY CO., 9386 I-5
Clear Creek, 350 K-4
Clear Fork, 150 L-3
Clearview, 565 D-6
Clendenin, 1227 I-4
Cleveland, 50 H-7
Clifftop, 60 K-5
Clifton Mills, 30 E-9
Clio I-4
Clothier, 270 K-3
Coalton, 250 H-8
Coalwood, 700 M-3
Coco, 50 J-4
Colliers, 600 C-6
Cool Ridge, 300 L-5
Copen, 45 H-6
Corinne, 362 L-4
Corinth, 150 F-9
Cottageville, 500 H-3
Cotton I-4
Cove Gap, 100 K-2
Cowen, 541 J-6
Coxs Mills, 50 G-5
Crab Orchard, 2678 L-4
Craigsville, 2213 J-6
Cranesville, 30 F-9
Crawley, 150 K-6
Creston, 100 H-4
Cross Lanes, 9995 I-3
Crossroads, 50 E-7
Crum, 182 K-1
Cucumber, 94 M-3
Culloden, 3061 I-2
Cunard, 400 K-5
Curtin, 75 I-7
Cyclone, 250 L-3
Czar, 20 H-7
Dailey, 114 H-8
Dallas, 350 D-6
Danese, 250 K-5
Daniels, 1881 L-5
Danville, 691 K-3
Davis, 660 G-9
Davis Creek, 600 M-8
Davy, 420 M-3
Dawson K-6
Daybrook, 225 E-7
Decota K-4
Deep Valley F-5
Delbarton, 579 L-2
Delorme, 300 L-2
Delray, 40 C-8
Denver, 100 F-8
Despard, 1004 G-7
Diana, 250 I-6
Dickson, 150 J-1
Dille, 260 I-5
Dingess, 200 K-2
Dixie, 291 J-4
DODDRIDGE CO., 8202 G-6
Dorcas, 50 H-10
Drennen, 40 J-5
Droop, 50 K-7
Dry Creek, 100 K-4
Duck, 40 I-5
Dudley Gap I-2
Dunbar, 7907 J-3
Dunlow, 125 K-1
Dunmore, 75 J-8
Durbin, 293 I-8
Durgon, 20 H-10
Dutchman, 50 G-5
Dyer J-6
E. Bank, 959 J-4
E. Lynn, 225 J-1
Eccles, 362 L-4
Eden D-3
Eglon, 120 G-9
Eleanor, 1518 I-3
Elizabeth, 823 G-4
Elk Forest, 600 L-10
Elk Gdn., 232 F-10
Elk Hills, 300 L-10
Elkins, 7094 H-8
Elkview, 1222 I-4
Ellamore, 125 H-7
Ellenboro, 363 G-5
Elm Grv. E-2
Elton, 90 K-5
Enon, 60 J-5
Enterprise, 961 F-7
Erbacon, 150 I-6
Erwin G-9
Eskdale, 300 K-4
Etam G-8
Ethel, 130 K-3
Eureka, 40 F-4
Evans, 700 H-3
Exchange, 40 H-6
Fairlea, 1747 L-6
Fairmont, 18704 F-7
Fairplain, 150 H-3
Fairview, 408 F-7
Falling Spr., 211 K-7
Falling Waters, 876 B-10
Farmington, 375 F-7
FAYETTE CO., 46039 K-5
Fayetteville, 2892 K-5
Fellowsville, 125 F-8
Fenwick, 116 J-6
Ferrellsburg, 150 K-2
Five Forks, 75 H-5
Flat Top, 100 L-5
Flatrock, 70 H-2
Flatwoods, 277 H-6
Flemington, 312 G-7
Follansbee, 2986 C-6
Folsom, 200 F-6
Forest Hill, 80 L-6
Forks of Cacapon B-8
Ft. Ashby, 1380 B-8
Ft. Gay, 705 J-1
Ft. Seybert I-10
Ft. Spring, 150 L-6
Fosterville, 200 K-3
Frame, 150 I-4
Frametown, 180 I-5
Frank, 90 I-8
Frankford, 175 K-7
Franklin, 721 I-9
Fraziers Bottom, 200 I-2
French Creek, 120 H-7
Frenchton, 150 H-7
Friars Hill K-6
Friendly, 132 F-5
Frost J-8
Gallipolis Ferry, 500 H-2
Gandeeville, 300 H-4
Gap Mills, 125 L-7
Gary, 968 M-3
Gassaway, 908 I-6
Gatewood, 250 K-5
Gauley Br., 614 J-4
Gay, 75 H-3
Gem H-6
Genoa, 100 J-1
Ghent, 457 L-5
Gilbert, 450 L-3
Gilboa, 150 J-5
Gilmer, 50 H-6
GILMER CO., 8693 G-5
Glace, 35 L-7
Glady, 60 H-8
Glen, 20 J-4
Glen Daniel, 600 L-4
Glen Easton, 120 E-6
Glen Fork, 487 L-4
Glen Jean, 210 K-5
Glendale, 1526 D-6
Glengary, 150 B-9
Glenhayes, 40 K-1
Glenville, 1537 H-5
Glenwood, 150 I-2
Glover Gap, 60 E-7
Goldtown, 100 I-3
Goodhope, 170 G-6
Gormania, 200 G-9
Grafton, 5164 F-8
GRANT CO., 11937 G-10
Grant Town, 613 F-7
Grantsville, 561 H-5
Granville, 781 J-9
Great Cacapon, 386 B-9
Green Bank, 143 I-8
Green Spr., 218 B-8
Green Sulphur Sprs., 75 L-5
GREENBRIER CO., 35480 K-6
Greenview, 378 K-3
Greenville, 150 L-6
Greenwood, 180 G-5
Greggsville D-2
Griffithsville, 350 J-2
Grimms, 75 I-2
Guardian I-6
Gum Spr. F-8
Guthrie, 600 L-9
Hacker Valley, 150 I-7
Halltown, 350 C-10
Hambleton, 232 G-9
Hamlin, 1142 J-2
Hampden, 150 L-2
HAMPSHIRE CO., 23964 C-8
Hancock, 35 A-9
HANCOCK CO., 30676 C-6
Hanover, 120 L-3
Harding, 90 H-8
HARDY CO., 14025 D-7
Harman, 143 H-9
Harmony I-4
Harpers Ferry, 286 B-10
HARRISON CO., 69099 F-6
Harrisville, 1876 G-5
Hartford City, 614 G-2
Hartland, 65 I-5
Harts, 656 K-2
Hastings, 50 F-6
Hazelton, 50 E-9
Heaters, 65 H-6
Hebron, 25 F-5
Hedgesville, 318 B-10
Helen, 219 L-4
Helvetia, 59 I-7
Henderson, 271 H-2
Hendricks, 272 G-9
Henlawson, 442 K-2
Herndon, 300 M-4
Hewett, 250 K-3
Hico, 272 J-5
High View, 30 C-8
Hillsboro, 260 J-7
Hines, 300 K-6
Hinton, 2676 L-5
Hodgesville, 150 G-7
Holden, 876 K-2
Hometown, 668 I-3
Hominy Falls J-6
Hooverson Hts., 2590 C-6
Hopeville, 20 H-10
Horner, 125 H-7
Horsepen, 50 M-4
Howesville, 125 F-8
Hundred, 299 E-6
Huntersville, 73 J-8
Huntington, 49138 I-1
Hurricane, 6284 I-2
Huttonsville, 221 H-8
Iaeger, 302 M-3
Ikes Fork, 300 L-3
Indian Mills L-5
Indore, 125 J-5
Institute, 1800 J-3
Inwood, 2954 B-9
Ireland, 130 H-6
Ivydale, 250 I-5
JACKSON CO., 29211 H-3
Jacksonburg, 182 F-6
Jane Lew, 409 G-7
Jarvisville G-6
JEFFERSON CO., 53498 C-10
Jeffrey, 500 K-3
Jesse, 250 L-3
Job, 40 H-9
Jodie, 180 J-5
Jolo, 500 M-3
Judy Gap I-9
Julian, 200 J-3
Junction, 15 C-7
Junior, 520 H-8
Justice, 412 L-3
Kanawha, 150 G-4
Kanawha City N-10
KANAWHA CO., 193063 J-4
Kanawha Drive H-5
Kausooth E-6
Kearneysville, 600 B-10
Kegley, 300 M-5
Kenna, 150 I-3
Kenova, 3216 I-1
Kent, 75 E-5
Kentuck I-3
Kerens, 100 G-8
Kermit, 406 K-1
Keyser, 5439 B-7
Keystone, 282 M-4
Kiahsville, 60 K-1
Kimball, 194 M-4
Kincaid, 260 K-4
Kingwood, 2939 F-8
Kirby, 30 C-8
Kistler, 528 L-3
Knob Fork E-6
Kopperston, 616 L-3
Landes H-10
Lansing, 400 K-5
Larkmead, 200 E-3
Laurel Pt., 80 K-9
Lavalette, 1073 J-1
Layland, 30 K-5
Leachtown G-4
Lead Mine, 30 G-9
Left Hand, 50 I-4
Leivasy, 150 J-6
Lenore, 300 L-2
Lenox, 50 F-9
Leon, 158 H-2
Leopold G-6
Lerona, 130 M-5
Lesage, 1358 I-2
Leslie, 250 K-6
Lester, 348 L-4
Letart, 100 H-2
Levels, 100 B-8
LEWIS CO., 16372 G-6
Lewisburg, 3830 L-6
Liberty, 30 I-3
Limestone, 200 D-6
LINCOLN CO., 21720 J-2
Linden, 50 H-4
Lindside, 200 M-6
Linn, 125 G-6
Littleton, 198 E-6
Liverpool, 60 H-4
Lizemores, 60 J-4
Lockwood, 50 J-5
Logan, 1779 K-2
LOGAN CO., 36743 L-2
Logansport, 30 F-7
Lookout, 250 K-5
Lorado, 300 L-3
Lorentz, 100 G-7
Lost City, 75 D-7
Lost Creek, 496 G-7
Lost River, 60 D-7
Loudenville, 50 E-6
Lubeck, 1311 G-3
Lumberport, 876 F-7
Lynn Camp, 40 E-6
Maben, 60 L-4
Mabie, 120 H-8
Mabscott, 1408 L-4
Macfarlan, 70 G-4
Macomber F-8
Madison, 3076 K-3
Malden, 850 J-3
Mallory, 1654 L-3
Man, 759 L-3
Mannings, 450 C-10
Mannington, 2063 F-7
MARION CO., 56418 F-7
Marlinton, 1054 J-7
Marlowe, 700 B-10
Marmet, 1503 J-3
Marrtown, 200 D-3
MARSHALL CO., 33107 E-6
Martinsburg, 17227 B-10
Maryland Jct., 977 *E-3
Mason, 968 G-2
MASON CO., 27324 I-2
Masontown, 546 F-8
Matewan, 499 L-2
Mathias, 140 D-7
Matoaka, 227 M-4
Maxwelton, 75 K-7
Maybeury, 234 M-4
Maysel, 300 I-5
Maysville, 150 G-10
MCDOWELL CO., 22113 M-3
McGee F-7
McKeefrey, 500 E-6
McMechen, 1926 D-6
McRoss, 150 K-6
Meadow Br., 379 K-5
Meadowbrook, 350 M-10
Medley, 20 G-10
MERCER CO., 62264 M-4
Metz, 120 F-7
Miami, 450 J-4
Middlebourne, 815 F-5
Midkiff, 250 J-2
Milam, 30 H-10
Mill Creek, 724 H-8
Mill Pt. J-7
Millstone, 60 H-5
Milton, 2423 I-2
Minden, 250 K-5
MINERAL CO., 28212 B-7
Mineralwells, 200 G-4
Mingo, 50 I-7
MINGO CO., 26839 K-1
Minnehaha Sprs., 50 J-8
Mitchell Hts., 323 K-2
Monongah, 1044 F-7
MONONGALIA CO., 96189 E-7
MONROE CO., 13502 L-6
Montcalm, 726 M-4
Montcoal, 150 K-4
Monterville, 100 I-7
Montgomery, 1638 J-4
Montrose, 156 G-8
Moorefield, 2544 C-7
MORGAN CO., 17541 B-9
Morgantown, 29660 E-8
Morrisvale, 100 J-3
Mossy K-4
Moundsville, 9318 D-6
Mt. Alto, 100 H-3
Mt. Gay, 700 K-2
Mt. Hope, 1414 K-5
Mt. Lookout, 400 J-5
Mt. Nebo, 150 J-5
Mt. Olivet, 250 E-2
Mt. Storm, 400 G-10
Mt. Zion, 40 H-5
Mountain, 40 F-5
Moyers I-9
Mozart E-2
Muddlety J-5
Mullens, 1559 L-4
Munday, 30 G-4
Murphytown, 130 G-4
Myrtle L-2
Nallen, 65 K-5
Napier, 40 H-6
Naugatuck, 250 L-1
Needmore C-8
Nellis, 300 J-3
Neola K-7
Nestorville, 75 G-8
Nettie, 568 J-6
New Creek, 350 F-10
New Cumberland, 1103 B-6
New England, 100 G-3
New Haven, 1560 H-2
New Manchester, 700 B-6
New Martinsville, 5366 E-5
New Milton, 30 G-6
Newburg, 329 F-8
Newell, 1376 B-6
Newton, 120 I-4
Newtown, 350 L-2
Newville, 60 I-6
NICHOLAS CO., 26233 J-5
Nimitz, 300 L-5
Nitro, 7178 I-3
Nolan, 500 L-1
Normantown, 50 H-5
N. Hills, 832 F-4
Northfork, 429 M-4
Norton, 400 H-8
Nutter Fort, 1593 G-7
Oak Flat, 25 I-10
Oak Hill, 7730 K-5
Oakvale, 121 M-5
Oceana, 1394 L-3
Odd, 200 L-4
OHIO CO., 44443 D-6

*, †, ‡, §, ◊ See explanation under state title in this index.
County and parish names are listed in capital letters & boldface type.
Independent cities (not included in a county) are listed in italics.

West Virginia (continued)

Old Fields, 50 — C-7
Omar, 552 — L-2
Ona, 500 — L-4
Onego, 30 — H-9
Orgas, 175 — K-3
Orma, 25 — J-9
Osage — G-5
Oxford — G-5
Paden City, 2633 — E-4
Pageton, 187 — M-4
Palestine, 135 — G-K
Panther, 200 — M-2
Parkersburg, 31492 — G-4
Parsons, 1485 — G-8
Paw Paw, 508 — C-9
Pax, 167 — K-4
Peewee — H-4
Pence Sprs., 100 — L-6
PENDLETON CO., 7695 — H-9
Pennsboro, 1171 — G-5
Pentress, 175 — E-7
Perkins, 20 — H-5
Petersburg, 2467 — H-10
Peterstown, 653 — M-5
Pettus, 75 — G-4
Pettyville, 500 — G-4
Peytona, 400 — J-3
Philippi, 2966 — G-8
Pickaway, 30 — L-6
Pickens, 66 — I-7
Pie, 50 — L-2
Piedmont, 876 — F-10
Pike, 40 — G-5
Pinch, 3262 — I-4
Pine Grv., 552 — F-6
Pineville, 668 — L-3
Piney View, 900 — B-3
Pipestem, 15 — L-5
Pleasant Valley, 3149 — F-7
Pleasant Valley, 60 — D-6
Pleasant View, 150 — J-9
PLEASANTS CO., 7605 — F-5
Pliny, 100 — J-3
Poca, 974 — I-3
POCAHONTAS CO., 8719 — J-8
Pocatalico, 1500 — I-3
Pt. Pleasant, 4350 — H-2
Points, 30 — B-8
Port Amherst, 350 — N-10
Porters Falls, 75 — F-6
Powellton, 619 — K-4
Pratt, 602 — K-4
Premier, 300 — M-3
Prenter, 300 — J-3
PRESTON CO., 33520 — F-8
Pricetown, 85 — F-6
Prichard, 527 — J-1
Prince, 116 — K-5
Princeton, 6432 — M-5
Procious, 125 — I-4
Proctor, 75 — E-5
Prosperity, 1498 — K-4
Pruntytown, 500 — F-7
Pullman, 154 — G-5
Purgitsville, 50 — C-7
PUTNAM CO., 55486 — I-3
Quick, 100 — J-4
Quiet Dell, 400 — G-7
Quinwood, 290 — K-6
Racine, 256 — J-3
Radnor, 40 — K-1
Ragland, 600 — L-2
Rainelle, 1505 — K-6
RALEIGH CO., 78859 — L-4
Ramage, 200 — K-3
Rand, 1631 — J-3
RANDOLPH CO., 29405 — H-8
Ranger, 180 — J-2
Ranson, 4440 — C-10
Raven Rock —
Ravenswood, 3876 — H-3
Reader, 397 — F-6
Red Creek, 80 — H-9
Red Jacket, 581 — L-2
Red Sulphur Sprs. — M-6
Reedsville, 593 — F-8
Reedy, 182 — H-4
Replete — I-7
Rhodell, 173 — L-4
Richwood, 2051 — J-6
Ridgeley, 675 — B-7
Ridgeway, 300 — M-6
Rig, 125 — G-10
Ringgold, 60 — H-6
Rio, 150 — C-8
Ripley, 3252 — H-3
Rippon, 25 — C-10
RITCHIE CO., 10449 — G-4
Riverton, 100 — H-9
Rivesville, 934 — F-7
ROANE CO., 14926 — H-4
Robertsburg, 140 — I-3
Robinette, 663 — L-3
Rock Cave, 400 —
Rock Creek, 980 — K-4
Rock View, 400 — L-3
Rocklick — K-4
Roderfield, 188 — M-3
Romney, 1848 — C-8
Ronceverte, 1765 — L-6
Rosedale, 175 — H-5
Rowlesburg, 584 — F-8
Rumble, 250 — J-3
Rupert, 942 — K-6
Ruth, 100 — N-8
Ruthdale, 65 — L-4
Sabine, 250 — L-4
St. Albans, 11044 — I-3
St. George, 60 — G-8
St. Joseph, 60 — I-4
St. Marys, 1900 — F-5
Salem, 1586 — G-6
Salt Rock, 388 — L-2
Sand Fork, 90 — H-5
Sand Ridge, 15 — H-5
Sandstone, 250 — L-5
Sandyville, 180 — H-4
Scherr, 25 — G-9
Schultz, 75 — J-3
Scott Depot, 1500 — I-3
Sedalia, 50 — J-4
Seebert, 30 — J-7
Seneca Rocks, 75 — H-9
Servia — I-6
Seth, 750 — K-3
Shady Spr., 2998 — L-5
Shanks, 100 — C-8
Shepherdstown, 1734 — B-10
Sherman, 60 — H-7
Shinnston, 2201 — F-7
Shirley, 135 — F-6
Shoals, 70 — I-1
Short Gap, 500 — B-7
Sias, 35 —
Silver Lake, 120 — G-9
Simpson, 250 — G-7
Sinks Grv., 75 — L-6
Sissonville, 4028 — I-3
Sistersville, 1396 — F-5
Slab Fork, 150 — L-4
Slanesville, 150 — B-8
Slate —
Slaty Fork, 100 — I-7
Smithburg, 120 — G-6
Smithers, 813 — J-4
Smithfield, 145 — F-6
Smithville, 200 — G-4
Smoot, 125 — K-6
Snow Hill, 275 — N-10
Sod, 150 — J-3
Sophia, 1344 — L-4
S. Charleston, 13450 — J-3
S. Hills — N-10
S. Park — N-10
Southside, 50 — H-2
Speed — H-4
Spencer, 2322 — H-4
Spring Hill — N-10
Spring Dale, 200 — K-5
Spring Valley, 900 — B-3
Springdale, 400 — K-5
Springfield, 477 — B-8
Spurlocksville, 25 — J-2
Squire, 450 — M-3
Star City, 1825 — E-8
Statts Mills, 25 — H-3
Steptown, 150 — K-1
Stonewood, 1806 — G-7
Stringtown, 120 — H-5
Stumptown, 100 — H-5
Sugar Grv., 35 —
SUMMERS CO., 13927 — L-5
Summersville, 3572 — J-5
Sundial, 90 — K-4
Sutton, 994 — H-6
Sweet Sprs., 150 — L-7
Swiss, 250 — J-5
Switzer, 595 — L-2
Sylvester, 160 — K-3
Tablers Sta., 100 — B-10
Talcott, 400 — L-5
Tallmansville, 120 — H-7
Tanner, 100 — H-5
Tariff, 20 — I-4
Taylorville, 350 — L-2
Taylorville, 350 —
Tennerton, 1800 — H-7
Terra Alta, 1477 — F-9
Tesla, 60 — I-6
Thomas, 586 — G-9
Thornton, 150 — F-8
Thornwood, 80 — I-8
Three Churches, 35 — B-8
Tioga, 90 —
Trout — K-6
Troy, 125 — H-5
Tunnelton, 294 — F-8
Tyler, 70 — F-5
TYLER CO., 9208 — F-5
Tyler Mtn., 450 — I-4
Uneeda, 65 — K-3
Unger, 100 — B-9
Union, 565 — L-6
Union City, 150 — M-3
Upper Falls, 3701 — J-3
Upper Tract, 90 — H-10
Uppergrade, 400 — J-6
UPSHUR CO., 24254 — H-7
Valley Bend, 485 — H-8
Valley Head, 267 — I-8
Valley Pt., 160 — F-9
Van, 211 — K-3
Varney, 250 — L-2
Verdunville, 687 — K-2
Vienna, 10749 — F-4
Volga, 140 — G-8
Vulcan, 100 — L-2
Wadestown, 150 — E-7
Waiteville, 40 — M-6
Walkersville, 150 — H-6
Wallace, 475 — F-6
Walton, 350 — I-4
Wana, 130 — E-7
War, 862 — M-3
Wardensville, 271 — C-8
Warwood —
Washington, 1175 — G-3
Waverly, 395 — F-4
Wayne, 1413 — L-1
Wayside, 40 — M-6
Webervood — M-9
Webster Sprs., 9154 — I-7
Weirton, 19746 — C-6
Welch, 2406 — M-3
Wellsburg, 2805 — C-6
W. Hamlin, 774 — J-2
W. Liberty, 1542 — D-6
W. Logan, 424 — L-2
W. Milford, 630 — G-7
W. Union, 825 — G-5
Weston, 4110 — G-6
Westover, 3983 — E-8
WETZEL CO., 16583 — F-6
Wheeling, 28486 — D-6
White Sulphur Sprs., 2444 — L-7
Whitehall, 648 — F-7
Whitesville, 514 — K-4
Whitman, 450 — K-2
Whitmer, 106 — H-9
Wick, 60 —
Widen, 200 — I-5
Wileyville, 100 — F-6
Williamsburg, 25 — K-6
Williamson, 3191 — L-1
Williamstown, 2908 — F-4
Willow Island —
Wilsondale, 40 — K-1
Windsor Hts., 423 — C-6
Winfield, 2301 — I-3

Wisconsin

Page locator
Map keys / Atlas pages
A–J / 228–229
K–T / 230–231
* City Keyed to p. 109
† City keyed to pp. 232–233

Abbotsford, 2310 — H-7
Abrams, 340 — I-12
Ada, 130 — L-11
Adams, 1967 — K-8
ADAMS CO., 20875 — K-9
Adell, 516 — L-13
Afton, 260 — P-10
Alaska, 30 — I-2
Albany, 1018 — O-9
Albion, 240 — O-10
Algoma, 3167 — J-13
Allen, 30 — J-11
Allens Grv., 180 — P-11
Allenton, 823 — M-3
Allouez, 13975 — J-3
Alma, 781 — J-3
Alma Ctr., 503 — J-6
Almena, 677 — E-3
Almond, 448 — J-9
Alpha, 50 — E-2
Alto, 200 — L-11
Altoona, 6706 — H-5
Alvin, 90 — E-11
Amberg, 180 — F-13
Amery, 2902 — G-2
Amherst, 1035 — J-10
Amherst Jct., 377 — J-10
Angelica, 92 — I-12
Angelo, 110 — K-6
Aniwa, 260 — H-10
Anson, 80 — I-12
Antigo, 8234 — G-10
Appleton, 72623 — J-12
Arbor Vitae, 220 — E-9
Arcadia, 2925 — J-4
Arena, 834 — N-8
Argonne, 160 — F-11
Argyle, 857 — O-8
Arkansaw, 177 — I-3
Arkdale, 158 — K-8
Arland, 40 — G-3
Arlington, 819 — M-9
Armstrong Creek, 200 — F-12
Arpin, 333 — I-8
Arthur, 70 — O-7
Ashippun, 333 — N-12
Ashland, 8216 — C-6
Athelstane, 110 — F-12
Athens, 1105 — H-8
Atlas, 70 — H-7
Atwood —
Auburndale, 703 — I-8
Augusta, 1510 — I-5
Aurora, 850 — L-13
Auroraville, 100 — K-10
Avalanche, 30 — L-6
Avalon, 200 — P-11
Avoca, 637 — N-7
Babcock, 126 — J-8
Bagley, 379 — O-5
Baileys Hbr., 257 — H-13
Bakerville, 50 — I-7
Baldwin, 3957 — H-2
Balsam Lake, 1009 — F-2
Bancroft, 535 — J-9
Bangor, 1459 — K-6
Baraboo, 12048 — M-9
Barneveld, 1231 — N-8
Barnum, 30 — I-6
Barron, 3423 — F-4
BARRON CO., 45870 — F-3
Barronett, 111 — F-3
Basco, 60 — O-9
Bay City, 500 — I-2
Bayfield, 487 — B-6
BAYFIELD CO., 15014 — B-5
Bayside, 4389 — C-6
Bear Creek, 448 — I-11
Bear Valley, 25 — M-7
Beaver, 90 — M-11
Beaver Dam, 16214 — M-11
Beecher, 35 — F-13
Beetown, 180 — O-6
Beldenville, 150 — I-2
Belgium, 2245 — M-13
Bell Ctr., 117 — M-6
Belleville, 2385 — O-9
Bellevue, 14570 — I-13
Bellinger —
Belmont, 986 — O-7
Beloit, 36966 — P-10
Benoit, 30 —
Benton, 973 — P-7
Berlin, 5524 — L-11
Bethel, 500 — P-3
Bevent, 100 — I-9
Big Bend, 1290 — N-1
Big Falls, 61 — I-10
Big Flats —
Big Spr., 40 — M-8
Billings Pk. — *C-9
Birchwood, 442 — E-4
Birnamwood, 818 — H-10
Biron, 839 — I-8
Black Creek, 1316 — I-12
Black Earth, 1338 — N-9
Black Hawk, 80 — N-7
Black River Falls, 3622 — J-6
Blackwell, 30 — F-11
Blair, 1366 — J-5
Blanchardville, 825 — O-8
Blenker, 120 — I-8
Bloom City, 80 — M-7
Bloomer, 3539 — G-4
Bloomfield, 3722 — P-12
Bloomingdale, 70 — L-7
Bloomington, 735 — O-6
Bloomville, 35 — J-12
Blue Mounds, 855 — N-8
Blue River, 434 — N-7
Bluff Siding, 40 — K-4
Bodman, 100 — M-7
Boaz, 156 — M-7
Boltonville, 200 — M-13
Bonduel, 1478 — I-11
Borth, 45 — K-11
Boscobel, 3231 — N-6
Boulder Jct., 183 — D-9
Bowler, 302 — H-10
Boyceville, 1086 — H-3
Boyd, 552 — H-6
Brackett, 120 — I-5
Branch, 160 — K-13
Brandon, 879 — L-11
Brantwood, 60 — F-8
Breed, 35 — H-12
Bridgeport, 60 — N-5
Briggsville, 380 — L-9
Brill, 130 — F-4
Brillion, 3148 — K-13
Bristol, 2583 — P-13
Brodhead, 3293 — P-9
Brokaw, 251 — H-9
Brookfield, 37920 — N-12
Brooklyn, 1401 — O-9
Brooks, 150 — L-9
Brookside, 75 — C-11
Brothertown, 200 — K-12
BROWN CO., 248007 — D-11
Brown Deer, 11999 — N-13
Brownsville, 581 — L-12
Browntown, 260 — P-8
Bruce, 779 — F-5
Brule, 254 — C-7
Brussels, 150 — C-12
Bryant, 100 — G-10
Buena Vista, 90 — J-8
Buffalo City, 1023 — J-4
BUFFALO CO., 13587 — J-4
Burke, 100 — N-10
Burlington, 10464 — O-12
Burnett, 226 — M-11
BURNETT CO., 15457 — E-2
Burton, 30 — O-6
Butler, 1841 — *D-3
Butte des Morts, 962 — K-11
Buttternut, 375 — D-7
Byron, 80 — L-12
Cable, 206 — D-5
Caddy Vista, 900 — *J-6
Cadott, 1437 — H-5
Caledonia, 24705 — O-13
Calamine, 70 — O-8
Camp, 250 — L-4
Cameron, 1783 — F-4
Camp Douglas, 601 — K-7
Campbellsport, 2016 — L-12
Canton, 50 — F-4
Carlsville, 50 — H-13
Carol Bch. Estates — *N-10
Caroline, 270 — G-11
Carter, 100 — G-11
Caryville, 50 — I-4
Cascade, 709 — L-13
Cashton, 1102 — L-6
Cassville, 947 — O-6
Cataract, 180 — K-6
Catawba, 162 — E-7
Cayuga, 30 — D-6
Cazenovia, 318 — M-7
Cecil, 570 — H-12
Cedar Falls, 40 — H-4
Cedar Grv., 2113 — M-13
Cedarburg, 11412 — M-13
Centerville, 120 — K-4
Centuria, 948 — F-2
Centennial, 111 — P-7
Chaseburg, 284 — L-6
Chelsea, 130 — F-8
Cherokee —
Chetek, 2221 — G-4
Chili, 226 — I-7
Chilton, 3933 — K-12
CHIPPEWA CO., 62415 — G-5
Chippewa Falls, 13661 — H-5
Christie, 30 — I-7
City Pt., 80 — J-7
Clam Falls, 80 — E-3
Clam Lake, 37 — D-6
CLARK CO., 34690 — I-6
Clayton, 571 — F-3
Clear Lake, 1070 — G-3
Clearwater Lake, 150 — E-10
Cleghorn, 75 — I-5
Cleveland, 1485 — L-13
Clifton, 40 —
Clinton, 2154 — P-11
Clintonville, 4559 — I-11
Clyman, 422 — M-11
Cobb, 455 — N-7
Cochrane, 450 — J-4
Colby, 1852 — H-7
Coleman, 724 — H-13
Colfax, 1158 — H-4
Colgate, 90 — *B-1
Collins, 164 — K-13
COLUMBIA CO., 56833 — M-10
Columbus, 4991 — M-10
Combined Locks, 3328 — K-12
Commonwealth — E-12
Comstock, 100 — F-3

Connorsville, 130 — G-3
Conover, 380 — D-10
Conrath, 95 — G-6
Coon Valley, 765 — L-6
Cooperstown, 50 — J-13
Cornell, 1467 — G-5
Cornucopia, 98 — B-5
Cottage Grv., 6192 — N-10
Couderay, 88 — E-5
County Line, 40 — I-11
Crandon, 1920 — F-11
CRAWFORD CO., 16644 — N-6
Cream, 30 — J-4
Crestview, 3500 — O-3
Crivitz, 984 — A-11
Cross Plains, 3538 — N-9
Cuba City, 2086 — P-7
Cudahy, 18267 — O-13
Cumberland, 2170 — F-3
Curtiss, 216 — H-7
Cushing, 200 — F-2
Custer, 170 — J-9
Dairyland — D-3
Dale, 245 — J-11
Dallas, 409 — G-4
Dalton, 206 — L-10
Danbury, 172 — D-2
Dancy, 80 — I-9
Dane, 995 — N-9
DANE CO., 488073 — O-9
Danville, 40 — N-8
Darboy, 350 — O-3
Darien, 1580 — P-11
Darlington, 2451 — P-8
Dayton, 150 — O-9
De Forest, 8936 — N-10
De Pere, 23800 — I-13
De Soto, 287 — M-5
Deer Pk., 216 — G-2
Deerbrook, 200 — G-10
Deerfield, 2319 — N-10
Delafield, 7085 — N-12
Delavan, 8463 — P-11
Dellwood, 563 — K-8
Denmark, 2123 — J-13
Deronda, 90 — G-2
Detroit Hbr., 400 — A-14
Dexterville, 50 — J-8
Diamond Bluff, 194 — I-2
Dickeyville, 1061 — P-6
Dodge, 121 — K-4
DODGE CO., 88759 — M-11
Dodgeville, 4693 — O-8
Doering — G-9
DOOR CO., 27785 — C-12
Dorchester, 876 — H-7
Dousman, 2302 — N-12
Downing, 265 — H-3
Downsville, 146 — I-3
Doylestown, 297 — M-10
Draper, 30 — E-6
Dresser, 895 — G-2
Drummond, 154 — C-5
Dunbar, 50 — F-12
Dundee, 140 — L-12
Duplainville — *B-1
Durand, 1931 — I-3
Dyckesville, 538 — C-12
Eagle, 1950 — O-12
Eagle River, 1398 — E-10
Eagleton, 40 — H-5
Earl, 60 — E-4
E. Farmington, 100 — G-2
E. Troy, 4281 — O-12
Eastman, 428 — N-5
East Troy —
Eau Claire, 65883 — H-4
EAU CLAIRE CO., 98736 — H-5
Eau Galle, 200 — I-3
Eden, 875 — L-12
Edgar, 1479 — H-8
Edgerton, 5461 — O-10
Edgewater, 100 — E-5
Edmund, 173 — O-7
Egg Hbr., 201 — B-13
El Paso, 90 — I-3
Eland, 202 — H-9
Elcho, 359 — F-10
Elderon, 179 — I-10
Eldorado, 250 — L-12
Eleva, 670 — I-4
Elk Mound, 878 — H-4
Elkhart Lake, 967 — L-13
Elkhorn, 10084 — P-12
Ella — E-3
Ellison Bay, 165 — A-13
Ellisville, 50 — J-12
Ellsworth, 3284 — I-2
Elm Grv., 5934 — *E-3
Elmhurst —
Elmore, 80 — M-4
Elmwood, 815 — I-3
Elmwood Pk., 497 — *I-10
Elroy, 1442 — L-7
Elton, 130 — G-11
Embarrass, 404 — I-11
Emerald, 161 — H-3
Emerald Grv., 90 — P-11
Endeavor, 468 — L-9
Enterprise, 40 — G-10
Ephraim, 288 — B-13
Erdman, 160 — *B-1
Ettrick, 524 — K-5
Eureka, 200 — K-11
Eureka, 40 — D-2
Evansville, 5012 — O-10
Excelsior, 70 — N-6
Exeland, 196 — E-5
Fairchild, 550 — I-6
Fairwater, 371 — L-11
Fall Creek, 1315 — I-5
Fall River, 1712 — M-10
Falun, 100 — F-2
Fayette, 40 — O-8
Fence, 100 — E-12
Fennimore, 2497 — O-6
Fenwood, 152 — H-8
Ferryville, 176 — M-5
Fifield, 330 — E-8
Finley, 40 — J-8
Fish Creek, 200 — B-13
Fitchburg, 25260 — N-9
Flintville, 60 — I-12
Florence, 592 — E-12
FLORENCE CO., 4423 — E-11
Fond du Lac, 43021 — L-12

FOND DU LAC CO., 101633 — L-11
Fontana, 1672 — P-11
Footville, 808 — P-10
Forest, 50 — G-3
FOREST CO., 9304 — F-11
Forest Jct., 616 — J-12
Forestville, 430 — C-12
Ft. Atkinson, 12368 — O-11
Foster, 90 —
Fountain City, 859 — K-4
Fox Lake, 1519 — M-11
Fox Pt., 6701 — †E-3
Foxboro, 100 — C-3
Francis Creek, 669 — J-13
Franklin, 35451 — O-13
Franklin, 30 —
Franksville, 1789 — †I-8
Frederic, 1137 — F-2
Fredonia, 2160 — M-13
Freedom, 400 — J-12
Fremont, 679 — J-11
French Island, 4410 — †K-8
Friendship, 725 — K-8
Friesland, 356 — M-10
Galesville, 1481 — K-5
Galloway, 120 — I-10
Gays Mills, 491 — M-6
Genesee, 450 — O-12
Genoa, 253 — M-5
Genoa City, 3042 — P-12
Germania, 60 — K-10
Germantown, 19749 — N-13
Gillett, 1386 — H-11
Gillingham, 100 — M-7
Gills Rock, 100 — A-13
Gilman, 410 — G-6
Gilmanton, 150 — J-4
Gleason, 200 — G-9
Glen Flora, 92 — F-6
Glen Haven, 73 — O-5
Glenbeulah, 463 — L-13
Glendale, 12872 — N-13
Glendale, 30 —
Glenwood City, 1242 — H-3
Glidden, 507 — D-7
Goodman, 271 — F-12
Goodrich, 40 — G-8
Gordon, 176 — D-4
Gotham, 191 — N-7
Grafton, 11459 — M-13
Grand Marsh, 127 — L-9
Grand View, 126 — C-5
Granton, 355 — I-7
Grantsburg, 1341 — E-2
Gratiot, 236 — P-8
Green Bay, 104057 — D-11
Green Lake, 960 — L-10
Green Valley, 30 — I-12
GREEN CO., 36842 — O-9
GREEN LAKE CO., 19051 — K-10
Green Valley, 133 — H-12
Greenbush, 100 — L-13
Greendale, 14046 — *G-5
Greenfield, 36720 — O-13
Greenleaf, 607 — J-12
Greenville, 300 — J-11
Greenwood, 1026 — I-7
Gresham, 586 — H-11
Gurney, 110 — C-7
Hager City, 338 — I-2
Halder, 40 —
Hales Cors., 7692 — *G-4
Hamburg, 100 — H-8
Hammond, 1922 — H-2
Hancock, 417 — K-9
Hannibal, 70 — F-6
Hanover, 181 — P-10
Harmony, 35 — B-11
Harrison, 30 —
Harrisville, 200 — K-9
Hartford, 14223 — M-12
Hartland, 9110 — N-12
Hatfield, 141 — J-6
Hatley, 574 — H-10
Haugen, 280 — F-4
Haven, 40 — L-13
Hawkins, 305 — F-6
Hawthorne, 40 — C-4
Hayes, 30 — H-7
Hayton, 100 — K-12
Hayward, 2318 — D-5
Hazel Green, 1256 — P-7
Hazelhurst, 500 — E-9
Heafford Jct., 200 — F-9
Hebron, 200 — O-11
Helenville, 249 — N-11
Herbster, 104 — B-5
Hersey, 85 — H-3
Hertel, 50 — E-3
Hewitt, 828 — I-8
High Br., 100 — C-6
Highland, 842 — N-7
Hilbert, 1132 — K-12
Hiles, 100 — E-10
Hillsboro, 1417 — L-7
Hillsdale, 180 — G-4
Hingham, 886 — L-13
Hixton, 433 — J-6
Hobart, 6182 — I-12
Holcombe, 75 — G-5
Holland, 100 — J-12
Hollandale, 288 — O-8
Hollister, 50 — J-7
Holmen, 9005 — K-5
Honey Creek, 400 — O-12
Horicon, 3655 — M-11
Hortonville, 2711 — J-11
Houlton, 386 — H-1
Howard, 17399 — D-11
Howards Grv., 3188 — L-13
Hub City, 100 — M-7
Hubertus, 170 — †A-1
Hudson, 12719 — H-1
Humbird, 266 — I-6
Hurley, 1547 — C-8
Hustisford, 1123 — M-11
Hustler, 194 — L-7
Independence, 1336 — J-5
Indianford, 250 — O-10
Ingram, 78 — F-6
Institute, 50 — *C-13
Iola, 1301 — I-10
Iowa, 23687 — N-7
IOWA CO., 23687 — N-7
Iron Belt, 173 — C-7
IRON CO., 5916 — D-7
Iron Ridge, 990 — M-12
Iron River, 761 — C-5
Ironton, 253 — M-8
Irvington, 120 — H-1
Island Lake, 30 — E-4
Ithaca, 100 — N-7
Ives Grv., 50 — †J-7
Ixonia, 1624 — N-11
JACKSON CO., 20449 — J-7
Jacksonport, 60 — B-13
Janesville, 63575 — P-10
Jefferson, 7973 — N-11
JEFFERSON CO., 83686 — N-11
Jennings, 40 — F-10
Jim Falls, 237 — H-5
Johnsburg, 180 — L-12
Johnson Creek, 2738 — N-11
Johnstown Ctr., 90 — O-11
Juda, 357 — P-9
Jump River, 52 — G-6
Junction City, 439 — I-9
Juneau, 2814 — M-11
JUNEAU CO., 26644 — K-7
Kaukauna, 15462 — J-12
Kekoskee, 161 — M-11
Kellner, 200 — I-9
Kellnersville, 332 — J-13
Kempster — G-10
Kendall, 472 — L-7
Kennan, 135 — F-7
Kenosha, 99218 — P-13
KENOSHA CO., 166426 — P-13
Keshena, 1262 — H-11
Kewaskum, 4004 — M-12
Kewaunee, 2952 — J-14
KEWAUNEE CO., 20574 — C-12
Kiel, 3738 — K-13
Kieler, 497 — P-6
Kimberly, 6468 — J-12
Kings, 150 — F-10
Kingston, 326 — L-10
Klondike, 50 — H-12
Knapp, 463 — H-3
Knowles, 160 — M-12
Knowlton, 120 — I-9
Kohler, 2120 — L-13
Kolberg — C-12
Krakow, 354 — I-12
Kronenwetter, 7210 — H-9
La Crosse, 51320 — L-5
La Farge, 746 — M-6
La Pointe, 100 — B-6
La Valle, 364 — M-8
Lac du Flambeau, 1646 — E-9
Lac La Belle, 290 — N-12
Lac Courte Oreilles —
Ladysmith, 3414 — F-5
Laona, 1050 — F-11
Land O' Lakes, 800 — D-10
Lannon, 1107 — †C-2
Laona, 583 — F-11
Lannon —
Lapham, 400 —
Larsen, 200 — K-11

Mather, 50 — K-7
Mattoon, 438 — H-10
Mauston, 4423 — L-8
Maxville, 30 — J-3
Mayville, 5016 — M-11
Mazomanie, 1652 — N-8
Mazon —
McAllister, 30 — A-12
McFarland, 7808 — N-10
McKinley —
McNaughton, 150 — E-9
Medford, 4326 — G-7
Medina, 250 — J-11
Mellen, 731 — C-7
Melrose, 503 — K-6
Melvina, 104 — L-6
Menasha, 17453 — J-12
Menchalville, 30 — J-13
Menomonee Falls, 35626 — N-13
MENOMINEE CO., 4232 — H-11
Mercer, 516 — D-8
Meridean, 80 — I-4
Merrill, 9661 — G-9
Merrillan, 542 — J-6
Merrimac, 450 — M-9
Merton, 3346 — N-12
Middle Inlet, 45 — A-11
Middle Ridge, 40 — L-6
Middleton, 17442 — N-9
Midway, 100 — K-5
Mikana, 250 — F-4
Milan, 130 — H-8
Milford, 80 — N-11
Milladore, 276 — I-8
Millston, 125 — K-6
Milltown, 917 — F-2
Milton, 5546 — O-11
Milwaukee, 594833 — N-13
MILWAUKEE CO., 947735 — O-13
Mindoro, 300 — K-5
Mineral Pt., 2487 — O-8
Minnesota Jct., 100 — M-11
Minocqua, 451 — E-9
Minong, 527 — D-4
Mishicot, 1442 — J-14
Mole Lake, 435 — F-10
Mondovi, 2777 — I-4
Monico, 150 — F-10
Monona, 7533 — N-10
Monroe, 10827 — P-9
Mt. Calvary, 762 — L-12
Mt. Hope, 225 — O-6
Mt. Horeb, 7009 — N-9
Mt. Ida, 45 — O-6
Mt. Morris, 130 — K-10
Mt. Pleasant —
Mt. Sterling, 211 — M-6
Mt. Tabor —
Mt. Vernon, 180 — O-9
Mt. Zion —
Mountain, 363 — G-12
Mukwonago, 7355 — O-12
Muscoda, 1299 — N-7
Muskego, 24135 — *H-2
Namur, 30 — C-12
Nashotah, 1395 — N-12
Navarino, 177 — I-12
Necedah, 916 — K-8
Neenah, 25501 — K-12
Neillsville, 2463 — I-6
Nekoosa, 2580 — J-8
Nelson, 374 — J-4
Nelsonville, 155 — J-10
Neopit, 690 — H-11
Neosho, 574 — M-12
Neshkoro, 434 — K-10
New Amsterdam, 150 — K-5
New Auburn, 548 — G-4
New Berlin, 39584 — *H-3
New Diggings, 100 — P-7
New Franken, 250 — I-13
New Glarus, 2172 — O-9
New Holstein, 3236 — K-13
New Lisbon, 2554 — L-8
New London, 7295 — I-11
New Munster —
New Post, 305 — E-5
New Richmond, 8375 — G-2
Newald, 90 — F-11
Newburg, 1254 — M-13
Reeseville, 708 — M-11
Reeve, 50 — K-12
Reserve, 428 — E-5
Retreat, 80 — M-5
Rewey, 292 — O-7
Rhinelander, 7798 — F-9
Rib Lake, 910 — G-7
Rice Lake, 8438 — F-4
Richfield, 11300 — N-13
Richford, 50 — K-9
Richland Ctr., 5184 — M-7
RICHLAND CO., 18021 — M-7
Ridgeland, 283 — G-3
Ridgeway, 653 — N-8
Ringle, 200 — H-9
Rio, 1059 — M-10
Rio Creek, 100 — C-12
Ripon, 7733 — L-11
Rising Sun, 30 — M-8
River Falls, 15000 — H-2
River Hills, 1590 — *D-3
Roberts, 1651 — H-2
Rochester, 3682 — O-12
ROCK CO., 160331 — O-10
Rock Falls, 1040 — I-3
Rock Spr., 362 — M-8
Rockbridge, 100 — M-7
Rockdale, 214 — O-10
Rockfield —
Rockland, 594 — K-6
Rockton, 35 — L-7
Rome, 689 — O-11
Oliver, 399 — B-3
Rosendale, 906 — L-11
Rosholt, 506 — I-10
Rosiere, 60 — C-12

Rothschild, 5269 — H-9
Rowleys Bay, 70 — A-13
Roxbury, 150 — N-9
Royalton, 250 — I-11
Rozellville, 250 — H-8
Rubicon, 110 — M-12
Rudolph, 439 — I-8
Rural, 200 — J-10
Rusk, 150 — G-5
RUSK CO., 14755 — F-5
St. Cloud, 477 — L-12
ST. CROIX CO., 84345 — H-2
St. Croix Falls, 2133 — F-2
St. Francis, 9365 — N-13
St. Germain, 400 — E-9
St. Joseph, 100 — M-11
St. Kilian, 80 — L-12
St. Lawrence, 200 — M-11
St. Marys, 25 — L-12
St. Michaels, 100 — L-12
St. Nazianz, 783 — K-13
Salem, 1150 — P-13
Sampson, 25 — J-12
Sanborn, 40 — C-6
Sand Bay — A-13
Sand Creek, 200 — G-4
Sarona, 100 — E-4
Sauk City, 3410 — N-9
SAUK CO., 61976 — M-8
Saukville, 4451 — M-13
Saxeville, 150 — K-10
Saxon, 90 — C-7
Sayner, 207 — E-9
Scandinavia, 363 — J-10
Schofield, 2169 — H-9
Sechlerville, 30 — J-5
Seeley, 80 — D-5
Seneca, 220 — N-6
Sextonville, 150 — N-7
Seymour, 3451 — I-12
Shamrock —
Shanagolden, 50 — D-7
Sharon, 1605 — P-11
Shawano, 9305 — I-11
SHAWANO CO., 41949 — H-10
Sheboygan, 49288 — L-13
SHEBOYGAN CO., 115507 — L-13
Sheboygan Falls, 7775 — L-13
Sheldon, 237 — G-6
Shell Lake, 1347 — E-3
Shennington, 45 — K-7
Sherry, 120 — I-8
Sherwood, 2713 — K-12
Shiocton, 921 — I-11
Shopiere, 200 — P-11
Shorewood, 13162 — N-13
Shorewood Hills, 1565 — *D-4
Shortville — J-7
Shullsburg, 1226 — P-7
Silver Lake, 2411 — P-12
Silver Lake, 300 — K-10
Sinsinawa, 250 — P-6
Siren, 800 — E-2
Sister Bay, 876 — A-13
Slinger, 5068 — M-12
Slovan, 30 — D-12
Sobieski, 259 — I-13
Soldiers Grv., 592 — M-6
Solon Sprs., 600 — C-4
Somers, 530 — P-13
Somerset, 2635 — G-2
S. Beaver Dam, 60 — M-11
S. Milwaukee, 21156 — O-13
S. Range, 120 — B-3
S. Superior — *D-9
S. Wayne, 489 — P-8
Sparta, 9522 — L-6
Spencer, 1925 — I-7
Spirit, 35 — F-8
Split Rock, 50 — I-10
Spooner, 2682 — E-4
Spread Eagle, 200 — E-12
Spring Green, 1628 — N-8
Spring Lake, 30 — K-10
Spring Valley, 1352 — I-3
Springbrook, 40 — E-4
Springfield, 158 — I-9
Springstead, 100 — E-8
Stangelville, 100 — J-13
Stanley, 3608 — H-6
Star Prairie, 561 — G-2
Starks, 50 — F-10
Stephensville, 250 — I-11
Stetsonville, 541 — H-7
Steuben, 131 — N-6
Stevens Pt., 26717 — I-9
Stevenson, 45 — O-12
Stiles, 100 — H-12
Stitzer, 200 — O-6
Stockbridge, 636 — K-12
Stockholm, 66 — I-3
Stoddard, 774 — L-5
Stone Lake, 178 — E-4
Stoughton, 12611 — O-10
Stratford, 1578 — H-8
Strum, 1114 — I-5
Sturgeon Bay, 9144 — C-13
Sturtevant, 6970 — O-13
Suamico, 11346 — D-11
Sugar Camp, 180 — E-10
Sullivan, 669 — N-11
Summit Lake, 144 — G-10
Sun Prairie, 29364 — N-10
Superior, 27368 — *D-9
Superior Vil., 664 — B-3
Sussex, 10518 — N-13
Symco, 100 — I-11
Taycheedah, 300 — L-12
Taylor, 476 — J-5
TAYLOR CO., 20689 — G-7
Tennyson, 330 — O-6
Theresa, 1262 — M-12
Thiensville, 3235 — *A-5
Thompsonville — P-11
Thornton, 50 — J-12
Thorp, 1621 — H-6
Three Lakes, 605 — E-10
Tigerton, 741 — H-10
Tilleda, 30 — H-11
Tipler, 50 — E-11
Tisch Mills, 200 — J-14
Tomah, 9093 — K-7
Tomahawk, 3397 — F-9
Tony, 113 — F-6
Townsend, 146 — G-11
Trade Lake, 60 — E-2
Trego, 227 — E-4
Trempealeau, 1529 — K-5
TREMPEALEAU CO., 28816 — J-5

Trimbelle, 30 — I-2
Tripoli, 70 — F-8
Tunnel City, 180 — K-7
Turtle Lake, 1050 — F-3
Tustin, 117 — K-11
Twin Bluffs, 80 — N-7
Twin Lakes, 5989 — P-12
Two Creeks, 90 — J-14
Two Rivers, 11712 — K-14
Underhill, 100 — H-12
Union Ctr., 200 — L-8
Union Grv., 4915 — O-13
Unity, 343 — H-7
Upson, 150 — C-7
Urne, 50 — J-4
Valders, 962 — K-13
Valley, 60 —
Valley Jct., 100 — K-7
Valmy, 30 — B-13
Van Dyne, 300 — L-12
VERNON CO., 29773 — L-5
Verona, 10619 — N-9
Vesper, 584 — I-8
Victory, 120 — M-5
VILAS CO., 21430 — D-9
Viola, 690 — M-7
Viroqua, 4362 — M-6
Wabeno, 575 — F-11
Waldo, 515 — L-13
Waldwick, 60 — O-8
Wales, 2549 — N-12
Walworth, 2816 — P-11
WALWORTH CO., 102228 — O-11
Wandawega, 500 — O-12
Wanderoos, 110 — G-2
Warrens, 363 — K-7
Wascott, 150 — D-4
Washburn, 2117 — B-6
WASHBURN CO., 15911 — E-4
Washington, 23861 — N-13
WASHINGTON CO., 131887 — M-12
Waterford, 5368 — O-12
Waterloo, 3333 — N-10
Waterville, 30 — M-12
Waubeka, 657 — M-13
Waukau, 150 — K-11
Waukesha, 70718 — N-12
WAUKESHA CO., 389891 — O-12
Waumandee, 68 — J-4
Waunakee, 12097 — N-9
Waupaca, 6069 — J-10
WAUPACA CO., 52410 — J-10
Waupun, 11340 — L-11
Wausau, 39106 — H-9
Wausaukee, 575 — A-11
Wautoma, 2218 — K-10
Wauwatosa, 46396 — *E-4
Wauzeka, 711 — N-6
Wayside, 200 — J-13
Webb Lake, 60 — D-3
Webster, 653 — E-2
Wentworth, 100 — B-3
W. Allis, 60411 — N-13
W. Baraboo, 1414 — M-9
W. Bend, 31078 — M-12
W. Bloomfield, 65 — L-9
W. Lima, 40 — M-7
W. Milwaukee, 4206 — *F-5
W. Salem, 4799 — K-5
Westboro, 190 — G-7
Westby, 2200 — L-6
Westfield, 1254 — L-9
Weston, 14868 — H-9
Weston, 30 — H-3
Weyauwega, 1900 — J-10
Weyerhaeuser, 238 — F-5
Wheeler, 348 — H-3
White Creek, 50 — L-8
Whitefish Bay, 14110 — N-13
Whitehall, 1558 — J-5
Whitelaw, 757 — J-13
Whitewater, 14390 — O-11
Whittlesey, 105 — G-7
Wild Rose, 725 — K-10
Williams Bay, 2564 — P-12
Willard, 60 — I-6
Willow Sprs., 120 — P-8
Wilmot, 450 — P-13
Wilson, 172 — H-3
Wilton, 504 — L-7
Winchester, 671 — J-11
Wind Lake, 5342 — O-12
Wind Pt., 1723 — O-13
Winnebago, 300 — K-11
WINNEBAGO CO., 166994 — K-11
Winneconne, 2383 — K-11
Wiota, 140 — P-8
Wisconsin Dells, 2678 — L-9
Wisconsin Rapids, 18367 — I-8
Withee, 487 — H-7
Wittenberg, 1081 — H-10
Wonewoc, 816 — L-8
WOOD CO., 74749 — I-9
Woodboro — F-9
Woodford, 69 — P-8
Woodland, 400 — M-12
Woodman, 132 — O-6
Woodruff, 90 — E-9
Woodville, 1365 — H-3
Wrightstown, 2827 — J-13
Wyeville, 167 — K-7
Wyocena, 768 — M-10
Yellow Lake, 70 — E-2
York, 40 — J-9
Zachow, 150 — H-12
Zenda, 200 — P-12
Zittau, 60 — K-11

Wyoming

Page locator
Map keys / Atlas pages
A–J / 234–235

Adkins Valley, 130 — B-10
Afton, 1911 — G-3
Airport Rd. —
Aladdin, 30 — B-13
Albany, 50 — G-10
ALBANY CO., 36299 — G-11
Albin, 181 — G-13

Allendale, 70 — H-3
Almy, 80 — H-4
Alpine, 828 — D-4
Alta, 394 — B-4
Little America, 68 — H-4
Lost Cabin, 30 — E-8
Lost Sprs., 4 — E-1
Lovell, 2361 — B-7
Lovern, 535 — B-4
Lusk, 1567 — E-1
Lyman, 2115 — H-3
Lysite, 60 —
Manderson, 114 — C-7
Manville, 95 — E-1
Marbleton, 1094 — F-4
McFadden, 80 — G-1
McKinley, 20 —
Medicine Bow, 284 — G-1
Meeteetse, 327 —
Meriden, 70 —
Midwest, 404 — D-9
Midwest Hts. —
Mills, 3461 — D-9
Moneta —
Moorcroft, 1009 — C-12
Moose, 180 —
Moran, 50 — C-2
Morton —
Mountain Home, 10 — H-4
Mountain View, 1286 —
Mountain View, 20 — C-2
Muddy Gap, 20 —
Natrona, 10 —
NATRONA CO., 75450 —
New Haven, 30 — B-12
Newcastle, 3532 — C-12
NIOBRARA CO., 2484 —
Old Faithful —
Opal, 96 —
Orchard Valley, 1800 —
Orin, 46 —
Orpha —
Osage, 208 — C-12
Oshoto, 30 — B-12
Osmond, 357 —
Otto, 52 —
Pahaska —
Paradise Valley —
Parkman, 111 —
Pavillion, 231 —
Pine Bluffs, 1129 — H-13
Pine Haven, 490 — C-12
Pinedale, 2030 — E-4
Pitchfork Ranch, 20 —
Point of Rocks, 30 —
Powder River, 50 —
Powell, 6314 —
Prospector Vil., 20 —
Quealy —
Ralston, 230 —
Ranchester, 855 —
Rawlins, 9259 —
Red Bank, 20 —
Red Desert, 30 —
Reliance, 714 —
Riverside, 52 —
Riverton, 10615 —
Robertson, 70 —
Rock Rvr., 245 —
Rock Sprs., 23036 —
Rockypoint —
Rolling Hills, 440 —
Rozet, 40 —
Ryan Pk., 38 —
Saddlestring, 10 —
Sand Draw —
Saratoga, 1690 —
Savery, 50 —
Seminole Dam, 40 —
Shawnee, 30 —
Shell, 83 —
Sheridan, 17444 —
SHERIDAN CO., 29116 —
Shirley Basin, 150 —
Shoshoni, 649 —
Sinclair, 433 —
Skull Creek, 30 —
Slater, 80 —
Smoot, 178 —
S. Laramie, 1560 —
S. Pass City, 30 —
S. Torrington, 380 —
Spotted Horse, 2 —
Story, 828 —
SUBLETTE CO., 10247 —
Sundance, 1182 —
Sunrise, 30 —
Superior, 336 —
Sussex —
SWEETWATER CO., 43806 —
Sweetwater Sta., 30 —
Table Rock —
Ten Sleep, 260 —
Teton —
TETON CO., 21294 —
Thayne, 366 —
Thermopolis, 3009 —
Thunder Basin, 100 —
Tie Siding, 30 —
Torrington, 6501 —
Tower Jct. —
Ucross —
UINTA CO., 21118 —
Upton, 1100 —
Urie, 262 —
Valley —
Van Tassell, 15 —
Veteran, 23 —
Veteran, 43 —
Vista West, 50 —
Walcott, 30 —
Waltman —
Wamsutter, 451 —
Wapiti, 60 —
WASHAKIE CO., 8533 —
W. Thumb —
Weston, 20 —
WESTON CO., 7208 —
Wheatland, 3627 —
Willwood, 80 —
Wilson, 1482 —
Winchester, 20 —
Woods, 20 —
Worland, 4907 —
Wright, 1801 —
Wyarno, 40 —
Wyodak, 80 —
Yoder, 151 —

LINCOLN CO., 18106 — G-
Lingle, 468 —
Lincoln —
Bear River, 518 — H-4
Bedford, 201 —
Beulah, 87 —
Big Horn, 490 — B-8
BIG HORN CO., 11668 — C-8
Big Piney, 552 — F-5
Bill, 10 — D-12
Bondurant, 93 — E-5
Bonneville — D-8
Boulder, 170 — E-6
Brookhurst, 185 —
Buffalo, 4585 — C-10
Burlington, 286 —
Burns, 301 — H-13
Burris, 80 — D-6
Byron, 593 — B-7
CAMPBELL CO., 46133 — C-11
Canyon —
CARBON CO., 15885 — H-9
Carlile, 30 — B-12
Carpenter, 94 — H-13
Carter, 10 — H-5
Casper, 55316 — E-10
Centennial, 270 — H-11
Cheyenne, 59466 — H-13
Chugwater, 212 — G-12
Clearmont, 142 — B-10
Cody, 9520 — B-7
Colony — A-13
Cora, 142 — E-5
Cowley, 655 — B-8
Crook —
CROOK CO., 7083 — B-13
Crowheart, 141 — D-7
Daniel, 150 — E-5
Dayton, 757 — B-9
Deaver, 178 — B-7
Devils Tower, 70 — B-13
Diamondville, 737 — G-5
Dixon, 97 — I-9
Douglas, 6120 — E-12
Dubois, 971 — D-6
Dwyer — E-12
Eden, 30 —
E. Thermopolis, 254 — D-8
Eden, 370 —
Edgerton, 195 — D-11
Egbert, 30 — H-13
Elk Mtn., 191 — G-10
Emblem, 70 — B-8
Encampment, 450 — H-10
Esterbrook, 52 — F-11
Ethete, 1553 — E-7
Etna, 164 — E-4
Evanston, 12359 — H-4
Evansville, 2544 — D-3
Fairview, 274 — C-8
Farson, 313 — G-6
Farthing, 30 — H-12
Fontenelle, 13 — G-6
Ft. Bridger, 345 — H-5
Ft. Laramie, 230 — F-13
Ft. Steele, 30 — G-10
Four Corners, 2 — B-13
Foxpark, 22 — H-11
Frannie, 157 — A-7
Freedom, 214 — E-4
Frontier —
FREMONT CO., 40123 — E-8
Ft. Washakie, 1759 — E-7
Gas Hills, 45 — E-9
Gillette, 29087 — C-11
Glendo, 205 — F-12
Glenrock, 2576 — E-11
GOSHEN CO., 13249 — F-13
Granger, 139 — H-5
Grant Vil. —
Grass Creek, 50 — C-7
Greybull, 1815 — B-8
Grover, 147 — F-3
Guernsey, 1147 — F-13
Halfway —
Hamilton Dome, 50 — C-7
Hanna, 841 — G-10
Harriman, 40 — H-12
Hartville, 62 — F-13
Hawk Sprs., 45 — G-13
Hiland, 10 — E-9
Hillsdale, 47 — H-13
Hoback, 1176 — D-4
Hobart, 20 —
Horse Creek, 120 — H-12
HOT SPRINGS CO., 4812 — D-7
Hudson, 458 — E-7
Hulett, 383 — B-13
Hyattville, 75 — C-8
Jackson, 9577 — C-4
Jay Em, 30 — F-13
James Town, 50 —
Jeffrey City, 58 — F-8
Jelm, 30 — I-11
Jenny Lake, 30 —
Jireh, 4 — F-1
Kaycee, 263 — D-10
Keeline, 10 —
Kelly, 138 — C-5
Kemmerer, 2656 — G-5
Kinnear, 90 — E-7
Kirby, 92 — D-8
La Barge, 448 — G-4
La Grange, 448 — G-13
Lance Creek, 43 — E-1
Lander, 7487 — E-7
Laramie, 30816 — H-11
LARAMIE CO., 91738 — H-13
Leiter, 5 — B-10
Linch, 100 — D-11

*, †, ‡, §, ◊ See explanation under state title in this index.
County and parish names are listed in capital letters & boldface type.
Independent cities (not included in a county) are listed in italics.